The PRENTICE HALL

American Nation

Independence Through 1914

Davidson ★ Castillo ★ Stoff

PRENTICE HALL
Upper Saddle River, New Jersey
Needham, Massachussetts

Authors

James West Davidson is coauthor of *After the Fact: The Art of Historical Detection* and *Nation of Nations: A Narrative History of the American Republic.* Dr. Davidson has taught at both the college and high school levels. He has also consulted on curriculum design for American history courses. In his spare time, Dr. Davidson is an avid canoeist and hiker. His published works on these subjects include *Great Heart,* the true story of a 1903 canoe trip in the Canadian wilderness.

Pedro Castillo teaches American history at the University of California, Santa Cruz, where he also co-directs the Chicano-Latino Research Center. He has earned a Rockefeller Foundation Research Fellowship and two Senior Fulbright-Hayes Lectureships in Latin America. Dr. Castillo's published works on American history and Chicano Latino history include *Mexico En Los Angeles* and *An Illustrated History of Mexican Los Angeles*. Dr. Castillo has also served as a curriculum design consultant for the California American History Framework.

Michael B. Stoff teaches history at the University of Texas at Austin, where he also directs the graduate program in history. He is the author of *Oil, War, and American Security: The Search for a National Policy on Foreign Oil, 1941–1947*, coauthor of *Nation of Nations: A Narrative History of the American Republic*, and co-editor of *The Manhattan Project: A Documentary Introduction to the Atomic Age*. Dr. Stoff has won numerous grants and fellowships. He has also served as a consultant for the development of secondary history curricula in Texas.

AmericanHeritage® *American Heritage* magazine was founded in 1954, and it quickly rose to the position it occupies today: the country's preeminent magazine of history and culture. Dedicated to presenting the past in incisive, entertaining narratives underpinned by scrupulous scholarship, *American Heritage* today goes to more than 300,000 subscribers and counts the country's very best writers and historians among its contributors. Its innovative use of historical illustration and its wide variety of subject matter have gained the publication scores of honors across more than forty years, among them the National Magazine Awards.

Senior Consultant Diane Hart is an education writer and consultant specializing in history and social studies. She is the author of several social studies textbooks as well as resource books for teachers, including *Authentic Assessment: A Handbook for Educators.* A former teacher and Woodrow Wilson Fellow, she remains deeply involved in social studies education through her active involvement in both the National and California Councils for the Social Studies.

Acknowledgments and Illustration Credits begin on page 792.

PRENTICE HALL

Printed in the United States of America.

ISBN 0-13-433634-8

1 2 3 4 5 6 7 8 9 10 03 02 01 00 99 98

Upper Saddle River, New Jersey Needham, Massachussetts

Program Reviewers

Academic Consultants

David Beaulieu, Ph.D.
Director of Office of Indian Education
U.S. Department of Education
Washington, D.C.

Richard Beeman, Ph.D.
Professor of History
University of Pennsylvania
Philadelphia, Pennsylvania

Wendy Gamber, Ph.D.
Assistant Professor of History
Indiana University
Bloomington, Indiana

Heidi Hayes Jacobs, Ed.D.
President, Curriculum Designs, Inc.
Rye, New York
Adjunct Professor of Curriculum and Teaching
Columbia University
New York, New York

Tetsuden Kashima, Ph.D.
Associate Professor of American Ethnic Studies
University of Washington
Seattle, Washington

Emma Lapsansky, Ph.D.
Professor of History and Curator of Special Collections
Haverford College
Haverford, Pennsylvania

Lyn Reese
Director, Women in World History Curriculum
Berkeley, California

Joel Silbey, Ph.D.
Professor of History
Cornell University
Ithaca, New York

Reading Specialist

Bonnie Armbruster, Ph.D.
Professor of Education
University of Illinois at Urbana–Champaign
Champaign, Illinois

Teacher Reviewers

Buckley Bangert
Social Studies Teacher
Ortega Middle School
Alamosa, Colorado

Clement R. Brown, III
Social Studies Teacher
Madison Junior High School
Naperville, Illinois

Lynn Castiaux
Social Studies Teacher/Mentor
Sylvan Middle School
Citrus Heights, California

Sandra Lee Eades, Ph.D.
Social Studies Content Leader
Ridgely Middle School
Lutherville, Maryland

Beverly Hooper
Social Studies Teacher
Dartmouth School
San Jose, California

Bill McElree
Social Studies Teacher
Vista Compana Middle School
Apple Valley, California

Denis O'Rourke
Chairman, Dept. of Social Studies
Hommocks Middle School
Larchmont, New York

Carol Philips
Social Studies Teacher
Colina Middle School
Thousand Oaks, California

Sharon L. Pope
Secondary Social Studies Coordinator
Spring Branch Independent School District
Houston, Texas

Jill Schumacher
Social Studies Teacher
Brown Middle School
McAllen, Texas

Pat Sitzler
Social Studies Teacher/Dept. Chair
Reed Middle School
Duncanville, Texas

Accuracy Panel

Esther Ratner
Greyherne Information Services
With
Marvin Beckerman, Ph.D., University of Missouri–St. Louis; Muriel Beckerman, University of Missouri–St. Louis; Lynn D. Hoover, The Hoover Associates; Jane B. Malcolm, Professional Research Services; Bennet J. Parstek, Ed.D., St. John's University, NY; Alice Radosh, Ph.D., Academy of Educational Development; Lorraine Rosenberg, Baldwin School District, NY (Ret.); Cathy S. Zazueta, California State University, Los Angeles.

Staff Credits

The people who made up ***The American Nation*** team—representing editorial, design services, market research, marketing, publishing processes, editorial services, production services, on-line services/multimedia development, electronic publishing technology, and marketing services—and their managers are listed below. Bold type denotes core team members.

Margaret Antonini, Tom Barber, Christopher Brown, Christina Burghard, **Sarah Carroll,** Lisa Charde, Lynda Cloud, Rhett Conklin, Martha Conway, Carlos Crespo, Kathy Dix, **Jim Doris,** Anne Falzone, Libby Forsyth, **Annemarie Franklin, Nancy Gilbert,** Holly Gordon, Linda Hardman, **Dorshia Johnson,** Carol Leslie, **Loretta Moe,** Gregory Myers, Rip Odell, Jim O'Shea, **Emily Rose,** Kirsten Richert, AnnMarie Roselli, Gerry Schrenck, Anne Shea, Annette Simmons, **Marilyn Stearns,** Frank Tangredi, Elizabeth Torjussen

UNIT 1 Connecting With Past Learnings: Reviewing Our Early Heritage xx

▲ Minuteman statue

Chapter Source Readings

▲ Plantation workers

UNIT 2 The Constitution of the United States 112

▲ *The Liberty Bell*

Chapter Source Readings

▲ *Signing the Constitution*

▼ *Quill and inkwell used at the Constitutional Convention*

UNIT 3 The Nation Takes Shape 168

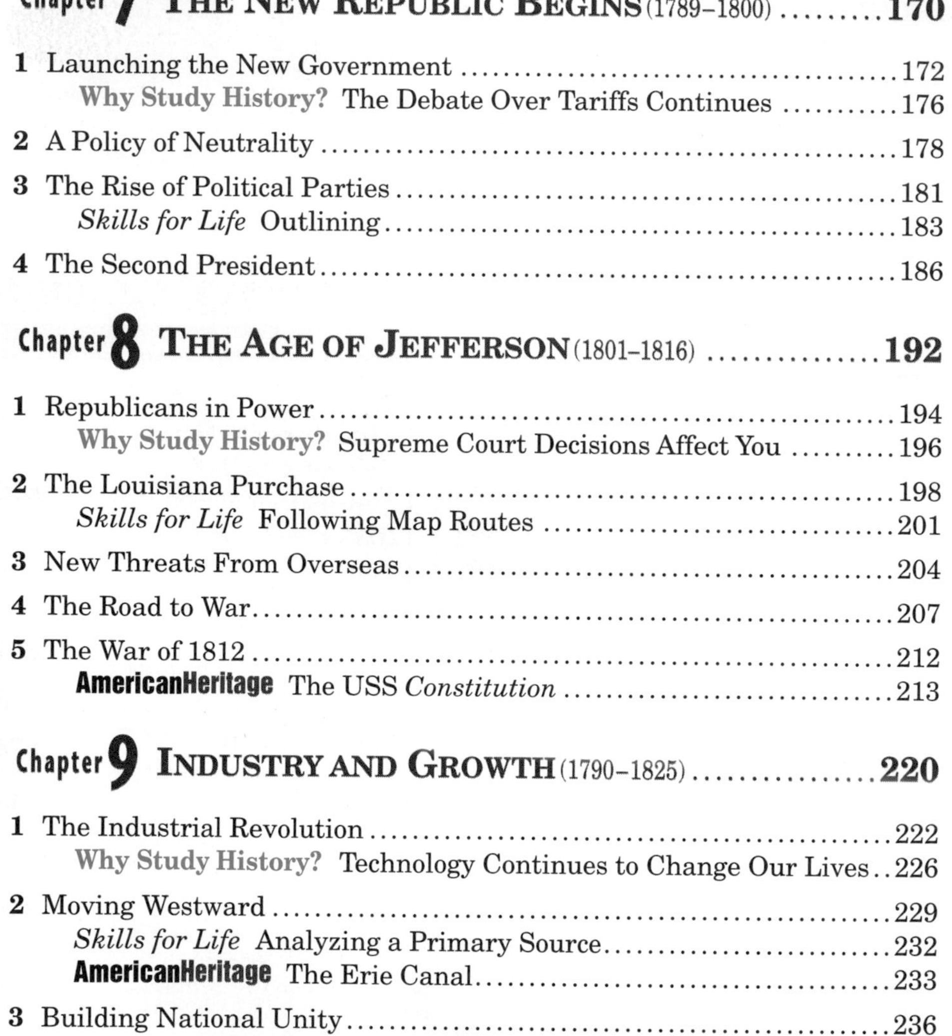

Women factory workers

Battle of New Orleans

The Louisiana Purchase

UNIT 4 The Nation Expands 248

▲ Miniature log cabin

Chapter Source Readings

▲ California Bear Flag

UNIT 5 Division and Reunion 348

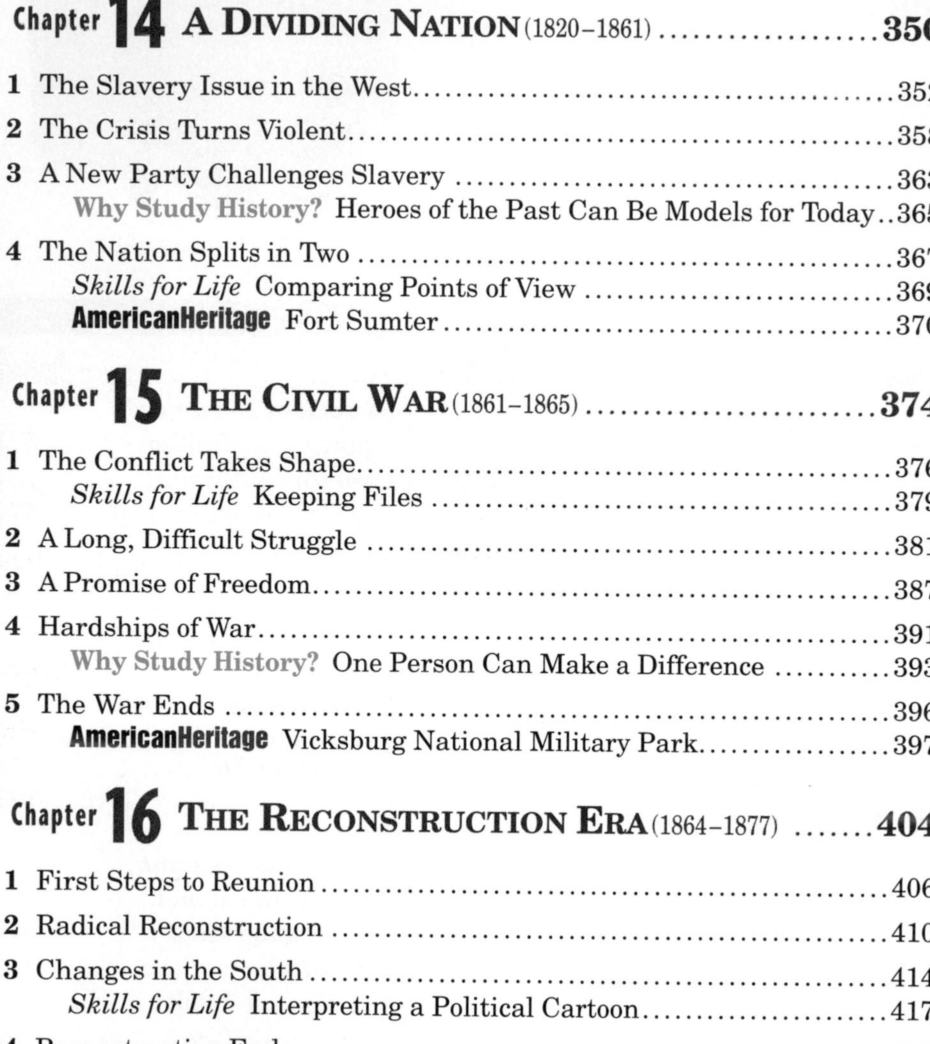

▲ Union drum

▲ Confederate canteen

Chapter Source Readings

▲ Copy of the Emancipation Proclamation

UNIT 6 Transforming the Nation 428

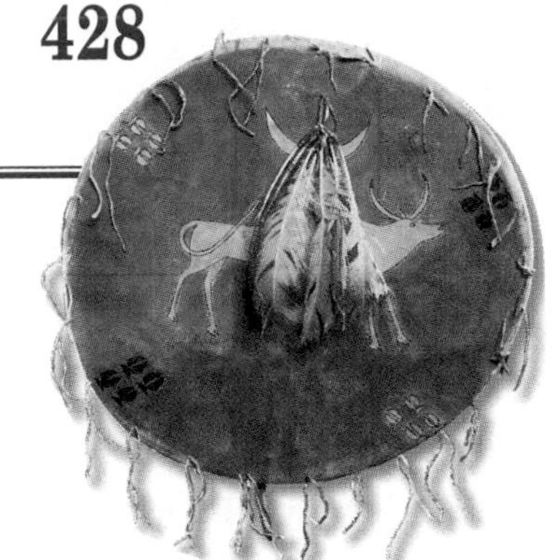
▲ Cheyenne shield

Chapter 17 An Era of Change in the West (1865–1914) 430

Chapter 18 The Rise of Industry and Unions (1865–1914) 458

Chapter 19 Immigration and the Growth of Cities (1865–1914) 484

Chapter Source Readings

▲ Early light bulb

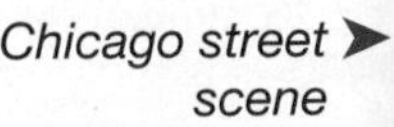
Chicago street scene ➤

UNIT 7

A New Role for the Nation 512

⮝ Wilson campaign button

Chapter Source Readings

⮝ Poster urging Americans to vote

Reference Section

Special Features

★ *These high-interest features show how history is relevant to American life today and to your life in particular.*

Poster urging conservation of water ➤

▲ *Registering to vote*

AmericanHeritage M A G A Z I N E

★ With the editors of American Heritage Magazine as your guides, you see and read about special sites where American history happened.

HISTORY HAPPENED HERE

▲ *Mission San Juan Capistrano*

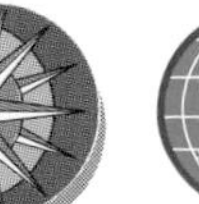

Linking Past and Present

★ *Pairs of pictures illustrate interesting connections between a condition or event in American history and a condition or event of today.*

Linking United States and the World

★ *Pairs of pictures show connections between historic events in the United States and in other countries of the world.*

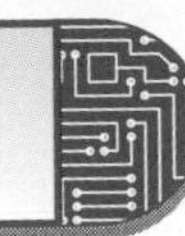

Linking History and Technology

★ *Detailed drawings and photographs illustrate major historical advances in technology.*

▲ *Cotton gin*

Biography

★ *Learn about the men and women who affected the course of American history and culture.*

★ *Learn and practice valuable skills that you will be able to use throughout your life.*

▲ *Using the Internet*

Viewpoints: Source Readings in American History

★ *Eyewitness accounts, historical documents, and literature selections provide you with different viewpoints on American history.*

Eyewitness Accounts

★ *Literature selections from different eras in American history provide a variety of viewpoints and insights into the American way of life. A literature selection appears at the end of each unit.*

★ Maps ★

Geographic Atlas

★ Charts, Graphs, and Time Lines ★

Graphic Organizers

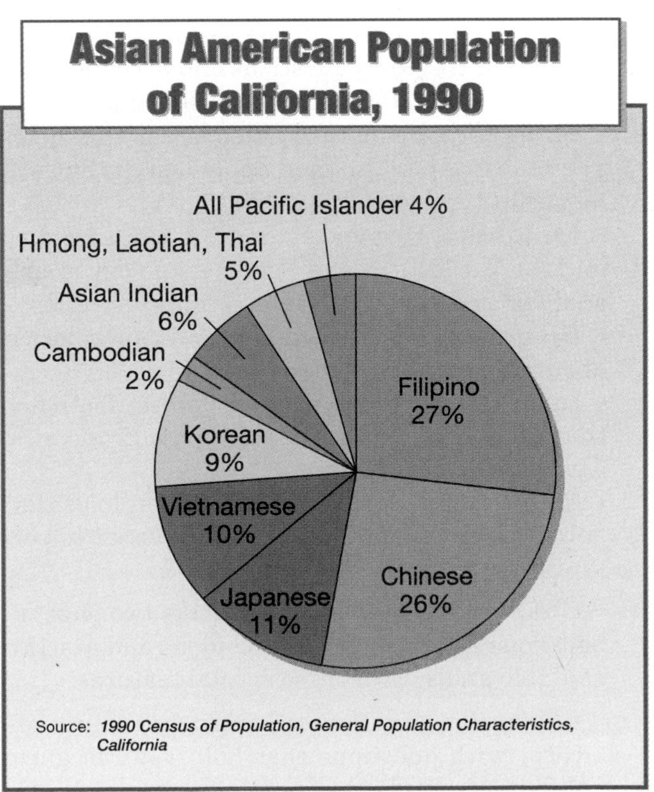

About This Book

The American Nation is organized into 7 units and 23 chapters, with "Viewpoints: Sources in American History" following the last chapter. The Table of Contents lists units, chapters, sections, and special features.

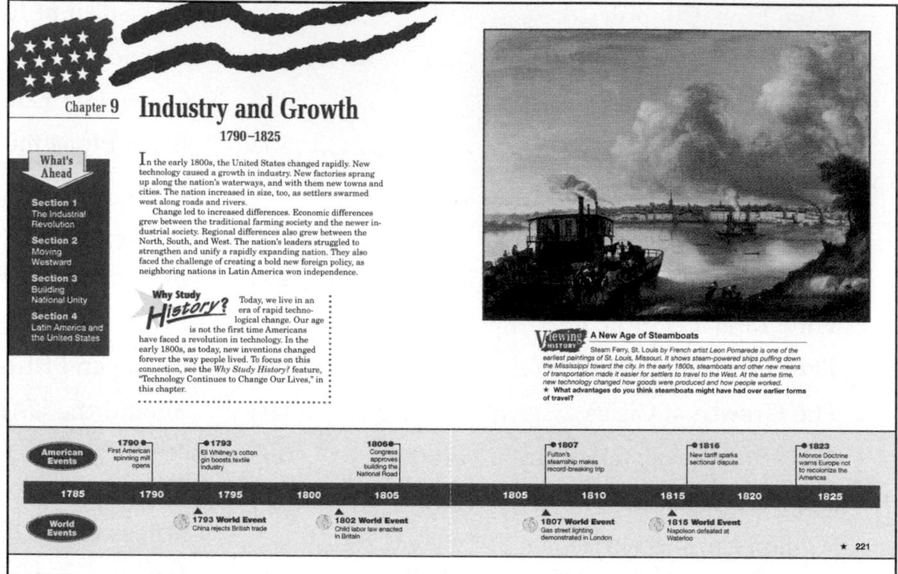

Chapter 9 **Industry and Growth**

1790–1825

What's Ahead

Section 1 The Industrial Revolution

Section 2 Moving Westward

Section 3 Building National Unity

Section 4 Latin America and the United States

In the early 1800s, the United States changed rapidly. New technology caused a growth in industry. New factories sprang up along the nation's waterways, and with them new towns and cities. The nation increased in size, too, as settlers swarmed west along roads and rivers.

Change led to increased differences. Economic differences grew between the traditional farming society and the newer industrial society. Regional differences also grew between the North, South, and West. The nation's leaders struggled to strengthen and unify a rapidly expanding nation. They also faced the challenge of creating a bold new foreign policy, as neighboring nations in Latin America won independence.

Why Study History? Today, we live in an era of rapid technological change. Our age is not the first time Americans have faced a revolution in technology. In the early 1800s, as today, new inventions changed forever the way people lived. To focus on this connection, see the *Why Study History?* feature, "Technology Continues to Change Our Lives," in this chapter.

Viewing History A New Age of Steamboats

Steam Ferry, St. Louis *by French artist Leon Pomarede is one of the earliest paintings of St. Louis, Missouri. It shows steam-powered ships puffing down the Mississippi toward the city. In the early 1800s, steamboats and other new means of transportation made it easier for settlers to travel to the West. At the same time, new technology changed how goods were produced and how people worked.*

★ **What advantages do you think steamboats might have had over earlier forms of travel?**

American Events

1790 First American spinning mill opens

1793 Eli Whitney's cotton gin boosts textile industry

1806 Congress approves building the National Road

1807 Fulton's steamship makes record-breaking trip

1816 New tariff sparks sectional dispute

1823 Monroe Doctrine warns Europe not to recolonize the Americas

1785 1790 1795 1800 1805 | 1805 1810 1815 1820 1825

World Events

1793 World Event China rejects British trade

1802 World Event Child labor law enacted in Britain

1807 World Event Gas street lighting demonstrated in London

1815 World Event Napoleon defeated at Waterloo

★ 221

In Each Unit

- **Unit Opener** a two-page introduction to the contents and major theme of the unit, with fine art and quotations offering viewpoints on the theme.
- **History Through Literature** a two-page excerpt from a significant and pertinent work of American literature.

In Each Chapter

- **Chapter Opener** a two-page introduction that includes a time line, art, and a description of the chapter's Why Study History? feature.
- **As You Read** an introduction to each section, including questions to guide your reading and lists of vocabulary terms and historical people.
- **Section Reviews** questions and activities that test your understanding of each section.
- **Skills for Life** a step-by-step lesson that helps you to learn, practice, and apply a skill that will be useful throughout your life.
- **Linking...** Past and Present, or United States and the World, or History and Technology is a visual feature that shows interesting connections.
- **Biographies** portraits of and information about key people in American history.
- **Interdisciplinary Connections** footnotes that give connections to Geography, Economics, Civics, Arts, or Science.
- **Maps, Graphs, and Charts** visual tools that help you understand history and practice important geography and thinking skills.
- **Chapter Review and Activities** two pages to help you review key terms and ideas and practice valuable skills, with these special features:
    - *Using Primary Sources,* a primary source excerpt with questions that help you recognize different points of view.
    - *Activity Bank,* Interdisciplinary Activity, Career Skills Activity, Citizenship Activity, Internet Activity.
    - *Eyewitness Journal,* a role-playing and writing activity that helps you understand differing viewpoints.
    - *Critical Thinking and Writing,* questions and exercises that go beyond simple recall.

Special Features

- **Why Study History?** This feature highlights the relevance of history. Historical ideas and events are linked to American life today and to your life in particular.
- **AmericanHeritage® Magazine History Happened Here** The editors of American Heritage Magazine are your guides to interesting historic sites throughout the nation.

Viewpoints: Sources in American History

- Located after the last unit, two readings per chapter, including eyewitness accounts, historical documents, and literature selections.

Reference Section

- Includes an Atlas, a Gazetteer, a Glossary, the Declaration of Independence, the Constitution of the United States, information about the fifty states, information about the Presidents of the United States, and an Index.

Researching on the Internet

The Internet and the World Wide Web

The **Internet** is a global computer network that began in the 1960s as a U.S. Department of Defense project linking university computer science departments. The Internet has since grown to include millions of business, governmental, educational, and individual computers around the world. The **World Wide Web,** or "the Web" for short, is a collection of linked electronic files. Using programs called browsers, Internet users can find out what files are available on the Web and then access those files.

Searching the Internet

There are two basic ways to find information on the Internet. The first is to go directly to the Web site that contains the information you want. Each Web site has its own address, called a **URL,** or Universal Resource Locator. (For example, http://www.phschool.com is the URL of the Prentice Hall Web site.) Of course, this method only works if you know the appropriate URL. Also, the Web sites sometimes change URLs or disappear altogether.

The second way is to search the Web for information on your chosen topic. Using a **search engine,** such as Infoseek or Yahoo!, you type the key words representing the topic you want to research. The search engine will then scan the Internet and list Web sites that pertain in some way to your topic.

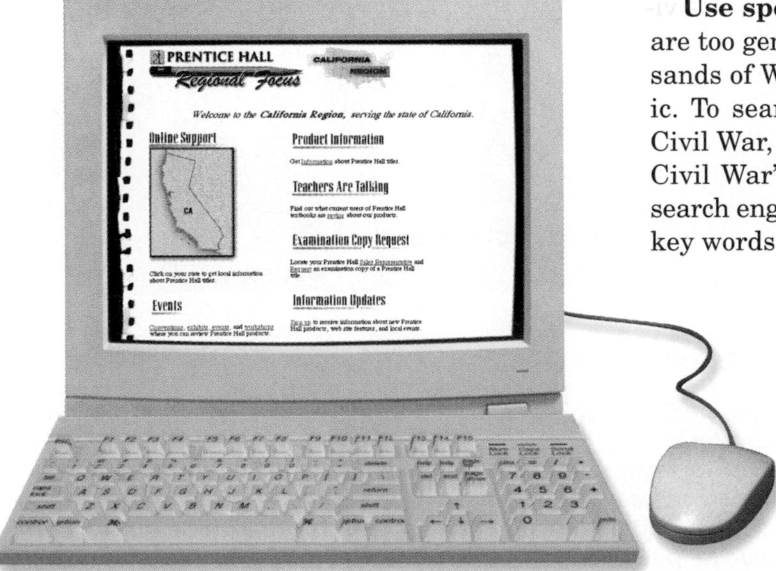

Whichever method you choose, you will encounter Web sites containing **hyperlinks.** These appear on your screen as colored or underlined text or as icons. Hyperlinks act as doorways to other documents. When you click your mouse on hyperlinked text or graphics, an entirely new document appears on your screen. That document may come from the same computer as the Web site you just left, or from one that is thousands of miles away.

As you search the Internet and arrive at various sites, you should pay careful attention to the source of the information you find. Is the source a government agency, or a university, or a private company, or an individual? Not all sources are equally accurate or reliable.

Tips for Successful Searches

Keep your search focused. Because the Internet contains so much interesting and varied information, it is easy to "wander off" into other parts of the Internet and forget about the information that you are trying to locate. To avoid this problem, it is a good idea to establish a specific research goal before you begin your Internet research.

Make bookmarks for your favorite Web sites. A bookmark is a note to your computer to "remember" the location of the Web site you may want to return to. You can reach any bookmarked site from any other site with a simple click of your mouse.

Use specific key words. If your key words are too general, your search might turn up thousands of Web sites. Make your key words specific. To search for information on the American Civil War, for example, the key words "American Civil War" are preferable to "Civil War." Many search engines have useful tips on searching with key words.

Evaluate the quality of Internet information. Not all of the information available on the Internet is appropriate for your research. Ask a teacher, parent, or librarian for help in evaluating the reliability and appropriateness of Web sites and information.

Unit 1

Connecting With Past Learnings: Reviewing Our Early Heritage

What's Ahead

Viewing UNIT THEMES **A Meeting of Different Cultures**

George Catlin, an American artist of the 1800s, painted LaSalle Claiming Louisiana for France, April 9, 1682. *As Native Americans watch, newly arrived French explorers gather around a flag and a cross. Encounters and exchanges between Europeans and Native Americans helped form the roots of American society.* ★ **In addition to Europeans and Native Americans, what other people have helped shape American society?**

Unit Theme Origins

Over thousands of years, Native Americans formed diverse societies throughout North America. In the 1500s and 1600s, Europeans and Africans began to arrive in the Americas. The blending and clashing of these three cultures helped shape the course of modern American life.

Along the Atlantic coast of North America, settlers from England established 13 colonies. English political traditions would form the basis for the American government today.

How did people of the time view American origins? They can tell you in their own words.

Viewpoints on American Origins

“Roots have spread out from the Tree of the Great Peace, one to the north, one to the east, one to the south, and one to the west.”

Treaty forming an alliance among Iroquois nations (1500s)

“The people are a collection of diverse nations in Europe as French, Dutch, Germans, Swedes, Danes, Finns, Scotch, Irish, and English.”

William Penn, founder of Pennsylvania (1685)

“A democracy... is when ... power is lodged in a council consisting of all the members and where every member has the privilege of a vote. ... Every man has the privilege freely to deliver his opinion concerning the common affairs.”

John Wise, Massachusetts minister (1717)

Activity **Writing to Learn** The peoples who first settled in North America came from many different backgrounds. Think about your school and your community. Then, make a list of the things that can help different people to live together without conflict.

Chapter 1

Focus on Geography

Prehistory–Present

What's Ahead

Section 1
Five Themes of Geography

Section 2
Maps and Mapmaking

Section 3
American Lands and Climates

The United States of America is blessed with a beautiful, diverse, and valuable natural environment. In this chapter, you will study geography in general and the geography of our nation in particular. You will learn about the landforms, physical regions, natural resources, and climates of the United States.

Several tools will aid you in your study. Geographers have developed five themes to help you understand the relationship between geography and history. Various kinds of maps will also prove useful.

Why Study History? In the months ahead, you will see how geography has influenced the history, the government, and the economy of the United States. You will also study how people's actions affect the natural environment. You can learn about the vital importance of one natural resource and how you can help preserve it by reading this chapter's *Why Study History?* feature, "We All Need Water."

American Events

1500s Early encounters between Europeans and Native Americans

1600s Growing numbers of enslaved Africans in the Americas

Prehistory | 1500 | 1600 | 1700

World Events

1500s World Event Europeans explore the Americas

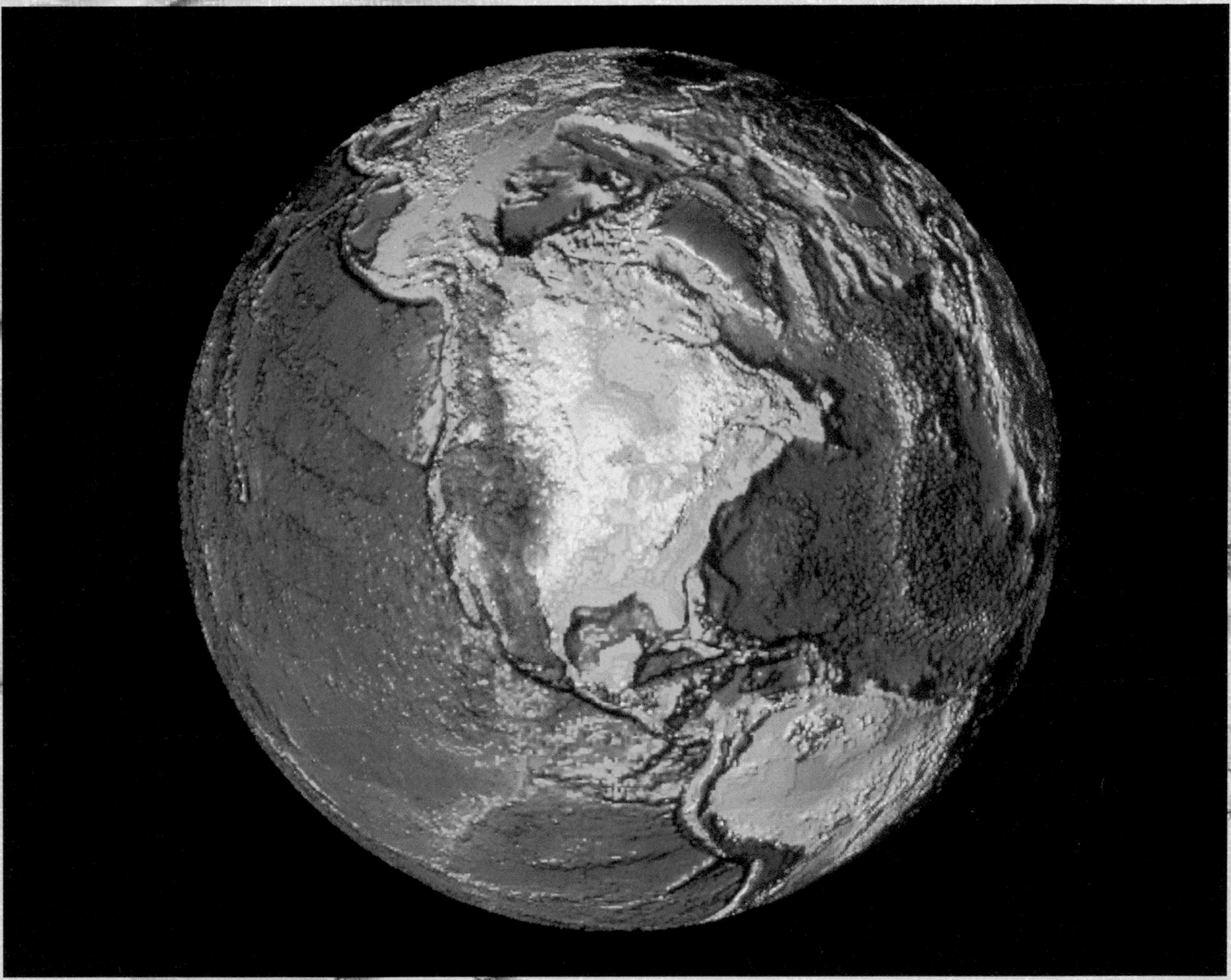

The View From Space

This picture was taken by a satellite in orbit around the Earth. You are looking directly at North America. The colors are enhanced to highlight the Earth's physical features. Green represents lowlands and orange represents highlands.

★ **What other continents are visible in this satellite photograph?**

1800s Migration to the Pacific Coast increases

1900s Industrialization affects the natural environment

Present Efforts to protect the environment increase

1700 **1800** **1900** **Present**

1700s World Event European states struggle for control of North America

1800s World Event Millions of immigrants move to the United States

Five Themes of Geography

As You Read

Explore These Questions

- What are the five themes of geography?
- How do people and their natural environment interact?
- What are some causes and effects of the movement of people?

Define

- geography
- history
- latitude
- longitude
- irrigate

SETTING the Scene If you read almost any newspaper, you will find stories about the land around you. One story might argue that building a dam will be harmful to a river. Another might announce the discovery of oil. To understand these and other issues, we need to understand geography.

Geography and History

Geography is the study of people, their environments, and their resources. Geographers ask how the natural environment affects the way we live and how we, in turn, affect the environment. By showing how people and the land are related, geography helps to explain both the past and the present.

Geography is closely linked to history. **History** is an account of what has happened in the lives of different peoples. Both historians and geographers want to understand how the characteristics of a place affect people and events.

To help show the connection between geography and history, geographers have developed five themes. The themes are location, place, interaction between people and their environment, movement, and region.

Location

Where did this event happen? Where is this place? Both historians and geographers often ask such questions. Finding the answers involves the geographic theme of location.

Exact location

As you study American history, you will sometimes need to know the absolute, or exact, location of a place. For example, where, exactly, is Washington, D.C., the nation's capital?

To describe the exact location of Washington, D.C., geographers use a grid of numbered lines on a map or globe that measure latitude and longitude. Lines of **latitude** measure distance north and south from the Equator. Lines of **longitude** measure distance east and west from the Prime Meridian, which runs through Greenwich (GREHN ihch), England.

The exact location of Washington, D.C., is 39 degrees (°) north latitude and 77 degrees (°) west longitude. In writing, this location is often shortened to 39°N/77°W. The Gazetteer in the Reference Section of this book provides the exact location of many important places in American history.

Relative location

Sometimes it is more useful to know the relative location of a place, or its location in relation to some other place. Is Washington, D.C., on the east or west coast of the United States? Is it north or south of Richmond, Virginia? These questions involve relative location.

Knowing relative locations will help you see the relationship between places. Is a place located near a lake, river, or other source of water and transportation? Is it inland or on the coast? Answers to such ques-

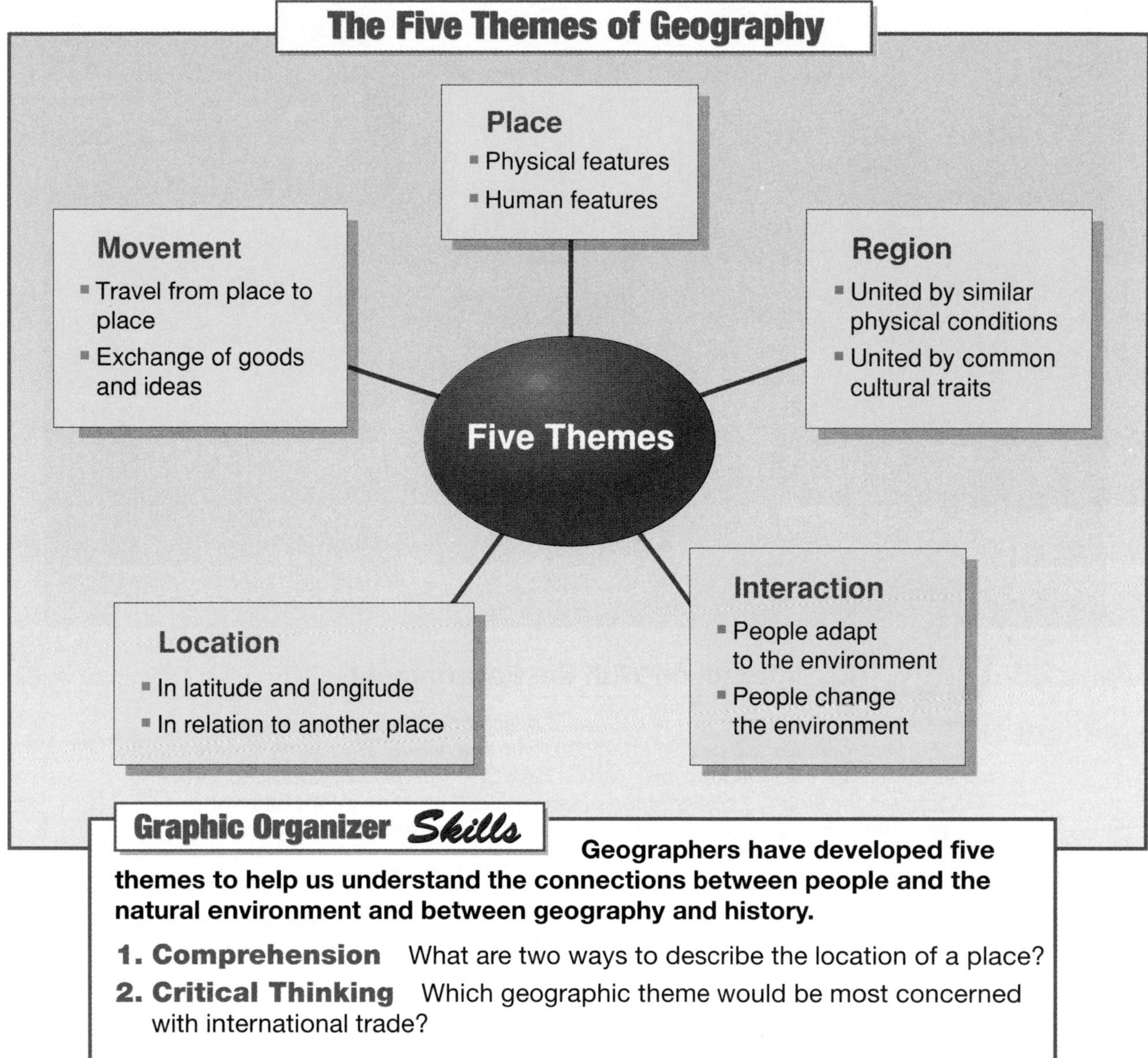

The Five Themes of Geography

Graphic Organizer *Skills* **Geographers have developed five themes to help us understand the connections between people and the natural environment and between geography and history.**

1. **Comprehension** What are two ways to describe the location of a place?
2. **Critical Thinking** Which geographic theme would be most concerned with international trade?

tions help explain why cities grew where they did. Chicago, Illinois, for instance, developed at the center of water, road, and railroad transportation in the Midwest.

Place

A second geography theme is place. Geographers generally describe a place in terms of both physical and human features.

The physical features of a place include climate, soil, plant life, animal life, and bodies of water. For example, New England has a hilly terrain, a rocky coast, and many deep harbors. Because of these physical features, early Native Americans of the region turned to fishing for a living.

People help to shape the character of a place through their ideas and actions. The human features of a place include the kinds of houses people build as well as their means of transportation, ways of earning a living, languages, and religions.

Think of the human features of the American frontier. In the forests of the frontier, early settlers built log cabins. On the grassy plains, where trees were scarce, some settlers built their homes out of sod, clumps of earth, and grass.

Viewing History **Interaction With the Environment**

Chicago is one of several major cities that dot the shores of Lake Michigan. Before people interacted with the natural environment, only dense forests encircled the lake. Notice how Chicago has extended into Lake Michigan through the construction of large piers. ★ **How might lakeshore cities like Chicago have a negative impact on the natural environment?**

Interaction

Interaction between people and their environment is a third theme of geography. Throughout history, people have adapted to and changed their natural environment.

For example, ancient hunters in the Americas learned to plant seeds and grow food crops. This adaptation greatly affected their lives. No longer did they have to move from place to place in search of food.

Agriculture was impossible in the arid Imperial Valley of southeastern California until irrigation canals were built in the 1900s. The canals bring water from the Colorado River. Today, the Imperial Valley is a very productive farming region.

Later, Native Americans in the Southwest found ways to **irrigate,** or bring water to, the desert. They dug ditches that channeled water from the Salt and Gila rivers. In this way, they were able to change arid, unproductive land into farmland.

In the 1860s, railroad builders in the United States changed the natural environment in order to improve transportation. They wanted to link the Atlantic and Pacific coasts. The railroad workers blasted through mountains and built bridges across rivers. When the project was completed, a railroad line stretched across the nation, linking the eastern and western parts of the United States.

Today, advanced technology allows people to alter their environment dramatically. People have invented ways to take oil from beneath the ocean floor. They have cut down forests to build communities. They have wiped out pests that destroy crops. Such changes have brought great benefits. They have also created new problems, such as air and water pollution.

Movement

A fourth geographic theme involves the movement of people, goods, and ideas. Movement occurs because people and resources are scattered unevenly around the globe. To get what they need or want, people travel from place to place. As they meet other people, they exchange ideas and technology as well as goods.

History provides many examples of the movement of people and ideas. The first people who came to the Americas were hunters following animal herds. Much later, people from all over the world moved to the United States in search of political and religious freedom. They brought with them customs and beliefs that have helped shape American life.

Today, the movement of goods links the United States with all parts of the world. For example, American producers ship goods such as grain and computers to Europe and Africa. Meanwhile, we rely on materials such as oil and tin from other parts of the world.

Region

Geographers study regions. A region is an area of the world that has similar, unifying characteristics. The characteristics of a region may be physical, such as its climate or landforms. For example, the Great Plains is considered a region because it has fairly level land, very hot summers, very cold winters, and little rainfall. The Pacific Coast region, meanwhile, is known for its rugged mountains, dense forests, and scenic ocean shore.

A region's characteristics may also be human and cultural. San Francisco's Chinatown is a region because Chinese Americans there have preserved their language and culture. In New York City, Broadway is a theater district where many plays are performed. In Chicago, the Loop is a downtown area where there are office buildings and museums.

A region can be any size. It can be as large as the United States or as small as a neighborhood. Within one city, there could be several regions. For example, there may be a parkland area known for its natural beauty. There may be a residential area where people live in homes and apartments. There also may be a business district, occupied mostly by office buildings and stores.

★ Section 1 Review ★

Recall

1. **Define** **(a)** geography, **(b)** history, **(c)** latitude, **(d)** longitude, **(e)** irrigate.

Comprehension

2. Briefly describe the five themes of geography.
3. **(a)** Describe two examples of how the natural environment can affect the way people live. **(b)** Give two examples of problems that can result when people change the natural environment.
4. How has the movement of people helped shape American life?

Critical Thinking and Writing

5. **Synthesizing Information** How does the picture of the New England coast on page 17 illustrate the theme of place?
6. **Understanding Causes and Effects** How does modern technology affect the movement of people, goods, and ideas?

Activity **Using Geographic Themes** Use the five themes of geography to describe the neighborhood, community, or state in which you live. Develop your description by writing one or two sentences for each of the five themes.

Maps and Mapmaking

As You Read

Explore These Questions

- What different types of maps do people use?
- How do latitude and longitude help us to locate places?
- Why are today's maps more accurate than maps of the past?

Define

- globe
- cartographer
- map projection
- hemisphere
- standard tlme zone

Identify

- Equator
- Prime Meridian

SETTING the Scene In a tiny Indian fishing village in the early 1600s, a small group gathered around Samuel de Champlain. They watched closely as the French explorer pointed to the shore and then drew a sweeping line on a deerskin spread out on the ground. The line represented the coastline where they stood. Quickly, the Native American chief drew other lines on the informal map. A young man added piles of rocks to represent the village and nearby settlements.

Champlain and the Native Americans he met on Cape Ann in Massachusetts did not understand each other's languages. Yet they found a way to communicate. Together, they created a map of the local area. Champlain later used the map to aid him in exploring the Massachusetts coast. People today use maps, too, to help them locate places, judge distances, and follow routes.

Maps and Globes

To locate places, geographers use maps and globes. A map is a drawing of the Earth's surface. A **globe** is a sphere with a map of the Earth printed on it. Because a globe is the same shape as the Earth, it shows sizes and shapes accurately.

Geographers often use flat maps rather than globes. Unlike a globe, a flat map of the world allows you to see all of the Earth's surface at one time. It is easier to handle and can show more detail. Still, a flat map has the disadvantage that it distorts, or misrepresents, some parts of the Earth.

Map Projections

Mapmakers, or **cartographers,** have developed dozens of different map projections. **Map projections** are ways of drawing the Earth on a flat surface.

Each map projection has benefits and disadvantages. Some projections show the sizes of landmasses correctly but distort their shapes. Others give continents their true shapes but distort their sizes. Still other projections distort direction or distances.

Mercator projection

In 1569, Gerardus Mercator developed the Mercator projection, the best map of its day. For hundreds of years, sailors depended on the Mercator map. Mercator himself boasted of his map:

> “If you wish to sail from one port to another, here is a chart, and a straight line on it, and if you follow this line carefully you will certainly arrive at your destination.”

A globe is a map of the world.

A Mercator map shows the true shapes of landmasses, but it distorts size, especially for places that are far from the Equator. On a Mercator map, for example, Greenland appears as big as all of South America, even though South America is more than eight times larger!

Robinson projection

Today, many geographers use the Robinson projection. It shows the correct sizes and shapes of landmasses for most parts of the world. The Robinson projection also gives a fairly accurate view of the relationship between landmasses and water.

Kinds of Maps

Maps are part of our daily lives. You have probably read road or bus maps. On television, you have seen weather maps and maps of places in the news.

As you study history, you will use various maps. Examine the Geographic Atlas in the Reference Section of this book. There, you will find maps showing national and state boundaries as well as the physical features and natural resources of the United States.

Each kind of map serves a specific purpose. A political map shows boundaries that people have set up to divide the world into countries and states. A physical map shows natural features, such as mountains and rivers. A population map lets you see how many people live in a particular area. An economic map shows how people of a certain region make a living. A natural resource map helps you see links between the resources of an area and the way people use the land.

Still other kinds of maps include election maps, product maps, and battle maps. These maps also help you to see the connections between geography and history.

Map Projections

Robinson Projection

Mercator Projection

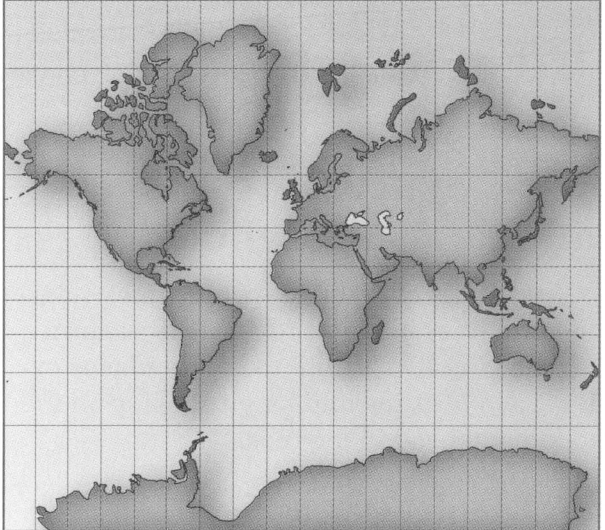

Geography *Skills* **Map projections make it possible for mapmakers to show a round world on a flat map.**

1. **Location** Use the map on page 10 to locate: **(a)** North America, **(b)** Africa, **(c)** Asia.
2. **Place** How does North America appear differently on the two projections?
3. **Critical Thinking** On the Mercator map, which areas are most distorted?

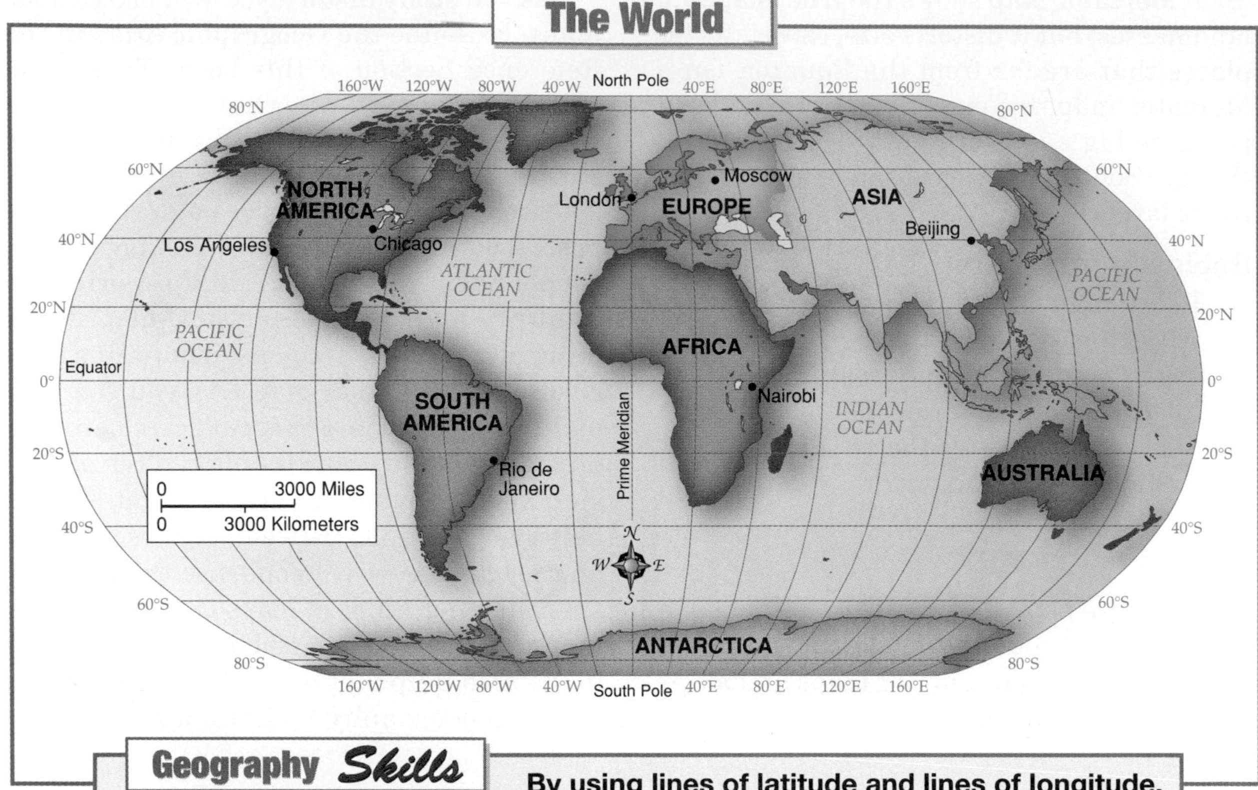

Geography *Skills* **By using lines of latitude and lines of longitude, one can locate any specific place in the world.**

1. **Location** On the map, locate: **(a)** Atlantic Ocean, **(b)** Pacific Ocean, **(c)** Europe, **(d)** North America, **(e)** Africa.
2. **Location** Which city is located at about 55°N/35°E?
3. **Critical Thinking** Which continents lie entirely in the Northern Hemisphere?

Latitude and Longitude

Most maps and globes include lines of latitude and lines of longitude. The lines form a grid, making it possible to locate places exactly. Each latitude and longitude line on the grid is measured in degrees (°).

Latitude

Look at the map of the world, above. Notice that lines of latitude run east and west. As you have read, lines of latitude measure distances north and south from the Equator.

The **Equator** is an imaginary line that lies at 0° latitude. It divides the Earth into two halves, called **hemispheres.**

The Northern Hemisphere lies north of the Equator. In the Northern Hemisphere, lines of latitude are numbered from 1°N to 90°N, where the North Pole is located.

The Southern Hemisphere lies south of the Equator. There, lines of latitude are numbered from 1°S to 90°S, where the South Pole is located.

Longitude

Lines of longitude on a map or globe run north and south between the two poles. They measure distances east and west from the **Prime Meridian,** which lies at 0º longitude and runs through the Royal Observatory in Greenwich, England. Unlike lines of latitude, lines of longitude are not parallel to each other. They converge at the North Pole and South Pole. The distance between longitude lines is greatest at the Equator. The distance

Skills FOR LIFE

Critical Thinking | Managing Information | Communication | **Maps, Charts, and Graphs**

Reading a Map

How Will I Use This Skill?

Maps are not used just to study history and geography. They can also help you plan a trip, understand current events, or find out about the weather. Knowing how to read a map can keep you from getting lost, or help you find your way again.

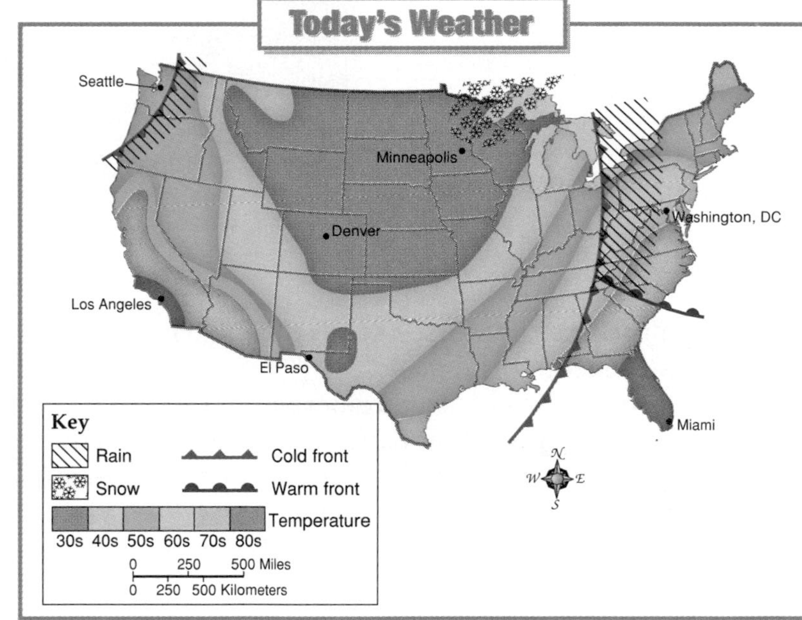

LEARN the Skill

You can read a map by following these three steps:

❶ Identify the topic of the map. The **title** will tell you the subject of the map. The **key** explains the meanings of the map's symbols and colors.

❷ Look at a map's **scale** to determine distances between places. The scale shows you how many inches on the map equal how many actual miles or kilometers.

❸ Study the **directional arrow** to identify north, south, east, and west on a map.

PRACTICE the Skill

Use the steps above and the map on this page to answer the following questions.

❶ (a) What is the title of the map? (b) How is a cold front shown on the map? (c) According to the color key, what is today's temperature in Los Angeles? In Denver?

❷ (a) On the scale, how many miles are represented by 3/4 of an inch? (b) What is the approximate distance from Washington, DC, to Miami in miles? In kilometers?

❸ (a) What is the northernmost city shown on the map? (b) What direction would you travel from El Paso to reach a place where it is snowing?

APPLY the Skill

With a group of classmates, create a map of your classroom. Include a title, plus a key that explains what symbols represent doors, windows, desks, and other features. Use a compass or the sun to determine north, south, east, and west. Use a tape measure to measure the room and create a scale.

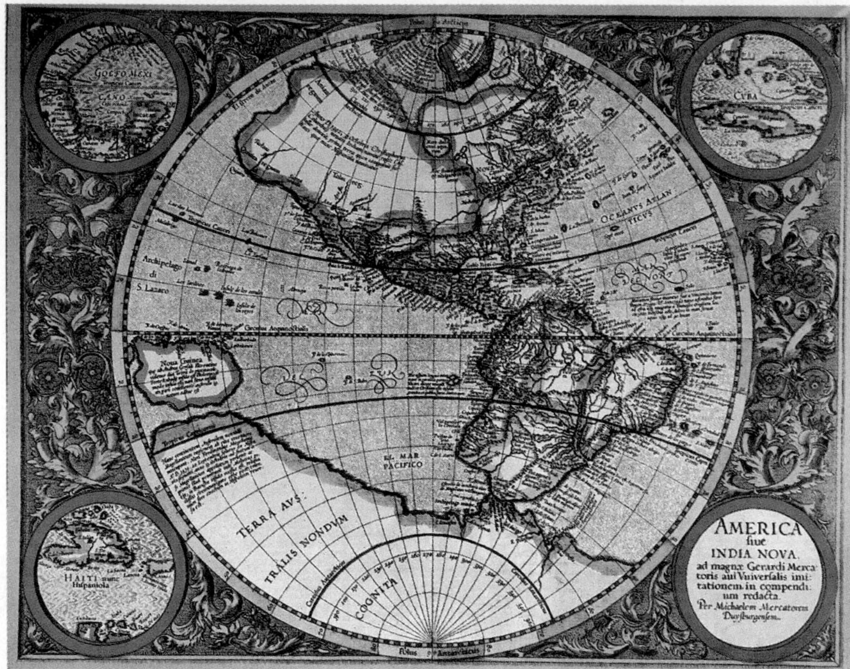

Viewing HISTORY **Early Map of the Americas**

This 1595 map distorts the true shapes of North America and South America. Gerardus Mercator, the map's creator, refers to the Americas as New India. Maps of the 1500s may not have been totally accurate, but they were very artistic. ★ **Why are today's maps much more accurate than those of several centuries ago?**

between the lines decreases as they approach and finally meet at the poles.

Lines of longitude are numbered from 1° to 179° east or west longitude. The line of longitude at 180° lies on the opposite side of the world from the Prime Meridian.

The circle formed by the Prime Meridian and 180° divides the Earth into the Eastern and Western hemispheres. The Eastern Hemisphere includes most of Europe, Africa, and Asia. The Western Hemisphere includes North America and South America.

Locating places

To locate places, you must combine latitude and longitude. Look at the map on page 10. Chicago is located north of the Equator at about 42°N latitude. It lies west of the Prime Meridian at about 88°W longitude. Its location is 42°N/88°W. Use the United States map in the Reference Section to find the exact location of your state capital.

Time Zones

Lines of longitude are also used to help us know what time it is around the world. When it is 11 A.M. in Miami, Florida, it is 8 A.M. in Portland, Oregon. In Lagos, Nigeria, it is 5 P.M.

Why does time differ from place to place? The answer is that the Earth rotates on its axis. As the Earth moves, the sun appears to rise in some places and to set in others. Throughout the world, people determine time by this rising and setting of the sun.

To make it easier to tell time around the world, a system of **standard time zones** was set up in 1884. Under this system, the world was divided into 24 times zones. Standard time is measured from the Prime Meridian, which runs through Greenwich, England.

When it is noon in Greenwich, it is before noon (A.M.) in places west of Greenwich. It is after noon (P.M.) in places east of Greenwich.

$ Connections With Economics

In the United States, the Daylight Saving Time system provides people with more usable hours of daylight. From April to October, clocks are set ahead one hour. The total amount of daylight remains the same, but more daylight hours are available for outdoor activities in the late afternoon and evening.

If you travel east from Greenwich across Europe, Africa, or Asia, you add one hour as you move through each time zone.

Making Accurate Maps

The oldest surviving map in the world today was created by an ancient cartographer on a clay tablet sometime around 2300 B.C. Ever since, geographers have worked to make maps more accurate.

Early mapmaking

Early cartographers relied on information from sailors and travelers as well as legends to create their maps. As a result, their maps included many errors. Five hundred years ago, European mapmakers did not even know that North America and South America existed!

Since the 1500s, mapmaking has improved greatly. Daring sailors gained information about uncharted lands. Explorers studied ocean currents and wind patterns around the world. Scientists learned more about the Earth itself.

Using satellites

Today, mapmakers depend on computers and satellites. By taking photographs from space, satellites provide information that no one on the ground can furnish. As a result, maps are more accurate than ever before.

Launched in 1972, Landsat 1 was the first satellite specially designed to study the Earth's surface from space. The unmanned spacecraft took pictures from about 570 miles (900 km) above the Earth. Each photo showed a land area that an airplane would need 1,000 pictures to depict. Within two years, Landsat photographed more than 80 percent of the Earth's surface.

Images from Landsat 1 and later satellites provided extraordinary help to mapmakers. They revealed uncharted islands. They enabled scientists to see entire mountain ranges and drainage basins at a single glance. They allowed surveys of remote areas, such as the polar regions and oceans. Based on these images, cartographers corrected old maps and mapped some places for the first time.

Today, geographers rely on satellites for more and more information about the Earth. Geographers can use satellite information to chart changes in population density and economic activity. They can also learn more about weather patterns, vegetation, pollution, and mineral resources.

★ Section 2 Review ★

Recall

1. **Locate** **(a)** North America, **(b)** South America, **(c)** Asia, **(d)** Arctic Ocean.
2. **Identify** **(a)** Equator, **(b)** Prime Meridian.
3. **Define** **(a)** globe, **(b)** cartographer, **(c)** map projection, **(d)** hemisphere, **(e)** standard time zone.

Comprehension

4. Why does a globe show the Earth more accurately than a flat map?
5. How can we use latitude and longitude to find the exact location of a place?
6. How have satellites made maps more accurate than ever before?

Critical Thinking and Writing

7. **Applying Information** Describe some of the special features of a road map.
8. **Understanding Causes and Effects** Before the 1500s, why were European maps of the world very inaccurate?

Activity **Making a Weather Map** You are the meteorologist for a local television news program. Make a map of your region, showing your forecast for tomorrow's weather conditions. You may wish to use the map on page 11 as a model.

3 American Lands and Climates

As You Read

Explore These Questions

- What are the eight physical regions of the United States?
- How are rivers and lakes important to the United States?
- What are the major climates of North America?

Define

- isthmus
- mountain
- elevation
- hill
- plain
- plateau
- tributary
- weather
- climate
- precipitation
- altitude
- El Niño

SETTING the Scene North America is the world's third largest continent. As the World map in the Reference Section shows, the Atlantic Ocean washes the eastern shore of North America. The Pacific Ocean laps at its western shore. To the north lies the icy Arctic Ocean. To the south, an **isthmus** (IHS muhs), or narrow strip of land, links North America to South America.

North America has many different features. For example, one of the world's highest mountains, Mount McKinley, is in Alaska. Yet one of the lowest points on the Earth is in Death Valley, California. You will find many examples of contrast as you read more about the American land.

Types of Landforms

North America has many landforms, or natural features. There are high mountains, rolling hills, and long rivers. There are grassy plains, dense forests, and barren deserts. Within these different landscapes are four basic landforms: mountains, hills, plains, and plateaus (pla TOHZ).

Mountains are high, steep, rugged land. They rise to an **elevation,** or height, of at least 1,000 feet (300 m) above the surrounding land. Few people live on steep mountainsides. Yet people often settle in valleys between mountains.

Hills are areas of raised land that are lower and more rounded than mountains. Farming is often possible on hilly land. Therefore, more people live in hilly areas than on mountains.

Plains are broad areas of fairly level land. Few plains are totally flat. Most are gently rolling. Plains do not usually rise much above sea level. People often settle on plains because it is easy to build farms, roads, and cities on the level land.

Plateaus are plains that range from a few hundred to many thousand feet above sea level. With enough rain, plateaus can be good for farming. Mountains surround some plateaus. Such plateaus are often very dry because the mountains cut off rainfall.

Mountains, hills, plains, and plateaus are only a few of the special words that geographers use. For definitions of other geographic terms, you may refer to the Dictionary of Geographic Terms on pages 24–25.

Physical Regions of North America

The landforms of North America form seven major physical regions. The United States also includes an eighth region, the Hawaiian Islands in the Pacific Ocean. (See the map on page 19.)

The seven physical regions of North America offer great

The red fox is native to North America.

contrasts. In some regions, the land is fertile. There, farmers plant crops and reap rich harvests. Other regions have natural resources such as coal and oil.

Pacific Coast

The westernmost region of North America is the Pacific Coast. It includes high mountain ranges that stretch from Alaska to Mexico. In the United States, some of these western ranges hug the Pacific Ocean. The Cascades and Sierra Nevada* stand a bit farther inland. Some important cities of the Pacific Coast are Seattle, Portland, San Francisco, and Los Angeles.

An important feature of the Pacific Coast region is the San Andreas Fault. This is a 600-mile (970 km) fracture in the Earth's crust. It runs through California from northwest to southeast. Movement of the Earth's crust along this fault causes earthquakes.

In 1906, a powerful earthquake in the city of San Francisco destroyed thousands of buildings and killed approximately 3,000 people. In 1994, another strong earthquake caused significant damage and loss of life in Los Angeles.

Intermountain region

East of the coast ranges is the Intermountain region. It is a very rugged region of mountain peaks, high plateaus, deep canyons, and deserts. The Grand Canyon, which is more than 1 mile (1.6 km) deep, and the Great Salt Lake are natural features of this region. Salt Lake City and Phoenix are among the few major cities of the Intermountain region.

*Sierra (see EHR uh) is the Spanish word for mountain range. Nevada is Spanish for snowy. Spanish explorers were the first to see these snow-covered mountains.

Viewing History **Mount Rainier**

The beauty of the Cascade Mountains can be seen at Mount Rainier National Park in the state of Washington. In spring, colorful wildflowers and evergreen trees contrast sharply with Mount Rainier's snowcap. ★ **In what physical region are the Cascades located?**

Rocky Mountains

The Rocky Mountains stretch from Alaska through Canada into the United States. They include the Bitterroot Range in Idaho and Montana, the Big Horn Mountains in Wyoming, and the Sangre de Cristo Mountains in Colorado and New Mexico. In Mexico, the Rocky Mountains become the Sierra Madre (MAH dray), or mother range.

The Rockies include some of the highest peaks in North America. Many peaks are more than 14,000 feet (4,200 m) high. Throughout history, people have described the mountains' rugged beauty and grandeur.

The Rockies, however, were a serious barrier to settlement of the United States. When settlers moved west in the 1800s, crossing the Rockies posed great hardships. Some people decided to stay and live in the Rockies. Today, Denver is a major city in the region.

Interior Plains

Between the Rockies in the West and the Appalachian Mountains in the East is a large lowland area called the Interior Plains. The dry western part of the Interior Plains is called the Great Plains. The eastern part is called the Central Plains.

According to scientists, a great inland sea once covered the Interior Plains. Today, some parts are rich in coal and petroleum.* Other parts offer fertile soil for farming and grassland for raising cattle. Chicago and Dallas are major cities on the Interior Plains.

Appalachian Mountains

The Appalachian Mountains run along the eastern part of North America. They stretch from Canada in the North to Georgia and Mississippi in the South. The Appalachians have different names in different places. For example, the Green Mountains, Alleghenies, and Great Smokies are all part of the Appalachian Mountains.

The Appalachians are lower and less rugged than the Rockies. The highest Appalachian peak is Mt. Mitchell in North Carolina, which is 6,684 feet (2,037 m) high. Still, early European settlers had a hard time crossing these heavily forested mountains.

Canadian Shield

The Canadian Shield is a lowland area that lies mostly in eastern Canada. The

*The Natural Resources map in the Reference Section shows where natural resources are located.

Viewing History: Interior Plains

Plains cover much of the central United States. They stretch from the Mississippi River to the Rocky Mountains and from Texas (shown at right) to Montana. The region is ideal for raising cattle. ★ **Why is this region ideal for raising cattle?**

▼ *Texas longhorn*

Viewing HISTORY **The Atlantic Coast**

In this picture, ocean waves crash against the rugged coast of Maine. The Atlantic puffin, native to the North Atlantic coast, is one example of the many sea birds that live in coastal regions. ★ **Why are so many cities built near an ocean?**

Atlantic puffin ➤

southern part extends into the United States. The region was once an area of high mountains. The mountains were worn away to low hills and plains. The Canadian Shield lacks topsoil for farming, but it is rich in minerals.

Coastal Plains

The region called the Coastal Plains is a fairly flat, lowland area that includes the Atlantic Plain and the Gulf Plain. The Atlantic Plain lies between the Atlantic Ocean and the foothills of the Appalachians. The Atlantic Plain is narrow in the North, where Boston and New York City are located. It broadens in the South to include all of Florida.

Another part of the Coastal Plains is the Gulf Plain, which lies along the Gulf of Mexico. The Gulf Plain has large deposits of petroleum. New Orleans and Houston are major cities of the Gulf Plain.

Hawaiian Islands

The Hawaiian Islands lie far out in the Pacific, about 2,400 miles (3,860 km) west of California. There are eight large islands and many small islands.

The islands are the visible tops of volcanoes that erupted through the floor of the Pacific Ocean. Some volcanoes are still active. Mauna Loa, on the island of Hawaii, is an active volcano that rises 13,680 feet (4,170 m) above sea level.

Rivers and Lakes

Great river systems crisscross North America. They collect runoff water from rains and melting snows and carry it into the oceans.

The mighty Mississippi

The Mississippi and Missouri rivers make up the longest and most important river system in the United States. This river system carries water through the Interior Plains into the Gulf of Mexico.

Many **tributaries,** or streams and smaller rivers, flow into the Mississippi-Missouri river system. Among these tributaries are the Ohio, Tennessee, Arkansas, and Platte rivers. These and other rivers provide water for the rich farmlands of the Interior Plains.

The Mississippi River also serves as a means of transportation. Today, barges carry freight up and down the river. As in the past, people travel by boat on the river.

Ansel Adams

Ansel Adams (1902–1984) is well known for his sharply focused black-and-white photographs of American landscapes. In 1946, the native Californian founded the California School of Fine Arts in San Francisco. From 1936 to 1973, he served as director of the Sierra Club, a group devoted to conservation of the natural environment. ★ **Why do you think Adams was so interested in conservation of the environment?**

Ansel Adams took this photo of the Grand Canyon.

The mighty Mississippi has inspired many admiring descriptions. Among them is this one from the 1937 film *The River:*

> “The Mississippi River runs to the Gulf.
> Carrying every drop of water, that flows down two thirds of the continent,
> Carrying every brook and rill, rivulet and creek,
> Carrying all the rivers that run down two thirds of the continent.
> The Mississippi runs to the Gulf of Mexico.”

The Colorado River

The Colorado River is another important river. It begins in the Rocky Mountains and flows through Colorado, Utah, Arizona, and Nevada. It forms the border between California and Arizona as it flows toward the Gulf of California. Smaller rivers feed into the Colorado. These include the Green River and the San Juan River.

The Colorado River created the Grand Canyon in Arizona. For millions of years, the river rushed over layers of rock, carving a deeper and deeper channel. Today, the Grand Canyon is one mile (1.6 km) deep and 18 miles (29 km) wide in some places.

There are several dams along the course of the Colorado River. These dams hold back the flow of the river. They help provide water and electricity to the people of the Southwest.

International borders

The Rio Grande and the St. Lawrence River serve as political boundaries. The Rio Grande is part of the border between the United States and Mexico. The St. Lawrence is part of the border with Canada.

Five large lakes, called the Great Lakes, also form part of the border between the United States and Canada. The Great Lakes are Superior, Michigan, Huron, Erie, and Ontario. Today, canals connect the Great Lakes, forming a major inland waterway that is important for commerce.

Weather and Climate

North America has a variety of weather patterns and climates. **Weather** is the condition of the Earth's atmosphere at any given time and place. It may be hot or cold, rainy or dry, or something in between.

Climate is the average weather of a place over a period of 20 to 30 years. Two main aspects of climate are temperature and **precipitation** (pree sihp uh TAY shuhn), or water that falls in the form of rain, sleet, hail, or snow.

Several factors affect climate. One factor is distance from the Equator. Lands near the Equator usually are hot and wet all year. Lands near the North and South poles are cold all year. **Altitude,** or height above sea

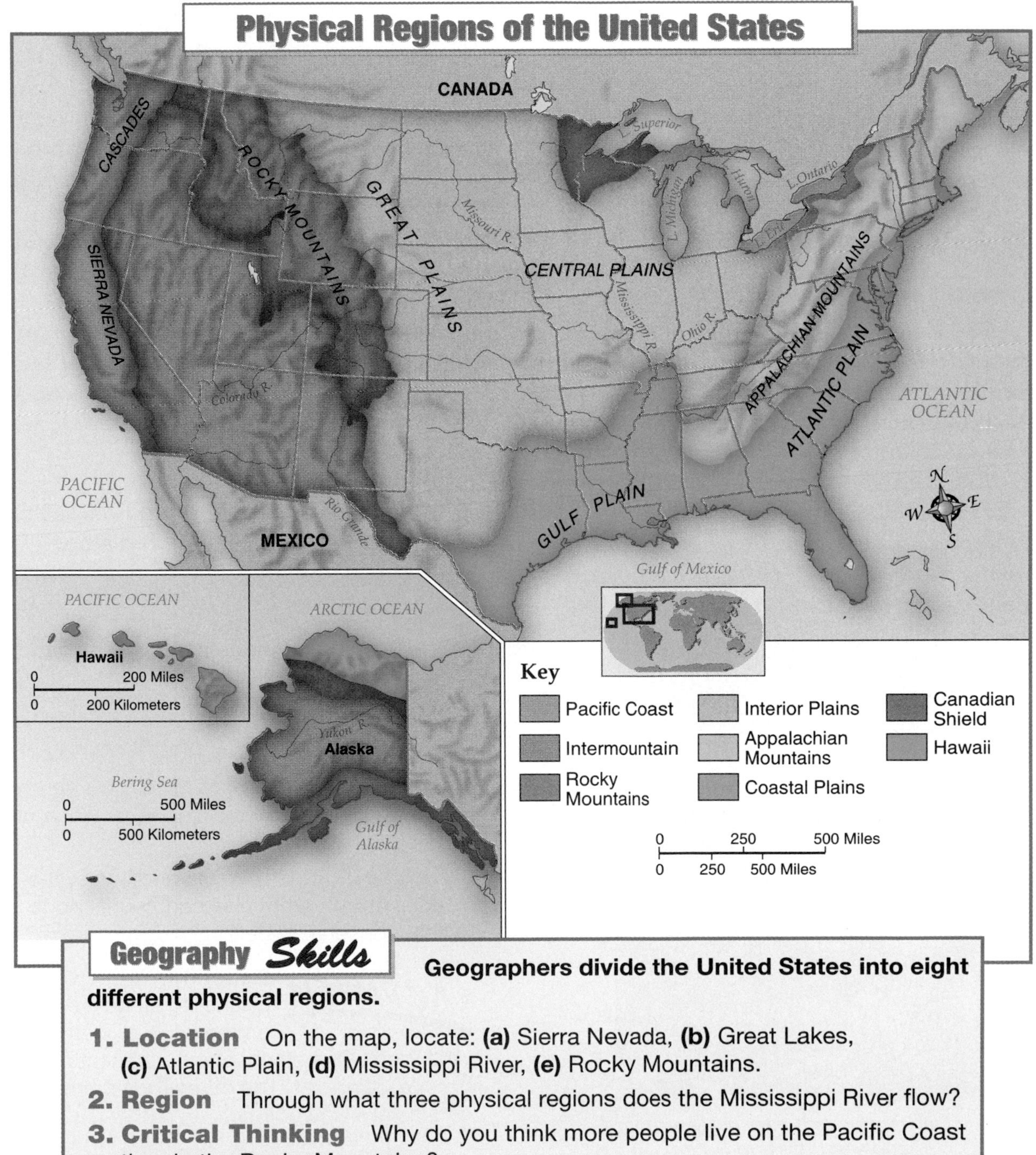

Geography *Skills* **Geographers divide the United States into eight different physical regions.**

1. **Location** On the map, locate: **(a)** Sierra Nevada, **(b)** Great Lakes, **(c)** Atlantic Plain, **(d)** Mississippi River, **(e)** Rocky Mountains.
2. **Region** Through what three physical regions does the Mississippi River flow?
3. **Critical Thinking** Why do you think more people live on the Pacific Coast than in the Rocky Mountains?

Why Study History?

Because We All Need Water

Historical Background

In the past century, the demand for water has risen greatly. More and more water is diverted from rivers to serve people's needs. As a result, some major rivers throughout the world have begun to run dry.

Connections to Today

The Colorado River is one of those rivers. (See page 18.) Today, the Colorado rarely empties into the Pacific Ocean. Instead, it gradually shrinks until its last traces evaporate in the desert heat of Mexico.

Today, the demand for Colorado River water is greater than the supply. In 1922, an agreement divided the river's water among seven western states. Other agreements guaranteed water rights to Native Americans and Mexico. Now, more than 20 million people rely on the Colorado River.

In California, this poster urges young people to conserve water.

Colorado River water disputes are often settled in court. Large cities such as Los Angeles and San Diego frequently accuse farmers of wasting water through old-fashioned irrigation methods. The farmers reply that cities are overbuilding and drawing too much water.

According to California Congressman George Miller, "The heart of the West is water. . . . It will be the most important commodity in dictating the future."

Connections to You

We all need water. You can help save water by taking these and other steps.

- Take short showers.
- Fix leaky faucets.
- Do only full loads in the dishwasher and clothes washer.
- Wash automobiles and water lawns infrequently.

1. **Comprehension** Why do past agreements on sharing Colorado River water not meet today's needs?
2. **Critical Thinking** In addition to the ideas above, what else can people do to help conserve water?

Debating Work with a partner to stage a debate on the issue of water rights in the West. One of you should present a farmer's viewpoint. The other should present a city official's viewpoint.

Linking United States and the World

The Philippines

United States

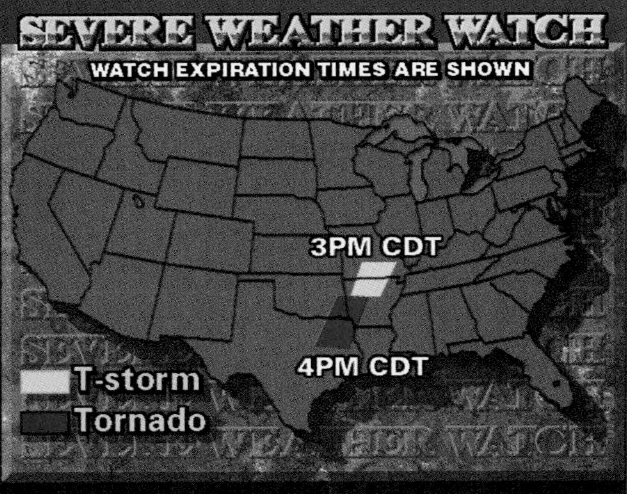

Weather Connections

Conditions around the world can affect your weather. Mount Pinatubo (above, left), a volcano in the Philippines, erupted in 1991. Gases and dust blocked some of the sun's rays and lowered temperatures in much of the world. In North America, though, the eruption led to a milder than average winter. ★ **What is the average winter like in the area where you live?**

level, also affects climate. In general, highlands are cooler than lowlands. Other factors that influence climate include ocean currents, wind currents, and mountains.

In the Pacific Ocean, wind and ocean currents interact to create the cyclical phenomenon called the **El Niño** (ehl NEEN yoh) Southern Oscillation. The temperature of Pacific Ocean water plays a major role in the phenomenon. During an El Niño period, the surface water of the eastern Pacific Ocean warms. During a La Niña (lah NEEN yah) period, ocean surface temperatures cool.

The Southern Oscillation affects weather patterns in nearly three quarters of the world. In the United States, for example, the warm ocean water of an El Niño helps to cause frequent and powerful storms in California and the Southwest. In Northeastern states, meanwhile, El Niño usually contributes to milder than normal winters.

North American Climates

The United States has 10 major climates. Look at the map on page 22 to see the locations of these climates.

Marine

The strip of land from southern Alaska to northern California is sometimes called the Pacific Northwest. This region has a mild, moist marine climate, with warm summers and cool winters. Moist winds from the Pacific Ocean bring mild temperatures and moisture that condenses and falls as rain or snow. The Pacific Northwest has many forests. This makes it the center of the lumber industry.

Mediterranean

Much of California has a Mediterranean climate. Winters are mild and wet. Summers are hot and dry. Farmers and fruit growers

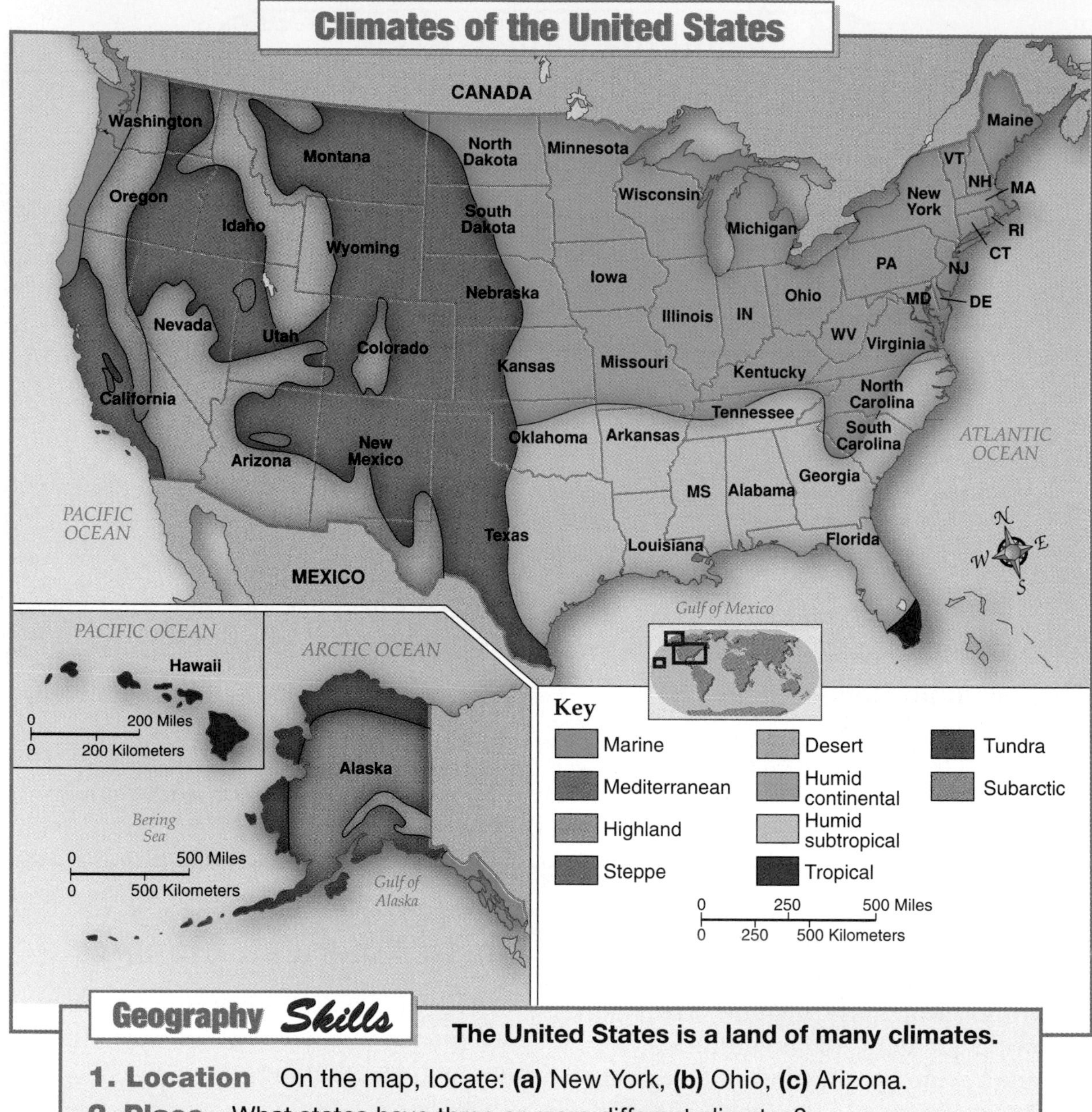

Geography Skills **The United States is a land of many climates.**

1. **Location** On the map, locate: **(a)** New York, **(b)** Ohio, **(c)** Arizona.
2. **Place** What states have three or more different climates?
3. **Critical Thinking** **(a)** Identify a state or part of a state where water is probably scarce. **(b)** Why is water in such short supply there?

must often irrigate the land. Because of the climate, this region produces crops that cannot be grown anywhere else in the country. For example, it produces almost all the nation's almonds, walnuts, olives, apricots, dates, and figs.

Highland

In the Cascades, Sierra Nevada, and Rocky Mountains, a highland climate brings cooler temperatures. Conditions in a highland climate vary according to altitude. For example, Mount Rainier in the state of Washington, at over 14,000 feet (4,200 m) above sea level, is snow-capped all year. During the spring and summer, runoff from melting snows provides water to the major rivers of the West. Many people vacation in the mountains so they can participate in winter sports. In summer, vacationers come to the mountains to escape the heat and enjoy the cool highland temperatures.

Desert and steppe

Much of the southwestern United States has a desert climate, with hot days and cold nights. This dry region stretches as far east as the Rockies. In the deserts of Nevada, Arizona, and southeastern California, there is almost no rainfall. In many areas, people irrigate the land so that they can grow crops.

East of the Rockies are the Great Plains. They have a steppe climate with limited rainfall. Summers are hot and winters are cold. Huge herds of buffaloes once grazed on the short grasses of the Great Plains. In the 1800s, settlers brought cattle to graze on the plains.

Humid continental

The Central Plains and the northeastern United States have a humid continental climate. This climate, with mild summers and cold winters, has more precipitation than the steppe. Tall prairie grasses once covered the Central Plains. Today, American farmers raise much of the world's food in this region.

At one time, the humid continental climate supported forests that covered much of the northeastern United States. Early European settlers cleared forests to build settlements and to grow crops. However, many forests remain, and the lumber industry thrives in some areas.

Tropical and humid subtropical

Southern Florida and Hawaii, located near the Equator, have tropical climates. The hot, humid conditions make these regions good for growing such crops as pineapples and citrus fruits. The warm tropical temperatures are also ideal for the tourism industry.

The southeastern United States has a humid subtropical climate. Warm temperatures and regular rainfall make this region ideal for growing crops such as cotton, soybeans, and peanuts.

Tundra and subarctic

Northern and western coastal regions of Alaska have a tundra climate. It is cold all year round. The rest of Alaska and northern Canada have a subarctic climate with long, cold winters and short summers. Farming is limited to a small fertile valley in southern Alaska. Almost one third of Alaska is covered by forest. Therefore, logging and the production of paper pulp are important industries.

★ Section 3 Review ★

Recall

1. **Locate** **(a)** North America, **(b)** Pacific Coast, **(c)** Intermountain region, **(d)** Rocky Mountains, **(e)** Interior Plains, **(f)** Appalachian Mountains, **(g)** Mississippi River, **(h)** Great Lakes.
2. **Define** **(a)** isthmus, **(b)** mountain, **(c)** elevation, **(d)** hill, **(e)** plain, **(f)** plateau, **(g)** tributary, **(h)** weather, **(i)** climate, **(j)** precipitation, **(k)** altitude, **(l)** El Niño.

Comprehension

3. Name the eight physical regions of the United States and describe one feature of each region.
4. How do rivers and lakes benefit the economy of the United States?
5. Describe the climate of the region where you live.

Critical Thinking and Writing

6. **Drawing Conclusions** Do you think more people live in the Appalachian Mountains or in the Rocky Mountains? Why?
7. **Making Decisions** If you could live anywhere in the United States, which physical region and climate would you choose? Explain.

★ ★

Activity **Making a Chart** You are the graphic designer for a popular vacation and travel magazine. Create a chart that lists and describes the 10 major climates of the United States.

Dictionary of Geographic Terms

The list below includes important geographic terms and their definitions. Sometimes, the definition of a term includes an example in parentheses. An asterisk (*) indicates that the term is illustrated above.

altitude height above sea level.

***archipelago** chain of islands. (Hawaiian Islands)

basin low-lying land area that is surrounded by land of higher elevation; land area that is drained by a river system. (Great Basin)

***bay** part of a body of water that is partly enclosed by land. (San Francisco Bay)

canal waterway made by people that is used to drain or irrigate land or to connect two bodies of water. (Eric Canal)

***canyon** deep, narrow valley with high, steep sides. (Grand Canyon)

***cape** narrow point of land that extends into a body of water. (Cape Cod)

climate pattern of weather in a particular place over a period of 20 to 30 years.

***coast** land that borders the sea. (Pacific Coast)

coastal plain lowland area lying along the ocean. (Gulf Plain)

continent any of seven large landmasses on the Earth's surface. (Africa, Antarctica, Asia, Australia, Europe, North America, South America)

continental divide mountain ridge that separates river systems flowing toward opposite sides of a continent.

***delta** land area formed by soil that is deposited at the mouth of a river. (Mississippi Delta)

desert area that has little or no moisture or vegetation. (Painted Desert)

directional arrow arrow on a map that always points north.

downstream in the direction of a river's flow; toward a river's mouth.

elevation the height above sea level.

fall line place where rivers drop from a plateau or foothills to a coastal plain, usually marked by many waterfalls.

foothills low hills at the base of a mountain range.

***gulf** arm of an ocean or sea that is partly enclosed by land, usually larger than a bay. (Gulf of Mexico)

hemisphere half of the Earth. (Western Hemisphere)

***hill** area of raised land that is lower and more rounded than a mountain. (San Juan Hill)

***island** land area that is surrounded by water. (Puerto Rico)

***isthmus** narrow strip of land joining two large land areas or joining a peninsula to a mainland. (Isthmus of Panama)

***lake** body of water surrounded entirely by land. (Lake Superior)

latitude the distance in degrees north and south from the Equator.

longitude the distance in degrees east or west from the Prime Meridian.

marsh lowland with moist soils and tall grasses.

***mountain** high, steep, rugged land that rises sharply above the surrounding land. (Mount McKinley)

mountain range chain of connected mountains. (Allegheny Mountains)

***mouth of a river** place where a river or stream empties into a large body of water.

ocean any of the four largest bodies of salt water on the Earth's surface. (Arctic, Atlantic, Indian, and Pacific Oceans)

***peninsula** piece of land that is surrounded by water on three sides. (Delmarva Peninsula)

piedmont rolling land along the base of a mountain range.

***plain** broad area of fairly level land that is generally close to sea level.

***plateau** large area of high, flat, or gently rolling land.

prairie large area of natural grassland with few or no trees or hills.

***river** large stream of water that empties into an ocean or lake or another river. (Pecos River)

***sea** large body of salt water that is smaller than an ocean. (Caribbean Sea)

sea level average level of the ocean's surface from which the height of land or depth of the ocean is measured.

***source of a river** place where a river begins.

steppe flat, treeless land with limited moisture.

***strait** narrow channel that connects two larger bodies of water. (Straits of Florida)

***tributary** stream or small river that flows into a larger stream or river.

upstream in the direction that is against a river's flow; toward a river's source.

***valley** land that lies between hills or mountains. (Shenandoah Valley)

***volcano** cone-shaped mountain formed by an outpouring of lava—hot, liquid rock—from a crack in the Earth's surface. (Mount St. Helens or Mauna Loa)

weather condition of the air at any given time and place.

Chapter 1 Review and Activities

★ Sum It Up ★

Section 1 Five Themes of Geography

- Geography is the study of people, their environments, and their resources.
- The five themes of geography help show the connection between geography and history.
- The five themes of geography are location, place, interaction, movement, and region.

Section 2 Maps and Mapmaking

- Each type of map projection has advantages and disadvantages.
- Latitude and longitude lines on maps enable us to locate places exactly.
- The use of computers and satellites has made modern mapmaking more accurate than the mapmaking of centuries ago.

Section 3 American Lands and Climates

- Mountains, plains, and many other types of landforms can be found in North America.
- There are eight major physical regions in the United States.
- Rivers and lakes provide many benefits to the people of the United States.
- A variety of factors interact to produce weather and climate conditions.
- The United States has 10 major climates.
- The climate of a region helps to determine some of the economic activities that take place in the region.

For additional review of the major ideas of Chapter 1, see ***Guide to the Essentials of American History*** or ***Interactive Student Tutorial CD-ROM,*** which contains interactive review activities, graphic organizers, and practice tests.

Reviewing the Chapter

Define These Terms

Match each term with the correct definition.

Column 1	Column 2
1. history	**a.** lines measuring distance east and west from the Prime Meridian
2. latitude	**b.** a mapmaker
3. longitude	**c.** lines measuring distance north and south from the Equator
4. cartographer	**d.** an account of what has happened in people's lives
5. precipitation	**e.** water that falls as rain, sleet, or snow

Explore the Main Ideas

1. How do geographers generally describe place?
2. How do people interact with their environment?
3. Why do all flat maps distort the shapes of continents and oceans?
4. Locate and describe three physical regions of the United States.
5. Why is the Mississippi River such an important waterway?
6. Locate and describe three climates found in the United States.

Geography Activity

Match the letters on the map with the following places:
1. North America, **2.** South America, **3.** Atlantic Ocean, **4.** Pacific Ocean, **5.** Isthmus of Panama, **6.** Great Lakes.
Location What ocean lies to the east of North America?

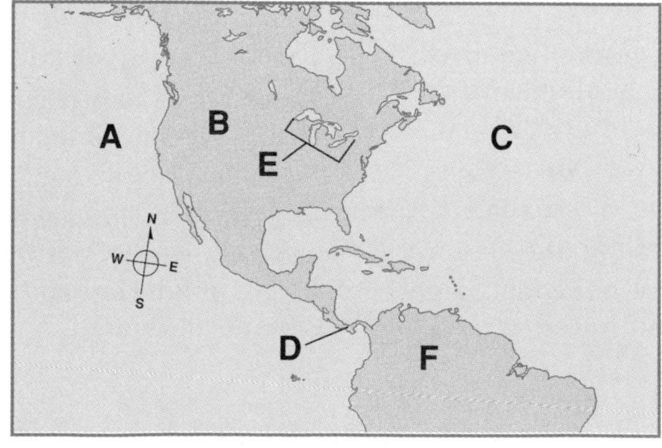

Critical Thinking and Writing

1. **Applying Information** Using the themes of geography, **(a)** describe the special geographic characteristics of the place where you live, **(b)** describe an example of how people in your community have adapted to or changed the natural environment.
2. **Evaluating Information** Which is more reliable: a map of North America from the 1500s or a map of North America from the 1900s? Explain the reasons for your choice.
3. **Synthesizing Information** Look at the picture of Mount Rainier that appears in Section 3 of this chapter. **(a)** Describe the physical region in which Mount Rainier is located. **(b)** Describe the climate of that region.
4. **Exploring Unit Themes** **Origins** How can the climate of a region affect people's economic activities in that region?

Using Primary Sources

In 1845, Lansford W. Hastings wrote a guide for people traveling to the West. In it he made the following predictions:

> “The time is not distant, when those wild forests, trackless plains, untrodden valleys . . . will present one grand scene of continuous improvements . . . when those vast forests shall have disappeared before the hardy pioneer; those extensive plains shall abound with innumerable herds of domestic animals; those fertile valleys shall groan under the weight of their abundant products.”

Source: *The Emigrants' Guide to Oregon and California*, Lansford W. Hastings, 1845.

Recognizing Points of View **(a)** What changes did Hastings expect from human interaction with the environment? **(b)** How did he feel about the predicted changes?

Activity Bank

Interdisciplinary Activity

Exploring the Arts Do research to find a song or poem about an American river. Read or sing the composition to the class. Then lead a group discussion on what the song or poem says about the river.

Career Skills Activity

Cartographers On a large sheet of paper, create a map of the United States. On the map, draw and label the 50 states. Then label the major physical regions and landforms of the United States.

Citizenship Activity

Using a Political Map Find a map that shows the Congressional districts in your state. Identify the district in which you live. Through research, find out the name of your district's representative in Congress. If an issue or question concerns you, you can write about it to your Congressperson and ask for a response.

Internet Activity

Use the Internet to find the official site of NASA (National Aeronautics and Space Administration). There you will find images of the Earth taken by satellites orbiting the Earth. Select a picture that interests you and, if possible, print it out. In a written report, describe what the picture shows and explain why the picture might be useful to a cartographer.

You are traveling across the United States from somewhere on the Atlantic Coast to somewhere on the Pacific Coast. List all the states that you are traveling through. Also, list and describe all the physical regions that you are crossing.

Chapter 2

A Meeting of Different Worlds Prehistory–1650

What's Ahead

Section 1 The First Americans

Section 2 Europeans Reach the Americas

Section 3 Africans Come to the Americas

Section 4 Rival Claims in North America

Thousands of years ago, the first people arrived in the Americas from Asia. Native Americans gradually developed a wide variety of economies and social organizations. At the same time, unique societies were also developing in Europe and Africa.

In the late 1400s, Europeans in search of trade sailed across the Atlantic and made contact with Native Americans. Later, Spain began to transport enslaved Africans to work on American plantations. As a result, Africans, too, became part of the new mix of peoples in the Americas.

Why Study History? Today, we take contact among different parts of the world for granted. You can see African art in European museums, or eat tacos in Japan. The pace of global exchange picked up around 500 years ago. To focus on this connection, see the *Why Study History?* feature, "You Live in a Shrinking World," in this chapter.

American Events

30,000–15,000 years ago Hunters from Asia cross land bridge to Americas

1300s Aztecs build powerful empire in Mexico

1492 Christopher Columbus reaches Caribbean Sea

Prehistory | **1200** | **1300** | **1400**

World Events

1100–1300 World Event European nations launch Crusades to Holy Land

1200–1400 World Event West African kingdom of Mali reaches its height

Viewing History: Crossing the Atlantic

This illustration by Johann Theodor de Bry shows Portugese ships in an ocean filled with sea monsters and flying fish. Beginning in the late 1400s, European explorers and conquerors set sail across the Atlantic Ocean. Their voyages had a lasting impact, not only on Europe and the Americas, but on West Africa as well.

★ **What does the figure in the upper left corner represent? Why do you think the artist included it?**

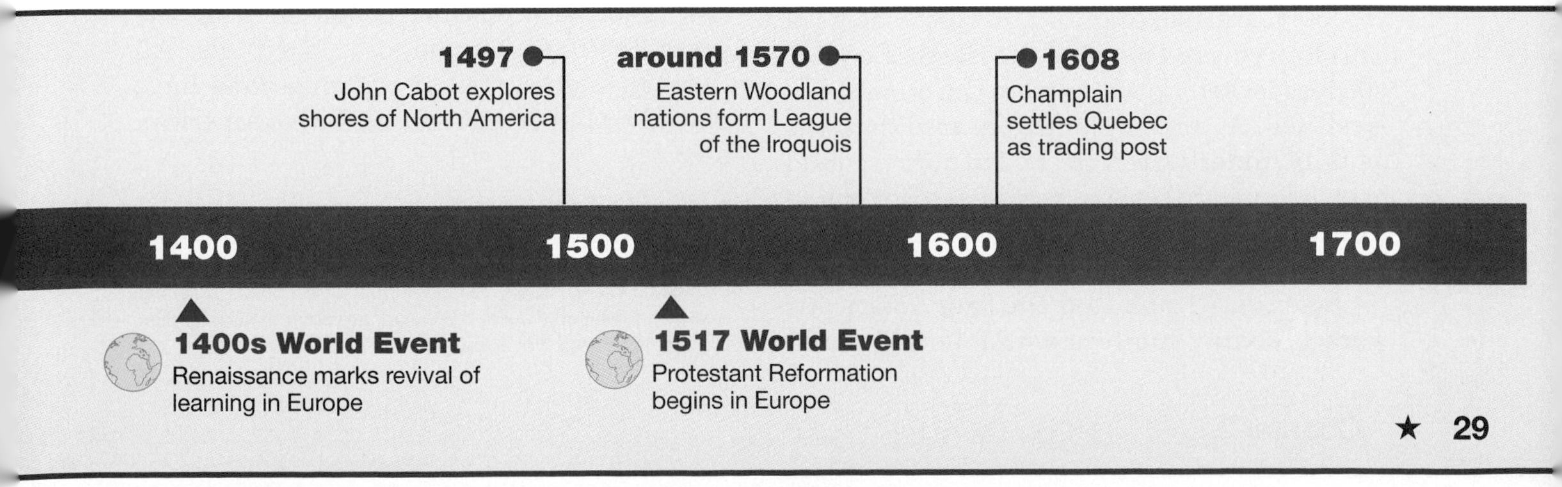

1497 John Cabot explores shores of North America

around 1570 Eastern Woodland nations form League of the Iroquois

1608 Champlain settles Quebec as trading post

1400 **1500** **1600** **1700**

1400s World Event Renaissance marks revival of learning in Europe

1517 World Event Protestant Reformation begins in Europe

The First Americans

As You Read

Explore These Questions

- What ways of life did Native Americans develop?
- What religious beliefs did Native American groups hold?
- How were Native American societies organized?

Define

- glacier
- culture
- tribe
- potlatch
- sachem

Identify

- Inuits
- Zuñis
- Hopis
- kachina
- Iroquois
- League of the Iroquois

Crouched low, the small band of hunters crept slowly forward. Ahead, a herd of bison grazed at the edge of a swamp. At a signal, the hunters leaped up, shouting loudly. The startled herd stampeded into the swamp. As the bison struggled in the deep mud, the hunters hurled their spears, bringing down many beasts.

Scenes much like this one took place on the Great Plains more than 10,000 years ago. Skillful hunters were among the first people to settle the Americas. Over many thousands of years, their descendants spread out across two continents. In the process, they developed many different ways of life.

Migration From Asia

Like other early peoples, the first Americans left no written records to tell us where they came from or when they arrived. However, scientists have found evidence that the first people reached the Americas sometime during the last ice age. Between 100,000 and 10,000 years ago, **glaciers,** or thick sheets of ice, often covered much of the Earth. Because glaciers locked up water from the oceans, sea levels fell. As a result land appeared that was usually under water. In the far north, a land bridge joined Siberia in northeastern Asia to Alaska in North America. Today, this land bridge is under the Bering Strait.

Scientists think that the first Americans were probably hunters who followed mammoths and other animals across the land bridge, from 30,000 to 15,000 years ago. Some time later, world temperatures rose. Glaciers melted, and water once again covered the land bridge. Over thousands of years, people spread throughout North America, Central America, and South America.

Culture Areas and Tribes

By the year 1500, a wide variety of Native American* cultures were thriving all across North America. A **culture** is the entire way of life developed by a people. It includes their homes, clothes, and government. It also includes the behavior, customs, ideas, beliefs, and skills that one generation passes to another.

The map to the right shows the 10 major culture areas of North America, north of Mexico. The peoples who lived within each area shared similar ways of living.

Within each culture area, many different tribes developed distinct ways of life. A **tribe** was a group of villages or settlements that saw itself as a distinct people sharing the same customs, language, and rituals. All through history, tribal organizations have played an important role in Native American life.

---

*Today, the earliest Americans and their descendants are known as Native Americans or Indians. As you will read, the name Indian came into use because Christopher Columbus, a European explorer, mistakenly believed he had arrived in the East Indies, islands off the coast of Asia.

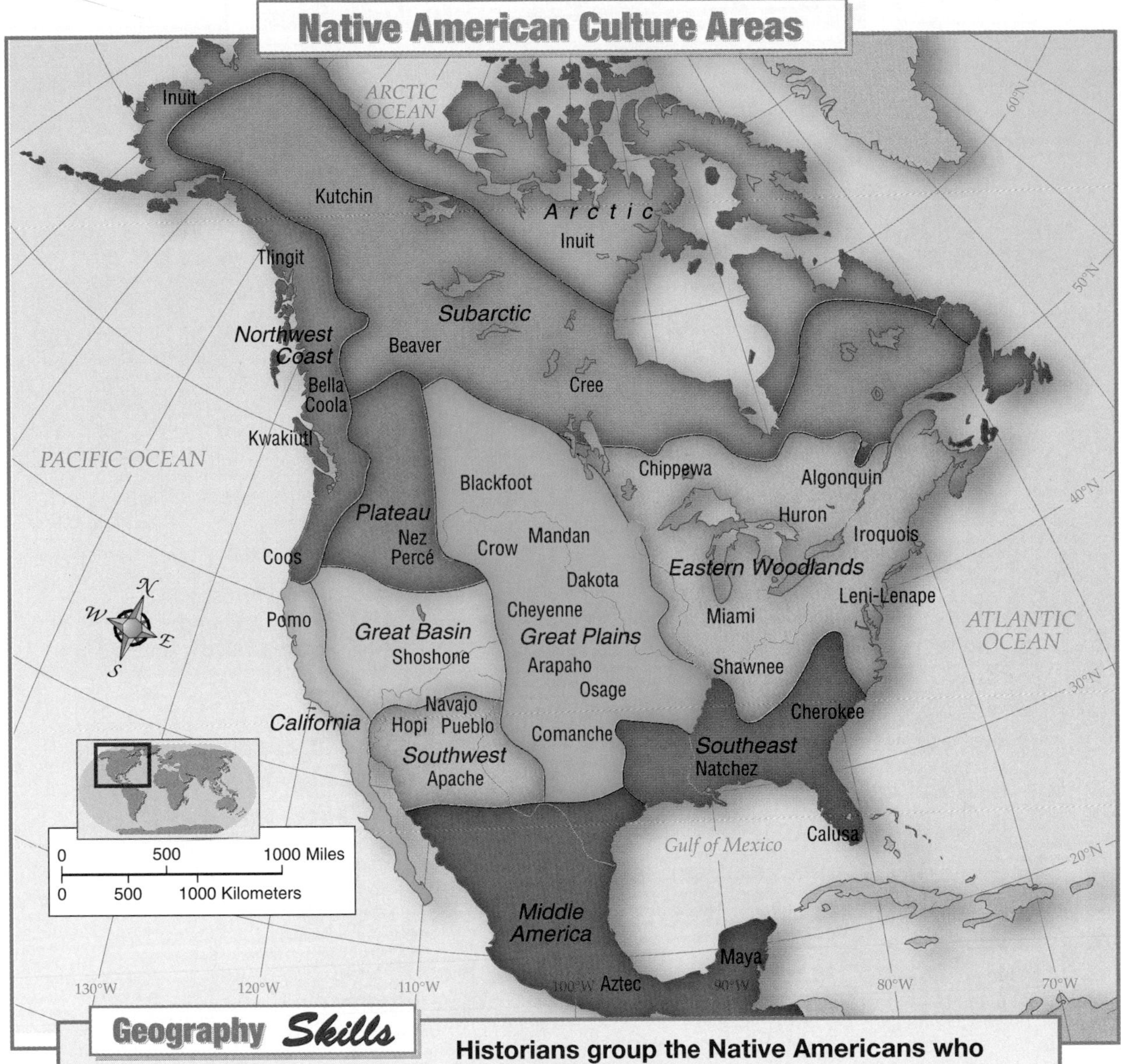

Geography *Skills* **Historians group the Native Americans who lived north of Mexico into ten major culture areas.**

1. **Location** On the map, locate the areas inhabited by the following groups: **(a)** Iroquois, **(b)** Inuit, **(c)** Pomo, **(d)** Hopi, **(e)** Shoshone.
2. **Place** Name two groups that lived in the coldest regions of North America.
3. **Critical Thinking** In which culture areas could Native Americans probably depend on the sea for food? Explain.

Economic Life

Native Americans developed many different means of living. Their economies took advantage of the geographic features of the varied regions where they lived.

Hunters and gatherers

Some Native Americans were hunter-gatherers. In forested regions, hunters used spears and bows and arrows to catch moose, bear, and deer. Near the ocean or along rivers, fishing peoples gathered rich harvests of seafood. For many groups in the California region, such as the Pomos, acorns were the basic food. Women harvested the nuts in autumn and later pounded them into flour.

Hunting and gathering supplied Native Americans with more than food. People of the Northwest Coast cut down majestic cedar trees to make houses and canoes. On the Great Plains, hunters used buffalo hides to make cone-shaped tents called tepees.

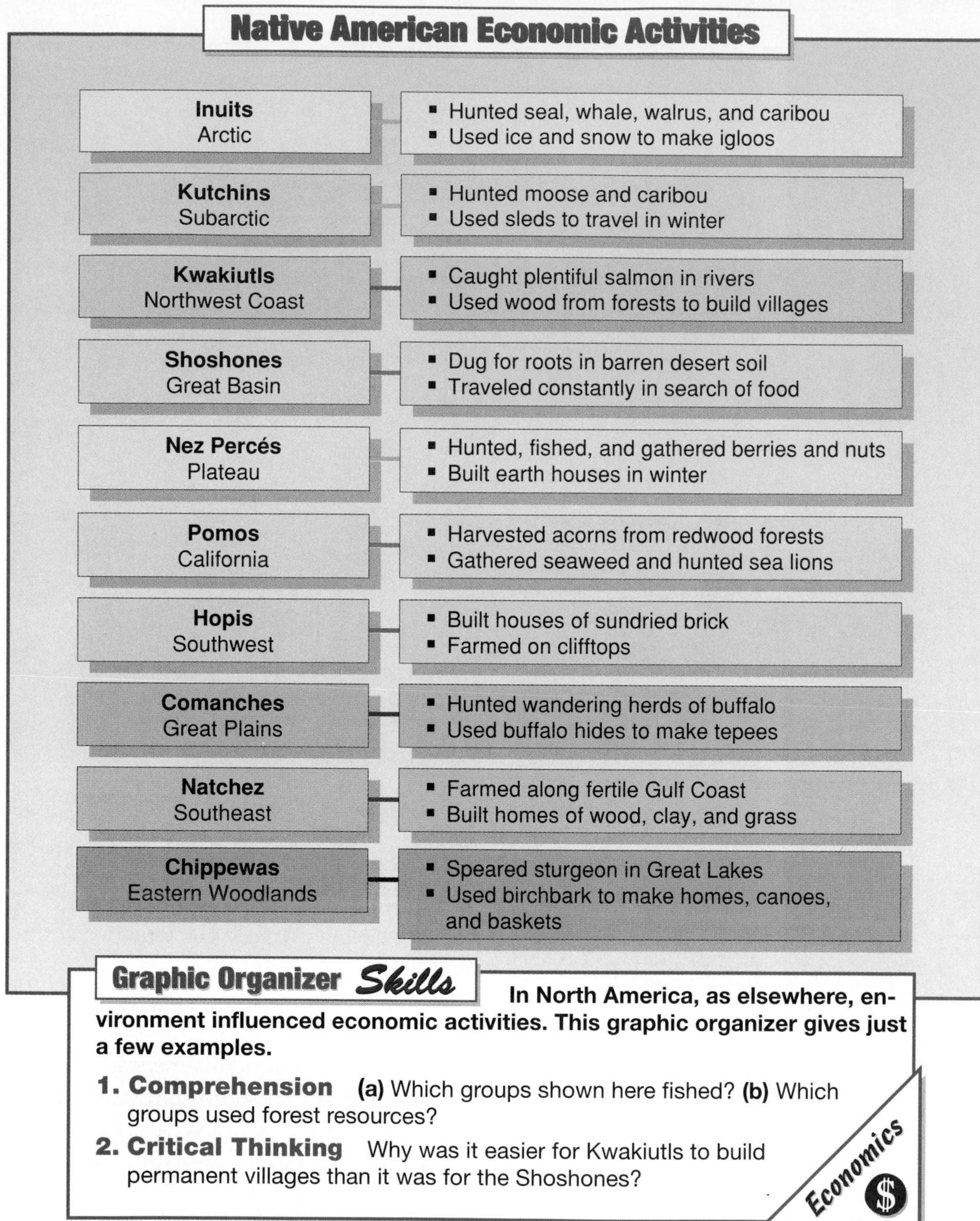

Graphic Organizer Skills **In North America, as elsewhere, environment influenced economic activities. This graphic organizer gives just a few examples.**

1. **Comprehension** **(a)** Which groups shown here fished? **(b)** Which groups used forest resources?
2. **Critical Thinking** Why was it easier for Kwakiutls to build permanent villages than it was for the Shoshones?

Economics $

In the Arctic region, far to the north, the **Inuits*** used all the limited resources of their environment to survive. They hunted seals from kayaks, small boats made from animal skins. In winter, they built igloos, houses of snow and ice.

*Inuit, meaning "humans," was the Arctic people's name for themselves. Neighboring people, the Crees, called the Inuits "Eskimos," meaning "Eaters of Raw Meat."

Agriculture

Other Native American groups learned to grow crops such as corn, beans, and squash. Unlike hunter-gatherers, farmers no longer had to move constantly in search of food. They built the first permanent villages in the Americas. As farming methods improved, villagers produced more food. In turn, the additional food supply allowed populations to grow.

Farming economies were often complex. In the dry Southwest, peoples like the **Zuñis** used a system of irrigation ditches to bring water from rivers to their fields. In the Southeast, Native American farmers planted corn and beans in the same field, so the bean vines could climb up the cornstalks. Fields were also used to grow squash, pumpkins, and sunflowers.

Religious Life

Native American peoples felt a strong bond with the land, plants, and animals around them. They hunted or raised crops or gathered wild plants for food. Native American religious ceremonies and daily customs were designed to honor the forces of the natural world.

On the Northwest Coast, people such as the Kwakiutls (kwah kee OOT 'lz) gathered rich harvests of salmon from the river. They took care to give thanks every year for the first fish they caught. The kwakiutls chanted this prayer:

> "We have come to meet alive,
> Swimmer,
> do not feel wrong about what I have
> done to you,
> friend Swimmer,
> for that is the reason why you came,
> that I may spear you, that I may eat
> you,
> Supernatural One, you, Long-Life-
> Giver,
> you Swimmer.
> Now protect us, me and my wife."

In the desert Southwest, Zuñi and **Hopi** Indians held religious ceremonies to ensure rainfall and good crops. At planting or harvest time, villages rang with the cry, "The kachinas are coming! The kachinas are coming!" **Kachinas** were masked dancers who represented the spirits. If the dance was pleasing, the spirits would return as rain for the next season's crops.

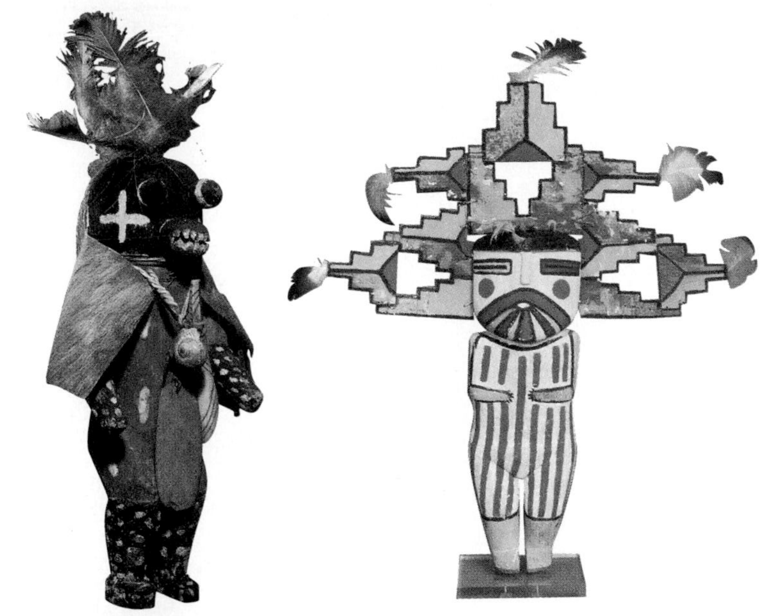

Viewing History — Kachina Dolls

To the Hopis of the Southwest, kachina dolls represented the spirits of the natural world. To create figures like these required great skill and care. For example, the kachina on the left is made of wood, cotton, fur, horsehair, feathers, shell, horn, and stone. ★ **Why do you think Hopi craftworkers took such care to create kachina dolls?**

Connections With Civics

While warrior chiefs led most Plains Indian societies, the Cheyennes had a complex civil, or nonmilitary, government. The ruling council included representatives from the 10 main Cheyenne bands. Any warrior chief sent to the council had to resign his military power.

Social Organization

The societies created by Indian peoples varied greatly. Some civilizations were complex, with different classes of people and elaborate systems of government. In other areas of North America, tribes developed simpler communities.

Simple and complex societies

Wandering hunters and gatherers usually formed simple societies. For example, in the Great Basin region, the Ute (YOOT) and Shoshone (shoh SHOH nee) Indians lived simply. In the region's harsh, dry climate, few plants or animals survived. Because the land offered so little, only a few related families traveled together in search of food. They had few possessions beyond digging sticks,

Linking History and Technology

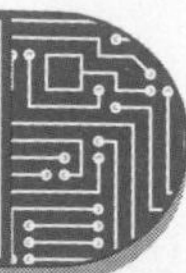

Pueblo

The walls are made of sandstone blocks plastered with adobe.

Kivas are rooms used for religious ceremonies.

Winter cooking room

Roofs are used as a center for work and socializing.

Storage room

Sleeping room

Drainspouts and splash blocks keep moisture away from roofs and walls.

Tepee

Lodge poles

Smoke flaps

Buffalo sinew

Inner lining

Buffalo hide

The entrance almost always faced the rising sun in the east.

Wooden stakes

Long House

Storage shelves

The stockade provided protection from enemies.

Each fire was shared by two families on either side of the center aisle.

Sleeping benches

The support posts divided the long house into separate rooms.

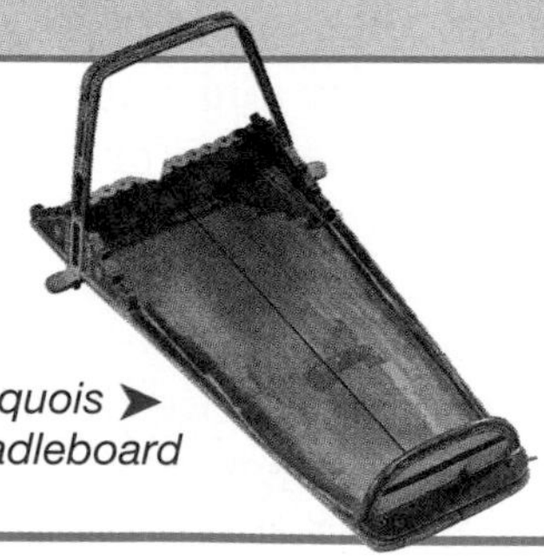

Elm bark walls

Iroquois ➤ cradleboard

Native American Dwellings

Native Americans developed a wide variety of dwellings to suit their different environments. Shown here are a pueblo from the Southwest, a tepee from the Great Plains, and a long house from the Eastern Woodlands. ★ **Describe one way each type of dwelling reflects the local environment.**

baskets, and other tools or weapons needed to hunt.

Groups who lived in permanent settlements generally formed a more complex social order. With plenty of food, peoples of the Pacific Northwest built villages and traded with nearby groups. Within a village, families gained status according to how much they owned. Families held **potlatches,** or ceremonial dinners, to show off their wealth. The family invited many guests and gave everyone gifts. The more gifts the family gave away, the higher their social status.

The Iroquois form a league

A complex society emerged among the **Iroquois** (IHR uh kwoi) of the Eastern Woodlands. The Iroquois included five nations: the Mohawk, Seneca, Onondaga (ahn uhn DAW guh), Oneida (oh NĪ duh), and Cayuga (kay YOO guh).

The basic unit of Iroquois society was the family, made up of a woman, her husband, and all her children. Two or more related families made up a clan. Several clans lived together in each village. Many villages made up each Iroquois nation. Each nation had its own ruling council.

Women held a special place in Iroquois society. They owned all household property and were in charge of planting and harvesting. When a couple married, the man moved in with his wife's family. Iroquois women also shared in political power because they chose the **sachems,** or chiefs, who made up the ruling council.

For many years, the five Iroquois nations fought with one another. Around 1570, the five nations formed an alliance to end the fighting. According to legend, a religious leader named Dekanawida (deh kan ah WEE dah) inspired Hiawatha, a Mohawk, to organize the alliance, which was known as the **League of the Iroquois.** Later, a sixth nation, the Tuscarora (tuhs kuh ROR uh) joined the League.

A council of 50 members, selected by women, made decisions for the League. Each nation had one vote. The council could take action only if all nations agreed.

★ Section 1 Review ★

Recall

1. **Locate** **(a)** Great Plains, **(b)** California, **(c)** Northwest Coast, **(d)** Arctic, **(e)** Southwest, **(f)** Southeast, **(g)** Great Basin, **(h)** Eastern Woodlands.
2. **Identify** **(a)** Inuits, **(b)** Zuñis, **(c)** Hopis, **(d)** kachina, **(e)** Iroquois, **(f)** League of the Iroquois.
3. **Define** **(a)** glacier, **(b)** culture, **(c)** tribe, **(d)** potlatch, **(e)** sachem.

Comprehension

4. How did hunting-gathering societies differ from farming societies?
5. How were Native American religions linked to the natural world?
6. **(a)** Describe the social organization of the Iroquois. **(b)** Why was the League of the Iroquois formed?

Critical Thinking and Writing

7. **Synthesizing Information** Review the feature Linking History and Technology in this section. **(a)** Which of the three kinds of homes shown here would you expect to find in a hunting-gathering society? Explain. **(b)** Which would be most suited to a settled farming community? Explain.
8. **Linking Past and Present** The Iroquois League helped settle disputes and keep the peace. What institutions perform this role in our society today?

Activity **Writing a Survival Plan** Unplug that computer! Circumstances have forced you to live for a year in a natural environment such as a northern forest, or an icy Arctic tundra, or a southwestern desert. Write a plan explaining how you might adapt to your environment, as early Native American societies did. Consider all your options.

Europeans Reach the Americas

As You Read

Explore These Questions

- Why did Europeans begin to expand overseas?
- How did Spain conquer and rule its American empire?
- What effects did the arrival of Europeans have on Native Americans?

Define

- colony
- conquistador
- viceroy
- pueblo
- presidio
- mission

Identify

- Crusades
- Renaissance
- Johannes Gutenberg
- Christopher Columbus
- Hernando Cortés
- Francisco Pizarro
- Juan de Oñate
- Eusebio Francisco Kino
- Columbian Exchange

Setting the Scene During the Middle Ages, a period from about 500 to 1350, most Europeans knew little about lands outside their small villages. Even mapmakers called the waters beyond Europe the Sea of Darkness. Sailors who strayed into these waters often returned with tales of fearsome creatures:

> “One of these sea monsters has terrible tusks. Another has horns, flames, and huge eyes 16 or 20 feet across.”

Toward the end of the Middle Ages, European explorers began to sail unfamiliar seas. These voyages brought amazing changes both to Europe and to the Americas.

Spanish sailing ship of the 1400s

A Changing Europe

Even during the Middle Ages, Europeans had some contact with distant lands. From about 1100 to 1300, the Roman Catholic Church fought a series of religious wars with Turkish Muslims to gain control of the Middle East. The wars were known as the **Crusades.**

European crusaders were unable to win control of the Middle East. However, they returned home with tales of strange foods, such as rice, oranges, and dates. Arab merchants offered silks and colorful rugs from Asia. Soon, European merchants began a lively trade in these goods. Arabs also taught Europeans how to use a device called an astrolabe to calculate a ship's position at sea.

A revival of learning

Trade and travel made Europeans more curious about the world. Scholars translated ancient Greek, Roman, and Arab works. They then made advances of their own in fields such as art, medicine, and astronomy. This burst of learning was known as the **Renaissance** (REHN uh sahns), a French word for rebirth. The Renaissance lasted from the late 1300s to about 1600.

A new invention, the printing press, helped to spread the Renaissance spirit. It was invented in the mid-1400s by German printer **Johannes Gutenberg** (GOOT uhn berg). During the Middle Ages, monks wrote out books by hand. As a result, only a few copies could be produced. With the printing press, large numbers of books could be printed at low cost. As more books became available, more people learned to read. The more people read, the more they found out about the world.

Monarchs increase their power

As trade brought new prosperity to Europe, kings and queens fought to gain greater control over their lands. During the Middle Ages, European monarchs had been weak. Most lands were divided among powerful nobles. Arab armies had conquered parts of Spain and Portugal.

Gradually, western European monarchs began to take back powers from nobles. Spanish and Portuguese rulers drove Arab forces back into Africa. The monarchs of the Renaissance era built the foundations of the European nations we know today.

The Search for Trade

Rulers of Portugal, Spain, England, and France all looked for ways to increase their wealth. They could make huge profits by trading with China and other Asian lands. However, Arab and Italian merchants controlled the trade routes across the Mediterranean Sea. To win a share of the trade, European rulers had to find another route to Asia.

Portugal led the way. During the 1400s, Portuguese sea captains sailed farther and farther south along the coast of West Africa. In 1498, Vasco da Gama passed the southern tip of Africa and continued on to India. Later, other Portuguese ships pressed on to the East Indies, source of a rich spice trade.

Spain Builds an Empire

As Portugal built a trading empire, the Spanish watched with envy. They, too, wanted a share of the spice trade. In 1492, King Ferdinand and Queen Isabella of Spain agreed to finance a voyage by **Christopher Columbus,** an Italian sea captain. Columbus planned to reach Asia by sailing west across the Atlantic.

Biography **Christopher Columbus**

Christopher Columbus grew up in Genoa, one of the busiest seaports in Italy. As a young sailor, he heard how Portuguese sea captains were sailing around the coast of Africa toward the Indies. After studying Portuguese charts and maps, Columbus slowly formed his own ideas about reaching the Indies—by sailing west. ★ **Today, some people consider Columbus a hero, while others condemn his actions. List one argument in favor of each viewpoint.**

Columbus sails west

Taking three ships and a crew of 90 sailors, Columbus set sail in August 1492. For a month, the crew saw no land. Finally, at 2 A.M. on October 12, a lookout spotted white cliffs shining in the moonlight. "*Tierra! Tierra!*" he shouted. "Land! Land!"

Columbus believed he had reached the East Indies. In fact, he had reached islands in the Caribbean Sea.

Columbus made three more voyages to the Caribbean. On his second voyage, in 1493, he founded the first Spanish colony in the Americas, on an island he called Hispaniola. A **colony** is a group of people who settle

AmericanHeritage MAGAZINE

Castillo de San Marcos

Castillo de San Marcos was built to last! The Spanish started work on the fort after pirates raided St. Augustine, Florida, in 1668. The stone structure took almost 25 years to complete. Today, you can walk across the moat and look over stone walls that survived invasions almost 300 years ago. You can also visit nearby St. Augustine—the oldest city in the United States.

★ ***To learn more about this historic site, write:*** *Castillo de San Marcos National Park, 1 South Castillo Drive, St. Augustine, FL 32084.*

Cannon at Castillo de San Marcos

in a distant land and are ruled by the government of their native land.

Over the next 25 years, the Spanish explored and settled other islands in the Caribbean Sea. Europeans called the islands the West Indies.

Spanish conquerors

Columbus was the first of many Spanish **conquistadors** (kahn KEES tuh dorz), or conquerors. The conquistadors were a bold lot. "We came here to serve God and the king and also to get rich," explained one. In their search for glory and gold, the conquistadors helped make Spain one of the richest nations in Europe.

In 1518, **Hernando Cortés** (kor TEHZ) led an expedition into the interior of Mexico. There, he found the powerful Aztec empire. With the help of neighboring peoples whom the Aztecs had conquered, Cortés triumphed over the Aztecs.

A few years later, **Francisco Pizarro** (pee ZAR oh) matched Cortés's conquest. Sailing along the Pacific coast of present-day Chile, Pizarro invaded the Inca empire. In a surprise attack, he captured and later killed its ruler, Atahualpa (at ah WAHL pah). By 1535, Pizarro controlled much of the vast territory that had been ruled by the Incas.

Aztec and Incan treasures made the conquistadors rich. Spain grew rich, too, especially after the discovery of rich deposits of gold and silver in Mexico and Peru. Treasure ships sailed regularly across the Atlantic to Spain.

Spanish settlements

At first, Spain let conquistadors govern its American lands. However, the conquistadors were poor rulers. When gold and silver began to flow into Spain from the Americas, the Spanish king set up stronger, more stable governments.

In 1535, the king divided his lands into New Spain and Peru. He put a viceroy in charge of each region to rule in his name. A **viceroy** is a person who rules in the place of a king or queen. In the new empire, three kinds of settlements were permitted: pueblos, presidios (prih SIHD ee ohz), and missions.

Pueblos, or towns, were centers of farming and trade. In the middle of each pueblo was a plaza where townspeople and farmers gathered on important occasions. They also came to worship at the church.

Presidios were forts with high adobe walls, where soldiers lived. Inside were shops, stables for horses, and storehouses for food. Most soldiers lived in large barracks. Soldiers protected the farmers who settled around the presidios.

Missions were religious settlements run by Catholic priests and friars. Like other Europeans who settled in the Americas, the Spanish believed that they had a duty to convert Indians to the Christian religion. Throughout New Spain, missionaries forced Indians to live and work on mission grounds.

The Spanish borderlands

During their first 100 years in the Americas, the Spanish did not build settlements in the borderlands north of Mexico. The only exception was a presidio built at St. Augustine, Florida, in 1565. Spanish explorers in the borderlands were unable to find gold and silver. They also faced strong resistance from Native Americans in the region.

In time, however, Spanish interest in the borderlands grew. In 1598, **Juan de Oñate** founded the colony of New Mexico, among the adobe villages of the Pueblo Indians. Later, Spanish missionaries moved into other areas of the present-day Southwest. The first mission in Texas was founded at El Paso in 1659.

Father **Eusebio Francisco Kino** (KEE noh) crossed into present-day Arizona in 1691. During the next 20 years, he set up 24 missions. Missionaries also moved into California. By the late 1700s, a string of Spanish missions dotted the California coast from present-day San Diego to San Francisco. (See the map at right.)

The Columbian Exchange

Spain's settlement in the Americas dramatically changed the course of history. The first contact between Europeans and Native Americans in the Caribbean set off a chain of events whose effects are felt throughout the world even to this day. The **Columbian Exchange,** as modern historians call it, transformed people's lives around the globe.

A tragic pattern

Like later Europeans who came to America, the Spanish were convinced that their civilization was superior to that of Native

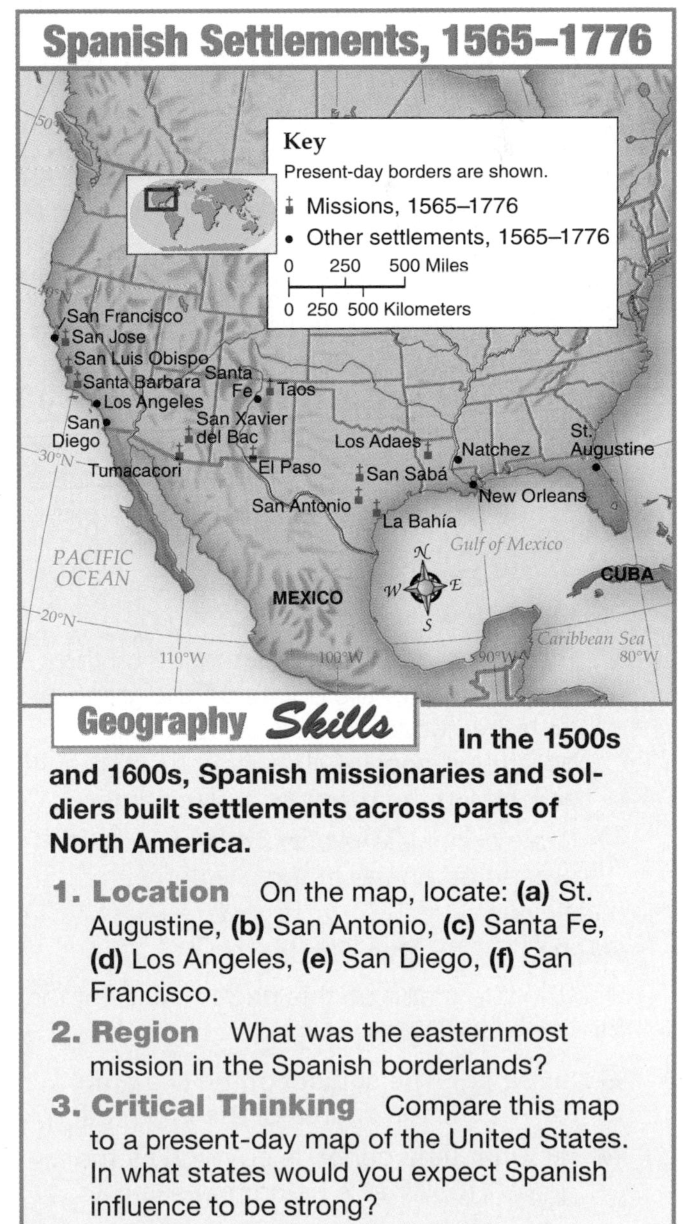

Spanish Settlements, 1565–1776

Geography Skills **In the 1500s and 1600s, Spanish missionaries and soldiers built settlements across parts of North America.**

1. **Location** On the map, locate: **(a)** St. Augustine, **(b)** San Antonio, **(c)** Santa Fe, **(d)** Los Angeles, **(e)** San Diego, **(f)** San Francisco.
2. **Region** What was the easternmost mission in the Spanish borderlands?
3. **Critical Thinking** Compare this map to a present-day map of the United States. In what states would you expect Spanish influence to be strong?

Skills FOR LIFE

Critical Thinking | Managing Information | Communication | **Maps, Charts, and Graphs**

Reading a Line Graph

How Will I Use This Skill ?

Graphs present statistics, or number facts, in a visual way. A line graph can show you at a glance how statistics change over time—from the population of the world to your batting average.

LEARN the Skill

You can read a line graph by following these four steps:

❶ Use the title to identify the subject of the graph. The source line will tell you where the information was found.

❷ Study the labels on the graph. The horizontal (or side-to-side) axis usually tells you the time period covered by the graph. The vertical (or up-and-down) axis tells you what is being measured.

❸ Practice reading the information on the graph. Line up the points on the graph with the horizontal and vertical axes to determine how much or how many of something there was at a given time.

❹ Draw conclusions about the information presented on the graph.

PRACTICE the Skill

Use the line graph on this page to answer the following questions.

❶ (a) What is the subject of the line graph? (b) What is the source of the information?

❷ (a) What time period is covered by the graph? (b) What is being measured?

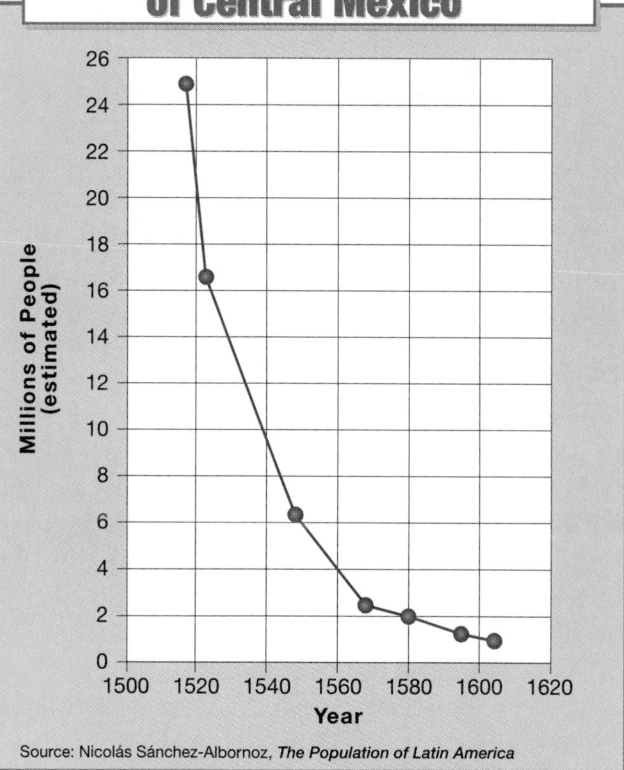

❸ About how many Native Americans lived in central Mexico before 1520? In 1580?

❹ Using the information on the graph, make a generalization about the Indian population of central Mexico.

APPLY the Skill

For the next week, keep track of the number of hours you spend each day performing a certain activity. Use your statistics to make a line graph.

Americans. They claimed Indian lands for themselves. They forced Native Americans to work in gold mines, on ranches, or in Spanish households. Many Indians died from harsh conditions.

European diseases took an even greater toll. Indians had no resistance to smallpox, chicken pox, measles, and influenza. Within 50 years of Cortés's conquest, the native population of Mexico dropped by about 90 percent. Some historians believe that disease alone would have ensured Spanish victory over the Indians.

Conquest, overwork, and disease created a tragic pattern for Native Americans in New Spain. Later colonists, such as the French and English, used Indian forced labor much less often. However, their arrival would still have tragic consequences for Indians.

Cultural exchange

The 1492 encounter had other effects. It started a worldwide exchange of goods and ideas. This exchange covered a wide range of areas. It included food, medicine, government, technology, the arts, and language.

The exchange went in both directions. Europeans contributed in many ways to the culture of the Americas. They introduced domestic animals such as chickens, goats, and horses. They taught Native Americans how to use metals to make copper pots and iron knives. Indians eagerly bought European firearms, which helped them both in hunting and in war.

Native American influences

For their part, Native Americans introduced Europeans to valuable crops like corn, potatoes, beans, tomatoes, squash, peanuts, pineapples, and blueberries. Today, almost half the world's food crops come from plants that first grew in the Americas.

Europeans also adopted Indian clothing, including ponchos, moccasins, and parkas. They used Indian inventions like hammocks, toboggans, and snowshoes. Europeans also learned to respect Native American medical knowledge. Indians often treated the newcomers with medicines that were unknown to Europeans.

In time, all Native Americans felt the effects of European conquest. Still, despite attacks on their cultures, Indians survived throughout the two continents. They have played a central role in American history.

★ Section 2 Review ★

Recall

1. **Locate** **(a)** Spain, **(b)** Portugal, **(c)** Mexico, **(d)** St. Augustine, **(e)** Caribbean Sea.
2. **Identify** **(a)** Crusades, **(b)** Renaissance, **(c)** Johannes Gutenberg, **(d)** Christopher Columbus, **(e)** Hernando Cortés, **(f)** Francisco Pizarro, **(g)** Juan de Oñate, **(h)** Eusebio Francisco Kino, **(i)** Columbian Exchange.
3. **Define** **(a)** colony, **(b)** conquistador, **(c)** viceroy, **(d)** pueblo, **(e)** presidio, **(f)** mission.

Comprehension

4. Describe three changes that led Europeans to look beyond their borders.
5. **(a)** Describe how Spain built an empire in the Americas. **(b)** What benefits did Spain get from its empire?
6. Describe two effects of the Columbian Exchange on **(a)** Native Americans, and **(b)** Europeans.

Critical Thinking and Writing

7. **Drawing Conclusions** In what way were the Crusades both a success and a failure?
8. **Recognizing Points of View** For many years, American schoolchildren were taught that Christopher Columbus "discovered America." In what way is this an accurate statement? In what way is it inaccurate?

Activity **Exploring Cultural Exchange** List three items or activities in your life that came from outside the United States. Items might include foods, articles of clothing, styles of music, sports, or holidays. Write one or two sentences explaining how your life would be different without each item or activity.

Africans Come to the Americas

As You Read

Explore These Questions
- What kinds of societies emerged in West Africa?
- How did the slave trade develop?
- What were conditions like for slaves on the way to the Americas?

Define
- city-state
- kinship network
- caravan
- plantation

Identify
- Mali
- Mansa Musa
- Songhai
- Timbuktu
- Affonso
- Bartolomé de Las Casas
- Middle Passage

Setting the Scene In the late afternoon, the peace of a West African village was disrupted by the sound of a horn in the distance, blowing repeatedly. Children ran to the village outskirts. *"Batafo! Batafo!"* the children cried. "Traders! Traders!"

Soon the traders arrived. A long line of porters and camels carried precious goods. Some brought sacks of salt or fish. Others sold gold dust, gold nuggets, fine cloths, jewelry, or brass basins.

West African artists produced fine ivory carvings, like this one showing Portuguese traders.

Trade played a vital role in African life. Complex trade routes across the Sahara, a vast desert, linked African villages and kingdoms. For many centuries, Europeans played little or no role in most African trade. After the 1400s, however, new trading patterns drew Africa into closer contact with both Europe and the Americas.

African States

Africa is a vast continent, the second largest on Earth. Like Europe and the Americas, it contains a wide variety of peoples and societies.

Trading states of West Africa

Several advanced trading states rose in West Africa, south of the Sahara. The kingdom of **Mali** reached its height between 1200 and 1400. In 1324, **Mansa Musa,** the Muslim emperor of Mali, journeyed from Mali across North Africa to Egypt and on to the Middle East. His wealth so dazzled Egyptians that news of his visit reached Europe. A caption on a Spanish map pays tribute to Mansa Musa's magnificent reputation:

> "So abundant is the gold in his country that he is the richest and most noble king in all the land."

In the late 1400s, **Songhai** (sawng HĪ) became the most powerful kingdom in West Africa. **Timbuktu,** located on the Niger River, was one of Songhai's thriving cities. There, thousands of people bought and sold grain, livestock, gold, ivory, and fine crafts. Timbuktu boasted over 100 religious schools as well as a university.

City-states of East Africa

A thriving commerce also developed in East Africa. Where the coast offered good harbors, small villages expanded into bustling trading centers. Cities like Mogadishu and Kilwa conducted a lively trade with other ports along the Indian Ocean. Gold from Zimbabwe, a powerful inland state, made its way to the coastal city of Sofala. From there, ships carried the gold up the African coast as well as to India.

Trade helped local rulers build strong city-states in East Africa. A **city-state** is a large town that has its own independant government and controls the surrounding countryside. As Africans mingled with traders from other lands, a rich and varied mix of cultures developed.

Village and Family Life

Families living in small villages farmed throughout Africa. In rainforests closer to the coast, they grew yams. In the grasslands, they raised grains, including rice. In the 1400s, many farmers began clearing forest lands in order to raise more crops. During the 1500s, Africans also began to grow corn, imported from the Americas.

Family relations played an important part in African life. Children owed duties not only to their parents, but to aunts, uncles, and cousins. Grandparents were entitled to special respect. Such close family ties are called a **kinship network.**

African religions emphasized the importance of kinship, too. Many farmers had worked the same land as their parents and grandparents before them. Religious ceremonies honored their ancestors and the spirits of the earth. Farmers believed that by farming the land properly, they brought honor on their families.

The Slave Trade

Trading caravans played a vital role in African life. A **caravan** is a group of traders and their animals journeying together across a long distance. From Timbuktu, many caravans began a long march across the Sahara toward markets along the Mediterranean Sea. Other caravans went from village to village within West Africa.

Often, the cargoes of these caravans included slaves. Since ancient times, Africans as well as Europeans, Asians, and Arabs had enslaved and sold people. Most slaves in Africa were people who had been captured in war. African traders often transported and sold these prisoners as laborers. Muslim merchants from North Africa also carried African slaves into Europe and the Middle East.

A new direction

During the 1400s, slave trade took a dramatic new turn. As Portuguese explorers visited the coast of West Africa, they began buying slaves as well as gold, ivory, and other trade goods. By 1500, as many as 2,500 Africans were being sold to the Portuguese each year.

As the slave trade increased, Africans from kingdoms along the coast made raids into the interior, seeking captives to sell to the Portuguese. After 1600, Dutch, Spanish, English, and French traders also bought slaves from Africans.

Failed protests

Some African leaders protested the expansion of the slave trade. **Affonso,** the king of the Central African kingdom of Kongo, wrote to the king of Portugal:

Mansa Musa

During his 25-year reign, Mansa Musa worked to bring peace and order to the kingdom of Mali. A visitor noted, "There is complete and general safety throughout the land." This detail from a French map of the 1300s shows Mansa Musa sitting on his throne. ★ **How does this picture suggest the economic prosperity of Mali?**

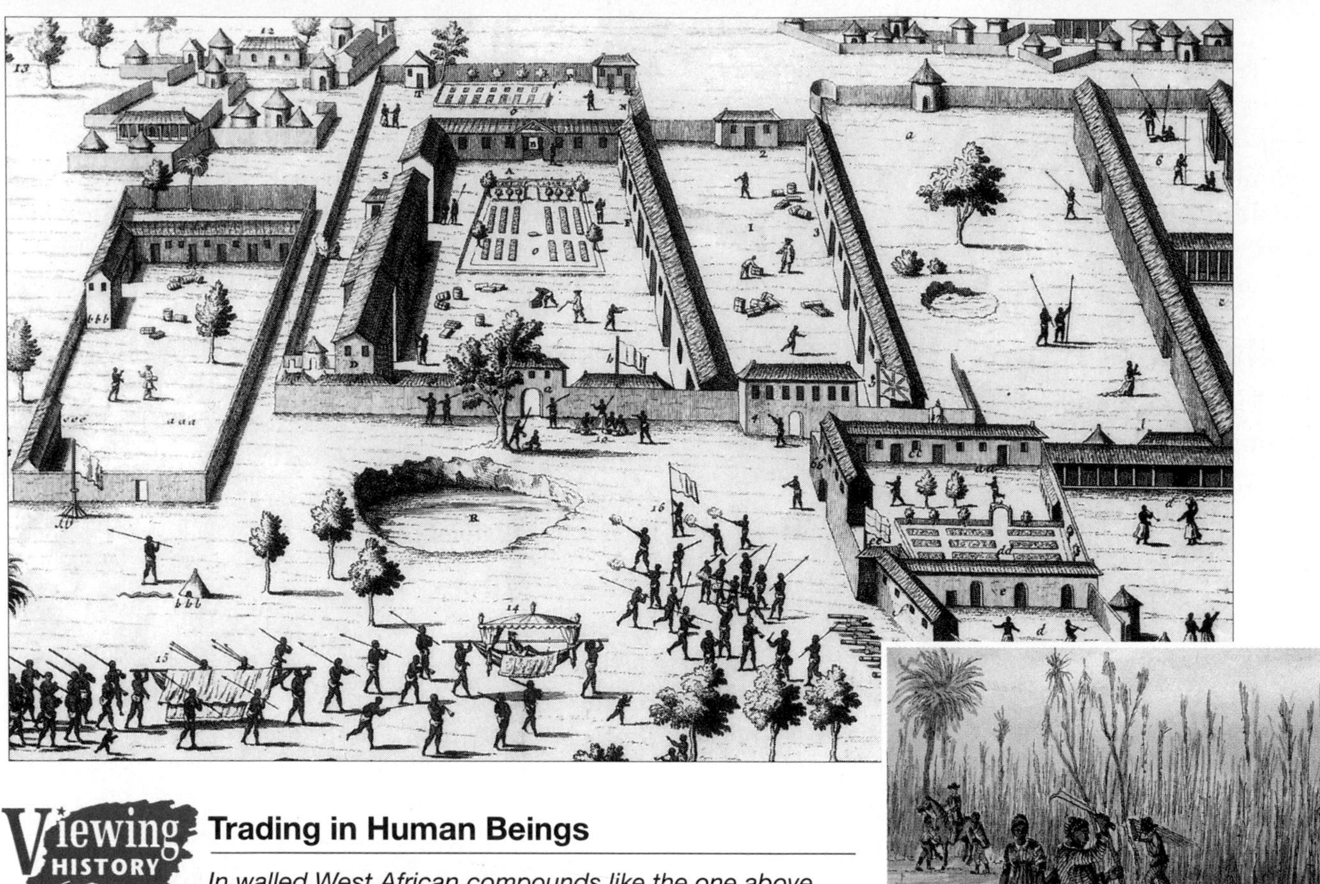

Viewing HISTORY **Trading in Human Beings**

In walled West African compounds like the one above, Portuguese, French, Dutch, and English merchants competed for a share of the profitable slave trade. African traders also made fortunes from the captives they sold. Across the Atlantic, many West Africans performed the backbreaking work of the sugar harvesting (right).

★ **How did the plantation system encourage the growth of slavery in the Americas?**

> "Merchants are taking every day our natives, sons of the land and sons of our nobles and vassals and our relatives, because the thieves and men of bad conscience . . . grab them and get them to be sold."

Such protests, however, had little effect. With many Europeans, as well as Africans, making huge profits, the slave trade grew rapidly.

Slavery in New Spain

The new African slave trade did not develop during the early years of New Spain. At first, the Spanish forced Indians to work in mines and on **plantations,** large estates that required many workers to farm. As you have read, however, thousands of Native Americans died from overwork. European diseases killed millions more. These harsh conditions led one priest, **Bartolomé de Las Casas** (day lahs KAH sahs), to campaign for reform.

Protesting Indian slavery

Traveling through New Spain, Las Casas saw Indians dying of hunger, disease, and mistreatment. "Even beasts enjoy more freedom when they are allowed to graze in the field," he wrote.

Horrified, Las Casas journeyed to Spain and asked the king to protect the Indians. In the 1540s, the royal government did pass laws stating that Native Americans could not be enslaved. The laws also allowed Indians to own cattle and grow crops. Few officials in New Spain enforced the new laws, however.

Slaves from Africa

As more and more Native Americans died from disease and mistreatment, the Spanish looked for other workers. Las Casas suggested that Africans be brought as slaves to replace Indian laborers. Unlike Indians, he claimed, Africans did not catch European diseases. In addition, the farming skills Africans had developed in their homeland made them attractive as workers on American plantations. In 1517, Spanish colonists began importing Africans as slaves.

By the time he died, Las Casas came to regret his suggestion. He saw that Africans suffered as much as Indians. By then, however, the plantation system had taken hold. In the years that followed, the African slave trade grew, not only in the Spanish colonies but elsewhere in the Americas.

The Passage West

Over the next 400 years, as many as 11 million Africans were enslaved and sent across the Atlantic Ocean. The vast majority came from West Africa. European slave traders set up posts along the African coast. They offered guns and other goods to African traders who brought them slaves. They loaded the captives aboard Spanish, Portuguese, Dutch, English, and French ships headed for the Americas.

Most slave ships went to Brazil and the Caribbean. However, by the 1720s, between 2,000 and 3,000 Africans were arriving each year in England's North American colonies. (In the next chapter, you will read about the English colonies.)

The trip from Africa to the Americas was called the **Middle Passage.** Slaves were crammed into small spaces below deck. "Each had scarcely room to turn himself, [and the heat] almost suffocated us," recalled Olaudah Equiano (oh LAW dah ehk wee AH noh), an African who made the voyage in the 1700s. The crew rarely, if ever, allowed the captives up on deck for fresh air and exercise.

Some Africans fought for their freedom. Others refused to eat. Equiano recalled:

> "One day... two of my wearied countrymen who were chained together... jumped into the sea; immediately another... followed their example.... Two of the wretches were drowned, but [the ship's crew] got the other, and afterwards flogged him unmercifully for thus attempting to prefer death to slavery."

Records of slave voyages show that about 10 percent of all Africans shipped to North America in the 1700s did not survive the Middle Passage. On some tragic voyages, the number of deaths was much higher.

★ Section 3 Review ★

Recall

1. **Identify** **(a)** Mali, **(b)** Mansa Musa, **(c)** Songhai, **(d)** Timbuktu, **(e)** Affonso, **(f)** Bartolomé de Las Casas, **(g)** Middle Passage.
2. **Define** **(a)** city-state, **(b)** kinship network, **(c)** caravan, **(d)** plantation.

Comprehension

3. What role did caravans play in African trade?
4. Why did the Spanish decide to import Africans to the Americas as slaves?
5. Describe conditions for enslaved Africans on the Middle Passage.

Critical Thinking and Writing

6. **Linking Past and Present** Kinship networks played a major role in West African society. In what ways are families important in modern American society?
7. **Drawing Conclusions** Why do you think protests against the slave trade were unsuccessful?

Activity **Drawing a Political Cartoon** You are helping King Affonso protest the growth of the slave trade. Create a political cartoon that could be included along with the king's letter of protest to the king of Portugal.

Rival Claims in North America

Explore These Questions
- How did competition grow among European nations?
- How did trappers and missionaries help New France grow?
- How did the Dutch gain colonies in North America?

Define
- northwest passage
- coureurs de bois

Identify
- Ferdinand Magellan
- Martin Luther
- Protestant Reformation
- New France
- Jacques Marquette
- Louis Joliet
- Peter Minuit
- New Netherland

In August 1497, the royal court of England buzzed with excitement. Italian sea captain Giovanni Caboto and a crew of English sailors had just returned from a 79-day Atlantic voyage. Caboto, called John Cabot by the English, told the king he had reached a "new-found" island in Asia where fish were plentiful.

Cabot was one of many European explorers who crossed the Atlantic in the late 1400s and early 1500s. England, France, and the Netherlands all envied Spain's new empire. They wanted American colonies of their own.

Exploration Continues

Throughout the 1500s, European nations continued looking for ways to reach the riches of Asia. In 1519, **Ferdinand Magellan** began a voyage around the southern tip of South America to Asia. His ships became the first to circle the globe.

Other explorers sought a **northwest passage,** or waterway through or around North America. (See the map on the next page.) John Cabot believed he had found a northwest passage in 1497. In fact, his "new-found" island off the Asian coast lay off the shore of North America.

France, too, sent explorers to seek a northwest passage. In 1524, Giovanni da Verrazano (vehr rah TSAH noh) journeyed along the North American coast from the Carolinas up to Canada. During the 1530s, Jacques Cartier (KAR tee yay) spotted the broad opening where the St. Lawrence River flows into the Atlantic. Cartier sailed a good distance up the St. Lawrence.

In 1609, the English captain Henry Hudson sailed for the Dutch. His ship, the *Half Moon,* entered what is today New York harbor. Hudson continued some 150 miles (240 km) up the river that now bears his name.

None of these explorers ever found a northwest passage to Asia. Yet as they searched, they mapped and explored many parts of North America. Now, rulers began thinking about how to profit from the region's rich resources.

European Rivalries

As European nations competed for riches, religious differences heightened their rivalry. Until the 1500s, the Roman Catholic Church was the only Christian church in western Europe. After that, however, a new reform movement sharply divided Christians.

Jacques Cartier used the Iroquis word *kanata,* meaning "settlement," to name the vast land in North America that he claimed for France. Today, our neighbor to the north still bears that name with a different spelling: Canada.

Catholics versus Protestants

In 1517, a German monk named **Martin Luther** challenged many practices of the Catholic Church. Luther believed that the Church had become too worldly and greedy. He also argued that people could be saved only by their faith in God.

Other reformers also protested against the Church. Their supporters became known as Protestants. The **Protestant Reformation,** as the new movement was known, divided Europe. Before long, the Protestants also began to split into many churches.

Rivalries in the Americas

European religious rivalries spread to the Americas. In the late 1500s, Catholic monarchs ruled Spain and France. England's Protestant queen, Elizabeth I, encouraged English adventurers to raid Spanish treasure fleets near New Spain. In North America, England competed for territory with France.

Not all rivalries were religious. The Netherlands, like England, was a Protestant nation. Yet the Dutch and the English would become rivals in North America.

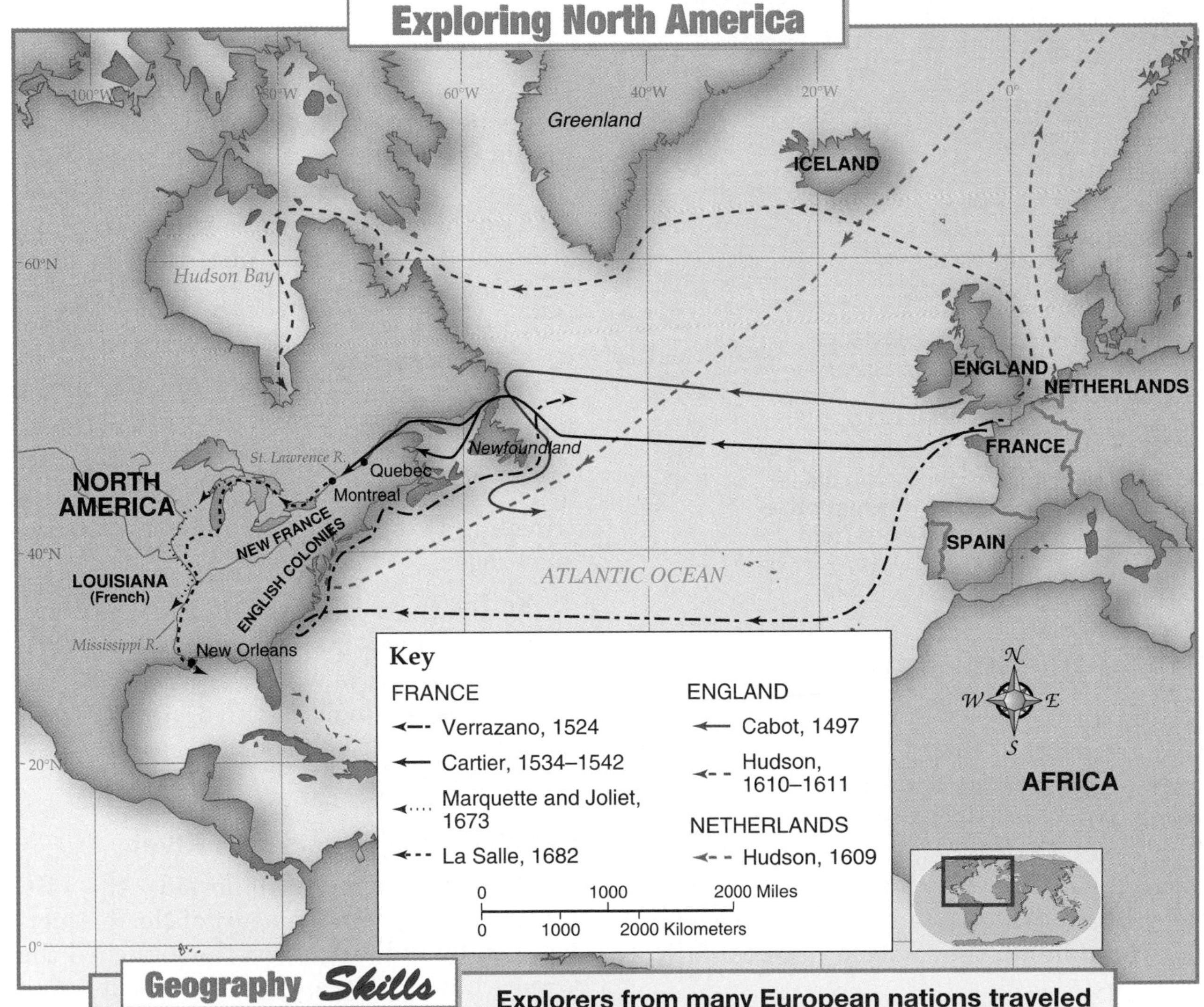

Geography Skills Explorers from many European nations traveled across North America. Many were seeking a northwest passage to Asia.

1. **Location** On the map, locate: **(a)** England, **(b)** France, **(c)** the Netherlands, **(d)** New France, **(e)** Newfoundland, **(f)** Quebec, **(g)** St. Lawrence River.
2. **Movement** Name the bodies of water La Salle traveled on or crossed.
3. **Critical Thinking** Identify two areas of North America where conflicts over land claims were likely to arise.

Viewing History **A "Runner of the Woods"**

French fur trappers like this one could make a fortune in New France. Still, they could not have survived without skills and technology they learned from Native Americans. For example, snowshoes helped them travel over frozen country and locate traps hidden in deep snow. ★ **What other skills did coureurs de bois learn from Indians?**

Building New France

Early voyages of exploration convinced the French that they could not build an empire of gold in the Americas, as Spain had done. Instead, they profited from riches of the sea. Every year, French fishermen braved winter gales and dangerous icebergs to sail across the Atlantic. Off the coasts of Newfoundland, they netted huge catches of codfish.

French ships brought knives, kettles, cloth, and other items for trade with Native Americans. In return, the French took home beaver skins. These furs sold for high prices in Europe.

The man who did the most to boost the French fur trade was Samuel de Champlain (sham PLAYN). Champlain founded the first permanent settlements in what was soon known as **New France.**

The first colony took root at Port Royal, Nova Scotia, in 1605. Three years later, Champlain led another group of settlers up the St. Lawrence River. On a rocky cliff, Champlain built a trading post known as Quebec (kwee BEHK).

Trappers, traders, and missionaries

Most French colonists were trappers and traders. Because they lived in the thick forests, they became known as **coureurs de bois** (koo RYOOR duh BWAH), or runners of the woods.

Coureurs de bois learned trapping and survival skills from Native Americans. Many trappers married Indian women. Indians taught the French how to build and use canoes. Each fall, Indians and trappers paddled up the St. Lawrence to winter trapping grounds. In the springtime, they paddled back down the river with the furs they had collected.

Catholic missionaries often traveled with fur traders. The missionaries were determined to convert Native Americans to Christianity. Life was difficult for the missionaries, especially in winter. One priest recalled traveling through deep snow using Indian snowshoes:

> "If a thaw came, dear Lord, what pain!... I was marching on an icy path that broke with every step I took; as the snow softened... we often sunk in it up to our knees and a few times up to the waist."

Reaching the Mississippi River

French trappers followed the St. Lawrence deep into the heart of North America. Led by Indian guides, they reached the Great Lakes. Here, Indians spoke of a mighty river, which they called Mississippi, or "Father of the Waters."

In 1673, a French missionary, Father **Jacques Marquette** (mar KEHT), and a fur trader, **Louis Joliet** (JOH lee eht), set out with Indian guides to reach the Mississippi. They followed the river for more than 700

Why Study History?

Because You Live in a Shrinking World

Food	Description	Place of Origin
borscht	Cold beet soup	Russia, Ukraine
chutney	Sauce or relish made of fruits, herbs, and spices	India
couscous	Tiny grains of wheat cooked until fluffy	North Africa
feta cheese	White, crumbly cheese	Greece
gazpacho	Chilled tomato soup	Spain
homous	Spread made from chickpeas	Middle East
salsa	Hot sauce made from tomatoes, chilies, peppers, herbs, and spices	Mexico
egg rolls	Shredded vegetables in fried dough wrapper	China
sushi	Raw fish and rice, often wrapped in seaweed	Japan

Plate of tacos ➤

Historical Background

Among the Aztecs in Mexico 600 years ago, a typical meal included corn porridge, beans, tortillas, and tomato or pepper sauce. In Europe, meanwhile, most people ate dark bread, cheese, and cabbage or turnip soup.

Then in the 1500s, contacts grew between the Americas and the rest of the world. Europeans got their first taste of potatoes, corn, and cocoa from the Americas. Native Americans began eating wheat bread, bananas, and citrus fruit from Europe, Africa, and Asia.

Connections to Today

Our world continues to get smaller. Today, people around the world watch American movies and television shows. They wear American styles of clothing and listen to American forms of music. At the same time, new ideas and goods travel from other lands to become part of American culture. New dance styles have come from Latin America, new clothing fashions from France, and new advances in communication from Japan. Due to modern communication and transportation, exchanges take place more quickly than ever before.

Connections to You

You can see—and taste—examples of cultural exchange in the international foods aisle of your local supermarket. The chart above lists some foods from other lands that have become popular in the United States.

1. **Comprehension**
   (a) Name two foods that Native Americans introduced to Europeans.
   (b) Name two Mexican foods that are popular in the United States today.
2. **Critical Thinking** How do you think communication via the Internet affects cultural exchange today?

Planning a Food Festival Working with other students, plan a festival of popular international foods. For ideas on what foods to include, visit your local supermarket or consult an international cookbook.

Viewing History

A View of Manhattan

From a tiny group of 30 houses, New Amsterdam grew into a busy port where ships docked from all over the world. This painting shows the Dutch settlement as it looked in the 1600s. Windmills, like the one on the far left, were a common source of power in the Netherlands. ★ **What city is now located on the island of Manhattan? What would this view look like today?**

miles (1,100 km) before turning back. In 1682, another explorer, Robert de La Salle (lah SAHL), completed the journey to the Gulf of Mexico. La Salle named the region around the Mississippi Louisiana in honor of the French king, Louis XIV.

To keep Spain and England away from Louisiana, the French built forts along the Mississippi. One fort, at the mouth of the river, was named New Orleans. New Orleans soon grew into a busy trading center. The French also built forts along the Great Lakes, in the north. Among them was Fort Detroit, near Lake Erie.

Government of New France

New France was governed much like New Spain. The French king controlled the government directly, and people in settled areas had little political freedom. A council appointed by the king made all decisions.

In the 1660s, to encourage farming, Louis XIV sent about a thousand farmers to the colony. The newcomers included many young women. Most of the women were single, but they soon found husbands. Peasant women were in greatest demand because they were used to hard work.

Despite Louis's efforts, New France grew slowly. By 1680, only about 10,000 settlers lived in the colony. Most continued to be coureurs de bois, who lived largely free of government control.

Building New Netherland

The Dutch also sought to profit from their discoveries in America. In 1626, **Peter Minuit** (MIHN yoo wiht) led a group of Dutch settlers to the mouth of the Hudson River. There, he bought Manhattan Island from local Indians. Minuit called his settlement New Amsterdam. (Today, it is the site of New York City.) Other Dutch colonists settled farther up the Hudson River. The entire colony was known as **New Netherland.**

Rivalry over furs

From the start, Dutch traders sent furs back to the Netherlands. The packing list for the first shipment included "the skins of 7,246 beaver, 853 otter, 81 mink, 36 cat lynx, and 34 small rats."

In the hunt for furs, the Dutch became fierce rivals of the French and their Indian allies, the Algonquins (al GAHN kwihnz). The Dutch made friends with the Iroquois, long-time enemies of the Algonquins. The Iroquois helped the Dutch bring furs down the Hudson. The French and Algonquins tried to block them. For years, fighting raged among Europeans and their Indian allies.

Dutch ways in North America

By the mid-1600s, New Amsterdam was a bustling port. The Dutch welcomed people of many nations and religions to their colony. A Dutch governor boasted that more than 15 languages could be heard in the streets of New Amsterdam.

Many Dutch customs became part of American culture. For example, every year on Saint Nicholas's birthday, children put out their shoes to be filled with presents. Later, "Saint Nick" became Santa Claus.

Some Dutch words entered the English language. A Dutch master was a "boss." The people of New Amsterdam sailed in "yachts." Dutch children munched on "cookies."

Impact on Native Americans

The coming of Europeans to North America brought major changes for Native Americans. European diseases killed many Native Americans, although the death rate was much smaller than in New Spain. Rivalry over the fur trade increased Indian warfare as European settlers encouraged their Indian allies to attack one another. The scramble for furs also led to overtrapping. By 1640, trappers had almost wiped out the beavers on Iroquois lands in New York.

The arrival of European settlers affected Native Americans in other ways. Missionaries tried to convert Indians to Christianity. Indians eagerly adopted European trade goods, such as copper kettles and knives, as well as muskets and gunpowder for hunting. Alcohol sold by European traders had a harsh effect on Native American life.

The French, Dutch, and English all seized Indian lands. As Indians were forced off their lands, they moved westward onto lands of other Indians. At one time or another, each of these European nations also enslaved Native Americans and sold them to plantations in the West Indies. The conflict between Native Americans and Europeans would continue for many years.

★ Section 4 Review ★

Recall

1. **Locate** **(a)** Newfoundland, **(b)** St. Lawrence River, **(c)** New France, **(d)** Quebec, **(e)** Mississippi River, **(f)** Louisiana, **(g)** New Orleans.
2. **Identify** **(a)** Ferdinand Magellan, **(b)** Martin Luther, **(c)** Protestant Reformation, **(d)** New France, **(e)** Jacques Marquette, **(f)** Louis Joliet, **(g)** Peter Minuit, **(h)** New Netherland.
3. **Define** **(a)** northwest passage, **(b)** coureurs de bois.

Comprehension

4. How did religious differences divide European nations?
5. **(a)** How did French trappers learn from Native Americans? **(b)** Why did missionaries often travel with fur traders?
6. How did competition arise between the French and Dutch in North America?

Critical Thinking and Writing

7. **Comparing** **(a)** Identify two ways in which New France was similar to New Spain. **(b)** Identify two ways in which the two colonies were different.
8. **Making Generalizations** **(a)** Based on what you have read, make a generalization about how the arrival of French and Dutch settlers affected Native Americans. **(b)** List three facts to support your generalization.

Activity **Making a Map** You have the chance to send a map back through time to Robert de La Salle. On your map, show him how he can journey from Nova Scotia to the mouth of the Mississippi over the land and waterways of North America.

Chapter 2 Review and Activities

★ Sum It Up ★

Section 1 The First Americans

- The ways of life of Native Americans varied widely depending on the geographic features of their location.
- Some Native American societies were small and simple, while others, such as that of the Iroquois, were complex.

Section 2 Europeans Reach the Americas

- During the Renaissance, Europeans began to explore the world outside Europe.
- European powers began to conquer or colonize much of North America and South America.
- European voyages to the Americas started a global exchange of products and ideas that continues today.

Section 3 Africans Come to the Americas

- Busy trade routes linked wealthy kingdoms and small villages across West Africa.
- European traders brought enslaved Africans to the Americas to work on plantations.

Section 4 Rival Claims in North America

- European nations such as France and the Netherlands were rivals for the wealth of resources in the Americas.
- Native Americans traded with Europeans, but also suffered bitterly from disease and warfare.

For additional review of the major ideas of Chapter 2, see ***Guide to the Essentials of American History*** or ***Interactive Student Tutorial CD-ROM,*** which contains interactive review activities, graphic organizers, and practice tests.

Reviewing the Chapter

Define These Terms

Match each term with the correct definition.

Column 1	Column 2
1. culture	**a.** group of settlers ruled by the government of their native land
2. colony	**b.** system of family ties
3. conquistador	**c.** Spanish conqueror
4. kinship network	**d.** French trapper and trader
5. coureur de bois	**e.** entire way of life developed by a people

Explore the Main Ideas

1. What was one important purpose of the religious ceremonies of Native Americans?
2. What role did women play in Iroquois society?
3. Why did Spain send explorers and conquerors to the Americas?
4. How did Bartolomé de Las Casas contribute to the growth of the African slave trade?
5. What role did Native Americans play in the rivalry between the French and the Dutch?

Geography Activity

Match the letters on the map with the following places: **1.** Africa, **2.** Asia, **3.** Europe, **4.** North America, **5.** East Indies, **6.** West Indies, **7.** South America. **Location** Why did Europeans want to reach Asia?

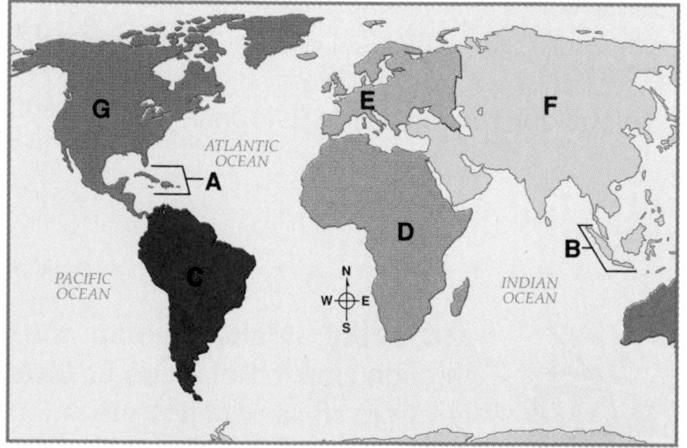

Critical Thinking and Writing

1. **Linking Past and Present** In what ways is the Iroquois government similar to our government today?
2. **Understanding Chronology** **(a)** Place the following events in their correct order: Columbus crosses the Atlantic; the Renaissance begins; Spain builds missions in the borderlands; Cortés conquers the Aztecs. **(b)** How did the earliest event on your list contribute to the other three?
3. **Understanding Points of View** Describe how you think each of the following people might have felt about Bartolomé de Las Casas: **(a)** an enslaved Native American in New Spain; **(b)** a Spanish plantation owner; **(c)** King Affonso of Kongo.
4. **Exploring Unit Themes** **Origins** Choose one event or development discussed in this chapter. Explain why you think that event or development had an impact on the present-day United States.

Using Primary Sources

In 1687 the French planned an attack on the Iroquois, who by then were the allies of the English. Part of the plan says:

> “The Iroquois force consists of two thousand picked warriors—brave, active, more skillful in the use of the gun than our Europeans and all well armed. . . . If they be [surrounded] on both sides, all their plantations of Indian corn will be destroyed, their villages burnt, their women, children, and old men captured, and their warriors driven into the woods, where they will be pursued and [destroyed] by the other Indians.”

Source: *Memoir for the Marquis de Seignelay, 1687,* Department of Alfa-Information, University of Groningen, 1996.

Recognizing Points of View **(a)** How did the French plan to destroy the Iroquois? **(b)** Does this selection suggest that the French respected the Iroquois? Explain.

Activity Bank

Interdisciplinary Activity

Exploring the Arts Choose one of the cultures described in this chapter—Native American, European, or African. Research its artwork. Choose a piece of art from the time period before 1700. Present and describe your work to the class.

Career Skills Activity

Biologists Find out which American mammals were hunted in the fur trade. Then prepare a fact sheet for one animal. Include what the animal eats, where it lives, its natural enemies, and whether today it faces extinction.

Citizenship Activity

Forming a League Forming the League of the Iroquois required cooperation, organization, and commitment. Sketch out a plan for a league that would meet a need in your school. Suggest what kind of body would make decisions and what groups would need to be represented.

Internet Activity

Use the Internet to find sites dealing with California's Native Americans. Save the information you have found as a text file. Work with other members of your class to print out and bind the text files in an attractive format.

Eyewitness Journal

In your Eyewitness Journal, write an account of Columbus's arrival in the Americas from the point of view of a Spanish sailor, a member of the Spanish court, or a Native American. If you prefer, you can write about the life of a coureur de bois in the North American woods.

Chapter 3

The 13 English Colonies

1587–1750

What's Ahead

Section 1
Establishing the Colonies

Section 2
Different Ways of Life

Section 3
The English Heritage

In the 1600s and 1700s, English settlers founded a string of colonies on the eastern coast of what is now the United States. Many colonists came in search of wealth. Others sought religious freedom. Over time, colonies in different parts of North America developed different economies and ways of life.

Despite differences, English settlers in all of the colonies shared certain traditions of liberty and law. Not everyone in the colonies enjoyed these basic rights. Still, Americans came to develop an independent spirit and a tradition of self-government.

Why Study History? The United States grew from the 13 English colonies. As a result, many of our traditions have English roots. One of the most important is representative government—the right to elect the people who govern us. To focus on this connection, see the *Why Study History?* feature, "You Have a Say in Government," in this chapter.

American Events

- **1607** English colony begins at Jamestown
- **1620** Pilgrims sign the Mayflower Compact
- **1647** Massachusetts sets up first public schools

1600 — 1625 — 1650 — 1675

World Events

- **1611 World Event** King James version of Bible is published
- **1666 World Event** Laws of gravity discovered by Isaac Newton

The Beginning of a New Society

Viewing HISTORY

The Pilgrims, the first English settlers in Massachusetts, crossed the Atlantic in search of religious freedom. Before leaving their ship, the Mayflower, *Pilgrim men signed an agreement promising to work together "for the general good of the colony." This painting shows the signing of the Mayflower Compact in 1620.*

★ **What does this painting suggest about the roles of women and men in Pilgrim society?**

1682
William Penn begins the colony of Pennsylvania

1732
James Oglethorpe founds colony of Georgia

1675 **1700** **1725** **1750**

1689 World Event
William and Mary sign English Bill of Rights

1700s World Event
Age of Enlightenment begins in Europe

Establishing the Colonies

Explore These Questions

- Why did early English settlers come to North America?
- What was William Penn's "holy experiment"?
- How did Georgia differ from other colonies?

Define

- charter
- representative government
- proprietary colony
- proprietor

Identify

- Jamestown
- House of Burgesses
- Pilgrims
- Mayflower Compact
- Puritans
- William Penn
- Quakers
- Lord Baltimore
- James Oglethorpe

In 1584, an English geographer named Richard Hakluyt urged Queen Elizabeth I to set up colonies in North America. Hakluyt wrote:

> "If England possesses these places in America, Her Majesty will have good harbors, plenty of excellent trees for masts, good timber to build ships. . . . all things needed for a royal navy, and all for no price."

In his letter, Hakluyt appealed to English pride. England's rival, Spain, had built a great empire in the Americas during the 1500s. During the 1600s, England won a place there, too.

The First English Colonies

English explorers tried several times to establish colonies in North America. In 1587, a group of men and women attempted to start a farming community on the island of Roanoke, off the coast of present-day North Carolina. Three years later, a supply ship from England found the settlement deserted. To this day, the fate of the Roanoke colonists remains unknown.

Founding Jamestown

In 1606, the Virginia Company of London received a charter from King James I. A **charter** is a legal document giving certain rights to a person or company.

The charter gave the Virginia Company the right to settle land in the area of Chesapeake Bay, to the north of Roanoke. The land was called Virginia. The charter guaranteed colonists of Virginia the same rights as English citizens.

In the spring of 1607, a group of 105 colonists sailed up the James River from Chesapeake Bay. They built a settlement and named it **Jamestown,** after their king.

Tobacco saves Virginia's economy

Virginia's early years were hard ones. Jamestown was located in a swampy area, where mosquitoes spread malaria. Many settlers died from disease. Those who survived seemed more interested in digging for gold than in raising crops. For the next few years, the colony suffered terribly. Desperate settlers cooked "dogs, cats, snakes, [and] toadstools" to survive.

Virginia's economy improved after 1612, when colonists began to grow tobacco. Europeans had learned about tobacco and pipe smoking from Native Americans. James I considered smoking "a vile custom." Still, the new practice caught on quickly in Europe. By 1620, England was importing more than 30,000 pounds (13,500 kg) of tobacco a year.

A representative government

In 1619, the Virginia Company sent a governor with orders to consult settlers on all important matters. Male settlers were allowed to elect burgesses, or representatives. The burgesses met in an assembly called the **House of Burgesses.** Together with the governor, they made laws for the colony.

The House of Burgesses marked the beginning of **representative government** in the English colonies. In a representative government, voters elect representatives to make laws for them. (You will learn more about English traditions of representative government later in this chapter.)

The Plymouth Colony

In 1620, another band of English settlers, the **Pilgrims,** sailed for the Americas. Unlike the Virginians or the Spanish, these colonists sought neither gold nor silver. All they wanted was to practice their religion freely.

In England, the Pilgrims belonged to a religious group known as Separatists. They got this name because they wanted to separate themselves from the official church, the Church of England. The English government fined, jailed, and sometimes even executed Separatists.

Voyage to America

In September 1620, more than 100 Separatists—men, women, and children—set sail from Plymouth, England, aboard a small ship called the *Mayflower*. After a stormy two-month voyage, the Pilgrims landed on the cold, bleak shore of Cape Cod, in present-day Massachusetts.

Before leaving the *Mayflower*, however, the Pilgrims drew up rules for their new home. Their agreement became known as the **Mayflower Compact.** The 41 men who signed it agreed to consult one another about laws for the colony and promised to work together to make the colony succeed.

Hardships and survival

The Pilgrims named the colony Plymouth. During their first winter there, nearly half the settlers died of disease or starvation. Then in the spring, the Pilgrims received help from neighboring Wampanoag (wahm puh NOH ahg) Indians. A Wampanoag man named Squanto brought the Pilgrims seeds of native plants—corn, beans, and pumpkins—and showed them how to plant them. He also taught the settlers to stir up eels from river bottoms and then snatch them with their hands. The grateful Pilgrims called Squanto "a special instrument sent of God."

Biography **Pocahontas**

Pocahontas, the daughter of a powerful Native American chief, brought food to the starving colonists at Jamestown. She later married colonist John Rolfe and visited England with him. This portrait shows Pocahontas in English dress. It is the only genuine painting of Pocahontas. ★ **Why do you think later Americans have honored Pocahontas?**

Connections With Civics

The first strike for civil rights may have taken place in Jamestown in 1619. Only English men could vote for the House of Burgesses. Polish settlers who had helped build the colony protested. "No vote, no work," they threatened. In the end the Virginia Company gave the Poles the right to vote.

Viewing History **The New England Puritan**

Augustus Saint-Gaudens, the leading American sculptor of the 1800s, captured the Puritan spirit in his bronze statue The Puritan, *below. The meetinghouse was the center of the Puritan community. Here, families attended services several times a week and all day on Sunday. The meetinghouse at left has been in use since 1681.* ★ **How does the architecture of this meetinghouse reflect what you have learned about the Puritans?**

In the fall, the Pilgrims had a good harvest. Because they believed that God had given them this harvest, they set aside a day for giving thanks. In later years, the Pilgrims celebrated every harvest with a day of thanksgiving. Americans today celebrate Thanksgiving as a national holiday.

The New England Colonies

In 1629, a much larger English colony was founded in Massachusetts Bay, north of Plymouth. This settlement was created by a different religious group, known as the Puritans.

Puritans in Massachusetts

Unlike the Pilgrims, the **Puritans** did not want to separate entirely from the Church of England. Instead, they hoped to reform the church by making its worship services simpler.

By 1629, some Puritan leaders were convinced that England had fallen on "evil and declining times." They persuaded royal officials to grant them a charter to form the Massachusetts Bay Company. The company's bold plan was to build a new society in New England. They vowed to base their new society on biblical laws and teachings.

One of the Puritan leaders, John Winthrop, boldly predicted that the new colony would set an example to the world:

> "The Lord will make our name a praise and glory, so that men shall say of succeeding [colonies]: 'The Lord make it like that of New England.' For we must consider that we shall be like a City upon a Hill. The eyes of all people are on us."

Under the leadership of Winthrop and other Puritans, the Massachusetts Bay Colony prospered. Between 1629 and 1640, more than 20,000 men, women, and children journeyed from England to Massachusetts. This movement of people is known as the Great Migration. Many newcomers settled in Boston, which grew into the colony's largest town. Most newcomers, however, settled in small villages all along the eastern coastal plain.

Over the next 100 years, English settlers built towns and farms throughout New England. Settlers dissatisfied with Puritan rule in Massachusetts Bay founded two new colonies—Rhode Island and Connecticut. (See Section 3.) In 1680, the king of England combined Massachusetts coastal settlements into a fourth New England colony, New Hampshire.

Economic interests

Some settlers came to New England for economic rather than religious reasons. Such people were attracted by cheap land or a chance to start their own businesses.

Some towns in New England were founded almost entirely for economic reasons. For example, the settlers in Marblehead, Massachusetts, made their town a center of

Founding of the Colonies

Colony / Date Founded	Leader	Reasons Founded
New England Colonies		
▪ Massachusetts Plymouth / 1620 Massachusetts Bay / 1630	William Bradford John Winthrop	Religious freedom Religious freedom
▪ New Hampshire / 1622	Ferdinando Gorges John Mason	Profit from trade and fishing
▪ Connecticut Hartford / 1636 New Haven / 1639	Thomas Hooker	Expand trade; religious and political freedom
▪ Rhode Island / 1636	Roger Williams	Religious freedom
Middle Colonies		
▪ New York / 1624	Peter Minuit	Expand trade
▪ Delaware / 1638	Swedish settlers	Expand trade
▪ New Jersey / 1664	John Berkeley George Carteret	Expand trade; religious and political freedom
▪ Pennsylvania / 1682	William Penn	Profit from land sales; religious and political freedom
Southern Colonies		
▪ Virginia / 1607	John Smith	Trade and farming
▪ Maryland / 1632	Lord Baltimore	Profit from land sales; religious and political freedom
▪ The Carolinas / 1663 North Carolina / 1712 South Carolina / 1712	Group of eight proprietors	Trade and farming; religious freedom
▪ Georgia / 1732	James Oglethorpe	Profit; home for debtors; buffer against Spanish Florida

Chart *Skills* **English settlers founded 13 separate colonies along the Atlantic coast of North America. The colonies were founded for many different reasons.**

1. **Comprehension** **(a)** Identify two colonies founded by people seeking religious freedom. **(b)** Identify two colonies founded by people seeking to expand trade.
2. **Critical Thinking** How long did it take for England to establish its American colonies?

shipbuilding. For its first fifty years, Marblehead did not even have a church.

Conflict with Native Americans

As more colonists settled in New England, they took over lands used by Native Americans for thousands of years. As a result, fighting often broke out between white settlers and Indian nations.

The largest conflict came in 1675. Wampanoag Indians attacked colonial villages throughout New England. Other Indian groups allied themselves with the Wampanoags. Fighting lasted 15 months. Finally, the settlers won the war. The English sold about 1,000 Native Americans into slavery in the West Indies. Other Indians were forced from their homelands.

This pattern of expansion followed by war happened again and again throughout the colonies. It would continue for many years to come.

The Middle Colonies

Another group of English colonies became known as the Middle Colonies because they were located between New England and the Southern Colonies. The Middle Colonies included New York, New Jersey, Pennsylvania, and Delaware.

Originally, the Middle Colonies were founded as proprietary (proh PRĪ uh tuhr ee) colonies. In setting up a **proprietary colony,** the king gave land to one or more people, called **proprietors.** Proprietors were free to divide the land and rent it to others. They made laws for the colony but had to respect the rights of colonists under English law.

New York and New Jersey

In 1664, the rivalry between England and the Netherlands for trade and colonies led to war in Europe. During the war, England took over the Dutch colony of New

Viewing HISTORY **William Penn Greets an Indian**

Unlike most colonial leaders, William Penn insisted that settlers pay Native Americans for their land. As a result of such fair policies, colonists in Pennsylvania enjoyed many years of peace with their Indian neighbors. This painting shows Penn greeting an Indian. ★ **How do you think Penn's Quaker beliefs influenced his relations with Native Americans?**

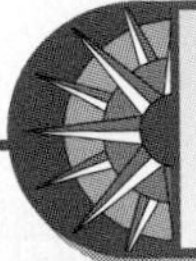

Linking Past and Present

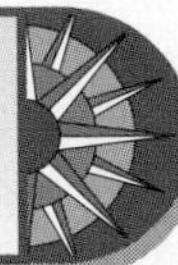

Past

Present

A Simple Country Life

Horses and buggies were a common sight in colonial Pennsylvania. Today, in some parts of Pennsylvania, they still are. The Amish, a Christian sect, have lived in Pennsylvania since the 1700s. They continue to farm the land, use horses, and dress as plainly as their ancestors did. ★ **Why do you think the Amish chose Pennsylvania as their home?**

Netherland, along the Hudson River. (See Chapter 2.) King Charles II of England then gave the colony to his brother, the Duke of York. He renamed the colony New York in the duke's honor.

At the time, New York stretched as far south as the Delaware River. The Duke of York realized that it was too large to govern easily. He gave some of the land to two of his friends, Lord Berkeley and Sir George Carteret. This land became the proprietary colony of New Jersey.

Pennsylvania and Delaware

In 1682, **William Penn** founded the colony of Pennsylvania. Penn came from a wealthy English family. At age 22, however, Penn shocked family and friends by joining the **Quakers,** one of the most despised religious groups in England.

Like the Pilgrims and Puritans, the Quakers were Protestant reformers. They believed that all people—men and women, nobles and commoners—were equal in God's sight. Quakers allowed women to preach in public and would not remove their hats in the presence of the nobility. Quakers also refused to serve in the army.

Because Quakers faced persecution in England, Penn persuaded King Charles II to grant him land in North America. The new colony became known as Pennsylvania, or Penn's woodlands.

William Penn thought of his colony as a "holy experiment." He wanted it to be a model of religious freedom, peace, and Christian living. Protestants, Catholics, and Jews went to Pennsylvania to escape persecution. Later, though, English officials forced Penn to turn away Catholic and Jewish settlers.

Most new settlers landed at Philadelphia, the colony's capital. By 1750, Philadelphia had become the most populous city in the English colonies.

For a time, Pennsylvania included some lands along the lower Delaware River. The

Growing Tobacco in the South

In the Southern Colonies, tobacco was so valuable that colonists used it as money. For example, a doctor might charge up to 2,500 pounds of tobacco for the care of a patient. In this drawing, wealthy planters look on while enslaved African Americans pack a cargo of tobacco. ★ **Why do doctors today oppose the use of tobacco?**

region was known as Pennsylvania's Lower Counties. Eventually, the Lower Counties broke away to form the colony of Delaware.

The Southern Colonies

In addition to Virginia, the English founded several other colonies to the south of Delaware. These settlements became known as the Southern Colonies. They included Maryland, North and South Carolina, and Georgia.

Lord Baltimore's Maryland

In the spring of 1634, 200 colonists landed along the upper Chesapeake Bay, across from Virginia. The land was rich and beautiful. Across the bay, Virginians were already growing tobacco for profit. These settlers hoped to do the same.

The new colony, Maryland, was the creation of Sir George Calvert. Calvert, a Roman Catholic, persuaded King Charles I in 1632 to grant him land in America. He planned to build a colony where Catholics could practice their religion freely. When Sir George died, his son Cecil, **Lord Baltimore,** pushed on with the project.

As proprietor of the colony, Lord Baltimore gave colonists a role in government by creating an elected assembly. To ensure Maryland's continued growth, he welcomed Protestants as well as Catholics to the colony.

Virginia expands

Meanwhile, new settlers continued to go to Virginia, lured by the promise of profits from tobacco. Wealthy planters quickly took the best lands near the coast. Newcomers had to push inland onto Indian lands.

As in New England, conflict over land led to fighting between settlers and Indians. After several bloody clashes, settlers called on the colonial governor to take action against Native Americans. The governor refused, in part because he profited from his own fur trade with the Indians. Frontier settlers were furious.

In 1676, a young planter, Nathaniel Bacon, led raids on Native American villages. Then, he led his followers to Jamestown and burned the capital. The uprising, known as Bacon's Rebellion, lasted only a short time. Bacon died suddenly. The governor hanged 23 of Bacon's followers. Still, the failure of

Bacon's Rebellion did not stop English settlers from moving onto Indian lands along the frontier.

The Carolinas

South of Virginia and Maryland, English colonists settled in a region called the Carolinas. Settlers in what became North Carolina were mostly poor tobacco farmers who had drifted south from Virginia. They tended to have small farms.

Farther south, in what was to become South Carolina, a group of eight English nobles set up a proprietary colony on land granted by King Charles II in 1663. The largest settlement was Charles Town, later shortened to Charleston.

Around 1685, planters discovered that rice grew well in the swampy lowlands along the coast. Before long, Carolina rice was a valuable crop traded around the world.

Carolina planters needed large numbers of workers to grow rice. At first, they tried to enslave local Native Americans. Many Indians died of disease or mistreatment, while others escaped into the forests. Planters then looked to Africa. By 1700, most people coming to Charleston were enslaved African men and women.

Georgia: a haven for debtors

The last of England's 13 colonies was carved out of the southern part of South Carolina. **James Oglethorpe,** an energetic reformer, founded Georgia in 1732. He wanted to create a place where people jailed for debt in England could make a new start. Oglethorpe offered to pay for debtors and other poor people to travel to Georgia. "In America," he said, "there are enough fertile lands to feed all the poor of England."

In 1733, Oglethorpe and 120 colonists built the colony's first settlement at Savannah. Oglethorpe set strict rules for the colony. Farms could be no bigger than 50 acres, and slavery was forbidden.

At first, Georgia grew slowly. Later, however, the rules changed to allow large plantations and slave labor. After that, the colony grew more quickly.

★ Section 1 Review ★

Recall

1. **Locate** **(a)** Virginia, **(b)** Massachusetts, **(c)** New Hampshire, **(d)** Rhode Island, **(e)** Connecticut, **(f)** New York, **(g)** New Jersey, **(h)** Pennsylvania, **(i)** Delaware, **(j)** Maryland, **(k)** North Carolina, **(l)** South Carolina, **(m)** Georgia.
2. **Identify** **(a)** Jamestown, **(b)** House of Burgesses, **(c)** Pilgrims, **(d)** Mayflower Compact, **(e)** Puritans, **(f)** William Penn, **(g)** Quakers, **(h)** Lord Baltimore, **(i)** James Oglethorpe.
3. **Define** **(a)** charter, **(b)** representative government, **(c)** proprietary colony, **(d)** proprietor.

Comprehension

4. Describe the reasons English settlers founded each of the following colonies: **(a)** Jamestown, **(b)** Massachusetts.
5. Why did the Quakers seek a new home in North America?
6. What were the goals of the founders of **(a)** Maryland, **(b)** the Carolinas, **(c)** Georgia?

Critical Thinking and Writing

7. **Comparing** **(a)** How was William Penn's "holy experiment" similar to the Puritan idea of a "City upon a Hill"? **(b)** How was it different?
8. **Making Inferences** In Oglethorpe's time, debtors could be thrown into prison until they repaid their debts. Why do you think many people objected to this law?

★ ★

Activity **Making Decisions** The time is 1750. You are a young person in Britain looking for a chance to succeed in life—so you plan to move to the American colonies. Choose a colony and write a letter to your parents explaining your choice.

Different Ways of Life

As You Read

Explore These Questions

- What role did religion play in New England society?
- How did farming in the Middle Colonies differ from farming in the Southern Colonies?
- How was colonial society structured?

Define

- common
- cash crops
- backcountry
- gentry
- middle class
- indentured servant

Identify

- Yankee
- Great Wagon Road
- Tidewater
- Gullah

Wooden codfish from a colonial Massachusetts home

Setting the Scene In the late 1700s, a soldier from New England was marching through the streets of Philadelphia. One local woman stared at this **"Yankee,"** as New Englanders were called. "La! Is he a Yankee?" she exclaimed in surprise. "I thought he was a Pennsylvanian. I don't see any difference between him and other people."

The woman was so surprised because she had never before met anyone from New England. The villages and farms only a few hundred miles to the north were as strange to her as if they were across the ocean.

For much of the 1600s and 1700s, the English colonies in America remained fairly isolated from one another. Each region developed in its own way.

New England's Farms, Forests, and Seas

New England's rocky soil was poor for farming. After a time, however, settlers learned to grow many Native American crops, such as Indian corn, beans, squash, and pumpkins.

Although the soil was poor, the forests were full of riches. New Englanders hunted wild turkey and deer. Settlers also cut down trees. They then floated the cut logs to sawmills near port cities such as Boston, Massachusetts, and Portsmouth, New Hampshire. These cities grew into major shipbuilding centers.

Other New Englanders fished the coastal waters for cod and halibut. New Englanders also hunted whales to supply them with ivory and with oil for lamps.

Tightly knit towns and villages

Puritans believed that people should worship and take care of local matters as a community. For this reason, New England became a land full of tightly knit towns and villages.

At the center of each village was the **common,** an open field where cattle grazed. Nearby stood the meetinghouse, where Puritans worshiped and held town meetings. Wooden houses with steep roofs lined both sides of the town's narrow streets.

The Puritans took their Sabbath, or holy day of rest, very seriously. On Sundays, no one was allowed to play games or visit taverns to joke, talk, and drink. The law required all citizens to attend church services, which on Sunday lasted all day.

At town meetings, settlers discussed and voted on many issues. What roads should be built? How much should the schoolmaster be paid? Town meetings gave New Englanders a chance to speak their minds. This early experience encouraged the growth of democratic ideas in New England.

Home and family

The average family had seven or eight children. The healthy climate allowed New Englanders to live long lives. As a result, children often grew up knowing both their parents and their grandparents. This did much to make New England towns closely knit communities.

During the 1700s, Puritan traditions declined. Fewer families left England for religious reasons. Ministers had less influence on colonial government. Even so, the Puritans stamped New England with their distinctive customs and their dream of a religious society.

Viewing History **A New England Mother and Daughter**

In New England, as elsewhere, women had the major responsibility for raising children. This 1674 painting shows a mother and daughter in Boston. Generally, the clothing worn by colonial children was just a miniature version of what their parents wore. ★ **How did close-knit families strengthen New England?**

The Diverse Middle Colonies

The Middle Colonies had a much greater mix of peoples than either New England or the Southern Colonies. One visitor from Maryland was amazed at the variety of people he met in Philadelphia. He wrote:

> "I dined at a tavern with a very mixed company of different nations and religions. There were Scots, English, Dutch, Germans, and Irish. There were Roman Catholics, Church [of England] men, Presbyterians, Quakers, . . . and one Jew."

Throughout the 1700s, immigrants from the British Isles and Europe continued to come to the Middle Colonies. Also, greater numbers of Africans arrived in Philadelphia and New York.

Commercial farms

Unlike New England's thin and rocky soil, the broad Hudson and Delaware river valleys were rich and fertile. On such promising land, farmers in the Middle Colonies produced surplus, or extra, wheat, barley, and rye. These were **cash crops,** or crops that are sold for money on the world market.

Farmers also raised cattle and pigs. Every year, they sent tons of beef, pork, and butter to the ports of New York and Philadelphia. From there, the goods went by ship to New England and the South, to colonies in the West Indies, or to England and other parts of Europe.

Farms in the Middle Colonies were usually larger than those in New England. Because houses tended to be fairly far apart in the Middle Colonies, towns there were less important than in New England. Counties, rather than villages, became the center of local government.

The backcountry

From Philadelphia, thousands of German and Scotch-Irish immigrants headed west into the **backcountry,** the area of land along the eastern slopes of the Appalachian Mountains. Settlers followed an old Iroquois trail that became known as the **Great Wagon Road.**

Many of these settlers moved onto Native American lands. "The Indians . . . are alarmed

Skills FOR LIFE

Reading a Pie Graph

How Will I Use This Skill?

When you read textbooks, newspapers, or magazines, you will often find important statistics presented as part of a pie graph. A pie graph is in the shape of a circle that represents 100% of the group you are examining. Pie graphs present statistics in wedges, like pieces of a pie. The wedges represent percentages of the whole, helping you better compare the groups.

LEARN the Skill

You can learn to understand pie graphs by using the steps below.

1. Identify the topic of the pie graph. Remember that the circle represents 100% of the group you are examining.
2. Identify which groups are represented by the various wedges of the pie. Some groups which are few in number or not easily identified may be shown as "others."
3. Compare the sizes of the various groups. The largest wedge will correspond to the largest group.

PRACTICE the Skill

Use the steps below to read the pie graph. The graph does not include Indians.

1. (a) What is the topic of this graph? (b) What entire group does the circle as a whole represent?
2. (a) List the population groups represented by the wedges. (b) Are all groups identified individually on the graph?
3. (a) Which group made up the largest percentage of the colonial population? (b) What percentage of the population had Swedish roots? (c) What was the largest non-European group shown here?

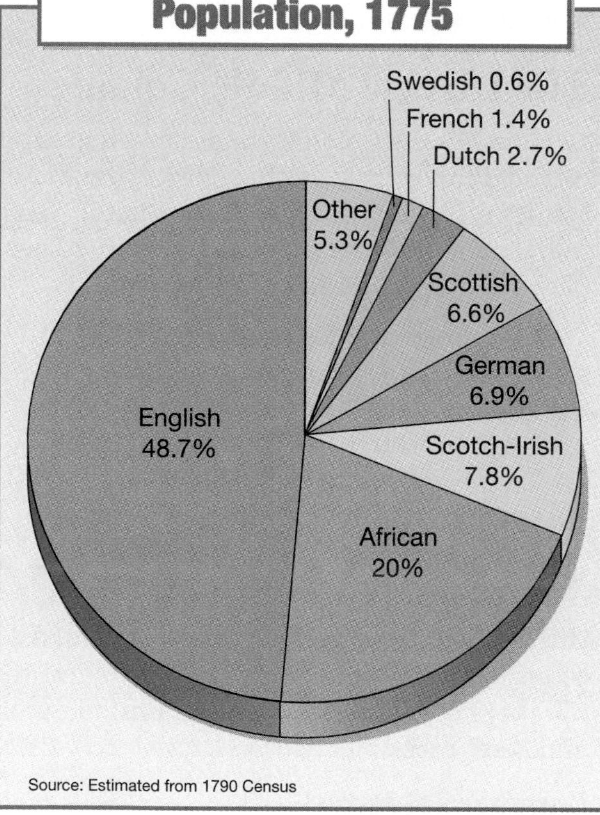

APPLY the Skill

Take a poll to determine in which month each member of your class was born. Turn the numbers into percentages and show the information on a pie graph. To figure out percentages, divide the number in each group by the total number of the class.

at the swarm of strangers," one Pennsylvania official reported. "We are afraid of a [fight] between them for the [colonists] are very rough to them." On more than one occasion, disputes between settlers and Indians resulted in violence.

The Southern Colonies

The Southern Colonies enjoyed warmer weather and a longer growing season than the colonies to the north. Virginia, Maryland, and parts of North Carolina all became major tobacco-growing areas. Settlers in South Carolina and Georgia raised rice and indigo, a plant used to make a blue dye.

A plantation economy

Southern colonists soon found that it was most profitable to raise tobacco and rice on large plantations. On a plantation, from 20 to 100 enslaved Africans did most of the work. Most slaves worked in the fields. Others were skilled workers, such as carpenters, barrelmakers, or blacksmiths. Still other slaves worked in the main house as cooks, servants, or housekeepers.

On plantations throughout the Southern Colonies, enslaved Africans used farming skills they had brought from West Africa. They showed English settlers how to grow rice. They also knew how to use wild plants unfamiliar to the English. They made water buckets out of gourds, and they used palmetto leaves to make fans, brooms, and baskets.

The earliest plantations were located along rivers and creeks of the coastal plain. Because these lowlands were washed by ocean tides, the region was known as the **Tidewater.** Farther inland, planters settled along rivers.

Most large coastal plantations had their own docks, where planters loaded their crops on ships bound for the West Indies and Europe. For this reason, few large seaport cities developed in the Southern Colonies.

The backcountry South

Life was very different west of the Tidewater. As in the Middle Colonies, this inland area at the base of the Appalachians was called the backcountry. Attracted by rich soil, settlers journeyed into the backcountry of Maryland, Virginia, and the Carolinas.

The backcountry was more democratic than the Tidewater. Settlers there were more likely to treat one another as equals. Men tended smaller fields of tobacco or corn or hunted game. Women cooked meals and fashioned simple clothing out of wool or deerskins.

A Southern Colonial Plantation

This painting provides a view of an early southern plantation. In the center is the main house, where the planter's family lived. Around it are rows of slave cabins. Not all slave cabins were as neat and orderly as these. ★ **Why did planters make use of enslaved laborers from Africa?**

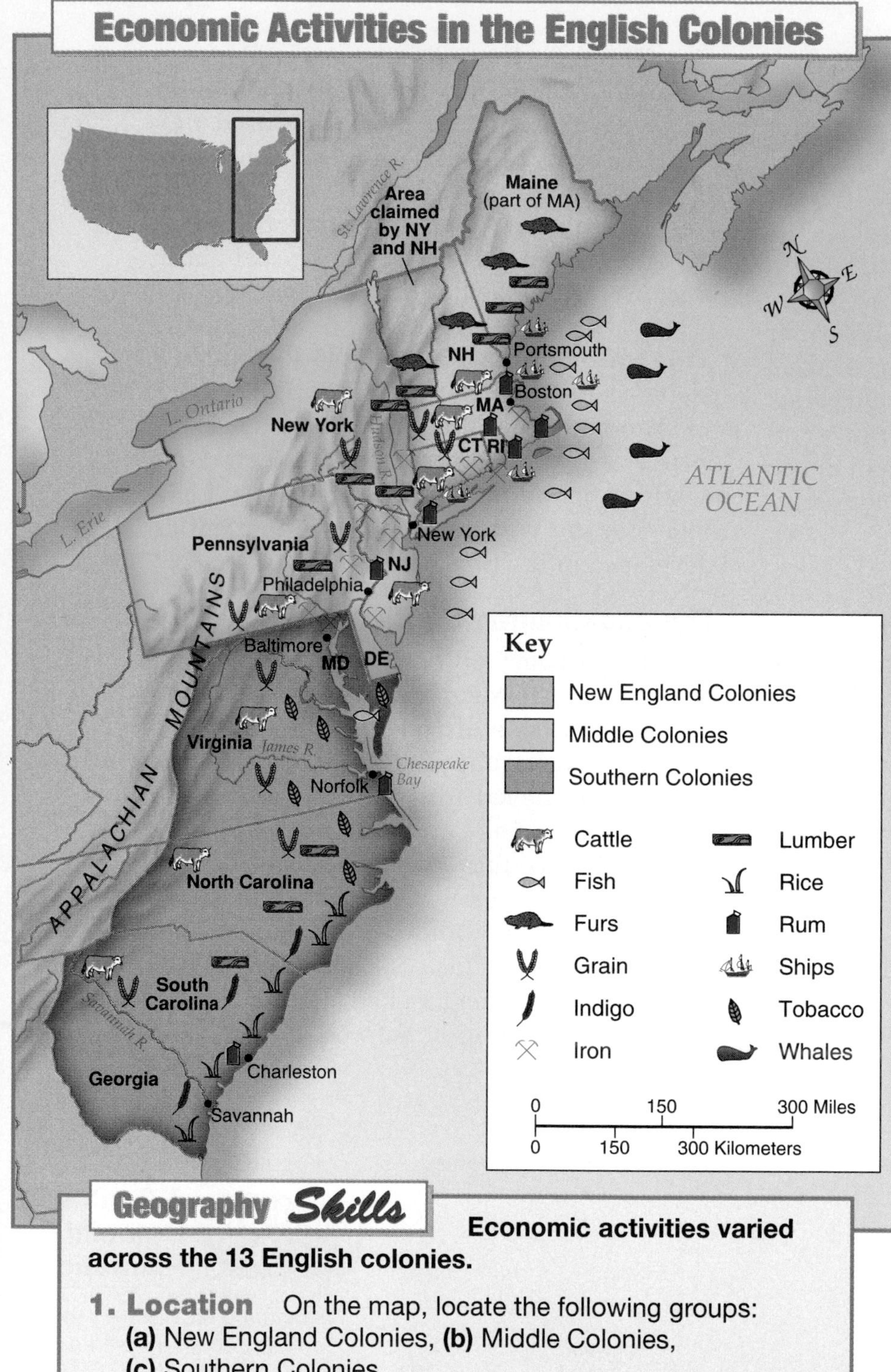

Geography *Skills* **Economic activities varied across the 13 English colonies.**

1. **Location** On the map, locate the following groups: **(a)** New England Colonies, **(b)** Middle Colonies, **(c)** Southern Colonies.
2. **Interaction** **(a)** Name two colonies where settlers mined for iron. **(b)** Name two colonies where settlers grew rice.
3. **Critical Thinking** How did New England's geography encourage the growth of shipbuilding?

Colonial Social Classes

Even in the backcountry, however, ordinary folk recognized that colonial society contained different social classes. Like Europeans, Americans in the colonies thought it only natural for some people to rank more highly than others.

At the top of society stood the **gentry.** The gentry included wealthy planters, merchants, ministers, successful lawyers, and royal officials. They could afford to dress in elegant clothes and follow the latest fashions from London.

Below the gentry were the **middle class,** the largest group of white settlers in the colonies. The middle class was made up of skilled craftsworkers, farmers who worked their own land, and some tradespeople.

The lowest social class included hired farmhands, indentured servants, and slaves. **Indentured servants** were settlers who signed contracts to work without wages for four to seven years for anyone who would pay their ocean passage.

Women's Work in the Colonies

From New Hampshire to Georgia, colonial women did many of the same tasks. A wife took care of her household, husband, and family. By the kitchen fire, she cooked the family's meals. She milked the cows, watched the children, and made clothing.

In the backcountry, wives and husbands often worked side by side in the fields at harvest time. A visitor from the East described a backcountry woman's activities:

> ❝ She will carry a gun in the woods and kill deer, turkeys &c., shoot down wild cattle, catch and tye hoggs, knock down [cattle] with an ax,

and perform the most manfull Exercises as well as most men. ❞

In cities, women sometimes worked outside the home. A young single woman from a poorer family might work as a maid, a cook, or a nurse for one of the gentry. Other women were midwives, delivering babies. Still others sewed fine hats, dresses, or cloaks to be sold to women who could afford them.

Women also worked as shoemakers, silversmiths, and butchers. Quite a few women became printers. Then, too, a woman might take over her husband's business when he died.

African Cultural Influences

By the mid-1700s, the culture of Africans in the colonies varied greatly. On plantations in South Carolina, slaves saw few white colonists. As a result, African customs remained strong. For example, parents often chose African names for their children, such as Quosh or Juba or Cuff. In some coastal areas, African Americans spoke a distinctive combination of English and West Indian languages, known as **Gullah.**

In Charleston and other South Carolina port towns, more than half the population had African roots. Skilled craftsworkers made fine wooden cabinets or silver plates. Many of their designs reflected African artistic styles.

In Virginia and Maryland, African traditions were weaker. Africans in the Chesapeake region were less isolated from white farmers and planters. Also, by the 1750s, the number of new slaves arriving in the region each year had begun to decline. Even so, many old customs survived. One traveler observed an African-style funeral. Mourners took part in a ceremony to speed a dead man's spirit to his home, which they believed was in Africa.

Fewer Africans lived in the Middle Colonies and New England. Most lived in such cities as Philadelphia, New York, and Newport. Often, the men outnumbered the women. As a result, the number of African families remained small.

★ Section 2 Review ★

Recall

1. **Locate** Appalachian Mountains.
2. **Identify** **(a)** Yankee, **(b)** Great Wagon Road, **(c)** Tidewater, **(d)** Gullah.
3. **Define** **(a)** common, **(b)** cash crops, **(c)** backcountry, **(d)** gentry, **(e)** middle class, **(f)** indentured servant.

Comprehension

4. How did the Puritans govern Massachusetts Bay?
5. **(a)** How did the land and climate of the Middle Colonies help farmers to prosper? **(b)** Why did southerners build large plantations?
6. **(a)** Describe the classes of colonial society. **(b)** What role did women play in the colonies?

Critical Thinking and Writing

7. **Forecasting** Why do you think tensions might have developed between people who lived in the backcountry and those who lived in the Tidewater region?
8. **Analyzing a Primary Source** "The sale of human beings in the market on board ship goes like this. English, Dutch, and Germans come on board to choose among the healthy passengers.... Adults bind themselves to serve anywhere from 3 to 6 years. Young people must serve until they are 21 years old." Does this passage refer to indentured servants or to enslaved Africans? How can you tell?

Activity **Creating Flashcards** Do you get confused about the English colonies? Use the text, including the maps and charts, to create 13 flashcards. On one side, write the name of a colony. On the other, write three facts about that colony. You may later use these cards for review.

The English Heritage

Explore These Questions
- What English political traditions influenced the American colonies?
- How did the Great Awakening influence the colonies?
- How did colonists educate their children?

Define
- legislature
- bill of rights
- slave code
- toleration
- established church
- public school
- apprentice
- dame school

Identify
- Magna Carta
- Parliament
- English Bill of Rights
- Roger Williams
- Anne Hutchinson
- Great Awakening
- Jonathan Edwards
- Enlightenment
- Benjamin Franklin

During the 1740s, a Swedish traveler named Peter Kalm was astonished by the clothes sometimes worn by workers in England. In France, Kalm observed, workers dressed simply, like peasants. English working men liked to put on knee breeches and wigs, especially on Sundays and holidays. Working women wore bonnets and puffed dresses.

Such habits shocked many Europeans. How could ordinary people dare to dress like the gentry! Europeans were convinced that the English loved liberty all too much. Even King George III once remarked that "the glory of Britain, and the direct end of its constitution is political liberty." American colonists shared in this love of liberty.

Political Liberties

The idea that people had political rights was not new to the English. In 1215, English nobles had forced King John to sign the **Magna Carta,** or Great Charter. This document said that the king could not raise taxes without first consulting the Great Council of nobles and church leaders. The Magna Carta showed that even the king had to obey the law.

Over time, the rights won by nobles were extended to other English people. The Great Council grew into a representative assembly, called **Parliament.** By the 1600s, Parliament was divided into the House of Lords, made up of nobles and high church leaders, and an elected House of Commons. The English system was not democratic. Only a few rich men had the right to vote. Still, the English had established the principle that their king or queen must consult Parliament on money matters and must respect the law.

Colonial charters

Each of England's 13 North American colonies had its own government. In Virginia, a charter established the House of Burgesses in 1619. Virginians later referred to this document as their own "great charter."

Other colonies also had charters, which they valued highly. Even more than most English people, American colonists believed that it was important to set down in writing the limits of a government. These "laws and liberties," explained one Pennsylvanian, were "framed and delivered down to us by our careful ancestors." Such charters, he boasted, listed the rights "belonging to all the King's subjects in America."

Governors and legislatures

Governments varied from colony to colony. Still, they had much in common. In each colony, a governor directed the colony's affairs and enforced the laws. Usually, the governor was appointed by the king or the colony's proprietor.

Why Study *History?*

Because You Have a Say in Government

★★★★★★★★★★★★★★★★★★★★★★★★★★★★★★★★★★★★

Historical Background

In 1295, King Edward I of England needed money for a war with France. To get the funds, he summoned Parliament, including representatives of the "common people," lords, and clergy. "What touches all should be approved by all," the king said. Over the years, the power of Parliament grew.

The idea of representative government passed on to England's American colonies. In 1619, King James I gave the Virginia colonists the right to form the House of Burgesses. Other colonies developed their own legislatures. Finally, the colonies became the United States of America. The English tradition of electing officials to make laws became the basis of American democracy.

Connections to Today

Today, Americans participate in government at many levels. On the national level, citizens elect representatives to Congress. Each state has its own legislature. In counties, cities, and towns, residents elect councils and boards to pass laws and make regulations. In some small towns, especially in New England, citizens still come together at town meetings to make their own laws.

Connections to You

Representative government affects you in a direct way. Do you attend a public school? If so, an elected school board probably governs your school district. School boards make decisions that affect everything from the books you use to your school's dress code and code of conduct.

You may also participate in representative government right now, by electing or serving on the student council. A student council may seem a long way from the English Parliament. Yet they are part of the same proud tradition.

1. **Comprehension** **(a)** How did the English tradition of representative government come to the colonies? **(b)** List two types of representative government in the United States today.
2. **Critical Thinking** "What touches all should be approved by all," said King Edward I. How do the king's words reflect one basic idea behind representative government?

Writing a Speech You have decided to run for a seat on your school's student council. Write a campaign speech. Describe what policies you would support. Explain why other students should elect you as their representative.

Representative government starts early.

A Tradition of Liberty

Sources of Rights

Magna Carta

- Monarch must consult Great Council to raise taxes
- Even rulers must obey laws
- Great Council grows into Parliament over time

English Bill of Rights

- Individual rights are guaranteed
- People accused of crime have right to trial by jury
- Ruler cannot raise taxes or an army without approval of Parliament

Colonial Charters

- Colonies ruled by governors and legislatures
- Legislature must approve tax requests from governor
- White male property owners have right to vote

Graphic Organizer *Skills* **The political rights of the 13 English colonies came from a variety of sources.**

1. **Comprehension** What were two features of the Magna Carta?
2. **Critical Thinking** Why do you think it is important for rights and liberties to be written down?

Civics

Each colony also had a legislature. A **legislature** is a group of people who have the power to make laws. In most colonies, the legislature had an upper house and a lower house. The upper house was also known as the governor's council. The council was made up of advisers appointed by the governor.

The lower house was an elected assembly. It approved laws and protected the rights of citizens. Just as important, it gained the right to approve or disapprove any taxes the governor asked for. This "power of the purse," or right to raise or spend money, was an important check on the governor's power. Any governor who ignored the assembly risked losing his salary.

The right to vote

Each colony had its own rules about who could vote. By the 1720s, however, all the colonies had laws that restricted the right to vote to white Christian men over the age of 21. All voters had to own property. Colonial leaders believed that only property owners knew what was best for a colony.

On election day, voters and their families gathered in towns and villages. Smiling candidates shook hands with voters and, in many places, offered to buy them drinks. After a while, the sheriff called the voters together. As the sheriff read out the roll, each man announced his vote aloud. Candidates personally thanked those who voted for them.

The rights of citizens

Colonists took great pride in their elected assemblies. In 1689, colonists won still more rights as a result of the Glorious Revolution in England.

The Glorious Revolution took place in 1688. Parliament removed King James II from the throne and asked William and Mary of the Netherlands to rule. In return for Parliament's support, William and Mary signed the **English Bill of Rights** in 1689. A

bill of rights is a written list of freedoms that a government promises to protect.

The English Bill of Rights guaranteed the rights of individuals and gave anyone accused of a crime the right to a trial by jury. Just important, the English Bill of Rights said that a ruler could not raise taxes or an army without the approval of Parliament.

Limits on Liberties

In many ways, English colonists in America enjoyed more freedoms than the English themselves. More ordinary men could vote. Colonial legislatures increased their powers over time. Still, the rights of English citizens did not extend to everyone in the colonies. Africans and Indians had almost no rights. Women and servants had more rights in the colonies than in Europe, but far fewer rights than did free white males.

Limited rights of women

Like women in Europe, colonial women had limited legal rights. A woman's father or husband was supposed to protect her. A married woman could not start her own business or sign a contract unless her husband approved it. In most colonies, unmarried women and widows had more rights than married women. They could make contracts and sue in court. In Maryland and the Carolinas, women settlers who headed families could buy land on the same terms as men.

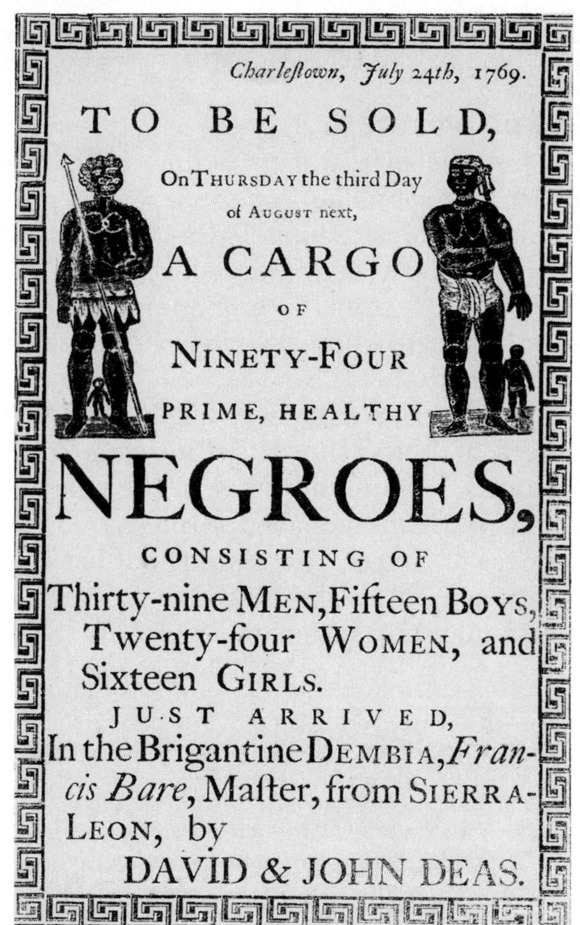

Viewing History **The Growth of Slavery**

Colonial rights and liberties did not extend to enslaved Africans. As this poster shows, colonial law permitted slaves to be bought and sold as property.
★ **Where did the slaves advertised on this poster come from? Where would they end up?**

The growth of slavery

The first Africans in the English colonies included free people and servants as well as slaves. During the 1600s, even those Africans who were enslaved enjoyed some freedom. In South Carolina, for example, some enslaved Africans worked as cowboys, herding cattle to market.

As the importance of slavery increased, however, greater limits were placed on the rights of slaves. Colonists passed laws that set out rules for slaves' behavior and denied slaves their basic rights. These **slave codes** treated enslaved African Americans not as human beings, but as property.

By 1750, the slave trade to North America was at its height. Sadly, slavery existed side by side with the English liberties so many colonists admired. The conflict between freedom and slavery would not be resolved until more than 100 years later, when the United States was divided by the Civil War.

Religion and Liberty

During the 1500s and 1600s, European Protestants and Catholics fought each other fiercely. Protestants themselves often disagreed about how to reform their church.

These disagreements spilled over into the American colonies. Gradually, however, the debates over religion produced a growing belief in an individual's freedom to worship without interference from the government.

Religious liberty became an important part of the American tradition.

Church and state

Many colonists did not believe in the freedom of religion. The Puritans, for example, founded the Massachusetts Bay Colony in order to worship as they pleased. However, they formed a government that punished or expelled colonists whose religious views seemed dangerous to them.

One Puritan who was expelled by the leaders of Massachusetts Bay was **Roger Williams,** a young minister in the village of Salem. Williams believed strongly that the business of church and state should be completely separate. The state, said Williams, should maintain order and peace. It should not support a particular church. Williams also believed in religious **toleration,** the willingness to let others practice their own beliefs.

In 1635, the Massachusetts General Court ordered Williams to leave the colony. He made his way to nearby Narragansett Bay, where he bought land from the Indians. Williams's settlement at Narragansett later became the English colony of Rhode Island.

In Rhode Island, Williams put into practice his ideas about religious toleration. He allowed complete freedom of religion for all Protestants, Catholics, and Jews. He did not set up a state church or require settlers to attend services.

Among those who fled to Rhode Island was a woman named **Anne Hutchinson.** Hutchinson was a popular Boston midwife and the mother of 14 children. She often met with friends at her home after church to discuss the minister's sermon. Puritan officials, however, argued that only clergymen were qualified to explain the word of God. When Hutchinson challenged the teachings of many ministers, she was put on trial.

During the 1700s most colonies still had **established churches.** That is, the colony's government gave official support to a particular religion. Still, with so many different religions being practiced within the colonies, the idea of religious toleration continued to grow.

George Whitefield

George Whitefield's preaching drew huge crowds throughout the colonies. One witness reported, "I have seen upwards of a thousand people hang on his words with breathless silence, broken only by an occasional half-suppressed sob." Whitefield also encouraged the building of colleges such as Princeton. ★ **Why did some Americans oppose the impact of preachers like Whitefield?**

The Great Awakening

In the 1730s and 1740s, a religious movement known as the **Great Awakening** swept through the colonies. Its drama and emotion touched women and men of all ages and backgrounds.

Powerful preachers

A New England preacher, **Jonathan Edwards,** set off the Great Awakening in the colonies. Edwards called on colonists, especially young people, to examine their lives. In powerful sermons, Edwards preached of the sweetness and beauty of God. At the same time, Edwards warned listeners that unless they heeded the Bible's teachings, they would be "sinners in the hands of an angry God," headed for the fiery torments of hell.

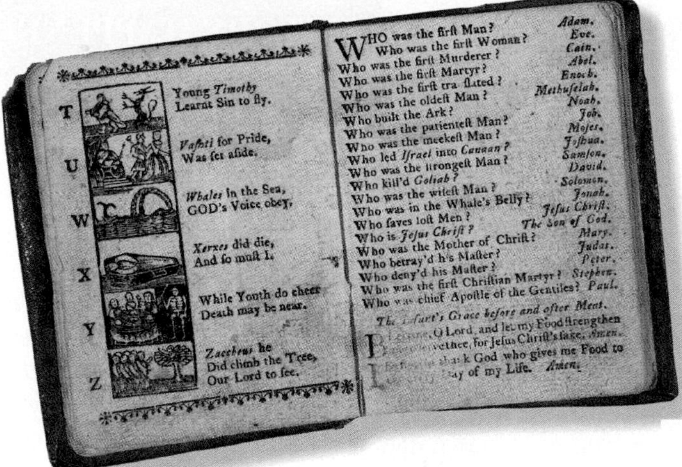

T Young *Timothy*
Learnt Sin to fly.

U *Vaſhti* for Pride,
Was ſet aſide.

W *Whales* in the Sea,
GOD's Voice obey.

X *Xerxes* did die,
And ſo muſt I.

Y While Youth do cheer
Death may be near.

Z *Zaccheus* he
Did climb the Tree,
Our Lord to ſee.

WHO was the firſt Man? *Adam.*
Who was the firſt Woman? *Eve.*
Who was the firſt Murderer? *Cain.*
Who was the firſt Martyr? *Abel.*
Who was the firſt tranſlated? *Enoch.*
Who was the oldeſt Man? *Methuſelah.*
Who built the Ark? *Noah.*
Who was the patienteſt Man? *Job.*
Who was the meekeſt Man? *Moſes.*
Who led *Iſrael* into *Canaan*? *Joſhua.*
Who was the ſtrongeſt Man? *Samſon.*
Who kill'd *Goliah*? *David.*
Who was the wiſeſt Man? *Solomon.*
Who was in the Whale's Belly? *Jonah.*
Who ſaves loſt Men? *Jeſus Chriſt.*
Who is *Jeſus Chriſt*? *The Son of God.*
Who was the Mother of Chriſt? *Mary.*
Who betray'd his Maſter? *Judas.*
Who deny'd his Maſter? *Peter.*
Who was the firſt Chriſtian Martyr? *Stephen.*
Who was chief Apoſtle of the Gentiles? *Paul.*

The Infant's Grace before and after Meat.

B ... O Lord, and let my Food ſtrengthen ... for Jeſus Chriſt's ſake. *Amen.*
... thank God who gives me Food to ... day of my Life. *Amen.*

Viewing HISTORY Education in the Colonies

Education and values were closely linked in the colonies. The picture below shows apprentices learning beekeeping and carpentry. The writing around the picture says that "at the working man's house, hunger looks in but dares not enter." The New England Primer, left, taught Bible tales and moral lessons along with the alphabet. ★ **Examine the page from the primer. What moral lesson is taught with the letter *y*? What does this suggest about the Puritan attitude toward childhood?**

In 1739, when an English minister named George Whitefield arrived in the colonies, the movement spread like wildfire. Whitefield drew huge crowds to outdoor meetings from Massachusetts to Georgia. His voice rang with feeling as he called on sinners to repent.

Impact of the Awakening

The Great Awakening aroused bitter debate. People who supported the movement often split away from their old churches to form new ones. Opponents warned that the movement was too emotional. Still, the growth of so many new churches forced colonists to become more tolerant of people with different beliefs.

The Great Awakening contributed in another way to the spread of democratic feelings in the colonies. Many of the Awakening's new preachers were not as well educated as most ministers. They argued that book learning was less important than preaching from a heart filled with the holy spirit.

This sense of independence encouraged many believers to challenge people in authority when their religious liberties were at stake. In years to come, many of the same American colonists were willing to challenge the authority of British officials during the American Revolution.

$ Connections *With* Economics

The earliest New England schools did not have large budgets. Parents paid the schoolteacher with corn, peas, or other crops. Each child was expected to bring a share of wood to burn in the stove. Students who forgot might find themselves seated in the coldest corner of the room.

A Tradition of Education

Education was another tradition that grew stronger in America. Among the colonists, New Englanders were most concerned about education. Puritans believed that all people had a duty to study the Bible. If settlers did not learn to read, how would they fulfill this duty?

Public schooling

In 1647, the Massachusetts assembly passed a law ordering all parents to teach their children "to read and understand the principles of religion." Beyond that, they required all towns with 50 or more families to hire a schoolteacher. Towns with 100 families

AmericanHeritage
M A G A Z I N E

HISTORY HAPPENED HERE

Colonial Williamsburg

In the 1700s, Williamsburg was one of the most important cities in Virginia. Today, it is one of the state's most popular attractions. As you walk down the restored streets, you can watch people bake bread, print newspapers, or make shoes as they did in colonial times.

★ ***To learn more about this historic site, write:*** *Colonial Williamsburg Foundation, P.O. Box 627, Williamsburg, VA 23187.*

➤ *A wigmaker in Colonial Williamsburg demonstrates her trade.*

or more also had to set up a grammar school that prepared boys for college.

In this way, Massachusetts set up the first **public schools,** or schools supported by taxes. Public schools allowed both rich and poor children to get an education.

In the Middle Colonies, churches and individual families set up private schools. Pupils paid to attend. As a result, only wealthy families could afford to educate their children.

In the Southern Colonies, people lived too far from one another to bring together children in one school building. Some planters hired tutors, or private teachers. The wealthiest planters sent their sons to school in England. As a rule, slaves were denied education of any kind.

Apprentices and dame schools

Boys whose parents wished them to learn a trade or a craft served as apprentices (uh PREHN tihs ehz). An **apprentice** worked for a master who taught him the necessary skills. In return, the apprentice worked without pay in the master's shop until he learned the skills he needed to set up his own shop. Boys were apprenticed in many trades, including papermaking, printing, and leather tanning.

In New England, some girls attended **dame schools,** or private schools run by women in their own homes. Most schools in the colonies accepted only boys, however. Girls learned skills from their mothers, who taught them to spin wool, weave, and embroider. A few colonial girls were also taught to read and write.

The Spread of New Ideas

During the 1600s, European scientists tried to use reason and logic to understand the world. They developed theories and then performed experiments to test them. In doing so, they discovered many laws of nature. The English scientist Isaac Newton, for example, explained how the force of gravity kept planets from flying out of their orbits.

The Enlightenment in Europe

European thinkers of the late 1600s and 1700s believed that reason and scientific methods could be applied to the study of society. Because these thinkers believed in the light of human reason, the movement they began is known as the **Enlightenment.**

In the colonies, the Enlightenment spread among better educated colonists. They included wealthy merchants, lawyers, ministers, and others who had the leisure to read the latest books from Europe.

The best example of the Enlightenment spirit in the 13 colonies was **Benjamin Franklin.** A believer in self-improvement, Franklin worked his way from poverty to become a successful printer and an important colonial leader.

Like other Enlightenment thinkers, Franklin wanted to use reason to improve the world around him. He invented practical devices such as a lightning rod, a stove, and bifocal glasses. As a community leader, Franklin persuaded city officials to pave Philadelphia's streets and to organize a fire company. With his help, local leaders also set up the first lending library in the Americas. Ben Franklin's inventions and his public service earned him worldwide fame.

Communication, transportation, and cities

Improved transportation and communication in the colonies helped the spread of new ideas. In 1717, it took one month or more for a letter to travel from Boston to Williamsburg, Virginia. By the mid-1700s, better roads between colonial cities allowed mail to move much more quickly. News and ideas also spread through pamphlets, newspapers, and books turned out on colonial printing presses.

The growth of colonial cities also helped new ideas to spread. Pamphlets and books from Europe arrived first in seaports like Boston, New York, Philadelphia, or Charleston. In cities, people met in great numbers. There, they exchanged news and ideas that would help shape a revolution in the years ahead.

★ Section 3 Review ★

Recall

1. **Identify** **(a)** Magna Carta, **(b)** Parliament, **(c)** English Bill of Rights, **(d)** Roger Williams, **(e)** Anne Hutchinson, **(f)** Great Awakening, **(g)** Jonathan Edwards, **(h)** Enlightenment, **(i)** Benjamin Franklin.
2. **Define** **(a)** legislature, **(b)** bill of rights, **(c)** slave code, **(d)** toleration, **(e)** established church, **(f)** public school, **(g)** apprentice, **(h)** dame school.

Comprehension

3. **(a)** Describe three political rights and liberties that the colonies inherited from England. **(b)** Describe two ways these rights and liberties were limited.
4. How did the Great Awakening encourage a spirit of independence?
5. Why did the Puritans support public education?

Critical Thinking and Writing

6. **Linking Past and Present** Which rights granted by the English Bill of Rights are similar to rights Americans enjoy today?
7. **Making Inferences** Why do you think slaveholders tried to prevent enslaved African Americans from receiving an education?

Activity **Explaining Ideas** You have received a letter from a teenager in another country. She tells you her family is not allowed to practice their religion openly. "If we come to the United States," she asks, "will we really be able to worship as we choose?" Write a reply in which you explain the long American tradition of religious freedom.

Chapter 3 Review and Activities

★ Sum It Up ★

Section 1 Establishing the Colonies

- The Pilgrims and the Puritans came to the Americas seeking a place in which they could worship as they wished.
- The Middle Colonies were settled by people seeking economic opportunity or religious freedom.
- Most of the Southern Colonies were proprietary colonies, settled by people seeking economic gain.

Section 2 Different Ways of Life

- In New England, people supported themselves by harvesting forest products and fishing offshore.
- Farms in the Middle Colonies produced cash crops such as grain and cattle.
- Southern colonists, raising cash crops such as tobacco and rice, began importing enslaved people to work their fields.
- African traditions remained strong among enslaved workers on plantations or in coastal cities.

Section 3 The English Heritage

- Settlers brought with them from Britain the idea that they had political rights.
- Most colonial governments consisted of an appointed governor and an elected legislature.
- The Great Awakening inspired religious feeling and increased the belief that people should have equal rights no matter what their social class.

For additional review of the major ideas of Chapter 3, see ***Guide to the Essentials of American History*** or ***Interactive Student Tutorial CD-ROM,*** which contains interactive review activities, graphic organizers, and practice tests.

Reviewing the Chapter

Define These Terms

Match each term with the correct definition.

Column 1	Column 2
1. charter	**a.** highest class of colonial society
2. gentry	**b.** document giving certain rights
3. indentured servants	**c.** group of people who have the power to make laws
4. legislature	**d.** young person who learns a trade or craft by working for a master
5. apprentice	**e.** settlers who promised to work without wages for a period in exchange for ocean passage

Explore the Main Ideas

1. How did the Jamestown colony survive hard times and gain prosperity?
2. Give two reasons why the towns and villages in the New England colonies were closely knit.
3. What were the social classes of colonial America?
4. What control did colonial legislatures have over the governor?
5. Why did colonies pass slave codes?

Geography Activity

Match the letters on the map with the following places: **1.** New England Colonies, **2.** Middle Colonies, **3.** Southern Colonies, **4.** Massachusetts, **5.** Pennsylvania, **6.** Virginia. **Region** Name the five Southern Colonies.

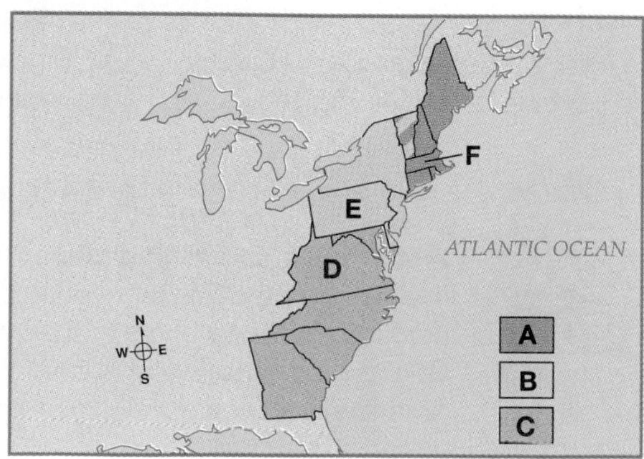

Critical Thinking and Writing

1. **Analyzing Ideas** "The Puritans came to America in search of religious freedom." **(a)** In what sense is this statement accurate? **(b)** In what sense is this statement inaccurate?
2. **Understanding Chronology** **(a)** For each of the following pairs of colonies, indicate which was formed out of the other: New York and New Jersey; Delaware and Pennsylvania; South Carolina and Georgia. **(b)** Why do you think many colonies were formed out of other colonies?
3. **Linking Past and Present** Are the New England, Middle Atlantic, and Southern Atlantic regions as different today as they were in colonial times? Explain.
4. **Exploring Unit Themes** **Origins** What do you think are the two most important traditions the United States got from England? Explain your reasoning.

Using Primary Sources

Nathan Cole, a Connecticut farmer, saw George Whitefield preach in 1740. Cole gave the following description:

> "He looked almost angelical, a young, slim, slender youth before some thousands of people.... My hearing how God was with him everywhere as he came along...put me in a trembling fear before he began to preach, for he looked as if he was clothed with authority from the great God, and a sweet solemn solemnity sat upon his brow and my hearing him preach gave me a heart wound."

Source: *The Great Awakening: Documents on the Revival of Religion, 1740–1745,* ed. Richard Bushman, 1989.

Recognizing Points of View **(a)** Summarize in your own words Cole's reaction to hearing Whitefield preach. **(b)** Why do you think preachers of the Great Awakening tried to stir such feelings?

Activity Bank

Interdisciplinary Activity

Exploring Sciences Do research on the inventions of Benjamin Franklin. Make a model and create a display that explains how one of his inventions worked.

Career Skills Activity

Playwrights Read more about the life of women in the British colonies. Write a short play in which a city woman, a backcountry woman, and the mistress of a plantation meet and compare their lives.

Citizenship Activity

Learning About Education In this chapter you read about the beginnings of public education in America. One of the responsibilities of citizens is being informed about and participating in education in the community. Arrange to visit a school board session or a meeting of your local parent-teacher association. Write a report on your visit.

Internet Activity

Use the Internet to find sites dealing with William Penn. After you have done research to find out more about him, write a letter from Penn to the President of the United States today, advising the President on how to handle some of the challenges facing our nation. Use information from your research in your letter.

Eyewitness Journal

You are a Puritan, a Pennsylvania Quaker, a southern plantation owner, or an enslaved African American. In your EYEWITNESS JOURNAL, describe a visit to another colony and compare it with your own. Remember, your viewpoint will be influenced by the colony in which you live.

Chapter 4

The American Revolution

1754–1783

What's Ahead

Section 1
The Road to Revolution

Section 2
The Fighting Begins

Section 3
Declaring Independence

Section 4
Winning the War

Before the 1760s, American colonists were proud of their connection with Britain. As Britain tried to tax colonists without their consent, however, Americans protested. Slowly, protests led to violence. In 1775, a confrontation between colonists and British troops in Massachusetts marked the start of the American Revolution.

In 1776, representatives of the colonies called for separation from Britain. With the bold words of the Declaration of Independence, the United States became a nation. Led by George Washington, America's army fought a life-and-death struggle for the new nation. With French help, the Americans defeated Britain and won their independence.

"Taxation without representation is tyranny!" This protest sparked a revolution in the 13 colonies. Today, American citizens have representation. Still, attempts to raise taxes always stir heated debate. To focus on this connection, look at the *Why Study History?* feature, "You Pay Taxes," in this chapter.

American Events

1754 French and Indian War begins in North America

1765 Stamp Act taxes goods to raise money for Britain

1767 Townshend Acts lead to widespread protest

1750 | 1760 | 1770

World Events

1763 World Event Treaty of Paris ends French power in North America

A Nation Wins Its Independence

This painting, Surrender of Lord Cornwallis, *is by John Trumbull, one of the greatest early American artists. It shows British troops surrendering to a colonial army at Yorktown, Virginia, in 1781. The Battle of Yorktown marked the end of the American Revolution. The six-year struggle freed the colonies from British rule.*

★ **Why do you think Great Britain was unwilling to give up its colonies?**

1775 Fighting at Lexington and Concord ends hope of peaceful compromise

1776 Declaration of Independence is issued

1783 Treaty of Paris ends the war

1770 **1780** **1790**

1772 World Event British court frees any slave who enters England

1778 World Event France recognizes American independence

The Road to Revolution

Explore These Questions

- What were the results of the French and Indian War?
- How did Britain try to regulate colonial trade?
- Why did the colonists protest new taxes?

Define

- triangular trade
- boycott
- repeal
- nonimportation agreements
- committee of correspondence

Identify

- French and Indian War
- Navigation Acts
- Stamp Act
- Townshend Acts
- Sons of Liberty
- Daughters of Liberty
- Samuel Adams
- John Adams
- Boston Massacre

SETTING the Scene In 1763, most Americans in the 13 colonies were proud to be part of the British empire. The empire was "our indulgent Mother," said Thomas Barnard, a New England minister. Barnard predicted that grateful Americans would serve Britain "with all Duty, Love, and Gratitude till Time shall be no more."

Yet only two years later, angry mobs were marching in the streets of colonial cities. They strongly protested new taxes and policies that Britain put into place in America. By 1776, the 13 colonies were ready to declare their independence. The kingdom that so many colonists had long admired was about to become their enemy.

Conflict Along the Frontier

During the 1600s, England, France, Spain, and the Netherlands competed for trade and colonies throughout much of the world. In North America, England's most serious rival was France. French forts and settlements stretched from the St. Lawrence River west to the Great Lakes and south to the Gulf of Mexico.

French and Indian War

Three times between 1689 and 1748, France and Great Britain fought for power in Europe and North America. Each war ended with an uneasy peace. In 1754, fighting broke out again in the Ohio Valley. English colonists called the conflict that followed the **French and Indian War** because it pitted them against France and its Native American allies.

At first, France won several victories. In 1759, the tide turned in Britain's favor. British soldiers climbed the steep cliffs along the St. Lawrence River. There, they defeated French troops and captured Quebec, the capital of New France.

In 1763, Britain and France signed the Treaty of Paris. It marked the end of French power in North America. Britain gained Canada and all French lands east of the Mississippi River. Spain, France's ally, gave up Florida to Britain. In return, Spain received all French land west of the Mississippi.

Pontiac's War

Indian nations in the Ohio Valley were shocked that Britain was taking over nearby French forts. In general, the French had more friendly relations with the Indians than the British did. The new British commanders also allowed English settlers to build farms on Indian lands.

Pontiac, an Ottawa chief who had fought with the French, led a series of attacks on British forts. Pontiac's War failed, however, when the French did not come to the Indians' aid. One by one, the Indian nations stopped fighting and returned home. Even more English settlers moved into the Ohio River valley.

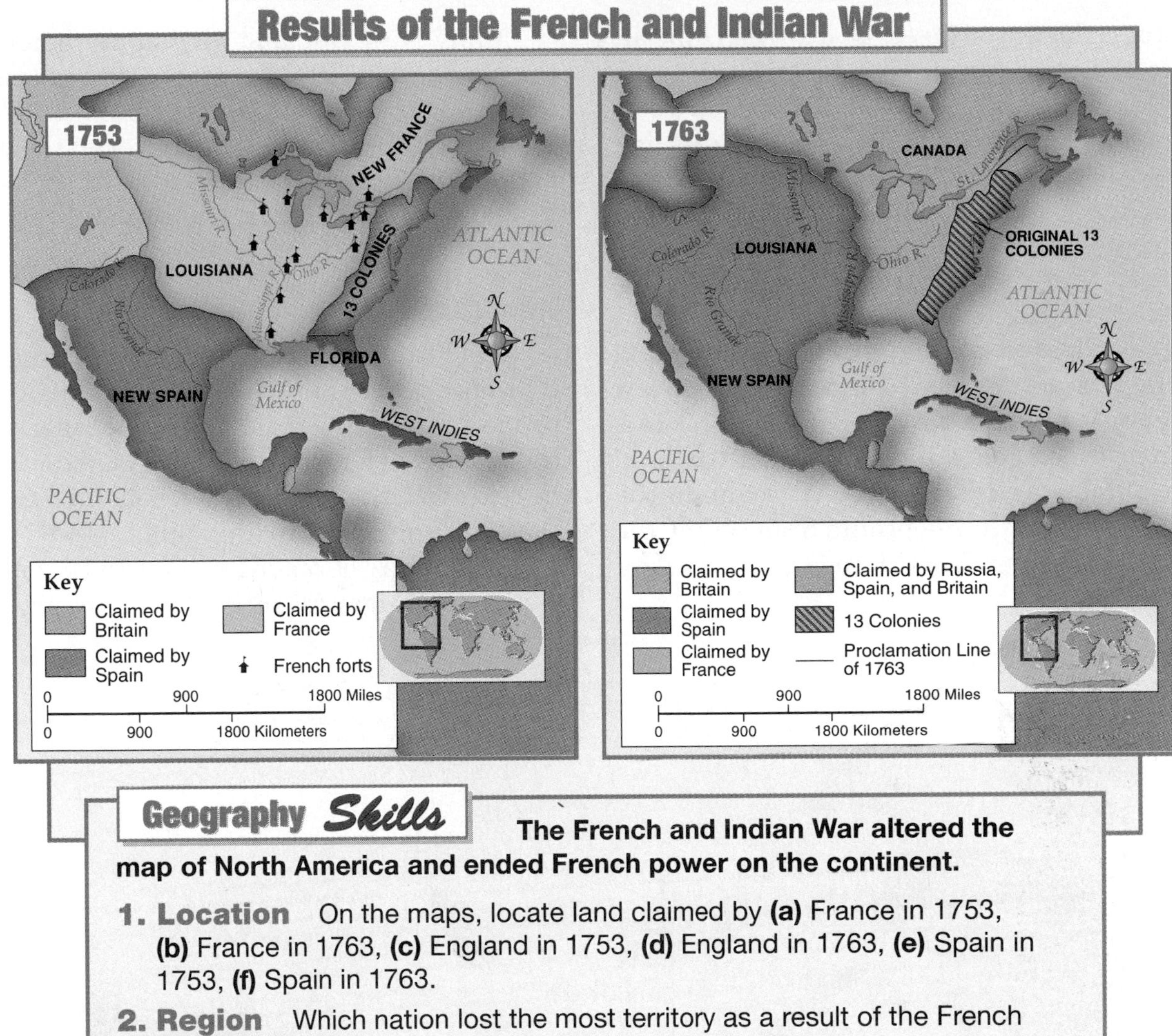

Geography *Skills* **The French and Indian War altered the map of North America and ended French power on the continent.**

1. **Location** On the maps, locate land claimed by **(a)** France in 1753, **(b)** France in 1763, **(c)** England in 1753, **(d)** England in 1763, **(e)** Spain in 1753, **(f)** Spain in 1763.
2. **Region** Which nation lost the most territory as a result of the French and Indian War?
3. **Critical Thinking** Note the location of French forts in 1753. Why do you think France built forts in these locations?

Pontiac's War convinced British officials that they should stop British subjects from settling on the Indian frontier. To do this, the government issued the Proclamation of 1763. It forbade colonists to settle west of the Appalachian Mountains. The proclamation angered colonists. Many settlers simply ignored it and moved west anyway.

Britain Reforms Its Colonial System

The Proclamation of 1763 was part of a larger effort to reform Great Britain's colonial system. Since the 1650s, Parliament had passed a series of laws to regulate trade between England and its colonies. Their goal was to ensure that trade within the empire benefited England. The laws were known as the **Navigation Acts.**

Trade regulations

Under the Navigation Acts, only colonial or English ships could carry goods to and from the colonies. At the same time, colonial merchants were forbidden to ship certain products, such as tobacco and cotton, to any nation but England.

The Navigation Acts helped the colonies as well as England. Because of the acts, colonial merchants did not have to compete with foreign merchants. Still, colonists complained that the Navigation Acts favored the English. Most of all, they did not like the customs duties, or taxes, that British officials collected on sugar and molasses.

Many New England ships traveled a regular trade route known as the **triangular trade** because its three legs formed a triangle. On the first leg, ships carried fish, lumber, and other goods to the West Indies. There, they bought sugar and molasses, which New Englanders used to make rum.

On the second leg, ships carried rum, guns, gunpowder, cloth, and tools from New England to West Africa. In Africa, merchants traded these goods for slaves. On the final leg, ships carried enslaved Africans to the West Indies. With the profits from selling the slaves, traders bought more sugar and molasses.

Many New England merchants ignored the Navigation Acts. Traders were supposed to buy sugar and molasses only from English colonies in the West Indies. However, the demand for molasses was so high that New Englanders bought from the Dutch, French, and Spanish West Indies, too.

New taxes

The French and Indian War had plunged Britain deeply into debt. The new British prime minister, George Grenville, insisted that colonists help pay off the debt. After all, he reasoned, the colonists had benefited from the war as much as Britain had.

As one way of raising money, Parliament passed the Sugar Act of 1764. The act placed

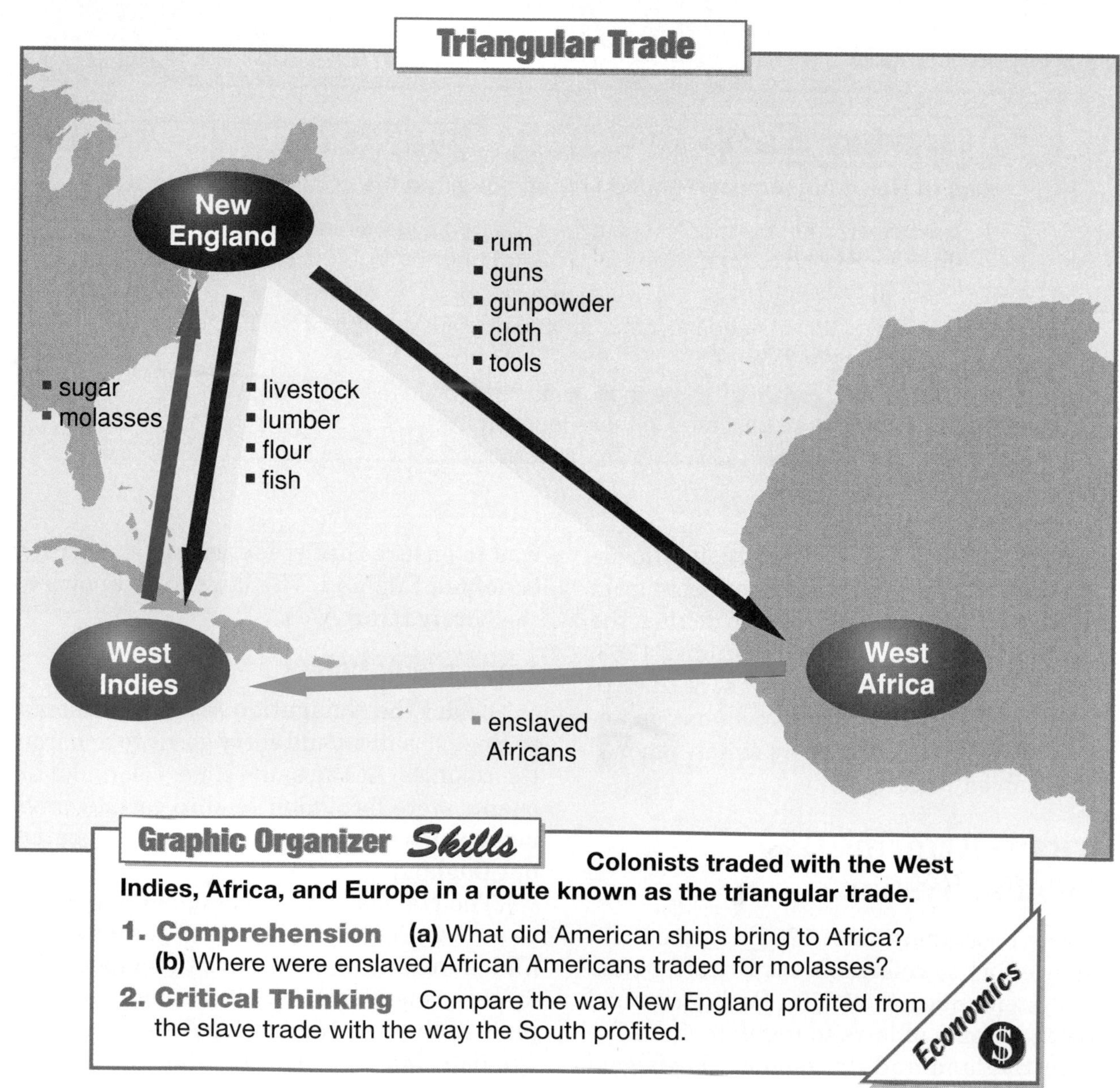

Graphic Organizer *Skills* **Colonists traded with the West Indies, Africa, and Europe in a route known as the triangular trade.**

1. **Comprehension** **(a)** What did American ships bring to Africa? **(b)** Where were enslaved African Americans traded for molasses?
2. **Critical Thinking** Compare the way New England profited from the slave trade with the way the South profited.

new duties on molasses and sugar. Even more important, it made it easier for British officials to bring colonial smugglers to trial.

The following year, Parliament enacted another law to raise money. The **Stamp Act** put a tax on legal documents such as wills and marriage papers. It also taxed newspapers, almanacs, playing cards, and even dice. All items named in the law had to carry a stamp showing that the tax had been paid.

Colonists Protest

Colonists greeted the new taxes with stormy protests. Riots broke out in Boston, New York, Newport, and Charleston. Angry colonists threw rocks at agents trying to collect the tax. Some mobs even tarred and feathered the agents or destroyed their homes and property.

The fury of the colonists shocked the British. Why, they asked, were colonists so angry about the Stamp Act?

Colonists replied that only they or their elected representatives had the right to tax them. Since the colonists did not elect representatives to Parliament, Parliament could not tax them.

Stamp Act Congress

In October 1765, nine colonies sent delegates to what became known as the Stamp Act Congress. Meeting in New York City, the delegates drew up petitions to King George III and to Parliament. In these petitions, they rejected the Stamp Act and declared that Parliament had no right to tax the colonies. Parliament paid little attention.

The colonists took other steps to change the law. They joined together to **boycott,** or refuse to buy, British goods. The boycott took its toll. Trade fell off, hurting British merchants and workers. Finally, in 1766, Parliament **repealed,** or canceled, the Stamp Act.

The Townshend Acts

In May 1767, however, Parliament reopened the debate over taxes. In one fiery exchange, George Grenville, now a member of Parliament, clashed with Charles Townshend. Townshend was in charge of the British treasury:

Biography **Mercy Otis Warren**

Mercy Otis Warren used her pen and sharp wit to stir feelings against the British. Warren wrote plays that ridiculed British officials. Her home in Massachusetts was a meeting place for colonists who opposed British policies. ★ **How do writers influence public opinion today?**

> “*Grenville:* You are cowards, you are afraid of the Americans, you dare not tax America!
> *Townshend:* Fear? Cowards? I dare tax America!”

The next month, Parliament passed the **Townshend Acts,** which taxed goods such as glass, paper, paint, lead, and tea. The taxes were low, but colonists still objected. The principle, they felt, was the same: Parliament did not have the right to tax them without their consent.

The Townshend Acts allowed customs officials to inspect a ship's cargo without giving a reason. Colonists protested that such actions violated their rights. Under British law, an official could not search a person's property without a good reason for suspecting the owner of a crime.

Why Study History?

Because You Pay Taxes

Many Americans protest that their taxes are too high.

Historical Background

In the 1760s and 1770s, colonists charged that taxes levied on them by the British government were unfair because Americans did not elect representatives to Parliament. “No taxation without representation!” American patriots cried. In protest, they boycotted British goods and attacked tax collectors. They even tarred and feathered a few agents. The furor over taxes helped cause the American Revolution.

Connections to Today

Fortunately, we no longer tar and feather tax collectors, but many people do still object to taxes. The most frequent complaint is that taxes are too high. In the mid-1990s, the average American worked from January to May just to pay taxes!

The size of the tax bill is not the only complaint. Some people charge that the tax system is unfair. They say that the poor pay too much while the rich pay too little. Others say that the tax system is too complicated and that the rules are hard to understand. Recently, one sentence in a tax instruction was 436 words long—longer than the entire Gettysburg Address. As a result, nearly half of all Americans pay someone else to prepare their taxes.

Taxes pay for essential services, such as fire protection.

Connections to You

If your state has a sales tax, you already pay taxes whenever you buy a taxable item. When you get a job, you will pay income taxes. Some day, you may pay property taxes on a home. As a voter, you will help to choose the legislators who decide our nation's tax laws.

Do you think taxes should be drastically reduced? Before you decide, remember that taxes pay for important services. Tax cuts could mean less money for national defense, health care, education, and transportation. There would also be less money for fire and police protection, recreation facilities, and the environment. So when you consider taxes, consider carefully.

1. **Comprehension** Describe three reasons some Americans complain about taxes today.
2. **Critical Thinking** Taxes spread the cost of services across the entire population. What are the benefits of this system? What are the disadvantages?

Debating Organize a classroom debate on taxes. One side should argue in favor of lower tax rates and the benefits to be gained from them. The other side should oppose tax cuts because of the possible negative effects on the community.

Colonial Protests Widen

As British officials began to enforce the Townshend Acts, colonial protests grew. From north to south, merchants and planters signed **nonimportation agreements.** In these agreements, they promised to stop importing goods taxed by the Townshend Acts.

Sons and Daughters of Liberty

To protest British policies, some angry colonists formed the **Sons of Liberty.** From Boston to Charleston, Sons of Liberty hanged of cloth or straw figures dressed like British officials. The hangings were meant to show tax collectors what might happen to them if they tried to collect the unpopular taxes.

Some women joined the **Daughters of Liberty.** They paraded, signed petitions, and organized a boycott of fine British cloth. They urged colonial women to raise more sheep, prepare more wool, and spin and weave their own cloth. A slogan of the Daughters of Liberty stated, "It is better to wear a Homespun coat than to lose our Liberty."

New leaders emerge

During the struggle over taxes, new leaders emerged in all of the colonies. People in Massachusetts and Virginia were especially active in the colonial cause.

Samuel Adams of Boston seemed an unlikely leader. He was a failure in business and a poor public speaker. Still, he was always present at Boston town meetings and at Sons of Liberty rallies. Adams knew how to work behind the scenes, organizing protests and stirring public support.

John Adams, cousin of Sam, was another important Massachusetts leader. John Adams was a skilled lawyer. More cautious than Sam, he weighed evidence carefully before acting. His knowledge of British law earned him much respect.

In Virginia, planters and others protested the Townshend Acts. In the House of Burgesses, a young lawyer named Patrick Henry gave speeches that moved listeners to anger. Once, Henry attacked Britain with such fury that some listeners cried out, "Treason!" Henry boldly replied, "If this be treason, make the most of it!"

The Boston Massacre

Port cities such as Boston and New York were centers of protest. Britain sent soldiers to both cities to protect customs officers from angry local citizens. To many Bostonians, the soldiers' tents set up on Boston Common were a daily reminder that Britain was trying to bully them into paying unjust taxes. When British soldiers walked along the streets of Boston, they risked insults or even beatings.

On the night of March 5, 1770, a crowd gathered outside the Boston customs house. Colonists jeered at the "lobsterbacks," as they called the redcoated British soldiers who guarded the building. Then the Boston crowd began to throw snowballs, oyster shells, and chunks of ice at the soldiers.

Suddenly, the soldiers fired into the crowd. When the smoke from the musket volley cleared, five people lay dead or dying. Among them was Crispus Attucks, a black sailor who was active in the Sons of Liberty.

Viewing History **The Boston Massacre**

Paul Revere's engraving of the Boston Massacre helped whip up colonial fury against the British. In fact, the picture is very inaccurate. No British officer ever gave an order to fire, as shown here. The redcoats, faced with an unruly mob, fired on their own. ★ **Why do you think Revere distorted the event in his engraving?**

Bostonians were quick to protest the incident, which they called the **Boston Massacre.** Silversmith Paul Revere created and spread an engraving that showed British soldiers firing on unarmed colonists. Sam Adams wrote letters to other colonists to stir outrage about the shooting. Later, he expanded this idea by organizing a **committee of correspondence.** Members of the committee regularly wrote letters and pamphlets reporting on events in Massachusetts. Before long, committees of correspondence became an important tool of protest in every colony.

Samuel Adams

The British soldiers were arrested and tried for firing on the crowd. John Adams agreed to defend them, saying that they deserved a fair trial. He wanted to show the world that the colonists believed in justice, even if the British government did not. At the trial, Adams brought in evidence to show that the crowd had provoked the soldiers. His arguments convinced the jury. In the end, the heaviest punishment any soldier received was a branding on the hand.

Repeal of the Townshend Acts

By chance, on the very day of the Boston Massacre, Parliament repealed most of the Townshend Acts. British merchants, hurt by the nonimportation agreements, had pressured Parliament to end the taxes. Still, King George III persuaded Parliament to keep the tax on tea. "There must always be one tax to keep up the right [to tax]," argued the king. Parliament agreed.

News of the repeal delighted the colonists. Most people dismissed the remaining tax on tea as not important and ended their boycott of British goods. For a few years, calm returned. Yet the underlying issue—Britain's power to tax the colonies—remained unsettled. For the first time, the colonists were thinking more clearly about their political rights.

★ Section 1 Review ★

Recall

1. **Identify** (a) French and Indian War, **(b)** Navigation Acts, **(c)** Stamp Act, **(d)** Townshend Acts, **(e)** Sons of Liberty, **(f)** Daughters of Liberty, **(g)** Samuel Adams, **(h)** John Adams, **(i)** Boston Massacre.
2. **Define** **(a)** triangular trade, **(b)** boycott, **(c)** repeal, **(d)** nonimportation agreements, **(e)** committee of correspondence.

Comprehension

3. What did Britain gain as a result of the French and Indian War?
4. **(a)** What was the purpose of the Navigation Acts? **(b)** Why did colonists resent them?
5. **(a)** List three ways Parliament tried to tax the colonies. **(b)** How did colonists respond to each?

Critical Thinking and Writing

6. **Defending a Position** Do you think that Britain had the right to tax the colonies? Defend your position.
7. **Drawing Conclusions** A "massacre" is the cruel and violent killing of large numbers of people. **(a)** Do you think the incident in Boston was a "massacre"? **(b)** Why do you think Sam Adams used this word to describe it?

Activity **Drawing a Cartoon** You work for a colonial printer. Choose one of Britain's actions between 1763 and 1770. Draw a political cartoon to illustrate colonial opinions about the action you have chosen.

The Fighting Begins

As You Read

Explore These Questions

- What were the causes and effects of the Boston Tea Party?
- Why did colonists clash with the British at Lexington and Concord?
- What steps did the Second Continental Congress take in 1775?

Define

- quarter
- militia
- minuteman

Identify

- Tea Act
- Boston Tea Party
- Intolerable Acts
- First Continental Congress
- Green Mountain Boys
- Battle of Bunker Hill
- Continental Army
- George Washington
- Olive Branch Petition

SETTING the Scene On a night in July 1774, John Adams stopped at a tavern in eastern Massachusetts. After riding for more than 30 miles, he was hot and dusty, and his body ached with fatigue.

Adams asked the innkeeper for a cup of tea. The innkeeper, though, refused his request. She did not serve tea, she informed him. He would have to drink coffee instead.

Chests of tea, like this one, sparked a storm of protest in the colonies.

Adams later praised the innkeeper's conduct. In a letter to his wife, Abigail, he wrote that tea must be given up by all colonists. He promised to break himself of the habit as soon as possible.

Why did colonists like John Adams give up tea? The answer was taxes. Ever since Parliament passed the Sugar Act in 1764, colonists and Great Britain had engaged in a battle of wills over taxation. Twice, Parliament passed taxes and then repealed them after colonial protests. In 1773, when Parliament decided to enforce a tax on tea, the quarrel with Britain could not be smoothed over.

The Crisis Over Tea

By 1773, the British East India Company was in deep financial trouble. The company sold tea to colonial merchants, and the merchants were not buying. Even though Parliament's tax on tea was small, many colonists resented it. They refused to buy tea. More than 15 million pounds of tea sat unsold in the East India Company's warehouses.

Parliament tried to help the company by passing the **Tea Act** of 1773. The act let the company sell directly to colonists at a very low price. Although colonists would still have to pay the tax, the tea itself would cost less than before.

To the surprise of Parliament, colonists protested the Tea Act. Colonial tea merchants were angry because they had been cut out of the tea trade. If Parliament ruined tea merchants today, they warned, what would prevent it from turning on other businesses tomorrow? Colonial tea drinkers believed the act was a British trick to make them accept Parliament's right to tax the colonies.

Once again, colonists responded to the tax with a boycott. One colonial newspaper warned:

> “Do not suffer yourself to sip the accursed, dutied STUFF. For if you do, the devil will immediately enter into you, and you will instantly become a traitor to your country.”

Viewing HISTORY **Boston Tea Party**

Disguised as Indians, some 50 or 60 Bostonians attacked British tea ships. A crowd watched silently as the colonists dumped tea into Boston harbor. British officials called the Boston Tea Party "the most wanton and unprovoked insult offered to the civil power that is recorded in history." ★ **Why did colonists attack the tea ships?**

Daughters of Liberty led the boycott. They served coffee or made "liberty tea" from raspberry leaves. At some ports, Sons of Liberty prevented British East India ships from unloading their cargoes of tea.

Boston Tea Party

Three ships loaded with tea reached Boston harbor in late November 1773. The colonial governor of Massachusetts, Thomas Hutchinson, insisted that they unload their cargo as usual.

Sam Adams and the Sons of Liberty had other plans. On the night of December 16, they met in Old South Church. They sent a message to the governor, demanding that the ships leave the harbor. When the governor rejected the demand, Adams stood up and declared, "This meeting can do nothing further to save the country."

Adams's words seemed to be a signal. As if on cue, a group of men burst into the meetinghouse. Dressed like Mohawk Indians, they waved hatchets in the air. From the gallery above, voices cried, "Boston harbor a teapot tonight! The Mohawks are come!"

The disguised colonists left the meetinghouse and headed for the harbor. Others joined them on the way. In the cold, crisp night, under a nearly full moon, the men boarded the ships, split open the tea chests, and dumped the tea into the harbor. By 10 P.M., the **Boston Tea Party,** as it was later called, was over. Its effects would be felt for a long time to come.

Britain strikes back

The British were outraged by Boston's behavior. In 1774, Parliament, encouraged by King George III, acted to punish Massachusetts. Colonists called the four laws they passed the **Intolerable Acts** because they were so harsh.

First, Parliament shut down the port of Boston. No ship could enter or leave the harbor—not even a small boat. The harbor would remain closed until the colonists paid for the tea.

Second, Parliament forbade Massachusetts colonists to hold town meetings more than once a year without the governor's permission. In the past, colonists had called town meetings whenever they wished.

Third, Parliament said that an official charged with a major crime would be tried in Britain instead of in Massachusetts. Colonists protested. They said that a dishonest official could break the law in the colonies and avoid punishment "by being tried, where no evidence can pursue him."

Fourth, Parliament passed a Quartering Act. No longer would British soldiers camp in tents on Boston Commons. Instead, under the new law, British commanders could force citizens to **quarter,** or house, the troops in their homes.

First Continental Congress

In response to the Intolerable Acts, colonial leaders called a meeting in Philadelphia.

In September 1774, delegates from 12 colonies gathered in what became known as the **First Continental Congress.** Only Georgia did not send delegates.

After much debate, the delegates passed a resolution backing Massachusetts in its struggle against the Intolerable Acts. They agreed to boycott all British goods and to stop exporting goods to Britain until the harsh laws were repealed. The Continental Congress also urged each colony to prepare its **militia** (mə LISH ə) for action. A militia is an army of citizens who serve as soldiers during an emergency.

Before leaving Philadelphia, the delegates agreed to meet again the following May. Little did they know that before May 1775, an incident in Massachusetts would change the fate of the colonies forever.

Lexington and Concord

In Massachusetts, colonists were already preparing to resist. Militia volunteers known as **minutemen** trained regularly. Minutemen got their name because they kept their muskets at hand, prepared to fight at a minute's notice.

In 1775, General Thomas Gage, the British commander, heard that minutemen had a large store of arms in Concord, a village outside of Boston. On April 18, General Gage sent about 700 British troops on a surprise march to Concord to seize the colonists' weapons.

"The British are coming!"

However, the Sons of Liberty were watching. As soon as the British set out, they hung two lamps from the Old North Church in Boston to signal that the redcoats were on the move.

Across the Charles River, colonists saw the signal. Messengers mounted their horses and galloped toward Concord. One midnight rider was Paul Revere. "The British are coming! The British are coming!" he shouted as he passed through each sleepy village.

The shot heard round the world

At daybreak on April 19, the redcoats reached Lexington, a town near Concord. On the village green, some 70 minutemen were waiting, commanded by Captain John Parker. The British ordered the minutemen to go home. Suddenly, a shot rang out. No one knows who fired it. In the brief struggle that followed, eight colonists were killed and one British soldier was wounded.

The British pushed on to Concord. Finding no arms in the village, they turned back to Boston. On a bridge outside Concord, they met 300 minutemen. Again, fighting broke out. This time, the British were forced to retreat. As they withdrew, colonial sharpshooters took deadly aim at them from the woods and fields. Local women also fired at the British from their windows. By the time they reached Boston, the redcoats had lost 73 men. Another 200 British soldiers were wounded or missing.

The events of that day left the British stunned. How had a handful of rebels forced 700 highly trained redcoats to retreat? That night, British soldiers grew even more uneasy as they watched rebels set up campfires all around Boston.

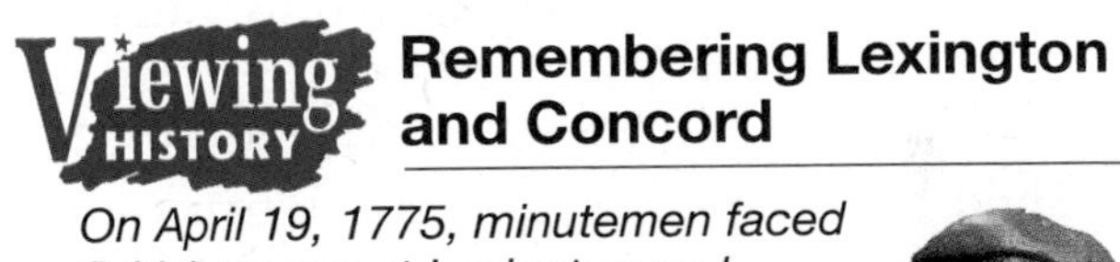

Remembering Lexington and Concord

On April 19, 1775, minutemen faced British troops at Lexington and Concord. The bronze statue, right, and the engraved boulder, below, honor the colonial militias whose courage launched the American Revolution. ★ **Read the words carved on the stone. What do they suggest about the minutemen?**

In the months ahead, the campfires remained. They were a clear sign that only war would decide the future of the 13 colonies.

Early Fighting in the North

During the first year of fighting, Boston remained at the center of the conflict. About 6,000 British troops were stationed there. The colonial militia surrounded the city, but they were not well organized. Just as important, they did not have the weapons they needed to drive out the British.

Massachusetts officials knew that the British had a large supply of cannons at Fort Ticonderoga. The fort was located at the southern tip of Lake Champlain. Massachusetts sent an expedition to attack the fort.

The Green Mountain Boys at Ticonderoga

As it turned out, another group of rebels were already marching toward Ticonderoga. Known as the **Green Mountain Boys,** they were commanded by a fiery Vermont blacksmith named Ethan Allen.

In early May, the Green Mountain Boys stole quietly through the morning mists at Fort Ticonderoga. They quickly surprised the guard on duty and entered the fort. Allen rushed to the room where the British commander slept. "Come out, you old rat!" he shouted.

The commander demanded to know on whose authority Allen acted. "In the name of the Great Jehovah and the Continental Congress!" Allen replied. The commander had no choice but to surrender Fort Ticonderoga. The Americans gained control of the fort's cannons and its valuable supply of gunpowder.

Connections With Arts

More than 60 years after the battles of Lexington and Concord, Massachusetts writer Ralph Waldo Emerson wrote a poem honoring the minutemen. Emerson's "Concord Hymn" contains these famous lines: "Here once the embattled farmers stood / And fired the shot heard round the world."

The Battle of Bunker Hill

Meanwhile, outside of Boston, the Americans were planning a surprise for the British. At sunset on June 16, 1775, Colonel William Prescott led 1,200 minutemen up Bunker Hill in Charlestown. From there, they could fire on British ships in Boston harbor.

Prescott soon saw that nearby Breed's Hill was a better position. He had his men dig trenches there. Prescott knew that if the trenches were not ready before dawn, the British could force him off the hill.

At sunrise, the British general William Howe spotted the Americans. He ferried about 2,400 redcoats across the harbor to Charlestown. Carrying heavy packs, the British slowly made their way across rough fields to climb Breed's Hill.

From their trenches, the Americans watched the British approach. Because the colonists had very little gunpowder, their commanders warned them to hold their fire as long as they could: "Don't shoot until you see the whites of their eyes!"

When the British did charge, the Americans drove them back twice. On the third try, the British pushed over the top. By then, the colonists had run out of powder. Finally, the British took both Bunker Hill and Breed's Hill. Still, the cost of victory was high. More than 1,000 redcoats lay dead or wounded. American losses numbered 400.

The **Battle of Bunker Hill** was the first major battle of the Revolution. It proved that the Americans could fight bravely. It also showed that the British would not be easy to defeat.

Last Efforts for Peace

On May 10, 1775, delegates in Philadelphia opened the Second Continental Congress. Most who attended still hoped to avoid a final break with Britain. Yet the news of fighting in New England pushed the Congress to prepare for war.

Forming an army

Delegates to the Second Continental Congress already knew of the clashes at Lexington and Concord. Letters had arrived from

Viewing HISTORY **Advancing on Bunker Hill**

This early painting shows British ships bombarding the village of Charlestown, Massachusetts. Bunker Hill lies just beyond Breed's Hill, shown at the upper right. Redcoats succeeded in taking the two hills, but at a great cost. ★ **Why was Bunker Hill important to the Americans?**

Drum carried at Bunker Hill ➤

Massachusetts asking them to create a "powerful Army." Then, even as Congress debated this request, new riders galloped into Philadelphia with reports of Ethan Allen's success at Ticonderoga.

In June, Congress took the bold step of setting up the **Continental Army.** Their next task was to select a commander. John Adams shrewdly decided to propose a southerner for the position, rather than someone from Massachusetts. His goal was to widen support for what was up until then considered largely a New England struggle. Adams told the delegates:

> "I [have] in mind for that important command . . . a gentleman whose skill and experience as an officer, whose independent fortune, great talents, and excellent universal character would command the [approval] of all America."

Adams's choice was **George Washington** of Virginia. Washington brought valuable qualities to the job of commander. He was from a wealthy, respected family. During the French and Indian War, he had led British troops in the Ohio Valley. A natural

Biography **Thomas Paine**

A poor English boy with little schooling, Tom Paine grew up to become a powerful voice for liberty. In Common Sense, *he explained in blunt language why American colonists should seek independence. A later pamphlet,* The Crisis, *helped raise the morale of American troops. Still later, Paine went to France to support a revolt against the French king.* ★ **Why did Paine title his pamphlet *Common Sense?***

◀ Common Sense

king at official dinners. After reading Paine's pamphlet, he ended this practice.

Congress Breaks From Britain

By June 1776, the Continental Congress was ready to make the final break with Britain. For the delegates, this was a difficult decision. There could be no turning back once they declared independence. If captured, they would be hanged as traitors. A **traitor** is a person who betrays his or her country.

Writing the Declaration

In July, the Congress took the fateful step. They chose a committee of five delegates to draw up a declaration of independence. The committee included John Adams, Benjamin Franklin, and **Thomas Jefferson.** Their job was to tell the world why the colonies were breaking away from Britain.

The committee asked Jefferson, a Virginian, to write the document. Jefferson was one of the youngest delegates. A quiet man, he spoke little at formal meetings. However, his ability to write clearly and gracefully earned him great respect.

On July 2, the Continental Congress voted that the 13 colonies were "free and independent States." Two days later, on July 4, 1776, the delegates accepted Jefferson's **Declaration of Independence,** making only a few changes. Since then, Americans have celebrated the Fourth of July as Independence Day.

John Hancock, president of the Continental Congress, signed the Declaration first. He penned his signature boldly, in large clear letters. "There," he said, "I guess King George will be able to read that."

Natural rights

Across the colonies, people read the Declaration of Independence. The document has three main parts. (The complete Declaration is printed on pages 728–731.)

The first part of the Declaration stressed the idea of **natural rights,** or rights that belong to all people from birth. In bold, ringing words, Jefferson declared:

> "We hold these truths to be self-evident, that all men are created equal, that they are endowed by their Creator with certain unalienable rights, that among these are life, liberty, and the pursuit of happiness."

Connections With Civics

As the Continental Congress debated independence, Abigail Adams wrote to her husband, John: "In the new code of laws that I suppose you will make, I wish you would remember the ladies." She warned that women would rebel against "any laws in which we have had no voice or representation."

How do people protect these God-given rights? By forming governments, the Declaration says. Governments can exist only if they have the "consent of the governed." If a government fails to protect the rights of its citizens, then it is the people's "right [and] duty, to throw off such government."

The Declaration's stress on natural rights was revolutionary. In 1765, when colonists protested the Stamp Act, they claimed to have the "rights and liberties of [the king's] natural-born subjects." In contrast, the Declaration insisted that the people's rights did not come from the king. Neither could they be granted by Parliament or by any other government.

The twin ideas of natural rights and the equality of men had two sources. First, they reflected the work of Enlightenment thinker John Locke, who declared that all people had natural rights to life, liberty, and property. Second, they had roots in the Christian teaching that all souls are equal in the eyes of God. In the more democratic society of the colonies, this belief was soon translated into the notion that all people are of equal worth.

Reasons for independence

The second part of the Declaration lists the wrongs committed by Britain. Jefferson carefully showed how George III had abused his power. For example, he condemned the

Viewing HISTORY **Signing the Declaration**

Thomas Jefferson labored many hours perfecting the Declaration of Independence. Here, Jefferson and other committee members present the Declaration to the Continental Congress. This painting, like the one on page 81, is by John Trumbull.

★ **What was the purpose of the Declaration of Independence?**

Copy of the Declaration of Independence

Viewing History **Patriots Protest**

In July 1776, angry New Yorkers tore down a statue of King George III. Patriots, including women and children, used the lead from the statue to make cartridges for George Washington's army. ★ **Summarize two complaints Patriots had against the king.**

king for disbanding colonial legislatures and for sending troops to the colonies in times of peace. Jefferson listed many other wrongs to show why the colonists had the right to rebel against the king.

The last part of the Declaration announces that the colonies had become "the United States of America." All ties with Britain were cut. As a free and independent nation, the United States could make alliances and trade with other countries.

The People Respond to the Declaration

The Continental Congress had acted. Still, what would ordinary Americans think of their decision? Would they support the delegates in their move to declare independence from Britain?

Congress sent express riders and coaches and packet ships to distribute copies of the Declaration of Independence throughout the colonies. In squares and coffeehouses, crowds gathered to hear the document read aloud and to debate its merits.

Patriots

Opinion was divided. Some colonists were **Patriots,** people who supported independence. Patriots rejoiced at the Declaration, often responding with loud cheers and hurrahs. Abigail Adams wrote her husband from Boston that, despite the gunpowder shortage, troops fired cannon and muskets in celebration.

In New York, an excited crowd pulled down a statue of King George. It was later melted down to make musket balls for use in the fight against the British.

Loyalists

A smaller number of colonists were **Loyalists,** people who remained loyal to Britain. Many families were split. Ben Franklin, for example, was a Patriot. His son, the royal governor of New Jersey, supported King George.

During the American Revolution, tens of thousands of people supported the British. Loyalists included most wealthy merchants and former officials of the royal government. However, many farmers and craftsworkers were Loyalists as well. There were more Loyalists in the Middle States and in the South than in New England.

Life was difficult for Loyalists everywhere. Patriots tarred and feathered people known to favor the British. Many Loyalists fled to England or Canada. They lost their homes, stores, and farms. Others found shelter in cities controlled by the British.

The Two Armies

The colonial forces who fought the British faced a difficult task. The British army was one of the best in the world. It had highly trained, experienced troops. Britain's powerful navy could move soldiers quickly up and down the Atlantic coast.

Colonial forces were largely untrained. Except for Virginia, southern militias during the 1700s had little experience fighting during wartime. True, New England militias had served in the wars against France. However, they were used to enlisting only for short terms. General Washington faced an uphill battle trying to build a Continental Army whose men would stay to fight for long periods of time.

Britain faced problems of its own. Its armies were 3,000 miles from home. News and supplies took months to travel from Britain to North America. Also, British soldiers risked attacks by colonists once they marched out of the cities into the surrounding countryside.

The Americans had certain advantages. They were fighting to defend their land, homes, farms, and shops. Reuben Stebbins of Massachusetts was typical of many American farmers. When he heard that the British were nearby, he rode off to battle. "We'll see who's goin' t'own this farm!" he cried.

Although few Americans had military training, many owned rifles and were good shots. Also, the colonists had a brilliant leader in General George Washington. He demanded—and received—respect from his troops.

★ Section 3 Review ★

Recall

1. **Identify** **(a)** *Common Sense,* **(b)** Thomas Paine, **(c)** Thomas Jefferson, **(d)** Declaration of Independence, **(e)** Patriot, **(f)** Loyalist.
2. **Define** **(a)** traitor, **(b)** natural rights.

Comprehension

3. What arguments did Thomas Paine offer in favor of independence?
4. Describe the three main parts of the Declaration of Independence.
5. Why was life difficult for Loyalists?

Critical Thinking and Writing

6. **Analyzing Ideas** Review the subsection Natural Rights. **(a)** In your own words, what are natural rights? **(b)** Why was the stress on natural rights in the Declaration of Independence revolutionary?
7. **Comparing** Compare the strengths and weaknesses of the British and Americans at the start of the Revolution.

★ ★

Activity **Rephrasing** You are in charge of teaching your friends what the Declaration of Independence means. Rewrite the first two paragraphs of the Declaration in the language you and your friends would use if you were creating the Declaration today.

Winning the War

Explore These Questions

- What were the major battles of the American Revolution?
- How did Washington force the British to surrender at Yorktown?
- What were the terms of the Treaty of Paris?

Define

- neutral
- ratify

Identify

- Charles Cornwallis
- Battle of Saratoga
- Valley Forge
- Marquis de Lafayette
- George Rogers Clark
- Yorktown
- Treaty of Paris

One morning in June 1776, Daniel McCurtin glanced out his window at New York harbor. As he watched, amazed, a "wood of pine trees" moved across the water. He realized that the trees were the masts of ships!

> "In about ten minutes, the whole bay was full of shipping as ever it could be. I declare that I thought all London was afloat."

By noon, a British fleet was anchored offshore. General William Howe and his redcoats had arrived in force.

The arrival of the British in New York marked a new stage in the war. Most early battles of the American Revolution were fought in New England. In mid-1776, the heavy fighting shifted to the Middle States.

Desperate Days in the Middle States

Washington had expected Howe's attack and had led his forces south from Boston to New York City. His raw army, however, was no match for the British.

Washington retreats

In August, Howe's army pushed ashore. In the Battle of Long Island, more than 1,400 Americans were killed, wounded, or captured. To avoid capture, Washington hurried north with the troops that remained.

Throughout the autumn, the Americans fought a series of battles with Howe's army. In November, they crossed the Hudson River into New Jersey. Pursued by the British, the Americans retreated across the Delaware River into Pennsylvania.

Months of campaigning took a toll on the Continental Army. In December 1776, Washington described his troops as sick, dirty, and "so thinly clad as to be unfit for service."

Victory at Trenton

Desperate for a victory, Washington decided to launch a surprise attack on Trenton, New Jersey. On Christmas night, Washington secretly led his troops across the icy Delaware River. Early on the morning of December 26, the Americans surprised the troops guarding Trenton and took most of them prisoner.

British general **Charles Cornwallis** set out to retake Trenton and capture Washington. Late on January 2, 1777, he saw the lights of Washington's campfires. "At last we have run down the old fox," Cornwallis boasted.

Washington fooled Cornwallis. He left the fires burning and slipped behind British lines to attack Princeton. There, the Continental Army won another victory. From Princeton, Washington moved to Morristown, where the army spent the winter. The victories at Trenton and Princeton gave the Americans new hope.

The Turning Point

In London, British officials were dismayed by the army's failure to crush the rebels. Early in 1777, General John Burgoyne presented the king with a new plan for victory. If British troops cut off New England from the other colonies, he argued, the war would soon be over.

Burgoyne wanted three armies to march on Albany, New York, and crush American forces there. In control of the Hudson River, the British could then stop the flow of soldiers and supplies from New England to Washington's army.

Two British victories

Burgoyne's plan called for General Howe to march on Albany from New York City. George III, however, wanted Howe to capture Philadelphia first.

In July 1777, Howe sailed from New York to the Chesapeake Bay. Despite Washington's efforts to stop him, Howe captured Philadelphia. He also won victories over the Americans at the battles of Brandywine and Germantown. Howe retired to comfortable quarters in Philadelphia for the winter. Washington set up a makeshift camp at Valley Forge.

Battle of Saratoga

Meanwhile, a strong American army beat back two other British armies that were marching from Canada toward Albany. Only Burgoyne was left to march on Albany. Despite valiant efforts by the Patriots to stop his progress, Burgoyne retook Fort Ticonderoga. He then sent troops into Vermont to find food and horses. Patriots met these troops at the Battle of Bennington, where they wounded or captured nearly 1,000 men.

Burgoyne's troubles grew. The Green Mountain Boys hurried into New York to help the American forces. At the village of Saratoga, the Americans surrounded the

Viewing HISTORY **Victory at Princeton**

This painting depicts the battle at Princeton, New Jersey, in January 1777. Victories at Trenton and Princeton boosted American morale. Still, difficult times lay ahead for Washington's troops. ★ **How was Washington able to surprise the British at Princeton?**

British. Realizing he was trapped, Burgoyne surrendered his army to the Americans on October 17, 1777.

France: A Powerful Ally

The American victory at the **Battle of Saratoga** was a turning point in the war. It ended the British threat to New England. It also boosted American spirits at a time when Washington's army was suffering defeats in Pennsylvania. Most important, it persuaded France to become an ally of the United States.

Congress had long sought French aid. They wanted the French to give them weapons and other supplies. Congress also wanted France to declare war on Britain. France had a strong navy.

King Louis XVI of France did not want to help the colonists openly unless he was sure they could win. Saratoga provided that proof. In February 1778, France became the first country to sign a treaty with the United States. Louis XVI recognized the new nation and agreed to provide military aid.

Winter at Valley Forge

French aid arrived too late to help Washington's ragged army at **Valley Forge.** During the long, cold winter of 1777–1778, the Continental Army suffered severe hardships in Pennsylvania.

American soldiers shivered in damp, drafty huts. Many slept on the frozen ground and suffered from frostbite and disease. An army surgeon from Connecticut described the suffering:

> “There comes a Soldier, his bare feet are seen through his worn-out stockings, his Breeches not sufficient to cover his nakedness . . . his whole appearance pictures a person forsaken & discouraged.”

When Americans learned about conditions at Valley Forge, they sent help. Women collected food, medicine, warm clothes, and ammunition for the army.

Volunteers from Europe also strengthened the American army. The **Marquis de Lafayette** (lah fee YEHT), a young French noble, became one of Washington's most trusted friends. Friedrich von Steuben (STOO buhn) from Prussia helped train Continental troops to march and drill. Two Polish officers, Thaddeus Kosciusko (kahs ee UHS koh) and Casimir Pulaski, also provided valuable aid.

The War in the West

When the Revolution began, most Indians tried to stay out of the conflict. An Iroquois chief told whites that he preferred "to sit still and see you fight it out." Yet Native Americans could not avoid becoming involved in the struggle.

Indians choose sides

As the war spread, Native Americans began to take sides. Loyalties varied from group to group and even from village to village. Most Iroquois helped the British. In Massachusetts, the Algonquins supported the Patriots. In the West, many Indians joined the British to protect their lands from American settlers.

In Tennessee and Kentucky, Cherokees were alarmed by white settlers pushing onto Indian lands. As a result, the Cherokees joined the British.

George Rogers Clark

In 1778, **George Rogers Clark** led Virginia frontier fighters against the British in the Ohio Valley. With help from Miami Indians, Clark captured the British forts at Kaskaskia and Cahokia.

Clark then plotted a surprise winter attack on the British fort at Vincennes. Clark's small band of men spread out through the woods around the fort to make their numbers appear greater. Convinced he was outnumbered, the British commander surrendered Vincennes without a fight in February 1779.

Spanish aid

Americans received help from New Spain, too. At first, Spain was **neutral**—that is, it did not take sides in the war. Still, Bernardo de Gálvez, governor of Spanish Louisiana, favored the Patriots. He secretly sent supplies to the Americans, including cattle to feed the Continental Army.

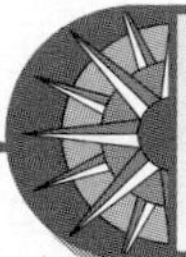

Linking Past and Present

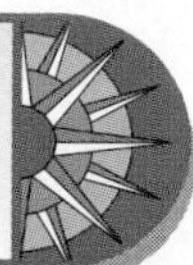

Past

Present

Women in Arms

During the American Revolution, few women took part directly in battle. Those who did became legendary. At left, Mary Ludwig Hays—known as "Molly Pitcher"—loads and fires a cannon in place of her fallen husband. By the 1990s, there were more than 70,000 women on active duty in the United States armed forces. ★ **Why do you think so many young women have volunteered to serve in the military?**

Spain entered the war against Britain in 1779. Gálvez then seized British forts along the Mississippi and Gulf of Mexico. He drove the British out of West Florida.

Women in the War

Women played an important role in the struggle for independence. When men went off to war, women took on added work. They planted and harvested the crops that fed the Continental Army. They made guns and other weapons. One woman, nicknamed "Handy Betsy the Blacksmith," was famous for supplying cannons and guns to the army. Other women made shoes and wove cloth for blankets and uniforms.

Many women also joined their soldier-husbands at the front. There, they washed clothes, cooked, and cared for the wounded. Martha Washington joined her husband whenever she could.

A few women acted as spies for the Patriots. Others even took part in battle. Deborah Sampson of Massachusetts dressed as a man and fought in several battles. She later wrote about her life in the army. Sybil Luddington, a 16-year-old Connecticut girl, rode 40 miles through a rainy night to warn the militia that British troops had set fire to a supply base.

African Americans in the Battle for Freedom

By 1776, more than a half million African Americans were living in the colonies. At first, the Continental Congress refused to let blacks, whether free or enslaved, join the army. However, when the British offered freedom to any male slave who served the king, Washington decided to allow free African Americans to enlist.

Biography **James Armistead**

Though enslaved, James Armistead of Virginia faithfully served the Patriot cause. In 1781, he acted as a spy for the French commander Lafayette, reporting on the actions of British officers. After winning his freedom, Armistead took a new name: James Lafayette. ★ **Why did Washington decide to allow African Americans to join the army?**

Taking up arms

About 5,000 African Americans fought against the British. At least nine black minutemen saw action at Lexington and Concord. Two of them, Peter Salem and Salem Poor, went on to fight bravely at Bunker Hill.

Some African Americans formed special regiments. Others served in white regiments as drummers, fifers, spies, and guides. Thousands of black sailors served on American ships.

Enslaved African Americans faced difficult choices. If they tried to flee toward the British army to gain freedom, they risked being hanged by angry Patriots. If they continued to work on Patriot-owned plantations, the British might capture them and sell them. In South Carolina alone, the British rounded up over 5,000 slaves.

A move to end slavery

Black Patriots hoped that the Revolution would bring an end to slavery. After all, the Declaration of Independence proclaimed that "all men are created equal." In Massachusetts and elsewhere, enslaved African Americans sent petitions to lawmakers asking for freedom.

Some whites also hoped the war would end slavery. James Otis wrote that "the colonists are by the law of nature free born, as indeed all men are, white or black." Quakers in particular spoke out against this "great evil."

By the 1770s, slavery was declining in the North. During the Revolution, several northern states moved to outlaw slavery, including Vermont, Massachusetts, New Hampshire, and Pennsylvania. Other states debated the issue.

As they gained their freedom, many African Americans moved to the seaport cities of Boston, Philadelphia and New York. There, African American men could get jobs as seamen or dockworkers. Women often worked as servants in homes of prosperous city dwellers.

War in the South

Scattered fighting had taken place in the South throughout the Revolution. Not until France entered the war, however, did the British focus their efforts on that region. Sir Henry Clinton, the new British commander-in-chief, knew that many Loyalists lived in the southern backcountry. He hoped that if British troops marched through the South, Loyalists would join them.

Connections With Geography

Almost 100,000 Loyalists fled the United States after the Revolution. Among them were more than 10,000 African Americans who had supported Britain in hopes of winning freedom. They moved to Canada, England, Spanish Florida, Jamaica in the West Indies, and Sierra Leone in Africa. There, they lived as free men and women.

Skills FOR LIFE

Managing Information | Communication | Maps, Charts, and Graphs

Understanding Causes and Effects

How Will I Use This Skill ?

Some causes and effects are easy to see. A frost in Florida causes the price of orange juice to rise. An accident at a busy intersection leads the town to put up a new stop sign. Recognizing the relationship between causes and effects can help you understand what has happened and predict future events.

LEARN the Skill

1. Identify the primary event or condition that you will examine.
2. Determine which events had a role in causing the primary event.
3. Determine which events occurred as a result of the primary event.
4. Explain the relationship between causes and effects.

PRACTICE the Skill

At right are a list of events and a partially filled-in cause-and-effect chart. After reading this section, answer the following questions:

1. What primary event is the focus of the chart?
2. Which events on the list would you include in the chart as causes? Why?
3. Which events on the list would you include in the chart as effects? Why?
4. (a) Why was taxation one cause of the American Revolution? (b) Do you think the United States of America could have been formed without the American Revolution?

Cause and Effect

Causes

- Parliament taxes the colonies
- ____________________
- ____________________

The American Revolution

Effects

- United States of America is formed
- ____________________
- ____________________

George Washington emerges as national leader

Proclamation of 1763 stops colonists from moving west

Intolerable Acts set up harsh rule in Massachusetts

United States borders extend to Florida and Mississippi River

APPLY the Skill

Select an event that affected you. Create a chart that identifies at least two causes and two effects of that event.

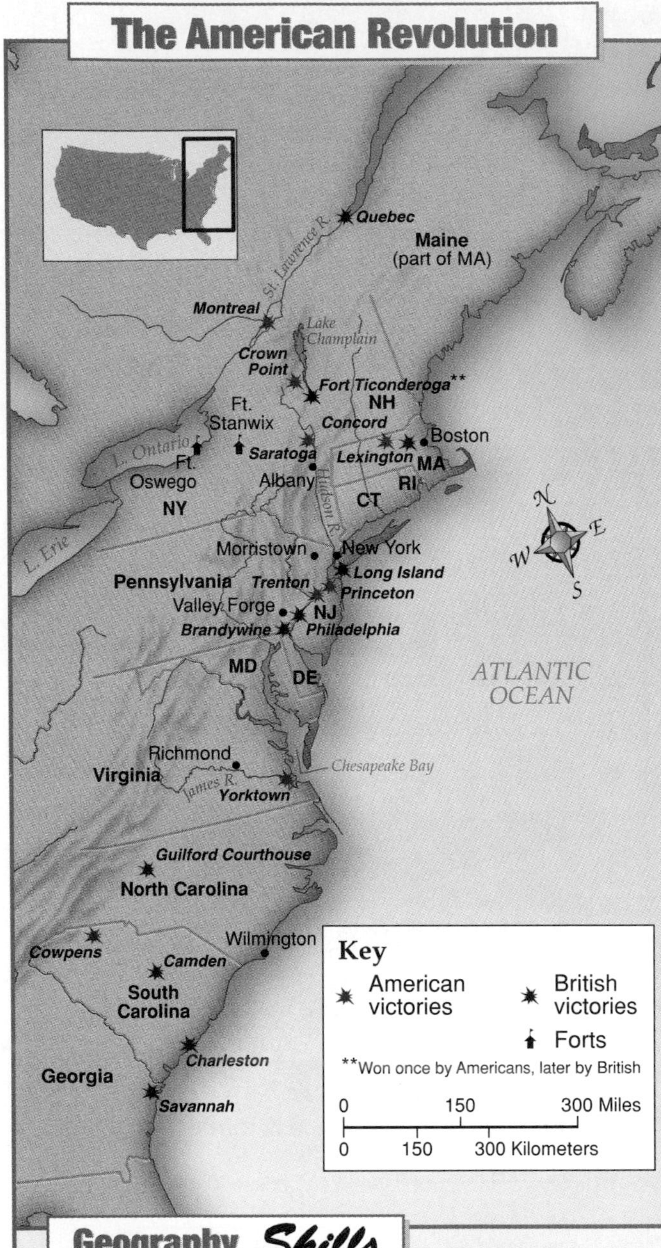

Geography *Skills* During the American Revolution, the main fighting moved from New England to the Middle States to the South.

1. **Location** On the map, locate: **(a)** Boston, **(b)** Fort Ticonderoga, **(c)** Long Island, **(d)** Trenton, **(e)** Princeton, **(f)** Saratoga, **(g)** Valley Forge, **(h)** Cowpens, **(i)** Yorktown.
2. **Movement** Name three British victories in the South.
3. **Critical Thinking** How did the geography of Yorktown help the French fleet trap British troops?

At first, Clinton's plan seemed to work. In December 1778, the British seized Savannah, Georgia. A year and a half later, they took Charleston, South Carolina.

Yet, in the long run, Clinton's strategy failed. Small bands of Loyalists launched savage attacks that angered many Americans who until then had remained neutral. British tactics also stirred anger. One Loyalist officer boasted that the army marched through the country "destroying furniture, breaking windows, taking . . . cattle, horses, mules, etc."

Many southerners responded by joining the Patriot cause. Bands of militia soon roamed the countryside. Neighbors—and even families—fought and killed one another in bitter fighting.

Francis Marion of South Carolina led a small Patriot band of white and black militia. They would appear suddenly out of the swamps, attack the British, and then retreat into the brush. Marion became known as the Swamp Fox. His attacks kept the British off balance.

The Patriots rally

Two able American generals, Daniel Morgan and Nathanael Greene, helped turn the tide in the South. Morgan's Virginia Riflemen had served well in the Battle of Saratoga. In January 1781, Morgan defeated the British at the Battle of Cowpens in South Carolina.

General Greene was a New Englander, but he quickly learned his way around the Carolinas. His small army engaged the British only when they had a sure advantage, then quickly retreated. General Cornwallis wore out his army trying to catch the quick-moving Greene. In the spring of 1781, Cornwallis moved his troops out of the Carolinas north into Virginia.

Victory at Last

Cornwallis set up camp at **Yorktown,** on a strip of land that juts into the Chesapeake Bay. He felt safe there, knowing that British ships could supply his troops from the sea.

Washington knew the area well. He realized that he could trap Cornwallis at Yorktown. As a French fleet sailed toward the Chesapeake, Washington marched south from New York. French troops joined him on the way to Virginia.

Meanwhile, the French fleet kept British ships out of the Chesapeake. Cornwallis was cut off. He could neither get supplies nor escape by sea.

Still, Cornwallis held out for three weeks. Finally, on October 17, 1781, he surrendered. Two days later, the defeated British turned their weapons over to the Americans.

Making Peace

Americans rejoiced when they heard the news from Yorktown. The defeat shocked the British, however. "It is all over," cried the prime minister, Lord North. Left with no choice, he agreed to peace talks.

Treaty of Paris

The delegates met in Paris. Because Britain was eager to end the war, the Americans got most of what they wanted. In the **Treaty of Paris,** the British agreed to recognize the United States as an independent nation. The borders of the new nation extended from the Atlantic Ocean to the Mississippi River. The southern border stopped at Florida, which was returned to Spain.

For their part, the Americans agreed to ask state legislatures to pay Loyalists for property they lost in the war. In the end, however, most states ignored the Loyalist claims.

John Adams used this seal at the signing of the Treaty of Paris.

On April 15, 1783, Congress voted to **ratify,** or approve, the Treaty of Paris. It was almost eight years to the day since the minutemen had faced the redcoats at Lexington and Concord.

Washington retires

In December 1783, General Washington bid farewell to his officers in New York City. He looked forward to retirement at his estate at Mount Vernon, Virginia. As Washington rode home, crowds gathered along the road to cheer the beloved hero of American independence.

The new nation faced difficult days ahead. Before long, Americans would again call on George Washington to lead them.

★ Section 4 Review ★

Recall

1. **Locate** **(a)** Long Island, **(b)** Delaware River, **(c)** Trenton, **(d)** Valley Forge, **(e)** Vincennes, **(f)** Yorktown.
2. **Identify** **(a)** Charles Cornwallis, **(b)** Battle of Saratoga, **(c)** Valley Forge, **(d)** Marquis de Lafayette, **(e)** George Rogers Clark, **(f)** Yorktown, **(g)** Treaty of Paris.
3. **Define** **(a)** neutral, **(b)** ratify.

Comprehension

4. Describe three results of the Battle of Saratoga.
5. Why was Cornwallis forced to surrender at Yorktown?
6. Describe the major points of the Treaty of Paris of 1783.

Critical Thinking and Writing

7. **Drawing Conclusions** Why do you think people from other lands, such as Lafayette, Kosciusko, and Pulaski were willing to risk their lives for the American cause?
8. **Making Decisions** If you had been a free African American in the North, would you have supported the Patriots or the British? Explain.

Activity **Summarizing** You are in charge of telling King George III the news of Cornwallis's surrender to Washington. Explain what happened—and how it happened—in as much detail as you can. Keep in mind, though, how the king will greet your news!

Chapter 4 Review and Activities

★ Sum It Up ★

Section 1 The Road to Revolution

- As a result of the French and Indian War, Britain won control of France's claims in North America.
- American colonists strongly protested efforts by the British Parliament to impose new taxes on the colonies.

Section 2 The Fighting Begins

- Conflict over taxes gradually increased until colonists staged the Boston Tea Party and Britain passed the Intolerable Acts.
- The first major fighting of the American Revolution broke out in April 1775 at the battles of Lexington and Concord.

Section 3 Declaring Independence

- In his pamphlet *Common Sense,* Thomas Paine argued that colonists did not owe loyalty to the king.
- The Continental Congress declared in 1776 that the American colonies had become the independent United States of America.

Section 4 Winning the War

- An American victory at the Battle of Saratoga helped persuade France to support the American side.
- After years of fighting, the British army finally surrendered at Yorktown.
- In the peace settlement, the United States established borders that stretched from the Atlantic Ocean to the Mississippi River.

For additional review of the major ideas of Chapter 4, see ***Guide to the Essentials of American History*** or ***Interactive Student Tutorial CD-ROM,*** which contains interactive review activities, graphic organizers, and practice tests.

Reviewing the Chapter

Define These Terms

Match each term with the correct definition.

Column 1	Column 2
1. traitor	**a.** militia volunteer
2. boycott	**b.** cancel
3. repeal	**c.** person who betrays his or her country
4. minuteman	**d.** refuse to buy
5. ratify	**e.** approve

Explore the Main Ideas

1. How did American colonists respond to the Townshend Acts?
2. Why did many colonists refuse to drink tea after 1773?
3. Where did most of the fighting take place **(a)** in the early part of the American Revolution, and **(b)** in the later part of the war?
4. What was the result of the capture of Ticonderoga?
5. **(a)** What advantages did the British have during the American Revolution? **(b)** What advantages did Americans have?
6. What role did African Americans play in the war?

Geography Activity

Match the letters on the map with the following places: **1.** Boston, **2.** Trenton, **3.** Saratoga, **4.** Cowpens, **5.** Savannah, **6.** Yorktown. **Movement** Why was control of the Chesapeake Bay important to Cornwallis at Yorktown?

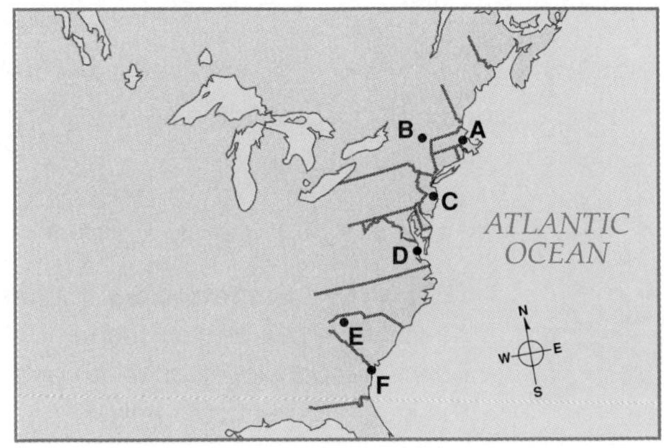

Critical Thinking and Writing

1. **Ranking** Which of the Intolerable Acts would have been most alarming to the Americans throughout the colonies? Explain.
2. **Exploring Unit Themes Origins** The battles of Lexington and Concord marked the start of the American Revolution. Why do you think Americans celebrate July 4, 1776, rather than April 19, 1775, as the birthdate of the United States?
3. **Understanding Chronology** Suppose you are reading two official documents from the American colonies in the 1700s. One refers to the rights colonists have as subjects of the king. The other refers to the natural rights given to colonists by God. Which would you guess was written later? Explain.
4. **Linking Past and Present** Why do you think the United States has maintained close ties with Britain in spite of the conflict that led to the Revolution?

Using Primary Sources

During the difficult winter of 1776–1777, Thomas Paine wrote *The Crisis* to inspire Americans to fight the British. Washington had the essay read aloud to his discouraged soldiers. Paine's work began with these now-famous words:

> "These are the times that try [test] men's souls. The summer soldier and the sunshine patriot will, in this crisis, shrink from the service of their country; but he that stands it now, deserves the love and thanks of man and woman."

Source: *The Crisis*, Thomas Paine, 1777.

Recognizing Points of View (a) How did Paine describe the difficult period through which the nation was passing? **(b)** What do you think Paine meant by "the summer soldier and the sunshine patriot"? **(c)** How do you think Washington's soldiers would have reacted to Paine's words?

Activity Bank

Interdisciplinary Activity

Exploring Sciences Compile statistics on major battles of the American Revolution. Include dates of the battles, the number of soldiers who fought in each, and the number of soldiers killed and wounded. Put your information in chart form.

Career Skills Activity

Graphic Artist Make a diagram of the events leading up to the Olive Branch Petition. Use graphic arts techniques to show how events built toward the final outcome.

Citizenship Activity

Testing Alternative Courses of Action Review the events of the Boston Tea Party. List reasons why citizens of the colonies should have supported the actions of the protesters. Then, list reasons why they should condemn the protesters' actions.

Internet Activity

Choose a field of the arts that interests you. Then, use the Internet to find information on an aspect of the American Revolution. After researching on the Internet, use your artistic interest to express what you have learned. For example, you might perform a skit about women in the Revolution, or paint a picture of the Battle of Yorktown.

You are a soldier in the American, British, or French army; a Native American; a free or enslaved African American; a woman at the battle front; a parent whose son is away fighting with the Continental Army; or a Loyalist. In your EYEWITNESS JOURNAL, describe three events of 1775–1781 as they affected you.

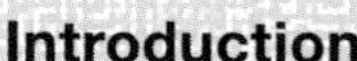

Valley Forge

by Maxwell Anderson

Introduction

For 30 years, Maxwell Anderson was one of the most respected American playwrights. Many of his dramas were based on history. His 1934 play *Valley Forge* describes the hardships the Continental Army faced during the winter of 1777–1778. In this scene, George Washington hears some of the complaints of his troops.

Vocabulary

Before you read the selection, find the meaning of these words in a dictionary: **lenient, commissary, savvy, munitions.**

TEAGUE: General Washington!

WASHINGTON: What is it?

TEAGUE: These here new regulations about men going home. Going home without leave. They say it's seventy-five lashes if they catch you now. Why is that?

WASHINGTON: The traditional penalty for desertion is shooting at sunrise. We've been more lenient here.

TEAGUE: But look, General Washington, it don't make sense. It don't stand to reason—

NICK: Do you want to talk your neck into a rope?

WASHINGTON: Let him say what's on his mind.

TEAGUE: Well, here it is: I'm going hungry here and my woman's going hungry at home. You let me go home for the winter, and you won't have to feed me, and that relieves the commissary. I rustle some wild meat for the younguns and the old woman, and they don't starve and I don't starve. More'n that, everybody knows there's two or three thousand men gone home already for that same reason, and if they was here now they'd be chewing the bark off the second-growth birch like so many cottontails. I don't hold it against you and I don't hold it against anybody because I don't know who in thunder to hold it against, but there's nothing to eat here.

ALCOCK: Stow it, will you? The dog ate the stuff, and he isn't dead yet.

TEAGUE: It ain't that I'm afraid of a good fight. A good fight's ham and eggs to me. Me and my boy here, we make for home every winter when the grub gets scarce, and we come back every spring when the fighting starts. We're coming back next spring, and every spring, till we chase the . . . redcoats clear out of Chesapeake Bay, and across the Atlantic Ocean and right up a lamppost in London town! Fightin's fine, but sitting here and starving down to a hide and buttons—I don't savvy it.

WASHINGTON: What is your name, sir?

TEAGUE: Teague, sir. Teague's my name.

WASHINGTON: Well, Master Teague, if they catch you they'll give you seventy-five

Viewing HISTORY Hard Winter at Valley Forge

The March to Valley Forge by William B. Trego shows General George Washington on horseback, reviewing his troops. At Valley Forge, Washington had to plead with local merchants and farmers for food supplies. ★ **Why does Trego show one of the soldiers taking off his hat to Washington?**

lashes, and that's a good deal to take and live. On the other hand you're quite right from your own angle, and if I were you I'd feel as you do.—But this you should know, sir: if you go home, and we all go home this winter, you won't need to bother about coming back in the spring. There'll be no fighting to come back to.—General Howe will march out of Philadelphia and take over these states of ours. If he knew now how many have deserted, how many are sick, how many unfit for duty on account of the lack of food and clothes and munitions, he'd come back in force and wring our necks one by one, and the neck of our sickly little revolution along with us.... What are we in this war for? Do we want to quit?

THE MEN: No, sir. No.

WASHINGTON: I can't blame you if you sound a bit half-hearted about it.

TEAGUE: I'm not half-hearted about it! Not me! I'm fighting to keep King George out of my backyard! I moved west three times to get away from his... tax-collectors, and every time they caught up to me! I'm sick of tax-collectors, that's why I'm in it!

WASHINGTON: Then it may be you're here in error, and the sooner you discover it the better. You'll get death and taxes under one government as well as another. But I'll tell you why I'm here, and why I've hoped you were here, and why it's seemed to me worthwhile to stick with it while our guns rust out for lack of powder, and men die around me for lack of food and medicine, and women and children sicken at home for lack of clothing and the little they need to eat.... [W]hat I fight for is your right to do what you please with your government and with yourselves without benefit of kings.—It's for you to decide, Master Teague—you, and your son, and the rest of you.... But if we lose you—if you've lost interest in this cause of ours—we've lost our war, lost it completely, and the men we've left lying on our battlefields died for nothing whatever—for a dream that came too early—and may never come true....

TEAGUE: I guess the old woman'll get along. She's brought in her own bear meat before.

NICK: Well, it's all right with me.

Analyzing Literature

1. What were some of the hardships that Washington's troops faced?
2. Summarize one argument Teague gives in favor of going home.
3. **Critical Thinking Comparing** How do Washington's reasons for fighting differ from Teague's?

Unit 2

The Constitution of the United States

Viewing UNIT THEMES **Freedom of Religion: A Basic American Right**

Since colonial days, American women have used the craft of quilt-making to express their values and depict their daily life. This detail from a New England quilt from the late 1700s portrays a church as the center of the community. Americans of the time expected their new government to safeguard freedom of religion. ★ **List two other freedoms that Americans enjoy.**

Unit Theme Rights and Liberties

In 1787, American leaders issued the Constitution of the United States. However, many people insisted that the Constitution must include a written guarantee of basic liberties, such as freedom of the press, freedom of religion, and the right to trial by jury. In the end, the new government created a Bill of Rights. It spelled out those rights and liberties we still enjoy as American citizens today.

How did Americans of the time feel about basic rights and liberties? They can tell you in their own words.

Viewpoints on Rights and Liberties

"If we separate from Britain, what code of laws will be established? How shall we be governed so as to retain our liberties?"

Abigail Adams, wife of John Adams (1775)

"By reason of long bondage and hard slavery, we have been deprived of the profits of our labor or the advantage of inheriting estates from our parents as our neighbors the white people do."

Paul Cuffe, African American ship owner (1783)

"Were it left to me to decide whether we should have a government without newspapers, or newspapers without a government, I should not hesitate a moment to prefer the latter."

Thomas Jefferson, Virginia political leader (1787)

Activity Writing to Learn Turn to the First Amendment in the Reference Section and read the Constitution. List the freedoms guaranteed by the First Amendment. Then, choose one of those freedoms. Write a skit showing what life might be like if that freedom were not protected.

Chapter 5

Creating a Republic

1776–1791

What's Ahead

Section 1
A Confederation of States

Section 2
The Constitutional Convention

Section 3
A More Perfect Union

Section 4
Ratifying the Constitution

After the American Revolution ended, the new nation struggled to create a workable government. At first, the states were knit together only by a loose set of laws. When this central government proved too weak, representatives of 12 states gathered in 1787. They created a new framework for government: the Constitution of the United States.

During nearly four exhausting months of debate, the representatives hammered out a set of laws that would make the nation strong, yet protect the rights of the people. After fiery arguments in each state, the Constitution was finally approved. It lives on as the framework of our government today.

Why Study History?

While the new nation was taking shape, American leaders were also creating many symbols and traditions. Today, as in the past, emblems such as the flag and the eagle bind the American people together. To focus on this connection, see the *Why Study History* feature, "National Symbols Unite Us," in this chapter.

American Events

1777 Continental Congress completes the Articles of Confederation

1783 Treaty of Paris formally ends the American Revolution

1776 **1780** **1784**

World Events

1778 World Event
British Captain Cook becomes first European to reach Hawaii

1784 World Event
Emperor Joseph II forces Czechs to use German language

Viewing HISTORY **Signing the Constitution**

In 1787, representatives from 12 states gathered in Philadelphia to create a new national government. The result of their work was the Constitution, which still governs the nation today. This painting by Howard Chandler Christy shows delegates to the Constitutional Convention, including George Washington (standing right) and Benjamin Franklin (seated center). Washington served as the president of the Convention. ★ **Why do you think the representatives chose Washington as their president?**

1787 Northwest Ordinance sets up method to admit new states to the United States

1788 The Constitution is ratified

1791 Bill of Rights guarantees individual rights and freedoms

1784 — **1788** — **1792**

1785 World Event
Russians settle in Aleutian Islands off coast of Alaska

1789 World Event
French Revolution begins

A Confederation of States

As You Read

Explore These Questions
- What ideas guided the new state governments?
- What problems did the nation face under the Articles of Confederation?
- How did the Northwest Ordinance benefit the nation?

Define
- constitution
- execute
- confederation
- ordinance
- economic depression

Identify
- Articles of Confederation
- Land Ordinance of 1785
- Northwest Ordinance
- Shays' Rebellion

SETTING the Scene In 1776, the Declaration of Independence created a new nation made up of 13 independent states. The former colonies, though, had little experience working together. In the past, Britain had made the major decisions. Now, the Americans set about the business of establishing 13 state governments. Furthermore, they hoped to create a central government that all the states would follow.

State Governments

In forming a government, most states wrote a constitution. A **constitution** is a document that sets out the laws and principles of a government. States created written constitutions for two reasons. First, a written constitution would spell out the rights of all citizens. Second, it would set limits on the power of government.

The new state governments were similar to the colonial governments. The states divided political power between an executive and a legislature. The legislature was elected by the voters to pass the laws. Most legislatures had an upper house, called a senate, and a lower house. All states except Pennsylvania had a governor who **executed,** or carried out, the laws.

Articles of Confederation

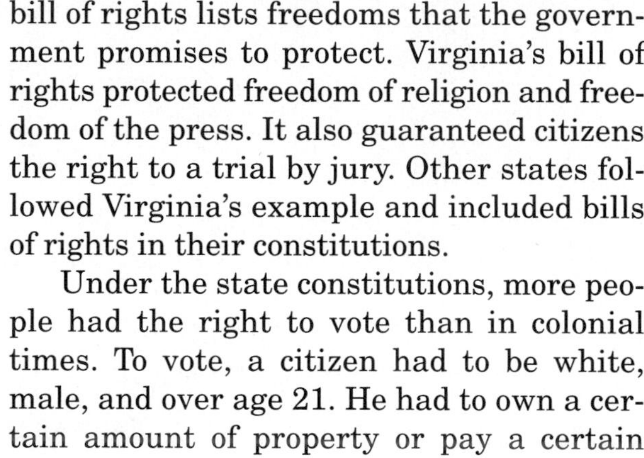

Virginia limited government power by including a bill of rights in its constitution. A bill of rights lists freedoms that the government promises to protect. Virginia's bill of rights protected freedom of religion and freedom of the press. It also guaranteed citizens the right to a trial by jury. Other states followed Virginia's example and included bills of rights in their constitutions.

Under the state constitutions, more people had the right to vote than in colonial times. To vote, a citizen had to be white, male, and over age 21. He had to own a certain amount of property or pay a certain amount of taxes.

For a time, some women in New Jersey could vote. In a few states, free black men could vote. In no state did enslaved African Americans have the right to vote.

A Weak Confederation

In 1776, as citizens were forming state governments, the Continental Congress was drafting a plan for the nation as a whole. Delegates believed that the colonies needed to be united by a central government in order to win independence.

It was difficult to write a constitution that all of the states would approve. They were reluctant to give up power to a national government. In 1776, few Americans saw themselves as citizens of one nation. Instead, they felt loyal to their own states. Also, people were fearful of replacing the "tyranny" of British rule with another strong government. Still, in 1777, after much debate, the Continental Congress completed the **Articles of Confederation**—the first American constitution. It created a **confederation,** or alliance of independent states.

Government under the Articles

Under the Articles of Confederation, the states sent delegates to a Confederation Congress. Each state had one vote in Congress. Congress could declare war, appoint military officers, and coin money. It was also responsible for foreign affairs. However, these powers were few compared with those of the states.

The Articles limited the powers of Congress and preserved the powers of the states. Congress could pass laws, but at least 9 of the 13 states had to approve a law before it could go into effect.

Congress had little economic power. It could not regulate trade between states nor could it regulate trade between states and foreign countries. It could not pass tax laws. To raise money, Congress had to ask the states for it. No state could be forced to contribute funds.

The new confederation government was weak. There was no president to carry out laws. It was up to the states to enforce the laws passed by Congress. There was no system of courts to settle disputes between states. The Articles created a very loose alliance of 13 states.

Dispute over western lands

A dispute arose even before the Articles of Confederation went into effect. Maryland refused to ratify the Articles unless Virginia and other states gave up their claims to lands west of the Appalachian Mountains. Maryland wanted these western lands turned over to Congress. In this way, the "landed" states would not become too powerful.

One by one, the states gave up their western claims. Only Virginia held out. However, Thomas Jefferson and other leading Virginians saw a great need for a central government. They persuaded state lawmakers to give up Virginia's claims in the West. At last, in 1781, Maryland ratified the Articles of Confederation, and the first American government went into effect.

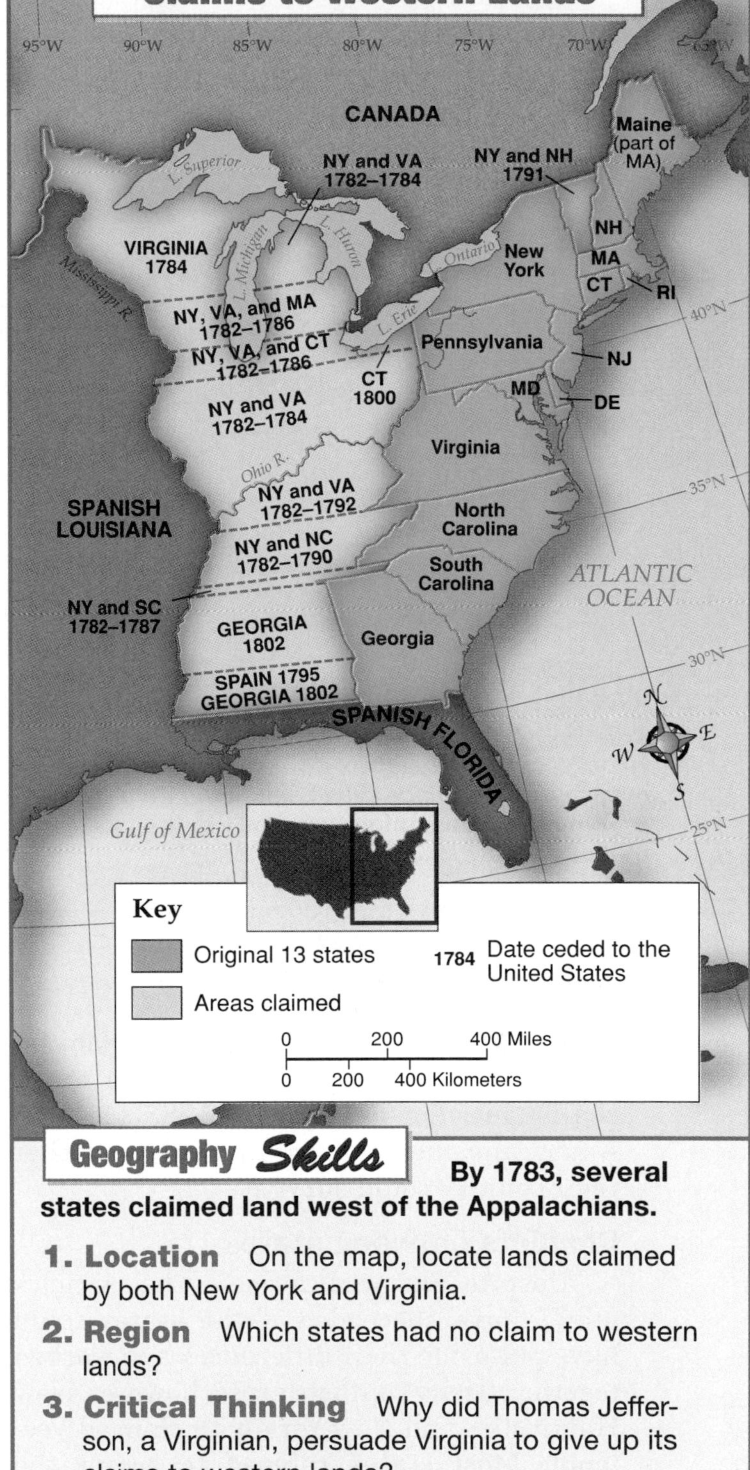

Geography *Skills* **By 1783, several states claimed land west of the Appalachians.**

1. **Location** On the map, locate lands claimed by both New York and Virginia.
2. **Region** Which states had no claim to western lands?
3. **Critical Thinking** Why did Thomas Jefferson, a Virginian, persuade Virginia to give up its claims to western lands?

Viewing HISTORY **State Banknotes**

During and after the American Revolution, each state issued its own money. The bills here came from Rhode Island and South Carolina.
★ **What problems might arise due to the fact that each state issued its own money?**

Troubles for the New Nation

By 1783, the United States had won independence. The new nation faced many challenges, however. From 1783 to 1787, Americans had reason to doubt whether their country could survive.

Conflicts between states

Despite its weaknesses, the Articles might have succeeded if the states could have put aside their differences and worked together. Many conflicts arose, however. New Hampshire and New York both claimed Vermont. Most states refused to accept the money of other states.

The Articles did not provide a way for states to settle such disputes. Noah Webster, a teacher from New England, warned:

> “So long as any individual state has power to defeat the measures of the other twelve, our pretended union is but a name, and our confederation, a cobweb.”

Money problems

As a result of borrowing during the Revolution, the United States owed millions of dollars to individuals and foreign nations. Since Congress did not have the power to tax, it had no way to repay these debts. Congress asked the states for money, but the states had the right to refuse. Often, they did.

During the Revolution, the Continental Congress solved the problem of raising funds by printing paper money. However, the money had little value because it was not backed by gold or silver. Before long, Americans began to describe any useless thing as "not worth a Continental."

As Continental dollars became worthless, states printed their own paper money. This caused confusion. How much was a North Carolina dollar worth? Was a Virginia dollar as valuable as a Maryland dollar? As a result, trade became difficult.

Other nations take advantage

Foreign countries took advantage of the confederation's weakness. Britain, for example, refused to withdraw its troops from the Ohio Valley, as it had agreed to do in the Treaty of Paris. Spain closed its port in New Orleans to American farmers. This was a serious blow to western farmers, who depended on the port to ship their products to the East.

Organizing the Northwest Territory

Despite its troubles, Congress did pass two important **ordinances,** or laws, concerning the Northwest Territory, the name for lands lying north of the Ohio River and east of the Mississippi. The principles established in the two laws were later applied to other areas of settlement.

Townships and sections

The first law, the **Land Ordinance of 1785,** set up a system for settling the Northwest Territory. The law called for the territory to be surveyed and then divided into townships.

Each township would have 36 sections. A section was 1 square mile and contained 640 acres. (See the diagram below.) Congress planned to sell sections to settlers for $640 each. One section in every township was set aside to support public schools.

A plan for new states

The second law, passed in 1787, was the **Northwest Ordinance.** It set up a government for the Northwest Territory, guaranteed basic rights to settlers, and outlawed slavery there. It also provided for the vast region to be divided into separate territories in the future.

Once a territory had a population of 60,000 free settlers, it could ask Congress to be admitted as a new state. The newly admitted state would be "on an equal footing with the original states in all respects whatsoever."

The Northwest Ordinance was the finest achievement of the national government under the Articles. It provided a way to admit new states to the nation. It guaranteed that new states would be treated the same as the original 13 states. In time, the states of Ohio, Indiana, Illinois, Michigan, and Wisconsin were created from the Northwest Territory.

The Northwest Territory

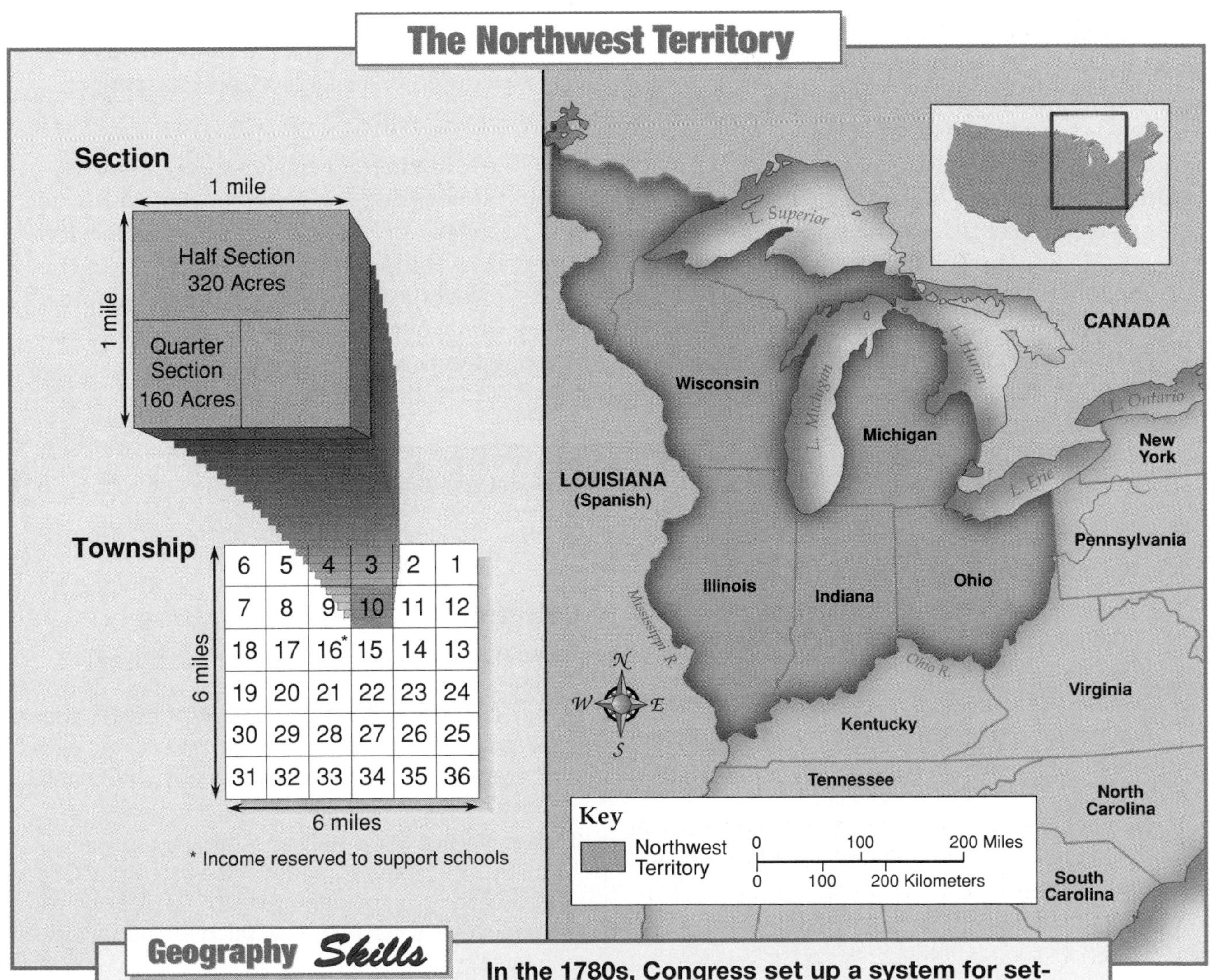

Geography *Skills* **In the 1780s, Congress set up a system for settling and governing the Northwest Territory.**

1. **Location** On the map, locate: **(a)** Ohio River, **(b)** Mississippi River, **(c)** Michigan, **(d)** Indiana, **(e)** Illinois, **(f)** Wisconsin, **(g)** Ohio.
2. **Place** What was the size of **(a)** a township, **(b)** a section?
3. **Critical Thinking** Did the state of Wisconsin have public education when it joined the Union? Explain.

A Farmers' Revolt

While Congress dealt successfully with the Northwest Territory, it failed to solve its economic problems. After the Revolution, the nation suffered an economic depression. An **economic depression** is a period when business activity slows, prices and wages fall, and unemployment rises.

The depression hit farmers hard. During the Revolution, there had been high demand for farm products. To increase production, farmers had borrowed money for land, seed, animals, and tools. However, when the war ended and soldiers returned home, demand for farm goods weakened. Prices fell, and many farmers could not repay their loans.

In Massachusetts, matters worsened when the state raised taxes. The courts seized the farms of those who could not pay their taxes or loans. Angry farmers felt they were being treated unfairly.

In 1786, Daniel Shays, a Massachusetts farmer who had fought at Bunker Hill and Saratoga, organized an uprising. Nearly 2,000 farmers took part in **Shays' Rebellion.** They attacked courthouses and prevented the state from seizing farms. They even tried to capture an arsenal filled with guns. Finally, the Massachusetts legislature sent the militia to drive them off.

A Change Is Needed

Many Americans saw Shays' Rebellion as a sign that the Articles of Confederation did not work. George Washington warned that a terrible crisis was at hand:

> "No day was ever more clouded than the present.... I predict the worst consequences from a half-starved, limping government, always moving upon crutches and tottering at every step."

To avoid such a crisis, leaders from several states called for a convention to revise the Articles of Confederation. They decided to meet in Philadelphia in May 1787. In the end, however, this convention would do much more than just revise the Articles. It would change the course of the nation.

★ Section 1 Review ★

Recall

1. **Locate** Northwest Territory.
2. **Identify** **(a)** Articles of Confederation, **(b)** Land Ordinance of 1785, **(c)** Northwest Ordinance, **(d)** Shays' Rebellion.
3. **Define** **(a)** constitution, **(b)** execute, **(c)** confederation, **(d)** ordinance, **(e)** economic depression.

Comprehension

4. **(a)** How were the new state governments similar to the old colonial governments? **(b)** How were they different?
5. Describe three problems the nation faced under the Articles of Confederation.
6. How did the Northwest Ordinance affect the future growth of the United States?

Critical Thinking and Writing

7. **Analyzing Ideas** When Thomas Jefferson heard about Shays' Rebellion, he wrote: "The spirit of resistance to government is so valuable on occasion that I wish it to be always kept alive." Do you think Shays' Rebellion was good for the United States? Explain.
8. **Identifying Main Ideas** After only 10 years, many Americans agreed that the Articles of Confederation did not work. Why did the Articles fail to serve as a lasting constitution for the United States?

Activity **Drawing a Political Cartoon** You have been asked to create a political cartoon about Shays' Rebellion. The purpose is to help explain to younger students the reasons why farmers like Daniel Shays were angry and what happened as a result of their rebellion.

2 The Constitutional Convention

As You Read

Explore These Questions

- How did the Virginia Plan and the New Jersey Plan differ?
- How did the Great Compromise satisfy both large and small states?
- What compromises were made on the issue of slavery?

Define

- legislative branch
- executive branch
- judicial branch
- compromise

Identify

- Constitutional Convention
- James Madison
- Virginia Plan
- New Jersey Plan
- Roger Sherman
- Great Compromise
- Three-Fifths Compromise

The Liberty Bell, a symbol of freedom, originally hung in the Pennsylvania State House.

SETTING the Scene An air of mystery hung over the Pennsylvania State House in Philadelphia during the summer of 1787. Philadelphians watched as the nation's greatest leaders passed in and out of the building. Eleven years earlier, some of the same men had signed the Declaration of Independence there. What was going on now? Susannah Dillwyn wrote to her father about the excitement:

> ❝ There is now sitting in this city a grand convention, who are to form some new system of government or mend the old one. I suppose it is a body of great consequence, as they say it depends entirely upon their pleasure whether we shall in the future have a congress. ❞

What would this "grand convention" decide? No one knew. For almost four months, Americans waited for an answer.

The Convention Opens

On May 25, 1787, the **Constitutional Convention** opened in Philadelphia. Every state except Rhode Island sent representatives. Their mission was to revise the Articles of Confederation.

The 55 delegates gathered for the convention were a remarkable group. At age 81, Benjamin Franklin was the oldest delegate. He was wise in the ways of government and human nature. George Washington was a representative from Virginia. Washington was so well respected that the delegates at once elected him president of the Convention.

Perhaps the best-prepared delegate to the Constitutional Convention was young **James Madison** of Virginia. For months, Madison had secluded himself on his father's plantation. There, he read many books on history, politics, and commerce. He arrived in Philadelphia with a case bulging with volumes of research.

Many delegates were young men in their twenties and thirties. Among them was Alexander Hamilton of New York. During the Revolution, Hamilton served for a time as Washington's private secretary. Hamilton despised the Articles of Confederation. "The nation," he wrote, "is sick and wants powerful remedies." The powerful remedy he prescribed was a strong national government.

When the Convention began, the delegates decided to keep their talks secret. They wanted to be able to speak their minds freely. They wished to explore issues and solutions without pressures from outside.

Biography Roger Sherman

Roger Sherman was a shoemaker, shopkeeper, surveyor, lawyer—and one of the most respected early leaders of the United States. Thomas Jefferson once said that Sherman "never said a foolish thing in his life." Sherman was one of only four people to sign both the Declaration of Independence and the Constitution. ★ **What major contribution did Roger Sherman make to the Constitutional Convention?**

To ensure secrecy, guards stood at the door. The windows were left closed to keep passersby from overhearing the debates. The closed windows made the room very hot, however. New Englanders in their woolen suits suffered terribly in the summer heat. Southerners, with clothing more suited to warm temperatures, were less bothered.

Hopelessly Divided

Soon after the meeting began, the delegates decided to do more than revise the Articles of Confederation. They chose instead to write an entirely new constitution for the nation. They disagreed, however, about what form the national government should take.

The Virginia Plan

Edmund Randolph and James Madison, both from Virginia, proposed a plan for the new government. This **Virginia Plan** called for a strong national government with three branches. The **legislative branch** would pass the laws. The **executive branch** would carry out the laws. The **judicial branch,** or system of courts, would decide if laws were carried out fairly.

According to the Virginia Plan, the legislative branch would consist of two houses. Seats in both houses would be awarded on the basis of population. Thus, in both houses, larger states would have more representatives than smaller ones. This differed from the Articles of Confederation, which gave every state, regardless of population, one vote in Congress.

The New Jersey Plan

Small states objected strongly to the Virginia Plan. They feared that the large states could easily outvote them in Congress. In response, supporters of the Virginia Plan said that it was only fair for a state with more people to have more representatives.

After two weeks of debate, William Paterson of New Jersey presented a plan that had the support of the small states. Like the Virginia Plan, the **New Jersey Plan** called for three branches of government. However, it provided for a legislature that had only one house. Each state, regardless of its population, would have one vote in the legislature.

The Great Compromise

For a while, no agreement could be reached. With tempers flaring, it seemed that the Convention would fall apart without adopting any plan. Finally, **Roger Sherman** of Connecticut worked out a compromise that he hoped would satisfy both large and small states. A **compromise** is a settlement in which each side gives up some of its demands in order to reach an agreement.

Sherman's compromise called for a two-house legislature. Members of the lower house, known as the House of Representatives, would be elected by popular vote. As

Skills FOR LIFE

Critical Thinking | Managing Information | Communication | Maps, Charts, and Graphs

Identifying Main Ideas

How Will I Use This Skill?

Every day you get huge quantities of information—from print materials, radio, television, the Internet, and other sources. Sometimes, excessive details make it easy to miss the main point. Learning to identify main ideas saves you time and makes it easier to understand the information you receive.

LEARN the Skill

When dealing with written information, such as in this textbook, use the structure that is provided. Take note of topic headings. In each paragraph, look for the main idea, usually found in a topic sentence at the beginning or end of the paragraph. Details and examples support the topic sentence. To identify main ideas, follow these steps.

1. Identify main topic headings and subtopic headings.
2. Identify the topic sentence found in each paragraph.
3. Identify the supporting details in each paragraph. Determine how each relates to the topic sentence.
4. Review the topic headings and main ideas of each paragraph to determine the main idea of the entire section or chapter.

PRACTICE the Skill

Review the subsection Hopelessly Divided on page 122.

1. Identify the two subtopic headings under Hopelessly Divided.
2. Identify the topic sentence of each of the five paragraphs in this subsection.
3. Identify two supporting details from the first paragraph. How does each support the main idea?
4. Review the main ideas of each paragraph. In your own words, restate the main idea of the entire subsection.

APPLY the Skill

Our mailboxes are often stuffed with business letters. Choose a letter from today's mail. Using the skills that you have learned, determine the main idea.

Quill and inkwell used at the Constitutional Convention

AmericanHeritage
M A G A Z I N E

HISTORY HAPPENED HERE

Independence Hall

For many, the birthplace of the United States is the old Pennsylvania State House, known today as Independence Hall. Here, the Declaration of Independence was signed, the Articles of Confederation were approved, and the Constitution was adopted. The site is now part of a national park. Visitors to the park can tour the building, learn about the Constitution, and see the Liberty Bell.

★ ***To learn more about this historic site, write:*** *Independence National Historical Park, 313 Walnut Street, Philadelphia, PA 19106.*

▲ *Chamber where the Constitution was debated*

the larger states wished, seats in the lower house would be awarded to each state according to its population.

Members of the upper house, called the Senate, would be chosen by state legislatures. Each state, no matter what its size, would have two senators. This part of Sherman's compromise appealed to the smaller states.

On July 16, the delegates narrowly approved Sherman's plan. It became known as the **Great Compromise.** Each side gave up some demands to preserve the nation.

Northern and Southern States Compromise

Just as there were disagreements between large and small states, there were also disagreements between northern and southern states. These disagreements concerned the issue of slavery. Would slaves be counted as part of a state's population? Would the slave trade continue to bring enslaved African Americans into the United States?

The Three-Fifths Compromise

Southerners wanted to include slaves in the population count even though they would not let slaves vote. If slaves were counted, southern states would have more representatives in the House of Representatives. Northerners argued that since slaves could not vote, they should not be counted.

Once again, the delegates compromised. They agreed that three fifths of the slaves in any state would be counted. In other words, if a state had 5,000 slaves, 3,000 of them would be included in the state's population count. This agreement became known as the **Three-Fifths Compromise.**

The slave trade

There was another disagreement over slavery. By 1787, some northern states had banned the slave trade within their borders. They urged that the slave trade be banned in the entire nation. Southerners warned that such a ban would ruin their economy.

In the end, the two sides compromised once more. Northerners agreed that Congress could not outlaw the slave trade for at least 20 years. After that, Congress could regulate the slave trade if it wished. Northerners also agreed that no state could stop a fugitive slave from being returned to an owner who claimed that slave.

Signing the Constitution

As summer drew to a close, the weary delegates struggled with other difficult questions. How many years should the President, head of the executive branch, serve? How should the courts be organized? Would members of Congress be paid?

Finally, on September 17, 1787, the Constitution was ready. Gathering for the last time, delegates listened quietly as Benjamin Franklin rose to plead that the document be accepted:

> "I doubt... whether any other Convention... may be able to make a better Constitution.... I cannot help expressing a wish, that every member of the Convention, who may still have objections to it, would with me, on this occasion, doubt a little of his own infallibility, and... put his name to this instrument."

One by one, delegates came forward to sign the document. Of the 42 delegates remaining in Philadelphia, 39 signed the document. Edmund Randolph and George Mason of Virginia, along with Elbridge Gerry of Massachusetts, refused to sign. They felt that the new Constitution gave too much power to the national government.

The Constitution required each state to hold a state convention to decide if the plan for the new government should be accepted. Once 9 of the 13 states endorsed it, the Constitution would go into effect. Before that occurred, the new Constitution was discussed and debated in all the states.

★ Section 2 Review ★

Recall

1. **Identify (a)** Constitutional Convention, **(b)** James Madison, **(c)** Virginia Plan, **(d)** New Jersey Plan, **(e)** Roger Sherman, **(f)** Great Compromise, **(g)** Three-Fifths Compromise.
2. **Define (a)** legislative branch, **(b)** executive branch, **(c)** judicial branch, **(d)** compromise.

Comprehension

3. Why did New Jersey and other small states oppose the Virginia Plan?
4. **(a)** How did the Great Compromise satisfy large states? **(b)** How did it satisfy small states?
5. What compromise did the North and South reach on the slave trade?

Critical Thinking and Writing

6. **Defending a Position** James Madison said that "no Constitution would ever have been adopted by the Convention if the debates had been made public." Do you agree or disagree? Defend your position.
7. **Predicting Consequences** Some historians refer to the issue of slavery as the Constitutional Convention's "unfinished business." How do you think the issue of slavery would continue to divide North and South in the years after the Convention?

Activity **Writing a Letter** You are the editor of a Philadelphia newspaper in 1787. Decide whether you agree or disagree with the Convention's decision to keep its talks secret. Explain your viewpoint in a letter to the delegates of the Constitutional Convention.

3 A More Perfect Union

As You Read

Explore These Questions

- What ideas helped shape the Constitution?
- How did the framers of the Constitution divide power between the national government and the states?
- How did they limit the power of government?

Define

- republic
- separation of powers
- federalism
- electoral college
- checks and balances
- bill
- veto
- override
- impeach

Identify

- Magna Carta
- English Bill of Rights
- House of Burgesses
- Mayflower Compact
- Enlightenment
- John Locke
- Montesquieu

SETTING the Scene Jonathan Smith, a Massachusetts farmer, wanted to learn the results of the Constitutional Convention. During Shays' Rebellion, he had seen how weak government could lead to violence and tyranny. Smith noted:

> "When I saw this Constitution, I found that it was a cure for these disorders. It was just such a thing as we wanted. I got a copy of it and read it over and over. I had been a member of the convention to form our state constitution, and had learnt something of the checks and balances of power; and I found them all here. I formed my own opinion, and I was pleased with this Constitution."

The framers of the Constitution had designed a **republic,** a government in which citizens rule themselves through elected representatives. The Constitution outlined a new government that would be strong. At the same time, it protected the people from excessive power in government. As Smith hoped, it also prevented any one branch of government from becoming too powerful.

Origins of the Constitution

The framers of the Constitution were well-educated men. They were familiar with the traditions of British and American government. Many of them had read the latest works of Europe's leading political philosophers. In creating the Constitution, the framers made good use of their rich knowledge and experience.

British government

As you learned in Chapter 3, the **Magna Carta** limited the power of English rulers. The Magna Carta contained two basic ideas that helped to shape both British and American government. First, it stated that English nobles had certain rights—rights that were later extended to other classes of people as well. Second, the Magna Carta made clear that English monarchs themselves had to obey the law.

When King John signed the Magna Carta, he agreed not to raise taxes without first consulting the Great Council of nobles and church officials. Eventually, the Great Council grew into the representative body known as Parliament. Parliament consisted

Connections With Civics

Benjamin Franklin admired the government formed by Indian nations in the Iroquois League. The nations in the League governed their own affairs, but joined together for mutual defense.

of two bodies—the House of Lords and the House of Commons.

In the Magna Carta, King John was also forced to recognize that citizens had legal rights. One of the most important of these was the right to a trial by jury:

> “No freeman shall be arrested or imprisoned or dispossessed or... in any way harmed... except by the lawful judgment of his peers or by the law of the land.”

In 1689, the **English Bill of Rights** went further in limiting the monarchy and protecting the rights of citizens. The document said that parliamentary elections should be held regularly. It reaffirmed the right to a trial by jury, while protecting people from excessive fines and cruel or unjust punishment. It allowed citizens to bear arms. It also affirmed the right of habeas corpus, the idea that no person could be held in prison without first being charged with a specific crime.

The American experience

Americans enjoyed a long tradition of elected representative government. In 1619, the Virginia colonists set up the **House of Burgesses.** Eventually, each of Britain's thirteen American colonies had its own representative legislature.

Another American tradition was having written documents that clearly identified the powers and limits of government. In 1620, the Pilgrim leaders at Plymouth drew up and signed the **Mayflower Compact,** the first document of self-government in North America. They agreed to "join together in a civil body politic" in order to establish "just and equal laws." Each of the 13 colonies had a written charter granted by the monarch or Parliament.

The framers of the Constitution also drew on their own experiences. They were very familiar with the workings of the Second Continental Congress, the Articles of Confederation, and their own state governments. Much that went into the Constitution came from either the Articles or from one of the state constitutions.

The Enlightenment

The Constitution was also based on the ideas of the European **Enlightenment.** Enlightenment thinkers believed that people could improve society through the use of reason. Many of the Constitution's framers had read the works of Enlightenment thinkers, such as John Locke and the Baron de Montesquieu (MOHN tehs kyoo).

In 1690, **John Locke** published *Two Treatises on Government.* In it, he stated two important ideas.

First, Locke declared that all people had natural rights to life, liberty, and property. Second, he suggested that government is an agreement between the ruler and the ruled. The ruler must enforce the laws and protect the people. If a ruler violates the people's natural rights, the people have a right to rebel.

Biography **Baron de Montesquieu**

Montesquieu studied European, Chinese, and Native American governments. His ideas influenced the framers of the Constitution to divide government power among three separate branches. He said that "government should be set up so that one man need not be afraid of another." ★ **Why do you think the framers of the Constitution did not want to place all power into a single branch of government?**

The Federal System

Powers Delegated to the National Government

- Regulate interstate and foreign trade
- Set standard weights and measures
- Create and maintain armed forces
- Make copyright and patent laws
- Establish postal offices
- Establish foreign policy
- Create federal courts
- Coin money
- Declare war
- Admit new states

Shared Powers

- Provide for public welfare
- Administer criminal justice
- Charter banks
- Raise taxes
- Borrow money

Powers Reserved to the States

- Create corporation laws
- Regulate trade within state
- Establish and maintain schools
- Establish local governments
- Make laws about marriage and divorce
- Conduct elections
- Provide for public safety

Graphic Organizer *Skills* **The system of federalism divides power between the national government and state governments.**

1. **Comprehension** **(a)** List two powers shared by national and state governments. **(b)** List two powers reserved to the states.
2. **Critical Thinking** Why do you think the power to create and maintain armed forces was delegated to the federal government?

Locke's ideas were popular among Americans. The framers of the Constitution wanted to protect people's natural rights and limit the power of government. They saw the Constitution as a contract between the people and their government.

In 1748, the French thinker Baron de **Montesquieu** published *The Spirit of the Laws.* He urged that the power of government be divided among three separate branches: the legislative, executive, and judicial. This idea, known as the **separation of powers,** was designed to keep any person or group from gaining too much power.

Montesquieu stressed the importance of the rule of law. The powers of government, he said, should be clearly defined. This would prevent individuals or groups from using government power for their own purposes. In the Constitution, the framers set out the basic laws of the nation, defining and limiting the powers of the government.

A Federal System

The framers had to decide how to divide power between the national government and the states. Under the Articles of Confederation, states had more power than Congress. Under the Constitution, states delegated, or gave up, some of their powers to the national government. At the same time, the states reserved, or kept, other powers. This division of power between the states and the national government is called **federalism.**

Federal powers

The Constitution spells out the powers of the federal government. For example, only the federal government can coin money or declare war. The federal government can also regulate trade between the states and with other countries.

State powers

Under the Constitution, states have the power to regulate trade within their borders. They decide who can vote in state elections. They also have power to establish schools and local governments.

In addition, the Constitution says that those powers not clearly given to the federal government belong to the states or the people. This point pleased people who were afraid that the federal government might become too powerful.

Shared powers

The Constitution lists some powers that are to be shared by federal and state governments. Both governments, for example, can build roads and raise taxes.

The framers of the Constitution had to decide how the state governments and the federal government would settle disagreements. They did so by making the Constitution "the supreme law of the land." This means that the Constitution is the final authority in any dispute between the states and the federal government.

Separation of Powers

The framers of the Constitution set up a strong federal government. However, they also took steps to prevent any one branch from becoming too powerful. James Madison said that this was necessary in order to prevent tyranny:

> "The accumulation of all powers, legislative, executive, and judiciary, in the same hands, whether one, a few, or many... may justly be pronounced the very definition of tyranny."

To prevent such a tyranny, the framers relied on Montesquieu's idea of separation of powers. In the Constitution, they created three branches of government and then defined the powers of each.

The legislative branch

The legislative branch of government is Congress. Its main function is to make laws. Congress consists of the House of Representatives and the Senate. Members of the House are elected for two-year terms. Senators are elected for six-year terms.

Under the Constitution, voters in each state elect members of the House of Representatives. Delegates to the Constitutional Convention wanted the House to represent the interests of ordinary people.

At first, the Constitution provided for senators to be chosen by state legislatures. In 1913, this was changed. Today, senators are elected in the same way as House members.

Article 1 of the Constitution sets out the powers of Congress. These include the power to collect taxes and to regulate foreign and interstate trade. In foreign affairs, Congress has the power to declare war and to "raise and support armies."

The executive branch

Article 2 of the Constitution sets up the executive branch of government. It is headed by the President. The executive branch also includes the Vice President and any advisers appointed by the President. The President and Vice President serve four-year terms.

The President is responsible for carrying out all laws passed by Congress. The President is also commander in chief of the armed forces and is responsible for directing foreign relations. Over the years, the power of the presidency has greatly increased.

The judicial branch

Article 3 of the Constitution calls for a Supreme Court. The article also allows Congress to set up other federal courts. The Supreme Court and other federal courts hear cases that involve the Constitution or any laws passed by Congress. They also hear cases arising from disputes between two or more states.

Separation of Powers

Legislative Branch (Congress)	Executive Branch (President)	Judicial Branch (Supreme Court and Other Federal Courts)
Passes laws Can override President's veto Approves treaties and presidential appointments Can impeach and remove President and other high officials Creates lower federal courts Appropriates money Prints and coins money Raises and supports the armed forces Can declare war Regulates foreign and interstate trade	**Carries out laws** Proposes laws Can veto laws Negotiates foreign treaties Serves as commander in chief of the armed forces Appoints federal judges, ambassadors, and other high officials Can grant pardons to federal offenders	**Interprets laws** Can declare laws unconstitutional Can declare executive actions unconstitutional

Chart Skills **The Constitution set up three branches of government. Each of the branches has its own powers.**

1. **Comprehension** **(a)** Who heads the executive branch? **(b)** What is the role of the legislative branch?
2. **Critical Thinking** Based on this chart, describe the relationship between the judicial branch and the executive branch.

Electing the President

The framers of the Constitution wanted to ensure that the President would not become too strong. Some feared that a President elected directly by the people might become too independent of Congress and the states.

Others opposed direct election because they worried that voters would not know a candidate from outside their area. In the late 1700s, news traveled slowly. New Englanders would probably know little about a candidate from the South. A candidate from Pennsylvania might be unknown to voters in Vermont or Georgia.

As a result of these concerns, the Constitution calls for an **electoral college.** It is made up of electors from every state. Every four years, the electors vote for the President and Vice President of the United States.

The framers of the Constitution expected that the electors would be well informed and familiar with the national government. They believed that such people would choose a President and Vice President wisely.

Checks and Balances

The Constitution set up a system of **checks and balances.** Under this system, each branch of the federal government has some way to check, or control, the other two branches. The system of checks and balances is another way in which the Constitution limits the power of government. (See the chart on page 148.)

Checks on Congress

To do its work, Congress passes **bills,** or proposed laws. A bill then goes to the President to be signed into law. The President can check the power of Congress by **vetoing,** or rejecting, a bill.

The Supreme Court checks the power of Congress by reviewing laws. If a law violates the Constitution, the Court can declare the law unconstitutional.

Checks on the President

After the President vetoes a bill, Congress can **override,** or overrule the veto. To override a veto, two thirds of both houses of Congress must vote for the bill again. In this way, a bill can become law without the President's signature.

Congress has other checks on the President. The President appoints officials such as ambassadors to foreign countries and federal judges. The Senate must approve these appointments. The President can negotiate treaties with other nations; however, a treaty becomes law only if two thirds of the Senate approve it.

Congress also has the power to remove a President from office if it finds the President guilty of a crime or serious misbehavior. First of all, the House of Representatives must **impeach,** or bring charges against, the President. A trial is then held in the Senate. If two thirds of the senators vote for conviction, the President must leave office.

Checks on the courts

Congress and the President have checks on the courts. The President appoints judges, who must be approved by the Senate. If judges misbehave, Congress may remove them from office. Congress establishes the number of justices in the Supreme Court. Congress can also propose changes to the Constitution to overturn Court decisions.

A Living Document

The Constitution carefully balances power among the three branches of the federal government. It also divides power between the federal government and the states. This balance has helped keep it alive for more than 200 years, longer than any other written constitution in the world. The Constitution has lasted because it is a living document. As you will read, it can be changed to meet new conditions.

★ Section 3 Review ★

Recall

1. **Identify** **(a)** Magna Carta, **(b)** English Bill of Rights, **(c)** House of Burgesses, **(d)** Mayflower Compact, **(e)** Enlightenment, **(f)** John Locke, **(g)** Montesquieu.
2. **Define** **(a)** republic, **(b)** separation of powers, **(c)** federalism, **(d)** electoral college, **(e)** checks and balances, **(f)** bill, **(g)** veto, **(h)** override, **(i)** impeach.

Comprehension

3. Describe three traditions or ideas that helped to shape the Constitution.
4. Why did the framers of the Constitution set up a system of federalism?
5. Describe one check on each of the following: **(a)** Congress, **(b)** the President, **(c)** the courts.

Critical Thinking and Writing

6. **Analyzing Ideas** On page 128, you read that the framers "... saw the Constitution as a contract between the people and their government." What do you think is meant by this statement?
7. **Comparing** Was the national government stronger under the Articles of Confederation or the Constitution? Explain.

Activity **Summarizing** You have been shipwrecked on a far-off island! The islanders want to set up a government like that of the United States. Write a summary for them in which you explain the basic ideas behind the Constitution.

Ratifying the Constitution

As You Read

Explore These Questions

- What arguments did Americans raise for and against the Constitution?
- How can the Constitution be amended?
- What rights does the Bill of Rights protect?

Define

- ratify
- amend
- due process

Identify

- Federalist
- Antifederalist
- *The Federalist Papers*
- Bill of Rights

SETTING the Scene In homes and in town squares across the nation, Americans discussed the new Constitution. Many supported it. Many others did not. Its critics especially worried that the Constitution had no bill of rights. In Virginia, Patrick Henry sounded the alarm:

> ❝ Show me an age and country where the rights and liberties of the people were placed on the sole chance of their rulers being good men, without a consequent loss of liberty! ❞

Was a bill of rights needed? Did the Constitution give too much power to the federal government? In the fall of 1787, citizens began to debate the document sentence by sentence. The Convention had done its work. Now the states had to decide whether or not to ratify the new frame of government.

The Constitution Goes to the Nation

The framers of the Constitution sent the document to Congress. With it, they sent a letter from George Washington, as president of the Constitutional Convention. In the letter, Washington described how the framers had struggled to make the Constitution meet the varied needs of the different states. He wrote:

> ❝ In our deliberations, we kept steadily in view... the greatest interests of every true American. That [the Constitution] will meet the full and entire [approval] of every state is not perhaps to be expected; but each will doubtless consider that had her interest been alone consulted, the consequences might have been... disagreeable or [harmful] to others. ❞

Washington warmly endorsed the document and called on Congress to support it. It was his belief, he said, that the Constitution would "promote the lasting welfare of that country so dear to us all, and secure her freedom and happiness."

The framers of the Constitution had set up a process for the states to decide on the new government. At least 9 of the 13 states had to **ratify**, or approve, the Constitution before it could go into effect. In 1787 and 1788, voters in each state elected delegates to special state conventions. These delegates then met to decide whether or not to ratify the Constitution.

Connections With Science

Today, the Constitution is publicly displayed. For protection against damage due to light, insects, and impurities in the air, each page is in a glass case filled with helium. Levels of light and humidity are carefully controlled.

Heated Debate

In every state, heated debates took place. Supporters of the Constitution called themselves **Federalists.** They called people who opposed the Constitution **Antifederalists.**

The Federalist position

The Federalists argued that the Articles of Confederation had produced an excessively weak central government. It had placed the nation in grave danger because it left too much power with the individual states. Disputes among the states, Federalists said, had made it too difficult for the Confederation government to function.

According to the Federalists, the Constitution gave the national government the authority to function effectively. At the same time, it still protected the rights of the individual states.

Among the best-known Federalists were James Madison, Alexander Hamilton, and John Jay. They wrote a series of essays, called ***The Federalist Papers,*** defending the Constitution. They used pen names, but most people knew who they were. Today, *The Federalist Papers* remains one of the best discussions of the political theory behind the American system of government.

Biography **James Madison**

Historians call James Madison the "Father of the Constitution" because much of the document was based on his ideas. When the Constitution was being debated, Madison was only in his 30s. He went on to serve the nation as a member of Congress, as Secretary of State, and as the fourth President of the United States . ★ **Was Madison a Federalist or an Antifederalist?**

The Antifederalist position

Antifederalists opposed the Constitution for many reasons. They felt that it made the national government too strong and left the states too weak. They thought that the Constitution gave the President too much power. Patrick Henry was among those who voiced such concerns:

> " This Constitution is said to have beautiful features, but . . . they appear to me horribly frightful. . . . Your President may become king . . . If your American chief be a man of ambition and abilities, how easy is it for him to render himself absolute! "

Most people expected George Washington to be elected President. Antifederalists admired Washington, but they warned that future Presidents might lack Washington's honor and skill. For this reason, they said, the office should not be too powerful.

Need for a bill of rights

The chief argument used by Antifederalists against the Constitution was that it had no bill of rights. Americans had just fought a revolution to protect their freedoms. They wanted a bill of rights in the Constitution that spelled out basic freedoms such as freedom of speech and freedom of religion.

Federalists replied that the Constitution protected citizens very well without a bill of rights. Anyway, they argued, it was impossible to list all the natural rights of people. Antifederalists responded that if rights were not written into the Constitution, it would be easy to ignore them. Several state conventions refused to ratify the Constitution unless they received a firm promise that a bill of rights would be added.

The Nation Celebrates

When the Constitution was ratified, celebrations were held across the nation. Shown here is a celebration parade in New York City. The three-masted ship on the float represented the "ship of state." ★ **Why do you think Alexander Hamilton's name is displayed so visibly?**

The States Vote to Ratify

One by one, states voted to ratify the Constitution. Delaware was the first, in December 1787. In June 1788, New Hampshire became the ninth state to ratify. The new government could now go into effect.

Still, the future of the United States remained in doubt. It was important that all the states support the Constitution. However, New York and Virginia, two of the largest states, had not yet ratified the plan. In both states, Federalists and Antifederalists were closely matched.

In Virginia, Patrick Henry strongly opposed the Constitution. Henry charged that the document gave the government too much power. "There will be no checks, no real balances in this government," he cried. In the end, however, Washington, Madison, and other Virginia Federalists prevailed. In late June, Virginia approved the Constitution.

In New York, the struggle went on for another month. At last, in July 1788, the state convention voted to ratify. North Carolina ratified in November 1789. Rhode Island was the last state to approve the Constitution, finally doing so in May 1790.

The Nation Celebrates

Throughout the land, Americans celebrated the news that the Constitution was ratified. The city of Philadelphia set its festival for July 4, 1788. At sunrise, church bells rang. In the harbor, the ship *Rising Sun* boomed a salute from its cannons. Horses wore bright ribbons, and bands played popular tunes.

A festive parade filed along Market Street, led by soldiers who had fought in the Revolution. Thousands cheered as six colorfully outfitted horses pulled a blue carriage shaped like an eagle. Thirteen stars and stripes were painted on the front, and the Constitution was raised proudly above it.

That night, even the skies seemed to celebrate. The northern lights, vivid bands of color, lit up the sky above the city. Benjamin Rush, a Philadelphia doctor and strong supporter of the Constitution, wrote to a friend: "'Tis done. We have become a nation."

Adding a Bill of Rights

Americans voted in the first election under the Constitution in January 1789. As

Why Study History?

Because National Symbols Unite Us

★ ★

Historical Background

The Constitution changed a loose alliance of states into a more unified nation. It takes more than a document, however, to create a nation. Shared ideals and symbols also help to bring people together. In 1789, the bald eagle was declared a symbol of the United States by Congress.

The presidential seal

Today, the eagle and other symbols appear on the Great Seal of the United States and on the Seal of the President of the United States. On both seals, the American eagle holds an olive branch representing peace and a bundle of arrows representing military readiness. In its beak, it holds a scroll with the Latin phrase *"E pluribus Unum."* These words, which mean "Out of many, one," are our nation's motto. They refer to the union of states and to the union of the diverse American people.

Connections to Today

Almost 200 years after Congress declared it an American symbol, the American bald eagle was in serious trouble. Only about 400 breeding pairs of eagles remained in the lower 48 states. Hunting, loss of habitat, and pollution were some causes of the decline. In the 1960s, President John F. Kennedy made an urgent appeal. "The fierce beauty and proud independence of this great bird aptly symbolize the strength and freedom of America," he said, "and we shall have failed a trust if we allow the eagle to disappear."

The nation took action. Congress banned the use of DDT, an insecticide that damaged the birds' eggs. Also, it declared the eagle an endangered species. This step prohibited the hunting of eagles and protected their habitat. By the mid-1990s, the eagle population had recovered.

Connections to You

The bald eagle is only one of the emblems that represent you and all citizens of the United States. The foremost symbol of the nation is the American flag. Others include the Liberty Bell, the Statue of Liberty, and Uncle Sam. Such images have a long and interesting history as symbols of our nation.

1. **Comprehension** **(a)** Why was the bald eagle endangered in the 1960s? **(b)** How did government help the eagle to recover?
2. **Critical Thinking** Why do you think Congress chose the eagle as a symbol of the United States?

Researching and Writing Conduct research to learn about the origins and meaning of the American flag, the Liberty Bell, or other symbols of the United States. Write an essay summarizing your findings.

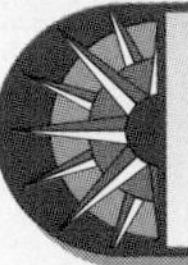

Linking Past and Present

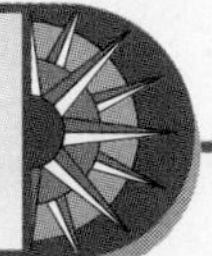

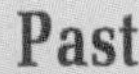

Past

Present

Trial by Jury

Trial by jury is part of the nation's English heritage. Yet in colonial times, British officials sometimes suspended jury trials. Therefore, many Americans wanted the new Constitution to guarantee this right. The members of a jury promise to give an impartial verdict based on evidence. ★ **Turn to the Reference Section and read the Sixth Amendment. List three rights guaranteed to Americans accused of crimes.**

expected, George Washington was elected President, while John Adams was chosen Vice President.

The first Congress was made up of 59 representatives and 22 senators. It met in New York City, which was chosen as the nation's first capital. The first Congress quickly turned its attention to adding a bill of rights to the Constitution.

The amendment process

The framers had set up a way to **amend,** or change, the Constitution. They did not want people to make changes lightly, however. Thus, they made the process of amending the Constitution fairly difficult.

To start the amendment process, an amendment must be proposed. This can be done in two ways. Two thirds of both houses of Congress can vote to propose an amendment, or two thirds of the states can request special conventions to propose amendments.

Next, the amendment must be ratified. Three fourths of the states must approve the amendment before it becomes part of the Constitution.

In the more than 200 years since the Constitution was adopted, only 27 amendments have been approved. Ten of those amendments were added in the first years after the Constitution was ratified.

The first 10 amendments

The first Congress proposed a series of amendments to the Constitution of the United States in 1789. By December 1791, three fourths of the states had ratified 10 amendments. Those 10 amendments became known as the **Bill of Rights.**

James Madison, who wrote the amendments, insisted that the Bill of Rights does not give Americans any rights. People already have the rights listed in the amendments. They are natural rights, said Madison, that belong to all human beings. The Bill of Rights simply prevents the government from taking these rights away.

Protecting individual rights

The 10 amendments that make up the Bill of Rights ensure the basic freedoms of American citizens. The First Amendment guarantees individual liberties, including freedom of religion, freedom of speech, and freedom of the press. It also guarantees the right to assemble peacefully and the right to petition the government.

The next three amendments came out of the colonists' struggle with Britain. The Second Amendment guarantees the right of citizens to keep and bear arms. The Third Amendment was included because the framers remembered Parliament's efforts to make colonists house and feed British soldiers. The amendment prevents Congress from forcing citizens to quarter, or house, troops in their homes. The Fourth Amendment protects citizens from unreasonable searches and seizures. Before the Revolution, you will remember, British customs officials had often searched and seized the property of colonists without their permission.

The Fifth Amendment guarantees due process of law. **Due process** means that the government must follow the same fair rules in all cases brought to trial. Under the Fifth Amendment, the accused must be notified of the charges brought against him or her. The accused must also be given the chance to present a defense in court. Also, the government cannot require self-incriminating testimony nor may it try a defendant twice for the same crime if the defendant has already been acquitted.

Amendments 6 through 8 provide other protections for citizens accused of crimes. The Sixth Amendment guarantees a jury trial in criminal cases and the right to be defended by a lawyer. The Seventh Amendment requires jury trials in civil cases. The Eighth Amendment prevents judges from ordering "excessive bail" or imposing "cruel and unusual punishment" on a convicted criminal.

The Ninth Amendment assures that the rights listed in the Constitution are not the only ones that exist. The Tenth Amendment states that all powers not given to the national government and not denied to the states are reserved for the states or for the people. This assured that the power of the national government would be limited.

With the Bill of Rights in place, the new framework of government was complete. Over time, the Constitution became a living document that grew and changed along with the nation.

★ Section 4 Review ★

Recall

1. **Identify** **(a)** Federalist, **(b)** Antifederalist, **(c)** *The Federalist Papers,* **(d)** Bill of Rights.
2. **Define** **(a)** ratify, **(b)** amend, **(c)** due process.

Comprehension

3. **(a)** Why did Federalists favor ratification of the Constitution? **(b)** Why did Antifederalists oppose it?
4. Describe the process for adding amendments to the Constitution.
5. Describe three specific rights protected by the first 10 amendments to the Constitution.

Critical Thinking and Writing

6. **Defending a Position** Imagine that you are a citizen of the United States in 1789. Would you argue for or against the Constitution? How would you defend your position?
7. **Analyzing Ideas** **(a)** List five rights protected by the Bill of Rights. **(b)** Which do you think is most important? Explain.

Activity **Making Illustrations** You are the illustrator for a handbook on the rights of American citizens. Draw a series of sketches to illustrate the rights that are guaranteed by the First Amendment.

Chapter 5 Review and Activities

★ Sum It Up ★

Section 1 A Confederation of States

- During the American Revolution, most states wrote constitutions providing for a governor and legislature.
- The Articles of Confederation created a weak alliance of states.
- Under the Articles of Confederation, the government set up a system for forming and governing new territories.

Section 2 The Constitutional Convention

- The Constitutional Convention met in Philadelphia in 1787 to revise the nation's government.
- The delegates created the Constitution by making important compromises on several divisive issues.

Section 3 A More Perfect Union

- The framers of the Constitution drew ideas from British government, colonial and state governments, and the Enlightenment.
- A federal system divides power between the national and state governments.
- The separation of powers prevents any branch of government from becoming too strong.

Section 4 Ratifying the Constitution

- After many debates, the separate states approved the Constitution.
- The first 10 amendments form a Bill of Rights designed to protect the rights of individuals.

For additional review of the major ideas of Chapter 5, see ***Guide to the Essentials of American History*** or ***Interactive Student Tutorial CD-ROM,*** which contains interactive review activities, graphic organizers, and practice tests.

Reviewing the Chapter

Define These Terms

Match each term with the correct definition.

Column 1	Column 2
1. constitution	**a.** system of courts
2. judicial branch	**b.** to bring charges against
3. republic	**c.** nation in which voters elect representatives to govern them
4. legislative branch	**d.** branch that passes laws
5. impeach	**e.** document that sets out the laws and principles of a government

Explore the Main Ideas

1. Describe three reasons for the failure of the Articles of Confederation.
2. **(a)** Why was the Great Compromise necessary? **(b)** Why was the Three-Fifths Compromise necessary?
3. Describe three ideas that shaped the Constitution.
4. What is one benefit of a federal system of government?
5. **(a)** Describe one reason why Federalists favored the Constitution. **(b)** Describe one reason why Antifederalists opposed it.

Chart Activity

Use the chart below to answer the following questions:
1. Which state was the first to ratify the Constitution?
2. Which state was the last? **Critical Thinking** In which three states was support for the Constitution strongest?

Ratification of the Constitution

State	Date	Vote
Delaware	Dec. 7, 1787	30–0
Pennsylvania	Dec. 12, 1787	46–23
New Jersey	Dec. 19, 1787	38–0
Georgia	Jan. 2, 1788	26–0
Connecticut	Jan. 9, 1788	128–40
Massachusetts	Feb. 6, 1788	187–168
Maryland	Apr. 28, 1788	63–11
South Carolina	May 23, 1788	149–73
New Hampshire	June 21, 1788	57–46
Virginia	June 25, 1788	89–79
New York	July 26, 1788	30–27
North Carolina	Nov. 21, 1789	184–77
Rhode Island	May 29, 1790	34–32

Critical Thinking and Writing

1. **Understanding Chronology** Arrange the following documents in chronological order: **(a)** the Constitution, **(b)** Articles of Confederation, **(c)** the First Amendment, **(d)** Magna Carta, **(e)** Mayflower Compact.
2. **Making Inferences** Benjamin Franklin said that Americans had a republic, if they could keep it. Why do you think Franklin was unsure whether the government would last?
3. **Predicting Consequences** What do you think might happen if the government was not required to follow due process?
4. **Exploring Unit Themes** **Rights and Liberties** The nation has changed a great deal since 1787. Does the Bill of Rights still protect individual rights in the United States today? Explain.

Using Primary Sources

During the American Revolution, Johann David Schoepf was a physician for Britain's Hessian troops. After the war, he traveled about the United States, recording his observations. Here, he comments on the government created by the Articles of Confederation:

> "The Congress has neither the necessary weight nor the necessary solidity.... It was to be expected of a people so enthusiastic for liberty that they should grant their Congress only a shadow of dignity, and watch its proceedings with a jealous eye."

Source: *Travels in the Confederation,* Johann David Schoepf, 1911.

Recognizing Points of View **(a)** Did Schoepf consider the new American Congress to be strong or weak? **(b)** Schoepf wrote that Americans watched Congress "with a jealous eye." What do you think he meant by this? **(c)** How do you think Schoepf's background affected his point of view?

Activity Bank

Interdisciplinary Activity

Exploring Geography Find out more about the early settlement of one of the five states carved out of the Northwest Territory. Report on how people traveled there, what obstacles they faced, and how they lived. Include a map showing geographic features of the area.

Career Skills Activity

Teachers Every immigrant who wants to become an American citizen has to learn about the Constitution. Suppose you were teaching a citizenship class. With a partner, prepare a presentation on one part the Constitution. Use visual aids such as diagrams and pictures in your presentation.

Citizenship Activity

Identifying Community Issues The process of amending the Constitution often starts with a petition—a statement signed by many members of a community and presented to lawmakers to show public support for a change. Working with others in your class, choose a problem in your community. Prepare a petition that suggests a solution.

Internet Activity

On the Internet, find information on one of the leading figures at the Constitutional Convention. Write a brief biography of the person, noting especially his role in producing the Constitution.

Eyewitness Journal

You are a delegate to the Constitutional Convention. In your EYEWITNESS JOURNAL, *describe the debate over the Virginia Plan and the New Jersey Plan. Also, describe the debates that took place over issues of slavery.*

★ CIVICS OVERVIEW ★

Chapter 6

The Constitution at Work 1789–Present

What's Ahead

The goal of the Constitution is to create a single, united nation with a fair government and system of laws. It ensures peace within the nation, provides for the defense of the country, and guarantees people's rights and liberties. The principles behind the Constitution include the people's right to rule themselves and the careful division of power among three separate branches of the government.

Changing the Constitution is not easy. For this reason, the basic framework of government has grown slowly. One key change over the centuries has been to extend the rights of citizenship to more and more Americans.

Why Study History?

As you study American history, you will see how different people won greater rights. Such rights carry with them responsibilities. Americans meet their responsibilities as citizens in many ways, such as voting or serving in the military. There are also individuals who see a problem in their community and work to solve it. To meet one such person, see this chapter's *Why Study History?* feature, "Citizens Have Responsibilities."

American Events

1788 Constitution of the United States is ratified

1791 Bill of Rights is approved

1700 **1750** **1800** **1850**

World Events

1700s World Event Age of Enlightenment begins

1789 World Event French Revolution begins

Voting: A Right and a Responsibility

Voting is one of the most important duties of an American citizen. Two hundred years ago, only white male property owners over the age of 21 could vote in most states. Today, as this painting shows, every citizen over the age of 18 has the right to vote. ★ **List three other rights that American citizens enjoy.**

1870
Fifteenth Amendment gives African American men the right to vote

1920
Nineteenth Amendment gives women the right to vote

1971
Twenty-sixth Amendment extends voting rights to Americans 18 to 21 years old

1850 **1900** **1950** **2000**

1893 World Event
New Zealand is first nation to give vote to women

1948 World Event
United Nations approves Universal Declaration of Human Rights

Goals of the Constitution

As You Read

Explore These Questions

- How does the national government help to unify the nation?
- What are the benefits of a national system of courts?
- How does the Constitution protect the basic rights of the people?

Define

- federal
- justice
- domestic tranquillity
- general welfare
- liberty

Identify

- Preamble
- Bill of Rights

SETTING the Scene In 1787, Benjamin Franklin was 81 years old. As long ago as the French and Indian War, he had urged the 13 colonies to unite for their mutual interest. Now, he was serving as the oldest delegate to the Constitutional Convention.

At the end of the convention, Franklin commented on the new Constitution. The document, he admitted, was not perfect:

> “When you assemble a number of men, to have the advantage of their joint wisdom, you inevitably assemble with those men all their prejudices, their passions, their errors of opinion, their local interests, and their selfish views.... It therefore astonishes me, Sir, to find this system approaching so near to perfection as it does.”

Constitution of the United States

He expressed his hope that the Constitution would unite the nation and be “a blessing to the people.” The Constitution has lived up to Franklin's hopes. It has remained the framework of our government for more than 200 years. It endures in part because it guarantees people their rights and liberties. Ensuring liberty is just one of the main goals of the Constitution.

Preamble to the Constitution

The opening statement, of the Constitution is called the **Preamble.** In it the American people proudly announce that they have established the Constitution to achieve certain goals:

> “We the people of the United States, in order to form a more perfect Union, establish justice, ensure domestic tranquillity, provide for the common defense, promote the general welfare, and secure the blessings of liberty to ourselves and our posterity, do ordain and establish this Constitution for the United States of America.”

As you read about these six goals, think about their importance to you.

“Form a More Perfect Union”

Under the Articles of Confederation, the United States was a loose alliance of independent, quarreling states. Many states acted like separate nations. One of the main goals of the framers of the Constitution was to get the states to work together as part of a single, united nation.*

* *E pluribus unum,* the official motto of the United States, also expresses this principle of unity. The Latin phrase means, “Out of many, one.”

To achieve this goal of unity, the Constitution gives a broad range of powers to the national government. For example, only Congress—the national legislature—has the power to tax all the people. The President—the national executive—is responsible for carrying out all the laws of the nation. And **federal,** or national, courts enforce one system of law for the entire nation.

"Establish Justice"

A second goal of the Constitution is to establish **justice,** or fairness. Justice requires that the law be applied fairly to every American, regardless of that person's race, religion, gender, country of origin, political beliefs, or financial situation. The Constitution gives this task to a federal system of courts.

Federal courts deal with a broad range of issues. They hear cases involving the Constitution, national laws, treaties, foreign ambassadors, and ships at sea. They also decide disputes between individuals, between individuals and the national government, and between the states.

When federal courts decide cases, they must often interpret, or explain, the law. The Supreme Court, the highest court in the land, can rule that a law passed by Congress or a state legislature is not permitted by the Constitution.

Why is a national system of courts necessary? Without it, state or local courts would interpret national laws. Judges in some states might refuse to enforce national laws they did not like. Disputes about the meaning of certain laws would remain unsettled. Confusion, and even injustice, might result.

"Ensure Domestic Tranquillity"

In 1786, Daniel Shays marched on a Massachusetts courthouse with nearly 1,200 other protesters. Upon hearing about Shays' Rebellion, George Washington warned, "We are fast verging to [absence of government] and confusion!" The uprising made it clear that the national government must have the power to ensure **domestic tranquillity,** or peace at home.

Contents of the Constitution

Chart *Skills*

The Constitution of the United States includes a preamble, 7 articles, and 27 amendments.

1. **Comprehension** **(a)** What is the subject of Article 4? **(b)** On what pages would you find the Bill of Rights?
2. **Critical Thinking** **(a)** Identify as many amendments as you can that deal with voting or elections. **(b)** Why do you think so many amendments are concerned with this issue?

Civics

Logo of the FDA

Biography **Frances Kelsey**

In the early 1960s, a prescription drug named thalidomide caused birth defects in hundreds of children in Europe and Canada. Thanks to Frances Kelsey (left), the drug was never sold in the United States. As an official at the Food and Drug Administration (FDA), Kelsey refused to approve thalidomide without more tests. For her work, Kelsey received a medal from President John Kennedy (right). ★ **How did Kelsey's work fulfill one of the goals of the Constitution?**

The Constitution gives the national government certain powers that allow it to keep the peace. State and local governments can use their own police to enforce national laws within their borders. When crime crosses state borders, however, national police agencies, such as the Federal Bureau of Investigation (FBI), can step in to help protect life and property.

Have you ever seen a news report about a civil emergency, such as a riot or a flood? If so, you probably saw the National Guard keeping the peace. The President can summon such aid if a state or community cannot or will not respond to the emergency.

"Provide for the Common Defense"

After the American Revolution, the United States had no armed forces to defend itself. Without an army, it could not force British troops to leave the western frontier. Without a navy, it could not prevent Spain from closing part of the Mississippi River to American trade.

The framers of the Constitution realized that armed forces are vital to a nation's survival. Military power helps not only to prevent attack by other nations, but also to protect economic and political interests.

The Constitution gives Congress the power to "raise and support Armies" and to "provide and maintain a Navy." Today, the armed forces include the army, navy, air force, marine corps, and coast guard.

At the same time, the Constitution establishes the principle that the military is under civilian, or nonmilitary, control. Article 2 of the Constitution states that the President is Commander in Chief of the armed forces. Thus, even the highest-ranking military officer must answer to an elected official.

"Promote the General Welfare"

The Constitution gives the national government the means to promote the **general welfare,** or well-being of all the people. The national government has the power to collect taxes. It also has the power to set aside money for programs that will benefit the people.

$ Connections With Economics

Government spending for defense and the general welfare has grown dramatically. In 1795, government outlays totaled $7.5 million for a population of 4.6 million people—an average of $1.63 per person. In 1995, the government's outlays totaled $1.5 billion for a population of 263 million people—an average of $5.70 per person.

The workplace provides many examples of how the national government—often in cooperation with state governments—has acted to promote the general welfare. Factory owners are required to meet safety standards for work areas. Workers who are disabled or unemployed receive financial support. Thanks to the Social Security system, all workers are entitled to income upon retirement.

Another way in which the national government helps to promote the general welfare is by supporting education. Education helps to prepare people to become responsible citizens. It also provides tools and training for employment.

Support for education takes many forms. The national government pays for school nutrition programs in local school districts. Many students receive money to help pay the costs of a college education.

The national government also supports scientific research and development to improve the quality of life. For example, researchers at the National Institutes of Health lead the fight against many diseases. Scientists at the Department of Agriculture help farmers to improve their crops and develop better livestock.

"Secure the Blessings of Liberty"

Protection of liberty was a major reason that colonists fought the American Revolution. It is no wonder, then, that the framers made securing liberty a major goal of the Constitution. **Liberty** is the freedom to live as you please, as long as you obey the laws and respect the rights of others.

One way that the Constitution ensures liberty is by limiting the powers of government. For example, the **Bill of Rights,** the first 10 amendments to the Constitution, lists basic rights and freedoms that the government may not take away.

The Constitution provides yet another safeguard of liberty—the right to vote. The people select the leaders who make the laws. At the same time, they can remove from office those leaders who abuse their power.

The "blessings of liberty" have been extended to more Americans since the Constitution was written. Changes in the Constitution have been made to ensure that all Americans—no matter what their sex, religion, or race—have the same rights regarding voting, education, housing, employment, and other opportunities in life.

★ Section 1 Review ★

Recall

1. **Identify** **(a)** Preamble, **(b)** Bill of Rights.
2. **Define** **(a)** federal, **(b)** justice, **(c)** domestic tranquillity, **(d)** general welfare, **(e)** liberty.

Comprehension

3. **(a)** List two goals of the Constitution. **(b)** Describe one way that the national government helps to achieve each of these goals.
4. How does the national system of courts help to ensure justice for all Americans?
5. List two ways the Constitution safeguards the people's liberty.

Critical Thinking and Writing

6. **Evaluating Information** Which goal of the Constitution do you think is most important? Explain.
7. **Linking Past and Present** Are the goals of the nation today the same as those set out in the Preamble to the Constitution?

Activity **Teaching Through Pictures** A fifth-grader in your school has to recite the Preamble to the Constitution in a speaking contest. When you hear him practice, you realize he doesn't understand what it means. Draw six pictures with captions that will explain the goals of the Constitution for him.

Five Principles of the Constitution

As You Read

Explore These Questions

- What are the five basic principles of the Constitution?
- Why do people adopt a system of representative government?
- How did the framers try to strike a balance between too much and too little government?

Define

- popular sovereignty
- representative government
- bill
- veto
- line item veto
- unconstitutional
- override

SETTING the Scene In 1787, when American leaders were struggling to create the new Constitution, every government in Europe was a monarchy. In most cases, a king or queen made, enforced, and interpreted the laws. Many European rulers would have agreed with Louis XIV, an earlier king of France. *"L'état, c'est moi,"* declared Louis. "I am the state."

The framers of the Constitution knew they had to set up a strong government. At the same time, they sought to keep power from falling into the hands of a privileged few. To achieve this delicate balance, they rested the Constitution on five basic principles: popular sovereignty, limited government, federalism, separation of powers, and checks and balances.

The People Rule

The first three words of the Constitution, "We the people," express the principle of **popular sovereignty.** According to this principle, the people hold the final authority in government.

The Constitution is a contract between the American people and their government. In it, the people grant the government the powers it needs to achieve its goals. At the same time, they limit the power of government by spelling out what the government may not do.

Poster urging Americans to vote

In a large society, not all citizens can take part directly in government. Instead, they exercise their ruling power indirectly by electing public officials to make laws and other decisions for them. This system is called **representative government.**

The people elect public officials by voting in free and frequent elections. Americans today have the constitutional right to vote for members of the House of Representatives (Article 1, Section 2) and for members of the Senate (Amendment 17). The people also elect the members of the electoral college, who, in turn, choose the President (Article 2, Section 1).

The right to vote has been gradually expanded over time. When the Constitution was ratified, only white men over age 21 who owned property could vote. Over the years, other Americans have won the right to vote. Today, all citizens are eligible to vote at the age of 18.

Limited Government

The framers of the Constitution had lived under the harsh rule of the British king. They feared tyranny, or cruel and unjust government. However, the failures of the Articles of Confederation made it clear that the national government had to be strong. How could the framers strike a balance between too much government and too little?

The answer was limited government. According to this principle, the government has only the powers that the people grant it. The Constitution clearly states the powers of the national government. It also states what powers the government does not have.

Guarantees of liberty

The most important limits on government are set out in the Bill of Rights. It guarantees that the government may not take away the individual freedoms of the people. These liberties include freedom of speech, freedom of the press, and freedom of religion.

The Ninth Amendment goes beyond these specific guarantees. It states that the people have rights that are not listed in the Constitution. The Tenth Amendment gives the states or the people any powers not formally granted by the Constitution to the national government.

Federalism

The framers of the Constitution created a strong central government. Yet they also wanted the states to retain much of their power. Like most Americans, they believed that state governments would best understand the special needs and concerns of their citizens. As one defender of the Constitution stated in 1788:

> “The two governments act in different manners, and for different purposes—the general government in great national concerns, in which we are interested in common with other members of the Union; the state legislature in our mere local concerns.”

The principle of federalism divides power between the federal government and state governments. The federal government has the power to deal with national issues. The states have the power to meet local needs.

The Constitution delegates, or assigns, certain powers to the national government. Other powers are reserved, or left, to the states. Still other powers, sometimes called concurrent powers, are shared by the federal and state governments. The chart on page 130 shows how government powers are divided under federalism.

Powers of the states

The Constitution does not list the powers of the states. Instead, it says that all powers not specifically granted to the federal government are reserved to the states (Tenth Amendment). At the same time, it makes clear exactly what powers the states do not have (Article 1, Section 10).

In addition to the reserved powers, the Constitution makes several guarantees to the states. All states must be treated equally in matters of trade (Article 1, Section 9). Each state must respect the laws of other states (Article 4, Section 1). Perhaps most important, all states have representation in the national government.

State License Plates

Under federalism, each state makes its own traffic laws and issues its own drivers' licenses and car registrations. At the same time, a driver's license issued by one state is valid in every other state. ★ **Name two other powers reserved to the states.**

System of Checks and Balances

Executive Branch (President carries out laws) 	**Checks on the Legislative Branch** Can propose laws Can veto laws Can call special sessions of Congress Makes appointments Negotiates foreign treaties	**Checks on the Judicial Branch** Appoints federal judges Can grant pardons to federal offenders
Legislative Branch (Congress makes laws) 	**Checks on the Executive Branch** Can override President's veto Confirms executive appointments Ratifies treaties Can declare war Appropriates money Can impeach and remove President	**Checks on the Judicial Branch** Creates lower federal courts Can impeach and remove judges Can propose amendments to overrule judicial decisions Approves appointments of federal judges
Judicial Branch (Supreme Court interprets laws) 	**Check on the Executive Branch** Can declare executive actions unconstitutional	**Check on the Legislative Branch** Can declare acts of Congress unconstitutional

Chart *Skills* **Through the system of checks and balances, each branch of government controls the powers of the other two.**

1. **Comprehension** **(a)** Name one check the President has on Congress. **(b)** How can the Supreme Court check Congress?
2. **Critical Thinking** Why do you think the framers of the Constitution gave Congress so many checks on the power of the President?

Civics

The "law of the land"

Federalism creates a working partnership between the national government and the state governments. However, when a dispute arises between them, there is no doubt where the final authority lies. The Constitution is the "supreme law of the land" (Article 6, Section 2). Only federal courts can settle the dispute.

Separation of Powers

The framers wanted to prevent the abuse of power by one person or group. To do so, the Constitution divides the national government into three branches: the legislative, the executive, and the judicial. Each branch has its own powers and responsibilities. This division of the national government is known as separation of powers.

Article 1 of the Constitution sets up the legislative branch. This branch, called Congress, makes the laws. Congress has two houses: the House of Representatives and the Senate. Its many powers include the power to tax, to coin money, and to declare war.

Article 2 describes the executive branch, which carries out the laws. The President heads the executive branch and appoints officials to help carry out the duties of the office.

Article 3 creates the Supreme Court to head the judicial branch. The Supreme Court interprets and explains laws. Congress may set up lower courts as needed.

Checks and Balances

To prevent one branch of government from gaining too much power, the Constitution sets up a system of checks and balances. Each branch can check, or control, the power of the other two branches. (See the chart on page 148.)

Checks on Congress

Congress has the power to pass **bills,** or proposed laws. However, the President can check Congress by **vetoing,** or rejecting, a bill. Until 1997, a President either had to sign or veto an entire bill. Then, a new law gave the President a **line item veto** in limited cases. It allows a President to veto part of a bill related to the spending of money.

The Supreme Court has the power to rule whether a law is **unconstitutional,** or not permitted by the Constitution. The power to declare laws unconstitutional is one check the Supreme Court has on Congress. Any law declared unconstitutional by the Court cannot take effect.

Checks on the President

Congress has several checks on the powers of the President. For example, the President is commander in chief of the armed forces, but only Congress has the power to declare war. In addition, the President has the power to make treaties with foreign nations. However, the Senate must ratify all treaties.

Congress may also check the President by **overriding,** or setting aside, a presidential veto. In this way, a bill can become a law without the President's signature. Two thirds of each house must vote to override a veto. The Supreme Court can also check the President by declaring that an act of the President is unconstitutional.

Checks on the courts

Both the President and Congress have several checks on the power of the judicial branch. The President appoints all federal judges, while the Senate must approve the President's court appointments. In addition, Congress has the power to remove federal judges from office if they are found guilty of wrongdoing. Congress may also propose a constitutional amendment to overrule a judicial decision.

★ Section 2 Review ★

Recall

1. **Define** **(a)** popular sovereignty, **(b)** representative government, **(c)** bill, **(d)** veto, **(e)** line item veto, **(f)** unconstitutional, **(g)** override.

Comprehension

2. **(a)** Identify the five basic principles of the Constitution. **(b)** Describe two of them.
3. **(a)** Explain how representative government works. **(b)** Why do people in a democracy adopt this system?
4. **(a)** Why did the framers of the Constitution set up three branches of government? **(b)** How does the Constitution prevent any branch from becoming too powerful?

Critical Thinking and Writing

5. **Synthesizing Information** How are the principles of popular sovereignty and limited government related?
6. **Analyzing Ideas** Explain the following statement: The Constitution sets up a government of laws, not of people.

Activity **Making a Chart** Working with a partner or your class, create a chart that gives examples of ways in which the five basic principles of the Constitution protect you and your community.

A Living Document

As You Read

Explore These Questions

- What is the formal process for changing the Constitution?
- What is the purpose of the Bill of Rights?
- What informal changes have been made to the Constitution?

Define

- amendment
- precedent
- Cabinet
- judicial review

Identify

- First Amendment
- Fourth Amendment
- Sixth Amendment
- Elastic Clause
- Commerce Clause

SETTING the Scene The framers of the Constitution realized that the nation would grow and change. With this in mind, they created a living Constitution—one that could be altered and improved to meet new conditions and challenges as they arose. As George Washington commented:

> "I do not think we are more inspired, have more wisdom, or possess more virtue than those who will come after us."

Formal Changes to the Constitution

The framers spelled out a process for making **amendments,** or formal written changes, to the Constitution. Amending the Constitution is not easy, however. It requires two difficult steps: proposal and ratification. (See the chart on page 151.)

Proposing an amendment

Article 5 describes two methods for proposing amendments. Two thirds of each house of Congress can vote to propose an amendment. Or two thirds of the state legislatures can demand that Congress summon a national "convention for proposing amendments."

So far, only the first method—a vote by Congress—has been used. As experts have pointed out, the Constitution does not give guidelines for a national convention. Who should set the agenda? How should delegates be selected? Such questions probably would cause much delay and confusion.

Ratifying an amendment

Article 5 also outlines two methods of ratifying a proposed amendment. Either three fourths of the state legislatures or three fourths of the states meeting in special conventions must approve the amendment. Congress decides which method of ratification to use.

So far, only the Twenty-first Amendment was ratified by state conventions. All other amendments were ratified by state legislatures. In recent years, Congress has set a time limit for ratification. The limit today is seven years, but it may be extended.

The 27 Amendments

As you can see, the amendment process is a difficult one. Since 1789, more than 9,000 amendments have been introduced in Congress. Yet, only 27 amendments have been ratified!

The Bill of Rights

The original Constitution did not list basic freedoms of the people. In fact, several states refused to ratify the Constitution until they were promised that a bill of rights would be added. Those states wanted to ensure that the national government would not be able to take away people's basic freedoms.

The Bill of Rights, the first 10 amendments to the Constitution, was ratified in 1791. (See the chart on page 143.)

You will recognize many of the freedoms in the Bill of Rights. The **First Amendment** protects your right to worship and speak freely and to hold peaceful meetings. The **Fourth Amendment** protects you from "unreasonable" search and seizure of your home and property. The **Sixth Amendment** guarantees you the right to a trial by jury.

The protections of the Bill of Rights extend into many areas of your life. Suppose that you sent a letter to a newspaper criticizing the governor. Without the First Amendment protection of free speech, the governor might order your arrest. Without the Sixth Amendment, you might even be imprisoned for years without a trial.

Amendments 11 through 27

Only 17 amendments have been ratified since 1791. Several of these amendments reflect changing ideas about equality.

Amendments 13 through 15—the so-called Civil War amendments—were passed to protect the rights of former slaves. The Thirteenth Amendment ended slavery. The Fourteenth Amendment guaranteed citizenship and constitutional rights to African Americans. The Fifteenth Amendment guaranteed African Americans the right to vote.

Equality was also the goal of two later amendments. The Nineteenth Amendment gave women the right to vote. The Twenty-sixth Amendment set age 18 as the minimum voting age. The chart on page 143 lists Amendments 11 through 27. For more information about the amendments, refer to the page numbers shown on the chart.

Informal Changes

The language of the Constitution provides a general outline rather than specific details about the national government. Over time, this flexible language has allowed the government to adapt to the changing needs of the nation.

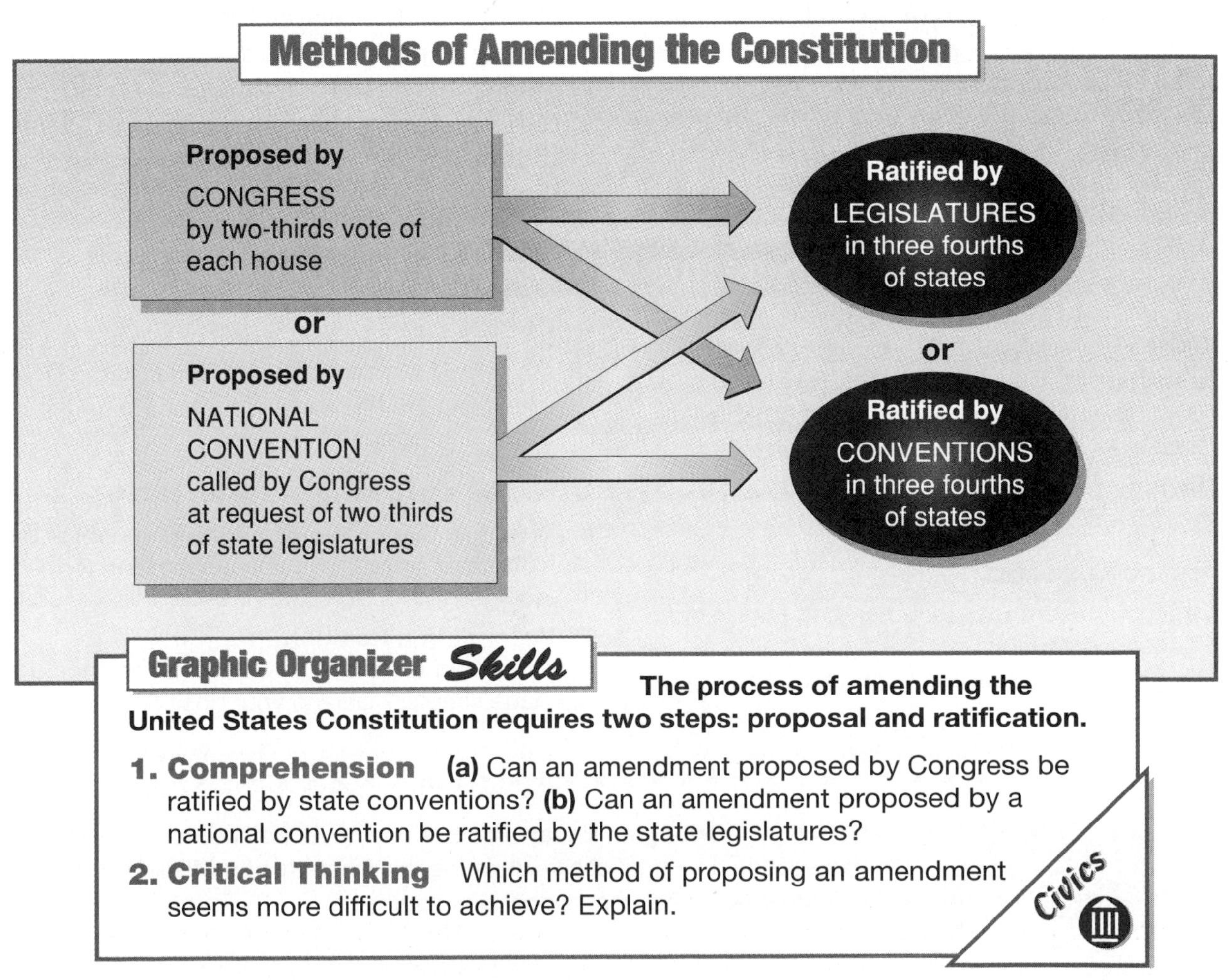

Graphic Organizer *Skills* **The process of amending the United States Constitution requires two steps: proposal and ratification.**

1. **Comprehension** **(a)** Can an amendment proposed by Congress be ratified by state conventions? **(b)** Can an amendment proposed by a national convention be ratified by the state legislatures?
2. **Critical Thinking** Which method of proposing an amendment seems more difficult to achieve? Explain.

New powers for Congress

The framers knew that they could not foresee the future. To deal with this problem, Article 1, Section 8, Clause 18, gives Congress the power to make all laws that shall be "necessary and proper" to carry out the powers of the national government. This so-called **Elastic Clause** has allowed Congress to stretch its power to pass laws.

Still another clause of the Constitution has allowed Congress to extend its powers. Article 1, Section 8, Clause 3, gives Congress the power to "regulate" trade with other nations and between the states.

Armed with the **Commerce Clause** and the Elastic Clause, Congress has been able to keep pace with change. For example, it has passed laws that regulate the airline industry, television, nuclear energy, and genetic engineering.

A more powerful executive

The Constitution does not describe in detail the powers of the President. Some Presidents, however, have taken actions or made decisions that set a **precedent,** or example, for later Presidents.

George Washington set one such precedent. The Constitution does not state that the President may appoint a **Cabinet,** or group of close advisers. President Washington assumed the power to do so on his own. Every President since then has followed his lead.

In national emergencies, Presidents have expanded their constitutional role. During the Great Depression, President Franklin Roosevelt expanded the size and power of the executive branch to propose and carry out programs that would restore the national economy.

A broader role for the judiciary

The Supreme Court can decide whether acts of a President or laws passed by Congress are unconstitutional. This power is known as **judicial review.**

The Constitution does not list judicial review as a power of the judicial branch. Like the unstated powers of the President, judicial review is implied in the words and structure of the Constitution. Article 3, Section 2, states that the Supreme Court has the right to hear "all cases . . . arising under this Constitution." In the case of *Marbury* v. *Madison,* an early Supreme Court decision interpreted Article 3, Section 2, to mean that the Supreme Court has the right to decide whether any law violates the Constitution.

★ Section 3 Review ★

Recall

1. **Identify** **(a)** First Amendment, **(b)** Fourth Amendment, **(c)** Sixth Amendment, **(d)** Elastic Clause, **(e)** Commerce Clause.
2. **Define** **(a)** amendment, **(b)** precedent, **(c)** Cabinet, **(d)** judicial review.

Comprehension

3. Describe the process for amending the United States Constitution.
4. List four rights protected by the Bill of Rights.
5. **(a)** How did George Washington expand the powers of the President? **(b)** How did Franklin Roosevelt expand the President's powers during the Great Depression?

Critical Thinking and Writing

6. **Drawing Conclusions** Why do you think there have been more informal changes than formal changes to the Constitution?
7. **Defending a Position** Do you think the process of amending the Constitution should be made simpler? Defend your position.

Activity **Writing an Essay** Choose one of the amendments described in this section. In a brief essay, describe your thoughts and feelings about that amendment and what it means to you.

The National Government at Work

Explore These Questions

- What are the roles of Congress?
- What jobs does the President do?
- How is the federal court system organized?

Define

- appropriate
- standing committee
- joint committee
- impeach
- constituent
- executive agreement
- appeal
- opinion
- dissenting opinion

Identify

- House of Representatives
- Senate
- Supreme Court

Vol. 143 WASHINGTON, MONDAY, DECEMBER 15, 1997 No. 161

Congressional Record

PROCEEDINGS AND DEBATES OF THE 105th CONGRESS, FIRST SESSION

The Congressional Record *reports events in Congress.*

SETTING the Scene On October 10, 1788, the last Congress under the Articles of Confederation transacted its final business. By September of the following year, the Presidential electors had chosen George Washington as the first President of the United States, the first Congress under the Constitution had met in New York City, and the Federal Judiciary Act had provided for the organization of the United States Supreme Court. The government of the United States, as set up by the Constitution, was in place.

More than 200 years later, Americans still live under this three-branched government set up by the Constitution. Each branch has its own clearly defined powers. Together, they provide us with a government of laws.

The Legislative Branch

Congress, the legislative branch of government, is made up of two houses: the House of Representatives and the Senate. Together, the two houses have the power to make the laws that govern all 50 states. At the same time, the states have a say in making those laws.

Two houses of Congress

The larger house, the **House of Representatives,** currently seats 435 members. The number of representatives for each state is determined according to that state's population. The more people who live in a state, the greater its number of representatives. Each state, however, is guaranteed at least one representative.*

Representatives serve for two-year terms. As a result, the entire House is up for election every even-numbered year. Congressional terms are numbered consecutively. The Congress that served from 1789 to 1791 is known as the First Congress. The Congress serving from 1999 to 2001 is the One Hundred Sixth Congress.

The **Senate,** the smaller house, has 100 members. Each state, no matter how large or small its population, has two senators. Senators serve for six-year terms. The terms are staggered, however. As a result, one third of the Senate are up for election every two years.

Powers of Congress

The chief job of Congress is to make the nation's laws. A new law first appears as a

*Guam, the Virgin Islands, American Samoa, and Washington, D.C., each elect a delegate to the House, while Puerto Rico elects a resident commissioner. However, these delegates are not voting members of the House.

Federal Officeholders

Office	Number	Term	Selection	Requirements
Representative	At least 1 per state; based on population	2 years	Elected by voters of congressional district	Age 25 or over Citizen for 7 years Resident of state in which elected
Senator	2 per state	6 years	Original Constitution—elected by state legislature Amendment 17—elected by voters	Age 30 or over Citizen for 9 years Resident of state in which elected
President and Vice President	1	4 years	Elected by electoral college	Age 35 or over Natural-born citizen Resident of U.S. for 14 years
Supreme Court Justice	9	Life	Appointed by President	No requirements in Constitution

Chart *Skills* **The Constitution details the number, length of term, method of selection, and requirements for officeholders in the three branches of government.**

1. **Comprehension** **(a)** At what age can you be elected to the Senate? The House of Representatives? **(b)** How long may a Supreme Court Justice remain in office?
2. **Critical Thinking** Why do you think the requirements for President and Vice President are the same?

Civics

proposal called a bill. The bill must be passed by both houses of Congress and signed by the President to become law. The chart on page 155 shows the steps a bill must pass through before becoming a law.

Congress has another equally important power. It decides what laws or programs will receive funds. The federal government cannot spend money on any program unless Congress **appropriates** it, or sets it aside for a special purpose. In this way, Congress controls how much money the government spends, whether for military aircraft, national highways, or school lunches.

Congressional committees

During the first session of Congress, 31 bills were proposed by both houses. Today, thousands of bills are introduced every year in Congress. Clearly, it would be impossible for each member of Congress to study and make recommendations about every bill. This job is reserved for committees.

The House of Representatives and the Senate each have **standing committees.** These are permanent committees assigned to study specific issues such as agriculture, labor, and energy. They are often broken up into subcommittees that examine certain problems in depth.

Congress may sometimes create a **joint committee,** or committees that include both House and Senate members. One of the most important kinds of joint committee is the conference committee. Its task is to settle differences between the House and the Senate versions of the same bill. Members of a conference committee try to find a middle ground and to agree on the language of the bill. Compromise is often difficult.

Skills FOR LIFE

Critical Thinking | Managing Information | Communication | **Maps, Charts, and Graphs**

Reading a Flowchart

How Will I Use This Skill ?

A flowchart is a type of graphic organizer. It uses boxes and arrows to guide you step by step through a development or process. Learning to read a flowchart can help you understand even the most complicated processes—from programming a VCR to running for public office.

LEARN the Skill

❶ Identify the process described by the flowchart.

❷ Locate the starting point of the process. (This is the box with no arrow leading toward it.) Some flowcharts may have more than one starting point, since more than one part of a process is being tracked to the end point.

❸ Follow the steps of the process by following the arrows to the end point.

PRACTICE the Skill

❶ What process does the flowchart below describe?

❷ (a) Where can a bill be introduced? (b) Why are there two starting points on this flowchart?

❸ (a) What happens to a bill after it is introduced? (b) At what point in the process do the work of the Senate and the House come together? (c) What happens next?

APPLY the Skill

Create a flowchart to describe the steps of a process you know well. You might show how to play a game, how to repair something, or how to prepare a meal. Show your flowchart to some friends. See if they can understand the process by looking at your chart.

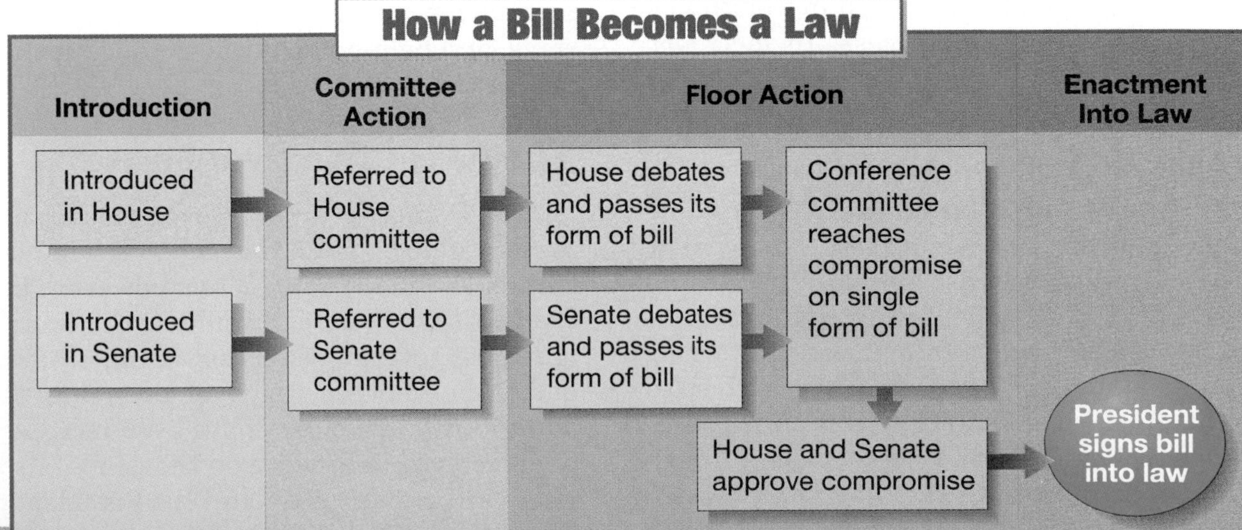

AmericanHeritage
M A G A Z I N E

HISTORY HAPPENED HERE

The United States Capitol Building

History is still happening at the Capitol Building. Since November 1800, the Capitol has been the meeting place of the United States Congress. Each year, millions of people visit the parts of the Capitol open to the public. If you have a pass from your representative or senator, you can even visit the House or Senate chambers and watch lawmakers in action. Funeral ceremonies for Presidents and other outstanding Americans are held in the Great Rotunda under the famous Capitol dome.

★ ***To learn more about this historic site, write:*** *The Capitol, Washington, DC 19106.*

◀ *The Capitol Building in Washington, D.C.*

Passing a bill requires the cooperation of many individuals. For example, a recent trade bill was 1,000 pages long. It required the efforts of 200 members of Congress, working in 17 subcommittees, to get it passed. Most bills introduced in Congress do not meet with such success. In fact, more than 90 percent of all the bills introduced are defeated in committees.

Other roles of Congress

Members of Congress have duties other than serving on committees and making laws. They also guard the public trust. For example, the House of Representatives can **impeach,** or bring a formal charge of wrongdoing against, the President or another federal official. The Senate acts as a court to try the accused. Congress also acts as a "watchdog" by supervising the way the executive branch carries out the laws.

Members of Congress must also respond to the special needs of their states. Responsible representatives and senators must remember their **constituents,** or the people who elected them. They do this by supporting bills that have a direct impact on the people "back home." Such bills might include promoting new post offices, improving highways, and helping to pay for local education programs.

The Executive Branch

The framers created an executive branch to carry out the laws. However, they left out details about the President's powers. They thought that Congress would be the central branch of government except in times of war and other emergencies. Over the years, the powers of the President have been increased or decreased, depending on the needs of the time. Still, Americans expect the President to fill certain roles.

Roles of the President

The main role of the President is to carry out the nation's laws. As chief executive, the President oversees the many departments, agencies, and commissions that help to accomplish this task.

The President directs the nation's foreign policy. Three important powers allow the President to influence relations with other countries. They are the powers to appoint ambassadors, make treaties, and enter into **executive agreements.** Executive agreements are informal agreements with other heads of state, usually dealing with trade. Unlike treaties, they do not require Senate approval.

The President is the highest-ranking officer in the armed forces. As commander in chief, the President can appoint and remove top military commanders. The President may also use the armed forces to deal with crises both at home and abroad. (However, only Congress has the power to declare war on another country.)

As the nation's chief legislator, the President suggests new laws and works for their passage. In this role, the President often meets with members of Congress to win their support. Sometimes, the President campaigns for public support through television or radio speeches and press conferences. The President also can use persuasion to oppose a bill. In this case, however, the President's most powerful weapon is the power to veto a bill.

The President is the living symbol of the nation. In this role, the President represents all American citizens at many occasions. For example, the President welcomes visiting foreign leaders, makes speeches to commemorate national holidays, and gives medals to national heroes. (See the photograph on page 144.)

The American people also see the President as the chief symbol of the condition of the nation, even though this responsibility is shared with Congress and the judiciary. In describing this situation, former President Jimmy Carter declared that "When things go bad you get entirely too much blame," and "when things go good, you get entirely too much credit."

Executive agencies and departments

The nation's laws cover a broad range of concerns—defense, housing, crime, and pollution, to name a few. To carry out these laws and to perform other duties, the President needs the help of millions of government workers and assistants.

Presidents at Work

Under the Constitution, the President commands the armed forces and directs foreign policy. At left, President Bill Clinton meets with Tony Blair, prime minister of Great Britain. Above, President George Bush visits American troops in Saudi Arabia. ★ **Describe two other roles of the President.**

The Supreme Court

Here, the 1998 Justices of the Supreme Court pose for an annual photograph. Standing, left to right, are Ruth Bader Ginsburg, David Souter, Clarence Thomas, and Stephen Breyer. Sitting, left to right, are Antonin Scalia, John Paul Stevens, Chief Justice William Rehnquist, Sandra Day O'Connor, and Anthony Kennedy.
★ **What kinds of cases does the Supreme Court hear?**

One group of assistants, the Executive Office, includes many agencies and individuals. They range from the Vice President to the Office of Management and Budget, which prepares the total budget of the United States.

The President's Cabinet, called secretaries, are the heads of executive departments. Today, the President relies on 14 executive departments—among them, the Departments of Defense, Commerce, Justice, Labor, and Energy. Each department has many concerns. For example, the Department of Agriculture deals with food quality, crop improvement, and nutrition. The Department of Transportation establishes rules for speed limits, automobile exhaust systems, and highway and vehicle safety.

More than 30 independent executive agencies also help the President carry out duties. For example, the Central Intelligence Agency (CIA) provides the President with secret information about the world's trouble spots. The National Aeronautics and Space Administration (NASA) is in charge of the nation's space program.

Eleven independent regulatory commissions enforce national laws. They establish rules, rates, and standards for trade, business, science, and transportation. For example, the Federal Trade Commission (FTC) enforced the federal law banning "false or misleading advertising" by ruling that cigarettes may not be advertised as "kind" to your throat.

Finally, there are government corporations. There are at least 60 government corporations today. They include the United States Postal Service, the Tennessee Valley Authority, and Amtrak.

The Judicial Branch

Article 3 of the Constitution gives the judicial power of the United States to the Supreme Court and to lower courts that Congress may set up. Under the Judiciary Act of 1789, Congress created the system of federal courts that still operates today.

Lower courts

Most federal cases are first heard in the district courts. These courts are located in more than 90 districts around the country. Cases brought to these courts may involve matters of criminal law, such as kidnapping and murder, or matters of civil law, such as bankruptcy and divorce. In district courts, decisions are made by either a judge or a jury, which is a panel of citizens.

Every citizen has the right to **appeal** a decision, or ask that it be reviewed by a higher court. These higher courts of appeal are called circuit, or appellate, courts. The United States has 13 circuit courts of appeal.

Circuit courts operate differently from district courts. A panel of three judges reviews each case. The judges decide if rules of trial procedure were followed in the original trial. If errors did occur, the circuit court may reverse, or overturn, the original decision. Or it may send back the case to the district court for a new trial.

Supreme Court

The **Supreme Court** is the highest court in the United States. Americans depend upon the Supreme Court to settle disputes, interpret the law, and protect their guaranteed rights. The Court is made up of a Chief Justice and eight Associate Justices. The President appoints the Supreme Court Justices, but Congress must approve the appointments. In about one out of five cases, Congress rejects the President's appointment and a new nomination must be made. Appointments to the Supreme Court are for life.

Only two kinds of cases can begin in the Supreme Court. One kind involves disputes between states. The other involves foreign ambassadors. In other cases, the Supreme Court serves as a final court of appeals. It hears cases that have been tried and appealed as far as law permits in lower courts.

The Supreme Court hears only issues about the Constitution, federal law, or treaties. It selects only about 120 cases from the 4,000 or more requests it receives each year. Most of the cases involve laws written in unclear language. The Court must decide what each law means, whom it affects, and whether it is constitutional.

A Supreme Court decision rests on a simple majority vote of at least five Justices. A member of the majority writes an **opinion,** or official statement of the legal reasons for the Court's decision. Sometimes, a member of the minority strongly disagrees with the majority ruling. That Justice may write a **dissenting opinion,** explaining the reasons for the disagreement. Justice Oliver Wendell Holmes, Jr., wrote so many dissenting opinions that he became known as the "Great Dissenter."

Supreme Court decisions are final. There are no other courts of appeal. If Congress strongly disagrees with a Supreme Court decision, however, it can take other action. It can pass a modified version of the law that will meet the Court's objections. Congress can also propose an amendment to the Constitution.

★ Section 4 Review ★

Recall

1. **Identify** **(a)** House of Representatives, **(b)** Senate, **(c)** Supreme Court.
2. **Define** **(a)** appropriate, **(b)** standing committee, **(c)** joint committee, **(d)** impeach, **(e)** constituent, **(f)** executive agreement, **(g)** appeal, **(h)** opinion, **(i)** dissenting opinion.

Comprehension

3. What are the two most important powers of Congress?
4. **(a)** How does the President influence legislation? **(b)** What three powers enable the President to direct foreign policy?
5. **(a)** What is the role of circuit courts? **(b)** What is the role of the Supreme Court?

Critical Thinking and Writing

6. **Ranking** Review the subsection "Roles of the President." List the President's roles. Then rank the roles in order of importance. Be prepared to support your ranking.
7. **Analyzing Ideas** Why is it important for Congress to approve the President's choices for Supreme Court Justices?

Activity **Making a Diagram** Make a graphic organizer with three branches. Fill in the chart to show the roles of each branch of government and the smaller parts that make them up.

Good Citizenship

Explore These Questions
- How was the Bill of Rights limited?
- How did the Supreme Court use the Fourteenth Amendment to expand citizens' rights?
- What are the rights and responsibilities of citizens?

Define
- due process

Identify
- *Gideon* v. *Wainwright*

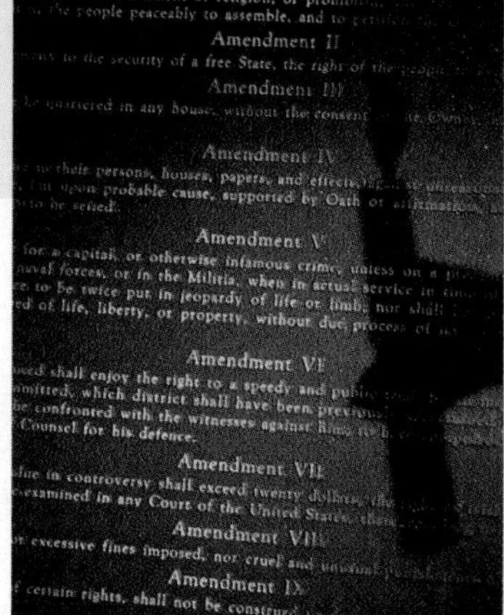

Plaque listing the Bill of Rights ➤

SETTING the Scene Americans first proclaimed their rights in the Declaration of Independence. In it, they declared boldly:

> ❝All men are created equal;. . . they are endowed by their Creator with certain unalienable rights, that among these are life, liberty, and the pursuit of happiness.❞

Since the birth of the nation, Americans have struggled to reach this ideal of basic rights for all. They have learned, however, that along with the rights of citizenship come responsibilities.

Citizens' Rights

The Constitution originally protected some individual rights by limiting government actions. For example, Article 6, Section 3, prevents the government from making religion a requirement for public service. Article 1, Section 9, prohibits Congress from passing a law punishing an act that was not illegal at the time it was committed.

Bill of Rights

Many Americans, however, demanded a more specific list of rights. In response, the first Congress drew up and the states ratified the Bill of Rights.

Still, the Bill of Rights applied only to the federal government. States were free to restrict or deny basic rights of many people, including women, African Americans, and Asian Americans. At times, the federal government also restricted rights through laws and court decisions.

Fourteenth Amendment

An amendment passed in 1868 paved the way for a major expansion of rights. The Fourteenth Amendment states that persons born or naturalized in the United States are citizens of both the nation and their state. No state may limit the rights of citizens or deny citizens **due process,** or a fair hearing or trial. States are also forbidden to deny citizens "equal protection of the laws."

Over the years, the Supreme Court has decided that the Fourteenth Amendment's guarantee of due process and equal protection includes rights listed in the Bill of Rights. States cannot deny citizens the protections of the Bill of Rights.

For example, in the 1960s, the Supreme Court ruled that due process includes the Sixth Amendment right to representation by a lawyer. The case of ***Gideon* v. *Wainwright*** involved a poor Florida man who had been convicted of breaking and entering. The judge hearing the case had refused the defendant's request for a lawyer. The Supreme Court ruled that a state court must appoint a lawyer for any defendant who cannot afford to hire one.

What are basic rights?

As the Ninth Amendment states, the people have rights beyond those listed in the Constitution. Americans still strive to define these rights. Some people believe that a citizen's basic rights include the opportunity to get a good education and to find a job. Others argue that these rights are not guaranteed by the Constitution.

Citizens' Responsibilities

Like every citizen, you must do your part to safeguard your rights. At the same time, you must accept the civic responsibilities that are a part of living in a free and democratic society.

Know your rights

You cannot protect your rights unless you know what they are. Books, government pamphlets, and groups such as the League of Women Voters, the National Association for the Advancement of Colored People (NAACP), and the Legal Aid Society can give you information about your rights and the law.

You must also know the limits of your rights. A popular saying states, "Your right to swing your fist ends where my nose begins." As part of your civic responsibilities, you must respect the rights of others. After all, your rights are only as safe as your neighbor's. If you abuse or allow abuse of another citizen's rights, your own rights may be at risk someday.

Become involved

Good government depends on good leaders. Therefore, citizens have the responsibility to exercise their right to vote. A good citizen studies the candidates and the issues in order to make responsible choices.

Linking United States and the World

United States

South Africa

Getting Out the Vote

Voting is both a right and a responsibility. Yet, many take this right for granted. In 1996, only 48.8 percent of Americans who were eligible to vote actually voted. In 1994, when South Africa's black majority won the right to vote for the first time (right), 86.9 percent of eligible voters cast their ballots. ★ **Why do you think South Africans were so eager to vote? What point is the cartoon on the left making?**

Why Study History?

Because Citizens Have Responsibilities

Historical Background

For many Americans, providing unpaid community service is an important civic responsibility. As far back as 1717, Boston had a volunteer fire department. During the Revolution, thousands of Americans volunteered to serve in state militias. By the mid-1800s, women took a leading role in charitable organizations that cared for the sick and needy.

In April 1997, the Presidents' Summit for America's Future encouraged a national spirit of volunteerism. At the meeting, President Bill Clinton said good citizenship meant that you "serve in your community to help make it a better place."

Connections to Today

Adults are not the only volunteers. Young people can also find ways to serve their community. Consider, for example, the story of David Levitt.

David Levitt was a sixth grader in Florida when he read about Kentucky Harvest. This organization collected leftover food from restaurants and distributed it to people in need. David had an idea. He had seen how much unused food was thrown out in his school cafeteria. Why not start a similar program himself?

David presented his plan to the local school board and got permission to start a food distribution program. His first delivery was cartons of milk and bags of salad. Over the next few years, David sent more than 250,000 pounds of cafeteria leftovers to

David Levitt collects food for the needy.

shelters and food banks all over Florida. While still in middle school, he was invited to the White House and awarded a medal for his volunteer work.

Connections to You

There are many ways for you to volunteer in your community. You can participate in a food or clothing drive. You can help clean up a neighborhood park. Perhaps you would like to tutor a younger child or help at a local hospital or senior citizen center. To learn more about these and other opportunities, look up community organizations in your local telephone directory.

1. **Comprehension** **(a)** How did President Clinton define good citizenship? **(b)** How did David Levitt help his local community?
2. **Critical Thinking** How might volunteering affect the cost of government?

Writing a Proposal Decide on a volunteer program that might be helpful in your community. Describe the benefits of the program and how it could be set up. Write your plan as a formal written proposal.

The First Amendment guarantees you the freedom to speak, write, sign petitions, and meet with others freely. You can use those freedoms not only to defend your rights but also to take a stand on political and community issues. It is important to remember that such expressions should be truthful and peaceful. Supreme Court Justice Oliver Wendell Holmes, Jr., once warned:

> “The most [strict] protection of free speech would not protect a man in falsely shouting fire in a theater and causing a panic.”

Responsible citizens keep informed about national and community issues. In addition to reading newspapers, you can attend local meetings. At a town council meeting, for example, you might learn about proposed solutions to local health issues or pollution problems. Groups such as the League of Women Voters may sponsor debates by candidates for political office.

The Bill of Rights guarantees citizens the right to a trial by jury. Every citizen, in turn, has the responsibility to serve on juries when called. Serving on a jury is a serious duty. Jurors must take time out from their work and personal lives. Deciding the guilt or innocence of the accused can be difficult.

Civic Values

Citizens enter into a contract with the government. They give the government the power to make certain laws. In return, they expect government to protect the well-being of society. As part of this contract, the government has the power to set penalties if laws are broken.

Like other citizens, you have a responsibility to obey the laws and respect the rights of others. For example, you should not steal, damage property, or harm someone.

Volunteer

Responsible citizens offer their time and talents to help others and to improve the community. For example, you can join or start a group to clean up parks or to serve food to senior citizens. You can also take part in a walk-a-thon or bike-a-thon to raise money for a worthy cause. Many volunteer fire departments have junior divisions.

Defend the nation

At age 18, all men must report their name, age, and address to the government. In time of war, the government may call them to serve in the armed forces. Many young citizens feel the duty to enlist in the military on their own.

★ Section 5 Review ★

Recall

1. **Identify** *Gideon* v. *Wainwright.*
2. **Define** due process.

Comprehension

3. Why were some states able to ignore the guarantees of the Bill of Rights?
4. **(a)** What does the Fourteenth Amendment guarantee? **(b)** How did the Supreme Court expand the guarantees of this amendment?
5. List three responsibilities of citizenship.

Critical Thinking and Writing

6. **Analyzing Ideas** Reread the words of Justice Holmes, above. How does this statement relate to the need to balance the rights of the individual and civic responsibility?
7. **Solving Problems** Why must a citizen of a democracy learn how to compromise?

Activity **Making a Poster** Help people in your school and community become better citizens. Create a poster that encourages people to do one of the following: know their rights, vote, become involved in government, volunteer in the community, or join the armed services.

Chapter 6 Review and Activities

★ Sum It Up ★

Section 1 Goals of the Constitution

- The goals of the Constitution include establishing justice, keeping peace at home, and defending the nation.
- The Constitution helps guarantee the rights and liberties of American citizens.

Section 2 Five Principles of the Constitution

- The five basic principles of the Constitution are popular sovereignty, limited government, federalism, separation of powers, and checks and balances.

Section 3 A Living Document

- The process for amending the Constitution was made difficult on purpose.
- Flexible language has allowed informal changes to the Constitution.

Section 4 The National Government at Work

- Congress, made up of the Senate and House of Representatives, makes the nation's laws.
- The duties of the President include carrying out the nation's laws, directing foreign policy, and commanding the armed forces.
- The judicial branch, headed by the Supreme Court, interprets the laws.

Section 5 Good Citizenship

- Over time, the protections of the Bill of Rights were extended to all Americans.
- Citizens have responsibilities, including obeying the law and voting.

For additional review of the major ideas of Chapter 6, see ***Guide to the Essentials of American History*** or ***Interactive Student Tutorial CD-ROM,*** which contains interactive review activities, graphic organizers, and practice tests.

Reviewing the Chapter

Define These Terms

Match each term with the correct definition.

Column 1	Column 2
1. federal	**a.** proposed law
2. bill	**b.** put money aside
3. general welfare	**c.** set aside a veto
4. appropriate	**d.** national
5. override	**e.** well-being of all the people

Explore the Main Ideas

1. How may the government promote the general welfare?
2. Describe how the Constitution is a contract.
3. How does the Elastic Clause allow for informal changes in the Constitution?
4. Give three examples of checks and balances.
5. What rights and responsibilities do citizens have in the justice system?

Chart Activity

Look at the chart and answer the following questions: **1.** What percentage of Americans vote in presidential elections? In local elections? **2.** Are people more likely to know the names of their representatives or their senators? **Critical Thinking** Why do you think so few Americans attend public meetings? What can happen if citizens do not participate in government?

Political Participation and Awareness

Percentage of Americans who...	
Vote in presidential elections	50%
Vote in congressional elections	35–40
Know name of congressional representative	36
Know names of both U.S. senators	29
Occasionally contact local officials	28
Vote in local elections	10–30
Occasionally attend public meetings	19
Give money to candidate or party	13

Source: Selected polls, including Gallup, *Denver Post* Poll, University of Michigan, and *The New York Times, 1989.*

Critical Thinking and Writing

1. **Exploring Unit Themes Rights and Liberties** How might our government be different today if there were no Tenth Amendment?
2. **Understanding Chronology (a)** In what order did the following groups win the right to vote: women; people 18 to 21 years old; African American men? **(b)** Who could vote for President in 1964 who could not do so in 1960?
3. **Linking Past and Present** The federal government recently adopted rules about a new type of nationwide television broadcasting that will provide sharper, clearer pictures. Explain how the government gets its power to make such rules.
4. **Defending a Position** Why is keeping informed an important responsibility of citizenship? Give reasons and examples.

Using Primary Sources

Long after the Constitution was ratified, Thomas Jefferson commented:

> "As the [human mind] becomes more developed, . . . as new discoveries are made, . . . and manners and opinions changed with the change of circumstances, [constitutions] must advance also, and keep pace with the times. We might as well require a man to wear still the coat which fitted him when a boy, as civilized society to remain ever under the [government] of their . . . ancestors."

Source: *Patterns in American History,* ed. Alexander De Conde et al., 1965.

Recognizing Points of View (a) What did Jefferson think happens as time goes on? **(b)** How do you think he felt about the process of amending the Constitution? Explain.

Activity Bank

Interdisciplinary Activity

Exploring the Arts Find out more about the procedure of a courtroom. If possible, visit a courthouse or watch a trial on television. Then, with several classmates, write a script and conduct a mock trial.

Career Skills Activity

Fiction Writer Write a short story about what might happen if people had no political rights. Set the story in the United States or in another country.

Citizenship Activity

Holding a Panel Discussion Organize a panel discussion to consider a proposal for a new constitutional amendment. You might examine the idea of limiting the President to a single six-year term, changing the voting age, or another issue.

Internet Activity

Use the Internet to find sites dealing with the agencies of the United States government. Choose one agency and prepare a report on its activities. Questions you should answer are: When was the agency founded? What does it do? What branch does it serve? How many employees does it have? How much money does it spend every year?

You are the President of the United States. In three EYEWITNESS JOURNAL entries, describe some of the kinds of activities you have to perform and what you think about your job. Use information from the chapter to help think up events.

The Great Little Madison

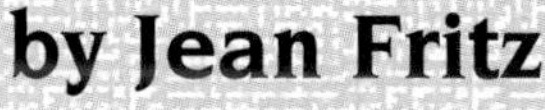

by Jean Fritz

Introduction

James Madison firmly believed in the unity of the American nation. He refused to let his weak voice or small stature keep him from defending the Constitution. In this scene from Jean Fritz's book *The Great Little Madison,* Madison attends the ratification convention in Virginia. He faces a powerful opponent, Antifederalist Patrick Henry.

Vocabulary

Before you read the selection, find the meaning of these words in a dictionary: **whit, spellbinder, confederated.**

Because of the crowds, the convention was moved to the largest room in Richmond. Even then it was packed —170 delegates and hordes of spectators, many of them curious to see if Patrick Henry, who was against the Constitution, was really as fabulous a speaker as everyone said he was. He had not given a public speech in twelve years. He was fifty-two years old now and wore a wig which would have covered his baldness if he'd let it. But no, as soon as he got excited, he shoved that wig up and down, back and forth as if it might burst into flames at any minute if allowed to lie still.

His years had not slowed Patrick Henry down one whit. As soon as he stood up, people sighed with satisfaction. Yes, he was the same old spellbinder. He pushed his glasses up on his forehead, raised one shoulder a notch, looked intensely at his audience with what people called his "Patrick flash," and before he said a word, people could sense the entire force of his contempt for the Constitution.

"We the people!" he snorted. Since when had they become "We the *people*"? Were they not still first and foremost, "We the States" as they had been under the good old Articles of Confederation? And what was wrong with those Articles? Hadn't the people lived in perfect tranquillity under them? Once Patrick Henry spoke eight times in a single day, once he spoke all day long, but no matter how long he spoke or how often, no one moved while he was on stage. During other speeches the audience felt free to shift about and whisper. Stretch their legs. And sometimes leave. It wasn't just what Patrick said that kept everyone so transfixed, it was the way he said it. When he talked of the new government as an empire reducing its citizens to slavery, he raised his arms in such a way that a person could almost see his chains. One member of the audience tested his own wrists to see if they too were shackled. Then there was the time when Patrick pretended to be the state of Virginia, balancing the fate of America on the scales of justice. Eight states were in favor of the Constitution, he said, wiggling those imaginary scales. But what had that to do with justice? If twelve

Viewing HISTORY Opposing Views of the Constitution

In 1775, Patrick Henry (left) rose in the Virginia House of Burgesses to speak out for independence from Britain. (See Chapter 4.) In the same hall, 13 years later, he spoke against ratification of the Constitution. Opposing him were Virginia Federalists like James Madison (right) and George Washington. ★ **Why was Virginia a key state in the debate over ratification?**

and a half states voted for the Constitution, he cried, still he would "with manly firmness . . . reject it."

No one enjoyed Patrick Henry's theatrics more than Patrick himself, and he had even more reason to be pleased with himself when in the middle of a speech one of his older sons approached the platform with a whispered message. Patrick's wife, Dorothea, had just given birth to Patrick's twelfth child, a boy. There was no stopping Patrick Henry now and no one tried.

When he finally sat down, the Federalists wanted only to get rid of the emotion in the room, set the debate back on firm ground, and let reason take over. But Mr. Madison wasn't the man to do it. Not yet. Let Edmund Randolph start off for the Federalists; he was always impressive. Not until the third day of the debate did James Madison take his turn. He never faced this many people at one time, but he stood his ground, his hat in his hand, his notes in his hat. He must have expected the audience to walk out because he knew he couldn't be heard in the back of the room and probably not even seen. Sometimes his voice sank so low, not even the secretary recording the meeting could hear it. But people didn't walk out. Those in the back began to move forward and before long much of the audience was standing in front of him, trying to catch his every word. Rocking back and forth, on his feet, James Madison poured out his conviction. Firmly, evenly, he talked of checks and balances, pointing out that the Senate, elected by the state legislatures, was really a confederated body while the House, elected by the people, was more national. It was a mixed government. How could it be called an empire, as Mr. Henry had claimed? Only the House had the power to spend money and declare war, and if ever the Congress got out of hand, the President could veto its measures. And if Congress thought the President was wrong, it could over-ride his veto. Where was the slavery in that?

Analyzing Literature

1. How did Henry describe the government under the Constitution?
2. According to Madison, what part of the Constitution would prevent the new government from becoming a tyranny?
3. **Critical Thinking Comparing (a)** According to this passage, how did Madison's style of speaking differ from that of Henry? **(b)** Which style do you think is more persuasive? Why?

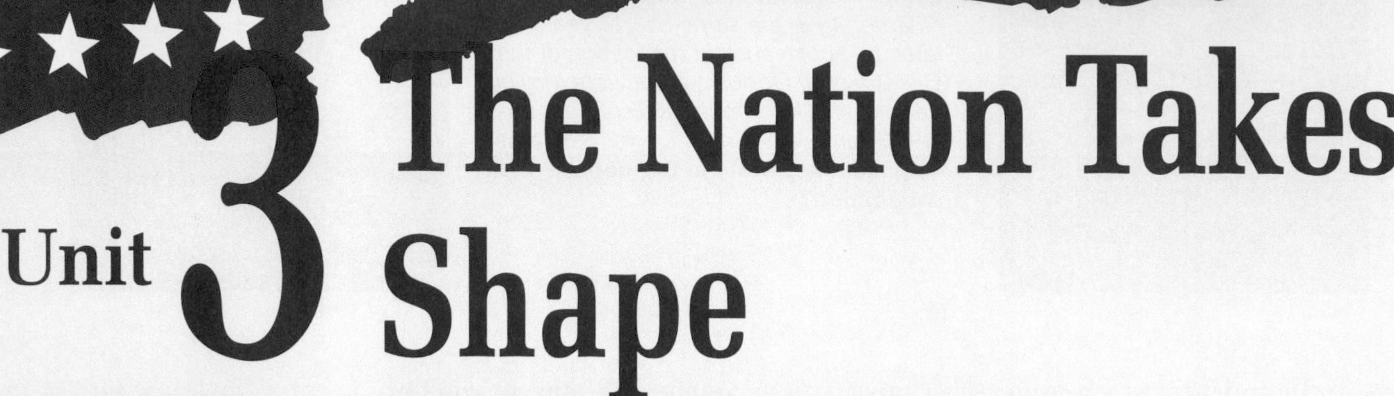

Unit 3 The Nation Takes Shape

What's Ahead

Chapter 7
The New Republic Begins (1789–1800)

Chapter 8
The Age of Jefferson (1801–1816)

Chapter 9
Industry and Growth (1790–1825)

Viewing UNIT THEMES

Celebrating the Nation

American artist John Lewis Krimmel painted this election celebration in 1815. This detail shows people of all ages enjoying parades and public debate in the streets of Philadelphia. By this time, Americans had developed strong feelings of pride in their young nation. ★ **Why do you think Americans at this time felt that an election was cause for celebration?**

Unit Theme Nationalism

In the years after winning independence and adopting a new Constitution, the United States grew and prospered. As the nation took shape, so did American nationalism. Nationalism is a feeling of loyalty and devotion to one's country. Proud Americans sought to identify qualities that set the United States apart from older nations.

How did Americans of the time describe their feelings about their country? They can tell you in their own words.

★ ★

Viewpoints on American Nationalism

"Britain, whose children we are, and whose language we speak, should no longer be *our* standard.... Customs, habits, and language, as well as government, should be national. America should have her *own* distinct from all the world."

Noah Webster, scholar and dictionary writer (1789)

"We have learned to love our country... because the sweat of our fathers' brows has subdued its soil;... because it embraces our fathers and mothers."

John Thornton Kirkland, Boston minister (1798)

"Our country! In her [dealings] with foreign nations, may she always be in the right; but our country, right or wrong."

Stephen Decatur, naval hero (1816)

★ ★

Activity Writing to Learn Another word for nationalism is patriotism. Many things might stir patriotic feelings, including holidays like the Fourth of July, symbols like the flag, or songs like "The Star-Spangled Banner." List 5 or 6 other things that may stir patriotic feelings. Then, choose one of the items from your list. Write a paragraph describing what you think it represents.

Chapter 7 The New Republic Begins

1789–1800

What's Ahead

In this chapter, you will learn about the early years of the United States. The new nation faced many decisions about how it would govern itself. Everything was a fresh issue, from what the President should be called to how the nation should pay its bills. The young republic also had to meet violent challenges inside its borders and on the high seas.

In these confusing times, leaders clashed over what policies to follow. Some wanted a stronger national government. Others felt the states should have more power. Before long, two political parties formed. Despite powerful feelings on both sides, the nation successfully elected its second President and moved into the 1800s.

Why Study History? Again and again, as you study American history, you will find people arguing about something called "the tariff." Tariffs may not seem very exciting. However, they can directly affect how much we pay for the things we buy. To focus on a recent issue involving tariffs, see the *Why Study History?* feature, "The Debate Over Tariffs Continues," in this chapter.

American Events

1789 George Washington becomes first President of the United States

1791 Congress creates the Bank of the United States

1793 Washington issues Neutrality Proclamation to keep the United States out of war

1788 — **1790** — **1792** — **1794**

World Events

1789 World Event French Revolution begins

1792 World Event Denmark is first European nation to abolish slave trade

Viewing History: Symbols of a Proud New Nation

In the late 1700s, paper cutouts like this one were a popular form of artwork. This design shows an eagle holding a flag under the word LIBERTY—symbols of the new nation's patriotism. As President George Washington took office in 1789, Americans looked to the future with pride and hope. ★ **If you were an American in 1789, what hopes and worries might you have about the new government?**

1795
Jay's Treaty keeps peace between the United States and Britain

1797
John Adams becomes second President of the United States

1798
Sedition Act makes it a crime to criticize the government

1794 | **1796** | **1798** | **1800**

1794 World Event
Thaddeus Kosciusko leads Polish uprising

1797 World Event
British sailors mutiny to demand better conditions

Launching the New Government

Explore These Questions

- How did George Washington's actions set an example for future Presidents?
- How did Alexander Hamilton plan to strengthen the nation's economy?
- Why did some people oppose Hamilton's economic plan?

Define

- inauguration
- precedent
- Cabinet
- national debt
- bond
- speculator
- tariff
- protective tariff

Identify

- Judiciary Act
- District of Columbia
- Bank of the United States
- Whiskey Rebellion

SETTING the Scene The new Congress met for the first time in the spring of 1789. Vice President John Adams brought up a curious question. How should people address the President?

For three weeks, members of Congress debated the issue. Some favored the simple title "President Washington." Others felt that it lacked dignity. Instead, they suggested titles such as "His Elective Highness" or "His Highness the President of the United States and Protector of the Rights of the Same."

Finally, Washington let Congress know he was content with "President of the United States." By choosing a simple title, Washington showed he was not interested in the kind of power that European monarchs had. In this decision, like many others, Washington set an example for later Presidents.

The New Government

George Washington was inaugurated in New York City on April 30, 1789. A President's **inauguration** is the ceremony at which the President officially takes the oath of office. A witness reported that the new President looked "grave, almost to sadness." Washington no doubt was feeling the awesome responsibility of his office. He knew that Americans were looking to him to make their new government work.

As the first President, Washington had no one to imitate. While the Constitution provided a framework for the new government, it did not explain how the President should govern from day to day. Washington knew he was setting an example for future generations. "There is scarcely any part of my conduct," he said, "which may not hereafter be drawn into precedent." A **precedent** (PREHS uh dehnt) is an act or decision that sets an example for others to follow.

Washington set one important precedent at the end of his second term. In 1796, he decided not to run for a third term. Not until 1940 did any President seek a third term.

The first Cabinet

The Constitution said little about how the executive branch should be organized. It was clear, however, that the President needed talented people to help him carry out his duties.

The President who finally broke Washington's two-term precedent was Franklin D. Roosevelt. In 1940, he ran for and won a third term. Four years later, Roosevelt was elected yet again. Today, the Twenty-Second Amendment to the Constitution prohibits any President from being elected more than twice.

Viewing HISTORY **The First President**

George Washington traveled on horseback to his inauguration in New York City. Along the way, crowds gathered to cheer their new President. Here, women and children scatter flower petals in Washington's path. ★ **How can you tell this painter greatly admired Washington?**

Mug honoring President Washington's inauguration ➤

In 1789, the first Congress created five executive departments. They were the departments of State, Treasury, and War and the offices of Attorney General and Postmaster General. The heads of these departments made up the President's **Cabinet.** Members of the Cabinet gave Washington advice and directed their departments.

Washington set a precedent by carefully choosing well-known leaders to serve in his Cabinet. The two most influential were the Secretary of State, Thomas Jefferson, and the Secretary of the Treasury, Alexander Hamilton.

The federal court system

The Constitution called for a Supreme Court. Congress, however, had to organize the federal court system. In 1789, Congress passed the **Judiciary Act.** It called for the Supreme Court to have one Chief Justice and five Associate Justices.* Washington named John Jay to serve as the first Chief Justice of the United States.

The Judiciary Act also set up a system of district courts and circuit courts across the nation. Decisions made in these lower courts could be appealed to the Supreme Court, the highest court in the land.

Battling the National Debt

As Secretary of the Treasury, Alexander Hamilton wanted to build a strong economy. He faced many major problems, however. Among the most pressing was the large national debt. The **national debt** is the total sum of money a government owes to others.

* Today, the Supreme Court has eight Associate Justices.

Biography **Alexander Hamilton**

Alexander Hamilton was born on the Caribbean island of Nevis in 1755. As a boy, he faced poverty, but he worked his way up in a local trading company. He later came to New York, served as an officer in the American Revolution, and became the first Secretary of the Treasury. This portrait was painted by John Trumbull, one of the most famous early American artists.

★ **How did Alexander Hamilton help strengthen the new nation?**

During the Revolution, both the national government and the individual states needed money to pay soldiers and buy supplies. They borrowed money from foreign countries and ordinary citizens.

Then, as now, governments borrowed money by issuing bonds. A **bond** is a certificate which promises to repay the money loaned plus interest on a certain date. For example, if a person pays $100 for a bond, the government agrees to pay back $100 plus interest in five or ten years.

By 1789, most southern states had paid off their debts from the Revolution. Other states and the federal government had not. Hamilton insisted that all these debts be repaid. After all, he asked, who would lend money to the United States in the future if the country did not pay its old debts?

Hamilton's Plan

Hamilton developed a two-part plan to repay both the national and state debts. First, he wanted to buy up all the bonds issued by the national and state governments before 1789. He planned to sell new bonds to pay off those old debts. When the economy improved, the government would be able to pay off the new bonds. Second, he wanted the national government to pay off debts owed by the states.

Many people, including bankers and investors, welcomed Hamilton's plan. Others attacked it.

Madison leads the opposition

James Madison led the opposition to Hamilton's plan. Madison argued that the plan was unfair because it would reward speculators. A **speculator** is someone willing to invest in a risky venture in the hope of making a large profit.

During the Revolution, the government had paid soldiers and citizens who supplied goods with bonds. Many of these bondholders needed cash to survive. They sold their bonds to speculators. Speculators paid only 10 or 15 cents for bonds that had an original, or face, value of one dollar.

If the government repaid the bonds at face value, speculators stood to make great fortunes. Madison thought that speculators did not deserve to make such profits.

Hamilton disagreed. The United States had to repay its bonds in full, he said, in order to gain the trust and help of investors. The support of investors, he argued, was crucial for building the new nation's economy. After much debate, Hamilton convinced Congress to accept his plan of repaying the national debt.

As a southerner, James Madison also led the fight against the other part of Hamilton's plan. It called for the federal government to pay state debts. Many southern states had already paid their own debts in full. They thought other states should do the same. As a result, southerners bitterly opposed Hamilton's proposal.

Hamilton's compromise

To win support for his plan, Hamilton suggested a compromise. He knew that many southerners wanted to move the nation's capital to the South. He offered to persuade his northern friends to vote for a capital in the South if southerners supported the repayment of state debts.

Madison and other southerners accepted this compromise. In July 1790, Congress passed bills taking over state debts and providing for a new capital city.

The capital would not be part of any state. Instead, it would be built on land along the Potomac River between Virginia and Maryland. Congress called this area the **District of Columbia.** It is known today as Washington, D.C. Congress hoped that the new capital would be ready by 1800. Meanwhile, the nation's capital was moved from New York to Philadelphia.

Building Up the Economy

Hamilton's compromise with the South had resolved the problem of the national debt. Now he took steps to build up the new nation's economy.

A national bank

Hamilton called on Congress to set up a national bank. In 1791, Congress passed a bill creating the first **Bank of the United States.** The national government deposited the money it collected in taxes in the Bank. The Bank, in turn, issued paper money. The government used the paper money to make loans to farmers and businesses. By making loans to citizens, the Bank encouraged the growth of the economy.

The Bank also used the paper money to pay government bills. The new government had many expenses. It had to pay its employees, build the new capital, and keep up the army and navy.

Protecting American industry

Another part of Hamilton's economic program was designed to give American manufacturing a boost. He proposed that Congress pass a **tariff,** or tax, on all foreign goods brought into the country. Hamilton called for a very high tariff. He wanted to make imported goods more expensive to buy than goods made in the United States. Because such a tariff was meant to protect American industry from foreign competition, it was called a **protective tariff.**

In the North, where factories were growing, many people supported Hamilton's plan. Southern farmers, however, bought more imported goods than northerners did. They did not want a protective tariff that would make these goods more expensive.

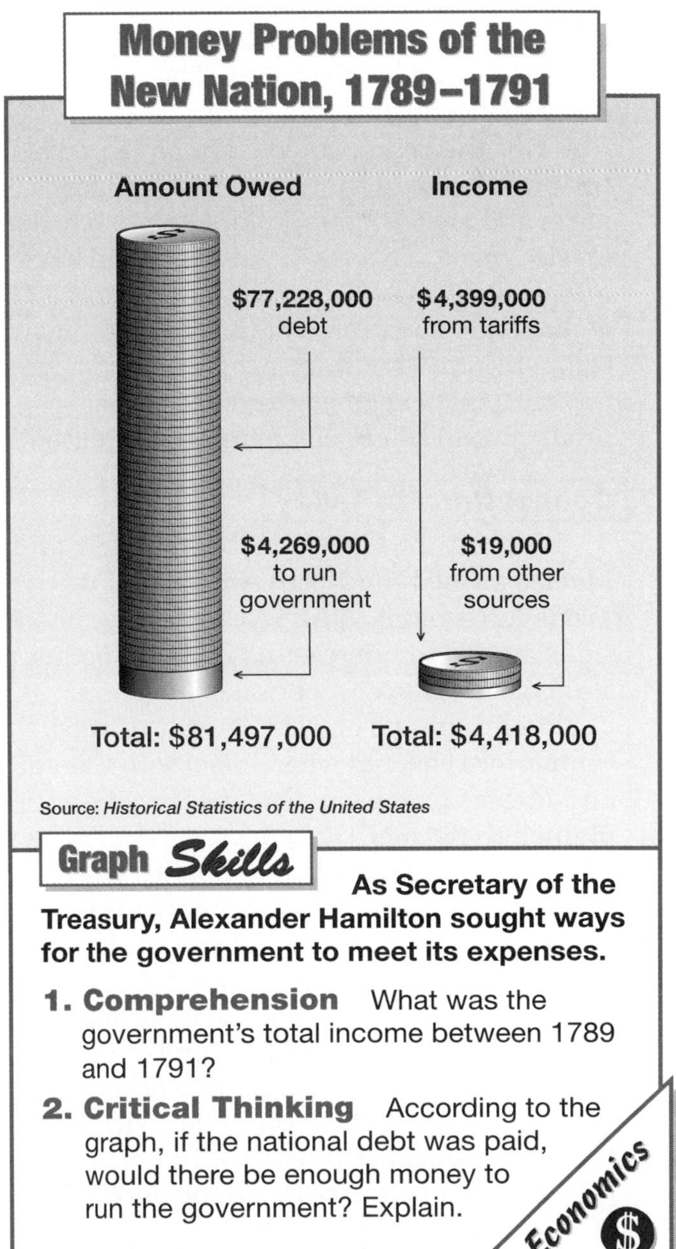

As Secretary of the Treasury, Alexander Hamilton sought ways for the government to meet its expenses.

1. **Comprehension** What was the government's total income between 1789 and 1791?
2. **Critical Thinking** According to the graph, if the national debt was paid, would there be enough money to run the government? Explain.

Why Study History?

Because the Debate Over Tariffs Continues

Tariffs can increase the cost of the goods you buy.

Historical Background

In the 1790s, Alexander Hamilton wanted protective tariffs placed on imports. Other American leaders disagreed. The national debate over tariffs had begun.

Over the years, supporters have praised tariffs for raising the price of foreign imports and encouraging Americans to buy domestic goods. They say that American businesses and workers prosper as a result. Opponents, however, feel that tariffs limit competition. They want people to be free to buy the least expensive and best-made product, regardless of where it is produced.

Connections to Today

By 1993, the United States, Canada, and Mexico formed the North American Free Trade Agreement (NAFTA). The three nations agreed to remove all tariffs and other trade barriers over a period of 15 years.

Public opinion on NAFTA was divided. Supporters cheered when exports to Canada and Mexico increased. Opponents complained that American workers were losing jobs as companies moved to Mexico where labor costs were lower. Opponents also charged that Mexico did not enforce laws banning child labor, ensuring safety in the workplace, and protecting the environment.

The opponents of NAFTA and similar agreements urged consumers to boycott, or not buy, goods made in countries with unfair or unsafe labor practices. In particular, they urged consumers to boycott foreign goods made by young children.

Connections to You

In one case, students in American schools made an impact. Manufacturers in Pakistan were using children to stitch soccer balls. In protest, American and European students threatened a boycott of soccer balls made in Pakistan. As a result, the manufacturers agreed to stop using child labor.

1. **Comprehension** **(a)** Explain one argument in favor of tariffs. **(b)** Explain one argument against tariffs.
2. **Critical Thinking** It can cost less to make some products in Mexico than in the United States. Why do you think this is so?

Debating Work with other students to stage a debate on NAFTA. One group will support the treaty. Another group will oppose it. Do additional research to find information supporting your position.

In the end, Congress did pass a tariff bill. However, its purpose was to raise money for operating the government, rather than protect American industries. For this reason, it was much lower than the protective tariff called for by Hamilton.

The Whiskey Rebellion

Congress also passed a bill that taxed all liquor made and sold in the United States. Hamilton wanted this tax to raise money for the Treasury. Instead, the whiskey tax led to a rebellion that tested the strength of the new government.

A hated tax

Like many other Americans, farmers in the backcountry grew corn. However, corn was bulky to haul over rough backcountry roads. Instead, farmers converted their corn into whiskey, which they could easily ship in barrels to markets in the East.

Backcountry farmers protested the whiskey tax. They compared it to the hated taxes Britain had forced on the colonies in the 1760s. Many farmers refused to pay the tax. A backcountry poet wrote:

> "Some chaps whom freedom's spirit warms
> Are threatening hard to take up arms....
> Their liberty they will maintain,
> They fought for't, and they'll fight again."

In 1794, officials in western Pennsylvania tried to collect the tax. Farmers rebelled. Soon, thousands were marching through Pittsburgh. They sang Revolutionary songs and tarred and feathered tax officials.

A show of strength

Washington responded quickly to this challenge to authority. He called up the militia and sent them to Pennsylvania. When the rebels heard that 15,000 troops were marching against them, they scattered. Washington later pardoned the leaders of the rebellion.

The **Whiskey Rebellion** was a critical test of the strength of the new government. Washington had shown those who disagreed with the government that violence would not be tolerated. The President's quick response proved to Americans that their new government would act firmly in times of crisis.

★ Section 1 Review ★

Recall

1. **Identify** **(a)** Judiciary Act, **(b)** District of Columbia, **(c)** Bank of the United States, **(d)** Whiskey Rebellion.
2. **Define** **(a)** inauguration, **(b)** precedent, **(c)** Cabinet, **(d)** national debt, **(e)** bond, **(f)** speculator, **(g)** tariff, **(h)** protective tariff.

Comprehension

3. Describe one precedent that George Washington set for future governments of the United States.
4. **(a)** Why did Alexander Hamilton think it was important to pay off government bonds? **(b)** Why did James Madison oppose Hamilton's repayment plan?
5. Describe two proposals Hamilton made to raise money for the new government.

Critical Thinking and Writing

6. **Linking Past and Present** By the late 1990s, the Cabinet included the heads of 13 separate departments. Why do you think the Cabinet has grown so much since Washington's time?
7. **Forecasting** What do you think might have happened if Washington had not taken strong action to put down the Whiskey Rebellion?

Activity **Acting a Scene** The year is 1789. Your family owns government bonds, but you are not sure whether the bonds will be repaid at full value. With a partner, act out a scene between two members of the family. Discuss whether you should hold onto the bonds or sell them to a speculator.

A Policy of Neutrality

Explore These Questions

- How did Americans react to the French Revolution?
- What policy did the United States adopt when war broke out in Europe?
- How did Washington's Farewell Address influence American foreign policy?

Define

- foreign policy

Identify

- French Revolution
- Neutrality Proclamation
- Jay's Treaty
- Farewell Address

Late in 1789, French ships arriving at American seaports brought startling news. On July 14, an angry mob in Paris, France, had destroyed the Bastille (bahs TEEL), a huge fort that was being used as a prison. The attack on the Bastille was one of several events that launched the **French Revolution**.

The French Revolution broke out a few years after Americans won independence. Like the Americans, the French fought for liberty and equality. As the French Revolution grew more violent, however, it ignited political quarrels that had been smoldering in the United States.

Revolution in France

The French had many reasons to rebel against their king, Louis XVI. Peasants and the middle class paid heavy taxes, while nobles paid none. Reformers called for a constitution to limit the power of the king. They also wanted a guarantee of rights like that in the American Constitution.

Americans support the revolution

At first, most Americans supported the French Revolution. Americans knew what it meant to struggle for liberty. Then, too, France had been the first ally of the United States in the war against Great Britain. Many Americans wanted to rally behind the Marquis de Lafayette, a leading French reformer. They remembered that Lafayette had fought side by side with them in the American Revolution.

In the 1790s, however, the French Revolution entered a very violent stage. A radical group gained power. In 1793, they beheaded Louis XVI and his wife, Queen Marie Antoinette. During a "reign of terror," tens of thousands of French citizens were executed.

Violence divides American opinion

The violence in France divided Americans. Some, like Thomas Jefferson, continued to support the French. He condemned the killings of the king and queen. Still, he felt that the French had the right to use violence to win freedom.

Alexander Hamilton, John Adams, and others disagreed with Jefferson's view. They thought that the French Revolution was doomed to fail. One could no more create democracy through violence, claimed Adams, "than a snowball can exist in the streets of Philadelphia under a burning sun."

Remaining Neutral

The French Revolution shocked rulers and nobles across Europe. They feared the spread of revolutionary ideas to their own

Viewing HISTORY **The French Revolution**

At the start of the French Revolution, famine gripped Paris. Thousands of angry women (above) marched on the palace of the king shouting, "Bread! Bread!" The statue at right honored the army of ragged peasants that rose up against long years of injustice. ★ **Why would the French expect Americans to support their revolution?**

lands. Britain, Spain, Prussia, Austria, and the Netherlands sent armies to overpower the revolutionaries in France. Europe was soon plunged into a war that continued on and off for more than 20 years.

A difficult decision

Faced with the war in Europe, Washington had to form a foreign policy for the nation. **Foreign policy** refers to the actions and stands that a nation takes in relation to other nations. An old treaty, signed during the American Revolution, allowed French ships to use American ports. As the war in Europe continued, the French wanted to use American ports to supply their ships and launch attacks on British ships.

"It is the sincere wish of United America," said the President, "to have nothing to do with . . . the squabbles of European nations." How could the United States honor its treaty with France and still remain neutral?

Divisions in the Cabinet

The issue of the treaty deepened divisions within Washington's Cabinet. Hamilton pointed out that the United States had signed the treaty with Louis XVI. Since the king was dead, he argued, the treaty was no longer valid. Jefferson, however, supported the French cause. He was suspicious of Hamilton, who wanted friendlier relations with Britain, the nation's old enemy.

After much debate, Washington issued the **Neutrality Proclamation** in April 1793. In it, he stated that the United States would not support either side in the war. It also forbade Americans to aid either Britain or France in any way.

Many viewed the Neutrality Proclamation as a defeat for Jefferson. Eventually, this and other conflicts with Hamilton caused Jefferson to leave the Cabinet.

An Unpopular Treaty

Declaring neutrality was easier than enforcing it. American merchants wanted to trade with both Britain and France. However, those warring nations ignored the rights of neutral ships. They seized American cargoes headed for each other's ports.

In 1793, the British captured more than 250 American ships trading in the French

West Indies. Americans clamored for war. Washington, however, knew that the United States was too weak to fight. He sent Chief Justice John Jay to Britain for talks.

Jay worked out a treaty. It called for Britain to pay damages for American ships seized in 1793. At the same time, Americans had to pay debts to British merchants, owed from before the Revolution. Britain agreed to give up forts it still held in the Ohio Valley. However, the treaty did nothing to protect the rights of neutral American ships.

George Washington retired to Mount Vernon, his Virginia home, where he died in 1799.

Jay's Treaty sparked a storm of protest. Many Americans felt they were giving up more than Britain was. After a furious debate, the Senate finally approved the treaty in 1795. Washington accepted the treaty because he wanted to avoid war.

Washington Retires

In 1796, George Washington published his **Farewell Address**. In it, he announced he would retire. He urged the United States to remain neutral in its relations with other countries:

> "Observe good faith and justice toward all nations.... Nothing is more essential than that permanent, [habitual hatred] against particular nations and passionate attachments for others should be excluded."

Washington warned Americans to avoid becoming involved in European affairs. "'Tis our true policy to steer clear of permanent alliances with any portion of the foreign world," said the retiring President. Such alliances, he felt, would pull the United States into war. That advice guided American foreign policy for many years.

★ Section 2 Review ★

Recall

1. **Identify** **(a)** French Revolution, **(b)** Neutrality Proclamation, **(c)** Jay's Treaty, **(d)** Farewell Address.
2. **Define** foreign policy.

Comprehension

3. How did the revolution in France divide Americans?
4. Describe two actions Washington took to avoid war.
5. What advice did Washington give in his Farewell Address?

Critical Thinking and Writing

6. **Recognizing Points of View** Writing about the French Revolution, Thomas Jefferson said he was willing to see "half the earth devastated" in order to win the "liberty of the whole." **(a)** Restate Jefferson's main idea in your own words. **(b)** What does this statement tell you about Jefferson's values?
7. **Analyzing Information** How did geographic location help the United States to "steer clear of permanent alliances" with European nations for many years?

Activity **Giving an Introduction** President Washington has chosen to deliver his Farewell Address in your school auditorium. You have been asked to introduce him. Prepare a two-minute introduction naming what you consider to be Washington's greatest achievements.

The Rise of Political Parties

As You Read

Explore These Questions

- How did political differences lead to the rise of two political parties?
- What role did newspapers play in politics?
- How did the election of 1796 increase political tensions?

Define

- faction
- unconstitutional

Identify

- Democratic Republicans
- Federalists

SETTING the Scene When President Washington took office in 1789, the United States had no political parties. In fact, most American leaders opposed the very idea of forming parties. "If I could not go to heaven but with a party," said Thomas Jefferson, "I would not go at all."

Still, deep divisions began to form in the Cabinet and Congress. Jefferson described the unpleasant mood:

> ❝ Men who have been [friends] all their lives cross streets to avoid meeting, and turn their heads another way, lest they should be obliged to touch their hats. ❞

By the time Washington left office in 1789, there were two parties competing for power.

A Distrust of Political Parties

Americans had reason to distrust political parties. They had seen how **factions,** or parties, worked in Britain. British factions were made up of a few people who schemed to win favors from the government. Most were more interested in personal gain than in the public good.

Americans also saw political parties as a threat to national unity. They agreed with George Washington, who warned Americans that parties would lead to "jealousies and false alarms."

Despite the President's warning, parties grew up around two members of his Cabinet, Alexander Hamilton and Thomas Jefferson. The two men differed in background, looks, and personality as well as in politics. Born in the West Indies, Hamilton had worked his way up from poverty. He dressed in fine clothes and spoke forcefully. Energetic, brilliant, and restless, Hamilton enjoyed political debate.

Jefferson was tall and lanky. Although he was a wealthy Virginia planter, he dressed and spoke informally. One senator recalled:

> ❝ His clothes seem too small for him. He sits in a lounging manner, on one hip commonly, and with one of his shoulders elevated much above the other. His face has a sunny aspect. His whole figure has a loose, shackling air.... He spoke almost without ceasing. [His conversation] was loose and rambling; and yet he scattered information wherever he went. ❞

Differing Views

Alexander Hamilton did not agree with Thomas Jefferson on many issues. At the root of their quarrels were different views about what was best for the young United States.

Manufacturing or farming

First, Hamilton and Jefferson disagreed about economic policy. Hamilton thought the United States should model itself on Britain. He felt the government should encourage

Viewing HISTORY **Two Views of the Nation**

Federalists and Republicans disagreed. Should the new nation build its future mainly on agriculture or on manufacturing? The farmer, above, and the ironworker, right, represent these two viewpoints.
★ **Which of these pictures represents Hamilton's view? Which picture represents Jefferson's view?**

manufacturing and trade. He also favored the growth of cities and the merchant class who helped make cities prosperous.

Jefferson believed that farmers, rather than merchants, were the backbone of the new nation. "Cultivators of the earth," he wrote, "are the most valuable citizens." He feared that a manufacturing economy would corrupt the United States by concentrating power in the hands of a small group of wealthy Americans.

Federal or state governments

Hamilton and Jefferson disagreed about the power of the federal government. Hamilton wanted the federal government to have greater power than state governments. A strong federal government, he argued, could encourage the growth of commerce. It would also have the power needed to restrain unruly mobs, such as the protesters who led the Whiskey Rebellion.

In contrast, Jefferson hoped to make the government as small as possible. Then, citizens would have the freedom to act as they pleased. Jefferson feared that a strong federal government might take over powers that the Constitution gave to the states.

Strict or loose interpretation of the Constitution

These disagreements led the two leaders to clash over the Bank of the United States. Jefferson worried that a national bank would give too much power to the federal government and the wealthy investors who helped run it.

To oppose Hamilton's proposal, Jefferson argued that the law creating the bank was **unconstitutional,** that is, not permitted by the Constitution. Nowhere did the Constitution give Congress the power to create a Bank, he argued. Jefferson thought that any power not specifically given to the federal government belonged to the states.

Hamilton did not agree with Jefferson's strict interpretation of the Constitution. He preferred a looser interpretation. The Constitution gave Congress the power to make all laws "necessary and proper" to carry out

Skills FOR LIFE

Critical Thinking | **Managing Information** | Communication | Maps, Charts, and Graphs

Outlining

How Will I Use This Skill?

In school and, later, at work, you may be asked to write a report or give a presentation. You will find the job easier if you prepare an outline. An outline helps you arrange information in logical order. In addition, when you speak in public, an outline can keep you from fumbling for words!

LEARN the Skill

Make an outline by following these four steps.

1. Use the theme or topic as the title of your outline.
2. Identify and list the main ideas in order. Label them with Roman numerals.
3. Identify subtopics for each main idea. Label these with capital letters and list them under the main ideas.
4. Identify details that support each subtopic. Label and list these with Arabic numerals as shown.

PRACTICE the Skill

The sample at right is a partial outline of the subsection Differing Views. Study the sample. Then, using the steps above, make an outline of the subsection Party Rivalry.

1. Take notes as you read the subsection.
2. Using your notes and the headings in the text, write down the main ideas.
3. Using the topic sentences of the paragraphs in the text, identify the subtopics for your outline.
4. Find and list supporting details from the text.

The Clash of Jefferson and Hamilton

I. Jefferson's Views
  A. Preferred farm economy
  B. Favored strict interpretation of Constitution
    1. Against Bank of United States
      a. Too much power to federal government
      b. Unconstitutional
    2. Favored state power
  C. Favored France in foreign policy
II. Hamilton's Views
  A. Supported manufacturing economy
  B. Favored loose interpretation of Constitution
    1. Planned Bank of United States
      a. Way to collect taxes
      b. Way to pay government bills
    2. Favored federal power
  C. Supported Britain in foreign policy

APPLY the Skill

Choose a topic that interests you. Make an outline for a short talk on this subject.

Federalists vs. Republicans

FEDERALISTS	REPUBLICANS
① Led by Alexander Hamilton	① Led by Thomas Jefferson
② Wealthy and well educated should lead nation	② People should have political power
③ Strong central government	③ Strong state governments
④ Emphasis on manufacturing, shipping, and trade	④ Emphasis on agriculture
⑤ Loose interpretation of Constitution	⑤ Strict interpretation of the Constitution
⑥ Pro-British	⑥ Pro-French
⑦ Favored national bank	⑦ Opposed national bank
⑧ Favored protective tariff	⑧ Opposed protective tariff

Graphic Organizer Skills **By the 1790s, there were two political parties in the United States—the Federalist party and the Republican party.**

1. **Comprehension** Describe two ways the Republicans and Federalists differed on economic issues.
2. **Critical Thinking** "The average person is far too ignorant to make wise political decisions." Do you think a Republican or a Federalist would be more likely to agree with this statement? Explain.

Civics

its duties. Hamilton argued that the Bank was necessary for the government to collect taxes and pay its bills.

Britain or France

Finally, the two leaders clashed over foreign policy. Hamilton wanted to form close ties with Britain, an important trading partner. Jefferson favored France, the first ally of the United States and a nation struggling for its own liberty.

Party Rivalry

At first, Hamilton and Jefferson clashed in private. However, when Congress began to pass many of Hamilton's programs, Jefferson and James Madison decided to organize public support for their views.

Madison and Jefferson moved cautiously at first. In 1791, they went to New York, telling people that they were going to study its wildlife. In fact, Jefferson was interested in nature and did travel far into upstate New York. Their main purpose, though, was to meet with important New York politicians like Governor George Clinton and Aaron Burr, a strong critic of Hamilton. Jefferson asked Clinton and Burr to help defeat Hamilton's program by getting New Yorkers to vote for Jefferson supporters.

Republicans and Federalists

Soon, leaders in other states began organizing to support either Hamilton or Jefferson. Jefferson's supporters called themselves **Democratic Republicans,** often shortened to Republicans.* Republicans included small farmers, craftworkers, and some wealthy planters.

*Jefferson's Republican party was not the same as today's Republican party. In fact, his party later grew into the Democratic party.

Hamilton and his supporters were called **Federalists** because they wanted a strong federal government. Federalists drew most of their support from merchants and manufacturers in cities such as Boston and New York. They also gained the backing of some southern planters.

Newspapers take sides

In the late 1700s, the number of American newspapers more than doubled. This growth met a demand for information. A visitor from Europe noted with surprise that so many Americans could read:

> "The common people [in the United States] are on a footing, in point of literature with the middle ranks of Europe. They all read and write, and understand arithmetic; almost every little town now furnishes a circulating library."

As party rivalry grew, newspapers took sides. In the *Gazette of the United States*, publisher John Fenno printed articles in favor of Alexander Hamilton and the Federalists. Philip Freneau (frih NOH), a friend of Thomas Jefferson, started a rival paper, the *National Gazette*. Freneau vigorously supported Republicans.

Newspapers had great influence on public opinion. In stinging language, they raged against opponents. Often, articles mixed rumor and opinion with facts. Emotional attacks and counterattacks fanned the flames of party rivalry. Still, newspapers performed a needed service. They kept people informed and helped shape public opinion.

Election of 1796

Political parties played a major role in the election of George Washington's successor. In 1796, Republicans backed Thomas Jefferson for President and Aaron Burr for Vice President. Federalists supported John Adams for President and Thomas Pinckney for Vice President.

The election had an unexpected outcome, which created new tensions. Under the Constitution, the person with the most electoral votes became President. The person with the next highest total was made Vice President. John Adams, a Federalist, won office as President. The leader of the Republicans, Thomas Jefferson, came in second and became Vice President.

With the President and the Vice President from different parties, political tensions remained high. Future events would further increase the distrust between the two men. Meanwhile, John Adams took office in March 1797 as the second President of the United States.

★ Section 3 Review ★

Recall

1. **Identify** **(a)** Democratic Republicans, **(b)** Federalists.
2. **Define** **(a)** faction, **(b)** unconstitutional.

Comprehension

3. Describe two issues on which Thomas Jefferson and Alexander Hamilton disagreed.
4. How did newspapers contribute to the rivalry between political parties?
5. What role did parties play in the 1796 election?

Critical Thinking and Writing

6. **Drawing Conclusions** Why do you think political parties emerged even though most Americans opposed them?
7. **Ranking** Which of the disagreements between Jefferson and Hamilton do you think was the most serious? Explain.

Activity **Writing a Newspaper Headline** You are the publisher of either the *Gazette of the United States* or the *National Gazette.* Write three headlines about the election of 1796. Be sure your headlines express the point of view of your own newspaper.

The Second President

Explore These Questions

- Why did many Americans favor war with France?
- Why did the Federalist party split in two?
- Why did the Alien and Sedition acts outrage many Americans?

Define

- immigrant
- sedition
- nullify

Identify

- XYZ Affair
- High Federalists
- Napoleon Bonaparte
- Alien and Sedition acts
- Kentucky and Virginia resolutions

Late in his life, John Adams looked back on his career with mixed feelings. He knew that leaders such as Washington and Jefferson were more widely admired than he was. Still, Adams wrote proudly of his life's work:

> ❝ I have done more labor, run through more and greater dangers, and made greater sacrifices than any man . . . living or dead, in the service of my country. ❞

At the same time, Adams found it hard to boast of his achievements. In the end, he concluded: "I am not, never was, and never shall be a great man."

Although he was not a popular hero, like Washington, Adams was an honest and able leader. As President, he tried to act in the best interests of the nation, even when his actions hurt him politically.

Conflict With France

No sooner did Adams take office than he faced a crisis with France. The French objected to Jay's Treaty because they felt that it favored Britain. In 1797, French ships began to seize American ships in the West Indies, as the British had done.

Once again, Americans called for war, this time against France. Adams tried to avoid war by sending diplomats to Paris to discuss the rights of neutral nations.

The XYZ Affair

France's foreign minister, Charles Maurice de Talleyrand, did not deal directly with the Americans. Instead, he sent three secret agents to offer the Americans a deal. Before Talleyrand would begin talks, the agents said, he wanted $250,000 for himself, as well as a loan to France of $10 million. "Not a sixpence!" replied one of the American diplomats angrily.

The diplomats informed Adams about the offer. Adams, in turn, told Congress. He did not reveal the names of the French agents, referring to them only as X, Y, and Z.

Many Americans were outraged when they heard about the **XYZ Affair** in 1798. They took up the slogan, "Millions for defense, but not one cent for tribute!" They were willing to spend money to defend their country, but they refused to pay a bribe to another nation.

Adams avoids war

Despite growing pressure, Adams refused to ask Congress to declare war on France. Still, he could not ignore French attacks on American ships. He moved to strengthen the navy. Shipyards built frigates—fast-sailing ships with many guns.

This show of strength helped convince Talleyrand to stop attacking American ships. He also promised Adams that if American ambassadors came to France, they would be treated with respect.

Linking United States and the World

France

United States

On the Brink of War

After the XYZ Affair, many Americans called for war with France. War fever led the nation to build up its navy. At left, a cartoon shows France as a five-headed monster asking for "Money, Money, Money." At right, Americans construct a new warship. ★ **Why did the XYZ affair outrage Americans?**

The Federalist Party Splits

Many Federalists, led by Hamilton, criticized Adams's actions. They hoped a war would weaken the Republicans, supporters of France. War would also force the United States to build up its military. A stronger army and navy would increase federal power, a major Federalist goal.

Although John Adams was a Federalist, he would not give in to Hamilton. Their disagreement created a split in the Federalist party. Hamilton and his supporters were called **High Federalists**.

Over Hamilton's opposition, Adams again sent diplomats to France. When they arrived, they found an ambitious young army officer, **Napoleon Bonaparte**, in charge. Napoleon did not have time for a war with the United States. He signed an agreement to stop seizing American ships.

Like Washington, Adams kept the nation out of war. His success, however, cost him the support of many Federalists.

Alien and Sedition Acts

During the crisis with France, Federalists pushed several laws through Congress. Passed in 1798, the laws were known as the **Alien and Sedition acts**.

The Alien Act allowed the President to expel any alien, or foreigner, thought to be dangerous to the country. Another law made it harder for immigrants to become citizens. An **immigrant** is a person who enters another country in order to settle there. Before, white immigrants could become citizens after living in the United States for 5 years. Under the new law, immigrants had to wait 14 years. This law was meant to keep new settlers, who often supported the Republicans, from voting.

Republican anger grew when Congress passed the Sedition Act. **Sedition** means stirring up rebellion against a government. Under this law, citizens could be fined or jailed if they criticized the government or its officials.

Locket given by John to Abigail Adams

Biography **John and Abigail Adams**

Throughout 54 years of marriage, John Adams valued the advice and support of his wife, Abigail. A brilliant woman and fine writer, Abigail Adams supported greater rights for women. They were the first President and First Lady to live in the White House. Their son, John Quincy Adams, also became President. ★ **Why would it have been hard for Abigail Adams to pursue her own political career?**

Republicans protested that the Sedition Act violated the Constitution. After all, they argued, the First Amendment protected freedom of speech and freedom of the press. Jefferson warned that the new laws threatened American liberties:

> “If this goes down, we shall immediately see attempted another act of Congress, declaring that the President shall continue in office during life, and after that other laws giving both the President and the Congress life terms in office.”

Under the Sedition Act, several Republican newspaper editors, and even members of Congress, were fined and jailed for expressing their opinions.

The Rights of States

Outraged, Jefferson urged the states to take strong action against the Alien and Sedition acts. He argued that the states had the right to **nullify,** or cancel, a law passed by the federal government. In this way, states could resist the power of the federal government.

With the help of Jefferson and Madison, Kentucky and Virginia passed resolutions in 1798 and 1799. The **Kentucky and Virginia resolutions** claimed that each state "has an equal right to judge for itself" whether a law is constitutional. If a state decides a law is unconstitutional, said the resolutions, it has the power to nullify that law within its borders.

Connections With Arts

The picture of Abigail Adams, above, is by Gilbert Stuart, one of the greatest American portrait painters. In fact, you may have a Gilbert Stuart painting in your pocket right now. His portrait of George Washington appears on the one dollar bill.

The Kentucky and Virginia resolutions raised a difficult question. Did a state have the right to decide on its own that a law was unconstitutional?

The question remained unanswered in Jefferson's lifetime. Before long, the Alien and Sedition acts were changed or dropped. Still, the issue of a state's right to nullify federal laws would come up again.

Election of 1800

By 1800, the cry for war against France was fading. As the election approached, the Republicans hoped to sweep the Federalists from office. Republicans focused on two issues. First, they attacked the Federalists for raising taxes to prepare for war. Second, they opposed the unpopular Alien and Sedition acts.

Republicans supported Thomas Jefferson for President and Aaron Burr for Vice President. Despite the bitter split in the Federalist party, John Adams was again named the Federalist candidate.

A deadlock

In the race for President, the Republicans won the popular vote. However, when the electoral college voted, Jefferson and Burr each received 73 votes. At the time, the electoral college did not vote separately for President and Vice President. Each Republican elector cast one vote for Jefferson and one vote for Burr.

Under the Constitution, if no candidate wins the electoral vote, the House of Representatives decides the election. The House vote, however, was also evenly split between Jefferson and Burr. After four days, and 36 votes, the tie was finally broken. The House chose Jefferson as President. Burr became Vice President.

Congress afterward passed the Twelfth Amendment. It required electors to vote separately for President and Vice President. The states ratified the amendment in 1804.

End of the Federalist era

The Republican victory set an important precedent for the nation. To this day, power continues to pass peacefully from one party to another.

After 1800, the Federalist party began to decline. Federalists won fewer seats in Congress. In 1804, the Federalist party was further weakened when their leader, Alexander Hamilton, was killed in a duel with Aaron Burr. Despite their decline, the Federalist party had helped shape the new nation. Republican Presidents eventually kept most of Hamilton's economic programs.

★ Section 4 Review ★

Recall

1. **Identify** **(a)** XYZ Affair, **(b)** High Federalists, **(c)** Napoleon Bonaparte, **(d)** Alien and Sedition acts, **(e)** Kentucky and Virginia resolutions.
2. **Define** **(a)** immigrant, **(b)** sedition, **(c)** nullify.

Comprehension

3. Why did many Americans want to declare war on France?
4. Why did John Adams lose the support of many Federalists?
5. **(a)** Why did Federalists favor the Alien and Sedition acts? **(b)** Why did Republicans oppose these laws?

Critical Thinking and Writing

6. **Applying Information** How did the Kentucky and Virginia resolutions reflect Jefferson's view of government?
7. **Analyzing Information** How did the Twelfth Amendment help prevent deadlocks like the one that took place in the election of 1800?

Activity **Drawing a Political Cartoon** Suppose that the Sedition Act of 1798 were passed by Congress today. Draw a political cartoon expressing your opinion of the law.

Chapter 7 Review and Activities

★ Sum It Up ★

Section 1 Launching the New Government

- George Washington set many precedents that determined how future Presidents would govern the nation.
- Alexander Hamilton formed a plan to improve the nation's finances.
- A rebellion against the national government quickly melted away when President Washington responded forcefully.

Section 2 A Policy of Neutrality

- Americans were sharply divided in their reaction to the French Revolution.
- Washington responded to war between Britain and France by declaring that the United States would remain neutral.

Section 3 The Rise of Political Parties

- Because of widely differing views on national issues, two major political parties soon formed in the new republic.
- Federalists supported a strong federal government, while Republicans opposed policies that made the national government too strong.

Section 4 The Second President

- Despite pressure, President John Adams avoided war with France.
- The unpopular Alien and Sedition acts led the states to consider ways to take power back from the federal government.
- In the election of 1800, power passed from the Federalists to the Republicans.

For additional review of the major ideas of Chapter 7, see ***Guide to the Essentials of American History*** or ***Interactive Student Tutorial CD-ROM,*** which contains interactive review activities, graphic organizers, and practice tests.

Reviewing the Chapter

Define These Terms

Match each term with the correct definition.

Column 1	Column 2
1. national debt	**a.** political party
2. tariff	**b.** type of tax
3. speculator	**c.** person who enters a country in order to settle there
4. faction	**d.** someone who invests in a risky venture to make a profit
5. immigrant	**e.** total a government owes

Explore the Main Ideas

1. Why did many southerners oppose Hamilton's plan to settle state debts?
2. How did Britain and France make Washington's neutrality policy difficult to enforce?
3. Describe the people who supported: **(a)** the Federalist party; **(b)** the Republican party.
4. How did President Adams avoid war?
5. How was the Sedition Act used to silence Republicans?

Graph Activity

Look at the graph below and answer the following questions: **1.** How many people served in the navy in 1798? **2.** What had happened to the navy by 1800? **Critical Thinking** Why did the size of the navy change?

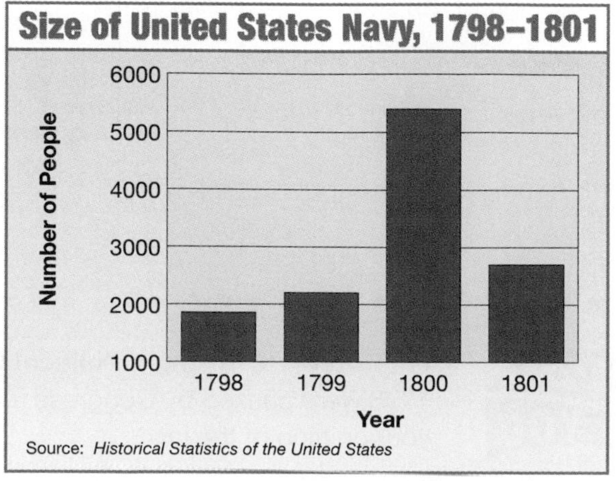

Critical Thinking and Writing

1. **Exploring Unit Themes Nationalism** How did each of the following strengthen the nation: **(a)** the presidency of Washington; **(b)** Hamilton's plan to pay off state debts; **(c)** Washington's response to the Whiskey Rebellion?
2. **Linking Past and Present** Washington urged the United States never to take sides in the world's wars. Do you think this policy would make sense in today's world? Explain.
3. **Defending a Position** Do you think the Constitution should be interpreted strictly or loosely? Give reasons for your position.
4. **Understanding Chronology** **(a)** Place the following events in chronological order: XYZ Affair; Neutrality Proclamation; French Revolution begins; Adams builds up American navy; Washington's Farewell Address. **(b)** Describe the relationship between two of these events.

Using Primary Sources

In its early years, Washington, D.C., was little more than a clearing in the wilderness. First Lady Abigail Adams described its location in a letter to a friend in 1800:

> "Woods are all you see, from Baltimore until you reach the city. . . . Here and there is a small [hut], without a glass window, [all alone] amongst the forests, through which you travel miles without seeing any human being. . . . But, surrounded with forests, can you believe that [fire]wood is not to be had, because people cannot be found to cut and cart it!"

Source: *Letters of Mrs. Adams,* edited by Charles Francis Adams, 1840.

Recognizing Points of View **(a)** Why was Abigail Adams unable to get firewood? **(b)** Why did she consider this surprising? **(c)** Do you think Abigail Adams approved of the new city? Explain.

Activity Bank

Interdisciplinary Activity

Exploring Economics Use library resources to locate information on our current national debt in newspapers or magazines. Prepare a three-minute presentation in which you explain what economic problems may arise because of the national debt.

Career Skills Activity

Reporters Early newspapers often mixed rumor and opinion with facts. Today, reporters have to keep facts and opinions apart. Practice this skill by writing a brief account of the election of 1796 as it might have appeared in a paper of the time. Then, write another account based only on facts.

Citizenship Activity

Researching Political Parties Learn about the political organizations in your area. Most groups will be glad to tell you about the rights and responsibilities of membership. Prepare a one-page data sheet covering at least two political parties. Describe their views and some of their recent or planned activities.

Internet Activity

Today, as in the 1790s, the United States has a special government bank. Use the Internet to find information about the Federal Reserve Bank. Then, write a reaction to the Federal Reserve Bank from the point of view of a Federalist or of a Democratic Republican.

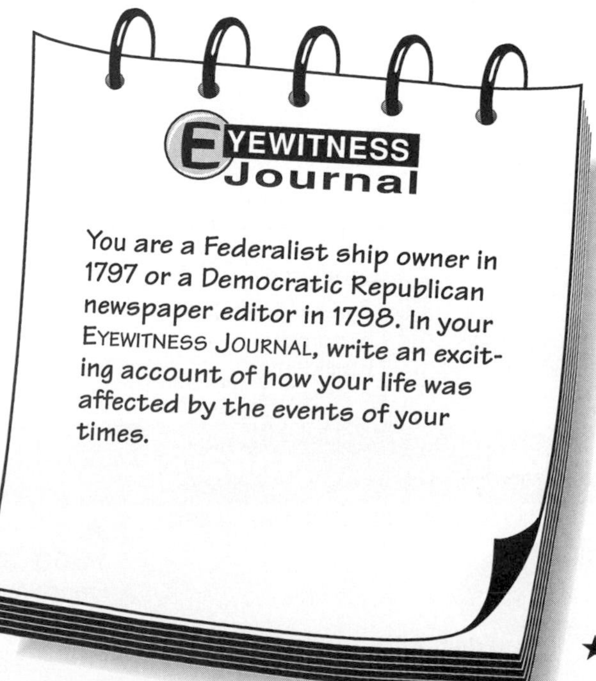

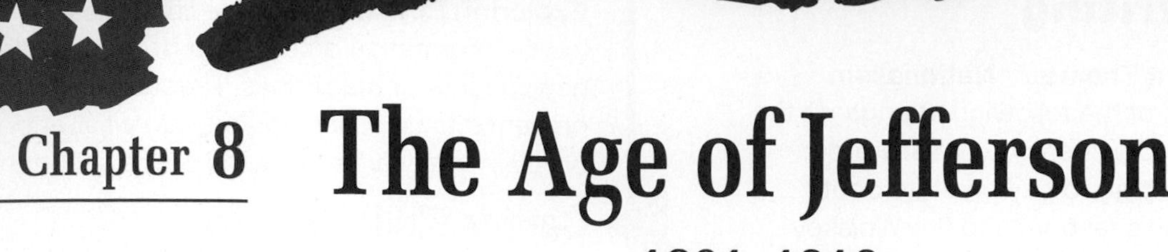

Chapter 8 The Age of Jefferson

1801–1816

What's Ahead

Section 1
Republicans in Power

Section 2
The Louisiana Purchase

Section 3
New Threats From Overseas

Section 4
The Road to War

Section 5
The War of 1812

Republican Presidents in the early 1800s tried to serve the needs of ordinary Americans while limiting the role of government. During this time, events that affected France and Britain reached beyond their borders. As a result, the United States had the opportunity to double its size by purchasing the Louisiana territory from France. The young nation also faced war with Britain again. Although there was no clear winner in the war, many Americans became more proud of their growing nation.

Why Study History?

During the early 1800s, each branch of the new government was learning its responsibilities and limits. It was at this time that the power and importance of the Supreme Court began to emerge. To learn more about the powerful influence of the "highest court in the land," see this chapter's *Why Study History?* feature, "Supreme Court Decisions Affect You."

American Events

1801 Thomas Jefferson becomes President

1804 Lewis and Clark begin to explore Louisiana

1807 Embargo Act bans trade with foreign nations

1800 | 1802 | 1804 | 1806 | 1808

World Events

1803 World Event France and Britain go to war

Viewing HISTORY **Lewis and Clark on the Lower Columbia**

In 1803, President Thomas Jefferson doubled the size of the United States by purchasing the Louisiana territory. He sent Meriwether Lewis and William Clark to explore the land and establish friendship with Native Americans. In this painting by Charles M. Russell, Lewis (right) stands by the Native American Sacajawea as she addresses Chinook Indians. ★ **Do you think Native Americans welcomed Lewis and Clark? Explain.**

1811 Harrison fights Native Americans at Tippecanoe

1812 War begins between United States and Britain

1815 Jackson defeats British at New Orleans

1808	1810	1812	1814	1816

1810 World Event
Simón Bolívar leads revolt against Spanish rule in South America

Republicans in Power

As You Read

Explore These Questions

- What were Jefferson's ideas about government?
- How did he reduce the power of government?
- Why was *Marbury* v. *Madison* important?

Define

- democratic
- laissez faire
- judicial review

Identify

- John Marshall
- *Marbury* v. *Madison*

When Thomas Jefferson became President of the United States in 1801, nearly nine out of ten Americans were farmers. This fact gave Jefferson confidence in the nation's future. Even though Jefferson came from a wealthy family, he believed in the importance of ordinary people, especially farmers. In a letter to James Madison, he expressed his faith in the American people:

> ❝ Educate and inform the whole mass of the people. Enable them to see that it is their interest to preserve peace and order, and they will preserve them. . . . They are the only [ones to rely on] for the preservation of our liberty.❞

A More Democratic Style

As President, Jefferson tried to protect and expand the rights of ordinary citizens. He felt that the Federalists promoted the interests of the wealthy few, but neglected the needs of others. Jefferson was determined to make the government more democratic. **Democratic** means ensuring that all people have the same rights.

Jefferson's personal style matched his democratic beliefs. The new President preferred quiet dinners to the formal parties that Washington and Adams had given. He wore casual clothes and greeted people by shaking hands instead of bowing. With his informal manner, Jefferson showed that the President was an ordinary citizen.

Some Federalists worried about Jefferson's democratic beliefs. They knew that he supported the French Revolution and they feared that he might bring revolutionary change to the United States. They were also afraid that he might punish Federalists who had used the Alien and Sedition acts to jail Republicans.

In his inaugural address, Jefferson tried to quiet Federalists' fears. Though a minority, Federalists "possess their equal rights, which equal laws must protect," he told the nation. He called for an end to the political disputes of past years. "We are all Republicans, we are all Federalists," the President said. Jefferson was determined to unite the country, not divide it further.

Reduced Role of Government

Jefferson had no plan to punish Federalists. He did, however, want to change their policies. In his view, the Federalists had made the national government too large and too powerful. Jefferson wanted to reduce government power by cutting the federal budget and by reducing the federal debt.

Connections With Civics

When Jefferson became President in 1801, there were fewer than 1,000 federal employees. Today, the United States government employs more than 2 million people—not counting those in the military.

Jefferson believed in an idea known as **laissez faire** (lehs ay FAYR), from the French term for "let alone." According to laissez faire, government should play as small a role as possible in economic affairs. Laissez faire was very different from the Federalist idea of government. Alexander Hamilton, you recall, wanted government to promote trade and manufacturing.

President Jefferson tried to reduce the role of government in people's lives. He decreased the size of government departments and cut the federal budget. With the approval of Congress, he reduced the size of the army and navy. He also asked Congress to repeal the unpopular whiskey tax.

The Sedition Act expired the day before Jefferson took office. Jefferson hated the law, and he pardoned those who were in jail because of it. He also asked Congress to restore the law allowing foreign-born people to become citizens after only a five-year waiting period. Jefferson acted to change other Federalist policies as well.

Jefferson did not discard all Federalist programs, however. He kept the Bank of the United States, which he had once opposed. The federal government also continued to pay off state debts that it had taken over when Washington was President. In addition, Jefferson let many Federalists keep their government jobs.

A Stronger Supreme Court

The election of 1800 gave Republicans control of Congress. Federalists, however, remained powerful in the courts.

Several months passed between Jefferson's election and his inauguration on March 4, 1801. During that time, Federalists in the old Congress passed a law increasing the number of federal judges. President Adams then appointed Federalists to fill these new judicial positions.

One of the judges that Adams appointed was **John Marshall,** the Chief Justice of the Supreme Court. Like Jefferson, Marshall

Biography Thomas Jefferson

Jefferson, author of the Declaration of Independence and third President of the United States, was a man of many talents. A skilled architect, he designed his own home, Monticello, in the classical style of ancient Greece and Rome. Jefferson felt that it was important for citizens in a democracy to be well educated. ★ **Why do you think Jefferson placed so much value on education?**

Monticello, home of Thomas Jefferson

Why Study History?

Because Supreme Court Decisions Affect You

Historical Background

In the early 1800s, the Supreme Court was not as respected as it is today. In fact, for a while, the justices met in the basement of the Capitol because the designers of Washington, D.C., had not provided a meeting place for the Court. However, under the strong leadership of Chief Justice John Marshall, the Supreme Court gained respect and power.

Connections to Today

Today, the Supreme Court is very important as the final authority on cases involving the Constitution. By exercising its power of judicial review (see page 197), the Supreme Court decides whether or not laws are constitutional. Supreme Court justices interpret the Constitution and define and limit our constitutional rights.

Connections to You

Supreme Court cases often involve young people like you. One recent example is the case of *Veronia School District* v. *Acton*.

In 1991, a seventh grader in Oregon wanted to join his school football team. The school required that he submit to a drug test. The student refused, and the school did not allow him to play on the team. The boy's parents sued, arguing that the school had violated the Fourth Amendment's protection against unreasonable searches. The case eventually went to the Supreme Court.

In a 6–3 decision, the Court agreed with the school. It ruled that schools can require athletes to undergo drug tests, just as they require physical examinations and vaccinations. The Court said that schools have a special responsibility to prevent drug abuse and to protect students' health.

This 1995 decision did not affect just one student in one school. The Court's ruling applied to student athletes across the nation. Indirectly, it also had an impact on other issues regarding the rights of students in American schools.

1. **Comprehension** **(a)** How did *Veronia School District* v. *Acton* involve the Constitution? **(b)** Why did the Supreme Court agree with the Oregon school's policy?
2. **Critical Thinking** How do you think the decision affected sports programs in other schools?

Researching Use library or Internet sources to research a recent Supreme Court case. Report to the class on the issue, the Court's decision, and possible effects of the decision.

was a rich Virginia planter with a brilliant mind. Unlike Jefferson, however, Marshall was a Federalist. He wanted to make the federal government stronger.

The framers of the Constitution expected the courts to balance the powers of the President and Congress. However, John Marshall found the courts to be very weak. In his view, it was not clear what powers the federal courts had.

Marbury v. *Madison*

In 1803, Marshall decided a case that increased the power of the Supreme Court. The case involved William Marbury, another one of the judges appointed by Adams. Adams made the appointment on his last night as President.

The Republicans refused to accept this "midnight judge." They accused Federalists of using unfair tactics to keep control of the courts. Jefferson ordered Secretary of State James Madison not to deliver the official papers confirming Marbury's appointment.

Marbury sued Madison. According to the Judiciary Act of 1789, only the Supreme Court could decide a case that was brought against a federal official. Therefore, the case of ***Marbury* v. *Madison*** was tried before the Supreme Court.

An important precedent

In its decision, the Supreme Court ruled against Marbury. Chief Justice Marshall wrote the decision, stating that the Judiciary Act was unconstitutional. The Constitution, Marshall argued, did not give the Supreme Court the right to decide cases brought against federal officials. Therefore, Congress could not give the Court that power.

The Supreme Court's decision in *Marbury* v. *Madison* set an important precedent. It gave the Supreme Court the power to decide whether laws passed by Congress were constitutional and to reject laws that it considered to be unconstitutional. This power of the Court is called **judicial review**.

Jefferson was displeased that the decision gave more power to the Supreme Court. He felt that the decision upset the balance of power that existed among the three branches of government. Even so, the President and Congress accepted the right of the Court to overturn laws. Today, judicial review remains one of the most important powers of the Supreme Court.

★ Section 1 Review ★

Recall

1. **Identify** **(a)** John Marshall, **(b)** *Marbury* v. *Madison.*
2. **Define** **(a)** democratic, **(b)** laissez faire, **(c)** judicial review.

Comprehension

3. Explain how Jefferson's ideas on government differed from Federalist ideas.
4. Describe three steps Jefferson took to reduce the power of government.
5. **(a)** What precedent did *Marbury* v. *Madison* set? **(b)** How did the precedent affect the balance of power in American government?

Critical Thinking and Writing

6. **Analyzing a Primary Source** "We are all Republicans, we are all Federalists." **(a)** What did Jefferson mean by these words? **(b)** Why did he need to make such a statement?
7. **Drawing Conclusions** Today, the federal government protects consumers by regulating the quality of certain goods. Would a laissez-faire economist agree with this policy? Why or why not?

Activity **Writing a Letter** Welcome to the United States! You are a newly arrived immigrant from Europe. Write a letter to your friends in Europe describing your feelings about President Jefferson and the Republican government.

The Louisana Purchase

As You Read

Explore These Questions

- Why was control of the Mississippi River important to western farmers?
- How did the United States gain Louisiana?
- What did the Lewis and Clark expedition achieve?

Define

- expedition
- Continental Divide

Identify

- Pinckney Treaty
- Toussaint L'Ouverture
- Louisiana Purchase
- Lewis and Clark
- Sacajawea
- Zebulon Pike

William Clark's journal

Setting the Scene One day, President Jefferson received several packages. Inside, he found hides and skeletons of animals, horns of a mountain ram, and a tin box full of insects. There were also cages of live birds and squirrels, as well as gifts from the Mandan and Sioux Indians.

All of these packages were from Meriwether Lewis and William Clark. Jefferson had sent the two to explore the land west of the Mississippi River. Almost two years before, President Jefferson had purchased the territory for the United States. The packages confirmed his belief that the new lands were a valuable addition to the nation.

Control of the Mississippi

By 1800, almost one million Americans lived between the Appalachian Mountains and the Mississippi. Most were farmers.

With few roads west of the Appalachians, western farmers relied on the Mississippi to ship their wheat and corn. First, they sent their produce down the river to New Orleans. From there, oceangoing ships carried the produce to ports along the Atlantic coast.

Threats from Spain and France

Spain sometimes threatened to close the port of New Orleans to Americans. In 1795, President Washington sent Thomas Pinckney to find a way to keep the vital port open. In the **Pinckney Treaty**, Spain agreed to let Americans ship their goods down the Mississippi and store them in New Orleans. The treaty also settled a dispute over the northern border of Spanish Florida.

For a time, Americans sent their goods to New Orleans without a problem. Then, however, Spain signed a treaty with Napoleon Bonaparte, the ruler of France. The treaty gave Louisiana back to France. President Jefferson was alarmed. Napoleon had already set out to conquer Europe. Jefferson feared that Napoleon might now try to build an empire in North America.

Revolt in Haiti

President Jefferson had good reason to worry. Napoleon wanted to grow food in Louisiana and ship it to French islands in the West Indies. However, events in Haiti soon ruined Napoleon's plan.

Haiti was the richest French colony in the Caribbean. There, enslaved Africans worked sugar plantations that made French planters wealthy. Inspired by the French Revolution, the African slaves in Haiti decided to fight for their liberty. **Toussaint L'Ouverture** (too SAN loo vehr TYOOR) led the revolt. By 1801, Toussaint and his followers had nearly forced the French out of Haiti.

Napoleon sent troops to retake Haiti. Although the French captured Toussaint, they did not regain control of the island. In 1804, Haitians declared their independence. Napoleon's dream of an empire in the Americas ended with the loss of Haiti.

Buying Louisiana

Meanwhile, President Jefferson decided to try to buy the city of New Orleans from Napoleon. Jefferson wanted to be sure that American farmers would always be able to ship their goods through the port. The President sent Robert Livingston and James Monroe to buy New Orleans and West Florida from the French. Jefferson said they could offer as much as $10 million.

A surprising deal

Livingston and Monroe negotiated with Talleyrand, the French foreign minister. At first, Talleyrand showed little interest in their offer. However, changing conditions in Haiti and in Europe were causing Napoleon to alter his plans for the future.

After losing Haiti, Napoleon had abandoned his plan for an empire in the Americas. He also needed money to pay for his very costly wars in Europe. Suddenly Talleyrand asked Livingston if the United States wanted to buy all of Louisiana, not just New Orleans.

Livingston and Monroe carefully debated the matter. They had no authority to buy all of Louisiana. However, they knew that Jefferson wanted control of the Mississippi. They agreed to pay the French $15 million for Louisiana. When he signed the treaty with France, Livingston proudly declared,

> “We have lived long, but this is the noblest work of our whole lives. . . . From this day the United States take their place among the powers of the first rank.”

Viewing History **A View of New Orleans**

New Orleans, shown here in an 1803 painting by John L. Boqueta de Woiseri, grew prosperous by controlling trade on the Mississippi River. The city's strategic location near the Gulf of Mexico was one reason for the Louisiana Purchase.

★ **How does this 1803 painting show the prosperity of New Orleans?**

Was the purchase constitutional?

Jefferson was pleased by the news from France, but he was not sure that he in fact had the constitutional power to purchase Louisiana. He had always insisted that the federal government had only those powers spelled out in the Constitution. The document said nothing about a President's power to buy land.

After giving it much thought, Jefferson decided that he did have the authority to buy Louisiana. The Constitution, he reasoned, allowed the President to make treaties. At his request, the Senate quickly approved a treaty making the **Louisiana Purchase.** In 1803, the United States took control of the vast lands west of the Mississippi.

Jefferson Plans an Expedition

The United States owned Louisiana now, but few Americans knew anything about the territory. In 1803, Congress provided money for a team of explorers to study the new lands. Jefferson chose Meriwether Lewis, his private secretary, to head the expedition. An **expedition** is a long journey or voyage of exploration. Lewis asked William Clark, another Virginian, to go with him. About 50 men made up the original band.

Jefferson gave Lewis and Clark careful instructions. He asked them to map a route to the Pacific Ocean. He also told them to study the climate, wildlife, and mineral resources of the new lands. The President requested a detailed report on the following:

> ❝ Climate as characterized by the thermometer, by the proportion of rainy, cloudy, and clear days, by lightning, hail, snow, ice... by the winds prevailing at different seasons, the dates at which particular plants put forth or lose their flower, or leaf, times of appearance of particular birds, reptiles or insects. ❞

Jefferson also instructed Lewis and Clark to learn about the Indian nations who lived in the Louisiana Purchase. For decades, these Native Americans had carried on a very busy trade with English, French, and Spanish merchants. Jefferson hoped that the Indians might trade with American merchants instead. Therefore, he urged Lewis and Clark to tell the Indians of "our wish to be neighborly, friendly, and useful to them."

The Lewis and Clark Expedition

In May 1804, **Lewis and Clark** started up the Missouri River from St. Louis. In time, their trip would take them to the Pacific Ocean. (Follow their route on the map on page 201.)

Across the plains

At first, the expedition's boats made slow progress against the Missouri's swift current. One night, the current tore away the riverbank where they were camping. The party had to scramble into the boats to avoid being swept downstream.

Lewis and Clark kept journals on their travels. They marveled at the broad, grassy plains that stretched "as far as the eye can reach." Everywhere, they saw "immense herds of buffalo, deer, elk, and antelopes."

As they traveled across the plains, the expedition met people of various Indian nations. Lewis and Clark had brought many gifts for Native Americans. They carried medals stamped with the United States seal. They also brought mirrors, beads, knives, blankets, and thousands of sewing needles and fishhooks.

During the first winter, Lewis and Clark stayed with the Mandans in present-day North Dakota. The explorers planned to continue up the Missouri in the spring. However, they worried about how they would cross the steep Rocky Mountains.

Connections With Science

Acting as botanist for the expedition, Meriwether Lewis collected and preserved many plants. He carefully dried and pressed each specimen. Of the more than 200 specimens Lewis brought back, 39 still remain at the Academy of Natural Sciences in Philadelphia.

Skills FOR LIFE

Critical Thinking | Managing Information | Communication | **Maps, Charts, and Graphs**

Following Map Routes

How Will I Use This Skill?

You can use map routes to find your way through a school or office building. With a road map, you can chart a route from home to other places. You can also give directions to others.

LEARN the Skill

You can follow a map route by using the steps below.

1. Identify the map's subject and symbols that indicate routes.
2. Use the directional arrow that identifies N, S, E, and W to determine in what direction a route goes. Recognize other directions, such as northeast (NE), the direction between N and E. Other directions are southeast (SE), southwest (SW), and northwest (NW).
3. Use the scale of miles to determine the distance of a route.
4. Choose the map route you will follow and describe it in terms of direction and distance.

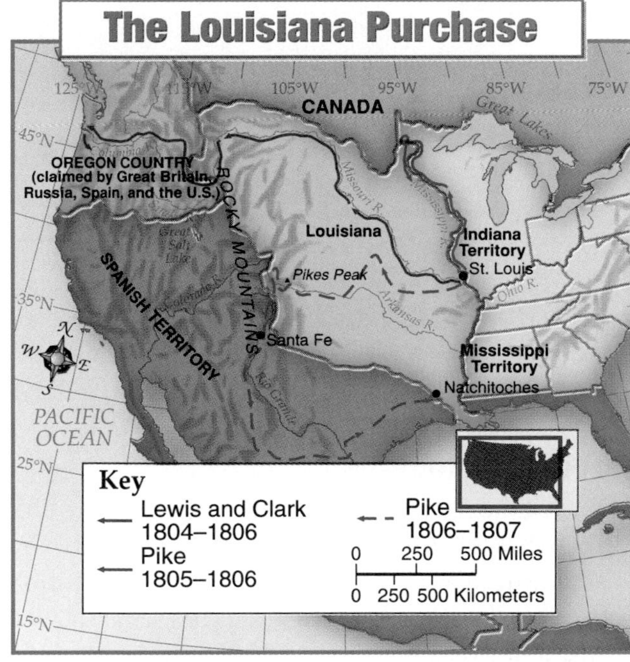

PRACTICE the Skill

Using the steps and the map above, answer the following questions.

1. What does the map show? What symbols represent routes?
2. In what general direction did Lewis and Clark travel from St. Louis?
3. About how many miles did Lewis and Clark travel in order to reach the Pacific Ocean?
4. Describe Pike's route from St. Louis to Natchitoches.

APPLY the Skill

Using a map of your community, describe the route that you follow to travel from home to school or to any other destination, such as a library or a park.

Antelope

Viewing HISTORY **The Way West**

In this painting, Lewis, Clark, and Sacajawea stand at the Great Falls of the Missouri River in 1804. Accompanying them is York, an enslaved African American in the service of Clark. After serving as a valuable member of the Lewis and Clark expedition, York was freed. He returned to the West to live with the Native Americans.

★ **Why did Lewis and Clark include Sacajawea in the expedition?**

Over the Rockies

A Shoshone woman, **Sacajawea** (sahk uh juh WEE uh), was also staying with the Mandans that winter. The Shoshones (shoh SHOH neez) lived in the Rockies. Sacajawea and her French Canadian husband agreed to accompany Lewis and Clark and serve as translators.

In early spring, the party set out. In the foothills of the Rockies, the landscape and wildlife changed. Bighorn sheep ran along the high hills. The thorns of prickly pear cactus jabbed the explorers' moccasins. One day, a grizzly bear chased Lewis while he was exploring alone.

Sacajawea contributed greatly to the success of the expedition. She gathered wild vegetables and advised the men where to fish and hunt. She knew about the healing qualities of plants and herbs, so the expedition relied on her for medical help.

In the mountains, Sacajawea recognized the lands of her people. One day, Lewis met some Shoshone leaders and invited them back to camp. Sacajawea began to "dance and show every mark of the most extravagant joy." One of the men, she explained, was her brother. The Shoshone people supplied the expedition with food and horses. The Shoshones also advised Lewis and Clark about the best route to take over the Rockies.

In the Rocky Mountains, Lewis and Clark crossed the **Continental Divide.** A continental divide is a mountain ridge that separates river systems flowing toward opposite sides of a continent. In North America, some rivers flow east from the Rockies into the Mississippi, which drains into the Gulf of Mexico. Other rivers flow west from the Rockies and empty into the Pacific Ocean.

To the Pacific

After building canoes, Lewis and Clark's party floated down the Columbia River. It carried them into the Pacific Northwest.

On November 7, 1805, Lewis and Clark finally reached their goal. Lewis wrote in his journal: "Great joy in camp. We are in view of the ocean, this great Pacific Ocean which we have been so long anxious to see." On a nearby tree, Clark carved, "By Land from the U. States in 1804 & 5."

The return trip to St. Louis took another year. In 1806, Americans celebrated the return of Lewis and Clark. The explorers brought back much useful information about the Louisiana Purchase.

Pike Explores the West

Before Lewis and Clark returned, another explorer set out from St. Louis. From 1805 to 1807, **Zebulon Pike** explored the upper Mississippi River, the Arkansas River, and parts of present-day Colorado and New Mexico. In November 1806, Pike viewed a mountain peak rising above the Colorado plains. Today, this mountain is known as Pikes Peak.

Continuing further westward into the Rocky Mountains, Pike came upon a small river. It was the Rio Grande. Pike had entered into Spanish territory. Spanish troops soon arrested Pike and his men and took them into Mexico.

After being questioned and detained for a while, the Americans were escorted through Texas back into the United States. Pike's maps and journals had been confiscated by the Spanish. Still, Pike was able to remember enough to write a report. The report greatly expanded Americans' knowledge about the Southwest.

The journeys of Zebulon Pike and Lewis and Clark excited Americans. It was a number of years, however, before settlers moved into the rugged western lands. As you will read, they first settled the region closest to the Mississippi River. Soon, the territory around New Orleans had a large enough white population for the settlers to apply for statehood. In 1812, this territory entered the Union as the state of Louisiana.

★ Section 2 Review ★

Recall

1. **Locate** **(a)** Mississippi River, **(b)** St. Louis, **(c)** Missouri River, **(d)** Rocky Mountains, **(e)** Columbia River, **(f)** Pikes Peak.
2. **Identify** **(a)** Pinckney Treaty, **(b)** Toussaint L'Ouverture, **(c)** Louisiana Purchase, **(d)** Lewis and Clark, **(e)** Sacajawea, **(f)** Zebulon Pike.
3. **Define** **(a)** expedition, **(b)** Continental Divide.

Comprehension

4. Why did western farmers oppose Spanish and French control of New Orleans?
5. Why was the United States able to buy Louisiana at a very low price?
6. Did Lewis and Clark accomplish what President Jefferson had asked them to do? Explain.

Critical Thinking and Writing

7. **Drawing Conclusions** Was Jefferson's purchase of Louisiana based on a strict or loose interpretation of the Constitution? Explain.
8. **Making Decisions** If you had been a Native American leader of the time, would you have welcomed Lewis and Clark in friendship? Explain the reasons for your decision.

Activity **Writing a Diary** Westward Ho! You are with Lewis and Clark as they travel to the Pacific. Write several diary entries describing what you see and feel as you explore Louisiana and meet the Native Americans who live there.

New Threats From Overseas

As You Read

Explore These Questions

- How did overseas trade grow in the late 1700s?
- How did war in Europe hurt American trade?
- Why was the Embargo Act a failure?

Define

- impressment
- embargo
- smuggler

Identify

- Barbary States
- Stephen Decatur
- Embargo Act
- Nonintercourse Act

SETTING the Scene James Brown, a young American sailor, wrote a letter. It was smuggled from a British ship and carried to the United States. The message described a desperate situation:

> “Being on shore one day in Lisbon, Portugal, I was [seized] by a gang and brought on board the [British ship] *Conqueror,* where I am still confined. Never have I been allowed to put my foot on shore since I was brought on board, which is now three years.”

Brown's situation was not unusual. In the early 1800s, the British navy forced thousands of American sailors to serve on their ships. This was only one of many dangers that Americans faced as their sea trade began to thrive.

The British navy seized American sailors.

Trading Around the World

After the Revolution, American overseas trade grew rapidly. Ships sailed from New England ports on voyages that sometimes lasted three years. Everywhere they went, Yankee captains kept a sharp lookout for new goods to trade and new markets in which to sell. One clever trader sawed up the winter ice from New England ponds, packed it deep in sawdust for insulation, and carried it to India. There, he traded the ice for silk and spices.

In 1784, the *Empress of China* became the first American ship to trade with China. Before long, New England merchants built up a profitable trade with China. Yankee traders took ginseng, a plant that grew wild in New England, and exchanged it for Chinese silks and tea. The Chinese used the roots of the ginseng plant for medicines.

Yankee merchants sailed up the Pacific coast of North America in the 1790s. In fact, Yankee traders visited the Columbia River more than 10 years before Lewis and Clark. So many traders from Boston visited the Pacific Northwest that Native Americans called every white man “Boston.” Traders bought furs from Native Americans. Then they sold the furs for large profits in China.

War With Tripoli

American traders ran great risks, especially in the Mediterranean Sea. For many years, pirates from nations along the coast of

North Africa attacked vessels from Europe and the United States. The North African nations were called the **Barbary States.** To protect American ships, the United States paid a yearly tribute, or bribe, to the rulers of the Barbary States.

In the early 1800s, Tripoli, one of the Barbary States, demanded a larger bribe than usual. When President Jefferson refused to pay, Tripoli declared war on the United States. In response, Jefferson ordered the navy to blockade the port of Tripoli.

During the blockade, the American ship *Philadelphia* ran aground near Tripoli. Pirates boarded the ship and hauled the crew to prison. The pirates planned to use the *Philadelphia* to attack other ships.

Then, **Stephen Decatur,** a United States Navy officer, took action. Very late one night, Decatur and his crew quietly sailed a ship into Tripoli harbor. When they reached the captured American ship, they set it on fire so that the pirates could not use it.

In the meantime, American marines landed on the coast of North Africa. They then marched 500 miles (805 km) to launch a surprise attack on Tripoli. The war with Tripoli lasted until 1805. In the end, the ruler of Tripoli signed a treaty promising not to interfere with American ships.

American Neutrality Is Violated

During the early 1800s, American ships faced another problem. In 1803, Britain and France went to war again. At first, Americans profited from the war. British and French ships were too busy fighting to engage in trade. American merchants took advantage of the war to trade with both sides. As trade increased, American shipbuilders hurried to build new ships.

Of course, neither Britain nor France wanted the United States to sell supplies to its enemy. As in the 1790s, they ignored American claims of neutrality. Each nation tried to stop American trade with the other. Napoleon seized American ships bound for England, and the British stopped Yankee traders on their way to France. Between

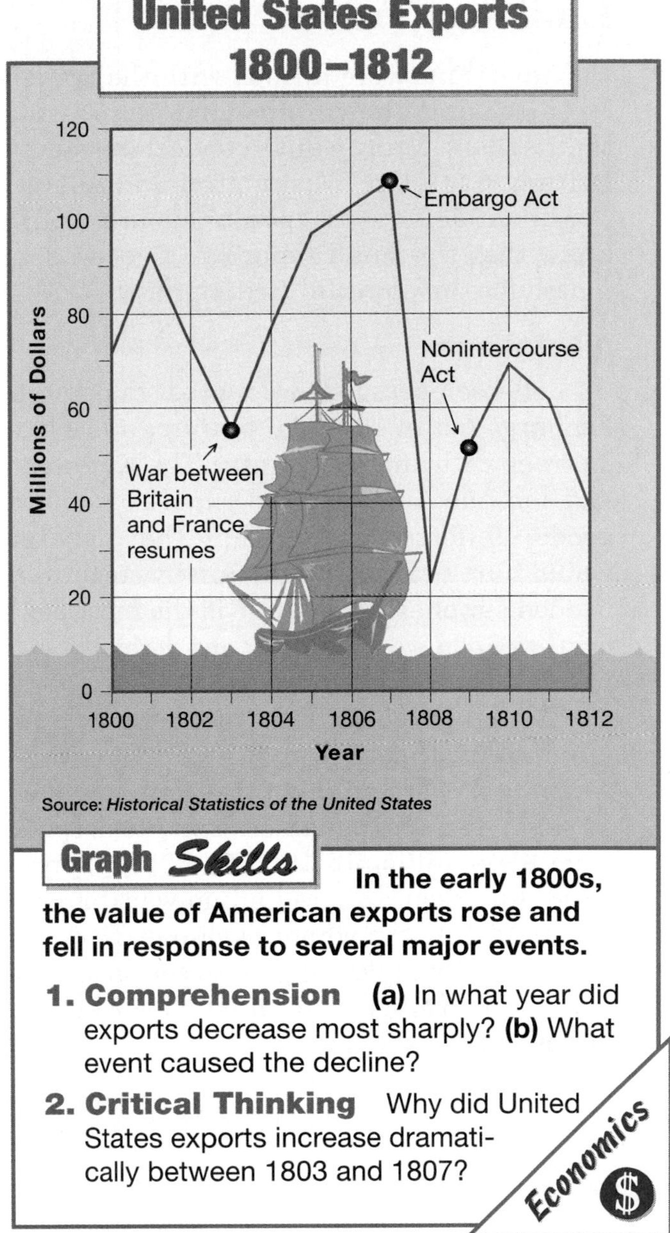

Graph *Skills* **In the early 1800s, the value of American exports rose and fell in response to several major events.**

1. **Comprehension** **(a)** In what year did exports decrease most sharply? **(b)** What event caused the decline?
2. **Critical Thinking** Why did United States exports increase dramatically between 1803 and 1807?

1805 and 1807, hundreds of American ships were captured.

The British navy also seized American sailors and forced them to serve on British ships. This practice of forcing people into service, called **impressment,** was common in Britain. For centuries, impressment gangs had raided villages and forced young men to serve in the navy.

Because the British navy needed more men to fight France, British ships stopped and searched American vessels. British officers seized all British sailors serving on American ships. They also impressed thousands of American sailors.

Limits on Trade

Americans were furious with the British for attacking their ships and impressing their sailors. Many wanted to declare war on Britain. Still, like Washington and Adams, President Jefferson hoped to avoid war. He knew that the small American fleet was no match for the powerful British navy.

A total ban

Jefferson persuaded Congress to pass the Embargo Act in 1807. An **embargo** is a ban on trade with another country. The **Embargo Act** forbade Americans to export or import goods. Jefferson hoped that the embargo would hurt France and Britain by cutting off needed supplies. "Our trade is the most powerful weapon we can use in our defense," one Republican newspaper wrote.

The embargo hurt Britain and France, but it hurt the United States even more. Americans were unable to get imports such as sugar, tea, and molasses. Exports dropped from $108 million in 1807 to $22 million in 1808. American sailors had no work. Farmers could not ship wheat overseas. Docks in the South were piled high with cotton and tobacco. The Embargo Act hurt New England merchants most of all.

Merchants from New England and other parts of the country protested loudly against the embargo. Some went a step further and became smugglers. A **smuggler** is a person who violates trade laws by illegally sneaking goods into or out of a country.

To stop defiance of the law, President Jefferson began using the navy and federal troops to enforce the embargo. On the border between New York and Canada, smugglers fought back. Some engaged in skirmishes with federal troops. Others, disguised as Indians, fired on federal ships.

A limited ban

After more than a year, Jefferson admitted that the Embargo Act had failed. In 1809, Congress replaced it with the less severe **Nonintercourse Act**. It allowed Americans to carry on trade with all nations except Britain and France.

The embargo was the most unpopular measure of Jefferson's years in office. Still, the Republicans remained strong. In 1808, Jefferson followed the precedent set by Washington and refused to run for a third term. James Madison, his fellow Republican, easily won the presidential election. Madison hoped that Britain and France would soon agree to stop violating American neutrality.

★ Section 3 Review ★

Recall

1. **Identify** **(a)** Barbary States, **(b)** Stephen Decatur, **(c)** Embargo Act, **(d)** Nonintercourse Act.
2. **Define** **(a)** impressment, **(b)** embargo, **(c)** smuggler.

Comprehension

3. How did American merchants expand their trading operations in the 1780s and 1790s?
4. How did war in Europe affect American overseas trade?
5. **(a)** What was the purpose of the Embargo Act? **(b)** Why did it fail?

Critical Thinking and Writing

6. **Making Generalizations** How can war both benefit and hurt the economy of a neutral nation? Explain.
7. **Predicting Consequences** What do you think the United States will do if Britain and France continue to violate American neutrality after 1809?

Activity **Drawing a Cartoon** Suppose the United States were under a limited or total embargo today. Draw a cartoon showing how such an embargo might affect you.

The Road to War

As You Read

Explore These Questions

- Why did the Prophet and Tecumseh unite Native Americans?
- How did fighting on the frontier lead to war with Britain?
- Why did War Hawks want war with Britain?

Define

- neutral
- nationalism

Identify

- Treaty of Greenville
- Tecumseh
- the Prophet
- William Henry Harrison
- Battle of Tippecanoe
- War Hawks
- Henry Clay

James Madison was a quiet, scholarly man. He had helped to write the Constitution and to pass the Bill of Rights. As President, he hoped to keep the United States out of war.

Many Americans, however, felt that Madison's approach was too timid. They argued that the United States must stand up to Native Americans and foreign countries. How could the nation grow if Native Americans stood in the way? How could the nation win respect if it allowed the British and French navies to seize American ships? The cost of war might be great, said one member of Congress. Yet, he continued, who would count in money "the slavery of our impressed seamen"?

This kind of talk aroused the nation. In the early 1800s, the United States went to war with several Native American nations. By 1812, many Americans were also calling for war with Britain.

Conflict With Native Americans

Thousands of white settlers had moved into the Northwest Territory in the 1790s. The large number of newcomers caused problems for Native Americans. The settlers ignored treaties the United States had signed with Indian nations of the region. They built farms on Indian lands. They hunted the animals that Indians depended on for food.

In the 1790s, U.S. infantry soldiers wore coats such as the one shown here.

Fighting often broke out between the Native Americans and settlers. Isolated acts of violence led to larger acts of revenge. As a result, both sides killed innocent people who had not taken part in acts of violence. In this way, warfare spread and minor conflicts grew into larger ones.

In 1791, the Miamis of Ohio joined with other Indian nations. Little Turtle, a skilled fighter, led the Miami nation. Armed with muskets and gunpowder supplied by the British, the Miamis drove white settlers from the area.

In 1794, President Washington sent General Anthony Wayne with a well-trained army into Miami territory. The Native American forces gathered at a place called Fallen Timbers. They thought that Wayne would have trouble fighting there because fallen trees covered the land. However, Wayne's army pushed through the tangle of logs and defeated the Indians.

In 1795, leaders of the Miamis and a number of other Indian nations signed the **Treaty of Greenville.** They gave up land that would later become part of Ohio. In return, they received $20,000 and the promise of more money if they kept the peace.

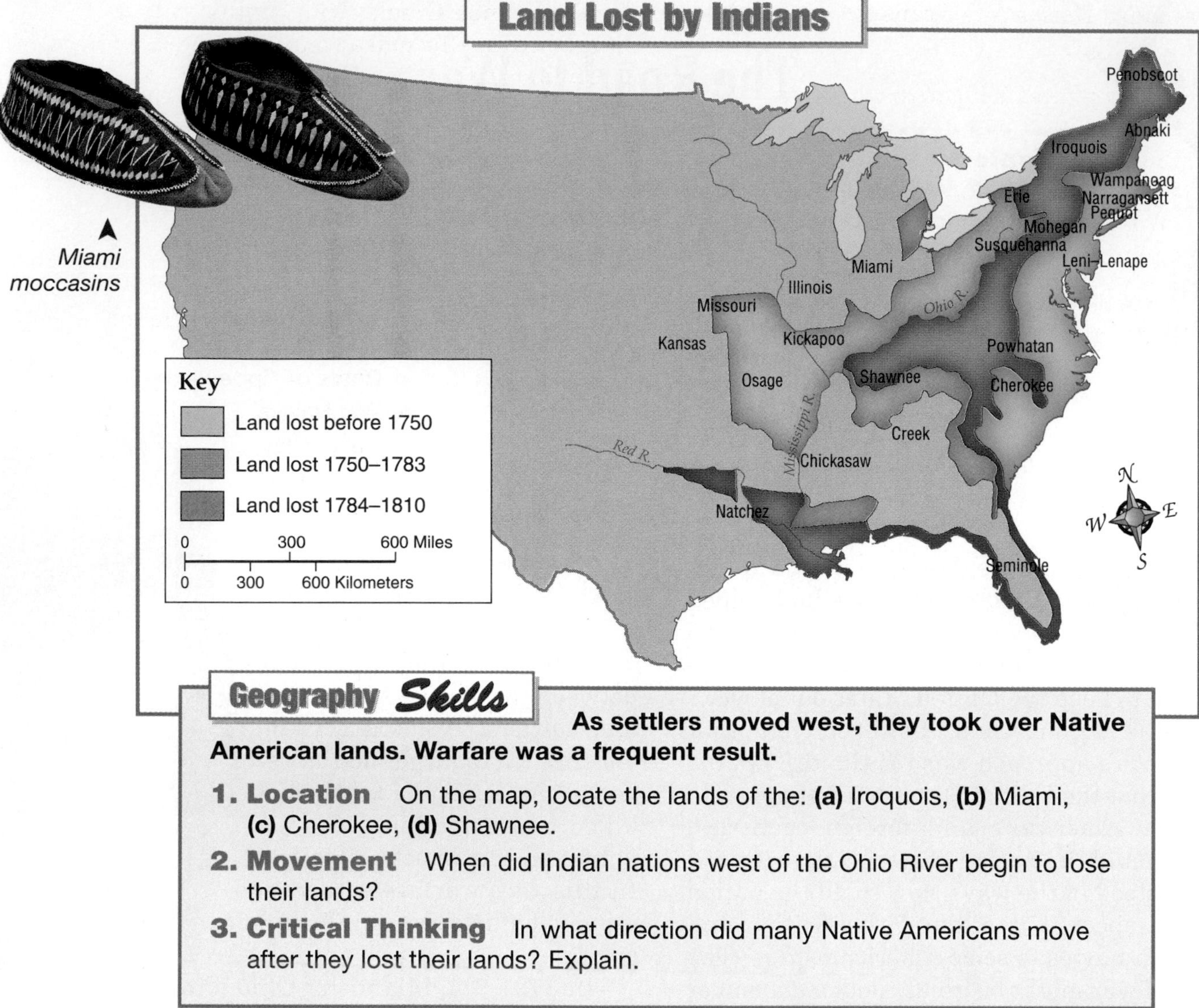

Miami moccasins

Geography Skills **As settlers moved west, they took over Native American lands. Warfare was a frequent result.**

1. **Location** On the map, locate the lands of the: **(a)** Iroquois, **(b)** Miami, **(c)** Cherokee, **(d)** Shawnee.
2. **Movement** When did Indian nations west of the Ohio River begin to lose their lands?
3. **Critical Thinking** In what direction did many Native Americans move after they lost their lands? Explain.

Tecumseh's Confederation

Ohio joined the Union in 1803. By then, white settlers were pushing beyond Ohio into Indiana Territory. Many Native Americans grew angry. They wanted to keep settlers from taking more Indian land. Among those who felt this way were two Shawnee leaders: **Tecumseh** (tih KUHM suh) and his brother, called **the Prophet**.

Unity and the Old Ways

The Prophet said that he had journeyed to the spirit world. There, he learned the path that Indians must take if they were to live happily. Both the Prophet and Tecumseh said that white customs corrupted the Native American way of life. They said that many Indians depended on white trade goods, such as muskets, cloth, cooking pots, and whiskey. They believed that by returning to the old ways, Indians could gain the power to resist white invaders.

In 1808, the Prophet built a village for his followers along Tippecanoe Creek in Indiana Territory. Indians traveled from lands as far away as Missouri, Iowa, and Minnesota to hear his message. His teachings brought hope to many.

In the early 1800s, Tecumseh and the Prophet organized many Native American nations into a confederation, or league. The Prophet was the spiritual leader of the confederation and Tecumseh was its spokesperson. Tecumseh and the Prophet persuaded Native Americans to unite against white settlers:

> “The whites have driven us from the great salt water, forced us over the mountains. . . . The way. . . to check and stop this evil is for all red men to unite in claiming a common equal right in the land.”

Tecumseh also impressed white leaders. **William Henry Harrison,** governor of Indiana Territory, grudgingly admitted, “He is one of those uncommon geniuses which spring up occasionally to produce revolutions and overturn the established order of things.”

Showdown at Tippecanoe

Rivalries among Native American nations kept Tecumseh from uniting all Indians east of the Mississippi River. Still, white settlers were alarmed at his success.

In 1811, Governor Harrison marched 1,000 soldiers against Tecumseh's town on the Tippecanoe Creek. The Prophet was in charge because Tecumseh was away organizing Indians in the South. The Prophet led a surprise night attack on Harrison's troops. Neither side won a clear victory in the battle that followed. Still, whites celebrated the **Battle of Tippecanoe** as a major victory.

Growing Conflict With Britain

The fighting with Native Americans caused relations between the United States and Britain to worsen. The British were supplying guns and ammunition to the Native Americans on the frontier. They were also encouraging Indians to attack United States' settlements.

Meanwhile, the United States and Britain also continued to disagree over trade. When the embargo against Britain and France was set to expire in 1810, the United States made a very daring offer. If either the British or French would stop seizing

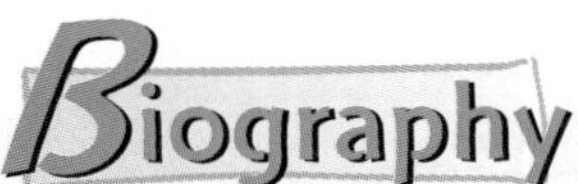

Tecumseh and the Prophet

Tecumseh (left) and the Prophet (right) felt that no Indian nation could sell land unless all other Indian nations agreed. Tecumseh said, “Sell a country! Why not sell the air, the great sea, as well as the earth?” ★ **Why did Tecumseh and the Prophet dislike the Treaty of Greenville?**

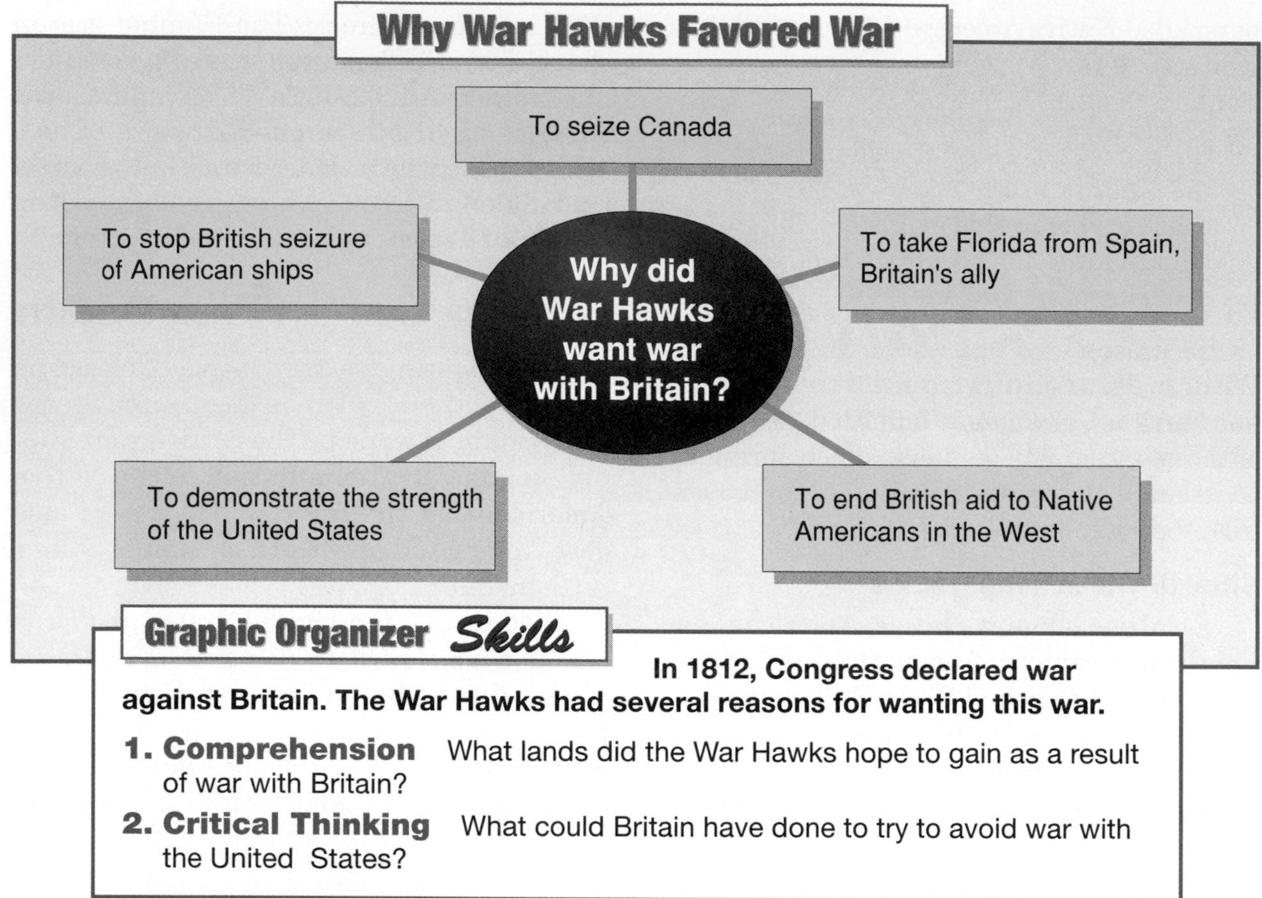

Graphic Organizer *Skills* **In 1812, Congress declared war against Britain. The War Hawks had several reasons for wanting this war.**

1. **Comprehension** What lands did the War Hawks hope to gain as a result of war with Britain?
2. **Critical Thinking** What could Britain have done to try to avoid war with the United States?

American ships, the United States would halt trade with the other nation.

Seizing the chance, Napoleon quickly announced that France would respect the United States' policy of staying **neutral,** or uninvolved in the war between Britain and France. As promised, the United States continued trade with France, but stopped all shipments to Britain.

The War Hawks

While President Madison did not want war, other Americans were not as cautious. Except in New England, where many merchants wanted to restore trade with Britain, anti-British feeling ran strong. Members of Congress from the South and the West called for war with Britain. They were known as **War Hawks**.

War Hawks had a strong sense of nationalism. **Nationalism** is pride in or devotion to one's country. War Hawks felt that Britain was treating the United States as if it were still a British colony. They were willing to fight a war to defend American rights.

Arguments for war

Henry Clay of Kentucky was the most outspoken War Hawk. Clay wanted war for two reasons. He wanted revenge on Britain for seizing American ships. He also wanted to conquer Canada. "The militia of Kentucky are alone [able] to place Montreal and Upper Canada at your feet," Clay boasted to Congress. Canadians, Clay believed, would be happy to leave the British empire and join the United States.

War Hawks saw other advantages of war with Britain. South of the United States, Florida belonged to Spain, Britain's ally. If Americans went to war with Britain, War Hawks said, the United States could seize Florida from Spain.

War Hawks had yet another reason to fight Britain. They pointed out that Britain was arming Native Americans on the frontier and encouraging them to attack settlers. The War Hawks felt that winning a war against Britain would bring lasting peace and safety to American settlers on the frontier.

Congress Declares War

In 1811, the United States and Britain drifted closer to war. To prevent Americans from trading with France, British warships blockaded some American ports. The British continued to board American ships and impress American seamen. In May 1811, near New York Harbor, a brief battle broke out between an American frigate and a British warship. The Americans crippled the British ship and left 32 British dead or wounded.

The War Hawks urged that Congress prepare for a war against Britain. One of the most radical and outspoken of the War Hawks was Felix Grundy, a Congressman from Tennessee. In December 1811, he gave a very emotional speech describing what he saw as the benefits of war:

> “This war... will have its advantages. We shall drive the British from our continent—they will no longer have an opportunity of intriguing with our Indian neighbors.”

Grundy hoped that a war with Britain would achieve other more ambitious goals. Like most War Hawks, he dreamed of winning additional land for the United States. He closed his speech with these words: "I therefore feel anxious not only to add the Floridas to the South, but the Canadas to the North of this empire."

Others in Congress opposed the strong views of the War Hawks. John Randolph of Virginia warned that the people of the United States would "not submit to be taxed for this war of conquest and dominion." Representatives of New England were especially concerned. They feared that the British navy would attack New England seaports.

President Madison at last gave in to war fever. In June 1812, he asked Congress to declare war on Britain. The House voted 79 to 49 in favor of war. The Senate vote was 19 to 13. Americans soon discovered, however, that winning the war would not be as easy as declaring it.

Cannon used in the war against Britain

★ Section 4 Review ★

Recall

1. **Locate** Native American lands lost **(a)** from 1750 to 1783, **(b)** from 1784 to 1810.
2. **Identify** **(a)** Treaty of Greenville, **(b)** Tecumseh, **(c)** the Prophet, **(d)** William Henry Harrison, **(e)** Battle of Tippecanoe, **(f)** War Hawks, **(g)** Henry Clay.
3. **Define** **(a)** neutral, **(b)** nationalism.

Comprehension

4. Why was there conflict between Native Americans and white settlers?
5. How did the Battle of Tippecanoe help lead to war between Britain and the United States?
6. What did the War Hawks hope to gain from a war with Britain?

Critical Thinking and Writing

7. **Identifying Main Ideas** What ideas did the Prophet and Tecumseh use to unite many Native Americans?
8. **Defending a Position** In 1812, would you have favored or opposed war with Britain? Explain the reasons for your position.

Activity **Writing a Speech** You are a Native American leader of the early 1800s. Write a speech explaining why you are against white settlement and what you think Native Americans can do to stop it. Deliver your speech to the class.

The War of 1812

As You Read

Explore These Questions

- How was the United States unready for war with Britain?
- What were the major turning points of the war in the West?
- What were the results of the war?

Identify

- Oliver Hazard Perry
- Battle of Lake Erie
- Andrew Jackson
- Battle of Horseshoe Bend
- Dolley Madison
- Battle of New Orleans
- Richard Allen
- Hartford Convention
- Treaty of Ghent

Many Americans welcomed the news of war with Britain. In some cities, they fired cannons and guns and danced in the streets. One New Jersey man wrote a song calling for a swift attack on Canada:

> "On to Quebec's embattled halls!
> Who will pause, when glory calls?
> Charge, soldiers, charge, its lofty
> walls. And storm its strong artillery."

Other Americans were less enthusiastic. New Englanders, especially, talked scornfully of "Mr. Madison's war." In fact, before the war ended, some New Englanders would threaten to leave the Union and make a separate peace with Britain.

Unready for War

The American declaration of war took the British by surprise. They were locked in a bitter struggle with Napoleon, and could not spare troops to fight the United States. As the war began, however, the United States faced difficulties of its own.

Because Jefferson believed in a small federal government and had reduced spending on defense, the United States was not ready for war. The navy had only 16 ships to fight against the huge British fleet. The army was small and ill equipped. Moreover, many of the officers knew little about the military. "The state of the Army," commented a member of Congress, "is enough to make any man who has the smallest love of country wish to get rid of it."

Since there were few regular troops, the government relied on volunteers to fight the war. Congress voted to give them $124 and 360 acres of land for their service. The money was high pay at the time—equal to a year's salary for most workers.

Attracted by money and the chance to own their own farm, young men eagerly enlisted. They were poorly trained, however, and did not know how to be good soldiers. Many deserted after a few months.

Fighting at Sea

The British navy blockaded American ports to stop Americans from trading with other countries. The small American navy was unable to break the blockade. Still, several sea captains won stunning victories.

One famous battle took place early in the war, in August 1812. As he was sailing near Newfoundland, Isaac Hull, captain of the *Constitution*, spotted the British ship *Guerrière* (gai ree AIR). For nearly an hour, the two ships jockeyed for position.

At last, the guns of the *Constitution* roared into action. They tore holes in the sides of the *Guerrière* and shot off both masts. When the smoke cleared, Hull asked the British captain if he had "struck" his flag—that is, lowered his flag in surrender. "Well, I don't know," replied the stunned British captain. "Our mizzenmast is gone, our mainmast

AmericanHeritage
MAGAZINE

HISTORY HAPPENED HERE

The USS Constitution

The USS Constitution *became known as "Old Ironsides" because British cannonballs often bounced off her thick wooden hull. In 1905, the ship was docked in Boston and opened to the public. In 1997, the ship underwent major restoration. Today, the United States Navy invites you to come aboard and tour "Old Ironsides." In the nearby museum, you can relive history by commanding a ship, hoisting a sail, or firing a cannon.*

★ ***To learn more about this historic ship, write:*** *USS* Constitution *Museum, Charlestown Navy Yard, Charlestown, MA 02129.*

is gone. And, upon the whole, you may say we *have* struck our flag."

American sea captains won other victories at sea. These victories cheered Americans, but did little to win the war.

War in the West

One goal of the War Hawks was to conquer Canada. They were convinced that Canadians would welcome the chance to throw off British rule and join the United States. The United States planned to invade Canada at three different points: Detroit, the Niagara River, and Montreal.

Invasion of Canada

General William Hull moved American troops into Canada from Detroit. The Canadians had only a few untrained troops to ward off the invasion. However, they were led by a clever and skillful British leader, General Isaac Brock.

Brock paraded his soldiers in red coats to make it appear that experienced British troops were helping the Canadians. He also let a message with false information fall into American hands. It exaggerated the number of Indians who were fighting with the Canadians. Brock's scare tactics worked. Hull retreated from Canada.

Other attempts to invade Canada also failed. Americans were wrong in thinking that the Canadians would welcome them as liberators from British rule. Instead, the Canadians fought fiercely and forced the Americans into retreat.

Battle of Lake Erie

In 1813, the Americans set out to win control of Lake Erie. Captain **Oliver Hazard Perry** had no fleet, so he designed and built his own ships. In September 1813, he sailed his tiny fleet against the British.

During the **Battle of Lake Erie**, the British battered Perry's own ship and left it

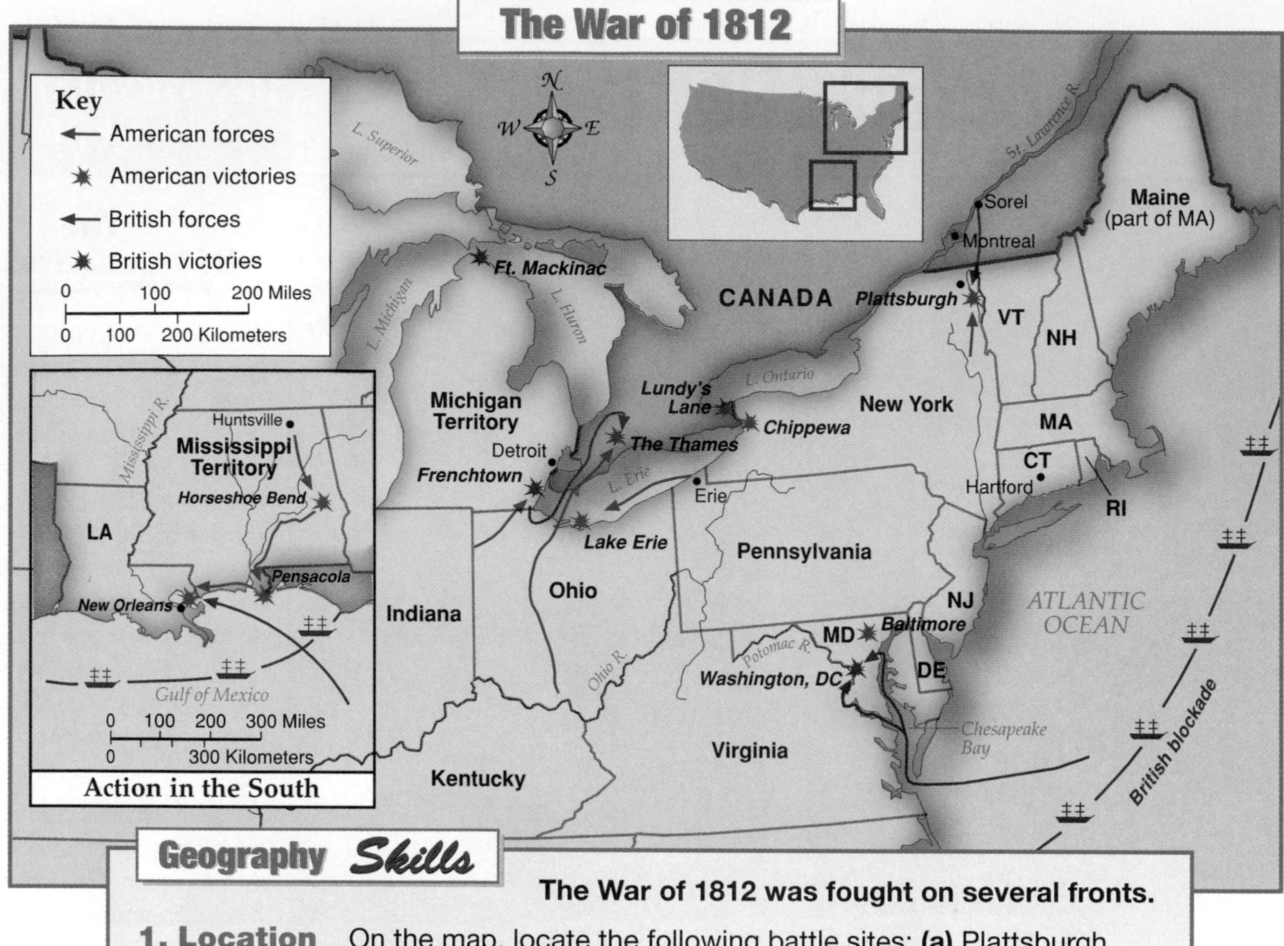

Geography Skills

The War of 1812 was fought on several fronts.

1. **Location** On the map, locate the following battle sites: **(a)** Plattsburgh, **(b)** Lake Erie, **(c)** The Thames, **(d)** Horseshoe Bend, **(e)** Washington, D.C., **(f)** Baltimore, **(g)** New Orleans.
2. **Movement** Using the inset map, describe the route that American forces followed from Huntsville to New Orleans
3. **Critical Thinking** How did the British blockade hurt the economy of the United States?

helpless. Perry took his flag down and rowed over to another American ship. There, he raised the colors again and continued to fight. Finally, the Americans won the battle. Captain Perry wrote his message of victory on the back of an envelope: "We have met the enemy and they are ours."

Native American losses

After losing control of Lake Erie, the British and their ally Tecumseh retreated from Detroit into Canada. General William Henry Harrison, veteran of Tippecanoe, pursued them. The Americans won a decisive victory at the Battle of the Thames. Tecumseh died in the fighting. Without Tecumseh's leadership, the Indian confederation soon fell apart.

Still, the Creeks, Tecumseh's allies in the South, continued their fight against the settlers. **Andrew Jackson,** a Tennessee officer, took command of American troops in the Creek War. In 1814, with the help of the Cherokees, Jackson won a crushing victory at the **Battle of Horseshoe Bend.** The leader of the Creeks walked alone into Jackson's camp to surrender:

> "I am in your power. Do unto me as you please.... If I had an army I would yet fight, and contend to the last.... But your people have destroyed my nation."

For the time being, the fighting ended. Once again, Native Americans had to give up land to whites.

Final Battles

In 1814, Britain and its allies defeated France. With the war in Europe over, Britain could send more troops and ships against the United States.

The British burn Washington

In the summer of 1814, British ships sailed into Chesapeake Bay and landed an invasion force about 30 miles (48 km) from Washington, D.C. American troops met the British at Bladensburg, Maryland. President Madison himself watched the battle. To his dismay, the battle-hardened British quickly scattered the untrained Americans. The British met little further resistance as they continued their march to the capital.

In the White House, **Dolley Madison** waited for her husband to return. Hastily, she scrawled a note to her sister:

> “Will you believe it, my sister? We have had a battle or skirmish near Bladensburg and here I am still within sound of the cannon! Mr. Madison comes not. May God protect us. Two messengers covered with dust come bid me fly. But here I mean to wait for him.”

Soon after, British troops marched into the capital. Dolley Madison gathered up important papers of the President and a portrait of George Washington. Then, she fled south. She was not there to see the British burn the White House and other buildings.

From Washington, the British marched north toward the city of Baltimore. The key to Baltimore's defense was Fort McHenry.

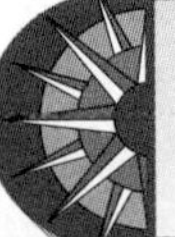

Linking Past and Present

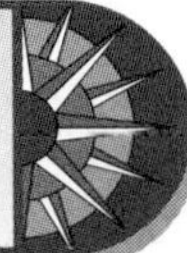

Past

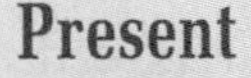

Present

The White House

After capturing Washington in August 1814, the British burned the White House. Margaret Smith, a resident of the city, recalled the sad scene: “Who would have thought that this mass so solid, so magnificent, so grand... [should] be thus irreparably destroyed.” In fact, the White House was not destroyed. A torrential thunderstorm put out the flames and saved the structure. Today, the White House continues to serve as the official residence of Presidents of the United States.” ★ **How do you think the burning of the White House affected American morale?**

Viewing HISTORY **Battle of New Orleans**

In this engraving, Andrew Jackson stands atop the American defense works as he spurs his troops to victory. The Battle of New Orleans was the bloodiest engagement of the War of 1812. Neither side knew that the war had ended two weeks earlier. ★ **Why did it take so long for the news of war's end to reach New Orleans?**

From evening on September 13 until dawn on September 14, British rockets bombarded the harbor.

When the early morning fog lifted, the "broad stripes and bright stars" of the American flag still waved over Fort McHenry. The British withdrew. Francis Scott Key, who witnessed the battle, wrote a poem about the bombardment. Later, "The Star-Spangled Banner" was set to music and adopted as the national anthem of the United States.

Battle of New Orleans

In late 1814, the British prepared to attack New Orleans. From there, they hoped to sail up the Mississippi. However, Andrew Jackson was waiting for the British. Jackson had turned his frontier fighters into a strong army. He took Pensacola in Spanish Florida to keep the British from using it as a base. He then marched through Mobile and set up camp in New Orleans.

Jackson's force included thousands of frontiersmen. Many of them were expert riflemen. In addition, citizens of New Orleans joined the army to defend their city from the approaching British. Among the volunteers were hundreds of African Americans.

The American soldiers dug trenches to defend themselves. On January 8, 1815, the British attacked. Again and again, British soldiers marched toward the American trenches. More than 2,000 British fell under the deadly fire of American sharpshooters and cannons. Only seven Americans died.

All over the United States, Americans cheered the victory at the **Battle of New Orleans**. Andrew Jackson became a national hero. His fame did not dim even when Americans later learned that the battle could have been avoided. It took place two weeks after the United States and Britain had signed a treaty in Europe ending the war.

African Americans in the War

African Americans served alongside other Americans in the fight against the British. African American soldiers helped win the Battle of New Orleans. Following the British attacks on Washington and Baltimore, African American volunteers helped defend Philadelphia against a possible attack. Bishop **Richard Allen** and the Reverend Absalom Jones recruited more than 2,000 men to help build Philadelphia's fortifications. The state of New York, meanwhile, organized two regiments of black volunteers to serve in the army.

African Americans also served with distinction in the United States Navy. They helped win the Battle of Lake Erie as well as other naval battles. Commander Nathaniel Shaler praised one particular black sailor who was killed in battle: "When America has such [sailors], she has little to fear from the tyrants of the ocean."

Peace at Last

In the early 1800s, news took weeks to cross the Atlantic Ocean. By late 1814, Americans knew that peace talks had begun, but they did not know how they were progressing or how long they would last. As Jackson was preparing to fight the British at New Orleans, New Englanders were meeting to protest "Mr. Madison's war."

New Englanders protest

The British blockade had hurt New England's sea trade. Also, many New Englanders feared that the United States might win land in Florida and Canada. If new states were carved out of these lands, the South and the West would become more influential than New England.

Delegates from around New England met in Hartford, Connecticut, in December 1814. Most were Federalists. They disliked the Republican President and the war. The delegates to the **Hartford Convention** threatened to leave the Union if the war continued.

Then, while the delegates debated what to do, news of the peace treaty arrived. The Hartford Convention ended quickly. With the war over, the protest was meaningless.

"Nothing was settled"

The **Treaty of Ghent** was signed in the city of Ghent, Belgium, on December 24, 1814. John Quincy Adams, one of the Americans at Ghent, summed up the treaty in one sentence: "Nothing was adjusted, nothing was settled."

Britain and the United States agreed to restore prewar conditions. The treaty said nothing about impressment or neutrality. These issues had faded due to the end of the Napoleonic Wars in Europe. Other issues were settled later. In 1818, for example, the two nations settled a dispute over the border between Canada and the United States.

Looking back, some Americans felt that the War of 1812 had been a mistake. Others argued that Europe would now treat the young republic with more respect. The victories of heroes like Oliver Hazard Perry and Andrew Jackson gave Americans new pride in their country. As one Republican leader remarked, "The people are now more American. They feel and act more as a nation."

★ Section 5 Review ★

Recall

1. **Locate** **(a)** Lake Erie, **(b)** Detroit, **(c)** Chesapeake Bay, **(d)** Washington, D.C., **(e)** Baltimore, **(f)** New Orleans.
2. **Identify** **(a)** Oliver Hazard Perry, **(b)** Battle of Lake Erie, **(c)** Andrew Jackson, **(d)** Battle of Horseshoe Bend, **(e)** Dolley Madison, **(f)** Battle of New Orleans, **(g)** Richard Allen, **(h)** Hartford Convention, **(i)** Treaty of Ghent.

Comprehension

3. What military problems did the United States face as the War of 1812 began?
4. How did the death of Tecumseh affect the war in the West?
5. What were the results of the War of 1812?

Critical Thinking and Writing

6. **Understanding Causes and Effects** How do you think the War of 1812 helped Andrew Jackson to later become the President of the United States?
7. **Applying Information** Why did the results of the War of 1812 please some Americans, but disappoint others?

★ ★

Activity **Writing a Song** Keep your head down! You are in the trenches at the Battle of New Orleans. Write a song describing what you see, hear, and feel as you help Andrew Jackson defeat the British and save New Orleans.

Chapter 8 Review and Activities

★ Sum It Up ★

Section 1 Republicans in Power

- President Jefferson tried to help ordinary citizens and limit government power.
- The Supreme Court established its power to decide if laws are constitutional.

Section 2 The Louisiana Purchase

- In 1803, the United States bought the vast western territory of Louisiana from France.
- Lewis and Clark explored Louisiana and tried to establish friendly relations with Native Americans.

Section 3 New Threats From Overseas

- American trade increased but was threatened by France and Britain.
- The Embargo Act hurt the United States more than Britain and France.

Section 4 The Road to War

- Native Americans fought to preserve their lands and culture.
- War Hawks wanted war with Britain to protect American trade and to gain new lands.

Section 5 The War of 1812

- Though poorly prepared, American forces defeated the British in key battles.
- Not all Americans supported the war. For many, however, the war brought a new sense of national pride.

For additional review of the major ideas of Chapter 8, see ***Guide to the Essentials of American History*** or ***Interactive Student Tutorial CD-ROM,*** which contains interactive review activities, graphic organizers, and practice tests.

Reviewing the Chapter

Define These Terms

Match each term with the correct definition.

Column 1	Column 2
1. laissez faire	**a.** forcing people into naval service
2. judicial review	**b.** ban on trade with another country
3. impressment	**c.** government should play a very limited role in economic affairs
4. embargo	**d.** pride in one's country
5. nationalism	**e.** Supreme Court's power to decide if laws are constitutional

Explore the Main Ideas

1. Describe two of President Jefferson's ideas about the proper role of government.
2. Why did the United States buy Louisiana from France?
3. What were the goals of the Lewis and Clark expedition?
4. How did war between Britain and France affect the United States?
5. Why did many Native Americans unite under Tecumseh and the Prophet?
6. **(a)** Describe one major turning point in the War of 1812. **(b)** Explain one result of the war.

Geography Skills

Match the letters on the map with the following places: **1.** Canada, **2.** Battle of the Thames, **3.** Battle of Horseshoe Bend, **4.** Battle of New Orleans, **5.** Baltimore, **6.** British blockade.

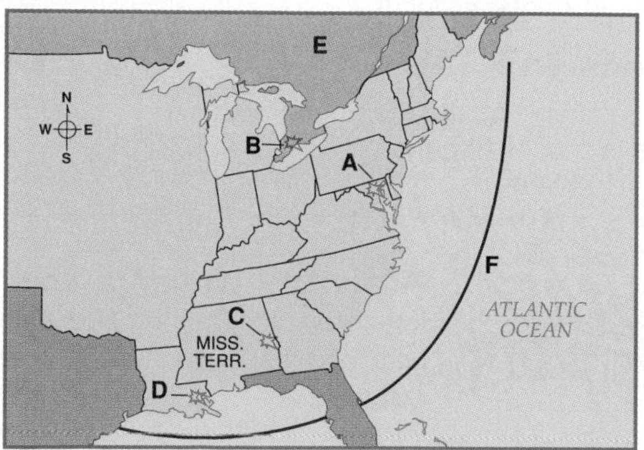

Critical Thinking and Writing

1. **Defending a Position** Do you agree or disagree with Jefferson's idea that federal power should be limited? Explain the reasons for your position.
2. **Understanding Chronology** How did a British-French war help lead to a British-American war?
3. **Solving Problems** Describe a treaty that might have satisfied both Native Americans and white settlers in the early 1800s.
4. **Exploring Unit Themes Nationalism** Describe two events or developments that caused many Americans to become more nationalistic during the Age of Jefferson.

Using Primary Sources

Soon after passage of the Embargo Act, President Jefferson received this letter from Jonathan Hall, a resident of New Hampshire:

> "Sir: I have respected your laws and your government for the United States of America and I wish to have you continue your laws and government and keep the embargo on till you see fit to take it off, though it is very trying to the people in this country about their debts.... I have a father and a mother and they can't take care of themselves and as times are I can't pay for their place so... I hope that... your [honor] will do a little for me, Jonathan Hall."

Source: *Jefferson Papers*. "Capt. Jonathan Hall to Jefferson." August 12, 1808.

Recognizing Points of View **(a)** Did Hall approve of the Embargo Act? **(b)** How did the embargo affect Hall? **(c)** Explain how the embargo might have caused this effect.

Activity Bank

Interdisciplinary Activity

Exploring Civics Create a chart comparing the different ideas of the Federalists and Republicans during the Age of Jefferson. Include categories such as ideas about democracy, economic policy, military policy, and foreign policy.

Career Skills Activity

Political Leaders Write a persuasive speech supporting or opposing war with Britain in 1812. The purpose of the speech is to persuade listeners to agree with your point of view. Deliver your speech to the class. Then, invite students to express their own views. If there is disagreement, you might wish to debate the issue.

Citizenship Activity

Creating a Poster "We are all Republicans, we are all Federalists," said President Jefferson. Create a poster describing and illustrating four goals you think all Americans should agree on, regardless of their political party.

Internet Activity

Use the Internet to find information about current or recent embargoes. In a written report, describe two of these modern embargoes and the reason for each. Explain whether or not each has been successful.

You are a War Hawk in Congress, or a Native American at the Battle of Horseshoe Bend, or a British soldier attacking Washington, D.C., or an American soldier at New Orleans. In your EYEWITNESS JOURNAL, record your participation in and feelings about the War of 1812.

Chapter 9

Industry and Growth

1790–1825

What's Ahead

In the early 1800s, the United States changed rapidly. New technology caused a growth in industry. New factories sprang up along the nation's waterways, and with them new towns and cities. The nation increased in size, too, as settlers swarmed west along roads and rivers.

Change led to increased differences. Economic differences grew between the traditional farming society and the newer industrial society. Regional differences also grew between the North, South, and West. The nation's leaders struggled to strengthen and unify a rapidly expanding nation. They also faced the challenge of creating a bold new foreign policy, as neighboring nations in Latin America won independence.

Why Study History?

Today, we live in an era of rapid technological change. Our age is not the first time Americans have faced a revolution in technology. In the early 1800s, as today, new inventions changed forever the way people lived. To focus on this connection, see the *Why Study History?* feature, "Technology Continues to Change Our Lives," in this chapter.

American Events

1790 First American spinning mill opens

1793 Eli Whitney's cotton gin boosts textile industry

1806 Congress approves building the National Road

1785 | 1790 | 1795 | 1800 | 1805

World Events

1793 World Event China rejects British trade

1802 World Event Child labor law enacted in Britain

Viewing HISTORY

A New Age of Steamboats

Steam Ferry, St. Louis by French artist Leon Pomarede is one of the earliest paintings of St. Louis, Missouri. It shows steam-powered ships puffing down the Mississippi toward the city. In the early 1800s, steamboats and other new means of transportation made it easier for settlers to travel to the West. At the same time, new technology changed how goods were produced and how people worked.

★ **What advantages do you think steamboats might have had over earlier forms of travel?**

1807 Fulton's steamship makes record-breaking trip

1816 New tariff sparks sectional dispute

1823 Monroe Doctrine warns Europe not to recolonize the Americas

1805 — **1810** — **1815** — **1820** — **1825**

1807 World Event Gas street lighting demonstrated in London

1815 World Event Napoleon defeated at Waterloo

The Industrial Revolution

As You Read

Explore These Questions

- What were the effects of the Industrial Revolution?
- How did the Industrial Revolution come to the United States?
- What was life like in early factories?

Define

- spinning jenny
- capitalist
- factory system
- interchangeable parts
- urbanization

Identify

- Industrial Revolution
- Samuel Slater
- Moses Brown
- Francis Cabot Lowell
- Boston Associates
- "Lowell girls"
- Eli Whitney

Setting the Scene At dawn, the factory bell woke 11-year-old Lucy Larcom. Rising quickly, she ate her breakfast, and hurried to her job at a spinning mill in Lowell, Massachusetts. Years later, Larcom described her workplace:

> "I never cared much for machinery. The buzzing and hissing and whizzing of pulleys and rollers and spindles and flyers around me often grew tiresome.... I could look across the room and see girls moving backward and forward among the spinning frames, sometimes stooping, sometimes reaching up their arms, as their work required."

Factories and machinery were part of a revolution that reached the United States in the early 1800s. Unlike the American Revolution, this one had no battles or fixed dates. The new **Industrial Revolution** was a long, slow process which completely changed the way goods were produced.

The Industrial Revolution Begins

Before the 1800s, most people were farmers and most goods were produced by hand. As a result of the Industrial Revolution, this situation gradually began to change. Machines replaced hand tools. New sources of power, such as steam, replaced human and animal power. While most Americans continued to farm for a living, the economy began a gradual shift toward manufacturing.

New technology

The Industrial Revolution started in Britain in the mid-1700s. British inventors developed new technologies that transformed the textile industry.

Since early times, workers used spinning wheels to make thread. A spinning wheel, however, could spin only one thread at a time. In 1764, James Hargreaves developed the **spinning jenny,** a machine that could spin several threads at once. Later, Richard Arkwright invented a machine that could hold 100 spindles of thread. It was called the water frame because it required water power to turn its wheels.

Other inventions speeded up the process of weaving thread into cloth. In the 1780s, Edmund Cartwright built a loom powered by water. It allowed a worker to produce 200 times more cloth in a day than was possible before.

The factory system

New inventions led to a new method of production. Before the Industrial Revolution, most spinning and weaving took place in the home. Machines like the water frame, however, had to be housed in large mills near rivers. Water flowing downstream or over a waterfall turned a wheel that produced the power to run the machines.

To set up and operate a spinning mill required large amounts of capital, or money.

Linking History and Technology

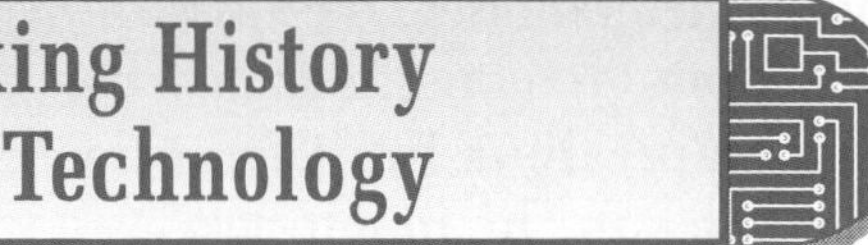

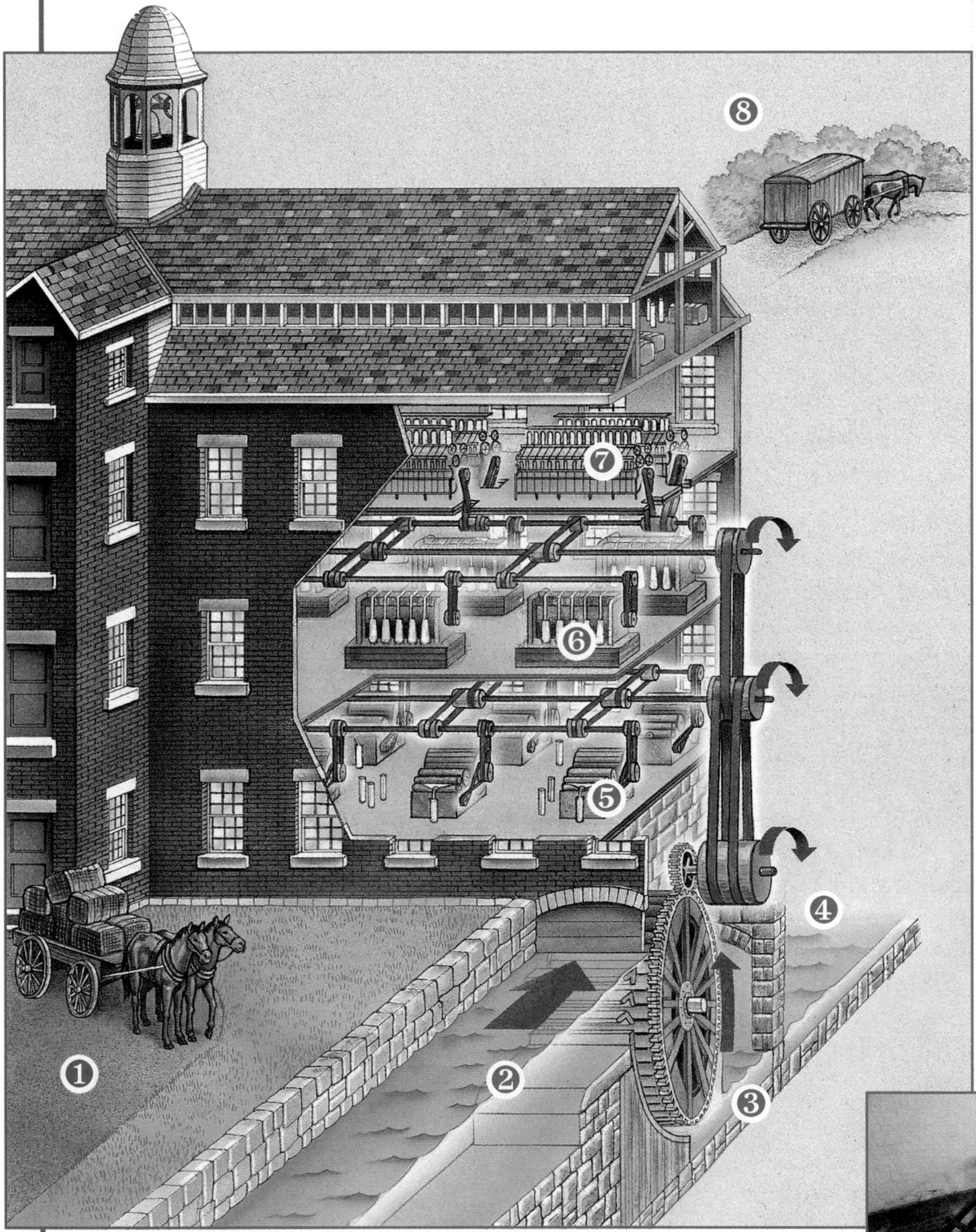

❶ *Wagons bring raw cotton to the mill to be spun into thread.*

❷ *Fast-moving water causes the water wheel to turn.*

❸ *The turning water wheel powers the mill's main shaft.*

❹ *The main shaft drives pulleys, which turn belts that drive the mill machinery.*

❺ *Carding machines comb the raw cotton fiber.*

❻ *Drawing machines pull the combed cotton fibers into ropelike strands.*

❼ *Spinning frames twist combed and drawn cotton strands into thread and wind them onto a bobbin.*

❽ *Wagons carry spun thread to weavers who use it to make cloth.*

Spinning Mill

New technology in the textile industry sparked the Industrial Revolution. As shown here, rapidly moving water turned a water wheel, like the one above. The wheel produced the power to run the machines. ★ **Would your town or community have been a suitable place for a spinning mill like this one? Why or why not?**

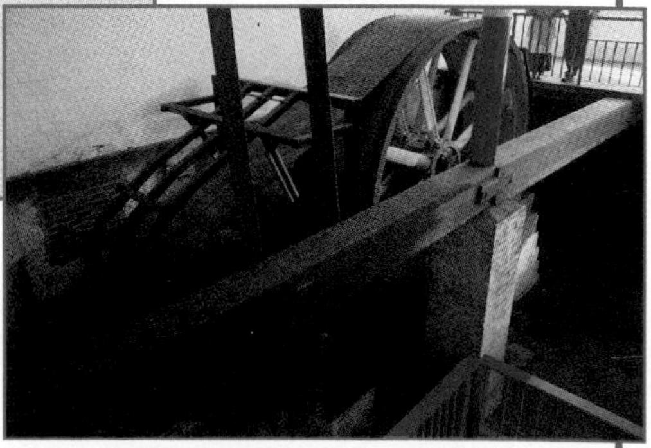

Main shaft of a spinning mill

Capitalists supplied this money. A **capitalist** is a person who invests in a business in order to make a profit. Capitalists built factories and hired workers to run the machines.

The new **factory system** brought workers and machinery together in one place to produce goods. Factory workers earned daily or weekly wages. They had to work a set number of hours each day.

A Revolution Crosses the Atlantic

Britain wanted to keep its new technology secret. It did not want rival nations to copy the new machines. The British Parliament passed a law forbidding anyone to take plans of Arkright's water frame out of the country. It also tried to prevent factory workers from leaving Britain.

Slater breaks the law

Samuel Slater soon showed that the law could not be enforced. Slater was a skilled mechanic in one of Arkwright's mills. When he heard that Americans were offering large rewards for plans of British factories, he decided to leave England.

In 1789, Slater boarded a ship bound for New York City. He knew that British officials searched the baggage of passengers sailing to the United States. To avoid getting caught, he memorized the design of the machines in Arkright's mill. He even used a false name when he traveled.

In New York, Slater learned that **Moses Brown**, a Quaker merchant, wanted to build a spinning mill in Rhode Island. Slater wrote confidently to Brown:

> “If I do not make as good yarn as they do in England, I will have nothing for my services, but will throw the whole of what I have attempted over the bridge.”

Brown replied at once: "If thou canst do what thou sayest, I invite thee to come to Rhode Island."

The first American mill

In 1790, Slater and Brown opened their first mill in Pawtucket, Rhode Island. In the following years, Slater continued to work on improvements. His wife, Hannah Slater, also contributed to the success of the mill. She discovered how to make thread stronger so that it would not snap on the spindles.

The first American factory was a huge success. Before long, other American manufacturers began to build mills using Slater's ideas.

Lowell, Massachusetts: A Model Factory Town

The War of 1812 provided a boost to American industries. The British blockade cut Americans off from their supply of foreign goods. As a result, they had to produce more goods themselves.

Francis Cabot Lowell

During the war, **Francis Cabot Lowell,** a Boston merchant, found a way to improve on British textile mills. In Britain, one factory spun thread while a second factory wove it into cloth. Why not, Lowell wondered, combine spinning and weaving under one roof?

To finance his project, Lowell joined with several partners in 1813 to form the **Boston Associates.** They built a textile factory in Waltham, Massachusetts. The new mill had all the machines needed to turn raw cotton into finished cloth.

After Lowell's death, the Boston Associates took on a more ambitious project. They built an entire factory town and named it after him. In 1821, Lowell, Massachusetts, was a village of five farm families. By 1836, it boasted more than 10,000 people. Visitors to Lowell described it as a model community made up of "small wooden houses, painted white, with green blinds, very neat, very snug, very nicely carpeted."

"Lowell girls"

To work in their new mills, the Boston Associates hired young women from nearby farms. The **"Lowell girls,"** as they came to be called, usually worked for a few years in the mills before returning home to marry. Most sent their wages home to their families. Some saved part of their wages to help set up their own homes.

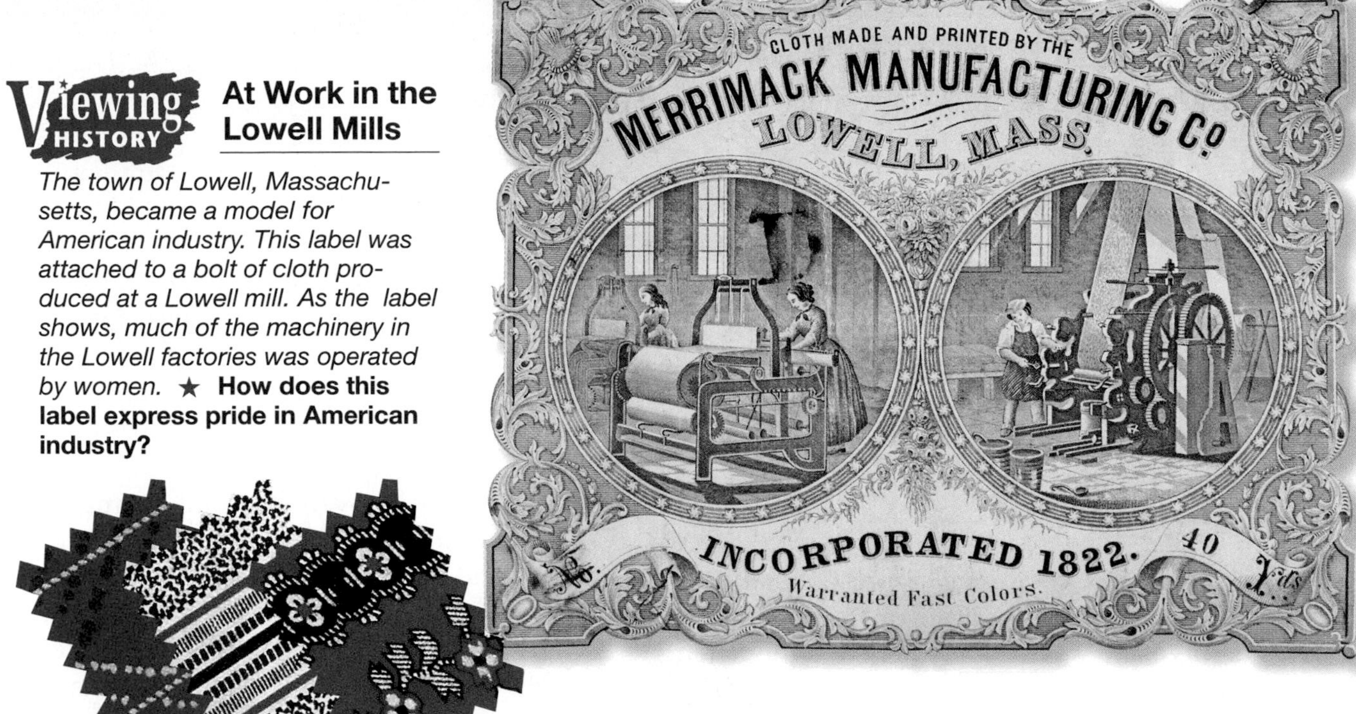

Viewing History **At Work in the Lowell Mills**

The town of Lowell, Massachusetts, became a model for American industry. This label was attached to a bolt of cloth produced at a Lowell mill. As the label shows, much of the machinery in the Lowell factories was operated by women. ★ **How does this label express pride in American industry?**

Cloth from a Lowell factory

At first, parents hesitated to let their daughters work in the mills. To reassure parents, the Boston Associates built boarding houses for their workers. The company also built a church and made rules to protect the young women.

Factory work was often tedious and hard. However, many women valued the economic freedom they got from working in the mills. The *Lowell Offering*, a magazine by and for workers in the Lowell mills, printed a song that began:

> “Despite of toil we all agree
> Out of the mills, or in,
> Dependent on others we ne'er will be
> So long as we're able to spin.”

Impact on Daily Life

In Lowell and elsewhere, mill owners mostly hired women and children. They did this because they could pay women and children half of what they would have had to pay men.

Child labor

Boys and girls as young as seven years of age worked in factories. Small children were especially useful in textile mills because they could squeeze around the large machines to change spindles. “I can see myself now,” recalled a woman who had worked in a mill as a child, “carrying in front of me a [spindle] bigger than I was.”

Today, most Americans look upon child labor as cruel. Yet in the 1800s, farm children also worked hard from an early age. Most people did not see much difference between children working in a factory or on a farm. Often, a child's wages were needed to help support the family.

Long hours

Working hours in the mills were long—12 hours a day, 6 days a week. True, farmers also put in long hours. However, farmers worked shorter hours in winter. Mill workers, by contrast, worked nearly the same hours all year round.

In the early 1800s, conditions in American mills were generally much better than in most factories in Europe. As industries grew, however, competition increased and employers took less interest in the welfare of their workers. In later chapters, you will read how working conditions grew worse.

Why Study History?

Because Technology Continues to Change Our Lives

Historical Background

Inventors like James Hargreaves and Richard Arkwright were not trying to change the world. They just wanted a better way to spin thread. (See page 222.) In the end, though, the Industrial Revolution changed forever how people worked, where they lived, and even how they spent their leisure time. Later inventions, such as the telephone and the automobile, have also transformed the world we live in.

Connections to Today

Not long before you were born, another revolution in technology began: the computer revolution. The earliest computers were not the kind you could have in your bedroom. One early model weighed 30 tons and filled an entire room!

Slowly, computers got smaller and spread out—to schools, businesses, hospitals, arcades, homes. Computers can help keep records, diagnose illnesses, or take people into outer space.

Connections to You

You already know some of the advantages of computers. You can research a report online and revise it on screen. You can enjoy a video game or create your own greeting cards. You can chat with people living in Sweden or Korea or Egypt.

Not every change is positive, though. Sitting at a computer screen for hours may cause severe headaches or hand injuries.

Some critics even fear that computers may lead to isolation. People can work, shop, and even make friends without leaving their homes. You may spend more time chatting with someone halfway around the world than going bowling with friends in your own neighborhood.

1. **Comprehension** **(a)** Name one result of the Industrial Revolution. **(b)** Name two results of the computer revolution.
2. **Critical Thinking** Do you think computers will lead to greater or less contact between people? Explain.

Making a Concept Web Make a concept web to show some of the ways that computers affect you. Then, review your web and decide whether each effect is positive, negative, or both.

What point is this cartoon making about the impact of computers?

Changes in home life

The Industrial Revolution had a great impact on home life. On farms or in home workshops, families worked together as a unit. As the factory system spread, more family members left the home to earn a living.

These changes affected ideas about the role of women. In poorer families, women often had to go out to work. In wealthier families, husbands supported the family while women stayed at home. For many husbands, having a wife who stayed at home became a sign of a success.

Interchangeable Parts

Manufacturers benefited from the pioneering work of American inventor **Eli Whitney**. Earlier, skilled workers made goods by hand. For example, a gunsmith spent days making the barrel, stock, and trigger for a single musket. Because the parts were handmade, each musket differed a bit from the next. If a part broke, a gunsmith had to fashion a new part to fit that gun.

Whitney wanted to speed up gunmaking by having machines manufacture each part. Machine-made parts would all be alike—for example, one trigger would be identical to another. **Interchangeable parts** would save time and money.

Because the government bought many guns, Whitney went to Washington, D.C., to demonstrate his method. At first, officials laughed at his plan. Whitney paid them no attention. Carefully, he sorted parts for 10 muskets into separate piles. He then asked an official to choose one part from each pile. In minutes, the first musket was assembled. Whitney repeated the process until 10 muskets were complete.

The idea of interchangeable parts spread rapidly. Inventors designed machines to produce interchangeable parts for clocks, locks, and many other goods. With such machines, small workshops grew into factories.

Cause and Effect

Causes

- British ideas of a spinning mill and powerloom reach the United States
- War of 1812 prompts Americans to make their own goods
- Eli Whitney introduces the idea of interchangeable parts

The Industrial Revolution in the United States

Effects

- Factory system spreads
- Young women and children from nearby farms work in mills
- Growing cities face problems of fire, sewage, garbage, and disease

Effects Today

- United States becomes leader in industrialized world
- Oil is a highly valued natural resource

Graphic Organizer *Skills*

The Industrial Revolution brought with it many immediate and long-term changes.

1. **Comprehension** What inventions and ideas contributed to the spread of the Industrial Revolution?
2. **Critical Thinking** Do you think the impact of the Industrial Revolution was positive or negative? Give reasons.

Economics

Growing Cities

Since colonial times, cities played an important role in American life. The vast majority of people lived in rural areas. However, farmers often sent crops to cities for sale or shipment. Cities were also centers of finance and manufacturing.

During the Industrial Revolution, many people left farms to work in factories. Older cities expanded rapidly, while new cities sprang up around factories. This movement of the population from farms to cities is called **urbanization**.

Urbanization was a steady but gradual process. In 1800, only 6 percent of the nation's population lived in urban areas. By 1850, the number had risen to 15 percent. Not until 1920 did more Americans live in cities than on farms.

By today's standards, these early cities were small. A person could walk from one end of any American city to the other in 30 minutes. Buildings were only a few stories tall. As the factory system spread, the nation's cities grew.

Hazards

Growing cities had many problems. Dirt and gravel streets turned into mudholes when it rained. Cities had no sewers, and people threw garbage into the streets. A visitor to New York reported:

> "The streets are filthy, and the stranger is not a little surprised to meet the hogs walking about in them, for the purpose of devouring the vegetables and trash thrown into the gutter."

In these dirty, crowded conditions, disease spread easily. Epidemics of yellow fever or cholera (KAHL er uh) raged through cities, killing hundreds.

Fire posed another threat to safety. If a sooty chimney caught fire, the flames quickly spread from one wooden house to the next. Rival volunteer companies often competed to get to a blaze first. Sometimes, they fought each other instead of the fire!

Attractions

Cities had attractions, too. Theaters, museums, and circuses created an air of excitement. In New York City, P. T. Barnum exhibited rare animals at his American Museum.

In rural areas, people depended on door-to-door peddlers for ready-made goods. In cities, people could shop in fine stores that sold the latest fashions from Europe. Some offered modern "ready-to-wear" clothing. One store in New York City advertised that "gentlemen can rely upon being as well fitted from the shelves as if their measures were taken."

Most women continued to sew their own clothes. However, they enjoyed visiting hat shops, china shops, shoe stores, and "fancy-goods" stores.

★ Section 1 Review ★

Recall

1. **Identify** **(a)** Industrial Revolution, **(b)** Samuel Slater, **(c)** Moses Brown, **(d)** Francis Cabot Lowell, **(e)** Boston Associates, **(f)** "Lowell girls," **(g)** Eli Whitney.
2. **Define** **(a)** spinning jenny, **(b)** capitalist, **(c)** factory system, **(d)** interchangeable parts, **(e)** urbanization.

Comprehension

3. Describe three ways the Industrial Revolution changed life.
4. How did industry move from Britain to the United States?
5. What were conditions like in the Lowell mills?

Critical Thinking and Writing

6. **Drawing Conclusions** Why were both inventors and capitalists needed to bring about the Industrial Revolution?
7. **Understanding Causes and Effects** How did the building of factories encourage the growth of cities?

Activity **Writing a Letter** The time is 160 years ago. You are the same age you are now, but instead of being in school, you are working in the Lowell mills. Write a letter home describing how you feel about working in a factory to help support your family.

Moving Westward

As You Read

Explore These Questions

- How did settlers travel westward in the early 1800s?
- What steps did Americans take to improve roads?
- How did steamboats and canals affect transportation?

Define

- turnpike
- corduroy road
- canal

Identify

- Lancaster Turnpike
- National Road
- John Fitch
- Robert Fulton
- *Clermont*
- Henry Shreve
- Erie Canal
- DeWitt Clinton

An Irish visitor to the United States described a stagecoach trip through Maryland:

> “The driver frequently had to call to the passengers in the stage, to lean out of the carriage first at one side, then at the other, to prevent it from oversetting in the deep ruts with which the road abounds: 'Now gentlemen, to the right,'... 'Now gentlemen, to the left,' and so on.”

In the 1790s, travel was as difficult as it had been in colonial times. Most roads were mud tracks. River travel could be difficult, too, when boats had to push their way upstream against the current. As the young nation grew westward, Americans saw the need to improve transportation.

To the Mississippi

Settlers had been moving steadily westward since the 1600s. By the early 1800s, “the West” referred to the land between the Appalachians and the Mississippi.

In the early 1800s, the stream of pioneers turned into a flood. By 1820, so many people had moved west that the population in some of the original 13 states had actually declined!

Western routes

Settlers took a number of routes west. One well-traveled path was the Great Wagon Road across Pennsylvania. It dated back to colonial days. Some settlers continued south and west along the trail opened by Daniel Boone before the Revolution. Known as the Wilderness Road, it led through the Cumberland Gap into Kentucky. (See the map on page 231.)

Other settlers pushed west to Pittsburgh. There, they loaded their animals and wagons onto flatboats and journeyed down the Ohio River into Indiana, Kentucky, and Illinois. Flatboats were well suited to the shallow waters of the Ohio. Even when carrying heavy cargoes, these raftlike barges rode high in the water.

Pioneers from Georgia and South Carolina followed other trails west to Alabama and Mississippi. Enslaved African Americans

Many settlers headed west in covered wagons, such as this Conestoga wagon.

Viewing History: A Need for Better Roads

This painting, by a visitor from Russia, shows a stagecoach on its run between Philadelphia, Pennsylvania, and Trenton, New Jersey. Passengers traveling on rocky, muddy, unpaved roads could expect to be "crushed, shaken, thrown about... and bumped." ★ **What details in this painting suggest that these passengers were having a rough ride?**

helped to carve plantations in the rich, fertile soil of these territories.

People from New England, New York, and Pennsylvania pushed into the Northwest Territory. Some settlers traveled west from Albany, New York, along the Mohawk River and across the Appalachians. Some settlers then followed Indian trails around Lake Erie. Others sailed across the lake into Ohio.

New states

Before long, some western territories had populations large enough to apply for statehood. Between 1792 and 1819, eight states joined the Union: Kentucky (1792), Tennessee (1796), Ohio (1803), Louisiana (1812), Indiana (1816), Mississippi (1817), Illinois (1818), and Alabama (1819).

Better Roads

Settlers faced a difficult journey. Many roads were narrow trails, barely wide enough for a single wagon. One pioneer wrote of "rotten banks down which horses plunged" and streams that "almost drowned them." Tree stumps stuck up through the road and often broke the axles on the wagons of careless travelers. The nation badly needed better roads.

Turnpikes and bridges

In the United States, as in Europe, private companies built gravel and stone roads. To pay for these roads, the companies collected tolls from travelers. At various points along the road, a pike, or pole, blocked the road. After a wagon driver paid a toll, the pike keeper turned the pole aside to let the wagon pass. As a result, these toll roads were called **turnpikes.**

Probably the best road in the United States was the **Lancaster Turnpike**. Built in the 1790s by a private company, the road linked Philadelphia and Lancaster, Pennsylvania. Because the road was set on a bed of gravel, water drained off quickly. It was topped with smooth, flat stones.

In swampy areas, roads were made of logs. These roads were known as **corduroy roads** because the lines of logs looked like corduroy cloth. Corduroy roads kept wagons from sinking into the mud, but they made for a bumpy ride.

Bridges carried travelers across streams and rivers. Stone bridges were costly to build, but wooden ones rotted quickly. A clever Massachusetts carpenter designed a wooden bridge with a roof to protect it from the weather. Covered bridges lasted much longer than open ones.

The National Road

Some states set aside money to build or improve roads. In 1806, for the first time, Congress approved funds for a national road-building project. The **National Road** was to run from Cumberland, Maryland, to Wheeling, in western Virginia.

Work on the National Road began in 1811 and was completed in 1818. Later, the road was extended into Illinois. As each new section of road was built, settlers eagerly used it to drive their wagons west.

Steam Transport

Whenever possible, travelers and freight haulers used river transportation. Floating downstream on a flatboat was both faster and more comfortable than bumping along rutted roads. It also cost less.

Yet, river travel had its own problems. Moving upstream was difficult. People used paddles or long poles to push boats against the current. Sometimes, they hauled boats from the shore with ropes. Both methods were slow. A boat could travel downstream from Pittsburgh to New Orleans in about six weeks. The return trip upstream took at least 17 weeks!

Fitch and Fulton

A new invention, the steam engine, improved river travel. **John Fitch** improved on steam engines that had been built in Britain.

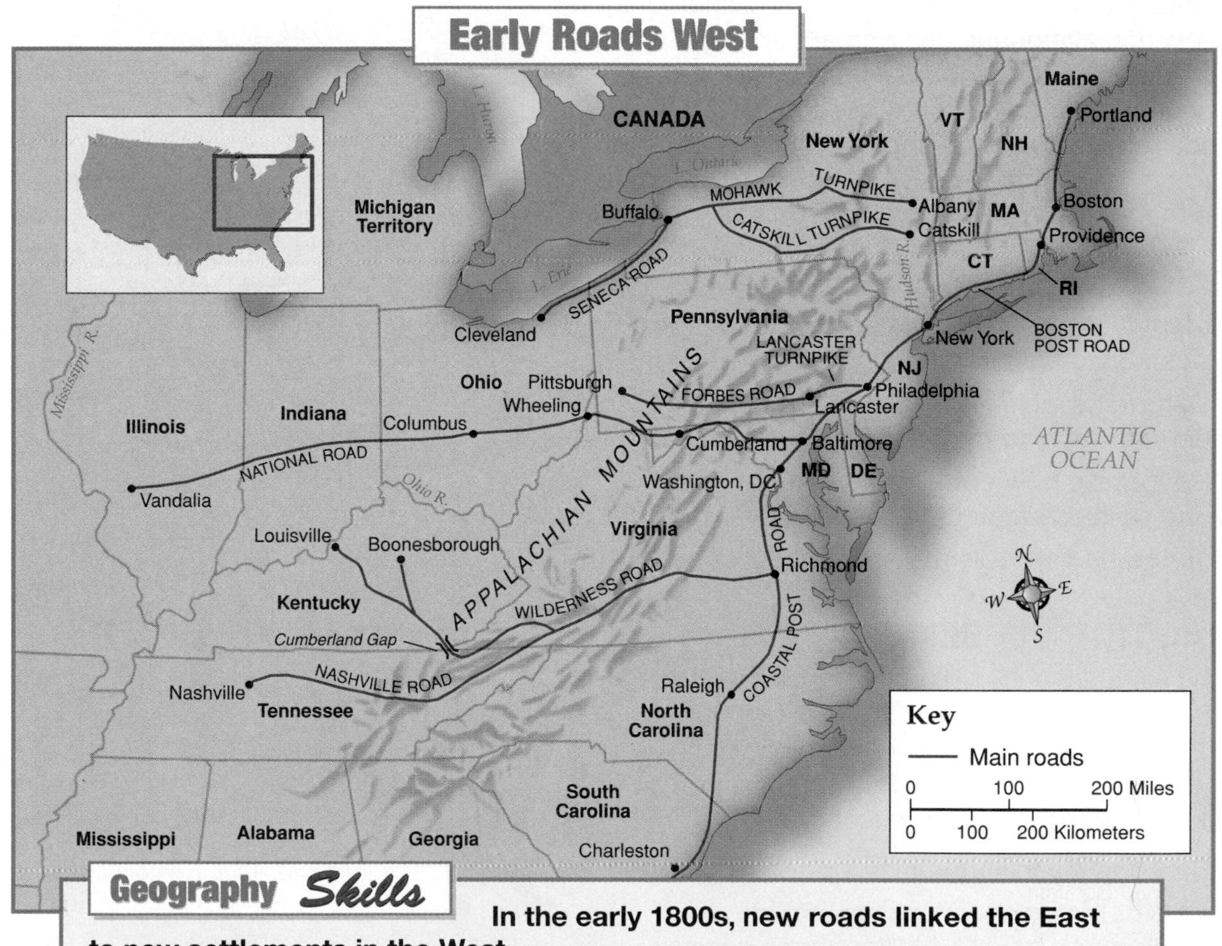

Geography Skills **In the early 1800s, new roads linked the East to new settlements in the West.**

1. **Location** On the map, locate: **(a)** Appalachian Mountains, **(b)** Cumberland Gap, **(c)** Wilderness Road, **(d)** Lancaster Turnpike, **(e)** National Road.
2. **Movement** What major roads would settlers use to travel from Boston, Massachussetts, to Nashville, Tennessee?
3. **Critical Thinking** Based on this map, what effect do you think roadbuilding had on cities like Philadelphia, Baltimore, and Richmond?

Skills FOR LIFE

Critical Thinking | Managing Information | Communication | Maps, Charts, and Graphs

Analyzing a Primary Source

How Will I Use This Skill ?

A **primary source** is firsthand information about people and events. Historians use primary sources to learn about the past. You, too, use primary sources—when you watch an interview on television, or listen to two friends tell their sides of something that happened. Learning to analyze primary sources helps you determine the reliability of the information that you get.

LEARN the Skill

1. Identify the source of the account. Decide if he or she has firsthand knowledge of the event.
2. Determine which words indicate facts. Are there enough facts to make the speaker reliable?
3. Recognize how emotions, points of view, and opinions affect the telling of the story.
4. Judge how reliable the source is.

PRACTICE the Skill

Fanny Kemble, an English actress, visited the United States in the early 1800s. In her journal, she described a stagecoach ride with her father and some Americans. Read the excerpt, then answer the following questions:

1. Explain why this journal is a primary source.
2. (a) What facts does Kemble include about stagecoach travel? (b) What facts does she include about American rural life?
3. What effect do you think Kemble's nationality and her discomfort may have had on her account?
4. Would you consider this journal a reliable source of information? Explain.

"Bones of me! what a road! Even my father's solid proportions...were jerked up to the roof and down again every three minutes. Our companions...laughed and talked [constantly], the young ladies, at the very top of their voices, and with the national nasal twang....The few cottages and farmhouses which we passed reminded me of similar dwellings in France and Ireland; yet the peasantry here have not the same excuse for disorder and [ruin] as either the Irish or French....The farms had the same desolate, untidy, untended look; the gates broken, the fences carelessly put up."

Excerpt from Journal by Frances Anne Kemble Butler

APPLY the Skill

Watch or read an interview given by an eyewitness to an event. Using the steps above, decide whether you think the interview is a reliable source of information.

HISTORY HAPPENED HERE

The Erie Canal

The opening of the Erie Canal in 1825 launched an age of canal building. Today, at the Erie Canal Village in Rome, New York, you can relive life along the old Erie Canal. Here, passengers ride atop a canal boat, pulled along by a team of mules, just as they did 150 years ago. Riding up top could be risky, though. When the boatmen yelled "Low bridge!" passengers who did not duck could bump their heads.

★ ***To learn more about this historic site, write:*** *Erie Canal Village, 5789 New London Road, Rome, NY 13440.*

Canal boat lantern

In 1787, he showed members of the Constitutional Convention how a steam engine could power a boat. He then opened a ferry service on the Delaware River. However, few people used the ferry, and Fitch went out of business.

Inventor **Robert Fulton** may have seen Fitch's steamboat in Philadelphia. In 1807, Fulton launched his own steamboat, the ***Clermont,*** on the Hudson River. On its first run, the *Clermont* carried passengers from New York City to Albany and back. The 300-mile (480-km) trip took just 62 hours—a record at the time.

The age of steamboats

Fulton's success ushered in the age of steamboats. Soon, steamboats were ferrying passengers up and down the Atlantic coast. More important, they revolutionized travel in the West. Besides carrying people, steamboats on the Mississippi, Ohio, and Missouri rivers gave farmers and merchants a cheap means of moving goods.

Because western rivers were shallow, **Henry Shreve** designed a flat-bottomed steamboat. It could carry heavy loads without getting stuck on sandbars.

Still, steamboat travel could be dangerous. Sparks from smokestacks could cause fires. As steamboat captains raced each other along the river, high-pressure boilers sometimes exploded. Between 1811 and 1851, 44 steamboats collided, 166 burned, and more than 200 exploded.

The Canal Boom

Steamboats and improved roads did not help western farmers get their goods directly to markets in the East. To meet this need, Americans dug canals. A **canal** is an artificial channel filled with water that allows boats to cross a stretch of land.

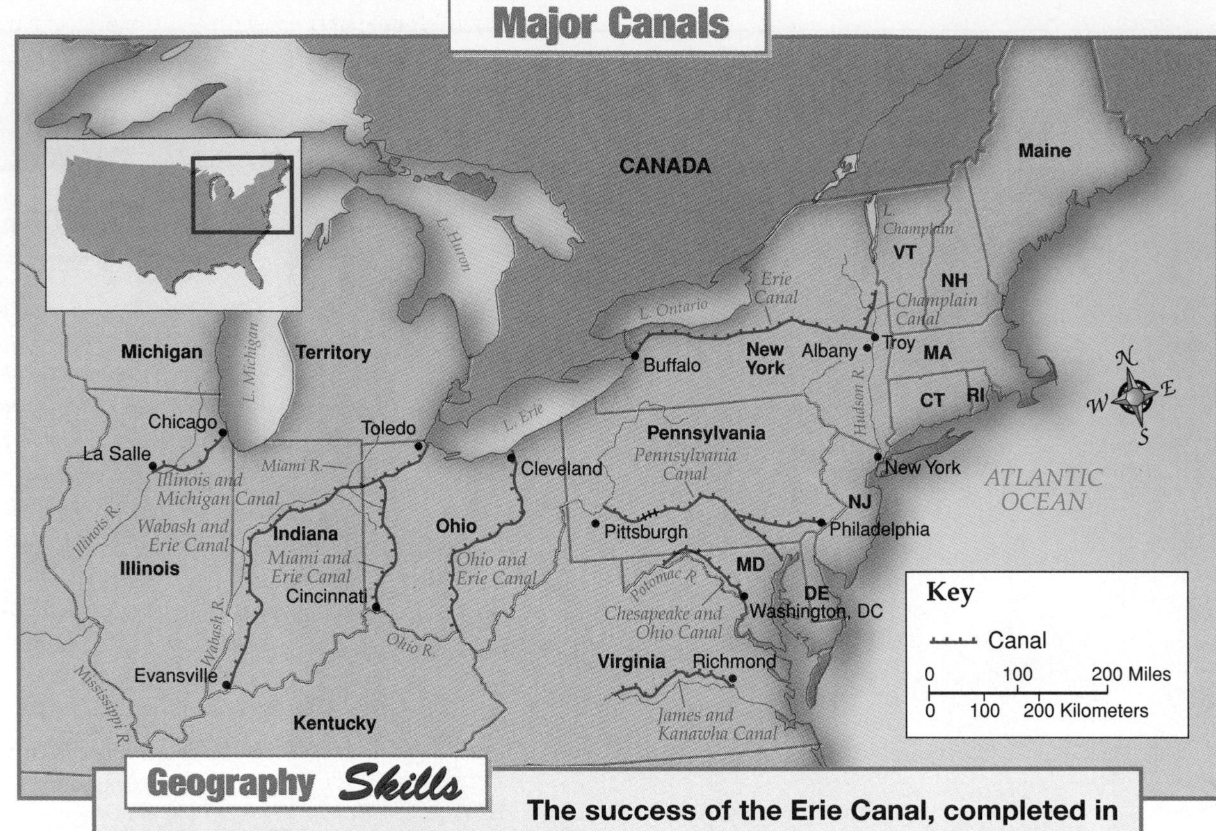

Geography Skills **The success of the Erie Canal, completed in 1825, set off an age of canal building.**

1. **Location** On the map, locate: **(a)** New York City, **(b)** Troy, **(c)** Buffalo, **(d)** Lake Erie, **(e)** Erie Canal.
2. **Movement** What two bodies of water were linked by the Illinois and Michigan Canal?
3. **Critical Thinking** Use the map to describe an all-water route from Evansville, Indiana, to New York City.

The earliest American canals were no more than a few miles long. Some provided routes around waterfalls on a river. Other canals linked a river to a nearby lake. By the early 1800s, however, Americans were building longer canals.

Building the Erie Canal

Some New Yorkers had a bold idea. They wanted to build a canal linking the Great Lakes with the Mohawk and Hudson rivers. The **Erie Canal** would let western farmers ship their goods to the port of New York. It would also bring business to towns along the route.

To many people, the idea of such a canal seemed farfetched. When Thomas Jefferson heard of the plan, he exclaimed:

> “Why, sir, you talk of making a canal 350 miles through the wilderness—it is little short of madness to think of it at this day!”

New York governor **DeWitt Clinton** ignored such criticism. He persuaded state lawmakers to provide money for the Erie Canal. Scoffers referred to the project as “Clinton's Ditch.”

Work on the Erie Canal began in 1817. At first, workers dug the waterway by hand. To speed up progress, inventors developed new equipment. One machine, a stump-puller, could pull out nearly 40 tree stumps a day. In two places, workers had to find ways to build stone bridges to carry the canal over other rivers along the way.

An instant success

By 1825, the immense job was finished. On opening day of the Erie Canal, a cannon fired a volley in Buffalo, New York. When the sound got to the next town along the route, it, too, fired a cannon. Town after town fired their cannons—all the way to New York City. The thunderous salute took 80 minutes to complete.

The Erie Canal was an instant success. It reduced travel time. The cost of shipping goods dropped to about 1/20 of what it was before the canal was built. The canal also helped to make New York City a center of commerce.

The success of the Erie Canal led other states to build canals. (See the map on the opposite page.) These canals created vital economic links between western farms and eastern cities.

Transportation Builds Prosperity

In 1831, a young Frenchman, Alexis de Tocqueville (TOHK vihl), made a nine-month tour of the United States. In his writings, Tocqueville described what he admired about the young nation. One of the things that impressed him most was the American transportation system.

"Of all the countries in the world," Tocqueville wrote, "America is that in which the spread of ideas and of human industry is most continual and most rapid." Tocqueville was amazed by "immense canals" and roads built in the middle of the wilderness. He also praised the American postal system:

> "In America one of the first things done in a new state is to make the post go there. In the forests of Michigan there is no cabin so isolated, no valley so wild but that letters and newspapers arrive at least once a week."

Tocqueville noted that Americans could easily ship goods from the western frontier to any part of the country. (By contrast, in his native France—a much smaller country—many large towns could not be reached by road at all!) Faster, easier transportation thus contributed to the growing prosperity of the United States.

★ Section 2 Review ★

Recall

1. **Locate** **(a)** Kentucky, **(b)** Tennessee, **(c)** Ohio, **(d)** Louisiana, **(e)** Indiana, **(f)** Mississippi, **(g)** Illinois, **(h)** Alabama.
2. **Identify** **(a)** Lancaster Turnpike, **(b)** National Road, **(c)** John Fitch, **(d)** Robert Fulton, **(e)** *Clermont,* **(f)** Henry Shreve, **(g)** Erie Canal, **(h)** DeWitt Clinton.
3. **Define** **(a)** turnpike, **(b)** corduroy road, **(c)** canal.

Comprehension

4. What means of transportation did settlers take to the West in the early 1800s?
5. **(a)** Why did the nation need better transportation in the early 1800s? **(b)** Describe two ways that travel improved.

Critical Thinking and Writing

6. **Linking Past and Present** Today, airplanes provide a faster means of travel than land transportation. Why do you think roads are still important to the nation?
7. **Identifying Alternatives** Examine the maps in this section. Then, describe two alternate ways a farmer might have shipped a cargo of grain from Cleveland, Ohio, to New York City.

Activity **Designing a Monument** You have been asked to design a monument honoring the two-hundredth anniversary of the Erie Canal. Draw a rough sketch of the monument, showing what design you would use. You may also include an inscription describing the importance of the canal.

3 Building National Unity

As You Read

Explore These Questions

- How did Congress try to strengthen the national economy?
- What were the goals of Henry Clay's American System?
- How did the Supreme Court strengthen national unity?

Define

- dumping
- sectionalism
- interstate commerce

Identify

- James Monroe
- John C. Calhoun
- Daniel Webster
- Henry Clay
- American System
- *McCulloch* v. *Maryland*
- *Gibbon* v. *Ogden*

SETTING the Scene After his visit to the United States, Alexis de Tocqueville described what he saw as the character of the American people. He wrote:

> "The American . . . is less afraid than any other inhabitant of the globe to risk what he has gained in the hope of a better future. . . . There is not a country in the world where man more confidently takes charge of the future, or where he feels with more pride that he can fashion the universe to please himself."

Tocqueville echoed the confidence Americans felt in themselves. After the War of 1812, the country grew rapidly. New lands opened to settlers with improved transportation. New industries appeared. In Congress, a new generation of political leaders sought to direct this expansion.

An Era of Good Feelings

In 1816, the Republican candidate for President, **James Monroe**, easily defeated the Federalist, Rufus King. Once in office, Monroe spoke of creating a new sense of national unity.

Monroe was the last of three Presidents in a row to come from Virginia. He was also the last Revolutionary War officer to become President.

In 1817, Monroe made a goodwill tour of the country. Not since George Washington had a President made such a tour. In Boston, crowds cheered Monroe. Boston newspapers expressed surprise at this warm welcome for a Republican from Virginia. After all, Boston had been a Federalist stronghold. One newspaper wrote that the United States was entering an "Era of Good Feelings."

By the time Monroe ran for a second term in 1820, no candidate opposed him. The Federalist party had disappeared.

Three Sectional Leaders

While conflict between political parties declined, disputes between different sections of the nation sharpened. In Congress, three ambitious young men took center stage. All three played key roles in Congress for more than 30 years, as well as serving in other offices. Each represented a different section of the country.

Calhoun of the South

John C. Calhoun spoke for the South. He had grown up on a frontier farm in South Carolina. Later, he went to Yale College in Connecticut. Calhoun's immense energy and striking features earned him the nickname "young Hercules." His intense way of speaking sometimes made people uncomfortable in his presence.

Calhoun had supported the War of 1812. Like many southerners, though, he generally opposed policies that would strengthen the power of the federal government.

Webster of the North

Daniel Webster of New Hampshire was perhaps the most skillful public speaker of his time. With eyes flashing and shoulders thrown back, Webster was an impressive sight when he stood up to speak in Congress. An observer described him as a "great cannon loaded to the lips."

Like many New Englanders, Webster had opposed the War of 1812. He even refused to vote for taxes to pay for the war effort. After the war, he wanted the federal government to take a larger role in building the nation's economy.

Clay of the West

Henry Clay spoke for the West. You have already met Clay as a leader of the War Hawks who pushed for war against Britain in 1812.

Clay was born in Virginia, the seventh of 20 children. He later moved to Kentucky. As a young lawyer, he was once fined for brawling with an opponent. Usually, however, he charmed both friends and rivals. Supporters called him "Gallant Harry of the West." Like Webster, Clay strongly favored a more active role for the central government.

A New National Bank

After the War of 1812, leaders like Calhoun, Webster, and Clay had to deal with the nation's economic weakness. The problem was due in part to the lack of a national bank.

The charter for the Bank of the United States ran out in 1811. Without the Bank to lend money and regulate the nation's money supply, the economy suffered. State banks made loans and issued money. Often, they put too much money into circulation. With so much money available to spend, prices rose rapidly.

In the nation's early years, Republicans like Jefferson and Madison had opposed a national bank. By 1816, however, many Republicans believed that a bank was needed. They supported a law to charter the second Bank of the United States. By lending money and restoring order to the nation's money supply, the Bank helped American businesses grow.

Protection From Foreign Competition

Another economic problem facing the nation was foreign competition, especially from

Viewing HISTORY **Three Sectional Leaders**

Henry Clay, left, was the first major political leader to emerge from the new states of the West. Along with Daniel Webster and John C. Calhoun, below, Clay played a major role in government for more than 30 years. ★ **What role did sectional politics play in the rise of Webster, Calhoun, and Clay?**

Effect of a Protective Tariff

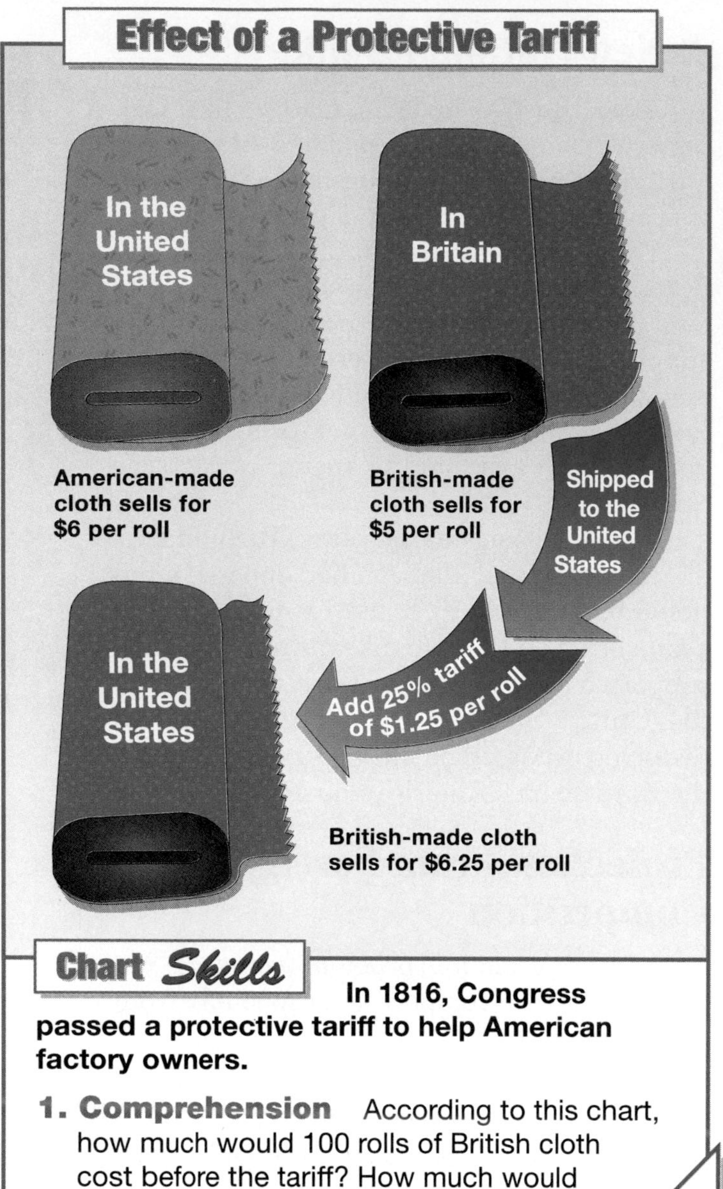

Chart Skills **In 1816, Congress passed a protective tariff to help American factory owners.**

1. **Comprehension** According to this chart, how much would 100 rolls of British cloth cost before the tariff? How much would they cost after the tariff?
2. **Critical Thinking** Why did southerners object to the tariff?

Economics $

Britain. In the early 1800s, the Embargo Act and then the War of 1812 kept most British goods out of the United States. In response, ambitious American business leaders like Francis Cabot Lowell set up their own mills and factories.

A flood of British goods

In 1815, British goods again poured into the United States. The British could make and sell goods more cheaply than Americans. Most British factories and machines were older and had already been paid for. By contrast, Americans still had to pay for building their new factories.

Sometimes, British manufacturers sold cloth in the United States for less than it cost to make. The practice of selling goods in another country at very low prices is today called **dumping.** Through dumping, British manufacturers hoped to put American rivals out of business.

Congress passes a protective tariff

Dumping caused dozens of New England businesses to fail. Angry owners asked Congress to place a protective tariff on all goods imported from Europe. As you recall, the purpose of a protective tariff is to protect a country's industries from foreign competition.

Congress responded by passing the Tariff of 1816. It greatly raised tariffs on imports. This increase made imported goods far more expensive than similar American-made goods. In 1818 and 1824, Congress passed even higher tariffs.

Higher tariffs led to angry protests, especially from southerners. Southerners had built few factories. As a result, they did not benefit from the tariff. Also, southerners bought many British goods. The new tariff drove up the price of British-made goods. Southerners complained that the tariff made northern manufacturers rich at the expense of the South.

Clay's American System

The bitter dispute over tariffs reflected the growth of sectionalism. **Sectionalism** is loyalty to one's state or section rather than to the nation as a whole. Americans identified themselves as southerners, northerners, or westerners. In Congress, representatives from different sections often clashed.

Henry Clay wanted to promote economic growth for all sections. He set out a program that became known as the **American System.** It called for high tariffs on imports, which would help northern factories. With wealth from industry, northerners would buy farm products from the West and the South. High tariffs would also reduce American dependence on foreign goods. Clay argued:

“Every nation should... be able to feed and clothe and defend itself. If it rely upon a foreign supply that may be cut off... it cannot be independent.”

Clay also urged Congress to use money from tariffs to build roads, bridges, and canals. A better transportation system, he believed, would make it easier and cheaper for farmers in the West and the South to ship goods to city markets.

Clay's American System never went fully into effect. Tariffs did remain high. However, Congress spent little on internal improvements. Southerners in particular disliked Clay's plan. The South had many fine rivers to transport goods. Many southerners opposed paying for roads and canals that brought them no direct benefits.

The Supreme Court Expands Federal Power

Under Chief Justice John Marshall, the Supreme Court strengthened the power of the federal government to promote economic growth. After Congress chartered the second Bank of the United States, Maryland tried to tax the bank in order to drive it out of the state. James McCulloch, the bank cashier, refused to pay the tax.

In the case of ***McCulloch* v. *Maryland*** (1819), the Court ruled that states had no right to interfere with federal institutions within their borders. “The power to tax involves the power to destroy,” warned Marshall. The ruling strengthened federal power. It also allowed the National Bank to continue, which helped the economy to expand.

In another case, ***Gibbon* v. *Ogden*** (1824), the Supreme Court upheld the power of the federal government to regulate commerce. The Court struck down a New York law that tried to control steamboat travel between New York and New Jersey. The Court ruled that a state could only regulate trade within its own borders. Only the federal government had the power to regulate **interstate commerce,** or trade between different states. This decision helped the national economy by making it easier for the government to regulate trade.

★ Section 3 Review ★

Recall

1. **Identify** **(a)** James Monroe, **(b)** John C. Calhoun, **(c)** Daniel Webster, **(d)** Henry Clay, **(e)** American System, **(f)** *McCulloch* v. *Maryland,* **(g)** *Gibbon* v. *Ogden.*
2. **Define** **(a)** dumping, **(b)** sectionalism, **(c)** interstate commerce.

Comprehension

3. How did Congress try to solve each of the following problems: **(a)** the money supply, **(b)** foreign competition?
4. Describe Clay's program to promote economic growth.
5. Describe one way the Supreme Court upheld the authority of the federal government.

Critical Thinking and Writing

6. **Analyzing a Primary Source** In 1816, a member of Congress said, “I will buy where I can get [manufactured goods] cheapest.... It is unjust to aggravate the burdens of the people for the purpose of favoring the manufacturers.” Do you think this speaker favored or opposed the Tariff of 1816? Explain.
7. **Drawing Conclusions** Based on your reading, do you think sectional differences were a serious threat to national unity? Give examples to support your conclusion.

Activity **Conducting an Interview** You are a political reporter assigned to interview a Congressional leader around 1820. Choose either Clay, Calhoun, or Webster. List three or four questions you would ask about the issues facing the nation.

Latin America and the United States

Explore These Questions

- How did Latin American nations win independence?
- How did the United States gain Florida?
- What was the purpose of the Monroe Doctrine?

Define

- creole
- intervention

Identify

- Miguel Hidalgo
- Simón Bolívar
- José de San Martín
- "black Seminoles"
- John Quincy Adams
- Adams-Onís Treaty
- Monroe Doctrine

On a quiet Sunday in September 1810, the church bell rang in the Mexican village of Dolores. In the square, people found their priest, **Miguel Hidalgo** (mee GEHL ee DAHL goh), making a stirring speech. No one knows the exact words, but Mexicans remembered and passed along his message:

> "My children.... Will you be free? Will you recover the lands stolen 300 years ago from your forefathers by the hated Spaniards? We must act at once!"

Thousands of Mexicans rallied to Father Hidalgo's call for freedom.

South of the United States, Spanish colonies in Latin America* fought wars for independence in the early 1800s. As new nations emerged, President Monroe formed a bold new foreign policy.

Revolution in Latin America

By 1810, many people in Spain's American colonies were eager for independence. They had many reasons for discontent. Most people, even wealthy creoles, had little or no say in government. **Creoles** were people born in Latin America to Spanish parents. Harsh laws ruled Indians and the poor. The French and American revolutions inspired colonists to seek self-rule.

Mexican independence

As you read, Miguel Hidalgo sounded the call for Mexican independence. Rebel forces won control of several provinces before Father Hidalgo was captured. In 1811, he was executed.

Another priest, José Morelos (hoh ZAY moh RAY lohs), took up the fight. Because he called for a program to give land to peasants, wealthy creoles opposed him. Before long, Morelos, too, was captured and killed by the Spanish.

Slowly, creoles began to support the revolution. In 1821, creole forces won control of Mexico. A few years later, Mexico became a republic with its own constitution.

The Liberator

In South America, too, a series of revolutions freed colonies from Spanish rule. The best-known revolutionary leader was **Simón Bolívar** (see MOHN boh LEE vahr). He became known as the Liberator for his role in the Latin American wars of independence.

Bolívar came from a wealthy creole family in Venezuela. As a young man, he took up the cause of Venezuelan independence. Bolívar promised, "I will never allow my hands to be idle, nor my soul to rest until I have broken the shackles which chain us to Spain."

Bolívar rose to become a leader of the rebel forces. In a bold move, he led an army

*Latin America refers to the region of the Western Hemisphere where Latin-based languages such as Spanish, French, and Portuguese are spoken. It includes Mexico, Central and South America, and the West Indies.

Biography **Simón Bolívar**

As a young man, Simón Bolívar enjoyed a life of wealth and privilege. He studied the republican form of government of the United States. He also admired the military genius of Napoleon. Later, Bolívar's democratic ideals and military skills helped him free several South American nations from Spanish rule.

★ **Which nations did Bolívar help to liberate?**

Crown given to Bolívar by South American Indians ➤

from Venezuela over the high Andes Mountains into Colombia. There, Bolívar took the Spanish forces by surprise and defeated them in 1819.

Soon after, Bolívar became president of the independent Republic of Great Colombia. It included the present-day nations of Venezuela, Colombia, Ecuador, and Panama.

Other new nations

Other independent nations emerged in Latin America. **José de San Martín** (san mahr TEEN) led Argentina to freedom in 1816. He then helped the people of Chile, Peru, and Ecuador win independence.

In 1821, the peoples of Central America declared independence from Spain. Two years later, they formed the United Provinces of Central America. It included the present-day nations of Nicaragua, Costa Rica, El Salvador, Honduras, and Guatemala. By 1825, Spain had lost all its colonies in Latin America except Puerto Rico and Cuba.

The Portuguese colony of Brazil won independence peacefully. Prince Pedro, son of the Portuguese king, ruled the colony. The king advised his son, "If Brazil demands independence, proclaim it yourself and put the crown on your own head." In 1822, Pedro became emperor of the new independent nation of Brazil.

The New Republics

Spain's former colonies modeled their constitutions on that of the United States. Yet their experience after independence was very different from that of their neighbor to the north.

Unlike the people of the 13 British colonies, the peoples of Latin America did not unite into a single country. In part, geography made unity difficult. Latin America covered a much larger area than the English colonies. Mountains like the high, rugged Andes acted as a barrier to travel and communication.

The new republics had a hard time setting up stable governments. Under Spanish rule, the colonists had little or no experience in self-government. Economic problems and deep divisions between social classes increased discontent. Powerful leaders took advantage of the turmoil to seize control. As a result, the new nations were often unable to achieve democratic rule.

Connections With Civics

Like the United States, new Latin American nations created national flags. Venezuela's flag of yellow, blue, and red symbolized the gold of the Americas separated from Spain by the blue ocean. Argentina's blue-white-blue flag was the same flag flown by pirates who attacked Spanish ports and ships along the coasts of South and Central America.

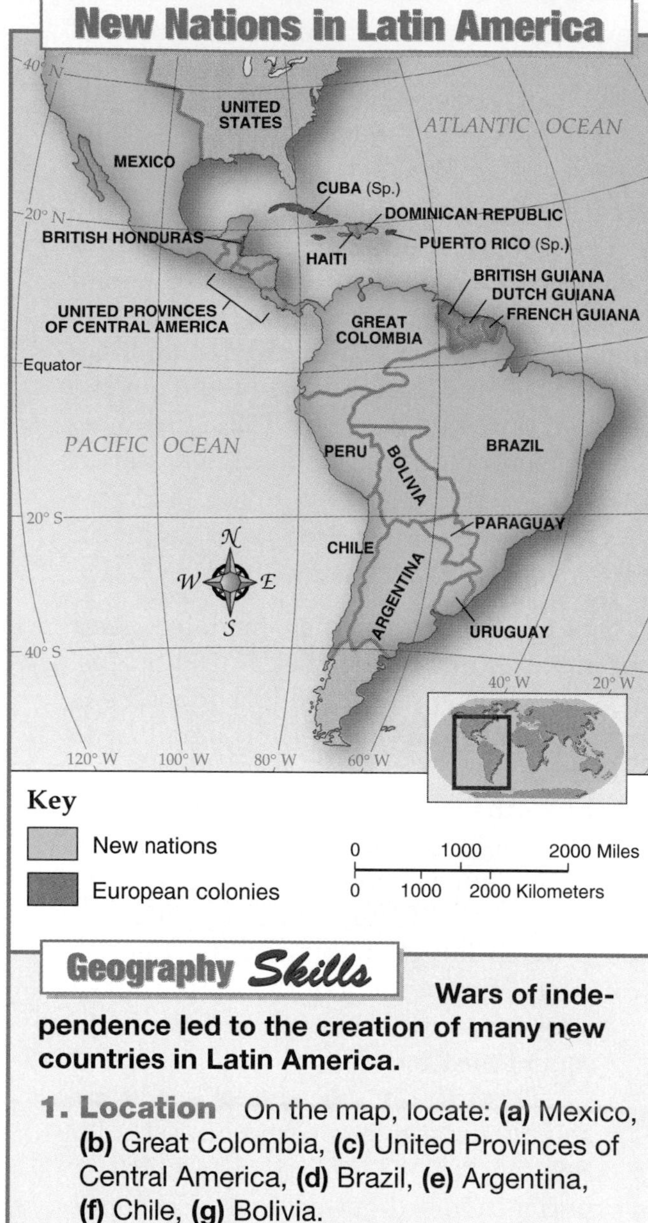

Geography Skills **Wars of independence led to the creation of many new countries in Latin America.**

1. **Location** On the map, locate: **(a)** Mexico, **(b)** Great Colombia, **(c)** United Provinces of Central America, **(d)** Brazil, **(e)** Argentina, **(f)** Chile, **(g)** Bolivia.
2. **Region** What parts of Latin America remained European colonies?
3. **Critical Thinking** Use the world map in the Reference Section to identify the modern nations that were eventually carved out of the United Provinces of Central America.

The United States Gains Florida

Spain lost another one of its colonies, Florida—not to independence, but to the United States. Many Americans wanted to gain possession of Florida. As early as 1810, President Madison tried to claim West Florida for the United States.

Concern over Florida grew, especially among Southerners. Creek and Seminole Indians in Florida sometimes raided settlements in Georgia. Also, Florida was a refuge for many enslaved African Americans.

"Black Seminoles"

Since the 1700s, Spanish officials had protected slaves who fled from plantations in Georgia and South Carolina. Seminole Indians allowed African Americans to live near their villages. In return, these **"black Seminoles"** gave the Indians a share of the crops they raised every year. The black Seminoles adopted many Indian customs. In addition, some African Americans married Seminoles.

After the War of 1812, African Americans occupied a fort on the Apalachicola River. They invited runaway slaves to settle nearby. Soon, some 1,000 African Americans farmed on the banks of the Apalachicola, protected by the "Negro Fort."

American gunboats attack

General Andrew Jackson demanded that Spain demolish the Negro Fort. The Spanish governor refused. In 1816, Jackson's gunboats invaded Spanish territory and sailed up the Apalachicola.

Inside the Negro Fort, a force of free African Americans waited, cannons ready. They knew that the Americans had come to return them to slavery. After a spirited fight, the gunboats destroyed the fort. Black settlers along the Apalachicola were forced to flee. Many joined nearby Seminoles. Together, they continued to resist American raids into Florida.

Spain gives up Florida

In 1818, Jackson headed to Florida again with a force of over 3,000 soldiers. Spain protested, but it was busy fighting rebels in Latin America. It could not risk war with the United States.

In the end, Spain agreed to peace talks. Secretary of State **John Quincy Adams** worked out a treaty with Spain. In it, Spain agreed to give Florida to the United States in exchange for $5 million. The **Adams-Onís Treaty** took effect in 1821.

The Monroe Doctrine

Americans cheered as Latin American nations won independence. The actions of European powers, however, worried American officials. Prussia, France, Russia, and Austria seemed ready to help Spain regain its colonies in Latin America. In addition, Russia claimed lands on the Pacific coast of North America.

The British, too, were concerned about European nations meddling in the Western Hemisphere. They suggested issuing a joint statement with the United States. It would guarantee the freedom of the new nations.

Monroe decided to act independently of Britain. In a message to Congress in 1823, he made a bold foreign policy statement, known as the **Monroe Doctrine.** Monroe declared that the United States would not interfere in the affairs of European nations or colonies. At the same time, he warned European nations not to interfere with newly independent nations of Latin America:

> ❝ The American continents . . . are henceforth not to be considered as subjects for future colonization by any European powers. . . . We should consider any attempt on their part to extend their system to any portion of this hemisphere as dangerous to our peace and safety. ❞

The Monroe Doctrine also stated that the United States would oppose any attempt to build new colonies in the Americas. Monroe's message showed that the United States was determined to keep European powers out of the Western Hemisphere.

The United States did not have the military power to enforce the Monroe Doctrine. Britain, however, supported the statement. With its strong navy, it could stop Europeans from interfering in the Americas.

As the United States became stronger, the Monroe Doctrine grew in importance. On several occasions, the United States successfully challenged European **intervention,** or direct involvement, in Latin America. In the early 1900s, Presidents also used the Monroe Doctrine to justify sending troops to Caribbean nations. Thus, Monroe's bold statement helped shape United States foreign policy for more than 100 years.

★ Section 4 Review ★

Recall

1. **Locate** **(a)** Mexico, **(b)** Great Colombia, **(c)** Argentina, **(d)** United Provinces of Central America, **(e)** Brazil.
2. **Identify** **(a)** Miguel Hidalgo, **(b)** Simón Bolívar, **(c)** José de San Martín, **(d)** "black Seminoles," **(e)** John Quincy Adams, **(f)** Adams-Onís Treaty, **(g)** Monroe Doctrine.
3. **Define** **(a)** creole, **(b)** intervention.

Comprehension

4. **(a)** Why did Latin American nations seek independence in the early 1800s? **(b)** What problems did the new republics face?
5. Why did many Americans want to gain control of Florida?
6. Why did President Monroe issue the Monroe Doctrine?

Critical Thinking and Writing

7. **Making Inferences** How do you think the defenders of the Negro Fort in Florida might have inspired enslaved African Americans in the United States?
8. **Predicting Consequences** What do you think might have happened if Spain had sent an army to regain control of Mexico in the late 1820s?

Activity **Designing a Poster** Your school is participating in a "Know Your Neighbors" fair. The goal is to promote friendly relations with Latin American nations. Design a poster honoring how one neighboring nation gained independence.

Chapter 9 Review and Activities

★ Sum It Up ★

Section 1 The Industrial Revolution

- The Industrial Revolution spread to the United States from Britain in the late 1700s.
- Though factory work was hard, many people moved from farms to work in factories in cities and towns.

Section 2 Moving Westward

- Westward movement was so heavy that eight new states joined the nation between 1789 and 1819.
- Improved roads, steamboats, and canals reduced travel time and lowered the cost of moving goods and people.

Section 3 Building National Unity

- As disputes between different sections of the nation grew more intense, great sectional leaders emerged.
- Political leaders tried to use their power to make the United States stronger economically.

Section 4 Latin America and the United States

- In the early 1800s, almost all of Spain's Latin American colonies won their independence.
- The Monroe Doctrine stated that the United States would oppose European efforts to create new colonies in the Western Hemisphere.

For additional review of the major ideas of Chapter 9, see ***Guide to the Essentials of American History*** or ***Interactive Student Tutorial CD-ROM,*** which contains interactive review activities, graphic organizers, and practice tests.

Reviewing the Chapter

Define These Terms

Match each term with the correct definition.

Column 1	Column 2
1. capitalist	**a.** channel that allows boats to cross a stretch of land
2. urbanization	**b.** person who invests in a business to make a profit
3. turnpike	**c.** practice of selling goods in another country at low prices
4. canal	**d.** movement of populations from farms to cities
5. dumping	**e.** toll road

Explore the Main Ideas

1. Describe the factory system.
2. Why was river travel better than travel by road?
3. Identify the great leader who spoke for each of the three sections of the United States.
4. Why did Congress pass the Tariff of 1816?
5. What two important points did Monroe make in the Monroe Doctrine?

Geography Activity

Match the letters on the map with the following places: **1.** Wheeling, Virginia, **2.** New York City, **3.** Cumberland Gap, **4.** Lancaster Turnpike, **5.** National Road, **6.** Erie Canal. **Interaction** What obstacles did Americans overcome in building the Erie Canal?

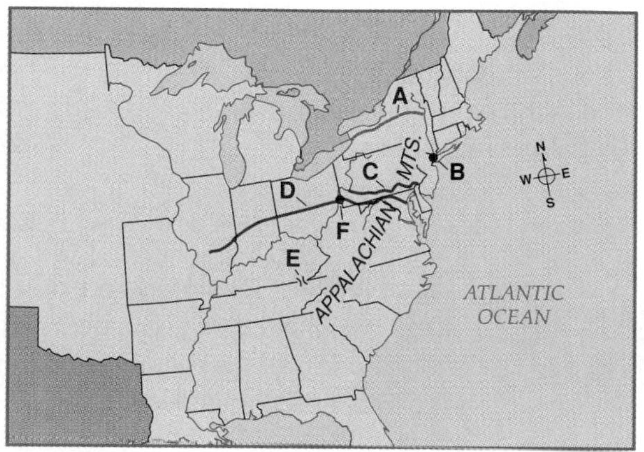

Critical Thinking and Writing

1. **Understanding Chronology** **(a)** Did the War of 1812 begin before or after the formation of the Boston Associates? **(b)** How were these two events linked?
2. **Linking Past and Present** Do cities today have the same kinds of problems as cities in the early 1800s? Explain.
3. **Evaluating Information** What information do you have that suggests that "The Era of Good Feelings" did not last?
4. **Exploring Unit Themes** **Nationalism** Henry Clay has been called the "most nationalistic" of the great congressional leaders. What facts support this opinion?

Using Primary Sources

Davy Crockett was a Tennessee settler who became a representative in Congress. He toured the city of Lowell in 1834 and gave this description:

> "The dinner bells were ringing, and the folks pouring out of the [work] houses like bees out of a gum [tree]. I looked at them as they passed, all well dressed, lively, genteel in their appearance.... I went in among the young girls, and talked with many of them. No one expressed herself as tired of her employment, or oppressed with work: all talked well, and looked healthy."

Source: *An Account of Col. Crockett's Tour to the North and Down East,* Davy Crockett, 1835.

Recognizing Points of View **(a)** What was the condition of the workers at Lowell, according to Crockett? **(b)** Why do you think a representative from Tennessee would have been interested in conditions at mills in Massachusetts?

Activity Bank

Interdisciplinary Activity

Exploring the Arts With a partner, create a skit, dance, or song about the difficulties of travel in the early 1800s.

Career Skills Activity

Engineers Draw a diagram or prepare a demonstration to show how early factories harnessed the force of water to create power to run machines.

Citizenship Activity

Understanding Regional Politics Sectional politics is still an issue in the United States. Prepare a report in which you describe the needs of your own region. Consider such questions as: Does your region have special resource or energy needs? How do the needs of your region compare with the needs of other regions? What policies would benefit your region?

Internet Activity

Use the Internet to find sites dealing with the National Road, now called Route 40. Using your Web research, create a tourist map of the road showing the towns it passes through, nearby hotels and restaurants, and historic or interesting information about it.

Eyewitness Journal

Take one of the following roles: a young woman working at the Lowell mills; a mayor of a frontier town; a settler living in the New York wilderness near the route of the Erie Canal; a black Seminole in Florida. In your Eyewitness Journal, record three events that affected your life between 1800 and 1825.

Rip Van Winkle

by Washington Irving

Introduction

Washington Irving (1783–1859) was the first American to make a living as a popular writer. "Rip Van Winkle" is Irving's best-loved tale. The story is a humorous fantasy about a lazy farmer in a small New York village. One night in the early 1770s, Rip Van Winkle wanders up into the Catskill Mountains, falls asleep—and does not wake up for 20 years! In the selection below, Rip returns to his old village after his long nap.

Vocabulary

Before you read the selection, find the meaning of these words in a dictionary: **yore, assemblage, incomprehensible, metamorphosed, buff, disputatious, tranquillity, haranguing, vehemently.**

He had now entered the skirts of the village. A troop of strange children ran at his heels, hooting after him and pointing at his gray beard. The dogs, too, not one of which he recognized for an old acquaintance, barked at him as he passed. The very village was altered; it was larger and more populous. There were rows of houses which he had never seen before, and those which had been his familiar haunts had disappeared. . . .

He now hurried forth and hastened to his old retreat, the village inn—but it too was gone. A large, rickety, wooden building stood in its place, with great gaping windows, some of them broken and mended with old hats and petticoats, and over the door was painted, "the Union Hotel, by Jonathan Doolittle." Instead of the great tree that used to shelter the quiet little Dutch town of yore, there now was reared a tall, naked pole, with something on the top that looked like a red nightcap,* and from it was fluttering a flag, on which was a singular assemblage of stars and stripes—all this was strange and incomprehensible. He recognized on the sign, however, the ruby face of King George . . . but even this was singularly metamorphosed. The red coat was changed for one of blue and buff, a sword was held in the hand instead of a scepter, the head was decorated with a cocked hat, and underneath was painted in large characters, GENERAL WASHINGTON.

There was, as usual, a crowd of folk about the door, but none that Rip recollected. The very character of the people seemed changed. There was a busy, bustling, disputatious tone about it, instead of the accustomed . . . drowsy tranquillity. He looked in vain for the sage Nicholas Vedder, with his broad face, double chin, and fair long pipe . . . or Van Bummel, the schoolmaster, doling forth the contents of an ancient newspaper. In place of these, a lean . . . fellow, with his pockets full of handbills, was haranguing vehemently about rights of citizens—elections—members of congress—liberty—Bunker's Hill—heroes of seventy-six—and other words, which were [strange] to the bewildered Van Winkle.

*"Liberty poles" and "liberty caps" were popular symbols of both the American and French revolutions.

Viewing HISTORY Rip Van Winkle Comes Home

Painter John Quidor was a personal friend of Washington Irving. His painting, Return of Rip Van Winkle *(detail), shows Rip coming home to his village. Rip's long white beard and tattered clothing show the effects of his 20-year nap.*
★ Identify two objects in this picture that confused Rip when he returned home. Why were they unfamiliar to him?

The appearance of Rip, with his long, grizzled beard . . . and an army of women and children at his heels, soon attracted the attention of the tavern politicians. They crowded around him, eyeing him from head to foot with great curiosity. The orator bustled up to him and, drawing him partly aside, inquired "on which side he voted?" Rip stared in vacant stupidity. Another short but busy little fellow pulled him by the arm and, rising on tiptoe, inquired in his ear, "whether he was Federal or Democrat?" Rip was equally at a loss to comprehend the question. . . . "Alas! Gentlemen," cried Rip, somewhat dismayed, "I am a poor, quiet man, a native of this place, and a loyal subject of the king, God bless him!"

Here a general shout burst from the bystanders. "A tory! A tory! A spy! A refugee! Hustle him! Away with him!" It was with great difficulty that [a] self-important man in [a] cocked hat restored order; and . . . demanded again of the unknown culprit what he came there for and whom he was seeking. The poor man humbly assured him that he meant no harm, but merely came there in search of some of his neighbors, who used to keep about the tavern.

"Well—who are they? Name them."

Rip bethought himself a moment, and inquired . . . "Where's Brom Dutcher?"

"Oh, he went off to the army at the beginning of the war; some say he was killed at the storming of Stony Point—others say he was drowned in a squall at the foot of Antony's Nose. I don't know—he never came back again."

"Where's Van Bummel, the schoolmaster?"

"He went off to the wars, too, was a great militia general, and is now in congress."

Rip's heart died away at hearing of these sad changes in his home and friends, and finding himself thus alone in the world. Every answer puzzled him, too, by treating of such enormous lapses of time and of matter which he could not understand: war—congress—Stony Point. He had no courage to ask after any more friends, but cried out in despair, "Does nobody here know Rip Van Winkle?"

Analyzing Literature

1. Describe three changes Rip Van Winkle sees when he returns to his village.
2. Why does Rip get into trouble with the men gathered outside the tavern?
3. **Critical Thinking Making Inferences** According to the story, the very nature of the people seemed different to Rip. **(a)** How does Rip think the people changed? **(b)** What do you think may have caused this change?

Unit 4 The Nation Expands

What's Ahead

Viewing UNIT THEMES **Wagon Trains to the West**

William Henry Jackson, who later became a famous photographer, painted this dramatic scene. It shows long lines of wagons carrying settlers westward across Nebraska toward Oregon. In the mid-1800s, wagon trains like this carried thousands of American families from the East to newly acquired territories in the West. ★ **Based on this painting, jot down four words or phrases that you would use to describe a journey to the West by wagon train.**

Unit Theme Expansion

From 1820 to 1860, the United States grew in several ways. The most dramatic growth was in the size of the nation. It gained vast western territories, including California, Texas, Oregon, and New Mexico. For the first time, an American could travel by land from the Atlantic Ocean to the Pacific without leaving the country.

How did people of the time feel about westward expansion? They can tell you in their own words.

★ ★

Viewpoints on Westward Expansion

"Our population is rolling toward the shores of the Pacific. . . . It will soon . . . reach the Rocky Mountains and be ready to pour into the Oregon territory."

John C. Calhoun, South Carolina senator (1843)

"We traveled till 11 o'clock with the hope of finding water for the weary cattle. The sun was excessively oppressive."

Susan Shelby Magoffin, New Mexico pioneer (1846)

"The white man comes and cuts down the trees, building houses and fences and the buffaloes get frightened and leave and never come back, and the Indians are left to starve."

Muguara, Chief of the Penateka Comanche Indians (1840s)

★ ★

Activity Writing to Learn Thousands of families left their homes in the East to make the long journey westward. What if your family was thinking of moving to another part of the country? List what you might gain by moving. Then, make another list of what you might lose. Use your lists to decide whether you want to move.

Chapter 10

Democracy in the Age of Jackson 1824–1840

What's Ahead

In this chapter, you will learn that the Age of Jackson was a time of expanding democracy and political conflict. As more and more white males gained the right to vote, two political parties, the Whigs and Democrats, competed for their support. Nomination conventions and heated election campaigns became part of American politics. Not all, however, shared in democracy's growth. Women, Native Americans, African Americans, and others had to wait for political and social equality.

Why Study History? Soon, you will have a right and a responsibility of all American citizens—voting. Learning more about how politics worked in past elections may help you make wise voting decisions in the future. To learn more about politics and your right to vote, see this chapter's *Why Study History?* feature, "You Will Choose Our Nation's Leaders."

American Events

1820s Right to vote extended to most white men

1828 Andrew Jackson is elected President

1830 Indian Removal Act forces Native Americans to move west of the Mississippi

1824 1826 1828 1830 1832

World Events

1824 World Event Simón Bolívar becomes president of Peru

1829 World Event Swiss adopt universal male suffrage

Viewing HISTORY **Election Day**

The Age of Jackson was a time of expanding democracy. During the 1820s and 1830s, more and more Americans gained the right to vote. In his painting County Election, *George Caleb Bingham shows that Election Day was a time for voting, socializing, and celebrating.* ★ **How does this painting suggest that women were not allowed to participate fully in American democracy?**

1832 President Jackson vetoes charter of the Bank of the United States

1835 Seminole War begins

1840 William Henry Harrison is elected President

1832 1834 1836 1838 1840

1832 World Event Reform Act doubles number of eligible voters in Britain

1837 World Event Canadian colonists revolt, demanding democratic reform

A New Era in Politics

As You Read

Explore These Questions

- Why was John Quincy Adams an unpopular President?
- How did voting rights change in the 1820s and 1830s?
- How did political parties become more democratic?

Define

- majority
- suffrage
- caucus
- nominating convention

Identify

- John Quincy Adams
- Whigs
- Democrats
- Alexis de Tocqueville

SETTING the Scene Harry Ward, a New England teacher, made a visit to Cincinnati, Ohio, during the 1824 presidential election campaign. Writing to a friend, he described how Ohioans felt about Andrew Jackson, who was running for President. "Strange! Wild! Infatuated! All for Jackson!" he observed.

On election day, more people voted for Andrew Jackson than for any of the other candidates. Oddly enough, Jackson did not become President that year.

The Disputed Election of 1824

There were four candidates for President in 1824. All four were members of the old Republican party. However, each had support in different parts of the country. **John Quincy Adams** was strong in New England. Henry Clay and Andrew Jackson had support in the West. William Crawford was favored in the South but became too ill to campaign.

The candidates

John Quincy Adams of Massachusetts was the son of Abigail and John Adams, the second President. The younger Adams was a graduate of Harvard University. He had served as Secretary of State and had helped end the War of 1812. People admired Adams for his intelligence and high morals. Adams, however, was uncomfortable campaigning among the common people.

Henry Clay, by contrast, was charming. A Kentuckian, Clay was a shrewd politician who had become Speaker of the House of Representatives. In Congress, Clay was a skillful negotiator. He worked out several important compromises. Despite his abilities, Clay was less popular than the other candidate from the West, Andrew Jackson.

Most Americans knew Andrew Jackson for his military victories in the War of 1812. He was the "Hero of New Orleans." Though he was a landowner and a slave owner, many saw him as a man of the people. Jackson was born in a log cabin and his parents were poor farmers. He was admired by small farmers and others who felt left out of the growing economy in the United States.

The "corrupt bargain"

No clear winner emerged from the election of 1824. Jackson won the popular vote, but no candidate won a **majority,** or more than half, of the electoral votes. As a result, the House of Representatives had to choose the President from among the top three candidates. Because he finished fourth, Clay was out of the running. As Speaker of the House, though, he was able to influence the results.

Clay urged members of the House to vote for Adams. After Adams became President, he made Clay his Secretary of State. Jackson and his backers were furious. They accused Adams and Clay of making a "corrupt bargain" and stealing the election from Jackson. As Jackson was riding home to Tennessee, he met an old friend. "Well, General," said the friend, "we did all we could for you here, but the rascals at Washington cheated you out of it."

"Indeed, my old friend," replied Jackson, "there was *cheating* and *corruption,* and *bribery,* too." In fact, such charges were not true. The election had been decided as the Constitution stated. Still, the anger of Jackson and his supporters seriously hampered President Adams's efforts to unify the nation.

An Unpopular President

Adams knew that the election had angered many Americans. To "bring the whole people together," he pushed for a program of economic growth through internal improvements. His plan backfired, however, and opposition to him grew.

Promoting economic growth

Similar to Alexander Hamilton and Henry Clay, Adams thought that the federal government should promote economic growth. He called for the government to pay for new roads and canals. These internal improvements would help farmers to transport goods to market.

Adams also favored projects to promote the arts and the sciences, as governments in Europe did. He suggested building a national university and an observatory from which astronomers could study the stars.

Most Americans objected to spending money on such programs. They feared that the federal government would become too powerful. Congress approved money for a national road and some canals, but turned down most of Adams's other programs.

A bitter campaign

In 1828, Adams faced an uphill battle for reelection. This time, Andrew Jackson was Adams's only opponent.

The campaign was a bitter contest. Jackson supporters renewed charges that Adams had made a "corrupt bargain" after the 1824 election. They attacked Adams as an aristocrat, or member of the upper class. Adams supporters replied with similar attacks. They called Jackson a dangerous "military chieftain." If Jackson became President, they warned, he could become a dictator like Napoleon Bonaparte of France.

Jackson won the election easily. His supporters cheered the outcome as a victory for common people. By common people, they meant farmers in the West and South and city workers in the East.

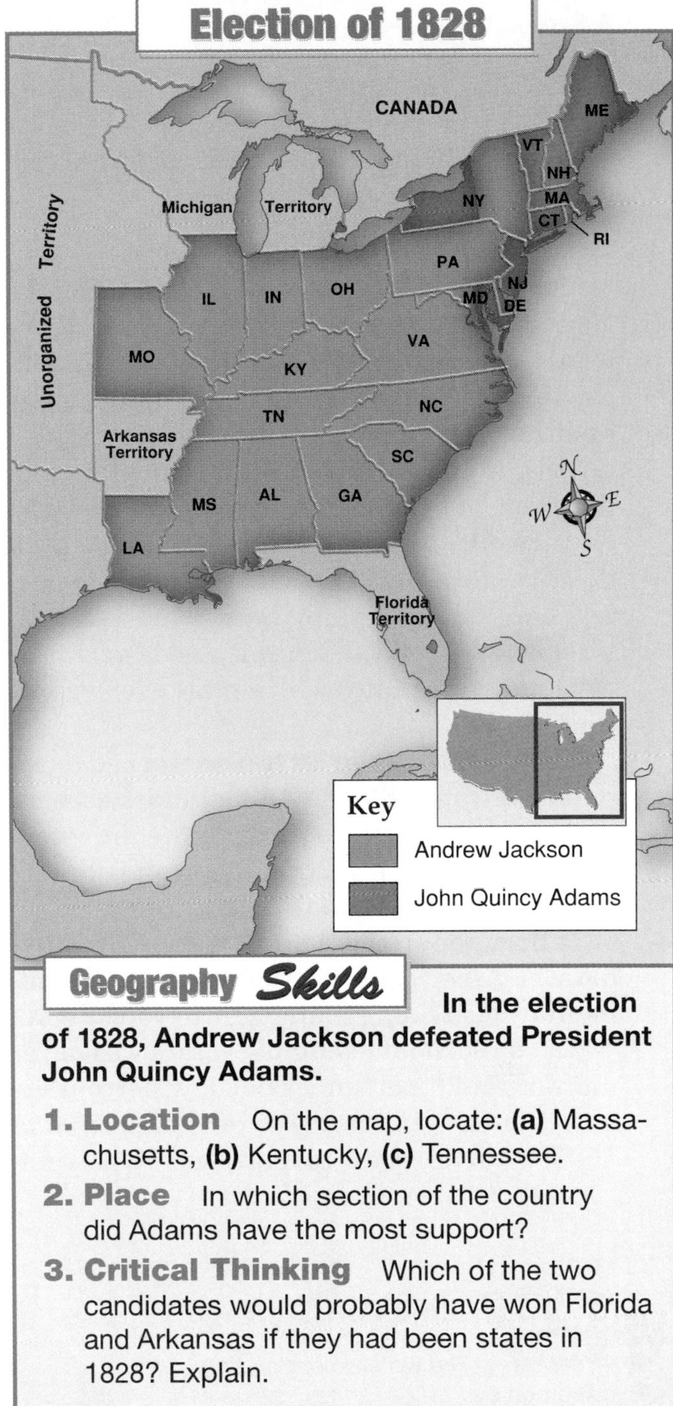

Geography *Skills* **In the election of 1828, Andrew Jackson defeated President John Quincy Adams.**

1. **Location** On the map, locate: **(a)** Massachusetts, **(b)** Kentucky, **(c)** Tennessee.
2. **Place** In which section of the country did Adams have the most support?
3. **Critical Thinking** Which of the two candidates would probably have won Florida and Arkansas if they had been states in 1828? Explain.

More Voters

During the 1820s, more people gained **suffrage,** or the right to vote. Others, however, were denied full participation in the growing democracy.

Expanding suffrage

The United States was growing rapidly. New states were joining the Union and there were many new voters. Many of them lived in western states between the Appalachians and the Mississippi.

In the West, many frontier people began life poor, but prospered through hard work. As a result, westerners commonly believed that it was possible to achieve success by being honest and working hard. This democratic spirit was reflected in suffrage laws. In the western states, any white man over age 21 could vote.

Reformers in the East also worked to expand suffrage. By the 1830s, most eastern states dropped the requirement that voters own land. In this way, many craftsworkers and shopkeepers won the right to vote.

Throughout the country, growing numbers of Americans participated in government by exercising their right to vote. Before 1828, the turnout of eligible voters was never more than 25 percent. That low percentage rose to nearly 55 percent in the election of 1828. By 1840, voter turnout was 78 percent.

Limits on suffrage

Despite the growing democratic spirit, many Americans did not have the right to vote. They included women, Native Americans, and most African Americans. Slaves had no political rights.

In fact, as more white men were winning suffrage, free African Americans were losing it. In the early years of the nation, most northern states had allowed free African American men to vote. In the 1820s, many of these states took away that right. By 1830, only a few New England states permitted African American men to vote on equal terms with white men. In New York, African American men had to own property in order to vote. White men did not.

New Political Practices

By 1820, the disappearance of the Federalist party temporarily ended party differences. In the 1830s, new political parties took shape. They grew out of the conflict between John Quincy Adams and Andrew Jackson.

Two new parties

People who supported Adams and his programs for national growth called themselves National Republicans. In 1834, they became known as **Whigs.** Whigs wanted the federal government to spur the economy. Whigs included eastern business people, some south-

Viewing History **Limits on Suffrage**

The watercolor painting Two Women *by Eunice Pinney shows two women engaged in conversation. During the Age of Jackson, women could not vote in a single state. Most men of the time thought that women should take care of household responsibilities.*

★ **How do you think women were able to influence the outcome of elections?**

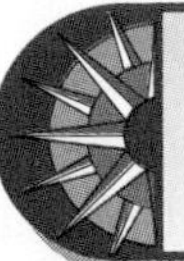

Linking Past and Present

Past

Present

The People and the Presidency

In 1829, President Jackson held a party at the White House to celebrate his inauguration. Cheerful guests helped themselves to slices of a huge cheese. Today, Presidents invite Americans into their home for tours or special events. One example is the Easter egg roll, held each year on the White House lawn. ★ **Why did some people criticize Jackson for opening the White House to the common people?**

ern planters, and former Federalists. Jackson and his supporters called themselves **Democrats.** Today's Democratic party traces its roots to Andrew Jackson's time. Democrats included frontier farmers, as well as factory workers in the East.

New ways to choose candidates

The two new political parties developed more democratic ways to choose candidates for President. In the past, powerful members of each party held a **caucus,** or private meeting. There, they chose their candidate. Critics called the caucus system undemocratic because only a few powerful people were able to take part in it.

In the 1830s, each party began to hold a **nominating convention,** where delegates from all the states chose the party's candidate for President. Nominating conventions gave people a more direct voice in choosing future leaders. Party leaders might still dominate a particular convention, but the nominating process was becoming subject to the will of the people. Today, the major political parties still hold conventions.

Growing Spirit of Equality

The spirit of democracy affected American ideas about social classes. Most Americans did not feel that the rich deserved special respect. "Does a man become wiser, stronger or more virtuous and patriotic because he has a fine house?" asked a Democrat.

Wealthy European visitors to the United States were surprised that American servants expected to be treated as equals. Others were amazed that butlers and maids refused to be summoned with bells, as in Europe. **Alexis de Tocqueville** (tohk VEEL), a visitor from France, became especially well known for his observations on American democracy.

Alexis de Tocqueville

In 1831, Alexis de Tocqueville arrived in the United States. The French government had sent him to study the American prison system. Over a period of several months, Tocqueville toured much of the United States. He observed much more than prisons. He observed a society that was becoming more and more democratic.

After his return to France, Tocqueville recorded his experiences and observations in a book titled *Democracy in America.* In it, he admired the American democratic spirit and its goals of equality and freedom.

> ❝ Although the revolution that is taking place in the social condition, laws, ideas, and feelings of men is still far from coming to an end, yet its results are already incomparably greater than anything which has taken place in the world before. ❞

Jacksonian democracy

Andrew Jackson's inauguration in 1829 reflected the spirit of Jacksonian democracy. As Jackson traveled to Washington, large crowds cheered him along the way. For the first time, thousands of ordinary people flooded the capital to watch the President take the oath of office.

After Jackson was sworn in, the crowd followed the new President to a reception at the White House. The appearance and behavior of the "common people" shocked an onlooker:

> ❝ A rabble, a mob, of boys, negros, women, children, scrambling, fighting, romping. What a pity, what a pity! No arrangements had been made, no police officers on duty, and the whole house had been [filled] by the rabble mob. ❞

The President, he continued, was "almost suffocated and torn to pieces by the people in their eagerness to shake hands."

Jackson's critics said the scene showed that "King Mob" was ruling the nation. Amos Kendall, a loyal Jackson supporter, viewed the inauguration celebration in a more positive way: "It was a proud day for the people. General Jackson is *their own* President."

★ Section 1 Review ★

Recall

1. **Locate** **(a)** Massachusetts, **(b)** Kentucky, **(c)** Tennessee.
2. **Identify** **(a)** John Quincy Adams, **(b)** Whigs, **(c)** Democrats, **(d)** Alexis de Tocqueville.
3. **Define** **(a)** majority, **(b)** suffrage, **(c)** caucus, **(d)** nominating convention.

Comprehension

4. Why did voters not reelect John Quincy Adams to the Presidency in 1828?
5. **(a)** How did suffrage expand in the 1820s and 1830s? **(b)** What Americans were denied suffrage?
6. How were nominating conventions more democratic than the caucus system?

Critical Thinking and Writing

7. **Applying Information** Based on what you learned about the election of 1824, if no candidate won a majority of electoral votes in the next presidential election, how would the President be chosen?
8. **Defending a Position** Do you agree or disagree with John Quincy Adams's position that the government should spend money to support the arts and sciences? Explain the reasons for your position.

Activity **Writing an Advertisement** Suffrage has expanded greatly since the Age of Jackson. Still, many Americans do not exercise their right to vote. Write a radio or television advertisement urging people to get out and vote next Election Day.

Jackson in the White House

As You Read

Explore These Questions

- What qualities helped Jackson succeed?
- Why did Jackson replace many office-holders?
- Why did Jackson fight against the Bank of the United States?

Define

- spoils system
- pet bank

Identify

- Old Hickory
- kitchen cabinet
- Nicholas Biddle

SETTING the Scene During the 1828 election campaign, many stories about Andrew Jackson spread. Like the one that follows, they often showed Jackson's courage and determination.

Years before he ran for President, Jackson was a judge in Tennessee. One day, a disorderly lawbreaker, Russell Bean, refused to appear before the court. The story tells how Jackson strutted out of the courthouse. "Surrender, you infernal villain," he roared, "or I'll blow you through." Bean looked into Jackson's blazing eyes and quietly surrendered. The iron will that made Russell Bean surrender also made Jackson a powerful President.

A young Andrew Jackson

Andrew Jackson

Like many who admired him, Jackson was born in a log cabin on the frontier. His parents had left Ireland to settle on the Carolina frontier. Both died before Jackson was 15. Young Andrew had to grow up quickly.

A tough fighter

Like many other boys who grew up on the frontier, young Andrew Jackson was a determined fighter. Even though he had a slight build, he was strong and determined. A friend who wrestled with him recalled, "I could throw him three times out of four, but he would never stay throwed."

Jackson showed his toughness during the American Revolution. At age 13, he joined the Patriots but was captured by the British. When a British officer ordered the young prisoner to clean his boots, Jackson refused. The officer took a sword and slashed the boy's hand and face. The memory of that attack stayed with Jackson for the rest of his life.

A self-made man

After the Revolution, Jackson studied law in North Carolina. Later, he moved to Tennessee and set up a successful law practice. He became very wealthy by buying and selling land in Georgia and Alabama. While still in his twenties, he was elected to Congress.

Jackson won national fame for his achievements during the War of 1812. He commanded the American forces to a major victory over the British at the Battle of New Orleans. He also defeated the Creek Indians and forced them to give up vast amounts of land in Georgia and Alabama.

A man of many qualities

Andrew Jackson was a man of many qualities. He had led a violent and adventurous life. He was no stranger to brawls, gambling, and duels. He was quick to lose his temper and he dealt with his enemies harshly.

Jackson's supporters admired his ability to inspire and lead others. They considered him a man of his word and a champion of the common people. The soldiers who served under Jackson called him **Old Hickory.** To them, he was as tough as the wood of a hickory tree.

To the Creek Indians, however, Jackson was an enemy who showed no mercy. After defeating them, Jackson had threatened to kill their leaders if they did not give up lands that earlier treaties had guaranteed them. As a result, the Creeks had no affection for Jackson. Their name for him was Sharp Knife.

The Spoils System

In 1828, President Jackson knew that Americans wanted change. "The people expected reform," he said. "This was the cry from Maine to Louisiana."

Reward for victory

After taking office, Jackson fired many government employees. He replaced them with his own supporters. Most other Presidents had done the same, but Jackson did it on a larger scale.

Critics accused Jackson of rewarding Democrats who had helped elect him instead of choosing qualified men. Jackson replied that he was serving democracy by letting more citizens take part in government. He felt that ordinary Americans could fill government jobs. "The duties of all public officers are ... so plain and simple that men of intelligence may readily qualify themselves for their performance," he said.

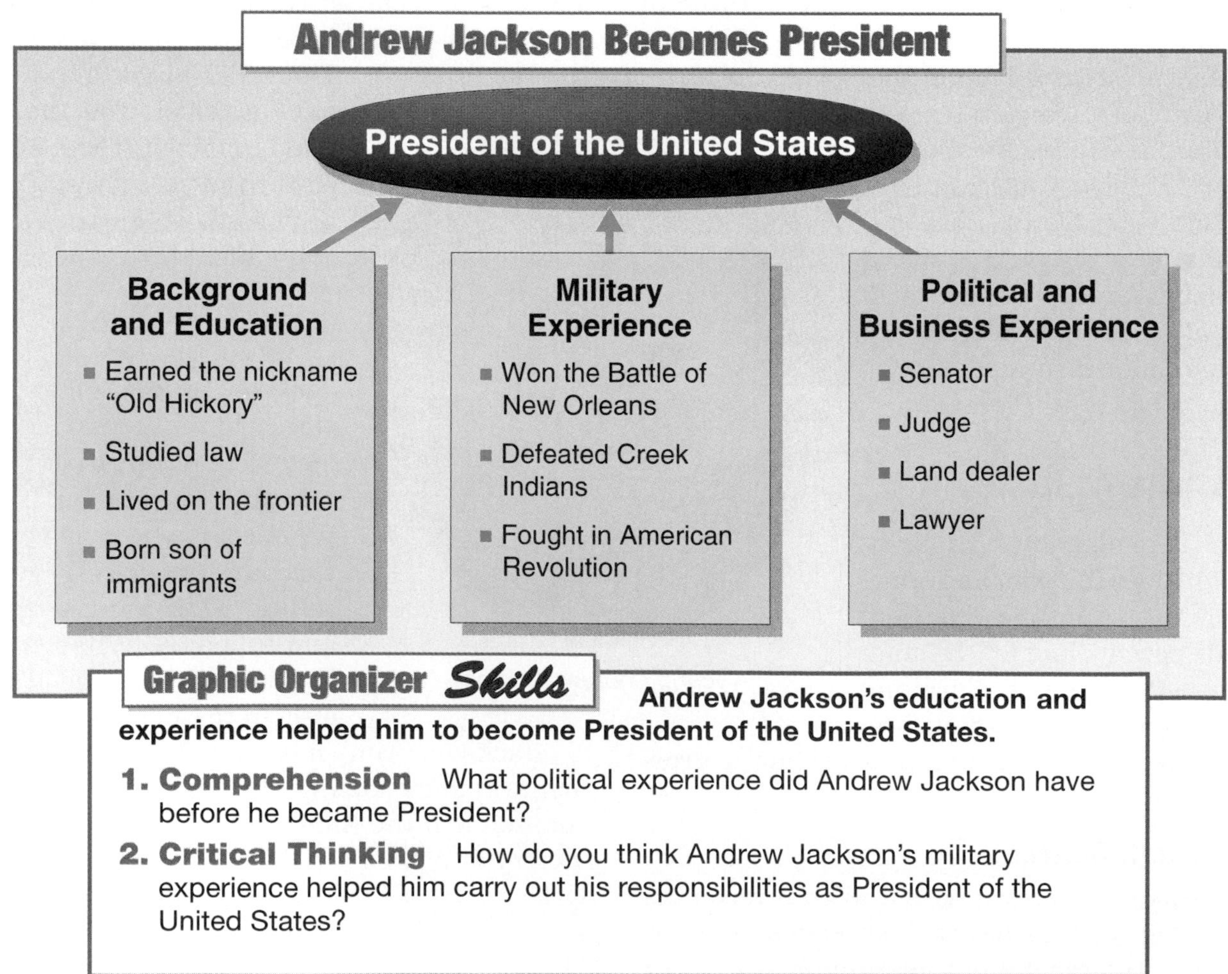

Graphic Organizer *Skills* **Andrew Jackson's education and experience helped him to become President of the United States.**

1. **Comprehension** What political experience did Andrew Jackson have before he became President?
2. **Critical Thinking** How do you think Andrew Jackson's military experience helped him carry out his responsibilities as President of the United States?

Viewing History **A Kitchen Cabinet Dispute**

President Jackson often asked for advice from an unofficial group of advisers. This cartoon presents one artist's view of Jackson's "kitchen cabinet." ★ **What was the cartoonist's opinion of the kitchen cabinet? Explain.**

A Jackson supporter explained the system another way. "To the victor belong the spoils," he declared. Spoils are profits or benefits. From then on, the practice of rewarding supporters with government jobs became known as the **spoils system.**

The kitchen cabinet

Jackson rewarded a number of his supporters with Cabinet jobs. Only Secretary of State Martin Van Buren was truly qualified for his position.

As a result, Jackson seldom met with his official Cabinet. Instead, he relied on a group of unofficial advisers. They included Democratic leaders and newspaper editors. These men had a good sense of the nation's mood. Because Jackson met with them in the White House kitchen, the group became known as the **kitchen cabinet.**

The Bank War

President Jackson waged war on the Bank of the United States. Like many westerners, he thought that it was too powerful.

Mr. Biddle's bank

From the first, the Bank of the United States had been a subject of dispute. (See page 175.) The Bank had great power because it controlled loans made by state banks. When the Bank's directors thought that state banks were making too many loans, they limited the amount these banks could lend. The cutbacks angered farmers and merchants who borrowed money to buy land or finance new businesses.

President Jackson and other leading Democrats saw the Bank as undemocratic. Although Congress had created the Bank, it was run by private bankers. Jackson condemned these men as agents of "special privilege" who grew rich with public funds. He especially disliked **Nicholas Biddle,** president of the Bank since 1823.

Biddle came from a wealthy Philadelphia family. He was well qualified to run the bank, but he was also arrogant and vain. Jackson felt that Biddle used the Bank to benefit only the rich. He also resented Biddle's influence over certain members of Congress.

$ Connections With Economics

Today, the Federal Reserve Board supervises a national system of banks and has much influence over the economy. It can tighten the money supply and reduce inflation by raising interest rates. By lowering interest rates on loans, it can encourage economic growth.

The war begins

Biddle and other Whigs worried that the President might try to destroy the Bank. Two Whig senators, Henry Clay and Daniel Webster, thought of a way to save the Bank and defeat Jackson at the same time.

The Bank's charter was not due for renewal by Congress until 1836. However, Clay and Webster wanted to make the Bank an issue in the 1832 election. They persuaded Biddle to apply for renewal early.

The Whigs believed that most Americans supported the Bank of the United States. If Jackson vetoed the bill to renew the charter, they felt sure that he would anger voters and lose the election. Clay pushed the charter renewal bill through Congress in 1832. Jackson was sick in bed when he heard that Congress had renewed the Bank's charter. "The Bank... is trying to kill me," Jackson fumed, "but I will kill it!"

Jackson's veto

In an angry message to Congress, Jackson vetoed the Bank bill. He gave two reasons for his veto. First, he declared the Bank unconstitutional, even though the Supreme Court had ruled in the Bank's favor. Jackson believed that only states, not the federal government, had the right to charter banks. Second, Jackson felt that the Bank helped aristocrats at the expense of the common people. He warned:

> ❝ When the laws undertake... to make the rich richer and the potent more powerful, the humble members of society—the farmers, mechanics, and laborers—... have a right to complain of the injustice of their government. ❞

As planned, the Whigs made the Bank a major issue in the election of 1832. They chose Henry Clay as their candidate to run against Andrew Jackson. When the votes were counted, Jackson won a stunning election victory. The common people had supported Jackson and rejected the Bank of the United States.

The Bank closes

Without a new charter, the Bank would have to close in 1836. Jackson refused to wait. He ordered Secretary of the Treasury Roger Taney to stop putting government money in the Bank. Instead, Taney deposited federal money in state banks. They became known as **pet banks** because Taney and his friends controlled many of them.

The loss of federal money crippled the Bank of the United States. Its closing in 1836 contributed to an economic crisis.

★ Section 2 Review ★

Recall

1. **Identify** **(a)** Old Hickory, **(b)** kitchen cabinet, **(c)** Nicholas Biddle.
2. **Define** **(a)** spoils system, **(b)** pet bank.

Comprehension

3. How did Andrew Jackson's education and experience help prepare him for the Presidency of the United States?
4. Why did critics object to the spoils system?
5. Why did many farmers and merchants dislike the Bank of the United States?

Critical Thinking and Writing

6. **Understanding Causes and Effects** How did the spoils system lead to the creation of the kitchen cabinet?
7. **Analyzing Information** What do you think the Creeks were saying about Jackson when they called him Sharp Knife?

Activity **Writing a Script** Write the script for a television drama in which Andrew Jackson and Nicholas Biddle discuss the Bank of the United States and pet banks.

Struggles Over States' Rights

As You Read

Explore These Questions

- How did John C. Calhoun and Daniel Webster disagree on states' rights?
- How did Jackson deal with the Nullification Crisis?
- Why did Native Americans of the Southeast have to leave their lands?

Define

- nullification
- states' rights
- secede

Identify

- Tariff of Abominations
- Nullification Crisis
- Sequoyah
- Indian Removal Act
- Trail of Tears
- Osceola
- Seminole War

SETTING the Scene As President, Andrew Jackson had to deal with a tariff crisis that threatened to split the nation. He also played a major role in deciding the future of many Native Americans. At the heart of both cases was a question that challenged the nation. Did states or the federal government have greater authority?

A Crisis Over Tariffs

In 1828, Congress passed the highest tariff in the nation's history. Southerners called it the **Tariff of Abominations.** An abomination is something that is hated.

Just like earlier tariffs, the new law protected manufacturers from foreign competition. Most manufacturers lived in the North. Southern planters, however, were hurt by the tariff. They sold their cotton in Europe and bought European goods in return. The high tariff meant that southerners had to pay more for these imports.

Calhoun vs. Webster

A leader in the South's fight against the tariff was Vice President John C. Calhoun. He used an argument that Thomas Jefferson had made in the Kentucky and Virginia resolutions. (See page 188.) Like Jefferson, Calhoun claimed that a state had the right to nullify, or cancel, a federal law that it considered to be unconstitutional. This idea is called **nullification.**

A tariff collector used this stencil to mark goods.

Calhoun supported **states' rights,** the right of states to limit the power of the federal government. He argued that the states had final authority because the states had created the national government.

Daniel Webster disagreed. In 1830, he made a speech in the Senate attacking the idea of nullification. The Constitution, he said, united the American people, not just the states. If states had the right to nullify federal laws, the nation would fall apart. Webster ended his speech with stirring words: "Liberty and Union, now and forever, one and inseparable."

Calhoun resigns

Southerners and westerners strongly supported states' rights. They expected Jackson, who had been born in the South and lived in the West, to support their view.

The President's position soon became clear. Jackson and Calhoun attended a political dinner in 1830. Several guests made toasts in favor of states' rights. Finally, Jackson rose. The room fell silent. Old Hickory

Skills FOR LIFE

Critical Thinking | Managing Information | **Communication** | Maps, Charts, and Graphs

Reaching a Compromise

How Will I Use This Skill?

When individuals or groups disagree, they can solve the problem and avoid conflict by reaching a compromise. In a compromise, the opposing sides give up some of their demands in order to forge an agreement that both can accept. Knowing how to reach a compromise will help you settle disagreements, solve problems, and get along with others.

A compromise is often sealed by a handshake.

LEARN the Skill

You can reach a compromise by following these four steps:

1. Understand the positions of the opposing sides.
2. Recognize the probable effects of not reaching compromise.
3. Determine what each side might give up or concede in order to reach an agreement.
4. Negotiate a deal by discussing the conflicting issues and offering possible concessions. Compromise is reached when an agreement is acceptable to both sides.

PRACTICE the Skill

Using the steps above, review the compromise concerning the Tariff of Abominations and the Nullification Crisis in this section.

1. Explain the positions of northern manufacturers and southern planters on the two issues.
2. What did each side threaten to do if a compromise was not reached?
3. What did each side give up in order to reach an agreement?
4. With a partner, reenact a negotiation as it might have occurred between representatives of the North and South.

APPLY the Skill

Working with a partner, role-play a dispute that might occur today between an employer and an employee. Identify various issues that they might disagree on. Then, apply what you have learned in order to reach a compromise.

raised his glass, looked straight at the Vice President, and proclaimed, "Our Federal Union—it must be preserved!"

The drama continued. Calhoun raised his glass and answered the President's challenge: "The Union—next to our liberty, most dear." To him, the liberty of a state was more important than the Union.

Because Calhoun strongly disagreed with Jackson, he resigned from the office of Vice President. He was then elected senator from South Carolina. The debate over states' rights would rage for years.

The Nullification Crisis

Anger against the tariff increased in the South. In 1832, Congress passed a new tariff that lowered the rate slightly. South Carolina was not satisfied. It passed the Nullification Act, declaring the new tariff illegal. It also threatened to **secede,** or withdraw, from the Union if challenged.

Jackson was furious. He knew that nullification could lead to civil war. In private, he raged:

> "If one drop of blood be shed there in defiance of the laws of the United States, I will hang the first man of them I can get my hands on to the first tree I can find."

Publicly the President supported a lower compromise tariff proposed by Henry Clay. Jackson also asked Congress to pass the Force Bill. It allowed him to use the army, if necessary, to enforce the tariff.

Faced with Jackson's firm stand, no other state chose to support South Carolina. Calhoun supported the compromise tariff that Clay had proposed. South Carolina repealed the Nullification Act and the **Nullification Crisis** passed. However, sectional tensions between the North and South would increase in the years ahead.

Tragedy for Native Americans

Jackson took a firm stand on another key issue. It affected the fate of Native Americans. Since the early colonial era, white settlers had forced Native Americans off their land. Indian leaders like Pontiac and Tecumseh had failed to stop the invasion of white settlers.

Biography **Sequoyah**

Sequoyah adapted Greek, Hebrew, and English letters to create the 86 symbols of his Cherokee alphabet. The Cherokees used Sequoyah's alphabet to write a constitution. ★ **Why would the lack of a written language be a disadvantage to a society?**

Indian nations in the Southeast

The Creek, Choctaw, Chickasaw, Cherokee, and Seminole nations lived in the Southeast. Many hoped to live in peace with their white neighbors. Their fertile land, however, was ideal for growing cotton. Settlers wanted the land for themselves.

Like earlier Presidents, Jackson sided with the white settlers. At his urging, the government set aside lands beyond the Mississippi River and then persuaded or forced Indians to move there. Jackson believed that this policy would provide land for white settlers as well as protect Native Americans from destruction.

Few Indians wanted to move. Some, like the Cherokee nation, had adopted customs of

Geography *Skills* **In the 1830s, the United States government forced thousands of Native Americans to leave their homelands and to resettle in western lands.**

1. **Location** On the map, locate: **(a)** Georgia, **(b)** Cherokee homeland, **(c)** Indian Territory, **(d)** Seminole homeland.
2. **Movement** What five southeastern nations moved to Indian Territory?
3. **Critical Thinking** Why were many Americans willing to give Native Americans lands west of the Mississippi?

white settlers. The Cherokees lived in farming villages. They had a constitution that set up a republican form of government.

In 1821, **Sequoyah** (sih KWOI uh) created a written alphabet for his people. Using Sequoyah's letters, Cherokee children learned to read and write. The Cherokees also published a newspaper.

A legal battle

In 1828, Georgia claimed the right to make laws for the Cherokee nation. The Cherokees went to court to defend their rights. They pointed to treaties with the federal government that protected their rights and property. The Cherokee case reached the Supreme Court. In the 1832 case of *Worcester v. Georgia,* Chief Justice John Marshall ruled in favor of the Cherokees. The Court declared Georgia's action unconstitutional and stated that Native Americans were protected by the United States Constitution.

However, President Jackson refused to enforce the Court's decision. In the Nullification Crisis, Jackson defended the power of the federal government. In the Cherokee case, he backed states' rights. He said that the federal government could not stop Georgia from extending its authority over Cherokee lands. "John Marshall has made his decision," Jackson reportedly said. "Now let him enforce it."

Forced to Leave

In 1830, Jackson supporters in Congress pushed through the **Indian Removal Act.** It forced many Native Americans to move west of the Mississippi. Whites did not mind turning this land over to Indians because they thought the region was a vast desert. During the 1830s, thousands of southeastern Indians were driven from their homes and forced to march to Indian Territory, west of the Mississippi.

A tragic march

In 1838, the United States Army drove more than 15,000 Cherokees westward to a land they had never seen. The Cherokees trekked hundreds of miles over a period of several months. They had little food or shelter. Thousands perished during the march, mostly children and the elderly. In all, about one fourth of the Indians died.

The Cherokees' long, sorrowful journey west became known as the **Trail of Tears.** An eyewitness described the suffering:

> "The Cherokees are nearly all prisoners. They had been dragged from their homes and encamped at the forts and military places, all over the nation. In Georgia especially, multitudes were allowed no time to take anything with them except the clothes they had on."

The Seminoles resist

In Florida, the Seminole Indians resisted removal. Led by Chief **Osceola** (ahs ee OH luh), they fought the United States Army. The **Seminole War** lasted from 1835 to 1842. It was the costliest war waged by the government to gain Indian lands. More than 1,500 soldiers died in the war and about 20 million dollars were spent in the war effort.

In the end, the Seminoles were defeated. The government forced the Seminole leaders and most of their people to leave Florida. By 1844, only a few thousand Native Americans remained east of the Mississippi River.

★ Section 3 Review ★

Recall

1. **Locate** **(a)** South Carolina, **(b)** Georgia, **(c)** Cherokee homeland, **(d)** Indian Territory, **(e)** Seminole homeland.
2. **Identify** **(a)** Tariff of Abominations, **(b)** Nullification Crisis, **(c)** Sequoyah, **(d)** Indian Removal Act, **(e)** Trail of Tears, **(f)** Osceola, **(g)** Seminole War.
3. **Define** **(a)** nullification, **(b)** states' rights, **(c)** secede.

Comprehension

4. Why did northerners and southerners disagree on the tariff issue?
5. How did Andrew Jackson respond to South Carolina's Nullification Act?
6. Why did Jackson support the policy of using force to move Native Americans beyond the Mississippi River?

Critical Thinking and Writing

7. **Forecasting** What do you think might have happened if other southern states supported South Carolina in the Nullification Crisis?
8. **Drawing Conclusions** Why do you think Andrew Jackson supported states' rights in the Cherokee case but not in the Nullification Crisis?

Activity **Writing a Protest Letter** You are a Cherokee on the Trail of Tears. Write a protest letter to President Jackson explaining why you consider his policy of Indian removal to be unjust.

The Presidency After Jackson

Explore These Questions

- What economic problems did Martin Van Buren face?
- How did Whigs and Democrats compete for the Presidency in 1840?
- Why did John Tyler have little success as President?

Define

- speculator
- depression
- laissez faire
- mudslinging

Identify

- Martin Van Buren
- Panic of 1837
- William Henry Harrison
- John Tyler

Andrew Jackson retired from office after two terms. Americans then elected **Martin Van Buren** to the Presidency. Van Buren had served as Jackson's Vice President since the resignation of John C. Calhoun in 1833.

As Van Buren took the oath of office in March 1837, Jackson stood at his side. Onlookers watched the outgoing President, not Van Buren. As Old Hickory left the platform, a rousing cheer rose from the crowd. In that moment, the people expressed their loyalty and respect for Andrew Jackson, the "Hero of New Orleans."

Van Buren and Hard Times

Martin Van Buren was very different from Andrew Jackson. He was a politician, not a war hero. Davy Crockett, a Congressman from Tennessee, once described Van Buren as "an artful, cunning, intriguing, selfish, speculating lawyer." As President, however, Van Buren needed more than sharp political instincts.

The Panic of 1837

Two months after taking office, Van Buren faced the worst economic crisis the nation had known. It was called the **Panic of 1837.** The panic had several causes. During the 1830s, the government sold millions of acres of public land in the West. Farmers bought some land, but **speculators** bought even more, hoping that their risky investment would earn them huge profits. To pay for the land, speculators borrowed money from state banks. After the Bank of the United States closed, the state banks could lend money without limit.

To meet the demand for loans, state banks printed more and more paper money. Often, the paper money was not backed by gold or silver. Paper money had value only if people trusted the banks that issued it.

Before leaving office, Jackson had grown alarmed at the wild speculation in land. To slow it down, he ordered that anyone buying public land had to pay for it with gold or silver. Speculators and others rushed to state banks to exchange their paper money for gold and silver. Many banks did not have enough gold and silver and had to close.

Economic depression

The panic worsened when cotton prices went down because of an oversupply. Cotton planters often borrowed money, which they repaid when they sold their crop. Low cotton prices meant that planters could not repay their loans. As a result, more banks failed.

The nation plunged into a deep economic **depression,** a period when business declines and many people lose their jobs. The depression lasted three years. In the worst days, 90 percent of the nation's factories were closed. Thousands of people were out of work. In some cities, hungry crowds broke into warehouses and stole food.

Van Buren's response

It was easy for people to blame President Van Buren for the country's economic depression. Van Buren took little action because he believed in **laissez faire**—the idea that government should play as small a role as possible in the nation's economic affairs. "The less the government interferes with private pursuits," he said, "the better for the general prosperity."

Van Buren's limited actions did little to help the economy. He tried to set up a more stable banking system. He also cut back on government expenses. For example, when he entertained visitors at the White House, they were served simple dinners. Still, the depression wore on. As a result, criticism of Van Buren increased.

Campaigns of 1840

Even though Van Buren had lost support, the Democrats chose him to run for reelection in 1840. The Whigs, learning from the Democrats, chose a candidate who would appeal to the common people. He was **William Henry Harrison** of Ohio. Harrison was known as the hero of the Battle of Tippecanoe. (See page 209.) To run for Vice President, the Whigs chose John Tyler.

Log cabin campaign

Most Americans knew very little about Harrison's stand on the issues. To appeal to voters, the Whigs focused on his war record. "Tippecanoe and Tyler too" became their campaign slogan.

The Whigs created an image for Harrison as a "man of the people." They presented him as a humble farmer who had been born in a log cabin. Harrison was actually a wealthy, educated man who lived in a large mansion. Still, the Whigs made the log cabin their campaign symbol. In a typical Whig cartoon, Harrison stands outside a log cabin, greeting Van Buren and his aides:

> "Gentlemen, . . . If you will accept the [simple food] of a log cabin, with a western farmer's cheer, you are welcome. I have no champagne but can give you a mug of good cider, with some ham and eggs, and good clean beds. I am a plain backwoodsman. I have cleared some land, killed some Indians, and made the Red Coats fly in my time."

A new sort of politics

The campaigns of 1840 reflected a new sort of politics. Harrison traveled across the land, making speeches and greeting voters. Both parties competed for votes with rallies, banquets, and entertainment. Ordinary citizens participated by giving speeches and singing campaign songs like this one:

> "The times are bad, and want
> curing;
> They are getting past all enduring:
> So let's turn out Martin Van Buren
> And put in old Tippecanoe!"

Viewing History **Log Cabin Campaign**

Harrison's log cabin symbol swept the nation in 1840. Marchers in parades often carried miniature cabins such as the one shown here. The cabin was attached to a pole and raised aloft for all to see. ★ **Why was the log cabin image appealing to many voters?**

Why Study History?

Because You Will Choose Our Nation's Leaders

Historical Background

In the political campaigns of 1840, Democrats and Whigs showed little concern for the key issues of the day. Instead, they organized parades, chanted slogans, offered free cider, and participated in name-calling. Candidates also used newspapers, posters, and even whisky jugs to carry their political messages. In 1840, the Whigs' log cabin campaign was a success and William Henry Harrison was elected President. (See page 267.)

Connections to Today

When election day draws near today, politicians flood the radio, television, Internet, and various other media with campaign sound bites. Like politicians of the 1840s, some candidates try to avoid the issues. Some candidates may even use questionable or inappropriate campaign tactics to win votes.

Responsible voters are familiar with the workings of political campaigns. They make their voting decisions based on a clear understanding of the candidates' past performance and stand on the issues. They want to vote for the most qualified candidate. Other voters, however, may be swayed more by clever campaign tactics and political advertisements.

Connections to You

Right now, you may participate in school elections. In a few years, you will have the right and responsibility of voting for our nation's leaders. You will help to choose leaders of your nation, state, and community. Politicians of today, like those of the 1840s, will sometimes use aggressive campaign tactics to try to win your vote. Learning about politics during the Age of Jackson and during other eras of American history can help you to become a knowledgeable and responsible voter.

1. Comprehension

(a) What campaign tactics did the Whigs use in the election of 1840?

(b) What role does advertising play in political campaigns today?

2. Critical Thinking
How can you learn more about a candidate's past performance and stand on major issues?

★Activity **Interviewing** Write several questions to help you learn how people make their voting decisions. Then, use your questions to interview people you know who voted in a recent election. Keep a written or taped record of their responses. What conclusions can you draw from your interviews?

Along the campaign trail, Whigs organized colorful parades in both small towns and big cities. At every stop, they served plenty of free cider. The log cabin symbol appeared on banners, quilts, and even packages of shaving soap.

Name-calling, half-truths, and lies

In their campaigns, both Whigs and Democrats engaged in **mudslinging,** or the use of insults to attack an opponent's reputation. They used name-calling, half-truths, and lies to win votes.

The Whigs attacked the President. One newspaper falsely reported that Van Buren spent thousands of dollars to install a bathtub in the White House. They blamed "Martin Van Ruin" for the depression. Daniel Webster charged that the Democrats had replaced "Old Hickory" Jackson with "Slippery Elm" Van Buren.

The Democrats responded with their own attacks and name-calling. They revealed that "Granny Harrison, the Petticoat General," had resigned from the army before the War of 1812 ended. They accused "General Mum" of not speaking on the issues. "Should Harrison be elected?" they asked voters. "Read his name spelled backwards," they advised. "No sirrah."

Whigs in the White House

Harrison won the election of 1840 easily. As a result, a Whig was in the White House for the first time in 12 years. "We have taught them how to conquer us!" complained one Democrat.

The Whigs had a clear-cut program. They wanted to create a new Bank of the United States and improve roads and canals. Also, they wanted a high tariff.

However, Whig hopes soon crashed. Just weeks after taking office, President Harrison died of pneumonia. **John Tyler** became the first Vice President to succeed a President who died in office.

President Tyler failed to live up to Whig expectations. A former Democrat, he opposed some Whig plans for developing the economy. When the Whigs in Congress passed a bill to recharter the Bank of the United States, Tyler vetoed it.

In response, most of Tyler's Cabinet resigned and the Whigs threw Tyler out of their party. Democrats welcomed the squabbling. "Tyler is heartily despised by everyone," reported an observer. "He has no influence at all." With few friends in either the Whig or Democratic party, Tyler could do little during his term in office.

★ Section 4 Review ★

Recall

1. **Identify** **(a)** Martin Van Buren, **(b)** Panic of 1837, **(c)** William Henry Harrison, **(d)** John Tyler.
2. **Define** **(a)** speculator, **(b)** depression, **(c)** laissez faire, **(d)** mudslinging.

Comprehension

3. Describe the economic depression that occurred after the Panic of 1837.
4. Describe some of the campaign tactics Democrats and Whigs used in the election of 1840.
5. Why did the Whigs throw President Tyler out of their party?

Critical Thinking and Writing

6. **Solving Problems** What do you think President Van Buren could have done to ease the economic crisis of the 1830s?
7. **Comparing** How do campaign tactics of today compare with those of 1840?

Activity **Researching** If you had money in a bank that failed today, would you lose your money just as people did in the 1830s? To find the answer, conduct research on the Federal Deposit Insurance Corporation, also known as the FDIC.

Chapter 10 Review and Activities

★ Sum It Up ★

Section 1 A New Era in Politics

- The 1828 election of Andrew Jackson for President was seen as a victory for the common people.
- In the 1820s, democracy expanded as more and more white males gained the right to vote.
- Women and African Americans did not share in the growth of democracy.

Section 2 Jackson in the White House

- Jackson rewarded his supporters with government jobs and relied on the advice of his unofficial kitchen cabinet.
- Jackson fought against the national bank, which he saw as a tool of the wealthy.

Section 3 Struggles Over States' Rights

- In his second term, Jackson used compromise and strong leadership to end a crisis over tariffs and states' rights.
- Jackson's Indian removal policy forced thousands of Native Americans to leave their homelands and move west.

Section 4 The Presidency After Jackson

- The Panic of 1837 brought an economic depression that caused President Van Buren to lose popular support.
- In 1840, Whigs used new political campaign tactics to get William Henry Harrison elected President.

For additional review of the major ideas of Chapter 10, see ***Guide to the Essentials of American History*** or ***Interactive Student Tutorial CD-ROM,*** which contains interactive review activities, graphic organizers, and practice tests.

Reviewing the Chapter

Define These Terms

Match each term with the correct definition.

Column 1	Column 2
1. suffrage	**a.** private meeting to choose candidates
2. caucus	**b.** right to vote
3. nominating convention	**c.** practice of rewarding supporters with government jobs
4. spoils system	**d.** meeting where state delegates choose candidates
5. kitchen cabinet	**e.** Jackson's group of unofficial advisers

Explore the Main Ideas

1. Why were there more voters in 1828 than in 1824?
2. What role did each of the following play in the struggle over the Bank: **(a)** Nicholas Biddle, **(b)** Henry Clay, **(c)** Andrew Jackson.
3. Why did South Carolina want to nullify the tariffs of 1828 and 1832?
4. Describe President Jackson's Indian removal policy.
5. What were the causes of the Panic of 1837?

Geography Activity

Match the letters on the map with the following places: **1.** Indian Territory, **2.** Chickasaw, **3.** Choctaw, **4.** Creek, **5.** Cherokee, **6.** Seminole. **Place** Why did settlers want Cherokee lands in the Southeast?

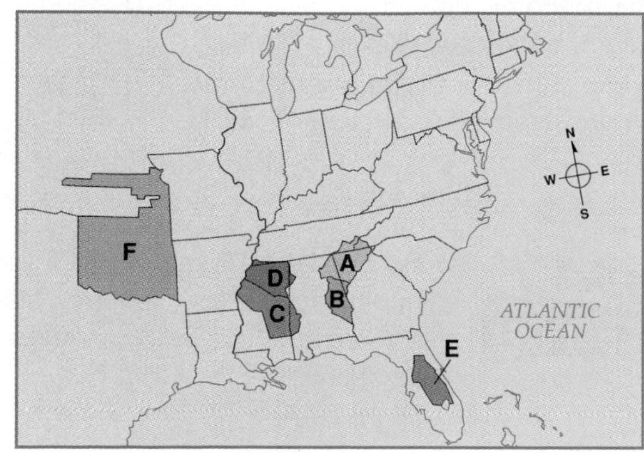

Critical Thinking and Writing

1. **Defending a Position** Do you think more Americans should have supported John Quincy Adams's plans to promote economic growth? Why or why not?
2. **Understanding Chronology** Place these events in chronological order: **(a)** Jackson becomes President, **(b)** the Cherokees are ordered off their land, **(c)** the Seminole War begins.
3. **Linking Past and Present** How are today's political tactics similar to those of the Jackson era? How are the tactics different?
4. **Exploring Unit Themes Expansion** We often think of the Age of Jackson as a time of expanding democracy. In what ways did American democracy expand during the Age of Jackson?

Using Primary Sources

President Jackson wanted to move all Native Americans west of the Mississippi River. In 1835, when it seemed that the Seminoles would resist, Jackson wrote a forceful letter to them.

> "My Children—
>
> I am sorry to have heard that you have been listening to bad counsel. . . . I have ordered a large military force to be sent among you. . . . If you listen to the voice of friendship and truth, you will go quietly and voluntarily. But should you listen to the bad birds that are always flying about you and refuse to move, I have then directed the commanding officer to remove you by force. This will be done. I pray the Great Spirit, therefore, to incline you to do what is right.
>
> Your friend,
>
> A. Jackson"

Source: "President Andrew Jackson's Letter to the Seminoles" in *History of the Indian Wars,* ed. Henry Trumbull, 1841.

Recognizing Points of View (a) How did President Jackson suggest that he was a friend of the Seminoles? **(b)** How do you think the Seminoles felt about Jackson after reading this letter?

Activity Bank

Interdisciplinary Activity

Exploring Economics Review the Tariff of Abominations. Then do research to learn about the North American Free Trade Agreement of the 1990s. In an oral report, explain the differences between these two national economic policies.

Career Skills Activity

Artists Select an issue or incident related to Andrew Jackson's presidency. Then create a political cartoon based on your selection. Remember that political cartoonists represent a point of view by using various symbols. Be prepared to explain your cartoon and its symbolism.

Citizenship Activity

Running a Food Drive Thousands of Cherokees died of starvation on the Trail of Tears. Today, in many communities, some people do not have enough food to eat. Form a student group to plan and run a food drive. Work with a charitable organization to deliver food to those in need.

Internet Activity

Search the Internet to find sites dealing with Cherokee culture and history. Continue exploring until you find Cherokee viewpoints on the Indian Removal and the Trail of Tears. Use the Cherokee viewpoints to write a poem about how people suffered on the Trail of Tears.

You are a frontier settler, a Whig politician, a Southern planter, an enslaved African American, or a Seminole. In your EYEWITNESS JOURNAL, record how key events and issues of the Jackson era affect your life.

Chapter 11 Westward Expansion

1820–1860

What's Ahead

By the mid-1800s, Americans began to dream of extending their territory to the Pacific Ocean. In this chapter, you will see how that dream came true.

First, the United States secured the Pacific Northwest by signing a treaty with Britain. Next, after American settlers declared independence from Mexico, the United States brought Texas into the Union. Americans then won California and the Southwest by fighting a war with Mexico. As settlers poured into the Southwest, a new culture developed that blended American, Mexican, and Indian cultures.

Why Study History?

Every year, millions of Americans visit historic memorials, from battlefields to the homes of famous people. To many Texans, for example, the best-loved historic site is a San Antonio mission called the Alamo. Why do so many Americans work to preserve the places where history happened? To explore this question, see this chapter's *Why Study History?* feature, "History Is All Around You."

American Events

1821 First white American traders arrive in Santa Fe, New Mexico

1836 Republic of Texas is formed

1820 | 1825 | 1830 | 1835 | 1840

World Events

1833 World Event Santa Anna comes to power in Mexico

Viewing HISTORY A Growing Texas City

This painting by William G. Samuel shows a street in San Antonio, Texas, in 1849. Texas had joined the Union a few years before, after winning independence from Mexico. In the mid-1800s, the United States gained vast western territories, including Texas, California, Oregon, and New Mexico. As a result, the nation stretched from the Atlantic Ocean to the Pacific. ★ **How does this painting show the Mexican roots of the Southwest?**

1845 James K. Polk becomes President

1846 Americans in northern California declare independence from Mexico

1859 Oregon is admitted to the Union

1840 **1845** **1850** **1855** **1860**

1840 World Event
Britain recognizes Texas as an independent nation

1854 World Event
Japan and United States sign trade agreement

Oregon Country

As You Read

Explore These Questions

- How did rival claims to Oregon Country develop?
- How did fur trappers and missionaries help open up the Far West?
- What hardships did settlers face?

Define

- mountain man
- rendezvous

Identify

- John Jacob Astor
- James Beckwourth
- Marie Dorion
- Marcus and Narcissa Whitman

SETTING the Scene In 1851, Horace Greeley, a New York newspaper editor, published an article titled "To Aspiring Young Men." In it, Greeley offered the following advice:

> "If you have no family or friends to aid you, . . . turn your face to the great West and there build up your home and fortune."

The public soon came to know Greeley's message as a simple, four-word phrase: "Go West, young man." His advice exactly suited the spirit of the times. Thousands of young men—and women—rallied to the cry "Westward Ho!"

The Lure of Oregon

By the 1820s, white settlers had occupied much of the land between the Appalachians and the Mississippi River. Families in search of good farmland continued to move west. Few, however, settled on the Great Plains between the Mississippi and the Rockies. Instead, they went onward to lands in the Far West.

Americans first heard about the area known as Oregon Country in the early 1800s. Oregon Country was the huge area beyond the Rocky Mountains. Today, this land includes Oregon, Washington, Idaho, and parts of Wyoming, Montana, and Canada.

The varied geography of Oregon Country attracted both farmers and trappers. Along the Pacific coast, the soil is fertile. Temperatures are mild all year round and rainfall is plentiful. Early white settlers found fine farmland in the Willamette River valley and the lowlands around Puget Sound.

Farther inland, dense forests covered a coastal mountain range. Beaver and other fur-bearing animals roamed these forests, as well as the Rocky Mountains on the eastern boundary. As a result, trappers flocked to Oregon Country.

Between the coastal mountains and the Rockies is a high plateau. This intermountain region is much drier than the coast and has some desert areas. This region of Oregon had little to attract early settlers.

Competing Claims

In the early 1800s, four countries had claims to Oregon. These countries were the United States, Great Britain, Spain, and Russia. Of course, several Native American groups had lived in Oregon for thousands of years. The land rightfully belonged to them. However, the United States and competing European nations gave little thought to Indian rights.

The United States based its claim to Oregon on several expeditions to the area. For example, Lewis and Clark had journeyed through the area in 1805 and 1806.

The British claim to Oregon dated back to a visit by the English explorer Sir Francis Drake in 1579. Also, Fort Vancouver, built by the British, was the only permanent outpost in Oregon Country.

In 1818, the United States and Britain reached an agreement. The two countries would occupy Oregon jointly. Citizens of each nation would have equal rights in Oregon. Spain and Russia had few settlers in the area and agreed to drop their claims.

Fur Trappers in the Far West

At first, the few Europeans or Americans who traveled to Oregon Country were mostly fur traders. Since furs could be sold at tremendous profits in China, merchants from New England stopped along the Oregon coast before crossing the Pacific. In fact, so many Yankee traders came to Oregon that, in some areas, the Indian name for a white man was "Boston."

Only a few hardy trappers actually settled in Oregon. These adventurous men hiked through Oregon's vast forests, trapping animals and living off the land. They were known as **mountain men.**

Mountain men won admiration as rugged individualists, people who follow their own independent course in life. Even their colorful appearance set them apart from ordinary society. They wore shirts and trousers made of animal hides and decorated with porcupine quills. Their hair reached to their shoulders. Pistols and tomahawks hung from their belts.

Lives filled with danger

Mountain men could make a small fortune trapping beaver in Rocky Mountain streams. They led dangerous lives, however. The long, cold mountain winters demanded special survival skills. In the thick forests, trappers had to be on the lookout for attacks by bears, wildcats, or other animals.

During the harsh winters, game was scarce. Facing starvation, trappers would eat almost anything. "I have held my hands in an anthill until they were covered with ants, then greedily licked them off," one mountain man recalled.

Trappers often spent winters in Native American villages. They learned many trapping skills from Indians. Many mountain men married Indian women who taught the newcomers how to find their way and survive in the mountains.

Relations with Native Americans were not always friendly, however. Indians, like the Blackfeet, sometimes attacked mountain men who trapped on Indian hunting grounds without permission.

Trading furs

During the fall and spring, mountain men tended their traps. Then in July, they

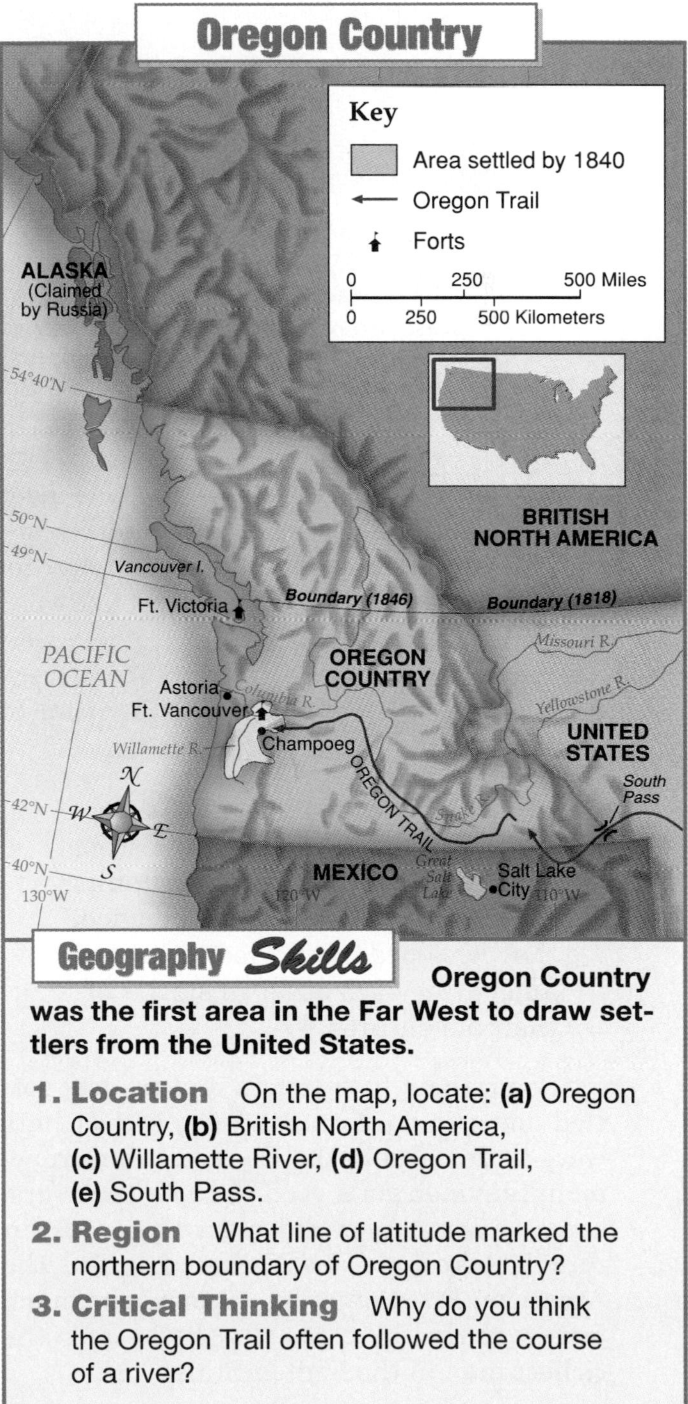

Geography Skills **Oregon Country was the first area in the Far West to draw settlers from the United States.**

1. **Location** On the map, locate: **(a)** Oregon Country, **(b)** British North America, **(c)** Willamette River, **(d)** Oregon Trail, **(e)** South Pass.
2. **Region** What line of latitude marked the northern boundary of Oregon Country?
3. **Critical Thinking** Why do you think the Oregon Trail often followed the course of a river?

Viewing History **The Fur Trade**

Alfred Miller painted this watercolor, Fort Laramie, *in 1837. Located in present-day Wyoming, Fort Laramie was originally built as a fur-trading post. Once a year, mountain men and Indian trappers gathered at trading posts like this one to sell their furs and have fun.* ★ **How did Native Americans help fur trappers?**

tramped out of the wilderness, ready to meet the fur traders. They headed to a place chosen the year before, called the **rendezvous** (RAHN day voo). Rendezvous is a French word meaning get-together.

For trappers, the first day of the rendezvous was a time to have fun. A visitor to one rendezvous captured the excitement:

> “[They] engaged in contests of skill at running, jumping, wrestling, shooting with the rifle, and running horses.... They sang, they laughed, they whooped; they tried to out-brag and out-lie each other in stories of their adventures.”

Soon, though, trappers and traders settled down to bargain. Because beaver hats were in demand in the East and in Europe, mountain men got a good price for their furs. Trading companies did even better. **John Jacob Astor,** a New Yorker, founded the American Fur Company. He made so much money in the fur trade that he became the richest man in the United States.

By the late 1830s, the fur trade was dying out. Trappers had killed so many beavers that the animals had grown scarce. Also, beaver hats went out of style. Even so, the mountain men's skills were still in demand. Some began leading settlers across the rugged trails into Oregon.

Exploring New Lands

In their search for furs, mountain men explored much new territory in the West. They followed Indian trails across the Rockies and through mountain passes. Later, they showed these trails to settlers moving west.

Jedediah Smith led white settlers across the Rockies through South Pass, in present-day Wyoming. Manuel Lisa, a Spanish American fur trader, led a trip up the Missouri River in 1807. He founded Fort Manuel, the first outpost on the upper Missouri.

James Beckwourth, an African American, headed west from Virginia to escape slavery. He was accepted as a chief by the Crow Indians. As a guide, Beckwourth discovered a mountain pass through the

Sierra Nevadas that later became a major route to California.

At least one mountain "man" was a woman. **Marie Dorion,** an Iowa Indian, first went to Oregon with fur traders in 1811. She won fame for her survival skills.

Missionaries in Oregon

The first white Americans to build permanent homes in Oregon Country were missionaries. Among them were **Marcus and Narcissa Whitman**. The couple married in 1836 and set out for Oregon, where they planned to convert local Native Americans to Christianity.

The Whitmans built their mission near the Columbia River and began to work with Cayuse (KI oos) Indians. They set up a mission school. Soon, other missionaries and settlers joined the Whitmans. As more settlers arrived and took over Cayuse lands, conflicts arose. Even worse, the newcomers brought diseases that often killed the Indians.

In 1847, tragedy struck. An outbreak of measles among the settlers spread to the Cayuses. Many Cayuse children died. Blaming the settlers, a band of angry Indians attacked the mission, killing the Whitmans and 12 others.

Wagon Trains West

Despite the killing of the Whitmans, other bold pioneers set out on the long trek to Oregon. Missionaries sent back glowing reports about the land. Farmers back East marveled at tales of wheat that grew taller than a man and turnips five feet around. Stories like these touched off an outbreak of "Oregon fever."

Oregon fever spread quickly. Soon, pioneers clogged the trails west. Beginning in 1843, wagon trains left every spring for Oregon. They followed a route called the Oregon Trail. (See the map on page 275.)

Families planning to go west met at Independence, Missouri, in the early spring. When enough families had gathered, they formed a wagon train. Each group elected leaders to make decisions along the way.

The Oregon-bound pioneers hurried to leave Independence in May. Timing was important. Travelers had to reach Oregon by early October, before snow began to fall in the mountains. This meant that pioneers had to cover 2,000 miles (3,200 km) on foot in five months!

Life on the trail

Once on the trail, pioneer families woke to a bugle blast at dawn. Each person had a job to do. Young girls helped their mothers prepare breakfast. Men and boys harnessed the horses and oxen. By 6 A.M., the cry of "Wagons Ho!" rang out across the plains.

Biography **Narcissa Whitman**

Narcissa Prentiss married Marcus Whitman in 1836. They then set out on a seven-month journey to Oregon. When they finally reached the Columbia River valley, she wrote, "The beauty of this extensive valley at the hour of twilight was enchanting and [turned] my mind from the fatigue under which I was laboring."

★ **Why did Narcissa Whitman journey to Oregon?**

China trunk brought to Oregon by eastern pioneers ➤

Wagon trains stopped for a brief meal at noon. Then it was back on the trail until 6 or 7 P.M. At night, wagons were drawn up in a circle to keep the cattle from wandering.

Most pioneer families set out on the journey west with a lot of heavy gear. When it came time to cross rivers and scale mountains, however, many possessions were left behind to lighten the load. One traveler found the Oregon Trail littered with objects such as "blacksmiths' anvils, ploughs, large grindstones, baking ovens, kegs, barrels, harness [and] clothing."

The long trek west held many dangers. During spring rains, travelers risked their lives floating wagons across swollen rivers. In summer, they faced blistering heat on the treeless plains. Early snowstorms often blocked passes through the mountains.

The biggest threat was sickness. Cholera and other diseases could wipe out whole wagon trains. Because the travelers lived so close together, germs spread quickly.

Trading with Native Americans

As they moved west toward the Rockies, pioneers often saw Indians. The Indians seldom attacked the whites trespassing on their land. A guidebook published in 1845 warned that pioneers had more to fear from their own guns than from Indians: "We very frequently hear of emigrants being killed from the accidental discharge of firearms; but we very seldom hear of their being killed by Indians."

Many Native Americans traded with the wagon trains. Hungry pioneers were grateful for food the Indians sold. A traveler noted:

> "Whenever we camp near any Indian village, we are no sooner stopped than a whole crowd may be seen coming galloping into our camp. The [women] do all the swapping."

Oregon at last!

Despite the many hardships, more than 50,000 people reached Oregon between 1840 and 1860. Their wagon wheels cut so deeply into the plains that the ruts can still be seen today.

By the 1840s, Americans greatly outnumbered the British in parts of Oregon. As you have read, the two nations agreed to occupy Oregon jointly in 1818. Now, many Americans began to feel that Oregon should belong to the United States alone.

★ Section 1 Review ★

Recall

1. **Locate** **(a)** Oregon Country, **(b)** Willamette River, **(c)** South Pass, **(d)** Oregon Trail.
2. **Identify** **(a)** John Jacob Astor, **(b)** James Beckwourth, **(c)** Marie Dorion, **(d)** Marcus and Narcissa Whitman.
3. **Define** **(a)** mountain man, **(b)** rendezvous.

Comprehension

4. How did the United States and Britain settle their claims to Oregon Country?
5. **(a)** Why did mountain men first go to Oregon? **(b)** How did they contribute to later settlement?
6. **(a)** Why did settlers flock to Oregon after the 1840s? **(b)** Describe two difficulties along the way.

Critical Thinking and Writing

7. **Linking Past and Present** **(a)** What qualities helped the mountain men survive in the wilderness? **(b)** Do you think such qualities are still important today? Explain.
8. **Analyzing Ideas** Economists talk about the "law of supply and demand." It states that when people want a product that is hard to get, the price goes up. How does the Oregon fur trade illustrate the idea of supply and demand?

Activity **Writing a Letter to the Editor** You are one of the young people Horace Greeley told to "go West." You took his advice. Now, write him a letter and tell him what it was like traveling to the West!

Texas Wins Independence

As You Read

Explore These Questions

- Why did many Americans settle in Texas?
- How did Texas become an independent nation?
- What challenges did the new Republic of Texas face?

Define

- siege
- annex

Identify

- Stephen Austin
- Antonio López de Santa Anna
- Tejanos
- Sam Houston
- Alamo
- William Travis
- Battle of San Jacinto
- Lone Star Republic

Setting the Scene In late 1835, the word spread: Americans in Texas had rebelled against Mexico! Joseph Barnard, a young doctor, recalled:

> "I was at Chicago, Illinois, practicing medicine, when the news of the Texan revolt from Mexico reached our ears.... They were in arms for a cause that I had always been taught to consider sacred,... Republican principles and popular institutions."

Along with hundreds of other Americans, Dr. Barnard made his way to Texas. Their fight led to the creation of a new nation.

Americans in Mexican Texas

Since the early 1800s, American farmers, especially from the South, had looked eagerly at the vast region called Texas. At the time, Texas was part of the Spanish colony of Mexico.

At first, Spain refused to let Americans move into the region. Then in 1821, Spain gave Moses Austin a land grant in Texas. Austin died before he could set up a colony. His son Stephen took over the project.

Meanwhile, Mexico won its independence from Spain. The new nation let **Stephen Austin** lead settlers into Texas. Only about 4,000 Mexicans lived there. Mexico hoped that the Americans would help develop the area and control Indian attacks.

This seal from Mexican Texas shows an eagle, serpent, and cactus—symbols of Mexico.

Mexico gave each settler a large grant of land. In 1821, Austin and 300 families moved to Texas. Many of these newcomers were slaveowners who brought their slaves with them. Under Austin's leadership, the colony grew rapidly. By 1830, about 20,000 Americans had resettled in Texas.

Conflict With Mexico

In return for land, Austin and the original settlers agreed to become citizens of Mexico and worship in the Roman Catholic Church. However, later American settlers felt no loyalty to Mexico. They spoke only a few words of Spanish. Also, most of the Americans were Protestants. Conflict soon erupted with the Mexican government.

Mexico enforces its laws

In 1830, Mexico forbade any more Americans to move to Texas. Mexico feared that the Americans wanted to make Texas part of

Independence for Texas

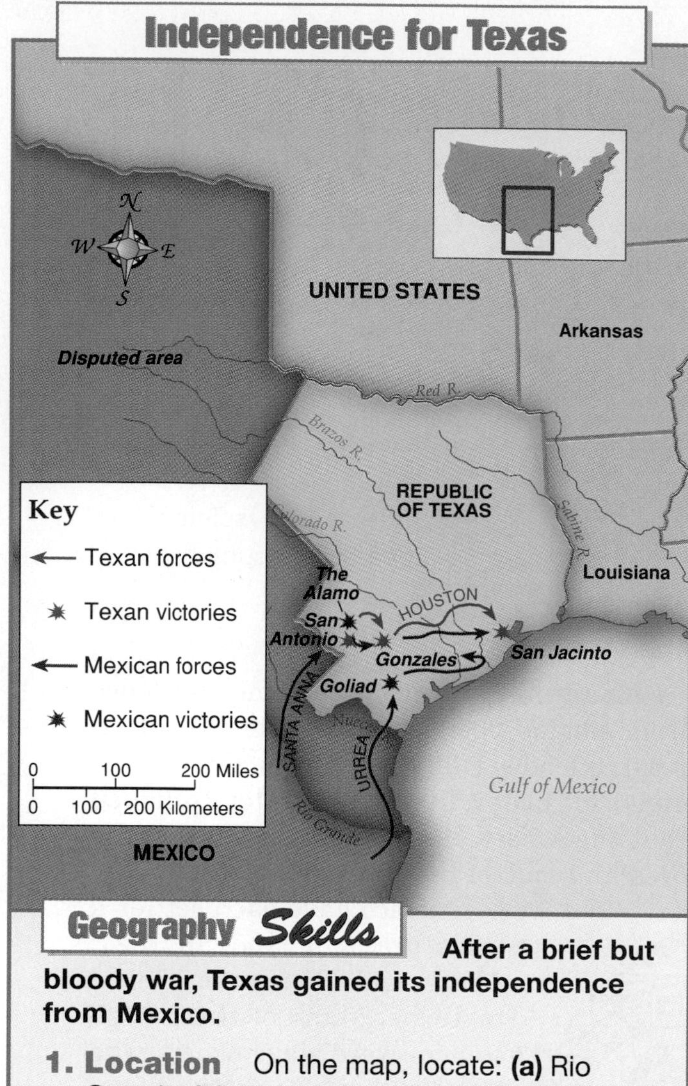

Geography *Skills* **After a brief but bloody war, Texas gained its independence from Mexico.**

1. **Location** On the map, locate: **(a)** Rio Grande, **(b)** Nueces River, **(c)** Gonzales, **(d)** San Antonio, **(e)** the Alamo, **(f)** Goliad, **(g)** San Jacinto.
2. **Movement** **(a)** Where did Santa Anna's army first fight the Texans? **(b)** Describe the movement of Mexican and Texan forces after the Alamo.
3. **Critical Thinking** Refer to the map of the United States in the Reference Section. How do the boundaries of the Republic of Texas compare with the boundaries of Texas?

the United States. Mexico had some reason for this fear. The United States had already tried twice to buy Texas.

Mexico also decided to make Texans obey Mexican laws that they had ignored for years. One was the law requiring Texans to worship in the Catholic Church. Another law banned slavery in Texas. Texans resented the laws and the Mexican troops who came north to enforce them.

In 1833, General **Antonio López de Santa Anna** came to power in Mexico. Two years later, he threw out the Mexican constitution. Rumors spread that Santa Anna intended to drive all Americans out of Texas.

Texans take action

Texans felt that the time had come for action. In this, they had the support of many **Tejanos** (teh HAH nohs), Mexicans who lived in Texas. Tejanos did not necessarily want independence from Mexico. However, they did want to be rid of Santa Anna, who ruled as a military dictator.

In October 1835, Texans in the town of Gonzales (gahn ZAH lehs) clashed with Mexican troops. The Texans forced the Mexicans to withdraw. Inspired by the victory, Stephen Austin vowed to "see Texas forever free from Mexican domination." Two months later, Texans stormed and took San Antonio. Determined to stamp out the rebellion, Santa Anna marched north with a large army.

While Santa Anna assembled his troops, Texans declared independence on March 2, 1836. They set up a new nation called the Republic of Texas and appointed **Sam Houston** commander of the army. Volunteers of many nationalities, as well as African Americans and Tejanos, joined the fight for Texan independence from Mexico.

Siege at the Alamo

By the time Santa Anna arrived in San Antonio, many of the Texans who had taken the city had drifted away. Fewer than 200 Texans remained as defenders.

In spite of the tremendous odds against them, the Texans refused to give up. Instead, they retired to an old Spanish mission called the **Alamo.**

Against tremendous odds

Texans who gathered in the Alamo in the winter of 1835–1836 were poorly equipped for a battle. Supplies of ammunition and medicine were low. Food consisted of some beef and corn, and access to water was limited. Worst of all, there were only about 150

Why Study History?

Because History Is All Around You

Historical Background

Did you know that we almost lost the Alamo? After 1836, it was used as an army supply depot, a warehouse, and a general store. For a time, its neighbors included a beer garden and a meat market. In 1903, there was even talk that it might be turned into a hotel.

Then, the Daughters of the Republic of Texas stepped in. They urged the state government to save the Alamo from destruction. Adina De Zavala gained public attention by barricading herself inside the old mission. In 1905, the state of Texas entrusted the Alamo to the Daughters of the Republic.

The Alamo

Connections to Today

Each year, thousands of tourists visit the Alamo. They walk the same ground where Texans fought for independence.

Throughout the nation, government and citizens work to save and restore important historic sites. Federal laws protect a variety of places, including ruins of Native American towns, homes of famous Americans, and even old factories. The National Trust for Historic Preservation, a nonprofit educational group, helps people to acquire and preserve historic properties.

Today, ordinary people are restoring and living in historic buildings. Some have transformed old train stations, schools, or factories into restaurants, shops, or apartment buildings. Several cities have revitalized old run-down neighborhoods and warehouse districts. These historic areas attract new businesses and residents.

Connections to You

History is all around you. It is there for you to visit and explore. Check out the *National Register of Historic Places* in your local library. It lists thousands of places and structures that have played a role in your nation's history. To find out how you can help preserve American history, contact your local historical society or the National Trust for Historic Preservation.

1. **Comprehension** What have ordinary citizens and local government done to save important historic sites?
2. **Critical Thinking** How can visiting an historic site be more interesting and informative than reading about it?

Visiting an Historic Site Visit a nearby historic site. In a brief presentation, explain the site's importance and describe how it has been preserved and restored.

▲ Republic of Texas flag

Viewing HISTORY **Winning Texas Independence**

Sam Houston was wounded in the leg during the Battle of San Jacinto. Despite tremendous pain and a boot full of blood, Houston fought on to victory. This painting shows Houston accepting the surrender of Mexican commander Santa Anna.
★ **Why was San Jacinto a turning point in Texas history?**

Texans to defend the Alamo against 6,000 Mexican troops!

Young **William Travis** commanded the Texans inside the mission. Among the volunteers were the famous frontiersmen Jim Bowie and Davy Crockett. Several Tejano families, two Texan women, and two young male slaves were also present.

"Victory or Death!"

On February 23, 1836, Mexican troops began a siege of the Alamo. In a **siege**, enemy forces try to capture a city or fort by surrounding and bombarding it. The Texan defenders fought bravely. Still, Travis knew that unless he received help, he and his troops were doomed. He sent a messenger through the Mexican lines with a letter addressed "to the People of Texas and all the Americans in the World":

> "The enemy have demanded a surrender. . . . I have answered the demand with a cannon shot and our flag still waves proudly from the walls.
>
> *I shall never surrender or retreat.*
>
> I call on you in the name of Liberty, of patriotism, and of everything dear to the American character to come to our aid with all dispatch. . . . *Victory or Death!*"

Travis also sent scouts to seek additional soldiers and provisions. About 40 men were able to sneak through enemy lines and join the fighters in the Alamo. However, no large force ever arrived.

For 12 days, the defenders held off Mexican bombardment. Then, at dawn on March 6, Mexican cannon fire broke through the Alamo walls. Thousands of Mexican soldiers poured into the mission. When the bodies were counted, 183 Texans and almost 1,500 Mexicans lay dead. The Texan survivors, including Davy Crockett, were executed.

Connections With Geography

Santa Anna crossed the Rio Grande on February 16, 1836, in the middle of a harsh Texas winter. Many of the army's cattle died from the brutal cold and inadequate grazing land. For the final thirty days before reaching the Alamo, soldiers ate only eight ounces of corn cake per day.

Texan Independence

The fall of the Alamo set off cries for revenge. The fury of the Texans grew even stronger three weeks later, when Mexican forces killed several hundred Texan soldiers at Goliad after they had surrendered. Volunteers flooded into Sam Houston's army. Men from the United States also raced south to help the Texan cause.

On April 21, 1836, Houston decided that the moment had come to attack. Santa Anna was camped with his army near the San Jacinto (jah SEEN toh) River. With cries of "Remember the Alamo!" the Texans charged the surprised Mexicans.

The **Battle of San Jacinto** lasted only 18 minutes. Although they were outnumbered, Texans killed 630 Mexicans and captured 700 more. The following day, Texans captured Santa Anna himself. They forced the general to sign a treaty granting Texas its independence.

The Lone Star Republic

In battle, Texans had carried a flag with a single white star. After winning independence, they nicknamed their nation the **Lone Star Republic.** They drew up a constitution based on the Constitution of the United States and elected Sam Houston as their president.

The new country faced several problems. First, Mexico refused to accept the treaty signed by Santa Anna. Mexicans still claimed Texas as part of their country. Second, Texas was nearly bankrupt. Most Texans thought that the best way to solve both problems was for Texas to become part of the United States.

In the United States, Americans were divided about whether to **annex,** or add on, Texas. Most white southerners were in favor of the idea. Many northerners, however, were against it. At issue was slavery.

In the 1830s, antislavery feelings were growing in the North. Because many Texans owned slaves, northerners did not want to allow Texas to join the Union. President Andrew Jackson also worried that annexing Texas would lead to war with Mexico. As a result, Congress refused to annex Texas.

Over the next 10 years, the Lone Star Republic prospered under Houston's leadership. During the Panic of 1837, thousands of Americans moved to Texas to find land and start businesses. Settlers from Germany and Switzerland also swelled the population. By the 1840s, there were about 140,000 people in Texas, including many Mexicans and African Americans.

★ Section 2 Review ★

Recall

1. **Locate** **(a)** Mexico, **(b)** Gonzales, **(c)** Goliad, **(d)** Republic of Texas.
2. **Identify** **(a)** Stephen Austin, **(b)** Antonio López de Santa Anna, **(c)** Tejanos, **(d)** Sam Houston, **(e)** Alamo, **(f)** William Travis, **(g)** Battle of San Jacinto, **(h)** Lone Star Republic.
3. **Define** **(a)** siege, **(b)** annex.

Comprehension

4. Why did Mexico encourage Americans to move to Texas?
5. **(a)** Why did Texans seek independence from Mexico? **(b)** How did they finally achieve their goal?
6. Why did northerners and southerners disagree about annexing Texas?

Critical Thinking and Writing

7. **Drawing Conclusions** Why was the fall of the Alamo both a defeat and a victory for Texans?
8. **Solving Problems** Why do you think many Texans believed that annexation by the United States would help them solve their problems?

Activity **Writing an Appeal** You are trapped in the Alamo with the rebel Texans and Tejanos. Write an appeal to people in the United States to come help you—make it quick!

3 California and the Southwest

As You Read

Explore These Questions

- What brought the first white settlers to New Mexico?
- What was life like for Native Americans in California?
- Why did Americans want to expand to the Pacific Ocean?

Identify

- New Mexico Territory
- William Becknell
- Santa Fe Trail
- Junípero Serra
- Manifest Destiny
- James K. Polk

SETTING the Scene In 1819, John Quincy Adams made a bold claim. The world, he said, would have to accept the fact that the United States would one day possess all of North America:

> "From the time we became an independent nation, it was as much a law of nature that this would become our claim as that the Mississippi should flow to the sea."

By the 1840s, many Americans agreed. They, too, believed that it was the mission of the United States to expand all the way to the Pacific Ocean. Americans began to look with interest to the vast, rich lands of California and the Southwest.

New Mexico Territory

The entire Southwest belonged to Mexico in the 1840s. This huge region was called **New Mexico Territory.** It included most of the present-day states of Arizona and New Mexico, all of Nevada and Utah, and parts of Colorado.

Much of the Southwest is hot and dry. In some areas, thick grasses grow. There are also desert and mountain areas. Before the Spanish arrived, Pueblo and Zuñi Indians irrigated and farmed the land. Other Native Americans, such as the Apaches, lived by hunting.

A Spanish explorer, Juan de Oñate, had claimed the territory of New Mexico for Spain in 1598. In the early 1600s, the Spanish built Santa Fe as the capital of the territory. Under the Spanish, Santa Fe grew into a busy trading town. However, Spain refused to let Americans settle in New Mexico. Only after Mexico won its independence in 1821 were Americans welcome in Santa Fe.

William Becknell, a merchant and adventurer, was the first American to head for Santa Fe. In 1821, Becknell led a group of traders from Franklin, Missouri, across the plains. When they reached Santa Fe, they found Mexicans eager to buy their cloth and other goods. Other Americans soon followed Becknell's route. It became known as the **Santa Fe Trail.** (See the map on page 294.)

Early Years in California

California, too, belonged to Mexico in the early 1840s. Spain had claimed the region 100 years before English colonists settled in Jamestown. In the years that followed, Spanish and Native American cultures shaped life in California.

Land and climate

California is a land of dramatic contrasts. Two tall mountain ranges slice through the region. One range hugs the coast. The other sits inland on the border of Nevada and Arizona. Between these two ranges is California's fertile Central Valley.

Northern California receives plenty of rain. In the south, though, water is scarce and much of the land is desert. California enjoys mild temperatures all year, except for areas high in the mountains.

HISTORY HAPPENED HERE

Mission San Juan Capistrano

In 1776, Father Junípero Serra founded Mission San Juan Capistrano in southern California. Today, you can still walk among its adobe walls, enjoy its peaceful gardens, and listen to its old bells. These mission bells told the priests and Native Americans who lived there when to wake up, when to eat, when to pray, when to work, and when to go to bed.

★ ***To learn more about this historic site, write:*** *Mission San Juan Capistrano, P.O. Box 697, San Juan Capistrano, CA 92693.*

◀ *Mission bells*

A string of missions

As you have read, Spanish soldiers and priests built the first European settlements in California. In 1769, Captain Gaspar de Portolá led a group of soldiers and missionaries up the Pacific coast. The chief missionary was Father **Junípero Serra** (hoo NEE peh roh SEHR rah). Father Serra built his first mission at San Diego. He went on to build eight others.

Eventually, there were 21 Spanish missions along the California coast. Each mission claimed the surrounding land and soon was able to take care of all its own needs. Spanish soldiers built forts near the missions. The missions supplied meat, grain, and other foods to the forts.

Mission life for Native Americans

California Indians lived in small, scattered groups rather than large, organized nations. As a result, they were not able to offer much organized resistance to soldiers who forced them to work for the missions.

Native Americans herded sheep and cattle and raised crops for the missions. In return, they lived at the missions and learned about the Roman Catholic religion. Many Spanish missionaries were truly concerned with converting the Indians to Christianity. However, mission life was hard. Thousands of Native Americans died from overwork and diseases.

Sometimes, Indians did resist mission life. Many were baptized as Christians but continued to follow their traditional beliefs. Others simply ran away. Still, most continued to live and labor at the missions.

After Mexico won its independence, conditions for Native Americans in California grew even worse. The new Mexican government offered mission land to ranchers. On some ranches, Indians faced cruel mistreatment. If they tried to run away, the ranchers hunted them down. An American observer reported that California Indians lived in a state "even more degrading, and more oppressive than that of our slaves in the South."

Skills FOR LIFE

Critical Thinking | Managing Information | Communication | Maps, Charts, and Graphs

Distinguishing Fact From Opinion

How Will I Use This Skill?

A fact is a statement that can be observed or proven. An opinion is a judgment that reflects a person's beliefs or feelings. To get a true picture of events, even in everyday conversation, you must be able to distinguish between facts and personal opinions.

LEARN the Skill

To tell fact from opinion, follow these steps:

1. Identify facts. Look at each phrase or sentence and ask, "Can this be observed or proven?"
2. Identify words that express the writer's opinion. Some opinions are clearly indicated with phrases like "I think," or "In my opinion." Others are not so easy to identify. Watch for words that express or inspire emotion.
3. Decide whether the facts can support the writer's opinions. (Remember, this does not mean that you must *agree* with the opinion.)

PRACTICE the Skill

The excerpt to the right is from an 1846 newspaper article urging the United States to gain possession of California.

1. List three facts that are included in this article. What makes them facts?
2. (a) What words show that the first sentence is an opinion? (b) Identify two other opinions expressed in this excerpt.
3. How do the facts presented by the writer support his opinion about gaining California? Give two examples.

We do regard it as extremely desirable that California—a part, at least, of the province known by that name—should become the property of the United States. Lower California, embracing the long, narrow peninsula between the Gulf and the Pacific, stretching from the 21° to 33° latitude, a distance of about 800 miles, is universally represented by travelers as sterile and hopelessly desolate. It consists, indeed, of a chain of volcanic, treeless, barren mountains of rock, broken only by still more dreary plains of sand. It may well, therefore, be left to Mexico.

The remaining part of Upper California—that which lies nearest the Pacific coast—is not only by far the best portion of the province but one of the most beautiful regions on the face of the earth. Among the highlands which enclose this valley are vast forests filled with the loftiest and finest cedars and pines in the world, with every variety of soil, freshwater lakes, and every element of unbounded agricultural wealth, except a good climate.

Source:
Adapted from the *American Review,* January 1846.

APPLY the Skill

Choose an article in your local newspaper that includes opinions. Circle facts and underline opinions. Write a paragraph stating whether you think the facts in the article support the opinion.

These harsh conditions had a deadly effect. From 1770 to 1850, the Native American population of California declined from about 310,000 to 100,000.

Expansion: A Right and a Duty

As late as the mid-1840s, only about 700 people from the United States lived in California. Every year, however, more and more Americans began to look toward the West. The United States government even tried to buy California from Mexico several times. Officials were especially interested in gaining the fine ports at San Francisco and San Diego.

The nation's destiny

Many Americans saw the culture and the democratic government of the United States as the best in the world. They believed that the United States had the right and the duty to spread its rule all the way to the Pacific Ocean.

In the 1840s, a newspaper in New York coined a phrase for this belief. The phrase was **Manifest Destiny.** Manifest means clear or obvious. Destiny means something that is sure to happen. Americans who believed in Manifest Destiny thought that the United States was clearly meant to expand to the Pacific.

Manifest Destiny had another side, too. Many Americans believed that they were superior to Native Americans and Mexicans. For these Americans, racism justified taking over lands belonging to Indians and Mexicans.

Election of 1844

Manifest Destiny played an important part in the election of 1844. The Whigs nominated Henry Clay for President. Clay was a famous and respected national leader. The Democrats chose a little-known candidate, **James K. Polk**.

Voters soon came to know Polk as the candidate who favored expansion. Polk demanded that Texas and Oregon be added to the United States. Clay, on the other hand, opposed the annexation of Texas.

The Democrats made Oregon a special campaign issue. As you read, Britain and the United States held Oregon jointly. Polk demanded the whole region all the way to its northern border at latitude 54°40′N. "Fifty-four forty or fight!" became the Democrats' campaign cry. On election day, Americans showed their support for expansion by choosing Polk as President.

★ Section 3 Review ★

Recall

1. **Locate** **(a)** Sante Fe, **(b)** Santa Fe Trail, **(c)** California, **(d)** San Diego, **(e)** San Francisco.
2. **Identify** **(a)** New Mexico Territory, **(b)** William Becknell, **(c)** Santa Fe Trail, **(d)** Junípero Serra, **(e)** Manifest Destiny, **(f)** James K. Polk.

Comprehension

3. Describe how American settlers first went to New Mexico.
4. How did mission life affect Native Americans?
5. How did belief in Manifest Destiny affect the election of 1844?

Critical Thinking and Writing

6. **Making Inferences** How do you think missionaries justified forcing Indians to live and work on missions?
7. **Analyzing Ideas** "The irresistible army of [American settlers] has begun to pour down upon [California], armed with the plough and the rifle, and marking its trail with schools and colleges, courts and representative halls, mills and meetinghouses." What does this quotation show you about people's belief in the idea of Manifest Destiny?

Activity **Drawing a Political Cartoon** Draw a political cartoon from the point of view of Native Americans about conditions on California missions or ranches before 1845.

War With Mexico

As You Read

Explore These Questions

- How did the United States gain Oregon?
- What were the causes and results of the Mexican War?
- How did cultures blend in the new American territories?

Define

- cede

Identify

- Zachary Taylor
- Mexican War
- Winfield Scott
- Stephen Kearny
- Bear Flag Republic
- John C. Frémont
- Chapultepec
- Mexican Cession
- Gadsden Purchase

Setting the Scene American troops marched off to war with Mexico in 1846. Many Americans were eager to fight. Soldiers proudly sang new words to the popular tune "Yankee Doodle":

> "They attacked our men upon our land,
> And crossed our river too, sir.
> Now show them all with sword in hand
> What yankee boys can do, sir."

Not all Americans supported the war against Mexico. Some even accused President Polk of provoking the war himself in order to win Texas.

The bloody Mexican War lasted 20 months. In the end, it helped the United States achieve its dream of Manifest Destiny.

Dividing Oregon

James K. Polk took office in March 1845. Acting on his campaign promise, he moved to gain control of Oregon. War with Britain threatened.

Polk did not really want a war with Britain. In 1846, he agreed to a compromise. Oregon was divided at latitude 49°N. Britain got the lands north of the line, and the United States got the lands south of the line. The United States named its portion the Oregon Territory. Later, the states of Oregon (1859), Washington (1889), and Idaho (1890) were carved out of the Oregon Territory.

Annexing Texas

Texas proved a more dangerous problem. As you read, the United States at first refused to annex Texas. In 1844, Sam Houston, president of Texas, signed a treaty of annexation with the United States. The Senate again refused to ratify the treaty. Senators feared that annexing Texas would cause a war with Mexico.

Sam Houston would not give up. To persuade the Americans to annex Texas, he pretended that Texas might become an ally of Britain. Houston's trick worked. Americans did not want Europe's greatest power to gain a foothold on their western border. In 1845, Congress passed a joint resolution admitting Texas to the Union.

Sam Houston

Conflict With Mexico

The annexation of Texas made Mexicans furious. They had never accepted the independence of Texas. They also were concerned that the example set by Texas would encourage Americans in California and New Mexico to rebel.

At the same time, Americans resented Mexico. President Polk offered to pay Mexico \$30 million for California and New Mexico. However, Mexico strongly opposed any further loss of territory and refused the offer. Many Americans felt that Mexico stood in the way of Manifest Destiny.

The war begins

A border dispute finally sparked war. The United States claimed that the southern border of Texas was the Rio Grande. Mexico argued that it was the Nueces (noo AY says) River, some 200 miles (320 km) to the north. Both nations claimed the land between the two rivers.

In January 1846, Polk ordered General **Zachary Taylor** to cross the Nueces River and set up posts in the disputed area along the Rio Grande. (See the map below.) Polk knew that the move might lead to war. In April 1846, Mexican troops crossed the Rio

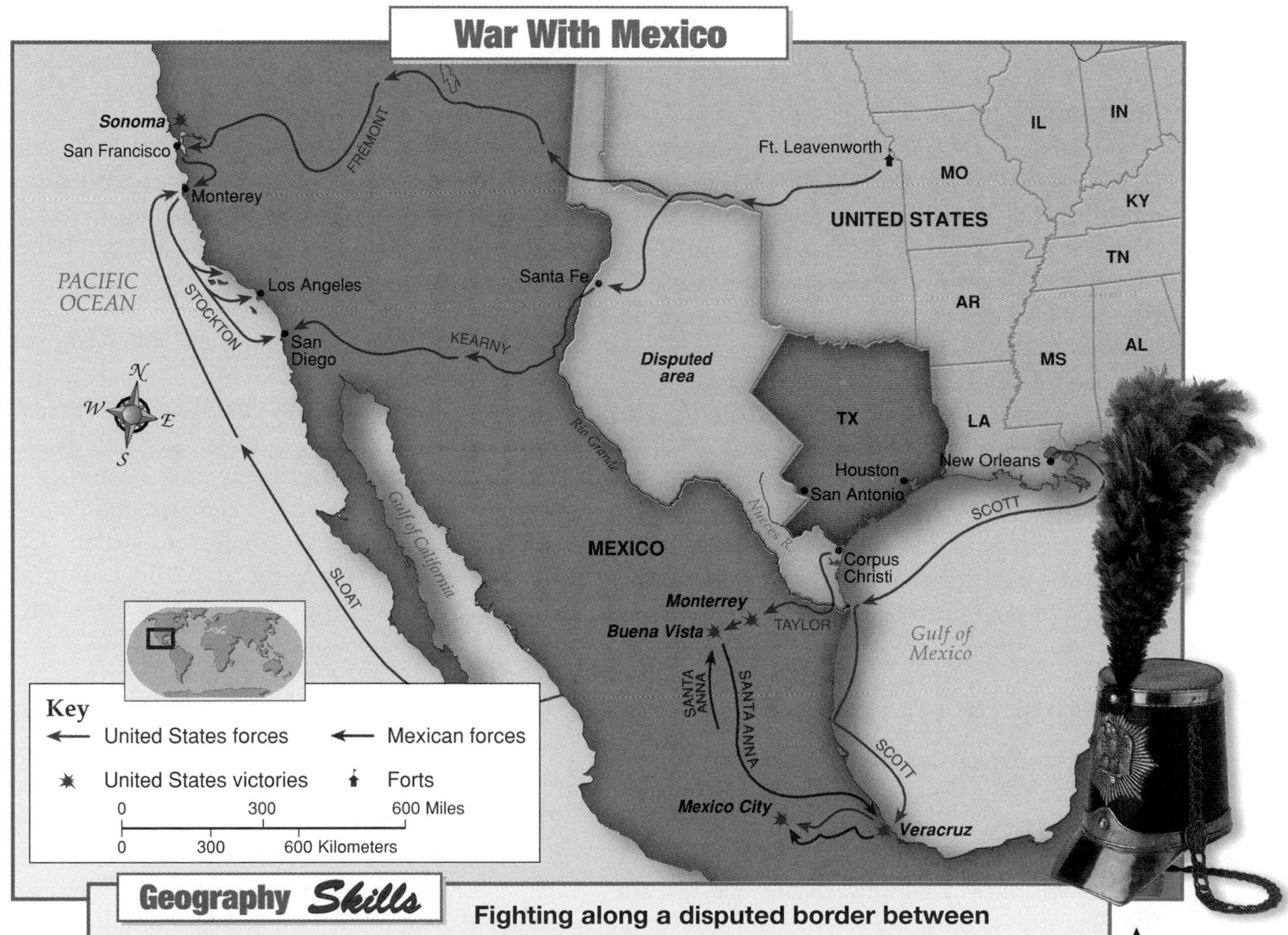

Geography *Skills* Fighting along a disputed border between Texas and Mexico triggered the Mexican War.

1. **Location** On the map, locate: **(a)** Rio Grande, **(b)** Nueces River, **(c)** Buena Vista, **(d)** Veracruz, **(e)** Mexico City.
2. **Movement** Describe the movements of each of the following American commanders: **(a)** Winfield Scott, **(b)** Stephen Kearny, **(c)** John Frémont.
3. **Critical Thinking** Based on the map, was sea power important to the United States in the Mexican War? Explain.

Cap of a United States soldier in the Mexican War

Grande and fought briefly with the Americans. Soldiers on both sides were killed.

President Polk was already considering going to war with Mexico. When he heard about the fighting at the Rio Grande, he asked Congress to issue a declaration of war. Polk told Congress:

> “Mexico has passed the boundary of the United States, has invaded our territory, and shed American blood upon American soil.”

Not everyone supported Polk's request. Abraham Lincoln, a young Whig Congressman, disputed Polk's claim that the fighting actually took place “upon American soil.” Still, at Polk's urging, Congress declared war on Mexico.

Americans respond

Americans were divided over the war. Many people in the South and West wanted more land and so were eager to fight. Many northerners, however, opposed the war. They saw it as a southern plot to add slave states to the Union. “Fresh markets of human beings are to be established,” claimed Charles Sumner, a Massachusetts opponent of slavery. “Further opportunities for this hateful traffic are to be opened.”

Still, many Americans joined the war effort. Since the nation's standing army was small, thousands of volunteers were needed. When the call for recruits went out, the response was overwhelming, especially in the South and West.

Fighting in Mexico

As the **Mexican War** began, the United States attacked on several fronts at the same time. President Polk hoped this strategy would allow American forces to win a quick victory. General Zachary Taylor crossed the Rio Grande into northern Mexico. There, he won several battles against the Mexican army. In February 1847, Taylor met Santa Anna at the Battle of Buena Vista. The Mexican troops greatly outnumbered the American forces, but the Americans were better armed and led. After fierce fighting, Santa Anna retreated. A major in Taylor's army later recalled feeding wounded Mexican soldiers after the battle:

> “We collected the wounded, who were suffering awfully from hunger and thirst as well as their wounds, and sent them to hospitals in town. . . . When coffee and biscuit were placed before them, they showed even in their famished state some signs of surprise and gratitude. This was the greatest victory of all, a victory unstained by blood. . . .”

Meanwhile, General **Winfield Scott** had landed another American army at the Mexican port of Veracruz. After a long battle, the Americans took the city. Scott then marched west toward the capital, Mexico City.

Rebellion in California

A third army, led by General **Stephen Kearny**, captured Santa Fe without firing a shot. Kearny hurried on to San Diego. After several battles, he took control of southern California early in 1847.

Even before hearing of the war, Americans in northern California had risen up against Mexican rule. The rebels declared California an independent republic on June 14, 1846. They called their new nation the **Bear Flag Republic.** At that time, a dashing young American explorer, **John C. Frémont,** was traveling in California on a scientific expedition for the army. Frémont quickly rushed to support the rebellion. Taking command of the rebel forces, he drove the Mexican governor's troops out of northern California. Frémont later joined forces with United States troops.

The final battle

By 1847, the United States controlled all of New Mexico and California. Meanwhile, General Scott had reached the outskirts of Mexico City.

Before they could take the Mexican capital, Scott's troops faced a fierce battle. Mexican soldiers made a heroic last stand at **Chapultepec** (chah POOL tuh pehk), a fort just outside Mexico City. Like the Texans who died at the Alamo, the Mexicans at Cha-

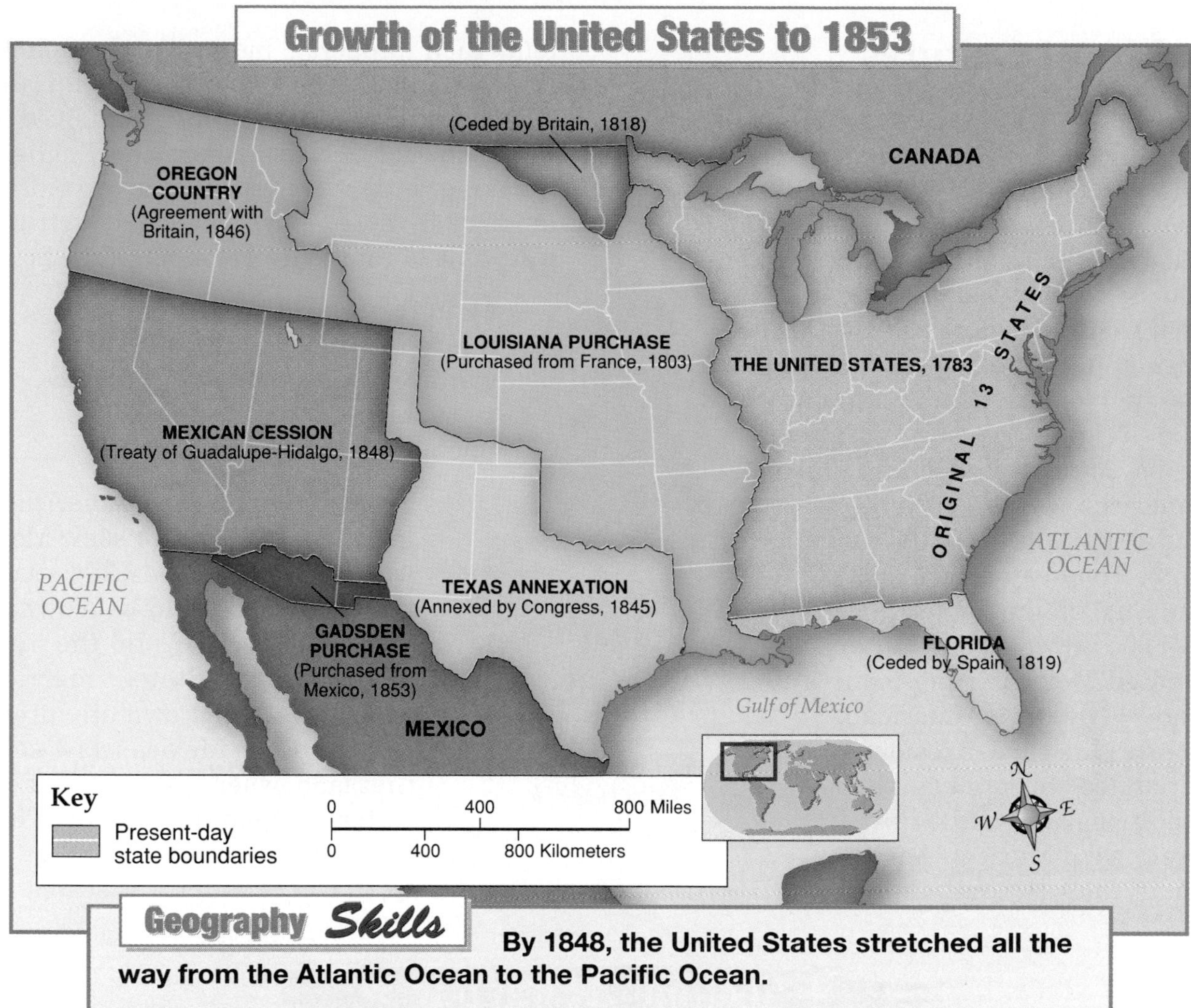

Geography Skills **By 1848, the United States stretched all the way from the Atlantic Ocean to the Pacific Ocean.**

1. **Location** On the map, locate: **(a)** Mexican Cession, **(b)** Gadsden Purchase, **(c)** Oregon Country.
2. **Region** Which of the territories shown on this map did the United States purchase from other nations?
3. **Critical Thinking** Refer to the map of the United States in the Reference Section. **(a)** Is your home state included on the map above? **(b)** If so, when and how did it become part of the United States?

pultepec fought to the last man. Today, Mexicans honor these young soldiers as heroes.

Achieving Manifest Destiny

With their capital in American hands, the Mexican government had no choice but to make peace. In 1848, Mexico signed the Treaty of Guadalupe-Hidalgo (gwah duh LOOP ay-ih DAHL goh). The treaty forced Mexico to **cede,** or give, all of California and New Mexico to the United States. These lands were called the **Mexican Cession.** (See the map above.)

In return, the United States paid Mexico $15 million. Americans also agreed to respect the rights of Spanish-speaking people in the Mexican Cession.

A few years after the end of the Mexican War, the United States completed its expansion across the continent. In 1853, it agreed to pay Mexico $10 million for a strip of land in present-day Arizona and New Mexico. The Americans needed this land to complete the building of a railroad. The land was called the **Gadsden Purchase.** The dream of Manifest Destiny was now complete.

A Mix of Cultures in the Southwest

English-speaking settlers poured into the Southwest. They brought their own culture with them, including their ideas about democratic government. The newcomers also learned a great deal from the older residents of the region. Mexican Americans taught the newcomers how to mine silver and irrigate the soil for growing crops. Many Spanish and Native American words—such as stampede, buffalo, tortilla, soda, and tornado—became part of the English language.

The new settlers often treated Mexican Americans and Native Americans poorly. The earlier residents struggled to protect their traditions and rights. However, when Mexican Americans went to court to defend their property, judges rarely upheld their claims. The family of Mariano Guadalupe Vallejo (vah YAY hoh) had lived in California for decades before the English-speaking settlers arrived. Vallejo, a wealthy landowner, noted how some new settlers were able to gain control of much of the land:

> “In their dealings with the rancheros, [Americans] took advantage of laws which they understood, but which were new to the Spaniards.”

Many Mexican homes in the Southwest contained religious statuettes like this one.

At the same time, Americans in the Southwest kept some Mexican laws. One of these laws said that a husband and wife owned property together. In the rest of the United States, married women could not own any property. Another Mexican law said that landowners could not cut off water to their neighbors. This law was important in the Southwest, where water was scarce.

★ Section 4 Review ★

Recall

1. **Locate** **(a)** Rio Grande, **(b)** Nueces River, **(c)** Buena Vista, **(d)** Veracruz, **(e)** Mexico City.
2. **Identify** **(a)** Zachary Taylor, **(b)** Mexican War, **(c)** Winfield Scott, **(d)** Stephen Kearny, **(e)** Bear Flag Republic, **(f)** John C. Frémont, **(g)** Chapultepec, **(h)** Mexican Cession, **(i)** Gadsden Purchase.
3. **Define** cede.

Comprehension

4. How did President Polk avoid war with Britain over Oregon?
5. **(a)** What event sparked the beginning of the Mexican War? **(b)** What were the final results of the war?
6. **(a)** Name two things that English-speaking settlers learned from Mexican Americans in the Southwest. **(b)** Name one tradition that settlers brought with them.

Critical Thinking and Writing

7. **Identifying Alternatives** Do you think the United States could have avoided going to war with Mexico in 1846? Explain.
8. **Recognizing Points of View** Frederick Douglass, an African American who fought to end slavery, wrote of the Mexican War that Americans “ought [to] blush and hang our heads for shame.” **(a)** Why do you think Douglass opposed the war? **(b)** Who might have agreed with his statement? Who might have disagreed?

Activity **Roleplaying** With your classmates, choose among the following roles: a citizen of Mexico; a white American living in Texas; a Mexican living in Texas; an American Californian; a northerner; a southerner; President Polk. Hold a debate about whether the United States should go to war with Mexico.

A Rush to the West

As You Read

Explore These Questions

- How did the Mormons settle Utah?
- How did the discovery of gold affect life in California?
- Why did California have a diverse population?

Define

- forty-niner
- vigilante

Identify

- Mormons
- Joseph Smith
- Brigham Young
- Sutter's Mill

SETTING the Scene In 1848, exciting news reached Toishan, a district in southern China. Mountains of gold had been discovered across the Pacific Ocean, in a place called California. It was there just for the digging!

The penalty for trying to leave China was harsh and sure—a swift beheading. Still, tens of thousands of Chinese risked the executioner's axe to cross the Pacific. Like other prospectors from Europe to Boston to South America, they were eager to join the California Gold Rush.

Gold was not the only thing that attracted settlers to the West in the mid-1800s. California, New Mexico, Oregon, and Texas were all now part of the United States. Restless pioneers, always eager to try something new, headed into these lands to build homes and a new way of life.

A Refuge for the Mormons

The largest group of settlers to move into the Mexican Cession were the **Mormons.** Mormons belonged to the Church of Jesus Christ of Latter-day Saints. The church was founded by **Joseph Smith** in 1830. Smith, a farmer who lived in upstate New York, attracted many followers.

Troubles with neighbors

Smith was an energetic and popular man. His teachings, however, angered many non-Mormons. For example, Mormons at first believed that property should be owned in common. Smith also said that a man could have more than one wife. Angry neighbors forced the Mormons to leave New York for Ohio. From Ohio, they were forced to move to Missouri, and from there to Illinois. In the 1840s, the Mormons built a community called Nauvoo on the banks of the Mississippi River in Illinois.

Before long, the Mormons again clashed with their neighbors. In 1844, an angry mob killed Joseph Smith. The Mormons chose **Brigham Young** as their new leader.

Brigham Young realized that the Mormons needed to find a home where they would be safe. He had read about a valley between the Rocky Mountains and the Great Salt Lake in Utah. Young decided that the isolated valley would make a good home for the Mormons.

A difficult journey

To move 15,000 men, women, and children from Illinois to Utah in the 1840s was an awesome challenge. Relying on religious faith and careful planning, Brigham Young achieved his goal.

In 1847, Young led an advance party into the Great Salt Lake valley. Wave after wave of Mormons followed. For the next few years, Mormon wagon trains struggled across the plains and over the Rockies to Utah. When they ran short of wagons and oxen, thousands made the long trip pulling their gear in handcarts.

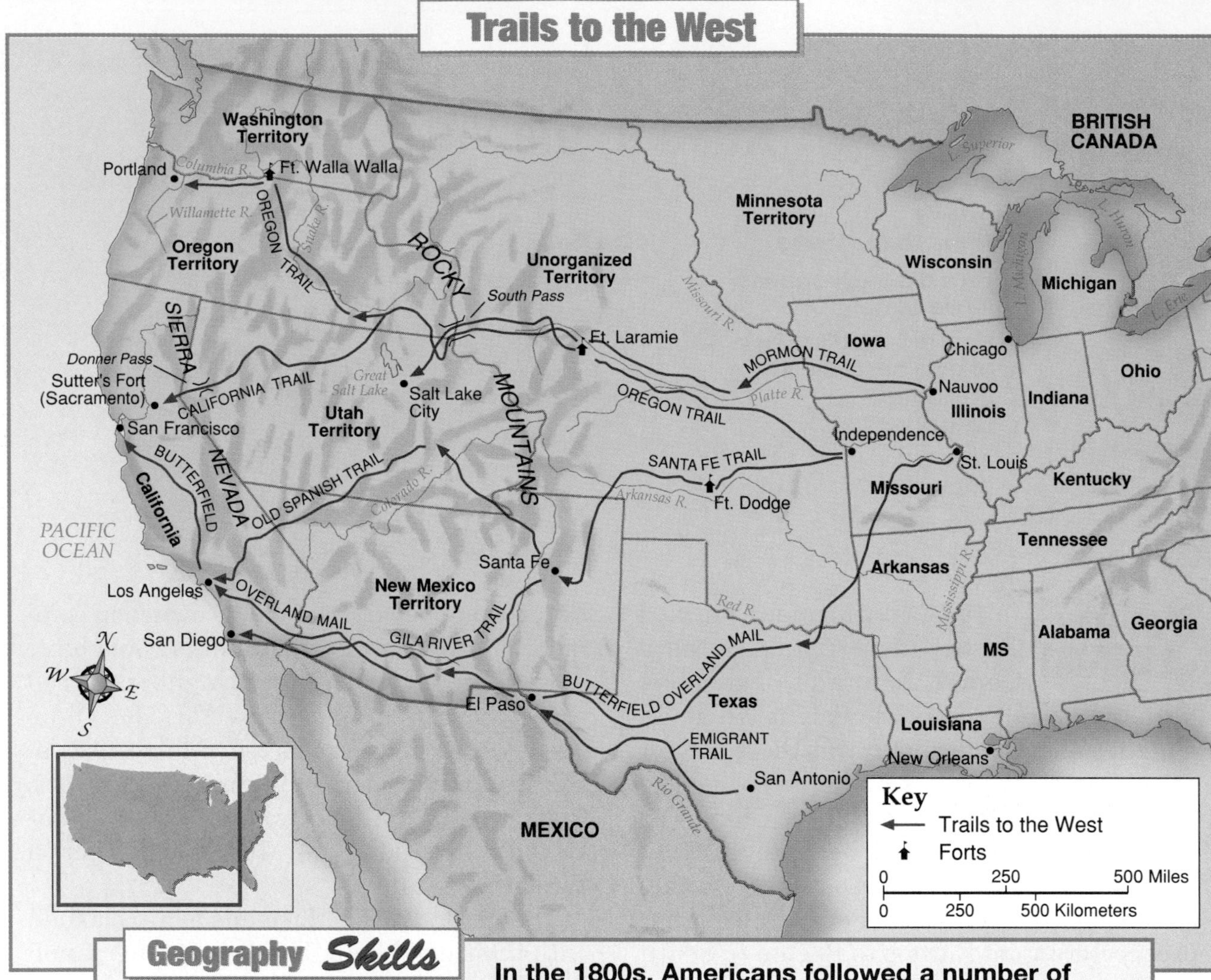

Geography *Skills* **In the 1800s, Americans followed a number of different trails to the West. Mountain passes allowed settlers to cross the Rockies and Sierra Nevada.**

1. **Location** On the map, locate: **(a)** Santa Fe, **(b)** Santa Fe Trail, **(c)** Sierra Nevada, **(d)** Rocky Mountains, **(e)** San Diego, **(f)** San Francisco, **(g)** Salt Lake City.
2. **Movement** Which trails ended in cities in California?
3. **Critical Thinking** **(a)** What would be the best route for a pioneer family to take from Independence, Missouri, to Sutter's Fort, California? **(b)** What mountains would they have to cross? **(c)** In which town might they seek shelter along the way?

Prospering in the desert

In Utah, the Mormons had to survive in a harsh desert climate. Still, Young was convinced that, for the Mormons, Utah was Zion, or the promised land:

> “We will raise our wheat, build our houses, fence our farms, plant our vineyards and orchards, and produce everything that will make our bodies comfortable and happy and in this manner we intend to build up Zion on the earth.”

To meet his goals, Young planned an irrigation system to bring water to farms. He also drew up plans for a large city, called Salt Lake City, to be built in the desert.

The Mormon settlement in Utah grew quickly. Like other whites, Mormons took over thousands of acres of Native American land, usually paying nothing for it.

Congress recognized Brigham Young as governor of the Utah Territory in 1850. Trouble later broke out when non-Mormons moved to the area. In the end, peace was restored, and Utah became a state in 1896.

California Gold Rush

While the Mormons trekked to Utah, thousands of other Americans were racing to California. These adventurous men and women all had a single objective: Gold!

Sutter's Mill

In 1848, John Sutter was building a sawmill on the American River, north of Sacramento, California. James Marshall was in charge of the job. On the morning of January 24, Marshall set out to inspect a ditch his crew was digging. He later told a friend what he saw that day:

> "It was a clear, cold morning; I shall never forget that morning. As I was taking my usual walk, . . . my eye was caught with the glimpse of something shining in the bottom of the ditch. There was about a foot of water running then. I reached my hand down and picked it up; it made my heart thump, for I was certain it was gold."

In a few days, word of the gold strike at **Sutter's Mill** spread to San Francisco. Carpenters threw down their saws. Bakers left bread in their ovens. Schools emptied as teachers and students joined the rush to the gold fields.

From San Francisco, the news spread across the United States and to the rest of the world. Thousands of Americans caught gold fever. People from Europe, China, Australia, and South America joined the rush as well. More than 80,000 people made the long journey to California in 1849. They became known as **forty-niners.**

In the gold fields

The first miners needed little skill. Because the gold was near the surface of the Earth, they could dig it out with knives. Later, the miners found a better way. They loaded sand and gravel from the riverbed into a washing pan. Then, they held the pan under water and swirled it gently. The water washed away lighter gravel, leaving the heavier gold in the pan. This process was known as "panning for gold."

Cause and Effect

Causes

- Oregon has fertile land
- Texas is ideal for raising cattle and growing cotton
- Many Americans believe in Manifest Destiny
- Mormons seek a safe home
- Gold is discovered in California

Westward Movement

Effects

- Texas wins war for independence
- United States annexes Texas
- Britain and United States divide Oregon
- United States defeats Mexico in war
- Cotton Kingdom spreads

Effects Today

- United States stretches from sea to sea
- California and Texas are the most populous states
- Mexican American culture enriches the United States

Graphic Organizer *Skills*

Westward movement increased at a tremendous rate in the mid-1800s.

1. **Comprehension** List two attractions that drew Americans to the West.
2. **Critical Thinking** According to this chart, was Manifest Destiny successful? Explain.

Economics $

Only a few miners actually struck it rich. Most went broke trying to make their fortunes. Still, although many miners left the gold fields, they stayed in California.

Linking United States and the World

China

United States

From China to the Golden Mountain

Some 25,000 Chinese left their ordered society for the rough-and-tumble world of the California gold fields. Few struck it rich, but their knowledge of farming helped the territory prosper. At left, Chinese peasants tend a rice field. At right, Chinese miners work at a gold claim. ★ **What qualities did the Chinese and other forty-niners need to succeed?**

Women joined the gold rush. Some staked claims and mined for gold. Others took advantage of economic opportunities in the mining camps. Women ran boarding houses, took in laundry, sewed, and ran bakeries.

A new state

The Gold Rush changed life in California. Almost overnight, San Francisco grew from a sleepy town to a bustling city.

Greed led some forty-niners to become criminals. Murders and robberies plagued many mining camps. To fight crime, miners formed vigilance committees. **Vigilantes** (vihj uh LAN teez), self-appointed law enforcers, dealt out punishment even though they had no legal power to do so. Sometimes an accused criminal was lynched, that is, hanged without a legal trial.

Californians realized they needed a government to stop the lawlessness. In 1849, they drafted a state constitution. They then asked to be admitted to the Union. Their request caused an uproar in the United States. Americans wondered whether the new state would allow slavery. As you will read, after a heated debate, California was admitted to the Union in 1850 as a free state.

Connections With Arts

The California Gold Rush provided the background for the still-popular folk song "My Darling Clementine." The song begins: "In a canyon, in a cavern / Excavating for a mine / Lived a miner, forty-niner / And his daughter Clementine."

California's Unique Culture

Most mining camps in California included a mix of peoples. A visitor to a mining town might meet runaway slaves from the South, Native Americans, and New Englanders. There were also people from Hawaii, China, Peru, Chile, France, Germany, Italy, Ireland, and Australia.

Most of the miners, however, were white Americans. During the wild days of the Gold Rush, they often ignored the rights of other Californians.

Mexican Americans and Indians

California included many Mexicans and Native Americans who had lived there long before the Gold Rush. In many instances, Mexican Americans lost land they had owned for generations. Still, they fought to preserve the customs of their people. José Carrillo (cah REE yoh) was from one of the oldest families in California. In part through his efforts, the state's first constitution was written in both Spanish and English.

Indians fared worst of all. Many Native Americans were driven off their lands and later died of starvation or diseases. Others were murdered. In 1850, about 100,000 Indians lived in California. By the 1870s, there were only 17,000 Indians left in the state.

Chinese Americans

Attracted by the tales of a "mountain of gold," thousands of Chinese began arriving in California in 1848. Because California needed workers, the Chinese were welcomed at first. When the Chinese staked claims in the gold fields, however, white miners often drove them off.

Discrimination against Chinese Americans and, later, other Asians would continue in California for many decades. Still, many Chinese Americans stayed in California and helped the state to grow. They farmed, irrigated, and reclaimed vast stretches of land.

African Americans

Free blacks, too, rushed to the California gold fields hoping to strike it rich. Some did become wealthy. By the 1850s, in fact, California had the richest African American population of any state. Yet African Americans were also denied certain rights. For example, California law denied blacks and other minorities the right to testify against whites in court. After a long struggle, blacks gained this right in 1863.

In spite of these problems, California thrived and grew. Settlers continued to arrive in the state. By 1860, it had 100,000 citizens. The mix of peoples in California gave it a unique culture.

★ Section 5 Review ★

Recall

1. **Locate** **(a)** Nauvoo, **(b)** Salt Lake City, **(c)** Sacramento, **(d)** San Francisco.
2. **Identify** **(a)** Mormons, **(b)** Joseph Smith, **(c)** Brigham Young, **(d)** Sutter's Mill.
3. **Define** **(a)** forty-niner, **(b)** vigilante.

Comprehension

4. Why did Brigham Young lead the Mormons to Utah?
5. Describe two effects of the Gold Rush on California.
6. Explain the problems that each of the following faced in California: **(a)** Mexican Americans, **(b)** Native Americans, **(c)** Chinese Americans, **(d)** African Americans.

Critical Thinking and Writing

7. **Comparing** Compare the settling of Utah with the settling of California. How were they similar? How were they different?
8. **Linking Past and Present** In the 1990s, almost 30 percent of immigrants to the United States settled in California. The largest group were from Asia. **(a)** Why do you think California still attracts many immigrants? **(b)** Why do so many Asian immigrants come to California?

Activity **Writing a Speech** There's trouble ahead! You and your friend went to California in the Gold Rush. Now, vigilantes are accusing your friend of a crime he didn't commit—stealing a horse. Write a speech in which you declare his innocence and call upon the vigilantes to wait until your friend can receive a legal trial.

Chapter 11 Review and Activities

★ Sum It Up ★

Section 1 Oregon Country

- The first white people to live in Oregon Country were hardy fur trappers.
- Settlers traveling by wagon train braved great dangers to reach Oregon Country.

Section 2 Texas Wins Independence

- Americans living in Texas, as well as Tejanos, rebelled against the Mexican government in 1835.
- After winning several battles, Texans set up an independent republic.

Section 3 California and the Southwest

- In the early years of white settlement, California was dotted with Spanish missions, forts, and ranches.
- In the 1840s, many Americans came to believe that the United States was destined to expand to the Pacific.

Section 4 War With Mexico

- The United States made Texas a part of the Union, and then went to war with Mexico in a border dispute.
- After defeating Mexico, the United States gained the Southwest and California.

Section 5 A Rush to the West

- Seeking religious freedom, the Mormons built a community in the Utah desert.
- A gold rush in California drew many newcomers to that region.

For additional review of the major ideas of Chapter 11, see ***Guide to the Essentials of American History*** or ***Interactive Student Tutorial CD-ROM,*** which contains interactive review activities, graphic organizers, and practice tests.

Reviewing the Chapter

Define These Terms

Match each term with the correct definition.

Column 1	Column 2
1. rendezvous	**a.** get-together for trappers
2. annex	**b.** person who joined the California Gold Rush
3. cede	**c.** to give something up
4. forty-niner	**d.** to add something on
5. vigilante	**e.** self-appointed law enforcer

Explore the Main Ideas

1. Describe the way of life of the mountain men in Oregon Country.
2. How did Texans force Santa Anna to grant them independence?
3. What role did the Catholic Church play in the settlement of California?
4. Describe one cause and one effect of the Mexican War.
5. Name the groups that made up the mixed culture of California in the mid-1800s.

Geography Activity

Match the letters on the map with the following places: **1.** Louisiana Purchase, **2.** Gadsden Purchase, **3.** Oregon Country, **4.** Florida, **5.** The United States in 1783, **6.** Texas Annexation, **7.** Mexican Cession. **Location** At what latitude did the United States and Britain agree to divide Oregon?

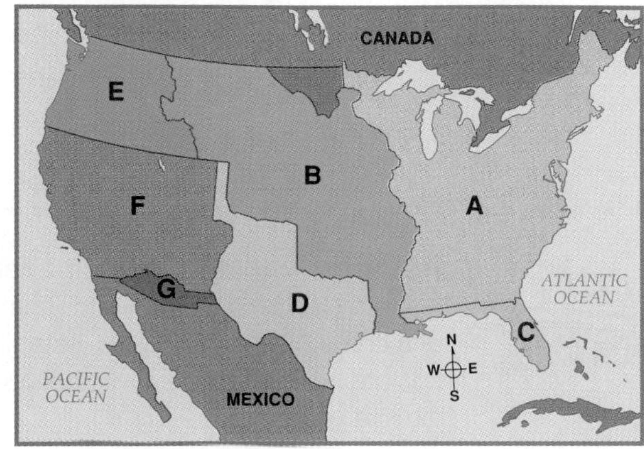

Critical Thinking and Writing

1. **Linking Past and Present** If you were Horace Greeley today, what advice would you give to young people seeking opportunity?
2. **Understanding Chronology** **(a)** List the following events in their correct order: Mexican War; annexation of Texas; founding of the Lone Star Republic; Battle of San Jacinto; Treaty of Guadalupe-Hidalgo. **(b)** Why was it unlikely that the United States would go to war with Mexico *before* Texas joined the Union?
3. **Understanding Causes and Effects** **(a)** What was the immediate cause of the war with Mexico? **(b)** Identify two long-range causes.
4. **Exploring Unit Themes** **Expansion** **(a)** Describe the idea of Manifest Destiny. **(b)** Explain how the nation achieved this goal. **(c)** What do you think were some of the positive and negative effects of Manifest Destiny?

Using Primary Sources

In a letter written in 1844, Henry Clay explained his thoughts about the annexation of Texas:

> "Annexation and war with Mexico are identical. Now, for one, I certainly am not willing to involve this country in a foreign war for the object of acquiring Texas. I know there are those who regard such a war... as a trifling affair, on account of the weakness of Mexico.... But I do not look upon it thus lightly. I regard all wars as great calamities, to be avoided, if possible, and honorable peace as the wisest and truest policy of this country."

Source: *National Intelligencer*, April, 17, 1844.

Recognizing Points of View **(a)** What did Clay predict would happen if the United States annexed Texas? **(b)** Why did he oppose the idea? **(c)** How do you think Sam Houston would have responded to Clay's letter?

Activity Bank

Interdisciplinary Activity

Exploring Science Working with a partner, give a presentation on how a geologic feature of the West influenced history. For example, you might choose the Rio Grande, the Great Salt Lake, the Rocky Mountains, the Central Valley of California, or the gold in California.

Career Skills Activity

City Planner You are a city official of San Francisco in 1849. You know that thousands of people will be moving to your city over the next few years. Write a report in which you propose a plan for growth.

Citizenship Activity

Exploring Immigration Like Californians, most Americans today are immigrants or descended from immigrants. Do you know when any of your ancestors first came to this country? If so, prepare a chart tracing your ancestors back to the first people in your family to come to the United States.

Internet Activity

Use the Internet to find sites dealing with the early history of the Mormons. Take notes on what you find and use them to compose a two-paragraph report on early Mormon history.

Eyewitness Journal

You are a mountain man or a missionary in Oregon; an American or Tejano in Texas; an American or Mexican in California; a Mormon in Utah; or a forty-niner. In your Eyewitness Journal, describe your participation in whatever was, for you, the single most important event of the years 1820–1860.

Chapter 12 The Worlds of North and South 1820–1860

What's Ahead

Section 1
Industry in the North

Section 2
Life in the North

Section 3
Cotton Kingdom in the South

Section 4
Life in the South

As the 1800s progressed, the North and the South continued to develop differently. In many ways, the two regions were like separate worlds. The North based its economy largely on industry. The South, meanwhile, developed an agricultural system that relied primarily on cotton. The industry of the North depended on paid workers. These workers struggled to make a living and endured hard working conditions. Still, they were free. In contrast, cotton production in the South depended on the labor of enslaved African Americans. These enslaved people had no rights or freedoms.

Why Study *History?* In the mid-1800s, many Americans could trace their roots to one of the British Isles, to Spain, or to a particular region of Africa. New immigrants were arriving from Germany, Ireland, and other European nations. Americans of all backgrounds were proud of their rich heritage. To learn about cultural influences that helped to shape several styles of American music, see this chapter's *Why Study History?* feature, "Music Is Part of Our Culture."

American Events

1820s Skilled workers begin to organize unions

1830s Railroads allow goods to be shipped quickly and cheaply

1820 | 1825 | 1830 | 1835 | 1840

World Events

1829 World Event Steam-powered locomotive travels 30 miles per hour in England

Viewing HISTORY **Different Worlds**

By the mid-1800s, the North and South had different economies. The North developed a variety of industries based on the labor of free workers. The South depended largely on agriculture and the labor of enslaved African Americans. A typical southern scene appears in William Aiken Walker's painting Plantation Economy in the Old South, *shown above.* ★ **What other economic differences between North and South do the pictures above suggest?**

1840s Cotton boom in South leads to spread of slavery

1844 Morse receives patent for telegraph

1850s Millions of Irish and German immigrants settle in the United States

1840 | 1845 | 1850 | 1855 | 1860

1840 World Event
World Anti-Slavery Convention held in Great Britain

1848 World Event
Revolutions in Germany

Industry in the North

As You Read

Explore These Questions

- How did new inventions change manufacturing and farming in the North?
- How did new means of communication and transportation benefit business?
- How did steam power help industry grow?

Define

- telegraph
- locomotive
- clipper ship

Identify

- Elias Howe
- John Deere
- Cyrus McCormick
- Samuel F. B. Morse
- John Griffiths

Elias Howe sewing machine

SETTING the Scene In 1834, a young French engineer, Michel Chevalier, toured the North. He was most impressed by the burst of industry there—the textile factories, shipyards, and iron mills. He wrote:

> "Everywhere is heard the noise of hammers, of spindles, of bells calling the hands to their work, or dismissing them from their tasks. . . . It is the peaceful hum of an industrious population, whose movements are regulated like clockwork."

Northern industry grew steadily in the mid-1800s. Most northerners still lived on farms. However, more and more of the northern economy centered on manufacturing and trade.

New Machines

The 1800s brought a flood of new inventions in the North. "In Massachusetts and Connecticut," a European visitor exclaimed, "there is not a laborer who has not invented a machine or a tool."

In 1846, **Elias Howe** patented a sewing machine. A few years later, Isaac Singer improved on Howe's machine. Soon, clothing makers bought hundreds of the new sewing machines. Workers could now make dozens of shirts in the time it took a tailor to sew one by hand.

Some new inventions made work easier for farmers. **John Deere** invented a lightweight steel plow. Earlier plows made of heavy iron or wood had to be pulled by slow-moving oxen. A horse could pull a steel plow through a field more quickly.

In 1847, **Cyrus McCormick** opened a factory in Chicago that produced mechanical reapers. The reaper was a horse-drawn machine that mowed wheat and other grains. McCormick's reaper could do the work of five people using hand tools.

The reaper and the steel plow helped farmers raise more grain with fewer hands. As a result, thousands of farm workers left the countryside. Some went west to start farms of their own. Others found jobs in new factories in northern cities.

$ Connections With Economics

Cyrus McCormick used a new business practice to help struggling farmers buy a reaper. He let farmers put some money down and pay the rest in installments. This practice is known as the installment plan or buying on credit.

The Telegraph

In 1844, **Samuel F. B. Morse** received a patent for a "talking wire," or telegraph. The **telegraph** was a device that sent electrical signals along a wire. The signals were based on a code of dots, dashes, and spaces. Later, this system of dots and dashes became known as the Morse code.

Congress gave Morse funds to run wire from Washington, D.C., to Baltimore. On May 24, 1844, Morse set up his telegraph in the Supreme Court chamber in Washington. As a crowd of onlookers watched, Morse tapped out a short message: "What hath God wrought!" A few seconds later, the operator in Baltimore tapped back the same message. The telegraph worked!

Morse's invention was an instant success. Telegraph companies sprang up everywhere. Thousands of miles of wire soon stretched across the country. As a result of the telegraph, news could now travel long distances in a matter of minutes.

The telegraph helped many businesses to thrive. Merchants and farmers could have quick access to information about supply, demand, and prices of goods in different areas of the country. For example, western farmers might learn of a wheat shortage in New York and ship their grain east to meet the demand.

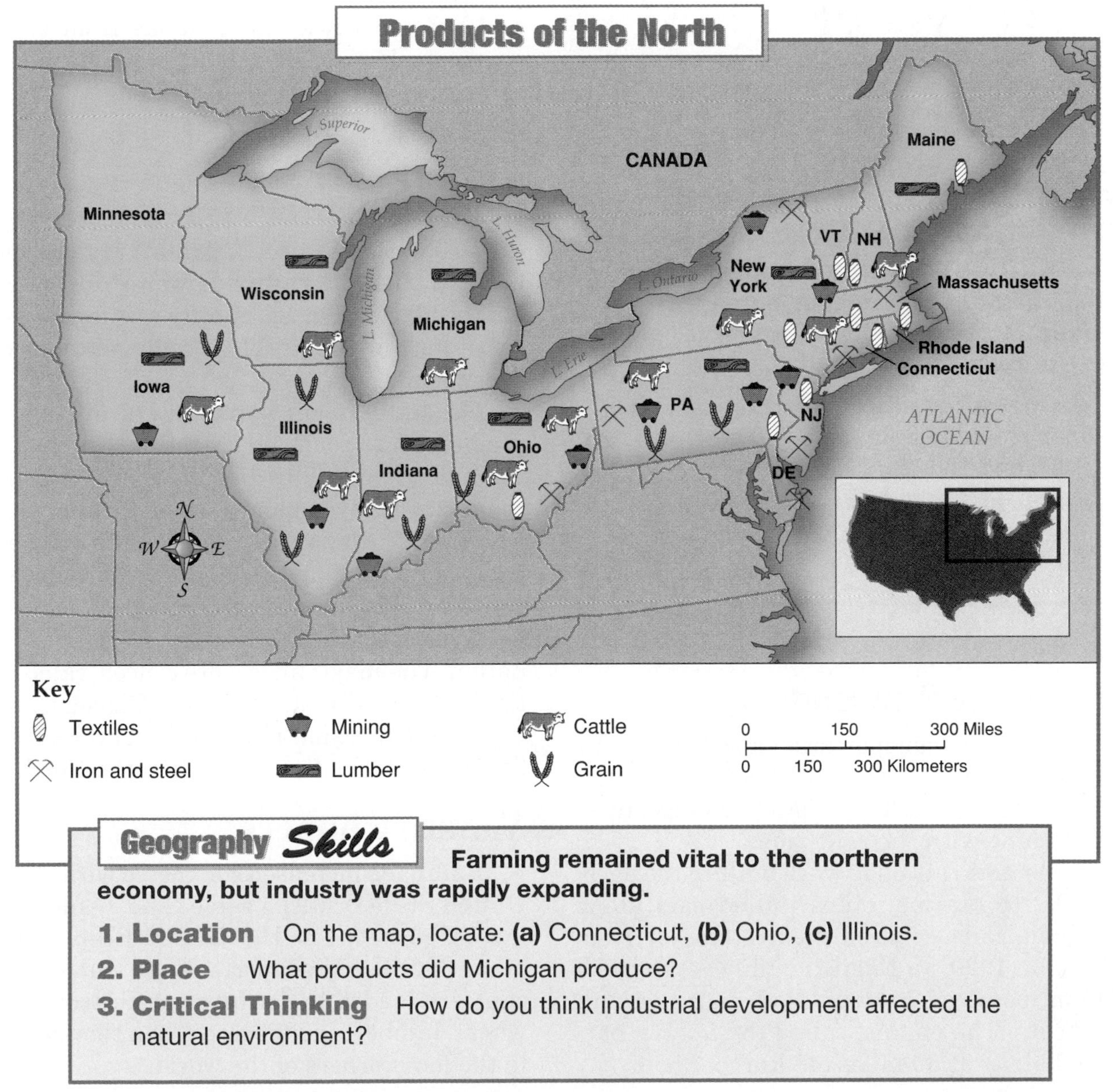

Geography Skills Farming remained vital to the northern economy, but industry was rapidly expanding.

1. **Location** On the map, locate: **(a)** Connecticut, **(b)** Ohio, **(c)** Illinois.
2. **Place** What products did Michigan produce?
3. **Critical Thinking** How do you think industrial development affected the natural environment?

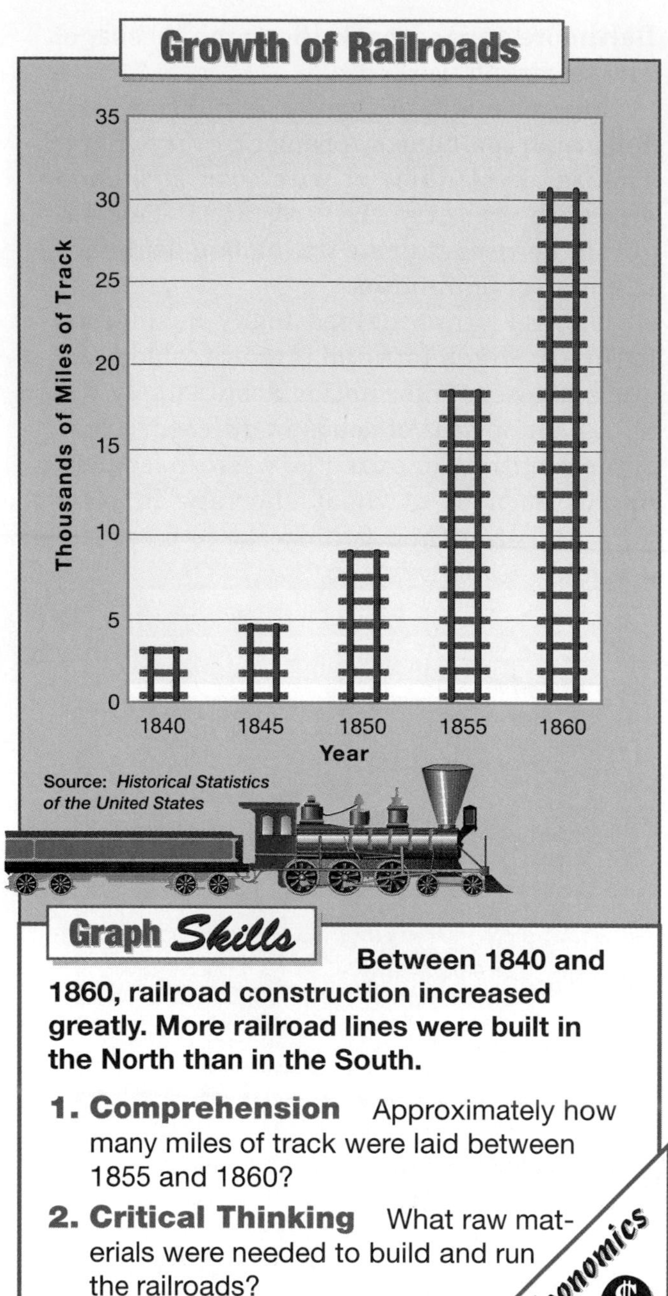

Graph Skills **Between 1840 and 1860, railroad construction increased greatly. More railroad lines were built in the North than in the South.**

1. **Comprehension** Approximately how many miles of track were laid between 1855 and 1860?
2. **Critical Thinking** What raw materials were needed to build and run the railroads?

The First Railroads

Improved transportation also boosted the economy. Americans continued to build new roads and canals. The greatest change, however, came with the railroads.

The first railroads were built in the early 1800s. Horses or mules pulled cars along wooden rails covered with strips of iron. Then, in 1829, an English family developed a steam-powered **locomotive** engine to pull rail cars. The engine, called the *Rocket,* barreled along at 30 miles (48 km) per hour.

Early difficulties

In the United States, there was some initial opposition to railroads. Farmers did not want railroads running through their fields. Teamsters who moved freight on horse-drawn wagons feared that they would lose their jobs. Likewise, people who invested in canals worried that competition from the railroads might cause them to lose their investments. Some states protected the canals by placing limits on railroads. One such limit was that railroads could carry freight only when canals were frozen.

Another problem for the railroads was concern over reliability and safety. Early steam locomotives often broke down. Soft roadbeds and weak bridges contributed to accidents. Locomotives were extremely noisy and belched thick black smoke from their smokestacks. Hot embers from smokestacks sometimes burned holes in passengers' clothing or set nearby buildings on fire.

A railroad boom

Despite these problems, promoters believed in the future of train travel. One boasted that the railroads were "unrivaled for speed, cleanliness, civility of officers and servants, and admirable accommodations of every kind."

Gradually, railroad builders overcame problems and removed obstacles. Engineers learned to build sturdier bridges and solid roadbeds. They replaced wooden rails with iron rails. Such improvements made railroad travel safer and faster. Meanwhile, legal restrictions on railroad building were removed.

By the 1850s, railroads crisscrossed the nation. The major lines were concentrated in the North and West. New York, Chicago, and Cincinnati became major rail centers. The South had much less track than the North.

Yankee Clippers

Railroads increased commerce within the United States. At the same time, trade also increased between the United States and other nations. At seaports in the Northeast, captains loaded their ships with cotton, fur, wheat, lumber, and tobacco. Then they sailed to the four corners of the world.

Speed was the key to successful trade at sea. In 1845, an American named **John Griffiths** launched the *Rainbow,* the first of the **clipper ships.** These sleek vessels had tall masts and huge sails that caught every gust of wind. Their narrow hulls clipped swiftly through the water.

In the 1840s, American clipper ships broke every speed record. One clipper sped from New York to Hong Kong in 81 days, flying past older ships that took five months to reach China. The speed of the clippers helped the United States win a large share of the world's sea trade in the 1840s and 1850s.

The golden age of the clipper ship was brief. In the 1850s, Britain launched the first oceangoing steamships. These sturdy iron vessels carried more cargo and traveled even faster than clippers.

The Northern Economy Expands

By the 1830s, factories began to use steam power instead of water power. Machines that were driven by steam were powerful and cheap to run. Also, factories that used steam power could be built almost anywhere, not just along the banks of swift-flowing rivers. As a result, American industry expanded rapidly.

At the same time, new machines made it possible to produce more goods at a lower cost. These more affordable goods attracted eager buyers. Families no longer had to make clothing and other goods in their homes. Instead, they could buy factory-made products.

Railroads allowed factory owners to transport large amounts of raw materials and finished goods cheaply and quickly. Also, as railroads stretched across the nation, they linked distant towns with cities and factories. These towns became new markets for factory goods.

The growth of railroads also affected northern farming. Railroads brought cheap grain and other foods from the West to New England. New England farmers could not compete with this new source of cheap foods. Many left their farms to find new jobs as factory workers, store clerks, and sailors. More and more, New Englanders turned to manufacturing and trade.

★ Section 1 Review ★

Recall

1. **Identify** **(a)** Elias Howe, **(b)** John Deere, **(c)** Cyrus McCormick, **(d)** Samuel F. B. Morse, **(e)** John Griffiths.
2. **Define** **(a)** telegraph, **(b)** locomotive, **(c)** clipper ship.

Comprehension

3. What new inventions made work easier for farmers?
4. Explain how each of the following helped industry grow: **(a)** telegraph, **(b)** railroads, **(c)** clipper ships.
5. How did steam power and new machines change northern industry?

Critical Thinking and Writing

6. **Linking Past and Present** What technology of today helps businesses in the same way that the telegraph helped businesses in the 1800s?
7. **Understanding Causes and Effects** How did the building of railroads cause many New Englanders to abandon farming?

Activity **Creating an Advertisement** It is the mid-1800s and you are working at an advertising agency. Create an advertisement poster urging people to buy or use one of the new inventions of the period. Use both words and pictures to make your advertisement persuasive.

Life in the North

Explore These Questions

- What conditions caused northern workers to organize?
- Why did many Europeans move to the United States in the mid-1800s?
- What was life like for African Americans in the North?

Define

- artisan
- trade union
- strike
- famine
- nativist
- discrimination

Identify

- Sarah Bagley
- Know-Nothing party
- Henry Boyd
- Macon Allen
- John Russworm

Alzina Parsons never forgot her thirteenth birthday. The day began as usual, with work in the local spinning mill. Suddenly, Alzina cried out. She had caught her hand in the spinning machine, badly mangling her fingers. The foreman summoned the factory doctor. He cut off one of the injured fingers and sent the girl back to work.

In the early 1800s, such an incident probably would not have happened. Factory work was hard, but mill owners treated workers like human beings. By the 1840s, however, there was an oversupply of workers. Many factory owners now treated workers like machines.

Factory Conditions Worsen

Factories of the 1840s and 1850s were very different from the mills of the early 1800s. The factories were larger, and they used steam-powered machines. More laborers worked longer hours for lower wages. Workers lived in dark, dingy houses in the shadow of the factory.

Families in factories

As the need for workers increased, entire families labored in factories. In some cases, a family agreed to work for one year. If even one family member broke the contract, the entire family might be fired.

The factory day began when a whistle sounded at 4 A.M. Father, mother, and children dressed in the dark and headed off to work. At 7:30 A.M. and at noon, the whistle sounded again to announce breakfast and lunch breaks. The workday did not end until 7:30 P.M., when a final whistle sent the workers home.

Hazards at work

During their long day, factory workers faced discomfort and danger. Few factories had windows or heating systems. In summer, the heat and humidity inside the factory were stifling. In winter, the extreme cold chilled workers' bones and contributed to frequent sickness.

Factory machines had no safety devices, and accidents were common. Owners ignored the hazards. There were no laws regulating factory conditions. Injured workers often lost their jobs.

In 1855, a visitor to a textile mill in Fall River, Massachusetts, asked the manager of the mill how he treated his workers. In his reply, the manager was harsh but honest. He described his feelings about the workers.

> “I regard people just as I regard my machinery. So long as they can do my work for what I choose to pay them, I keep them, getting out of them all I can.”

Workers Join Together

Poor working conditions and low wages led workers to organize. The first to do so were **artisans.** Artisans are workers who have learned a trade, such as carpentry or shoemaking.

Trade unions and strikes

In the 1820s and 1830s, artisans in each trade united to form **trade unions**. The unions called for a shorter workday, higher wages, and better working conditions. Sometimes, unions went on strike to gain their demands. In a **strike**, union workers refuse to do their jobs.

At the time, strikes were illegal in many parts of the United States. Strikers faced fines or jail sentences. Employers often fired strike leaders.

Progress for artisans

Slowly, however, workers made progress. In 1840, President Van Buren approved a 10-hour workday for government employees. Other workers pressed their demands until they won the same hours as government workers. Workers celebrated another victory in 1842 when a Massachusetts court declared that they had the right to strike.

Artisans won better pay because factory owners needed their skills. Unskilled workers, however, were unable to bargain for better wages. Unskilled workers held jobs that required little or no training. Because these workers were easy to replace, employers did not listen to their demands.

Women Workers Organize

The success of trade unions encouraged other workers to organize. Workers in New England textile mills especially were eager to protest cuts in wages and unfair work rules. Many of these workers were women.

Women workers faced special problems. First, they had always earned less money than men did. Second, most union leaders did not want women in their ranks. Like many people at the time, they believed that women should not work outside the home. In fact, the goal of many unions was to raise men's wages so that their wives could leave their factory jobs.

Viewing History **Working in a Factory**

Factory employees faced crowded and dangerous working conditions. Many were injured on the job. The workers in this scene are making McCormick reapers. ★ **What kinds of accidents could occur in a factory such as this?**

▼ *A worker's lunch pail*

Skills FOR LIFE

Critical Thinking | Managing Information | **Communication** | Maps, Charts, and Graphs

Teaching Others

How Will I Use This Skill?

You already use it. You may teach others how to do school work, how to make something, how to play a sport, or how to use a computer program. In the future, you may teach job skills to co-workers. If you become a parent, you will teach your child. We are all teachers.

LEARN the Skill

You can teach others by following these four steps:

1. Make sure you know the material you will teach.
2. Prepare a teaching plan that is interesting, informative, and at the proper level of difficulty.
3. Present your lesson. Encourage your students to participate and to ask questions.
4. Check that your students have learned the material and reteach if necessary.

PRACTICE the Skill

Using the steps above, teach some classmates about the immigrants who came to the United States in the mid-1800s.

1. Study and take notes on the material in this section under the heading "Millions of New Americans."
2. Prepare the teaching plan that you will use for your lesson. You might make an outline or chart or write a skit. You might use additional books or videotapes.
3. Present your lesson. Keep your students involved! Ask interesting questions and encourage your students to participate.
4. Provide a quiz or activity to check for student understanding. If your students did not learn the lesson well enough, use a different method and try again.

Teaching and learning

APPLY the Skill

You can apply this skill by volunteering to tutor a classmate or younger student who is having difficulty with reading, mathematics, or another school subject. You might also teach a friend about a hobby or game that interests you.

Despite these problems, women workers organized. They staged several strikes at Lowell, Massachusetts, in the 1830s. In the 1840s, **Sarah Bagley** organized the Lowell Female Labor Reform Association. The group petitioned the state legislature for a 10-hour workday.

Millions of New Americans

By the late 1840s, many factory workers in the North were immigrants. An immigrant is a person who enters a new country in order to settle there. In the 1840s and 1850s, about 4 million immigrants arrived in the United States.

From Ireland and Germany

In the 1840s, a disease destroyed the potato crop across Europe. The loss of the crop caused a **famine**, or severe food shortage, especially in Ireland. Between 1845 and 1860, over 1.5 million Irish fled to the United States.

Most Irish immigrants were too poor to buy farmland. They settled in the cities where their ships landed. In New York and Boston, thousands of Irish crowded into poor neighborhoods.

In the 1850s, nearly one million German immigrants arrived in the United States. In 1848, revolutions had broken out in several parts of Germany. The rebels fought for democratic reforms. When the revolts failed, thousands had to flee.

Many other German immigrants came to the United States simply to make a better life for themselves.

Enriching the nation

Immigrants supplied much of the labor that helped the nation's economy to grow. Many Irish immigrants worked in northern factories because they did not have enough money to buy farmland. Other Irish workers helped build the canals and railroads that were crisscrossing the nation.

Immigrants from Germany often had enough money to move west and buy good farmland. Many of them were artisans and merchants. Towns of the Midwest often had German grocers, butchers, and bakers.

A Reaction Against Immigrants

Not everyone welcomed the flood of immigrants. One group of Americans, called **nativists**, wanted to preserve the country for native-born, white citizens. Using the slogan "Americans must rule America," they called for laws to limit immigration. They also wanted to keep immigrants from voting until they had lived in the United States for 21 years. At the time, newcomers could vote after only 5 years in the country.

Some nativists protested that newcomers "stole" jobs from native-born Americans by working for lower pay. Others blamed immigrants for crime in the growing cities. Still others mistrusted Irish and German newcomers because many of them were Catholics. Until the 1840s, nearly all Americans were Protestants.

In the 1850s, nativists formed a new political party. It was known as the **Know-Nothing party** because members answered, "I know nothing," when asked about the party. Many meetings and rituals of the party were kept secret. In 1856, the Know-Nothing candidate for President won 21 percent of the popular vote. Soon after, however, the party died out. Still, many Americans continued to blame the nation's problems on immigrants.

African Americans in the North

During the nation's early years, slavery was legal in the North. By the early 1800s, however, all the northern states had outlawed slavery. As a result, thousands of free African Americans lived in the North.

Denied equal rights

Free African Americans in the North faced discrimination. **Discrimination** is a policy or an attitude that denies equal rights to certain groups of people. As one writer pointed out, African Americans were denied "the ballot-box, the jury box, the halls of the legislature, the army, the public lands, the school, and the church."

Biography **John Jones**

In the 1840s, John Jones ran a profitable tailoring business in Chicago. He helped runaway slaves and opposed Illinois laws that discriminated against African Americans. In the 1870s, he would help to integrate Chicago's public schools.

★ **What obstacles did Jones probably have to overcome?**

Even skilled African Americans had trouble finding good jobs. One black carpenter was turned away by every furniture maker in Cincinnati. At last, a shop owner hired him. However, when he entered the shop, the other carpenters dropped their tools. Either he must leave or they would, they declared. Similar experiences occurred throughout the North.

Some success

Despite the obstacles in their way, some African Americans achieved notable success in business. William Whipper grew wealthy as the owner of a lumber yard in Pennsylvania. He devoted much of his time and money to help bring an end to slavery. **Henry Boyd** operated a profitable furniture company in Cincinnati.

African Americans made strides in other areas as well. Henry Blair invented a corn planter and a cotton seed planter. In 1845, **Macon Allen** became the first African American licensed to practice law in the United States. After graduating from Bowdoin College in Maine, **John Russworm** became one of the editors of *Freedom's Journal*, the first African American newspaper.

★ Section 2 Review ★

Recall

1. **Identify** (a) Sarah Bagley, (b) Know-Nothing party, (c) Henry Boyd, (d) Macon Allen, (e) John Russworm.
2. **Define** (a) artisan, (b) trade union, (c) strike, (d) famine, (e) nativist, (f) discrimination.

Comprehension

3. How did working conditions in factories worsen in the 1840s and 1850s?
4. In the mid-1800s, why did so many immigrants to the United States come from Ireland and Germany?
5. How did discrimination affect free African Americans in the North?

Critical Thinking and Writing

6. **Making Inferences** Who do you think were the strongest supporters of laws that made strikes illegal? Explain.
7. **Recognizing Points of View** Make a graphic organizer that identifies the reasons for the nativist point of view.

Activity **Writing a Petition** You are a female mill worker of the 1840s. You are unhappy about the harsh working conditions in the mills. Write a petition to the state legislature listing your complaints and asking for better working conditions.

Cotton Kingdom in the South

As You Read

Explore These Questions

- Why did cotton planters begin to move westward?
- How did the cotton gin affect slavery in the South?
- Why did the South have less industry than the North?

Identify

- Eli Whitney
- Cotton Kingdom
- William Gregg

Setting the Scene In 1827, an Englishman, Basil Hall, traveled through much of the South aboard a riverboat. He complained that the southerners he met were interested in only one thing—cotton:

> “All day and almost all night long, the captain, pilot, crew and passengers were talking of nothing else; and sometimes our ears were so wearied with the sound of cotton! cotton! cotton! that we gladly hailed fresh . . . company in hopes of some change—but alas! . . . 'What's cotton at?' was the first eager inquiry.”

Cotton became even more important to the South in the years after Hall's visit. Even though southerners grew other crops, cotton was the region's leading export. Cotton plantations—and the slave system on which they depended—shaped the way of life in the South.

Cotton Gin, Cotton Boom

The Industrial Revolution greatly increased the demand for southern cotton. Textile mills in the North and in Britain needed more and more cotton to make cloth. At first, southern planters could not meet the demand. They could grow plenty of cotton because the South's soil and climate were ideal. However, removing the seeds from the cotton by hand was a slow process. Planters needed a better way to clean cotton.

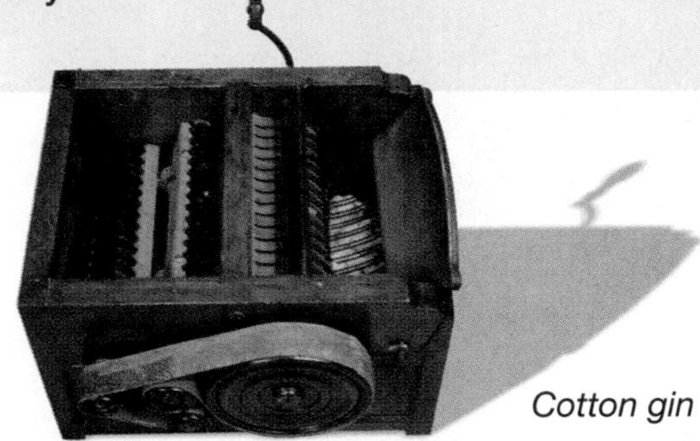

Cotton gin

Eli Whitney's invention

In 1793, **Eli Whitney**, a young Connecticut schoolteacher, was traveling to Georgia. He was going to be a tutor on a plantation. When Whitney learned of the planters' problem, he decided to build a machine to clean cotton.

In only 10 days, Whitney came up with a model. His cotton engine, or gin, had two rollers with thin wire teeth. When cotton was swept between the rollers, the teeth separated the seeds from the fibers. (See Linking History and Technology on page 312.)

The cotton gin was simple, but its effects were enormous. A worker using a gin could do the work of 50 people cleaning cotton by hand. Because of the gin, planters could now grow cotton at a huge profit.

Connections With Science

Technology thieves stole Eli Whitney's first cotton gin. Before Whitney could build another, someone filed a patent for a machine that copied his invention. To receive the profits that were due to him, Whitney went to court. He filed more than 50 lawsuits.

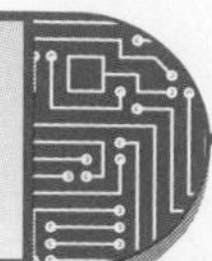

Linking History and Technology

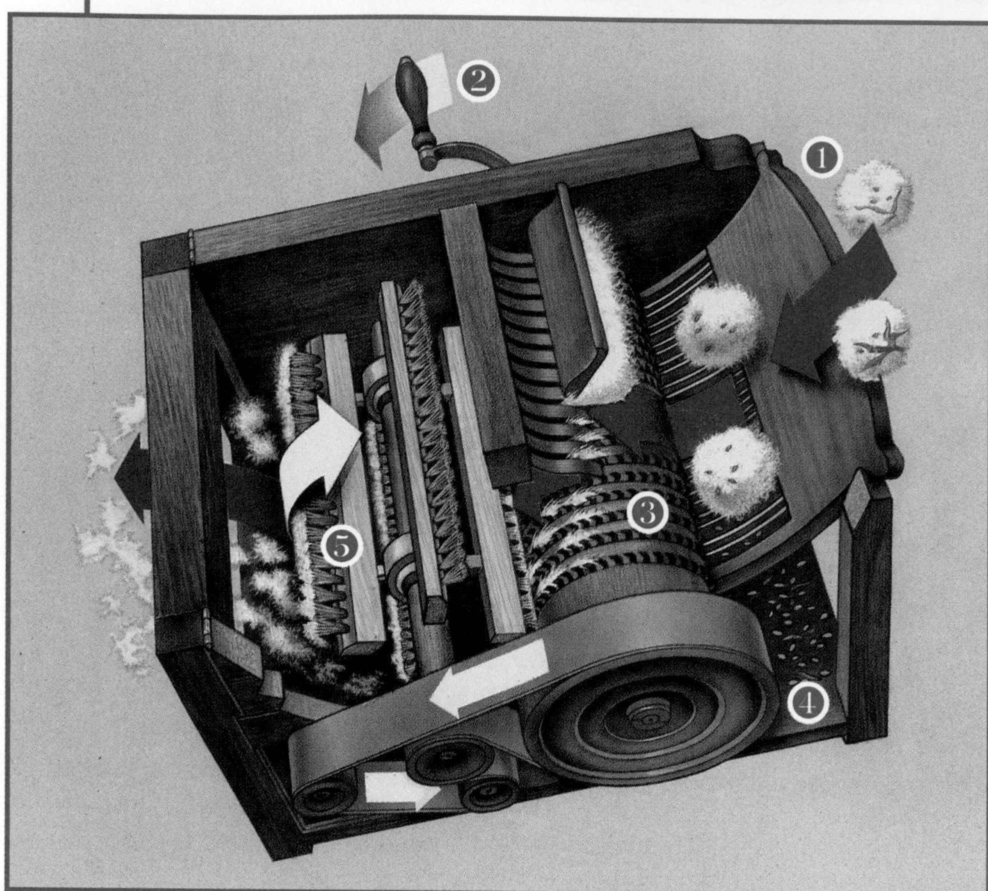

❶ *Cotton bolls, made up of fiber and seeds, are fed into the cotton gin. The red arrows show the path of the cotton through the gin.*

❷ *As the handle is turned, the cylinder and brushes rotate.*

❸ *Wire teeth catch the cotton bolls and pull them through narrow wire slots.*

❹ *The seeds are too large to pass through the slots. They fall to the bottom of the gin.*

❺ *Rotating brushes pull cleaned cotton fiber from the wire teeth and sweep it out of the gin.*

The Cotton Gin

The cotton gin separated unwanted seeds from cotton fiber. With the help of a gin, a worker was able to process as much as 50 pounds of cotton in a single day. As a result, cotton production became a very profitable business.

★ **How did the gin separate the seeds from the fiber?**

▲ *A cotton boll*

Cotton Kingdom and slavery

The cotton gin led to a boom in cotton production. In 1792, planters grew only 6,000 bales of cotton a year. By 1850, the figure was over 2 million bales.

Planters soon learned that soil wore out if planted with cotton year after year. They needed new land to cultivate. After the War of 1812, cotton planters began to move west.

By the 1850s, there were cotton plantations extending in a wide band from South Carolina through Alabama and Mississippi to Texas. (See the map on page 314.) This area of the South became known as the **Cotton Kingdom**.

Tragically, as the Cotton Kingdom spread, so did slavery. Even though cotton could now be cleaned by machine, it still had to be planted and picked by hand. The result was a cruel cycle. The work of slaves brought profits to planters. Planters used the profits to buy more land and more slaves.

An Agricultural Economy

Cotton was the South's most profitable cash crop. However, the best conditions for growing cotton could be found mostly in the southernmost portion of the South. In other areas of the South, rice, sugar cane, and tobacco were major crops. In addition, Southerners raised much of the nation's livestock.

Rice was an important crop along the coasts of South Carolina and Georgia. Sugar cane was important in Louisiana and Texas. Growing rice and sugar cane required expensive irrigation and drainage systems. Cane growers also needed costly machinery to grind their harvest. Small-scale farmers could not afford such expensive equipment, however. As a result, the plantation system dominated areas of sugar and rice production just as it did areas of cotton production.

Tobacco had been an export of the South since 1619, and it continued to be planted in Virginia, North Carolina, and Kentucky. However, in the early 1800s, the large tobacco plantations of colonial days had given way to small tobacco farms. On these farms, a few field hands tended five or six acres of tobacco.

In addition to the major cash crops of cotton, rice, sugar, and tobacco, the South also led the nation in livestock production. Southern livestock owners profited from hogs, oxen, horses, mules, and beef cattle. Much of this livestock was raised in areas that were unsuitable for growing crops, such as the pine woods of North Carolina.

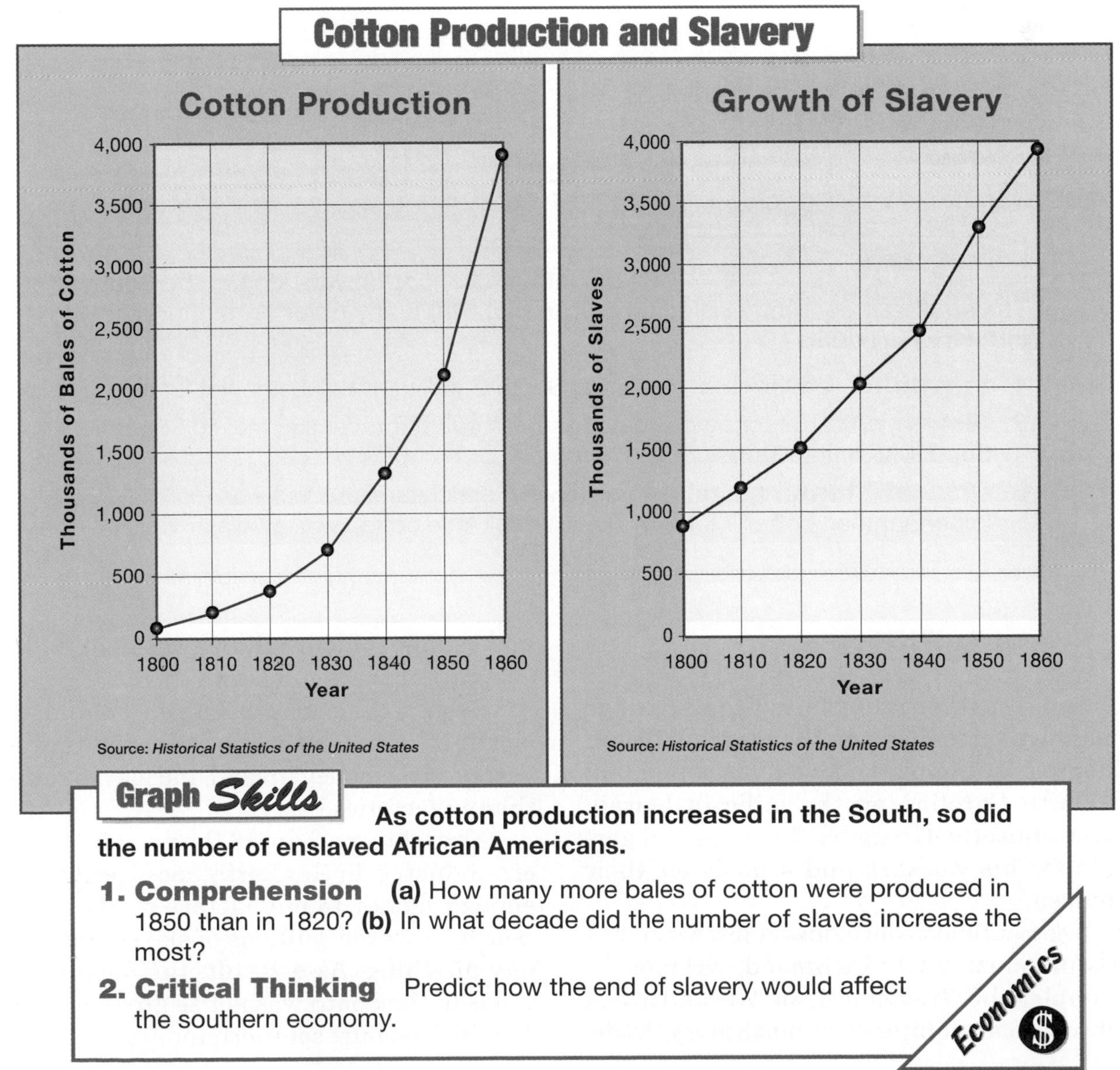

Graph *Skills* **As cotton production increased in the South, so did the number of enslaved African Americans.**

1. **Comprehension** **(a)** How many more bales of cotton were produced in 1850 than in 1820? **(b)** In what decade did the number of slaves increase the most?
2. **Critical Thinking** Predict how the end of slavery would affect the southern economy.

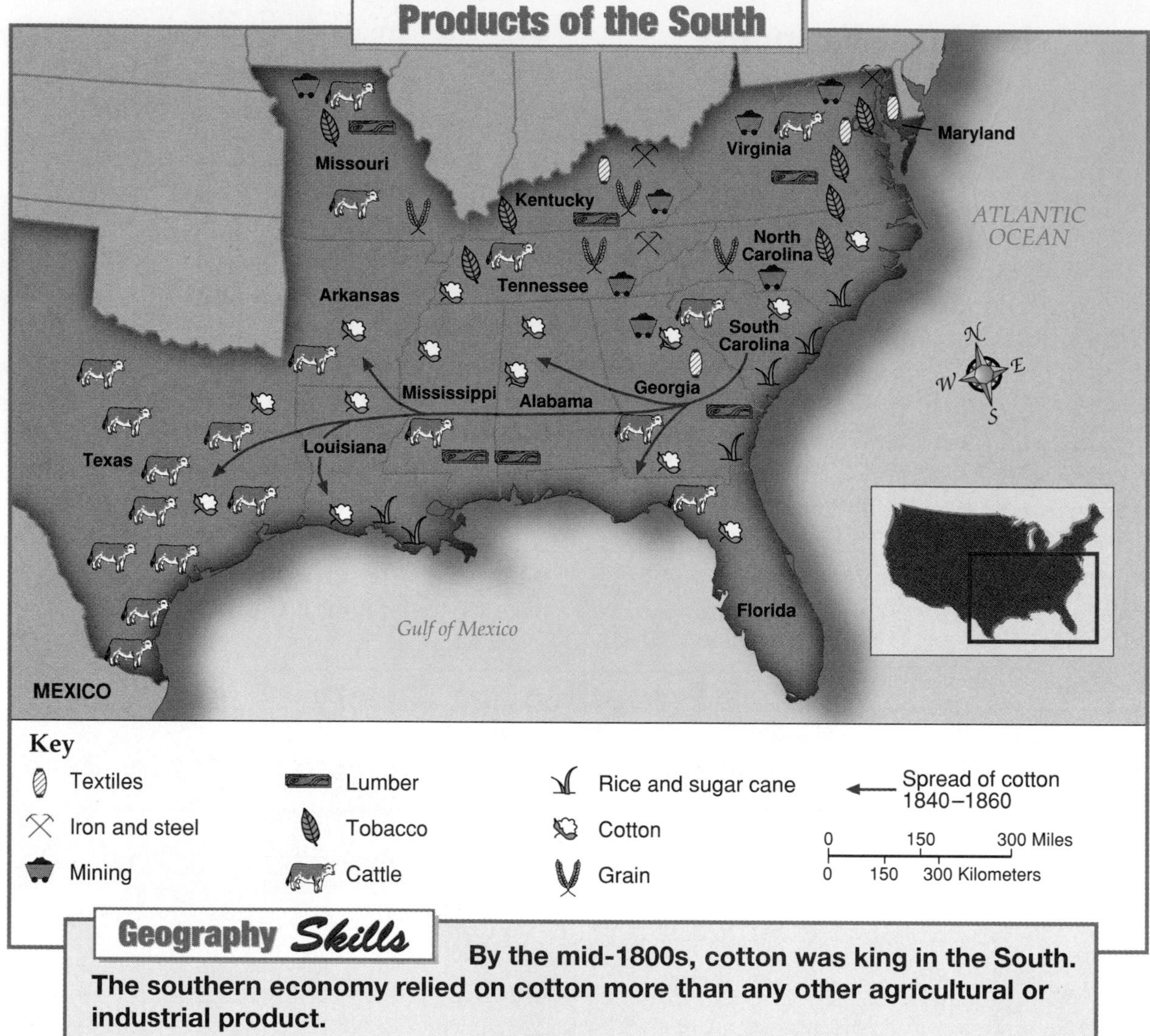

Geography *Skills* **By the mid-1800s, cotton was king in the South. The southern economy relied on cotton more than any other agricultural or industrial product.**

1. **Location** On the map, locate: **(a)** South Carolina, **(b)** Alabama, **(c)** Louisiana.
2. **Movement** Describe the route by which cotton production moved from South Carolina to Texas.
3. **Critical Thinking** **(a)** In Virginia, what agricultural product was more important than cotton? **(b)** Why do you think little cotton was grown in Virginia?

Limited Industry

Some southerners wanted to encourage the growth of industry in the South. **William Gregg**, for example, modeled his cotton mill in South Carolina on the mills in Lowell, Massachusetts. Gregg built houses and gardens for his workers and schools for their children.

The South also developed a few other successful industries. In Richmond, Virginia, for example, the Tredegar Iron Works turned out railroad equipment, machinery, tools, and cannons. Flour milling was another important southern industry.

Even so, the South lagged behind the North in manufacturing. Rich planters invested their money in land and slaves rather than in factories.

Also, slavery reduced the need for southern industry. In the North, most people had enough money to buy factory goods. In the South, however, millions of slaves could not buy anything. As a result, the demand for goods in the South was not as great as in the North. This hurt southern industry.

Viewing HISTORY **Economically Dependent**

Many southerners ordered goods from northern and European manufacturers. This advertisement appeared in the mail-order catalog of a store located in Milledgeville, Illinois. ★ **Why were there so few factories in the South?**

Economically Dependent

With little industry of its own, the South came to depend more and more on the North and on Europe. Southern planters often borrowed money from northern banks in order to expand their plantations. They also purchased much of their furniture, farm tools, and machines from northern or European factories.

Many southerners resented this situation. One southerner described a burial to show how the South depended on the North for many goods in the 1850s:

> “The grave was dug through solid marble, but the marble headstone came from Vermont. It was in a pine wilderness but the pine coffin came from Cincinnati. An iron mountain overshadowed it but the coffin nails and the screws and the shovel came from Pittsburgh. . . . A hickory grove grew nearby, but the pick and shovel handles came from New York. . . . That country, so rich in underdeveloped resources, furnished nothing for the funeral except the corpse and the hole in the ground.”

Still, most southerners were proud of the booming cotton industry in their region. As long as cotton remained king, southerners believed, they could look to the future with confidence.

★ Section 3 Review ★

Recall

1. **Locate** **(a)** South Carolina, **(b)** Alabama, **(c)** Mississippi, **(d)** Texas.
2. **Identify** **(a)** Eli Whitney, **(b)** Cotton Kingdom, **(c)** William Gregg.

Comprehension

3. Why did the Cotton Kingdom spread westward?
4. How did the cotton gin cause slavery to expand in the South?
5. Why did the South not develop as much industry as the North?

Critical Thinking and Writing

6. **Predicting Consequences** How might the southern economy have developed differently if the cotton gin had never been invented?
7. **Analyzing Primary Sources** Review the quotation that appears at the end of the section. Is the southerner praising or criticizing the economy of the South? Explain.

Activity **Linking Past and Present** The cotton gin had a major impact on the South's way of life. In a chart, list some modern inventions, describe what they do, and explain how they are changing the way you live today.

Life in the South

Explore These Questions

- What five groups made up society in the South?
- How did African Americans suffer under slavery?
- How did African Americans struggle against slavery?

Define

- slave code
- extended family

Identify

- "cottonocracy"
- Norbert Rillieux
- Henry Blair
- Denmark Vesey
- Nat Turner

Setting the Scene

"I was born in 1844.... First [thing] I remember was my ma and us [children] being sold off the [auction] block to Mistress Payne. When I was... too little to work in the field, I stayed at the big house most of the time and helped Mistress Payne feed the chickens, make scarecrows to keep the hawks away and put wood on the fires. After I got big enough to hoe, I went to the field same as the other[s]."

In this excerpt, Jack Payne recalls his life as an enslaved person in Texas. Payne was only one of millions of African Americans throughout the South who suffered the anguish of slavery. Toiling from dawn till dusk, they had neither freedom nor rights.

White Southerners

The Old South is often pictured as a land of vast plantations worked by hundreds of slaves. Such grand estates did exist in the South. However, most white southerners were not rich planters. In fact, most whites owned no slaves at all.

The "cottonocracy"

A planter was someone who owned at least 20 slaves. In 1860, there were about 2 million white families in the South. Of them, less than 2 percent, or a total of about 50,000, were families of planters. These wealthy families were called the **"cottonocracy"** because they made their money from cotton. Though few in number, their views and way of life dominated the South.

The richest planters built elegant homes and filled them with expensive furniture from Europe. They entertained lavishly. They tried to dress and behave like European nobility.

Planters had responsibilities, too. Because of their wealth and influence, many planters became political leaders. They devoted many hours to local, state, and national politics. Planters hired overseers to run day-to-day affairs on their plantations and to manage the work of slaves.

Small farmers

About 75 percent of southern whites were small farmers. These "plain folk" owned the

In later years, both literature and film gave a false view of plantation life. Writers and film producers focused on the "gentility" of the planters and largely ignored the injustices of slavery. The most successful of these fictional works is the 1939 film *Gone With the Wind.* Based on Margaret Mitchell's novel, the film won 10 Academy Awards, including Best Picture.

AmericanHeritage
M A G A Z I N E

HISTORY HAPPENED HERE

Rosedown Plantation

Rosedown Plantation, built in 1835, is located in St. Francisville, Louisiana. It was owned by the wealthy cotton planter, Daniel Turnbull, and his wife Martha. The Turnbulls filled their mansion with beautiful furniture and art from Europe. They surrounded their home with avenues of trees and formal gardens. Today, visitors can tour Rosedown, its gardens, and its many outbuildings. You can even stay overnight and recall the luxurious lifestyle of the southern aristocracy.

★ ***To learn more about this historic site, write:*** *Rosedown Plantation, 12501 Highway 10, St. Francisville, LA 70775.*

Original bedroom furniture at Rosedown

land they farmed. They might also own one or two slaves. Unlike planters, plain folk worked with their slaves in the fields.

Among small farmers, helping each other was an important duty. "People who lived miles apart counted themselves as neighbors," wrote a farmer in Mississippi. "And in case of sorrow or sickness, there was no limit to the service neighbors provided."

Poor whites

Lower on the social ladder was a small group of poor whites. They did not own the land they farmed. Instead, they rented it, often paying the owner with part of their crop. Many barely made a living.

Poor whites often lived in the hilly, wooded areas of the South. They planted crops such as corn, potatoes, and other vegetables. They also herded cattle and pigs. Poor whites had hard lives, but they enjoyed rights denied to all African Americans, enslaved or free.

African American Southerners

Both free and enslaved African Americans lived in the South. Although free under the law, free African Americans faced harsh discrimination. Enslaved African Americans had no rights at all.

Free African Americans

Most free African Americans were descendants of slaves freed during and after the American Revolution. Others had bought their freedom. In 1860, over 200,000 free blacks lived in the South. Most lived in Maryland and Delaware, where slavery was

Southern Society in 1860

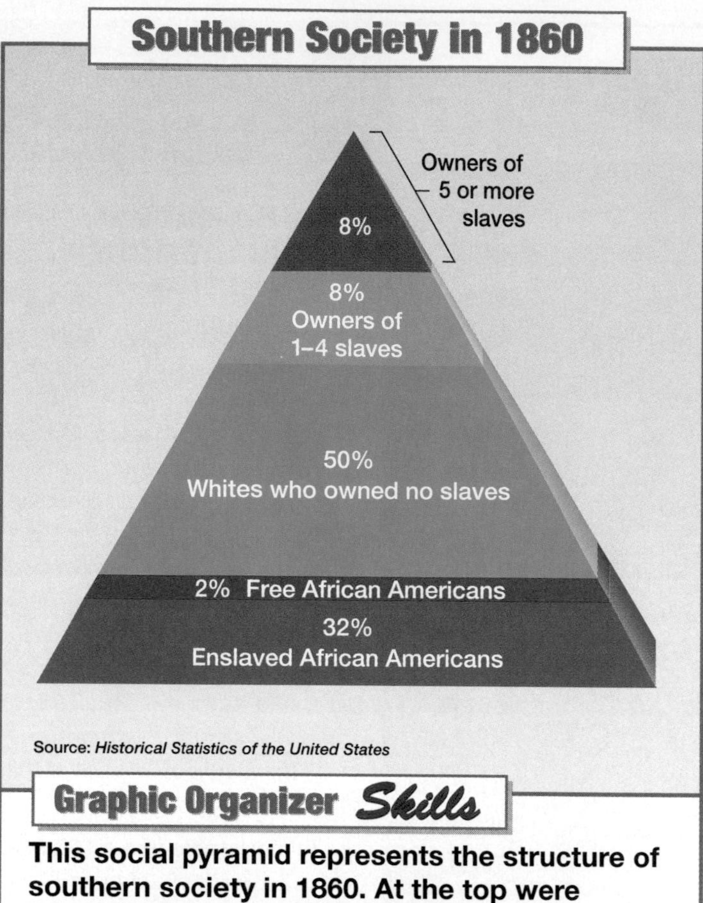

Source: *Historical Statistics of the United States*

Graphic Organizer *Skills*

This social pyramid represents the structure of southern society in 1860. At the top were wealthy and powerful planters. At the bottom were millions of enslaved African Americans.

1. **Comprehension** Which group in southern society was most numerous?
2. **Critical Thinking** Many white southerners owned no slaves but still supported the institution of slavery. Why do you think they did so?

in decline. Others lived in cities such as New Orleans, Richmond, and Charleston.

Slave owners did not like free African Americans living in the South. They feared that free African Americans set a bad example, encouraging slaves to rebel. Also, slave owners justified slavery by claiming that African Americans could not take care of themselves. Free African American workers proved this idea wrong.

To discourage free African Americans, southern states passed laws that made life even harder for them. Free African Americans were not allowed to vote or travel. In some southern states, they either had to move out of the state or allow themselves to be enslaved.

Despite these limits, free African Americans made valuable contributions to southern life. For example, **Norbert Rillieux** (RIHL yoo) invented a machine that revolutionized the way sugar was made. Another inventor, **Henry Blair,** patented a seed planter.

Enslaved African Americans

By 1860, enslaved African Americans made up one third of the South's population. Most worked as field hands on cotton plantations. Both men and women cleared new land and planted and harvested crops. Children helped by pulling weeds, collecting wood, and carrying water to the field hands. By the time they were teenagers, they too worked between 12 and 14 hours a day.

On large plantations, some African Americans became skilled workers, such as carpenters and blacksmiths. A few worked in cities and lived almost as if they were free. Their earnings, however, belonged to their owners.

Life Without Freedom

The life of enslaved African Americans was determined by strict laws and the practices of individual slave owners. Conditions varied from plantation to plantation. Some owners made sure their slaves had clean cabins, decent food, and warm clothes. Other planters spent as little as possible on their slaves.

Slave codes

Southern states passed laws known as **slave codes** to keep slaves from either running away or rebelling. Under the codes, enslaved African Americans were forbidden to gather in groups of more than three. They could not leave their owner's land without a written pass. They were not allowed to own guns.

Slave codes also made it a crime for slaves to learn how to read and write. Owners hoped that this law would make it hard for African Americans to escape slavery. They reasoned that uneducated runaway slaves would not be able to use maps or read train schedules. They would not be able to find their way north.

Why Study History?

Because Music Is Part of Our Culture

▲ Gospel singers

▲ Country music singer

Historical Background

From the colonial era on, southerners of diverse backgrounds shared their music with one another. As a result, a variety of rich musical traditions developed in the American South.

African Americans built on the musical heritage of their ancestral homelands. One common technique was the "call and response" in which a soloist sang a line and the group responded. African American music stressed varied rhythms and improvisation, the spontaneous creation of new lyrics and melodies. In the 1800s, these qualities were typical of African American work songs, religious songs, and folk songs.

The early musical traditions of most white southerners were rooted in the tunes and melodies of the British Isles. German, Mexican, Cajun, and other traditions also enriched Southern folk music. The sounds of fiddles and banjos often celebrated house raisings, harvest feasts, and other major events.

Connections to Today

Several American music styles of today are firmly rooted in the South. Blues, jazz, and gospel music emerged from the traditions of African American southerners. Country music and rock-and-roll developed from the folk music of both white and black southerners. In fact, most early rock performers of the 1950s came from the South.

Connections to You

The sounds of jazz, country, and rock are all around you. The next time you pop in your favorite CD, consider the roots of the music you hear. When you watch a television show, note its theme music. When you go to the movies, listen to the soundtrack. You will discover that American music owes much to the rich and diverse traditions of the American South.

1. **Comprehension** What music styles of today can be traced to traditions in the American South?
2. **Critical Thinking** Why do you think jazz and blues music developed in the South rather than in the North?

Planning a Documentary Research the history of a music style discussed here. Then, outline a television documentary on that style. List the topics and pictures that will appear in your documentary.

Viewing HISTORY **African American Community**

The painting Plantation Burial *by John Antrobus is unusual for providing a realistic portrait of life on a southern plantation. The central figures are African Americans. To the left, a white couple keeps a respectful distance from the religious ceremony.* ★ **What role did religion play in the life of enslaved African Americans?**

Some laws were meant to protect slaves, but only from the worst forms of abuse. However, enslaved African Americans did not have the right to testify in court. As a result, they were not able to bring charges against owners who abused them.

Enslaved African Americans had only one real protection against mistreatment. Owners looked on their slaves as valuable property. Most slave owners wanted to keep this human property healthy and productive.

Hard work

Even the kindest owners insisted that their slaves work long, hard days. Slaves worked from "can see to can't see," or from dawn to dusk, up to 16 hours a day. Frederick Douglass, who escaped slavery, recalled his life under one harsh master:

> ❝ We were worked in all weathers. It was never too hot or too cold; it could never rain, blow, hail, or snow too hard for us to work in the field. Work, work, work. . . . The longest days were too short for him and the shortest nights too long for him. ❞

Some owners and overseers whipped slaves to get a full day's work. However, the worst part of slavery was not the beatings. It was the complete loss of freedom.

Family life

It was hard for enslaved African Americans to keep their families together. Southern laws did not recognize slave marriages or slave families. As a result, owners could sell a husband and wife to different buyers. Children were often taken from their parents and sold.

On large plantations, many enslaved families did manage to stay together. For those African Americans, the family was a source of strength, pride, and love. Grandparents, parents, children, aunts, uncles, and cousins formed a close-knit group. This idea of an **extended family** had its roots in Africa.

Enslaved African Americans preserved other traditions as well. Parents taught their children traditional African stories and songs. They used folk tales to pass on African history and moral beliefs.

Religion offers hope

By the 1800s, many enslaved African Americans were devout Christians. Planters often allowed white ministers to preach to their slaves. African Americans also had their own preachers and beliefs.

Religion helped African Americans cope with the harshness of slave life. Bible stories about how the ancient Hebrews had escaped from slavery inspired many spiritual songs. As they worked in the fields, slaves sang about a coming day of freedom. One spiritual, "Go Down, Moses," includes these lines:

> "We need not always weep and
> moan,
> Let my people go.
> And wear these slavery chains
> forlorn,
> Let my people go."

Resistance Against Slavery

Enslaved African Americans struck back against the system that denied them both freedom and wages. Some broke tools, destroyed crops, and stole food.

Many enslaved African Americans tried to escape to the North. Because the journey was long and dangerous, very few made it to freedom. Every county had slave patrols and sheriffs ready to question an unknown black person.

A few African Americans used violence to resist the brutal slave system. **Denmark Vesey**, a free African American, planned a revolt in 1822. Vesey was betrayed before the revolt began. He and 35 other people were executed.

In 1831, an African American preacher named **Nat Turner** led a major revolt. Turner led his followers through Virginia, killing more than 57 whites. Terrified whites hunted the countryside for Turner. They killed many innocent African Americans before catching and hanging him.

Nat Turner's revolt increased southern fears of an uprising of enslaved African Americans. Revolts were rare, however. Since whites were cautious and well armed, a revolt by African Americans had almost no chance of success.

★ Section 4 Review ★

Recall

1. **Identify** (a) "cottonocracy," (b) Norbert Rillieux, (c) Henry Blair, (d) Denmark Vesey, (e) Nat Turner.
2. **Define** (a) slave code, (b) extended family.

Comprehension

3. How did the "cottonocracy" dominate economics and politics in the South?
4. Describe three ways that African Americans suffered under slavery.
5. How did African Americans struggle against the slave system?

Critical Thinking and Writing

6. **Applying Information** How were successful free African Americans a threat to the slave system?
7. **Making Decisions** If you had been an enslaved African American, would you have decided to live under slavery, to try to escape, or to rebel? Explain the reasons for your decision.

Activity **Writing a Speech** You are an enslaved African American living in the South in the 1850s. Write a speech encouraging people to resist slavery and explaining ways in which they can do it.

Chapter 12 Review and Activities

★ Sum It Up ★

Section 1 Industry in the North

- During the mid-1800s, new inventions helped industry grow in the North.
- Railroads linked the Northeast with Chicago and other midwestern cities.
- With produce coming in from western farms, agriculture declined in the Northeast.

Section 2 Life in the North

- Northern factory workers endured long hours, dangerous conditions, and low pay.
- As millions of immigrants arrived in the United States, nativist fears grew.
- Free African Americans faced discrimination. Still, some became very successful.

Section 3 Cotton Kingdom in the South

- Due to the invention of the cotton gin, growing cotton became very profitable.
- As the Cotton Kingdom spread from the Atlantic coast to Texas, so did slavery.
- As planters invested in land and slaves, the South developed an agricultural economy rather than an industrial one.

Section 4 Life in the South

- Southern society consisted of rich planters, small farmers, poor whites, and free and enslaved African Americans.
- Enslaved people lacked freedoms and rights and were forced to work for no pay.
- Some enslaved African Americans resisted slavery by rebelling or running away.

For additional review of the major ideas of Chapter 12, see ***Guide to the Essentials of American History*** or ***Interactive Student Tutorial CD-ROM,*** which contains interactive review activities, graphic organizers, and practice tests.

Reviewing the Chapter

Define These Terms

Match each term with the correct definition.

Column 1	Column 2
1. clipper	**a.** a policy or attitude that denies equal rights to certain groups
2. nativist	**b.** a swift ship with tall masts, huge sails, and a narrow hull
3. discrimination	**c.** a person who has learned a trade
4. skilled worker	**d.** someone who favors native-born citizens

Explore the Main Ideas

1. Describe three developments that caused the North's economy to expand.
2. **(a)** Why did workers form unions in the early and mid-1800s? **(b)** Describe two reasons for immigration to the United States in the 1840s and 1850s.
3. How did the cotton gin change life in the South?
4. Describe two ways that slaves resisted slavery.
5. What were two key differences between the North's economy and the South's economy?

Graph Activity

Use the graph below to answer the following questions: **1.** In what year did Irish immigration to the United States double? **2.** How many Irish immigrants came to the United States in 1851? **Critical Thinking** Why did increasing immigration alarm some Americans?

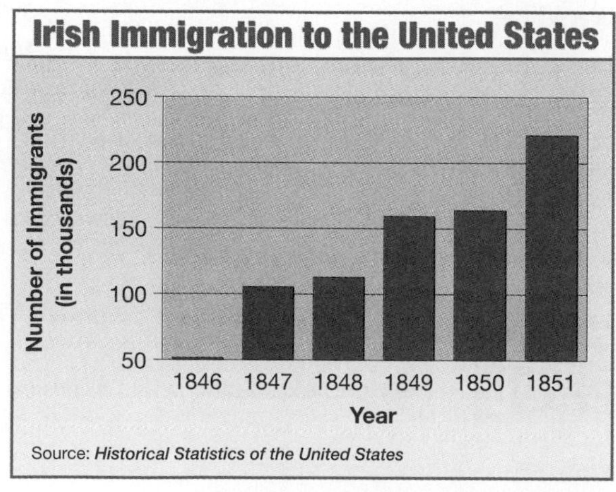

Source: *Historical Statistics of the United States*

Critical Thinking and Writing

1. **Using Chronology** Place these events in chronological order: **(a)** over 1.5 million Irish enter the United States, **(b)** the Know-Nothing party forms, **(c)** famine breaks out in Ireland.
2. **Ranking** In your opinion, what two inventions had the greatest impact on American life in the early and mid-1800s? Explain.
3. **Making Decisions** If you were directing a nation's economy, would you develop agriculture more than industry or industry more than agriculture? Explain.
4. **Exploring Unit Themes Expansion** **(a)** Why did slavery spread west during the early 1800s? **(b)** How did economic differences between the North and South grow?

Using Primary Sources

Solomon Northrup was a free African American until he was kidnapped and sold as a slave in 1845. For the next twelve years, he worked on a cotton plantation in Louisiana. Below, he describes the start of a typical workday.

> " [My bed]... was a plank twelve inches wide and ten feet long. My pillow was a stick of wood. The bedding was a coarse blanket.... The cabin is constructed of logs, without floor or window.... In stormy weather, the rain drives through [spaces between the logs].... An hour before daylight the horn is blown. Then the slaves arouse, prepare their breakfast... and hurry to the field again. It is an offense invariably followed by a flogging, to be found at the quarters after daybreak. "

Source: *Twelve Years a Slave* by Solomon Northrup, 1853.

Recognizing Points of View **(a)** How does Northrup show his home to be uncomfortable? **(b)** How does he feel about the start of each day? Explain.

Activity Bank

Interdisciplinary Activity

Exploring Science It is fairly easy to make a telegraph. In your school or local library, find a science book with information on how to build one. Working with other students, create your own telegraph and transmit a message using Morse code.

Career Skills Activity

Musicians Learn a spiritual sung by enslaved people in the South in the 1800s. Possible songs are "Go Down, Moses," "Deep River," and "Swing Low, Sweet Chariot." Perform the spiritual for the class and then explain the meaning of the song.

Citizenship Activity

Protecting Religious Freedom Nativists of the mid-1800s discriminated against Catholics even though Americans are guaranteed religious freedom. Create a poster encouraging citizens to respect the religious beliefs of all Americans.

Internet Activity

Use the Internet to find primary sources on enslaved African Americans in the 1800s. Use the information you find to write a short story about a typical day in the life of an enslaved African American.

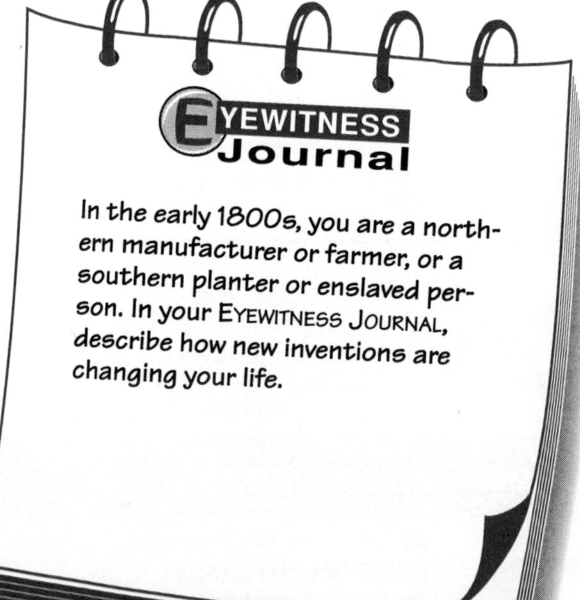

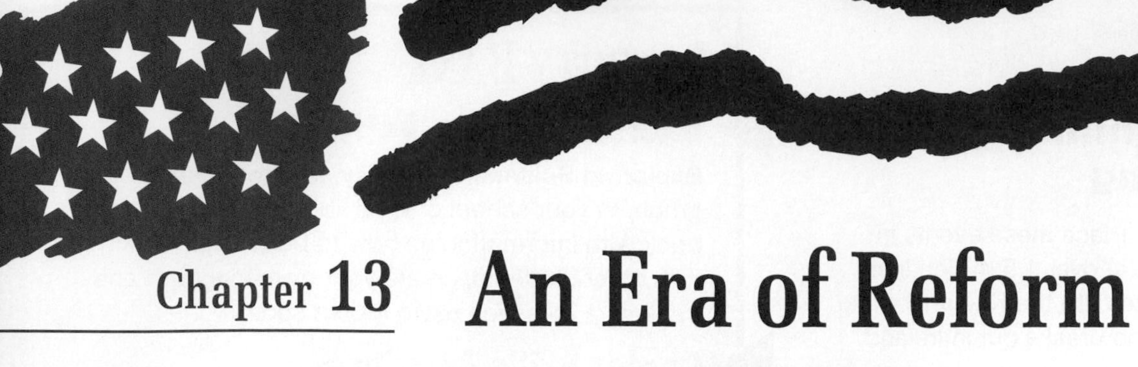

Chapter 13

An Era of Reform

1820–1860

What's Ahead

Section 1
The Spirit of Reform

Section 2
The Fight Against Slavery

Section 3
Struggle for Women's Rights

Section 4
American Literature and Art

In the mid-1800s, dedicated reformers sought to better American society. Many of these reformers acted out of political ideals. They wanted the nation to live up to its promise of "liberty and equality for all." Religious feeling also spurred many reformers.

Reform took many directions. Two of the most sweeping goals were equal rights for women and the abolition of slavery. Reformers often faced opposition, criticism, and even threats. Yet, they continued to struggle and slowly gained support. In this chapter, you will read about the individuals who contributed to this era of reform.

Why Study *History?*

Today, as in the 1800s, the reforming impulse is strong in the United States. Americans still work to correct many types of social problems. To learn more about one reform movement that has attracted many Americans, young and old, see the *Why Study History?* feature, "The Fight Against Alcohol Abuse Continues," in this chapter.

American Events

1826 James Fenimore Cooper publishes *The Last of the Mohicans*

1831 William Lloyd Garrison begins antislavery newspaper

1837 Horace Mann begins educational reforms in Massachusetts

1820 **1825** **1830** **1835** **1840**

World Events

1822 World Event Liberia is established in Western Africa

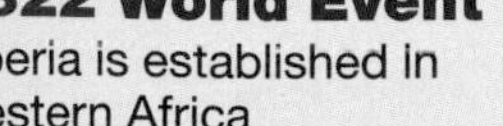

1837 World Event First kindergarten opens in Germany

Viewing HISTORY

Spirit of Religion

This painted tray honors Lemuel Haynes, a famous African American preacher. From the nation's earliest years, religion was a powerful influence in the United States. In the early 1800s, a religious revival movement fed a new spirit of reform. ★ **Why would religious feelings lead some people to try to find ways to improve society?**

1848 Women's Rights Convention is held at Seneca Falls

1851 Maine bans the sale of alcohol

1840 | 1845 | 1850 | 1855 | 1860

1843 World Event
Charles Dickens publishes *A Christmas Carol*

1848 World Event
First women's college in Great Britain opens

The Spirit of Reform

Explore These Questions

- What were the political and religious roots of reform?
- What goals did social reformers pursue?
- How did Americans improve public education in the mid-1800s?

Define

- social reform
- predestination
- revival
- penal system
- temperance movement

Identify

- Second Great Awakening
- Charles Grandison Finney
- Dorothea Dix
- Horace Mann
- Prudence Crandall
- Thomas Gallaudet
- Samuel Gridley Howe
- Laura Bridgman

In 1840, New England philosopher Ralph Waldo Emerson wrote about Americans' growing passion for improving society:

> “We are all a little wild here with numberless projects for social reform. But what is man born for but to be a Reformer... a restorer of truth and good?”

Many idealistic Americans shared Emerson's beliefs. Between 1820 and 1860, a wide variety of reform movements sprang up to cure the nation's ills.

The Reforming Impulse

Social reform is an organized attempt to improve what is unjust or imperfect in society. The reforming impulse had both political and religious roots. The political roots went back to the ideals of liberty and equality expressed in the Declaration of Independence. The religious reform involved new teachings about salvation and the individual.

Political ideals

The election of Andrew Jackson in 1828 unleashed a wave of democratic change in the nation. More people could vote and take part in government than ever before.

Still, some critics argued that “Jacksonian democracy” was far from democratic. Many said that a true democracy would not allow slavery. Others questioned why women had fewer rights than men. Reformers hoped that by changing such injustices, they might move the nation closer to its political ideals.

A new religious movement

Many early American Protestants believed that God decided in advance which people would gain salvation in heaven. This idea is known as **predestination.** Belief in predestination led many people to think that society could not be changed. In fact, they felt it was sinful to want to improve the world.

In the early 1800s, a dynamic religious movement, known as the **Second Great Awakening,** swept the nation. Its leaders stressed free will rather than predestination. They taught that individuals could choose by their own actions to save their own souls.

Throughout the nation, preachers held huge outdoor meetings. The goal of these **revivals** was to stir religious feelings. Revivals often lasted for days and attracted thousands of people. A witness described the excitement of a revival in Kentucky:

> “The vast sea of human beings seemed to be agitated as if by storm. I counted seven ministers all preaching at once.... Some of the people were singing, others praying, some crying for mercy.”

Deeply affected, converts vowed to reform their lives.

One of the leaders of the Second Great Awakening was a Presbyterian minister named **Charles Grandison Finney.** A powerful speaker, Finney wrote articles giving tips on effective preaching. He also taught that individual salvation was the first step toward improving society. He told followers that their goal was "the complete reformation of the whole world." Through teachings like these, the Second Great Awakening encouraged the growing spirit of reform.

Helping the Mentally Ill

Some reformers turned their attention to what one minister called the "outsiders" in society—criminals and the mentally ill. One of the most vigorous of these reformers was a Boston schoolteacher named **Dorothea Dix.**

One day in 1841, Dix visited a jail for women near Boston. She was shocked to discover that some of the prisoners had committed no crime. These women were in jail because they were mentally ill.

The jailer locked the mentally ill prisoners in small, dark, unheated cells. The women were half frozen. Dix demanded to know why these women were treated so cruelly. The jailer replied that "lunatics" did not feel the cold.

That moment changed Dix's life forever. During the next 18 months, Dix visited every jail, poorhouse, and hospital in Massachusetts. Her report shocked state legislators:

> ❝ I proceed, gentlemen, briefly to call your attention to the present state of Insane Persons confined . . . in cages, closets, cellars, stalls, pens! Chained, naked, beaten with rods, and lashed into obedience. ❞

Eventually, legislators agreed to fund a new mental hospital. Dix then went on to inspect jails in states as far away as Louisiana and Illinois. In nearly every state, her reports persuaded legislatures to treat the mentally ill as patients, not criminals.

Biography **Dorothea Dix**

Dorothea Dix was shocked by the sight of "harmless lunatics" shackled in dark cells. When she was told that "nothing" could be done, Dix replied, "I know no such word." Largely through her efforts, more than 15 states established special hospitals for the care of the mentally ill by 1860. ★ **How did Dix go about achieving reform?**

Reforming Prisons

Dix also joined others in trying to reform the **penal system,** or system of prisons. Prisons were at the time fairly new to the United States. In colonial days, states generally imposed the death penalty for serious offenses. People who committed minor offenses received some form of physical punishment, such as a public whipping.

In the early 1800s, imprisonment gradually replaced physical punishment. In the early prisons, men, women, and children were often crammed together in cold, damp rooms. When food supplies were low, prisoners might go hungry—unless they had money to buy meals from jailers. Some jailers even made extra money selling rum to prisoners.

Five out of six people in northern jails were in jail because they could not pay their debts. While behind bars, debtors had no way to earn money to pay back their debts.

Why Study History?

Because the Fight Against Alcohol Abuse Continues

Historical Background

Americans in the early 1800s consumed more alcohol per person than at any other time in American history. Some American reformers grew concerned about the impact of alcohol on society. The temperance movement that began in the 1820s hoped to end alcohol abuse.

In the late 1800s, the temperance movement grew. Groups like the Women's Christian Temperance Union attracted many followers. Finally, in 1919, the states ratified the Eighteenth Amendment, prohibiting the production and sale of alcoholic drinks. However, law enforcement officials found it nearly impossible to enforce Prohibition. It was repealed in 1933 by the Twenty-first Amendment.

Connections to Today

Reformers now focus on the problems of underage and excessive drinking. Today, the legal drinking age in every state is 21 years. A variety of organizations and programs exist to help people who suffer from alcoholism. Still, as many as 40 million Americans are problem drinkers—people whose drinking causes harm to themselves or their family and friends.

One of the most destructive forms of alcohol abuse is drinking and driving. In the early 1990s, more than 25,000 Americans died each year in accidents involving drunk drivers. Young people were often the victims. In fact, alcohol-related accidents were the number-one killer of teenagers.

Students organize to warn about the dangers of alcohol.

Connections to You

If you or someone you know has a problem with alcohol, there are several things you can do. You can seek support from your parents or other family members. You can get information from school counselors or a family physician. Also, your school may participate in the Students Against Drunk Driving (SADD) program. Students who belong to SADD promise to call their parents if they cannot get a safe ride with a sober driver.

1. **Comprehension** Name and describe the two constitutional amendments related to the use of alcohol in the United States.
2. **Critical Thinking** Why do you think some people make the irresponsible decision to drink and drive?

★Activity **Making a Poster** Construct a poster that warns people about the dangers of underage drinking, excessive drinking, or drinking and driving.

As a result, many debtors remained in prison for years.

Dorothea Dix and others called for changes in the penal system. Some states built prisons with only one or two inmates to a cell. Cruel punishments were banned, and people convicted of minor crimes received shorter sentences. Slowly, states stopped treating debtors as criminals.

Battling "Demon Rum"

Alcohol abuse was widespread in the early 1800s. At political rallies, weddings, and funerals, men, women, and sometimes even children drank heavily. Men could buy whiskey in candy stores or barber shops as easily as at taverns.

During the late 1820s, reformers began the **temperance movement,** a campaign against alcohol abuse. Women often took a leading role in the temperance movement. They knew that "demon rum" could lead to wife beating, child abuse, and the breakup of families.

Some temperance groups urged people to drink less. Others sought to wipe out all drinking of alcohol. They won a major victory in the 1850s, when Maine banned the sale of alcohol. Eight other states passed "Maine laws." Although most states later repealed the laws, temperance crusaders pressed on. They gained new strength in the late 1800s.

Pages from McGuffey's First Eclectic Reader

Mug to reward good performance

Viewing History — A Better Education

The painting Homework *by Winslow Homer shows an elementary school student of the mid-1800s. This boy may be reading a lesson from one of William McGuffey's* Eclectic Readers. *First published in 1836, McGuffey's popular textbooks used rhymes and stories to teach spelling, grammar, and good behavior.* ★ **What methods are used today to teach children to read?**

Improving Education

In 1816, Thomas Jefferson wrote, "If a nation expects to be ignorant and free, it expects what never was and never will be." He knew that a republic needed educated citizens. As more men won the right to vote, reformers acted to improve education.

Before the 1820s, few American children attended school. Public schools were rare. Those that did exist were usually old and run-down. Teachers were poorly trained and ill paid. Students of all ages crowded together in a single room.

Growth of public schools

New York State took the lead in improving public education. In the 1820s, the state ordered every town to build a grade school. Before long, other northern states required towns to support public schools.

$ Connections With Economics

The temperance movement got a lot of support from factory owners. They thought workers would be more productive if they did not drink. Today, many businesses pay for programs to combat alcohol and drug abuse among their employees. In what ways do you think drug or alcohol abuse can hurt the economy?

In Massachusetts, **Horace Mann** led the fight for better schools. Mann became head of the state board of education in 1837. He hounded legislators to provide more money for education. Under his leadership, Massachusetts built new schools, extended the school year, and raised teacher pay. The state also opened three colleges to train teachers.

Reformers in other states urged their legislatures to follow the lead of Massachusetts and New York. By the 1850s, most northern states had set up free tax-supported elementary schools. Schools in the South improved more slowly. In both the North and South, schooling usually ended in the eighth grade. There were few public high schools.

Education for African Americans

In most areas, African Americans had little chance to attend school. A few cities, like Boston and New York, set up separate schools for black students. However, these schools received less money than schools for white students did.

Some attempts to educate African Americans met with great hostility. In the 1830s, **Prudence Crandall,** a Connecticut Quaker, began a school for African American girls. The community was outraged. Crandall continued to teach even when rocks crashed through the classroom window. She was jailed three times. Finally, a band of men broke in one night and destroyed the school.

Despite such obstacles, some free African Americans attended private colleges such as Harvard, Dartmouth, and Oberlin. In the 1850s, several colleges for African Americans opened in the North. The first was Lincoln University, in Pennsylvania.

Meeting special needs

Some reformers took steps to improve education for people with disabilities. In 1817, **Thomas Gallaudet** (gal uh DEHT) set up a school for the deaf in Hartford, Connecticut.

A few years later, **Samuel Gridley Howe** became director of the first American school for blind students. Howe created a system of raised letters that allowed blind students to read with their fingers. One of Howe's pupils, **Laura Bridgman,** was the first deaf and blind student to receive a formal education. She later assisted Howe in teaching other blind students.

★ Section 1 Review ★

Recall

1. **Identify** **(a)** Second Great Awakening, **(b)** Charles Grandison Finney, **(c)** Dorothea Dix, **(d)** Horace Mann, **(e)** Prudence Crandall, **(f)** Thomas Gallaudet, **(g)** Samuel Gridley Howe, **(h)** Laura Bridgman.
2. **Define** **(a)** social reform, **(b)** predestination, **(c)** revival, **(d)** penal system, **(e)** temperance movement.

Comprehension

3. Describe two reasons the reforming spirit grew in the mid-1800s.
4. What were the goals of **(a)** prison reformers, and **(b)** leaders of the temperance movement?
5. What improvements were made in public education after the 1820s?

Critical Thinking and Writing

6. **Linking Past and Present** Do churches and religious leaders still take an active role in promoting social reform today? Give examples.
7. **Understanding Causes and Effects** How would lack of educational opportunities for African Americans contribute to prejudice against them?

Activity **Acting a Scene** The year is 1843. You are a legislator. You are unwilling to raise taxes to improve conditions for prisoners while tax money is needed to improve conditions for law-abiding citizens. With a partner, act out a scene between you and Dorothea Dix. For each argument for prison reform given by Dix, present an opposing argument.

The Fight Against Slavery

As You Read

Explore These Questions
- How did reformers try to end slavery?
- How did the underground railroad work?
- How did Americans react to the antislavery movement?

Define
- colonization
- abolitionist
- underground railroad

Identify
- Henry Highland Garnet
- David Walker
- Maria Stewart
- Frederick Douglass
- William Lloyd Garrison
- Angelina and Sarah Grimké
- Harriet Tubman

This medallion was a popular emblem of the antislavery movement.

SETTING the Scene In 1848, a group of reformers met to listen to a minister named **Henry Highland Garnet.** Garnet had once escaped slavery himself. He told the crowd:

> ❝ America is my home, my country.... I mourn because the accursed shade of slavery rest[s] upon it. I love my country's flag, and I hope that soon it will be cleansed of its stains, and be hailed by all nations as the emblem of freedom and independence. ❞

A growing number of Americans—black and white—spoke out against slavery. Only by ending slavery, they believed, could the United States become truly democratic.

Roots of the Antislavery Movement

In the Declaration of Independence, Thomas Jefferson wrote that "all men are created equal." Yet, many white Americans, including Jefferson, did not think the statement applied to enslaved African Americans. In the 1800s, many reformers disagreed.

Religious beliefs led some Americans to speak out against slavery. Since colonial times, Quakers had said that it was a sin for one human being to own another. They preached that all men and women were equal in the eyes of God. Later, ministers like Charles Grandison Finney called on other Christians to join a crusade to stamp out slavery.

In the North, slavery came to an early end. By 1804, all states from Pennsylvania to New England had promised to free their slaves. Still, there were only 50,000 slaves in the North in 1800, compared to nearly one million in the South.

A Colony in Africa

Some Americans proposed to end slavery by setting up an independent colony in Africa for freed slaves. Supporters of **colonization** founded the American Colonization Society in 1817. Five years later, President Monroe helped the society found the nation of Liberia in western Africa. The name Liberia comes from the Latin word for free.

Many white southerners supported the colonization movement because it did not call for an end to slavery. The society promised to pay slave owners who freed their slaves.

Some African Americans also favored colonization. They felt they would never have equal rights in the United States. Most African Americans, however, opposed the movement. Nearly all, enslaved or free, were born in the United States. They wanted to stay in their homeland. In the end, only a few thousand Americans settled in Liberia.

Biography **William Lloyd Garrison**

To William Lloyd Garrison, slavery was a disease that threatened the whole nation. He once even burned a copy of the Constitution because the document permitted slavery. Garrison refused to back down even after a mob in Boston almost killed him. ★ **How did Garrison spread his antislavery message?**

Garrison's vow

A Call to End Slavery

Supporters of colonization did not attack slavery directly. Another group of Americans, known as **abolitionists,** wanted to end slavery in the United States completely.

Some abolitionists favored a gradual end to slavery. They expected slavery to die out if it were kept out of the western territories. Other abolitionists demanded that slavery end everywhere, at once.

African American abolitionists

African Americans played an important part in the abolitionist movement. Some tried to end slavery through lawsuits and petitions. James Forten and other wealthy African Americans gave generously to antislavery efforts. In the 1820s, Samuel Cornish and John Russwurm set up an abolitionist newspaper, *Freedom's Journal.* They hoped to turn public opinion against slavery by printing stories about the brutal treatment of enslaved African Americans.

David Walker called for stronger measures. In 1829, he published *Appeal to the Colored Citizens of the World.* He encouraged enslaved African Americans to free themselves by any means necessary. Walker's friend **Maria Stewart** also spoke out against slavery. Stewart was the first American woman to make public political speeches.

Douglass speaks out

The best known African American abolitionist was **Frederick Douglass.** Douglass was born into slavery in Maryland. As a child, he defied the slave codes and taught himself to read.

In 1838, Douglass escaped and made his way to Boston. One day at an antislavery meeting, he felt a powerful urge to speak. Rising to his feet, he talked about the sorrows of slavery and the meaning of freedom. The audience was moved to tears. Soon, Douglass was lecturing across the United States and Britain. In 1847, he began publishing an antislavery newspaper, the *North Star.*

Garrison and *The Liberator*

The most outspoken white abolitionist was a fiery, young man named **William Lloyd Garrison.** Garrison launched his antislavery paper, *The Liberator,* in 1831. In it, he proclaimed that slavery was an evil to be ended immediately. On the very first page of the first issue, Garrison revealed his commitment:

> “I will be as harsh as truth, and as uncompromising as justice . . . I am in earnest . . . I will not excuse—I will not retreat a single inch—and I WILL BE HEARD.”

A year later, Garrison helped to found the New England Anti-Slavery Society. Members included Theodore Weld, a young minister connected with Charles Grandison Finney. Weld brought the energy of a religious revival to antislavery meetings.

The Grimké sisters

Women also played an important role in the abolitionist cause. **Angelina and Sarah Grimké** were the daughters of a wealthy slaveholder in South Carolina. They came to hate slavery and moved to Philadelphia to work for abolition. Their lectures drew large crowds.

Some people, including other abolitionists, objected to women speaking out in public. Sarah Grimké replied that "whatsoever it is morally right for a man to do, it is morally right for a woman to do." As you will see, this belief led the Grimkés and others to crusade for women's rights.

The Underground Railroad

Some abolitionists, black and white, risked prison and death to help African Americans escape slavery. These bold men and women formed the **underground railroad.** It was not a real railroad, but a network of abolitionists who secretly helped slaves reach freedom in the North or Canada.

"Conductors" guided runaways to "stations" where they could spend the night. Some stations were homes of abolitionists. Others were churches, or even caves. Conductors sometimes hid runaways under loads of hay in wagons with false bottoms.

One daring conductor, **Harriet Tubman,** had escaped slavery herself. Risking her freedom and her life, Tubman returned to the South 19 times. She led more than 300 slaves, including her parents, to freedom.

Admirers called Tubman the "Black Moses," after the ancient Hebrew leader who

Viewing HISTORY **Conductor on the Underground Railroad**

"There was one of two things I had a right to," declared Harriet Tubman, "liberty or death. If I could not have the one, I would have the other." After escaping slavery, Tubman became a fearless conductor on the underground railroad. Here, Tubman (left) poses with some of the hundreds of people she led to freedom.

★ **Why was Tubman called the "Black Moses"?**

Skills FOR LIFE

Critical Thinking | Managing Information | Communication | Maps, Charts, and Graphs

Analyzing Visual Evidence

How Will I Use This Skill?

Today, newspapers and television present us with a world full of images. A photograph of a bombing victim or a sketch of a courtroom can have a powerful impact. Still, artists and photographers can be influenced by their own viewpoints. We must analyze visual evidence to determine the reliability of what we see.

LEARN the Skill

1. Identify the subject matter of the drawing, painting, or photograph.
2. Note the details of the picture. Pay attention to facial expressions, actions, objects, and clothing.
3. What is the artist's point of view? How does the artist use details to stir sympathy or anger?
4. Determine the reliability of the visual evidence. Is it an accurate picture of what is shown? What may have been left out?

PRACTICE the Skill

The painting at right depicts a scene of the underground railroad. Look at the picture and answer the following questions.

1. (a) Where do you think this scene is taking place? (b) Who are the two people in the center of the picture? (c) Describe what is happening in this scene.
2. (a) What is the man holding in his right hand? What does this tell you about him? (b) What does the expression on the woman's face tell you about her? (c) Why is there a hay wagon in the background?
3. Do you think the artist was sympathetic toward the underground railroad? How can you tell?
4. Based on your reading, do you think this picture is reliable? Explain.

APPLY the Skill

Analyze a news photograph that had an emotional impact on you. List the details of the photograph that added to the emotional effect.

led the Israelites out of slavery in Egypt. Slave owners offered a $40,000 reward for Tubman's capture.

Reaction in the North

Abolitionists like Douglass and Garrison made enemies in both the North and the South. Northern mill owners, bankers, and merchants depended on cotton from the South. They saw attacks on slavery as a threat to their livelihood. Some northern workers also opposed abolition. They feared that African Americans might come north and take their jobs by working for low pay.

In New York and other northern cities, mobs sometimes broke up antislavery meetings or attacked homes of abolitionists. At times, the attacks backfired and won support for the abolitionists. One night, a Boston mob dragged William Lloyd Garrison through the streets at the end of a rope. A witness wrote, "I am an abolitionist from this very moment."

Reaction in the South

Not all white southerners favored slavery. Some bravely spoke out against it. Others, such as the Grimké sisters, moved north rather than live in a slaveholding state.

Most white southerners, however, were disturbed by the growing abolitionist movement. They accused abolitionists of preaching violence. Many southerners blamed Nat Turner's revolt on William Lloyd Garrison. (See page 311.) Garrison had founded *The Liberator* in 1831, only a few months before Turner's rebellion. David Walker's call for a slave revolt seemed to confirm the worst fears of southerners.

Many slave owners reacted to the abolitionist crusade by defending slavery even more. One slave owner wrote that if slaves were treated well, they would "love their master and serve him . . . faithfully." Other owners argued that slaves were better off than northern workers who labored long hours in dusty, airless factories.

Even some southerners who owned no slaves defended slavery. To them, slavery was essential to the southern economy. Many southerners believed northern support for the antislavery movement was greater than it really was. They began to fear that northerners wanted to destroy their way of life.

★ Section 2 Review ★

Recall

1. **Locate** Liberia.
2. **Identify** **(a)** Henry Highland Garnet, **(b)** David Walker, **(c)** Maria Stewart, **(d)** Frederick Douglass, **(e)** William Lloyd Garrison, **(f)** Angelina and Sarah Grimké, **(g)** Harriet Tubman.
3. **Define** **(a)** colonization, **(b)** abolitionist, **(c)** underground railroad.

Comprehension

4. Choose two abolitionists. Describe how each contributed to the antislavery movement.
5. **(a)** Why did some northerners oppose abolition? **(b)** Describe two effects of the abolitionist movement in the South.

Critical Thinking and Writing

6. **Drawing Conclusions** Why do you think slavery ended more easily in the North than in the South?
7. **Defending a Position** **(a)** Why do you think some abolitionists favored a gradual end to slavery? **(b)** How do you think William Lloyd Garrison or Frederick Douglass would have replied?

★ ★

Activity **Writing a Letter** You are a conductor on the underground railroad. You have a cousin in New Jersey whom you need to hide runaway slaves. Write a letter to the cousin describing who will be coming, what signals they will use to gain entry, and how they can be helped. (You might want to disguise your message in case it gets into the wrong hands.)

Struggle for Women's Rights

As You Read

Explore These Questions

- What rights did women lack in the early 1800s?
- What were the goals of the Seneca Falls Convention?
- How did opportunities for women improve in the mid-1800s?

Define

- women's rights movement

Identify

- Sojourner Truth
- Lucretia Mott
- Elizabeth Cady Stanton
- Seneca Falls Convention
- Susan B. Anthony
- Emma Willard
- Mary Lyon
- Elizabeth Blackwell

SETTING the Scene As you have read, Sarah and Angelina Grimké became powerful speakers against slavery. However, the boldness of their activities shocked many people. Some New England ministers even scolded the sisters in a newspaper. "When [a woman] assumes the place and tone of a man as a public reformer," they wrote, "her character becomes unnatural."

Unmoved by such criticism, Angelina Grimké asked, "What then can woman do for the slave, when she herself is under the feet of man and shamed into silence?" More determined than ever, the Grimkés continued their crusade. Now, however, they had a second topic to lecture about—women's rights.

Seeking Equal Rights

Women had few political or legal rights in the mid-1800s. They could not vote or hold office. When a woman married, her husband became owner of all her property. If a woman worked outside the home, her wages belonged to her husband. A husband also had the right to hit his wife as long as he did not seriously injure her.

Many women, like the Grimkés, had joined the abolitionist movement. As these women worked to end slavery, they became aware that they lacked full social and political rights themselves. Both black and white abolitionists joined the struggle for women's rights.

Truth speaks out

One of the most effective women's rights leaders was born into slavery in New York. Her original name was Isabella Baumfree. After gaining her freedom, she came to believe that God wanted her to crusade against slavery. Vowing to sojourn, or travel, across the land speaking the truth, Baumfree took the name **Sojourner Truth.**

Truth was a spellbinding speaker. Her exact words were rarely written down. However, her powerful message spread by word of mouth. According to one witness, Truth ridiculed the idea that women were inferior to men by nature:

> "I have as much muscle as any man, and can do as much work as any man. I have plowed and reaped and husked and chopped and mowed, and can any man do more than that?"

Connections With Science

In the mid-1800s, women wore tightly laced corsets to make the waist as tiny as possible. Doctors warned that these "tightlacers" caused fainting, squeezed the internal organs, and could even crush the rib cage. Instead, reformers supported a looser, trouserlike garment known as bloomers.

Mott and Stanton

Other abolitionists also turned to the cause of women's rights. The two most influential were Lucretia Mott and Elizabeth Cady Stanton.

Lucretia Mott was a Quaker and the mother of five children. A quiet speaker, she won the respect of many listeners with her persuasive logic. Mott also used her organizing skills to set up petition drives across the North.

Elizabeth Cady Stanton was the daughter of a New York judge. As a child, she was an excellent student as well as an athlete. However, her father gave his gifted daughter little encouragement. Stanton later remarked that her "father would have felt a proper pride had I been a man." In addition, clerks in her father's law office used to tease her by reading laws that denied basic rights to women. Such experiences made her a lifelong foe of inequality.

In 1840, Stanton and Mott joined a group of Americans at a World Antislavery Convention in London. However, convention officials refused to let women take an active part in the proceedings. Female delegates were even forced to sit behind a curtain, hidden from view. After returning home, Mott and Stanton took up the cause of women's rights with new energy.

A Historic Meeting

While they were still in London, Mott and Stanton decided to hold a convention to draw attention to the problems women faced. "The men . . . had [shown] a great need for some education on that question," Stanton later recalled.

Eight years later, in 1848, in Seneca Falls, New York, the meeting finally took place. About 200 women and 40 men attended the **Seneca Falls Convention.**

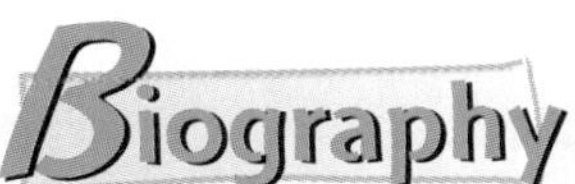

Elizabeth Cady Stanton and Sojourner Truth

Elizabeth Cady Stanton (left) was born into a well-to-do, middle-class family and raised her own children in comfort. Sojourner Truth (right) was born into slavery and saw at least one of her children sold. Despite their vastly different backgrounds, the two women became allies in the fight for women's rights. ★ **Both Truth and Stanton were abolitionists. How was abolition linked to the movement for women's rights?**

The Spirit of Reform

Reform Movements

Social Reform	Antislavery Movement	Women's Rights Movement
▪ Humane treatment for mentally ill ▪ Prison reform ▪ Temperance movement against alcohol ▪ Improvements in education	▪ End of slavery in the North ▪ Establishment of Liberia ▪ Abolitionist speeches, books, and newspapers ▪ Underground railroad	▪ Seneca Falls Convention ▪ Schools for women ▪ New legal rights in some states ▪ New work opportunities

Graphic Organizer *Skills*

The spirit of reform of the 1800s motivated some people to try to improve American society.

1. **Comprehension** What were two types of social reform addressed by reformers in the mid-1800s?
2. **Critical Thinking** What did the reforms shown in this graphic organizer have in common?

Civics

"Women are created equal"

At the meeting, leaders of the women's rights movement presented a Declaration of Sentiments. Modeled on the Declaration of Independence, it proclaimed, "We hold these truths to be self-evident: that all men and women are created equal."

The women and men at Seneca Falls voted for resolutions that demanded equality for women at work, at school, and in church. Only one resolution met any opposition at the convention. It demanded that women be allowed to vote. Even the bold women at Seneca Falls hesitated to take this step. In the end, the resolution narrowly passed.

A long struggle

The Seneca Falls Convention marked the start of an organized campaign for equal rights, or **women's rights movement.** Other leaders took up the struggle. **Susan B. Anthony** built a close-working partnership with Elizabeth Cady Stanton. While Stanton usually had to stay at home with her seven children, Anthony was free to travel across the country. Anthony was a tireless speaker. Even when audiences heckled her and threw eggs, she always finished her speech.

In the years after 1848, women worked for change in many areas. They won additional legal rights in some states. For example, New York passed laws allowing married women to keep their own property and wages. Still, many men and women opposed the women's rights movement. The struggle for equal rights would last many years.

New Opportunities

In the early 1800s, women from poor families had little hope of learning even to read. Middle-class girls who went to school learned dancing and drawing rather than science or mathematics. After all, people argued, women were expected to care for their families. Why did they need an education?

The women at Seneca Falls believed that education was a key to equality. Elizabeth Cady Stanton said:

> “The girl must be allowed to romp and play, climb, skate, and swim. Her clothes must be more like those of the boy—strong, loose-fitting garments, thick boots. . . . Like the boy, she must be taught to look forward to a life of self-dependence and to prepare herself early for some trade profession.”

The American Medical Women's Association gives this annual medal in honor of Elizabeth Blackwell.

Schools for women

Reformers worked to improve education for women. **Emma Willard** opened a high school for girls in Troy, New York. Here, young women studied “men's” subjects, such as mathematics and physics.

Mary Lyon opened Mount Holyoke Female Seminary in Massachusetts in 1837. She did not call the school a college because many people thought it was wrong for women to attend college. In fact, Mount Holyoke was the first women's college in the United States.

New careers

At about this time, a few men's colleges began to admit women. As their education improved, women found jobs teaching, especially in grade schools.

A few women entered fields such as medicine. **Elizabeth Blackwell** attended medical school at Geneva College in New York. To the surprise of school officials, she graduated first in her class. Women had provided medical care since colonial times, but Blackwell was the first woman in the United States to earn a medical degree. She later set up the nation's first medical school for women.

Women made their mark in other fields as well. Maria Mitchell became a noted astronomer. In the 1850s, Antoinette Blackwell was the first American woman to be ordained as a minister. She also campaigned for abolitionism, temperance, and women's right to vote.

★ Section 3 Review ★

Recall

1. **Identify** **(a)** Sojourner Truth, **(b)** Lucretia Mott, **(c)** Elizabeth Cady Stanton, **(d)** Seneca Falls Convention, **(e)** Susan B. Anthony, **(f)** Emma Willard, **(g)** Mary Lyon, **(h)** Elizabeth Blackwell.
2. **Define** women's rights movement.

Comprehension

3. Describe three ways that laws discriminated against women in the early 1800s.
4. What resolutions did the delegates at Seneca Falls make?
5. **(a)** What type of education did most women receive in the mid-1800s? **(b)** How did reformers change women's education?

Critical Thinking and Writing

6. **Understanding Causes and Effects** How was the women's rights movement a long-term effect of the antislavery movement?
7. **Predicting Consequences** How do you think the growth of educational opportunities affected the future of the women's rights movement?

Activity **Designing a T-shirt** It is four weeks before the Seneca Falls Convention. You have been asked to create a T-shirt for all the attendees. Draw a clever and attractive design that expresses the feelings and demands of the women's rights movement.

American Literature and Art

As You Read

Explore These Questions

- What themes did American novelists and poets explore?
- What ideas did Emerson and Thoreau express?
- How did American painters create their own styles?

Define

- transcendentalism

Identify

- Washington Irving
- James Fenimore Cooper
- Ralph Waldo Emerson
- Henry David Thoreau
- Walt Whitman
- Emily Dickinson
- Hudson River School

In 1820, a Scottish minister named Sydney Smith blasted what he saw as a lack of culture in the United States:

> ❝ In the four quarters of the globe, who reads an American book? Or goes to an American play? Or looks at an American picture or statue? What does the world yet owe to Americans? ❞

Even as Smith wrote these words, American writers and artists were breaking free of European traditions. These men and women created a voice and a vision that were truly American.

American Storytellers

Until the early 1800s, most American writers depended on Europe for their ideas and inspiration. In the 1820s, however, a new crop of writers began to write stories with American themes.

Two early writers

One of the most popular American writers was **Washington Irving,** a New Yorker. Irving first became known for *The Sketch Book,* a collection of tales published in 1820. Two of the best-loved tales are "Rip Van Winkle" and "The Legend of Sleepy Hollow." (See page 246.)

Irving's stories gave Americans a sense of the richness of their past. His appeal went beyond the United States, however. Irving was the first American writer to also enjoy fame in Europe.

James Fenimore Cooper also published novels set in the past. In *The Deerslayer* and *The Last of the Mohicans,* Cooper created the character Natty Bumppo, a heroic model of a strong, silent, solitary frontiersman. The novels also gave an idealized view of relations between whites and Native Americans on the frontier. The stories were so exciting, however, that few readers cared if they were true to life.

Later writers

Nathaniel Hawthorne drew on the history of Puritan New England to create his novels and short stories. Hawthorne was fascinated by Puritan notions of sin and guilt. His best-known novel, *The Scarlet Letter,* was published in 1850.

In 1851, Herman Melville published *Moby-Dick.* The novel tells the story of Ahab, the crazed captain of a whaling ship. Ahab vows revenge against the white whale that years earlier bit off his leg. *Moby-Dick* had only limited success when it was first published. Today, however, critics rank it among the finest American novels.

Edgar Allan Poe became famous for his many tales of horror. His short story "The Tell-Tale Heart" tells of a murderer, driven mad by guilt, who imagines he can hear his victim's heartbeat. Poe is also called the "father of the detective story" for his mystery stories, such as "The Murders in the Rue Morgue."

William Wells Brown published *Clotel,* a novel about slave life, in 1853. Brown was the first African American to earn his living as a writer.

Women writers

Many best-selling novels of the period were written by women. Some novels told about young women who gained wealth and happiness through honesty and self-sacrifice. Others showed the hardships faced by widows and orphans.

Few of these novels are read today. However, writers like Catherine Sedgwick and Fanny Fern earned far more than Hawthorne or Melville. Hawthorne complained about the success of a "mob of scribbling women."

The "Inner Light"

In New England, a small group of writers and thinkers, known as Transcendentalists, emerged. **Transcendentalism** was the belief that the most important truths in life transcended, or went beyond, human reason. Transcendentalists stressed emotions over reason. They believed that each individual had control over his or her life. This belief influenced many transcendentalists to support social reform.

One Transcendentalist, Margaret Fuller, wrote *Woman in the Nineteenth Century.* The book strongly influenced the movement for women's rights.

Emerson

The leading Transcendentalist was **Ralph Waldo Emerson.** Emerson was the most popular essayist and lecturer of his day. Audiences flocked to hear him talk on subjects such as self-reliance and character. Emerson believed that the human spirit was reflected in nature. Civilization might provide material wealth, he said, but nature held higher values that came from God.

An Enduring American Tale

In 1826, James Fenimore Cooper's frontier tale The Last of the Mohicans *(left) was a best-seller. In 1992, a film version of Cooper's novel (right) was one of the year's most popular movies. The works of other early American writers, such as Hawthorne and Melville, have also been turned into movies or television miniseries.* ★ **Why do you think modern audiences would still enjoy a movie version of *The Last of the Mohicans?***

The Hudson River School

Thomas Cole wrote that "it is of the greatest importance for a painter always to have his mind upon Nature." In paintings like Kaaterskill Falls, *left, Cole captured the beauty and power of New York's Hudson River valley.*

★ **What kinds of emotion might a painting like this stir?**

In his essays and lectures, Emerson stressed the importance of the individual. Each person, Emerson said, has an "inner light." He urged people to use this inner light to guide their lives and improve society.

Thoreau

Henry David Thoreau (thuh ROW), Emerson's friend and neighbor, believed that the growth of industry and the rise of cities were ruining the nation. He urged people to live as simply as possible. In *Walden,* his best-known work, Thoreau describes spending a year alone in a cabin on Walden Pond in Massachusetts.

Like Emerson, Thoreau believed that each individual must decide what is right or wrong. He wrote:

> "If a man does not keep pace with his companions, perhaps it is because he hears a different drummer. Let him step to the music he hears."

Thoreau's "different drummer" told him that slavery was wrong. He was a fierce abolitionist and served as a conductor on the underground railroad.

Poetic Voices

Henry Wadsworth Longfellow was the favorite poet of Americans in the mid-1800s. Longfellow based many poems on events from the past. "Paul Revere's Ride" honored the Revolutionary War hero. "The Song of Hiawatha" idealized Native American life.

Other poets spoke out on social issues. John Greenleaf Whittier, a Quaker from Massachusetts, and Frances Watkins Harper, an African American woman from Maryland, used their pens to make readers aware of the evils of slavery.

Walt Whitman published only one book of poems, *Leaves of Grass.* However, he added to it over a period of 27 years. Whitman had great faith in the common people. His poetry celebrated democracy and the diverse people who made the nation great. He wrote proudly of being part of a "Nation of many nations":

Connections With Civics

In his essay *Civil Disobedience,* Thoreau argued that people had a right to disobey unjust laws if their consciences demanded it. He once went to jail for refusing to pay taxes to support the Mexican War, which he felt promoted slavery. Thoreau's ideas on nonviolent protest later influenced Mohandas Gandhi and Martin Luther King, Jr.

“A Southerner soon as a
Northerner...
At home on the hills of Vermont or
in the woods of Maine, or the
Texan ranch,
Comrade of Californians, comrade of
free North-Westerners....
Of every hue and caste am I, of
every rank and religion,
A farmer, mechanic, artist, gentle-
man, sailor, quaker,
Prisoner, fancy-man, rowdy, lawyer,
physician, priest.”

Today, critics consider **Emily Dickinson** one of the nation's greatest poets. Yet, only seven of her more than 1,700 poems were published in her lifetime. A shy woman who rarely left her home, Dickinson called her poetry "my letter to the world / That never wrote to me."

American Painters

Before the 1800s, most American painters studied in Europe. In 1772, Benjamin West of Philadelphia was appointed historical painter to King George III. Many American painters journeyed to London to study with West, including Charles Willson Peale and Gilbert Stuart. Both Peale and Stuart painted famous portraits of George Washington.

By the mid-1800s, American artists began to develop their own style. The first group to do so became known as the **Hudson River School** because they painted landscapes of New York's Hudson River region. Two of the best-known painters of the Hudson River School were Thomas Cole and Asher B. Durand. African American artist Robert S. Duncanson also reflected the style of the Hudson River School.

Other American artists painted scenes of hardworking country people. George Caleb Bingham was inspired by his native Missouri. His paintings show frontier life along the rivers that feed the great Mississippi.

Several painters tried to capture the culture of Native Americans on canvas. George Catlin and Alfred Jacob Miller traveled to the Far West. Their paintings record the daily life of Indians on the Great Plains and in the Rockies.

★ Section 4 Review ★

Recall

1. **Identify** (a) Washington Irving, **(b)** James Fenimore Cooper, **(c)** Ralph Waldo Emerson, **(d)** Henry David Thoreau, **(e)** Walt Whitman, **(f)** Emily Dickinson, **(g)** Hudson River School.
2. **Define** Transcendentalism.

Comprehension

3. Describe the subjects explored by each of the following writers: **(a)** Nathaniel Hawthorne, **(b)** Edgar Allan Poe, **(c)** William Wells Brown, **(d)** Henry Wadsworth Longfellow.
4. What did Emerson and Thoreau think about the importance of the individual?
5. **(a)** Where did early American painters get their inspiration? **(b)** How did this situation change in the mid-1800s?

Critical Thinking and Writing

6. **Drawing Conclusions** Why do you think writers and artists did not develop a unique American style until the mid-1800s?
7. **Linking Past and Present** **(a)** What do you think Walt Whitman meant when he called the United States a "Nation of many nations"? **(b)** Do you think these words can still be used to describe the nation today? Explain.

Activity **Creating a Chart** Henry David Thoreau is returning to look at today's society. He will spend a week in your community. Make a two-column chart. In the left column, list things, places, and activities he will probably criticize. On the right, list things, places, and activities he will appreciate.

Chapter 13 Review and Activities

★ Sum It Up ★

Section 1 The Spirit of Reform

- ▶ Political and religious ideals encouraged a spirit of reform.
- ▶ Reformers worked for many goals, including temperance, improved education, and better treatment for the mentally ill.

Section 2 The Fight Against Slavery

- ▶ Abolitionists fought to end slavery in many ways, including publishing newspapers, lecturing, and helping runaway slaves escape on the underground railroad.
- ▶ Slavery was defended by northerners who depended on cotton for their livelihood and by Southerners who felt their economy depended on slavery.

Section 3 Struggle for Women's Rights

- ▶ Many women joined the struggle for women's rights after fighting for abolition of slavery.
- ▶ The Seneca Falls Convention in 1848 marked the beginning of an organized women's rights movement.

Section 4 American Literature and Art

- ▶ In the 1820s, American writers began to explore American themes in their stories and poems.
- ▶ American artists gradually broke away from European models and developed their own styles.

For additional review of the major ideas of Chapter 13, see ***Guide to the Essentials of American History*** or ***Interactive Student Tutorial CD-ROM,*** which contains interactive review activities, graphic organizers, and practice tests.

Reviewing the Chapter

Define These Terms

Match each term with the correct definition.

Column 1	Column 2
1. revival	**a.** system of prisons
2. temperance movement	**b.** network of people who helped runaway slaves reach freedom
3. abolitionist	**c.** campaign against drinking
4. underground railroad	**d.** person who wanted to end slavery
5. penal system	**e.** huge outdoor religious meeting

Explore the Main Ideas

1. What were two goals of the Second Great Awakening?
2. What goals did Dorothea Dix pursue?
3. Why was Harriet Tubman called the "Black Moses"?
4. Why did supporters of the women's rights movement seek better education for women?
5. Name two writers in the 1800s who wrote about American experiences.

Graph Activity

Look at the graph below and answer the following questions: **1.** About how many students were enrolled in American schools in 1840? In 1860? **2.** How much did school enrollment increase between 1850 and 1870? **Critical Thinking** Based on what you have read, why did school enrollment increase steadily in the mid-1800s?

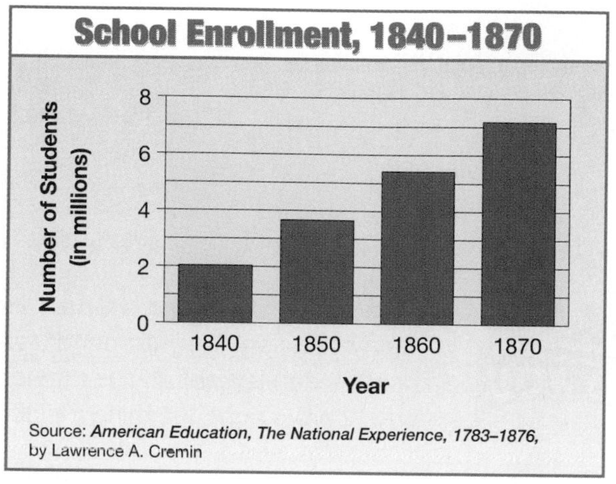

Source: *American Education, The National Experience, 1783–1876,* by Lawrence A. Cremin

Critical Thinking and Writing

1. **Linking Past and Present** **(a)** How did reformers in the 1800s try to gain public support? **(b)** What methods do people use to win public support today?
2. **Analyzing Ideas** In his *Appeal to the Colored Citizens of the World,* David Walker wrote that "all men are created equal; that they are endowed by their Creator with certain inalienable rights." **(a)** From which document did Walker borrow this idea? **(b)** What point do you think he was making by including these words?
3. **Ranking** In the mid-1800s, women like Sojourner Truth, the Grimké sisters, Lucretia Mott, and Elizabeth Cady Stanton organized to fight for abolition and women's rights. Make a list of the demands of these women. Then rank the demands from most important to least important. Give reasons for this ranking.
4. **Exploring Unit Themes** **Expansion** How do you think westward expansion increased concerns about slavery?

Using Primary Sources

Frederick Douglass denounced the slave trade in the South:

> "Fellow citizens, this murderous traffic is, today, in active operation in this boasted republic. I see the bleeding footsteps; I hear the doleful wail of [chained] humanity on the way to the slave markets where the victims are to be sold like horse, sheep, and swine.... My soul sickens at the sight."

Source: Frederick Douglass, speech to New York abolitionist society, 1852.

Recognizing Points of View **(a)** What words did Douglass use to stir up anger against the slave trade? **(b)** What did he mean when he called the United States a "boasted republic"? **(c)** How did Douglass's background make him an effective speaker on the subject of slavery?

Activity Bank

Interdisciplinary Activity

Exploring the Arts Do research on one of the American painters discussed in this chapter. Then, prepare a guidebook for a museum exhibit of that painter's work. Include a brief biographical note and descriptions of two or three paintings.

Career Skills Activity

Musicians Write and perform a marching song to be used at one of the following events: a temperance rally; an abolitionist meeting; the Seneca Falls Convention. You may work alone or with a group.

Citizenship Activity

Creating a Campaign Today, as in the past, communities are concerned with making sure all students get a good education. Plan a campaign designed to encourage students to stay in school. Your campaign may include posters, speeches, or other public events.

Internet Activity

Use the Internet to find information on any five of the following women: Antoinette Blackwell, Emily Blackwell, Amelia Bloomer, Myra Bradwell, Margaret Fuller, Matilda Joslyn Gage, Maria Mitchell, Lucy Stone. Write a one-sentence summary of the contribution each woman made to the women's rights movement.

Eyewitness Journal

You are one of the reformers discussed in this chapter. In your EYEWITNESS JOURNAL, write three entries that express your views on a major issue and the actions you are taking. You may choose to do further research before writing your journal.

Nightjohn

by Gary Paulsen

Introduction

Nightjohn, set in the 1850s, is told by Sarny, a 12-year-old slave on a southern plantation. When John comes to live there, Sarny's life is changed forever. John had escaped to the North. Yet, he came back—to teach others to read. As this excerpt begins, Sarny is talking to John late at night in the slave quarters. She is deciding whether to let John teach her some letters.

I knew about reading. It was something that the people in the white house did from paper. They could read words on paper. But we weren't allowed to be reading. We weren't allowed to understand or read nothing but once I saw some funny lines on the side of a feed sack. It said:

100 lbs.

I wrote them down in the dirt with a stick and mammy gave me a smack on the back of the head that like to drove me into the ground.

"Don't you take to that, take to writing," she said.

"I wasn't doing it. I was just copying something I saw on a feed sack."

"Don't. They catch you doing that and they'll think you're learning to read. You learn to read and they'll whip you. . . . Or cut your thumb off. Stay away from writing and reading."

So I did. But I remembered how it had looked, the drawings on the sack and in the dirt, and it still puzzled me. . . .

[Sarny then speaks to John.]

"You saying you can read?"

He nodded.

"I give you something to read, you can read it? Just like that?"

"I can.". . .

"Way it works," he said, "is you got to learn all the letters and numbers before you can learn to read. You got to learn the alphabet."

"Alphabet?"

He nodded. "There be lots of letters, and each one means something different. You got to learn each one."

. . . Then he made a drawing with his thumb.

A

"Tonight we just do *A.*" He sat back on his heels and pointed. "There it be.". . .

"What does it mean?"

"It means *A*—just like I said. It's the first letter in the alphabet. And when you see it you make a sound like this: *ayyy,* or *ahhhh.*"

Viewing History: Learning to Read—In Secret

This illustration from the novel Nightjohn *shows John teaching Sarny to read. By the mid-1800s, many southern states had made it illegal for enslaved African Americans to learn to read and write. Yet many slaves risked severe punishment to learn anyway.*

★ **Why do you think enslaved African Americans valued education so highly?**

"That's reading? To make that sound?" He nodded. "When you see that letter on paper or a sack or in the dirt you make one of those sounds. That's reading."

"Well, that ain't hard at all."

He laughed. That same low roll. Made me think of thunder long ways off, moving in a summer sky. "There's more to it. Other letters. But that's it."

"Why they be cutting our thumbs off if we learn to read—if that's all it is?"

"'Cause to know things, for us to know things, is bad for them. We get to wanting and when we get to wanting it's bad for them. They thinks we want what they got.... That's why they don't want us reading." He sighed. "I got to rest now. They run me ten miles in a day and worked me into the ground. I need some sleep."

He moved back to the corner and settled down and I curled up to mammy in amongst the young ones again.

A, I thought, *ayyy, ahhhh.* There it is. I be reading.

"Hey there in the corner," I whispered.

"What?"

"What's your name?"

"I be John."

"I be Sarny."

"Go to sleep, Sarny."

But I didn't. I snuggled into mammy and pulled a couple of the young ones in for heat and kept my eyes open so I wouldn't sleep and thought:

A.

Analyzing Literature

1. Why did Sarny's mother tell her to stay away from reading and writing?
2. According to John, why did the slave owners want to keep the slaves from learning to read and write?
3. **Critical Thinking Making Inferences** Based on this excerpt, what are some of John's qualities? How can you tell?

Unit 5 Division and Reunion

What's Ahead

Viewing UNIT THEMES **War Divides the Nation**

In 1861, conflict between the North and the South erupted into war. Winslow Homer, one of the country's greatest artists, painted Prisoners From the Front. *It shows a northern officer (right) inspecting captured southern troops (left). The opposing soldiers look on each other with pride and hostility.* ★ **Based on what you have learned in earlier units, identify two differences between the North and South.**

Unit Theme Sectionalism

Sectionalism is loyalty to a state or region rather than to the country as a whole. From colonial days, Americans felt strong loyalties to the regions where they lived. By the mid-1800s, several issues increased sectional differences between the North and South. The most dramatic of these issues was slavery. Extreme sectionalism eventually led to war.

How did people of the time feel about sectional divisions? They can tell you in their own words.

Viewpoints on Sectional Divisions

"We have always been taught to look upon the people of New England as a selfish, cunning set of fellows."

Davy Crockett, Tennessee member of Congress (1835)

"I have heard something said about allegiance to the South. I know no South, no North, no East, no West, to which I owe any allegiance.... The Union, sir, is my country."

Henry Clay, senator from Kentucky (1848)

"Union! I can more easily conceive of the Lion and Lambs lying down together, than of a union of the North and South."

Sarah Chase, Massachusetts teacher in the South (1866)

★ ★

Activity Writing to Learn Today, the United States is often divided into these geographic regions: the Northeast; the Midatlantic; the Southeast; the Midwest; the Rocky Mountain states; the Southwest; the Pacific Coast states. List three features, other than location, that make the region you live in special. Then, write a paragraph explaining whether you feel more loyal to your region or to the United States as a whole.

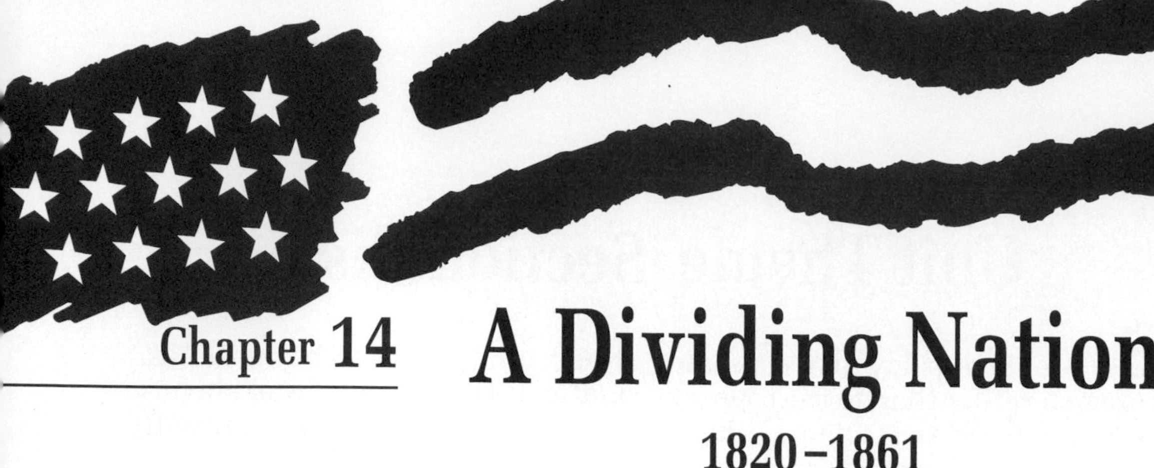

Chapter 14 A Dividing Nation

1820–1861

What's Ahead

Section 1
The Slavery Issue in the West

Section 2
The Crisis Turns Violent

Section 3
A New Party Challenges Slavery

Section 4
The Nation Splits in Two

Between 1820 and 1861, the nation grew increasingly divided as it struggled to answer difficult questions concerning slavery. Should slavery be allowed to spread to the West? Should slavery be abolished throughout the nation? For a time, northerners and southerners settled their differences through compromises. Gradually, however, violence became more and more common. In 1860, voters elected Abraham Lincoln, a member of the anti-slavery Republican party, to be the next President of the United States. In response, southern states withdrew from the Union. The North and the South then prepared for war.

Why Study History?

Many consider Abraham Lincoln to be one of the greatest leaders in American history. Some call him an American hero. Frequently, therefore, he is held as a role model for others to imitate. Could Lincoln be a role model for you? To answer this question, see this chapter's *Why Study History?* feature, "Heroes of the Past Can Be Models for Today."

American Events

1820 Missouri Compromise allows slavery in some western territories

1850 Fugitive Slave Law requires citizens to help catch runaway slaves

1852 *Uncle Tom's Cabin* increases support for abolitionism

1820 | 1848 | 1850 | 1852 | 1854

World Events

1833 World Event Slavery is abolished in British empire

1850 World Event Taiping Rebellion begins civil war in China

Viewing History: From Slavery to Freedom

In the painting On to Liberty *by Theodor Kaufmann, fugitive slave families try to reach the North and freedom. In the 1850s, many northerners protested against a law requiring all citizens to help return runaway slaves. Disagreement over slavery heightened the growing division between North and South.* ★ **How do you think enslaved African Americans felt as they tried to escape to the North?**

1854 Kansas-Nebraska Act leads to violence

1857 Supreme Court says Congress cannot outlaw slavery in territories

1861 Abraham Lincoln becomes President

1854 | 1856 | 1858 | 1860 | 1862

1857 World Event
New constitution in Mexico prohibits slavery

Other moderates supported the idea of **popular sovereignty,** or control by the people. In other words, voters in a new territory would decide for themselves whether or not to allow slavery in the territory. Slaves, of course, could not vote.

The Free Soil Party

The debate over slavery led to the birth of a new political party. By 1848, many northerners in both the Democratic party and the Whig party opposed the spread of slavery. However, the leaders of both parties refused to take a stand on the question. They did not want to give up their chance of winning votes in the South. Some also feared that the slavery issue would split the nation.

In 1848, antislavery members of both parties met in Buffalo, New York. There, they founded the **Free Soil party.** Their slogan was "Free soil, free speech, free labor, and free men." The main goal of the Free Soil party was to keep slavery out of the western territories. Only a few Free Soilers were abolitionists who wanted to end slavery in the South.

In the 1848 presidential campaign, Free Soilers named former President Martin Van Buren as their candidate. Democrats chose Lewis Cass of Michigan. The Whigs selected **Zachary Taylor,** a hero of the Mexican War.

For the first time, slavery was an important election issue. Van Buren called for a ban on slavery in the Mexican Cession. Cass supported popular sovereignty. Because Taylor was a slave owner from Louisiana, many southern voters assumed that he supported slavery.

Zachary Taylor won the election, but Van Buren took 10 percent of the popular vote. Thirteen other Free Soil candidates won seats in Congress. The success of the new Free Soil party showed that slavery had become a national issue.

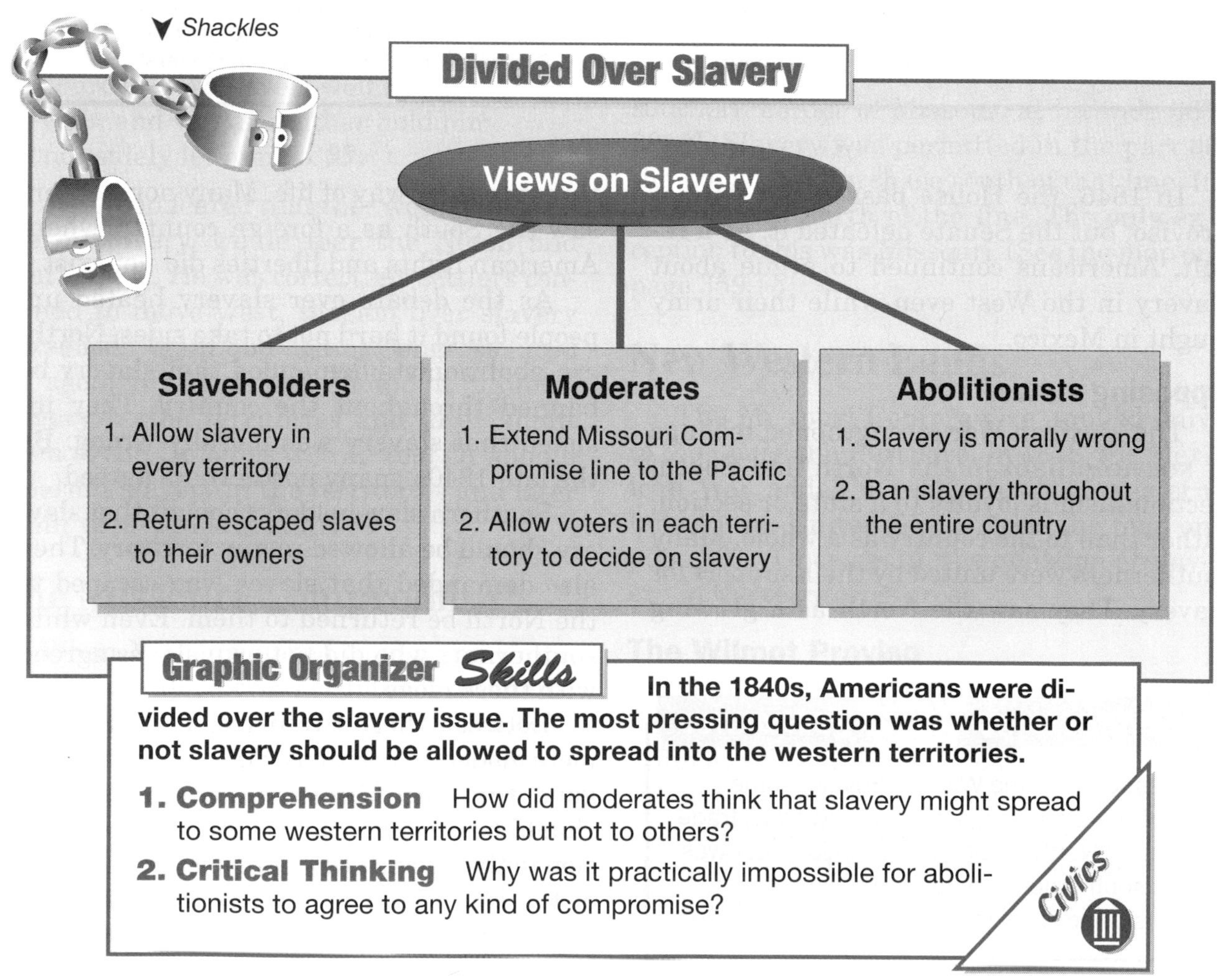

Graphic Organizer *Skills* **In the 1840s, Americans were divided over the slavery issue. The most pressing question was whether or not slavery should be allowed to spread into the western territories.**

1. **Comprehension** How did moderates think that slavery might spread to some western territories but not to others?
2. **Critical Thinking** Why was it practically impossible for abolitionists to agree to any kind of compromise?

Need for a New Compromise

For a time after the Missouri Compromise, both slave and free states entered the Union peacefully. However, when California requested admission to the Union as a free state in 1850, the balance of power in the Senate was once again threatened. (See the graph to the right.)

California's impact

In 1849, there were 15 slave states and 15 free states in the nation. If California entered the union as a free state, the balance of power would be broken. Furthermore, it seemed quite possible that Oregon, Utah, and New Mexico might also join the Union as free states.

Many Southerners feared that the South would be hopelessly outvoted in the Senate. Some even suggested that southern states might want to **secede,** or remove themselves, from the United States. Northern congressmen, meanwhile, argued that California should enter the Union as a free state because most of the territory lay north of the Missouri Compromise line.

As Congress tried to reach a new compromise, tempers raged. One frightening incident involved Senators Thomas Hart Benton of Missouri and Henry Foote of Mississippi. Benton supported California's entry as a free state even though he himself was a slave owner. He denounced Foote for opposing California's admission. In response, Foote rose angrily from his seat and aimed a pistol at Benton. As other senators watched in horror, Benton roared, "Let him fire. Stand out of the way and let the assassin fire!"

No blood was shed in the Senate that day. However, it was clear that the nation faced a crisis. Many in Congress looked to Senator Henry Clay for a solution.

Clay vs. Calhoun

Clay had won the nickname "the Great Compromiser" for working out the Missouri Compromise. Now, nearly 30 years later, the 73-year-old Clay was frail and ill. Still, he pleaded for the North and South to reach an agreement. If they failed to do so, Clay warned, the nation could break apart.

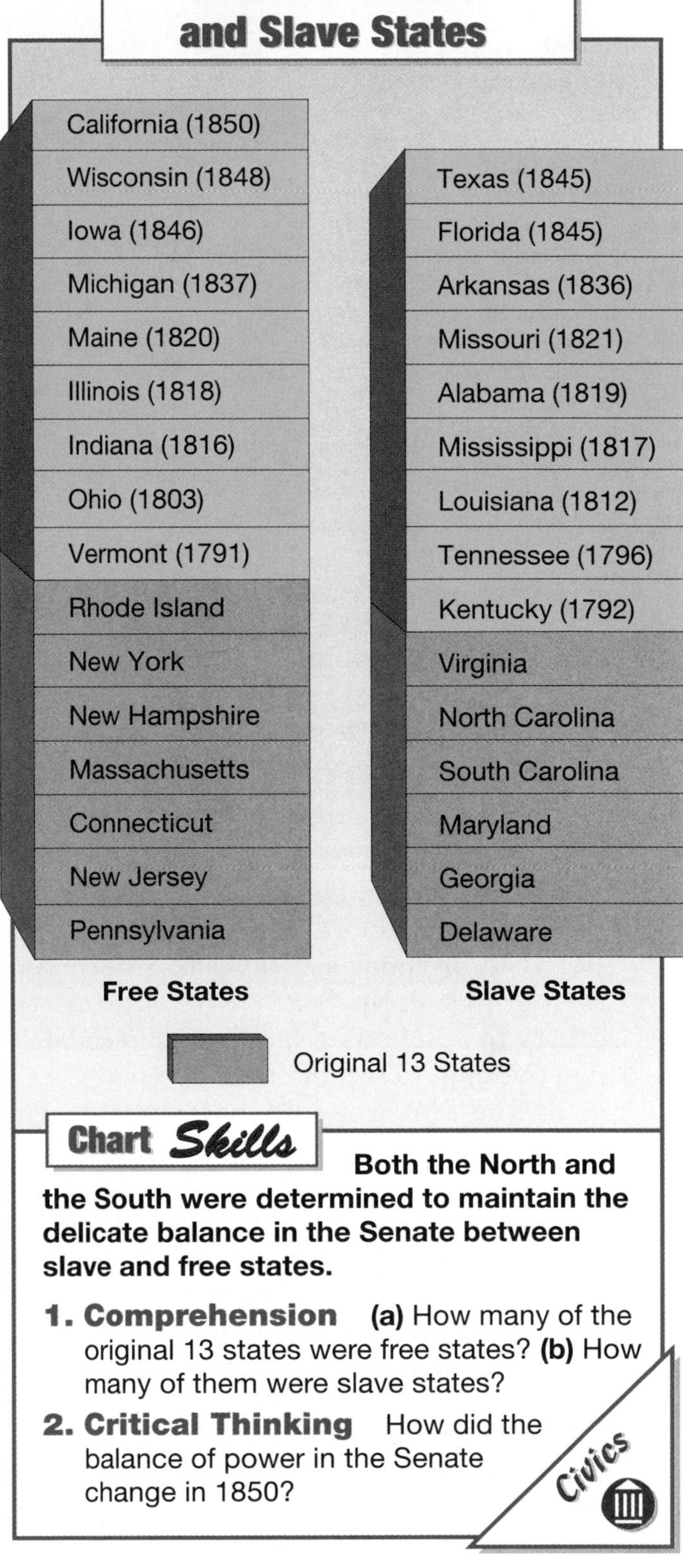

Chart Skills **Both the North and the South were determined to maintain the delicate balance in the Senate between slave and free states.**

1. **Comprehension** **(a)** How many of the original 13 states were free states? **(b)** How many of them were slave states?
2. **Critical Thinking** How did the balance of power in the Senate change in 1850?

Civics

Senator John C. Calhoun of South Carolina prepared the South's reply to Clay. Calhoun was dying of tuberculosis and could not speak loudly enough to address the Senate. He stared defiantly at his northern foes while Senator James Mason of Virginia read his speech.

Viewing HISTORY **Protest!**

In 1854, a Boston court ordered that fugitive slaves Anthony Burns and Thomas Sims be returned to their owners in the South. Public outcry against the decision was so great that United States marines and artillery were sent into Boston. Angry protesters lined the streets as the two were led to the ship that would return them to slavery.

★ **Do you think the court made the right decision in this case? Explain.**

Calhoun refused to compromise. He insisted that slavery be allowed in the western territories. Calhoun also demanded that **fugitive,** or runaway, slaves be returned to their owners in the South. He wanted northerners to admit that southern slaveholders had the right to reclaim their "property."

If the North would not agree to the South's demands, Calhoun told the Senate, "let the states . . . agree to part in peace. If you are unwilling that we should part in peace, tell us so, and we shall know what to do." Everyone knew what Calhoun meant. If an agreement could not be reached, the South would secede from the Union.

Webster calls for unity

Daniel Webster of Massachusetts spoke next. He supported Clay's plea to save the Union. Webster stated his position clearly:

> "I speak today not as a Massachusetts man, nor as a northern man, but as an American. . . . I speak today for the preservation of the Union. . . . There can be no such thing as a peaceable secession. Peaceable secession is an utter impossibility."

Webster feared that the states could not separate without a **civil war.** A civil war is a war between people of the same country.

Like many northerners, Webster viewed slavery as evil. Disunion, however, he believed was worse. To save the Union, Webster was willing to compromise with the South. He would support the South's demand that northerners be required to return fugitive slaves.

Compromise of 1850

In 1850, as the debate raged, Calhoun died. His last words reportedly were "The South! The South! God knows what will become of her!" President Taylor also died in 1850. The new President was Millard Fillmore. Unlike Taylor, he supported Clay's compromise plan. An agreement finally seemed possible.

Henry Clay gave more than 70 speeches in favor of a compromise. At last, however, he became too sick to continue. **Stephen Douglas,** an energetic senator from Illinois, took up the fight for him. Douglas tirelessly guided each part of Clay's plan, called the **Compromise of 1850,** through Congress.

The Compromise of 1850 had four parts. First, California was allowed to enter the Union as a free state. Second, the rest of the

Mexican Cession was divided into the territories of New Mexico and Utah. Voters in each territory would decide the slavery question according to popular sovereignty. Third, the slave trade was ended in Washington, D.C., the nation's capital. Congress, however, declared that it had no power to ban slave trade between slave states. Fourth, a strict fugitive slave law was passed.

Fugitive Slave Law of 1850

Most northerners had ignored the Fugitive Slave Law of 1793. As a result, fugitive slaves often lived as free citizens in northern cities. The **Fugitive Slave Law of 1850** was harder to ignore. It required all citizens to help catch runaway slaves. People who let fugitives escape could be fined $1,000 and jailed for six months.

The new law also set up special courts to handle the cases of runaways. Judges received $10 for sending an accused runaway to the South. They received only $5 for setting someone free. Lured by the extra money, some judges sent African Americans to the South whether or not they were runaways.

The Fugitive Slave Law enraged antislavery northerners. By forcing them to catch runaways, the law made northerners feel they were part of the slave system. In several northern cities, crowds tried to rescue fugitive slaves from their captors.

Martin R. Delany, an African American newspaper editor, spoke for many northerners, black and white:

> "My house is my castle.... If any man approaches that house in search of a slave—I care not who he may be, whether constable or sheriff, magistrate or even judge of the Supreme Court... if he crosses the threshold of my door, and I do not lay him a lifeless corpse at my feet, I hope the grave may refuse my body a resting place."

The North and South had reached a compromise. Still, tensions remained because neither side got everything that it wanted. The new Fugitive Slave Law was especially hard for northerners to accept. Each time the law was enforced, it convinced more northerners that slavery was evil.

★ Section 1 Review ★

Recall

1. **Locate** **(a)** Missouri, **(b)** Maine, **(c)** Missouri Compromise Line, **(d)** California, **(e)** New Mexico Territory, **(f)** Utah Territory.
2. **Identify** **(a)** Missouri Compromise, **(b)** Wilmot Proviso, **(c)** Free Soil party, **(d)** Zachary Taylor, **(e)** Stephen Douglas, **(f)** Compromise of 1850, **(g)** Fugitive Slave Law of 1850.
3. **Define** **(a)** sectionalism, **(b)** popular sovereignty, **(c)** secede, **(d)** fugitive, **(e)** civil war.

Comprehension

4. Describe three different views on the issue of slavery in the West.
5. Why did some people leave the Whig and Democratic parties and create the Free Soil party?
6. Explain the four parts of the Compromise of 1850.

Critical Thinking and Writing

7. **Analyzing Ideas** Why might the goals of the Free Soil party have pleased some northerners but not others?
8. **Analyzing Visual Evidence** Based on your understanding of the painting on page 356, how did the Compromise of 1850 create new conflict over the slavery issue?

Activity **Making a Decision** You are a northerner of the 1850s. There is a knock at your door. It's a fugitive slave! Will you help the runaway or will you turn the person in to the authorities? Write a brief statement explaining the reasons for your decision.

The Crisis Turns Violent

As You Read

Explore These Questions

- How did *Uncle Tom's Cabin* affect attitudes toward slavery?
- Why did a civil war break out in Kansas?
- How did the Dred Scott decision divide the nation?

Define

- repeal
- guerrilla warfare
- lawsuit

Identify

- Harriet Beecher Stowe
- *Uncle Tom's Cabin*
- Kansas-Nebraska Act
- Franklin Pierce
- Border Ruffians
- John Brown
- Bleeding Kansas
- Charles Sumner
- Dred Scott decision

SETTING the Scene In the mid-1850s, proslavery and antislavery forces battled for control of the territory of Kansas. An observer described election day in one Kansas district in 1855:

> "On the morning of the election, before the polls were opened, some 300 or 400 Missourians and others were collected in the yard... where the election was to be held, armed with bowie-knives, revolvers, and clubs. They said they came to vote, and whip the... Yankees, and would vote without being sworn. Some said they came to have a fight, and wanted one."

Hearing of events in Kansas, Abraham Lincoln, then a young lawyer in Illinois, predicted that "the contest will come to blows, and bloodshed." Once again, the issue of slavery in the territories divided the nation.

An Antislavery Bestseller

An event in 1852 added to the growing antislavery mood of the North. That year, **Harriet Beecher Stowe** published a novel called ***Uncle Tom's Cabin.*** Stowe wrote the novel to show the evils of slavery and the injustice of the Fugitive Slave Law. She had originally published the story as a serial in an abolitionist newspaper.

A powerful story

Stowe told the story of Uncle Tom, an enslaved African American noted for his kindness and his devotion to his religion. Tom is bought by Simon Legree, a cruel planter who treats his slaves brutally. In the end, Uncle Tom refuses to obey Legree's order to whip another slave. Legree then whips Uncle Tom to death.

Uncle Tom's Cabin had wide appeal in the North. The first 5,000 copies that were printed sold out in two days. In its first year, Stowe's novel sold 300,000 copies. The book was also published in many different languages. Soon, a play based on the novel appeared in cities not only in the North but around the world.

Nationwide reaction

Although *Uncle Tom's Cabin* was popular in the North, southerners objected to the book. They claimed that it did not give a true picture of slave life. Indeed, Stowe had seen little of slavery firsthand.

Even so, the book helped to change the way northerners felt about slavery. No longer could they ignore slavery as a political problem for Congress to settle. They now saw the slavery issue as a moral problem facing every American. For this reason, *Uncle Tom's Cabin* was one of the most important books in American history.

Kansas-Nebraska Act

Americans had hoped that the Compromise of 1850 would end debate over slavery in the West. In 1854, however, the issue of slavery in the territories surfaced yet again.

In January 1854, Senator Stephen Douglas introduced a bill to set up a government for the Nebraska Territory. This territory stretched from Texas north to Canada, and from Missouri west to the Rockies.

Douglas knew that white southerners did not want to add another free state to the Union. He proposed that the Nebraska Territory be divided into two territories, Kansas and Nebraska. (See the map below.) The settlers living in each territory would decide the issue of slavery by popular sovereignty. Douglas's bill was known as the **Kansas-Nebraska Act.**

Support for the act

The Kansas-Nebraska Act seemed fair to many people. After all, the Compromise of 1850 had applied popular sovereignty in New Mexico and Utah.

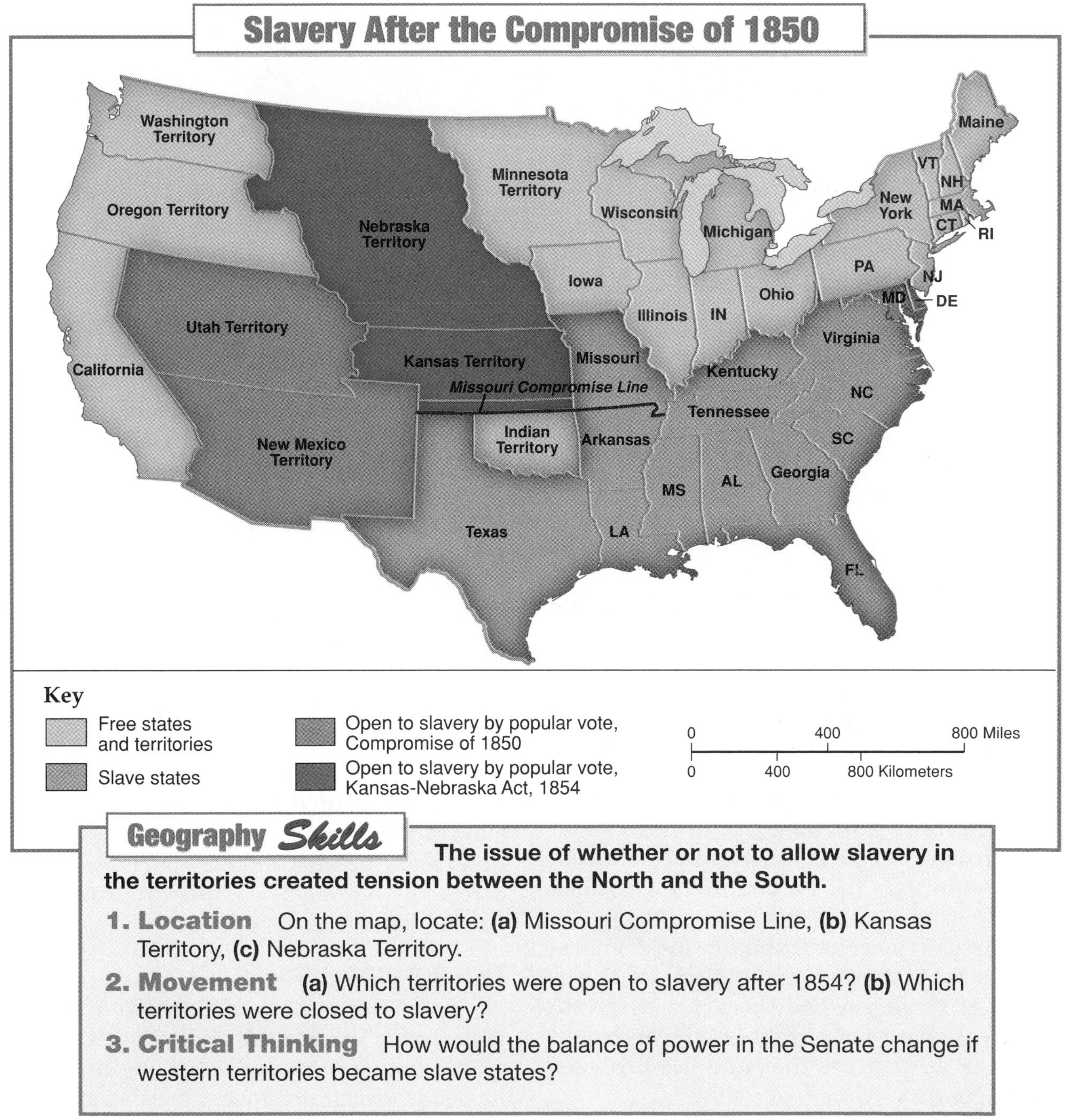

Geography *Skills* **The issue of whether or not to allow slavery in the territories created tension between the North and the South.**

1. **Location** On the map, locate: **(a)** Missouri Compromise Line, **(b)** Kansas Territory, **(c)** Nebraska Territory.
2. **Movement** **(a)** Which territories were open to slavery after 1854? **(b)** Which territories were closed to slavery?
3. **Critical Thinking** How would the balance of power in the Senate change if western territories became slave states?

Abolitionist's saber

Viewing HISTORY **Bleeding Kansas**

In 1856, a bloody civil war broke out in Kansas. Proslavery and antislavery forces fought for control of the territory. The battle depicted here took place at Hickory Point, 25 miles north of Lawrence. ★ **How was the violence in Kansas related to the Kansas-Nebraska Act?**

Southern leaders especially supported the Kansas-Nebraska Act. They were sure that slave owners from neighboring Missouri would move across the border into Kansas. In time, they hoped, Kansas would become a slave state.

President **Franklin Pierce,** a Democrat elected in 1852, also supported the bill. With the President's help, Douglas pushed the Kansas-Nebraska Act through Congress. He did not realize it at the time, but he had lit a fire under a powder keg.

Northern outrage

Other people were unhappy with the new law. The Missouri Compromise had already banned slavery in Kansas and Nebraska, they insisted. In effect, the Kansas-Nebraska Act would **repeal,** or undo, the Missouri Compromise.

The northern reaction to the Kansas-Nebraska Act was swift and angry. Opponents of slavery called the act a "criminal betrayal of precious rights." Slavery could now spread to areas that had been free for more than 30 years.

Bleeding Kansas

Kansas now became a testing ground for popular sovereignty. Stephen Douglas hoped that settlers would decide the slavery issue peacefully on election day. Instead, proslavery and antislavery forces sent settlers to Kansas to fight for control of the territory.

Most of the new arrivals were farmers from neighboring states. Their main interest in moving to Kansas was to acquire cheap land. Few of these settlers owned slaves. At the same time, abolitionists brought in more than 1,000 settlers from New England.

Proslavery settlers moved into Kansas as well. They wanted to make sure that antislavery forces did not overrun the territory. Proslavery bands from Missouri often rode across the border. These **Border Ruffians** battled the antislavery forces in Kansas.

Two governments

In 1855, Kansas held elections to choose lawmakers. Hundreds of Border Ruffians crossed into Kansas and voted illegally. They helped to elect a proslavery legislature.

The new legislature quickly passed laws to support slavery. One law said that people could be put to death for helping slaves escape. Another made speaking out against slavery a crime punishable by two years of hard labor.

Antislavery settlers refused to accept these laws. They elected their own governor and legislature. With two rival governments, Kansas was in chaos. Armed gangs roamed the land looking for trouble.

A bloody battleground

In 1856, a band of proslavery men raided the town of Lawrence, an antislavery stronghold. The attackers destroyed homes and smashed the press of a Free Soil newspaper.

John Brown, an abolitionist, decided to strike back. Brown had moved to Kansas to help make it a free state. He claimed that God had sent him to punish supporters of slavery.

Brown rode with his four sons and two other men to the town of Pottawatomie (paht uh WAHT uh mee) Creek. In the middle of the night, they dragged five proslavery settlers from their beds and murdered them.

The killings at Pottawatomie Creek led to more violence. Both sides fought fiercely and engaged in **guerrilla warfare,** or the use of hit-and-run tactics. By late 1856, more than 200 people had been killed. Newspapers called the territory **Bleeding Kansas.**

Violence in the Senate

Even before John Brown's attack, the battle over Kansas had spilled into the Senate. **Charles Sumner** of Massachusetts was the leading abolitionist senator. In one speech, the sharp-tongued Sumner denounced the proslavery legislature of Kansas. He then viciously criticized his southern foes, singling out Andrew Butler, an elderly senator from South Carolina.

Butler was not in the Senate on the day Sumner spoke. A few days later, however, Butler's nephew, Congressman Preston Brooks, marched into the Senate chamber. Using a heavy cane, Brooks beat Sumner until he fell down, bloody and unconscious, to the floor.

Many southerners felt that Sumner got what he deserved for his verbal abuse of another senator. Hundreds of people sent canes to Brooks to show their support. To northerners, however, the brutal act was just more evidence that slavery led to violence.

The Dred Scott Case

With Congress in an uproar, many Americans looked to the Supreme Court to settle the slavery issue and restore peace. In 1857, the Court ruled on a case involving a slave named Dred Scott. Instead of bringing harmony, however, the Court's decision further divided North and South.

Dred Scott had lived for many years in Missouri. Later, he moved with his owner to Illinois and then to the Wisconsin Territory,

Dred Scott

Dred Scott filed a lawsuit for his freedom. He argued that he should be a free man because he had lived in a free territory. The Supreme Court, however, ruled that he had no right to sue because he was property and not a citizen. After the decision, Scott's new owner granted freedom to Scott and his family. Just one year later, Scott died of consumption. ★ **How did the Dred Scott decision overturn the Missouri Compromise?**

where slavery was not allowed. After they returned to Missouri, Scott's owner died. Antislavery lawyers helped Scott to file a **lawsuit,** a legal case brought by a person or group against another to settle a dispute between them. Scott's lawyers argued that since Scott had lived in a free territory, he was a free man.

The Supreme Court's decision

In time, the case reached the Supreme Court. The Court's decision startled Americans who opposed slavery. The Court ruled that Scott could not file a lawsuit because, as an enslaved person, he was not a citizen. Also, the Court clearly stated that slaves were property.

The Court's ruling did not stop there. Instead, the Justices went on to make a sweeping decision about the larger issue of slavery in the territories. According to the Court, Congress did not have the power to outlaw slavery in any territory. The Court's ruling meant that the Missouri Compromise was unconstitutional.

The nation reacts

White southerners rejoiced at the **Dred Scott decision.** It meant that slavery was legal in all the territories. This was just what white southerners had been demanding for years.

African Americans responded angrily to the Dred Scott decision. In the North, many held public meetings to condemn the ruling. At a meeting in Philadelphia, a speaker hoped that the Dred Scott decision would lead more whites to "join with us in our efforts to recover the long lost boon of freedom."

White northerners were also shocked by the ruling. Many had hoped that slavery would eventually die out if it were restricted to the South. Now, however, slavery could spread throughout the West. Even northerners who disliked abolitionists felt that the Dred Scott ruling was wrong. A newspaper in Cincinnati declared, "We are now one great . . . slaveholding community." In New England, another newspaper asked, "Where will it all end?"

★ Section 2 Review ★

Recall

1. **Locate** **(a)** Kansas Territory, **(b)** Nebraska Territory.
2. **Define** **(a)** repeal, **(b)** guerrilla warfare, **(c)** lawsuit.
3. **Identify** **(a)** Harriet Beecher Stowe, **(b)** *Uncle Tom's Cabin,* **(c)** Kansas-Nebraska Act, **(d)** Franklin Pierce, **(e)** Border Ruffians, **(f)** John Brown, **(g)** Bleeding Kansas, **(h)** Charles Sumner, **(i)** Dred Scott decision.

Comprehension

4. **(a)** How did *Uncle Tom's Cabin* portray slavery? **(b)** How did the book affect people's attitudes toward slavery?
5. How did the Kansas-Nebraska Act lead to violence in Kansas?
6. Explain how each of the following reacted to the Dred Scott decision: **(a)** white southerners, **(b)** African Americans, **(c)** white northerners.

Critical Thinking and Writing

7. **Analyzing Primary Sources** After the Kansas-Nebraska Act was passed, Stephen Douglas stated, "The struggle for freedom was forever banished from the halls of Congress to the western plains." **(a)** What did Douglas mean? **(b)** Do you agree or disagree with his statement? Explain.
8. **Comparing** Compare Harriet Beecher Stowe's and John Brown's contributions to the abolitionist movement.

Activity **Writing a Protest Letter** You are outraged by the Dred Scott decision! Write a protest letter to the justices of the Supreme Court explaining why you think their decision in this case was wrong.

3 A New Party Challenges Slavery

As You Read

Explore These Questions

- Why did the Republican party come into being in the mid-1850s?
- What were Abraham Lincoln's views on slavery?
- How did northerners and southerners respond differently to the raid on Harpers Ferry?

Define

- arsenal
- martyr

Identify

- Republican party
- John C. Frémont
- James Buchanan
- Abraham Lincoln

SETTING the Scene In the mid-1850s, people who opposed slavery in the territories needed a new political voice. Neither Whigs nor Democrats would take a strong stand against slavery. "We have submitted to slavery long enough," an Ohio Democrat declared.

Free Soilers, northern Democrats, and antislavery Whigs met in towns and cities across the North. In 1854, a group gathered in Michigan to form the **Republican party.** The new party grew quickly. By 1856, it was ready to challenge the older parties for power.

The Republican Party

In the 1850s, the main goal of the Republican party was to keep slavery out of the western territories. A few Republicans were abolitionists. They hoped to end slavery in the South as well. Most Republicans, however, wanted only to stop the spread of slavery.

In 1856, Republicans selected **John C. Frémont** to run for President. Frémont was a frontiersman who had fought for California's independence. (See page 290.) He had little political experience, but he opposed the spread of slavery.

John C. Frémont

Frémont's main opponent was Democrat **James Buchanan** of Pennsylvania. He had served as a senator and as Secretary of State. Many Democrats considered Buchanan to be a "compromise" candidate because he was a "northern man with southern principles." They hoped that he would attract voters in both the North and the South.

Buchanan won the election with support from a large majority of southerners and many northerners. Still, the Republicans made a strong showing in the election. Without the support of a single southern state, Frémont won one third of the popular vote. Southerners worried that their influence in the national government was fading.

Abe Lincoln of Illinois

The next test for the Republican party came in 1858 in the state of Illinois. **Abraham Lincoln,** a Republican, challenged Democrat Stephen Douglas for his seat in the Senate. The election captured the attention of the whole nation. The race was important because most Americans thought that Douglas would run for President in 1860.

Viewing HISTORY **The Lincoln-Douglas Debates**

In this painting, Stephen Douglas sits to Lincoln's right during a debate held at Charleston, Illinois, in September 1858. Thousands of people attended the Lincoln-Douglas debates. ★ **What was the most important issue discussed in the debates?**

A self-starter from Kentucky

Abraham Lincoln was born in the backcountry of Kentucky. Like many frontier people, his parents moved often to find better land. The family lived in Indiana and later in Illinois. As a child, Lincoln spent only a year in school. Still, he taught himself to read and spent many hours reading by firelight.

After Lincoln left home, he opened a store in Illinois. There, he studied law on his own and launched a career in politics. After spending eight years in the state legislature, Lincoln served one term in Congress. Bitterly opposed to the Kansas-Nebraska Act, he decided to run for the Senate in 1858.

"Just folks"

When the race began, Lincoln was not a national figure. Still, people in Illinois knew him well and liked him. To them, he was "just folks"—someone who enjoyed picnics, wrestling contests, and all their other favorite pastimes.

People also admired his honesty and wit. His plainspoken manner made him a good speaker. Even so, a listener once complained that he could not understand one of Lincoln's speeches. "There are always some fleas a dog can't reach" was Lincoln's reply.

Lincoln-Douglas Debates

During the Senate campaign, Lincoln challenged Douglas to a series of debates. Douglas was not eager to accept, but he did. During the campaign, the two debated seven times. Slavery was the important issue.

Views on slavery

Douglas wanted to settle the slavery question by popular sovereignty. He disliked slavery, but he thought that people in the territories should be able to vote "down or up" for it.

Lincoln, like nearly all whites of his day, did not believe in "perfect equality" between blacks and whites. He did, however, believe that slavery was a "moral, social, and political wrong." He believed that blacks were entitled to the rights named in the Declaration of Independence—"life, liberty, and the pursuit of happiness."

Since slavery was wrong, said Lincoln, Douglas and other Americans should not treat it as an unimportant question to be voted "down or up." Lincoln was totally opposed to slavery in the territories. Still, he was not an abolitionist. He had no wish to interfere with slavery in the states where it already existed.

Lincoln believed that the nation could not survive if it remained divided by slavery. On June 16, 1858, Lincoln spoke in a crowded hall in Springfield, Illinois:

> "A house divided against itself cannot stand. I believe this government cannot endure permanently half slave and half free. I do not expect the Union to be dissolved—I do not expect the house to fall—but I do expect it will cease to be divided. It will become all one thing, or all the other."

Why Study History?

Because Heroes of the Past Can Be Models for Today

Historical Background

Many consider Abraham Lincoln one of the truly heroic figures in American history. Through education and hard work, "Honest Abe" rose from humble beginnings to national leadership. As President, he would lead the nation through the horrors of a civil war and help bring an end to slavery.

Lincoln Memorial

Connections to Today

Today, we still honor Lincoln. Each year, we remember him on Presidents' Day. His image is on the money we use every day. In addition, thousands of people show their respect by visiting the Lincoln Memorial in Washington, D.C.

Admirers of Lincoln consider him a model for others to imitate. They point to his easygoing manner, keen wit, high sense of morality, and ability to make wise decisions in tough situations.

Connections to You

Do you think Lincoln is an American hero? Should you look to him as a role model? To help you decide, read the following excerpts from Lincoln's conversations, speeches, and writings.

"I have no other [ambition] so great as that of being truly esteemed of my fellow men, by rendering myself worthy of their esteem."—June 13, 1836

"The better part of one's life consists in his friendships."—May 19, 1849

"Let us have faith that Right makes Might, and in that faith, let us to the end, dare to do our duty."—February 27, 1860

"I want every man to have a chance—and I believe a black man is entitled to it—in which he can better his condition."—March 6, 1860

"The people's will, constitutionally expressed, is the ultimate law for all."—October 19, 1864

"Whenever I hear anyone arguing for slavery, I feel a strong impulse to see it tried on him personally."—March 17, 1865

1. Comprehension How do Americans show their respect for Abraham Lincoln today?

2. Critical Thinking **(a)** Which quotation deals most directly with the idea of racial equality? **(b)** What was Lincoln's position on equality?

Writing an Essay Do you consider Lincoln an American hero and role model? Develop your answer in a brief essay, using the quotations above to describe some of Lincoln's ideas and values.

A leader emerges

Week after week, both men spoke nearly every day to large crowds. Newspapers reprinted their campaign speeches. The more northerners read Lincoln's speeches, the more they thought about the injustice of slavery.

In the end, Douglas won the election by a slim margin. However, Lincoln was a winner, too. He was now known throughout the country. Two years later, the two rivals would again meet face to face—both seeking the office of President.

John Brown's Raid

In the meantime, more bloodshed pushed the North and South farther apart. In 1859, John Brown carried his antislavery campaign from Kansas to the East. He led a group of followers, including five African Americans, to Harpers Ferry, Virginia.

There, Brown planned to raid a federal **arsenal,** or gun warehouse. He thought that enslaved African Americans would flock to him at the arsenal. He would then give them weapons and lead them in a revolt.

Sentenced to death

Brown quickly gained control of the arsenal. No slave uprising took place, however. Instead, troops led by Robert E. Lee killed 10 of the raiders and captured Brown.

Most people, in both the North and the South, thought that Brown's plan to lead a slave revolt was insane. After all, there were not many enslaved African Americans in Harpers Ferry. At his trial, however, Brown seemed perfectly sane. He sat quietly as the court found him guilty of murder and treason and sentenced him to death.

Hero or villain?

Brown became a hero to many northerners. Some considered him a **martyr** because he was willing to give up his life for his beliefs. On the morning he was hanged, church bells rang solemnly throughout the North. In years to come, New Englanders would sing a popular song: "John Brown's body lies a mold'ring in the grave, but his soul is marching on."

To white southerners, the northern response to John Brown's death was outrageous. People were singing the praises of a man who had tried to lead a slave revolt! Many southerners became convinced that the North wanted to destroy slavery—and the South along with it. The nation was poised for a violent clash.

★ Section 3 Review ★

Recall

1. **Identify** **(a)** Republican party, **(b)** John C. Frémont, **(c)** James Buchanan, **(d)** Abraham Lincoln.
2. **Define** **(a)** arsenal, **(b)** martyr.

Comprehension

3. What was the main goal of the Republican party?
4. How did Abraham Lincoln's opinions on slavery differ from those of Stephen Douglas?
5. **(a)** How did Northerners respond to John Brown's execution? **(b)** How did Southerners respond?

Critical Thinking and Writing

6. **Identifying Main Ideas** Reread the subsection on page 364 called "Just folks." State the main idea of this subsection.
7. **Analyzing Ideas** Lincoln said the nation could not "endure permanently half slave and half free." Do you agree that slavery was too great an issue to allow differences among the states? Explain.

Activity **Writing Headlines** You are a journalist in the 1850s. Choose three events discussed in Section 3. Write two headlines for each event—one for a northern newspaper, the other for a southern newspaper.

The Nation Splits in Two

As You Read

Explore These Questions

- Why was Abraham Lincoln able to win the election of 1860?
- How did the South react to Lincoln's election victory?
- What events led to the outbreak of the Civil War?

Identify

- John Breckinridge
- John Bell
- John Crittenden
- Confederate States of America
- Jefferson Davis
- Fort Sumter

SETTING the Scene In May 1860, thousands of people swarmed into Chicago for the Republican national convention. They filled the city's 42 hotels. When beds ran out, they slept on billiard tables. All were there to find out one thing. Who would win the Republican nomination for President—William Seward of New York or Abraham Lincoln of Illinois?

On the third day of the convention, a delegate rushed to the roof of the hall. There, a man stood waiting next to a cannon. "Fire the salute," ordered the delegate. "Old Abe is nominated!"

As the cannon fired, crowds surrounding the hall burst into cheers. Amid the celebration, a delegate from Kentucky struck a somber note. "Gentlemen, we are on the brink of a great civil war."

The Election of 1860

The Democrats held their convention in Charleston, South Carolina. Southerners wanted the party to support slavery in the territories. However, Northern Democrats refused to do so.

In the end, the party split in two. Northern Democrats chose Stephen Douglas to run for President. Southern Democrats picked **John Breckinridge** of Kentucky.

Some Americans tried to heal the split between North and South by forming a new party. The Constitutional Union party chose **John Bell** of Tennessee, a Whig, to run for President. Bell was a moderate who wanted to keep the Union together. He got support only in a few southern states that were still trying to find a compromise.

Republican campaign banner

Senator Douglas was sure that Lincoln would win the election. However, he believed that Democrats "must try to save the Union." He pleaded with southern voters to stay with the Union, no matter who was elected.

When the votes were counted, Lincoln had carried the North and won the election. Southern votes did not affect the outcome at all. Lincoln's name was not even on the ballot in 10 southern states. Northerners outnumbered southerners and outvoted them.

The Union Is Broken

Lincoln's election brought a strong reaction in the South. A South Carolina woman described how the news was received:

> ❝ The excitement was very great. Everybody was talking at the same time. One... more moved than the others, stood up saying... 'The die is cast—No more vain regrets—Sad forebodings are useless. The stake is life or death—'... No doubt of it. ❞

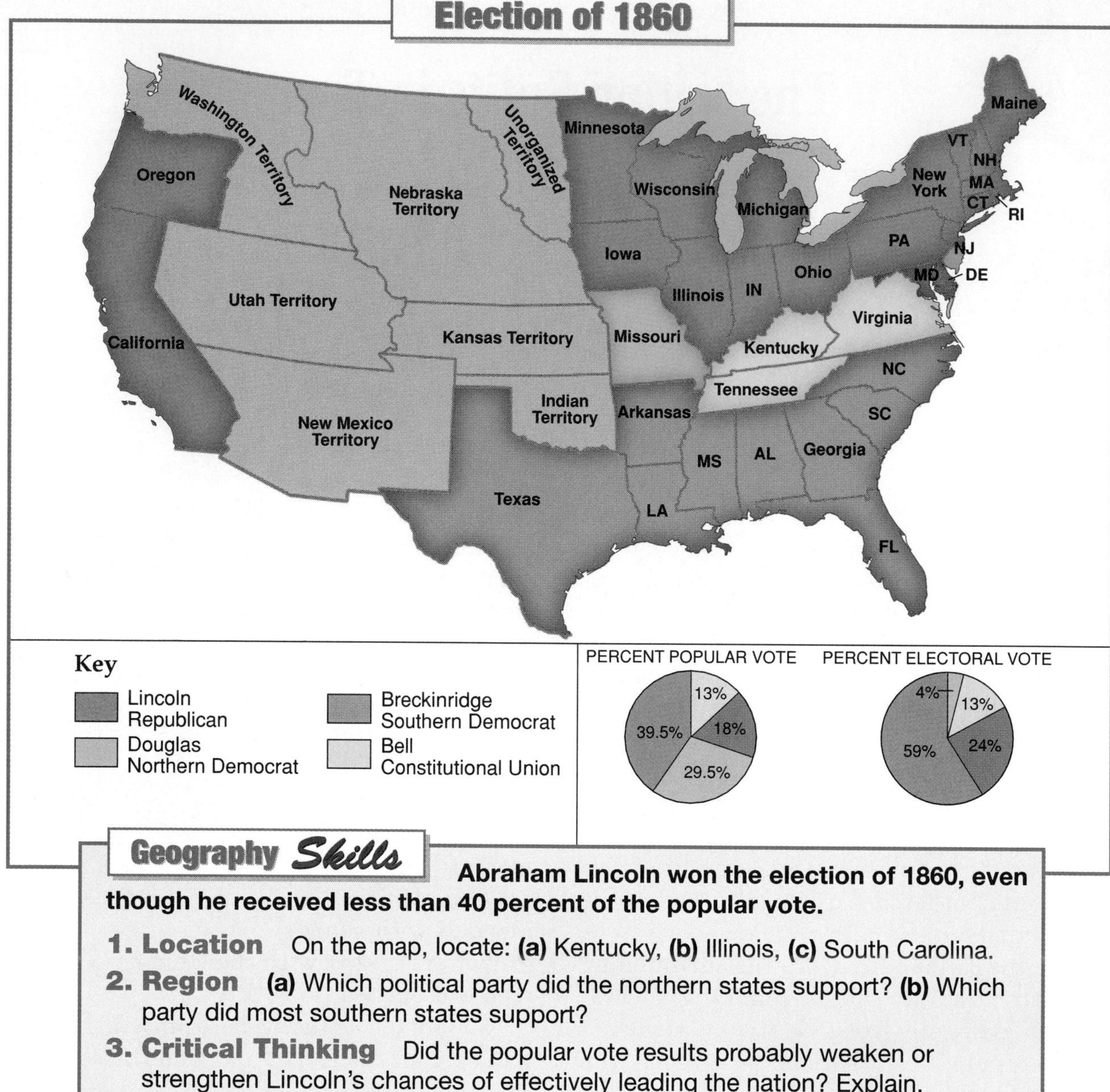

Geography *Skills* **Abraham Lincoln won the election of 1860, even though he received less than 40 percent of the popular vote.**

1. **Location** On the map, locate: **(a)** Kentucky, **(b)** Illinois, **(c)** South Carolina.
2. **Region** **(a)** Which political party did the northern states support? **(b)** Which party did most southern states support?
3. **Critical Thinking** Did the popular vote results probably weaken or strengthen Lincoln's chances of effectively leading the nation? Explain.

To many southerners, Lincoln's election meant that the South no longer had a voice in national government. They believed that the President and Congress were now set against their interests—especially slavery. Even before the election, South Carolina's governor had written to other southern governors. If Lincoln won, he wrote, it would be their duty to leave the Union.

Secession

Senator **John Crittenden** of Kentucky made a last effort to save the Union. In December 1860, he introduced a bill to extend the Missouri Compromise line to the Pacific. He also suggested adding an "unamendable" amendment to the Constitution to forever guarantee the right to hold slaves in states south of the compromise line.

The compromise bill received little support. Slavery in the West was no longer the issue. Many southerners believed that the North had put an abolitionist in the White House. They felt that secession was their only choice. Most Republicans also refused to compromise. They were unwilling to surrender what they had won in the national election.

Skills FOR LIFE

Critical Thinking | Managing Information | Communication | Maps, Charts, and Graphs

Comparing Points of View

How Will I Use This Skill?

When two or more people describe the same event, their descriptions of the event often differ. That is because each person's point of view is subjective, or influenced by personal experiences and feelings. By comparing different sources, you can learn objective information, or facts, as well as subjective points of view regarding those facts.

Bullying the Free States

November 19, 1860
The New York Tribune

Abraham Lincoln has been designated for next President of this Republic by the popular vote of nearly every Free State, and the ruling politicians of the Slave States are not pleased with the selection. We can fancy their feelings, as we felt much the same when they put a most undesired President upon us four years ago. Moreover, we...advise them to do as we did—Bear it with fortitude, and hope to do better next time.

Devotion to the Union Is Treason to the South

November 19, 1860
Oxford Mississippi Mercury

We have at last reached that point in our history when it is necessary for the South to withdraw from the Union....

[A] powerful sectional majority are now about to seize upon the Government...to destroy the institution of Slavery....We cannot stand still and quietly see the Government pass into the hands of such an infamous crew.

South Carolina,...Georgia, Mississippi, Alabama, Louisiana, Texas, and Arkansas, will soon be united as brothers to defend each other from the inroads of the fanatics of the North.

LEARN the Skill

You can compare points of view by following the steps below.

1. Identify the author of each source. Consider how each report might be affected by the author's point of view.
2. Find objective information common to two or more sources.
3. Identify subjective statements that reflect the author's point of view.
4. Draw conclusions about the historical event and different points of view on it.

PRACTICE the Skill

The newspaper articles above give different viewpoints on Abraham Lincoln's victory in the election of 1860. Compare the two viewpoints by answering the following questions.

1. (a) Which source is a southern newspaper? (b) Which source is a northern newspaper? (c) Why would you expect the two to have different opinions about Lincoln?
2. What factual information do you find in both articles?
3. How do the two articles describe the election result differently?
4. (a) Why did the election cause conflict between North and South? (b) What did the *Tribune* think the South should do? (c) What did the *Mercury* recommend?

APPLY the Skill

In two or more newspapers or news magazines, find different points of view on some issue or event. Use the steps you have learned to compare the various viewpoints.

AmericanHeritage
M A G A Z I N E

HISTORY HAPPENED HERE

Fort Sumter

The Civil War began in 1861 when Confederate forces bombarded and captured Fort Sumter in Charleston Harbor, South Carolina. Later in the war, Union gunships reduced Sumter to rubble. The fort was rebuilt, and it remained part of the seacoast defenses until 1947. Today, Fort Sumter is a national monument. Tour boats to the fort leave regularly from downtown Charleston.

★ ***To learn more about this historic site, write:*** *Fort Sumter National Monument, Sullivan's Island, SC 29482.*

◄ *Union flag from Fort Sumter*

The first state to secede was South Carolina. On December 20, 1860, delegates to a convention in Charleston voted for secession. "The state of South Carolina has resumed her position among the nations of the world," the delegates proudly declared. By February 1, 1861, Alabama, Florida, Georgia, Louisiana, Mississippi, and Texas had seceded.

The Confederacy

The seven states that had seceded held a convention in Montgomery, Alabama. There, the southern states formed a new nation, the **Confederate States of America.** To lead the new country, they named **Jefferson Davis** of Mississippi as the first president of the Confederacy.

Most southerners believed that they had every right to secede. After all, the Declaration of Independence said that "it is the right of the people to alter or to abolish" a government that denies the rights of its citizens. Lincoln, they believed, would deny white southerners their right to own slaves.

Lincoln Speaks to the Nation

When Abraham Lincoln took office on March 4, 1861, he faced a national crisis. Crowds gathered in Washington, D.C., to hear him take the presidential oath of office. In his Inaugural Address, the new President assured Americans of both the North and the South that he had two goals. He hoped to maintain the Union and avoid war.

On the first goal, preserving the Union, Lincoln would not compromise. Secession of states from the Union, he said, was unconstitutional. Lincoln believed that his duty as

Connections With Civics

Texas voters chose secession, but Governor Sam Houston refused to swear allegiance to the new Confederacy. He was replaced by a new governor. Houston sadly warned his fellow Texans that the North would "move with the steady momentum and perseverance of a mighty avalanche; and...overwhelm the South."

President was clear. He would take strong action to preserve national union.

> "In view of the Constitution and the law, the Union is unbroken;... I will take care... that the laws of the Union be faithfully executed in all the States."

At the same time, however, Lincoln tried to reassure the South. He promised that there would not be war with the South unless southern states started it:

> "We are not enemies, but friends. We must not be enemies. Though passion may have strained, it must not break our bonds of affection."

Civil War

The Confederacy, however, had already started seizing federal forts in the South. It felt that the forts were a threat because the United States was now a "foreign power."

Lincoln's difficult decision

President Lincoln faced a difficult decision. Should he let the Confederates take over federal property? If he did, he would seem to be admitting that states had the right to leave the Union. On the other hand, if he sent troops to hold the forts, he might start a civil war. He might also lose the support of the eight slave states that had not seceded from the Union.

In April, the Confederacy forced Lincoln to make up his mind. By then, Confederate troops controlled nearly all forts, post offices, and other federal buildings in the South. The Union held only three forts off the Florida coast and Fort Sumter in South Carolina. **Fort Sumter** was important to the Confederacy because it guarded Charleston Harbor.

Bombardment of Fort Sumter

President Lincoln learned that food supplies at Fort Sumter were running low. He notified the governor of South Carolina that he was going to ship food to the fort. Lincoln promised not to send troops or weapons.

The Confederates could not leave the fort in Union hands, however. On April 12, 1861, they asked for Fort Sumter's surrender.

Major Robert Anderson, the Union commander, refused to give in. Confederate guns then opened fire. Anderson and his troops quickly ran out of ammunition. On April 13, Anderson surrendered the fort.

When Confederate troops shelled Fort Sumter, people in Charleston had gathered on their rooftops to watch. To many, it was like a fireworks display. No one knew that the fireworks marked the beginning of a civil war that would last four terrible years.

★ Section 4 Review ★

Recall

1. **Identify** **(a)** John Breckinridge, **(b)** John Bell, **(c)** John Crittenden, **(d)** Confederate States of America, **(e)** Jefferson Davis, **(f)** Fort Sumter.

Comprehension

2. Why were there two Democratic candidates for President in 1860?
3. Why did many southerners feel that secession was necessary after Lincoln won the Presidency in 1860?
4. How did the Civil War begin at Fort Sumter in 1861?

Critical Thinking and Writing

5. **Making Inferences** How do you think the split in the Democratic party helped Lincoln win the election of 1860?
6. **Solving Problems** Write a compromise plan that tries to save the Union in 1861. Your plan should offer advantages to both the North and the South.

Activity **Writing Slogans** You are a famous political campaign manager of the mid-1800s. Write a campaign slogan for each of the four candidates in the presidential election of 1860.

Chapter 14 Review and Activities

★ Sum It Up ★

Section 1 The Slavery Issue in the West

- Americans disagreed on whether slavery should be allowed in the western territories.
- The new Free Soil party wanted to limit the spread of slavery.
- The Compromise of 1850 settled the issue for a time, but the new Fugitive Slave Law angered many.

Section 2 The Crisis Turns Violent

- The novel *Uncle Tom's Cabin* turned many northerners against slavery.
- After the Kansas-Nebraska Act of 1854, proslavery and antislavery settlers battled for control of Kansas.
- In the Dred Scott case, the Supreme Court ruled that Congress could not outlaw slavery in any territory.

Section 3 A New Party Challenges Slavery

- The Republican party wanted to keep slavery out of the western territories.
- Abraham Lincoln emerged as a leader of the Republican party.
- John Brown's raid on Harpers Ferry brought the nation to the brink of war.

Section 4 The Nation Splits in Two

- Abraham Lincoln won the presidential election of 1860.
- Southern states seceded from the Union and formed a new nation.
- A civil war broke out between the North and the South.

For additional review of the major ideas of Chapter 14, see ***Guide to the Essentials of American History*** or ***Interactive Student Tutorial CD-ROM,*** which contains interactive review activities, graphic organizers, and practice tests.

Reviewing the Chapter

Define These Terms

Match each term with the correct definition.

Column 1

1. sectionalism
2. fugitive
3. civil war
4. arsenal
5. Wilmot Proviso

Column 2

a. a law to ban slavery in any lands won from Mexico
b. a runaway
c. a gun warehouse
d. a war between people of the same country
e. loyalty to a part of a nation rather than the whole

Explore the Main Ideas

1. What were the four parts of the Compromise of 1850?
2. Why was Kansas referred to as Bleeding Kansas in the 1850s?
3. What effect did the Dred Scott decision have on the Missouri Compromise?
4. What groups combined to form the new Republican party?
5. Why did South Carolina secede from the Union in 1860?

Geography Activity

Match the letters on the map with the following places: **1.** Missouri, **2.** Maine, **3.** California, **4.** Kansas Territory, **5.** Nebraska Territory, **6.** New Mexico Territory, **7.** Utah Territory. **Region** Which area listed above was admitted to the Union as a free state in 1850?

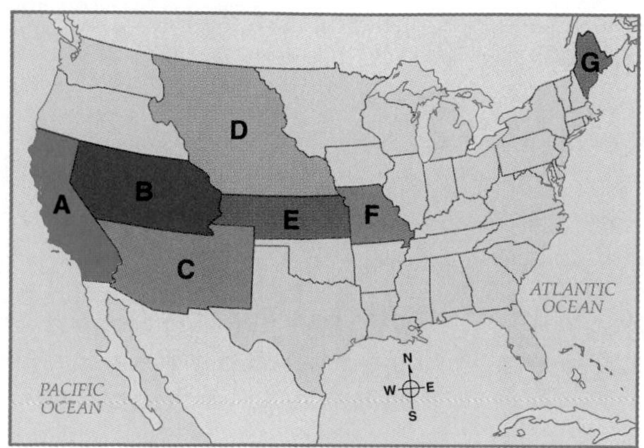

Critical Thinking and Writing

1. **Understanding Chronology** Place the following events in chronological order: **(a)** Kansas-Nebraska Act, **(b)** Compromise of 1850, **(c)** Lincoln becomes President, **(d)** Dred Scott decision.
2. **Understanding Cause and Effect** **(a)** What caused the Democratic party to split in 1860? **(b)** How did the split affect the election of 1860?
3. **Identifying Alternatives** Describe one alternative to secession that the slave states could have chosen.
4. **Exploring Unit Themes** **Sectionalism** The 1860 Republican convention was held in Illinois, then considered a western state. How did this help bring victory for Lincoln in the national election?

Using Primary Sources

In 1860, Abraham Lincoln was elected to succeed James Buchanan as President. As his term of office came to an end, President Buchanan offered his thoughts on the possibility of secession and civil war:

> “Our Union rests upon public opinion, and can never be cemented by the blood of its citizens shed in civil war. If it cannot live in the affections of the people, it must one day perish. Congress may possess many means of preserving it by [compromise], but the sword was not placed in their hand to preserve it by force.”

Source: *The Rise and Fall of the Confederate Government* by Jefferson Davis, 1881.

Recognizing Points of View **(a)** Was Buchanan in favor of a war to prevent southern states from leaving the Union? Explain. **(b)** Do you agree or disagree with Buchanan? Defend your position.

Activity Bank

Interdisciplinary Activity

Exploring the Arts In a painting, drawing, collage, sculpture, or other form of art, express the reaction of the North or the South to one event described in this chapter. Display your work to the class. Ask other students to identify the event and point of view that your art work reflects.

Career Skills Activity

Lawyer Choose the role of prosecutor or defense lawyer at the trial of John Brown. Depending on the role you have chosen, write a speech declaring Brown to be either guilty or not guilty. Present your speech to the class and ask them to reach a verdict.

Citizenship Activity

Reaching a Compromise Find an issue in your community that is the subject of heated debate between two groups. Then brainstorm solutions to the problem that will offer something to both sides. Type up your suggestions and offer them to a neutral party who might be able to mediate between the two groups.

Internet Activity

Use the Internet to find sites dealing with Abraham Lincoln. Use your research to write a biography or a character sketch. Use as many quotations as possible. Make a bibliography by writing down the title, author, and address of each Web site that you use.

Eyewitness Journal

You are an African American or white American living in the North or the South between 1820 and 1861. In your EYEWITNESS JOURNAL, describe your reaction to the important events of these years: 1820, 1850, 1859, 1860, 1861.

Chapter 15 The Civil War

1861–1865

What's Ahead

For more than four years, Americans fought Americans in the Civil War. The South wanted to exist as an independent nation. The North wanted to force the South back into the Union. The war was also linked closely to the question of slavery. President Lincoln made this clear when he issued the Emancipation Proclamation.

Throughout the North and the South, both soldiers and civilians experienced much suffering. The Union's armies struggled in the early years of the war. However, the North's superior resources wore heavily on the South. By the end of 1863, the South was in retreat. In 1865, the South surrendered and the Civil War came to an end.

Why Study *History?* During the Civil War, millions of northerners and southerners served their nation well. Their efforts, as both soldiers and civilians, affected the course of the war. To see an example of how one person can affect the course of history, see this chapter's *Why Study History?* feature, "One Person Can Make a Difference." The feature focuses on the achievements of Clara Barton.

American Events

- **1861** Civil War begins with attack on Fort Sumter
- **1862** Union gunboats capture New Orleans and Memphis
- **1863** Abraham Lincoln issues Emancipation Proclamation

1861 **1862** **1863**

World Events

1861 World Event Russian czar frees serfs

1862 World Event Britain refuses to recognize the Confederacy

Viewing HISTORY **The Soldiers of the Civil War**

In A Rainy Day in Camp *by Winslow Homer, Civil War soldiers find time to gather around a campfire. It is estimated that more than 2,500,000 men served as soldiers in the Civil War. Over 600,000 of them died—more than in any other American war.* ★ **What emotions do you think soldiers felt on the eve of a battle? Explain.**

1863
Battle of Gettysburg ends Confederate drive into the North

1864
General Grant becomes commander of Union army

1865
General Lee surrenders at Appomattox Courthouse

1863 **1864** **1865**

1864 World Event
First Red Cross societies established in Europe

The Conflict Takes Shape

As You Read

Explore These Questions

- What strengths and weaknesses did the Confederacy have?
- What strengths and weaknesses did the Union have?
- What special qualities did Presidents Abraham Lincoln and Jefferson Davis possess?

Define

- racism
- martial law

Identify

- border states
- Robert E. Lee

Confederate canteen

SETTING the Scene In April 1861, President Abraham Lincoln called for 75,000 volunteers to serve as soldiers for 90 days in a campaign against the South. The response was overwhelming. Throughout the North, crowds cheered the Stars and Stripes and booed the southern "traitors."

Southerners were just as enthusiastic for the war. They rallied to the Stars and Bars, as they called the new Confederate flag. Volunteers flooded into the Confederate army.

With flags held high, both northerners and southerners marched off to war. Most felt certain that a single, gallant battle would bring a quick end to the conflict. Few suspected that the Civil War would last four terrible years and be the most destructive war in the nation's history.

A Nation Divided

As the war began, each side was convinced that its cause was just. Southerners believed that they had the right to leave the Union. In fact, they called the conflict the War for Southern Independence. Southerners wanted independence so that they could keep their traditional way of life—including the institution of slavery.

Northerners, meanwhile, believed that they had to fight to save the Union. At the outset of the war, abolishing slavery was not an official goal of the North. In fact, many northerners, guided by feelings of racism, approved of slavery. **Racism** is the belief that one race is superior to another.

In April 1861, eight slave states were still in the Union. They had to make the difficult decision of which side to join. Virginia,* North Carolina, Tennessee, and Arkansas joined the Confederacy. The four **border states** of Delaware, Kentucky, Missouri, and Maryland remained in the Union. (See the map on page 377.)

Still, some citizens of the border states supported the South. For example, in April 1861, pro-Confederate mobs attacked Union troops in Baltimore, Maryland. In response, President Lincoln declared **martial law,** or rule by the army instead of the elected government. Many people who sided with the South were arrested.

Strengths and Weaknesses

Both sides in the conflict had strengths and weaknesses as the war began. The South had the strong advantage of fighting a defensive war. It was up to the North to go on the offensive, to attack and defeat the South. If the North did not move its forces into the South, the Confederacy would remain a separate country.

*Many people in western Virginia supported the Union. When Virginia seceded, westerners formed their own government. West Virginia became a state of the Union in 1863.

The South

Southerners believed that they were fighting a war for independence, similar to the American Revolution. Defending their homeland and their way of life gave them a strong reason to fight bravely. "Our men must prevail in combat," one Confederate said, "or they will lose their property, country, freedom—in short, everything."

Also, many southerners had skills that made them good soldiers. Hunting was an important part of southern life. From an early age, boys learned to ride horses and use guns. Wealthy young men often went to military school. Before the Civil War, many of the best officers in the United States Army were from the South.

The South, however, had serious economic weaknesses. (See the chart on page 378.) It had few factories to produce weapons and other vital supplies. It also had few railroads to move troops and supplies. The railroads that it did have often did not connect to one another. The South also had political problems. The Confederate constitution favored states' rights and limited the authority

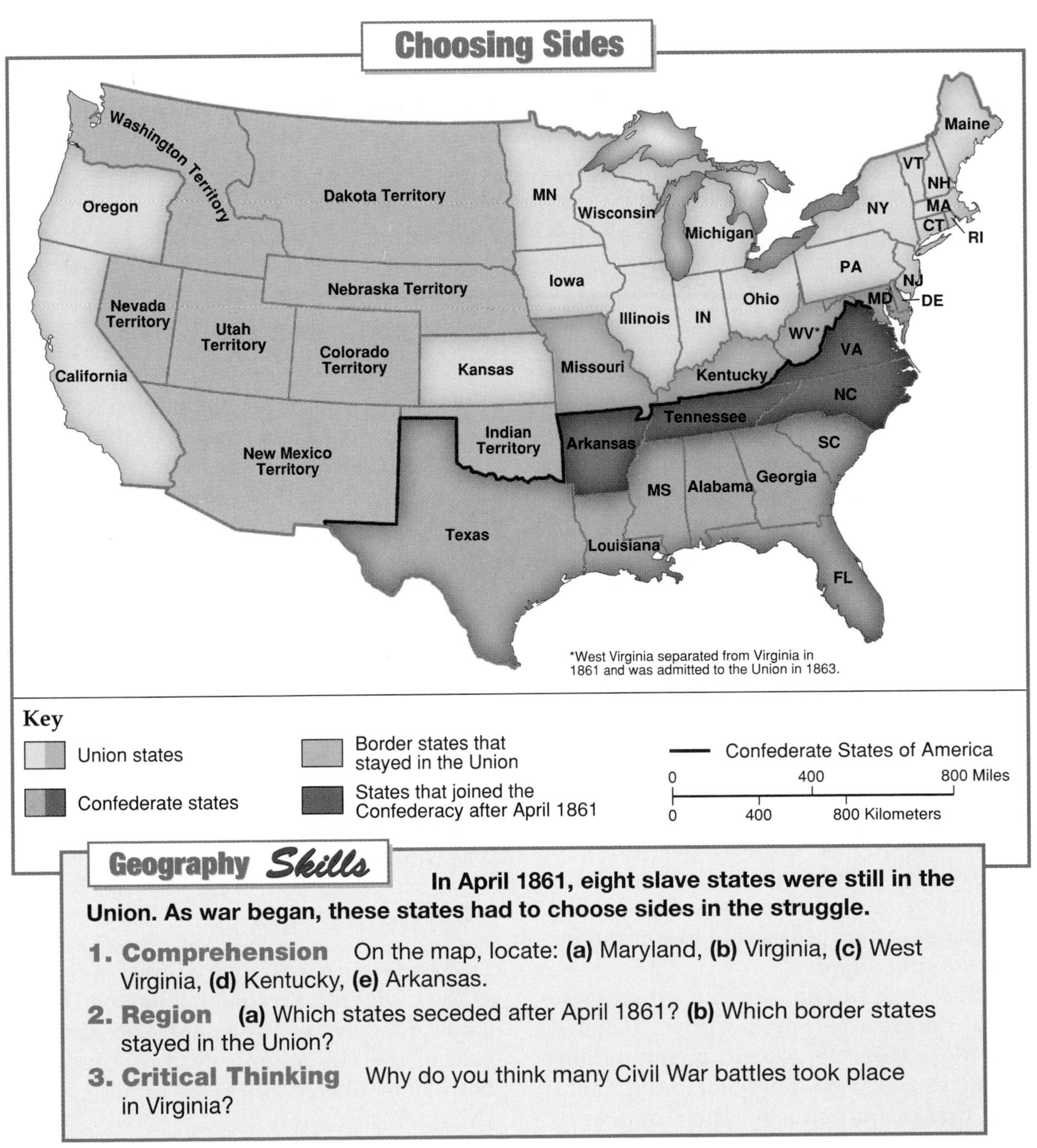

Geography Skills **In April 1861, eight slave states were still in the Union. As war began, these states had to choose sides in the struggle.**

1. **Comprehension** On the map, locate: **(a)** Maryland, **(b)** Virginia, **(c)** West Virginia, **(d)** Kentucky, **(e)** Arkansas.
2. **Region** **(a)** Which states seceded after April 1861? **(b)** Which border states stayed in the Union?
3. **Critical Thinking** Why do you think many Civil War battles took place in Virginia?

Resources of the North and South, 1861

Resources	North		South	
	Number	Percent of Total	Number	Percent of Total
Farmland	105,835 acres	65%	56,832 acres	35%
Railroad Track	21,847 miles	71%	8,947 miles	29%
Value of Manufactured Goods	$1,794,417,000	92%	$155,552,000	8%
Factories	119,500	85%	20,600	15%
Workers in Industry	1,198,000	92%	111,000	8%
Population	22,340,000	63%	9,103,000 (3,954,000 slaves)	37%

Source: *Historical Statistics of the United States*

Chart Skills **As the Civil War began, the North enjoyed a number of economic advantages over the South. These advantages affected the war's outcome.**

1. **Comprehension** **(a)** How many acres of farmland did each side have? **(b)** What percentage of the nation's factories did the South have?
2. **Critical Thinking** **(a)** Which side had more railroad track? **(b)** How do you think this advantage affected the war?

Economics $

of the central government. As a result, it was often difficult for the Confederate government to get things done. On one occasion, for example, the governor of Georgia insisted that only Georgia officers be in command of Georgia troops.

Finally, the South had a small population. Only about 9 million people lived in the Confederacy, compared with 22 million in the Union. More than one third of the southern population were enslaved African Americans. As a result, the South did not have enough people to serve as soldiers and to support the war effort.

The North

The North had almost four times as many free citizens as the South. Thus, it had a large source of volunteers. It also had many people to grow food and to work in factories making supplies.

Industry was the North's greatest resource. Before the war, northern factories made more than 90 percent of the nation's manufactured goods. These factories quickly began making supplies for the Union army. The North also had more than 70 percent of the nation's rail lines, which it used to transport both troops and supplies.

The North also benefited from a strong navy and a large fleet of trading ships. With few warships and only a small merchant fleet, the South was unable to compete with the North at sea.

Despite these advantages, the North faced a difficult military challenge. To bring the South back into the Union, northern soldiers had to conquer a huge area. Instead of defending their homes, they were invading unfamiliar land. As Union armies invaded the South, their lines of supply would be much longer than those of the Confederates and thus more open to attack.

Wartime Leaders

Leadership was a very important factor in the Civil War. President Jefferson Davis of the Confederacy, President Abraham Lincoln of the Union, and military leaders on both sides played key roles in determining the war's outcome.

Skills FOR LIFE

Critical Thinking | **Managing Information** | Communication | Maps, Charts, and Graphs

Keeping Files

How Will I Use This Skill ?

A file system is a method for organizing and storing information, usually in a cabinet or on a computer disk. By keeping files, you can save and retrieve information quickly and easily. In school, this skill is useful for research projects. At home, a file system can help organize recipes, coupons, or documents and bills. Finally, you will probably use a file system in your future job or career.

Recipe file

LEARN the Skill

❶ Set up and name various file sections. For example, a recipe file would need separate sections for appetizers, entrees, and desserts.

❷ Create and label file folders for each section of the file. For example, a dessert section of a recipe file might need one folder for pies and another for cakes.

❸ Create or collect the information or material that will be filed.

❹ File the informtion or material in the appropriate folders.

PRACTICE the Skill

Read the subsection titled "Strengths and Weaknesses" on pages 376–378. Use the following steps to file information on the North and South.

❶ Create a file system with two sections. Label one section "The South." What should you label the other section?

❷ For each of the two sections, create a file folder labeled "Economy." Create and name two other file folders for each section. (You will have a total of six folders.)

❸ For each of the two sections, record two or three facts to go into the "Economy" file folders. Write each fact on a separate sheet of paper. Place each sheet of paper in the appropriate folder.

❹ In the same way, record and file other facts about the North and South.

APPLY the Skill

Create a file system for discount grocery coupons. You might start by making a section for dairy products that includes a folder for yogurt, another for cheese, and a third for butter. Offer your completed file system to someone who uses discount coupons.

President Jefferson Davis

Many people thought Davis was a stronger leader than Lincoln. Davis had attended the United States Military Academy at West Point. He had served as an officer in the Mexican War. Later, he served as Secretary of War. He was widely respected for his honesty and courage.

Davis, however, did not like to turn over to others the details of military planning. When he made a decision, according to his wife, he "could not understand any other man coming to a different conclusion." As a result, Davis spent much time arguing with his advisers.

President Abraham Lincoln

At first, some northerners had doubts about Abraham Lincoln's ability to lead. He had little experience in national politics or military matters. In time, however, Lincoln proved to be a patient but strong leader and a fine war planner.

Day by day, Lincoln gained the respect of those around him. Many especially liked his sense of humor. They noted that Lincoln even accepted criticism with a smile. When Secretary of War Edwin Stanton called Lincoln a fool, Lincoln commented, "Did Stanton say I was a fool? Then I must be one, for Stanton is generally right and he always says what he means."

Military leaders

As the war began, army officers in the South had to make a choice. They could stay in the Union army and fight against their home states, or they could join the Confederate forces.

Robert E. Lee faced this dilemma when his home state of Virginia seceded. President Lincoln asked Lee to command the Union army. Lee refused. He explained in a letter to a friend:

> "I cannot raise my hand against my birthplace, my home, my children. I should like, above all things, that our difficulties might be peaceably arranged.... What ever may be the result of the contest, I foresee that the country will have to pass through a terrible ordeal."

Later, **Robert E. Lee** became commander of the Confederate army. In fact, many of the best officers served for the Confederacy. As a result, President Lincoln had trouble finding generals to match those of the South.

★ Section 1 Review ★

Recall

1. **Locate** **(a)** West Virginia, **(b)** Delaware, **(c)** Kentucky, **(d)** Missouri, **(e)** Maryland.
2. **Identify** **(a)** border states, **(b)** Robert E. Lee.
3. **Define** **(a)** racism, **(b)** martial law.

Comprehension

4. Describe two advantages that the South had over the North at the start of the Civil War.
5. Describe two advantages that the North had over the South at the start of the Civil War.
6. Explain one strength and one weakness of each of the following leaders: **(a)** President Abraham Lincoln, **(b)** President Jefferson Davis.

Critical Thinking and Writing

7. **Identifying Alternatives** List arguments for and against a border state's staying in the Union in 1861.
8. **Analyzing Ideas** Jefferson Davis said this of the Confederacy: "All we ask is to be left alone." **(a)** What do you think Davis meant? **(b)** Why was the Union unwilling to agree to Davis's wish?

Activity **Making a Decision** You are the captain of your hometown school basketball team. A rival school's coach has offered you a scholarship if you will play for them. Write the coach a letter informing him of your decision and the reasons for your decision. As you write your letter, keep in mind Robert E. Lee's difficult choice at the start of the Civil War.

A Long, Difficult Struggle

As You Read

Explore These Questions

- What were the military plans of each side?
- Which of its military goals did the Union achieve?
- Why did the Union fail to win major battles in the East?

Identify

- Stonewall Jackson
- Battle of Bull Run
- George McClellan
- *Merrimack*
- *Monitor*
- Battle of Antietam
- Battle of Fredericksburg
- Battle of Chancellorsville
- Ulysses S. Grant
- Battle of Shiloh

Union infantry drum

SETTING the Scene In the summer of 1861, the armies of the North and the South marched off to war with flags flying and crowds cheering. Each side expected a quick victory. However, the reality of war soon shattered this dream. Abner Small, a volunteer from Maine, described a scene that would be repeated again and again:

> "I saw... the dead and hurt men lying limp on the ground. From somewhere across the field a battery [heavy guns] pounded us. We wavered, and rallied, and fired blindly; and men fell writhing."

It soon became clear that there would be no quick, easy end to the war. Leaders on both sides began to plan for a long, difficult struggle.

Strategies for Victory

The North and South had different strategies for victory. The Union planned to use its naval power to cripple the South's economy. At the same time, Union armies would invade southern territory. The South, meanwhile, planned to defend itself until the North lost the will to fight.

Union plans

First, the Union planned to use its navy to blockade southern ports. This would cut off the South's supply of manufactured goods by halting its trade with Europe.

In the East, Union generals wanted to seize Richmond, Virginia, the Confederate capital. They thought that they might end the war quickly by capturing the Confederate government.

In the West, the Union planned to seize control of the Mississippi River. This would prevent the South from using the river to supply its troops. It would also separate Arkansas, Texas, and Louisiana from the rest of the Confederacy.

Confederate plans

The South's strategy was simpler: The Confederate army would fight a defensive war until northerners tired of the fighting. If the war became unpopular in the North, President Lincoln would have to stop the war and recognize the South's independence.

The Confederacy counted on European money and supplies to help fight the war. Southern cotton was important to the textile mills of England and other countries. Southerners were confident that Europeans would quickly recognize the Confederacy as an

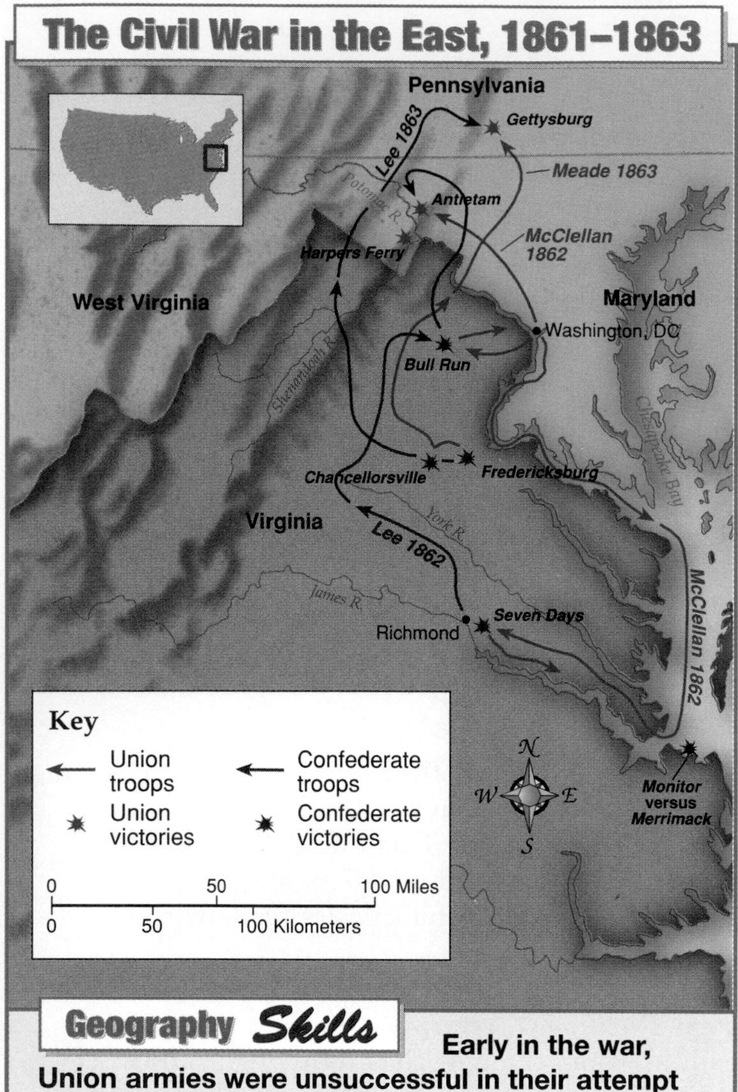

The Civil War in the East, 1861–1863

Geography Skills **Early in the war, Union armies were unsuccessful in their attempt to capture Richmond, the Confederate capital.**

1. **Location** On the map, locate: **(a)** Washington, DC, **(b)** Richmond, **(c)** Bull Run, **(d)** Chancellorsville, **(e)** Potomac River.
2. **Movement** Describe the route that General McClellan took when he tried to capture Richmond in 1862.
3. **Critical Thinking** Do you think the Confederacy made a wise decision in locating its capital at Richmond? Explain.

independent nation and continue to buy southern cotton for their factories.

Forward to Richmond!

"Forward to Richmond! Forward to Richmond!" Every day for more than a month, the influential *New York Tribune* blazed this "Nation's War Cry" across its front page. Responding to popular pressure for a quick victory, President Lincoln ordered the attack.

Battle of Bull Run

In July 1861, Union troops set out from Washington, D.C., for Richmond, about 100 miles (160 km) away. They met with Confederate soldiers soon after they left. The battle that followed took place near a small stream called Bull Run, in Virginia.

July 21, 1861, was a lovely summer day. Hundreds of Washingtonians rode out to watch their army crush the Confederates. Many carried picnic baskets. In a holiday mood, they spread out on a grassy hilltop overlooking Bull Run and awaited the battle.

The spectators, however, were shocked. Southern troops did not turn and run as expected. Inspired by the example of General Thomas Jackson, they held their ground. A Confederate officer remarked that Jackson stood his ground "like a stone wall." From that day on, the general was known as **"Stonewall" Jackson.**

In the end, it was Union troops who panicked and ran. A congressman who witnessed the retreat reported,

> ❝ Off they went . . . across fields, toward the woods, anywhere, everywhere, to escape. . . . To enable them better to run, they threw away their blankets, knapsacks, canteens, and finally muskets, cartridge-boxes, and everything else. ❞

The Confederates did not pursue the fleeing Union army. Had they done so, they might even have captured Washington, D.C. Instead, they remained behind to gather the gear thrown away by the Union troops.

The **Battle of Bull Run** showed both the Union and the Confederacy that their soldiers needed training. It also showed that the war would be long and bloody.

Caution, delay, and retreat

After the shocking disaster at Bull Run, President Lincoln appointed General **George McClellan** as commander of the Union army of the East, known as the Army of the Potomac. McClellan, a superb

Biography

Robert E. Lee and Stonewall Jackson

Robert E. Lee (left) was perhaps the greatest general of the Civil War. Earlier, he had served admirably in the Mexican War and as superintendent of the United States Military Academy. Stonewall Jackson (right) was one of Lee's most skillful generals. Jackson's clever tactics and swift troop movements contributed to many victories.

★ **How did Jackson earn the nickname of "Stonewall" Jackson?**

organizer, transformed inexperienced recruits into an army of trained soldiers prepared for battle.

McClellan, however, was very cautious. He delayed leading his troops into battle. Newspapers reported "all quiet along the Potomac" so often that the phrase became a national joke. Finally, President Lincoln lost patience. "If McClellan is not using the army," the President snapped, "I should like to borrow it."

Finally, in March 1862, McClellan was ready to move. He and most of his troops left Washington by steamboat and sailed down the Potomac River for Richmond. The rest of the army stayed in Washington.

Landing south of Richmond, McClellan began inching slowly toward the Confederate capital. General Robert E. Lee launched a series of brilliant counterattacks. Lee also sent General Stonewall Jackson north to threaten Washington. Lincoln was thus prevented from sending the rest of the Union army to help McClellan. Cautious as usual, McClellan abandoned the attack and retreated. Once again, there was a lull in the war in the East.

Naval Action

Early in the war, Union ships blockaded southern ports. At first, some small, fast ships slipped through the blockade. These "blockade runners" brought everything from matches to guns into the Confederacy.

In time, however, the blockade became more effective. Trade through southern ports dropped by more than 90 percent. The South desperately needed a way to break the Union blockade. One method it tried was the ironclad ship.

At the start of the war, the Union abandoned a warship named the ***Merrimack*** near Portsmouth, Virginia. Confederates covered the ship with iron plates 4 inches (10.2 cm) thick and sent it into battle against the Union navy. On March 8, 1862, the *Merrimack* sank one Union ship, drove another aground, and forced a third to surrender. The Union vessels' cannonballs bounced harmlessly off the *Merrimack's* metal skin.

The Union countered with its own ironclads. One of these, the ***Monitor,*** battled the *Merrimack* in the waters off Hampton Roads, Virginia. The Confederate ship had more firepower, but the *Monitor* maneuvered more easily. In the end, neither ship seriously damaged the other, and both withdrew.

Ironclad ships changed naval warfare. Both sides rushed to build more of them. However, the South never mounted a serious attack against the Union navy. The Union blockade held throughout the war.

Linking History and Technology

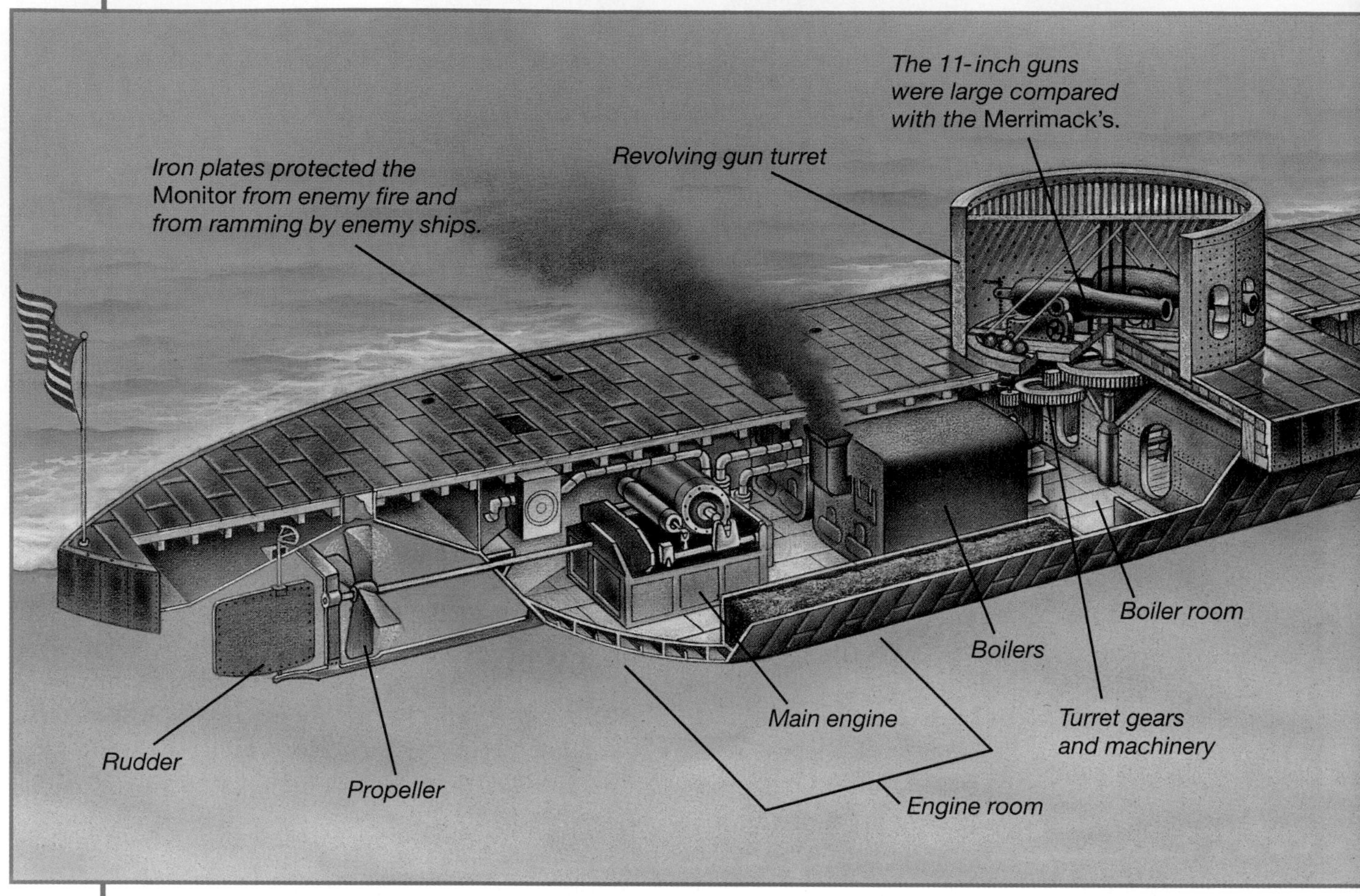

Antietam

In September 1862, General Lee took the offensive and marched his troops north into Maryland. He believed that a southern victory on northern soil would be a great blow to northern morale.

Luck was against Lee, however. A Confederate messenger lost Lee's battle plans. Two Union soldiers found them and turned them over to General McClellan.

Even with Lee's battle plan before him, however, McClellan was slow to act. After waiting a few days, he finally attacked Lee's main force at Antietam (an TEE tuhm) on September 17. In the day-long battle that followed, more than 23,000 Union and Confederate soldiers were killed or wounded.

On the night of September 18, Lee ordered his troops to slip back into Virginia. The Confederates breathed a sigh of relief when they saw that McClellan was not pursuing them.

Neither side was a clear winner at the **Battle of Antietam.** The North was able to claim victory, though, because Lee had ordered his forces to withdraw. As a result, northern morale increased. Still, President Lincoln was keenly disappointed. The Union army had suffered more casualties than the Confederate army. Furthermore, General McClellan had failed to follow up his victory by

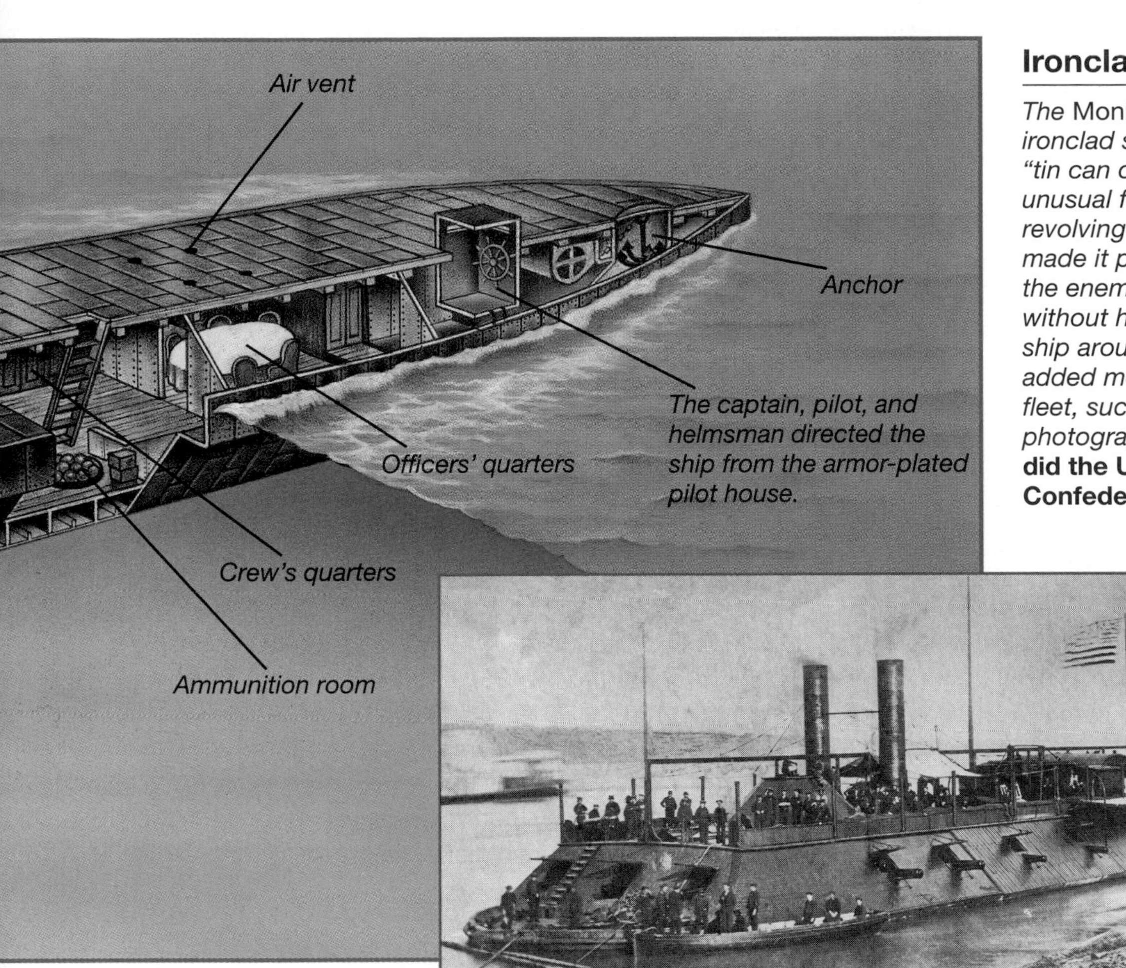

Ironclad Warship

The Monitor, *the first Union ironclad ship, looked like a "tin can on a raft." Its most unusual feature was the revolving gun turret, which made it possible to fire at the enemy from any angle without having to turn the ship around. The Union added more ironclads to its fleet, such as the one in the photograph below.* ★ **How did the Union navy hurt the Confederate economy?**

pursuing the Confederates. In November, Lincoln appointed General Ambrose Burnside to replace McClellan as commander of the Army of the Potomac.

Confederate Victories

Two stunning victories for the Confederacy came in late 1862 and 1863. (See the map on page 382.) General Robert E. Lee won by outsmarting the Union generals who fought against him.

Fredericksburg

In December 1862, Union forces set out once again toward Richmond. This time, they were led by General Ambrose Burnside.

Meeting Lee's army outside Fredericksburg, Virginia, Burnside ordered his troops to attack. Lee pulled back and left the town to Burnside. The Confederates dug in at the crest of a treeless hill above Fredericksburg. There, in a strong defensive position, they waited for the Union attack.

As the Union soldiers advanced, Confederate guns mowed them down by the thousands. Six times Burnside ordered his men to charge. Six times the rebels drove them back. "We forgot they were fighting us," one southerner wrote, "and cheer after cheer at their fearlessness went up along our lines." The **Battle of Fredericksburg** was one of the Union's worst defeats.

Chancellorsville

In May 1863, Lee, aided by Stonewall Jackson, again outwitted the Union army. This time, the battle took place on thickly wooded ground near Chancellorsville, Virginia. Lee and Jackson defeated the Union troops in three days.

Although the South won the **Battle of Chancellorsville,** it paid a high price for the victory. At the end of one day, nervous Confederate sentries fired at what they thought was an approaching Union soldier. The "Union soldier" was General Stonewall Jackson. Jackson died as a result of his injuries several days later.

The War in the West

While Union forces struggled in the East, those in the West met with success. As you have read, the Union strategy was to seize control of the Mississippi River. General **Ulysses S. Grant** began moving toward that goal. (See the map on page 398.) In February 1862, Grant attacked and captured Fort Henry and Fort Donelson in Tennessee. These Confederate forts guarded two important tributaries of the Mississippi.

Grant now pushed south to Shiloh, a village on the Tennessee River. At Shiloh, on April 6, he was surprised by Confederate forces. The Confederates won the first day of the **Battle of Shiloh.** They drove the Union troops back toward the river.

Grant now showed the toughness and determination that would enable him to win many battles in the future. "Retreat?" he replied to his doubting officers after that first day. "No. I propose to attack at daylight and whip them."

With the aid of reinforcements, Grant was able to win his victory and beat back the Confederates. However, the Battle of Shiloh was one of the bloodiest encounters of the Civil War. More Americans were killed or wounded at Shiloh than in the American Revolution, the War of 1812, and the Mexican War combined.

While Grant was fighting at Shiloh, the Union navy moved to gain control of the Mississippi River. In April 1862, Union gunboats captured New Orleans. Other ships seized Memphis, Tennessee. By capturing these two cities, the Union controlled both ends of the Mississippi. No longer could the South use the river as a supply line.

★ Section 2 Review ★

Recall

1. **Locate** **(a)** Richmond, **(b)** Washington, D.C., **(c)** Potomac River, **(d)** Fort Henry, **(e)** Fort Donelson, **(f)** New Orleans, **(g)** Memphis.
2. **Identify** **(a)** Stonewall Jackson, **(b)** Battle of Bull Run, **(c)** George McClellan, **(d)** *Merrimack,* **(e)** *Monitor,* **(f)** Battle of Antietam, **(g)** Battle of Fredericksburg, **(h)** Battle of Chancellorsville, **(i)** Ulysses S. Grant, **(j)** Battle of Shiloh.

Comprehension

3. **(a)** Describe the North's three-part plan for defeating the South. **(b)** Which part of the plan did the North achieve first?
4. Why was President Lincoln unhappy with General McClellan's performance as commander of the Union armies?
5. How did the loss of New Orleans and Memphis affect the South?

Critical Thinking and Writing

6. **Analyzing Primary Sources** In response to Stonewall Jackson's death, General Lee said, "I have lost my right arm." What did Lee mean by this statement?
7. **Analyzing Visual Evidence** Study the iron-clad ships on pages 384–385. Explain how such ships were superior to wooden sailing ships.

Activity **Making a Map** You are the chief cartographer for the Union army. Your assignment is to make a map illustrating the Union's three-part plan for defeating the South.

A Promise of Freedom

As You Read

Explore These Questions

- Why did Lincoln issue the Emancipation Proclamation?
- What were the effects of the Proclamation?
- How did African Americans contribute to the Union war effort?

Define

- emancipate
- discrimination

Identify

- Emancipation Proclamation
- 54th Massachusetts Regiment
- Fort Wagner

Antislavery potholders

SETTING the Scene At first, the Civil War was not a war against slavery. Yet wherever Union troops went, enslaved African Americans eagerly rushed to them, expecting to be freed. Most were sorely disappointed. Union officers often held these runaways until their masters arrived to take them back to slavery.

Some northerners began to raise questions. Was slavery not the root of the conflict between North and South? Were tens of thousands of men dying so that a slaveholding South would come back into the Union? Questions like these led Northerners to wonder what the real aim of the war should be.

Lincoln Was Cautious

The Civil War began as a war to restore the Union, not to end the institution of slavery. President Lincoln made this clear in the following statement.

> "If I could save the Union without freeing any slave, I would do it; and if I could save it by freeing all the slaves, I would do it; and if I could do it by freeing some and leaving others alone, I would also do that."

Lincoln had a reason for handling the slavery issue cautiously. As you have read, four slave states remained in the Union. The President did not want to do anything that might cause these states to shift their loyalty to the Confederacy. The resources of the border states might allow the South to turn the tide of the war.

The Emancipation Proclamation

By mid-1862, however, Lincoln came to believe that he could save the Union only by broadening the goals of the war. He decided to **emancipate**, or free, enslaved African Americans living in the Confederacy. In the four loyal slave states, however, slaves would not be freed. Nor would slaves be freed in Confederate lands that had already been captured by the Union, such as the city of New Orleans.

Motives and timing

Lincoln had practical reasons for his emancipation plan. At the start of the Civil War, more than 3 million enslaved people labored for the Confederacy. They helped grow the food that fed Confederate soldiers. They also worked in iron and lead mines that were vital to the South's war effort. Some served as nurses and cooks for the army. Lincoln knew that emancipation would weaken the Confederacy's ability to carry on the war.

However, Lincoln did not want to anger slave owners in the Union. Also, he knew that many northerners opposed freedom for

Viewing History The Emancipation Proclamation

The Emancipation Proclamation meant that Union troops were now fighting to end slavery. Lincoln's action, however, did not please all northerners. Opposition to the preliminary proclamation contributed to Republican party losses in the Congressional elections of 1862.

★ **How does this poster make use of symbolism?**

enslaved African Americans. Lincoln therefore hoped to introduce the idea of emancipation slowly, by limiting it to territory controlled by the Confederacy.

The President had another very important motive, too. As you read in Chapter 14, Lincoln believed that slavery was wrong. When he felt that he could act to free slaves without threatening the Union, he did so.

Lincoln was concerned about the timing of his announcement. The war was not going well for the Union. He did not want Americans to think he was freeing slaves as a desperate effort to save a losing cause. He waited for a victory to announce his plan.

Freedom proclaimed

On September 22, 1862, five days after the Union victory at Antietam, Lincoln issued a preliminary proclamation. It warned that on January 1, 1863, anyone held as a slave in a state still in rebellion against the United States would be emancipated.

Then, on January 1, 1863, Lincoln issued the formal Emancipation Proclamation. The **Emancipation Proclamation** declared:

> "On the 1st day of January, in the year of our Lord 1863, all persons held as slaves within any state or... part of a state [whose] people... shall then be in rebellion against the United States, shall be then, thenceforward, and forever free."

Impact of the Proclamation

Because the rebelling states were not under Union control, no slaves actually gained their freedom on January 1, 1863. Nevertheless, as a result of the Emancipation Proclamation, the purpose of the war changed. Now, Union troops were fighting to end slavery as well as to save the Union.

The opponents of slavery greeted the proclamation with joy. In Boston, African American abolitionist Frederick Douglass witnessed one of the many emotional celebrations that took place:

> "The effect of this announcement was startling... and the scene was wild and grand.... My old friend Rue, a Negro preacher,... expressed the heartfelt emotion of the hour, when he led all voices in the anthem, 'Sound the loud timbrel o'er Egypt's dark sea, Jehovah hath triumphed, his people are free!'"

Connections With Arts

Many northerners greeted the Emancipation Proclamation with music and song. At Boston's Music Hall, people celebrated with performances of Mendelssohn's *Hymn of Praise,* and Handel's *Hallelujah Chorus*.

The Proclamation won the Union the sympathy of people in Europe, especially workers. As a result, it became less likely that Britain or any other European country would come to the aid of the South.

African Americans Help

When the war began, thousands of free blacks volunteered to fight for the Union. At first, federal law forbade African Americans to serve as soldiers. When Congress repealed that law in 1862, however, both free African Americans and escaped slaves enlisted in the Union army.

In the Union army

The army assigned these volunteers to all-black units, commanded by white officers. At first, the black troops served only as laborers. They performed noncombat duties such as building roads and guarding supplies. Black troops received only half the pay of white soldiers.

African American soldiers protested against this policy of **discrimination** that denied them the same rights and treatment as other soldiers. Gradually, conditions changed. By 1863, African American troops were fighting in major battles against the Confederates. In 1864, the United States War Department announced that all soldiers would receive equal pay. By the end of the war, about 200,000 African Americans had fought for the Union. Nearly 40,000 lost their lives.

Acts of bravery

One of the most famous African American units in the Union army was the **54th Massachusetts Regiment.** The 54th accepted African Americans from all across the

Viewing HISTORY **Assault on Fort Wagner**

In this painting by Tom Lovell, African American soldiers of the 54th Massachussetts Regiment charge against Confederate troops at Fort Wagner. Nearly half the regiment died in the failed attack, including the regiment's commander, Colonel Robert Gould Shaw. ★ **Why do you think the Union army was reluctant to appoint African American officers?**

North. Frederick Douglass helped recruit troops for the regiment, and two of his sons served in it.

On the night of July 17, 1863, the 54th Massachusetts Regiment launched an attack on **Fort Wagner** near Charleston. Under heavy fire, nearly 100 soldiers forced their way into the fort and engaged the Confederate troops in hand-to-hand combat. The commander, most of the officers, and almost half the regiment were killed.

The courage of the 54th Massachusetts and other regiments helped to win respect for African American soldiers. Sergeant William Carney of the 54th Massachusetts was awarded the Congressional Medal of Honor for acts of bravery. He was the first of 16 African American soldiers to be so honored during the Civil War. In a letter to President Lincoln, Secretary of War Stanton praised African American soldiers.

> “[They] have proved themselves among the bravest of the brave, performing deeds of daring and shedding their blood with a heroism unsurpassed by soldiers of any race.”

Behind Confederate lines

In the South, despite the Emancipation Proclamation, African Americans still had to work as slaves on plantations. However, many enslaved African Americans slowed down their work. Others refused to work at all or to submit to punishment. In so doing, they knew they were helping to weaken the South's war effort. They knew that when victorious Union troops arrived in their area, they would be free.

Throughout the South, thousands of enslaved African Americans also took direct action to free themselves. Whenever a Union army appeared in an area, the slaves from all around would flee their former masters. They crossed over to the Union lines and to freedom. By the end of the war, about one fourth of the enslaved population in the South had escaped to freedom.

The former slaves helped Union armies achieve victory in a variety of ways. They used their knowledge of the local terrain to serve as guides and spies. Many more enlisted in African American regiments of the Union army.

★ Section 3 Review ★

Recall

1. **Identify** **(a)** Emancipation Proclamation, **(b)** 54th Massachusetts Regiment, **(c)** Fort Wagner.
2. **Define** **(a)** emancipate, **(b)** discrimination.

Comprehension

3. **(a)** Why was President Lincoln cautious about making emancipation a goal of the war? **(b)** Why did he finally decide to issue the Emancipation Proclamation?
4. Why were no slaves actually freed when the Proclamation was issued?
5. **(a)** How did the 54th Massachussetts Regiment's attack on Fort Wagner affect public opinion about enslaved African American soldiers? **(b)** How did African Americans help to weaken the Confederacy?

Critical Thinking and Writing

6. **Drawing Conclusions** What did the Union army's policy toward all-black regiments reveal about northern attitudes toward African Americans? Explain.
7. **Analyzing Primary Sources** In 1861, Frederick Douglass said, "This is no time to fight with one hand when both hands are needed. This is no time to fight with only your white hand, and allow your black hand to remain tied!" **(a)** What did Douglass mean by this statement? **(b)** Did the United States Congress agree with Douglass? Explain.

Activity **Writing a Poem** A monument is being built to honor the courageous African American soldiers of the Civil War. Write a poem to be engraved on the monument, mentioning some of the facts you have learned in this section.

Hardships of War

As You Read

Explore These Questions
- What was life like for soldiers in the Civil War?
- How did women contribute to the war effort?
- What problems did each side face during the war?

Define
- civilians
- draft
- habeas corpus
- income tax
- inflation
- profiteer

Identify
- Copperheads
- Loreta Janeta Velazquez
- Rose Greenhow
- Dorothea Dix
- Clara Barton
- Sojourner Truth
- Sally Tompkins

The Civil War caused hardships not only for soldiers but for people at home as well. Southerners, especially, suffered from the war, because most of the fighting took place in the South.

On both sides, **civilians,** or people who were not in the army, worked on farms and labored in factories to support the war effort. They used their mules to move troops and supplies. They tended the wounded. As their hardships increased, so did opposition to the war.

The Hard Life of Soldiers

On both sides, most soldiers were under age 21. However, war quickly turned gentle boys into tough men. Soldiers drilled and marched for long hours. They slept on the ground even in rain and snow. In combat, boys of 18 learned to stand firm as cannon blasts shook the earth and bullets whizzed past their ears.

New technology added to the horror of war. Cone-shaped bullets, which made rifles twice as accurate, replaced round musket balls. New cannons could hurl exploding shells several miles. The new weapons had deadly results. In most battles, one fourth or more of the soldiers were killed or wounded.

Sick and wounded soldiers faced other horrors. Medical care on the battlefield was crude. Surgeons routinely cut off injured

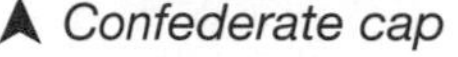

▲ *Confederate cap*

▲ *Union cap*

arms and legs. Minor wounds often became infected. With no medicines to fight infection, half the wounded died. Diseases like pneumonia and malaria killed more men than guns or cannons did.

On both sides, prisoners of war faced horrifying conditions. At Andersonville, a prison camp in Georgia, more than one Union prisoner out of three died of disease or starvation. One prisoner wrote:

> "There is no such thing as delicacy here.... In the middle of last night I was awakened by being kicked by a dying man. He was soon dead. I got up and moved the body off a few feet, and went to sleep to dream of the hideous sights."

Discontent in the North

Some northerners opposed using force to keep the South in the Union. Supporters of the war called these people **Copperheads,** after the poisonous snake. Other northerners supported the war but opposed the way Lincoln was conducting it. In some northern cities, this opposition led to riots.

Viewing HISTORY **The Faces of War**

Confederate soldiers wore gray uniforms and were sometimes called Johnny Rebs. Union soldiers wore blue and were called Billy Yanks. During the Civil War, about 1 of every 10 soldiers deserted from service. ★ **Why do you think desertion rates were high in both armies?**

The draft law

As the war dragged on, public support dwindled. Soon, not enough men were volunteering to serve in the Union army. The government took action.

In 1863, Congress passed a **draft** law. It required all able-bodied males between the ages of 20 and 45 to serve in the military if they were called.

Under the law, a man could avoid the draft by paying the government $300 or by hiring someone to serve in his place. This angered many people. They began to see the Civil War as "a rich man's war and a poor man's fight."

Riots in the cities

Opposition to the draft law led to riots in several northern cities. The draft law had gone into effect soon after Lincoln issued the Emancipation Proclamation. As a result, some northerners believed that they were being forced to fight to end slavery. This idea angered some white workers, especially recent immigrants in the cities. Like many other northerners, some of these immigrants held racist beliefs. They also feared that free African Americans would be employed at jobs that they needed, too.

The worst riot took place in New York City during July 1863. For four days, white workers attacked free blacks. Rioters also attacked rich New Yorkers who had paid to avoid serving in the army. At least 74 people were killed during the riot.

President Lincoln moved to stop the riots and other "disloyal practices." Several times, he denied **habeas corpus** (HAY bee uhs KOR puhs), the right to have a hearing before being jailed. Lincoln defended his actions by saying that the Constitution gave him the right to deny people their rights "when in the cases of rebellion or invasion, the public safety may require it."

Problems in the South

President Davis, meanwhile, struggled to create a strong federal government for the Confederacy. Many southerners were strong supporters of states' rights. They resisted paying taxes to a central government. At one point, Georgia threatened to secede from the Confederacy!

Like the North, the South had to pass a draft law to fill its army. However, men who owned or supervised more than 20 slaves did not have to serve in the army. Southern farmers who owned few or no slaves resented this law.

Near war's end, the South no longer had enough white men to fill the ranks. Robert E. Lee urged that enslaved African Americans be allowed to serve as soldiers. Desperate, the Confederate congress finally agreed. However, the war ended before any enslaved people put on Confederate uniforms.

Why Study History?

Because One Person Can Make a Difference

Historical Background

In the early days of the Civil War, Clara Barton and other women provided medical care to wounded soldiers. However, the government required women to stay far from battle. As a result, many soldiers received treatment too late and died of their wounds. Barton therefore sought permission to work directly on the fields of battle.

After some initial refusals, the government gave in. Through the remainder of the war, Clara Barton served as a battlefield nurse. Because of her courageous efforts, she became known as the "Angel of the Battlefield."

Connections to Today

After the Civil War, Barton continued to make a difference. In Europe, she worked with the International Red Cross, an organization that aided victims of war. In 1881, after returning to the United States, she founded the American Red Cross. This new organization served both victims of war and victims of natural disaster.

Today, disaster relief remains a primary service of the Red Cross. The Red Cross helps people recover from natural disasters such as fires, floods, and hurricanes. It provides victims with medical assistance, food, clothing, and shelter.

The American Red Cross provides other services as well. It helps homeless people and seniors in need. It supervises donations of blood and other organs. It also provides instruction in a variety of safety programs.

Connections to You

Like Clara Barton, you too can make a difference. You can learn about first aid and safety procedures in a Red Cross educational course. Courses include first aid, water safety, fire prevention, and even babysitting. Some local Red Cross chapters invite teens to serve as volunteers. You might also organize or participate in a drive to help raise funds for the Red Cross. Red Cross disaster relief services are provided free of charge because of contributions made by caring Americans.

▲ Clara Barton

▲ Red Cross book

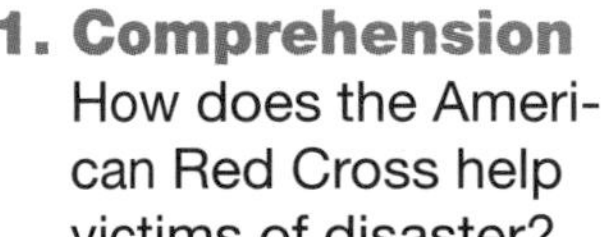

1. **Comprehension** How does the American Red Cross help victims of disaster?
2. **Critical Thinking** At the start of the Civil War, why do you think government officials allowed men, but not women, to aid wounded soldiers on the field of battle?

★Activity Making an Advertisement Create an advertisement that seeks public support for the Red Cross by informing people about the many services the Red Cross provides.

Viewing HISTORY **Nursing the Wounded**

In this Civil War scene, painted by Allyn Cox in 1974, women are nursing the wounded in the rotunda of the Capitol building. During the war, many public buildings served as temporary hospitals. The painting decorates a corridor of the Capitol today.

★ How else did women help in the war effort?

The Northern Economy

The Civil War cost far more than any earlier war. The Union had to use several strategies to raise money. In some ways, though, war helped the North's economy.

Taxation and inflation

In 1861, to pay for the war, Congress established the nation's first **income tax** on people's earnings. In addition, the Union issued bonds worth millions of dollars. Still, taxes and bonds did not raise enough money. To get the funds it needed, the North printed more than $400 million in paper money.

As the money supply increased, each dollar was worth less. In response, businesses charged more for their goods. The North was experiencing **inflation,** a rise in prices and a decrease in the value of money. During the war, prices for goods nearly doubled in the North.

Economic benefits

In some ways, the war helped the North's economy. Because many farmers went off to fight, more machines were used to plant and harvest crops. As a result, farm production actually went up during the war.

The wartime demand for clothing, shoes, guns, and other goods helped many northern industries. Some manufacturers made fortunes by profiteering. **Profiteers** charged excessive prices for goods the government desperately needed for the war.

The Southern Economy

For the South, war brought economic ruin. The South had to struggle with the cost of the war, the loss of the cotton trade, and severe shortages brought on by the Union blockade.

The economy suffers

To raise money, the Confederacy imposed an income tax and a tax-in-kind. The tax-in-kind required farmers to turn over one tenth of their crops to the government. The government took crops because it knew that southern farmers had little money.

Like the North, the South printed paper money. It printed so much, in fact, that wild inflation set in. By 1865, one Confederate dollar was worth only two cents in gold.

The war did serious damage to the cotton trade, the South's main source of income. Early in the war, President Davis halted cotton shipments to Britain. He hoped that Britain would side with the South in order to get cotton. The tactic backfired. Britain simply bought more cotton from Egypt and

$ Connections With Economics

As inflation in the South worsened, it became more and more difficult to feed and clothe a family. Near the end of the war, a barrel of flour cost $1,000 and a pair of shoes cost $400.

India. Davis succeeded only in cutting the South's income.

Effects of the blockade

The Union blockade created severe shortages in the South. Confederate armies sometimes had to wait weeks for supplies of food and clothing. Guns and ammunition were also in short supply. With few factories of its own, the South bought many of its weapons in Europe. However, the blockade cut off most deliveries from Europe.

For civilians, the blockade brought food shortages. Even the wealthy went hungry. "I had a little piece of bread and a little molasses today for my dinner," wrote plantation mistress Mary Chesnut in her diary. By 1865, there was widespread famine in the Confederacy.

Women at War

Women of both the North and South played vital roles during the war. As men left for the battlefields, women took jobs in industry, in teaching, and on farms.

Women and the military

Women's aid societies helped supply the troops with food, bedding, clothing, and medicine. Throughout the North, women held fairs and other fund-raising events to pay for the supplies. They succeeded in raising millions of dollars.

A few women disguised themselves so they could serve as soldiers. **Loreta Janeta Velazquez,** for example, fought for the South at Bull Run and Shiloh. Other women worked as spies. **Rose Greenhow** gathered information for the South while entertaining Union leaders in her Washington, D.C., home. She was caught, convicted of treason, and exiled.

Nursing the wounded

Women on both sides worked as nurses. Doctors were unwilling at first to permit even trained nurses to work in military hospitals. When wounded men began to swamp army hospitals, however, this attitude soon changed.

Dorothea Dix, famous for her work reforming prisons and mental hospitals, became superintendent of nurses for the Union army. **Clara Barton** earned fame as a Civil War nurse. She later founded the American Red Cross. **Sojourner Truth,** the African American antislavery leader, worked in Union hospitals and in camps for freed slaves. In the South, **Sally Tompkins** set up a hospital in Richmond, Virginia.

★ Section 4 Review ★

Recall

1. **Identify** **(a)** Copperheads, **(b)** Loreta Janeta Velazquez, **(c)** Rose Greenhow, **(d)** Dorothea Dix, **(e)** Clara Barton, **(f)** Sojourner Truth, **(g)** Sally Tompkins.
2. **Define** **(a)** civilians, **(b)** draft, **(c)** habeas corpus, **(d)** income tax, **(e)** inflation, **(f)** profiteer.

Comprehension

3. Describe three hardships faced by soldiers during the Civil War.
4. Describe three ways women contributed to the war effort.
5. How did the Union blockade affect the South?

Critical Thinking and Writing

6. **Linking Past and Present** **(a)** What advances in technology made Civil War battles deadly? **(b)** In what ways would a war today be even more deadly?
7. **Defending a Position** What facts support the charge that the Civil War was "a rich man's war and a poor man's fight"?

★ ★

Activity **Making a Chart** You are the graphic illustrator for an economics magazine. Create a flowchart or cause-and-effect chart to illustrate how the high cost of the Civil War led to high inflation.

The War Ends

Explore These Questions

- What was the significance of the Union victories at Vicksburg and Gettysburg?
- What ideals did Lincoln express in the Gettysburg Address?
- How did Union generals use a new type of war to defeat the Confederacy?

Define

- siege
- total war

Identify

- Battle of Gettysburg
- Gettysburg Address
- Ulysses S. Grant
- Philip Sheridan
- William Tecumseh Sherman

SETTING the Scene As you have read, Confederate armies won major battles at Fredericksburg in December 1862 and at Chancellorsville in May 1863. These were gloomy days for the North.

Then, in July 1863, the tide of war turned against the South. In the West, the Union extended its control of the Mississippi River and cut the South in two. At the Battle of Gettysburg, in Pennsylvania, both Union and Confederate forces suffered terrible losses. However, as President Davis later explained, "Theirs could be repaired, ours could not."

The following year, President Lincoln would appoint Ulysses S. Grant commander in chief of the Union army. In Grant, Lincoln had found the general who could lead the Union to victory.

The Fall of Vicksburg

After capturing New Orleans and Memphis, the Union controlled both ends of the Mississippi River. Still, the North could not safely use the river because Confederates held Vicksburg, Mississippi. Vicksburg sat on a cliff high above the river. Cannons there could shell boats traveling between New Orleans and Memphis.

Early in 1863, Grant's forces tried again and again to seize Vicksburg. The Confederates held out bravely. At last, Grant devised a brilliant plan. Marching his troops inland, he launched a surprise attack on Jackson, Mississippi. Then, he turned west and attacked Vicksburg from the rear. (See the map on page 398.)

For over six weeks, Grant's forces lay siege to Vicksburg. A **siege** is a military blockade of an enemy town or position in order to force it to surrender. Day after day, the Union soldiers pushed their lines closer to the town. Union artillery and gunboats on the Mississippi bombarded the besieged soldiers and inhabitants. As their food supplies ran out, the southerners began to use mules and rats as food. Finally, on July 4, 1863, the Confederates surrendered Vicksburg.

On July 9, Union forces also captured Port Hudson, Louisiana. The entire Mississippi was now under Union control. The Confederacy was split into two parts. Texas, Arkansas, and Louisiana were cut off from the rest of the Confederacy.

Union Victory at Gettysburg

In the East, after his victory at Chancellorsville, General Lee moved his army north into Pennsylvania. He hoped to take the Yankees by surprise. If he was successful, Lee planned to then swing south and capture Washington, D.C.

HISTORY HAPPENED HERE

Ohio regiment monument

Vicksburg National Military Park

You can learn about the siege of Vicksburg, Mississippi, by touring the actual battle site. The park includes a museum, miles of defensive earthworks, and more than 125 cannons. You can even walk the deck of a Union ironclad gunboat, raised from the Mississippi River in the 1960s. Throughout the park, numerous monuments honor the soldiers who fought and died for control of this small Mississippi River town.

★ ***To learn more about this historic site, write:*** *Vicksburg National Military Park, 3201 Clay Street, Vicksburg, MS 39180.*

On June 30, 1863, a Union force under General George C. Meade met part of Lee's army at the small town of Gettysburg, Pennsylvania. Both sides quickly sent in reinforcements. The three-day Battle of Gettysburg that followed was one of the most important battles of the Civil War.

At the start of the battle, the Confederates drove the Union forces out of Gettysburg. The Yankees took up strong positions on Cemetery Ridge, overlooking the town. On July 2, a Confederate attack failed with heavy casualties. Nevertheless, Lee decided to launch another attack. On July 3, he ordered General George Pickett to lead 15,000 men in a daring charge against the center of the Union line. To reach the Yankees, Pickett's men had to cross an open field and run up a steep slope.

Pickett gave the order to charge and the Union guns opened fire. Row after row of soldiers fell to the ground, bleeding. Still, the Confederate troops continued to rush forward against a rain of bullets and shells. Few were able to reach the Union lines. A Union soldier described the fighting at the crest of the ridge:

> ❝ Men fire into each other's faces not five feet apart. There are bayonet thrusts, saber strokes, pistol shots, men going down on their hands and knees... gulping blood, falling, legless, armless, headless.❞

Pickett's charge failed. As the survivors limped back, Lee rode among them. "It's all my fault," he admitted humbly. Lee had no choice but to retreat. After their defeat at the **Battle of Gettysburg,** the Confederates would never again invade the North.

The Union victories at Vicksburg and Gettysburg marked the turning point of the Civil War. On July 4, 1863, northerners had good reason to celebrate.

The Gettysburg Address

The Battle of Gettysburg left more than 40,000 dead or wounded. When the soldiers who died there were buried, their graves stretched as far as the eye could see. On November 19, 1863, northerners held a ceremony to dedicate this cemetery.

President Lincoln attended the ceremony, but he was not the main speaker. At the time, his popularity was quite low. Lincoln sat with his hands folded as another speaker talked for two hours. When it was his turn, the President rose and spoke for about three minutes.

In his **Gettysburg Address,** Lincoln said that the Civil War was a test of whether or not a democratic nation could survive. He reminded Americans that their nation was founded on the belief that "all men are created equal." Looking out at the thousands of graves, Lincoln told the audience:

> ❝ We here highly resolve that these dead shall not have died in vain—that this nation, under God, shall have a new birth of freedom—and that government of the people, by the people, for the people, shall not perish from the earth. ❞

Geography *Skills*

As the Civil War dragged on, Union armies advanced deeper and deeper into the South. General Sherman marched his troops through Georgia and the Carolinas.

1. **Location** On the map, locate: **(a)** Vicksburg, **(b)** Atlanta, **(c)** Savannah.
2. **Place** What three Confederate states were cut off from the rest of the Confederacy after Union forces gained control of the Mississippi River?
3. **Critical Thinking** Based on the map, why would the South be hurt more than the North—no matter who won the war?

Few people listened to Lincoln that day. Newspapers gave his speech little attention. Later generations, however, have honored Lincoln's brief address as a profound statement of American ideals.

The Union Wages Total War

For three years, Lincoln had searched for a general who could lead the Union to victory. More and more, he thought of **Ulysses S. Grant.** After capturing Vicksburg, Grant continued to win battles in the West. In 1864, Lincoln appointed him commander of the Union forces.

Some questioned the choice, but President Lincoln felt that "Unconditional Surrender" Grant was the general who would lead the Union to victory. "I can't spare this man," Lincoln said. "He fights."

Grant and other Union generals began to wage **total war** against the South. In total war, civilians as well as soldiers are affected. The Union army waged total war by destroying food and equipment that might be useful to the enemy. Civilians in the South suffered the same hardships as soldiers.

Sheridan in the Shenandoah

Grant had a plan for ending the war. He wanted to destroy the South's ability to fight. Grant sent General **Philip Sheridan** and his cavalry into the rich farmland of Virginia's Shenandoah Valley. He instructed Sheridan:

> "Leave nothing to invite the enemy to return. Destroy whatever cannot be consumed. Let the valley be left so that crows flying over it will have to carry their rations along with them."

Sheridan obeyed. In the summer and fall of 1864, he marched through the valley, destroying farms and livestock.

Sherman's march to the sea

Grant also ordered General **William Tecumseh Sherman** to capture Atlanta, Georgia, and then march to the Atlantic coast. Like Sheridan, Sherman had orders to destroy everything useful to the South.

Cause and Effect

Causes

- Issue of slavery in the territories divides the North and South
- Abolitionists want slavery to end
- South fears it will lose power in the national government
- Southern states secede after Lincoln's election
- Confederates bombard Fort Sumter

The Civil War

Effects

- Lincoln issues the Emancipation Proclamation
- Northern economy booms
- South loses its cotton trade with Britain
- Total war destroys the South's economy
- Hundreds of thousands of Americans killed

Effects Today

- Sectionalism is less of a force in American life and politics
- African Americans have equal protection under the Constitution
- Millions of Americans visit Civil War battlefields each year

Graphic Organizer *Skills*

The Civil War was a major turning point in the history of the United States.

1. **Comprehension** How did the war affect the northern and southern economies differently?
2. **Critical Thinking** Describe another cause or effect that could be added to this chart.

Sherman's troops captured Atlanta in September 1864. They burned the city in November. Then Sherman began his "march to the sea."

Sherman's troops ripped up railroad tracks, built bonfires from the ties, then heated and twisted the rails. They killed livestock and tore up fields. They burned barns, homes, and factories.

Lincoln Is Reelected

In 1864, Lincoln ran for reelection. At first, his defeat seemed, in his own words, "extremely probable." Before the capture of Atlanta, Union chances for victory looked bleak. Lincoln knew that many northerners were unhappy with his handling of the war. He thought that this might cost him the election.

The Democrats nominated General George McClellan to oppose Lincoln. Although he had commanded the Union army, McClellan was more willing than Lincoln to compromise with the South. If peace could be achieved, he was ready to restore slavery.

When Sherman took Atlanta in September, the North rallied around Lincoln. Sheridan's smashing victories in the Shenandoah Valley in October further increased Lincoln's popular support. In the election in November, the vote was close, but Lincoln remained President.

In his second Inaugural Address, Lincoln looked forward to the coming of peace:

> "With malice toward none, with charity for all . . . let us strive . . . to bind up the nation's wounds . . . to do all which may achieve a just and a lasting peace among ourselves and with all nations."

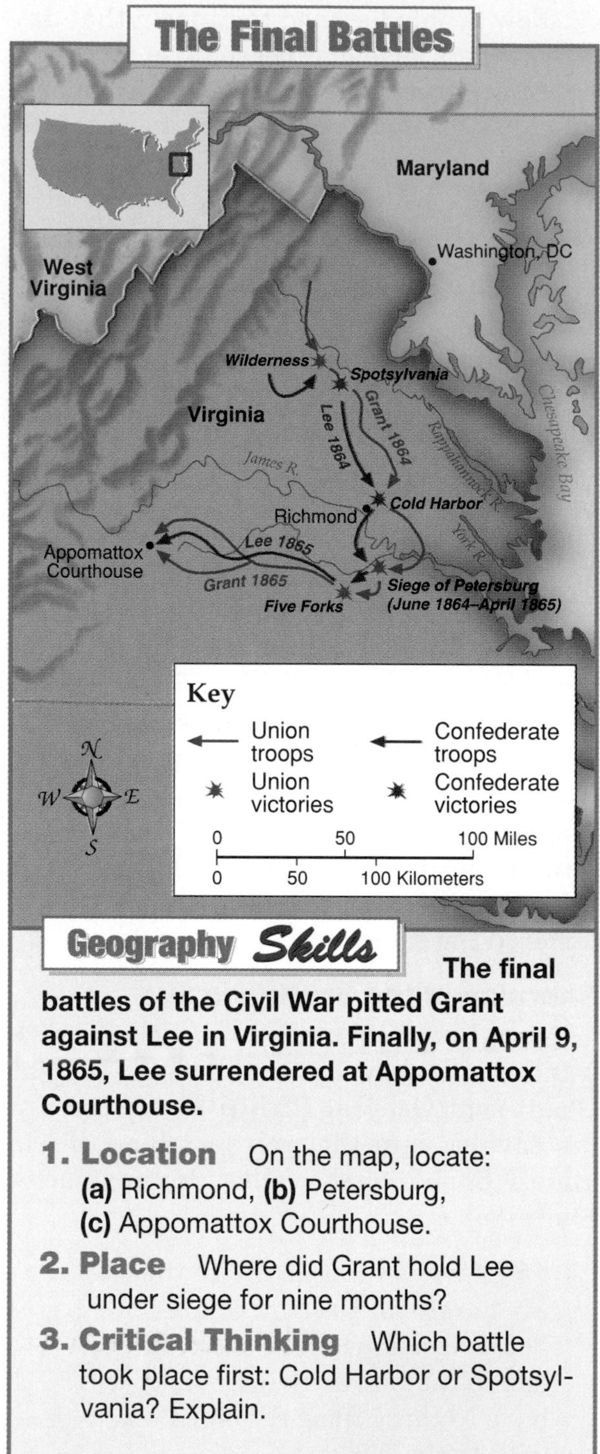

Geography Skills **The final battles of the Civil War pitted Grant against Lee in Virginia. Finally, on April 9, 1865, Lee surrendered at Appomattox Courthouse.**

1. **Location** On the map, locate: **(a)** Richmond, **(b)** Petersburg, **(c)** Appomattox Courthouse.
2. **Place** Where did Grant hold Lee under siege for nine months?
3. **Critical Thinking** Which battle took place first: Cold Harbor or Spotsylvania? Explain.

The War Ends

Grant had begun a drive to capture Richmond in May 1864. Throughout the spring and summer, he and Lee fought a series of costly battles.

Northerners read with horror that Grant had lost 60,000 dead and wounded in a single month at the battles of the Wilderness, Spotsylvania, and Cold Harbor. Still, Grant pressed on. He knew that the Union could replace men and supplies. The South could not.

Lee dug in at Petersburg, near Richmond. Here, Grant kept Lee under siege for nine months. At last, with a fresh supply of troops, Grant took Petersburg on April 2, 1865. The same day, Richmond fell.

General Lee surrenders to General Grant at Appomattox Courthouse.

Lee and his army withdrew to a small Virginia town called Appomattox Courthouse. There, a week later, they were trapped by Union troops. Lee knew that his men would be slaughtered if he kept fighting. On April 9, 1865, Lee surrendered.

At Appomattox Courthouse, Grant offered generous terms of surrender to the defeated Confederate army. Soldiers were required to turn over their rifles, but officers were allowed to keep their pistols. Soldiers who had horses could keep them. Grant knew that southerners would need the animals for spring plowing.

As the Confederates surrendered, Union soldiers began to cheer. Grant ordered them to be silent. "The war is over," he said. "The rebels are our countrymen again."

Effects of the War

More than 360,000 Union soldiers and 250,000 Confederate soldiers lost their lives in the Civil War. No war has ever resulted in more American deaths. As a result, feelings of bitterness remained among both northerners and southerners.

Southerners had special reasons to view the North with resentment. They had lost their struggle for independence. Their way of life had been forcibly changed. Union armies had destroyed much of their land. In addition, many southerners feared that the North would seek revenge against the South after the war.

Finally, the Civil War was a major turning point in American history. The Union was secure. States' rights had suffered a terrible blow. As a result, the power of the federal government grew. The war also brought freedom to millions of African Americans. Still, a long and difficult struggle for equality lay ahead.

★ Section 5 Review ★

Recall

1. **Locate** **(a)** Vicksburg, **(b)** Port Hudson, **(c)** Gettysburg, **(d)** Atlanta, **(e)** Petersburg, **(f)** Appomattox Courthouse.
2. **Identify** **(a)** Battle of Gettysburg, **(b)** Gettysburg Address, **(c)** Ulysses S. Grant, **(d)** Philip Sheridan, **(e)** William Tecumseh Sherman.
3. **Define** **(a)** siege, **(b)** total war.

Comprehension

4. Why did the Union victories at Vicksburg and Gettysburg mark a turning point in the war?
5. What ideals did Lincoln express in his Gettysburg Address and Second Inaugural Address?
6. How did Sheridan and Sherman use total war to destroy the South's ability to fight?

Critical Thinking and Writing

7. **Predicting Consequences** If Sherman and Sheridan had not won victories just before the election of 1864, how might the election and the war have turned out differently?
8. **Defending a Position** Some people have condemned Grant's decision to wage total war. Do you agree or disagree with this position? Explain.

Activity **Writing a Speech** It is a sad day for the South. You are a member of the Confederate Congress and you have just heard of Lee's surrender. Write a speech in which you reflect on the hardships of the war and offer hope for the future.

Chapter 15 Review and Activities

★ Sum It Up ★

Section 1 The Conflict Takes Shape

★ The Union's advantages included a greater population and superior industrial resources.

▶ The Confederacy's advantages included better military leaders and its position of defending the homeland.

Section 2 A Long, Difficult Struggle

▶ The Union navy blockaded southern ports. Union armies tried to take Richmond and the Mississippi Valley.

▶ The Confederates won major battles in the East. Union armies were more successful in the West.

Section 3 A Promise of Freedom

▶ The Emancipation Proclamation made the end of slavery a goal of the war.

▶ African Americans worked, fought, and died in the effort to preserve the Union and end slavery.

Section 4 Hardships of War

▶ Both men and women suffered hardships in their efforts to win the war.

▶ During the war, the Union and Confederacy both struggled with political and economic problems.

Section 5 The War Ends

▶ The North waged total war deep into the South, disrupting civilian lives and inflicting great losses.

▶ Lee surrendered his army at Appomattox Courthouse, Virginia, on April 9, 1865.

For additional review of the major ideas of Chapter 15, see ***Guide to the Essentials of American History*** or ***Interactive Student Tutorial CD-ROM,*** which contains interactive review activities, graphic organizers, and practice tests.

Reviewing the Chapter

Define These Terms

Match each term with the correct definition.

Column 1

1. emancipate
2. martial law
3. draft
4. profiteers
5. inflation

Column 2

a. rule by the army
b. set free
c. people who overcharge for desperately needed goods
d. a rise in prices
e. a law requiring people to serve in the military

Explore the Main Ideas

1. What advantages did the United States have over the Confederate States?
2. Why were Confederate armies in the East often victorious in the early years of the war?
3. What were the results of the Emancipation Proclamation?
4. How did women support the war effort?
5. Explain how total war affected the South.

Chart Activity

Use the chart below to answer the following questions: **1.** How many members of Company D were captured and imprisoned by the Union? **2.** How many soldiers were in Company D at the start of the war? **Critical Thinking** Why do you think so many soldiers died from disease?

Seventh Virginia Infantry, Company D

Original members	122
Killed in battle or died of wounds	17
Died of disease	14
Discharged	29
Transferred	6
Prisoners of war	27
On leave, hospitalized, or at home	8
Deserted	12
Surrendered at Appomattox	9

Source: David E. Johnston, *The Story of a Confederate Boy in the Civil War*

Critical Thinking and Writing

1. **Understanding Chronology** For each pair of events that follow, select the event that happened first: **(a)** Battle of Bull Run, Battle of Gettysburg; **(b)** fall of Richmond, Emancipation Proclamation; **(c)** Sherman's march to the sea, fall of Vicksburg.
2. **Linking Past and Present** How do you think Americans would react today if a general lost 60,000 soldiers in one month as General Grant once did? Explain your answer.
3. **Identifying Alternatives** Should African American men have volunteered to serve in the Union army in 1862? Explain two reasons for volunteering and two reasons for not volunteering.
4. **Exploring Unit Themes Sectionalism** Do you think sectional differences and conflicts continued even after the end of the Civil War? Explain the reasons for your answer.

Using Primary Sources

Confederate General John B. Gordon described how his troops felt at Appomattox Courthouse as General Lee was about to surrender:

> "The men cried like children. Worn, starved, and bleeding as they were, they had rather have died than have surrendered.... But I could not permit it.... That these men should have wept at surrendering so unequal a fight, at being taken out of this constant [bloodshed] and storm, at being sent back to their families... was [proof of bravery] and patriotism that might set an example."

Source: *Reminiscences of the Civil War* by John B. Gordon, 1903.

Recognizing Points of View **(a)** Why did General Gordon's troops cry? **(b)** How did Gordon feel about the behavior of the soldiers? **(c)** How do you think Confederate veterans felt about northern soldiers occupying southern lands after the war?

Activity Bank

Interdisciplinary Activity

Exploring Science Research and prepare a report on medical care during the Civil War. Include information on battlefield hospitals, common diseases, and people who cared for the sick and wounded.

Career Skills Activity

Cartographer Choose a Civil War battle and make a map showing the positions and movements of troops in the battle. Do research to find the information you need.

Citizenship Activity

Writing a Speech In the late 1860s, Memorial Day emerged as a day to honor soldiers who had died in the Civil War. Today, the holiday honors those whose lives were sacrificed in all American wars. Write a brief speech explaining why it is important to honor those who have died in American wars.

Internet Activity

On the Internet, find sites dealing with the Civil War. Choose a specific Civil War topic and prepare a five-minute presentation to give to the class. Possible topics include: a specific battle, a particular military or political leader, or the poetry and music of the Civil War.

Assume the role of an enslaved African American living in the Confederacy or an enslaved African American living in the Union. In your EYEWITNESS JOURNAL, describe your thoughts and feelings on January 1, 1863, the day the Emancipation Proclamation took effect.

Chapter 16 The Reconstruction Era

1864–1877

What's Ahead

Section 1 First Steps to Reunion

Section 2 Radical Reconstruction

Section 3 Changes in the South

Section 4 Reconstruction Ends

After the Civil War, rebuilding the ruined South was a tremendous job. Just as troubling was the task of bringing the former Confederate states back into the Union. Should southerners who had fought against the United States government be welcomed back or treated harshly? How could the nation protect the newly won rights of freed African Americans?

During a period called Reconstruction, North and South slowly reunited. At the same time, the economy of the South slowly recovered, and African Americans in the South gained several important rights and freedoms. However, in the years following Reconstruction, many of these rights were lost.

Why Study *History?* During Reconstruction and after, many African Americans became victims of violence. Groups like the Ku Klux Klan used terror to prevent black citizens from voting. Today, Americans continue to battle "hate crimes" and encourage tolerance, or acceptance of all people. To focus on this connection, see the *Why Study History?* feature in this chapter, "Tolerance Begins With You."

American Events

1865 Abraham Lincoln is assassinated

1867 Reconstruction Act imposes strict measures on southern states

1868 House of Representatives votes to impeach President Johnson

1864 | 1866 | 1868 | 1870

World Events

1865 World Event Maximillian becomes Emperor of Mexico

1867 World Event Dominion of Canada is formed

Viewing HISTORY **Reunion Begins**

This painting by Dennis Malone Carter shows Abraham Lincoln arriving in Richmond, Virginia. The President visited the captured Confederate capital during the final days of the Civil War. The painting shows Lincoln receiving a hero's welcome. In fact, though, many Richmond residents resented the visit by the leader of the victorious North. The reunion of the nation would not be easy. ★ **Predict two problems that the nation would face as the North and South reunited.**

1870
Fifteenth Amendment guarantees voting rights for African American men

1872
Congress pardons former Confederate officials

1877
Rutherford B. Hayes becomes President; Reconstruction ends

1870 | **1872** | **1874** | **1876**

1870 World Event
Italy is unified

1873 World Event
Abolition of slave markets in Zanzibar

Biography Charlotte Forten

Charlotte Forten came from a wealthy Philadelphia family. A strong abolitionist, she devoted her life to helping other African Americans improve their lives through education. When she was 25, she helped set up a school on the Sea Islands off South Carolina. Later, she helped recruit other teachers for the Freedmen's Bureau. ★ **Why do you think education was so important to freedmen?**

surrendered, Congress passed a bill creating the **Freedmen's Bureau.** Lincoln signed it.

The Freedmen's Bureau gave food and clothing to former slaves. It also tried to find jobs for freedmen. The bureau helped poor whites as well. It provided medical care for more than one million people. One former Confederate was amazed to see "a Government which was lately fighting us with fire, and sword, and shell, now generously feeding our poor and distressed."

One of the bureau's most important tasks was to set up schools for freed slaves in the South. By 1869, about 300,000 African Americans attended bureau schools. Most of the teachers were volunteers, often women, from the North.

Both old and young were eager to learn. Grandparents and grandchildren sat side by side in the classroom. One bureau agent in South Carolina observed that freedmen "will starve themselves, and go without clothes, in order to send their children to school." Charlotte Forten, an African American woman from Philadelphia, came south as a volunteer teacher. She wrote of her students:

> " I never before saw children so eager to learn.... It is wonderful how a people who have been so long crushed to the earth... can have so great a desire for knowledge, and such a capacity for attaining it. "

The Freedmen's Bureau laid the foundation for the South's public school system. It set up more than 4,300 grade schools. It also created colleges for African American students, including Howard, Morehouse, Fisk, and Hampton Institute. Many graduates of these schools became teachers themselves. By the 1870s, African Americans were teaching in grade schools throughout the South.

Lincoln Is Assassinated

President Lincoln hoped to persuade Congress to accept his Reconstruction plan. However, he never got the chance.

On April 14, 1865, just five days after Lee's surrender, the President attended a play at Ford's Theater in Washington, D.C. As Lincoln watched the play, **John Wilkes Booth,** a popular actor from the South, crept into the President's box and shot Lincoln in the head. Within a few hours, the President was dead. Booth was later caught and killed in a barn outside the city.

Connections With Arts

Walt Whitman's famous poem "O Captain! My Captain!" expresses his grief at the death of Lincoln. It begins, "O Captain! my Captain! our fearful trip is done, / The ship has weather'd every rack, the prize we sought is won." You can find this and other Civil War poems in Whitman's collection *Leaves of Grass.*

The nation plunged into grief. Millions who had been celebrating the war's end now mourned Lincoln's death. "Now he belongs to the ages," commented Secretary of War Edwin Stanton.

A New President

Vice President **Andrew Johnson** became President when Lincoln died. Johnson had served as governor of Tennessee and had represented that state in Congress. When Tennessee seceded, Johnson had remained loyal to the Union.

At first, many Republicans in Congress were pleased when Johnson became President. They believed that he would support a strict Reconstruction plan. As it turned out, Johnson's plan was much milder than expected.

Johnson called for a majority of voters in each southern state to pledge loyalty to the United States. He also demanded that each state ratify the **Thirteenth Amendment,** which banned slavery throughout the nation. (As you have read, Lincoln's Emancipation Proclamation did not free slaves in states that remained loyal to the Union.) Congress had approved the Thirteenth Amendment in January 1865.

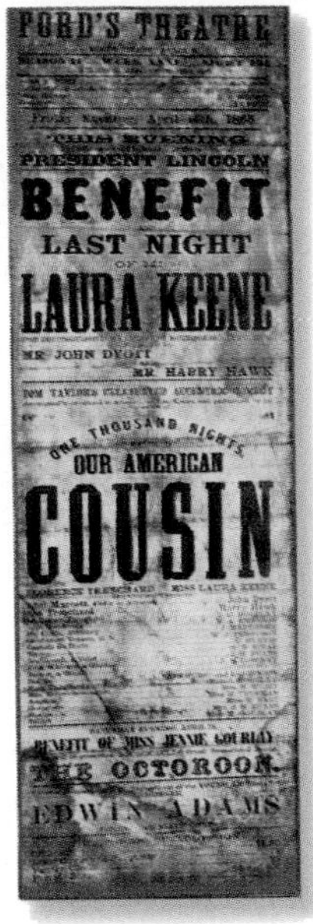

Playbill from Ford's Theater on the night Lincoln was shot

Rebellion in Congress

The southern states quickly met Johnson's conditions. As a result, the President approved their new state governments in late 1865. Voters in the South then elected representatives to Congress. Many of those elected had held office in the Confederacy. For example, Alexander Stephens, the former vice president of the Confederacy, was elected senator from Georgia.

Republicans in Congress were outraged. The men who had led the South out of the Union were being elected to the House and Senate. Also, no southern state allowed African Americans to vote.

When Congress met in December 1865, Republicans refused to let southern representatives take their seats. Instead, they set up a Joint Committee on Reconstruction to draw up a new plan for the South. The stage was set for a showdown between Congress and the President.

★ Section 1 Review ★

Recall

1. **Identify** **(a)** Reconstruction, **(b)** Ten Percent Plan, **(c)** Wade-Davis Bill, **(d)** Freedmen's Bureau, **(e)** John Wilkes Booth, **(f)** Andrew Johnson, **(g)** Thirteenth Amendment.
2. **Define** **(a)** freedmen, **(b)** amnesty.

Comprehension

3. Describe two problems the South faced after the Civil War.
4. **(a)** What was President Lincoln's Reconstruction plan? **(b)** How did it differ from the Wade-Davis Bill?
5. **(a)** What was President Johnson's plan for readmitting the former Confederate states to the Union? **(b)** How did Republicans in Congress react to Johnson's plan?

Critical Thinking and Writing

6. **Analyzing Information** The North lost more soldiers in the Civil War than the South did. Why was it easier for the North to recover from the war?
7. **Ranking** **(a)** What services did the Freedmen's Bureau provide? **(b)** Which do you think was most important? Explain.

Activity **Writing a Poem** President Lincoln has been shot! Taking the viewpoint of a northerner or southerner, write a poem about the death of Lincoln. If you like, you may set your poem to music.

Radical Reconstruction

As You Read

Explore These Questions

- What were the goals of the Radical Republicans?
- Why did Congress try to remove President Johnson from office?
- What were the Fourteenth and Fifteenth Amendments?

Define

- black codes
- radical
- impeach

Identify

- Radical Republicans
- Thaddeus Stevens
- Charles Sumner
- Fourteenth Amendment
- Radical Reconstruction
- Reconstruction Act
- Fifteenth Amendment

Setting the Scene In the spring of 1866, disturbing reports trickled into Congress. In some southern cities, peddlers were openly selling Confederate flags. Throughout the South, people sang a new song, "I'm a good old rebel / And I don't want no pardon for anything I done."

These reports confirmed what many Republicans had suspected. "The rebellion has not ended," declared one angry Republican. "It has only changed its weapons!"

Black Codes

After the war, most southern states had promptly ratified the Thirteenth Amendment, which banned slavery. At the same time, however, Southern legislatures passed **black codes,** laws that severely limited the rights of freedmen.

Black codes forbade African Americans to vote, own guns, or serve on juries. In some states, African Americans were permitted to work only as servants or farm laborers. In others, the codes required freedmen to sign contracts for a year's work. Those without contracts could be arrested and sentenced to work on a plantation.

Black codes did give African Americans some rights they did not have before the Civil War. For example, the codes permitted African Americans to marry legally and to own some kinds of property. Still, the codes were clearly meant to keep freedmen from gaining political or economic power.

The North Reacts

Republicans were angered by the black codes, as well as by the election of former Confederate leaders to Congress. The Joint Committee on Reconstruction sent the President a report accusing the South of trying to "preserve slavery in its original form as much and as long as possible." When Johnson ignored the report, members of Congress vowed to take Reconstruction out of the President's hands.

Those who led the opposition to President Johnson were called **Radical Republicans,** or Radicals. A **radical** wants to make drastic changes in society. **Thaddeus Stevens** of Pennsylvania led the Radicals in the House. **Charles Sumner** of Massachusetts was the chief Radical Republican in the Senate.

Radicals had two main goals. First, they wanted to break the power of wealthy planters who had long ruled the South. Radicals blamed these "aristocrats" for the Civil War. Second, Radicals wanted to ensure that freedmen received the right to vote.

Radical Republicans did not control Congress. To accomplish their goals, they needed the support of moderate Republicans, the largest group in Congress. Moderates and Radicals disagreed on many issues. However, they shared a strong political motive for endorsing strict treatment of the South. Most southerners were Democrats. With southerners barred from Congress, Republicans easily controlled both houses.

The President vs. Congress

The conflict between the President and Congress came to a head in 1866. In April, Congress passed the Civil Rights Act, giving citizenship to African Americans. Congress hoped to combat the black codes and secure basic rights for African Americans. When Johnson vetoed the bill, Congress overrode the veto.

The Fourteenth Amendment

Congressional Republicans worried that the Supreme Court might declare the Civil Rights Act unconstitutional. In the Dred Scott decision of 1857, the Court had ruled that African Americans were not citizens. Hoping to avoid a similar ruling, Republicans proposed the Fourteenth Amendment.

The **Fourteenth Amendment** granted citizenship to all persons born in the United States. This included nearly all African Americans. It also guaranteed all citizens "equal protection of the laws" and declared that no state could "deprive any person of life, liberty, or property without due process of law." This provision made it illegal for states to discriminate against an individual on unreasonable grounds, such as skin color.

The Fourteenth Amendment also provided that any state that denied African Americans the right to vote would have its representation in Congress reduced. Republicans believed that freedmen would be able to defend their rights if they could vote.

With the Fourteenth Amendment, Republicans hoped to secure basic political rights for African Americans in the South. In fact, the nation had far to go before all Americans achieved equality. Over the next 100 years, citizens would seek to obtain their rights by asking the courts to enforce the Fourteenth Amendment.

Election of 1866

President Johnson urged the former Confederate states to reject the Fourteenth Amendment. He also decided to make the amendment an issue in the November 1866 congressional elections. Traveling through the North, the President called on voters to reject the Radical Republicans.

Viewing History **New Rights for Freedmen**

Under the black codes, former slaves gained some new rights, such as the right to marry legally. Forms like this one helped freedmen keep their marriage and family records. ★ **Why were family records so valuable to freedmen?**

In many towns, audiences heckled the President. One heckler shouted that Johnson should hang Jefferson Davis. Losing his temper, Johnson yelled back, "Why not hang Thad Stevens?" Many northerners criticized Johnson for acting in an undignified manner.

In July, white mobs in New Orleans, Louisiana, killed 34 African Americans. This convinced many northerners that stronger measures were needed to protect freedmen.

In the end, the election results were a disaster for Johnson. Republicans won majorities in both houses of Congress. They also won every northern governorship and majorities in every northern state legislature.

The Radical Program

In 1867, Republicans in Congress prepared to take charge of Reconstruction. The period that followed is often called **Radical Reconstruction.** With huge majorities in

Rival Plans for Reconstruction

Plan	Ten Percent Plan	Wade-Davis Bill	Johnson Plan	Reconstruction Act
Proposed by	President Abraham Lincoln (1863)	Republicans in Congress (1864)	President Andrew Johnson (1865)	Radical Republicans (1867)
Conditions for former Confederate states to rejoin Union	▪ 10 percent of voters must swear loyalty to Union ▪ Must abolish slavery	▪ Majority of white men must swear loyalty ▪ Former Confederate volunteers cannot vote or hold office	▪ Majority of white men must swear loyalty ▪ Must ratify Thirteenth Amendment ▪ Former Confederate officials may vote and hold office	▪ Must disband state governments ▪ Must write new constitutions ▪ Must ratify Fourteenth Amendment ▪ African American men must be allowed to vote

Graphic Organizer *Skills* **In the early years of Reconstruction, federal leaders debated several plans for readmitting southern states.**

1. **Comprehension** **(a)** Identify one similarity between the Wade-Davis Bill and President Johnson's plan. **(b)** Identify one difference.
2. **Critical Thinking** If Lincoln had lived, do you think he would have supported the 1867 Reconstruction Act? Explain.

Civics

both the House and the Senate, Congress could easily override a presidential veto.

First Reconstruction Act

In March 1867, Congress passed the first **Reconstruction Act** over Johnson's veto. The Reconstruction Act threw out the southern state governments that had refused to ratify the Fourteenth Amendment—all the former Confederate states except Tennessee. The act also divided the South into five military districts under army control.

The Reconstruction Act required the former Confederate states to write new constitutions and to ratify the Fourteenth Amendment before rejoining the Union. Most important, the act stated that African Americans must be allowed to vote in all southern states.

Further Republican victories

Once the new constitutions were in place, the reconstructed states held elections to set up new state governments. To show their disgust with Radical Reconstruction policies, many white southerners stayed away from the polls. Freedmen, on the other hand, proudly turned out to exercise their new right to vote. As a result, Republicans gained control of all of the new southern state governments.

Congress passed several more Reconstruction acts. Each time, the Republicans easily overrode Johnson's veto.

Johnson Is Impeached

It was Johnson's duty, as President, to enforce the new Reconstruction laws. However, many Republicans feared he would not do so. Republicans in Congress decided to remove the President from office.

On February 24, 1868, the House of Representatives voted to impeach President Johnson. To **impeach** means to bring formal charges of wrongdoing against an elected official. According to the Constitution, the House can impeach the President only for "high crimes and misdemeanors." The Senate tries the case. The President is removed from office only if found guilty by two thirds of the senators.

During Johnson's trial, it became clear that he was not guilty of high crimes and misdemeanors. Even Charles Sumner, the President's bitter foe, admitted that the charges were "political in character."

Despite intense pressure, seven Republican senators refused to vote for conviction. The Constitution, they believed, did not allow a President to be removed from office simply because he disagreed with Congress. In the end, the Senate vote was 35 for and 19 against impeachment—one vote short of the two-thirds majority needed to remove the President from office. Johnson served out the few remaining months of his term.

A New President

In 1868, Republicans nominated General Ulysses S. Grant as their candidate for President. Grant was the Union's greatest hero in the Civil War.

By election day, most of the southern states had rejoined the Union. As Congress demanded, the new southern governments allowed African Americans to vote. About 700,000 blacks went to the polls in the 1868 election. Nearly all cast their votes for Grant. He easily defeated his opponent, Horatio Seymour.

The Fifteenth Amendment

In 1869, Republicans in Congress proposed another amendment to the Constitution. The **Fifteenth Amendment** forbade any state to deny African Americans the right to vote because of their race.

Many Republicans had moral reasons for supporting the Fifteenth Amendment. They remembered the great sacrifices that were made by African American soldiers in the Civil War. They also felt it was wrong to let African Americans vote in the South but not in the North.

Some Republicans also supported the Fifteenth Amendment for political reasons. African American votes had brought Republicans victory in the South. If African Americans could also vote in the North, they would help Republicans to win elections there, too.

The Fifteenth Amendment was ratified in 1870. At last, all African American men over age 21 had the right to vote.

★ Section 2 Review ★

Recall

1. **Identify** **(a)** Radical Republicans, **(b)** Thaddeus Stevens, **(c)** Charles Sumner, **(d)** Fourteenth Amendment, **(e)** Radical Reconstruction, **(f)** Reconstruction Act, **(g)** Fifteenth Amendment.
2. **Define** **(a)** black codes, **(b)** radical, **(c)** impeach.

Comprehension

3. Describe the Reconstruction plan enacted by Congress in 1867.
4. **(a)** Why did Congress impeach President Johnson? **(b)** What was the result?
5. Describe the goals of: **(a)** the Fourteenth Amendment; **(b)** the Fifteenth Amendment.

Critical Thinking and Writing

6. **Defending a Position** **(a)** Compare Johnson's plan for Reconstruction with the Radical Reconstruction plan. **(b)** Which plan would you have supported? Defend your position.
7. **Analyzing Ideas** A senator who voted against the removal of President Johnson later said that he did not vote in favor of Johnson but in favor of the presidency. What do you think he meant?

Activity **Writing a Speech** Write a speech from the point of view of a radical or moderate Republican. Present your position on Reconstruction and give reasons for your opinion.

3 Changes in the South

As You Read

Explore These Questions

- What groups dominated southern politics during Reconstruction?
- What did Reconstruction governments do to rebuild the South?
- Why did many southerners sink into a cycle of poverty?

Define

- scalawag
- carpetbagger
- sharecropper

Identify

- Hiram Revels
- Blanche K. Bruce
- Conservatives
- Ku Klux Klan

SETTING the Scene By 1867, life in the South had changed dramatically. African Americans were free to work for themselves, to vote, and to run for office. In Alabama, a political convention of freedmen drew up this ringing declaration:

> “We claim exactly the same rights, privileges and immunities as are enjoyed by white men. We ask nothing more and will be content with nothing less.”

Before the Civil War, a small group of rich planters controlled southern politics. During Reconstruction, however, new groups dominated state governments in the South. They tried to reshape southern politics. At the same time, others were taking strong action to reverse the gains made by African Americans.

New Forces in Southern Politics

The state governments created during Radical Reconstruction were different from any governments the South had known before. The old leaders had lost much of their influence. Three groups stepped in to replace them. These new groups were white southerners who supported the Republicans, northerners who moved south after the war, and African Americans.

Scalawags

Some white southerners supported the new Republican governments. Many were business people who had opposed secession in 1860. They wanted to forget the war and get on with rebuilding the South.

Many whites in the South felt that any southerner who helped the Republicans was a traitor. They called white southern Republicans **scalawags,** a word used for small, scruffy horses.

Carpetbaggers

Northerners who came south after the war were another important force. To white southerners, the new arrivals from the North were **carpetbaggers**—fortune hunters hoping to profit from the South's misery. Southerners claimed that these northerners were in such a hurry they had time only to fling a few clothes into cheap suitcases, or carpetbags.

To many southerners, the carpetbag became a hated symbol of Reconstruction.

In fact, northerners went south for a number of reasons. A few were fortune hunters who hoped to profit as the South was being rebuilt. Many more, however, were Union soldiers who had grown to love the South's rich land. Others, both white and

Viewing History **African Americans in Congress**

During Reconstruction, several African Americans won election to Congress. Here, Robert Brown Elliott of South Carolina stands in the House of Representatives to argue for a civil rights bill. Words from his speech appear on the banner above. "What you give to one class, you must give to all. What you deny to one class, you shall deny to all." ★ **Summarize Elliott's main point in your own words.**

black, were teachers, ministers, and reformers who sincerely wanted to improve the lives of the freedmen.

African Americans

Freedmen and other African Americans were the third major new group in southern politics. Before the war, African Americans had no voice in southern government. During Reconstruction, they not only voted in large numbers, but they also ran for and were elected to public office in the South.

African Americans became sheriffs, mayors, and legislators in the new state and local governments. Between 1869 and 1880, 16 African Americans were elected to Congress.

Two African Americans, both representing Mississippi, served in the Senate. **Hiram Revels,** a clergyman and teacher, became the nation's first black senator in 1870. He completed the unfinished term of former Confederate president Jefferson Davis. In 1874, **Blanche K. Bruce** became the first African American to serve a full term in the Senate. Born into slavery, Bruce escaped to freedom when the Civil War began and later served as a country sheriff.

Freedmen had less political influence than many whites claimed, however. Only in South Carolina did African Americans win a majority in one house of the state legislature. No state elected a black governor.

Conservatives Resist

From the start, most prominent white southerners resisted Reconstruction. These **Conservatives** wanted the South to change as little as possible. They were willing to let African Americans vote and hold a few offices. Still, they were determined that real power would remain in the hands of whites.

A few wealthy planters tried to force African Americans back onto plantations. Many small farmers and laborers wanted the government to take action against the millions of freedmen who now competed with them for land and power.

Most of these white southerners were Democrats. They declared war on anyone who cooperated with the Republicans. "This is a white man's country," they cried, "and white men must govern it."

Spreading terror

White southerners formed secret societies to help them regain power. The most dangerous was the **Ku Klux Klan,** or KKK. The Klan worked to keep blacks and white Republicans out of office.

Viewing HISTORY **Spreading Terror**

Wearing white hoods, the Ku Klux Klan used terror and violence to keep African Americans from voting. Famous cartoonist Thomas Nast attacked the Klan and other secret societies.

★ **Identify two Klan actions shown in the cartoon. Why do you think Nast labeled his cartoon "WORSE THAN SLAVERY"?**

Ku Klux Klan hood ➤

Dressed in white robes and hoods to hide their identity, Klansmen rode at night to the homes of African American voters, shouting threats and burning wooden crosses. When threats did not work, the Klan turned to violence. Klan members murdered hundreds of African Americans and their white allies.

Congress responds

Many moderate southerners condemned the violence of the Klan. Yet they could do little to stop the Klan's reign of terror. Freedmen turned to the federal government for help. In Kentucky, African American voters wrote to Congress:

> ❝ We believe you are not familiar with the Ku Klux Klan's riding nightly over the country spreading terror wherever they go by robbing, whipping, and killing our people without provocation. ❞

Congress tried to end Klan violence. In 1870, Congress made it a crime to use force to keep people from voting. As a result, Klan activities decreased. Yet the threat of violence lingered. Some African Americans continued to vote and hold office despite the risk. Many others were frightened away from the ballot box.

The Task of Rebuilding

Despite political problems, Reconstruction governments tried to rebuild the South. They built public schools for both black and white children. Many states gave women the right to own property. In addition, Reconstruction governments rebuilt railroads, telegraph lines, bridges, and roads. Between 1865 and 1879, the South put down 7,000 miles of railroad track.

Rebuilding cost money. Before the war, southerners paid very low taxes. Reconstruction governments raised taxes sharply. This created discontent among many southern whites.

Southerners were further angered by widespread corruption in the Reconstruction governments. One state legislature, for example, voted $1,000 to cover a member's bet on a horse race. Other items billed to the state included hams, perfume, and a coffin.

Corruption was not limited to the South. After the Civil War, dishonesty plagued northern governments as well. In fact, most southern officeholders served their states honestly.

A Cycle of Poverty

In the first months after the war, freedmen left the plantations on which they had

While the Ku Klux Klan carried out its program of violence, others used economic weapons to intimidate African Americans. Planters refused to rent land to blacks. Employers refused to hire them, and storekeepers denied them credit. What effect do you think such pressures had?

Skills FOR LIFE

Critical Thinking | Managing Information | Communication | Maps, Charts, and Graphs

Interpreting a Political Cartoon

How Will I Use This Skill?

Almost every newspaper today includes political cartoons. Cartoonists comment on current events through both visual imagery and words. Their pictures often use symbols and exaggeration to make their point. Learning to analyze cartoons can help you better understand views on current issues.

LEARN the Skill

1. Identify the characters and symbols used in the cartoon. Remember that a symbol is an object that represents something beyond itself. The eagle, for example, is often used as a symbol for the United States.
2. Note details in the drawing. Are some details larger or smaller than normal? Are any facial features or actions in the cartoon exaggerated?
3. Analyze the relationship between the pictures and any words in the cartoon.
4. Identify the cartoonist's point of view. Try to identify policies or actions that the cartoonist wants readers to support.

PRACTICE the Skill

The cartoon on the right appeared in a northern newspaper in the 1870s. Use the steps above to analyze the cartoon.

1. The figure at the top of the cartoon is President Grant. Explain what these other symbols represent: (a) the woman; (b) the soldiers; (c) the carpetbag.
2. (a) Note the size of the details in this drawing. Are any larger than normal? Why? (b) What do Grant's facial expression and the position of his arms suggest about his attitude toward the South?
3. (a) What words are written on the paper sticking out of the carpetbag? What do they mean? (b) What is the woman doing? (c) Is her task easy or difficult?
4. (a) How do you think this cartoonist felt about Radical Reconstruction? Explain. (b) What policy do you think the cartoonist would want his readers to support?

APPLY the Skill

Find a current political cartoon in the editorial section of a newspaper. Using the skills you have learned in this section, write a paragraph explaining the cartoon.

lived and worked. They found few opportunities, however.

"Nothing but freedom"

Some Radical Republicans talked about giving each freedman "40 acres and a mule." Thaddeus Stevens suggested breaking up big plantations and distributing the land. Most Americans opposed the plan, however. In the end, former slaves received—in the words of a freedman—"nothing but freedom."

Through hard work or good luck, some freedmen were able to become landowners. Most, however, had little choice but to return to where they had lived in slavery.

Sharecropping

Some large planters had held onto their land and wealth through the war. Now, they had land but no slaves to work it. During Reconstruction, many freedmen and poor whites went to work on the large plantations. These **sharecroppers** farmed the land, using seed, fertilizer, and tools provided by the planters. In return, the planters got a share of the crop at harvest time. Sharecroppers hoped to have their own land one day. Meanwhile, they were lucky to have enough food for themselves and their families.

Even farmers who owned land faced hard times. Each spring, the farmers received supplies on credit. In the fall, they had to repay what they had borrowed. Often, the harvest did not cover the debt. Unable to pay, many farmers lost their land and became sharecroppers themselves. Many southerners became locked in a cycle of poverty.

Sharecroppers growing cotton behind their cabin

★ Section 3 Review ★

Recall

1. **Identify** **(a)** Hiram Revels, **(b)** Blanche K. Bruce, **(c)** Conservatives, **(d)** Ku Klux Klan.
2. **Define** **(a)** scalawag, **(b)** carpetbagger, **(c)** sharecropper.

Comprehension

3. **(a)** What role did freedmen play in Reconstruction governments? **(b)** How was this different from the role of African Americans before the Civil War?
4. **(a)** What were two accomplishments of Reconstruction governments? **(b)** What were two problems?
5. Why did many freedmen and poor whites become sharecroppers?

Critical Thinking and Writing

6. **Understanding Causes and Effects** During Reconstruction, freedmen proved that, given the chance, they could do the same jobs as whites. Do you think this made southern Conservatives more willing or less willing to accept African Americans as equals? Explain.
7. **Linking Past and Present** Many southerners were angered by high taxes imposed by Reconstruction governments. **(a)** How do voters today feel about paying high taxes? **(b)** Do you think some services should be provided even if they require high taxes? Explain.

Activity **Drawing a Political Cartoon** Draw a political cartoon expressing your opinion about scalawags, carpetbaggers, the Ku Klux Klan, or another aspect of Reconstruction in the South.

Reconstruction Ends

Explore These Questions
- Why did Reconstruction end?
- How did the southern economy expand after Reconstruction?
- How did African Americans in the South lose rights?

Define
- poll tax
- literacy test
- grandfather clause
- segregation
- lynching

Identify
- Rutherford B. Hayes
- Henry Grady
- James Duke
- Jim Crow laws
- *Plessy* v. *Ferguson*

SETTING the Scene In 1876, millions of Americans visited a great Centennial Exposition held in Philadelphia. The fair celebrated the first hundred years of the United States. Visitors gazed at the latest wonders of modern industry—the elevator, the telephone, a giant steam engine.

As Americans looked to the future, they lost interest in Reconstruction. By the late 1870s, white Conservatives had regained control of the South.

Radicals in Decline

By the 1870s, Radical Republicans were losing power in Congress. Many northerners grew weary of trying to reform the South. It was time to forget the Civil War, they believed, and let southerners run their own governments—even if that meant African Americans might lose their rights.

Republicans were also hurt by disclosure of widespread corruption in the government of President Grant. The President had appointed many friends to office. Some used their position to steal large sums of money from the government. Grant won reelection in 1872, but many northerners had lost faith in Republican leaders and their policies.

Congress reflected the new mood of the North. In May 1872, it passed the Amnesty Act, which restored the right to vote to nearly all white southerners. As expected, they voted solidly Democratic. At the same time, southern whites terrorized African Americans who tried to vote.

White Conservatives were firmly in control once more. One by one, the Republican governments in the South fell. By 1876, only three southern states—Louisiana, South Carolina, and Florida—were still controlled by Republicans.

Election of 1876

The end of Reconstruction came with the election of 1876. The Democrats nominated Samuel Tilden, governor of New York, for President. Tilden was known for fighting corruption. The Republican candidate was **Rutherford B. Hayes,** governor of Ohio. Like Tilden, Hayes vowed to fight dishonesty in government.

Tilden won 250,000 more popular votes than Hayes. However, Tilden had only 184 electoral votes—one vote short of the number needed to win. Twenty other votes were in dispute. The outcome of the election hung on these votes. All but one of the disputed votes came from Florida, Louisiana, and South Carolina—the three southern states still controlled by Republicans.

As inauguration day drew near, the nation still had no one to swear in as President. Congress set up a special commission to settle the crisis. A majority of the commission members were Republicans. The commission decided to give all the disputed electoral votes to Hayes.

Southern Democrats could have fought the election of Hayes. Hayes, however, had privately agreed to end Reconstruction. Once in office, he removed all remaining federal troops from South Carolina, Louisiana, and Florida. Reconstruction was over.

Industry and the "New South"

During Reconstruction, the South made some progress toward rebuilding its economy. Cotton production, long the basis of the South's economy, slowly recovered. By 1880, planters were growing as much cotton as they had in 1860.

After Reconstruction, a new generation of southern leaders worked to expand the economy. **Henry Grady,** editor of the *Atlanta Constitution,* made stirring speeches calling for the growth of a "New South." Grady argued that the South should use its vast natural resources to build up its own industry, instead of depending on the North.

Agricultural industries

Southerners agreed that the best way to begin industrializing was to process the region's agricultural goods. Investors built textile mills to turn cotton into cloth. By 1880, the entire South was still producing fewer textiles than Massachusetts. In the next decade, though, more and more communities started building textile mills.

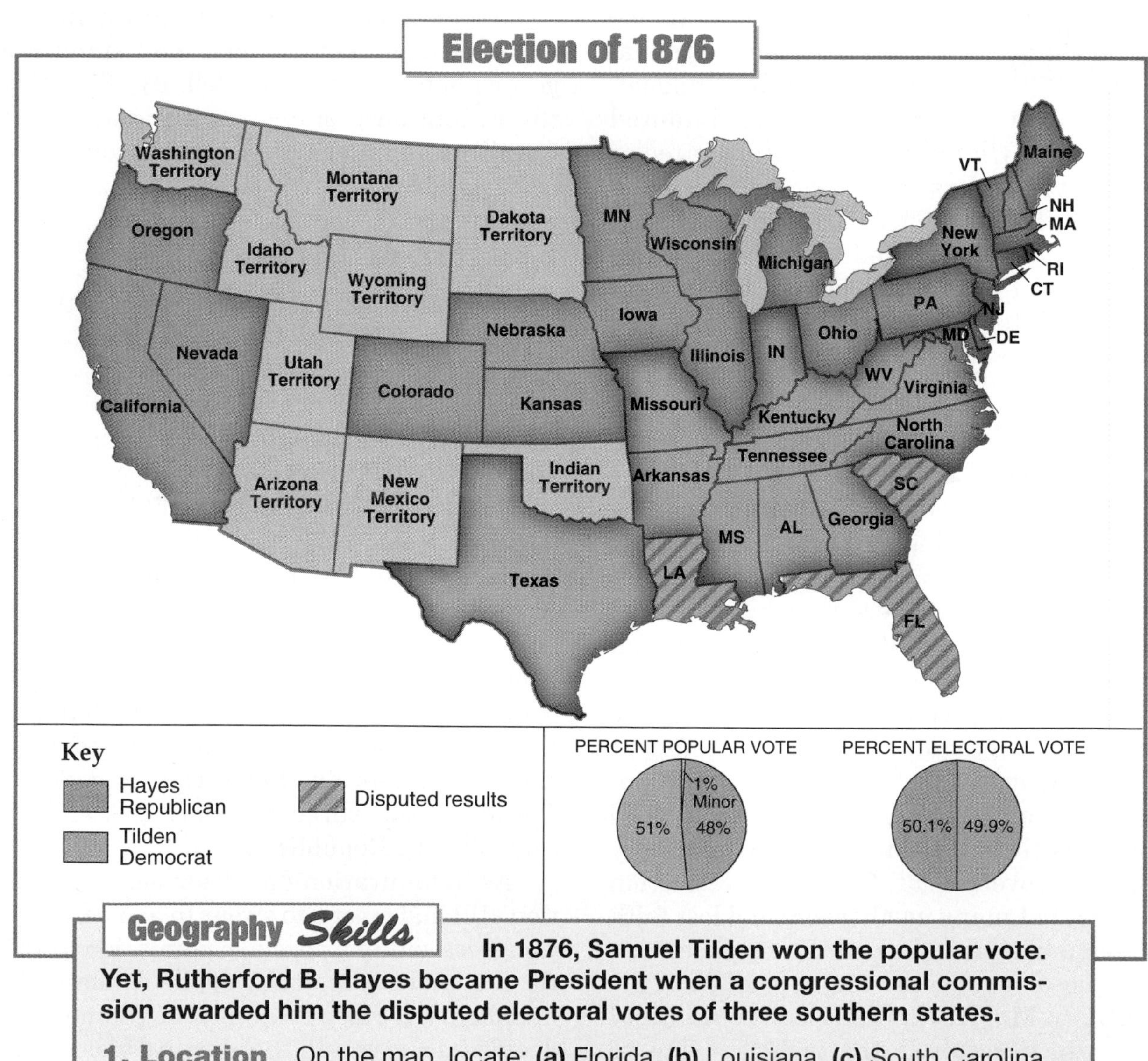

Geography *Skills* **In 1876, Samuel Tilden won the popular vote. Yet, Rutherford B. Hayes became President when a congressional commission awarded him the disputed electoral votes of three southern states.**

1. **Location** On the map, locate: **(a)** Florida, **(b)** Louisiana, **(c)** South Carolina.
2. **Movement** Which candidate carried the undisputed southern vote?
3. **Critical Thinking** Based on the map, do you think the Civil War ended sectionalism in the United States? Explain.

The tobacco industry also grew rapidly. In North Carolina, **James Duke** used new machinery to revolutionize production of tobacco products. In 1890, he bought out several competitors to form the American Tobacco Company. Duke eventually controlled 90 percent of the nation's tobacco industry.

New industries

The South also tapped its mineral resources. Local deposits of iron ore and coal, as well as low wages for workers, made steel production cheaper in Alabama than in Pennsylvania. Oil refineries developed in Louisiana and Texas. Other states became leading producers of coal, copper, granite, and marble.

By the 1890s, many northern forests had been cut down. The southern yellow pine was competing with the northwestern white pine as a lumber source. Some southern factories began to make cypress shingles and hardwood furniture.

A visitor from New England described what he found on a visit to the South in 1887:

> ❝ We find a South wide awake with business, excited and even astonished at the development of its own immense resources in metals, marbles, coal, timber, fertilizers, eagerly laying lines of communication, rapidly opening mines, building furnaces, foundries, and all sorts of shops for utilizing the native riches. ❞

By 1900, the South had developed a more balanced economy. Still, it failed to keep up with even more rapid growth in the North and the West.

Viewing HISTORY **Rise of the New South**

From Darkness to Light *by Grant Hamilton shows the New South rising from the ruins of war. Hamilton created this picture for one of several industrial expositions held in Atlanta, Georgia, in the late 1800s.* ★ **According to this picture, what products helped the southern economy grow?**

Restricting the Rights of African Americans

The years after Reconstruction brought prosperity to some southerners. For African Americans, though, the end of Reconstruction had tragic effects.

With the North out of southern affairs, white Conservatives tightened their grip on southern governments. Some groups continued to use violence to keep African Americans from voting. Southern states also found new ways to keep African Americans from exercising their rights.

Voting restrictions

In the 1880s, many southern states began passing new laws that restricted the right to vote. **Poll taxes** required voters to pay a fee each time they voted. As a result, poor freedmen could rarely afford to vote. **Literacy tests** required voters to read and explain a section of the Constitution. Since most freedmen had little education, such tests kept them away from the polls.

Many poor southern whites also could not pass the literacy test. To increase the number of eligible white voters, states passed **grandfather clauses.** If a voter's father or grandfather had been eligible to vote on January 1, 1867, the voter did not have to take

Why Study History?

Because Tolerance Begins With You

Historical Background

During and after Reconstruction, hate groups like the Ku Klux Klan used violence and terror to keep African Americans from voting or holding any political office. Angry mobs set fire to African American homes, churches, and schools. They even lynched people. Often, these tactics worked. Yet many whites and African Americans continued to speak out against injustice.

Artist Jim Osborn created this painting to encourage respect and tolerance.

Connections to Today

Discrimination and hate crimes have not been limited to African Americans in the South in the 1800s. Almost every group in this nation has suffered the pain of senseless hatred. People feel the sting of prejudice for many reasons: religion, race, economic status, age, or physical or mental abilities.

Acts of prejudice continue today. In recent years, Jewish cemeteries have been vandalized. African American churches have been burned. Asian American stores have been covered in racist graffiti. Mexican American or Arab American businesses have been attacked. In some areas, police have set up special "hate crime" units to investigate actions such as these.

Connections to You

Tolerance begins with you. You can fight prejudice by respecting and appreciating people's differences. Everyone in your class has different talents and experiences. You can get to know your classmates for who they are, rather than on the basis of what you think you know about them. You will find that you have much in common with students who seem different.

Many schools provide opportunities for you to increase your ability to get along with others. Human relations clubs promote understanding of diverse groups. Peer-mediation programs can teach you how to deal with anger and conflict. By keeping an open mind and educating yourself, you can help end discrimination and prejudice.

1. **Comprehension** **(a)** What tactics did hate groups use against African Americans in the South? **(b)** Identify two kinds of discrimination some people face today.
2. **Critical Thinking** How do prejudice and discrimination begin?

Making a Poster Make a list of three things that you could do to promote tolerance. Create a poster illustrating one of them.

a literacy test. Since no African Americans in the South could vote before 1868, grandfather clauses were a way to ensure that only white men could vote.

Racial segregation

Southern blacks lost more than the right to vote. After 1877, segregation became the law of the South. **Segregation** means separating people of different races in public places. Southern states passed laws that separated blacks and whites in schools, restaurants, theaters, trains, streetcars, playgrounds, hospitals, and even cemeteries. **Jim Crow laws,** as they were known, trapped southern blacks in a hopeless situation. In 1885, the Louisiana novelist George Washington Cable described segregation as:

> "... a system of oppression so rank that nothing could make it seem small except the fact that [African Americans] had already been ground under it for a century and a half."

African Americans brought lawsuits to challenge segregation. In 1896, in the case of ***Plessy* v. *Ferguson,*** the Supreme Court ruled that segregation was legal so long as facilities for blacks and whites were equal. In fact, facilities were rarely equal. For example, southern states spent much less on schools for blacks than for whites.

Violence

When Reconstruction ended, groups like the Ku Klux Klan declined. However, violent acts against African Americans continued. During the 1890s, almost 200 Americans were lynched each year. **Lynching** is the illegal seizure and execution of someone by a mob. Four out of five lynchings took place in the South, and the majority of the victims were African American.

Some lynching victims were accused of crimes. Others were simply considered troublemakers. Victims—including some women and children—were hanged, shot, or burned to death, often after painful torture. Members of lynch mobs rarely faced punishment. By the late 1800s, some reformers began to speak out against lynching.

Results of Reconstruction

Reconstruction was a time of both success and failure. Southerners faced hard times. Still, the South gained a public education system and expanded its rail lines.

As a result of Reconstruction, all African Americans became citizens for the first time. These rights eroded after Reconstruction ended. However, the laws passed during Reconstruction, such as the Fourteenth Amendment, became the basis of the civil rights movement almost 100 years later.

★ Section 4 Review ★

Recall

1. **Identify** **(a)** Rutherford B. Hayes, **(b)** Henry Grady, **(c)** James Duke, **(d)** Jim Crow laws, **(e)** *Plessy* v. *Ferguson.*
2. **Define** **(a)** poll tax, **(b)** literacy test, **(c)** grandfather clause, **(d)** segregation, **(e)** lynching.

Comprehension

3. Why did Radical Republicans' power decline?
4. How did the economy of the South change?
5. Describe two ways that African Americans lost their rights after Reconstruction ended.

Critical Thinking and Writing

6. **Evaluating Information** Do you think that Reconstruction was successful? Explain.
7. **Predicting Consequences** How do you think *Plessy* v. *Ferguson* affected later efforts to achieve equality for African Americans?

Activity **Acting a Scene** With a partner, act out a scene of an African American man trying to vote in the South in the late 1880s. Begin by considering how you might feel if you knew that you had the right to vote, yet someone was able to prevent you from voting.

Chapter 16 Review and Activities

★ Sum It Up ★

Section 1 First Steps to Reunion

- After the Civil War, the South faced the task of repairing tremendous destruction.
- The Freedmen's Bureau helped newly freed African Americans learn to read, and provided food and clothing to the needy.
- Presidents Lincoln and Johnson recommended mild plans for Reconstruction, but Congress refused to accept either one.

Section 2 Radical Reconstruction

- Radical Republicans wanted to break the power of rich planters in the South and make sure that freedmen could vote.
- Congress tried and failed to remove President Johnson from office.
- Republicans proposed the Fourteenth and Fifteenth amendments to ensure the civil rights of African Americans.

Section 3 Changes in the South

- Southern Republicans, whites from the North, and freed African Americans played important roles in southern governments.
- Landless black and white sharecroppers became locked in a cycle of poverty.

Section 4 Reconstruction Ends

- Reconstruction ended after presidential candidate Rutherford B. Hayes made a private deal with southern politicians.
- After Reconstruction, a new industrial economy began to emerge in the South.
- Southern whites passed new laws to deny African Americans equal rights.

For additional review of the major ideas of Chapter 16, see ***Guide to the Essentials of American History*** or ***Interactive Student Tutorial CD-ROM,*** which contains interactive review activities, graphic organizers, and practice tests.

Reviewing the Chapter

Define These Terms

Match each term with the correct definition.

Column 1

1. freedman
2. black codes
3. scalawag
4. poll tax
5. segregation

Column 2

- **a.** laws that severely limited the rights of freedmen
- **b.** tax required before someone could vote
- **c.** white southern Republican
- **d.** former slave
- **e.** separating people of different races in public places

Explore the Main Ideas

1. Describe the condition of the South after the war.
2. How did Republicans in Congress gain control of Reconstruction?
3. Give two reasons why Republicans supported the Fifteenth Amendment.
4. Describe the economic recovery of the South after the Civil War.
5. Why did most Americans lose interest in Reconstruction in the 1870s?
6. What was the purpose of Jim Crow laws?

Geography Activity

Match the letters on the map with the following places: **1.** South Carolina, **2.** Florida, **3.** Louisiana, **4.** Ohio, **5.** New York. **Region** Which southern states were under Republican control in 1876?

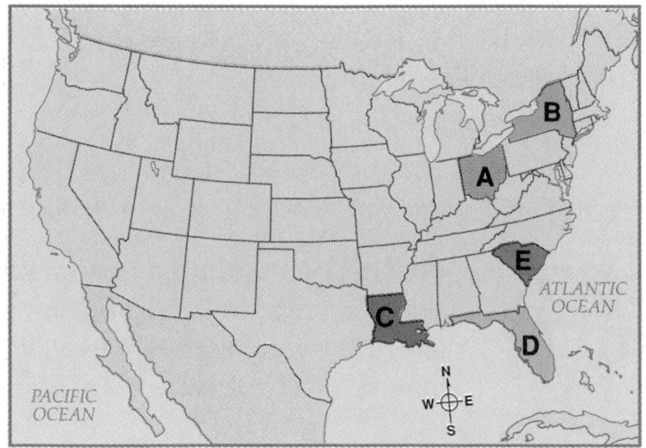

Critical Thinking and Writing

1. **Understanding Chronology** **(a)** Put the following in the order in which they were first proposed: the Reconstruction Acts; the Wade-Davis Bill; the Ten Percent Plan; Jim Crow laws. **(b)** Why did Lincoln have so little influence on Reconstruction?
2. **Exploring Unit Themes** **Sectionalism** Briefly state your own plan for repairing the bitter feelings between North and South.
3. **Analyzing Ideas** Most people call groups such as the Ku Klux Klan "un-American." Explain the reasons for this belief.
4. **Predicting Consequences** After the Civil War, the United States entered a period of industrial growth that made it the richest nation in the world. How do you think the South's experiences during Reconstruction affected its share in this industrial boom?

Using Primary Sources

Born into slavery, Booker T. Washington became a leading educator. Here, he describes one of the problems that came with emancipation:

> "Was it any wonder that within a few hours the wild rejoicing ceased and a feeling of deep gloom seemed to pervade the slave quarters? To some it seemed that, now that they were in actual possession of it, freedom was a more serious thing than they expected to find it. Some of the slaves were seventy or eighty years old; their best days were gone. They had no strength with which to earn a living in a strange place and among strange people, even if they had been sure where to find a new place of abode."

Source: *Up From Slavery,* Booker T. Washington, 1901.

Recognizing Points of View **(a)** What caused the "wild rejoicing" Washington mentions? **(b)** Why did the rejoicing end so quickly? **(c)** Why do you think many African Americans were unprepared for the realities of freedom?

Activity Bank

Interdisciplinary Activity

Connections With Arts Review the goals of the Freedmen's Bureau. Then create a poster advertising the Bureau's work and encouraging volunteers to participate.

Career Skills Activity

Playwrights and Actors Find out more about the events and issues leading up to the trial of President Andrew Johnson. Then prepare a skit in which you act out Johnson's trial in the United States Senate.

Citizenship Activity

Understanding the Constitution Study the text of the Fourteenth and Fifteenth amendments printed in the Reference Section. Create a graphic organizer for each amendment. Include the main ideas of each amendment and show how it affects the daily lives of Americans today. You may illustrate your work with original drawings or clippings.

Internet Activity

Use the Internet to find primary sources on Reconstruction. Then use the primary source to create a newspaper interview with the person who wrote the material you have found. Create questions that are answered by quotations taken from the primary source.

You are a freedman, a Radical Republican, a Conservative southern planter, or a northerner who went south during Reconstruction. In your EYEWITNESS JOURNAL, *describe your reaction to three important events of the Reconstruction era.*

The Red Badge of Courage

Stephen Crane

Introduction

Stephen Crane was born six years after the Civil War ended. He spent many hours reading about the war and talking to veterans. In 1895, he published his great Civil War novel, *The Red Badge of Courage.* It tells the story of Henry Fleming, a young volunteer in the Union Army. The following passage describes Henry's departure from home and his early days in the army.

Vocabulary

Before you read the selection, find the meaning of these words in a dictionary: **doggedly, shirking, monotonous, province, pickets, philosophical, reflectively, reproached, infantile, assurance.**

When [Henry] had stood in the doorway with his soldier's clothes on his back, and with the light of excitement and expectancy in his eyes almost defeating the glow of regret for the home bonds, he had seen two tears leaving their trails on his mother's scarred cheeks.

Still, she had disappointed him by saying nothing whatever about returning with his shield or on it.* He had privately primed himself for a beautiful scene. He had prepared certain sentences which he thought could be used with touching effect. But her words destroyed his plans. She had doggedly peeled potatoes and addressed him as follows: "You watch out, Henry, an' take good care of yerself in this here fighting business —you watch out, an' take good care of yerself. Don't go a-thinkin' you can lick the hull rebel army at the start, because yeh can't. Yer jest one little feller amongst a hull lot of others, and yeh've got to keep quiet an' do what they tell yeh. I know how you are, Henry.

"I've knet yeh eight pair of socks, Henry, and I've put in all yer best shirts, because I want my boy to be jest as warm and comf'able as anybody in the army. Whenever they get holes in 'em, I want yeh to send 'em rightaway back to me, so's I kin dern 'em.

"An' allus be careful an' choose yer comp'ny. There's lots of bad men in the army, Henry. The army makes 'em wild, and they like nothing better than the job of leading off a young feller like you, as ain't never been away from home much and has allus had a mother, an' a-learning 'em to drink and swear. Keep clear of them folks, Henry....

"I don't know what else to tell yeh, Henry, excepting that yeh must never do no shirking, child, on my account. If so be a time comes when yeh have to be kilt or do a mean thing, why, Henry, don't think of anything 'cept what's right, because there's many a woman has to bear up 'ginst sech things these times, and the Lord'll take keer of us all.

"Don' forget about the socks and the shirts, child; and I've put a cup of blackberry jam with yer bundle, because I know yeh like it

* The Spartan people of ancient Greece carried home their dead warriors on their shields.

Viewing History: A Soldier Says Goodbye

This anonymous painting, Off to the Front, 1861, *hangs in the museum of the United States Military Academy at West Point, New York. It shows a young soldier saying goodbye to his family in the first year of the Civil War. Scenes like this were common in homes throughout the North and South.* ★ **Choose one of the people in this painting. What do you think are that person's thoughts and feelings?**

above all things. Good-by, Henry. Watch out, and be a good boy."

He had, of course, been impatient under the ordeal of this speech. It had not been quite what he expected, and he had borne it with an air of irritation. He departed feeling vague relief.

Still, when he had looked back from the gate, he had seen his mother kneeling among the potato parings. Her brown face, upraised, was stained with tears, and her spare form was quivering. He bowed his head and went on, feeling suddenly ashamed....

After complicated journeyings with many pauses, there had come months of monotonous life in a camp. He had had the belief that real war was a series of death struggles with small time in between for sleep and meals; but since his regiment had come to the field the army had done little but sit still and try to keep warm....

He had grown to regard himself merely as a part of a vast blue demonstration. His province was to look out, as far as he could, for his personal comfort. For recreation he could twiddle his thumbs and speculate on the thoughts which must agitate the minds of the generals. Also, he was drilled and drilled and reviewed, and drilled and drilled and reviewed.

The only foes he had seen were some pickets along the river bank. They were a suntanned, philosophical lot, who sometimes shot reflectively at the blue pickets. When reproached for this afterward, they usually expressed sorrow, and swore by their gods that the guns had exploded without their permission. The youth, on guard duty one night, conversed across the stream with one of them. He was a slightly ragged man, who spat skillfully between his shoes and possessed a great fund of bland and infantile assurance. The youth liked him personally.

"Yank," the other had informed him, "yer a right dum good feller." This sentiment, floating to him upon the still air, had made him temporarily regret war.

Analyzing Literature

1. What advice did Henry's mother give him?
2. How was a soldier's life different than what Henry expected?
3. **Making Generalizations** What does Henry's experience with the enemy picket suggest about the special problems of fighting a civil war?

Unit 6 Transforming the Nation

What's Ahead

Viewing UNIT THEMES **A Triumph of Technology**

On May 24, 1883, New Yorkers celebrated the opening of the Brooklyn Bridge with fireworks and a boat parade. The bridge was one of the greatest feats of American engineering. At first, the Brooklyn Bridge carried pedestrians and horse-drawn carriages. Soon after, a new invention—the automobile—would appear.

★ **Name two earlier inventions that improved transportation in the United States.**

Unit Theme Industrialization

After the Civil War, the United States underwent a great transformation. Industrialists opened thousands of new factories. Shrewd business leaders made fortunes building railroads, manufacturing steel, or drilling for oil. New inventions, from the light bulb to the automobile, changed daily life. Industrialization fueled the rapid growth of cities.

How did people of the time feel about industrialization? They can tell you in their own words.

★ ★

Viewpoints on Industrialization

"In factories where labor-saving machinery has reached its most wonderful development, little children are at work."

Henry George, economist and journalist (1879)

"Better morals, better sanitary conditions, better health, better wages, these are the practical results of the factory system."

Carroll D. Wright, United States labor commissioner (1882)

"Law, I reckon I was born to work in a mill. I started when I was ten years old and I aim to keep right on just as long as I'm able. I'd a-heap rather do it than housework."

Alice Caudle, textile worker, recalling her childhood (1938)

★ ★

Activity Writing to Learn Industrialization transformed the way people worked. You are a young American of the late 1800s. You grew up in the country, working on the family farm. You have just moved to a big city where you are about to begin your new job in a factory making lawnmowers. Make a list of the ways in which your new job differs from your old one.

Chapter 17

An Era of Change in the West 1865–1914

What's Ahead

Section 1
The Plains Indians

Section 2
Miners and Railroaders

Section 3
Ranchers and Cowhands

Section 4
A Way of Life Ends

Section 5
The Farmers

After the Civil War, settlers flooded the West. Miners sought gold and silver. Railroad builders spanned the continent with rail lines. Ranchers raised great herds of cattle. Farmers changed grasslands into fields of wheat and corn. As these westerners gained political influence, they urged government leaders to address their needs and concerns.

Native Americans, meanwhile, were driven from their homelands. The Indians struggled to keep their way of life. In the end, however, they were defeated. On reservations, they were forced to learn new ways. Native Americans suffered greatly from the changes that swept the West.

Why Study History?

According to most historians, the cowhand was an important figure in the American West for only a short time. Nevertheless, the cowboy entered American culture as an enduring mythic hero. The image of the cowboy still speaks to people today. To learn more about this topic, see this chapter's *Why Study History?* feature, "The Cowboy Is Part of Our Culture."

American Events

1869 Nation's first transcontinental railroad is completed

1876 Sitting Bull defeats Custer during the Sioux War

1887 Dawes Act encourages Native Americans to change their lifestyle

1865 | 1870 | 1875 | 1880 | 1885 | 1890

World Events

1869 World Event
Suez canal opens in Egypt

1879 World Event
British and Zulus go to war in southern Africa

Viewing HISTORY **Cold Morning on the Range**

In the late 1800s, the West and its wide-open spaces captured the imagination of adventurers, settlers, business people, writers, and artists. They all saw the frontiers of the West as places of opportunity. Sadly, few people were concerned with the Native Americans who already lived there. In this colorful painting by Frederic Remington, a cowhand tries to ride a bucking bronco. ★ **How do you think this and similar paintings affected people's ideas about the West? Explain.**

1891
Farmers and labor unions join to form Populist Party

1897
William McKinley becomes President

1913
States ratify income tax amendment to the Constitution

1890 **1895** **1900** **1905** **1910** **1915**

1900 World Event
Trans-Siberian railroad opens to connect Moscow to Pacific coast

1910 World Event
China abolishes slavery

The Plains Indians

As You Read

Explore These Questions

- How did Plains Indians rely on the horse and the buffalo?
- What traditions were important to the Plains Indians?
- How did the roles of women and men differ?

Define

- tepee
- travois
- corral
- jerky

Identify

- Sun Dance

SETTING the Scene Standing Bear, a Lakota, or Sioux* Indian, recalled the buffalo-rib sled his father made for him when he was a boy living on the Plains:

> ❝ After all the meat had been cleaned from the bones, my father took six of the ribs and placed them together. He then split a piece of cherry wood and put the ends of the bones between the pieces of wood. The whole affair was then laced together with rawhide rope. ❞

Standing Bear's rib sled is only one example of the many uses that Plains Indians had for the buffalo that roamed their homeland. Indians had been living for centuries on the Great Plains. They developed ways of life that were well suited to the region.

Way of Life

Many different Native American nations lived on the Great Plains. (See the map on page 31.) A number of nations, such as the Arikaras, had lived on the Plains for hundreds of years. Others, like the Lakotas, did not move to the Plains until the 1700s.

Plains Indians had rich and varied cultures. They had well-organized religions, made fine handicrafts, and created much poetry. Each nation had its own language. People from different nations used sign language to talk to one another.

At one time, most Plains Indians were farmers who lived in semipermanent villages. From there, they sent out hunting parties that pursued herds of buffalo and other animals on foot. Agriculture, however, was their main source of food.

During the 1600s, the Plains Indians' way of life changed as they captured and tamed wild horses. These horses were descended from animals that the Spanish had brought to the Americas. On horseback, the Indians could travel farther and faster. As a result, buffalo hunting replaced farming as the basis of life for many Plains people.

Following the buffalo

Plains Indians followed the huge herds of buffalo that roamed the Plains. They began to live in **tepees** (TEE pees), or tents made by stretching buffalo skins on tall poles. The tepees could easily be carried on a **travois** (trə VOI), or sled pulled by a dog or horse.

Connections With Science

Plains Indians rubbed buffalo fat on their skin to protect themselves from the weather and from insects. They used paints made from clay, charred wood, and copper ore to decorate their faces.

*Sioux was the French name for these Indians. In fact, the Sioux included many different groups who had their own names for themselves, including Lakota, Dakota, and Nakota.

Viewing History **Following the Buffalo Run**

During buffalo hunts, Plains women packed, moved, and unpacked the group's possessions. In this painting by Charles M. Russell, women have loaded their belongings on a travois. They are following the buffalo to a new location, where they will set up camp. ★ **Do you think Plains Indians had many personal possessions? Why or why not?**

▲ *Kiowa baby carrier*

The migration of the Plains Indians mirrored the movement of the buffalo. In winter, small groups of buffalo moved off the Plains to protected valleys and forests. In summer, huge buffalo herds gathered on the Plains where the grass was growing high. In the same way, Plains Indians spent the winter in small bands and gathered in large groups during the summers. The people worked together and owned many things in common.

These groups often staged buffalo drives. Shouting and waving colored robes, hunters drove a herd of buffalo into a **corral,** or enclosure. There, they killed the trapped buffalo. After a kill, the band celebrated with a feast of roasted buffalo meat.

Uses of the buffalo

Plains Indians depended on the buffalo for food, clothing, and shelter. Buffalo meat, rich in protein, was a main item in the Indians' diet. Women cut up and dried the meat on racks. The dried meat was called **jerky.**

Women also tanned buffalo hides to make leather. They wove buffalo fur into coarse, warm cloth. Buffalo horns and bones were carved into tools and toys. The sinews of the buffalo could be used as thread or bowstrings.

Traditions

In summer, many Native American groups met on the Plains. They hunted together, played games, and staged foot and horse races.

Summer gatherings were also the time for councils. At the councils, leaders consulted with elders about problems that affected the whole nation. Indian doctors treated the sick.

One of the most important events was a religious ceremony known as the **Sun Dance.** Thousands of people attended the four-day ceremony to thank the Great Spirit for help in times of trouble.

The Sun Dance took place in a lodge made of tree branches. A sacred tree stood in the middle, and people hung their offerings from it. Dancers circled the tree and asked the Great Spirit for good fortune in the coming year.

A Well-Ordered Society

Women oversaw life in the home. They gathered foods and prepared meals for their families. They also performed such heavy work as raising and taking down tepees. Women cared for the children and taught them the traditions of their people.

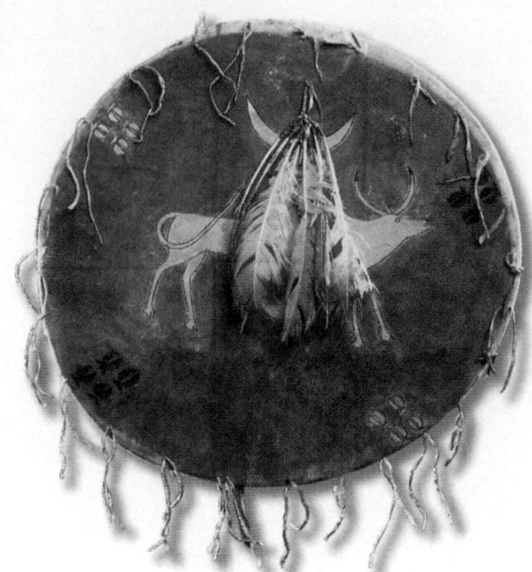

Cheyenne war shield

Women also engaged in many crafts. They sewed animal hides to make clothing and tepees. They made the baskets, pottery, and blankets that were essential to the community. Their work often displayed great artistic skill and design. In fact, a woman's ability in crafts established her rank in society. The woman who made the most beautiful clothing or prepared the greatest number of baskets gained much the same honor as a man who performed bravely in battle.

In some of the tribes, women helped men with the duties of hunting and governing. A Blackfoot woman, Running Eagle, led many hunting parties herself. In other bands, a woman respected for her wisdom made the final decisions about important matters.

The men of the Plains Indians had important responsibilities too. They hunted and traded. They passed on their valuable skills and knowledge to the boys. They supervised the spiritual life of the community by leading religious ceremonies. Men with special skills provided medical care for the sick and injured.

Another important responsibility of the men was to provide military leadership. They waged war to defend or extend territory, to gain horses and other riches, or to seek revenge. More than anything else, however, men waged war to protect their people and to prove their bravery and ability. The most successful warriors gained great respect and status among their nation.

★ Section 1 Review ★

Recall

1. **Identify** Sun Dance.
2. **Define** **(a)** tepee, **(b)** travois, **(c)** corral, **(d)** jerky.

Comprehension

3. **(a)** How did the use of horses change the way Plains Indians lived? **(b)** Why did Plains Indians live in different places at different times of the year?
4. Describe three ways in which Native Americans made use of buffalo.
5. What activities took place at the summer gatherings of Plains Indians?

Critical Thinking and Writing

6. **Making Inferences** How did the dependence on hunting buffalo affect the roles of Indian women and men on the Plains?
7. **Making Generalizations** Based on what you know about the Sun Dance ceremony, what were some religious beliefs of the Plains Indians?

Activity **Making a Graphic Organizer** Based on what you have learned in this section, make a graphic organizer to show the different ways in which the Plains Indians relied on the buffalo.

Miners and Railroaders

As You Read

Explore These Questions

- How did mining change the West?
- What was life like for miners and railroad workers?
- How did railroads help the West develop?

Define

- vigilante
- subsidy
- transcontinental railroad

Identify

- Comstock Lode
- Union Pacific Railroad
- Central Pacific Railroad
- Leland Stanford

Many Americans were lured west by the chance to strike it rich mining gold and silver. "What a clover-field is to a steer, the sky to the lark, a mudhole to a hog, such are new diggings to a miner," wrote one observer in 1862.

Miners reversed the traditional pattern of expansion. Instead of moving from east to west as the earlier pioneers had done, many journeyed from west to east. From the California coast, they fanned out eastward, ever in search of new ways to make their fortune.

The Mining Boom

The western mining boom had begun with the California Gold Rush of 1849. When the Gold Rush ended, miners looked for new opportunities. The merest rumor sent them racing east in search of new strikes.

Gold and silver strikes

In 1859, two young prospectors struck gold in the Sierra Nevada. Suddenly, another miner, Henry Comstock, appeared. "The land is mine," he cried, and demanded to be made a partner. From then on, Comstock boasted about "his" mine. The strike became known as the **Comstock Lode.** A lode is a rich vein of gold or silver.

Comstock and his partners often complained about the heavy blue sand that was mixed in with the gold. It clogged the devices used for separating the gold and made the gold hard to reach. When Mexican miners took the "danged blue stuff" to an expert in California, tests showed it was loaded with silver. Comstock had stumbled onto one of the richest silver mines in the world.

Miners moved into many other areas of the West. Some found valuable ore in Montana and Idaho. Others struck it rich in Colorado. In the 1870s, miners discovered gold in the Black Hills of South Dakota. (See the map on page 438.) In the late 1890s, thousands rushed north to Alaska after major gold strikes were made there.

Boom towns and ghost towns

Gold and silver strikes attracted thousands of prospectors. Miners came from across the United States, as well as from Germany, Ireland, Mexico, and China. Towns sprang up near all the major mining sites.

First, miners built a tent city near the diggings. Then, thousands of people came to supply the miners' needs. Traders brought mule teams loaded with tools, food, and clothing. Merchants hauled in wagonloads of supplies and set up stores.

Connections With Arts

After failing as a prospector, Samuel Clemens became a writer for a Nevada newspaper. His amusing articles appeared in papers throughout the West. In 1863, Clemens signed one of his articles with a new name, one well-known to readers today—Mark Twain.

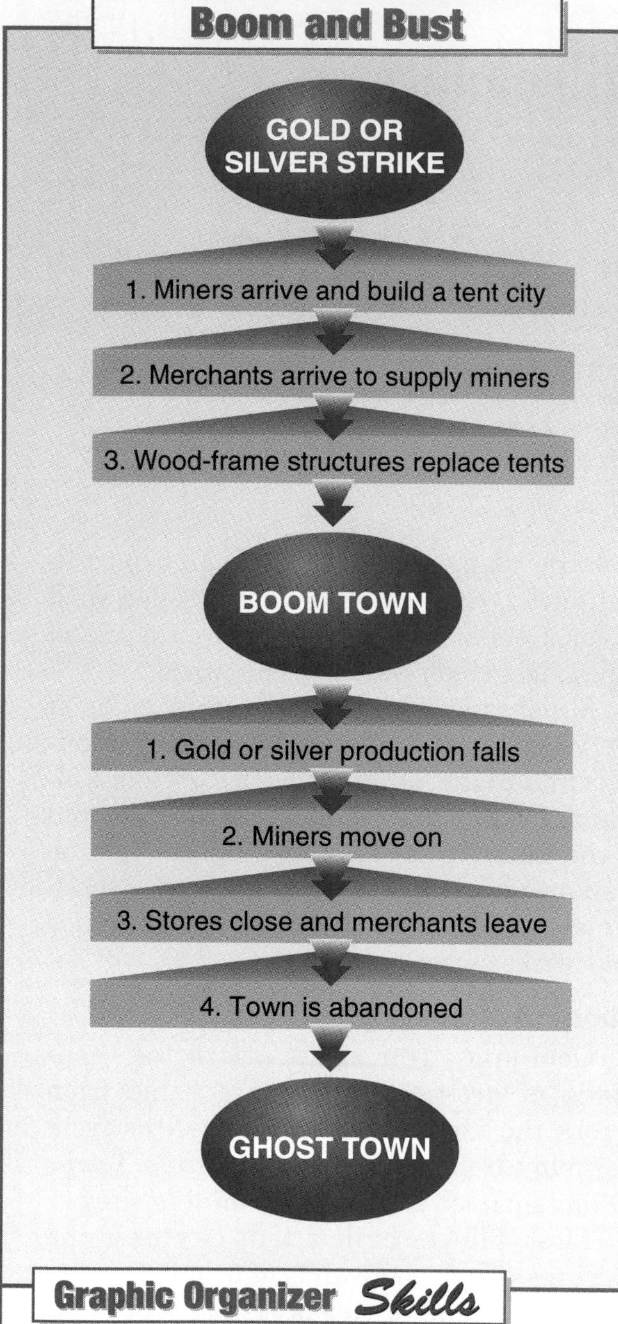

Graphic Organizer *Skills*

A gold or silver strike often led to the building of a boom town. However, many boom towns quickly became ghost towns.

1. **Comprehension** **(a)** Why did merchants often follow miners? **(b)** What caused large numbers of miners to suddenly leave a boom town?
2. **Critical Thinking** Based on this chart and on the map on page 438, why do you think there are more ghost towns today in Colorado than there are in Texas?

Economics $

Soon, wood frame houses, hotels, restaurants, and stores replaced the tents. For example, it took less than a year for the mining camp at the Comstock Lode to become the boom town of Virginia City, Nevada.

Most settlers in the boom towns of the mining frontier were men. However, enterprising women also found ways to profit. Some women ran boarding houses and laundries. Others opened restaurants, where miners gladly paid high prices for a home-cooked meal.

Many boom towns lasted for only a few years. When the gold or silver ore was gone, miners moved away. Without miners for customers, businesses often had to close. In this way, a boom town could quickly go bust and turn into a ghost town.

Still, some boom towns survived and prospered even after the mines shut down. In these towns, miners stayed and found new ways to make a living.

Impact of the boom

The surge of miners into the West created problems. Mines and towns polluted clear mountain streams. Miners cut down forests to get wood for buildings. As you will read, they also forced Native Americans from the land.

Foreign miners were often treated unfairly. In many camps, mobs drove Mexicans from their claims. Chinese miners were heavily taxed or forced to work claims abandoned by others.

Few miners got rich quickly. Much of the gold and silver lay deep underground. It could be reached only with costly machinery. Eventually, most mining in the West was taken over by large companies that could afford to buy this equipment.

Governing the mining frontier

Lawlessness and disorder often accompanied the rapid growth of a town. In response, miners sometimes resorted to organizing groups of **vigilantes.** These self-appointed law enforcers tracked down outlaws and punished them, usually without a trial. A common punishment used by vigilantes was lynching.

American Heritage
M A G A Z I N E

HISTORY HAPPENED HERE

Bannack State Park

In 1862, gold was found along Grasshopper Creek in Montana. The boom town of Bannack grew up at the site and became Montana's first territorial capital. Bannack was a wild frontier town, complete with saloons, gambling, and gunfights. But, when the gold disappeared, so did the people. Today, the ghost town is Bannack State Park. Visitors can walk among the remains of more than 50 buildings, including the Montana Territorial Capitol, the Hotel Meade, and the town jail.

★ ***To learn more about this historic site, write: Bannack State Park, 4200 Bannack Road, Dillon, MT 59725.***

Informal methods of government gradually gave way to more formal arrangements. In 1861, Colorado, Dakota, and Nevada were organized into territories. Idaho and Arizona followed in 1863 and Montana in 1864. The process of more permanent settlement and government had begun.

The Railroads

The people of the mining towns needed large amounts of supplies. They also needed to transport their gold and silver. As a result, railroad companies raced to lay track to the mines and boom towns.

Spanning the continent

The federal government helped the railroad companies because it felt that rail lines in the West would benefit the entire nation. The government's aid came in the form of subsidies. A **subsidy** is financial aid or a land grant from the government. Congress lent money to the railroad companies and gave them land. Often, both business and government ignored the fact that Native Americans lived on the land.

In 1863, two companies began a race to build the first transcontinental railroad. A **transcontinental railroad** is one that stretches across a continent from coast to coast. The **Union Pacific** started building a rail line from Omaha, Nebraska, westward. The **Central Pacific** began in Sacramento, California, and built eastward. The *Sacramento Union* of January 8, 1863, reported:

> "With rites appropriate to the occasion . . . ground was formally broken at noon for the commencement of the Central Pacific Railroad—the California link of the continental chain that is to unite American communities now divided by thousands of miles of trackless wilderness."

Ranchers and Cowhands

As You Read

Explore These Questions
- Why were there cattle drives?
- What was the life of a cowhand like?
- Why did the Cattle Kingdom end?

Define
- cattle drive
- cowhand
- vaquero
- cow town

Identify
- Chisolm Trail
- Cattle Kingdom

SETTING the Scene In the 1860s, a new group of Americans arrived in the West. These riders on horseback came from Texas, leading dusty lines of bellowing cattle. As they rode along, these cattle herders passed the time by singing songs like this one:

> "Well, come along, boys, and listen to my tale;
> I'll tell you of my troubles on the old Chisholm Trail.
> With a ten dollar horse and a forty dollar saddle,
> I started in herding these Texas cattle."

The Cattle Drives

Before the arrival of settlers from the United States, the Spanish and then the Mexicans set up cattle ranches in the Southwest. Over the years, strays from these ranches grew into large herds of wild cattle, known as longhorns. They roamed freely across the grassy plains of Texas.

After the Civil War, the demand for beef increased. Growing cities in the East needed more meat. Miners, railroad crews, and soldiers in the West added to the demand.

In response, Texas ranchers began rounding up herds of longhorns. They drove the animals hundreds of miles north to railroad lines in Kansas and Missouri. The long trips were called **cattle drives.**

Jesse Chisholm blazed one of the most famous cattle trails. Chisholm was half Scottish and half Cherokee. In the late 1860s, he began hauling goods by wagon between Texas and the Kansas Pacific Railroad. His route crossed rivers at the best places and passed by water holes. Ranchers began using the **Chisholm Trail** in 1867. Within five years, more than one million head of cattle had walked the road. (See the map on page 438.)

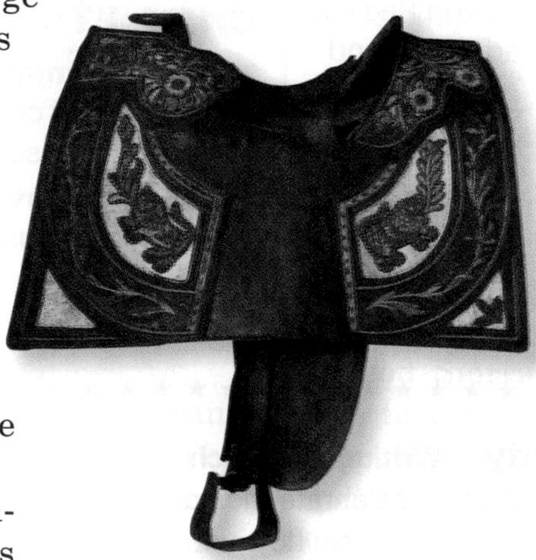

Saddle used by a Mexican vaquero

The Cowhands

Ranchers employed **cowhands** to tend their cattle and drive herds to market. These hard workers rode alongside the huge herds in good and bad weather. They kept the cattle moving and rounded up strays. It is estimated that nearly one in three cowhands was either Mexican American or African American.

Spanish heritage

American cowhands learned much about riding, roping, and branding from Spanish and Mexican **vaqueros** (vah KEHR ohs). Vaqueros were skilled riders who herded cattle on ranches in Mexico, California, and the Southwest.

California Vaqueros

Mexican American vaqueros were very important to the cattle industry of California, Texas, and the entire Southwest. The American artist James Walker painted this scene in the 1870s. ★ **Why did vaqueros and cowhands wear wide-brimmed hats?**

The gear used by American cowhands was modeled on the tools of the vaquero. Cowhands used the lariat—a leather rope—to catch runaway cattle. *Lariat* comes from the Spanish word for rope. Cowhands wore wide-brimmed hats like the Spanish sombrero. Their leather leggings, called chaps, were modeled on Spanish chaparreras (chap ah RAY rahs). Chaps protected a rider's legs from the thorny plants that grow in the Southwest.

On the trail

A cattle drive was hot, dirty, tiring work. Cowhands worked in all kinds of weather and faced many dangers. They had to prevent nervous cattle from drowning while crossing a fast-flowing river. They had to fight raging grass fires. They also faced attacks from cattle thieves who roamed the countryside.

One of the cowhand's worst fears on a cattle drive was a stampede. A clap of thunder or a gunshot could set thousands of longhorns off at a run. Cowhands had to ride into the crush of hoofs and horns. They slowed the stampeding herd by turning the cattle in a wide circle.

Most cowhands did not work for themselves. Instead, they were hired hands for the owners of large ranches. For all their hard work, cowhands were lucky to earn $1 a day! Even in the 1870s, this was low pay.

The Cow Towns

Cattle drives ended in **cow towns** that had sprung up along the railroad lines. The Chisholm Trail, for example, ended in Abilene, Kansas. (See the map on page 438.) In cow towns, cattle were held in great pens until they could be loaded on railroad cars and shipped to markets in the East.

In Abilene and other busy cow towns, dance halls, saloons, hotels, and restaurants catered to the cowhands. Sheriffs often had a hard time keeping the peace. Some cowhands spent wild nights drinking, dancing, and gambling.

Cow towns also attracted settlers who wanted to build stable communities where families could thrive. Doctors, barbers, artisans, bankers, and merchants helped to establish the cow towns.

The main street of a town was where people conducted business. Almost every town

Why Study History?

Because the Cowboy Is Part of Our Culture

Historical Background

In the late 1800s, writers and artists created the popular image of the American cowboy. The mythic and heroic cowboy was a hard worker—brave, dependable, and self-reliant. He helped the weak, fought for justice, and punished wrongdoers. He was a man of action.

People throughout the nation were captivated by the exciting adventures of this new American folk hero. They read about him in dime novels and magazines. They admired him in paintings and sculptures. They saw him in Wild West shows entertaining audiences with trick riding, fancy roping, and mock gunfights. In the early 1900s, people began watching their favorite cowboy stars in the motion pictures.

Pawnee Bill, shown here, is the popular cowboy star of a Wild West Show.

Connections to Today

Today, the cowboy remains an important part of American culture. Wild West shows are still popular, and rodeos are enjoying increasing attention. Some men and women try to take part in the action by vacationing on a dude ranch. Also, the heroic cowboy still rides the range in film and television. Sometimes, though, the cowboy is an "intergalactic starfighter," the West is outer space, and the outlaws are aliens bent on destroying the Earth.

Connections to You

The heroic cowboy image seems to capture the imagination of each new generation. Many young people enjoy listening to country-western music. Others like to wear western jeans and boots. Cowboys and western scenes often appear in commercial advertisements for a variety of products.

The heroic cowboy remains a popular figure in American culture today because of the ideals that are often associated with him. These ideals include independence, courage, hard work, and justice. The cowboy will probably remain an enduring American symbol as long as Americans cherish those values.

1. **Comprehension** **(a)** How was the heroic cowboy image created? **(b)** What were the key characteristics of the heroic cowboy?
2. **Critical Thinking** How are science-fiction films such as those of the *Star Wars* and *Star Trek* series similar to traditional movie westerns?

★Activity **Interviewing** Interview several people of different generations. Ask them to describe some ideals that they associate with the cowboy heroes of literature, film, and television. Share your findings in a report to the class.

had a general store that sold groceries, tools, clothing, and all sorts of goods. The general store also served as a social center where people could talk and exchange the latest news. As a town grew, more and more specialty shops lined its main street. These included drug stores, hardware stores, and even ice cream parlors.

Religion also played an important role for the townspeople. Throughout the West, places of worship grew in number and membership. They served as spiritual and social centers, and as symbols of progress and stability. "A church does as much to build up a town as a school, a railroad, or a fair," noted one New Mexico newspaper.

The Cattle Boom

In the 1870s, ranching spread north from Texas across the grassy Plains. Soon, cattle grazed from Kansas to present-day Montana. Ranchers had built a **Cattle Kingdom** in the West.

The open range

Ranchers let their cattle run wild on the open range. To identify cattle, each ranch had its own brand that was burned into the cattle's hide. Twice a year, young calves were rounded up and branded.

Sometimes, there were conflicts on the range. Since water was scarce, ranchers battled over rights to water holes and streams. When sheepherders moved onto the Plains, ranchers tried to drive them out. The ranchers complained that sheep nibbled the grass so low that cattle could not eat it.

End of an era

In the 1870s, farmers began moving onto the range. They fenced their fields with barbed wire. Sharp barbs kept cattle and sheep from pushing over fences and trampling plowed fields. As more farmers bought land and strung barbed wire, the open range began to disappear.

Bad weather on the Great Plains speeded the end of the Cattle Kingdom. The bitterly cold winters of 1886 and 1887 killed millions of cattle. By the spring of 1887, nine out of ten head of cattle on the northern Plains had frozen to death.

Cattle owners began to buy land and fence it in. Soon, farmers and ranchers divided the open range into a patchwork of large fenced plots. The days of the Cattle Kingdom were over.

★ Section 3 Review ★

Recall

1. **Locate** (a) Texas, (b) Kansas, (c) Abilene, (d) Dodge City, (e) Montana.
2. **Identify** (a) Chisolm Trail, (b) Cattle Kingdom.
3. **Define** (a) cattle drive, (b) cowhand, (c) vaquero, (d) cow town.

Comprehension

4. After the Civil War, why did Texas ranchers drive cattle herds to Kansas?
5. Describe some of the dangers that cowhands faced.
6. Explain two reasons why the Cattle Kingdom came to an end.

Critical Thinking and Writing

7. **Analyzing Visual Evidence** Study the painting of California vaqueros on p. 441. Then, identify and describe some of the equipment used by both vaqueros and cowhands.
8. **Predicting Consequences** How do you think the growth of the Cattle Kingdom affected the Plains Indians? Explain.

Activity **Writing a Song** Round 'em up! Move 'em out! You are driving cattle along the old Chisolm Trail. Review the song verse at the start of this section. Then, based on what you have learned about a cowhand's life, write a second verse to the song.

A Way of Life Ends

As You Read

Explore These Questions

- Why did Native Americans and settlers come into conflict?
- How did Native Americans try to preserve their way of life?
- How did government policies affect Native American culture?

Define

- reservation

Identify

- Sitting Bull
- Fort Laramie Treaty
- Chivington Massacre
- Battle of Little Bighorn
- Chief Joseph
- Geronimo
- Ghost Dance
- Susette La Flesche
- Helen Hunt Jackson
- Dawes Act

SETTING the Scene In 1876, **Sitting Bull,** a Lakota chief, wrote to the commander of United States Army troops, who had been sent to force him off his land:

> ❝I want to know what you are doing on this road. You scare all the buffalo away. I want to hunt in this place. I want you to turn back from here. If you don't, I will fight you.❞

After the Civil War, many Americans moved west. At first, the United States government promised to protect Indian hunting grounds. However, as settlers pushed westward, the government broke its promises. When Indians resisted the arrival of settlers, wars spread across the West. For Native Americans, tragedy was the result.

Broken Promises

Conflict began as early as the 1840s when settlers and miners began to cross Indian hunting grounds. The settlers and miners asked for government protection from the Indians.

Fort Laramie Treaty

In 1851, federal government officials met with Indian nations near Fort Laramie in Wyoming. The officials asked each nation to keep to a limited area. In return, they promised money, domestic animals, agricultural tools, and other goods. Officials told the Native Americans that the lands that were reserved for them would be theirs forever.

Native American leaders agreed to the terms in the **Fort Laramie Treaty.** However, in 1858, gold was discovered at Pikes Peak in Colorado. A wave of miners rushed to land that the government had promised to the Cheyennes and Arapahos.

Federal officials forced Indian leaders to sign a new treaty giving up the land around Pikes Peak. Some Native Americans refused to accept the agreement. They attacked white settlers.

The Chivington Massacre

The settlers struck back. In 1864, Colonel John Chivington led his militia against a peaceful Cheyenne village that the government had promised to protect. When Chivington attacked, the Indians raised a white flag of surrender. Chivington ignored the flag. He ordered his men to destroy the village and take no prisoners. In the **Chivington Massacre,** soldiers slaughtered about 150 men, women, and children.

People throughout the United States were outraged. "When the white man comes in my country he leaves a trail of blood behind him," said Lakota War Chief Red Cloud. Across the Plains, soldiers and Indians went to war.

Learning "American" ways

In 1867, federal officials established a peace commission. The commission wanted to end the wars on the Plains so that railroad builders and miners would be safe. The commission urged Native Americans to settle down and live as white farmers did. It also urged them to send their children to white schools to learn "American" ways.

At one white school in Indiana, Lakota children were horrified to hear that their hair would be cut short. Among the Lakotas, only cowards had short hair. One girl described her distress:

> "I cried aloud... I felt the cold blades of the scissors against my neck, and heard them gnaw off one of my thick braids. Then I lost my spirit."

Forced onto reservations

In 1867, the Kiowas, Comanches, and other southern Plains Indians signed a new treaty with the government. They promised to move to Indian Territory in present-day Oklahoma. The soil there was poor. Also, most Plains Indians were hunters, not farmers. The Indians did not like the treaty but knew they had no choice.

The Lakotas and Arapahos of the northern Plains also signed a treaty. They agreed to live on reservations in present-day South Dakota. A **reservation** is a limited area set aside for Native Americans.

End of the Buffalo

The Plains Indians suffered from lost battles and broken treaties. Even worse for them, however, was the destruction of the buffalo.

As the railroads moved west, buffalo hunting became a fashionable sport. Trainloads of easterners shot the animals from the comfort of railroad cars. Then, in the 1870s, buffalo hide blankets became popular in the East. Commercial hunters began shooting

Linking United States and the World

United States

New Zealand

Surrendering Their Land

In 1868, Sioux leaders met with United States government officials at Fort Laramie. The Indians signed a treaty agreeing to live on a reservation. In 1840, on the other side of the world, the Maori people of New Zealand signed the Treaty of Waitangi. By this treaty, the Maori leaders gave Great Britain control over New Zealand. ★ **Why do you think the United States and Britain both wanted more land?**

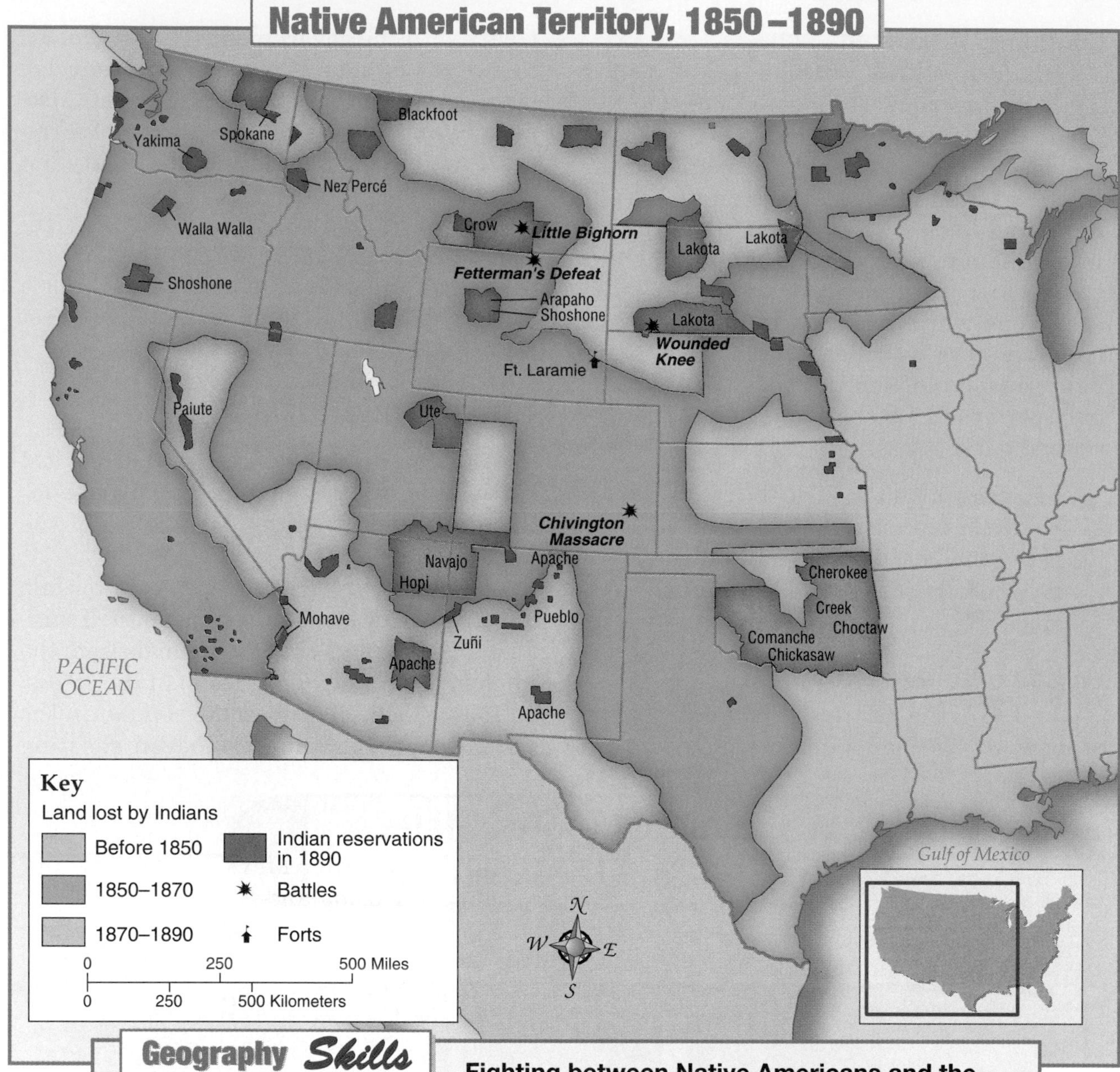

Geography *Skills*

Fighting between Native Americans and the United States government went on for years until most Indians were forced onto reservations.

1. **Location** On the map, locate: **(a)** Fort Laramie, **(b)** Little Bighorn, **(c)** Apache reservations, **(d)** Wounded Knee.
2. **Region** In which areas of the country did Native Americans still retain much of their land in 1870?
3. **Critical Thinking** Why do you think the Apaches of the desert Southwest were one of the last Indian nations to lose their land?

2 to 3 million buffalo every year. The number of buffalo fell from 13 million in 1860 to a few hundred in 1900.

Facing starvation, the Plains Indians had to struggle simply to survive. As the buffalo disappeared, so did the Plains Indians' way of life. Years later, Pretty Shield, a woman of the Crow nation, sadly recalled the tragedy. "When the buffalo went away the hearts of my people fell to the ground, and they could not lift them up again. . . . I [saw] dead buffalo scattered all over our beautiful country."

The Final Battles

Settlers and miners continued to move into the West. They wanted more and more land for themselves. Even on reservations, the Indians were not left in peace.

Sioux War of 1876

In 1874, prospectors found gold in the Black Hills region of the Lakota, or Sioux, reservation. Thousands of miners rushed to the area. Led by Sitting Bull and Crazy Horse, another Lakota chief, the Indians fought back in what became known as the Sioux War of 1876.

In June 1876, Colonel George A. Custer led a column of soldiers into the Little Bighorn Valley. Indian scouts warned Custer that there were many Lakotas and Cheyennes camped ahead. Custer did not wait for more soldiers. Instead, he attacked with only 225 men. Custer and all his men died in the **Battle of Little Bighorn.**

The Indian victory at the Little Bighorn was shortlived. The army soon defeated the Lakotas and Cheyennes. Then, Congress ordered that no food rations be distributed to the Indians until they agreed to the government's demands. To avoid starvation, the Lakotas gave up all claims to the Black Hills and other territory. In this way, they surrendered about one third of the lands that the United States government had guaranteed them by the Fort Laramie Treaty.

Chief Joseph

The Nez Percés lived in the Snake River valley, at a place where Oregon, Washington, and Idaho meet. In the 1860s, gold strikes brought miners onto Nez Percé land. The government ordered the Nez Percés to move to a reservation in Idaho.

At first, **Chief Joseph,** a Nez Percé leader, refused to leave. Then, in 1877, he and his people, including women and children, fled north toward Canada. Army troops followed close behind.

In the months that followed, Chief Joseph earned the respect and admiration of many. Again and again, he fought off or eluded pursuing army units. He set high standards for his soldiers, warning them not to injure women or children as the white soldiers did. He also made sure that his soldiers paid settlers for any supplies that they took.

Finally, after a tragic journey of more than 1,000 miles, Chief Joseph decided that he must surrender. Of the approximately 700 Nez Percés who had set out with him, fewer than 450 remained. As he lay down his weapons, he sadly said:

> “It is cold, and we have no blankets. The little children are freezing to death. . . . Hear me, my chiefs! I am tired. My heart is sick and sad. From where the sun now stands, I will fight no more forever.”

The Apache wars

In the arid lands of the Southwest, the Apaches fiercely resisted the loss of their lands. One leader, **Geronimo,** continued fighting the longest. In 1876, he assumed leadership of a band of Apache warriors when the government tried to force his people onto a reservation.

Geronimo waged war off and on for the next ten years. From Mexico, he led frequent raids into Arizona and New Mexico. In the end, 5,000 United States soldiers were trying to capture Geronimo, who, by this time, had less than forty followers. Geronimo finally surrendered in 1886. His capture marked the end of formal warfare between Indians and whites.

A Way of Life Lost

Many Indians longed for their lost way of life. On the reservations, the Lakotas and other Plains Indians turned to a religious ceremony called the **Ghost Dance.** It celebrated the time when Native Americans lived freely on the Plains.

The Ghost Dance

In 1889, word spread that a prophet named Wovoka had appeared among the Paiute people of the southern Plains. Wovoka said that the Great Spirit would make a new world for his people, free from whites and filled with plenty. To bring about this new

Biography **Geronimo**

For many years, Geronimo (on horseback) fought against both Mexico and the United States. He paid a high price for his fierce resistance. At a peace conference in the 1850s, Mexican soldiers murdered his mother, wife, and three children. After he surrendered to the United States Army, he was imprisoned for two years. ★ **Why do you think Geronimo refused to surrender for so long?**

world, all the Indians had to do was to dance the Ghost Dance.

Across the Plains, many Indians began preparing for the new world. Ghost Dancers painted their faces red and put on the sacred Ghost Dance shirt. Some believed that the shirt protected them from harm, even from the bullets of soldiers' guns.

In their ceremonies, Ghost Dancers joined hands in a large, spinning circle. As they danced, they all cried and laughed. A "growing happiness" filled them, said one. They saw a glowing vision of a new and perfect world.

Settlers react

Many settlers grew alarmed. The Ghost Dancers, they said, were preparing for war. The settlers persuaded the government to outlaw the Ghost Dance.

In December 1890, police officers entered a Lakota reservation to arrest Sitting Bull, who had returned from Canada and was living on the reservation. They claimed that he was spreading the Ghost Dance among the Lakotas. In the struggle that followed, Sitting Bull was accidentally shot and killed.

Wounded Knee

Upset by Sitting Bull's death, groups of Lakotas fled the reservations. Army troops pursued them to Wounded Knee Creek, in present-day South Dakota. On December 29, the Indians agreed to surrender. As nervous troops watched, they began to give up their guns.

Suddenly, a shot rang out. The army opened fire with rifles and artillery. By the time the shooting stopped, nearly 300 Native American men, women, and children lay dead. About 30 soldiers also died.

The fighting at Wounded Knee marked the end of the Ghost Dance religion. Years later, Black Elk, a former Ghost Dancer, remembered the events at Wounded Knee:

> "When I look back now from this high hill of my old age, I can still see the . . . women and children lying [on the ground there]. . . . And I can see that something else died there. . . . A people's dream died there."

Failed Reforms

The Native Americans were no longer able to resist the government. During the late 1800s, the army forced more Indians onto reservations every year.

Reformers speak out

Many people—Indian and white—spoke out against the tragedy that was occurring. **Susette La Flesche,** daughter of an Omaha chief, wrote and lectured about the destruction of the Native American way of life. Her work led others to take up the Indian cause.

One reformer influenced by La Flesche was **Helen Hunt Jackson.** In 1881, Jackson published *A Century of Dishonor.* The book vividly recounted the long history of broken treaties between the United States and the Native Americans. In her book, Jackson urged the United States government to end its policy of "cheating, robbing, [and] breaking promises."

Alice Fletcher was another reformer who worked for the Indians. She became an agent of the Indian Bureau, the government department that handled Indian affairs. To better understand Native American culture, Fletcher lived for a time with various Indian nations, including the Omahas and Winnebagos of Nebraska.

Ghost Dance shirt

The Dawes Act

Calls for reform led Congress to pass the **Dawes Act** in 1887. The act encouraged Native Americans to become farmers. Some tribal lands were divided up and given to individual Native American families.

The Dawes Act worked poorly. To Native Americans, land was an open place for riding and hunting—not something to divide into small parcels. As a result, Indians often sold their parcels to whites for low prices. In the end, Native Americans lost more than one half of the land that they had owned before the passage of the Dawes Act.

Life on the reservations changed Native American culture. The federal government took away the power of Indian leaders. In their place, it appointed government agents to make most decisions. These agents believed that Native Americans should give up their old ways, including their language, religion, and traditional customs.

Because Native Americans could no longer hunt buffalo, many had to depend on food and supplies guaranteed by treaties. Few Indians were content with life on the reservations.

★ Section 4 Review ★

Recall

1. **Locate** **(a)** Wyoming, **(b)** Colorado, **(c)** Oklahoma, **(d)** South Dakota, **(e)** Little Bighorn, **(f)** Wounded Knee.
2. **Identify** **(a)** Sitting Bull, **(b)** Fort Laramie Treaty, **(c)** Chivington Massacre, **(d)** Battle of Little Bighorn, **(e)** Chief Joseph, **(f)** Geronimo, **(g)** Ghost Dance, **(h)** Susette La Flesche, **(i)** Helen Hunt Jackson, **(j)** Dawes Act.
3. **Define** reservation.

Comprehension

4. Why did treaties between Native Americans and the United States fail to bring peace to the Plains?
5. Why were many Plains Indians attracted to Wovoka's teachings about the Ghost Dance?
6. How did each of the following affect Native Americans: **(a)** peace commission of 1867, **(b)** destruction of the buffalo, **(c)** establishment of reservations?

Critical Thinking and Writing

7. **Recognizing Points of View** Why do you think the government wanted Plains Indians to settle down and become farmers?
8. **Solving Problems** What do you think the federal government could have done to avoid wars with Native Americans in the West?

Activity **Writing a Poem** You are a Native American looking back at the changes that have occurred between 1865 and 1890. Write a poem describing your thoughts and feelings about those changes.

The Farmers

As You Read

Explore These Questions

- What were the different origins of western farmers?
- Why was life hard for Plains farmers?
- Why did farmers unite in the late 1800s?

Define

- sod house
- sodbuster
- cooperative
- wholesale

Identify

- Mary Elizabeth Lease
- Homestead Act
- Exodusters
- Hispanic-American Alliance
- National Grange
- Farmers' Alliance
- Populist party
- William Jennings Bryan
- William McKinley

SETTING the Scene Like miners and ranchers who arrived before them, farmers dreamed of a new life in the West. Mary Zimmerman and her family were among the first farmers on the Great Plains. She recalled their early struggle:

> "The soil was [new]. It had to be broken, turned, stirred, and taught to produce. With the simple means of the time, the process was slow, but . . . I helped my father on the farm and learned to do the work pretty well."

Later, western farmers would face other challenges. In the 1890s, **Mary Elizabeth Lease,** a fiery Kansas reformer, spoke bitterly of a struggle against low prices:

> "We raised the big crop . . . and what came of it? Eight-cent corn, ten-cent oats, two-cent beef. . . . Then the politicians told us we suffered from overproduction."

Farmers Settle in the West

Congress passed the **Homestead Act** in 1862. The law promised 160 acres of land to anyone who farmed it for five years. The government was encouraging farmers to settle the West. It also wanted to give poor easterners a chance to own a farm.

Homesteaders

Many easterners rushed to accept the offer of free land. They planted their 160 acres with wheat and corn. By 1900, half a million Americans had set up farms under the Homestead Act.

The Homestead Act had its problems. The land was free, but poor people did not have the money to move west and start a farm. Also, only about 20 percent of the homestead land went directly to small farmers. Land-owning companies took large areas of land illegally. They divided the land and resold it to farmers at a high price.

Exodusters

African Americans joined the rush for homestead land. The largest group moved west at the end of Reconstruction. At this time in the South, blacks were seeing many of their hard-won freedoms slip away.

In 1879, a group of African Americans moved to Kansas. They called themselves **Exodusters.** They took the name from Exodus, the book of the Bible that tells about the Jews escaping slavery in Egypt.

Some white southerners did not want to lose the cheap labor supplied by African Americans. They used force to stop boats from carrying Exodusters up the Mississippi. Nevertheless, between 40,000 and 70,000 African Americans moved to Kansas by 1881.

Mexicanos

Easterners who moved to the Southwest met a large Spanish-speaking population there. As you recall, the United States had gained the Southwest through the Mexican War. Spanish-speaking southwesterners called themselves Mexicanos. White Americans who lived in the region were known as Anglos.

Most Mexicanos lived in small villages. They farmed and raised sheep for themselves and their families. A few wealthy Mexicanos were large landowners and merchants.

As growing numbers of Anglos settled in the Southwest, they acquired the best jobs and land. Often, Mexicanos found themselves working as low-paid laborers on Anglo farms. Many Mexicanos ended up living in poverty.

Some Mexicanos fought back. In New Mexico, in the 1880s, angry farmers known as "Las Gorras Blancas," or "White Caps," demanded fair treatment. They protested the fencing of their grazing lands by cutting the barbed wire fences of Anglo cattle ranchers.

Other Mexicanos united in political organizations. In 1894, Mexicanos in Arizona founded the **Hispanic-American Alliance.** It vowed "to protect and fight for the rights of Spanish Americans" through political action.

A Final Rush for Land

As settlers spread across the West, free land began to disappear. The last major land rush took place in Oklahoma. Several Indian nations lived there, but the government forced them to sell their land. The government then announced that farmers could claim free homesteads in Oklahoma. They could not stake their claims, however, until noon on April 22, 1889.

On the appointed day, as many as 100,000 land seekers lined up at the Oklahoma border. At noon, a gunshot rang out. The "boomers" charged into Oklahoma, but they found that others were already there.

Viewing HISTORY **Exodusters**

In this photograph, Exodusters await the arrival of a steamboat to take them up the Mississippi River. Most Exodusters settled in Kansas. African American homesteaders also settled in Nebraska, Oklahoma, and other western states. ★ **Why did some white southerners try to prevent African Americans from moving west?**

Viewing HISTORY On the Homestead

These homesteaders posed for a family picture in front of their sod house. ★ **Why did people on the Plains build sod houses rather than wood houses?**

"Sooners" had sneaked into Oklahoma before the official opening and had staked out much of the best land.

Hard Life on the Plains

Farmers on the western plains faced many hardships. The first problem was shelter. Since wood was scarce on the Great Plains, many farmers built houses of sod—soil held together by grass roots. Rain was a serious problem for **sod houses.** One pioneer woman complained that her sod roof "leaked two days before a rain and for three days after."

Sodbusting

The fertile soil of the Great Plains was covered with a layer of thick sod that could crack wood or iron plows. A new sodbusting plow made of steel reached the market by 1877. It enabled **sodbusters,** as Plains farmers were called, to cut through the sod to the soil below.

Technology helped farmers in other ways. On the Great Plains, water often lay hundreds of feet underground. Farmers built windmills to pump the water to the surface. New reapers, threshing machines, and binders helped farmers to harvest crops.

Battling the climate

The dry climate was a constant threat. When too little rain fell, the crops shriveled and died. Dry weather also brought the threat of fire. In the strong winds that whipped across the land, a grass fire traveled "as fast as a horse could run."

The summers often brought swarms of grasshoppers that darkened the sky like a storm. Grasshoppers ate everything in their path—crops, food, tree bark, even clothing.

Pioneers dreaded the winters most. With few trees or hills to block the wind, icy gusts built huge snowdrifts. The deep snow buried farm animals and trapped families inside their homes. Wise sodbusters kept enough food on hand to help them survive during a long blizzard.

Women on the Plains

Women had to be strong to survive the hardships of life on the Great Plains. Since there were few stores, women made clothing, soap, candles, and other goods by hand. They also cooked and preserved food needed through the long winter.

Women served their families and their communities in many ways. They often helped with planting and harvesting. Most schoolteachers were women. When there were no doctors nearby, women treated the sick and injured.

Pioneer families usually lived miles apart. They relaxed by visiting with neighbors and gathering for church services. Picnics, dances, and weddings were eagerly awaited events. "Don't think that all of our time and thoughts were taken up with the problems of living," one woman wrote. "We were a social people."

Skills FOR LIFE

Critical Thinking | **Managing Information** | Communication | Maps, Charts, and Graphs

Working in Teams

How Will I Use This Skill ?

By forming a team, you bring together the skills, knowledge, and experience of a number of people. A team can often produce better results in less time than an individual. In the classroom, on the playing field, or in the workplace, people often work together on a team to achieve some common goal.

LEARN the Skill

You can work as a member of a team by following these four steps:

1. Organize a team and identify your goal.
2. Identify the tasks needed to complete the goal. Sometimes, team members work together for the entire project. Other times, they divide the tasks, work separately, and then come together to share their results.
3. The team members complete their tasks by working together, individually, or in smaller groups or committees.
4. The team develops a presentation to share their work with others.

A marching band relies on teamwork.

PRACTICE the Skill

Using the information on pages 454–455, work in teams to learn about efforts to help farmers in the late 1800s.

1. Organize three teams. One team will focus on the Grange, a second team will learn about the Farmers' Alliance, and a third team will study the Populist Party.
2. The members of each team should read and take notes on their assigned topic.
3. Each team should come together to discuss their findings and to make sure that everyone understands the material.
4. Each team should prepare a presentation that includes a poster and a speech. Some members should prepare the poster, while others prepare the speech. Finally, one member will present and explain the poster to the class. Another team member will make the speech.

APPLY the Skill

Organize a team to research and present information on a current issue. Use newspapers, magazines, or the Internet as sources.

Biography **Mary Elizabeth Lease**

Kansas lawyer Mary Elizabeth Lease won fame as an activist for the Farmers' Alliance and Populist party. She was a stirring, dynamic speaker. The way to fight falling grain prices, she told Kansan farmers, was to "raise less corn and more hell."

★ **Why were grain prices falling in the late 1800s?**

Crisis for farmers

Despite the harsh conditions, farmers began to thrive in the West. Before long, they were selling huge amounts of wheat and corn in the nation's growing cities and even in Europe.

Then, however, farmers faced a strange problem. The more they harvested, the less they earned. In 1881, a bushel of wheat sold for $1.19. By 1894, the price had plunged to 49 cents.

Western farmers were hurt most by low grain prices. They had borrowed money during good times to buy land and machinery. When wheat prices fell, they could not repay their debts. In the South, cotton farmers faced the same problem when the price of cotton dropped.

Farmers Take Action

As early as the 1860s, farmers began to work together. They learned that they could improve their condition through economic cooperation and political action.

The Grange

In 1867, farmers formed the **National Grange.** Grangers wanted to boost farm profits. They also wanted to reduce the rates that railroads charged for shipping grain.

Grangers helped farmers set up cooperatives. In a **cooperative,** a group of farmers pooled their money to buy seeds and tools wholesale. **Wholesale** means buying or selling something in large quantities at lower prices. Grangers built cooperative warehouses so that farmers could store grain cheaply while waiting for better selling prices.

Leaders of the Grange urged farmers to use their vote. In 1873, western and southern Grangers pledged to vote only for candidates who supported their aims. They elected officials who understood the farmers' problems.

As a result, several states passed laws limiting what could be charged for grain shipment and storage. Nevertheless, crop prices continued to drop. Farmers sank deeper and deeper into debt.

Farmers' Alliance

Another group, the **Farmers' Alliance,** joined the struggle in the 1870s. Like the Grange, the Alliance set up cooperatives and warehouses. The Farmers' Alliance spread from Texas through the South and into the Plains states. In the South, the Alliance tried to bring black and white farmers together. Alliance leaders also tried to join with factory workers and miners who were angry about their treatment by employers.

The Populist Party

In 1891, farmers and labor unions joined together to form the **Populist party.** At their first national convention, the Populists demanded government help with falling farm prices and regulation of railroad rates. They also called for an income tax, an eight-hour workday, and limits on immigration.

Another Populist party demand was "free silver." Populists wanted all silver mined in the West to be coined into money. They said that farm prices dropped because there was not enough money in circulation. Free silver would increase the money supply and make it easier for farmers to repay their debts.

Eastern bankers and factory owners disagreed. They argued that increasing the money supply would cause inflation, or runaway prices. Business people feared that inflation would wreck the economy.

Rise and Fall of the Populists

The Populist candidate for President in 1892 won one million votes. The next year, a severe depression brought the Populists new support. In 1894, they elected six senators and seven representatives to Congress.

Election of 1896

The Populists looked toward the election of 1896 with high hopes. Their program had been endorsed by one of the great orators of the age—**William Jennings Bryan.**

Bryan was a young Democratic congressman from Nebraska. He was called the "Great Commoner," because he championed the cause of common people. Like the Populists, he believed that the nation needed to increase the supply of money. He often spoke out on behalf of the farmers.

At the Democratic convention in 1896, Bryan made a powerful speech. Delegates cheered wildly as he thundered against the rich and powerful and for free silver.

Both Democrats and Populists supported Bryan for President. However, bankers and business people feared that Bryan would ruin the economy. They supported **William McKinley,** the Republican candidate.

Bryan narrowly lost the election of 1896. He carried the South and West, but McKinley won the heavily populated states of the East.

Populist Party Fades

The Populist party broke up after 1896. One reason was that the Democrats adopted several Populist causes. Also, prosperity returned in the late 1890s. People worried less about railroad rates and free silver.

Still, the influence of the Populists lived on. In the years ahead, the eight-hour workday became standard for American workers. In 1913, the states ratified an income tax amendment. Perhaps most important, the Populists had helped to tie the West more tightly to the politics of the nation.

★ Section 5 Review ★

Recall

1. **Identify** **(a)** Mary Elizabeth Lease, **(b)** Homestead Act, **(c)** Exodusters, **(d)** Hispanic-American Alliance, **(e)** National Grange, **(f)** Farmers' Alliance, **(g)** Populist party, **(h)** William Jennings Bryan, **(i)** William McKinley.
2. **Define** **(a)** sod house, **(b)** sodbuster, **(c)** cooperative, **(d)** wholesale.

Comprehension

3. **(a)** Why did Exodusters move to the Plains? **(b)** How did the arrival of white settlers affect Mexicano farmers in the Southwest?
4. Describe three hardships that farmers faced on the Great Plains.
5. Identify and explain two goals that the National Grange and Populist party shared.

Critical Thinking and Writing

6. **Analyzing Primary Sources** An army general wrote to President Hayes, "Every river landing is blockaded by white enemies of the colored exodus." Explain in fuller detail the event to which the general was referring.
7. **Understanding Causes and Effects** How did the amount of grain that farmers produced affect the price of that grain? Explain.

Activity **Drawing a Political Cartoon** You are a political commentator of the late 1800s. Draw a political cartoon to illustrate one of the problems that farmers faced during this period.

Chapter 17 Review and Activities

★ Sum It Up ★

Section 1 The Plains Indians

- On the Great Plains, Native American nations depended on the buffalo for survival.
- Plains Indians had a rich religious life and a well-ordered society.

Section 2 Miners and Railroaders

- With gold and silver strikes came a rush of miners and the building of boom towns.
- Transcontinental railroads brought rapid growth to the West.

Section 3 Ranchers and Cowhands

- In the 1860s and 1870s, cattle ranching spread across the Great Plains.
- The life of the cowhand was difficult and dangerous.

Section 4 A Way of Life Ends

- Native Americans struggled to keep their lands and their way of life.
- The United States government forced Indians to move onto reservations and to adopt new ways of life.

Section 5 The Farmers

- By 1900, despite many hardships, half a million farmers had settled on the Great Plains.
- To improve their condition, farmers united to form several economic and political organizations.

For additional review of the major ideas of Chapter 17, see ***Guide to the Essentials of American History*** or ***Interactive Student Tutorial CD-ROM,*** which contains interactive review activities, graphic organizers, and practice tests.

Reviewing the Chapter

Define These Terms

Match each term with the correct definition.

Column 1

1. travois
2. corral
3. reservation
4. sodbusters
5. cooperative

Column 2

- **a.** a limited area set aside for a group of people
- **b.** an enclosure for livestock
- **c.** early farmers on the Great Plains
- **d.** sled pulled by a dog or horse
- **e.** an organization in which people pool their resources for more buying power

Explore the Main Ideas

1. Why was the buffalo very important to the Plains Indians?
2. How did the mining boom lead to the growth of western towns?
3. **(a)** What caused the cattle boom of the 1870s? **(b)** Why did the Cattle Kingdom decline in the 1880s?
4. How did life change for the Plains Indians between the 1860s and 1880s?
5. **(a)** What problems did sodbusters and other farmers face? **(b)** How did the Grange help farmers?

Geography Activity

Match the letters on the map with the following places: **1.** Texas, **2.** Colorado, **3.** Nevada, **4.** Promontory Point, **5.** Omaha, **6.** San Francisco. **Interaction** What natural obstacles slowed the building of the first transcontinental railroad?

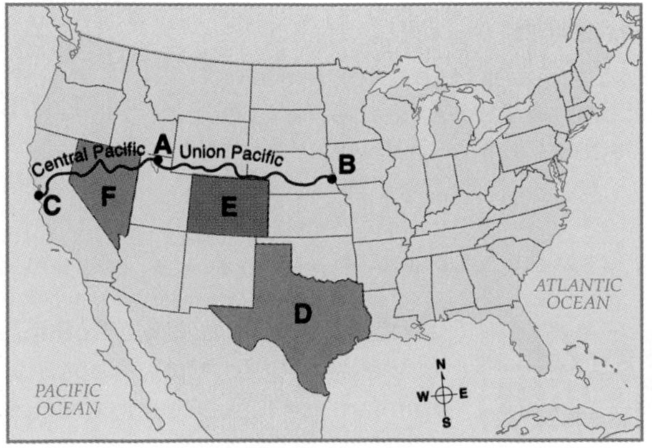

Critical Thinking and Writing

1. Understanding Chronology Place the following events in chronological order: **(a)** Dawes Act, **(b)** Fort Laramie Treaty, **(c)** Battle of Little Bighorn, **(d)** discovery of gold on Lakota land, **(e)** death of Sitting Bull, **(f)** fighting at Wounded Knee.

2. Linking Past and Present **(a)** What places are considered frontiers today? **(b)** How do these frontiers compare with the American frontiers of the 1800s?

3. Evaluating Information **(a)** What is inaccurate in the way movie westerns depict the life of the American cowhand? **(b)** Why do you think these inaccuracies exist?

4. Exploring Unit Themes **Industrialization** Why were easterners and westerners both eager to build transcontinental railroads?

Using Primary Sources

Hamilton Wicks was a "boomer" who staked a land claim during the Oklahoma land rush of April 1889. Years later, Wicks recalled the early days of Guthrie, Oklahoma—the town where he settled:

> "All that there was of Guthrie . . . on April 22, at 1:30 P.M., . . . was a water tank, a small station house, a shanty for the Wells Fargo Express, and a Government Land Office. . . . [By day's end] ten thousand people had [settled] upon a square mile of virgin prairie . . . and . . . [thousands] of white tents [had] suddenly appeared upon the face of the country. . . . Here indeed was a city laid out and populated in half a day."

Source: "The Opening of Oklahoma" by Hamilton Wicks, 1889, in *Voices of America,* 1963.

Recognizing Points of View **(a)** What happened to Guthrie, Oklahoma, on April 22, 1889? **(b)** Why did the town change so suddenly?

Activity Bank

Interdisciplinary Activity

Exploring the Arts Working with other students, prepare a skit about the hopes and dreams of the Exodusters. Perform the skit for the class.

Career Skills Activity

Farmer Do research to find out about the challenges facing farmers today. In a written report, compare conditions that exist today with those of the 1890s.

Citizenship Activity

Writing a Petition Citizens can bring about change by submitting petitions with many signatures to government leaders. Write a petition that Helen Hunt Jackson might have composed in the 1880s. In your petition, list the actions that you would like the government to take to improve conditions for Native Americans.

Internet Activity

Use the Internet to find sites dealing with one of the Native American nations discussed in this chapter. Gather information related to these questions: **(a)** How do Native Americans work to preserve their culture today? **(b)** What special problems still face Native Americans? Present your findings in a written or oral presentation.

Eyewitness Journal

Write three different eyewitness reports of what happened at Wounded Knee on December 29, 1890. Write one description as a United States soldier, a second description as a Lakota Ghost Dancer, and a third description as a white settler in South Dakota. You may wish to do additional research before completing this assignment.

Chapter 18

The Rise of Industry and Unions 1865–1914

What's Ahead

After the Civil War, American industry boomed. One reason for this tremendous growth was the rapid increase in the number of railways in the nation. Shrewd, energetic (and sometimes ruthless) business leaders created vast companies. A constant stream of new inventions also helped industry grow.

In the new economy, workers often faced long hours, unsafe conditions, and low pay. They soon banded together to win improvements in their lives. Slowly, organized labor became a powerful new force in American society.

Why Study History? In 1859, Americans discovered a valuable new natural resource—oil! This "black gold" became a major source of fuel, and a major source of wealth for those individuals who controlled it. Today, we use oil and oil products every day. Limits on the world's oil supply make it an even more valuable resource. To focus on this connection, see the *Why Study History?* feature, "The Need for Oil Affects You," in this chapter.

American Events

1876 Alexander Graham Bell develops first telephone

1882 Standard Oil trust controls oil industry

1886 American Federation of Labor is formed

1865 | 1870 | 1875 | 1880 | 1885 | 1890

World Events

1871 World Event Britain makes labor unions legal

1886 World Event Electricity is introduced to Japan

Viewing HISTORY

Business Was Booming!

In the 1880s, William Henry Jackson used a secret chemical process to create early colored photographs like this one. It shows a glass-roofed shopping arcade in Cleveland, Ohio. There, shoppers could buy anything from the latest fashions to new products such as the phonograph. In the late 1800s, new inventions, new industries, and new business practices helped the American economy to boom.

★ **Based on this picture, how was this arcade similar to a modern shopping mall? How was it different?**

1894
Federal court rules Pullman strike illegal

1911
Triangle Shirtwaist fire shows need for safety measures

1913
Henry Ford uses assembly line to mass produce automobiles

1890 **1895** **1900** **1905** **1910** **1915**

1901 World Event
FIrst transatlantic wireless message is sent

1909 World Event
French aviator makes first flight across English Channel

Railroads and Industry

As You Read

Explore These Questions

- How did railroads expand after the Civil War?
- What effects did competition have on the railroad industry?
- How did railroads spur the growth of industry?

Define

- network
- consolidate
- rebate
- pool

Identify

- George Westinghouse
- George Pullman
- Cornelius Vanderbilt
- James Hill

SETTING the Scene In 1873, Americans began singing a new folk song. "John Henry" tells the story of a legendary African American railroad worker who drives steel spikes into rock with a hammer. When the boss introduces a steam-powered drill, John Henry vows:

> "Before I'll let that steam drill
> beat me down
> I'll die with my hammer in my hand."

True to his word, John Henry dies after beating the steam drill in a contest.

Railroad workers loved singing of John Henry's victory over the machine. Still, nothing could slow down the nation's amazing industrial growth. Of the many factors spurring this growth, none was more important than the railroad.

A Railroad Network

The Civil War showed the importance of railroads. Railroads carried troops and supplies to the battlefields. They also moved raw materials to factories. After the war, railroad companies began to build new lines all over the country. (See page 437.)

Connecting lines

Early railroads were short lines that served local communities. Many lines ran for no more than 50 miles (80 km). When passengers and freight reached the end of one line, they had to move to a train on a different line to continue their journey.

Even if the lines had been connected, the problem would not have been solved. Different lines used rails of different gauges, or widths. As a result, the trains from one line could not run on the tracks of another line. In general, the tracks of northern and southern rail lines used different gauges .

In 1886, railroads in the South decided to adopt the northern gauge. On May 30, southern railroads stopped running so that work could begin. Using crowbars and sledgehammers, crews worked from dawn to dusk to move the rails a few inches farther apart. When they had finished, some 13,000 miles (20,800 km) of track had been changed.

Once the track was standardized, American railroads formed a **network,** or system of connected lines. The creation of a rail network brought benefits to shippers. Often, rail companies arranged for freight cars on one line to use the tracks of another. For example, goods loaded in Chicago could stay on the same car all the way to New York, instead of being transferred from one car to another. As a result, the shipper had to pay only one fare for the whole distance.

New rails knit the sprawling nation together. By 1900, there were more miles of tracks in the United States than in Europe and Russia combined.

Other improvements

To simplify train schedules, the railroad companies set up a system of standard time zones in 1883. Before that, each town kept its own time, based on the position of the sun. Towns in Illinois, for example, had 27 different local times! The new system divided the nation into four time zones: Eastern, Central, Mountain, and Pacific. Every place within the same time zone observed the same time.

New inventions helped make railway travel safer and faster. In 1868, **George Westinghouse** began selling his new air brake. On early trains, each railroad car had its own brakes and its own brake operator. If different cars stopped at different times, serious accidents could result. Westinghouse's air brake allowed a locomotive engineer to stop all the railroad cars at once.

The air brake increased safety and allowed for longer, faster trains. By 1900, a passenger could travel from New York to San Francisco in only six days, rather than months.

Long distance travel also became more comfortable. In 1864, **George Pullman** designed a railroad sleeping car. Pullman cars had convertible berths as well as lavatories. Rail lines also added dining cars. Porters, conductors, and waiters attended to the needs of passengers. A national magazine described the comforts of a rail trip in 1872:

> ❝From Chicago to Omaha your train will carry a dining car. . . . You sit at little tables which comfortably accommodate four persons; you order your breakfast, dinner, or supper from a bill of fare which contains a surprising number of dishes; you eat from snow-white linen . . . admirable cooked food, and pay a modest price.❞

Consolidation

As railroads grew, they looked for ways to operate more efficiently. Many companies began to **consolidate,** or combine. Larger

Viewing HISTORY **A Nation Linked by Rail**

By the late 1800s, a complex network of rail lines linked the nation. Freight trains, like the one below, hauled tons of coal and other resources needed by industry. Passenger lines advertised a new level of elegance and comfort (right).

★ **How were the nation's local rail lines transformed into a network?**

Viewing HISTORY **Farmers *vs.* Railroads**

In this 1873 cartoon, Thomas Nast portrayed railroads as a monster snaking through American farmland. A bearded farmer bravely opposes the monster. ★ **The building shown in the background is the Capitol building. Why do you think Nast showed the Capitol in the monster's coils?**

companies bought up smaller ones or forced them out of business. The Pennsylvania Railroad, for example, consolidated 73 companies into its system.

Tough-minded business people led the drive for consolidation. The most powerful of these "railroad barons" was **Cornelius Vanderbilt.** The son of a poor farmer, Vanderbilt earned his fortune in steamship lines. He then began to buy up railroad lines in New York State.

Vanderbilt sometimes used ruthless tactics to force smaller owners to sell to him. In the early 1860s, he decided to buy the New York Central Railroad. The owners refused to sell. Vanderbilt then announced that New York Central passengers would not be allowed to transfer to his trains. With their passengers stranded and business dropping sharply, the New York Central owners gave in and sold their line to Vanderbilt.

Vanderbilt then bought up most of the lines between Chicago and Buffalo. By the time of his death in 1877, his companies controlled 4,500 miles (7,200 km) of track and linked New York City to the Great Lakes region.

Other consolidations were soon underway. Before long, the major railroads of the nation were organized into systems directed by a handful of powerful men.

Building New Lines

Railroad builders raced to create thousands of miles of new tracks. In the years after Leland Stanford hammered in the golden spike in 1869, Americans built three more transcontinental railroads. **James Hill,** a Canadian-born railroad baron, finished the last major cross-country line in 1893. (See the map on page 438.) His Great Northern Railway wound from Duluth, Minnesota, to Everett, Washington.

Unlike other rail lines, the Great Northern was built without financial aid from Congress. To make his railroad succeed, Hill had to turn a profit from the start. He encouraged farmers and ranchers to settle near his railroad. He gave seed to farmers and helped them buy equipment. He even imported special bulls to breed hardier cattle. Not only was Hill's policy generous, it made good business sense.

Abuses

With builders rushing to share in the profits of the railroad boom, overbuilding occurred. Soon, there were too many rail lines in some parts of the country. Between Atlanta and St. Louis, for example, 20 different lines competed for business. There was not nearly enough rail traffic to keep all these lines busy.

Reducing competition

In the West, especially, there were too few people for the railroads to make a profit. Competition was fierce. Rate wars broke out as rival railroads slashed their fares to win customers. Usually, all the companies lost money as a result.

To win new business or keep old business, big railroads secretly offered **rebates,** or discounts, to their biggest customers. This practice forced many small companies out of business. It also hurt small shippers, such as farmers, who still had to pay the full price.

Railroad barons soon realized that cutthroat competition was hurting even their large lines. They looked for ways to end the competition. One method was pooling. In a **pool,** several railroad companies agreed to divide up business in an area. They then fixed their prices at a high level.

High prices for farmers

Railroad rebates and pools angered small farmers in the South and the West. Both practices kept shipping prices high for them. Indeed, rates were so high that at times farmers burned their crop for fuel rather than ship it to market.

As you read in Chapter 17, many farmers joined the Populist party. Populists called for government regulation of rail rates. Congress and several states passed laws regulating railroad companies. However, the laws did not end abuses. Railroad barons bribed officials to keep the laws from being enforced.

Spurring Economic Growth

Despite their problems, railroads made possible the rapid growth of industry after 1865. As railroads expanded, they stimulated the whole economy.

Building rail lines created thousands of jobs. Steelworkers turned millions of tons of iron into steel for tracks and engines. Lumberjacks cut down whole forests to supply wood for railroad ties. Miners sweated in dusty mine shafts digging coal to fuel railroad engines. The railroad companies themselves employed thousands of workers. They laid tracks, built trestles across rivers, and carved tunnels through mountains.

Because they were so large, railroads also pioneered new ways of managing business. Rail companies created special departments for shipping and accounting and for servicing equipment. Expert managers headed each department, while chains of command ensured that the organization ran smoothly. Other big businesses soon copied these management techniques.

Railroads opened every corner of the country to settlement and growth. They brought people together, especially in the West. New businesses sprang up, and towns sprouted where rail lines crossed. With rail lines in place, the United States was ready to become the greatest industrial nation the world had ever seen.

★ Section 1 Review ★

Recall

1. **Identify** **(a)** George Westinghouse, **(b)** George Pullman, **(c)** Cornelius Vanderbilt, **(d)** James Hill.
2. **Define** **(a)** network, **(b)** consolidate, **(c)** rebate, **(d)** pool.

Comprehension

3. Describe three changes that took place in the railroad industry after the Civil War.
4. **(a)** What methods did big railroads use to win and keep business? **(b)** How did these practices affect small businesses and farmers?
5. List three ways that railroads spurred the growth of industry.

Critical Thinking and Writing

6. **Synthesizing Information** After the Civil War, railroads consolidated as large railroad companies took over smaller ones. **(a)** What were the advantages of consolidation? **(b)** What were the disadvantages?
7. **Linking Past and Present** Are railroads as important today as they were in the 1800s? Why or why not?

Activity **Asking Questions** "Tonight's special guest: railroad baron Cornelius Vanderbilt. The phone lines are now open." Jot down three or four questions you would ask Vanderbilt if he appeared on a talk show. The questions may concern his goals, his business practices, and his achievements.

Big Business

As You Read

Explore These Questions

- Why did the steel industry become important after the Civil War?
- What new ways of doing business did Americans develop?
- What were the arguments for and against the growth of giant corporations?

Define

- vertical integration
- corporation
- stock
- dividend
- trust
- monopoly
- free enterprise system

Identify

- John D. Rockefeller
- Bessemer process
- Andrew Carnegie
- J. Pierpont Morgan
- Standard Oil Company
- Sherman Antitrust Act

SETTING the Scene On a February day in 1865, an unusual auction was held. The owners of an Ohio oil refinery stood toe to toe, the only two people in the room. Each was bidding to buy the other's share in the company.

Bidding opened at $500. The price swiftly jumped higher and higher. Finally, the bid reached $72,500. "I'll go no higher, John," said one of the men. "The business is yours." John paid the $72,500 and became sole owner of the company. It was a smart buy. When he died more than 70 years later, **John D. Rockefeller** was a multimillionaire who dominated the entire American oil industry.

Rockefeller was one of a new breed of American business leaders in the late 1800s. They were bold, imaginative—and sometimes ruthless. During the next 50 years, these leaders shaped the nation's emerging businesses and industries.

Growth of the American Steel Industry

The growth of railroads after the Civil War fueled the growth of the steel industry. Early trains ran on iron rails that wore out quickly. Railroad owners knew that steel rails were much stronger and not as likely to rust as iron. Steel, however, was costly and difficult to make.

A new way to make steel

In the 1850s, William Kelly in the United States and Henry Bessemer in England each discovered a new way to make steel. The **Bessemer process,** as it came to be called, enabled steelmakers to produce strong steel at a lower cost. As a result, railroads began to lay steel rails.

Other industries also took advantage of the cheaper steel. Manufacturers made steel nails, screws, needles, and other items. Steel girders supported the great weight of the new "skyscrapers."

Steel mills spring up

Steel mills sprang up in cities throughout the Midwest. Pittsburgh became the steelmaking capital of the nation. Nearby coal mines and good transportation helped Pittsburgh's steel mills to thrive.

The thriving steel mills brought jobs and prosperity to Pittsburgh and other steeltowns. They also caused problems. The mills belched thick black smoke that turned the air gray. Soot blanketed houses, trees, and streets. Waste polluted local rivers.

Andrew Carnegie

Many Americans made fortunes in the steel industry. Richest of all was a Scottish immigrant, **Andrew Carnegie.** Carnegie's ideas on how to make money—and how to spend it—had a wide influence.

Carnegie's career reads like a history of American industry. As a child, he went to work in a textile mill. Later, he became a telegraph operator. When the railroad boom started, Carnegie got a job with the Pennsylvania Railroad.

Traveling in England in the 1870s, Carnegie visited a factory and saw the Bessemer process at work. When he returned to the United States, he built a steel mill at Homestead, Pennsylvania, south of Pittsburgh. His friendships with railroad owners helped him win contracts for the steel he manufactured.

Controlling the steel industry

Within a short time, Carnegie was earning huge profits from his steel mill. He used the money to buy out rivals. He also bought iron mines, railroad and steamship lines, and warehouses.

Soon, Carnegie controlled all phases of the steel industry—from mining iron ore to shipping finished steel. Acquiring control of all the steps required to change raw materials into finished products is called **vertical integration.** Vertical integration gave Carnegie a great advantage over other steel companies.

In 1892, Carnegie combined all of his businesses into the Carnegie Steel Company. By 1900, it was turning out more steel than all of Great Britain.

The "gospel of wealth"

Like other business owners, Carnegie drove his workers hard, Still, he believed that the rich had a duty to help the poor and improve society. He called this idea the "gospel of wealth." He wrote:

> "Wealth, passing through the hands of the few, can be made a much more powerful force for the elevation of our race than if it had been distributed in small sums to the people themselves."

Carnegie himself gave millions to charities. He donated $60 million to build public libraries in towns all over the country. After selling Carnegie Steel in 1901, he spent his time and money helping people.

Rise of Corporations

Before the railroad boom, nearly every American town had its own small factories. They produced goods for people in the area. By the late 1800s, however, big factories were producing goods more cheaply than small factories could. Railroads distributed these goods to nationwide markets. As demand for local goods fell, many small factories closed. Big factories then increased their output.

Expanding factories needed capital, or money, for investment. Factory owners used the capital to buy raw materials, pay workers, and cover shipping and advertising costs. To raise capital, Americans adopted new ways of organizing their businesses.

Biography **Andrew Carnegie**

As a teenager, Andrew Carnegie worked in a textile mill for $1.20 a week. By the age of 50, he was the nation's "Steel King." Carnegie believed that the rich had a right to make money, and a duty to spend it for the public good. He gave away millions to schools, libraries, and the cause of world peace.

★ **What business methods did Carnegie use to build his steel company?**

Many expanding businesses became corporations. A **corporation** is a business that is owned by investors. A corporation sells **stock,** or shares in the business, to investors, who are known as stockholders. The corporation can use the money invested by stockholders to build a new factory or buy new machines.

In return for their investment, stockholders hope to receive **dividends,** or shares of a corporation's profit. To protect their investment, stockholders elect a board of directors to run the corporation.

Thousands of people bought stock in corporations. Stockholders faced fewer risks than owners of private businesses. If a private business goes bankrupt, the owner must pay all the debts of the business. By law, stockholders cannot be held responsible for a corporation's debts.

Banks and Industry

In the years after the Civil War, corporations attracted large amounts of capital from American investors. Corporations also borrowed millions of dollars from banks. These loans helped American industry grow at a rapid pace. At the same time, the banks made huge profits.

The most powerful banker of the late 1800s was **J. Pierpont Morgan.** Morgan's influence was not limited to banking. He used his banking profits to gain control of major corporations.

During economic hard times in the 1890s, Morgan and other bankers invested in the stock of troubled corporations. As large stockholders, they easily won seats on the boards of directors. They then adopted policies that reduced competition and ensured big profits. "I like a little competition, but I like combination more," Morgan used to say.

Between 1894 and 1898, Morgan gained control of most of the nation's major rail lines. He then began to buy up steel companies, including Carnegie Steel, and merge them into a single large corporation. By 1901, Morgan had become head of United States Steel Company. It was the first American business worth more than $1 billion.

Connections With Arts

J. Pierpont Morgan used much of his wealth to collect manuscripts and rare books—some of them more than 400 years old. By 1906, his collection could no longer fit into his private library. Morgan then had a separate building constructed. After Morgan's death, the Pierpont Morgan Library in New York City was opened to the public.

The Oil Industry

Industry could not have expanded so quickly in the United States without the nation's rich supply of natural resources. Iron ore was plentiful, especially in the Mesabi Range of Minnesota. Pennsylvania, West Virginia, and the Rocky Mountains had large deposits of coal. The Rockies also contained minerals such as gold, silver, and copper. Vast forests provided lumber for building.

In 1859, Americans discovered a valuable new resource—oil. Drillers near Titusville, Pennsylvania, made the nation's first oil strike. An oil boom quickly followed. Hundreds of prospectors rushed to western Pennsylvania ready to drill wells in search of a "gusher."

Rockefeller and Standard Oil

Among those who came to the Pennsylvania oil fields was young John D. Rockefeller. Rockefeller, however, did not rush to drill for oil. He knew that oil had little value until it was refined, or purified, to make kerosene. Kerosene was used as a fuel in stoves and lamps.

The son of a humble New York peddler, Rockefeller moved with his family to Ohio when he was 14. At 23, he invested in his first oil refinery.

Rockefeller believed that competition was wasteful. He used the profits from his refinery to buy up other refineries. He then combined the companies into the **Standard Oil Company** of Ohio.

Rockefeller was a shrewd businessman. He was always trying to improve the quality of his oil. He also did whatever he could to get rid of competition. Standard Oil slashed

Why Study History?

Because the Need for Oil Affects You

Historical Background

In 1859, drillers struck oil in Pennsylvania. At the time, most refined oil ended up as kerosene for lamps. Factories also used oil to lubricate machines.

By the early 1900s, new inventions like the automobile created a demand for gasoline—another oil product. Before long, filling stations sprang up in cities and towns. Oil was fueling a growing nation.

Connections to Today

You know that we use oil as fuel for cars, buses, airplanes, lawn mowers, and heaters. Did you also know that manufacturers use petroleum to make plastics, cloth, paints, and medicines? Oil also fuels generators that supply electricity.

This valuable resource is also limited. The world's supply of petroleum could eventually run out. Scientists are working to develop alternate sources of energy.

Connections to You

How would your future change if the use of oil was restricted? High fuel costs might limit your ability to travel. Expensive heating oil might force you to live in a colder home. Prices for other items would rise, too, as factories paid higher prices for oil.

Such extreme shortages are not likely to happen soon. However, saving energy in small ways can help stretch our precious oil resources. Here are some things you can do:

- Recycle plastics and other products.
- Turn off lights when you leave a room.
- Avoid wasting hot water.
- Whenever possible, take the bus or train.

1. **Comprehension** **(a)** How was oil used in the late 1800s? **(b)** List three ways you use oil and petroleum products.
2. **Critical Thinking** Today, the United States imports much of its oil supply from other countries. Why do you think many Americans worry about dependence on foreign oil?

Writing an Advertisement List the qualities that you would want a new fuel source to have. Then, create a name and write an advertisement for your new fuel.

Petroleum is used to make hundreds of products, from plastic combs to pool floats.

Linking Past and Present

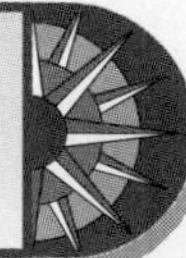

Past

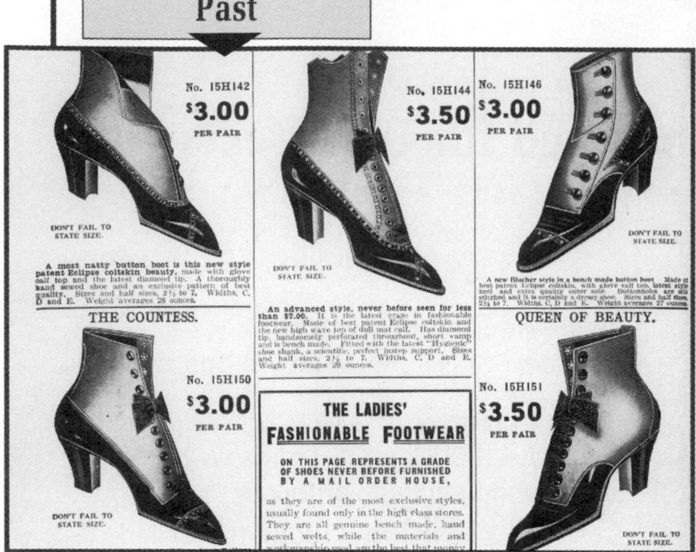

Present

Shopping at Home

In the late 1800s, manufacturers pioneered new ways to sell their products nationwide. Companies like Sears, Roebuck used mail order catalogs (left) to sell goods to isolated western farmers. Today, Americans can turn on their televisions and instantly order anything from jewelry to cookware (right). ★ **What are the advantages and disadvantages of shopping at home?**

its prices to drive rivals out of business. It pressured its customers not to deal with other oil companies. Rockefeller even persuaded railroad companies eager for his business to grant rebates to Standard Oil. Lower shipping costs gave Rockefeller an important edge over his competitors.

Creating a trust

To tighten his hold over the oil industry, Rockefeller formed the Standard Oil trust in 1882. A **trust** is a group of corporations run by a single board of directors.

Stockholders in dozens of smaller oil companies turned over their stock to Standard Oil. In return, they got stock in the newly created trust. The trust stock paid the stockholders high dividends. However, the stockholders gave up their right to choose the board of directors. The board of Standard Oil, headed by Rockefeller, managed all the companies, which before had been rivals.

The Standard Oil trust created a monopoly in the oil industry. A **monopoly** controls all or nearly all the business of an industry. The Standard Oil trust controlled 95 percent of all oil refining in the United States.

Other businesses followed Rockefeller's lead. They set up trusts and tried to build monopolies. By the late 1890s, monopolies and trusts controlled some of the nation's most important industries.

Big Business: Two Viewpoints

Some Americans charged that the leaders of giant corporations were abusing the free enterprise system. In a **free enterprise system,** businesses are owned by private citizens. Owners decide what products to make, how much to produce, where to sell products, and what prices to charge. Companies compete to win customers by making the best product at the lowest price.

Opposition to trusts

Critics argued that trusts and monopolies reduced competition. Without competition, there was no reason for companies to keep prices low or to improve their products. It was also hard for new companies to start up and compete against powerful trusts. Workers, moreover, often felt that large corporations treated them badly.

Critics were also upset about the political influence of trusts. Leaders of big business were richer than Americans had ever been before. Some people worried that millionaires were using their wealth to buy favors from elected officials. The *Chicago Tribune* warned that "liberty and monopoly cannot live together." John Reagan, a member of Congress from Texas, said:

> "There were no beggars till Vanderbilts and . . . Morgans . . . shaped the actions of Congress and molded the purposes of government. Then the few became fabulously wealthy, the many wretchedly poor."

Under pressure from the public, the government slowly moved toward controlling giant corporations. Congress approved the **Sherman Antitrust Act** in 1890. The act banned the formation of trusts and monopolies. However, it was too weak to be effective. Some state governments passed laws to regulate business, but the corporations usually sidestepped them. Later reformers began to demand even stronger measures.

Support for trusts

Naturally, business leaders defended trusts. Andrew Carnegie published articles arguing that too much competition ruined businesses and put people out of work. In an article titled "Wealth and Its Uses," he wrote:

> "It will be a great mistake for the community to shoot the millionaires, for they are the bees that make the most honey, and contribute most to the hive even after they have gorged themselves full."

Defenders of big business argued that the growth of giant corporations brought lower production costs, lower prices, higher wages, and a better quality of life for millions of Americans. By 1900, Americans enjoyed the highest standard of living in the world. Innovative business leaders also helped usher in a new age of technology and invention that revolutionized American life.

★ Section 2 Review ★

Recall

1. **Identify** **(a)** John D. Rockefeller, **(b)** Bessemer process, **(c)** Andrew Carnegie, **(d)** J. Pierpont Morgan, **(e)** Standard Oil Company, **(f)** Sherman Antitrust Act.
2. **Define** **(a)** vertical integration, **(b)** corporation, **(c)** stock, **(d)** dividend, **(e)** trust, **(f)** monopoly, **(g)** free enterprise system.

Comprehension

3. Name three uses for cheap steel in the 1800s.
4. Why did many American businesses become corporations?
5. Why did some Americans think that big business threatened the free enterprise system?

Critical Thinking and Writing

6. **Understanding Causes and Effects** **(a)** What were two causes of the growth of the steel industry? **(b)** What were two effects?
7. **Applying Information** Andrew Carnegie once said of people who held onto their fortunes, "The man who dies thus rich, dies disgraced." **(a)** Restate Carnegie's meaning in your own words. **(b)** Did Carnegie carry out this philosophy in his own life? Explain.

Activity **Creating a Business Plan** You are a clever business owner in the late 1800s. Describe the business you would choose to build. Then, outline a plan showing how you would go about doing it.

A Flood of Inventions

As You Read

Explore These Questions

- What inventions improved communication in the 1800s?
- Why was Menlo Park called an "invention factory"?
- How did Henry Ford revolutionize the automobile industry?

Define

- assembly line
- mass production

Identify

- Cyrus Field
- Alexander Graham Bell
- Thomas Edison
- Jan Matzeliger
- Gustavus Swift
- George Eastman
- Henry Ford
- Orville and Wilbur Wright

SETTING the Scene Josephine Cochrane was annoyed. The wife of an Illinois politician, she hosted many elegant dinners. Her fine china, though, often broke when being washed.

Cochrane took a hose, some wire, a motor, and a large copper boiler to the woodshed. There, she built the first automatic dishwasher. Soon, Cochrane was selling her machine to restaurants. She patented her invention in 1886.

A flood of invention swept the United States in the late 1800s. By the 1890s, Americans were patenting 21,000 new inventions a year. These inventions helped industry to grow and become more efficient. New devices also made daily life easier in many American homes.

Advanced Communication

Some remarkable new devices filled the need for faster communication. The telegraph had been in use since 1844. (See Chapter 12.) It helped people around the nation stay in touch. It also helped business. For example, a steelmaker in Pittsburgh could instantly order iron ore from a mine in Minnesota.

Transatlantic cable

The telegraph speeded communication within the United States. It still took weeks, however, for news from Europe to arrive by boat.

In 1866, **Cyrus Field** ran an underwater telegraph cable across the Atlantic Ocean. Field marveled at his success:

> "In five months... the cable had been manufactured, shipped... stretched across the Atlantic, and was sending messages... swift as lightning from continent to continent."

Field's transatlantic cable brought the United States and Europe closer together.

The telephone

Morse and Field used a dot and dash code to send messages over telegraph wires. Meanwhile, **Alexander Graham Bell,** a Scottish-born teacher of the deaf, was trying to transmit sound.

In March 1876, Bell was ready to test his "talking machine." Before the test, Bell accidentally spilled battery acid on himself. His assistant, Thomas Watson, was in another

Alexander Graham Bell's telephone

room. Bell spoke into the machine, "Watson, come here, I want you!" Watson rushed to Bell's side. "Mr. Bell," he cried, "I heard every word you said, distinctly!" The telephone worked.

Bell's telephone aroused little interest at first. Scientists praised the invention. Most people, however, saw it as a toy. Bell offered to sell the telephone to the Western Union Telegraph Company for $100,000. The company refused—a costly mistake. In the end, the telephone earned Bell millions.

Bell formed the Bell Telephone Company in 1877. By 1885, he had sold more than 300,000 phones, mostly to businesses. The telephone speeded up the pace of business even more. Instead of having to go to a telegraph office, people could find out about prices or supplies simply by talking on the telephone.

Thomas Edison

In an age of invention, **Thomas Edison** was right at home. In 1876, he opened a research laboratory in Menlo Park, New Jersey. There, Edison boasted that he and his 15 co-workers set out to create "minor" inventions every 10 days and "a big thing every 6 months or so."

The "invention factory"

The key to Edison's success lay in his approach. He turned inventing into a system. Teams of experts refined Edison's ideas and translated them into practical inventions. Menlo Park became an "invention factory."

The results were amazing. Edison became known as the "Wizard of Menlo Park" for inventing the light bulb, the phonograph, and hundreds of other devices.

One invention from Edison's laboratory launched a new industry—the movies. In 1893, Edison introduced his first machine for showing moving pictures. Viewers watched short films by looking through a peephole in a cabinet. Later, Edison developed a motion picture projector, making it possible for many people to watch a film at the same time. By 1905, thousands of silent movie houses called nickelodeons were opening in cities across the United States.

▲ *Electric light bulb* ▲ *Phonograph*

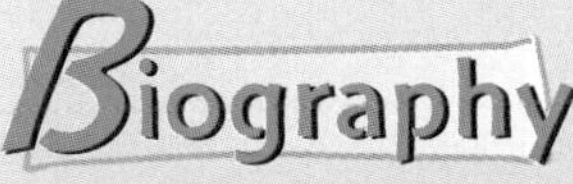

Thomas Alva Edison

A poor student, Thomas Edison grew up to invent the light bulb, the phonograph and dozens of other devices. The photo above was taken after Edison went without sleep for three days working on his phonograph. At last, he heard his own voice reciting "Mary Had a Little Lamb." ★ **Edison said, "Genius is one percent inspiration and ninety-nine percent perspiration." What do you think he meant?**

Electric power

One of Edison's most important creations was the electric power plant. Edison built the first power plant in New York City in 1882. He wired the business district first in hopes of attracting investors. With the flip of a switch, Edison set the district ablaze in light.

Within a year, Edison's power plant was supplying electricity to homes as well as businesses. Soon, more power plants were built. Factories replaced steam-powered engines with safer, quieter electric engines. Electric energy powered streetcars in cities and lighted countless homes. The modern age of electricity had begun.

Skills FOR LIFE

Critical Thinking | **Managing Information** | Communication | Maps, Charts, and Graphs

Using a Computerized Card Catalog

How Will I Use This Skill?

Whether you are hunting for information on the development of the automobile, or the newest bestseller, you may find yourself searching in a library. Today, most libraries are equipped with computerized catalogs to assist you during your search.

LEARN the Skill

1. Decide whether your search should start with a specific author, a title of a publication, or a subject.
2. Use the main menu to start your search. The main menu presents you with a list of options. From this list, choose the path to begin your search: Author, Title, or Subject.
3. Narrow your search. Follow the instructions on the computer screen to locate the books you need.
4. Select books that might be helpful. Write down the call numbers, titles, and authors of the books. The call numbers will allow you to find the books on the library shelves.

PRACTICE the Skill

Using the sample screens to the right, practice searching a typical library computer catalog.

1. Review screens 1 and 2. Which option has been chosen to begin the library search: Author, Title, or Subject?
2. Look at Screen 1, Main Menu. Which number would you type to begin the search documented on these diagrams?
3. Look at Screens 2 and 3. Identify the topic chosen for research. On Screen 3, note the books available on this topic.
4. Look at Screen 4. What are the title and call number of the chosen book?

APPLY the Skill

Use the computerized catalog in your school or community library to research the history of any invention discussed in this chapter.

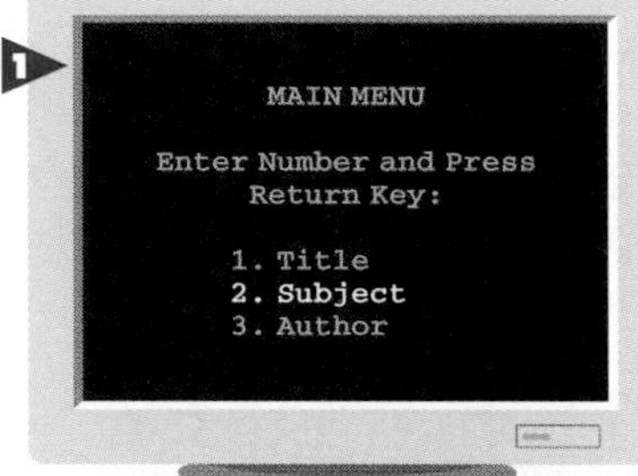

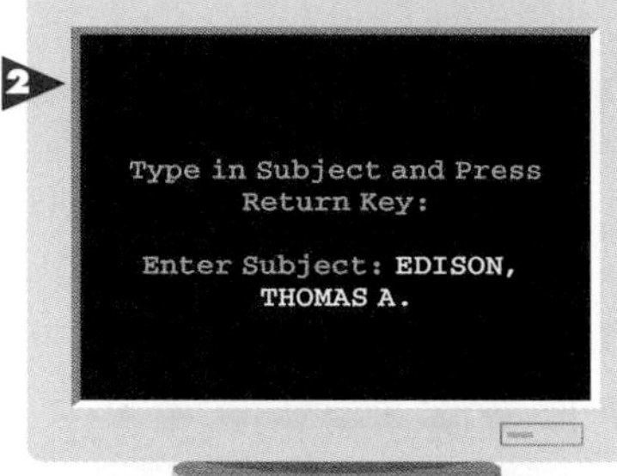

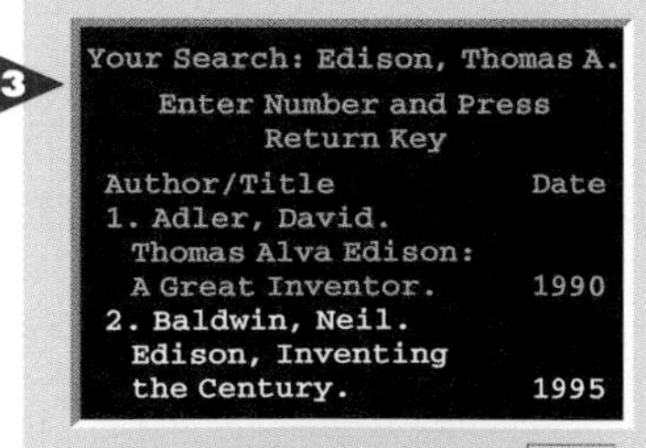

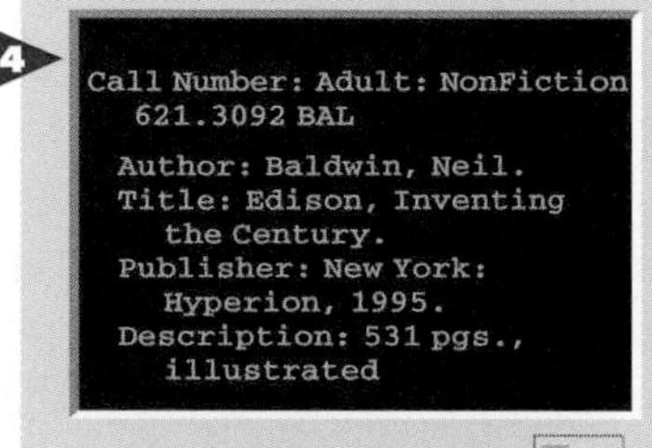

A Rush of Technology

Almost every day, it seemed, American inventors were creating new devices that made business more efficient and life more pleasant. The United States became known as the land of invention.

Inventions by African Americans

African Americans contributed to the flood of inventions. In 1872, Elijah McCoy created a special device that oiled engines automatically. It was widely used on railroad engines and in factories. Granville T. Woods found a way to send telegraph messages between moving railroad trains.

Jan Matzeliger invented a machine that could perform almost all the steps in shoemaking that had been done before by hand. Patented in 1883, Matzeliger's machine was eventually used in shoe factories everywhere.

Many African American inventors had trouble getting patents for their inventions. Even so, in 1900, an assistant in the patent office compiled a list of patents issued to African American inventors. The list, together with drawings and plans of all the inventions, filled four huge volumes.

Refrigeration

In the 1880s, **Gustavus Swift** came up with an idea that transformed the American diet. Swift introduced refrigeration to the meatpacking industry. In the past, cattle, pigs, and chickens had been raised and sold

A Time of Invention

Inventor	Date	Invention
Elisha Otis	1852	passenger elevator brake
George Pullman	1864	sleeping car
George Westinghouse	1868	air brake
Elijah McCoy	1872	automatic engine-oiling machine
Andrew S. Hallidie	1873	cable streetcar
Stephen Dudley Field	1874	electric streetcar
Alexander Graham Bell	1876	telephone
Thomas Alva Edison	1877	phonograph
Anna Baldwin	1878	milking machine
Thomas Alva Edison	1879	first practical incandescent light bulb
James Ritty	1879	cash register
Jan E. Matzeliger	1883	shoemaking machine
Lewis E. Waterman	1884	fountain pen
Granville T. Woods	1887	automatic air brake
Charles and J. Frank Duryea	1893	gasoline-powered car
King C. Gillette	1895	safety razor with throwaway blades
John Thurman	1899	motor-driven vacuum cleaner
Leo H. Baekeland	1909	plastic

Chart *Skills* **New inventions transformed daily life in the United States. They also helped the American economy grow.**

1. **Comprehension** **(a)** What did George Westinghouse invent? In what year? **(b)** Who improved on Westinghouse's invention? In what year?
2. **Critical Thinking** **(a)** Which of these inventions made transportation easier? **(b)** Which of these inventions might be found in a home today?

AmericanHeritage
MAGAZINE

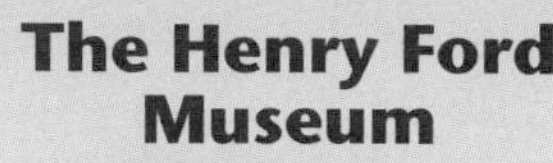

HISTORY HAPPENED HERE

The Henry Ford Museum

Not far from his Detroit auto plant, Henry Ford built a place to display "every household article, every kind of vehicle, every sort of tool." Today at the Henry Ford Museum, you can explore the world's largest transportation collection, from canoes to giant locomotives to classic cars. You can also see devices you might have had in your home 100 years ago.

★ ***To learn more about this historic site, write: Henry Ford Museum, P.O. Box 1970, Dearborn, MI 48121.***

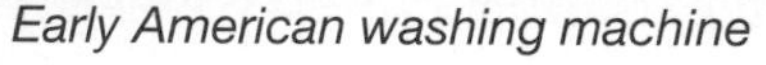

Early American washing machine ➤

locally. Meat spoiled quickly, so it could not be shipped over distances.

Swift set up a meatpacking plant in Chicago, a railroad hub midway between the cattle ranches of the West and the cities of the East. Cattle were shipped by train to Chicago. At Swift's plant, the animals were slaughtered and carved up into sides of beef. The fresh beef was quickly loaded onto refrigerated railroad cars and carried to market. Even in summer, Swift sent fresh meat to eastern cities. As a result, Americans began to eat more meat.

Inventions for home and office

New inventions also affected life at home and in the office. Christopher Sholes perfected the typewriter in 1868. This invention made office work easier.

In 1888, **George Eastman** introduced the lightweight Kodak camera. No longer did photography require bulky equipment and chemicals. The cost was only $25, including a roll of film. After 100 snaps of the shutter, the owner returned the camera to Kodak. The company developed the pictures and sent them back, along with a reloaded camera. Taking pictures became a popular pastime.

The Automobile

No single person invented the automobile. Europeans had produced motorized vehicles as early as the 1860s. Several Americans began building cars in the 1890s. Still, only the wealthy could afford them.

Ford and mass production

It was **Henry Ford,** with his "motor car for the multitude," who made the auto a part of everyday American life. In 1913, Ford introduced the **assembly line.** In this method of production, workers are stationed in one place as products edge along on a moving belt. At Ford's auto plant, one group of workers would bolt seats onto a passing car frame, the next would add the roof, and so on. The assembly line greatly reduced the time needed to build a car. Other industries soon adopted it.

Ford's assembly line allowed mass production of cars. **Mass production** means making large quantities of a product quickly and cheaply. Because of mass production, Ford could sell his cars at a lower price than other auto makers.

Cars become popular

At first, most people laughed at the "horseless carriage." Some thought automobiles were dangerous. A backfiring auto engine could scare a horse right off the road. Towns and villages across the nation posted signs: "No horseless carriages allowed."

Slowly, attitudes toward the automobile changed. No other means of travel offered such freedom. As prices dropped, more people could afford to buy cars. In 1900, only 8,000 Americans owned cars. By 1917, more than 4.5 million autos were chugging along American roads.

Automobiles were at first regarded as machines for men only. Auto makers soon realized, however, that women could drive—and buy—cars. Companies began to direct advertisements to women, stressing the comfort and usefulness of automobiles. Driving gave women greater independence.

A hit song from 1905 shows the growing popularity of the automobile. "In My Merry Oldsmobile" is a love story about a boy, a girl, and a car:

> "Johnnie Steel has an Oldsmobile;
> He loves a dear little girl:
> She is the queen of his gas machine;
> She has his heart in a whirl.
> Now when they go for a spin, you know,
> She tries to learn the auto, so
> He lets her steer while he gets her ear
> And whispers soft and low:
>
> 'Come away with me Lucile,
> In my merry Oldsmobile. . . .'"

The Airplane

Meanwhile, two Ohio bicycle mechanics, **Orville and Wilbur Wright,** were experimenting with another new method of transportation—flying. After trying out hundreds of designs, the Wright brothers tested their first "flying machine" on December 17, 1903. At Kitty Hawk, North Carolina, Orville took off. The plane, powered by a small gasoline engine, stayed in the air for 12 seconds and flew a distance of 120 feet (37m).

The Wrights' flight did not attract much attention. Most people saw little use for flying machines. Slowly, however, air pioneers built better planes and made longer flights. In time, the airplane changed the world.

★ Section 3 Review ★

Recall

1. **Identify** **(a)** Cyrus Field, **(b)** Alexander Graham Bell, **(c)** Thomas Edison, **(d)** Jan Matzeliger, **(e)** Gustavus Swift, **(f)** George Eastman, **(g)** Henry Ford, **(h)** Orville and Wilbur Wright.
2. **Define** **(a)** assembly line, **(b)** mass production.

Comprehension

3. Describe two inventions that transformed communication in the 1800s.
4. Why was Edison's electric power plant important?
5. How did the assembly line change auto making?

Critical Thinking and Writing

6. **Drawing Conclusions** Why might inventors be more creative working in an "invention factory" than working on their own?
7. **Ranking** Which invention discussed in this section had the greatest impact on American life? Explain your answer.

Activity **Playing a Role** Which invention mentioned in this section would have amazed you the most if you lived at that time? In a brief skit, play the role of a person seeing that invention for the first time.

Labor in the Age of Industry

As You Read

Explore These Questions
- How did the role of the worker change in the new industrial age?
- What were the goals of early unions?
- Why was progress slow for labor?

Define
- sweatshop
- strikebreaker
- anarchist
- collective bargaining
- injunction

Identify
- Knights of Labor
- Terence Powderly
- Haymarket Riot
- Samuel Gompers
- American Federation of Labor
- Mother Jones
- International Ladies' Garment Workers Union
- Triangle Fire
- Western Federation of Miners

SETTING the Scene In 1896, Frederick Taylor observed workers at a steel plant. He wrote down the number of times a worker picked up a shovel and the amount of time he took to swing it. Taylor then redesigned the shovels and work pattern in order to make the workers more productive.

Many factory owners adopted Taylor's system of "scientific management." Workers, however, often complained that they were being treated as parts of the machinery.

The rise of industry changed the workplace. By the late 1800s, harsh new conditions led workers to organize.

The American Federation of Labor and other unions fought to win workers an eight-hour day.

A Changing Workplace

Factories drew workers from many different backgrounds. Most workers were native-born white men. Many had left farms to take jobs in large cities.

Some northern factory workers were African Americans who had migrated from the South. Large numbers of immigrants from Europe, Asia, and Mexico also found jobs in factories. Women and children worked in factories, too. All of these groups earned lower wages than native-born white men.

Workers and employers

Workers had to adjust to the new kinds of factories of the late 1800s. Before the Civil War, most factories were small and family-run. Bosses knew their workers by name and chatted with them about their families. Because most workers had skills that the factory needed, they could bargain with the boss for wages.

By the 1880s, the relationship between worker and boss declined. Workers stood all day tending machines in a large, crowded, noisy room. Their skills were no longer needed, and they worked for wages fixed by their bosses. In the garment trade and other industries, sweatshops became common. A **sweatshop** is a workplace where people labor long hours in poor conditions for low pay. Most sweatshop workers were immigrants, young women, or children.

Child labor

The 1900 census reported nearly 2 million children under age 15 at work through-

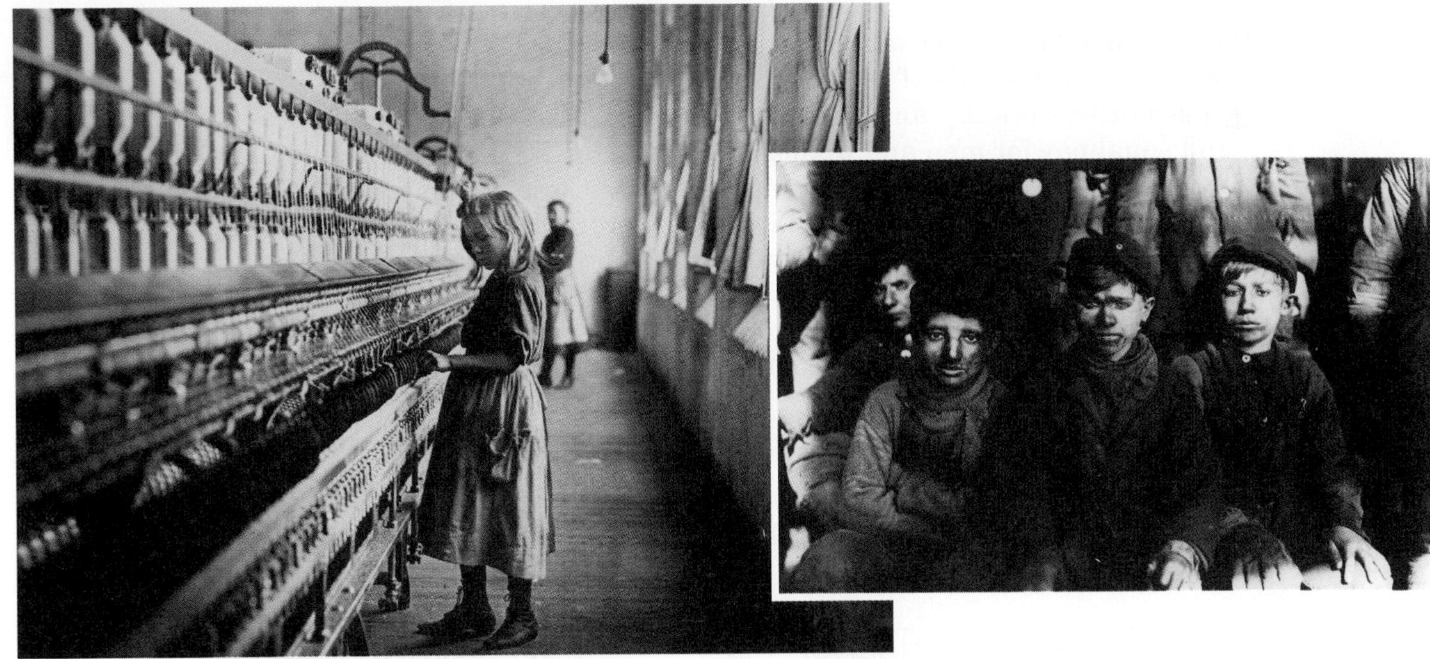

Viewing History **Children at Work**

Children—many of them from immigrant families—labored in the nation's industries. "Breaker boys," hand-sorted slate from coal in grimy mines (right). Young girls operated heavy machinery in textile mills (left). ★ **How do you think the lives of these children were affected by having to go to work at an early age?**

out the country. Boys and girls labored in hazardous textile mills, tobacco factories, and garment sweatshops. In coal mines, they picked stones out of the coal for 12 hours a day, 6 days a week.

Working children had little time for schooling. Lack of education reduced their chance to build a better life as adults.

Many Americans believed that child labor was wrong. However, as long as factory owners could hire children at low pay, and as long as their families needed the money, child labor continued.

Dangerous conditions

Factories brimmed with hazards. Lung-damaging dust filled the air of textile mills. Cave-ins and gas explosions plagued mines. In steel mills, vats of red-hot metal spilled without warning.

Owners were more concerned with profits than with worker safety. They spent little to improve working conditions. Some workers had their health destroyed. Others were severely injured or killed in industrial accidents. In one year, 195 workers died in the steel mills of Pittsburgh.

Workers Organize

Low pay, long hours, and unhealthful conditions threatened the well-being of workers. Many found ways to fight back. Some workers took days off or slowed their work pace. Others went on strike. Strikes were usually informal, organized by workers in individual factories.

Sometimes, workers banded together to win better conditions. Most early efforts to form unions failed, however. (See page 307.)

Knights of Labor

In 1869, workers formed the **Knights of Labor.** At first, the union was open to skilled workers only. Members held meetings in secret because employers fired workers who joined unions.

In 1879, the Knights of Labor selected **Terence Powderly** as their president. Powderly worked to strengthen the union by opening membership to immigrants, blacks, women, and unskilled workers.

Powderly wanted the Knights to make the world a better place for both workers and employers. He did not believe in strikes.

Rather, he relied on rallies and meetings to win public support. Goals of the Knights included a shorter workday, an end to child labor, and equal pay for men and women.

In 1885, some Knights of Labor launched a strike that forced the Missouri Pacific Railroad to restore wage cuts. The Knights did not officially support the strike. Still, workers everywhere saw the strike as a victory for the union. Membership soared to 700,000, including 60,000 African Americans.

Haymarket Riot

The following year, the Knights of Labor ran into serious trouble. Workers at the McCormick Harvester Company in Chicago went on strike. Again, the Knights did not endorse the strike.

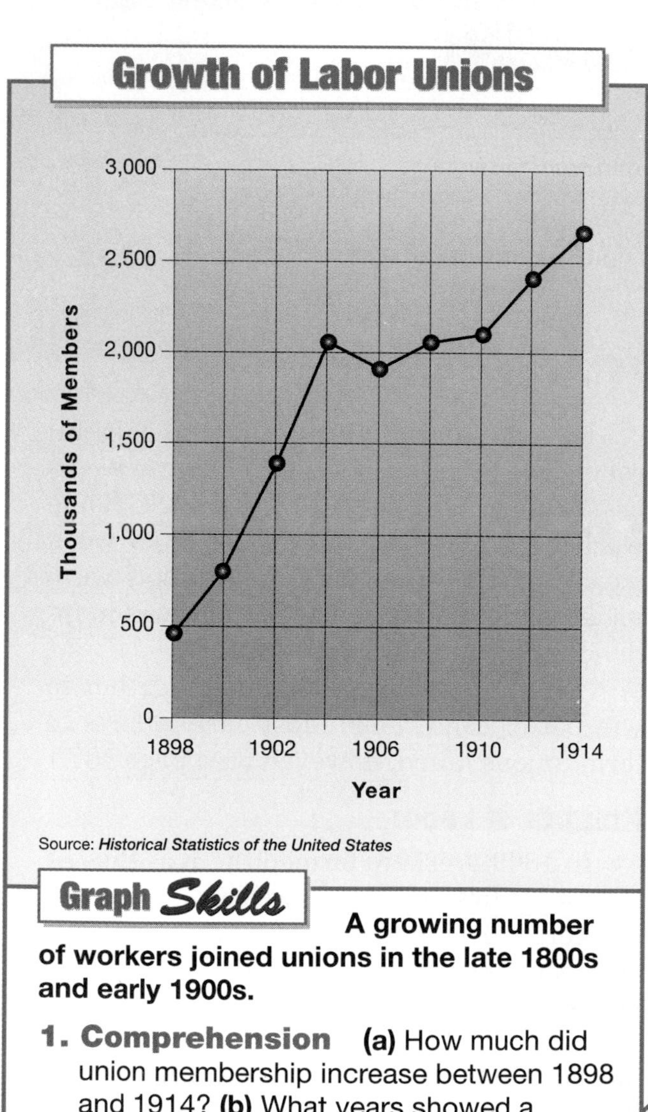

Graph Skills **A growing number of workers joined unions in the late 1800s and early 1900s.**

1. **Comprehension** **(a)** How much did union membership increase between 1898 and 1914? **(b)** What years showed a decrease in membership?
2. **Critical Thinking** Why did membership in unions grow so much?

Like many companies at the time, the McCormick company hired **strikebreakers,** or replacements for striking workers. On May 3, 1886, workers clashed with strikebreakers outside the factory. Police opened fire. Four workers were killed.

The next day, thousands of workers gathered in Haymarket Square to protest the killings. The rally was led by **anarchists,** people who oppose all forms of organized government. Suddenly, a bomb exploded, killing a police officer. Police peppered the crowd with bullets. Ten more people died, and 50 were injured.

Eight anarchists were arrested for their part in the **Haymarket Riot,** as the incident was called. No real evidence linked these men to the bombing, but four were tried, convicted, and hanged. A wave of anti-labor feeling swept the nation. Membership in the Knights of Labor dropped sharply.

American Federation of Labor

Despite the failure of the Knights of Labor, the labor movement continued to grow. In 1886, a British-born cigarmaker named **Samuel Gompers** organized a new union in New York City. The **American Federation of Labor,** or AFL, was open to skilled workers only.

Workers did not join the AFL directly. Rather, they joined a trade union, a union of persons working at the same trade. For example, a typesetter would join a typesetter's union. The union then joined the AFL. In effect, the AFL was a union made up of other unions.

Limited goals

Unlike the Knights of Labor, the AFL did not set out to change the world. It stressed practical goals. As one AFL leader said:

> “Our organization does not consist of idealists. We are going on from day to day. We are fighting only for immediate objects—objects that can be realized in a few years.”

The AFL stressed higher wages, shorter hours, and improved working conditions. It led the fight for **collective bargaining,** the right of unions to negotiate with management for workers as a group.

A powerful union

Unlike the Knights of Labor, the AFL supported the use of strikes to achieve its goals. The AFL collected money from its member unions. Some of it went into a strike fund. When AFL members went on strike, they were paid from the fund so that they could still feed their families.

Its practical approach helped the AFL become the most powerful union in the nation. Between 1886 and 1910, membership in the AFL swelled from 150,000 to one million. However, because African Americans, immigrants, and unskilled workers were barred from most trade unions, they could not join the AFL.

Biography **Mother Jones**

"Join the union, boys!" urged Mary Jones. Traveling from strike to strike, she moved in with miners' families, organized marches, and cared for the sick. She always urged strikers to avoid violence. When she died in 1930—at the age of 100—Mother Jones had become a legend. ★ **Jones was jailed many times. Why do you think this was so?**

Women in the Labor Movement

By 1890, one million women worked in American factories. In the textile mills of New England and the tobacco factories of the South, women formed the majority of workers. In New York City, women outnumbered men in the garment industry.

During the 1800s, women formed their own unions. A few, like the all-black Washerwomen's Association of Atlanta, struck for higher wages. None of these unions succeeded, however.

Mother Jones

The best-known woman in the labor movement was Irish-born Mary Harris Jones, known as **Mother Jones.** Jones worked as a dressmaker in Chicago until the Chicago fire of 1871 destroyed her business. Faced with the need to start all over again, she devoted the rest of her life to the cause of workers.

In 1877, Jones supported striking railroad workers in Pittsburgh. Later, she traveled around the country, organizing coal miners and campaigning for improved working conditions.

Jones spoke out about the hard lives of children in textile mills, "barefoot . . . reaching thin little hands into the machinery." By calling attention to such abuses, Mother Jones helped pave the way for reform.

Organizing garment workers

In 1900, garment workers organized the **International Ladies' Garment Workers Union,** or ILGWU. More than 20,000 women and men in the ILGWU walked off their jobs

$ Connections With Economics

Some immigrant workers banded together to demand higher wages. In 1903, Mexican and Japanese farm workers in Oxnard, California, organized the Japanese-Mexican Labor Association. Their strike forced farmers to pay them $5 per acre for thinning beets.

Cause and Effect

Causes

- Railroad boom spurs business
- Businesses become corporations
- Nation has rich supply of natural resources
- New inventions make business more efficient

The Rise of Industry

Effects

- Steel and oil become giant industries
- Monopolies and trusts dominate important industries
- Factory workers face harsh conditions
- Membership in labor unions grows

Effects Today

- United States is world's leading economic power
- American corporations do business around the world
- Government laws regulate monopolies

Graphic Organizer *Skills*

American industry boomed after the Civil War. The effects of industrial growth are still being felt today.

1. **Comprehension** List two causes for the rise of industry.
2. **Critical Thinking** Why do you think the government now tries to regulate monopolies?

Economics $

in 1910. After a few weeks, employers met union demands for better pay and shorter hours. The ILGWU became a key member of the AFL.

Despite the efforts of the ILGWU and other labor groups, most women with factory jobs did not join unions. They continued to work long hours for low pay. Many labored under unsafe conditions. Then, a tragic event focused attention on the dangers faced by women workers.

The Triangle Fire

In 1911, a fire broke out in the Triangle Shirtwaist Factory, a sweatshop in New York City. Within minutes, the upper stories were ablaze. Hundreds of workers raced for the exits, only to find them locked. The company had locked the doors to keep workers at their jobs. In their panic, workers ran headlong into the doors, blocking them with their bodies.

Fire trucks arrived almost immediately, but their ladders could not reach the upper floors. One after another, workers trying to escape the flames leaped to their deaths. One reporter wrote:

> "As I looked up . . . there, at a window, a young man was helping girls to leap out. Suddenly one of them put her arms around him and kiss[ed] him. Then he held her into space and dropped her. He jumped next. Thud . . . dead. Thud . . . dead."

Nearly 150 people, mostly young women, lost their lives in the **Triangle Fire.** The deaths shocked the public. As a result, New York and other states approved new safety laws to help protect factory workers.

Slow Progress for Labor

The new era of industry led to vast economic growth. At the same time, it created economic strain. In the rush for profits, many industries overexpanded. As goods flooded the market, prices dropped. To cover their losses, factory owners often fired workers. In time, factories geared up again, and the cycle was repeated.

The economy swung wildly between good times and bad. Between 1870 and 1900, two major depressions and three smaller recessions rocked the country. Workers lost their jobs or faced pay cuts. Often, they had no money to pay rent or buy food.

Violent strikes

During a severe depression in the 1870s, railroad workers were forced to take several cuts in pay. In July 1877, workers went on strike, shutting down rail lines across the country. Riots erupted in many cities as workers burned rail yards and ripped track from the ground. In Pittsburgh, a battle between strikebreakers and strikers left more than 20 people dead.

Violent strikes also broke out in the West. In the 1870s, miners in Idaho tried to shut down two large mines. Violence flared until the territorial governor threatened to bring in troops. In 1893, after another bitter strike, miners formed the **Western Federation of Miners.** This militant union gained great strength in the Rocky Mountain states. Between 1894 and 1904, it organized strike after strike when owners refused to negotiate.

A major setback

The federal government usually sided with factory owners. Several Presidents sent in troops to end strikes. Courts ruled against strikers, too.

In 1894, a Chicago court dealt a serious blow to unions. A year earlier, George Pullman had cut the pay of workers at his railroad car factory. Yet, he did not reduce the rents he charged them for company-owned houses. Workers walked off the job in protest.

A federal judge issued an injunction against the strikers. An **injunction** is a court order to do or not to do something. The judge ordered the Pullman workers to stop their strike. Leaders of the strike were jailed for violating the Sherman Antitrust Act. This act had been meant to keep trusts from limiting free trade. The courts, however, said that the strikers were limiting free trade. This decision was a major setback for unions.

Small gains

Union workers staged thousands of strikes during the late 1800s. Strikers won little sympathy at first. Few Americans supported unions. They believed that individuals who worked hard would be rewarded. Many were afraid that unions were run by foreign-born radicals. Because unions were unpopular, owners felt free to crush them.

Workers did make some gains. Skilled workers in the AFL won better conditions and higher pay. Overall, wages for workers rose slightly between 1870 and 1900. Still, progress was slow. In 1910, only one worker in 20 belonged to a union. Some 30 years would pass before large numbers of unskilled workers were able to join unions.

★ Section 4 Review ★

Recall

1. **Identify** **(a)** Knights of Labor, **(b)** Terence Powderly, **(c)** Haymarket Riot, **(d)** Samuel Gompers, **(e)** American Federation of Labor, **(f)** Mother Jones, **(g)** International Ladies' Garment Workers Union, **(h)** Triangle Fire, **(i)** Western Federation of Miners.
2. **Define** **(a)** sweatshop, **(b)** strikebreaker, **(c)** anarchist, **(d)** collective bargaining, **(e)** injunction.

Comprehension

3. How did factory work change in the late 1800s?
4. What were the goals of **(a)** the Knights of Labor? **(b)** the AFL?
5. How did the public view labor unions in the late 1800s?

Critical Thinking and Writing

6. **Making Inferences** Why did machines make some workers' skills useless?
7. **Drawing Conclusions** Why do you think workers gained so little from strikes in the late 1800s and early 1900s?

Activity **Drawing a Cartoon** Choose one of the events or issues you have read about in this section. Draw a political cartoon illustrating the topic you have chosen.

Chapter 18 Review and Activities

★ Sum It Up ★

Section 1 Railroads and Industry

- After the Civil War, thousands of miles of new railway lines were built, creating a nationwide rail network.
- Despite many abuses by large railroads, the growth of railroads stimulated the nation's economy.

Section 2 Big Business

- In the late 1800s, steelmaking became a huge source of wealth and power for American companies.
- Large corporations formed trusts and monopolies to control competition and maximize profit.

Section 3 A Flood of Inventions

- Advances in communication in the late 1800s included the laying of the first transatlantic telegraph cable and the invention of the telephone.
- At his research laboratory, Thomas Edison invented the light bulb, the phonograph, and hundreds of other useful devices.
- Through his use of the assembly line, Henry Ford made it possible for millions of Americans to afford automobiles.

Section 4 Labor in the Age of Industry

- Though various labor unions had differing ideals and methods, they all worked to improve conditions and pay for workers.
- Labor unions made slow progress at first because few Americans supported their goals.

For additional review of the major ideas of Chapter 18, see ***Guide to the Essentials of American History*** or ***Interactive Student Tutorial CD-ROM,*** which contains interactive review activities, graphic organizers, and practice tests.

Reviewing the Chapter

Define These Terms

Match each term in Column 1 with the correct definition in Column 2.

Column 1	Column 2
1. trust	**a.** discount
2. rebate	**b.** business owned by investors
3. corporation	**c.** court order
4. stock	**d.** share in a business
5. injunction	**e.** group of corporations run by a single board of directors

Explore the Main Ideas

1. What tactics did railroads use to fight competition?
2. What methods did American businesses use to raise capital in the late 1800s?
3. Summarize the arguments for and against monopolies.
4. Why was Edison's research laboratory an important development?
5. How did the Triangle Fire influence public opinion?

Chart Activity

Look at the table below and answer the following questions: **1.** During what five-year period did the government issue the most patents? **2.** How many patents were issued between 1881 and 1890? **Critical Thinking** Make two generalizations about American technology in the late 1800s.

United States Patents, 1861–1900

Five-Year Periods	Number of Patents
1861–1865	20,725
1866–1870	58,734
1871–1875	60,976
1876–1880	64,462
1881–1885	97,156
1886–1890	110,358
1891–1895	108,420
1896–1900	112,188

Source: *Historical Statistics of the United States*

Critical Thinking and Writing

1. **Understanding Chronology** Suppose you were asked to create a graphic organizer in the shape of a pyramid showing the growth of American industry. At the bottom you plan to place three items that began that growth. What three items would you choose?
2. **Linking Past and Present** Today, airlines often have "price wars" to attract customers. Judging from what you know about railroad competition, what do you think might be the long-term result of these "wars"?
3. **Exploring Unit Themes Industrialization** Describe one way each of the following transformed the nation: **(a)** steel, **(b)** new sources of power, **(c)** advances in communication, **(d)** new forms of transportation.
4. **Analyzing a Quotation** Jay Gould, a railroad owner, once said, "I can hire one half of the working class to kill the other half." **(a)** What do you think he meant? **(b)** Based on the statement, what do you think was Gould's opinion of unions? Explain.

Using Primary Sources

James J. Davis began working in the iron mills of Pittsburgh when he was twelve. He later described his job:

> "I had iron biscuits to bake; my forge fire must be hot as a volcano. There were five bakings every day and this meant the shoveling in of nearly two tons of coal. In summer I was stripped to the waist and panting while sweat poured down across my heaving muscles. My palms and fingers, scorched by the heat, became hardened like goat hoofs. . . . Do [weight-lifting exercises] ten hours in a room so hot it melts your eyebrows and you will know what it is like to be [an ironworker]."

Source: *The Life of an Iron Puddler*, James W. Davis, 1922.

Recognizing Points of View (a) To what did Davis compare the work of an ironworker? **(b)** How do you think Mother Jones would have reacted to this description? Explain.

Activity Bank

Interdisciplinary Activity

Exploring Economics Review the material on railroads and the growth of industry. Then make a concept map to show the industries that resulted from or were related to the growth of a railroad network in the United States.

Career Skills Activity

Advertising Writers Create advertisements for a mail-order catalog selling the new inventions discussed in the chapter. Write text and use pictures in your ads. Then organize your ads into a catalog.

Citizenship Activity

Learning About Corporate Citizenship Many corporations today make an effort to be good citizens in their communities. Interview the public relations officer at a large local corporation to find out what that company has done to help your community. Write up your interview and prepare a report.

Internet Activity

Use the Internet to find sites dealing with the Carnegie Foundation. After learning about the work of the foundation, write a proposal for a project that you would like to see the foundation support.

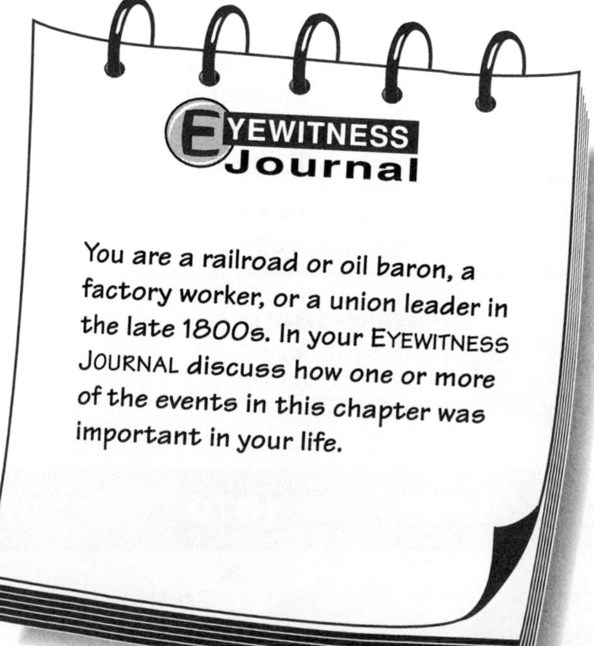

Chapter 19

Immigration and the Growth of Cities

1865–1914

What's Ahead

Section 1
The New Immigrants

Section 2
Booming Cities

Section 3
City Life Transformed

Section 4
Education and Culture

In the 50 years after the Civil War, 25 million immigrants poured into the United States. Most were driven by hunger and poverty and drawn by hope of a better life. They came from places such as Italy, Eastern Europe, Armenia, China, and Mexico. During this time, American cities grew rapidly.

Population growth brought problems including poor housing and strained city services. At the same time, it led to a rich mix of cultures. Cities fostered new leisure-time activities, such as sports. As education improved, newspapers, magazines, and new American fiction gained a larger audience.

Why Study History? In the late 1800s, educators made vast improvements in public education. Today, Americans continue to stress the role of education in producing good citizens and preparing them for a changing future. To focus on this connection, see the *Why Study History?* feature, "You Have a Right to an Education," in this chapter.

American Events

Mid-1800s Immigrants from Northern Europe flock to United States

1882 Chinese Exclusion Act bars Chinese immigrants

1886 Statue of Liberty is dedicated

1865 | 1870 | 1875 | 1880 | 1885 | 1890

World Events

1870 World Event Britain establishes compulsory education

1881 World Event Russia increases violent pogroms against Jews

A Busy City Street

Viewing History

In his painting Houston Street, *George Benjamin Luks captured the bustle of a crowded New York City street. Many of these pushcart vendors, shopping housewives, or playing children probably spoke Italian, Russian, or other foreign languages. In the late 1800s and early 1900s, a boom in immigration fed the rapid growth of American cities.* ★ **Why do you think many immigrants wanted to come to the United States at this time?**

1889 Jane Addams founds Hull House to help poor immigrants

1902 Macy's department store opens nine-story building

1904 New York opens its subway system

1890 | 1895 | 1900 | 1905 | 1910 | 1915

1891 World Event Arthur Conan Doyle publishes *Adventures of Sherlock Holmes*

1905 World Event Chinese in Shanghai boycott American goods to protest exclusion laws

HISTORY HAPPENED HERE

Ellis Island

In the harbor between New York and New Jersey, Ellis Island was the gateway for millions of European immigrants. Hopeful newcomers were crowded into pens in the main hall (left), nervously awaiting interviews with immigration officials. For years, Ellis Island fell into disrepair. In the 1980s, it was restored and is now a museum devoted to the immigrant experience. You can see hundreds of items carried by immigrants, like the ones shown here.

★ ***To learn more about this historic site, write:*** *Ellis Island National Monument, New York, NY 10004.*

▲ Czechoslovakian vest

Italian pasta pot ▲

Ellis Island

After 1892, ships entering New York harbor stopped at the new receiving station on **Ellis Island.** Here, immigrants faced a last hurdle, the dreaded medical inspection.

Doctors watched the newcomers climb a long flight of stairs. Anyone who appeared out of breath or walked with a limp might be stopped. Doctors also examined eyes, ears, and throats. The sick had to stay on Ellis Island until they got well. Those who failed to regain full health were sent home.

With hundreds of immigrants to process each day, officials had only minutes to check each new arrival. To save time, they often changed names that they found difficult to spell. Krzeznewski became Kramer. Smargiaso ended up as Smarga. One Italian immigrant found that even his first name had been changed—from Bartolomeo to Bill.

A few lucky immigrants went directly from Ellis Island into the welcoming arms of friends and relatives. Most, however, stepped into a terrifying new land whose language and customs they did not know.

Angel Island

On the West Coast, immigrants from China, and later from Japan, faced even harsher experiences than the Europeans in the East. By the early 1900s, many Asians were processed on **Angel Island** in San Francisco Bay.

Because Americans wanted to discourage Asian immigration, new arrivals often faced long delays. One immigrant from China scratched these lines on the wall:

> “Why do I have to languish in this jail?
> It is because my country is weak and my family poor.
> My parents wait in vain for news;
> My wife and child, wrapped in their quilt, sigh with loneliness.”

Changing Patterns of Immigration

Before 1885, most new immigrants to the United States were Protestants from Northern and Western Europe. Those from England and Ireland already spoke English. The Irish, English, Germans, and Scandinavians became known as "old immigrants." At first, the old immigrants faced some discrimination. As the nation grew, though, they were drawn into American life.

In the late 1800s, the patterns of immigration changed. Large numbers of people arrived from Southern and Eastern Europe. Millions of Italians, Poles, Greeks, Russians, and Hungarians landed in the eastern United States. On the West Coast, a smaller but growing number of Asian immigrants arrived, first from China, then from Japan. There were also a few immigrants from Korea, India, and the Philippines.

Few of these "new immigrants" spoke English. Many of the Europeans were Catholic, Eastern Orthodox, or Jewish. Immigrants from Asia might be Buddhist or Daoist. Their languages and religions set the new immigrants apart. As a result, they found it harder to adapt to a new life.

Adjusting to a New Land

Many immigrants had heard stories that the streets in the United States were paved with gold. Once in the United States, the newcomers had to adjust their dreams to reality. They immediately set out to find work. European peasants living on the land had little need for money, but it took cash to survive in the United States. Through friends, relatives, labor contractors, and employment agencies, the new arrivals found jobs.

Most immigrants stayed in the cities where they landed. The slums of cities soon became packed with poor immigrants. By 1900, one such neighborhood on the lower east side of New York City had become the most crowded place in the world.

Ethnic neighborhoods

Immigrants adjusted to their new lives by settling in neighborhoods with their own ethnic group. An **ethnic group** is a group of people who share a common culture. Across the United States, cities were patchworks of Italian, Irish, Polish, Hungarian, German, Jewish, and Chinese neighborhoods.

Within these ethnic neighborhoods, newcomers spoke their own language and celebrated special holidays with foods prepared as in the old country. Italians joined ethnic clubs such as the Sons of Italy. Hungarians bought and read Hungarian newspapers.

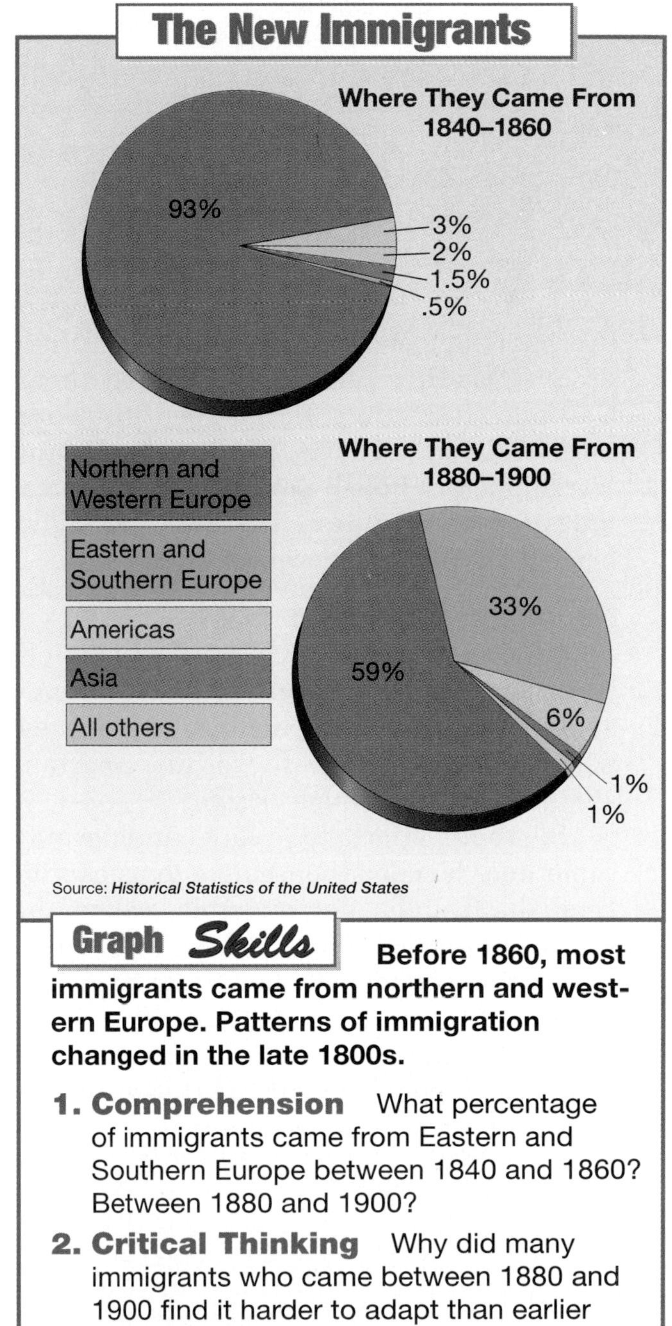

Source: *Historical Statistics of the United States*

Graph Skills **Before 1860, most immigrants came from northern and western Europe. Patterns of immigration changed in the late 1800s.**

1. **Comprehension** What percentage of immigrants came from Eastern and Southern Europe between 1840 and 1860? Between 1880 and 1900?
2. **Critical Thinking** Why did many immigrants who came between 1880 and 1900 find it harder to adapt than earlier immigrants?

◀ *Phrase book for Chinese immigrants*

Chinese Americans

This photograph shows Chinese children sitting on a stoop in San Francisco's Chinatown. For many immigrants like these, learning English was important. Books of useful phrases helped immigrants get through shopping and other activities of day-to-day life. ★ **Do you think these children had already assimilated into American culture when this picture was taken? How can you tell?**

Religion stood at the center of immigrant family life. Houses of worship sprang up in most neighborhoods. They brought ethnic groups together but also separated them. Catholics from Italy worshipped in Italian neighborhood parishes. Those from Poland worshipped in Polish parishes. Jewish communities divided into the older orthodox branch and the newer conservative wing.

Becoming Americans

Often, newcomers were torn between old traditions and American ways. Still, many struggled to learn the language of their new nation. Learning English was an important step toward becoming a citizen.

In their effort to adapt, immigrants sometimes blended their native tongues with English. Italians, for example, called the Fourth of July *"Il Forte Gelato,"* an Italian phrase that sounds like the holiday name but means "the great freeze." In El Paso, Texas, Mexican immigrants developed *Chuco,* a language that blended English and Spanish.

The process of becoming part of another culture is called **assimilation.** Children assimilated more quickly than their parents. They learned English in school and then helped their families learn to speak it. Because children wanted to be seen as Americans, they often gave up customs their parents honored. They played American games and dressed in American-style clothes.

Connections With Arts

One Russian Jewish immigrant became the nation's most popular songwriter. Israel Baline came to New York in 1893, when he was five years old. Under the name Irving Berlin, he went on to write such familiar tunes as "Easter Parade," "White Christmas," and "God Bless America."

A New Surge of Nativism

Many Americans opposed the increase in immigration. They felt the newcomers would not assimilate because their languages, religions, and customs were too different.

Even before the Civil War, **nativists** had wanted to limit immigration and preserve the country for native-born white Protestants. In the late 1800s, nativist feelings reached a new peak. Many workers resented the new immigrants because they took jobs for low pay. One newspaper complained:

> "The Poles, Slavs, Huns, and Italians come over without any ambition to live as Americans live and... accept work at any wages at all, thereby lowering the tone of American labor as a whole."

Nativist pressure grew wherever new immigrants settled. Nativists targeted Jews and Italians in the Northeast and Mexicans in the Southwest. On the West Coast, nativists worked to end immigration from China.

Chinese exclusion

Since the California Gold Rush and the building of the railroads, Chinese immigrants had helped build the West. Most lived in cities, in tight-knit communities called "Chinatowns." Others made their living as farmers.

Most Americans did not understand Chinese customs. Also, some Chinese did not try to learn American ways. Like many other immigrants, they planned to stay only until they made a lot of money. They then hoped to return home, to live out their lives as rich and respected members of Chinese society. When that dream failed, many Chinese settled in the United States permanently.

As the numbers of Chinese grew, so did the prejudice and violence against them. Gangs attacked and sometimes killed Chinese people, especially during hard times.

Congress responded to this anti-Chinese feeling by passing the **Chinese Exclusion Act** in 1882. Under it, no Chinese laborer could enter the United States. In addition, no Chinese living in the United States could return once they left the country.

The Chinese Exclusion Act was the first limit on immigration into the United States. Congress renewed the original 10-year ban several times. It was finally repealed in 1943.

Other limits

In 1887, nativists formed the American Protective Association. It soon had a million members. The group campaigned for laws to restrict immigration. Congress responded by passing a bill that denied entry to people who could not read their own language.

President Grover Cleveland vetoed the bill. It was wrong, he said, to keep out peasants just because they had never gone to school. Congress passed the bill again and again. Three more presidents vetoed it. In 1917, Congress overrode President Woodrow Wilson's veto, and the bill became law.

★ Section 1 Review ★

Recall

1. **Locate** **(a)** Italy, **(b)** Russia, **(c)** Armenia, **(d)** Greece, **(e)** China.
2. **Identify** **(a)** Statue of Liberty, **(b)** Emma Lazarus, **(c)** Ellis Island, **(d)** Angel Island, **(e)** Chinese Exclusion Act.
3. **Define** **(a)** push factor, **(b)** pull factor, **(c)** pogrom, **(d)** steerage, **(e)** ethnic group, **(f)** assimilation, **(g)** nativist.

Comprehension

4. Identify one push factor and one pull factor that caused people to come to the United States.
5. Why did children adjust more easily to the United States than their parents?
6. **(a)** Why did many Americans resent the new immigrants? **(b)** What steps did they take to limit immigration?

Critical Thinking and Writing

7. **Making Inferences** **(a)** How did the "old immigrants" differ from the "new immigrants"? **(b)** Why do you think the new immigrants faced greater problems when they first arrived in the United States than the old immigrants had?
8. **Distinguishing Facts From Opinions** Read the following statement: "Immigrants work for almost nothing and seem to be able to live on wind." **(a)** Is this a fact or an opinion? How do you know? **(b)** Who would most likely have made a statement like this? Explain.

Activity **Writing a Handbook** You are an immigrant to the United States in the 1880s. Write at least one page for a handbook for future immigrants from your country. Tell them what problems they should expect to have and how they can overcome those problems.

Booming Cities

As You Read

Explore These Questions

- Why did cities grow in the late 1800s?
- What hazards did city dwellers face?
- How did reformers help to improve city life?

Define

- urbanization
- tenement
- building code
- settlement house

Identify

- Jane Addams
- Hull House
- Mother Cabrini
- Social Gospel
- Salvation Army
- Young Men's Hebrew Association

A small fire started in the barn behind the O'Leary cottage. Within hours, dry winds had whipped the blaze into an inferno that raged across Chicago. A survivor described how panicked residents fled their homes:

> ❝ Everybody was running north. People were carrying all kinds of crazy things. A woman was carrying a pot of soup, which was spilling all over her dress. People were carrying cats, dogs, and goats. In the great excitement, people saved worthless things and left behind good things. ❞

Fire was a constant danger in cities. However, Americans agreed they had never seen anything like the great Chicago Fire of 1871. The blaze killed nearly 300 people, left almost 100,000 homeless, and destroyed the entire downtown.

Yet from the ashes, a new city rose. By the end of the century, Chicago was the fastest growing city in the world, with a population of over one million. Other American cities, too, underwent a population explosion. For new and old Americans alike, the golden door of opportunity opened into the city.

City Populations Grow

"We cannot all live in cities," declared the newspaper publisher Horace Greeley, "yet nearly all seem determined to do so." **Urbanization,** the movement of population from farms to cities, began slowly in the early 1800s. As the nation industrialized after the Civil War, urbanization became much more rapid. In 1860, only one American in six lived in a city. By 1890, one in three did.

Chicago street in the late 1800s

Jobs drew people to cities. As industries grew, so did the need for workers. New city dwellers took jobs in steel mills, meatpacking plants, and garment factories. They worked as sales clerks, waiters, barbers, bank tellers, and secretaries.

Immigrants and farmers

The flood of immigrants swelled city populations. Also, by the 1890s, most land in the West had been divided into farms and ranches. As a result, fewer pioneers went there to homestead. In fact, many Americans left farms to find a better life in the city. A young man in a story by western writer Hamlin Garland summed up the feelings of many farmers:

> ❝ I'm sick of farm life . . . it's nothing but fret, fret, and work the whole time, never going any place, never seeing *anybody.* ❞

African Americans migrate

African Americans, too, moved to cities to improve their lives. Most African Americans lived in the rural South. When hard times hit or prejudice led to violence, some blacks headed to northern cities. By the 1890s, the south side of Chicago had a thriving African American community. Detroit, New York, Philadelphia, and other northern cities also had growing African American neighborhoods. The migration to the north began gradually, but increased rapidly after 1915.

As with immigrants from overseas, black migration usually began with one family member moving north. Later, relatives and friends joined the bold pioneer. Like immigrants from rural areas in Europe, many African Americans faced the challenge of adjusting to urban life.

City Life

Cities grew outward from their old downtown sections. Before long, many took on a similar shape.

Poor families crowded into the city's center, the oldest section. Middle-class people lived farther out in row houses or new apartment buildings. Beyond them, the rich built fine homes with green lawns and trees.

The poor

Poor families struggled to survive in crowded slums. The streets were jammed with people, horses, pushcarts, and garbage.

Because space was so limited, builders devised a new kind of house to hold more people. They put up buildings six or seven stories high. They divided the buildings into small apartments, called **tenements.** Many tenements had no windows, heat, or indoor bathrooms. Often, 10 people shared a single room.

Typhoid and cholera raged through the tenements. Tuberculosis, a lung disease, was the biggest killer, accounting for thousands of deaths each year. Babies, especially, fell victim to disease. In one Chicago slum, more than half of all babies died before they were one year old.

Despite the poor conditions, the population of slums grew rapidly. Factory owners moved in to take advantage of low rents and cheap labor. They took over buildings for use as factories, thus forcing more and more people into fewer and fewer apartments.

The middle class

Beyond the slums stood the homes of the new middle class, including doctors, lawyers, business managers, skilled machinists, and office workers. Rows of neat houses lined tree-shaded streets. Here, disease broke out less frequently than in the crowded slums.

The Growth of Cities

Population Growth in Ten Selected Cities

City	Population in 1870	Population in 1900
New York	1,478,103	3,437,202
Chicago	298,977	1,698,575
Philadelphia	674,022	1,293,697
St. Louis	351,189	575,238
Boston	250,526	560,892
San Francisco	149,473	342,782
New Orleans	191,418	287,104
Denver	4,759	133,859
Los Angeles	5,728	102,479
Memphis	40,226	102,320

Rural and Urban Population in the United States, 1860–1920

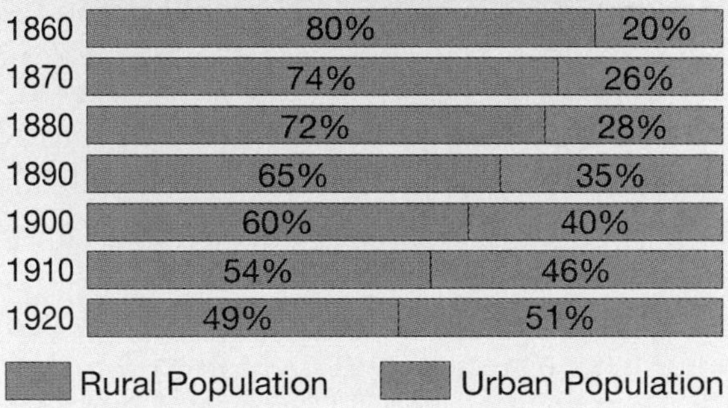

Year	Rural Population	Urban Population
1860	80%	20%
1870	74%	26%
1880	72%	28%
1890	65%	35%
1900	60%	40%
1910	54%	46%
1920	49%	51%

Source: *United States Census Bureau*

Graph Skills **City populations grew rapidly in the United States in the decades following the Civil War.**

1. **Comprehension** Between 1870 and 1900, which cities on the chart above more than doubled in population?
2. **Critical Thinking** Study the bar graphs above. Make one generalization about the population of the United States after 1870.

Viewing HISTORY **Lives of the Wealthy**

The Brown Family, *a painting by Eastman Johnson, suggests the elegance and fine manners of a wealthy American family. Many of the furnishings in this home, such as the crystal chandelier, were probably imported from Europe. Later, American manufacturers like Louis Tiffany produced fine glassware and other items for the rich.* ★ **In a typical American city, where did the rich live?**

Middle-class people joined singing societies, bowling leagues, and charitable organizations. Such activities gave them a sense of community and purpose. As one writer said, the clubs "bring together many people who are striving upward, trying to uplift themselves."

The wealthy

On the outskirts of the city, behind brick walls or iron gates, lay the mansions of the very rich. In New York, huge homes dotted Fifth Avenue, which was still on the city's outskirts. In Chicago, by the 1880s, 200 millionaires lived along the exclusive lake front. In San Francisco, wealthy residents lived nearer the center of the city, but they built their mansions in the exclusive Nob Hill area. ("Nob" is British slang for a person of wealth and position.)

Tiffany lamp

Rich Americans modeled their lives on European royalty. They filled their mansions with priceless artworks and gave lavish parties. At one banquet, the host handed out cigarettes rolled in hundred-dollar bills.

Cleaning Up the Cities

As more and more people crowded into cities, problems grew. Tenement buildings were deathtraps if fires broke out. One magazine reporter in 1888 wrote:

> "It would be impossible for the occupants of the crowded rooms to escape by the narrow stairways, and the flimsy fire-escapes . . . are so laden with broken furniture, bales, and boxes that they would be worse than useless."

Garbage rotted in the streets. Factories polluted the air. Crime flourished. Thieves and pickpockets haunted lonely alleys, especially at night.

By the 1880s, reformers were demanding change. They forced city governments to pass **building codes**—laws that set standards for how structures should be built. The codes required new buildings to have fire escapes and decent plumbing. Cities also hired workers to collect garbage and sweep the streets. To reduce pollution, zoning laws kept factories out of neighborhoods where people lived.

Safety improved when cities set up professional fire companies and trained police forces. Gas—and later electric—lights made streets less dangerous at night. As you will read, many cities built new systems of public transportation as well.

Pushed by reformers, city governments hired engineers and architects to design new water systems. New York City, for example,

Skills FOR LIFE

Critical Thinking | Managing Information | Communication | Maps, Charts, and Graphs

Synthesizing Information

How Will I Use This Skill ?

Most of the things we learn about in life do not come to us from just one source. When something happens in your community, you may see a report on local television, read an account in a newspaper, and hear what friends say about it. Then, you put together and analyze the different pieces of information to form a complete picture. This process is called synthesizing.

LEARN the Skill

1. Identify the different sources of information and the facts and ideas in each.
2. Compare the evidence from each source. Do the pieces support one another? Is there any contradictory evidence?
3. Synthesize the evidence so that you can draw conclusions.

PRACTICE the Skill

To practice the skill, use the following pieces of information: the photograph on this page; the painting on page 494; the quotation to the right; the information in your textbook.

1. (a) What is the subject of the photograph? (b) What does the painting show? (c) What topic is Riis talking about?
2. (a) How does the family in the painting differ from that in the photograph? List three details that show the differences. (b) Does the quotation describe the photograph or the painting? (c) What information in the text is supported by the painting? The photograph?
3. Based on the evidence, make two generalizations about city life in the late 1800s.

Tenement family in New York City

> "In this house, where a case of smallpox was reported, there were fifty-eight babies and thirty-eight children . . . over five years of age."
>
> —Journalist Jacob Riis, describing a Jewish community in New York City

APPLY the Skill

Research a current topic in a newsmagazine or newspaper. Synthesize the written information with evidence from a photograph.

Singing class at Hull House ➤

Biography Jane Addams

A wealthy woman, Jane Addams dedicated her life to serving the poor. She founded Hull House in Chicago, which provided many services to immigrants and others. Above, neighbors enjoy a singing class at Hull House. Addams also worked for world peace. In 1931, she became the first American woman to win the Nobel Peace Prize.

★ Addams insisted on living at Hull House herself. What does this tell you about her?

dug underground tunnels to the Catskill Mountains—100 miles to the north. The tunnels brought a clean water supply to the city every day.

The Settlement House Movement

Some people looked for ways to help the poor. By the late 1800s, individuals began to organize settlement houses. A **settlement house** is a community center that offers services to the poor. The leading figure of the settlement house movement was a Chicago woman named **Jane Addams.**

Connections With Civics

Most settlement houses did not admit African Americans, so some black women opened their own settlement houses. In New York City, Victoria Earle Matthews started the White Rose Mission and Verna Morton-Jones opened Lincoln House. They offered shelter, child care, and classes to their communities.

Hull House

Addams came from a well-to-do family but had strong convictions about helping the poor. After college, she moved into one of the poorest slums in Chicago. There, in an old mansion, she opened a settlement house in 1889. She called it **Hull House.**

Other idealistic young women soon joined Addams. They took up residence in Hull House so that they could experience firsthand some of the hardships of the slum community in which they worked. These women dedicated their lives to service and to sacrifice—"like the early Christians," in the words of one volunteer.

The Hull House volunteers provided day nurseries for children whose mothers worked outside the home. They organized sports and a theater for young people. They taught English to immigrants and gave classes in health care. They also launched investigations into social and economic conditions in the city.

Over the years, the settlement house movement spread. By 1900, about 100 such centers had opened in cities across the United States.

Working for reform

Jane Addams and her Hull House staff were an important influence in bringing about reform legislation to improve the living and working conditions of the poor. They studied the slum neighborhoods where they worked and lived. They realized that the problems were too big for any one person or group, and they urged the government to act.

Alice Hamilton, a Hull House doctor, campaigned for better health laws. Florence Kelley worked to ban child labor. Jane Addams herself believed that reform legislation would be speeded if women could vote. She campaigned tirelessly for women's suffrage.

Religious Organizations Help the Poor

Religious groups also provided services to the poor. The Catholic Church ministered to the needs of Irish, Polish, and Italian immigrants. An Italian nun, **Mother Cabrini,** helped found more than 70 hospitals in North and South America. These hospitals treated people who could not afford doctors.

In cities, Protestant ministers began preaching a new **Social Gospel.** They called on their well-to-do members to do their duty as Christians by helping society's poor. One minister urged merchants and industrialists to pay their workers enough to enable them to marry and have families. He also proposed that they grant their workers a half day off on Saturdays.

Protestant groups set up programs for needy slum dwellers. In 1865, a Methodist minister named William Booth created the **Salvation Army** in London. By 1880, it expanded to the United States. In addition to spreading Christian teachings, the Salvation Army offered food and shelter to the poor.

In Jewish neighborhoods, too, religious organizations provided community services. The first **Young Men's Hebrew Association** (YMHA) began in Baltimore in 1854. The YMHA provided social activities, encouraged good citizenship, and helped Jewish families preserve their culture. In the 1880s, the Young Women's Hebrew Association (YWHA) grew out of the YMHA.

Other groups—like the YMCA (Young Men's Christian Association) and the YWCA (Young Women's Christian Association)—taught classes, organized team sports, and held dances. Such activities offered young people a brief escape from the problems of slum life.

★ Section 2 Review ★

Recall

1. **Identify** **(a)** Jane Addams, **(b)** Hull House, **(c)** Mother Cabrini, **(d)** Social Gospel, **(e)** Salvation Army, **(f)** Young Men's Hebrew Association
2. **Define** **(a)** urbanization, **(b)** tenement, **(c)** building code, **(d)** settlement house.

Comprehension

3. Name three causes for the growth of city populations in the late 1800s.
4. What problems did cities face as their populations grew?
5. What reforms did cities make?

Critical Thinking and Writing

6. **Comparing** Compare and contrast the lives of the rich, the middle class, and the poor in American cities in the late 1800s.
7. **Linking Past and Present** How do the problems of city dwellers today compare to those of city dwellers in the late 1800s?

Activity **Writing a Grant Proposal** You are a modern-day reformer who wants to start a settlement house somewhere in a nearby city or town. Choose a good location. Then write a proposal in which you ask a charitable foundation for funds to start your settlement house. Explain why the settlement is needed and what kind of services you plan to offer.

City Life Transformed

As You Read

Explore These Questions

- How did cities change in the late 1800s?
- Why did newspapers grow in number and importance?
- How did Americans spend their leisure time?

Define

- yellow journalism
- vaudeville
- ragtime

Identify

- Joseph Pulitzer
- William Randolph Hearst
- Nellie Bly
- Will Rogers
- Scott Joplin
- John Philip Sousa
- James Naismith

SETTING the Scene Bells rang. Cannons thundered. Fireworks crackled in the afternoon sky. New Yorkers were celebrating the opening of the Brooklyn Bridge. In 1883, its soaring arches were a triumph of modern engineering. Linking Manhattan Island and Brooklyn, the bridge was soon carrying 33 million people each year across New York City's East River.

The Brooklyn Bridge was only one sign of the changing face of New York. Other American cities, too, underwent vast changes that transformed their appearance and their way of life.

A New Look for Cities

A building boom changed the face of American cities in the late 1800s. Cities like Chicago and New York ran out of space in their downtown areas. Resourceful city planners and architects decided to build up instead of out.

Skyscrapers

After fire leveled downtown Chicago, planners tried out many new building ideas. Using new technology, they designed tall buildings with many floors. Called skyscrapers, these high-rise buildings had frames of lightweight steel to hold the weight of the structure.

Newly invented electric elevators carried workers to upper floors. Elevators moved so quickly, according to one rider, that "the passenger seems to feel his stomach pass into his shoes."

Public transportation

As skyscrapers crowded more people into smaller spaces, cities began to face a new problem: the traffic jam. Downtown streets were choked with horse-drawn buses, carriages, and carts.

Electricity offered one solution. In 1887, Frank Sprague, an engineer from Richmond, Virginia, designed the first electric streetcar system. Streetcars, or trolleys, were fast, clean, and quiet. Many trolley lines ran out from the center of a city to the outlying countryside.

Other cities, such as New York, built steam-driven passenger trains on overhead tracks. In 1897, Boston led the way in building the first American subway, or underground electric railway. In 1904, New York opened the first section of its subway system. These trains carried workers rapidly to and from their jobs.

Open spaces

While cities grew up and out, some planners wanted to preserve open spaces. They believed that open land would calm busy city dwellers.

In the 1850s, architect Frederick Law Olmsted planned Central Park in New York City. Other cities followed this model. They

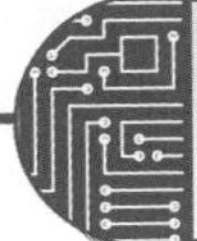

Linking History and Technology

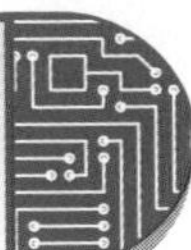

The Reliance Building in Chicago

Bay windows let in light and air. This was important at a time when few buildings had electric lights and no one had even heard of air conditioning.

The steel frame carried the weight of the building.

Clay tile walls protected the building from fire.

Elevators made it practical for buildings to have more than five or six stories.

The upper floors were used for offices. The ground floor held stores.

Skyscraper

As people crowded into American cities, architects began building up instead of out. Today, the Reliance Building in Chicago, shown here, does not look very tall. When it was built in the 1890s, however, its 16 stories made it a "skyscraper." ★ **Based on this drawing, what new kinds of technology made skyscrapers possible?**

set aside land for zoos and gardens so that city people could enjoy green grass and trees during their leisure time.

Department stores

Shopping areas also got a new look. In the late 1800s, department stores sprang up. In the past, people had bought shoes in one store, socks in another, and dishes in a third. The new department stores sold all kinds of goods in one building.

In 1902, R. H. Macy opened a nine-story building in New York. It had 33 elevators and a motto that became famous: "We sell goods cheaper than any house in the world." Soon, other cities had department stores. Shopping became a popular pastime. People browsed each floor, looking at clothes, furniture, and jewelry. On the street, "window shoppers" paused to enjoy elaborate window displays.

The Daily Newspaper

"Read all about it!" cried newsboys on city street corners. The number of newspapers grew dramatically after 1880. By 1900, half the newspapers in the world were printed in the United States.

The rapid growth in the number of newspapers was linked to the growth of cities. In towns and villages, neighbors shared news when they met. In the city, people had thousands of "neighbors." Also, there was so much news that people needed newspapers to be informed.

Newspapers reported on major events of the day. Most featured stories about local government, business, fashion, and sports. Many immigrants learned to read English by spelling their way through a daily paper. At the same time, they learned about life in the United States.

Two newspaper giants

Joseph Pulitzer created the first modern, mass-circulation newspaper. Pulitzer was a Hungarian immigrant. In 1883, he bought the New York *World.* He set out to make it lively and "truly democratic."

To win readers, Pulitzer slashed prices and added comic strips. He introduced bold "scare" headlines to attract reader attention and used pictures to illustrate stories. The *World* splashed crimes and political scandals across its front page. The paper's circulation jumped from 20,000 to one million.

William Randolph Hearst, who came to New York City from San Francisco, challenged Pulitzer. Hearst's New York *Journal* began to outdo the *World* in presenting scandals, crime stories, and gossip. Critics coined the term **yellow journalism** for the sensational reporting style of the *World* and the *Journal.* They complained that the papers offered less news and more scandal every day.

Women journalists

Newspapers competed for women readers. They added special sections on fashion, social events, health, homemaking, and family mat-

Viewing History **A Popular Newspaper**

This 1880 advertisement for the New York Sun *shows the growing popularity of newspapers. The ad suggests that* The Sun *covered everything from politics and shipping news to horse races and weddings. Readers could buy from a corner newsboy or get home delivery.* ★ **Why did newspapers become more important as cities grew?**

ters. Newspapers rarely pushed for women's rights, however. Most were afraid to take bold positions that might anger some readers.

A few women worked as reporters, like **Nellie Bly** of the *World*. Once, Bly pretended to be insane in order to find out about treatment of the mentally ill. Her articles about cruelty in mental hospitals led to reforms.

A World of Entertainment

By the late 1800s, American cities supported a wide variety of cultural activities. Talented Italian, German, Jewish, and other immigrants contributed to a new world of music and theater.

Music and other kinds of entertainment brought Americans together. People from different cultures sang the same songs and enjoyed the same shows. As railroads grew, circuses, acting companies, and "Wild West" shows toured the country. These traveling groups helped spread American culture beyond the cities to small towns throughout the United States.

Vaudeville

Many large cities organized symphony orchestras and opera companies. Generally, only the wealthy attended the symphony or the opera. For other city dwellers, an evening out often meant a trip to a vaudeville house. **Vaudeville** (VAWD vihl) was a variety show that included comedians, song-and-dance routines, and acrobats.

Vaudeville provided opportunities for people from many ethnic backgrounds, such as Irish American dancer-singer George M. Cohan and Jewish comedians like the Marx Brothers. **Will Rogers,** a performer of Cherokee descent, was one of the best-loved performers in the nation. Wearing a cowboy hat and twirling a rope, Rogers used gentle wit to comment about American life.

Popular music

Songwriters produced many popular tunes, such as "Shine On, Harvest Moon." Later, Thomas Edison's phonograph sparked a new industry. By 1900, millions of phonograph records had been sold.

Biography **Scott Joplin**

Fingers flying swiftly over the piano keys, Scott Joplin was the "King of Ragtime." By the age of 14, he was already making a living as a piano player. He went on to compose more than 60 pieces of music, including his popular "Maple Leaf Rag." Joplin also wrote an opera, Treemonisha, *which was not performed until more than 60 years after his death.* ★ **How did popular music styles like ragtime spread across the country?**

Ragtime was a new kind of music with a lively, rhythmic sound. **Scott Joplin,** an African American composer, helped make ragtime popular. His "Maple Leaf Rag" was a nationwide hit.

In towns and cities, marching bands played the military music of **John Philip Sousa.** Sousa wrote more than 100 marches, including "The Stars and Stripes Forever." His marches became favorites at Fourth of July celebrations.

Sports and Leisure

The rise of the factory split the worlds of work and play more sharply than ever. With less chance to socialize on the job, there was more interest in leisure. In sports, Americans found a great escape from factories, stores, and offices.

Baseball: the national pastime

Baseball was the most popular sport in the nation. The game was first played in New York in the 1840s. During the Civil War, New York soldiers showed other Union troops how to play the game. By the 1870s, the country had several professional teams and its first league.

Early baseball was very different from today's game. Pitchers threw underhanded. Catchers caught the ball after one bounce. Fielders did not wear gloves. As a result, high scores were common. One championship game ended with a score of 103 to 8!

At first, African Americans played professional baseball. In the 1880s, however, the major leagues barred black players. In 1885, Frank Thompson organized a group of waiters into the first African American professional team, the Cuban Giants of Long Island.

Football

Football grew out of soccer, which Americans had played since colonial times. Early football called for lots of muscle and little skill. On every play, the opposing teams crashed into each other like fighting rams. The quarterback ran or jumped over the tangle of bodies.

This toy bank shows three unhelmeted football players. If you drop in a coin, the players turn and collide.

Players did not wear helmets and were often hurt. In one brutal season, 44 college football players died from injuries. Some colleges banned the sport or drew up stricter rules of play for the game.

Basketball

In 1891, **James Naismith** invented a new sport: basketball. Naismith was teaching physical education at a YMCA in Springfield, Massachusetts. He wanted to find a sport that could be played indoors in winter. Naismith had two bushel baskets nailed to the gym walls. Players tried to throw a soccer ball into the baskets.

Basketball caught on quickly. It spread to other YMCAs and then to schools and colleges around the country.

★ Section 3 Review ★

Recall

1. **Identify** **(a)** Joseph Pulitzer, **(b)** William Randolph Hearst, **(c)** Nellie Bly, **(d)** Will Rogers, **(e)** Scott Joplin, **(f)** John Philip Sousa, **(g)** James Naismith.
2. **Define** **(a)** yellow journalism, **(b)** vaudeville, **(c)** ragtime.

Comprehension

3. How did new technology change the face of American cities?
4. Describe newspapers of the late 1800s.
5. **(a)** How did entertainment unite Americans? **(b)** What sports were popular in the late 1800s?

Critical Thinking and Writing

6. **Understanding Cause and Effect** Describe the cause-and-effect relationship between population growth and development of the skyscraper.
7. **Identifying Alternatives** Some journalists defend sensational stories by saying they are giving the public what it wants. What types of stories do you think newspapers and other media should provide? Explain your answer.

Activity **Creating a Poster** You are a printer in the early 1900s. Create an illustrated poster advertising one of the following: a new department store; a sporting event; a vaudeville show.

Education and Culture

As You Read

Explore These Questions

- How did public education improve in the late 1800s?
- How did American reading habits change?
- What themes did American writers and painters explore?

Define

- dime novel
- realist
- local color

Identify

- Chautauqua Society
- Horatio Alger
- Stephen Crane
- Paul Laurence Dunbar
- Mark Twain
- Winslow Homer
- Henry Tanner
- Mary Cassatt

SETTING the Scene The writer Mark Twain felt sure that the new mechanical typesetter would revolutionize publishing. The machine could do the work of four people. He invested $5,000 in it—a huge sum in 1880. "Very much the best investment I have ever made," he concluded.

In fact, Twain lost his investment. The company that he backed was a failure. The mechanical typesetter, however, did change publishing. It made printing easier and cheaper. Mass-produced, affordable books helped spread American culture.

Public Education

Before 1870, fewer than half of American children went to school. Many who did attended one-room schoolhouses, with only one teacher. Often, several students shared a single book.

Growth of schools

As industry grew after the Civil War, the nation needed an educated work force. As a result, states improved public schools at all levels. St. Louis created the first kindergarten in the United States in 1873. By 1900, there were 4,000 such programs serving children from ages 3 through 7 across the nation.

In the North, most states passed laws that required children to attend school, usually through sixth grade. In the South, the Freedmen's Bureau built grade schools for both African American and white students. However, most schools in the South were segregated.

In cities such as Boston and New York, public schools taught English to young immigrants. Native-born and immigrant children also learned about the duties and rights of citizens. In the 1880s, Catholic immigrants became worried that public schools stressed Protestant teachings. They opened their own, church-sponsored schools.

The school day

The typical school day lasted from 8:00 A.M. to 4:00 P.M. Pupils learned the "three Rs": reading, 'riting, and 'rithmetic. The most widely used textbook was *McGuffey's Eclectic Reader*. Students memorized and recited passages from *McGuffey's Reader*. With titles like "Waste Not, Want Not," the poems and stories taught not only reading but religion, ethics, and values.

Schools emphasized discipline and obedience. A 13-year-old boy complained:

> "They hits ye if yer don't learn and they hits ye if ye whisper, . . . and they hits ye if yer seat squeaks, and they hits ye if ye don't stan' up in time, and they hits ye if yer late, and they hits ye if ye ferget the page."

High schools and colleges

After 1870, many cities and towns built public high schools. By 1900, the United States had 6,000 high schools.

Why Study History?

Because You Have a Right to an Education

Historical Background

Today, it is easy to take education for granted. This was not true 150 years ago. Many states did not require children to go to school. If you were from a poor family, your chances of getting an education were slim. Then, reformers expanded American public education. They insisted that every child had a right to an education.

Schooling was especially valuable to young immigrants. Most had little opportunity for schooling in their homelands. Few could speak English. However, free public schools gave immigrant children the opportunity to succeed in their new homeland. They learned not only English, but American customs, laws, and history.

Graduation day

Connections to Today

In today's information age, education is more important than ever before. The modern world depends on advanced electronics, rapid communication, and computer technology. There are fewer and fewer good-paying, steady jobs for people who do not have at least a high school education.

Schools develop skills employers seek, such as creative thinking, organization, and public speaking. Schools also stress values like responsibility, self-discipline, and teamwork. Perhaps most important, schools prepare Americans for the duties of citizenship. Today, as in the past, democracy depends on an informed public.

Connections to You

It is your responsibility to get the most out of your education. The variety of classes you take give you an opportunity to explore your talents. A subject or activity may interest you enough for you to pursue a career in that field.

In addition, school gives you the opportunity to know and work with people who have different backgrounds and viewpoints. By taking advantage of what your school has to offer, you will prepare yourself for whatever your future brings.

1. **Comprehension** **(a)** How did immigrant children benefit from public schools? **(b)** List three skills that employers look for today.
2. **Critical Thinking** List three qualities that you need to do well in your classes. Write a sentence explaining how each quality can be important outside of school.

Making a Poster With a partner, create a poster that encourages students to stay in school. Use a catchy slogan as well as images.

To help meet the need for trained workers, the Chicago Manual Training School opened in 1884. It offered courses in "shop work" as well as a few academic subjects. Within a decade, almost every public school in the nation had programs aimed at educating students for jobs in business and industry.

Higher education also expanded. New private colleges for both women and men opened. Many states built universities that offered free or low-cost education. However, for women, African Americans and others, opportunities for a college education were often limited.

Adult education

A new form of family education grew up along Lake Chautauqua in New York State. There, in 1874, a Methodist minister opened a summer school for Bible teachers. So many people enrolled that the next year the camp was opened to the general public and nonreligious subjects were introduced.

By the 1880s, some 75,000 thousand people gathered at Lake Chautauqua each summer not only for spiritual guidance but for lectures about art, politics, philosophy, and other subjects. Reformers, religious leaders, and seven American presidents spoke there. The mostly middle-class audiences discovered that education could be fun as well as uplifting.

In 1904, the **Chautauqua Society** began to send out traveling companies. Before long, Chautauquas were reaching as many as 5 million people in 10,000 American towns every year.

New Reading Habits

As more Americans learned to read in the late 1880s, they read not only newspapers but also more books and magazines. New printing methods lowered the cost of magazines. Magazines also added eye-catching pictures to attract readers.

Each magazine had its special audience. The *Ladies' Home Journal* appealed mostly to middle-class women with articles about famous people and stories by well-known authors. By 1900, it had one million readers. Other magazines, such as *Harper's Monthly* and *The Nation,* specialized in politics and current events.

Dime novels

In the late 1800s, paperback books became popular. Bestsellers were often **dime novels.** These low-priced paperbacks offered thrilling adventure stories. Many told about the "Wild West." Young people loved dime novels, but parents often disapproved of the stories. One critic complained:

> "Stories for children used to begin, 'Once upon a time there lived—.' Now they begin, 'Vengeance, blood, death,' shouted Rattlesnake Jim."

Horatio Alger, a popular writer, produced more than 100 dime novels for children. Most told the story of a poor boy who became rich and respected through hard work, luck, and honesty. Americans snapped up these rags-to-riches stories. They offered

Biography **Horatio Alger, Jr.**

In the novels of Horatio Alger, virtue and hard work were always rewarded. Alger published more than 130 "rags-to-riches" tales, with titles such as Tattered Tom, Phil the Fiddler, *and* Paul the Peddler. *Alger devoted many of the profits from his books to a New York home for orphans and runaways.*

★ **How did Alger's books reflect an optimistic view of the United States?**

Viewing HISTORY **A Painting by Mary Cassatt**

Mothers and children were a favorite theme of Mary Cassatt. This 1880 painting is titled Mother About to Wash Her Sleepy Child. *Cassatt was influenced by new French styles as well as by Japanese prints, which were becoming popular in Europe.*
★ **Describe the work of one other American painter of the late 1800s.**

the hope that even the poorest person could become rich and successful in the United States.

New American writers

In the 1880s, a new crop of writers appeared. For the first time, Americans read more books by American authors than by British authors. One group of writers, known as **realists,** tried to show the harsh side of life as it was. Many realists had worked as newspaper reporters. They had seen the poverty and the growth of cities created by the Industrial Revolution.

Stephen Crane was best known for his Civil War novel *The Red Badge of Courage.* (See page 426.) Crane also wrote about the hard lives of young city slum dwellers in novels like *Maggie: A Girl of the Streets.* Hamlin Garland described the harsh lives of farmers in the 1890s. Jack London, born in California, wrote about the hardships of miners and sailors on the West Coast.

Kate Chopin found an audience for short stories about New Orleans life in women's magazines. Chopin's stories showed women breaking out of traditional roles.

Paul Laurence Dunbar was the first African American to make a living as a writer. He wrote poems, such as "We Wear the Mask," in a serious, elegant style. In other poems, short stories, and novels, he used everyday language to express the feelings of African Americans of the time.

Mark Twain

The most famous and popular author of this period was Samuel Clemens, better known by his pen name, **Mark Twain.** As a young man, Clemens worked on a Mississippi River steamboat. There, he heard the boatman's cry "Mark twain," meaning that the river was two "marks," or 12 feet, deep. He took it as his name when he sent out his first story.

Popular stories

Like many other American writers, Twain used local color to make his stories more realistic. **Local color** refers to the speech and habits of a particular region. Twain's novels captured the speech patterns of Southerners who lived and worked along the Mississippi. Twain used homespun, no-nonsense characters to poke fun at serious issues. Novels like *The Adventures of Tom Sawyer* and short stories like "The Celebrated Jumping Frog of Calaveras County" became so well known that people often quoted them to win arguments.

Huckleberry Finn

Twain's greatest work was probably *The Adventures of Huckleberry Finn.* The novel takes place along the Mississippi River before the Civil War. Huck is a country boy who helps an escaped slave named Jim. The two become good friends as they raft down the river together.

Twain filled his novel with humor and adventure to entertain his readers. At the same time, he made a serious point. In the beginning, Huck Finn accepts slavery. During the novel, Huck comes to respect Jim and decides that their friendship is more important than the unjust laws that enslaved Jim. In the following passage, Huck tells of Jim's longing to be reunited with his family:

> "He was saying how the first thing he would do when he got to a free state he would go to saving up money, . . . and when he got enough he would buy his wife, which was owned on a farm close to where Miss Watson lived; and then they would both work to buy the two children, and if their master wouldn't sell them, they'd get an Ab'litionist to go and steal them."

Although *Huckleberry Finn* became a classic American novel, some schools and libraries refused to buy the book. They claimed that Huck was a crude character who would have a bad influence on "our pure-minded lads and lasses."

Realism in Art

Like writers of the period, many artists sought to capture local color and the gritty side of modern life. In the late 1800s, leading artists painted realistic everyday scenes.

As a young man during the Civil War, **Winslow Homer** drew scenes of brutal battles for magazines. Later, he gained fame for realistic scenes of the New England coast. Painter Thomas Eakins learned anatomy and dissected dead bodies to be able to portray the human form accurately. Many of his paintings depicted sports scenes or medical operations. **Henry Tanner,** an African American student of Eakins, won fame for pictures of black sharecroppers. Later, Tanner moved to Paris to enjoy greater freedom.

Other American artists preferred to work in Europe, too. James Whistler left Massachusetts for Paris and London, where his use of color and light influenced young European artists. John Singer Sargent made money painting portraits of wealthy Europeans.

The painter **Mary Cassatt** (kuh SAT) was born in Pennsylvania but settled in Paris. She carved out a place for herself in the French art world. Cassatt painted bright, colorful scenes of people in everyday situations, especially mothers with their children.

★ Section 4 Review ★

Recall

1. **Identify** **(a)** Chautauqua Society, **(b)** Horatio Alger, **(c)** Stephen Crane, **(d)** Paul Laurence Dunbar, **(e)** Mark Twain, **(f)** Winslow Homer, **(g)** Henry Tanner, **(h)** Mary Cassatt.
2. **Define** **(a)** dime novel, **(b)** realist, **(c)** local color.

Comprehension

3. How did public education change after the Civil War?
4. Describe two new kinds of reading matter that became popular in the late 1800s.
5. What was Mark Twain's goal in *Huckleberry Finn?*

Critical Thinking and Writing

6. **Understanding Causes and Effects** How do you think the growth of public education was related to the popularity of newspapers, magazines, and books in the late 1800s?
7. **Drawing Conclusions** Why do you think many American artists and writers turned to realism in the late 1800s?

Activity **Writing a Short Story** Horatio Alger lives! Write the outline and first page for a "rags-to-riches" dime novel. Make your story begin with a thrilling "hook" that captures the attention of the reader.

Chapter 19 Review and Activities

★ Sum It Up ★

Section 1 The New Immigrants

- ▶ Immigrants from southern and eastern Europe, Asia, and Latin America poured into the United States after the Civil War.
- ▶ Most immigrants settled in ethnic neighborhoods in cities while they assimilated into American culture.
- ▶ A new surge of nativism arose in response to the so-called new immigrants.

Section 2 Booming Cities

- ▶ Cities grew rapidly in the late 1800s, and many poor people lived in crowded slums.
- ▶ Under pressure from reformers, cities passed building codes and improved city services.
- ▶ Church groups, along with idealistic reformers like Jane Addams, worked to improve the life of poor city residents.

Section 3 City Life Transformed

- ▶ Skyscrapers, public transportation, and public parks became a part of the city scene in the late 1800s.
- ▶ Newspaper circulation grew as publishers introduced new features, comics, and sensational "yellow journalism."
- ▶ Leisure activities such as sports and entertainment helped unite Americans.

Section 4 Education and Culture

- ▶ In the late 1800s, education improved in the United States.
- ▶ American literature and art ranged from dime novels to new works of realism.

For additional review of the major ideas of Chapter 19, see ***Guide to the Essentials of American History*** or ***Interactive Student Tutorial CD-ROM,*** which contains interactive review activities, graphic organizers, and practice tests.

Reviewing the Chapter

Define These Terms

Match each term with the correct definition.

Column 1	Column 2
1. ethnic group	**a.** process of becoming part of another culture
2. assimilation	**b.** apartment in a slum building
3. tenement	**c.** variety show
4. vaudeville	**d.** group of people who share a common culture
5. dime novel	**e.** low-priced paperback, usually offering thrilling adventure stories

Explore the Main Ideas

1. Why did many Armenians and Russian Jews immigrate to the United States in the late 1800s?
2. How did nativist reaction to immigration vary by region?
3. Describe the three sections of cities in the late 1800s.
4. How did church programs help the poor?
5. How did cities cope with traffic problems?

Chart Activity

Look at the graph below and answer the following questions: **1.** About how many daily newspapers were printed in the United States in 1860? in 1900? **2.** During what 10-year period did the number of newspapers increase the most? **Critical Thinking** List two causes for the rapid increase in the number of newspapers.

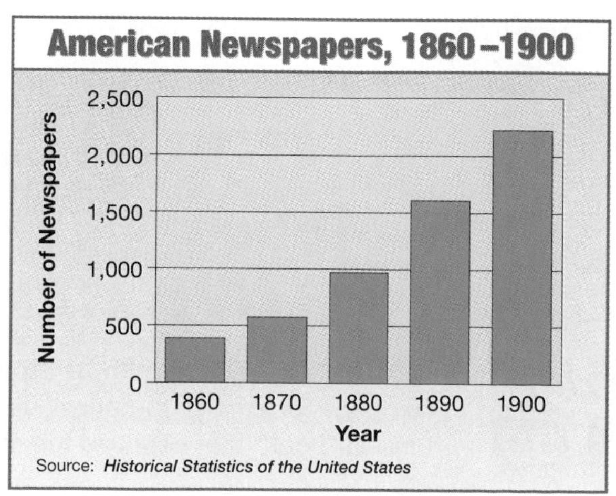

Critical Thinking and Writing

1. **Exploring Unit Themes Industrialization** What effect do you think the increased supply of immigrant workers in industry had on American industrial output?
2. **Understanding Chronology** Place the following events in their proper order: American cities boomed; city governments did not adequately serve their citizens; immigrants moved to the United States; reforms helped cities work better; Europeans and Asians were looking for economic opportunities.
3. **Linking Past and Present (a)** What did city dwellers in the 1800s do to escape the pressures of city life? **(b)** How do people in cities today relax?
4. **Making Decisions** If you had been alive in the late 1800s, would you have preferred to live in a large city like New York or Chicago, or on a ranch or farm in the West? Explain.

Using Primary Sources

A New York journalist reporting on Chicago in 1893 told his readers:

> "I do not know how many very tall buildings Chicago contains, but they must number nearly two dozen.... The best of them are very elegantly and completely [decorated], and the communities of men inside them might almost live their lives within their walls, so [varied] are the occupations and services of the tenants.... It is a great mistake to think that we in New York possess all the elegant, rich, and ornamental [products] of taste."

Source: *Harper's Chicago and the World's Fair,* Julian Ralph, 1893.

Recognizing Points of View (a) Does the reporter approve or disapprove of Chicago's buildings? **(b)** How does the writer think Chicago's buildings compare with those of New York?

Activity Bank

Interdisciplinary Activity

Exploring Geography Research population figures for San Francisco, Chicago, and New York between 1865 and 1910. Create a line graph that shows how the population of these cities grew during this period.

Career Skills Activity

Architects Find out more about the layout and the buildings of a city in the late 1800s. Then create a model of a city. Include skyscrapers, tenements, stores, theaters, parks, and other features.

Citizenship Activity

Understanding Reform Look for a problem in your community that is similar to the problems faced by reformers like Jane Addams. Consult with officials and action groups in your area. Then, work out a proposal for reform of the problem.

Internet Activity

Use the Internet to find sites dealing with Angel Island. Use the information you find to write a poem like the one on page 488. In your poem, refer to specific conditions described by sites you visited.

You are an immigrant living in an American city in the 1880s or 1890s. In your EYEWITNESS JOURNAL, describe a typical day in your life. You might describe work, education, the importance of family and religion, neighborhood life, and leisure activities.

My Ántonia

Willa Cather

Introduction

Willa Cather was one of the greatest American novelists. When she was nine, her family moved to Nebraska. Cather's experiences on the frontier inspired her 1918 novel *My Ántonia.* It tells the story of two young people growing up in Nebraska: the narrator, Jim, and his immigrant friend, Ántonia. In this passage, Jim describes a Nebraska winter on his family's farm.

Vocabulary

Before you read the selection, find the meaning of these words in a dictionary: **boisterously, bile, mottled.**

We had three weeks of this mild, open weather. The cattle in the corral ate corn almost as fast as the men could shell it for them, and we hoped they would be ready for an early market. One morning the two big bulls, Gladstone and Brigham Young, thought spring had come, and they began to tease and butt at each other across the barbed wire that separated them. Soon they got angry. They bellowed and pawed up the soft earth with their hoofs, rolling their eyes and tossing their heads. Each withdrew to a far corner of his own corral, and then they made for each other at a gallop. Thud, thud, we could hear the impact of their great heads, and their bellowing shook the pans of the kitchen shelves. Had they not been dehorned, they would have torn each other to pieces. Pretty soon the fat steers took it up and began butting and horning each other. Clearly, the affair had to be stopped. We all stood by and watched admiringly while Fuchs rode into the corral with a pitchfork and prodded the bulls again and again, finally driving them apart.

The big storm of the winter began on my eleventh birthday, the twentieth of January. When I went down to breakfast that morning, Jake and Otto came in white as snowmen, beating their hands and stamping their feet. They began to laugh boisterously when they saw me, calling:

"You've got a birthday present this time, Jim, and no mistake. They was a full-grown blizzard ordered for you."

All day the storm went on. The snow did not fall this time, it simply spilled out of heaven, like thousands of feather-beds being emptied. That afternoon the kitchen was a carpenter-shop; the men brought in their tools and made two great wooden shovels with long handles. Neither grandmother nor I could go out in the storm, so Jake fed the chickens and brought in a pitiful contribution of eggs.

Next day our men had to shovel until noon to reach the barn—and the snow was still falling! There had not been such a storm in the ten years my grandfather had lived in Nebraska. He said at dinner that we would

A Homestead in Nebraska

Like Willa Cather, Sallie Cover grew up in rural Nebraska. In her painting Homestead of Ellsworth L. Ball, *Cover shows a neighboring farm in the 1880s. Mrs. Ball tends to her baby in the doorway of the house. Her husband works with a team of horses in the field.* ★ **Compare this painting to the photograph on page 452. What differences can you see between the two homesteads?**

not try to reach the cattle—they were fat enough to go without their corn for a day or two; but to-morrow we must feed them and thaw out their water-tap so that they could drink. We could not so much as see the corrals, but we knew the steers were over there, huddled together under the north bank. Our ferocious bulls, subdued enough by this time, were probably warming each other's backs. "This'll take the bile out of 'em!" Fuchs remarked gleefully.

At noon that day the hens had not been heard from. After dinner Jake and Otto, their damp clothes now dried on them, stretched their stiff arms and plunged again into the drifts. They made a tunnel through the snow to the hen-house, with walls so solid that grandmother and I could walk back and forth in it. We found the chickens asleep; perhaps they thought night had come to stay. One old rooster was stirring about, pecking at the solid lump of ice in their water-tin. When we flashed the lantern in their eyes, the hens set up a great cackling and flew about clumsily, scattering down-feathers. The mottled, pin-headed guinea-hens, always resentful of captivity, ran screeching out into the tunnel and tried to poke their ugly, painted faces through the snow walls. By five o'clock the chores were done—just when it was time to begin them all over again! That was a strange, unnatural sort of day.

Analyzing Literature

1. How does Cather show that the blizzard was unusually harsh? Give two examples.
2. **(a)** Identify two extra chores that had to be done because of the blizzard. **(b)** What chore is Jim unable to do?
3. **Making Inferences** **(a)** What attitude do the men seem to have toward the storm? **(b)** What does this suggest about the people who settled the Plains?

Unit 7 A New Role for the Nation

What's Ahead

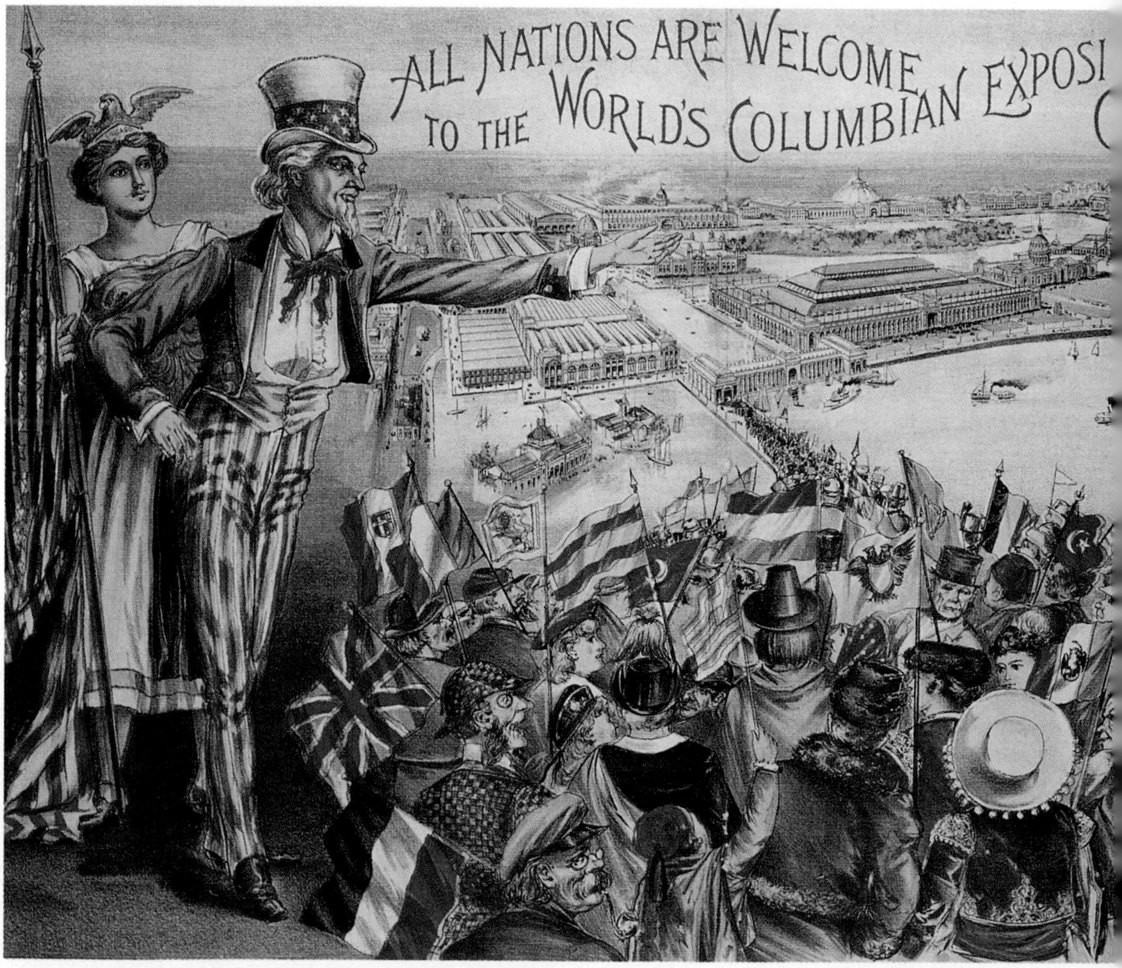

Viewing UNIT THEMES **Becoming a World Power**

J.R. Campbell created this poster to celebrate a giant industrial fair in Chicago. At left are Uncle Sam and Columbia, two symbols of the United States. They welcome representatives of many lands—from Britain and Turkey to Mexico and China. By the late 1800s, the United States was becoming a major force in world trade and politics. ★ **How does this poster express national pride?**

Unit Theme Global Interaction

George Washington had advised the United States to limit its involvement with other nations. By the late 1800s, however, many Americans wanted the country to become more involved in world affairs. American industry, they said, needed new markets for its products. National pride also led some Americans to push for overseas colonies and a stronger military.

How did Americans of the time feel about global interaction? They can tell you in their own words.

★★★★★★★★★★★★★★★★★★★★★★★★★★★★★★★★★★★

Viewpoints on Global Interaction

“Whether they will or no, Americans must begin to look outward. The growing production of the country demands it.”

Alfred Thayer Mahan, naval officer (1897)

“You cannot govern a foreign territory, a foreign people, another people than your own . . . you cannot [conquer] them and govern them against their will, because you think it is for their good.”

George Hoar, representative from Massachusetts (1899)

“This is the divine mission of America. . . . American law, American order, American civilization, and the American flag will plant themselves on shores hitherto bloody and [ignorant].”

Albert Beveridge, senator from Indiana (1900)

★★★★★★★★★★★★★★★★★★★★★★★★★★

Activity **Writing to Learn** Americans still disagree about how involved our country should be in global affairs. Conduct a survey of ten adults you know outside of school. Ask: “Do you think the United States should be more involved or less involved in foreign affairs?” Tally the responses in writing and share them with the class.

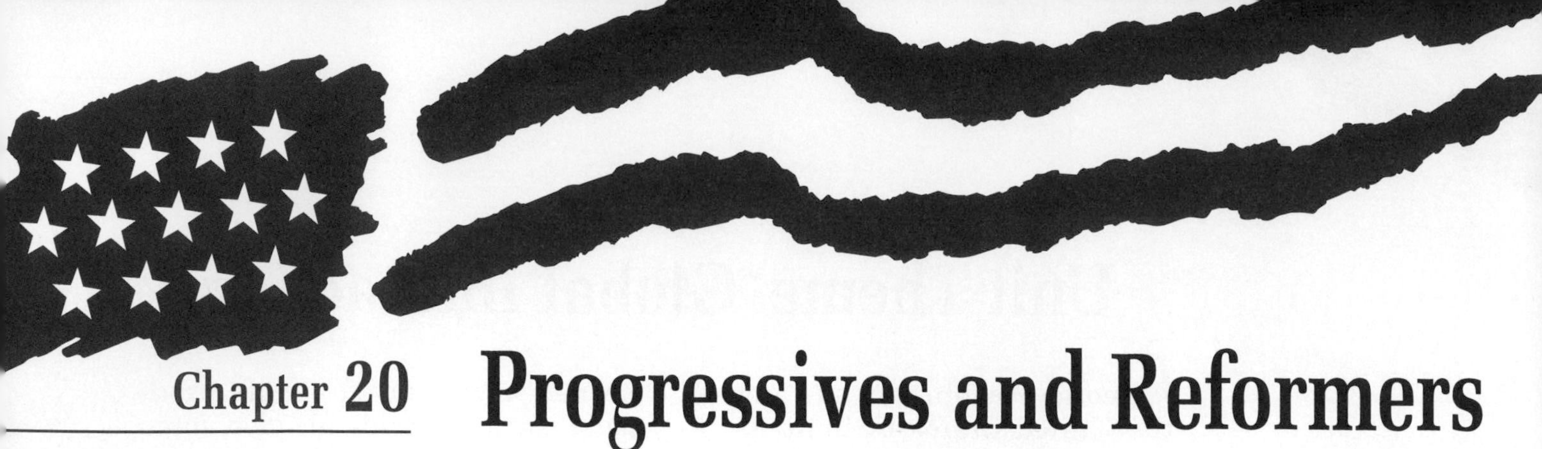

Chapter 20

Progressives and Reformers

1876–1914

What's Ahead

Section 1
Early Reforms

Section 2
The Progressives and Their Goals

Section 3
Presidents Support Reforms

Section 4
Progress for Women

Section 5
Fighting for Equality

A period of reform known as the Progressive Era took shape in the late 1800s. During this time, Americans worked to fight corruption in government, reduce the power of big business, and improve society. Government became more democratic as people in many states gained the power to pass laws directly. After years of effort, American women finally won the right to vote. From 1901 to 1921, three Presidents played a leading role in reform efforts.

African Americans and other minorities also took action against discrimination during the Progressive Era. Despite many setbacks, they laid the groundwork for future progress in civil rights.

Why Study *History?* During the Progressive Era, journalists helped expose a variety of social ills, from child labor to lynching. Today, investigative reporters still play an important role in society. Yet their methods are often subject to criticism. To explore this connection, see the *Why Study History?* feature, "Journalists Keep Us Informed," in this chapter.

American Events

1881 Booker T. Washington founds Tuskegee Institute

1888 Sherman Antitrust Act tries to stop businesses from limiting competition

1890 Wyoming is first state with women's suffrage admitted to union

1875 | 1880 | 1885 | 1890 | 1895

World Events

1875 World Event Japan reforms its courts of law

1893 World Event New Zealand gives vote to women

Viewing History: Fighting the Power of Trusts

Horace Taylor created this cartoon, The Trust Giant's Point of View, *in 1900. Taylor was one of several cartoonists who used his art to protest against the power of giant corporations. Here, oil tycoon John D. Rockefeller holds the White House in his hand.* ★ **What do the buildings in the background represent? Why do you think Taylor put smokestacks on top of them?**

1901 Theodore Roosevelt becomes President

1906 Food and Drug Act bans use of impure ingredients

1913 Federal Reserve Act regulates banks

1895 **1900** **1905** **1910** **1915**

1900 World Event
Chinese rebels seek to expel foreigners

1910 World Event
Revolution begins in Mexico

Early Reforms

Explore These Questions

- What was American politics like in the 1870s and 1880s?
- Why did many Americans oppose the spoils system?
- How did the government try to regulate business?

Define

- spoils system
- patronage
- civil service

Identify

- Gilded Age
- James Garfield
- Chester Arthur
- Grover Cleveland
- Interstate Commerce Commission
- Benjamin Harrison
- Sherman Antitrust Act

Setting the Scene In the 1870s, Mark Twain and Charles Dudley Warner wrote *The Gilded Age.* ("Gilded" means coated with a thin layer of gold paint.) The novel poked fun at greed and political corruption. In one scene, a land speculator describes how he gets funds from Congress:

> "A majority of the House committee, say, $10,000 apiece—$40,000; a majority of the Senate committee, the same each—say $40,000; . . . a lot of dinners to members—say $10,000 altogether; lot of [gifts] for Congressmen's wives and children—those go a long way. . . ."

Of course, Twain and Warner were exaggerating. Still, for many Americans, the novel captured the spirit of the time. Before long, the decades between the 1870s and 1890s became known as the **Gilded Age.** During this period, reformers began to take steps to combat political corruption.

The Gilded Age
by Twain and Warner

Gilded Age Politics

During the Gilded Age, political power was split between the two major parties. By and large, the North and Far West voted Republican, the South Democrat. In national elections, margins of victory were often paper-thin. Neither party could win control of Congress for more than a term or two. The Republican party did hold on to the White House for nearly 25 years. However, Presidents during the Gilded Age generally had less power than Congress.

For Americans of the Gilded Age, politics was mass entertainment. Campaigns featured brass bands, torchlight parades, free picnics, and three-hour speeches. Millions turned out to march, eat, drink, and listen. Voter turnout in presidential elections was higher than at any other time before or since: almost 80 percent.

Two concerns shaped the politics of the Gilded Age. Many Americans worried over the growing power of "special interests." Americans feared that bankers, industrialists, and other men of wealth were gaining control of politics and overpowering the interests of the public. A second worry was political corruption. Bribery and voter fraud angered voters. Reformers especially targeted the corrupt **spoils system,** the practice of rewarding supporters with government jobs.

Taming the Spoils System

Since the days of Andrew Jackson, the spoils system had grown. When a new President entered the White House, thousands of job seekers swarmed into Washington. They sought government jobs as rewards for their political support. Giving jobs to loyal supporters is called **patronage.** By handing out jobs, politicians cemented ties with their supporters and increased their control of government.

Patronage often led to corruption. Some officeholders helped themselves to public money. Many people appointed to government jobs had no skills for those jobs. For example, one man appointed as a court reporter in New York could not read or write.

Early reform efforts

Calls for reform slowly brought change. In 1877, President Rutherford Hayes took steps toward ending the spoils system. He refused to appoint his own supporters to office unless they were qualified for the job. Hayes also launched an investigation of the New York customs house. Investigators found that more than 200 appointed officials received high salaries for doing no work. Despite the protests of leading Republicans, Hayes dismissed two senior customs house officials.

James Garfield entered the White House in 1881. He thought that people should get government jobs on the basis of merit, or ability, rather than as a political reward. However, like other Presidents, Garfield found himself swamped by people seeking patronage.

One disappointed office seeker, Charles Guiteau, blamed Garfield for his failure. In July 1881, Guiteau shot the President in a train station. Two months later, Garfield died. The assassination outraged Americans and sparked new efforts to end the spoils system.

Exams for federal jobs

Upon Garfield's death, Vice President **Chester Arthur** became President. As a New York politician, Arthur had used the spoils system. In fact, he was one of the customs house officials dismissed by President Hayes only a few years earlier! "Elegant Arthur" was better known for his fine wardrobe than his political ideals. Yet, as President, he prosecuted corrupt politicians and worked with Congress to reform the spoils system.

In 1883, Congress passed the Pendleton Act. It created a Civil Service Commission to conduct exams for federal jobs. The **civil service** includes all federal jobs except elected positions and the armed forces. The aim of the civil service was to fill jobs on the basis of merit. People who scored highest on the civil service exams earned the posts.

At first, the Civil Service Commission controlled only a few federal jobs. Under pressure from reformers, however, later Presidents added more jobs to the civil service list. By 1900, the commission controlled about 40 percent of all federal jobs.

Viewing HISTORY **Wealthy Americans in a Gilded Age**

This painting by William T. Smedley shows a golf tournament at a country club near Washington, D.C. The Gilded Age was a time of great luxury for wealthy Americans like these. They built great mansions, dressed in the latest fashions, and enjoyed leisure activities like tennis and polo. Some also used their fortunes to buy political influence. ★ **Why were many Americans concerned about the power of the rich?**

Skills FOR LIFE

Managing Information | Communication | Maps, Charts, and Graphs

Solving Problems

How Will I Use This Skill?

Every day, you face problems and make decisions about how to solve them. Sometimes, the problem is so simple the solution is automatic. When the issue is more complex, you have to put more effort into considering possible solutions and the consequences of each alternative. In the community, leaders and citizens try to come up with practical solutions that not only solve problems but eliminate their causes as well.

LEARN the Skill

To solve a problem, you first have to define what the problem is. Use the following steps to help you in this process:

1. Identify the problem.
2. Determine the impact of the problem.
3. Identify alternate solutions to the problem.
4. Determine the effectiveness of the solution.

PRACTICE the Skill

Reread what you have learned about the spoils system. Then, answer the following questions:

1. Reformers during the Gilded Age considered the spoils system to be a problem. Describe how the spoils system worked.
2. (a) How did the spoils system lead to corruption? (b) Do you think the spoils system made government more or less efficient? Explain.
3. (a) What actions did Congress take to tame the spoils system? (b) Jot down two or three other alternatives you might have considered if you had been in Congress at the time.
4. How effective was Congressional action in solving the negative effects of the spoils system? Explain.

APPLY the Skill

Think about some problem that you or your classmates faced in school recently. Describe the problem. Give as many alternatives as you can to resolve the issue. Which do you think is the best solution? Explain your answer.

President Grover Cleveland supported reforms to expand the civil service.

Regulating Big Business

In 1877, Collis Huntington, builder of the Central Pacific Railroad, faced a problem. A bill before Congress aimed at breaking his control of rail routes to southern California. To Huntington, the solution was simple—bribe members of Congress to kill the bill. "It costs money to fix things," he explained.

The behavior of men like Huntington convinced many Americans that big businesses controlled the government. Public outcry against monopolies grew.

Interstate Commerce Act

The government responded by taking steps to regulate railroads and other large businesses. In 1887, President **Grover Cleveland** signed the Interstate Commerce Act. The new law forbade practices such as pools and rebates. (See pages 462–463.) It also set up the **Interstate Commerce Commission,** or ICC, to oversee the railroads.

At first, the ICC was weak. Richard Olney, an attorney for one of the railroad owners, explained:

> "The Commission . . . satisfies the popular clamor for a government supervision of the railroads, at the same time that supervision is almost entirely [ineffective]."

In court challenges, most judges ruled in favor of the railroads. Still, Congress had shown that it was ready to regulate big business. Later laws made the Interstate Commerce Commission more effective.

Sherman Antitrust Act

In 1888, President Cleveland lost his bid for reelection. **Benjamin Harrison** became President. In 1890, Harrison signed the **Sherman Antitrust Act.** The act prohibited trusts or other businesses from limiting competition.

The Sherman Antitrust Act sounded strong, but in practice trusts used the courts to block enforcement. Judges ruled that the law was an illegal attempt by government to control private property.

Instead of regulating trusts, the Sherman Antitrust Act was first used to stop labor unions. The courts said union strikes blocked free trade and thereby threatened competition. As the reform spirit spread, however, courts began to use the Sherman Act against monopolies.

★ Section 1 Review ★

Recall

1. **Identify** **(a)** Gilded Age, **(b)** James Garfield, **(c)** Chester Arthur, **(d)** Grover Cleveland, **(e)** Interstate Commerce Commission, **(f)** Benjamin Harrison, **(g)** Sherman Antitrust Act.
2. **Define** **(a)** spoils system, **(b)** patronage, **(c)** civil service.

Comprehension

3. What two concerns dominated Gilded Age politics?
4. Why did many Americans favor creation of a civil service?
5. **(a)** Why did Congress create the ICC? **(b)** Was the ICC effective? Explain.

Critical Thinking and Writing

6. **Making Inferences** The term "golden age" is used to describe a period of great progress and achievement. What point do you think Twain and Warner were making by calling the 1870s the Gilded Age?
7. **Synthesizing Information** Why do you think early efforts to regulate big business had little success?

Activity **Writing an Editorial** You are a newspaper editor in 1881. Write an editorial on President James Garfield's death. Explain the circumstances and tell why the assassination shows the need to reform the spoils system.

The Progressives and Their Goals

As You Read

Explore These Questions

- Why did reformers attack city governments?
- How did the press contribute to reform efforts?
- What new practices gave more power to voters?

Define

- muckraker
- public interest
- primary
- initiative
- referendum
- recall
- graduated income tax

Identify

- William Tweed
- Ida Tarbell
- Upton Sinclair
- Progressives
- John Dewey
- Robert La Follette
- Wisconsin Idea
- Sixteenth Amendment

Joseph Folk, city prosecutor of St. Louis, was furious. Local politicians had just ordered him to hire men he felt were dishonest.

"I and my office, the criminal law, was to be run by—criminals!" he complained to reporter Lincoln Steffens. Instead, Folk led a crusade against dishonest politicians and businessmen. Elsewhere, other reformers fought to oust corrupt politicians and to give voters greater power.

Reforming City Government

How had city governments become so corrupt? Growing cities needed many improvements, such as new sewers, better garbage collection, and more roads. In many cities, politicians traded these jobs for money. In some places, bribes and corruption became a way of life.

Boss rule

Powerful politicians, known as bosses, came to rule many cities. They controlled all work done in the city and demanded payoffs from businesses. Often, bosses did not hold office. Instead, they worked behind the scenes to influence officeholders. In California, for example, Abraham Ruef was the Republican boss for northern San Francisco. At one time, Boss Ruef controlled enough delegates to choose his party's nominee for governor.

City bosses were popular with the poor, especially with immigrants. Bosses provided jobs and made loans to the needy. They handed out extra coal in winter and turkeys at Thanksgiving. In exchange, the poor voted for the boss or his candidate.

Boss Tweed

In New York City, Boss **William Tweed** carried corruption to new heights. During the 1860s and 1870s, Tweed cheated New York out of more than $100 million. Reformers tried to have him jailed.

Journalists exposed Tweed's wrongdoings. Cartoonist Thomas Nast showed Boss Tweed as a vulture destroying the city. Nast's attacks upset Tweed. He complained that his supporters might be unable to read, but they could understand pictures.

Faced with prison, Tweed fled to Spain. There, local police arrested him when they recognized him from a Nast cartoon. Tweed died in jail in 1878. Thousands of poor New Yorkers mourned his death.

Good government leagues

Reformers in many cities formed good government leagues. Their goal was to replace corrupt officials with honest leaders.

The leagues met with some success. The good government league in Minneapolis sent a corrupt mayor to jail. In Cleveland, reformers elected Tom Johnson as mayor. Johnson improved garbage collection and sewage systems in the city. He also set up services to help the poor of Cleveland.

Muckrakers Rouse Public Opinion

To bring about change, reformers first had to ignite public anger. A major weapon was the press. Newspaper reporters visited the slums. They described burned-out tenements and exposed how corruption led to inadequate fire protection. They talked to mothers whose babies were dying of tuberculosis, a lung disease. Photographer Jacob Riis provided shocking images of slum life.

Crusading journalists like Riis became known as **muckrakers.** People said they raked the dirt, or muck, and exposed it to public view. One muckraker, **Ida Tarbell,** targeted the unfair practices of big business. Her articles about the Standard Oil Company led to demands for tighter controls on trusts.

In 1906, **Upton Sinclair** shocked the nation when he published *The Jungle.* This novel revealed gruesome details about the meatpacking industry in Chicago. Although the book was fiction, it was based on things Sinclair had seen. One passage described the rats in a meatpacking house:

> "These rats were nuisances, and the packers would put poisoned bread out for them: they would die, and then rats, bread, and meat would go into the hoppers together."

Muckrakers helped change public opinion. For years, middle-class people had ignored the need for reform. When they saw

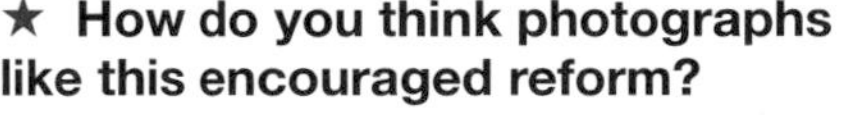

Rousing Public Anger

Danish-born muckraker Jacob Riis used a powerful weapon—the camera—to influence public opinion. In books like How the Other Half Lives, *he showed middle-class readers what poverty really looked like. This Riis photograph shows an Italian ragpicker and her baby in a New York City tenement.*

★ **How do you think photographs like this encouraged reform?**

Camera of the 1890s

how corruption menaced the nation, they joined with muckrakers to demand change.

Connections With Civics

Mayor Tom Johnson of Cleveland fought to make public parks more open to the public. Upper-class people protested, especially when Johnson ordered the removal of "Keep Off the Grass" signs. Eventually, Johnson created a citywide system of parks with hundreds of playgrounds and baseball fields.

The Progressives

By 1900, reformers were calling themselves **Progressives.** By that, they meant they were forward-thinking people who wanted to improve American life. They won many changes from 1898 to 1917. This period is often called the Progressive Era.

Progressives were never a single group with a single aim. They backed various causes. What united them was their faith that the problems of society could be solved.

Progressive beliefs

Progressives drew inspiration from two sources. One was religion. In the late 1800s, Protestant ministers had begun preaching a social gospel. (See page 497.) It stressed the duty of Christians to improve society.

Why Study History?

Because Journalists Keep Us Informed

Historical Background

During the Progressive Era, Josiah Flynt wrote about crime in American cities. His reports were accurate because Flynt had gone undercover. He had assumed the role of an urban thug and joined criminal gangs. To blend in, he committed crimes himself.

Some people found Flynt's methods inexcusable. Nevertheless, Flynt's muckraking articles exposed illegal gang activities and corruption among police and political officials. His work helped spark needed reforms.

Connections to Today

Today, investigative journalists are everywhere, from your local paper to national news programs such as *60 Minutes*. Like muckrakers of the past, today's reporters continue to provide information that can benefit the public. Some critics, though, say that reporters go too far.

In 1992, a television station used undercover reporters with hidden cameras to show unsanitary conditions at a supermarket. The reporters lied in order to be hired. They also took pictures without the store's permission. After the report aired, the supermarket sued. A jury found that reporters had trespassed and engaged in fraud to get their story. The court ordered the network to pay the supermarket $5.5 million.

Connections to You

We may disagree about the methods investigative journalists use. Yet these muckrakers of today often provide useful information that can have a direct effect on your community. Some journalists have exposed illegal dumping of toxic wastes. Others have uncovered facts about overcrowded classrooms or child labor in sweatshops. Such reports may bring about needed reforms.

Television news teams have exposed many public health violations, such as illegal dumping of dangerous chemicals.

1. **Comprehension** How did Josiah Flynt get the information to write his stories?
2. **Critical Thinking** Do you think journalists should be allowed to break some laws to expose wrongdoing? Explain.

Exploring Local News Read a local newspaper or watch a local television news program to find an example of investigative journalism. Write a brief summary of the story.

Advances in science also inspired Progressives. Like scientists, Progressives made use of careful analysis and statistics.

Progressive reformers believed that the **public interest,** or the good of the people, should guide government actions. The public interest, they said, must not be sacrificed to the greed of a few trusts and city bosses.

Progressives stressed the importance of education. **John Dewey,** a Progressive educator, wanted schools to promote reform. They must not only teach democratic values, he argued, but reflect them. Dewey encouraged students to ask questions and work together to solve problems. On college campuses, Progressive educators stressed the need to teach skills to help society. Colleges offered new courses in areas such as social work.

Women played leading roles in the Progressive Era. In the mid-1800s, a new view of women emerged. Many Americans believed that women were morally superior to men. In a world of corruption, they said, women had the moral force to bring about change. This view encouraged many women to work for reform. To increase their social influence, they also sought the right to vote.

The Wisconsin Idea

Progressivism got its start in the states of the Midwest. Among the leading Progressives was **Robert La Follette** of Wisconsin. "The will of the people shall be the law of the land," was his motto. His fighting spirit won him the nickname "Battling Bob."

In 1900, La Follette was elected governor. He introduced a statewide program of Progressive reforms, called the **Wisconsin Idea.** For example, he lowered railroad rates. The result was increased rail traffic, which helped both railroad owners and customers.

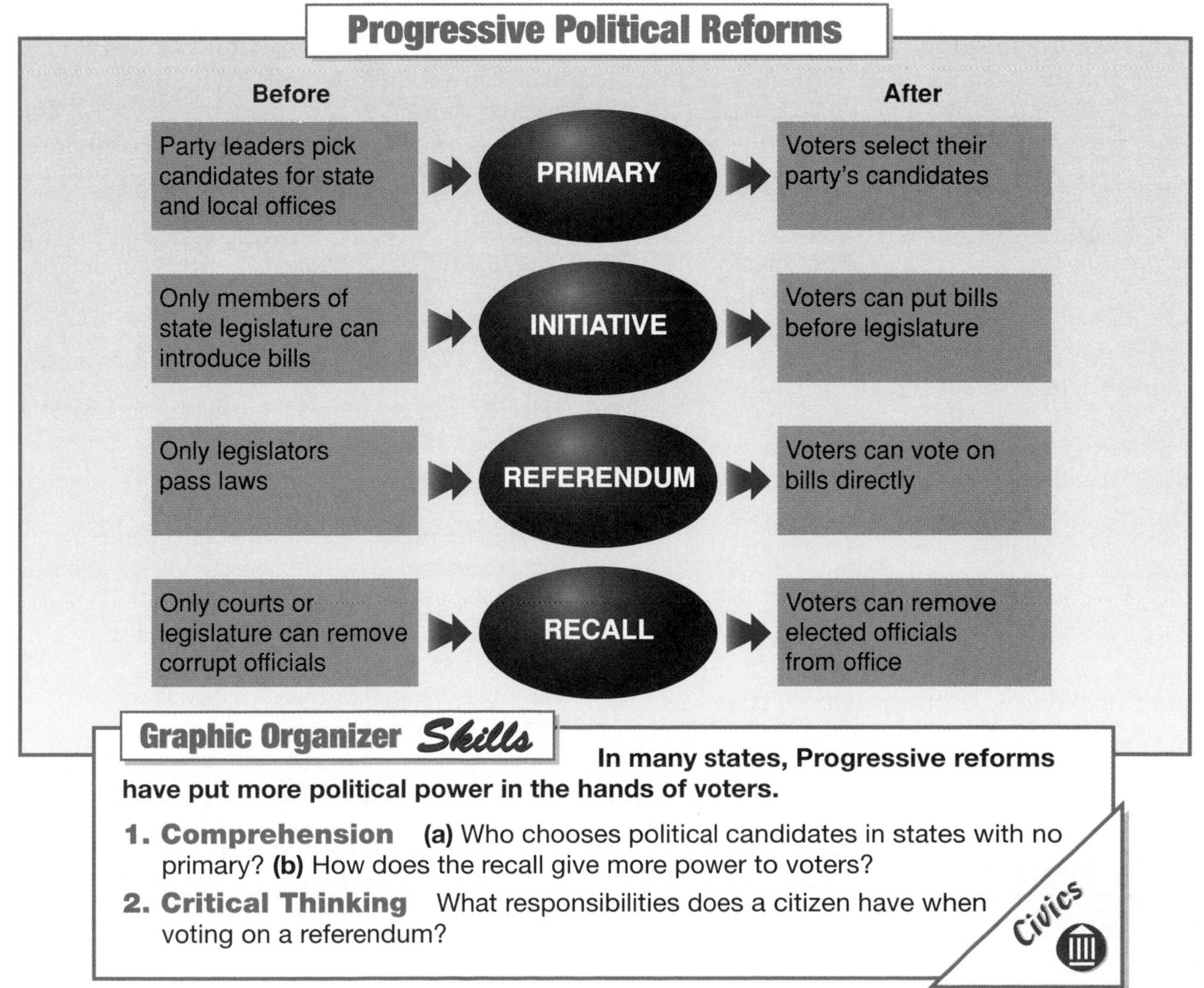

Graphic Organizer *Skills* In many states, Progressive reforms have put more political power in the hands of voters.

1. **Comprehension** **(a)** Who chooses political candidates in states with no primary? **(b)** How does the recall give more power to voters?
2. **Critical Thinking** What responsibilities does a citizen have when voting on a referendum?

Civics

Progressives from other states visited Wisconsin to study La Follette's system. Before long, voters in California, Indiana, Arkansas, Oregon, and New York were talking about the Wisconsin Idea. They, too, elected Progressive governors who introduced far-reaching changes.

The will of the people

LaFollette and other Progressives believed that the people would make the right decisions if given the chance. As a result, they pressed for reforms to give voters more power.

Since Andrew Jackson's time, party leaders had picked candidates for local and state offices. Instead, Progressives pressed for **primaries,** in which voters choose their party's candidate for the general election. In 1903, Wisconsin was the first state to adopt the primary. By 1917, all but four states had done so.

Progressives also urged states to adopt measures that allowed voters to participate directly in lawmaking. The **initiative** gave voters the right to put a bill directly before the state legislature. The **referendum** allowed them to vote the bill into law at the next election.

Another Progressive measure was the **recall.** The recall allowed voters to remove an elected official in the middle of his or her term. This gave ordinary people a chance to get rid of corrupt officials.

Other Reforms

Other Progressive reforms required federal action. Most Progressives supported a **graduated income tax,** which taxes people from different income levels at different rates. The wealthy pay taxes at a higher rate than the poor or the middle class.

In 1895, the Supreme Court had ruled that a federal income tax was unconstitutional. In response, Progressives campaigned to amend the Constitution. In 1913, the states ratified the **Sixteenth Amendment.** It gave Congress the power to impose an income tax.

Progressives backed another amendment. Since 1789, senators had been elected by state legislatures, rather than directly by voters. Special interests sometimes bribed lawmakers to vote for certain candidates. Progressives wanted to end such abuses. In 1913, the states ratified the Seventeenth Amendment for the direct election of senators.

★ Section 2 Review ★

Recall

1. **Identify:** **(a)** William Tweed, **(b)** Ida Tarbell, **(c)** Upton Sinclair, **(d)** Progressives, **(e)** John Dewey, **(f)** Robert La Follette, **(g)** Wisconsin Idea, **(h)** Sixteenth Amendment.
2. **Define** **(a)** muckraker, **(b)** public interest, **(c)** primary, **(d)** initiative, **(e)** referendum, **(f)** recall, **(g)** graduated income tax.

Comprehension

3. **(a)** How did city bosses win the support of the poor? **(b)** Why did reformers oppose bosses?
4. How did muckrakers help change public attitudes?
5. Describe two ways the Progressives increased the power of voters.

Critical Thinking and Writing

6. **Analyzing Ideas** Dewey thought school classes should reflect democratic values. What did he mean?
7. **Defending a Position** Do you agree with La Follette and other Progressives that the people will make the right decisions if given the chance? Why or why not?

Activity **Drawing a Political Cartoon** You are Thomas Nast. Boss Tweed and his pals are stealing millions from the city you love. Draw a political cartoon commenting on Tweed's corruption.

3 Presidents Support Reforms

As You Read

Explore These Questions

- How did Theodore Roosevelt try to control trusts?
- What other reforms did Roosevelt support?
- What were Woodrow Wilson's goals as President?

Define

- trustbuster
- conservation
- national park

Identify

- Theodore Roosevelt
- Square Deal
- Pure Food and Drug Act
- William Howard Taft
- Bull Moose party
- Woodrow Wilson
- New Freedom
- Federal Reserve Act
- Federal Trade Commission

SETTING the Scene In 1900, Republicans needed a reform-minded candidate to run with President William McKinley. They offered the job to **Theodore Roosevelt,** a New York politician. However, Roosevelt was not interested in serving as Vice President. "I will not accept under any circumstances," he replied.

As a loyal Republican, Roosevelt finally did accept the nomination. A year later, McKinley was shot and Roosevelt became President.

By 1901, Progressives were having success in many states. With Roosevelt in the White House, they hoped to push national reforms and turn the federal government into a protector of the people.

Teddy Roosevelt

Teddy Roosevelt—or "TR," as he was called—belonged to an old, wealthy New York family. As a child, he suffered from asthma and was often sick. To build his strength, he lifted weights, ran, and boxed.

Early career

The children of wealthy, old families were expected to live lives of ease and privilege. Instead, TR entered politics after college, determined to end corruption and protect the public interest.

Roosevelt's friends mocked his political ambitions. He later recalled:

> "They assured me that the men I met would be rough and brutal and unpleasant to deal with. I answered that I certainly would not quit until I...found out whether I was really too weak to hold my own in the rough and tumble."

By age 26, Roosevelt was serving in the New York state legislature. Then tragedy almost ended his political career. In 1884, his mother and his young wife died on the same day. Overcome by grief, Roosevelt quit the legislature. He went west to work on a cattle ranch in present-day North Dakota.

After two years, Roosevelt returned to the East and to politics. He served on the Civil Service Commission. Later on, he held posts as head of the New York City police department and as assistant secretary of the navy.

In 1898, when the United States went to war against Spain, Roosevelt fought in Cuba. He returned home to a hero's welcome. That same year, he was elected governor of New York.

Pitcher in the likeness of Theodore Roosevelt

Viewing HISTORY **TR on the Campaign Trail**

This photograph shows Theodore Roosevelt campaigning in Wyoming in 1903. TR put tremendous energy into his speeches, pounding his fists into the air as he spoke. Roosevelt's activities as an outdoorsman also helped his public image. After he refused to shoot a small captured bear, a toy company named a new product after the President: the Teddy bear. ★ **How did Roosevelt's actions as President support his image as an energetic fighter?**

▲ *Teddy bear of the early 1900s*

A progressive governor

Since his days in the legislature, Roosevelt had pushed for reform. Other legislators called him a "goo goo," a mocking name for someone who wanted good government. As governor, Roosevelt worked for Progressive reforms.

New York Republican bosses were relieved when Roosevelt became Vice President. Then, in September 1901, an assassin shot President McKinley. At age 42, Roosevelt became the nation's youngest President.

TR and Big Business

Roosevelt promised to continue McKinley's pro-business policies. Still, many business people worried about the new President's Progressive ideas.

Roosevelt believed that giant corporations were here to stay. He thought, however, that there were good trusts and bad trusts. Good trusts were efficient and fair and should be left alone, TR said. Bad trusts took advantage of their workers and cheated the public. The government should either control them or break them up.

Taking on the trusts

Roosevelt wanted to test the power of the government to break up bad trusts. In 1902, he ordered the Attorney General, the government's chief lawyer, to bring a lawsuit against the Northern Securities Company. Roosevelt argued that Northern Securities used unfair business practices in violation of the Sherman Act.

Stock prices on Wall Street, the New York center of business and finance, fell at news of the lawsuit. One newspaper editor noted:

> "Wall Street is paralyzed at the thought that a President of the United States would sink so low as to try to enforce the law."

While business leaders worried, ordinary people supported the President.

In 1904, the Supreme Court ruled that Northern Securities had violated the Sherman Antitrust Act by limiting trade. It ordered the trust to be broken up. The decision showed the effects of Progressive reform. In the 1890s, the Sherman Antitrust Act had been used to break up unions, not trusts.

President Roosevelt hailed the case as a victory. He then ordered the Attorney General to file suit against other trusts, including Standard Oil and the American Tobacco Company. The courts later ordered both trusts to be broken up on the grounds that they blocked free trade.

Some business leaders called Roosevelt a **trustbuster** who wanted to destroy all trusts. "Certainly not," replied Roosevelt, only those that "have done something we regard as wrong." He preferred to control or regulate trusts, not "bust" them.

Support for labor

Roosevelt also clashed with the nation's mine owners. In 1902, Pennsylvania coal miners went on strike. They wanted better pay and a shorter workday. Mine owners refused to talk to the miners' union.

As winter approached, schools and hospitals around the country ran out of coal. Furious at the stubbornness of mine owners, Roosevelt threatened to send in troops to run the mines. In response, owners sat down with the union and reached an agreement.

Working men and women around the country cheered. Earlier Presidents had used federal troops to break strikes. Roosevelt was the first to side with labor.

The Square Deal

In 1904, Roosevelt ran for President in his own right. During the campaign, he promised Americans a **Square Deal.** By this, he meant that many different groups—farmers and consumers, workers and owners—should have an equal opportunity to succeed. The promise of a Square Deal helped Roosevelt win a landslide victory.

Railroads were a key target of the Square Deal. Roosevelt knew that the Interstate Commerce Act of 1887 had done little to end rebates and other abuses. He urged Congress to pass the Elkins Act in 1903. It outlawed rebates. In 1906, Congress gave the ICC the power to set railroad rates.

Protecting consumers

Roosevelt had read Upton Sinclair's shocking novel, *The Jungle.* In response, he sent more government inspectors to meatpacking houses. The owners refused to let the inspectors in.

Roosevelt fought back. He gave the newspapers copies of a government report that supported Sinclair's picture of the meatpacking industry. As public rage mounted, Congress passed the Meat Inspection Act of 1906. It forced packers to open their doors to more inspectors.

Roosevelt supported other reforms to protect consumers. Muckrakers had revealed that the drug companies made false claims about their medicines. They also found that

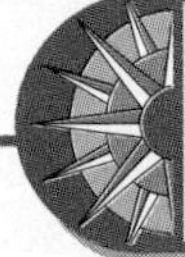

Linking Past and Present

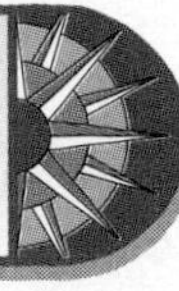

Past

Present

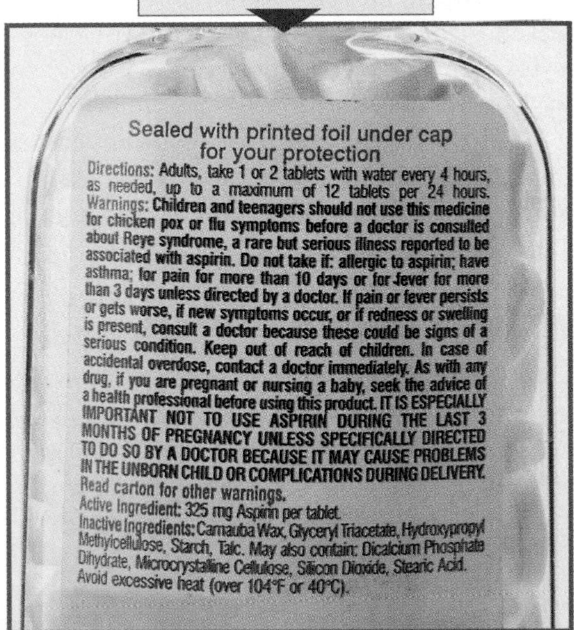

Protecting the Consumer

Before the Progressive Era, drug manufacturers were not controlled by the law. Advertisers often made wild, exotic claims for medicines that actually did nothing. Today, every medicine label must include a list of ingredients, exact directions for use, and warnings about possible side effects. ★ **How is the advertisement at the top different from a medicine ad you might see in a magazine today?**

the food industry added dangerous chemicals to canned foods. In 1906, Congress passed the **Pure Food and Drug Act.** It required food and drug makers to list ingredients on their packages. It also tried to end false advertising and the use of impure ingredients.

Protecting resources

Roosevelt grew alarmed about the destruction of the American wilderness. To fuel the nation's industrial growth, lumber companies were cutting down whole forests. Miners were taking iron and coal from the earth at a frantic pace and leaving gaping holes.

Roosevelt loved the outdoors and objected to this destruction of the land. He believed in **conservation,** the protection of natural resources. "The rights of the public to natural resources outweigh private rights," he said.

Roosevelt thought that natural resources could serve both the public interest and private companies. Some forest and mountain areas, he said, should be left as wilderness. Others could supply wood for lumber. He wanted lumber companies to replant trees in the forests they were clearing. Mining, too, should be controlled.

Under Roosevelt, the government created some 170,000 acres of national parkland. A **national park** is an area set aside and run by the federal government for people to visit.

Taft and the Reformers

In 1908, Roosevelt decided not to run for reelection. Instead, he threw his support behind **William Howard Taft,** his Secretary of War. With Roosevelt's backing, Taft won an easy victory. A confident Roosevelt said:

> "Taft will carry on the work... as I have. His policies, principles, purposes, and ideals are the same as mine. The Roosevelt policies will not go out with Roosevelt."

Roosevelt then set off for Africa to hunt big game for a year. He left behind an impressive record as a reformer. He also left the presidency more powerful than it had been at any time since the Civil War.

Taft was different from Roosevelt. Unlike the hard-driving, energetic Roosevelt, Taft was quiet and careful. Roosevelt loved power. Taft feared it.

Nevertheless, Taft supported many Progressive causes. He broke up even more trusts than TR. He supported the graduated income tax, approved new safety regulations for mines, and signed laws setting an eight-hour day for government employees. Under Taft, the Department of Labor set up a bureau to deal with the problems of working children.

Despite such successes, Taft lost Progressive support. In 1909, Taft signed a bill that raised most tariffs. Progressives opposed high tariffs because they felt tariffs raised prices for consumers. Also, Taft fired the chief of the United States Forest Service during a dispute over the sale of wilderness areas in Alaska. Progressives accused Taft of blocking conservation efforts.

Election of 1912

When Roosevelt returned from Africa, he found that reformers felt Taft had betrayed them. Roosevelt declared that Taft was "a flub-dub with a streak of the second-rate." TR decided to run against Taft for the Republican nomination in 1912.

The Bull Moose party

Roosevelt won wide public support. He won almost every state primary he entered. Still, many Republican business leaders distrusted Roosevelt. Also, Taft still controlled the party leadership. At the Republican convention, the party nominated Taft.

Right in the middle of Taft's nomination, angry Progressive Republicans stormed out

Connections With Geography

Theodore Roosevelt's conservation efforts encouraged Mexican immigration. In 1902, Congress passed the Newlands Act to finance construction of irrigation projects in arid states. The law created millions of acres of new farmland in California, Texas, and Arizona. As a result, many Mexicans entered the United States in search of work.

AmericanHeritage
MAGAZINE

Almost 100 years ago, President Theodore Roosevelt camped out in the Yosemite Valley in California. He viewed its majestic mountains and walked beneath its towering sequoia trees—the oldest living things on Earth. Today, thanks to the work of conservationists like Roosevelt, you can still enjoy Yosemite and other natural beauties. In fact, you can even see the very same redwoods Roosevelt saw!

★ To learn more about this historic site, write: Yosemite National Park, PO Box 577, Yosemite, CA 95389.

This sign welcomes you to Yosemite's sequoia forest.

of the convention. They set up a new Progressive party and chose Roosevelt as their candidate. He eagerly accepted. "I feel as strong as a bull moose," he boasted. Roosevelt and his supporters became known as the **Bull Moose party.**

A Democratic victory

Democrats picked **Woodrow Wilson,** a Progressive, as their candidate. Born in Virginia, Wilson was the son of a Presbyterian minister. His father taught him that the world was strictly divided between good and evil. As a boy, Wilson made up his mind always to fight for what he thought was right. Wilson had served as president of Princeton University and as governor of New Jersey. He was known as a brilliant scholar and a cautious reformer.

Together, Taft and Roosevelt won more votes than Wilson. However, they split the Republican vote. Their quarrel helped Wilson win the election of 1912.

President Wilson

Wilson took the oath of office in March 1913. His inaugural address reflected his strong, unbending sense of morality:

> "The nation has been deeply stirred, stirred by a solemn passion, stirred by the knowledge of wrong, of ideals lost, of government too often . . . made an instrument of evil. The feelings with which we face this new age of right and opportunity sweep across our heart-strings like some air out of God's own presence."

Wilson asked honest, forward-looking Americans to stand at his side. "God helping me," he pledged, "I will not fail them."

The New Freedom

At first, Wilson's goal was to break up trusts into smaller companies. By doing so, he hoped to restore the competition that had once existed in the American economy. "If America is not to have free enterprise, then she can have freedom of no sort whatever," he said. Wilson called his program the **New Freedom.**

Campaign song for Woodrow Wilson

Wilson worked with Congress for laws to spur competition. He pushed first for a lower tariff to create more competition from imports. After a struggle, Congress lowered the tariff. It also imposed a graduated income tax to make up for lost revenues.

To regulate banking, Congress passed the **Federal Reserve Act** in 1913. The act set up a nationwide system of federal banks. The system gave the government the power to raise or lower interest rates and control the money supply.

Regulating competition

To ensure fair competition, President Wilson persuaded Congress to create the **Federal Trade Commission** (FTC) in 1914. The FTC had power to investigate companies and order them to stop using business practices that destroyed all competitors.

That same year, Wilson signed the Clayton Antitrust Act. The law was weaker than he wanted. However, it did ban some business practices that limited free enterprise. It also barred antitrust laws from being used against unions—a major victory for labor.

Despite Wilson's successes, the Progressive movement slowed after 1914. By then, the Progressives had achieved many of their goals. In addition, the outbreak of war in Europe seized public attention. Americans became concerned that the fighting in Europe might soon involve the United States.

★ Section 3 Review ★

Recall

1. **Identify** **(a)** Theodore Roosevelt, **(b)** Square Deal, **(c)** Pure Food and Drug Act, **(d)** William Howard Taft, **(e)** Bull Moose party, **(f)** Woodrow Wilson, **(g)** New Freedom, **(h)** Federal Reserve Act, **(i)** Federal Trade Commission.
2. **Define** **(a)** trustbuster, **(b)** conservation, **(c)** national park.

Comprehension

3. **(a)** How did Roosevelt feel about trusts? **(b)** What action did he take in the Northern Securities case?
4. Describe one action Roosevelt took to achieve each of the following goals: **(a)** consumer protection, **(b)** protection of natural resources.
5. Describe two actions Wilson took to ensure competition.

Critical Thinking and Writing

6. **Analyzing Ideas** Reread the comment of the newspaper editor on page 526. **(a)** Why were many business leaders surprised by Roosevelt's actions in the Northern Securities case? **(b)** What point was the editor making about the role of the President?
7. **Making Inferences** "I'm glad to be going," commented William Howard Taft as he left the White House in 1913. "This is the lonesomest place in the world." Why do you think Taft might have felt this way?

Activity **Expressing an Opinion** You are the owner of a large area of wilderness. Theodore Roosevelt wants to use your land for a park. Write him a letter in which you explain your reaction to his proposal.

Progress for Women

As You Read

Explore These Questions

- How did women work for suffrage in the Progressive Era?
- What new opportunities did women earn?
- How did the temperance movement gain strength?

Define

- suffragist
- temperance movement

Identify

- Carrie Chapman Catt
- Alice Paul
- Nineteenth Amendment
- Florence Kelley
- Frances Willard
- Carry Nation
- Eighteenth Amendment

SETTING the Scene Susan B. Anthony had broken the law. Her crime was voting. Along with 14 other women, Anthony registered to vote in her home town of Rochester, New York, in 1872. When she cast her ballot, she was arrested.

At her trial, the judge directed that Anthony be found guilty. The judge then asked if she had anything to say. Anthony responded defiantly:

> “Yes, your honor, I have many things to say; for in your ordered verdict of guilty, you have trampled underfoot every vital principle of our government. My natural rights, my civil rights, my political rights, are all alike ignored. Robbed of the fundamental privilege of citizenship, I am degraded from the status of a citizen to that of a subject; and not only myself individually, but all of my sex, are . . . doomed to political subjection.”

Anthony refused to quiet down or to ask for mercy. The judge then ordered her to pay a fine of $100. “May it please your honor,” Anthony replied, “I shall never pay a dollar of your unjust penalty.” Anthony never did pay the fine. Her courageous stand won her many new followers.

Porcelain figure of a women's suffrage campaigner

During the Progressive Era, women continued their long battle to win the right to vote. They also worked for many other reforms. Women spoke out against trusts, supported pure food laws, and called for an end to child labor. They also led a renewed effort to ban the sale of alcohol.

Working for the Vote

The struggle to grant women the vote, or suffrage, went back many years. As you read in Chapter 13, the Seneca Falls Convention in 1848 was the start of an organized women's rights movement in the United States. Delegates at the convention called for many reforms, including women's suffrage.

After the Civil War, Elizabeth Cady Stanton and Susan B. Anthony led a renewed drive to win the vote. In 1869, they formed the National Woman Suffrage Association. This group worked to amend the Constitution to give women the vote. Stanton and Anthony opposed the Fifteenth Amendment because it gave the vote to African American men but not to women.

Women vote in the West

Few politicians favored women's suffrage. Still, in the late 1800s, women gained the right to vote in four western states: Wyoming, Utah, Colorado, and Idaho. Pioneer women had worked alongside men

Biography Carrie Chapman Catt

Carrie Chapman Catt was the only woman in Iowa State College's Class of 1880. She became a tireless lecturer and fighter for women's suffrage. In 1919, she visited 13 states in 8 weeks, urging listeners to ratify the Nineteenth Amendment. After ratification, she declared that women were finally "free and equal citizens." ★ **What strategy did Catt use to win the vote?**

to build the farms and cities of the West. By giving women the vote, these states recognized women's contributions.

When Wyoming applied for statehood in 1890, many members of Congress wanted the state to change its voting law. During the debate, Wyoming lawmakers wired Congress: "We may stay out of the Union for 100 years, but we will come in with our women." Wyoming barely won admission.

Suffragists

In the early 1900s, the women's suffrage movement gained strength. More than 5 million women were earning wages outside the home. Although women were paid less than men, wages gave women a sense of power. Many demanded a say in making the laws that governed them.

By 1906, Elizabeth Cady Stanton and Susan B. Anthony had died. A new generation of leaders took up their cause. **Carrie Chapman Catt** spoke powerfully in favor of suffrage. Catt had worked as a school principal and a reporter. Later, she became head of the National American Woman Suffrage Association.

Catt was an inspired speaker and a brilliant organizer. She devised a detailed battle plan for fighting the war for suffrage, state by state. Around the country, **suffragists,** or people who campaigned for women's right to vote, followed her strategy.

Slowly, the efforts of Catt and other suffragists succeeded. Year by year, more states in the West and Midwest gave women the vote. For the most part, women in these states were allowed to vote only in state elections. In time, more and more women called for an amendment to the Constitution to give them a voice in national elections.

Amending the Constitution

Some suffragists took strong measures to achieve their goal. **Alice Paul** was one of them. In 1907, Paul had gone to England. There, she had marched with suffragists in London. She had been jailed and gone on hunger strikes—all to help British women win the vote. Later, Paul returned home to support the cause of suffrage for American women.

Protest at the White House

Paul and other suffragists met with President Wilson soon after he took office in 1913. Wilson was not opposed to women's suffrage. He did not, however, support a constitutional amendment. Paul told the President what suffragists wanted:

> “We said we're going to try and get [a constitutional amendment] through Congress, that we would like to have his help and needed his support very much. And then we sent him another delegation and another and another and another and another and another and another—every type of women's group we could get.”

In January 1917, Paul and other women stopped sending delegations and began to picket at the White House. After several months of these silent demonstrations, police began arresting the protesters. Paul received a seven-month jail sentence for obstructing the sidewalk. To protest their arrest, Paul and others went on a hunger strike. Prison officials force fed the women in an attempt to end the strike. Upon release, Paul and the other women resumed their picketing.

Victory at last

By early 1918, the tide began to turn in favor of the suffrage cause. The tireless work of Catt, Paul, and others began to pay off. President Wilson agreed to support the suffrage amendment.

Finally, in 1919, Congress passed the **Nineteenth Amendment** guaranteeing women the right to vote. By August 1920, three fourths of the states had ratified the Nineteenth Amendment. The amendment doubled the number of eligible voters in the United States.

Women Win New Opportunities

For years, women struggled to open doors to jobs and education. Most states refused to grant women licenses to practice in professions such as law, medicine, or college teaching. Myra Bradwell taught herself law, just as Abraham Lincoln had done. Still, Illinois denied her a license in 1869 because she was a woman. In 1890, Illinois at last let Bradwell practice law.

Higher education

Despite obstacles, a few women managed to get the higher education needed to enter the professions. In 1877, Boston University granted the first Ph.D. to a woman. In the next decades, women made important advances. By 1900, about 1,000 women lawyers and 7,000 women doctors were in practice.

Women entered the sciences, too. Mary Engle Pennington earned a degree in chemistry. She became the nation's top expert on preserving foods.

Viewing History **Suffragists on the March**

Suffragists parading for the right to vote were a common sight in many cities and towns. These women, along with their children, are marching down a New York City street in 1912. ★ **Why do you think these suffragists carried American flags as they marched?**

Window banner from 1915

The Vote for Women by 1919

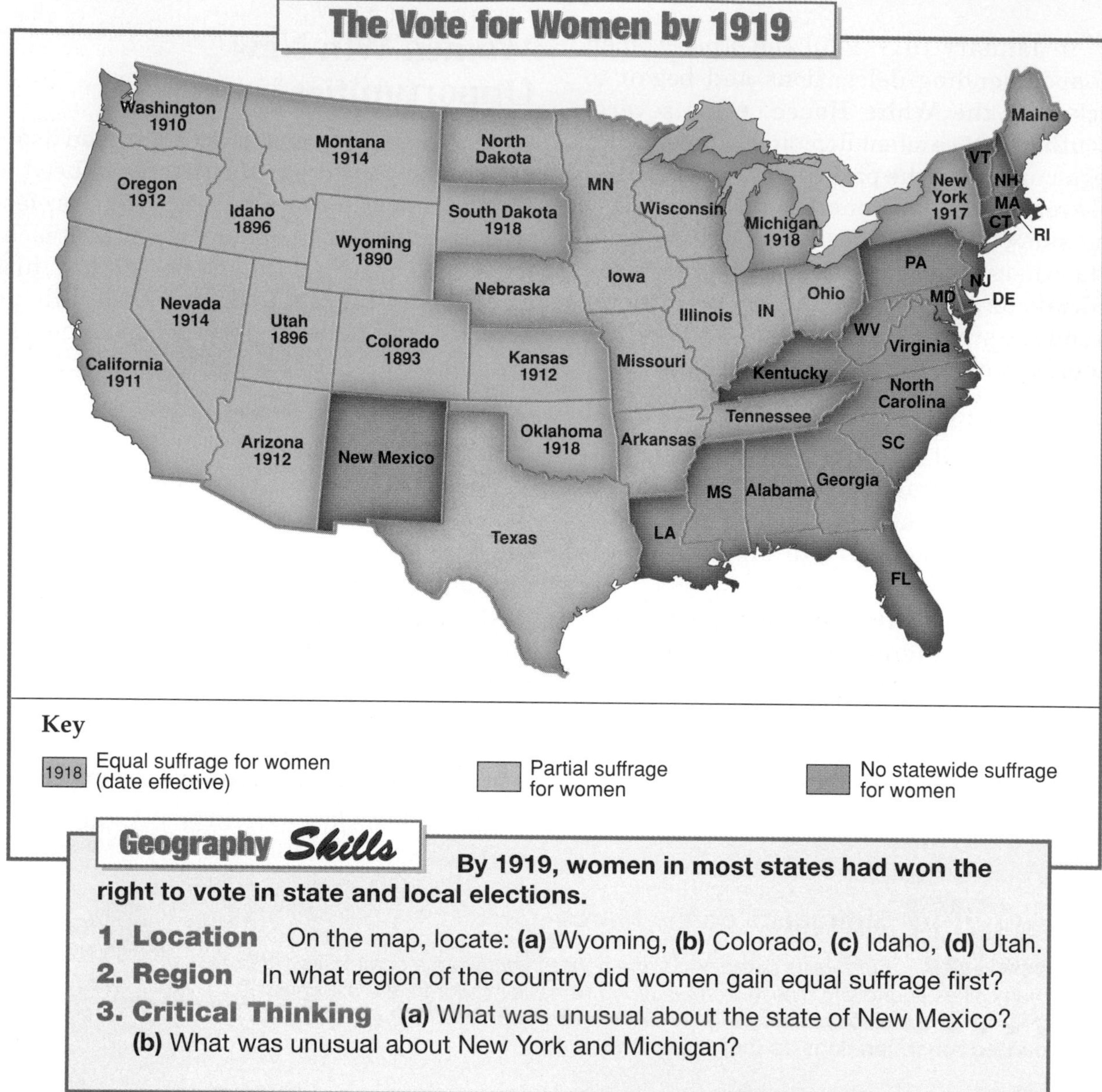

Geography *Skills* **By 1919, women in most states had won the right to vote in state and local elections.**

1. **Location** On the map, locate: **(a)** Wyoming, **(b)** Colorado, **(c)** Idaho, **(d)** Utah.
2. **Region** In what region of the country did women gain equal suffrage first?
3. **Critical Thinking** **(a)** What was unusual about the state of New Mexico? **(b)** What was unusual about New York and Michigan?

Commitment to reform

Women in the Progressive Era were committed to reform. Some entered the new profession of social work. Others worked to call attention to social ills. **Florence Kelley** investigated conditions in sweatshops. She became the first chief factory inspector for the state of Illinois.

Kelley's chief concern was child labor. As secretary of the National Consumer's League (NCL), she organized a boycott of products made with child labor. The NCL published a list of manufacturers whose factories met their approval. By 1907, many businesses vied to get the NCL "white label" of approval on their products.

Many women joined the women's clubs that had sprung up in the late 1800s. At first, clubwomen read books, went to plays, and sought other ways to improve their minds. By the early 1900s, they were caught up in the reform spirit. Clubwomen raised money for libraries, schools, and parks. They fought for laws to protect women and children, for pure food and drug laws, and for the right to vote.

Faced with racial barriers, African American women formed their own clubs, such as the National Association of Colored Women. These members crusaded against lynching and racial separation, as well as for suffrage and other causes.

The Temperance Crusade

The **temperance movement** against the use of alcoholic beverages began in the early 1800s. By the end of the century, the temperance movement was gaining strength.

Women reformers were the major force in the crusade against alcohol. Many wives and mothers recognized alcohol as a threat to their families. Drinking was a frequent cause of violence and economic hardship in the home. Other women campaigned against the saloon for political reasons. In saloons, male political bosses often decided matters of politics far from the reach of women. Most saloons refused entry to women.

Willard and Nation

In 1874, a group of women founded the Women's Christian Temperance Union, or WCTU. **Frances Willard** became a leader of the WCTU. Willard recalled joining temperance leaders as they entered a saloon in Pittsburgh:

> "The tall, stately lady who led us placed her Bible on the bar and read a psalm. . . . Then we sang "Rock of Ages" as I thought I had never sung it before. . . . This was my Crusade baptism. The next day I went on to the West."

In 1880, Willard became president of the WCTU. She worked to educate people about the evils of alcohol. She urged states to pass laws banning the sale of liquor. She also worked to outlaw saloons as a step toward strengthening democracy. Later, Willard joined the suffrage movement, bringing many WCTU members along with her.

A more radical temperance crusader was **Carry Nation.** After her husband died from heavy drinking, Nation dedicated her life to fighting "demon rum." Swinging a hatchet, she stormed into saloons where she smashed beer kegs and liquor bottles. Nation won publicity, but her actions embarrassed many WCTU members.

The Eighteenth Amendment

Temperance crusaders wanted to amend the Constitution to prohibit the sale of liquor. After 1917, support for such an amendment grew. In that year the United States entered World War I. Temperance forces argued that grain used to make liquor should go to feed American soldiers instead.

Temperance leaders finally persuaded Congress to pass the **Eighteenth Amendment** in 1917. By 1919, three fourths of the states had ratified the amendment. The amendment made it illegal to sell alcoholic drinks anywhere in the United States.

★ Section 4 Review ★

Recall

1. **Identify** **(a)** Carrie Chapman Catt, **(b)** Alice Paul, **(c)** Nineteenth Amendment, **(d)** Florence Kelley, **(e)** Frances Willard, **(f)** Carry Nation, **(g)** Eighteenth Amendment.
2. **Define** **(a)** suffragist, **(b)** temperance movement.

Comprehension

3. Describe two methods suffragists used to achieve their goal.
4. Describe two opportunities women gained during the Progressive Era.
5. Why did many women support temperance?

Critical Thinking and Writing

6. **Defending a Position** Do you think Alice Paul's tactics to win suffrage for women were necessary? Explain your position.
7. **Linking Past and Present** Frances Willard considered alcohol a threat to society. What threats does alcohol abuse pose today?

Activity **Writing a Song** You have worked for passage of the Nineteenth Amendment, and finally it has become law. Using a tune you know, write a song celebrating your success.

Fighting for Equality

As You Read

Explore These Questions

- What problems did African Americans face during the Progressive Era?
- How did African American leaders try to fight discrimination?
- What challenges faced other minorities?

Define

- barrio
- mutualista

Identify

- Ida B. Wells
- Booker T. Washington
- W.E.B. Du Bois
- NAACP
- George Washington Carver
- Society of American Indians
- Gentlemen's Agreement

The Thirteenth Amendment abolished slavery in 1865. Yet, 50 years later, life for many African Americans had not changed for the better. One woman declared:

> ❝ Whether in the cook kitchen, at the washtub, over the sewing machine, behind the baby carriage, or at the ironing board, we are but little more than pack horses, beasts of burden, slaves! ❞

In general, white Progressives did little for the needs of nonwhites. It was up to African Americans to help themselves. Mexican Americans, Native Americans, and Asian Americans, too, had to fight for justice.

African Americans

After the end of Reconstruction, African Americans in the South lost their hard-won political rights. Jim Crow laws led to segregation in schools, trains, and other public places. (See Chapter 16.)

Northern blacks also faced prejudice. Landlords in white neighborhoods refused to rent homes to African Americans. Many hotels and restaurants would not serve blacks. In the North and the South, African Americans were hired only for low-paying jobs.

In the 1890s, life grew worse for African Americans. The depression of 1893 threw many people out of work. In some areas, mainly in the South, unemployed whites took out their anger on blacks. In the 1890s, lynch mobs murdered more than 1,000 blacks.

Such violence outraged the African American journalist **Ida B. Wells.** In her newspaper, *Free Speech,* Wells published shocking statistics about lynching. She urged African Americans to protest by refusing to ride the streetcars or shop in white-owned stores. Wells spoke out despite threats to her life.

Washington's solution

Booker T. Washington offered one answer to the question of how to fight discrimination. In his autobiography, *Up From Slavery,* Washington told how he had succeeded. Born into slavery, he taught himself to read. In 1881, he founded Tuskegee Institute in Alabama. It became a center for black higher education.

Washington stressed living in harmony with whites. He urged African Americans to work patiently and move upward slowly. First, learn trades and earn money, advised Washington. Only then would African Americans have the power to insist on political and social equality.

In the meantime, Washington accepted segregation. "In all things that are purely social," he said, "we can be as separate as the fingers, yet one as the hand in all things essential to mutual progress."

Viewing History: Du Bois Fights for Equality

W.E.B. Du Bois refused to accept discrimination. As editor of The Crisis, *the journal of the NAACP, he spoke out against injustice and demanded equal rights for African Americans. Here, Du Bois is shown standing at right in the offices of* The Crisis. ★ **How did the view of Du Bois differ from those of Booker T. Washington?**

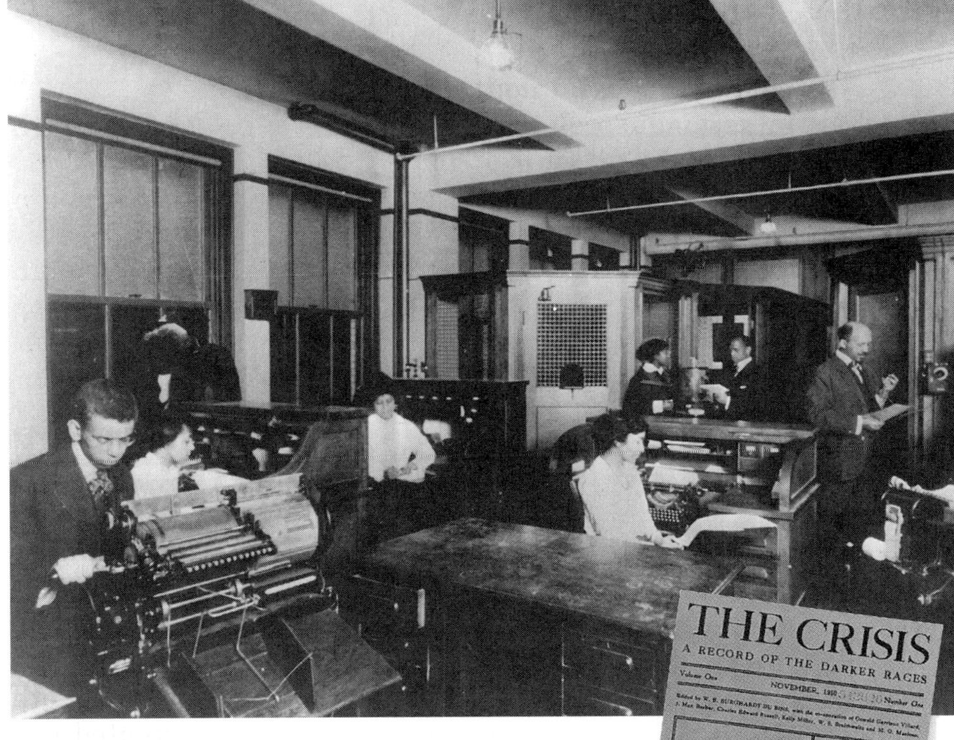

Journal of the NAACP ➤

Booker T. Washington was a spokesman for many African Americans. Business tycoons such as Andrew Carnegie and John D. Rockefeller gave him money to build trade schools for African Americans. Several Presidents sought his advice on racial issues.

Du Bois disagrees

Other African Americans disagreed with Washington. How could blacks move ahead, they asked, when whites denied them advanced education and jobs? Racial harmony was impossible when whites were lynching blacks and denying them the right to vote.

W.E.B. Du Bois (doo BOYS) was one leader who took this view. Du Bois was a professor, author, and public speaker. In 1895, he became the first African American to earn a Ph.D. from Harvard University.

Du Bois agreed with Booker T. Washington on the need for "thrift, patience, and industrial training." However, he added, "So far as Mr. Washington apologizes for injustice, we must firmly oppose him." Instead, Du Bois urged blacks to fight discrimination actively.

In 1909, Du Bois joined with Jane Addams, Lincoln Steffens, and other reformers to form the National Association for the Advancement of Colored People, or **NAACP.** Blacks and whites in the NAACP worked to gain equal rights for African Americans.

Obstacles and successes

Still, most Progressives thought little about the problems of African Americans. When black soldiers were accused of rioting in Brownsville, Texas, President Roosevelt ordered their whole regiment to be dishonorably discharged. Later, President Wilson ordered the segregation of black and white government workers. When black leaders protested, Wilson replied that "segregation is not humiliating, but a benefit." His action led hotels, restaurants, and stores in the nation's capital to enforce segregation.

Some African Americans succeeded despite huge obstacles. **George Washington Carver** discovered hundreds of new uses for peanuts and other crops grown in the South.

Connections With Science

George Washington Carver established a "school on wheels." In this traveling classroom, he taught Alabama farmers how intensive cultivation of cotton and tobacco depleted the soil, while growing peanuts and sweet potatoes helped to enrich it.

Chapter 21

Becoming a World Power

1865–1916

What's Ahead

Section 1
Across the Pacific

Section 2
The Spanish-American War

Section 3
Relations With Latin America

The United States increased its role in world affairs throughout the second half of the nineteenth century. As the nation became an industrial and commercial power, American leaders sought new trade opportunities in Asia. Alaska, Hawaii, and other overseas territories came under United States control.

As a result of the Spanish-American War of 1898, the United States acquired an overseas empire. After the war, the United States played an increasing role in the affairs of Latin America. As a result, many Latin Americans began to view the United States with distrust and anger.

Why Study History?

In 1898, the United States sent soldiers to Cuba to help Cubans gain independence from Spain. Today, the United States continues to send American soldiers to troubled spots around the world. To study some of the reasons for these actions, see this chapter's *Why Study History?* feature, "Americans Are Involved in World Affairs."

American Events

1867 United States buys Alaska from Russia

1898 United States defeats Spain in Spanish-American War

1899 Open Door Policy keeps trade with China open to all nations

1865 — 1890 — 1895 — 1900

World Events

1870s World Event Age of Imperialism begins

1895 World Event Cubans rebel against Spain

Viewing HISTORY

The Great White Fleet

In this painting by Henry Reuterdahl, the "Great White Fleet" of the United States steams into the harbor of San Francisco. The fleet, named for the fact that its ships were painted white, proclaimed the new role of the United States in the world. In his autobiography, President Theodore Roosevelt referred to the fleet as "the most important service that I rendered to peace." ★ **What do you think Roosevelt meant by his statement?**

1900
Hawaii becomes territory of United States

1904
President Roosevelt declares right of United States to intervene in Latin America

1914
Panama Canal opens

1900 **1905** **1910** **1915**

1904 World Event
Russo-Japanese war begins

1911 World Event
Revolution in China begins

Across the Pacific

Explore These Questions

- How did treaties with Japan and Russia benefit the United States?
- Why did some Americans favor imperialism in the late 1800s?
- How did United States policy concerning Hawaii differ from American policy in China?

Define

- isolationism
- expansionism
- annex
- imperialism
- sphere of influence

Identify

- Matthew Perry
- Treaty of Kanagawa
- William Seward
- Alfred Mahan
- Great White Fleet
- Liliuokalani
- John Hay
- Open Door Policy
- Boxer Rebellion

In 1880, the ruler of the Turkish empire thought of a way to save his country money. He would shut down his nation's embassies in "minor" countries. One of these minor countries was the United States, a nation known to play only a small role in world affairs.

Turkey's plan was badly timed. By 1880, the United States was making moves to increase its diplomatic contacts with the rest of the world. In fact, it was on the verge of becoming a world power.

Isolationism and Expansionism

In his Farewell Address, as you recall, George Washington had advised the nation to "steer clear of permanent alliances." He urged Americans to have "as little political connection as possible" with foreign nations. Later Presidents continued this policy of **isolationism,** or having little to do with the political affairs of other nations. Americans had no wish to be dragged into Europe's frequent wars.

Earlier in his career, however, Washington had also called the United States a "rising empire." Indeed, from its earliest existence, the American republic followed a policy of **expansionism,** or extending its national boundaries. The people of the United States were constantly pressing westward across the continent.

At the same time, Americans conducted a lively foreign trade. From the early 1700s, sailing ships carried American goods to Europe. American traders also traveled to Asia, including China and the Philippines. The Asian nation of Japan, however, refused to open its doors to American trade.

Opening Trade With Japan

Japan was a small island nation. Fearing outsiders, the Japanese had cut themselves off from the world in the 1600s. They expelled all Westerners* and allowed only one ship a year—from the Dutch East India Company—to trade at the port of Nagasaki. Foreign sailors wrecked on the shores of Japan were not allowed to leave.

Perry's mission

American merchants wanted to open Japan to trade. They also wanted the Japanese to help shipwrecked sailors who washed up on their shores. To achieve these goals, President Millard Fillmore sent Commodore **Matthew Perry** to Japan in the early 1850s.

With four warships, Perry entered Tokyo Bay in July 1853. The Japanese had never seen steam-powered ships. They denounced the Americans as "barbarians in floating volcanoes" and ordered them to leave.

* To the Japanese, Westerners were white people from Europe and North America.

Before departing, Perry presented Japanese officials with a letter from President Fillmore. In it, the President asked the Japanese to open trading relations with the United States. Perry said he would return the following year for an answer.

A new treaty

Perry returned in February 1854, this time with seven warships. Impressed by this show of strength, the Japanese emperor signed the **Treaty of Kanagawa.** The treaty accepted American demands to help shipwrecked sailors. It also opened two Japanese ports to trade.

Perry's visit had important effects. First, it launched trade between Japan and the West. Second, it made the Japanese aware of the power of the Western industrial nations. As a result, Japan soon set out to become a modern, industrial nation itself, with the United States as one of its models.

Viewing History **Opening Trade With Japan**

Perry's mission to Japan in 1853 is portrayed in the painting Perry's First Landing in Japan at Kurihama *by Gessan Ogata. Perry gave the Japanese many gifts, including several clocks, a telescope, and a toy train.* ★ **Why did the United States government send Perry to Japan?**

Toy train given as a gift to Japan

The Purchase of Alaska

American interest in Asia and the Pacific continued. In the 1860s, Secretary of State **William Seward** wanted the United States to dominate trade in the Pacific. In 1867, he persuaded Congress to **annex** Midway Island, in the middle of the Pacific Ocean. In this way, the island became part of the United States. In that same year, Seward made a deal to buy the vast territory of Alaska.

An amazing land deal

In the 1800s, Alaska belonged to Russia. The Russians, however, were eager to get rid of the territory, which was too far away to govern effectively. Seward saw Alaska as an important stepping stone for increasing United States commerce in Asia and the Pacific.

One night in 1867, Seward was playing cards in Washington, D.C. He was interrupted by a message from the Russian ambassador. The czar of Russia, said the ambassador, was willing to sell Alaska to the United States for $7.2 million. Seward did not hesitate. He agreed to buy the land then and there.

"But your Department is closed," said the ambassador. "Never mind that," Seward replied. "Before midnight you will find me at the Department, which will be open and ready for business."

Next morning, Seward completed the deal. The cost came to 2 cents an acre. The purchase of Alaska increased the area of the United States by almost one fifth.

"Seward's Folly"

To most Americans, the purchase of Alaska—which they thought of as a barren land of icy mountains and frozen fish—seemed foolish. They mockingly called Alaska "Seward's Ice Box" and referred to the purchase as "Seward's Folly."

AmericanHeritage
MAGAZINE

HISTORY HAPPENED HERE

White Pass and Yukon Railroad

This rail line was built during the mad gold rush of 1898. It carried miners and supplies from Skagway, Alaska, to the rich Klondike goldfields in Canada. Today, tourists can ride the train along the very trail that the miners used in 1898. As you view the spectacular natural beauty of Alaska's mountains, you pass Bridal Veil Falls, Inspiration Point, and Dead Horse Gulch.

★ ***To learn more about this historic site, write:*** *White Pass and Yukon Railroad, P.O. Box 435, Skagway, AK 99840.*

In fact, Seward was correct in considering Alaska a very valuable territory. The lowlands of southern Alaska are well suited to farming. The land is also rich in timber, copper, and other natural resources. In the 1890s, miners rushed to the territory after prospectors found gold in Alaska and nearby Canada. In 1959, Alaska was admitted as the forty-ninth state. Today, the state is a very important source of petroleum and natural gas.

Age of Imperialism

The period between 1870 and 1914 has often been called the Age of Imperialism. **Imperialism** is the policy of powerful countries seeking to control the economic and political affairs of weaker countries or regions. Between 1870 and 1914, European nations seized control of almost the entire continent of Africa and much of southern Asia. During this period, the United States and Japan also became imperial powers.

Reasons for imperialism

One reason for the growth of imperialism in the 1800s was economic. The industrial nations of Europe wanted raw materials from Africa and Asia. European factories would use the raw materials to manufacture goods. Some of these goods would then be sold to people in Africa and Asia.

Imperialism had other causes. Many Europeans believed that they had a duty to spread their religion and culture to people whom they considered to be less civilized. British writer Rudyard Kipling called this responsibility "the white man's burden." Such thinking ignored the fact that Africans and Asians already had rich cultures of their own.

A third cause was competition. When a European country colonized an area, it often closed the area's markets to other countries. A European nation might take over an area just to keep a rival nation from gaining control of it.

American interests in empire

Americans could not ignore Europe's race for colonies. By the 1890s, the United States was a world leader in both industry and agriculture. American factories turned out huge amounts of steel and other goods. American farms grew bumper crops of corn, wheat, and cotton. The nation was growing rapidly, and arguments in favor of expansion held great appeal.

Many people believed that the American economy would collapse unless the United States gained new foreign markets for its products. Alfred Beveridge, campaigning for the Senate from Indiana in 1898, summed up the arguments for commercial expansion:

> ❝ Today we are raising more than we can consume. Today we are making more than we can use. Today our industrial society is congested; there are more workers than there is work. . . . Therefore we must find new markets for our produce, new occupations for our capital, new work for our labor. ❞

Expansionists also argued that Americans had a right and a duty to bring Western culture to the "uncivilized" peoples of the world. Josiah Strong, a Congregational minister, declared that Americans were "divinely commissioned" to spread democracy and Christianity "down upon Mexico, down upon Central and South America, out upon the islands of the sea."

Other expansionists stressed the need to offset the vanishing frontier. For 100 years, the economy had boomed as Americans settled the western frontier. The 1890 census said, however, that the frontier was gone. People in crowded eastern cities had no new land to settle. The solution, said some, was to take new land overseas.

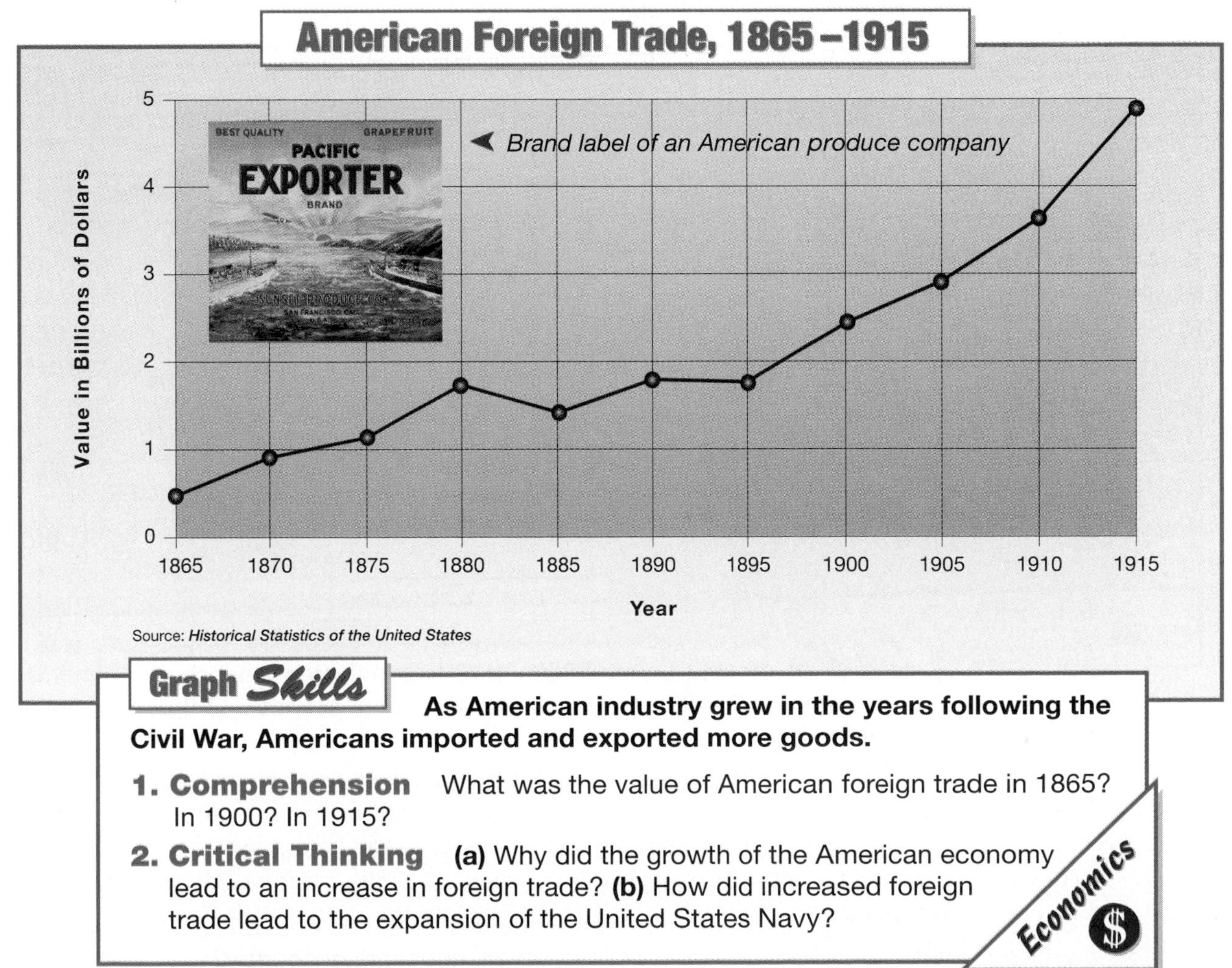

Graph Skills **As American industry grew in the years following the Civil War, Americans imported and exported more goods.**

1. **Comprehension** What was the value of American foreign trade in 1865? In 1900? In 1915?
2. **Critical Thinking** **(a)** Why did the growth of the American economy lead to an increase in foreign trade? **(b)** How did increased foreign trade lead to the expansion of the United States Navy?

American naval power

One leading supporter of American imperialism was Captain **Alfred Mahan** of the United States Navy. He argued that the prosperity of the United States depended on foreign trade. Furthermore, he said a bigger navy was needed to protect American merchant ships. "When a question arises of control over distant regions," Mahan wrote, "it must ultimately be decided by naval power."

In Mahan's view, the United States could not expand its navy unless it acquired overseas territories A bigger navy would need bases throughout the world. Mahan was especially interested in acquiring harbors in the Caribbean and the Pacific as stepping stones to Latin America and Asia.

Even before Mahan's appeal, Congress had begun to enlarge and modernize the navy. New steam-powered warships with steel hulls were already being built in the 1880s. By the late 1890s, a large and powerful American navy was ready for action. Its ships were called the **Great White Fleet** because they were all painted white.

A Naval Base in Samoa

In the 1880s, the United States began showing interest in Samoa, a chain of islands

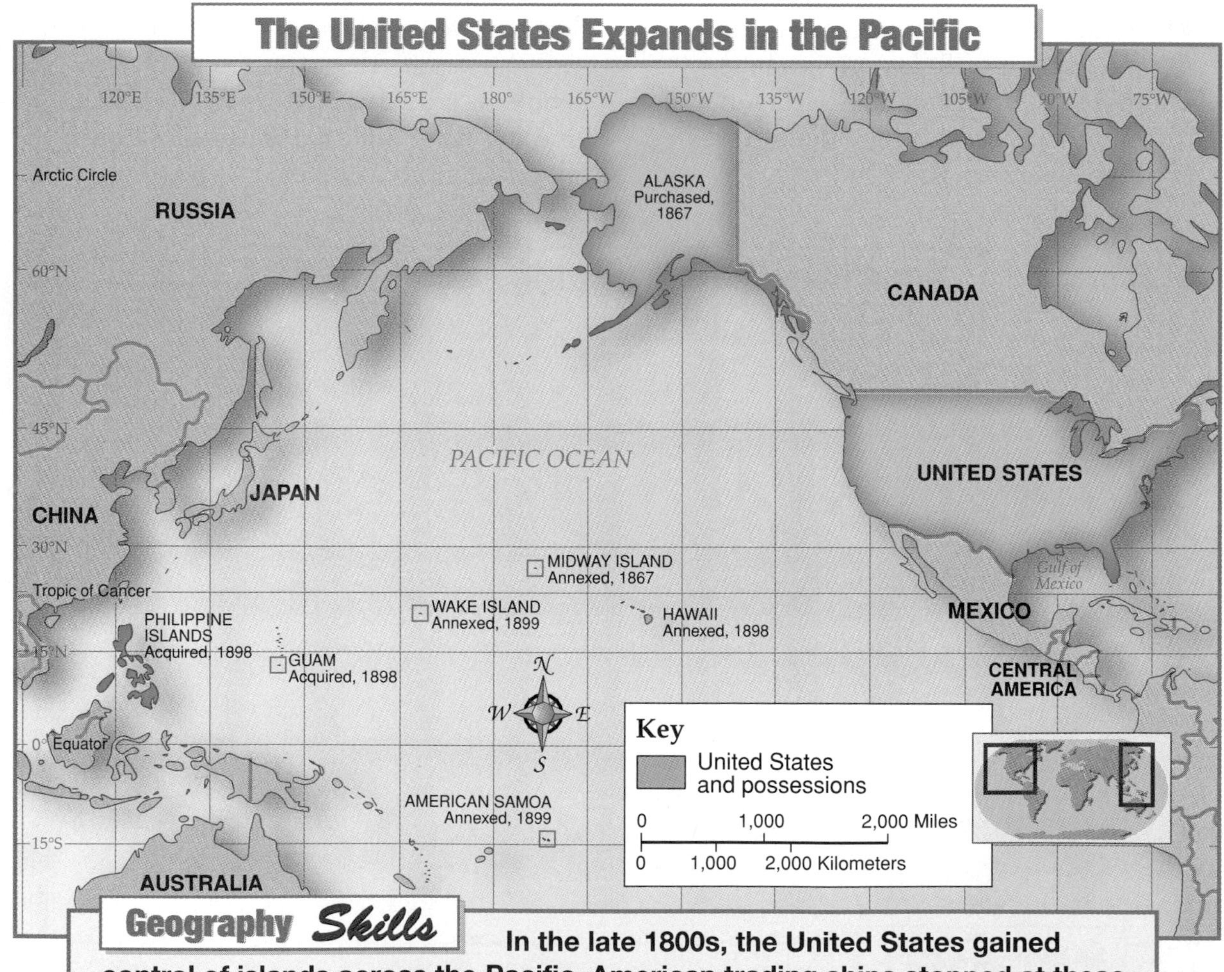

Geography Skills In the late 1800s, the United States gained control of islands across the Pacific. American trading ships stopped at these islands on their way to China and Japan.

1. **Location** On the map, locate: **(a)** Japan, **(b)** China, **(c)** Alaska, **(d)** Hawaii, **(e)** American Samoa.
2. **Region** **(a)** Which Pacific island did the United States acquire first? **(b)** Which territory was farthest from the United States mainland?
3. **Critical Thinking** Compare this map to the world map on pages 778–779. Which United States Pacific possession is now an independent country?

in the South Pacific. Samoa had a fine harbor that could serve as a naval base and commercial port. Germany and Great Britain, however, also realized the value of the harbor. As a result, the three nations competed for control of the islands.

In 1889, a military clash seemed very likely. German ships had fired upon Samoan villages that were friendly to the Americans. For months, German and American sailors eyed each other nervously from their warships. Then, just as tensions were at their highest, a powerful storm struck and sank ships of both countries.

Later, the three nations arranged a peaceful settlement. The United States and Germany divided Samoa, while Britain received territories elsewhere in the Pacific. The people of Samoa, meanwhile, had little say in the matter. The United States had demonstrated that it would assert its power in the Pacific Ocean.

Annexing Hawaii

Another territory that had long interested the United States was Hawaii. Hawaii is a chain of eight large islands and more than 100 smaller islands. They are located in the Pacific Ocean, about 2,400 miles (3,800 km) southwest of California. The islands have rich soil, a warm climate, and plenty of rainfall. These conditions make it possible to grow crops all year round.

About 2,000 years ago, people from Polynesia—islands in the Central and South Pacific—first settled Hawaii. Europeans and Americans first learned about Hawaii in 1778. That year, a British sea captain, James Cook, stopped at the islands for water on his way to China. In the early 1800s, American ships bound for China began stopping in Hawaii, and a few American sailors and traders settled there.

Missionaries and planters

In 1820, the first American missionaries arrived. Their goal was to convert the Hawaiians to Christianity. The missionaries and other Americans advised the rulers of Hawaii from the 1830s on. Americans also helped write Hawaii's first constitution in 1839.

Biography **Liliuokalani**

In her youth, Liliuokalani was educated by an American missionary. She also toured the United States and Europe. As queen of Hawaii, however, she worked to reduce foreign influence in her country. ★ **How did Liliuokalani oppose American influence in Hawaii?**

Hawaiian royal crown ➤

By the mid-1800s, Americans had set up large sugar plantations in Hawaii. The planters wanted cheap labor. They brought thousands of workers from China, Korea, the Philippines, and Japan. By 1900, one fourth of Hawaii's population had been born in Japan.

As the sugar industry grew, so did the power of American planters. In 1887, they forced the Hawaiian king, Kalakaua, to accept a new constitution. It reduced the king's power and increased the planters' influence.

Planters stage a revolt

In 1891, Kalakaua died, and his sister **Liliuokalani** (lih lee oo oh kah LAH nee) came to the throne. The new queen cherished Hawaiian independence and deeply resented the growing power of American planters. She

Viewing HISTORY **Rivalry in China**

In this cartoon, titled "Putting His Foot Down," Uncle Sam holds a copy of the treaty that put the Open Door Policy into effect. The figures holding scissors represent (left to right) Germany, Italy, Britain, Austria (background), Russia, and France.
★ **Why are the figures holding scissors?**

therefore rejected the new constitution. She hoped to reduce the influence and privileges of foreign merchants.

In early 1893, the American planters rebelled against the queen's attempt to limit their power. The American ambassador called for United States marines to land on Hawaii and protect American lives. In fact, the marines helped topple the queen.

Faced with American guns, Liliuokalani gave up her throne. However, she wrote a protest to the United States government:

> "I, Liliuokalani, . . . do hereby solemnly protest against any and all acts done against myself and the constitutional Government of the Hawaiian Kingdom. . . .
>
> I yield to the superior force of the United States of America, whose [ambassador] . . . has caused United States troops to be landed [on Hawaii]. . . .
>
> Now, to avoid any collision of armed forces and perhaps the loss of life, I do this under protest, and impelled by said force, yield my authority."

Connections With Civics

Liliuokalani later sued the United States government for losses totaling $450,000. The lawsuit was unsuccessful. However, the Hawaiian territorial government granted her a pension of $4,000 per year and allowed her some income from a sugar plantation.

A United States territory

With Liliuokalani gone, the planters quickly set up a republic and asked the United States to annex Hawaii. A debate raged in Congress for months. President Grover Cleveland blocked moves to take over the islands. "Our interference in the Hawaiian Revolution of 1893 was disgraceful," he later said. "I am ashamed of the whole affair."

Congress finally annexed Hawaii in 1898, after Cleveland left office. Two years later, Hawaii became a United States territory. In 1959, Hawaii became the fiftieth state.

Rivalry in China

By acquiring Hawaii and Samoa, the United States gained important footholds in the Pacific. Still, the United States was a latecomer in the race for Pacific and Asian territory. Britain, Germany, Japan, and other nations were already competing for colonies in Asia. Rivalry among the industrial nations was especially fierce in China.

China had once been the most advanced empire in the world. However, years of civil war had weakened the empire. In addition, China had failed to industrialize as other nations had in the 1800s. As a result, it was unable to fight off industrial nations that wanted to reap profits from its vast resources and markets.

The Open Door Policy

In the late 1800s, Britain, France, Germany, Russia, and Japan carved spheres of influence in China. A **sphere of influence** was an area, usually around a seaport, where a nation had special trading privileges. Each nation made laws for its own citizens in its own sphere.

American leaders feared that the Europeans and Japanese would try to bar the United States from trading in China. In 1899, therefore, Secretary of State **John Hay** sent a letter to all the nations that had spheres of influence in China. He urged them to follow an **Open Door Policy** in China. Under the policy, any nation could trade in the spheres of others.

Reluctantly, the imperialist powers accepted the Open Door Policy. The agreement allowed the United States to trade freely with the Chinese without interference from the foreign powers in China.

The Boxer Rebellion

Many Chinese opposed foreign influence in their country. In 1899, some of them set up a secret society called the Righteous Fists of Harmony, or Boxers. The Boxers wanted to rid China of "foreign devils."

In 1900, the Boxers rebelled. They attacked foreigners all over China, killing more than 200. The Boxers trapped hundreds of foreigners in Beijing, the Chinese capital. Foreign governments quickly organized an international army that included 2,500 Americans. Armed with modern weapons, the international army fought its way into Beijing. They freed the trapped foreigners and crushed the rebellion.

Several nations saw the **Boxer Rebellion** as an excuse to seize more land in China. Secretary of State Hay sent another Open Door letter, urging all nations to respect China's independence. Britain, France, and Germany accepted Hay's letter. Japan and Russia, fearing that any attempt to divide China might lead to war, quietly observed Hay's policy. Hay's Open Door letters showed that the United States was playing a new role in world affairs.

★ Section 1 Review ★

Recall

1. **Locate** **(a)** Japan, **(b)** Alaska, **(c)** Samoa, **(d)** Hawaii, **(e)** China.
2. **Identify** **(a)** Matthew Perry, **(b)** Treaty of Kanagawa, **(c)** William Seward, **(d)** Alfred Mahan, **(e)** Great White Fleet, **(f)** Liliuokalani, **(g)** John Hay, **(h)** Open Door Policy, **(i)** Boxer Rebellion.
3. **Define** **(a)** isolationism, **(b)** expansionism, **(c)** annex, **(d)** imperialism, **(e)** sphere of influence.

Comprehension

4. How did the United States benefit from: **(a)** the Treaty of Kanagawa; **(b)** the purchase of Alaska?
5. In the late 1800s, why did some Americans favor a policy of imperialism?
6. **(a)** How did United States policy concerning Hawaii differ from the policy concerning China? **(b)** Why did the United States pursue these different policies?

Critical Thinking and Writing

7. **Understanding Causes and Effects** What were the causes and effects of the 1893 rebellion against Hawaii's Queen Liliuokalani?
8. **Linking Past and Present** Do you think that the United States could follow a policy of isolationism today? Explain.

Activity **Summarizing Ideas** You are Secretary of State William Seward. Write a brief telegram to Congress and the President summarizing your reasons for buying Alaska and annexing Midway Island.

The Spanish-American War

As You Read

Explore These Questions
- What were the causes of the Spanish-American War?
- What were the major events of the war?
- What were the results of the war?

Define
- yellow journalism
- armistice
- protectorate

Identify
- Lola Rodríguez de Tió
- José Martí
- George Dewey
- Emilio Aguinaldo
- Rough Riders
- Battle of San Juan Hill
- Platt Amendment
- Foraker Act

Replica of 1890s United States Army hat

In the late 1890s, Americans opened their daily newspapers to find shocking tales of violence. The reports told about a revolution in Cuba, a Spanish-owned island just 90 miles off the Florida coast. A typical story cried out against Spanish actions toward the Cuban people:

> ❝ Blood on the roadsides, blood in the fields, blood on the doorsteps, blood, blood, blood! ❞

Such sensational reports were often inaccurate or one-sided. Yet they succeeded in stirring American anger against Spain. In 1898, the United States put aside its long policy of neutrality to intervene in the Cuban revolution. In the process, American power grew in the Caribbean and across the Pacific.

Trouble in Cuba

For many years, Americans had looked longingly at Cuba. In 1823, Secretary of State John Quincy Adams compared Cuba to a ripe apple. A storm, he said, might tear that apple "from its native tree"—the Spanish empire—and drop it into American hands.

By the 1890s, Spain's once-vast empire in the Western Hemisphere had shrunk to two islands in the Caribbean, Cuba and Puerto Rico. Then, Cuban rebels created the storm that Adams had hoped for.

Revolts against Spain

In 1868, the Cuban people had rebelled against Spanish rule. The revolution was finally crushed after 10 years of fighting. Some of the revolutionaries fled to New York where they kept up the battle for freedom. **Lola Rodríguez de Tió** wrote patriotic poems in support of Cuban independence. **José Martí** told of the Cuban struggle for freedom in his newspaper, *Patria*.

In 1895, Martí returned to Cuba. With cries of *Cuba Libre!*—Free Cuba!—rebels launched a new fight against Spain. Martí died early in the fighting, but the rebels won control of much of the island.

The rebels burned sugar cane fields and sugar mills all over Cuba. They hoped that this would make the island unprofitable for Spain, and convince the Spanish to leave. The rebels killed workers who opposed them. They even blew up some passenger trains.

In response, Spain sent a new governor to Cuba, General Valeriano Weyler (WAY ee lair). Weyler used brutal tactics to crush the revolt.

$ Connections With Economics

An American tariff helped cause the Cuban Revolution. The Wilson-Gorman Tariff of 1894 placed a high tariff on imported sugar. As Americans bought less Cuban sugar, the island's economy declined. Increasing poverty contributed to popular discontent.

His men moved about half a million Cubans into detention camps so they could not aid the rebels. At least 100,000 died from starvation and disease.

Americans react

In the United States, people watched the revolt in nearby Cuba with growing concern. Americans had invested about $50 million in the island. The money was invested in sugar and rice plantations, railroads, tobacco, and iron mines. American trade with Cuba was worth about $100 million a year.

Opinion split over whether the United States should intervene in Cuba. Many business leaders opposed American involvement. They thought that it might hurt trade. Other Americans sympathized with Cuban desires for freedom and wanted the government to take action.

War Fever

The press whipped up American sympathies for Cuba. Two New York newspapers—Joseph Pulitzer's *World* and William Randolph Hearst's *Journal*—competed to print the most grisly stories about Spanish cruelty. The publishers knew that war with Spain would boost sales of their newspapers.

Yellow journalism

To attract readers, Hearst and Pulitzer used **yellow journalism**, or sensational stories that were often biased or untrue. "You supply the pictures," Pulitzer told a photographer bound for Cuba. "I'll supply the war." News stories described events in Cuba in graphic and horrifying detail.

President Cleveland wanted to avoid war with Spain. He called the war fever in the United States an "epidemic of insanity." Stories in the press, he grumbled, were nonsense. When William McKinley became President in 1897, he also tried to keep the country neutral.

Sinking of the *Maine*

In 1898, fighting broke out in Havana, the Cuban capital. Acting promptly, President McKinley sent the battleship *Maine* to Havana to protect American citizens and property there.

On the night of February 15, the *Maine* lay at anchor. Just after the bugler played taps, a huge explosion ripped through the ship. The explosion killed at least 260 of the 350 sailors and officers on board.

The yellow press quickly pounced on the tragedy. "DESTRUCTION OF THE WARSHIP *MAINE* WAS THE WORK OF AN ENEMY," screamed one New York newspaper. "THE WARSHIP *MAINE* SPLIT IN TWO BY AN ENEMY'S SECRET INFERNAL MACHINE?" suggested another.

The real cause of the explosion remains a mystery. Most historians believe it was an accident. But Americans, urged on by Pulitzer and Hearst, clamored for war with Spain. "Remember the *Maine*!" they cried.

Viewing HISTORY **Yellow Journalism**

The front page of the New York Journal and Advertiser *shouted that an enemy had sunk the* Maine. *To the reading public, that enemy was Spain. Today, most historians believe that the explosion was accidental.* ★ **Why did newspaper publishers favor sensationalist headlines such as this?**

$50,000 REWARD.—WHO DESTROYED THE MAINE?—$50,000 REWAR

EDITION FOR GREATER NEW YORK

NEW YORK JOURNAL AND ADVERTISER.

NEW YORK, THURSDAY, FEBRUARY 17, 1898.—16 PAGES. PRICE ONE CENT

DESTRUCTION OF THE WAR SHIP MAINE WAS THE WORK OF AN ENEM

$50,000! $50,000 REWARD! For the Detection of the Perpetrator of the Maine Outrage!

Assistant Secretary Roosevelt Convinced the Explosion of the War Ship Was Not an Accident.

The Journal Offers $50,000 Reward for the Conviction of the Criminals Who Sent 258 American Sailors to Their Death. Naval Officers Unanimous That the Ship Was Destroyed on Purpose.

$50,000! $50,000 REWARD For the Detection of the Perpetrator of the Maine Outrage!

NAVAL OFFICERS THINK THE MAINE WAS DESTROYED BY A SPANISH MINE.

Hidden Mine or a Sunken Torpedo Believed to Have Been the Weapon Used Against the American Man-of-War---Of and Men Tell Thrilling Stories of Being Blown Into the Air Amid a Mass of Shattered Steel and Exploding Shells---Survivors Brought to Key West Scout the Idea of Accident---Spanish Officials Protest Too Much---Our Cabinet Orders a Searching Inquiry---Journal Sends Divers to Havana to Report Upon the Condition of the Wreck. Was the Vessel Anchored Over a Mine?

Still hoping to avoid war, McKinley tried to get Spain to talk with the Cuban rebels. In the end, however, he gave in to war fever. On April 25, 1898, Congress declared war on Spain.

The Spanish-American War

The Spanish-American War lasted only four months. The battlefront stretched from the nearby Caribbean to the distant Philippine Islands.

Fighting in the Philippines

Two months earlier, Assistant Secretary of the Navy Theodore Roosevelt had begun making preparations for a possible war with Spain. Roosevelt realized that a conflict with Spain would be fought, not only in the Caribbean, but wherever Spanish sea power lay. The Philippine Islands, a Spanish colony and Spain's main naval base in the Pacific, would be a major objective.

Roosevelt believed it was important to attack the Spanish in the Philippines as soon as war began. He wired secret orders to Commodore **George Dewey,** commander of the Pacific fleet:

> “Order the squadron . . . to Hong Kong. . . . [I]n the event of declaration of war [with] Spain, your duty will be to see that the Spanish squadron does not leave the Asiatic coast. And then [begin] offensive operations in Philippine Islands.”

Dewey followed Roosevelt's instructions. Immediately after war was declared, the Commodore sailed his fleet swiftly to Manila, the main city of the Philippines. On April 30, 1898, Dewey's ships slipped into Manila

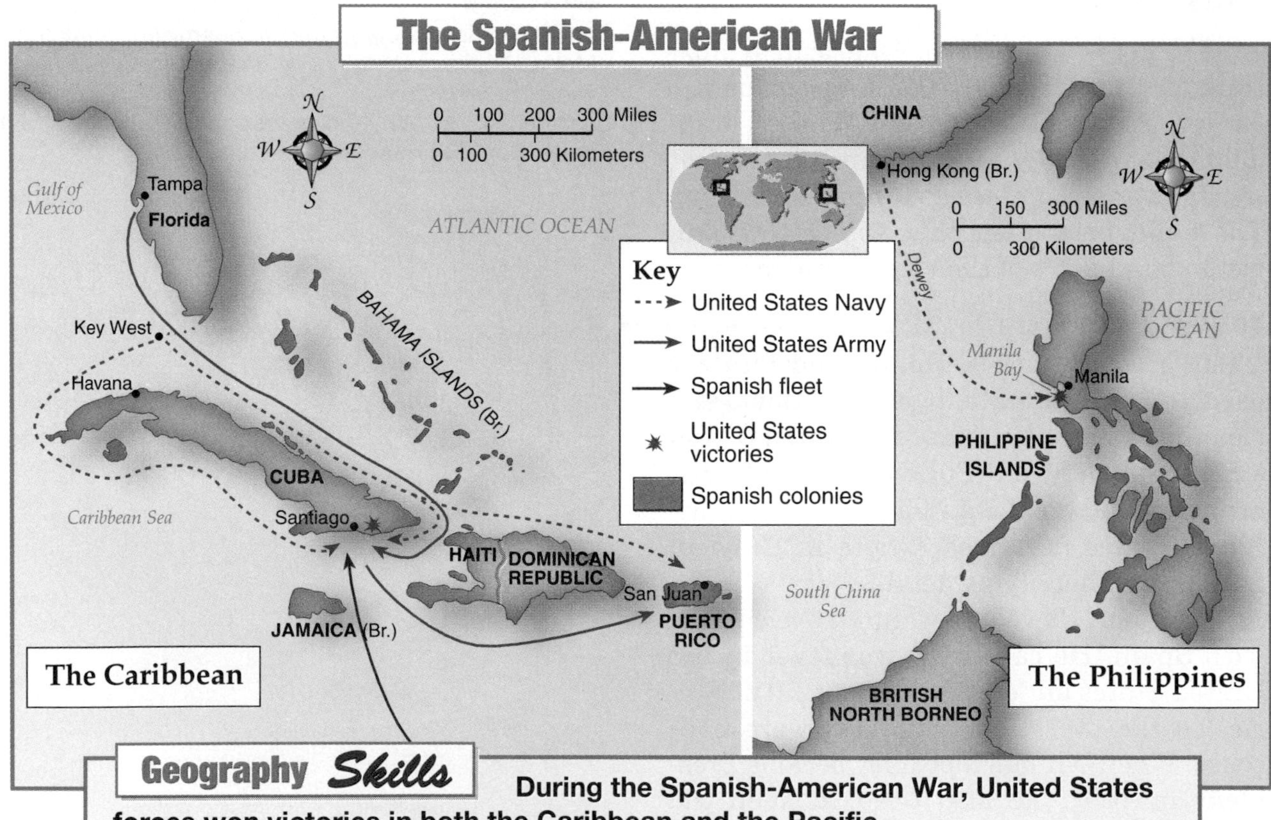

Geography *Skills* **During the Spanish-American War, United States forces won victories in both the Caribbean and the Pacific.**

1. **Location** On the map, locate: **(a)** Caribbean Sea, **(b)** Cuba, **(c)** Philippine Islands, **(d)** Manila Bay.
2. **Movement** **(a)** Describe the route Dewey took to reach the Philippines. **(b)** On what Caribbean islands did American forces land?
3. **Critical Thinking** Why do you think Dewey was able to trap the Spanish fleet in Manila Bay?

harbor under cover of darkness. There lay the Spanish fleet.

At dawn, Dewey told his flagship commander, Charles Gridley, "You may fire when you are ready, Gridley." Taking their cue, the Americans bombarded the surprised Spanish ships. By noon, the Spanish fleet had been destroyed.

In July, American troops landed in the Philippines. As in Cuba, local people had been fighting for independence from Spain for years. With the help of the rebels, led by **Emilio Aguinaldo** (ah gwee NAHL doh), the Americans captured Manila.

Fighting in the Caribbean

Meanwhile, American troops had also landed in Cuba. The expedition was badly organized. Soldiers wore heavy woolen uniforms in the tropical heat, and they often had to eat spoiled food. Yet, most were eager for battle.

None was more eager than Theodore Roosevelt. When the war broke out, Roosevelt resigned his position as Assistant Secretary of the Navy. He then organized the First Volunteer Cavalry Regiment, later called the **Rough Riders.** The Rough Riders were a mixed crew—ranging from cowboys to college students and adventurers.

During the battle for the key Cuban city of Santiago, Roosevelt led the Rough Riders in a charge up San Juan Hill. They were joined by African American soldiers of the 9th and 10th Cavalries. Under withering fire, American troops took the hill. Major John J. Pershing, commander of the 10th Cavalry, described how the troops united in the **Battle of San Juan Hill:**

> "White regiments, black regiments, regulars and Rough Riders, representing the young manhood of the North and South, fought shoulder to shoulder... mindful of their common duty as Americans."

Two days later, the Americans destroyed the Spanish fleet in Santiago Bay. The Spanish army in Cuba surrendered. American troops then landed on Puerto Rico and claimed the island.

Biography **Emilio Aguinaldo**

"Filipino citizens! Now is the occasion for shedding our blood for the last time, that we may achieve our beloved freedom." With these words, Aguinaldo urged Filipinos to throw off Spanish rule. Later, he led an unsuccessful revolt against United States rule. The Philippines did not become an independent nation until 1946. ★ **Was Aguinaldo an imperialist or an anti-imperialist? Explain.**

Spain was defeated. On August 12, Spain and the United States agreed to sign an **armistice,** thus ending the fighting. American losses in battle were fairly light—379 killed. However, more than 5,000 Americans died of other causes, such as yellow fever, typhoid, and malaria.

John Hay, who was soon to become Secretary of State, summed up American enthusiasm for the war. "It's been a splendid little war," he wrote. A malaria-ridden veteran of the war had a different view: "I was lucky—I survived."

Viewing HISTORY **American Soldiers in Cuba**

This United States Army cavalry unit served in Cuba during the Spanish-American War. A number of African American cavalry units also fought against Native Americans in the American West.
★ **How do you think these soldiers felt about fighting in Cuba?**

▲ *Army bugle*

The Fruits of Victory

In a peace treaty signed in Paris in December 1898, Spain agreed to grant Cuba its freedom. Spain also gave the United States two islands: Puerto Rico in the Caribbean and Guam in the Pacific. Finally, in return for $20 million, Spain handed over the Philippines to the United States.

Before the Senate approved the treaty, a great debate occurred. Many Americans objected to the treaty. They said it violated American principles of democracy by turning the United States into a colonial power.

Expansionists favored the treaty. They said that the navy needed bases in the Caribbean and the Pacific. They pointed out that the Philippines and Puerto Rico offered new territory for American businesses. Also, many Americans agreed with President McKinley, who said that the United States would "uplift and civilize and Christianize [the Filipinos]." In fact, most Filipinos already were Christians.

Urged on by McKinley, the Senate narrowly approved the treaty in early 1899. At last, the United States had an empire.

Ruling Cuba and Puerto Rico

Americans had to decide how to rule their new territories. When the war with Spain began, the United States had pledged to "leave the government and control of [Cuba] to its people." That promise was not kept.

After the war, American soldiers remained in Cuba while the nation debated. Many in Congress believed that Cuba was not ready for independence. American business leaders feared that an independent Cuba might threaten their investments there.

In the end, the United States let the Cuban people write their own constitution. However, Cuba had to accept the **Platt Amendment.** The amendment allowed the United States to intervene in Cuba and gave the United States control of the naval base at Guantanamo Bay.

Why Study History?

Because Americans Are Involved in World Affairs

★ ★

Historical Background

In 1897, American observer William Calhoun described the terrible situation in Cuba. "Every house had been burned... and everything in the shape of food destroyed. ... The country was wrapped in the stillness of death."

Both Cuban rebels and Spanish soldiers were responsible for the destruction. All over the island, rebels had burned sugar fields so that Cuba would not yield a profit for Spain. To prevent people from aiding the rebels, the Spanish moved 500,000 Cubans into detention camps. One hundred thousand people, including women and children, died from lack of food, shelter, and medicine.

Economic and humanitarian concerns fueled the drive for the United States to get involved. On April 19, 1898, the United States Congress recognized Cuban independence and authorized President McKinley to use military force to end the fighting in Cuba. On April 24, Spain declared war on the United States.

An American soldier in Somalia

Connections to Today

When should the United States intervene in conflicts within or between other nations? Some say only when vital American interests are at stake. Such was the case when Iraq invaded Kuwait and threatened the United States oil supply. In the Persian Gulf War that followed, American and United Nations military forces defeated Iraq.

Other people think that the United States should also intervene for humanitarian reasons. American peacekeeping forces were sent to Somalia in Africa to help the innocent victims of a civil war. The war itself did not provide a direct threat to the United States in this case.

Connections to You

What do you think? Under what circumstances should the United States commit American soldiers to foreign military conflicts? The question is one that each generation of Americans must answer for themselves by weighing the benefits of a policy against its costs. The answer is not always easy.

1. **Comprehension** Why did the United States get involved in the war in Cuba?
2. **Critical Thinking** How can American voters influence United States foreign policy decisions?

Writing an Editorial Do research to learn about a current or recent military intervention by the United States. Then write an editorial in which you agree or disagree with the use of American military power in this case.

In effect, the amendment made Cuba an American **protectorate**, a nation whose independence is limited by the control of a more powerful country. The United States pulled its army out of Cuba in 1904. However, American soldiers would return to Cuba in 1906 and again in 1917.

In Puerto Rico, the United States set up a new government under the **Foraker Act** of 1900. The act gave Puerto Ricans only a limited say in their own affairs. In 1917, Puerto Ricans were made citizens of the United States. Americans set up schools, improved health care, and built roads on the island. Even so, many Puerto Ricans wanted to be free of foreign rule.

Filipino War for Independence

Filipino nationalists had begun fighting for independence long before the Spanish-American War. When the United States took over their land after the war, Filipinos felt betrayed. Led by Emilio Aguinaldo, they now fought for freedom against a new imperial power—the United States.

Aguinaldo, who had fought beside the Americans against Spain, accused the United States of forgetting its beginnings. The United States, he said, was using military force to keep the Filipinos from attaining "the same rights that the American people proclaimed more than a century ago."

The war in the Philippines dragged on for years. At one point, more than 70,000 American troops were fighting there. Aguinaldo was captured in 1901, and the war finally came to an end.

The war against Aguinaldo's nationalists was longer and more costly than the original war against Spain in 1898. More than 4,000 Americans died in the Philippines. Nearly 20,000 Filipino soldiers were killed. Another 200,000 civilians died from shelling, famine, and disease.

In 1902, the United States set up a government in the Philippines similar to the one in Puerto Rico. Filipinos, however, were not made American citizens because the United States planned to give them independence in the future. It was not until 1946, however, that the United States allowed Filipinos to govern themselves.

★ Section 2 Review ★

Recall

1. **Locate** **(a)** Cuba, **(b)** Philippine Islands, **(c)** Puerto Rico.
2. **Identify** **(a)** Lola Rodríguez de Tió **(b)** José Martí, **(c)** George Dewey, **(d)** Emilio Aguinaldo, **(e)** Rough Riders, **(f)** Battle of San Juan Hill, **(g)** Platt Amendment, **(h)** Foraker Act.
3. **Define** **(a)** yellow journalism, **(b)** armistice, **(c)** protectorate.

Comprehension

4. Explain one long-term cause and one immediate cause of the Spanish-American War.
5. **(a)** How did the United States Navy help win the war? **(b)** How did Theodore Roosevelt contribute to American victory? **(c)** What role did African American soldiers play in the war?
6. How did the war affect the relationship between the United States and each of the following? **(a)** Cuba, **(b)** Puerto Rico, **(c)** Philippines

Critical Thinking and Writing

7. **Analyzing Primary Sources** Review the newspaper headlines that reported the sinking of the *Maine.* How are they examples of yellow journalism?
8. **Analyzing Ideas** Why did Emilio Aguinaldo fight alongside American soldiers as an ally, but later fight against them?

Activity **Drawing a Political Cartoon** You are a journalist covering international affairs after the Spanish-American War. Draw a cartoon about some topic related to the results of the war.

Relations With Latin America

As You Read

Explore These Questions

- Why did the United States build the Panama Canal?
- What policies did the United States adopt toward Latin America?
- Why did the United States invade Mexico in 1916?

Define

- isthmus
- dollar diplomacy
- moral diplomacy

Identify

- William Gorgas
- George Goethals
- Roosevelt Corollary
- Francisco "Pancho" Villa
- John J. Pershing

SETTING the Scene In 1889, Secretary of State James G. Blaine invited Latin American nations to a conference in Washington, D.C. He wanted to remove trade barriers between the United States and Latin America. He also wanted to ease concerns that the United States might extend its growing power across the Western Hemisphere.

The conference failed to remove the fears. The Latin American states refused to open their borders to trade with the United States for fear that a flood of American imports would ruin their own industries. Cuban patriot and writer José Martí charged that the real purpose of the conference was to achieve "an era of United States dominion over the nations of America."

U.S. postage stamp honoring the Panama Canal

Roosevelt and the Panama Canal

When Theodore Roosevelt became President in 1901, he was determined to build a canal through the Isthmus of Panama. (See the map on page 560.) An **isthmus** is a narrow strip of land connecting two larger bodies of land. Panama was a perfect place for a canal because of its location between the Caribbean Sea and the Pacific Ocean. Also, the isthmus was narrow—only about 50 miles (80 km) wide.

Roosevelt knew that a canal through the isthmus would greatly benefit American commerce and military capability. By avoiding the long trip around South America, ships could shorten the journey from New York City to San Francisco by nearly 8,000 miles (12,800 km). Thus, a canal would reduce the cost of shipping goods. In addition, in the event of a war, naval ships could move back and forth between the Pacific Ocean and Atlantic Ocean more quickly than ever before.

A failed deal

In order to build the canal, Roosevelt had to deal with Colombia, the Latin American country to which Panama belonged. Roosevelt asked Secretary of State John Hay to approach Colombia. Hay offered $10 million cash plus $250,000 a year to rent a strip of land across Panama. Colombian officials turned down the offer.

President Roosevelt was furious. He exclaimed to Secretary of State Hay:

> "I do not think the [Colombian] lot of obstructionists should be allowed permanently to bar one of the future highways of civilization."

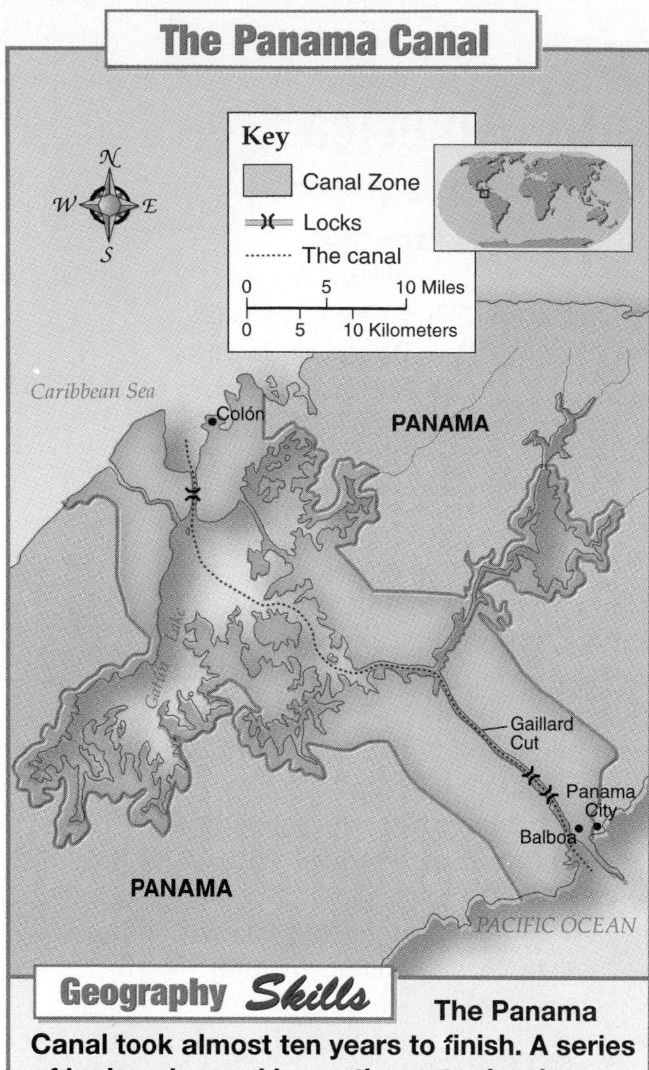

Geography *Skills* **The Panama Canal took almost ten years to finish. A series of locks raise and lower the water level so that ships can move through the canal.**

1. **Location** On the map, locate: **(a)** Panama, **(b)** Canal Zone, **(c)** Panama City.
2. **Movement** In what direction do ships travel to get from the Caribbean Sea to the Pacific Ocean?
3. **Critical Thinking** **(a)** Describe the location of the Canal Zone in relation to the country of Panama. **(b)** How do you think Panamanians felt about United States control of the zone?

At times like this, Roosevelt often quoted an African proverb: "Speak softly and carry a big stick, and you will go far." He meant that words should be supported by strong action.

Revolution in Panama

Roosevelt knew that some Panamanians wanted to rebel and break away from Colombia. He made it known that he would not help Colombia suppress the rebels. In fact, he might even support the rebellion.

On November 2, 1903, the American warship *Nashville* dropped anchor in the port of Colón, Panama. The next day, the people of Panama rebelled against Colombia. American forces stopped Colombian troops from crushing the revolt. On November 3, Panama declared itself an independent republic.

The United States recognized the new nation at once. Panama then agreed to let the United States build a canal on terms similar to those it had offered to Colombia.

Roosevelt's high-handed action in Panama angered many Latin Americans. It also upset some members of the United States Congress. The President, however, was proud of his action. "I took the Canal Zone," he said later, "and let Congress debate."

Battling disease

With its tropical heat, heavy rainfall, and plentiful swamps, Panama was a "mosquito paradise." This presented serious difficulties for the canal builders. Mosquitoes carry two of the deadliest tropical diseases: malaria and yellow fever.

Dr. **William Gorgas,** an army physician who had helped wipe out yellow fever in Cuba, arrived in Panama to help control the mosquitoes and the spread of disease. He ordered workers to locate all pools of water, where mosquitoes laid their eggs. Day after day, the workers drained swamps, sprayed tons of insecticide, and spread oil on stagnant water to kill mosquito eggs.

By 1906, Gorgas had won his battle. Yellow fever had disappeared from Panama. Malaria cases dropped dramatically. Work on the Panama Canal could proceed.

Digging the canal

Under the supervision of army engineer Colonel **George Goethals,** more than 40,000 workers struggled to dig the canal. Most were blacks from the West Indies. They blasted a path through mountains and carved out the largest man-made lake in the world. By the time they were done, they had removed more than 200 million cubic yards of earth. Then, they built gigantic locks to raise and lower

Skills FOR LIFE

Critical Thinking | Managing Information | **Communication** | Maps, Charts, and Graphs

Using the Internet

Students using the Internet ➤

How Will I Use This Skill?

The Internet is a global computer network. By "surfing the Net," you can link to millions of computer sites sponsored by businesses, governments, educational groups, and individuals all over the world. The Internet provides many services, including information, electronic mail, and on-line shopping.

LEARN the Skill

You can search the Internet by using an on-line search engine such as Yahoo, Lycos, or Excite, and by following these steps:

1. Choose a search engine and type in key words to describe your research topic.
2. Scan the site descriptions that the search engine provides and click on one that seems to apply best to your topic.
3. At each Internet site, you can take notes on the on-screen information. Usually, you can also print the information or copy and import it to your own computer. You can also click on highlighted hyperlinks to take you to other related Internet sites.
4. Return to the search engine. Continue your search by scanning more site descriptions, or start a new search by typing in new key words.

PRACTICE the Skill

Use these steps to learn about the economic importance of the Panama Canal today.

1. Choose a search engine. What key words should you type?
2. Based on the site descriptions you see, which site seems most pertinent to your topic? Go to the site by clicking on the description.
3. Look for information on the volume of goods and ships that travel through the canal. When you find the information, take notes, print, or import the data. What hyperlinks does the site provide to other sites?
4. Return to the search engine and continue scanning site descriptions. How could you start a new search on the history of the canal?

APPLY the Skill

Use a search engine to see if your state's department of education provides an Internet site. If it does, visit and explore the site. What kinds of useful information and hyperlinks do you find there? Do you have any ideas for improving the site? Perhaps, you could E-mail your suggestions directly to the department of education.

Linking United States and the World

Colombia

United States

Trading Partners

During the early 1900s, trade increased between the United States and Latin America. At left, young Colombian farm workers display a harvest of coffee beans. At right, an American coffee company advertises the finished product: packaged, ground coffee.

★ **Does Colombia import coffee or export coffee?**

ships as they passed through the canal. Finally, in 1914, the first ocean-going steamship traveled through the Panama Canal.

The new waterway helped the trade of many nations. American merchants and manufacturers benefited most. They could now ship goods cheaply to South America and Asia. However, many Latin American nations remained bitter about the way in which the United States had gained control of the canal.

Policing Latin America

The Panama Canal involved the United States more than ever in Latin America. Gradually, President Roosevelt and succeeding Presidents established a policy of intervening in Latin America to settle disputes and disturbances. The United States was especially concerned when disturbances threatened American lives, property, and interests in Latin America.

The Roosevelt Corollary

In 1902, several European countries sent warships to force Venezuela to repay its debts. The United States did not want Europeans to interfere in Latin America. President Roosevelt decided that the United States must step in to keep Europeans out. Roosevelt declared that it was the responsibility of the United States to prevent disorder and lawlessness in Latin America:

> “If we intend to say hands off to the powers of Europe, then sooner or later we must keep order ourselves.”

In 1904, Roosevelt announced an important addition to the Monroe Doctrine. In the **Roosevelt Corollary,** he claimed the right of the United States to intervene in Latin America to preserve law and order. By using this “international police power,” the United States could force Latin Americans to pay their debts to foreign nations. It would also keep those nations from meddling in Latin American affairs.

Over the next 20 years, several Presidents, including Roosevelt, used this police power. Most Latin Americans strongly resented this interference in their affairs.

Dollar diplomacy

Roosevelt's successor, William Howard Taft, also favored a strong American role in Latin America. Taft, however, wanted to "substitute dollars for bullets." He urged American bankers to invest in Latin America. It was better to use trade than warships to expand American influence in Latin America, he said. This policy of building strong economic ties to Latin America became known as **dollar diplomacy.**

American investors responded eagerly. They helped build roads, railroads, and harbors in Latin America. These improvements increased trade, benefiting both Americans and local governments. The new railroads, for example, brought minerals and other resources to Latin American ports. From there, they were shipped all over the world.

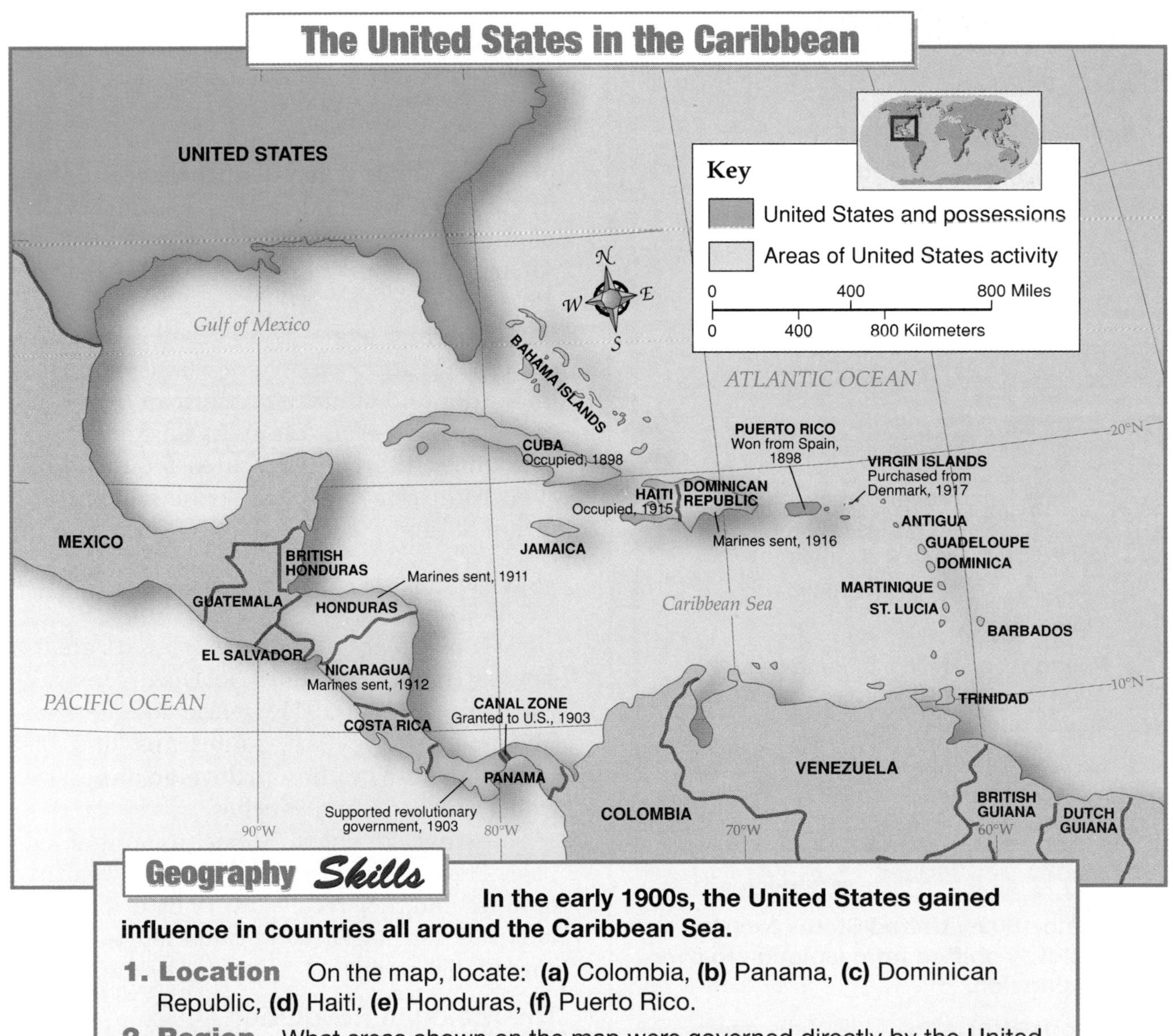

Geography *Skills* **In the early 1900s, the United States gained influence in countries all around the Caribbean Sea.**

1. **Location** On the map, locate: **(a)** Colombia, **(b)** Panama, **(c)** Dominican Republic, **(d)** Haiti, **(e)** Honduras, **(f)** Puerto Rico.
2. **Region** What areas shown on the map were governed directly by the United States?
3. **Critical Thinking** Review what you have learned about the Roosevelt Corollary. Identify three areas on the map where Presidents used the Roosevelt Corollary.

Cause and Effect

Causes

- Western frontier closes
- Businesses seek raw materials and new markets
- European nations compete for resources and markets

Overseas Expansion

Effects

- United States develops strong navy
- Open Door Policy protects trade with China
- United States governs lands in Caribbean and Pacific
- United States builds Panama Canal
- United States sends troops to Latin American nations to protect its interests

Effects Today

- United States is global superpower
- Alaska and Hawaii are 49th and 50th states
- Puerto Rico, American Samoa, Guam, and U.S. Virgin Islands remain United States territories
- United States has close economic ties with Latin America and Pacific Rim

Graphic Organizer *Skills*

In the late 1800s, United States foreign policy slowly shifted from isolation to overseas expansion.

1. **Comprehension** List three effects of expansion on Latin America.
2. **Critical Thinking** Which of the Effects Today listed here do you think is most important? Explain.

Dollar diplomacy created problems, too. American businesses, such as the United Fruit Company, often meddled in the political affairs of host countries. Sometimes, the United States used military force to keep order. In 1912, when a revolution erupted in Nicaragua, the United States sent in marines to protect American investments.

Wilson and moral diplomacy

Woodrow Wilson, elected President in 1912, disliked the heavy-handed foreign policy of his predecessors. He proposed instead a policy of **moral diplomacy.** "The force of America is the force of moral principle," he said. Wilson's goals were to condemn imperialism, spread democracy, and promote peace.

Nevertheless, Wilson ordered military intervention in Latin America more than any prior President. When disturbances erupted in Haiti in 1915 and in the Dominican Republic in 1916, Wilson sent in the marines. American troops remained in Haiti until 1934.

Again and again, the United States declared that its troops were restoring peace and order and guarding American lives and property. However, many Latin Americans denounced the United States for invading their countries and interfering in their internal affairs.

Relations With Mexico

Wilson's moral diplomacy faced its greatest test in Mexico. Porfirio Díaz, Mexico's ruler from 1877 to 1911, welcomed American investment. By 1912, Americans had invested about $1 billion to develop mines, oil wells, railroads, and ranches.

Meanwhile, most Mexicans remained poor. They worked the land of a few wealthy families and they received very little for their labor. These harsh conditions led to widespread discontent.

The Mexican Revolution

In 1910, Mexicans rebelled against Díaz. The new leader, Francisco Madero, promised democratic reform. Then, in 1913, Madero was himself overthrown and killed by General Victoriano Huerta (WEHR tuh). As civil war raged in Mexico, Wilson vowed that he would never recognize this "government of butchers."

Wilson tried to stay neutral. He hoped that Mexico would develop a democratic government without American interference. However, Huerta's dictatorship grew more brutal. In response, Wilson authorized the sale of arms to Huerta's rival, Venustiano Carranza.

Finally, a minor incident led to American intervention. In 1914, Huerta's troops arrested several American sailors. The sailors were quickly released and an apology issued. Still, Wilson ordered the United States Navy to occupy the Mexican port of Veracruz. Rallied by the American show of strength, Carranza's forces drove Huerta from power. The United States troops withdrew.

American soldiers in Mexico

Still, civil war continued in Mexico. Now, General **Francisco "Pancho" Villa** hoped to overthrow Carranza. The United States, meanwhile, supported Carranza.

In January 1916, Villa's soldiers removed 17 American citizens from a train in Mexico and shot them. In March, Villa raided the town of Columbus, New Mexico, killing 19 Americans. He hoped that his actions would weaken relations between the United States and the Carranza government. Villa's plan backfired.

To capture Villa, President Wilson sent General **John J. Pershing** with an army of several thousand soldiers into Mexico. When Mexico demanded that the "invasion" be halted, the United States refused. There were some calls for war, but both Wilson and Carranza opposed the idea. In 1917, after failing to capture Villa, Wilson ordered Pershing's army to withdraw.

Once again, the United States had demonstrated its willingness to use force to protect its interests. However, there was a cost. Like many other Latin Americans, Mexicans became more resentful of their powerful neighbor to the North.

As United States troops headed home from Mexico, many Americans realized that their nation's role in world affairs had dramatically changed over the years. Now the United States kept troops and ships in both Asia and Latin America. American business interests spanned the globe. It would be very difficult for the United States to ignore the war that had been raging in Europe since 1914.

★ Section 3 Review ★

Recall

1. **Locate** **(a)** Colombia, **(b)** Panama, **(c)** Panama Canal, **(d)** Venezuela, **(e)** Mexico.
2. **Identify** **(a)** William Gorgas, **(b)** George Goethals, **(c)** Roosevelt Corollary, **(d)** Francisco "Pancho" Villa, **(e)** John J. Pershing.
3. **Define** **(a)** isthmus, **(b)** dollar diplomacy, **(c)** moral diplomacy.

Comprehension

4. Why did President Roosevelt think it was important for the United States to build the Panama Canal?
5. How were the foreign policies of Roosevelt, Taft, and Wilson similar?
6. **(a)** Why did Mexicans rebel against their government in 1910? **(b)** Why did President Wilson send General Pershing into Mexico?

Critical Thinking and Writing

7. **Understanding Causes and Effects** How did geographic conditions in Panama make it difficult to build a canal there?
8. **Thinking Creatively** What do you think President Wilson could have done to help bring the Mexican Revolution to a peaceful end?

Activity **Preparing for an Interview** You are a historian about to interview President Theodore Roosevelt concerning his policy in Latin American countries. Write three questions you would ask him.

Chapter 21 Review and Activities

★ Sum It Up ★

Section 1 Across the Pacific

- In the mid-1800s, the United States increased its influence in the Pacific by opening trade with Japan and by buying Alaska from Russia.
- Americans began to favor imperialism because they wanted raw materials and markets in other regions.
- After American planters rebelled against the Hawaiian government, the United States annexed Hawaii.
- To protect American trading rights in China, the United States established the Open Door Policy.

Section 2 The Spanish-American War

- The Cuban revolt against Spain led to war between the United States and Spain.
- United States forces defeated the Spanish in Cuba, Puerto Rico, and the Philippines.
- After the war, the United States took control of Spain's former colonies in the Caribbean Sea and the Pacific Ocean.
- Filipino nationalists fought unsuccessfully against the United States Army.

Section 3 Relations With Latin America

- The United States built the Panama Canal through Central America.
- Roosevelt and succeeding Presidents intervened repeatedly in Latin American affairs.
- In response to events of the Mexican Revolution, President Wilson sent United States troops into Mexico.

For additional review of the major ideas of Chapter 21, see ***Guide to the Essentials of American History*** or ***Interactive Student Tutorial CD-ROM,*** which contains interactive review activities, graphic organizers, and practice tests.

Reviewing the Chapter

Define These Terms

Match each term with the correct definition.

Column 1	Column 2
1. isolationism	**a.** policy of having little to do with foreign nations
2. sphere of influence	**b.** agreement to end fighting
3. isthmus	**c.** part of a nation where another nation has special trading privileges
4. yellow journalism	**d.** sensational news reporting
5. armistice	**e.** narrow strip of land connecting two larger areas of land

Explore the Main Ideas

1. Why did many Americans favor imperialism in the late 1800s?
2. How did the United States extend its interests in Asia and the Pacific?
3. **(a)** What was one cause of the Spanish-American War? **(b)** What was one effect of the war?
4. How did the United States acquire the rights to build a canal in Panama?
5. Explain each of the following: **(a)** Roosevelt Corollary, **(b)** dollar diplomacy, **(c)** moral diplomacy.

Geography Activity

Match the letters on the map with the following places: **1.** United States, **2.** Puerto Rico, **3.** Panama Canal, **4.** Cuba, **5.** Nicaragua, **6.** Dominican Republic. **Place** Why was the Isthmus of Panama a good place to build a canal?

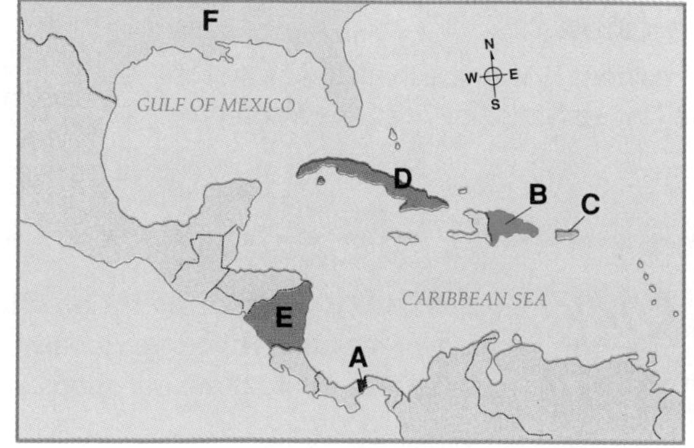

Critical Thinking and Writing

1. **Understanding Chronology** List the following events in chronological order: **(a)** Filipino War for Independence, **(b)** Spanish-American War, **(c)** Cuban rebellion against Spain, **(d)** the sinking of the battleship *Maine.*
2. **Linking Past and Present** What national projects today present challenges similar to those overcome in building the Panama Canal? Explain.
3. **Making Inferences** In the quotation on page 555, Pershing described the American forces at San Juan as being made up of men "of North and South." Why did he choose this way of describing the military?
4. **Exploring Unit Themes Global Interaction** Captain Mahan insisted that the navy was the decisive power that would control events in distant regions. **(a)** Give evidence to prove or disprove that his view was correct in his time. **(b)** Does his view hold true today?

Using Primary Sources

Naval Lieutenant John Blandin was on the *Maine* when it exploded. He later made this statement about the event:

> "I have no theories as to the cause of the explosion. I cannot form any. I, with others, had heard that the Havana harbor was full of [explosive mines], but the officers whose duty it was to examine into that reported that they found no signs of any. Personally, I do not believe that the Spanish had anything to do with the disaster. Time may tell. I hope so."

Source: *Memories of Two Wars: Cuban and Philippine Experiences,* Frederick Funston, 1911.

Recognizing Points of View **(a)** According to Blandin, what evidence was there that the Spanish were to blame for the sinking of the *Maine*? **(b)** Why did the views of Blandin and other witnesses have little effect on American public opinion about the explosion?

Activity Bank

Interdisciplinary Activity

Exploring Geography Choose one of the lands the United States acquired during its period of foreign expansion. Prepare a geographic fact sheet on its geography. Then, write a short essay explaining why the geography of the place you have chosen made it a target for American imperialists.

Career Skills Activity

Cartographers On a large sheet of paper, draw a map of the world. Indicate the following on the map: **(a)** the territory of the United States in 1850, **(b)** the territory gained by the United States between 1850 and 1914.

Citizenship Activity

Writing an Editorial The question of whether the United States should act as the police officer of the world arose many times during the early 1900s. Write an editorial in which you either support or oppose the use of United States military forces to settle disputes and disturbances in other parts of the world.

Internet Activity

Use the Internet to find sites dealing with the Spanish-American War. Gather information on a single event of the war. Then, write a newspaper story as it might have appeared in the yellow press of the time. How do the facts and your story differ?

You are an American farmer, industrialist, missionary, or naval officer during the Age of Imperialism. In your EYEWITNESS JOURNAL, describe your thoughts on the increasing role of the United States in world affairs.

Chapter 22

World War I

1914–1919

What's Ahead

Section 1
War Erupts in Europe

Section 2
The United States Enters the War

Section 3
Winning the War

Section 4
Wilson and the Peace

In 1914, long-standing rivalries among European nations exploded into war. At first, President Woodrow Wilson tried to keep the United States neutral. However, after several of Germany's actions affected American citizens, the United States entered the war against Germany in 1917.

World War I, as the war is now called, cost millions of lives. After the war ended, Wilson worked hard to build a lasting peace. However, because of conflicts at the peace conference and at home, he was unable to achieve all of his goals.

Why Study History? World War I ended on November 11, 1918. Today, Americans celebrate November 11 as Veterans Day. On this day, we remember and honor all the men and women who have served the nation in the armed services. To focus on this connection, see the *Why Study History?* feature, "We Honor Our Veterans," in this chapter.

American Events

1915 Americans die when Germany sinks the *Lusitania*

1916 Avoiding war helps President Wilson win reelection

1917 United States enters World War I

1914 — 1915 — 1916 — 1917

World Events

1914 World Event World War I begins in Europe

1916 World Event Hundreds of thousands die in Battle of Verdun

Viewing History: Americans Fight in Europe

During World War I, the government sent artists to the battleground in Europe. This painting, 18 on the Trail of the San Mihiel, *is by W. J. Aylward. It shows American troops in 1918 moving equipment to the front.* ★ **Why do you think the government sent artists to the front lines?**

1918 Armistice ends World War I fighting

1919 Senate rejects Treaty of Versailles

1921 United States signs peace treaty with Germany

1917 | **1918** | **1919** | **1920**

1917 World Event
Russian Revolution begins

1918 World Event
Influenza epidemic kills millions

▲ Sheet music for "Over There"

Biography George M. Cohan

A popular singer and dancer, George M. Cohan was also famous for his patriotism. He wrote such songs as "You're a Grand Old Flag" and "I'm a Yankee Doodle Dandy." During World War I, "Over There" boosted soldiers' morale and earned money for the war effort. In appreciation, Congress awarded Cohan a special medal. ★ **Why are patriotic songs important to a nation?**

an ally of an absolute ruler. Without the czar, it would be easier for Wilson to support the Allied cause.

Declaration of war

On April 2, President Wilson went before Congress to ask for a declaration of war. "The world must be made safe for democracy," he declared. His war message assured the American people that entering the war was not only just, it was noble. He concluded:

> ❝ It is a fearful thing to lead this great peaceful people into war, into the most terrible and disastrous of all wars, civilization itself seeming to be in the balance. But the right is more precious than peace, and we shall fight for the thing which we have always carried nearest our hearts—for democracy. ❞

Congress voted for war 455 to 56. Among those who voted against the declaration was **Jeannette Rankin** of Montana, the first woman elected to Congress. She hated war as much as she loved her country. "I want to stand by my country, but I cannot vote for war. I vote no!" she said.

On April 6, the President signed the declaration of war. It thrust Americans into the deadliest war the world had yet seen.

The Nation at War

The day after Congress declared war, George M. Cohan wrote a new song, "Over There." The patriotic tune swept the nation. Its opening lines expressed the confidence that Americans felt :

> ❝ Over there, over there,
> Send the word, send the word, over
> there,
> That the Yanks are coming . . . ❞

Its closing message promised, "We'll be over, we're coming over, And we won't come back till it's over over there."

Americans had to do more than sing patriotic tunes, however. They had to prepare to fight—and quickly. The Allies needed everything from food to arms. Britain and France were on the verge of collapse. In Russia, soldiers at the front were deserting to join the revolution.

Building an army

Before it could fight, the United States needed an army. On May 18, Congress passed the **Selective Service Act.** It required all young men from age 21 to 30 to register for the military draft. A **draft** is a law requiring people of a certain age to serve in the military.

In the next 18 months, 4 million men and women joined the armed forces. People from every ethnic group enlisted. About 20,000 Puerto Ricans served in the armed forces, as did many Filipinos. Scores of soldiers were immigrants who had recently arrived in the United States.

Many Native Americans were not citizens, so they could not be drafted. Large numbers of Native Americans enlisted anyway. One family of Winnebago Indians provided 35 volunteers! They served together in the same unit.

At first, the armed forces did not allow African Americans in combat. When the government abandoned this policy, more than 2 million African Americans registered for the draft. Nearly 400,000 were accepted for duty. They were forced into segregated "black-only" units that were commanded mostly by white officers.

Still, African Americans rallied behind the war effort. Blacks like W.E.B. Du Bois voiced strong support for the war's goals:

> "Let us, while the war lasts, forget our special grievances and close ranks . . . with our fellow citizens and the allied nations that are fighting for democracy."

In training

While men drilled for combat, women served as radio operators, clerks, and stenographers. At training camps, there were not always enough weapons for everyone. Until supplies increased, some recruits trained using broomsticks for guns.

Despite long hours of drill, soldiers got caught up in the war spirit. A young recruit wrote, "We don't know where we are going, but the band plays 'Over There' every day, and they can't send us any too soon." To many, the war seemed like a great adventure. "Here was our one great chance for excitement and risk," wrote a volunteer. "We could not afford to pass it up."

Educating the recruits

For many recruits, especially African Americans, southerners, and immigrants, the Army offered several firsts. It was their first exposure to military authority and discipline. It was the first time most had ventured outside their farms and villages, let alone outside their country. Some had never taken regular baths or eaten regular meals before. Others had never used indoor plumbing. About 25 percent were **illiterate**, that is, unable to read or write.

The Army became a great educator. It taught millions of young Americans not only how to fight but also how to read, how to eat nutritious meals, and how to care for their daily health needs.

Shocking rates of illiteracy and other low test scores among recruits fueled a drive to reform public education. State and local school boards lengthened the school day and

Building an Army

The Selective Service Act required young men between the ages of 21 and 30 to register for the draft. In this photograph, a blindfolded woman selects the numbers of men to be called for duty. ★ **Do you think a draft is a fair way to raise an army? Explain.**

required students to spend more years in school. They raised teacher training standards. More truancy officers patrolled the streets. By 1920, 75 percent of all school-age children were enrolled in school.

Organizing the War Effort

The United States reorganized its economy to produce food, arms, and other goods needed to fight the war. President Wilson set up government agencies to oversee the effort. A huge bureaucracy (byoo ROK ruh see) emerged to manage the war effort. A **bureaucracy** is a system of managing government through departments run by appointed officials.

"Food will win the war"

Wilson chose **Herbert Hoover** to head the Food Administration. Hoover's job was to boost food production. The nation had to feed its troops and help the Allies.

In keeping with the nation's democratic traditions, Hoover relied on cooperation rather than force. He tried to win support for his programs with publicity campaigns that encouraged Americans to act voluntarily. "Food Will Win the War," proclaimed one Food Administration poster. A magazine urged:

> "Do not permit your child to take a bite or two from an apple and throw the rest away; nowadays even children must be taught to be patriotic to the core."

Encouraged by rising food prices, farmers grew more crops. Families planted "victory gardens." People went without wheat on "wheatless Mondays," and without meat on "meatless Tuesdays." The food they saved helped the men in the trenches.

Connections With Economics

President Wilson also did his part for the war effort. He kept a herd of sheep to trim the White House lawn. The sheep replaced gardeners who had been drafted. In addition, Wilson raised $100,000 for the Red Cross by selling the wool of the White House sheep.

Wartime industry

War caught the nation short of supplies. The military had on hand only around 600,000 rifles, 2,000 machine guns, and fewer than 1,000 pieces of artillery. Disorder threatened as the military competed with private industry to buy scarce materials.

To meet this crisis, President Wilson set up a new government agency, the War Industries Board. It told factories what they had to produce. It also divided up limited resources.

Without the support of workers, industry could not mobilize. In 1918, Wilson created the War Labor Board. It settled disputes over working hours and wages and tried to prevent strikes. With workers in short supply, unions were able to win better pay and working conditions. With the President supporting workers, union membership rose sharply.

The Home Front

Americans on the home front united behind the war effort. Movie stars, such as Charlie Chaplin and Mary Pickford, helped sell **Liberty Bonds.** By buying bonds, American citizens were lending money to the government to pay for the war. The sale of Liberty Bonds raised $21 billion, just over half of what the United States spent on the war.

To rally public support for the war, the government sent out 75,000 speakers known as "Four-Minute Men." Their name reminded people of the heroic Minutemen of 1776. It also referred to the four-minute speeches the men gave at public events, movies, and theaters. The speakers urged Americans to make sacrifices for the goals of freedom and democracy.

Women at work

As men joined the armed forces, women stepped into their jobs. Women received better pay in war industries than they had in peacetime. Still, they earned less than the men they replaced.

In factories, women assembled weapons and airplane parts. Some women drove trol-

Viewing HISTORY **Women Support the War Effort**

Whether in uniform or on the job, American women rallied behind the war effort. The poster at right urged support for women serving in the military. The shipyard workers above hold the tongs and buckets they used to work with red-hot steel rivets. ★ **How do you think wartime work helped women win the right to vote?**

ley cars and delivered the mail. Others served as police officers. By performing well in jobs once reserved for men, women helped change the view that they were fit only for "women's work." Unfortunately, most of the gains made by women disappeared when the men returned to the work force at the end of the war.

Anti-German feelings

German Americans endured suspicion and intolerance during the war. Newspapers questioned their loyalty. Mobs attacked them on the streets. In 1918, a mob lynched Robert Prager, whose only crime was that he had been born in Germany. A jury later refused to convict the mob leaders.

Anti-German prejudice led some families to change their names. Schools stopped teaching the German language. Concert halls banned works by German composers. Americans began referring to German measles as "liberty measles" and sauerkraut as "liberty cabbage."

Other ethnic tensions

During the war, almost a half million African Americans and thousands of Mexican Americans embarked on a great migration. They left the South and Southwest for cities in the North, hoping to escape poverty and discrimination.

In northern cities, many blacks found better-paying jobs in war industries. At the

Skills FOR LIFE

Managing Information | Communication | Maps, Charts, and Graphs

Recognizing Propaganda

How Will I Use This Skill?

Propaganda is an attempt to spread ideas that support a particular cause or hurt an opposing cause. In our everyday lives, propaganda can be found in advertisements, in political posters and speeches, even in movies and television shows. Being aware of propaganda techniques can help us evaluate the messages we receive and make reasoned judgments.

LEARN the Skill

Propaganda often stresses emotional appeals. It may use half-truths, stressing some truths but ignoring others. In extreme cases, propaganda may even use outright lies. Other common propaganda techniques include name-calling and using symbols and words that show the opposition in the worst light. To recognize propaganda, look for these points:

1. Identify factual information, exaggerations, or misinformation.
2. Analyze the type of emotion the propaganda wants the reader to feel. Look for name-calling and the use of emotional symbols and words.
3. Try to determine the source of the propaganda. Identify the action or opinion the propaganda is trying to support or oppose.
4. Judge whether the propaganda is effective.

PRACTICE the Skill

The propaganda poster above appeared after the United States declared war on Germany in 1917. Look at the poster and answer the following questions.

1. Is any factual information about the war included in this poster? Explain.
2. (a) What image of the enemy do the words and picture convey? (b) What emotions is the poster trying to stir?
3. (a) Who do you think produced this poster? (b) What action do they want to encourage?
4. Do you think this poster was effective propaganda at the time? Why or why not?

APPLY the Skill

Advertisements, like propaganda, use emotions and facts to persuade us to perform certain actions. Choose an advertisement from a newspaper or magazine. Using the steps given above, analyze the advertisement as propaganda.

same time, they ran into prejudice and even violence. Competition for housing and jobs sometimes led to race riots. In 1917, 39 African Americans were killed during a riot in East St. Louis, Illinois. A New York parade protested the deaths. Marchers carried signs demanding, "Mr. President, Why Not Make AMERICA Safe for Democracy?"

In the Southwest, ranchers pressed the government to let more Mexicans cross the border. Almost 100,000 Mexicans entered the United States to work on farms, mostly in California and Texas. By 1920, Mexicans were the leading foreign-born group in California. Some Mexicans moved on to northern cities, where they worked in factories.

Throughout the war, Mexicans worked in cotton and beet fields, in copper mines, and in steel mills. All these jobs were important to the war effort. Yet after the war, when veterans returned and unemployment grew, the United States tried to force Mexican workers to return to Mexico.

Silencing protest

Some Americans opposed the war. Among them were Progressives such as Jane Addams. Many of these critics were **pacifists,** people who refuse to fight in any war because they believe war is evil.

Antiwar feeling also ran high among socialists and radical labor groups. A **socialist** believes that the people as a whole rather than private individuals should own all property and share the profits from all businesses. Socialists argued that the war benefited factory owners but not workers.

To encourage unity, Congress passed laws making it a crime to criticize the government or to interfere with the war. Nearly 1,600 men and women were arrested for breaking these laws. Eugene V. Debs, Socialist candidate for President five times, was jailed for protesting the draft. The government also jailed "Big Bill" Haywood, head of the Industrial Workers of the World (IWW), a radical union. Using special powers granted under the wartime laws, government authorities ransacked the IWW's offices.

A few people questioned these laws. They argued that silencing critics violated the Constitution's guarantee of freedom of speech. Most Americans, however, felt that the laws were necessary in wartime.

★ Section 2 Review ★

Recall

1. **Identify** **(a)** Zimmermann telegram, **(b)** Jeannette Rankin, **(c)** Selective Service Act, **(d)** Herbert Hoover, **(e)** Liberty Bonds.
2. **Define** **(a)** warmonger, **(b)** czar, **(c)** draft, **(d)** illiterate, **(e)** bureaucracy, **(f)** pacifist, **(g)** socialist.

Comprehension

3. Identify three events that moved the United States toward war.
4. **(a)** List three government agencies that were set up to organize the war effort. **(b)** What did each agency do?
5. What steps did the government take to silence critics of the war?

Critical Thinking and Writing

6. **Synthesizing Information** Review the account of the East St. Louis race riot on page 583. Why did the marchers carry signs demanding: "Mr. President, Why Not Make AMERICA Safe for Democracy?"
7. **Defending a Position** Do you think that the government should have the right to silence critics during wartime? Defend your position.

★ ★

Activity **Preparing a Speech** You have only four minutes. *GO!* As one of Wilson's "Four-Minute Men," you must give a speech urging Americans to make sacrifices for the war effort. Be sure to think about what kind of arguments would most appeal to your listeners.

Winning the War

As You Read

Explore These Questions

- Why did the Allies face hard times in 1917?
- How did Americans help defeat Germany?
- What were the human costs of the war?

Define

- armistice
- abdicate
- epidemic

Identify

- Bolsheviks
- V. I. Lenin
- Treaty of Brest-Litovsk
- John J. Pershing
- Harlem Hell Fighters
- Battle of Belleau Wood
- Ferdinand Foch
- Alvin York
- Battle of the Argonne Forest

American soldiers carried shaving kits like this one to the trenches in France.

Soon after war was declared, an official at the War Department asked the Senate for $3 billion for arms and other supplies. "And we may have to have an army in France," he added. "Good grief!" sputtered one senator. "You're not going to send soldiers over there, are you?"

The United States would send more than 2 million soldiers to France. The buildup took time. First, troops had to be trained and armed. By March 1918, fewer than 300,000 American troops had reached France. Then they poured in. Fresh and eager to fight, they gave the Allies a much-needed boost.

Hard Times for the Allies

The first American troops reached France in June 1917. They quickly saw the desperate situation of the Allies. The Allies had lost millions of soldiers. Troops in the trenches were exhausted and ill. Many civilians in Britain and France were near starvation.

Russia withdraws from the war

To make matters worse, Russia withdrew from the war. In November 1917, a group known as the **Bolsheviks** seized power from the Provisional Government. Under the leadership of **V. I. Lenin,** the Bolsheviks wanted to bring a communist revolution to Russia.

Lenin embraced the ideas of Karl Marx, a German thinker of the 1800s. Marx had predicted that workers around the world would unite to overthrow the ruling class. After the workers revolted, they would end private property and set up a classless society. Lenin was determined to lead such a revolution in Russia.

Once in power, Lenin opened talks with Germany. He had opposed the war, arguing that it benefited only the ruling class. In March 1918, Russia and Germany signed the **Treaty of Brest-Litovsk.** Although Russia had to give up land to Germany, Lenin welcomed peace. With war ended, he could focus on the communist revolution.

The Allies saw the treaty as a betrayal. It gave Germany coal mines and other resources in Russia. More important, with Russia out of the way, Germany could move its armies away from the Russian front and into France. In early 1918, Germany used these troops in an all-out attack on the Allies.

A new German offensive

By March 21, German forces had massed near the French town of Amiens. (See the map at right.) The Germans called this move a "peace offensive." They hoped that a final push would end the war.

Dozens of German divisions massed up against a small British force. Late at night, 6,000 German cannons began pounding the British troops camped at Amiens. Despite the heavy fire, the British held on. The battle lasted for two weeks. At last, on April 4, the Germans gave up their attack.

The Germans continued their offensive elsewhere. By late May, they had smashed through Allied lines along the Aisne (EHN) River. On May 30, they reached the Marne River, just east of Château-Thierry (sha TOH tee ER ee). Paris lay only 50 miles (80 km) away. At this point, American troops entered the war in force.

Americans in France

By June 1918, American troops were reaching France in record numbers. Commanding the American Expeditionary Force (AEF) was General **John J. Pershing.** Pershing was already well known at home for leading American troops into Mexico in 1916 to hunt for Mexican rebel leader Francisco "Pancho" Villa. (See page 565.)

Allied generals wanted the fresh troops to reinforce their own war-weary soldiers. Pershing refused. He insisted that American troops operate as separate units. The United States wanted to have an independent role in shaping the peace. Only by playing "a definite and distinct part" in the war would it win power at the peace table.

In the end, Pershing agreed to let some Americans fight with the British and French. At the same time, he set up an American operation to fight on its own.

Harlem Hell Fighters

Among the first American units attached to the French Army was the 369th United States Infantry. This African American unit became known as the **Harlem Hell Fighters.** Although the United States allowed few African Americans to train for combat, the French respected the bravery of African American soldiers and were glad to fight side by side with them.

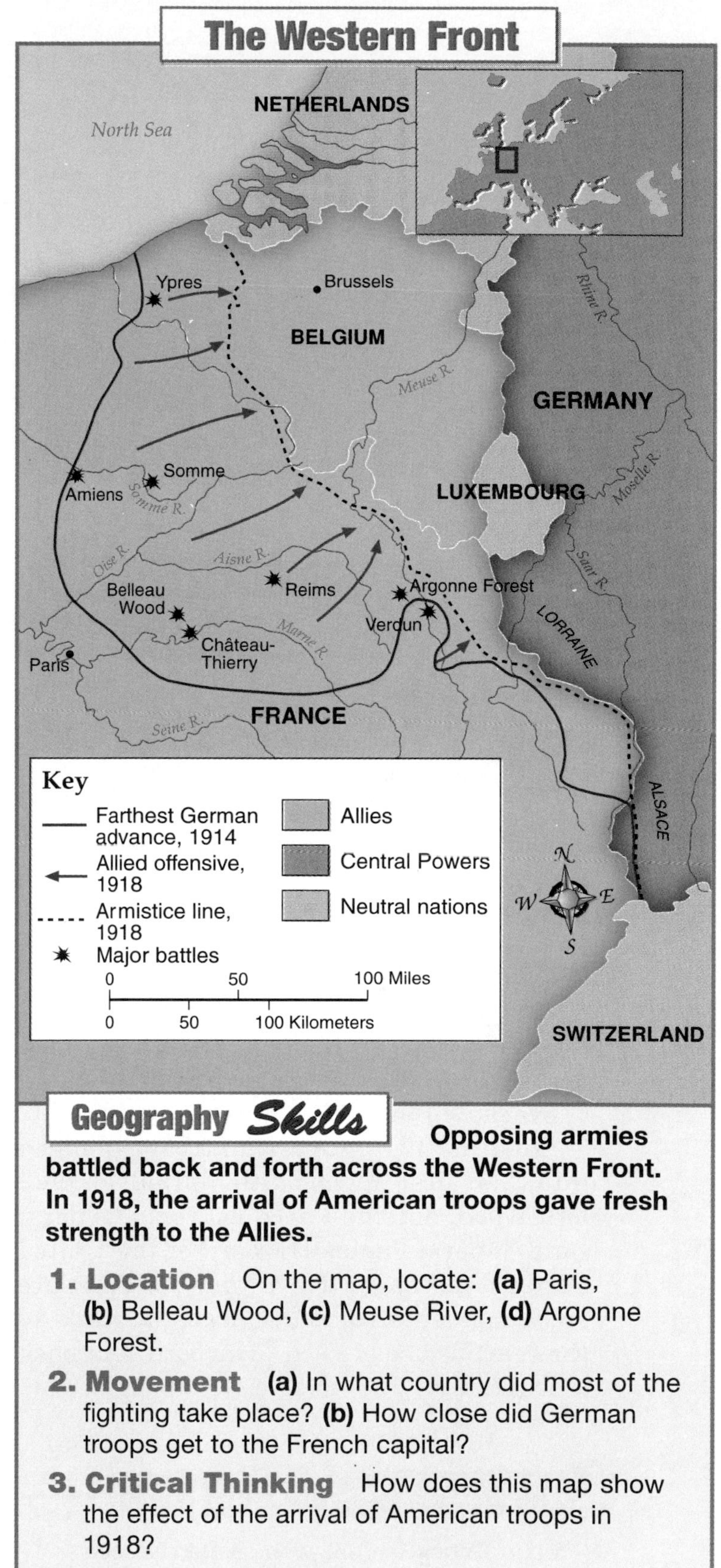

Geography *Skills* **Opposing armies battled back and forth across the Western Front. In 1918, the arrival of American troops gave fresh strength to the Allies.**

1. **Location** On the map, locate: **(a)** Paris, **(b)** Belleau Wood, **(c)** Meuse River, **(d)** Argonne Forest.
2. **Movement** **(a)** In what country did most of the fighting take place? **(b)** How close did German troops get to the French capital?
3. **Critical Thinking** How does this map show the effect of the arrival of American troops in 1918?

In the end, the Harlem Hell Fighters spent more time under fire than any other American unit. For their bravery, the French awarded them the Croix de Guerre, or Cross

Viewing HISTORY **Victims of Poison Gas**

Gassed, by John Singer Sargent, shows troops disabled by poison gas in 1918. Gas was one of the most feared weapons of World War I. Various gases caused choking, blindness, or severe skin blisters.
★ **Why do you think nations later agreed to ban the use of poison gas?**

◀ *World War I gas mask*

of War, and numerous other decorations. After the war, New Yorkers greeted them with a huge parade.

Belleau Wood

Meanwhile, the Germans were continuing their "peace offensive." As they rolled across the Aisne River, the French prepared to evacuate Paris.

In June 1918, American troops plunged into their first major battle in Belleau (BEH loh) Wood, outside Paris. A French general sent General James Harbord of the United States a message: "Have your men prepare entrenchments some hundreds of yards to the rear in case of need." Harbord sent back a firm reply:

> ❝ We dig no trenches to fall back on. The marines will hold where they stand. ❞

The **Battle of Belleau Wood** raged for three weeks. At last, on June 25, General Harbord passed along the good news: "Wood now exclusively U.S. Marine Corps."

Connections With Arts

John Singer Sargent, who painted *Gassed* (above), was one of the leading American artists of his time. Sargent gained fame for his portraits of elegant society women. Wealthy American and European women flocked to his Paris studio. Sargent was over 60 years old when he volunteered to serve as a war artist.

Final Battles

In mid-July, the Germans launched another drive to take Paris. They pushed the Allies back until they came up against American troops. Within three days, the Allies had forced the Germans to retreat.

The Allies now took the offensive. French Marshal **Ferdinand Foch** (FOHSH), commander of the Allied forces, ordered attacks along a line from Verdun to the North Sea. American forces stormed the area between the Meuse (MYOOZ) River and the Argonne Forest. (See the map on page 585.)

Into the Argonne Forest

On September 26, 1918, more than one million American soldiers pushed into the Argonne Forest. Years of fierce fighting had left the land scarred with trenches and shell

Why Study History?

Because We Honor Our Veterans

★ ★

Historical Background

In 1919, on the first anniversary of the end of World War I, President Wilson proclaimed a new holiday. November 11 would be celebrated as Armistice Day. In 1954, the holiday was renamed Veterans Day—the day we honor all men and women who have served in the nation's armed forces.

To honor the dead of World War I, the United States also dedicated the Tomb of the Unknown Soldier. In 1921, the body of an unidentified American soldier was brought from an unmarked grave in France to a military cemetery in Arlington, Virginia. Above his grave, a marble monument bears the inscription: "Here rests in honored glory an American soldier known but to God." Since then, unknown soldiers from three later wars have joined him.

VFW members salute as a Veterans Day parade passes.

Connections to Today

Today, the government and private organizations continue to honor and serve veterans. The Department for Veterans Affairs oversees veterans' pensions and benefits and runs veterans' hospitals. The Veterans of Foreign Wars (VFW), a nonprofit organization, offers support to veterans, as well as sponsoring community projects.

Each year, tourists visit the Tomb of the Unknown Soldier, the Vietnam War Memorial, and other monuments. Many families fly the flag on Veterans Day and Memorial Day.

Connections to You

How can you honor veterans? You might attend a parade or put flowers on a war memorial. Your local VFW post can supply a list of monuments in your area. You can enter the VFW's annual essay contest for seventh, eighth, and ninth graders. As you get older, you may do volunteer work in a veterans' hospital.

Mostly, you can honor veterans by remembering the past. As the Secretary of the Army said on Veterans Day 1996:

> "American veterans all . . . your nation and your Army honor you for your sacrifice and continuing selfless service."

1. **Comprehension** List three ways that Americans honor veterans.
2. **Critical Thinking** Why do you think groups like the VFW urge young people to learn more about American history?

Creating a Memory Book With your classmates, interview veterans in your community. Some students can write questions, while others set up the interviews. Write up your interviews and compile them in an illustrated binder. Ask your school or library to display your memory book on Veterans Day.

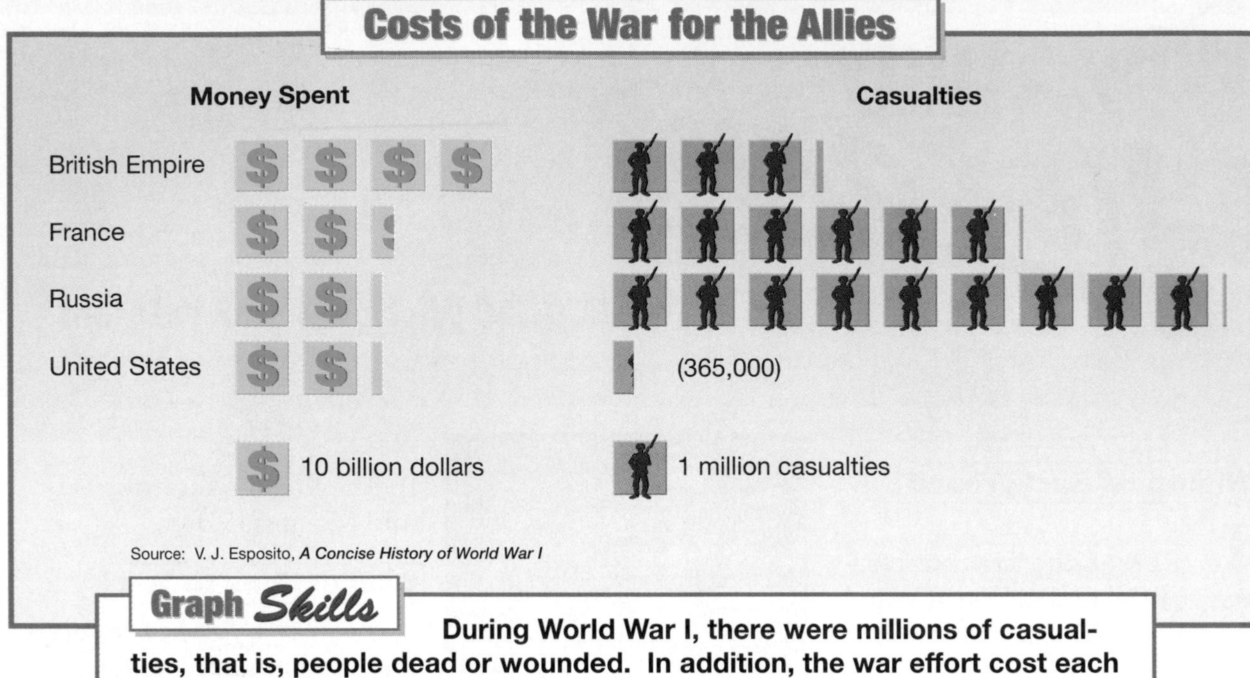

Graph Skills **During World War I, there were millions of casualties, that is, people dead or wounded. In addition, the war effort cost each side billions of dollars.**

1. **Comprehension** **(a)** Which Allied nation had the greatest number of casualties in World War I? **(b)** How much money did the United States spend on the war effort?
2. **Critical Thinking** **(a)** Which nation shown here had the fewest casualties? **(b)** Why was this so?

holes. The air still smelled of poison gas from earlier battles.

At first, the Americans advanced despite heavy German fire. Then, rains and the thick woods slowed their movement. Small units drove forward to capture deadly German positions. Armed with a single rifle, Sergeant **Alvin York** of Tennessee wiped out a nest of German machine gunners. His bravery helped clear the way for advancing American troops. York became the most decorated American soldier of the war.

Finally, after 47 days, the Americans broke through the German defense. They had won the **Battle of the Argonne Forest.** The cost was high on both sides. Americans and Germans each suffered more than 100,000 casualties in the battle.

British, French, and Belgian forces also smashed through the German lines in their areas. By November, German forces were in retreat. After more than four years of fighting, the Great War was finally nearing its end.

The war ends

In September, German generals told the kaiser that the war could not be won. On October 4, Prince Max of Baden, head of the German cabinet, secretly cabled President Wilson:

> “To avoid further bloodshed, the German government requests the President to arrange the immediate conclusion of an armistice on land, by sea, and in the air.”

An **armistice** is an agreement to stop fighting. Wilson set two conditions for an armistice. First, Germany must accept his plan for peace. Second, the German emperor must **abdicate,** that is, give up power.

While German leaders debated a response, rebellion simmered in the ranks. Daily, the German army lost ground. Morale plunged among the troops. German sailors mutinied. Several German cities threatened to revolt.

On November 9, the German emperor was forced to resign. He and his son fled to Holland, and Germany became a republic. The new German leaders agreed to the armistice terms. At 11 A.M. on November 11, 1918—the eleventh hour of the eleventh day of the eleventh month—World War I ended at last.

The costs of war

The costs of the war were staggering. A generation of young Europeans lost their lives. Between 10 million and 13 million people died in battle. Germany, alone, lost about 2 million men. More than 4 million Russian, French, and British soldiers were killed. The United States lost over 50,000 men. Many more died of diseases. More than 20 million soldiers on both sides were wounded.

Much of northern France lay in ruins. Millions of Germans were near starvation. In France and other nations, many children were left orphaned and homeless.

In 1918, a new disaster struck. A terrible influenza epidemic spread around the world. An **epidemic** is the rapid spread of a contagious disease among large numbers of people. Between 1918 and 1919, more than half a million Americans died in the flu epidemic. The death toll in other countries was even higher. All told, the epidemic killed more than 20 million people—twice as many as the war itself!

A wounded veteran and his family

★ Section 3 Review ★

Recall

1. **Locate** **(a)** Amiens, **(b)** Marne River, **(c)** Château Thierry, **(d)** Belleau Wood, **(e)** Argonne Forest.
2. **Identify** **(a)** Bolsheviks, **(b)** V. I. Lenin, **(c)** Treaty of Brest-Litovsk, **(d)** John J. Pershing, **(e)** Harlem Hell Fighters, **(f)** Battle of Belleau Wood, **(g)** Ferdinand Foch, **(h)** Alvin York, **(i)** Battle of the Argonne Forest.
3. **Define** **(a)** armistice, **(b)** abdicate, **(c)** epidemic.

Comprehension

4. Describe the situation of the Allies when the Americans arrived in June 1917.
5. What role did the Americans play in ending the war?
6. What conditions did Europeans face at the end of the war?

Critical Thinking and Writing

7. **Making Inferences** Why do you think General Pershing wanted American troops to fight as independent units rather than alongside the British and French?
8. **Analyzing Visual Evidence** Study the paintings on pages 569 and 586. **(a)** Describe what each painting shows. **(b)** How is the mood of the first picture different from that of the second picture?

Activity **Planning a Celebration** It is November 11, 1918. The armistice has just been signed. You have been asked to plan a community celebration in honor of the event. Prepare a schedule for the celebration, including at least four meaningful events.

Wilson and the Peace

As You Read

Explore These Questions

- What was Wilson's plan for peace?
- How did Wilson's goals for peace differ from those of the other Allies?
- Why did the Senate reject the Versailles Treaty?

Define

- self-determination
- reparation
- isolationist

Identify

- Fourteen Points
- League of Nations
- Big Four
- Treaty of Versailles
- Henry Cabot Lodge

SETTING the Scene Huge crowds cheered Woodrow Wilson when he arrived in France in December 1918. Some people cried with joy to see the American leader. After years of suffering, Europeans saw Wilson as a symbol of hope. He was the man who had promised to make the world "safe for democracy."

Wilson went to France determined to achieve a just and lasting peace. He believed that most Europeans shared his views. He soon learned, however, that his goals were often at odds with those of the other Allies.

Wilson's Peace Plan

In Europe, Wilson visited Paris, London, Milan, and Rome. Everywhere, cheering crowds welcomed him. To Wilson, this was a sign that Europeans supported his goal of "peace without victory." In fact, he was wrong. The people who greeted Wilson so warmly scoffed at his high-minded proposals. They and their leaders were determined to punish the Germans for the war.

In January 1918, even before the war ended, Wilson outlined his peace plan. Known as the **Fourteen Points,** it was meant to prevent international problems from causing another war.

President Woodrow Wilson

The first point in Wilson's plan called for an end to secret agreements. Secrecy, Wilson felt, had created the rival alliances that had helped lead to war. Next, he called for freedom of the seas, free trade, and a limit on arms. He urged peaceful settlement of disputes over colonies. He also supported the principle of national **self-determination,** that is, the right of national groups to their own territory and forms of government.

For Wilson, however, the fourteenth point was the most important. It called for a "general association of nations," or **League of Nations.** Its job would be to protect the independence of all countries—large or small. The goal was simple, he noted:

> "...justice to all peoples and nationalities, and their right to live on equal terms of liberty and safety with one another, whether weak or strong."

Wilson persuaded the Allies to accept the Fourteen Points as the basis for making peace. However, the plan soon ran into trouble. Some goals were too vague. Others conflicted with reality. In Paris,

Wilson faced a constant battle to save his Fourteen Points. He discovered that the Allies were more concerned with protecting their own interests.

The Peace Treaty

Diplomats from more than 30 nations met in Paris and Versailles (vuhr SI), hoping to make a lasting peace. Key issues were decided by the **Big Four**—Woodrow Wilson of the United States, David Lloyd George of Britain, Georges Clemenceau (kleh mahn SOH) of France, and Vittorio Orlando of Italy.

Conflicting goals

Each leader had his own aims. Wilson had called for "peace without victory." He opposed punishing the defeated powers.

The other Allies, however, ached for revenge. Germany must pay, they said. They insisted on large **reparations,** or cash payments, for the losses they had suffered during the war. Further, they wanted Germany to accept responsibility for the war.

The Allies were also determined to prevent Germany from rebuilding its military strength. In particular, Clemenceau wanted to weaken Germany so that it could never again threaten France. During the months of haggling, Wilson had to compromise on his Fourteen Points in order to save his key goals, especially the League of Nations.

Viewing History: Wilson at the Peace Conference

British artist William Orpen painted this scene at the 1919 Paris peace conference. The Big Four, including Woodrow Wilson, are seated center. Facing them, two German representatives read the treaty.
★ **How do you think the Germans responded to the Treaty of Versailles?**

The final treaty

By June 1919, the **Treaty of Versailles** was ready. None of the Allies was satisfied with it. Germany, which had not even been allowed to send delegates to the peace talks, was horrified by the terms of the treaty. Still, it had no choice but to sign.

Under the treaty, Germany had to take full blame for the war. It had to pay the Allies huge reparations, including the cost of pensions for Allied soldiers or their widows and children. The total cost of German reparations would come to over $300 billion.

Other provisions of the Treaty of Versailles were aimed at weakening Germany. The treaty severely limited the size of the German military. It returned Alsace-Lorraine to France. In addition, the treaty stripped Germany of its overseas colonies. However, instead of gaining independence, the colonies were put under the control of Britain or France.

Wilson's successes

Wilson had his way on a few issues, however. In Eastern Europe, the Allies provided for several new nations to be formed on the principle of national self-determination. They included Poland, Czechoslovakia, and Yugoslavia. They were created out of lands once ruled by Germany, Russia, and Austria-Hungary. (See the map on page 592.)

Still, some people were dissatisfied with the new boundaries. Many Germans, for example, had settled in Poland and Czechoslovakia. Before long, Germany would seek to

Geography *Skills* **A series of treaties ended World War I. The treaties created several new nations in Eastern Europe.**

1. **Location** On the map, locate: **(a)** Poland, **(b)** Czechoslovakia, **(c)** Yugoslavia.
2. **Region** **(a)** In what region of Europe were most of the new nations created? **(b)** Which new nations bordered Russia?
3. **Critical Thinking** Compare this map to the map on page 574. **(a)** What happened to Austria-Hungary? **(b)** What happened to Serbia? **(c)** What happened to the city of Sarajevo?

regain control of German-speaking peoples in Eastern Europe.

To Wilson, however, his greatest achievement was persuading the Allies to include the League of Nations in the treaty. Wilson was certain that the League would prevent future wars by allowing nations to talk over their problems. If talk failed, members would join together to fight aggressors. "A living thing is born," he declared. The League "is definitely a guarantee of peace."

Battle Over the Treaty

When President Wilson returned home, he faced a new battle. He had to persuade the Senate to approve the Versailles Treaty.

Opposition to the League

Most Americans favored the treaty. A vocal minority opposed it, however. Some said that it was too soft on the defeated powers. Many German Americans felt that it was too harsh. Some Republicans hoped to embarrass

President Wilson, a Democrat, by rewriting or defeating the treaty. **Isolationists,** people who wanted the United States to stay out of world affairs, opposed the League of Nations.

Critics of the treaty found a leader in **Henry Cabot Lodge** of Massachusetts. Lodge, a Republican, was chairman of the powerful Senate Foreign Relations Committee. Lodge accepted the idea of the League of Nations. However, he wanted changes in some provisions relating to the League.

Specifically, Lodge objected to Article 10 of the treaty. It called for the League to protect any member whose independence or territory was threatened. Lodge argued that Article 10 could involve the United States in future European wars. He wanted changes in the treaty that would ensure that the United States remained independent of the League. He also wanted Congress to have the power to decide whether the United States would follow League policy.

Wilson believed that Lodge's changes would weaken the League. Advisers urged the President to compromise, giving up some of his demands in order to save the League. Wilson replied, "Let Lodge compromise." He refused to make any changes.

A defeat for Wilson

As the battle grew hotter, the President took his case to the people. In early September 1919, Wilson set out across the country, making 37 speeches in 29 cities. He urged Americans to let their senators know that they supported the treaty.

Wilson kept up a killing pace. On September 25, the exhausted President complained of a headache. His doctors canceled the rest of the trip. Wilson returned to Washington. A week later, his wife found him unconscious. He had suffered a stroke that left him bedridden for weeks.

In November 1919, the Senate rejected the Versailles Treaty. "It is dead," Wilson mourned, "[and] every morning I put flowers on its grave." Gone, too, was Wilson's cherished goal—American membership in the League of Nations.

The United States did not sign a peace treaty with Germany until 1921. Many nations had already joined the League of Nations. Without the United States, though, the League failed to live up to its goals of protecting members against aggression. Wilson's dream of a world "safe for democracy" would have to wait.

★ Section 4 Review ★

Recall

1. **Identify** **(a)** Fourteen Points, **(b)** League of Nations, **(c)** Big Four, **(d)** Treaty of Versailles, **(e)** Henry Cabot Lodge.
2. **Define** **(a)** self-determination, **(b)** reparation, **(c)** isolationist.

Comprehension

3. **(a)** Describe the major points of Wilson's peace plan. **(b)** Which point did Wilson consider most important? Why?
4. Why did Wilson's peace plan run into trouble at Versailles?
5. **(a)** What changes did critics want to make in the peace treaty? **(b)** How did the President respond to their demands?

Critical Thinking and Writing

6. **Predicting Consequences** **(a)** List three ways that the Treaty of Versailles punished Germany. **(b)** What do you think the effects of this harsh treatment might be?
7. **Defending a Position** Many historians blame Wilson for the defeat of the Versailles Treaty in Congress. What reasons can you give to support this position?

Activity **Drawing a Political Cartoon** Draw a political cartoon expressing your feelings about the conflict over the League of Nations. If possible, include figures representing Henry Cabot Lodge and Woodrow Wilson.

Chapter 22 Review and Activities

★ Sum It Up ★

Section 1 War Erupts in Europe

- Nationalism, imperialism, and militarism increased tensions in Europe in the early years of the 1900s.
- After Austria-Hungary declared war on Serbia in 1914, the alliance system drew other nations into the conflict.
- While the United States remained neutral, German submarine warfare outraged Americans.

Section 2 The United States Enters the War

- After declaring war on Germany in 1917, the United States set up a military draft.
- A huge government bureaucracy built support for the war effort.
- The government silenced protests against the war by arresting people who criticized the government.

Section 3 Winning the War

- In the final battles of the war, American troops helped defeat German forces at Belleau Wood and the Argonne Forest.
- World War I was a costly war, with more than 30 million people killed or wounded.

Section 4 Wilson and the Peace

- Wilson's plan for peace included a call for a League of Nations to settle disputes between nations.
- The Senate rejected the peace treaty because critics believed that the League of Nations might draw the United States into future wars.

For additional review of the major ideas of Chapter 22, see ***Guide to the Essentials of American History*** or ***Interactive Student Tutorial CD-ROM,*** which contains interactive review activities, graphic organizers, and practice tests.

Reviewing the Chapter

Define These Terms

Match each term with the correct definition.

Column 1

1. nationalism
2. militarism
3. bureaucracy
4. armistice
5. self-determination

Column 2

a. system of managing government though departments
b. pride in one's country
c. right of a national group to its own territory and own form of government
d. policy of building up armed forces to prepare for war
e. agreement to stop fighting

Explore the Main Ideas

1. How did the alliance system help lead to World War I?
2. **(a)** What nations formed the Central Powers? **(b)** What nations formed the Allied powers?
3. How did the Russian Revolution affect the war?
4. **(a)** Describe the German "peace offensive" of 1918. **(b)** What were the results?
5. How did Britain and France feel about Germany during the Paris peace conference?

Geography Activity

Match the letters on the map with the following places: **1.** Allied Powers, **2.** Central Powers, **3.** Sarajevo, **4.** Great Britain, **5.** France, **6.** Russia, **7.** Germany, **8.** Austria-Hungary. **Movement** Why did European nations seek colonies in Asia and Africa?

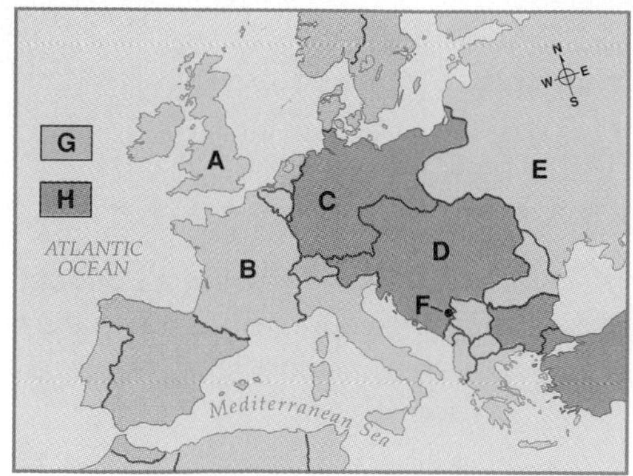

Critical Thinking and Writing

1. **Understanding Chronology** **(a)** List the following events in chronological order: Zimmermann telegram is discovered; U-boats sink the *Lusitania;* Archduke Franz Ferdinand is assassinated; United States declares war on Germany; armistice is signed. **(b)** Describe the relationship between any two events on the list.
2. **Linking Past and Present** During World War I, inventions such as submarines and machine guns changed the nature of the fighting. List two kinds of technology that are important in warfare today.
3. **Analyzing Ideas** Why do you think Americans accepted government controls on the economy during World War I?
4. **Exploring Unit Themes** **Global Interaction** Based on what you have learned, make two generalizations about American isolationism and global interaction before, during, and after World War I.

Using Primary Sources

President Wilson toured the nation in 1919, hoping to gain support for the Versailles Treaty. In one speech, he talked about how the sight of American soldiers impressed him:

> "I saw many fine sights in Paris, many gallant sights, many sights that quickened the pulse; but my pulse never beat so fast as when I saw groups of our boys [marching] along the street. They looked as if they owned something, and they did. They owned the finest thing in the world.... They owned the ideals... that will govern the world."

Source: "The Destiny of America," Woodrow Wilson, *Senate Document 120,* 1919–1920.

Recognizing Points of View **(a)** Why was Wilson thrilled to see American soldiers in Paris? **(b)** What did Wilson mean by his statement that American ideals would "govern the world"? **(c)** Do you think Georges Clemenceau would have agreed with Wilson's statement?

Activity Bank

Interdisciplinary Activity

Exploring the Arts Learn the song "Over There" by George M. Cohan. Write an additional stanza for the song or write a new song of your own. Perform the song for the class.

Career Skills Activity

Economists Find out more about the effects that the war had on the nation's economy. Then make a concept map showing these effects.

Citizenship Activity

Organizing a Debate Organize a classroom debate about freedom of speech during wartime. One team of students will argue that the government should be allowed to silence protests during wartime. The other team will argue that the government does not have the right to silence protests. Assign one student to act as moderator. After the debate, write a paragraph explaining your position.

Internet Activity

Use the Internet to find sites dealing with the causes of World War I. Then, use the results of your research to write a short essay on whether you think the war could have been avoided.

You are one of the following: an American isolationist in 1914; a Mexican immigrant working in America for the war effort; a German American; a woman working in a factory; an American soldier in Europe; President Wilson. In your EYEWITNESS JOURNAL, describe the events of the war years that had the greatest impact on you.

Picture Bride

Yoshiko Uchida

Introduction

In the early 1900s, many Japanese women who came to the United States were "picture brides." The marriages were arranged by relatives, with the bride and bridegroom seeing each other only through pictures. Yoshiko Uchida tells the story of one of these immigrants in her novel *Picture Bride.* Here, young Hana Omiya looks back on her decision to go to the United States.

Vocabulary

Before you read the selection, find the meaning of these words in a dictionary: **samurai, perpetuate, conscientious, affluence, latitude, tuberculosis.**

It was she who had first planted in her uncle's mind the thought that she would make a good wife for Taro Takeda, the lonely man who had gone to America to make his fortune in Oakland, California.

It all began one day when her uncle had come to visit her mother.

"I must find a nice young bride," he had said, startling Hana with this blunt talk of marriage in her presence. She blushed and was ready to leave the room when her uncle quickly added, "My good friend Takeda has a son in America. I must find someone willing to travel to that far land."

This last remark was intended to indicate to Hana and her mother that he didn't consider this a suitable prospect for Hana who was the youngest daughter of what once had been a fine family. Her father, until his death fifteen years ago, had been the largest landholder of the village and one its last *samurai.* They had once had many servants and field hands, but now all that was changed. Their money was gone. . . .

Her uncle spoke freely of Taro Takeda only because he was so sure Hana would never consider him. "He is a conscientious, hardworking man who has been in the United States for almost ten years. He is thirty-one, operates a small shop and rents some rooms above the shop where he lives." Her uncle rubbed his chin thoughtfully. "He could provide well for a wife," he added.

"Ah," Hana's mother said softly.

"You say he is successful in this business?" Hana's sister inquired.

"His father tells me he sells many things in his shop—clothing, stockings, needles, thread and buttons—such things as that. He also sells bean paste, pickled radish, bean cake and soy sauce. A wife of his would not go cold or hungry."

They all nodded, each of them picturing this merchant in varying degrees of success and affluence. There were many Japanese emigrating to America these days, and Hana had heard of the picture brides who went with nothing more than an exchange of photographs to bind them to a strange man.

Viewing HISTORY **A Workshop in Japan**

This 1897 woodblock print shows young women working in a Japanese clothing factory. The machinery and the clothing worn by the workers show the influence of American ways. ★ **Why were many young Japanese women permitted to come to the United States after 1907?**

Almost before she realized what she was doing, Hana spoke to her uncle. "Oji San, perhaps I should go to America to make this lonely man a good wife."

"You, Hana Chan?" Her uncle observed her with startled curiosity. "You would go all alone to a foreign land so far away from your mother and family?"

"I would not allow it." Her mother spoke fiercely. Hana was her youngest and she had lavished upon her the attention and latitude that often befall the last child. How could she permit her to travel so far, even to marry the son of Takeda who was known to her brother.

But now, a notion that had seemed quite impossible a moment before was lodged in his receptive mind, and Hana's uncle grasped it with pleasure that comes from an unexpected discovery....

"You know," he said looking at Hana, "it might be a very good life in America."

Hana felt a faint fluttering in her heart. Perhaps this lonely man in America was her means of escaping. . . .

Her uncle spoke with increasing enthusiasm of sending Hana to become Taro's wife. And the husband of Hana's sister, who was head of their household, spoke with equal eagerness. Although he never said so, Hana guessed he would be pleased to be rid of her, the spirited younger sister who stirred up his placid life with what he considered radical ideas about life and the role of women. He often claimed that Hana had too much schooling for a girl.

A man's word carried much weight for Hana's mother.... Finally, she agreed to an exchange of family histories and an investigation was begun into Taro Takeda's family, his education and his health, so they would be assured there was no insanity or tuberculosis or police records concealed in his family's past.

Analyzing Literature

1. What did Hana know about Taro Takeda before she left Japan?
2. Why did Hana's mother agree to let her go?
3. **Making Inferences** Give two reasons why Hana might have wanted to go to the United States.

Chapter 23

Linking Past to Present: A Century of Change

1914–Present

What's Ahead

Section 1 A Changing Economy

Section 2 A Changing Population

Section 3 The Civil Rights Movement

Section 4 Expanding Opportunities

Section 5 Understanding Citizenship

During the twentieth century, the United States saw tremendous changes. Although the nation struggled with periods of economic hard times, the middle class grew larger and the percentage of people who were poor grew smaller.

The nation saw social changes, too. Immigrants made the United States a land of rich cultural variety. African Americans waged a long struggle to secure their constitutional rights. Their successes inspired others, such as women and Mexican Americans. Now, more Americans than ever share the rights and responsibilities of citizenship.

Why Study History?

You have learned a lot about American history this year. Studying history can help you become an informed, responsible citizen. Did you know that a background in history can also prepare you for many jobs? To focus on this connection, see the *Why Study History?* feature, "Knowing History May Help Your Career," in this chapter.

American Events

1929 Stock Market crash sets off Great Depression

1950s Baby boom increases United States population

1954 Supreme Court rules that school segregation is illegal

1920 — 1940 — 1960

World Events

1922 World Event Soviet Union is formed

1939 World Event World War II begins

Viewing HISTORY **A Land of Liberty**

Taiwanese-born artist Tsing-fang Chen studied in Paris before coming to the United States. In his 1986 painting Liberty States, *Chen uses familiar images to stress the continuing importance of liberty to the American nation.* ★ **What does the figure in the lower left and right corners represent?**

1964 Civil Rights Act protects rights of all citizens to vote

1970 Widespread use of computers revolutionizes business

1990 Congress passes law to protect disabled Americans

1960 **1980** **2000**

1975 World Event Vietnam War ends

1991 World Event Soviet Union breaks up into 15 independent republics

A Changing Economy

As You Read

Explore These Questions

- What cycles has the American economy experienced since World War I?
- Why has the middle class grown?
- What changes have affected American workers?

Define

- productivity
- recession
- standard of living
- service industry

Identify

- Henry Ford
- Herbert Hoover
- Great Depression
- Franklin D. Roosevelt
- New Deal
- Henry J. Kaiser
- Lyndon Johnson

SETTING the Scene In 1950, George Yano opened an auto repair shop. His office shelves held repair manuals for all makes and models of cars. To fix a car, Yano consulted the right manual and used his own skills.

Today, Yano's son Andy runs the shop. The repair manuals are gone. Instead, Andy Yano uses a computer. He gets repair information off a CD-ROM or the Internet. He also attends night classes to acquire new skills. Andy Yano said:

> ❝ They used to call us grease monkeys. If anyone had told me I would have a computer in the garage, I'd have told them they were crazy. ❞

The rise of computer technology is just one of several developments that have transformed the American economy.

New Ways to Organize Work

Henry Ford helped revolutionize industry. Ford set out to build inexpensive cars that ordinary Americans could afford. In 1913, he introduced the assembly line. It divided the process of making a car into dozens of simple tasks. (See page 474.)

Assembly line technology

Ford's new method of production had dramatic results. In 1913, it took more than 12 hours to make a car. A year later, it took just 93 minutes to make the same car.

1913 Ford Model T

Still, performing the same task hour after hour was boring. Many workers quit their jobs. To attract loyal workers, Ford offered to double their wages:

> ❝ The Ford Motor Company, the greatest and most successful in the world, will on January 12 inaugurate the greatest revolution in the matter of rewards for its workers ever known to the industrial world. ❞

Many workers applied for these higher-paying jobs. Gradually, they got used to the routine of the assembly line. In time, Ford produced cars even more quickly. By 1925, a Ford Model T rolled off the assembly line every 10 seconds.

Rising productivity

During the early 1900s, many industries set up assembly lines. They also used Frederick Taylor's methods of "scientific management." (See page 476.) As a result, productivity rose rapidly. **Productivity** measures how much a given number of workers can produce in a given time.

Between 1919 and 1929, American industrial production nearly doubled. As time passed, businesses developed even more efficient methods. Today's workers are 50 times more productive than those of a century ago.

Economic Cycles

The American economy has always experienced cycles of growth and decline. After World War I, the economy boomed. When **Herbert Hoover** ran for President in 1928, he declared, "We in America are nearer to the final triumph over poverty than ever before."

Hoover won the election, but his confident prediction proved to be very wrong. In October 1929, a stock market crash set off a series of economic disasters that plunged the United States into the worst depression in its history. The **Great Depression** lasted from 1929 to 1941.

The Great Depression

As the depression spread, many businesses closed. Others cut back production and laid off workers. By 1932, one in four workers was unemployed. Many more had to work shorter hours or take pay cuts.

The number of homeless people soared as jobless workers lost their homes. Many people drifted from town to town looking for work. Desperately, parents and children searched city dumps for food. In one school, a teacher told a hungry-looking child to go home and eat. "I can't," the girl replied. "This is my sister's day to eat."

The New Deal

As hard times dragged on, a sense of despair spread. Then, in 1932, **Franklin D. Roosevelt** ran for President against Hoover. Roosevelt seemed to offer hope when he pledged "a new deal for the American people." Roosevelt won a landslide victory.

Once in office, Roosevelt sent a flood of bills to Congress. These laws became known as the **New Deal.** Roosevelt's New Deal program had three main goals: aid for the unemployed, plans to help the economy recover, and reforms to prevent another depression.

The New Deal did not end the Great Depression. Still, it had important long-term

MILESTONES: Economic Change

5,000 years ago
Farming in Americas

1600s
Farming and trade in colonies

1790
First factory

1800
Interchangeable parts

Early 1800s
Internal improvements

1869
Transcontinental railroad

Late 1800s
Rise of industry and big business

1890s
Overseas trade increases

1913
Assembly line

1930s
Government role increases

1970s
Computer age

1980s
Shift from manufacturing to services

1993
NAFTA

Graphic Organizer *Skills*

Economics refers to the ways a society produces, distributes, and uses goods and services. The American economy has undergone several major shifts.

1. **Comprehension** Identify two developments that affected the way goods were produced.
2. **Critical Thinking** Which event listed here has had the greatest effect on your everyday life? Explain.

Economics $

Viewing HISTORY **Boom or Bust**

The highs and lows of the economic cycle have had a great impact on American families. The boy at left is living in a temporary work camp during the Great Depression of the 1930s. At right, a family enjoys the prosperity of the 1950s. ★ **Examine the photograph on the left. Identify three details that show the effects of economic hard times.**

effects. The federal government grew larger. It greatly expanded its role in people's lives by regulating the economy and by undertaking to help needy citizens.

Wartime recovery

In 1941, the United States entered World War II on the Allied side.* As orders for war goods poured in, shipyards and defense plants expanded production with amazing speed. In California, shipbuilder **Henry J. Kaiser** used his organizing skills to speed up construction. Before the war, it took workers up to a year to build a cargo ship. During the war, Kaiser shipyards reduced that time to less than a week.

The wartime demand for goods ended the Great Depression. Unemployment fell as millions of people entered the armed services or took jobs in war industries.

Growth and recession

World War II ended in 1945. As the economy adjusted to peacetime, it entered a long period of growth called the postwar boom. Jobs were plentiful and wages rose.

Overall, the economy has continued to grow since 1945. At times, however, it has suffered periods of **recession.** A recession is a mild depression in which business slows down and some workers lose their jobs. Postwar recessions were never as severe as the Great Depression. Still, they brought hardships to those who lost jobs or businesses.

Wealth and Poverty

In 1956, *Fortune* magazine boasted that the United States had become the richest nation in the world. It proclaimed:

> “Never has a whole people spent so much money on so many expensive things in such an easy way as Americans are doing today.”

With the economy booming, millions enjoyed a higher standard of living. A nation's **standard of living** is based on the amount and quality of goods, services, education, and leisure time that people have.

The middle class grows

As the standard of living rose, millions of Americans lived better than ever before. In

* World War II began in 1939. It pitted the Allies (including Britain, France, and the Soviet Union) against the Axis (Germany, Italy, and Japan).

Why Study History?

Because Knowing History May Help Your Career

To become an archaeologist, you need more than a shovel—you need a knowledge of history!

Historical Background

"Those who cannot remember the past are condemned to repeat it." With these words, Spanish American philosopher George Santayana stressed the need to understand history. Yet not all Americans have placed the same value on the study of our past. Automaker Henry Ford proclaimed, "History is more or less bunk." Since 1957, when the Soviet Union launched the first artificial satellite, American schools have often emphasized science and mathematics.

Connections to Today

Can history be helpful in today's job market? The answer is yes! The United States Department of Labor lists more than 30 careers for people with a background in history, including:

- Antiques
- Banking
- Insurance
- Journalism
- Law
- Library science
- Museum operations
- Publishing
- Research
- Teaching
- Tourism

Connections to You

Current statistics say that in the next century, people will change jobs at least five to seven times. This means that your education must prepare you for change. You will have to be adaptable, flexible, and creative. The skills you need to study history—researching, creative thinking, understanding causes and effects, recognizing other viewpoints—can be valuable no matter what career you finally choose.

1. **Comprehension** Identify two skills that the study of history can help you develop.
2. **Critical Thinking** Choose one career from the Department of Labor list above. Explain why you think knowledge of history might be helpful in that career.

Investigating Careers Do further research into one of the careers listed above. (Your school librarian can suggest resources.) Prepare a fact sheet summarizing the responsibilities of the job, the average pay range, and future opportunities in that field.

1900, only 20 percent of American families earned enough money to enjoy a comfortable middle-class life. Most people were poor or lived on the edge of poverty.

By 1960, the numbers were reversed. Only 20 percent of Americans were poor. Most families belonged to the middle class. Higher wages for factory workers contributed to this change. The postwar economy also offered many more high-paying management and professional jobs.

Equally important, more women joined the labor force. During wartime, many women worked outside the home for the first time. After the war, as men returned from military service, women were encouraged to return to the home. Many women, however, kept their jobs. Their paychecks helped families rise into the middle class.

Poverty remains

Despite the postwar boom, millions of Americans remained poor. In the 1960s, President **Lyndon Johnson** declared a "War on Poverty." He believed that the government should use its power to wipe out poverty in the United States.

To achieve that goal, Johnson pushed 50 laws through Congress. They included Medicare, a plan to help pay hospital bills for citizens over age 65. Another law set up job training programs for the poor. New government welfare programs provided direct economic assistance to the poor. Such programs helped lower the poverty rate from 22 percent to 11 percent by 1973. The elderly benefited the most.

By the 1990s, the overall poverty rate had crept back up to about 15 percent, and

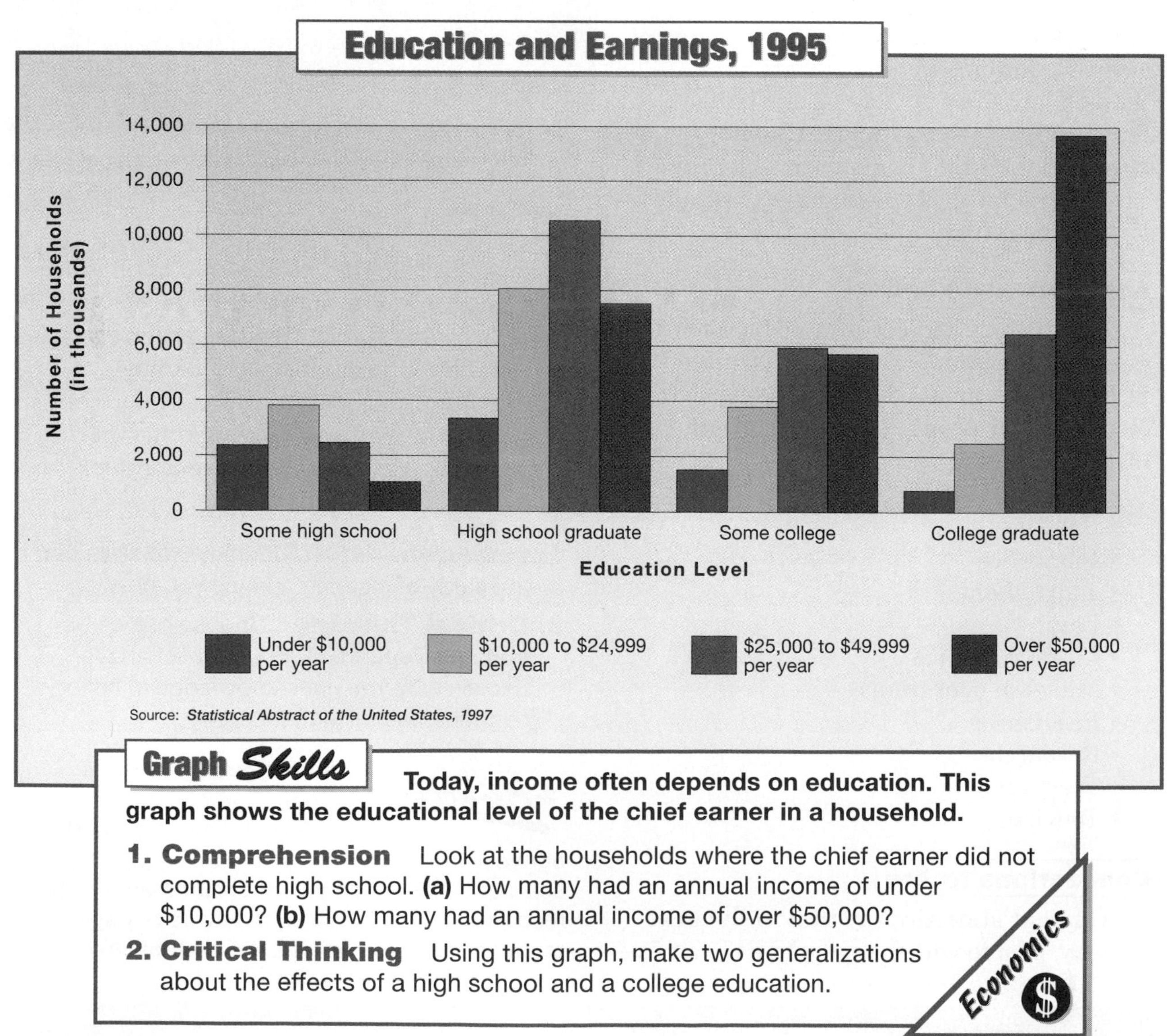

Graph Skills Today, income often depends on education. This graph shows the educational level of the chief earner in a household.

1. **Comprehension** Look at the households where the chief earner did not complete high school. **(a)** How many had an annual income of under $10,000? **(b)** How many had an annual income of over $50,000?
2. **Critical Thinking** Using this graph, make two generalizations about the effects of a high school and a college education.

the number of poor children was increasing at an alarming rate. By the late 1990s, about 40 million Americans still lived in poverty.

Many people believed that welfare was not an effective solution to the problem of poverty. These critics argued that welfare programs made people too dependent on government aid. In 1996, after much bitter debate, Congress passed reforms to get poor people off welfare and into jobs. The government continued to give assistance to children, the elderly, and the severely disabled.

Shift to a Service Economy

A century ago, 9 out of 10 American workers did manual labor. Most jobs were in farming, manufacturing, and mining.

In the 1960s, a great economic shift began. The number of manufacturing jobs declined. Many such jobs moved to factories overseas. By 1990, only one in five American workers held manufacturing jobs.

As manufacturing jobs disappeared, new jobs opened up in service industries. In a **service industry,** workers perform a service rather than produce goods. Service industries range from banking and education to recreation and transportation. In the 1950s, about one in three American workers was a service worker. Today, more than three out of four workers hold jobs in the service industry.

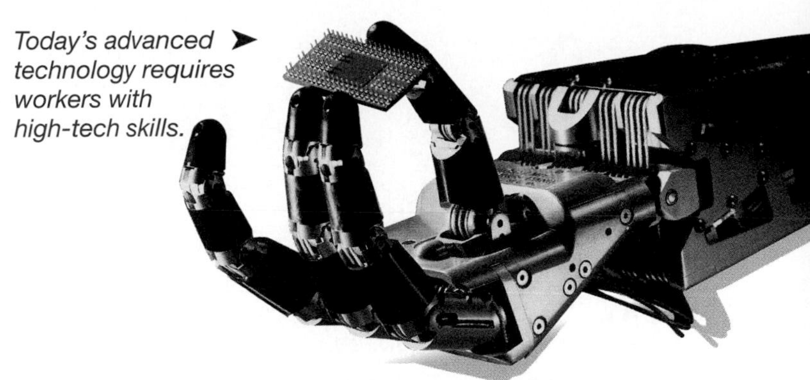
Today's advanced technology requires workers with high-tech skills.

Succeeding in Tomorrow's Workplace

People who perform high-tech jobs or provide information are part of the service economy. They include doctors, lawyers, computer programmers, engineers, and writers. Such workers generally earn more than other workers in the service economy.

In the past, a worker could get a good job with only a high school diploma. Today, many top jobs require advanced technical skills, knowledge of other languages, or creative thinking. Students are urged to stay in school because success in tomorrow's workplace will depend on a high level of education.

★ Section 1 Review ★

Recall

1. **Identify** **(a)** Henry Ford, **(b)** Herbert Hoover, **(c)** Great Depression, **(d)** Franklin D. Roosevelt, **(e)** New Deal, **(f)** Henry J. Kaiser, **(g)** Lyndon Johnson.
2. **Define** **(a)** productivity, **(b)** recession, **(c)** standard of living, **(d)** service industry.

Comprehension

3. Identify one economic effect of each of the following: **(a)** the Great Depression, **(b)** the New Deal, **(c)** World War II.
4. **(a)** Describe two reasons for the growth of the American middle class. **(b)** How has the government tried to combat poverty?
5. How has manufacturing changed?

Critical Thinking and Writing

6. **Defending a Position** Identify one argument for and one argument against welfare programs.
7. **Predicting Consequences** Based on what you have read, how do you think failure to graduate from high school might affect a young person's future?

Activity **Sharing Ideas** The changes in the economy after 1914 affect you *today*. With a partner, discuss how each of the following developments has already affected your own life: assembly lines, computers, the service economy.

A Changing Population

As You Read

Explore These Questions

- How did the baby boom affect the United States?
- How have American immigration laws changed over time?
- How has immigration affected California?

Define

- birth rate
- life expectancy
- quota system
- refugee
- illegal alien

Identify

- baby boom
- Sunbelt
- Amy Tan
- Immigration Reform and Control Act

Leave It to Beaver, popular 1950s television comedy

SETTING the Scene In 1946, a year after World War II ended, 3.4 million babies were born in the United States. The postwar **baby boom** was under way. Newspaper columnist Sylvia Porter predicted big changes:

> “Just imagine how much these extra people, these new markets, will absorb—in food, in clothing, in gadgets, in housing, in services. Our factories must expand just to keep pace.”

Because of the baby boom, new immigration patterns, and other changes, the American population is far different today from what it was a century ago.

The Baby Boom

The **birth rate** is usually figured as the number of babies born each year for every thousand members of the population. During the 1930s and 1940s, the birth rate was low. During the Great Depression, many parents were unable to support large families. During World War II, many couples had to wait until after the war to marry and start their families.

By 1946, the nation was at peace and the economy was growing. These changes contributed to the postwar baby boom. From 1946 to 1964, about 80 million Americans were born. Members of this generation were later called “boomers.”

Impact of the baby boom

The baby boom spurred the economy. Growing families needed homes. The demand for housing led to a building boom. Factories increased production to meet the demand for building materials, furniture, and other goods.

The need for schools grew. During the 1950s, California opened one new school a week. Between 1956 and 1965, Los Angeles hired 1,000 new teachers a year and still had a teacher shortage. The baby boom also reshaped colleges and universities. More baby boomers went on to higher education than their parents.

New leisure activities shaped the baby boomers. They were the first generation to grow up watching television. By the late 1960s, nearly every American home had a television set. As teenagers, boomers listened to rock 'n' roll, a new music that blended black rhythm-and-blues with country music.

Many older Americans criticized the new sound, but it won a worldwide audience. Rock 'n' roll of the 1950s and 1960s evolved into the popular music of today.

A generation gap?

New music was one sign of what many called the "generation gap." Some baby boomers rebelled against their parents' values and rules. They demonstrated for social and political causes. During the 1960s, opposition to a war in Vietnam sparked bitter protests that occasionally turned violent. Some young people turned to illegal drugs such as marijuana and LSD. Drug abuse became a growing social problem that continues today. Still, many baby boomers did not join protests or use drugs.

Like their parents and grandparents, baby boomers continued to raise their families in towns and cities. However, they generally had fewer children than their parents. The birth rate plunged to its lowest level in American history.

Family Life

Social and economic forces have long shaped family life. In colonial times, children often had stepparents because death rates were high. Slavery tore apart many African American families. After the Industrial Revolution, many poor children went to work in factories or mines. Attitudes toward children and family reflected the values of the times.

During the 1950s, peace and prosperity shaped family life. Television programs such as *Father Knows Best* reflected what many saw as an ideal image of the American family. Father, mother, and children lived in a middle-class suburb. The father worked in an office. The mother cooked, cleaned, and cared for the children.

Still, family life did not always match this image. Even in the prosperous 1950s, more than 25 percent of American children lived in poverty. Divorce, illness, and other problems disrupted many families.

Changing family patterns

Since the 1950s, family life has changed in some ways. Today, the average couple

MILESTONES: Changing Population

70,000–50,000 years ago
First Americans arrive from Asia

1500–1700s
Europeans found colonies

1619
Africans arrive in Virginia

1803
Louisiana Purchase doubles territory of United States

1840s
Immigration from Northern Europe continues

1840s–1900
People move westward

1880s
Immigration from Southern and Eastern Europe booms

1920
Census shows majority of Americans live in urban areas

1924
Emergency Quota Act limits immigration

1950s
Baby boom increases United States population

1980s
Immigration from Latin America, Asia, and Caribbean increases

Graphic Organizer *Skills*

Immigration and changing birth rates are two of the many factors that have shaped the American population.

1. **Comprehension** Identify two developments that are related to the geographic theme of movement.
2. **Critical Thinking** **(a)** Which developments shown here contributed to greater diversity? **(b)** Which development limited diversity?

Gray Panthers banner

Biography **Maggie Kuhn**

In 1970, Maggie Kuhn was forced to retire because she had turned 65. She spent the next 20 years fighting age discrimination. Kuhn founded the Gray Panthers, a group that works to protect the interests of older Americans. Kuhn said her goal was to see "young and old working together for a better world for the young to grow old in." ★ **Why should younger Americans be concerned about issues affecting older people?**

waits longer to marry and has fewer children. The divorce rate has also soared. As a result, about a quarter of all children grow up in single-parent families. Nearly as many live in stepfamilies. About half of all children live with both of their birth parents.

During the 1950s, a married man's income often supported a family's middle-class life. Low-interest government loans let families buy houses fairly easily. As a result, it was not a hardship for women to stay home and raise children.

Today, many more mothers work outside the home. Many of these women choose to continue the careers that they began before they had children. Other working mothers feel that economic changes make it difficult for their families to live on a single income. Still other women are the sole support of single-parent households.

Challenges and values

Today, families face diverse challenges. Drug abuse, unemployment, and a busier pace of life have put a strain on the family. Fewer families sit down together for regular meals than in earlier times.

Still, the vast majority of Americans remain deeply committed to family. One woman who is stepmother to several children said:

> "Family is people who love each other, living together and working it out day by day."

An Older Population

Americans are living longer than ever before. Their **life expectancy** has risen sharply since 1900. Life expectancy means the average number of years a newborn can expect to live. A child born in 1900 could expect to live to the age of 47 years. Today, the average life expectancy has risen to 75. Improvements in diet, sanitation, and education contributed to the change. Medical breakthroughs, from antibiotics to heart bypass surgery, further increased life expectancy.

Because Americans are living longer but having fewer children, our population is aging. At one time, only a small fraction of the population was 65 and over. By 2030, more than 20 percent of Americans will be 65 or over.

As baby boomers reach 65, their numbers will put a great strain on programs for the elderly. As children, boomers created needs for housing and schools. As they age, they will need medical care and other services.

People on the Move

Change comes partly as people move from place to place. At one time, the majority of the American population lived in rural areas. After the Industrial Revolution, population gradually shifted to cities.

Move to the suburbs

After World War II, the population shifted again. As more veterans bought their own homes, millions of families moved from city apartments to the suburbs.

Cities often suffered from the growth of the suburbs. As well-to-do Americans moved out, many urban neighborhoods were allowed to deteriorate. Today, the nation's cities are working on programs to revitalize inner-city neighborhoods.

Move to the Sunbelt

Population has also shifted nationwide. After the 1950s, many people moved from the Northeast to the **Sunbelt,** the band of states from Florida to California that have mild climates. In 1960, only 2 of the 10 largest American cities were in the South or West. By 1990, six of them were: Los Angeles, Houston, San Diego, Dallas, San Antonio, and Phoenix.

As a result of the move to the Sunbelt, California became the most populous state by far. Nearly one American in eight now lives in California.

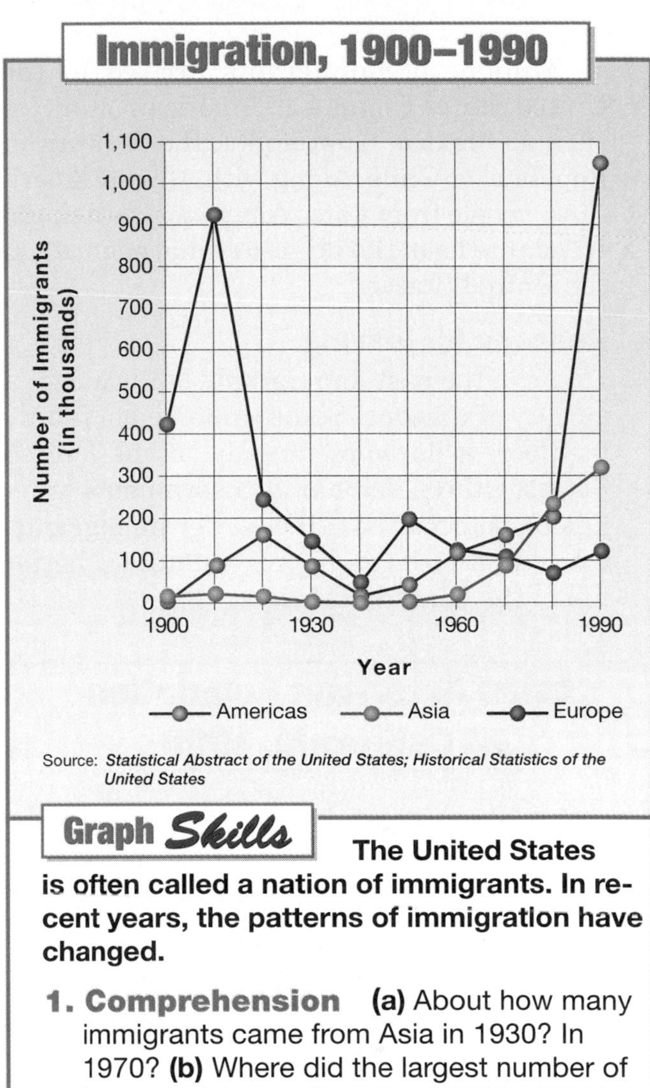

Source: *Statistical Abstract of the United States; Historical Statistics of the United States*

Graph Skills **The United States is often called a nation of immigrants. In recent years, the patterns of immigration have changed.**

1. **Comprehension** **(a)** About how many immigrants came from Asia in 1930? In 1970? **(b)** Where did the largest number of immigrants come from in 1900? In 1990?
2. **Critical Thinking** Why did the number of immigrants drop after the 1920s?

Immigration and Diversity

The American population, noted historian Ronald Takaki, "has been racially diverse since our very beginning on the Virginia shore." In colonial times, immigrants from Europe and Africa joined the Native American population. Later immigrants added to the nation's diversity. From 1890 to 1915, more than 18 million newcomers arrived.

In the 1920s, Congress decided to limit immigration. It set up a **quota system** that allowed only a certain number of immigrants per year from each country. The system favored people from Northern Europe. People from Eastern Europe, Africa, and Asia had a harder time entering the country. Earlier laws already excluded immigrants from Japan and China.

Connections With Geography

Picture the United States as a large, flat surface with all of its people standing where they live. The point where the weight of the people would balance is called the center of population. The center of population has moved steadily westward. In 1790, it was located in Maryland. By 1900, it had shifted to Indiana. In 1990, the center of the population was 9.7 miles northwest of Steelville, Missouri.

New immigration patterns

In 1965, Congress finally ended the quota system. New laws made it easier for non-Europeans to enter the country. Immigration soared as millions of newcomers arrived.

Most new immigrants came from Asia and Latin America. Asians came from such countries as the Philippines, China, Korea, Japan, Cambodia, Vietnam, and India. The Arab American population also grew rapidly.

Millions of immigrants arrived in the United States from Latin American countries such as Mexico, Guatemala, the Dominican Republic, or Chile. Along with African Americans, people from Latin America and their descendants form the largest ethnic minority in the United States.

Reasons for leaving

As in the past, immigrants left home for a variety of reasons. Some came to join family members who were already in the United States. Others fled harsh governments or religious persecution. Like earlier immigrants, many fled poverty, hoping to build a better life in the United States.

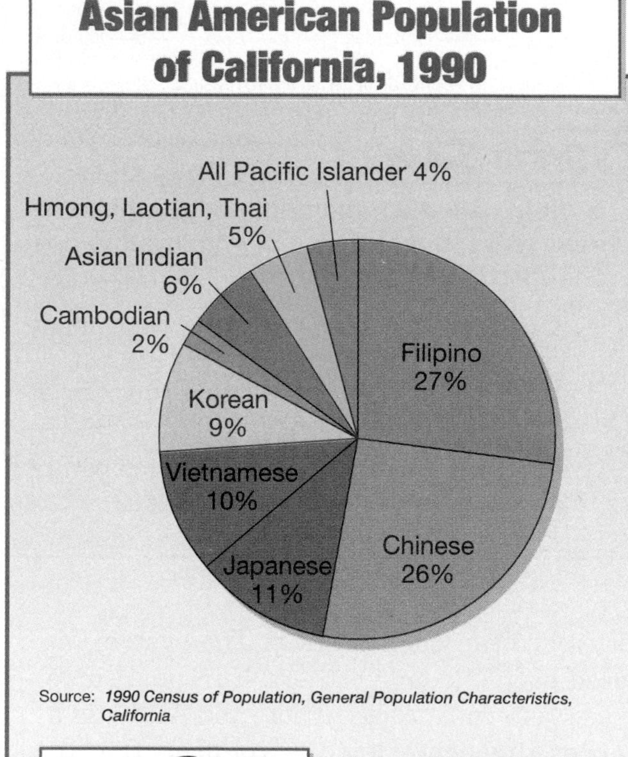

Source: *1990 Census of Population, General Population Characteristics, California*

Graph *Skills* **California has a very diverse Asian American population. This graph does not include Asians from Russia or the Middle East.**

1. **Comprehension** **(a)** What two groups make up more than half of California's Asian American population? **(b)** What percentage are of Vietnamese background?
2. **Critical Thinking** Why do you think California has a more diverse Asian American population than many other states?

Still other immigrants were **refugees,** people who flee their homelands to seek safety elsewhere. Fighting in the Southeast Asian nations of Vietnam, Laos, and Cambodia created millions of refugees. After the Vietnam War, some of these refugees were allowed to settle in the United States. Civil wars in Central America brought large numbers of refugees from Guatemala, El Salvador, and Nicaragua.

The immigrant experience

Today, as in the past, immigrants help shape our society. They contribute skills, talents, and hard work to their new homeland. Their foods, languages, and customs further add to the nation's diverse heritage.

Growing diversity fueled a debate over what it meant to be an American. Some argued that immigrants should try to assimilate into American society. Others felt that people should be free to retain their diverse cultures.

In *The Joy Luck Club,* California author **Amy Tan** looked at the lives and attitudes of Chinese-born mothers and their American-born daughters. The novel revealed the mixed feelings of immigrants. Many were eager to adopt American ways, but did not want to lose the traditions of their homeland.

Illegal immigration

Today, as in the past, large numbers of people have entered the United States illegally. An **illegal alien** is someone who enters a country without legal permission. To reduce illegal immigration, Congress passed new laws. The **Immigration Reform and Control Act** of 1986 allowed people who had arrived illegally before 1982 to apply for citizenship. To discourage further illegal immigration, the law imposed fines on employers who hired undocumented, or illegal, foreign workers.

In states like California, many people argued that the growing number of immigrants, both legal and illegal, placed a strain on state resources. Such critics pointed out that the state had to provide schooling, medical care, and other services to all newcomers. Burdened by a flood of illegal immigrants, California passed a controversial law in 1994. It banned schooling and health services for illegal aliens. The law faced challenges in the courts.

California's ethnic mosaic

Since 1965, more immigrants settled in California than in any other state, creating a highly diverse population. By 1990, about one third of all foreign-born newcomers lived in California. A high school student who recently immigrated from Mexico noted:

> "I was surprised when I arrived to see so many kinds of people—Black people, Asians. I found people from Korea and Cambodia and Mexico. In California I found not just America. I found the world."

Sign in a Korean American neighborhood

In its diversity, Los Angeles today resembles New York City in the early 1900s. It has the largest number of Mexicans outside of Mexico City and the most Koreans outside of Seoul, South Korea. In the city's public schools, students speak dozens of different languages. "We are all minorities," noted one Mexican American student, "but together we are a majority."

As in the past, newcomers from the same country often live in neighborhoods with others who speak their language and share their culture. In the Los Angeles area, immigrant neighborhoods have names such as "Little Saigon" or "Koreatown."

Although newcomers are often seen as separate groups, they are part of the whole. Like earlier immigrants, they will play a major rule in the prosperity of the state and the nation. "Anything will be possible here in the future," said an urban planner. "These people who are coming here can succeed or they can fail. They can be our hope or our downfall."

★ Section 2 Review ★

Recall

1. **Identify** **(a)** baby boom, **(b)** Sunbelt, **(c)** Amy Tan, **(d)** Immigration Reform and Control Act.
2. **Define** **(a)** birth rate, **(b)** life expectancy, **(c)** quota system, **(d)** refugee, **(e)** illegal alien.

Comprehension

3. How did the baby boom affect the economy?
4. What changes have taken place in the American family since the 1950s?
5. How has the United States changed its immigration policy over the years?

Critical Thinking and Writing

6. **Evaluating Information** How has a diverse population contributed to the strength of the United States?
7. **Comparing** How are the new immigrants different from those who came in earlier times? How are they similar?

Activity **Formulating Questions** You are an ace reporter writing an article on how the United States changed during the 1900s. Write five questions you would ask a baby boomer and five questions you would ask an immigrant as you gather information for your article.

The Civil Rights Movement

As You Read

Explore These Questions

- What were the main goals of the civil rights movement?
- What methods did civil rights leaders use?
- What successes have African Americans had?

Define

- civil rights
- civil disobedience
- affirmative action

Identify

- *Brown* v. *Board of Education of Topeka*
- Thurgood Marshall
- Rosa Parks
- Martin Luther King, Jr.
- Civil Rights Act of 1964
- Voting Rights Act of 1965
- Malcolm X

Setting the Scene In February 1960, four black college freshmen sat down at the lunch counter of a Woolworth's store in Greensboro, North Carolina. When they asked for coffee, the waitress told them to go downstairs, where African Americans were served. The students said that they would remain seated until they were served. When they were arrested for breaking segregation laws, the four students went peacefully to jail.

News of the Greensboro "sit-in" spread quickly. More students joined the peaceful protest. After a few months, Woolworth's ended its policy of racial segregation.

In the 1950s and 1960s, African Americans and their white supporters worked to ensure that black citizens received their rights under the Constitution. Their success would inspire other groups to seek justice.

Segregation North and South

During Reconstruction, Congress passed the Fourteenth Amendment. Its goal was to secure basic political rights for African Americans in the South. Yet these rights were quickly lost when Reconstruction ended. (See Chapter 16.)

In the South, Jim Crow laws set up a system of racial segregation. Chief Justice Earl Warren later noted:

> ❝ Segregation was enforced at all places of public entertainment, including libraries, auditoriums, and circuses. There was segregation in hospitals, prisons, mental institutions, and nursing homes. ❞

African Americans who protested segregation risked beatings, jail, or even death.

In the North, segregation was not written into the law. Still, many employers refused to hire qualified African Americans. Black families could not buy homes in white areas.

Fighting Segregation

During World War II, black soldiers fought bravely in segregated units. After the war, President Harry Truman ended segregation in the military. Also, segregation in major league baseball ended in 1947 when Jackie Robinson was hired to play for the Brooklyn Dodgers.

Jackie Robinson baseball card

By the 1950s, an organized civil rights movement was gaining force. **Civil rights** are the basic rights belonging to all American citizens—in particular, those rights guaranteed by the Fourteenth and Fifteenth Amendments. Civil rights leaders used the Fourteenth Amendment to challenge Jim Crow laws in the nation's courts.

Integrating schools

Civil rights lawyers targeted segregated schools. In 1896, in the case of *Plessy* v. *Ferguson*, the Supreme Court had ruled that "separate but equal" facilities were constitutional. (See page 423.) The ruling in *Plessy* v. *Ferguson* created a legal foundation for segregation laws.

By the 1940s, the National Association for the Advancement of Colored People (NAACP) had challenged the principle of "separate but equal" with some success. Yet 21 states and the District of Columbia allowed segregated public schools.

Oliver Brown of Topeka, Kansas decided to challenge the state's segregation law. He asked the local school board to let his daughter Linda attend the all-white school near their home rather than the distant, segregated school where she had been assigned. The school board refused Brown's request.

With the help of the NAACP, Brown filed a lawsuit against the school board. The case of ***Brown* v. *Board of Education of Topeka*** reached the Supreme Court. A brilliant African American lawyer, **Thurgood Marshall,** argued the case before the Supreme Court. "Separate," Marshall said, could never be "equal." Thus, segregated schools violated the Fourteenth Amendment, which promised all citizens "equal protection of the laws."

In 1954, the Supreme Court ruled in Brown's favor. In writing the decision, Chief Justice Warren noted that segregation affected the "hearts and minds" of black students "in a way unlikely ever to be undone." A year later, the Court ordered American schools to desegregate "with all deliberate speed."

At first, southern states strongly resisted school desegregation. Arkansas governor

MILESTONES: Civil Rights Movement

1619
20 Africans arrive in Virginia

1808
United States ends slave trade

1831
Nat Turner leads slave rebellion

1863
Emancipation Proclamation

1890s
Southern states pass Jim Crow laws

1909
NAACP is formed

1954
Brown v. *Board of Education* Supreme Court decision

1963
March on Washington

1964
Civil Rights Act

1983
Birthday of Martin Luther King, Jr., becomes national holiday

Graphic Organizer *Skills*

The African American struggle for civil rights has roots that stretch back to colonial days.

1. **Comprehension** Identify one development listed here that was a setback for African American rights.
2. **Critical Thinking** In 1903, W.E.B. DuBois predicted, "The problem of the twentieth century is the problem of the color line." **(a)** What do you think he meant? **(b)** How does this chart support his statement?

Civics

Viewing HISTORY **School Integration in Little Rock**

In 1957, African American students faced a hostile crowd in Little Rock, Arkansas. "The crowd came toward me," recalled one of the students, Elizabeth Eckford. "Somebody started yelling, 'Lynch her! Lynch her!' " President Eisenhower sent federal troops to integrate Central High. ★ **Why did the Supreme Court rule against school segregation?**

Orval Faubus vowed to block school integration. In 1957, he called out the National Guard to prevent African American students from attending Central High School in Little Rock. In response, President Dwight Eisenhower sent federal troops to Little Rock to enforce the Supreme Court's order. Protected by soldiers, nine black students entered Central High.

Connections With Civics

A California court case set an important precedent for *Brown* v. *Board of Education of Topeka*. In 1947, in the case of *Mendez* v. *Westminster,* the Supreme Court ruled that the practice of setting up separate schools for Mexican Americans was illegal. The ruling forced schools in Orange County to integrate.

Montgomery bus boycott

African Americans challenged other unjust laws during the 1950s. In Montgomery, Alabama, city buses were segregated. Whites sat in the front of the bus, blacks in the back. In December 1955, **Rosa Parks** refused to give up her seat to a white man. Parks was arrested and jailed.

In response, Montgomery's black leaders organized a bus boycott. They asked African Americans to stop riding the buses. Finally, the Montgomery bus company agreed to integrate its buses and to hire black drivers. In 1956, the Supreme Court ruled that segregation on buses was unconstitutional.

Martin Luther King, Jr.

One of the leaders of the Montgomery bus boycott was a young Baptist minister, **Martin Luther King, Jr.** King soon emerged as the nation's foremost civil rights leader.

King insisted that his followers limit their actions to **civil disobedience,** or nonviolent protest and refusal to obey laws that are seen as unjust. "We must use the weapon of love," King urged. "We must have compassion and understanding for those who hate us."

King's ideas on nonviolence were based on Christian teachings, as well as on *Civil Disobedience* by American writer Henry David Thoreau. (See page 342.) King was also influenced by the great Indian leader Mohandas Gandhi. Gandhi taught his followers that it was wrong to meet violence with violence. Using nonviolent techniques, Gandhi had helped free India from British rule in 1947.

In August 1963, King and other civil rights leaders organized a giant march on Washington, D.C. More than 200,000 Americans, both black and white, went to the capital to voice support for a civil rights bills before Congress. In his famous "I Have a Dream" speech, King described his vision for the United States:

> ❝ I have a dream that my four little children will one day live in a nation where they will be judged not by the color of their skins, but by the content of their character. ❞

King was shot to death in 1968. Today, his commitment to nonviolence and equality continues to inspire Americans. In 1983, his birthday became a national holiday.

Turbulent Times

The civil rights movement influenced the government to pass civil rights laws. The **Civil Rights Act of 1964** protected the right of all citizens to vote. It outlawed discrimination in hiring and ended segregation in public places. The Twenty-fourth Amendment banned poll taxes, which had been used in the South to keep African Americans from voting. The **Voting Rights Act of 1965** ended literacy tests and allowed federal officials to register voters. As a result of such laws, the number of African Americans voting in the South soared.

The civil rights movement toppled other barriers to equality. It pushed for an end to segregation in housing and hiring. In many places, the federal government used its authority to force states to end segregation and other forms of discrimination.

New voices and views

Despite victories, tensions remained high. Some African Americans rejected King's call for nonviolence. Radical groups such as the Black Panthers urged African Americans to arm themselves. The Panthers argued that blacks must be prepared to fight for their rights if necessary.

Black Muslims, such as **Malcolm X,** argued that African Americans could succeed only if they separated from white society. Malcolm X later modified his views. Before he was killed in 1965, he called for "a society in which there could exist honest white-black brotherhood."

Moderates as well as radicals talked about "black power." They urged African

Linking United States and the World

United States

Civil Disobedience

Mohandas Gandhi used nonviolent resistance to help free India from British rule. Gandhi and his followers refused to obey unjust laws. When arrested, they submitted peacefully. American civil rights workers later adopted civil disobedience. At right, protesters hold a sit-in at a "whites-only" lunch counter in North Carolina. ★ **Why do you think Gandhi and the American protesters were willing to be arrested?**

AmericanHeritage
M A G A Z I N E

HISTORY HAPPENED HERE

Ebenezer Baptist Church

In the 1960s, an unforgettable voice echoed through the Ebenezer Baptist Church in Atlanta, Georgia. At the height of the civil rights movement, it was the home church of Martin Luther King, Jr. Today, the church is part of the Martin Luther King, Jr., National Historic Site. You can sit in the hall where King called for equality and justice. You can also take a short walk to visit the birthplace, the childhood home, and the grave of the slain civil rights leader.

★ ***To learn more about this historic site, write:*** *Martin Luther King, Jr., National Historic Site, 450 Auburn Avenue NE, Atlanta, GA 30312-1525.*

Dr. King's tomb in Atlanta ➤

Americans to achieve economic independence by starting their own businesses and shopping in black-owned stores. Leaders also called for "black pride," encouraging African Americans to learn more about their heritage. Schools and universities began teaching about African civilizations and the achievements of African Americans.

Riots in the cities

During the 1960s, frustration over poverty and anger at the lack of economic gains exploded into violence. Riots broke out in cities across the country. In 1965, rioting lasted for days in Watts, a black neighborhood in Los Angeles. After Martin Luther King, Jr., was killed, riots shook Washington, Chicago, and other cities.

In response to urban riots, government reports called for the nation to address not only segregation but the causes of poverty as well. Programs were set up to improve conditions among the poor and unemployed, especially in the cities.

Progress and Problems

Prodded by the civil rights movement, businesses and universities opened their doors to African Americans. Many set up **affirmative action** programs. These programs were designed to encourage the hiring and promotion of African Americans, as well as women and others who had faced discrimination in the past. The government used economic pressure to promote affirmative action. For example, government agencies might refuse to give contracts to companies accused of practicing discrimination.

Critics later challenged affirmative action. They said such programs led to a form of "reverse discrimination," favoring one group over the other on the basis of race or gender. In the 1990s, Californians voted to end affirmative action on the state level. The debate over affirmative action continues to this day.

Success stories

Efforts to fight discrimination helped African Americans move into higher-paying jobs once closed to them. Some opened their own businesses. As a result, by the 1990s, the black middle class was steadily growing.

More and more African Americans attained public office. In 1967, Thurgood Marshall became the first African American to sit on the Supreme Court. For the first time since Reconstruction, voters elected African Americans to Congress. In the following decades, Los Angeles, San Francisco, New York, Detroit, and other cities elected black mayors. In 1989, General Colin Powell was appointed Chairman of the Joint Chiefs of Staff.

Continuing issues

Despite such successes, many African Americans continued to face problems. Unemployment among blacks was two times higher than for whites. Poor African Americans lacked adequate health care. Black babies were twice as likely to die in infancy as white babies. The number of African Americans attending college was dropping.

Poverty and lack of education trapped many African Americans in urban slums. Some leaders warned about a growing "underclass" of poorly educated, jobless blacks. They urged renewed attention to the problems of urban poverty and racism.

In 1992, rioting broke out in South Central Los Angeles after a jury acquitted white police officers accused of beating an African American. Some saw riots as a symbol of the problems facing the inner cities. *Business Week* noted:

> "Racism surely explains some of the carnage in Los Angeles. But the day-to-day living conditions with which many of America's urban poor must contend is an equally compelling story—a tale of economic injustice."

Still, the civil rights movement of the 1950s and 1960s had achieved many of its goals. It wiped out legal segregation in the United States. As you will read, it also set the stage for other groups of Americans to demand their rights.

★ Section 3 Review ★

Recall

1. **Identify** **(a)** *Brown* v. *Board of Education of Topeka,* **(b)** Thurgood Marshall, **(c)** Rosa Parks, **(d)** Martin Luther King, Jr., **(e)** Civil Rights Act of 1964, **(f)** Voting Rights Act of 1965, **(g)** Malcolm X.
2. **Define** **(a)** civil rights, **(b)** civil disobedience, **(c)** affirmative action.

Comprehension

3. **(a)** What was the goal of civil rights lawyers in the case of *Brown* v. *Board of Education of Topeka?* **(b)** What were the results of the case?
4. Describe two ways civil rights leaders worked for change.
5. Describe two achievements of the civil rights movement.

Critical Thinking and Writing

6. **Evaluating Information** Has Martin Luther King, Jr.'s, "dream" been achieved? Explain.
7. **Analyzing Ideas** How might the idea of "black pride" have helped African Americans achieve their goals?

★ ★

Activity **Creating Flashcards** Do you need a good way to learn about the civil rights movement? Use the text to create a set of flashcards. On one side of the cards, write the name of a person or event important in the movement. On the other, identify the person or event. You may later use these cards for review.

Expanding Opportunities

As You Read

Explore These Questions

- What were the goals of the women's movement?
- How did Mexican Americans and Native Americans fight for justice?
- How did Americans with disabilities gain greater opportunities?

Define

- bilingual
- migrant worker
- mainstream

Identify

- Betty Friedan
- National Organization for Women
- Title IX
- Equal Rights Amendment
- César Chávez
- Chicanos
- American Indian Movement
- Americans With Disabilities Act

SETTING the Scene Jessie Lopez de la Cruz spent her days picking lettuce under the hot sun. One day in 1962, César Chávez and two other men came to her door. Like her, they were Mexican American farm workers. She later recalled:

> "The next thing I knew, they were sitting around our table talking about a union.... César said, 'The women have to be involved.' So I sat up straight and said to myself, 'That's what I want!'"

Lopez eagerly joined the new Farm Workers Association. As a union leader, she worked to gain higher pay and improved conditions for her people.

Inspired by the civil rights movement, groups like the farm workers sought justice. In doing so, they opened new opportunities for all Americans.

Women

In 1920, the Nineteenth Amendment gave women the right to vote. Yet the amendment did not end all discrimination against women. Many jobs were closed to them. Law and medical schools accepted few women. Women workers were often paid less than men doing the same job.

From 1920 to 1945, women opened a few doors. Frances Perkins became the first woman to hold a Cabinet post in 1933. During World War II, many women worked in factories and offices.

1970s women's movement poster

A new women's movement

During the 1960s, a new women's rights movement took shape. In 1963, **Betty Friedan** wrote *The Feminine Mystique.* The book challenged the idea that a woman's status depended on her role as caregiver to her family.

Friedan's book, as well as the civil rights movement, led women to demand change. They called for equal access to education and jobs, as well as equal pay for equal work. In 1963, women won an equal pay law. The Civil Rights Act of 1964 banned discrimination in hiring based on gender. In 1966, leaders of the women's movement set up the **National Organization for Women** (NOW) to work for equal rights.

Equality in the schools

Some women's leaders called for greater educational opportunities. They argued that, from kindergarten through college, male and female students did not receive equal treatment. In high schools, for example, girls were not allowed to take wood shop or auto mechanics, while boys could not take home economics. Many colleges and universities required higher test scores and grades from women than from men.

In 1972, President Richard Nixon signed a major civil rights bill, known as **Title IX.** It banned discrimination in educational programs and activities that received federal funds. Partly as a result of Title IX, the number of women graduating from high school and going to college began to increase.

Perhaps the most direct impact of Title IX was on school sports. Under the law, schools increased spending for girls' athletics programs. Today, more than five times as many female high school students participate in sports than 25 years ago.

Debate over the ERA

Leaders of the women's movement called for a constitutional amendment to protect their rights. In 1972, Congress responded by approving the **Equal Rights Amendment** (ERA). It stated:

> "Equality of rights under the law shall not be denied or abridged by the United States or any state on account of sex."

To become part of the Constitution, the ERA had to be ratified by 38 states.

A debate soon raged. Supporters argued that the ERA was necessary to ensure equality for women. Opponents replied that the Constitution already protected equal rights. Some critics predicted that, if the ERA passed, women might be drafted into the military. In the end, the required number of states did not vote for the amendment.

Opportunities and obstacles

Even without the ERA, women made many advances. More women became mayors, governors, and members of Congress. In

MILESTONES: Expanding Opportunities

1791
Freedom of religion guaranteed in First Amendment

1848
Seneca Falls Convention

1917
Puerto Ricans given United States citizenship

1920
19th Amendment

1924
Indian Citizenship Act gives citizenship to every Indian born within United States territory

1964
Civil Rights Act

1965
National Immigration Quota System abolished; Voting Rights Act

1968
Bilingual Education Act

1990
Americans With Disabilities Act

Graphic Organizer *Skills*

Like African Americans, many other groups have worked to secure their rights as citizens of the United States.

1. **Comprehension** Identify three groups of Americans that gained greater rights after 1900.
2. **Critical Thinking** How long after the first women's rights convention did women win the right to vote?

Civics

"...and this hardhat will protect your head when you bump up against the glass ceiling."

Viewing HISTORY Hitting a "Glass Ceiling"?

In recent decades, a growing number of women have achieved success in American corporations. Still, many women claim that discrimination prevents them from attaining high executive positions. ★ **Explain the meaning of this cartoon in your own words.**

1981, Sandra Day O'Connor became the first woman on the Supreme Court. In 1997, Madeline Albright became the first woman to serve as secretary of state, the highest Cabinet position. Still, women today hold a relatively small percentage of public offices.

Women moved into jobs once reserved for men. The gap between the wages of women and men narrowed, but did not close. Large companies hired and promoted college-educated women. However, women in many companies complained that a "glass ceiling" of invisible discrimination kept them confined to jobs with low salaries and out of higher-paying positions.

In 1900, only one woman in five worked outside the home. Today three out of five women work for wages. Working women face the challenge of balancing the demands of jobs and family.

In 1997, the Lilith Fair toured the United States. A series of concerts celebrated women's achievements in music. Performers ranged from Sheryl Crow and Tracy Chapman to country singers Emmylou Harris and Mary Chapin Carpenter. The tour also raised money for various charities, including shelters for abused women.

Latinos

Across the United States, a growing number of residents trace their roots to the diverse nations of Latin America. These people are often referred to as Latinos or Hispanics. Many Latinos in the United States are from Spanish-speaking countries. Others are native-born citizens.

In the eastern United States, most Latinos are from Puerto Rico, Cuba, or the Dominican Republic. Cubans came to the United States to escape Fidel Castro's communist government. Most settled in southern Florida. Most Dominicans came to escape severe poverty and seek economic opportunity.

In the Southwest, Mexican Americans outnumber other Latinos. The region belonged to Mexico until 1848. When the United States annexed the region, thousands of Mexicans instantly became American citizens. (See Chapter 11.)

Campaign for change

Many Latinos settled in cities. There, they experienced discrimination in housing, jobs, and education. During the civil rights movement, Latino groups pressed for equality. Along with other minorities, they benefited from the Civil Rights Act of 1964. It prohibited discrimination in education, jobs, and public facilities on the basis of "race, color, religion, or national origin."

In 1975, the Voting Rights Act was extended to ensure voting rights for citizens who spoke Spanish or other languages. The law required bilingual elections in some places. **Bilingual** means in two languages. Ballots printed in English and Spanish made it easier for many Latinos to vote.

Other laws called for bilingual education. Public schools had to offer immigrant children courses in their own languages while they learned English. Supporters claimed that bilingual education made it easier for immigrants to adapt to American life. Opponents charged that it kept students from learning English, which they needed for future success.

Organizing farm workers

In the West and Southwest, a large number of Mexican Americans were **migrant workers.** They moved with the seasons, planting or harvesting crops. The pay was low, and conditions in the fields were bad. Children of migrant workers had little chance to go to school because their families were on the move so much.

As a child in a migrant family, **César Chávez** attended 65 schools. During the 1960s, Chávez became a labor leader in California. He set out to organize a union of farm workers to win better pay and improve working conditions.

Chávez adopted the nonviolent methods of Martin Luther King, Jr. He organized a boycott that forced farm owners to recognize the National Farm Workers Association (today the United Farm Workers). The union also won better pay for migrant workers.

Building Chicano pride

Like African Americans, Mexican Americans took new pride in their heritage. Young Mexican Americans began calling themselves **Chicanos.** The term comes from the Spanish version of an Indian word, *Mexicano.*

Activists promoted Chicano culture. Chicano artists painted colorful outdoor murals. Theater groups performed plays in English or Spanish about Latino issues. Poet Sergio Elizondo noted with pride:

> "Chicanos are singing, singing and
> revealing the reality of our lives
> that we have always kept relatively
> hidden."

Native Americans

Since the early 1900s, federal policy toward Indians has changed several times. During the 1930s, the government gave tribal leaders on reservations greater control over their own affairs. By the late 1940s, the government was encouraging Indians to leave the reservations. Thousands moved to the cities. Some Native Americans saw this policy

César Chávez

César Chávez traveled 300,000 miles in six months to sign up members for the National Farm Workers Association. When owners refused to talk to the union, he organized a nationwide boycott of grapes and other products. "The boycott of grapes was the most near-perfect of nonviolent struggles," Chávez later stated proudly. ★ **Why is a boycott an effective means of protest?**

Grape boycott button ➤

Preserving Native American Traditions

Today, as in the past, Indians pass on their cultural heritage from generation to generation. This rich heritage includes traditional languages and tribal histories, as well as many types of skills and crafts. Here, a Hoopa woman of northern California teaches a child how to weave baskets from straw. ★ **Why do you think many Indian activists encouraged the teaching of traditional crafts like basket weaving?**

Hoopa basket

as an effort to take their land and weaken their traditions.

Indian protests

During the 1960s, Indian activists protested government policies past and present. They wanted the United States to honor treaties it had broken in the past. They also wanted to protect and preserve Native American traditions.

To dramatize Native American issues, a group called Indians of All Tribes seized Alcatraz Island in San Francisco Bay in 1969. "The people of this country know little of the real history of and tragedy of the Indian people," stated the group:

> "What they do not know is the tragic story of the Indian people today. We intend to tell them that story. This is only the first stepping stone of the great ladder of Indian progress."

The events on Alcatraz made some Indians feel proud that they had stood up to the American government. "Alcatraz encouraged young people to become themselves, as opposed to hiding their Indianness," noted Joseph Myers, a California Pomo.

Another group called the **American Indian Movement** (AIM) pushed for change. In 1972, AIM led a march on Washington, D.C., called the Trail of Broken Treaties. Protesters occupied the Bureau of Indian Affairs building. AIM refused to leave the building until officials agreed to study their demands.

Victories

Prodded by groups such as the National Indian Education Association, the government gave Native Americans more freedom to direct their own lives and preserve their traditions. Congress passed the Indian Education Act in 1972. Under the law, Indian parents became more involved in developing programs for their children in schools both on and off reservations. Indian students began to learn about their ancient traditions and history. By taking such courses in school, predicted one parent, "our kids will grow up proud to be Indians."

In the courts, Native American nations tried to get the United States to honor treaty promises. Indian groups also developed their economic resources. On many reservations, they set up businesses. With profits from business ventures, they built schools and cultural centers. A number of tribes now operate their own colleges and universities.

Today, about 2.2 million Native Americans live in the United States. More than half live in urban areas. About 700,000 live on reservations. After many centuries of decline, the Indian population is growing. Still, Native Americans must deal with serious issues such as widespread poverty.

Americans With Disabilities

Americans with disabilities waged their own struggle for equal rights. In the past, many people in wheelchairs could not use public transportation or enter most buildings. Disabled rights groups organized to win access to public facilities. They backed laws requiring reserved parking spaces, ramped curbs, and wheelchair lifts on buses. Other groups pushed for accommodations such as closed captioning of television shows for deaf viewers.

A 1975 law ensured access to public schools for children with disabilities. Some students have been **mainstreamed,** or placed in regular classes. Others have been assigned to smaller classes where they can receive specialized help.

By law, many public places must set aside parking places for the disabled.

In 1990, Congress passed the **Americans With Disabilities Act.** It banned discrimination in hiring people with physical or mental disabilities. The law also required employers to make "reasonable accommodations," such as building ramps for workers in wheelchairs.

In 1998, golfer Casey Martin took the Professional Golf Association (PGA) to court. Martin has a disability that prevents him from walking long distances. The PGA refused to let Martin use a golf cart during tournaments. The PGA said that other competitors had to walk, so Martin must do the same.

In the end, a judge ruled in Martin's favor. Triumphantly, the golfer said:

> "I just hope that maybe 5 or 10 years from now, if I'm still able to play golf, the PGA Tour will just kind of lean back and scratch their heads and say: 'Now why did we fight this guy?'"

★ Section 4 Review ★

Recall

1. **Identify** **(a)** Betty Friedan, **(b)** National Organization for Women, **(c)** Title IX, **(d)** Equal Rights Amendment, **(e)** César Chávez, **(f)** Chicano, **(g)** American Indian Movement, **(h)** Americans With Disabilities Act.
2. **Define** **(a)** bilingual, **(b)** migrant worker, **(c)** mainstream.

Comprehension

3. What changes did the women's rights movement bring about?
4. Describe the major goals of: **(a)** César Chávez, **(b)** AIM.
5. What victories did Americans with disabilities win?

Critical Thinking and Writing

6. **Recognizing Points of View** How did supporters and opponents of the Equal Rights Amendment differ?
7. **Analyzing Ideas** Why is the idea of bilingual education controversial?

Activity **Writing a Speech** You are a leader of one of the civil rights movements described in this section. Write a speech to inspire other Americans to support your cause. Be sure to outline the goals you still need to achieve.

Understanding Citizenship

As You Read

Explore These Questions

- How do people become American citizens?
- What are some of the rights and responsibilities of citizens?
- What can we do to protect our rights and the rights of others?

Define

- naturalization
- deport
- initiative
- intern
- compensation

Identify

- McCarran-Walter Act

On an August day in 1997, the Los Angeles Convention Center was filled with 4,000 immigrants from 99 countries. All were about to become United States citizens. A judge asked the group to stand and take an oath of loyalty to their new country. Manik Bokchalian rose from her wheelchair. As cameras flashed, she smiled and waved a small American flag.

Bokchalian was the center of attention because of her age. She was 117 years old—perhaps the oldest person ever to become a United States citizen. Bokchalian had traveled a long way to see this moment. An Armenian, she was born in eastern Turkey. Her family fled Turkey when the army began killing Armenians. She lived in Syria and Lebanon before moving to the United States in 1980. When asked what she liked the most about the United States, she said:

> ❝ It would be a sin to say any one thing is the best thing. Everything about living here is wonderful. ❞

Every year, thousands of immigrants become citizens. For them, as for all Americans, citizenship is a privilege that brings both rights and responsibilities.

New citizen at a naturalization ceremony in Los Angeles

Who Is a Citizen?

The word *citizen* has special meaning in the United States. In many countries, only people who are born into the dominant racial or ethnic group can become citizens. Under the United States Constitution, a citizen is a person who by birth or by choice owes allegiance to this country.

By birth or by choice

Most Americans are citizens by birth. People born in the United States or its territories are citizens whether or not their parents are citizens. Children born outside the United States may be citizens by birth if either parent is a citizen.

Millions of Americans became citizens by choice. Like Manik Bokchalian, they immigrated from another country and became naturalized. **Naturalization** is the legal process of becoming a citizen.

To become naturalized, a person must live in the United States for a certain length of time. He or she must meet other requirements, such as having good moral character and pledging loyalty to the government of the United States.

Denial of citizenship

The government encourages immigrants to become citizens. Illegal aliens or immigrants with criminal records, however, are denied citizenship. The government also has the right to **deport,** or expel, immigrants for various reasons, such as breaking the law.

In the past, citizenship was also denied to whole groups of people, including African Americans and Indians. African Americans were finally recognized as citizens with the ratification of the Fourteenth Amendment in 1868. Not until 1924 did Congress grant full citizenship to all Indians.

As early as 1790, Congress had passed a law stating that only white immigrants could become naturalized citizens. This law and others prevented Asian immigrants from becoming citizens. In 1922, a Japanese immigrant named Takao Ozawa challenged these laws in court. Even though Ozawa met all the requirements for citizenship, the Supreme Court ruled that he could not become a citizen because he was not white.

During the 1940s and 1950s, groups such as the League of Women Voters of San Francisco called for an end to racial exclusions. In 1952, Congress passed the **McCarran-Walter Act.** It ended racial restrictions on naturalization. "The bill established our parents as the equal of other Americans," said Harry Takagi, a leader in the Asian American fight for citizenship.

Rights and Responsibilities

American citizens enjoy many rights. The Constitution protects basic rights such as freedom of speech and religion or the right to vote, hold public office, and receive a fair trial. Both the federal government and state governments must protect these constitutional rights. Federal, state, and local laws regulate other rights. (See Chapter 6.)

Citizens have responsibilities as well as rights. To the authors of the Constitution, citizens made a contract with the government. They gave the government power to make and enforce laws for the public good. In return, citizens accepted the responsibility to obey those laws.

MILESTONES: Democracy and Citizenship

1570
League of the Iroquois

1619
House of Burgesses

1620
Mayflower Compact

1788
United States Constitution

1791
Bill of Rights

1865–1870
13th, 14th, 15th Amendments

1913
17th Amendment

1920
19th Amendment

1964
Civil Rights Act

1971
26th Amendment

1978
American Indian Religious Freedom Act

1997
Summit conference on volunteerism

Graphic Organizer *Skills*

More than 200 years ago, the United States set up a government based on the ideals of justice, liberty, and equality. Today, Americans still work to perfect our democracy.

1. **Comprehension** Identify two documents that have helped shape American democracy.
2. **Critical Thinking** What do you think is the most important development listed above? Give reasons for your answer.

Civics

Skills FOR LIFE

Critical Thinking | Managing Information | **Communication** | Maps, Charts, and Graphs

Planning a Multimedia Presentation

How Will I Use This Skill?

Multimedia presentations combine both audio and visual formats, including music, moving and still pictures, and printed material. They are effective because most people remember what they see better than what they hear. By using a variety of methods, you can communicate your ideas clearly and more forcefully. Multimedia presentations are used not only in class but in government and the business world as well.

LEARN the Skill

Follow these steps to prepare your multimedia presentation:

1. Choose your topic.
2. Gather materials and information about your subject.
3. Decide what types of media will best convey your information. Arrange for any equipment you will need.
4. Develop an outline for the presentation. Indicate what audio and visual materials you will use, and when.
5. Practice and give your multimedia presentation.

You can use tools like these to create a multimedia presentation.

PRACTICE the Skill

1. Focus your presentation on this question: How does an immigrant become a naturalized citizen?
2. Research the topic. What books are available on the subject? Does the United States Immigration and Naturalization Service have a site on the Internet? What people might you interview in your family or community?
3. List answers to these questions: Will visuals include videotapes, overheads, interactive computer displays? Will audio include taped interviews, music, CD-ROMs? What equipment will you need?
4. Complete your outline, indicating where and how you will use audio and visual materials.
5. Make your presentation.

APPLY the Skill

Use the steps you have learned to create a multimedia presentation about your family history or cultural background. Consider using photos, taped interviews, family mementos, or antiques.

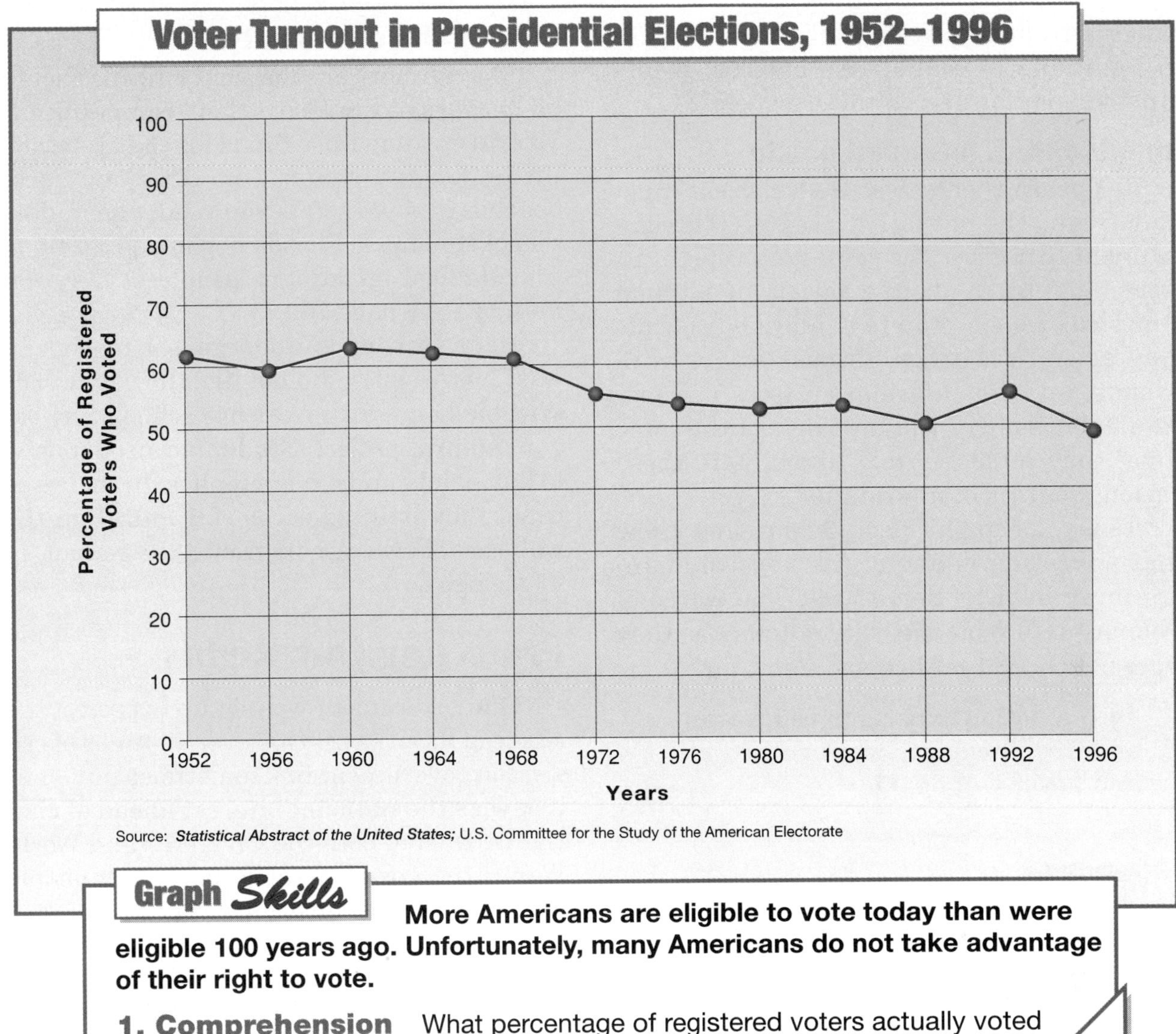

Graph Skills

More Americans are eligible to vote today than were eligible 100 years ago. Unfortunately, many Americans do not take advantage of their right to vote.

1. **Comprehension** What percentage of registered voters actually voted for President in 1952? In 1972? In 1996?
2. **Critical Thinking** What risks do citizens take if they do not exercise their right to vote?

Civics

Citizens may be required to defend the nation from internal or external threats. During wartime, the United States imposed a draft, calling men of a certain age to serve in the armed forces. Today's armed forces are made up of volunteers, both men and women. Other responsibilities of citizenship include paying taxes and serving on juries.

Participating in government

Good government depends upon good choices by voters. In a democracy, citizens have a responsibility to vote. People can also participate in elections by working for candidates they support. Even citizens who are too young to vote can work for the candidates of their choice.

Some citizens participate directly in government by running for office. They may serve on town councils or in state and national governments. Elected officials are expected to make the best decision possible for the people they represent.

In the early 1900s, reformers in California and other states argued that voters should be able to enact laws directly. They backed the **initiative** process, which lets citizens propose and vote on new state and local laws. In California today, ballots often include initiatives on a wide variety of issues, ranging from education to the environment to taxation. To make wise choices, voters must keep informed on these issues.

An educated, informed public

To govern themselves well, citizens must understand the nation's history and its commitment to democratic values. As voters, citizens must learn about a variety of national and local issues. To stay informed, people may attend meetings, discuss issues with friends, and get information from newspapers, television, or the Internet. At the same time, they must be able to evaluate these various sources of information.

Today, as in the past, Americans know that education is one of the keys to maintaining a healthy democracy. The words of Thomas Jefferson are as true today as they were nearly 200 years ago:

> "If a nation expects to be ignorant and free, it expects what never was and never will be."

Viewing HISTORY **Serving in the Schools**

Since 1963, a group called San Francisco School Volunteers has placed helpers from the community in elementary, middle, and high schools. Volunteers donate at least one hour of their time a week. One woman said of volunteering, "You will give, but you will just as certainly receive something back." ★ **Are there volunteer workers in your school? If so, what services do they perform?**

Serving the community

Many Americans feel that citizens should be encouraged to serve their communities. Volunteers may raise funds for charity, coach Little League teams, or clean up local beaches and parks. As you read, one middle school student in Florida began a program to provide food for hungry people in his community. (See page 162.)

Rena Harder, a kindergarten teacher in East Los Angeles, did not like the ugly words scribbled on a wall near her school. She began a mural project. Students raised money to buy paints and other supplies. In their free time, they painted a colorful mural on the wall that shows careers from A (astronaut) to Z (zoologist).

Protecting Our Rights

Our government was set up to protect the rights of its citizens. However, in times of crisis, the government has sometimes put what it saw as the national interest ahead of civil rights. During both the Civil War and World War I, the government jailed many people who spoke out against its war policies.

Case study: internment of Japanese Americans

On December 7, 1941, Japanese war planes bombed the United States fleet anchored at Pearl Harbor, Hawaii. The unexpected attack plunged the United States into World War II.

Even before the bombing, prejudice against Japanese Americans was widespread. The attack on Pearl Harbor unleashed a hysterical reaction against Japanese Americans. Newspapers, government officials, and others claimed that many Japanese were spies.

No evidence was ever found of Japanese spying or disloyalty. Still, President Franklin Roosevelt gave in to demands from West Coast states. He ordered Japanese Americans to be **interned,** or held, in special detention camps. About 110,000 Japanese Americans were forced to sell their homes, farms, or businesses and move with their families to the camps.

Most interned Japanese Americans were from California. The majority were American citizens. Norman Minetta, who later became a member of Congress from San Jose, recalled being sent to a detention camp:

> “I was 10 years old and wearing my Cub Scout uniform when we were packed onto a train in San Jose. . . . The camp was surrounded by barbed wire. Guards with machine guns were posted at watch towers, with orders to shoot anyone who tried to escape.”

During the war, Japanese Americans turned to the courts for justice. They argued that internment deprived them of their freedom and their property without due process of law. In 1944, however, the Supreme Court ruled that the internment camps were a necessary wartime measure.

For years after the war, Japanese Americans who had been interned pressed Congress for a presidential apology as well as symbolic **compensation**, or repayment, for their losses. Finally, in the late 1980s, Congress offered $20,000 to families who had been interned. Each check came with a letter from President George Bush:

> “We can never fully right the wrongs of the past. But we can take a clear stand for justice and recognize the serious injustices that were done to Japanese Americans during World War II. In enacting a law calling for [compensation] and offering a sincere apology, your fellow Americans have, in a very real sense, renewed their traditional commitment to the ideals of freedom, equality, and justice.”

Maintaining a healthy democracy

The case of Japanese American internment shows that citizens' rights may sometimes be violated, even in a democracy. At the same time, it demonstrates how citizens can work to seek justice and protect basic constitutional rights. The civil rights movement of the 1950s and 1960s had a similar outcome. Through peaceful efforts, Americans banded together to win change.

Even in a healthy democracy, people cannot take their basic rights for granted. Responsible citizens must take a stand if their rights or the rights of others are threatened. The noted American anthropologist Margaret Mead once wrote:

> “Never doubt that a small group of thoughtful, committed citizens can change the world; indeed, it is the only thing that ever has.”

★ Section 5 Review ★

Recall

1. **Identify** McCarran-Walter Act.
2. **Define** **(a)** naturalization, **(b)** deport, **(c)** initiative, **(d)** intern, **(e)** compensation.

Comprehension

3. How can an immigrant become an American citizen?
4. Describe two rights and two responsibilities of citizens.
5. **(a)** Why were Japanese Americans interned during World War II? **(b)** How did they work to correct this injustice?

Critical Thinking and Writing

6. **Making Generalizations** How have laws on citizenship changed over time?
7. **Ranking** Which responsibility of citizens do you think is most important? Why?

Activity **Doing a Citizenship Self-Check** How good a citizen are you? List two ways in which you are a good citizen. Then, list two things you could do to be a better citizen.

Chapter 23 Review and Activities

★ Sum It Up ★

Section 1 A Changing Economy
- The United States went through several cycles of growth and recession in the 1900s.
- Although many Americans still live in poverty, the size of the middle class has grown.
- As the economy shifts from manufacturing to service, the need for an educated work force is growing.

Section 2 A Changing Population
- The population of the United States grew dramatically after World War II.
- Immigrants continue to seek a better life in the United States, but patterns of immigration have changed.

Section 3 The Civil Rights Movement
- Civil rights leaders used the courts and the Constitution to fight segregation.
- Although African Americans have enjoyed many victories, challenges remain.

Section 4 Expanding Opportunities
- Through the women's rights movement, American women gained new opportunities.
- Latinos and Native Americans have worked to secure their rights as citizens.

Section 5 Understanding Citizenship
- Responsibilities of citizenship include being informed and participating in government.
- To maintain a healthy democracy, Americans must be ready to speak out when their rights or the rights of others are violated.

For additional review of the major ideas of Chapter 23, see ***Guide to the Essentials of American History*** or ***Interactive Student Tutorial CD-ROM,*** which contains interactive review activities, graphic organizers, and practice tests.

Reviewing the Chapter

Define These Terms

Match each term with the correct definition.

Column 1	Column 2
1. productivity	**a.** refusal to obey unjust laws
2. recession	**b.** repayment for losses
3. civil disobedience	**c.** mild economic depression
4. compensation	**d.** process of becoming a citizen
5. naturalization	**e.** amount of goods produced by workers in a given time

Explore the Main Ideas

1. Describe how the middle class changed during the 1900s.
2. Why is a good education more important now than ever before?
3. **(a)** In what ways is life better for African Americans than it was in 1900? **(b)** Describe two problems that still remain.
4. What changes occurred for women in the job market?
5. Why must people be watchful in a democracy?

Chart Activity

Look at the table below and answer the following questions: **1.** How much did the percentage of people working in manufacturing, construction, or mining drop since 1970? **2.** Which segment of the economy grew? **Critical Thinking** Give one reason for the decline in manufacturing jobs.

Changing Employment Patterns

Type of Work	Percentage of Work Force	
	1970	**1990**
Agriculture	4.4%	2.8%
Manufacturing, mining, construction	33.1%	23.0%
Service industries	62.5%	74.2%

Source: *United States Bureau of Labor Statistics*

Critical Thinking and Writing

1. **Understanding Chronology** **(a)** Place the following events in correct chronological order: Franklin Roosevelt elected President; World War II begins; New Deal begins; stock market crashes; Great Depression ends. **(b)** Describe a cause-and-effect relationship between two of the events on this list.
2. **Linking Past and Present** Choose one change in social conditions discussed in this chapter. Explain how your life might have been different today if that change had not taken place.
3. **Applying Information** How does the Constitution guarantee the rights of individuals? Give two examples since 1914.
4. **Analyzing Ideas** Why is it important for citizens to oppose discrimination, even when it does not affect them directly?

Using Primary Sources

In 1957, an angry crowd threatened African American students as they tried to enter Central High School in Little Rock. One of the students said of the crowd:

> “I think [this] is downright un-American. I think it’s the most terrible thing ever seen in America. I mean, I guess I’m sounding too patriotic or something, but I always thought all men were created equal.”

Source: *Eyes on the Prize: America’s Civil Rights Years, 1954–1965,* Juan Williams, 1987.

Recognizing Points of View **(a)** How did this student view the actions of the crowd? **(b)** What do the words “un-American” and “patriotic” suggest about this student’s attitude toward the United States?

Activity Bank

Interdisciplinary Activity

Exploring the Arts Choose one of the social issues described in this chapter. Create a poster, skit, or song relating to that issue.

Career Skills Activity

Business Leader Many business leaders believe that they have a duty to serve the communities in which they are located. Take on the role of the president of a local company. Write a statement to your customers explaining what action your company will take to improve the community.

Citizenship Activity

Exploring Religious Freedom Research the many religious groups in the United States. Create a chart showing the number of followers of each religion. Then, write a statement explaining why you think members of so many different religions live here.

Internet Activity

Use the Internet to find a Web site for a national or local news agency, newspaper, or television station. Report on what kinds of news you can get from that site, and how you can use that site to keep informed about current issues.

Eyewitness Journal

You are a young student attending an American school right now. In your Eyewitness Journal, describe three events of the past century that have had the biggest impact on your life. You may write as if you had the ability to go back in time to witness these events.

The Circuit

by Francisco Jiménez

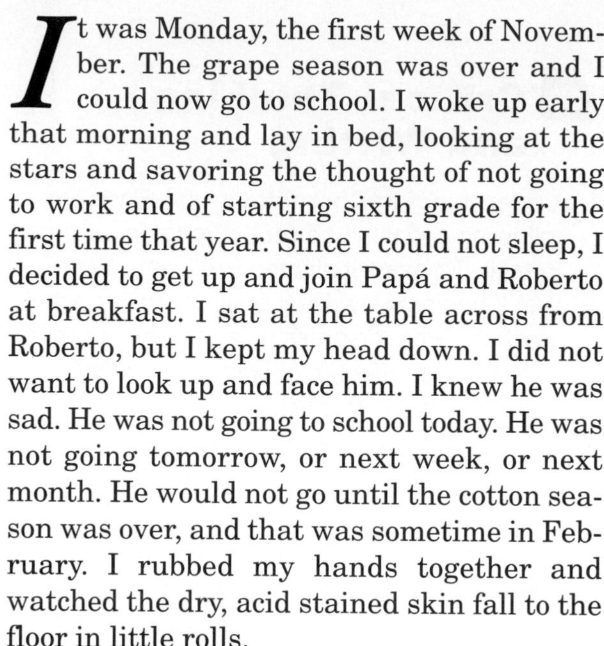

Introduction

As a child, Francisco Jiménez labored in the fields of California. He later became a writer and university teacher. Many of his stories describe "the joys and disappointments of growing up in a migrant setting." In his short story "The Circuit," Jiménez describes how being constantly on the move affects Panchito, a young migrant worker.

Vocabulary

Before you read the selection, find the meanings of these words in a dictionary: **savoring, instinct, enthusiastically.**

It was Monday, the first week of November. The grape season was over and I could now go to school. I woke up early that morning and lay in bed, looking at the stars and savoring the thought of not going to work and of starting sixth grade for the first time that year. Since I could not sleep, I decided to get up and join Papá and Roberto at breakfast. I sat at the table across from Roberto, but I kept my head down. I did not want to look up and face him. I knew he was sad. He was not going to school today. He was not going tomorrow, or next week, or next month. He would not go until the cotton season was over, and that was sometime in February. I rubbed my hands together and watched the dry, acid stained skin fall to the floor in little rolls.

When Papá and Roberto left for work, I felt relief. I walked to the top of a small grade next to the shack and watched the car disappear in the distance in a cloud of dust.

Two hours later, around eight o'clock, I stood by the side of the road waiting for school bus number twenty. When it arrived I climbed in. Everyone was busy either talking or yelling. I sat in an empty seat in the back.

When the bus stopped in front of the school, I felt very nervous. I looked out the bus window and saw boys and girls carrying books under their arms. I put my hands in my pant pockets and walked to the principal's office. When I entered I heard a woman's voice say: "May I help you?" I was startled. I had not heard English for months. For a few seconds I remained speechless. I looked at the lady who waited for an answer. My first instinct was to answer her in Spanish, but I held back. Finally, after struggling for English words, I managed to tell her that I wanted to enroll in the sixth grade. After answering many questions, I was led to the classroom.

Mr. Lema, the sixth grade teacher, greeted me and assigned me a desk. He then introduced me to the class. I was so nervous and scared at that moment when everyone's eyes were on me that I wished I were with Papá and Roberto picking cotton. After taking roll, Mr. Lema gave the class the assignment for

Viewing HISTORY **Chicano Art**

Tony Ortega painted Los Jovenes con Bicicleta *(Young People With Bicycles) in 1991. Ortega's use of bright colors shows the influence of Mexican artistic style. Art from many different cultures has enriched American culture.* ★ **How would you describe the mood of this painting? Explain.**

the first hour. "The first thing we have to do this morning is finish reading the story we began yesterday," he said enthusiastically. He walked up to me, handed me an English book, and asked me to read. "We are on page 125," he said politely. When I heard this, I felt my blood rush to my head; I felt dizzy. "Would you like to read?" he asked hesitantly. I opened the book to page 125. My mouth was dry. My eyes began to water. I could not begin. "You can read later," Mr. Lema said understandingly.

For the rest of the reading period I kept getting angrier and angrier with myself. I should have read, I thought to myself.

During recess I went into the restroom and opened my English book to page 125. I began to read in a low voice, pretending I was in class. There were many words I did not know. I closed the book and headed back to the classroom.

Mr. Lema was sitting at his desk correcting papers. When I entered he looked up at me and smiled. I felt better. I walked up to him and asked if he could help me with the new words. "Gladly," he said.

The rest of the month I spent my lunch hours working on English with Mr. Lema, my best friend at school.

One Friday during lunch hour Mr. Lema asked me to take a walk with him to the music room. "Do you like music?" he asked me as we entered the building. Yes, I like corridos,"* I answered. He then picked up a trumpet, blew on it and handed it to me. The sound gave me goose bumps. I knew that sound. I had heard it in many corridos. "How would you like to learn how to play it?" he asked. He must have read my face because before I could answer, he added: "I'll teach you how to play it during our lunch hours."

That day I could hardly wait to get home to tell Papá and Mamá the great news. As I got off the bus, my little brothers and sisters ran up to meet me. They were yelling and screaming. I thought they were happy to see me, but when I opened the door to our shack, I saw that everything we owned was neatly packed in cardboard boxes.

*Corridos are a form of dance music popular in Mexico.

Analyzing Literature

1. Why is Panchito able to go to school, but not Roberto?
2. How does Mr. Lema win Panchito's friendship?
3. **Making Inferences** **(a)** At the end of the story, what emotions do you think Panchito feels when he sees the packed boxes? **(b)** What is Jiménez suggesting about the education of young migrant workers?

Viewpoints: Source Readings in American History

Historical Documents, Literature, and Eyewitness Accounts

Reviewing Our Early Heritage

★ Chapter 1 ★ Focus on Geography

★ 1–1 ★ The Mountains of California

Introduction In the 1800s, Scottish naturalist John Muir walked across much of the United States making observations, taking notes, and describing the natural life found in each region. Muir wrote extensively about his observations of nature and stressed the importance of conservation. He launched a campaign urging the federal government to adopt a forest conservation policy. Through his efforts, Sequoia and Yosemite national parks were established in 1890. In 1892, Muir founded the Sierra Club, which began a national conservation movement. This excerpt about the Sierra Nevada is from Muir's book, *The Mountains of California,* published in 1894.

Vocabulary Before you read the selection, find the meaning of these words in a dictionary: **reposing, luminous, celestial, ineffably, adamant, composite, inaccessible, diversified, infinitely, anchorage, comprehensively, avalanches.**

★ ★ ★ ★ ★ ★ ★ ★ ★ ★

Making your way through the mazes of the Coast Range to the summit of any of the inner peaks or passes opposite San Francisco, in the clear springtime, the grandest and most telling of all California landscapes is outspread before you. At your feet lies the great Central Valley glowing golden in the sunshine, extending north and south farther than the eye can reach, one smooth, flowery, lake-like bed of fertile soil. Along its eastern margin rises the mighty Sierra, miles in height, reposing like a smooth, cumulous cloud in the sunny sky, and so gloriously colored, and so luminous, it seems to be not clothed with light, but wholly composed of it, like the wall of some celestial city. Along the top, and extending a good way down, you see a pale, pearl gray belt of snow; and below it a belt of blue and dark purple, marking the extension of the forests; and along the base of the range a broad belt of rose purple and yellow, where lie the miner's goldfields and the foot-hill gardens. All these colored belts blending smoothly make a wall of light ineffably fine, and as beautiful as a rainbow, yet firm as adamant.

When I first enjoyed this superb view, one glowing April day, from the summit of the Pacheco Pass, the Central Valley, but little trampled or plowed as yet, was one furred, rich sheet of golden composite, and the luminous wall of the mountains shone in all its glory. Then it seemed to me the Sierra should be called not the Nevada, or Snowy Range, but the Range of Light. And after ten years spent in the heart of it, rejoicing and wondering, bathing in its glorious floods of light, seeing the sunbursts of morning among the ivy peaks, the noonday radiance on the trees and rocks and snow, the flush of the alpenglow, and a thousand dashing waterfalls with their marvelous abundance of irised spray, it still seems to me above all others the Range of

Light, the most divinely beautiful of all the mountain-chains I have ever seen.

The Sierra is about 500 miles long, 70 miles wide, and from 7,000 to nearly 15,000 feet high. In general views no mark of man is visible on it, nor anything to suggest the richness of the life it cherishes, or the depth and grandeur of its sculpture. None of its magnificent forest-crowned ridges rises much above the general level to publish its wealth. No great valley or lake is seen, or river, or group of well-marked features of any kind, standing out in distinct pictures. Even the summit-peaks, so clear and high in the sky, seem comparatively smooth and featureless. Nevertheless, glaciers are still at work in the shadows of the peaks, and thousands of lakes and meadows shine and bloom beneath them, and the whole range is furrowed with canyons to a depth of from 2,000 to 5,000 feet, in which once flowed majestic glaciers, and in which now flow and sing a band of beautiful rivers.

Though of such stupendous depth, these famous canyons are not raw, gloomy, jagged-walled gorges, savage and inaccessible. With rough passages here and there they still make delightful pathways for the mountaineer, conducting from the fertile lowlands to the highest icy fountains, as a kind of mountain streets full of charming life and light, graded and sculptured by the ancient glaciers, and

Viewing History **Yosemite Valley**

In the late 1800s, German-born Albert Bierstadt traveled from New York City, across the Mississippi River and the Rocky Mountains, all the way to the Pacific Ocean. Bierstadt painted many landscapes of the American West, like this one. It shows the Sierra Nevada in central California. Viewers in the East paid high prices for his works. His paintings showed the huge, empty spaces and great beauty of the western land. ★ **What feelings did Bierstadt try to suggest in this painting? How can you tell?**

Albert Bierstadt, *Landscape*

presenting, throughout all their courses, a rich variety of novel and attractive scenery, the most attractive that has yet been discovered in the mountain-ranges of the world.

In many places, especially in the middle region of the western flank of the range, the main canyons widen into spacious valleys or parks, diversified like artificial landscape-gardens, with charming groves and meadows, and thickets of blooming bushes, while the lofty, retiring walls, infinitely varied in form and sculpture, are fringed with ferns, flowering plants of many species, oaks, and evergreens, which find anchorage on a thousands narrow steps and benches; while the whole is enlivened and made glorious with rejoicing streams that come dancing and foaming over the sunny brows of the cliffs to join the shining river that flows in tranquil beauty down the middle of each one of them.

The walls of these park valleys of the Yosemite kind are made up of rocks mountains in size, partly separated from each other by narrow gorges and side-canyons; and they are so sheer in front, and so compactly built together on a level floor, that, comprehensively seen, the parks they inclose look like immense halls and temples lighted from above. Every rock seems to glow with life. Some lean back in majestic repose; others, absolutely sheer, or nearly so, for thousands of feet, advance their brows in thoughtful attitudes beyond their companions, giving welcome to storms and calms alike, seemingly conscious yet heedless of everything going on about them, awful in stern majesty... yet associated with beauty of the frailest and most fleeting forms; their feet set in pine groves and gay emerald meadows, their brows in the sky; bathed in light, bathed in floods of singing water, while snow-clouds, avalanches, and the winds shine and surge and wreathe about them as they years go by, as if into these mountain mansions Nature had taken pains to gather their choicest treasures.

Source: *The Mountains of California,* John Muir, 1894.

Analyzing Primary Sources

1. What first impressed Muir about the Sierra Nevada?
   A. the light
   B. the height of the mountains
   C. the destruction of the land
   D. the mild weather
2. The rivers at the bottom of the canyons were formed by
   F. avalanches.
   G. irrigation.
   H. glaciers.
   J. earthquakes.
3. **Critical Thinking Recognizing Points of View** What do you think was the main reason that Muir wrote this description?

Historical Critique

Why is Muir's description of the Sierra Nevada an authentic historical document? What facts does Muir include here that could not have come from his own personal observations?

★ 1–2 ★ America the Beautiful

Introduction Katharine Lee Bates was an English professor at Wellesley College in Massachusetts. She wrote many poems and children's books during her long career. However, she is best known for writing the words to "America the Beautiful." Bates wrote the hymn in 1893 and revised it in 1911. Over the years, many people have suggested that this song should become the national anthem of the United States.

Vocabulary Before you read this selection, find the meaning of these words in a dictionary: **amber, strife, alabaster.**

★ ★ ★ ★ ★ ★ ★ ★ ★

O beautiful for spacious skies,
For amber waves of grain,
For purple mountain majesties
Above the fruited plain!
America! America!
God shed His grace on thee
And crown thy good with brotherhood
From sea to shining sea!

O beautiful for pilgrim feet,
Whose stern, impassioned stress
A thoroughfare for freedom beat
Across the wilderness!
America! America!
God mend thine every flaw,
Confirm thy soul in self-control,
Thy liberty in law!

O beautiful for heroes proved
In liberating strife,
Who more than self their country loved,
And mercy more than life!
America! America!
May God thy gold refine,
Till all success be nobleness
And every gain divine!

O beautiful for patriot dream
That sees beyond the years
Thine alabaster cities gleam
Undimmed by human tears!
America! America!
God shed his grace on thee,
And crown thy good with brotherhood
From sea to shining sea!

Source: *America the Beautiful and Other Poems,* Katharine Lee Bates, 1911.

Viewing History: Amber Waves of Grain

The scenic beauty of the United States has inspired not only poets and painters, but also photographers like Adam Jones. This photograph by Jones suggests the "amber waves of grain" in Katharine Lee Bates's song "America the Beautiful." ★ **In what region of the United States might this scene be located? Explain your answer.**

Analyzing Literature

1. What is the main idea expressed in the song?
  A. It describes the founding of the United States.
  B. It describes American farm life.
  C. It describes American city life.
  D. It describes our political system.

2. To what "heroes" does the third verse refer?
  F. Pilgrims
  G. soldiers
  H. explorers
  J. farmers

3. Critical Thinking Synthesizing Information Briefly list the historical events that the author mentions in the song.

Historical Critique

Patriotic songs are meant to stir feelings of pride in one's country. How does the first verse of "America the Beautiful" encourage feelings of pride? Why do you think Bates included the words "crown thy good with brotherhood"?

★ Chapter 2 ★ A Meeting of Different Worlds

★ 2–1 ★ The Spider Woman

Introduction The following folk tale tells how Navajo women learned to weave. Weaving is an important part of Navajo culture. The Kisani woman, the main character, is rejected by society because she is so ugly.

Vocabulary Before you read the selection, find the meaning of these words in a dictionary: **abode, hogan, loom.**

★ ★ ★ ★ ★ ★ ★ ★ ★ ★

Near the path up there among some rocks, she saw smoke rising up from the ground. "I wonder what that could be?" she asked herself, and decided to go there in search of food and warmth. To her surprise, when she reached her destination she found that the smoke was rising from the bottom of a little round hole. Waving the smoke away, she was able to look inside the hole. And much to her amazement she saw a strange looking old woman who was every bit as ugly as she was sitting by the warmth of the fire spinning a web. It was the Spider Woman, and when she saw a shadow over the hole she looked up and saw the Kisani woman staring down at her.

"Do not be afraid, my daughter. Come down into my house and visit with me," the old woman said.

"The hole is much too small for me to enter," replied the Kisani woman.

"It is big enough," replied the Spider Woman.

Then she blew her breath up the hole four times and it opened out bigger and bigger until it became a wide passageway, with four ladders leading up to the top. On the east was a white ladder, on the south a blue one, on the west a yellow one, and on the north a black one.

The Kisani woman climbed down the blue ladder into the abode of the Spider Woman who was weaving something. "Come down and sit here beside me and watch what I do, my grandchild," the old woman said. And the Kisani woman did as she asked.

The Spider Woman was using a stick about a foot long with a hole in one end like a needle, and with this she passed the thread in and out, making a blanket. "What is this that you do, grandmother?" the Kisani girl asked.

"It is a blanket I weave," the old woman replied.

"Does it have a name, my grandmother?"

"I will name it Black Design Blanket." And this became the Black Design Blanket, the first blanket of the Navajo. . . . Then Spider Woman told the girl the sun was low and it would soon be dark. . . .

"It is late and I must be leaving," the girl said.

"Please. Spend the night with me, my grandchild." This the Kisani woman agreed to and began to settle for the night. . . .

Spider Woman made some dumplings out of grass seeds and fed the girl and the next morning started weaving another blanket. She worked so fast that she finished it that day. It was square and as long as her arm and she named this new blanket Pretty Design Blanket. The girl watched her all day and stayed there a second night, and the following morning the Spider Woman started still another blanket. She finished this blanket, which she called White Striped Blanket, that day, and on the fourth morning she began another. This was a "Beautiful Design Skirt" such as Yeibichai dancers and Snake dancers wear, and was white with figures in black.

The next morning the Kisani girl went back to the hogan where she had been staying and asked the Navajos for some cotton in three colors—yellow, black, and white. After the cotton had been given to her, she put up a loom, but not like the Spider Woman's loom. She put it up the way Navajo women do now and began a blanket. Her blanket was about half done when another Kisani woman came in and looked at the loom and the design. The girl had made a picture of a bird on both sides of the blanket.

"Where did you learn to do that?" the Kisani woman asked. "I did this on my own thought," answered the girl. "It is called a Black Design Blanket."

She finished it in one day, and the next morning she put up her loom again and asked for more cotton to weave. She made a Beautiful Design Skirt the same day. It was finished when two Kisani men came to see what she was doing and asked to see the blankets she had made. One examined the Beautiful Design Blanket very carefully. The second man observed the Black Design weaving. They then returned to their homes and made looms, copying the designs they had learned. And this is why it is the Kisani men who are known for their beautiful weaving.

The girl only made two blankets and then went back to Spider Woman's house. Spider Woman was now weaving a wicker water jar and after that she wove a big carrying basket such as Navajo women used to carry on their backs. The Kisani girl learned to make the basket and then the water jar. "When I went back," she told Spider Woman, "I showed the people how to make blankets like yours. Now I will go back and make carrying baskets and water jars."

"That is good," said Spider Woman. "I am glad you have taught them. But whenever you make a blanket, you must leave a hole in

Viewing HISTORY **Navajo Blanket**

Blanket weaving was a valued tradition among the Navajo people of the Southwest. Designs varied from village to village and were handed down from one generation to the next. The blanket shown here was woven in the late 1800s. ★ **Why are Navajo blankets prized today?**

the middle the way I do. For if you do not, your weaving thoughts will be trapped within the cotton and not only will it bring you bad luck, but it will drive you mad."

The girl went back to her hogan and made a carrying basket and a water jar.

"Where do you learn all these things?" The People* asked.

"I just guessed it out," she said.

The Navajo women watched her, and soon they were all making carrying baskets and then they learned to make water jars and blankets too, just like those of the Spider Woman. Unlike the Kisani men, it is the Navajo women who kept on with their blanket weaving. And they always left the spider-hole in the center of a spider web. That keeps them from getting "blanket sickness" of the mind from keeping the weaving patterns inside their heads. Navajo women almost never draw their blanket patterns down but keep them inside as Spider Woman did.

And that's true, even today.

* "The People" is how the Navajo refer to themselves.

Source: *Sweet Salt: Navajo Folk Tales and Mythology,* edited by Raymond Friday Locke, 1990.

Analyzing Literature

1. What distinguishes a blanket woven by a Navajo?
   A. It contains three different colors.
   B. It is made on a loom.
   C. It contains a picture of the sun.
   D. It has a hole in the middle.
2. What is Kisani's obligation to the Spider Woman?
   F. to sell the Spider Woman's blankets
   G. to learn to weave much faster
   H. to take care of the Spider Woman
   J. to teach others how to weave
3. **Critical Thinking Making Generalizations** What role do you think folk tales play in a society?

Historical Critique

"Spider Woman" was first told in the Navajo language. Also, like many folk tales, the story was passed on orally for generations before it was ever written down. How might these two facts affect the authenticity of this version of the story?

★ 2–2 ★ Two Descriptions of the Middle Passage

Introduction Enslaved Africans were packed onto ships and brought to the Americas on a route known as the Middle Passage. The following two excerpts are the views and observations of men who witnessed it firsthand. John Newton was a former slave ship captain who later became a minister. Dr. Falconbridge was a surgeon who served on a slave ship during the time of the African slave trade.

Vocabulary Before you read these excerpts, find the meanings of this word in a dictionary: **ensue.**

★ ★ ★ ★ ★ ★ ★ ★ ★

The Reverend John Newton:

The cargo of a vessel of a hundred tons or a little more is calculated to purchase from 220 to 250 slaves. Their lodging rooms below the deck which are three (for the men, the boys, and the women) besides a place for the sick, are sometimes more than five feet high and sometimes less; and this height is divided toward the middle for the slaves lie in two rows, one above the other, on each side of the ship, close to each other like books upon a shelf. I have known them so close that the shelf would not easily contain one more.

The poor creatures, thus cramped, are likewise in irons for the most part which makes it difficult for them to turn or move or attempt to rise or to lie down without hurting themselves or each other. Every morning, perhaps, more instances than one are found of the living and the dead fastened together.

Viewing History: On Board a Slave Ship

An English officer created this painting, the only eyewitness picture of a slave ship. It shows how enslaved Africans were packed into the cargo hold. Captains often overloaded their ships, knowing that many people would die during the brutal Middle Passage. ★ **Why was the death rate so high during the Middle Passage?**

Dr. Falconbridge:

Some wet and blowing weather... having occasioned the port-holes to be shut and the grating to be covered,... fever among the Negroes ensued. While they were in this situation, I frequently went down among them till at length their rooms became so extremely hot as to be only bearable for a very short time.... The climate was too warm to admit the wearing of any clothing but a shirt and that I had pulled off before I went down; notwithstanding which, by only continuing among them for about a quarter of an hour, I was so overcome with the heat, stench and foul air that I nearly fainted; and it was only with assistance that I could get on deck. The consequence was that I soon after fell sick of the same disorder from which I did not recover for several months.

Source: *Black Cargoes: A History of the Atlantic Slave Trade 1518–1865,* Daniel P. Mannix, 1962.

Analyzing Primary Sources

1. What is the main subject of Dr. Falconbridge's account?
   - **A.** bad weather
   - **B.** living conditions on the ship
   - **C.** his illness
   - **D.** the ship's captain
2. According to Newton, what was his main job as captain of a slave ship?
   - **F.** to provide a safe and comfortable passage
   - **G.** to load the ship to maximum capacity
   - **H.** to keep the crew and passengers healthy
   - **J.** to avoid bad weather
3. **Critical Thinking Recognizing Point of View** Do you think that Dr. Falconbridge and Captain Newton have similar points of view about conditions aboard slave ships?

Historical Critique

Both of these reports, as well as the painting above, are by officers who worked on slave ships. Why do you think there are fewer eyewitness accounts from enslaved Africans on the Middle Passage? What kind of information could an African witness give that Newton and Falconbridge could not?

★ Chapter 3 ★ The 13 English Colonies

★ 3–1 ★ The Mayflower Compact

Introduction Before the *Mayflower* anchored in what is now Provincetown Harbor off Cape Cod, Massachusetts, the ship's 41 male passengers signed a binding agreement that established a basis for self-government. This agreement became known as the Mayflower Compact. Its signers promised to create a government based on the consent of the governed and ruled by law. Since women had no political rights, the women aboard the *Mayflower* were not asked to sign the Mayflower Compact.

Vocabulary Before you read the selection, find the meaning of these words in a dictionary: **sovereign, covenant.**

★ ★ ★ ★ ★ ★ ★ ★ ★

In the name of God Amen, We whose names are underwritten, the loyal subjects of the dread sovereign Lord King James by the grace of God, of Great Britain, France, and Ireland king, defender of the faith, etc.

Having undertaken for the glory of God, and advancements of the Christian faith and honor of our King and country, a voyage to plant the first colony in the northern parts of Virginia, do by these presents solemnly and mutually in the presence of God, and one of another, covenant and combine ourselves together into a civil body politic; for our better ordering and preservation and furtherance of the ends afore said; and by virtue hereof to enact, constitute, and frame such just and

Viewing History **Pilgrims Go to Church**

This painting shows Pilgrim families on their way to attend church services at the Plymouth colony. It was painted in the 1800s, many years after the signing of the Mayflower Compact. Faith in God and study of the Bible were central to Pilgrim life. ★ **What does the fact that the men are carrying weapons suggest about the lives of the Pilgrims?**

equal laws, ordinances, acts, constitutions, and offices, from time to time, as shall be thought most meet and convenient for the general good of the colony: unto which we promise all due submission and obedience.

In witness whereof we have here under subscribed our names at Cape Cod the 11 of November, in the year the reign of our sovereign Lord King James of England, France, and Ireland, the eighteenth and of Scotland the fifty-fourth Anno Domini 1620.

Source: *The American Reader: Words That Moved a Nation,* edited by Diane Ravitch, 1990.

Analyzing Primary Sources

1. What was the purpose of the Mayflower Compact?

A. to elect church members
B. to write a new constitution
C. to establish a governing body
D. to honor the English king

2. At what location was the Mayflower Compact signed?

F. England
G. France
H. Cape Cod
J. Virginia

3. Critical Thinking Linking Past and Present How are the ideas in the Mayflower Compact reflected in the form of government that exists in the United States today?

Historical Critique

Pilgrim men signed the Mayflower Compact while they were still on board ship. What can the document tell us about the government of the Plymouth colony? What can it not tell us?

★ 3–2 ★ How I Became a Printer

Introduction This excerpt from Benjamin Franklin's autobiography describes his early education and his apprenticeship to his brother James, a Boston printer. Franklin also writes about the role printers played in bringing attention to colonial opposition to British rule.

Vocabulary Before you read the selection, find the meaning of these words in a dictionary: **tithe, censure, admonishing, notwithstanding, satire, contrivance.**

★ ★ ★ ★ ★ ★ ★ ★ ★

I was put to the grammar-school at eight years of age, my father intending to devote me, as the tithe of his sons, to the service of the Church. My early readiness in learning to read (which must have been very early, as I do not remember when I could not read), and the opinion of all his friends, that I should certainly make a good scholar, encouraged him in this purpose of his....But my father, in the mean time, from the view of the expense of a college education, which having so large a family he could not well afford...took me from the grammar-school, and sent me to a school for writing and arithmetic....At ten years old I was taken home to assist my father in his business, which was that of a tallow-chandler and soapboiler....Accordingly, I was employed in cutting wick for the candles, filling the dipping mold and the molds for cast candles, attending the shop, going of errands etc.

I disliked the trade, and had a strong inclination for the sea, but my father declared against it. However, living near the water, I

Viewing HISTORY **Ben Franklin, Printer**

In 1723, young Ben Franklin left Boston for Philadelphia. Through hard work, he turned The Pennsylvania Gazette *into a successful newspaper. The* Gazette *allowed Franklin to share his ideas with a large audience.* ★ **How might Franklin's early experiences have helped him make *The Pennsylvania Gazette* prosper?**

was much in and about it, learned early to swim well, and to manage boats; and when in a boat or canoe with other boys, I was commonly allowed to govern, especially in any case of difficulty; and upon other occasions I was generally a leader among the boys....

From a child I was fond of reading, and all the little money that came into my hands was ever laid out in books....

This bookish inclination at length determined my father to make me a printer, though he had already one son (James) of that profession. In 1717 my brother James returned from England with a press and letters to set up his business in Boston. I liked it much better than that of my father, but still had a hankering for the sea. To prevent the apprehended effect of such an inclination, my father was impatient to have me bound to my brother. I stood out some time, but at last was persuaded, and signed the indenture when I was yet but twelve years old. I was to serve as an apprentice till I was twenty-one years of age, only I was to be allowed journeyman's wages during the last year. In a little time I made great proficiency in the business, and became a useful hand to my brother.

Though a brother, he considered himself as my master, and me as his apprentice, and accordingly, expected the same services from me as he would from another, while I thought he demeaned me too much in some he required of me, who from a brother expected more indulgence. Our disputes were often brought before our father, and I fancy I was either generally in the right, or else a better pleader, because the judgment was generally in my favor. But my brother was passionate, and had often beaten me, which I took extremely amiss; and, thinking my apprenticeship very tedious, I was continually wishing for some opportunity of shortening it, which at length offered in a manner unexpected.

One of the pieces in our newspaper on some political point, which I have now forgotten, gave offense to the Assembly. He [James] was taken up, censured, and imprisoned for a month, by the speaker's warrant, I suppose, because he would not discover [reveal] his author. I too was taken up and examined before the council; but, though I did not give them any satisfaction, they contented themselves with admonishing me, and dismissed me, considering me, perhaps, as an apprentice, who was bound to keep his master's secrets.

During my brother's confinement, which I resented a good deal, notwithstanding our private differences, I had the management of the paper; and I made bold to give our rulers some rubs in it, which my brother took very kindly, while others began to consider me in an unfavorable light, as a young genius that had a turn for libeling and satire. My brother's discharge was accompanied with an order of the House (a very odd one), that "James Franklin should no longer print the paper called the New England Courant."

There was a consultation held in our printing-house among his friends, what he should do in this case. Some proposed to evade the order by changing the name of the paper; but my brother, seeing inconveniences in that, it was finally concluded on as a better way, to let it be printed for the future under the name of BENJAMIN FRANKLIN; and to avoid the censure of the Assembly, that might fall on him as still printing it by his apprentice, the contrivance was that my old indenture should be returned to me, with full discharge on the back of it, to be shown on occasion, but to secure to him the benefit of my service, I was to sign new indentures for the remainder of the term, which were to be kept private. A very flimsy scheme it was; however, it was immediately executed, and the paper went on accordingly, under my name for several months.

Source: *Autobiography of Benjamin Franklin,* edited by John Bigelow, 1868.

Analyzing Primary Sources

1. Why did his father decide Benjamin Franklin should become a printer?
   - **A.** He liked books.
   - **B.** He did not do well in school.
   - **C.** His brother was a printer.
   - **D.** He thought that it was better than a tallow-chandler.
2. Why was James Franklin censured?
   - **F.** He published an offensive political statement.
   - **G.** He refused to pay his taxes.
   - **H.** He released Benjamin Franklin from his apprenticeship.
   - **J.** He permitted Benjamin Franklin to run his newspaper.
3. **Critical Thinking Recognizing Point of View** Based on this excerpt, how do you think Benjamin Franklin viewed the British?

Historical Critique

Benjamin Franklin wrote his autobiography when he was around 50 years old. How does an autobiography differ from a diary as a source of historical information?

⋆ Chapter 4 ⋆ The American Revolution

⋆ 4–1 ⋆ Common Sense

Introduction In January 1776, Patriot Thomas Paine published a pamphlet called *Common Sense.* In the following passage from that pamphlet, Paine presents several arguments for declaring independence from Britain. He also discusses representative government.

Vocabulary Before you read the selection, find the meaning of these words in a dictionary: **venture, duplicity, conquerors, expedience.**

⋆ ⋆ ⋆ ⋆ ⋆ ⋆ ⋆ ⋆ ⋆ ⋆

Another reason why the present time is preferable to all others, is, that the fewer our numbers are, the more land there is yet unoccupied, which instead of being lavished by the k__ on his worthless dependents, may be hereafter applied, not only to the discharge of the present debt, but to the constant support of government. No nation under heaven hath such an advantage as this.

The infant state of the colonies, as it is called, so far from being against, is an argument in favor of independence. We are sufficiently numerous, and were we more so, we might be less united. It is a matter worthy of observation, that the more a country is peopled, the smaller their armies are. In military numbers, the ancients far exceeded the moderns: and the reason is evident, for trade being the consequence of population, men become too much absorbed thereby to attend to anything else. Commerce diminishes the spirit, both of patriotism and military defense. And history sufficiently informs us, that the bravest achievements were always accomplished in the non-age of a nation.... The more men have to lose, the less willing are they to venture. The rich are in general slaves to fear, and submit to courtly power with the trembling duplicity of a spaniel.

Youth is the seed time of good habits, as well in nations as in individuals. It might be difficult, if not impossible, to form the continent into one government half a century hence. The vast variety of interests, occasioned by an increase in trade and population, would create confusion. Colony would be against colony. Each being able might scorn each other's assistance; and while the proud and foolish glorified in their little distinctions, the wise would lament that the union had not been formed before....

The present time, likewise, is that peculiar time, which never happens to a nation but once, [that is] the time of forming itself into a government. Most nations have let slip this opportunity, and by that means have been compelled to receive laws from their conquerors, instead of making laws for themselves. First, they had a king, and then a form of government; whereas, the articles or charter for government should be formed first, and men delegated to execute them afterward: but from the errors of other nations, let us learn wisdom, and lay hold of the present opportunity—to begin government at the right end....

In a former page I likewise mentioned the necessity of a large and equal representation; and there is no political matter which more deserves our attention. A small number of electors, or a small number of representatives, are equally dangerous. But if the number of representatives be not only small, but unequal, the danger is increased....

Immediate necessity makes many things convenient, which if continued would grow into oppressions. Expedience and right are different things. When the calamities of America required a consultation, there was no method so ready, or at that time so proper, as to appoint persons from the several Houses of Assembly for that purpose and the wisdom with which they have proceeded hath preserved this continent from ruin. But

Viewing History: Raising a Liberty Pole

In this picture by John McRae, Patriots in the colonies raise a liberty pole, symbol of freedom. Women, men, and children join to show their support for independence from Great Britain.
★ **Do you think Thomas Paine's writings encouraged scenes like this? Explain.**

as it is more than probable that we shall never be without a Congress, every well wisher to good order, must own, that the mode for choosing members of that body, deserves consideration. And I put it as a question to those who make a study of mankind, whether representation and election is not too great a power for one and the same body of men to possess? When we are planning for posterity, we ought to remember that virtue is not hereditary.

Source: *Common Sense,* Thomas Paine, edited by Isaac Kramnick, 1982.

Analyzing Primary Sources

1. According to Paine, what is one reason that the colonies should declare independence?
   - **A.** The population of the country is small.
   - **B.** Trade is flourishing.
   - **C.** There is a well-trained military.
   - **D.** Americans have many diverse interests.
2. In Paine's view, what is the first step in forming a government?
   - **F.** to write a constitution
   - **G.** to pass laws
   - **H.** to raise taxes
   - **J.** to elect representatives
3. **Critical Thinking Analyzing Primary Sources** To support what particular cause did Thomas Paine write this document?

Historical Critique

Common Sense was read and discussed throughout the 13 colonies. In evaluating a historical document, why is it important to know how popular and influential the document was?

★ 4–2 ★ Letters on Independence

Introduction John Adams and his wife, Abigail, corresponded through lengthy letters during John's many trips away from home. An avid letter writer, Abigail wrote to her family and friends about her life, including her observations of the political scene. She supported women's rights and opposed slavery. On March 31, 1776, Abigail Adams wrote to her husband while the Continental Congress discussed declaring independence. She reminded him that the legislators should "remember the ladies" when writing the new laws. John Adams responded jokingly to his wife's concerns.

Vocabulary Before you read the selection, find the meaning of these words in a dictionary: **fabricating, labyrinth, perplexities, surmounted, perseverance, tyrant, foment, impunity, insolent, despotism, oligarchy, ochlocracy.**

★ ★ ★ ★ ★ ★ ★ ★ ★

Abigail to John
November 27, 1775

I wish I knew what mighty things were fabricating. If a form of government is to be established here, what one will be assumed? Will it be left to our assemblies to choose one? And will not many men have many minds? And shall we not run into dissensions among ourselves?. . .

The building up of a great empire... may now, I suppose, be realized even by the unbelievers. Yet, will not ten thousand difficulties arise in the formation of it? The reins of government have been so long slackened that I fear the people will not quietly submit to those restraints which are necessary for the peace and security of the community. If we separate from Britain, what code of laws will be established? How shall we be governed so as to retain our liberties? Can any government be free which is not administered by general stated laws? Who shall frame these laws? Who will give them force and energy? It is true your [the Congress's] resolutions, as a body, have hitherto had the force of laws; but will they continue to have?

When I consider these things, and the prejudices of people in favor of ancient customs and regulations, I feel anxious for the fate of our monarchy or democracy, or whatever is to take place. I soon get lost in a labyrinth of

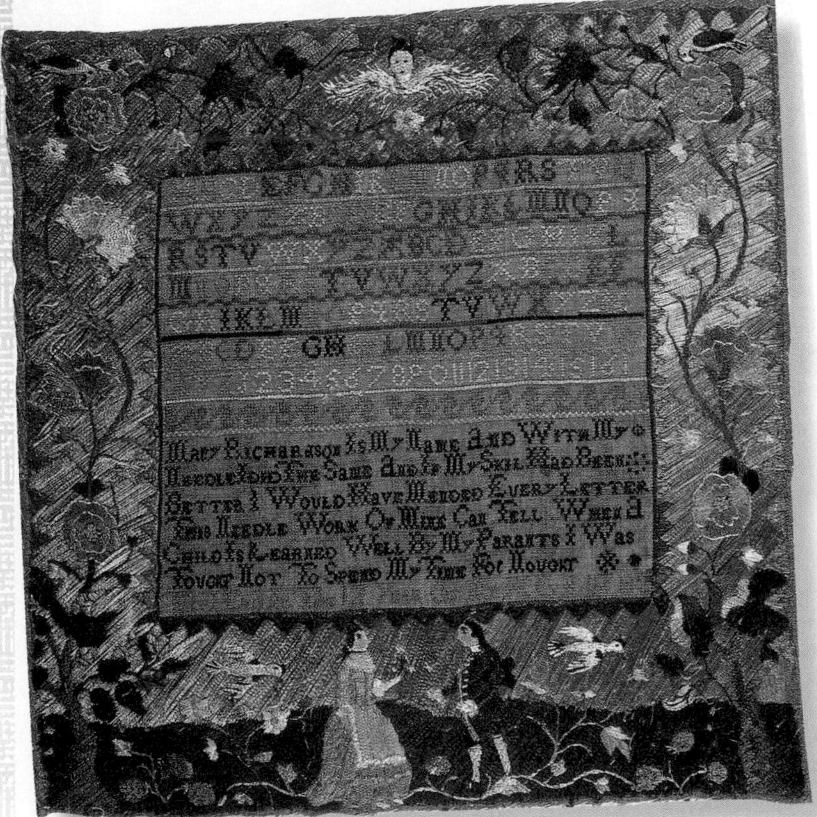

Viewing HISTORY **An American Sampler**

In colonial times, most well-bred New England women learned to stitch samplers. Mary Richardson made this sampler in 1783 when she was 11 years old. ★ **Besides teaching embroidery, how did samplers help educate girls?**

perplexities; but, whatever occurs, may justice and righteousness be the stability of out times, and order arise out of confusion. Great difficulties may be surmounted by patience and perseverance.

Abigail to John
March 31, 1776

I long to hear that you have declared an independency—and by the way in the new code of laws which I suppose it will be necessary for you to make I desire you would remember the ladies, and be more generous and favorable to them than your ancestors. Do not put such unlimited power into the hands of the husbands. Remember all men would be tyrants if they could. If particular care and attention is not paid to the ladies we are determined to foment a rebellion, and will not hold ourselves bound by any laws in which we have no voice, or representation.

That your sex are naturally tyrannical is a truth so thoroughly established as to admit of no dispute, but such of you as wish to be happy willingly give up the harsh title of master for the more tender and endearing one of friend. Why then, not put it out of the power of the vicious and the lawless to use with cruelty and indignity with impunity. Men of sense of all ages abhor those customs which treat us only as the vassals of your sex. Regard us then as beings placed by providence under your protection and in imitation of the supreme being make use of that power only for our happiness.

John to Abigail
April 14, 1776

As to your extraordinary code of laws, I cannot but laugh. We have been told that our struggle has loosened the bands of government everywhere. That children and apprentices were disobedient—that schools and colleges were grown turbulent. . . . But your letter was the first intimation that another tribe more numerous and powerful than all the rest were grown discontented. This is rather too coarse a compliment but you are so saucy, I won't blot it out.

Depend upon it, we know better than to repeal our masculine systems. Although they are in full force, you know they are little more than theory. We dare not exert our power in its full latitude. We are obliged to go fair, and softly, and in practice you know we are the subjects. We have only the name of masters, and rather than give up this, which would completely subject us to the despotism of the petticoat, I hope General Washington, and all our brave heroes would fight. I am sure every good politician would plot, as long as he would against despotism, empire, monarchy, aristocracy, oligarchy, or ochlocracy. A fine story indeed.

Source: *The American Reader: Words That Moved a Nation,* edited by Diane Ravitch, 1990.

Analyzing Primary Sources

1. What is Abigail Adams's main concern in her letter of November 27, 1775?
- **A.** women's rights
- **B.** the creation of a stable government
- **C.** her husband's safety
- **D.** freedom of speech

2. In her letter of March 31, 1776, Abigail Adams asks her husband to
- **F.** declare independence.
- **G.** write laws that ended slavery.
- **H.** write laws that treated women fairly.
- **J.** lower taxes.

3. Critical Thinking Recognizing Points of View How did John Adams reply to his wife's request? What does his response indicate about his thinking?

Historical Critique

Abigail and John Adams wrote hundreds of letters to each other. Would reading more of their letters help you to evaluate the ones printed above? Explain.

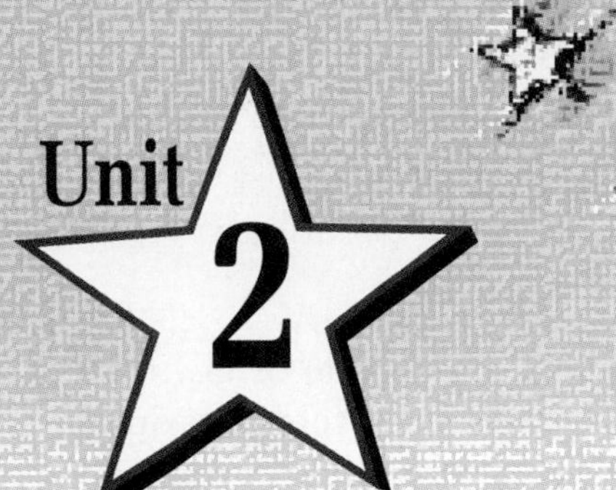

The Constitution of the United States

★ Chapter 5 ★ Creating a Republic

★ 5–1 ★ Delegates to the Constitutional Convention

Introduction William Pierce of Georgia, one of the delegates to the Constitutional Convention in 1787, wrote character sketches of some of the other delegates. His sketches include information about the age, occupation, war record, and political experience of the men who wrote the United States Constitution.

Vocabulary Before you read the selection, find the meaning of these words in a dictionary: **integrity, mercantile, perseverance, embellish.**

★ ★ ★ ★ ★ ★ ★ ★ ★

Mr. Gerry's character is marked for integrity and perseverance. He is a hesitating and laborious speaker: possesses a great degree of confidence and goes extensively into all subjects that he speaks on, without respect to elegance or flower of diction. He is connected and sometimes clear in his arguments, conceives well, and cherishes as his first virtue, a love for his country. Mr. Gerry is very much of a gentlemen in his principles and manners. He has been engaged in the mercantile line and is a man of property. He is about 37 years of age....

Mr. Sherman exhibits the oddest shaped character I ever remember to have met with. He is awkward, [expressionless], and unaccountably strange in his manner. But in his train of thinking there is something regular, deep, and comprehensive; yet the oddity of his address, the vulgarisms that accompany

Viewing History **The Liberty Bell**

The Liberty Bell hung in Philadelphia long before the Revolution. Written on it are words from the Bible: "Proclaim liberty throughout the land...." In the 1800s, the Liberty Bell became an honored symbol of the United States. Because of a crack in the bell, it was not rung.

★ **Why is Philadelphia a suitable place for the Liberty Bell?**

his public speaking, and that strange New England cant which runs through his public as well as his private speaking make everything that is connected with him grotesque and laughable. And yet he deserves infinite praise,—no man has a better heart or a clearer head. If he cannot embellish he can furnish thoughts that are wise and useful. He is an able politician, and extremely artful in accomplishing any particular object. It is remarked that he seldom fails. I am told that he sits on the bench in Connecticut, and is very correct in the discharge of his judicial functions.... He is about 60.

Mr. Elsworth is a judge of the supreme court in Connecticut. He is a gentleman of a clear, deep, and copious understanding; eloquent, and connected in public debate; and always attentive to his duty.... Mr. Elsworth is about 37 years of age, a man much respected for his integrity, and venerated for his abilities.

Colonel Hamilton is deservedly celebrated for his talents. He is a practitioner of the law, and reputed to be a finished scholar.... Hamilton requires time to think. He inquires into every part of his subject with the searchings of philosophy, and when he comes forward he comes highly charged with interesting matter, there is no skimming over the surface of a subject with him, he must sink to the bottom to see what foundation it rests on.... He is about 33 years old, of small stature, and lean....

Mr. Lansing is a practicing attorney at Albany, and mayor of that [city]. He has a hesitation in his speech, that will prevent his being an orator of any eminence. His legal knowledge I am told is not extensive, nor his education a good one. He is however a man of good sense, plain in his manners, and sincere in his friendships. He is about 32 years of age.

Mr. Patterson is one of those kind of men whose powers break in upon you, and create wonder and astonishment. He is a man of great modesty, with looks that bespeak talents of no great extent, but he is a classic, a lawyer, and an orator; and of a disposition so favorable to his advancement that everyone seemed ready to exalt him with their praises. He is very happy in the choice of time and manner of engaging in a debate, and never speaks but when he understands his subject well. This gentleman is about 34 years of age, of a very low stature....

Dr. Franklin is well known to be the greatest philosopher of the present age; all the operations of nature he seems to understand—the very heavens obey him, and the clouds yield up their lightning to be imprisoned in his rod. But what claim he has to the politician, posterity must determine.... He is 82 years old, and possesses an activity of mind equal to a youth of 25 years of age....

Robert Morris... [although] not learned, yet he is as great as those who are. I am told that when he speaks in the assembly of Pennsylvania, that he bears down all before him. What could have been his reason for not speaking in the convention I know not—but he never once spoke on any point. This gentleman is about 50 years old.

Source: *The Records of the Federal Convention of 1787,* edited by Max Farrand, 1911.

Analyzing Primary Sources

1. How does Pierce describe Dr. Franklin?
- **A.** as the greatest philosopher
- **B.** as a man of great modesty
- **C.** as being attentive to his duties
- **D.** as being respected for his integrity

2. Which one of the following men is not a lawyer?
- **F.** Colonel Hamilton
- **G.** Mr. Gerry
- **H.** Mr. Patterson
- **J.** Mr. Lansing

3. Critical Thinking Recognizing Points of View Based on this excerpt, how did William Pierce view these delegates to the Constitutional Convention?

Historical Critique

What information might help you decide if William Pierce's opinions of the other delegates is reliable?

★ 5–2 ★ *The Federalist Papers*

Introduction *The Federalist* is a name given to a collection of essays that were written by Alexander Hamilton, James Madison, and John Jay in 1787. They wrote the essays to persuade people in the separate states to accept the new federal Constitution. The first passage that follows is by Alexander Hamilton, and it introduces the series. The second passage is by James Madison. In it, Madison discusses the many advantages of the new system of government.

Vocabulary Before you read the selection, find the meaning of these words in a dictionary: **unequivocal, inefficiency, inducement, philanthropy, solicitude, formidable, diminution, emolument, aggrandize, faction, candid.**

★ ★ ★ ★ ★ ★ ★ ★ ★ ★

Number 1 (Hamilton)

After an unequivocal experience of the inefficiency of the subsisting federal government, you are called upon to deliberate on a new Constitution for the United States of America. The subject speaks its own importance; comprehending in its consequences nothing less than the existence of the UNION, the safety and welfare of the parts of which it is composed, the fate of an empire in many respects the most interesting in the world. It has been frequently remarked that it seems to have been reserved to the people of this country, by their conduct and example, to decide the important question, whether societies of men are really capable or not of establishing good government from reflection and choice, or whether they are forever destined to depend for their political constitutions on accident and force. If there be any truth in the remark, the crisis at which we are arrived may with propriety be regarded as the era in which that decision is to be made; and a wrong election of the part we shall act may, in this view, deserve to be considered as the general misfortune of mankind.

This idea will add the inducements of philanthropy to those of patriotism, to heighten the solicitude which all considerate and good men must feel for the event. Happy will it be if our choice should be directed by a judicious estimate of our true interests, unperplexed and unbiased by considerations not connected with the public good. But this is a thing more ardently to be wished than seriously to be expected. The plan offered to our deliberations affects too many particular interests, innovates upon too many local institutions, not to involve in its discussion a variety of objects foreign to its merits, and of views, passions, and prejudices little favorable to the discovery of truth.

Among the most formidable of the obstacles which the new Constitution will have to encounter may readily be distinguished the obvious interest of a certain class of men in every state to resist all changes which may hazard a diminution of the power, emolument, and consequence of the offices they hold under the state establishments; and the perverted ambitions of another class of men, who will either hope to aggrandize themselves by the confusions of their country, or will flatter themselves with fairer prospects of elevation from the subdivision of the empire into several partial confederacies than from its union under one government.

Number 10 (Madison)

Among the numerous advantages promised by a well constructed union, none deserves to be more accurately developed than its tendency to break and control the violence of faction. . . . The instability, injustice, and confusion introduced into the public councils have, in truth, been the mortal diseases under which popular governments have everywhere perished. . . . The valuable improvements made by the American Constitution on the popular models, both ancient and modern, cannot certainly be too much admired; but it would be an unwarranted partiality to contend that they have as effectually obviated the danger on this side, as was wished and expected. Complaints are

Viewing History **Celebrating Ratification**

When the Constitution was ratified, celebrations and parades were common throughout the nation. This parade in New York City featured a float representing the "ship of state." ★ **Why do you think the name Hamilton is included on the float?**

everywhere heard from our most considerate and virtuous citizens, equally the friends of public and private faith and of public and personal liberty, that our governments are too unstable, that the public good is disregarded in the conflicts of rival parties, and that measures are too often decided, not according to the rules of justice and the rights of the minor party, but by the superior force of an interested and overbearing majority. . . . It will be found, indeed, on a candid review of our situation, that some of the distresses under which we labor have been erroneously charged on the operation of our governments; but it will be found, at the same time, that other causes will not alone account for many of our heaviest misfortunes. . . . These must be chiefly, if not wholly, effects of the unsteadiness and injustice with which a factious spirit has tainted our public administrations.

Source: *Words That Made American History,* Volume 1, edited by Richard N. Current, 1972.

Analyzing Primary Sources

1. What is the main subject of *The Federalist?*
   A. the American Revolution
   B. the Constitution
   C. the Declaration of Independence
   D. the Articles of Confederation
2. What does Madison say is the main problem in forming a new government?
   F. conflicts of interest
   G. holding elections
   H. passing new laws
   J. choosing a good President
3. **Critical Thinking Comparing** How does Madison's view of government compare with Hamilton's?

Historical Critique

People often try to win support by attacking their opponents. Give one example of how Hamilton attacks the Antifederalists.

★ Chapter 6 ★ The Constitution at Work

★ 6–1 ★ The Magna Carta

Introduction On June 15, 1215, King John of England made peace with rebellious barons by agreeing to sign the Magna Carta. The Magna Carta contained the barons' demands for reforms that increased the barons' rights and limited the king's power. The document established the principle that the king has to obey the law of the land. The Magna Carta became the basis for democratic government in England. Later, in 1787, American statesmen used the democratic principles found in the Magna Carta in writing the Constitution of the United States.

Vocabulary Before you read the selection, find the meanings of these words in a dictionary: **inviolate, compelled, bailiffs, chattels, assessment, abbots, counsel, constable, provisions, tendering, postponement, credible, dispossessed, peers.**

★ ★ ★ ★ ★ ★ ★ ★ ★ ★

John, by the grace of God, king of England, lord of Ireland, duke of Normandy and Aquitaine, count of Anjou to the archbishops,

Viewing History **The British Parliament Meets**

This print shows the House of Commons meeting in London in the 1700s. The British parliamentary tradition was a major influence on the government of the United States. ★ **What branch of the American government is similar to Parliament?**

bishops, abbots, earls, barons, justiciars, foresters, sheriffs, reeves, servants, and all his bailiffs and his faithful people greeting....

1. In the first place we have granted to God and by this our present charter confirmed for us and our heirs forever that the English church shall be free, and shall hold its rights entire, and her liberties inviolate.... We have granted moreover to all free men of our kingdom for us and our heirs forever all the liberties written below, to be held by them and their heirs from us and our heirs forever....

8. No widow shall be compelled to marry, so long as she prefers to live without a husband; provided always that she gives security not to marry without our consent, if she holds of us,* or without the consent of the lord of whom she holds, if she holds of another.

9. Neither we nor our bailiffs shall seize any land or rent for any debt, so long as the chattels of the debtor are sufficient to repay the debt....

14. And for holding a common council of the kingdom concerning the assessment of an aid [tax]... we shall cause to be summoned the archbishops, bishops, abbots, earls, and greater barons... we shall cause to be summoned by our sheriffs and bailiffs, all others who hold of us in chief, for a fixed date... and at a fixed place; and in all letters of such summons we will specify the reason of the summons. And when the summons has thus been made, the business shall proceed on the day appointed, according to the counsel of such as are present, although not all who were summoned have come....

28. No constable or other bailiff of ours shall take corn or other provisions from any one without immediately tendering money therefor, unless he can have postponement thereof by permission of the seller....

30. No sheriff or bailiff of ours, or other person, shall take the horses or carts of any freeman for transport duty, against the will of the said freeman.

31. Neither we nor our bailiffs shall take, for our castles or for any other work of ours, wood which is not ours, against the will of the owner of that wood....

38. No bailiff for the future shall, upon his own unsupported complaint, put anyone to his "law," without credible witness brought for this purpose.

39. No free man shall be taken, or imprisoned, or dispossessed, or outlawed, or banished, or in any way destroyed, except by the legal judgment of his peers or by the law of the land.

40. To no one will we sell, to no one will we deny, or delay, right or justice.

* To "hold of" meant to live on land granted by the king or by another lord.

Source: *Readings in European History,* Volume 1, edited by James Harvey Robinson, 1904.

Analyzing Primary Sources

1. What is the purpose of the Magna Carta?
- **A.** to give more rights to the king
- **B.** to write a new constitution
- **C.** to reform the government
- **D.** to give more land to the common people

2. What part of the United States legal system is based on article 39?
- **F.** freedom of religion
- **G.** trial by jury
- **H.** election of representatives
- **J.** freedom of speech

3. Critical Thinking Drawing Conclusions What conclusions can you make about the importance of the reforms listed in the Magna Carta?

Historical Critique

The Magna Carta was originally written in an earlier form of English and has been translated into modern English. Why is it important to know whether a document has been translated?

★ 6–2 ★ The Volunteer Spirit: Three Views

Introduction Many young people decide to volunteer their time and talent by spending several years as members of the Peace Corps. The Peace Corps program, started in 1961 by President John Kennedy, gives young people the opportunity to live in another culture and teach skills to others. The first two passages below are from Peace Corps volunteers in the Philippines and in Paraguay. In the third account, a fish farmer in Thailand tells how the Peace Corps volunteers helped him.

Vocabulary Before you read the selection, find the meanings of these words in a dictionary: **illiteracy, materialistic, atypical.**

★ ★ ★ ★ ★ ★ ★ ★ ★

Dennis Drake:

My first introduction to the [Peace] Corps was via a television advertisement that ran under the slogan, "The toughest job you'll ever love." Perhaps it was partly the slogan that got me thinking about joining or just the chance to change my life and help people at the same time. Really a simplistic view but maybe common thinking for more than just a few volunteers. Just imagine a person thinking he can actually do something about world hunger, poverty, illiteracy, or disease. Those are not "just" problems, but problems the size of mountains, yet the average Peace Corps volunteer believes he can do his part

Viewing History **A Peace Corps Volunteer in Costa Rica**

This Peace Corps worker is helping students in a school in the Central American nation of Costa Rica. Volunteers do many different kinds of jobs, both in the United States and overseas. ★ **Why do you think many Americans volunteer their time and energy to help other people?**

by chipping away at those mountains . . . one person at a time.

Kathleen Maria Sloop:

At the time I received my assignment from Washington, I had just been promoted to a great position as a market analyst in the bank at which I was working. I was a recent college graduate, so it was hard to give up all the things I had recently acquired, like a car, a good job, a nice house that I was sharing with two roommates whom I loved. But, I also knew that I'd learn more as a PCV [Peace Corps volunteer], and I'd be "richer" as a person, if I lived and ate and shared with people who needed my help and friendship. I saw I was easily slipping into the easy, yet sometimes empty, materialistic life we Americans lead. I wanted to do something that would remind me for the rest of my life that Americans' lifestyles are atypical, not the norm in the world. It was hard to give up the convenience and comfort of the U.S., and I won't say there haven't been times when I wished I could blink and be home again, but I've also never regretted making the decision I did to serve.

Mr. Prakong:

Volunteers have helped me a lot in two different ways: first, with their labor, helping me to run the farm—just proving that they are willing to "get their feet wet" alongside me. They dress in jeans, they put on "farmer pants," sometimes they get diseases or infections, but that's the way they work. The other way they help is that volunteers know something about how to raise fish, the different species, what [food] they need. I never knew anything like that before volunteers came. They taught me induced fish spawning techniques, they helped me build signs on the road to market my fish. . . . Before the volunteers came, I was a "blind man" in terms of fish breeding. . . . If I had to rely on government administrations, I would be starving by now. They work from the top down, they are eager to show off their technical expertise, but they don't know the faces of the people they want to instruct. Peace Corps volunteers work from the bottom up. They have the theory, but they are not afraid to get their feet wet, to work one-on-one with the farmers.

Working this way with Volunteers, a very close relationship develops. I am the "older brother," the Volunteer is the "younger brother or sister." We suffer the same problems together, we sit together, we eat together—sometimes don't eat together if there's no food—joke together. We are family. I cried when the last Volunteer left. I will cry when Ron Rice (my Volunteer coworker) leaves.

Source: *Who Cares? Millions Do: A Book About Altruism,* Milton Meltzer, 1994.

Analyzing Primary Sources

1. Where do most Peace Corps volunteers work?
- **A.** in Washington, D.C.
- **B.** on fish farms
- **C.** in foreign countries
- **D.** in Thailand

2. According to Mr. Prakong, what did Peace Corps volunteers teach him?
- **F.** how to read
- **G.** fish farming methods
- **H.** how to stop infections
- **J.** television advertising

3. Critical Thinking Recognizing Points of View Based on this excerpt, what was Mr. Prakong's view of the Peace Corps volunteers?

Historical Critique

Author Milton Meltzer collected these three accounts for a book titled *Who Cares? Millions Do: A Book About Altruism.* (Altruism means unselfish concern for others.) Do you think Meltzer wanted to present a positive view of the Peace Corps? How might this have influenced what he included in his book?

The Nation Takes Shape

The New Republic Begins

★ 7–1 ★ A Description of George Washington

Introduction Thomas Jefferson, author of the Declaration of Independence, knew all the chief leaders of the Revolution and the new republic. He himself served as third President of the United States. He also wrote on many subjects ranging from philosophy, religion, and science to education and farming. As he grew older, he was often asked about leaders of the Revolutionary era. This excerpt is from a letter Jefferson wrote to Dr. Walter Jones, who had asked about George Washington.

Vocabulary Before you read the selection, find the meanings of these words in a dictionary: **delineate, acute, judiciously, prudence, colloquial, mediocrity, copiousness, fluency, indifferent, constellation, worthies.**

★ ★ ★ ★ ★ ★ ★ ★ ★ ★

I think I knew General Washington intimately and thoroughly; and were I called on to delineate his character, it should be in terms like these.

His mind was great and powerful, without being of the very first order; his penetration [keenness of mind] strong, though not so acute as that of a Newton, Bacon, or Locke; and as far as he saw, no judgment was ever sounder. It was slow in operation, being little aided by invention or imagination, but sure in conclusion. Hence the common remark of his officers, of the advantage he derived [gained] from councils of war, where hearing all suggestions, he selected whatever was best; and certainly no General ever planned his battles more judiciously. But if deranged [upset] during the course of the action, if any member of his plan was dislocated by sudden circumstances, he was slow in readjustment.

Viewing History **Honoring Washington**

An admirer said that George Washington was "first in war, first in peace, first in the hearts of his countrymen." This banner honors the first President. ★ **What symbols of the United States can you identify on this banner?**

The consequence was, that he often failed in the field, and rarely against an enemy in station, as in Boston and York.

He was incapable of fear, meeting personal dangers with the calmest unconcern. Perhaps the strongest feature in his character was prudence, never acting until every circumstance, every consideration, was maturely weighed; refraining if he saw a doubt, but, when once decided, going through with his purpose, whatever obstacles opposed....

His heart was not warm in its affections; but he exactly calculated every man's value, and gave him a solid esteem proportioned to it. His person, you know, was fine, his stature exactly what one would wish, his deportment [bearing] easy, erect and noble; the best horseman of his age, and the most graceful figure that could be seen on horseback. Although in the circle of his friends, where he might be unreserved with safety, he took a free share in conversation, his colloquial talents were not above mediocrity, possessing neither copiousness of ideas, nor fluency of words. In public, when called on for a sudden opinion, he was unready, short and embarrassed. Yet he wrote readily, rather diffusely [wordily], in an easy and correct style....

On the whole, his character was, in its mass, perfect, in nothing bad, in a few points indifferent; and it may truly be said, that never did nature and fortune combine more perfectly to make a man great, and to place him in the same constellation with whatever worthies have merited from man an everlasting remembrance.

Source: *The Complete Jefferson,* edited by Saul K. Padover, 1943.

Analyzing Primary Sources

1. What was Jefferson mainly describing in this passage?
- **A.** General Washington's greatest victories
- **B.** the first President's political ideas
- **C.** George Washington's character
- **D.** his long friendship with George Washington

2. In Jefferson's view, what was one of Washington's greatest strengths?
- **F.** his speaking ability
- **G.** his imagination
- **H.** his careful judgment
- **J.** his warmth

3. Critical Thinking Recognizing Points of View Based on this excerpt, does Jefferson think Washington's strengths outweigh his weaknesses? Explain your answer.

Historical Critique

Would you consider Thomas Jefferson to be a reliable source of information about George Washington? Why or why not?

★ 7–2 ★ Farewell Address

Introduction In 1796, after serving two terms as President, George Washington wrote his famous Farewell Address. In it, he announced that he would not seek a third term. As he retired from public service, the outgoing President gave his views on the best policies for the young republic to follow. As the nation's first President, he knew firsthand the great issues of the day. He was especially concerned about the rise of political parties and the danger of the nation becoming involved in European wars. Washington's advice about foreign policy influenced future Presidents for more than a century.The following excerpt is from Washington's Farewell Address.

Vocabulary Before you read the selection, find the meanings of these words in a dictionary: **apprise, baneful, enfeeble, agitate, animosity, foment, facilitate access, enjoin, magnanimous, benevolence, provocation, maxim.**

★ ★ ★ ★ ★ ★ ★ ★ ★ ★

Viewing History **The Nation's Capital**

When George Washington left office in 1797, the new nation's new capital city was still in the planning stages. As a result, Washington was the only President never to live in Washington, D.C. This photograph shows Washington today. The tall white tower is the Washington Monument. ★ **How was the location for the nation's capital chosen?**

FRIENDS AND FELLOW-CITIZENS:

The period for a new election of a citizen, to administer the executive government of the United States, being not far distant . . . , it appears to me proper, . . . that I should now apprise you of the resolution I have formed to decline being considered among the number of those out of whom a choice is to be made. . . .

I have already intimated [suggested] to you the danger of parties in the State, with particular reference to the founding of them on geographical discriminations [bases]. Let me now take a more comprehensive view, and warn you in the most solemn manner against the baneful effects of the spirit of party, generally. . . .

It serves always to distract the public councils and enfeeble the public administration. It agitates the community with ill-founded jealousies and false alarms, kindles the animosity of one part against another, foments occasionally riot and insurrection. It opens the door to foreign influence and corruption, which find a facilitated access to the government itself through the channels of party passions. Thus the policy and the will of one country, are subjected to the policy and will of another. . . .

Observe good faith and justice toward all nations. Cultivate peace and harmony with all. Religion and morality enjoin this conduct and can it be that good policy does not equally enjoin it? It will be worthy of a free, enlightened, and at no distant period, a great nation, to give to mankind the magnanimous and too novel example of a people always guided by an exalted justice and benevolence. . . .

The great rule of conduct for us in regard to foreign nations is, in extending our commercial relations to have with them as little political connection as possible. So far as we have already formed engagements let them be fulfilled, with perfect good faith. Here let us stop.

Europe has a set of primary interests which to us have none, or a very remote relation. Hence she must be engaged in frequent controversies, the causes of which are essentially foreign to our concerns. . . .

Our detached and distant situation invites and enables us to pursue a different course. If we remain one people, under an efficient government, the period is not far off when we may defy material injury from external [outside] annoyance; when we may take such an attitude as will cause the neutrality we may at any time resolve upon to be scrupulously [carefully] respected; when belligerent [warring] nations, under the impossibility of making acquisitions upon us, will not lightly hazard [risk] the giving us provocation; when we may choose peace or war, as our interest, guided by justice, shall counsel. . . .

It is our true policy to steer clear of permanent alliances with any portion of the foreign world, so far, I mean as we are now at liberty to do it; for let me not be understood as capable of patronizing [supporting] infidelity [unfaithfulness] to existing engagements. I hold the maxim no less applicable to public than to private affairs that honesty is always the best policy. I repeat, therefore, let those engagements be observed in their genuine sense. But in my opinion it is unnecessary and would be unwise to extend them.

Taking care always to keep ourselves by suitable establishments on a respectable defensive posture, we may safely trust to temporary alliances for extraordinary emergencies.

Source: *A Documentary History of the United States,* edited by Richard D. Heffner, 1952.

Analyzing Primary Sources

1. What was Washington's view of political parties?
   - **A.** They cost too much money.
   - **B.** They caused dangerous divisions within the nation.
   - **C.** They resulted in the rise of monarchs.
   - **D.** They weakened the system of checks and balances.
2. What advice about foreign policy did Washington give?
   - **F.** Seek trade but avoid other links with Europe.
   - **G.** Have no contact with European countries.
   - **H.** Cancel all treaties with European countries.
   - **J.** Build up a strong army and navy.
3. **Critical Thinking Understanding Cause and Effect** How does Washington think the United States should behave toward other nations? Why does he give that advice?

Historical Critique

Washington himself belonged to no political party. Do you think that fact increases or decreases the effectiveness of what he has to say about parties?

★ Chapter 8 ★ The Age of Jefferson

★ 8–1 ★ Traveling With Lewis and Clark

Introduction A Shoshone woman named Sacajawea, her husband, and her baby son Pomp accompanied Lewis and Clark on their expedition across the Louisiana Territory. As a child Sacajawea had been kidnapped from her Mandan village by the Minnetarees, a rival Native American group. She was adopted by a Minnetaree family and lived in their village. Sacajawea met Lewis and Clark when they camped at the Minnetaree village. Years later, Sacajawea told her life story to James Willard Schultz. This passage is from Sacajawea's autobiography, *Bird Woman.* In this passage, Sacajawea refers to Lewis and Clark as Long Knife and Red Hair.

Vocabulary Before you read the selection, find the meaning of this word in a dictionary: **abandon.**

★ ★ ★ ★ ★ ★ ★ ★ ★

Upon my man's return to the fort the boats were all loaded. We had two large ones and six small ones, and we abandoned the fort and headed up river. At the same time that we started, Long Knife and Red Hair sent their very large boat down the river in charge of some of their men. It was loaded with many skins, bones, and other

Viewing HISTORY **Wildlife of the American West**

Thomas Jefferson asked Lewis and Clark to explore lands west of the Mississippi. The President also asked them to send back information on the animal life they found. Clark sketched this bird and salmon in his journal. ★ **If you were sending an expedition into an unfamiliar land, what kind of information would you ask for?**

things, presents for the great chief of the whites. Counting in my son, we were thirty-three people in our eight boats. I was given a place in one of the two large ones.

As we went on and on up the river, sometimes making a long distance between the rising and the setting of the sun, I was, at times, I believe, happier than I had ever been in my life, for each day's travel brought me so much nearer my people whom I so much longed to see. Then at other times, whenever I thought of what was before us, I would become very unhappy. I would say to myself that we could not possibly survive the dangers we should be sure to encounter along the way. I may as well say it: my good, kind white chiefs were not cautious; they were too brave, too sure of themselves. From the very start they and their men would foolishly risk their lives by attacking all the mankilling bears that came in sight of us. At night they would build great fires and would be sure to attract to us any wandering war party that might be in the country. After we passed the mouth of the Yellowstone and entered the country of the Blackfeet, I begged my chiefs to be more cautious. I asked them to stop always a short time before dark and build little cooking-fires, and then, after our meal, to put out the fires, and then go on until dark and make camp in the darkness. But they only laughed at me and answered: "We have good guns and know how to use them."

I often said to myself: "Strange are these white men! Strange their ways! They have a certain thing to do, to make a trail to the west to the Everywhere-Salt-Water. Why, then, are we not on horseback and traveling fast and far each day? Here we are in boats, heavily loaded with all kinds of useless things, and when the wind is bad or the water swift, we make but little distance between sun and sun! We could have all got all the horses that we needed from the Earth House tribes, and had we done that, we should long since have arrived at the mountains. Yes, right now I should probably be talking with my own people!"

And those medicine packages of theirs, packages big and little piled all around me in the boat in which I rode, how my chiefs valued them! One day a sudden hard wind struck our sail and the boat began to tip and fill with water. More and more it filled, and the men in it and those on the shore went almost crazy with fear. But I was not afraid. Why should I be when I knew that I could cast off my robe and swim ashore with my little son? More and more water poured into the boat and the medicine packages began to float out of it. I seized them one by one as they were going, and kept seizing them and holding them, and when, at last, we reached the shore, my good white chiefs acted as though I had done a wonderful thing in saving their packages; it seemed as though they could not thank me enough for what I had done. Thinking about it, after it was all over, and when the things had been spread out to dry, I said to myself: "Although I cannot understand them, these little instruments of shining steel and these writings on thin white paper must be powerful medicine. Hereafter, whenever we run into danger, I shall, after my son, have my first thought for their safety, and so please my kind white chiefs."

After leaving the mouth of Little River, or, as my white chiefs named it, Milk River, we went up through a part of the Big River Valley that I had not seen. . . . When we arrived at the mouth of the stream my white chiefs named the Musselshell, some of the men went up it during the afternoon, and, returning, told of a stream coming into it from the plain on the right. My chiefs then told me that it should have my name, as they called it, Sah-ka-já-we-ah.

I asked my man to tell them that I wished they would give it my right name, Bo-í-naiv, Grass Woman.

Source: *Bird Woman,* James Willard Schultz, 1918.

Analyzing Primary Sources

1. Whom did Sacajawea help during the expedition?
   A. Lewis and Clark
   B. the Blackfeet
   C. the Minnetaree
   D. the Mandan

2. What transportation did the expedition use?
   F. mules
   G. wagons
   H. boats
   J. horses

3. **Critical Thinking Recognizing Points of View** Why do you think that Sacajawea thought that the ways of Lewis and Clark were strange?

Historical Critique

Sacajawea told her life story to writer James Willard Schultz, who published it in 1918. Identify two factors that might affect the reliability of the published account.

★ 8–2 ★ The Pioneers

Introduction James Fenimore Cooper wrote action-filled adventure stories that were very popular. The central character in five of his novels is a wilderness hunter named Natty Bumppo, or Leather-stocking, who lives between the Indian and white worlds. Bumppo has learned the forest skills of the Indians. This selection is from *The Pioneers.* In this scene, Leather-stocking realizes that the wilderness is fast falling to settlers.

Vocabulary Before you read the selection, find the meanings of these words in a dictionary: **species, sapling, gaunt, vain, prodigious, profusion, uneasy, sentiments, indignant.**

★ ★ ★ ★ ★ ★ ★ ★ ★

If the heavens were alive with pigeons, the whole village seemed equally in motion, with men, women, and children. Every species of fire-arms, from the French ducking-gun, with a barrel near six feet in length, to the common horseman's pistol, was to be seen in the hands of the men and boys; while bows and arrows, some made of the simple stick of a walnut sapling, and others in a rude [simple] imitation of the ancient cross-bows, were carried by many of the latter. . . .

Amongst the sportsmen was the tall, gaunt form of Leather-stocking, walking over the field, with his rifle hanging on his arm, his dogs at his heels; the latter now scenting the dead or wounded birds, that were beginning to tumble from the flocks, and then crouching under the legs of their master, as if they participated in his feelings, at this wasteful and unsportsmanlike execution.

The reports of the fire-arms became rapid, whole volleys rising from the plain, as flocks of more than ordinary numbers darted over the opening, shadowing the field, like a cloud; and then the light smoke of a single piece would issue from among the leafless bushes on the mountain, as death was hurled on the retreat of the affrighted birds, who were rising from a volley, in a vain effort to escape. Arrows, and missiles of every kind, were in the midst of the flocks; and so numerous were the birds, and so low did they take their flight, that even long poles, in the hands of those on the sides of the mountain, were used to strike them to the earth. . . .

So prodigious was the number of birds, that the scattering fire of the guns, with the hurling of missiles, and the cries of the boys, had no other effect than to break off small flocks from the immense masses that continued to dart along the valley, as if the whole of the feathered tribe were pouring through one pass. None pretended to collect the game, which lay scattered over the fields in such profusion, as to cover the very ground with the fluttering victims.

Leather-stocking was a silent, but uneasy spectator of all these proceedings [events], but was able to keep his sentiments to himself until he saw the introduction of the swivel [cannon] into the sports.

"This comes of settling a country!" he said—"here have I known the pigeons to fly for forty long years, and, till you made your clearings, there was nobody to skear [scare] or to hurt them. I loved to see them come into the woods, for they were company to a body; hurting nothing; being, as it was, as harmless as a garter-snake. But now it gives me sore thoughts when I hear the frighty things whizzing through the air, for I know it's only a motion to bring out all the brats in the village. Well! the Lord won't see the waste of his creaters for nothing, and right will be done to the pigeons, as well as others, by-and-by. . . ."

Among the sportsmen was Billy Kirby, who, armed with an old musket, was loading, and, without even looking into the air, was firing, and shouting as his victims fell even on his own person. He heard the speech of Natty, and took upon himself to reply—

"What! old Leather-stocking," he cried, "grumbling at the loss of a few pigeons! If you had to sow your wheat twice, and three times, as I have done, you wouldn't be so massy-fully [mercifully] feeling'd to'wards the divils.—Hurrah, boys! scatter the feathers. This is better than shooting at a turkey's head and neck, old fellow."

"It's better for you, maybe, Billy Kirby," replied the indignant old hunter, "and all them that don't know how to put a ball down a rifle-barrel, or how to bring it up ag'in with a true aim; but it's wicked to be shooting into flocks in this wastey manner; and none do it, who know how to knock over a single bird. If a body has a craving for pigeon's flesh, why! it's made the same as all other creater's, for man's eating, but not to kill twenty and eat one."

Source: *The Pioneers,* James Fenimore Cooper, 1823.

Settling the Wilderness

As they moved westward, settlers had to hack homes out of thick forests. This engraving shows a group of pioneers in the Ohio Valley. Even the smallest child had to work in order for the family to survive. ★ **Based on this picture, identify two reasons settlers chopped down many trees in the frontier forests.**

Analyzing Literature

1. Why did Natty Bumppo object to the killing of the pigeons?
   A. He disliked the sound of gunfire.
   B. He felt that eating pigeons was sinful.
   C. He thought the killing was wasteful.
   D. He was afraid people would get shot.
2. Why did the settlers shoot the pigeons?
   F. to sell the feathers
   G. to protect their wheat fields
   H. to show off their hunting skills
   J. to frighten the Indians
3. **Critical Thinking Linking Past and Present** How is Natty Bumppo's conflict with the settlers similar to that between environmentalists and developers today?

Historical Critique

Fiction writers often express their views through the mouths of their characters. Which character do you think expresses Cooper's view: Leather-stocking or Kirby? Give reasons for your answer.

★ Chapter 9 ★ Industry and Growth

★ 9–1 ★ Working in the Lowell Mills

Introduction In 1898, Harriet Hanson Robinson published a book, *Loom and Spindle,* which tells of her experiences working in the Lowell, Massachusetts, textile mills in the 1830s. In the following passage, Robinson describes life in Lowell, and tells about the first strike there.

Vocabulary Before you read the selection, find the meaning of these words in a dictionary: **modes, incendiary, consternation, ardent, irresolute, accede.**

★ ★ ★ ★ ★ ★ ★ ★ ★ ★

In 1831 Lowell was little more than a factory village. Several corporations were started, and the cotton-mills belonging to them were building. Help was in great demand; and stories were told all over the country of the new factory town, and the high wages that were offered to all classes of work-people—stories that reached the ears of mechanics' and farmers' sons, and gave new life to lonely and dependent women in distant towns and farmhouses. Into this Yankee El Dorado,* these needy people began to pour by the various modes of travel known to those slow old days. The stagecoach and the canal boat came everyday, always filled with new recruits for this army of useful people. The mechanic and machinist came, each with his home-made chest of tools, and oftentimes his wife and little ones. The widow came with her little flock and her scanty housekeeping goods to open a boarding-house or variety store, and so provided a home for her fatherless children. Many farmers' daughters came to earn money to complete their wedding outfit, or buy the bride's share of housekeeping articles. . . .

One of the first strikes of cotton factory operatives that ever took place in this country was that in Lowell, in October 1836. When it was announced that the wages were to be cut down, great indignation was felt, and it was decided to strike, *en masse.* This was done. The mills were shut down, and the girls went in procession from their several corporations to the "grove" on Chapel Hill, and listened to "incendiary" speeches from early labor reformers.

One of the girls stood on a pump, and gave vent to the feelings of her companions

*El Dorado refers to a place rich in opportunity to become wealthy.

Viewing HISTORY **The Lowell Offering**

The textile mills in Lowell, Massachusetts, employed mostly young, unmarried women. These "Lowell girls" published their own magazine, the Lowell Offering. ★ **What view of life in a factory town does this magazine cover suggest? Explain.**

in a neat speech, declaring that it was their duty to resist all attempts at cutting down the wages. This was the first time a woman had spoken in public in Lowell, and the event caused surprise and consternation among her audience.

Cutting down the wages was not their only grievance, nor the only cause of the strike. Hitherto the corporations had paid twenty-five cents a week towards the board of each operative, and now it was their purpose to have the girls pay the sum; and this, in addition to the cut in wages, would make a difference of at least one dollar a week. . . .

My own recollection of this first strike (or "turn out" as it was called) is very vivid. I worked in a lower room, where I had heard the proposed strike fully, if not vehemently, discussed; I had been an ardent listener to what was said against this attempt at "oppression" on the part of the corporation, and naturally I took sides with the strikers. When the day came on which the girls were to turn out, those in the upper rooms started first, and so many of them left that our mill was at once shut down. Then, when the girls in my room stood irresolute, uncertain what to do, asking each other, "Would you?" or "Shall we turn out?" and not one of them having the courage to lead off, I, who began to think they would not go out, after all their talk, became impatient, and started on ahead, saying, with childish bravado, "I don't care what you do, I am going to turn out, whether any one else does or not"; and I marched out, and was followed by the others. . . .

It is hardly necessary to say that so far as results were concerned this strike did no good. The dissatisfaction of the operatives subsided, or burned itself out, and though the authorities did not accede to their demands, the majority returned to their work, and the corporation went on cutting down the wages.

Source: *Loom and Spindle,* Harriet Hanson Robinson, 1898.

Analyzing Primary Sources

1. Why did the mill workers go on strike?
   - **A.** Children had been hired to work in the mills.
   - **B.** Factory owners wanted them to work longer hours.
   - **C.** Some workers had been fired.
   - **D.** Wages were going to be cut.
2. This passage is mainly about
   - **F.** transportation in Lowell.
   - **G.** working in a cottonmill.
   - **H.** women's rights.
   - **J.** child labor.
3. **Critical Thinking Recognizing Points of View** How did the author view the cotton-mill workers?

Historical Critique

How much of what Robinson reports did she witness herself? How much did she learn from other sources?

★ 9–2 ★ *The Monroe Doctrine*

Introduction In his State of the Union message to Congress in December 1823, James Monroe issued a warning to European powers not to try to extend their influence in the Western Hemisphere. His warning, which has come to be known as the Monroe Doctrine, had immediate implications. At the time, Russia threatened to encroach in the far Northwest, Great Britain showed some interest in acquiring Cuba, and it was thought that the Quadruple Alliance* wanted to help Spain recover its lost American colonies. The following passage includes relevant excerpts from the Monroe Doctrine.

Vocabulary Before you read the selection, find the meaning of these words in a dictionary: **amicable, acceded, solicitude, comport, felicity, candor, *de facto,* eminently.**

★ ★ ★ ★ ★ ★ ★ ★ ★

Annual Message

December 2, 1823

Fellow-citizens of the Senate and House of Representatives:

. . . At the proposal of the Russian Imperial Government, made through the minister of the Emperor residing here, a full power and instructions have been transmitted to the ministers of the United States at St. Petersburg to arrange by amicable negotiations the respective rights and interests of the two nations on the northwest coast of this continent. A similar proposal had been made by His Imperial Majesty to the government of Great Britain, which had likewise been acceded to. The government of the United States has been desirous, by this friendly proceeding, of manifesting the great value which they have invariably attached to the friendship of the Emperor and their solicitude to cultivate the best understanding with his government. In the discussions to which this interest has given rise and in the arrangements by which they may terminate, the occasion has been judged proper for asserting, as a principle in which the rights and interests of the United States are involved, that the American continents, by the free and independent condition which they have assumed and maintain, are henceforth not considered as subject for future colonization by any European powers. . . .

The citizens of the United States cherish sentiments the most friendly in favor of the liberty and happiness of their fellow men on that side of the Atlantic. In the wars of the European powers in matters relating to themselves we have never taken any part, nor does it comport with our policy so to do. It is only when our rights are invaded or seriously menaced that we resent injuries or make preparations for our defense. With the movements in this hemisphere we are of necessity more immediately connected, and by causes which must be obvious to all enlightened and impartial observers. The political system of the allied powers is essentially different in this respect from that of America. This difference proceeds from that which exists in their respective governments; and to the defense of our own, which has been achieved by the loss of so much blood and treasure, and matured by the wisdom of their most enlightened citizens, and under which we have enjoyed unexampled felicity, this whole nation is devoted. We owe it, therefore, to candor and to the amicable relations existing between the United States and those powers to declare that we should consider any attempt on their part to extend their system to any portion of this hemisphere as dangerous to our peace and safety. With the existing colonies or dependencies of any European power we shall not interfere. But with the governments who have declared their independence and maintained it, and whose independence we have, on great consideration and on just principles, acknowledged, we could not view any interposition for the purpose of oppressing them or

* The Quadruple Alliance was a group of European nations that worked together to achieve their goals. It included Britain, Austria, Prussia, and—later—France.

Viewing HISTORY **The Triumph of Mexico**

This painting uses symbols to celebrate Mexico's struggle for independence. Father Miguel Hidalgo, left, places a victory wreath on the head of a woman representing Mexico. The growth of new nations in Latin America led President James Monroe to issue the Monroe Doctrine. ★ **What do you think the man in the lower left represents?**

controlling in any other manner their destiny, by any European power in any other light than as the manifestation of an unfriendly disposition toward the United States. . . .

Our policy in regard to Europe, which was adopted at an early stage of the wars which have so long agitated that quarter of the globe, nevertheless remains the same, which is, not to interfere in the internal concerns of any of its powers; to consider the government *de facto* as the legitimate government for us; to cultivate friendly relations by a frank, firm, and manly policy, meeting in all instances the just claims of every power, submitting to injuries from none. But in regard to those continents circumstances are eminently and conspicuously different. It is impossible that the allied powers should extend their political system to any portion of either continent without endangering our peace and happiness; nor can anyone believe that our southern brethren, if left to themselves, would adopt it of their own accord. It is equally impossible, therefore, that we should behold such interposition in any form with indifference. If we look to the comparative strength and resources of Spain and those new governments, and their distances from each other, it must be obvious that she can never subdue them. It is still the true policy of the United States to leave the parties to themselves, in the hope that other powers will pursue the same course.

Source: *Words That Made American History,* Volume 1, Richard N. Current, 1972.

Analyzing Primary Sources

1. What is the main point of the Monroe Doctrine?
- **A.** It recognizes the independent nations in Latin America.
- **B.** It warns Europe against further colonization in the Americas.
- **C.** It permits Russia to settle in the Northwest.
- **D.** It warns Spain against invading Portugal.

2. What policy does the Monroe Doctrine apply to the wars in Europe?
- **F.** not to interfere in them
- **G.** to send aid when asked
- **H.** to help negotiate a peace treaty
- **J.** not to colonize European countries

3. Critical Thinking Evaluating Information Why did the United States issue the Monroe Doctrine?

Historical Critique

Monroe addressed this speech to "Fellow-citizens of the Senate and House of Representatives." What other audience did he intend his message to reach?

The Nation Expands

★ Chapter 10 ★ Democracy in the Age of Jackson

★ 10–1 ★ Against Nullification

Introduction In 1830, Senator Robert Y. Hayne of South Carolina, representing the southern states, spoke in the Senate in support of states' rights and nullification. Senator Daniel Webster of Massachusetts then replied to Hayne. His dramatic speech, given over two days, became famous throughout the nation. The following excerpt is from Webster's reply to Hayne.

Vocabulary Before you read the selection, find the meanings of these words in a dictionary: **sovereign, construe, interpolated, conscientiously, vigilantly.**

★ ★ ★ ★ ★ ★ ★ ★ ★ ★

If anything be found in the national Constitution . . . which ought not be in it, the people know how to get rid of it. If any construction is established unacceptable to them, so as to become practically a part of the Constitution, they will amend it, at their own sovereign pleasure. But while the people choose to maintain it as it is, while they are satisfied with it, and refuse to change it, who has given, or who can give, to the state legislatures a right to alter it, either by interference, construction, or otherwise? Gentlemen do not seem to recollect that the people have any power to do anything for themselves. They imagine there is no safety for them, any longer than they are under the close guardianship of the state legislatures. . . .

The people of the United States have at no time, in no way, directly or indirectly, authorized any state legislature to construe or interpret *their* high instrument of government; much less to interfere, by their own power, to arrest its course and operation.

Viewing History **Two Nationalist Leaders**

Massachusetts sculptor Thomas Ball created these bronze statuettes of Henry Clay (left) and Daniel Webster (right) in the 1850s. Ball greatly admired Clay and Webster for their efforts to preserve the union. ★ **What impression of Daniel Webster do you get from Ball's sculpture and from Webster's speech?**

If, sir, the people in these respects had done otherwise than they have done, their Constitution could neither have been preserved, nor would it have been worthy preserving. And if its plain provisions shall now be disregarded, and these new doctrines interpolated in it, it will become as feeble and helpless a being as its enemies, whether early or more recent, could possibly desire. It will exist in every state but as a poor dependent on state permission. . . .

But, sir, although there are fears, there are hopes also. The people have preserved this, their own chosen Constitution, for forty years, and have seen their happiness, prosperity, and renown grow with its growth, and strengthen with its strength. They are now, generally, strongly, attached to it. Overthrown by direct assault, it cannot be; evaded, undermined, *nullified,* it will not be, if we, and those who shall succeed us here, as agents and representatives of the people, shall conscientiously and vigilantly discharge the two great branches of our public trust, faithfully to preserve, and wisely to administer it. . . .

While the Union lasts, we have high, exciting, gratifying prospects spread out before us, for us and our children. . . . Liberty *and* Union, now and forever, one and inseparable!

Source: *American Reader: Words That Moved a Nation,* edited by Diane Ravitch, 1990.

Analyzing Primary Sources

1. According to Webster, the liberty of the American people is safeguarded by
   A. Congress.
   B. the Constitution.
   C. state legislatures.
   D. prosperity.
2. In his speech, Webster is supporting
   F. states' rights.
   G. the War of 1812.
   H. preservation of the Union.
   J. succession.
3. **Critical Thinking Identifying Main Ideas** What are the main ideas in Webster's speech?

Historical Critique

In their speeches, politicians often use emotional appeals to rally support for a particular cause. How do Webster's final words appeal to his listeners' emotions? How do you think he used his voice to increase the effect of his words?

★ 10–2 ★ The Cherokee Removal

Introduction The Indian Removal Act forced the Cherokee, the Creek, the Chickasaw, and the Choctaw to resettle west of the Mississippi. When it came time for the Cherokees to leave their homes in 1838, many resisted. Evan Jones, a Baptist missionary, worked among the Cherokee in North Carolina and joined them on their westward march. The following excerpt is from a series of letters written by Jones.

Vocabulary Before you read the selection, find the meanings of these words in the dictionary: **plunderers, wretches, agitation, consoling, disposition, perpetrated, manifests.**

★ ★ ★ ★ ★ ★ ★ ★ ★

Camp Hetzel, Near Cleveland, June 16

The Cherokees are nearly all prisoners. They have been dragged from their houses, and encamped at the forts and military posts, all over the nation. In Georgia, especially, multitudes were allowed no time to take anything with them, except the clothes they had on. Well-furnished houses were a prey to plunderers, who, like hungry wolves, follow in the train of the captors. These wretches rifle the houses, and strip the helpless, unoffending owners of all they have on earth. . . . The property of many has been taken, and sold before their eyes for almost nothing—the sellers and buyers, in many cases, being combined to cheat the poor Indians. . . . The poor captive, in a state of distressing agitation, his weeping wife almost frantic with terror, surrounded by a group of crying, terrified children, without a friend to speak a consoling word, is in a poor condition to make a good disposition of his property and is in most cases stripped of the whole, at one blow. Many of the Cherokees, who, a few days ago, were in comfortable circumstances, are now victims of abject poverty. Some, who have been allowed to return home, under passport, to inquire after their property, have found their cattle, horses, swine, farming tools, and house furniture all gone. And this is not a description of extreme cases. It is altogether a faint representation of the work which has been perpetrated on the unoffending, unarmed, and unresisting Cherokees. . . .

It is due to justice to say, that, at this station (and I learn the same is true of some others), the officer in command treats his prisoners with great respect and indulgence. But fault rests somewhere. They are prisoners, without a crime to justify the fact. . . .

July 10 and July 11

The work of war in time of peace, is commenced in the Georgia part of the Cherokee nation, and is carried on, in most cases, in the most unfeeling and brutal manner; no regard being paid to the orders of the commanding General, in regard to humane treatment of the Indians. I have heard of only one officer in Georgia (I hope there are

Viewing History **Along the Trail of Tears**

Robert Liudneux painted this view of Cherokee families traveling west on the Trail of Tears. Blue-coated soldiers force Cherokee families to move to Indian Territory. Some families carry their belongings in wagons, but many others must make the journey on foot. ★ **How does the painting suggest the hardships the Cherokees faced?**

more), who manifests anything like humanity, in his treatment of this persecuted people....

The work of capturing being completed, and about 3,000 sent off, the General had agreed to suspend the further transportation of the captives till the first of September. This arrangement, though but a small favor, diffused universal joy through the camps of the prisoners....

On our way, we met a detachment of 1,300 prisoners. As I took some of them by hand, the tears gushed from their eyes. Their hearts, however, were cheered to see us, and to hear a word of consolation. Many members of the church were among them. At Fort Butler, we found a company of 300, just arrived from the mountains, on their way to the general depot, at the agency. Several of our members were among these also.

Source: *The Cherokee Removal: A Brief History With Documents,* edited by Theda Perdue and Michael Green, 1995.

Analyzing Primary Sources

1. Where were the Cherokees living when Jones wrote these letters?
- **A.** in Georgia
- **B.** in California
- **C.** in Texas
- **D.** in Ohio

2. Where were the Cherokees being taken?
- **F.** to their homes
- **G.** to reservations
- **H.** to forts and military posts
- **J.** to Cleveland

3. Critical Thinking Recognizing Points of View Based on the excerpt, how did Evan Jones view the United States Army's treatment of the Cherokees?

Historical Critique

Did Evan Jones directly witness everything he describes in his letters? Explain.

★ Chapter 11 ★ Westward Expansion

★ 11–1 ★ Death Comes for the Archbishop

Introduction Many of the novels of Willa Cather focus on pioneer life on the Great Plains. In *Death Comes for the Archbishop,* however, her setting is the American Southwest during the 1850s. The book's main character, Bishop Jean Latour, journeys with his Native American guide, Jacinto, through Arizona and New Mexico. In the following selection, Latour and Jacinto camp for the night during a journey to a distant mission.

Vocabulary Before you read the selection, find the meanings of these words in a dictionary: **firmament, proposition, vehement.**

★ ★ ★ ★ ★ ★ ★ ★ ★

Jacinto got firewood and good water from the Lagunas, and they made their camp in a pleasant spot on the rocks north of the village. As the sun dropped low, the light brought the white church and the yellow adobe houses up into relief from the flat ledges. Behind their camp, not far away, lay a group of great mesas. The Bishop asked Jacinto if he knew the name of the one nearest them.

"No, I do not know any name," he shook his head. "I know Indian name," he added, as if, for once, he were thinking aloud.

"And what is the Indian name?"

"The Laguna Indians call Snow-Bird mountain." He spoke somewhat unwillingly.

"That is very nice," said the Bishop musingly. "Yes, that is a pretty name...."

The Bishop sat drinking his coffee slowly out of the tin cup, keeping the pot near the embers. The sun had set now, the yellow rocks were turning grey, down in the pueblo the light of the cook fires made red patches of the glassless windows, and the smell of [pine] smoke came softly through the still air.

The whole western sky was the color of golden ashes, with here and there a flush of red on the lip of a little cloud. High above the horizon the evening-star flickered like a lamp just lit, and close beside it was another star of constant light, much smaller. . . .

Viewing HISTORY **A Mission in California**

An unknown California artist painted Oriana Day, Mission Francisco Solano de Sonoma *in the mid-1800s. It shows Native Americans at a mission in northern California. Throughout the Southwest, the Spanish had forced many Indians into missions.* ★ **Study the picture. What seems to be the main building of the mission? Where on the mission grounds did Indians live?**

The two companions sat, each thinking his own thoughts as night closed in about them; a blue night set with stars, the bulk of the solitary mesas cutting into the firmament. The Bishop seldom questioned Jacinto about his thoughts or beliefs. He didn't think it polite, and he believed it to be useless. There was no way he could transfer his own memories of European civilization into the Indian mind, and he was quite willing to believe that behind Jacinto there was a long tradition, a store of experience, which no language could translate to him. A chill came with the darkness. Father Latour put on his old fur-lined cloak, and Jacinto, loosening the blanket tied about his loins, drew it up over his head and shoulders.

"Many stars," he said presently. "What do you think about the stars, Padre?"

"The wise men tell us they are worlds like ours, Jacinto. . . ."

"I think not," [Jacinto] said in the tone of one who has considered a proposition fairly and rejected it. "I think they are leaders—great spirits."

"Perhaps they are," said the Bishop with a sigh. "Whatever they are, they are great. Let us say *Our Father*, and go to sleep, my boy."

Kneeling on either side of the embers they repeated the prayer together and then rolled up in their blankets. The Bishop went to sleep thinking with satisfaction that he was beginning to have some sort of human companionship with his Indian boy. One called the young Indians "boys," perhaps because there was something youthful and elastic in their bodies. Certainly about their behavior there was nothing boyish in the American sense, nor even in the European sense. Jacinto was never, by any chance, [naive]; he was never taken by surprise. One felt that his training, whatever it had been, had prepared him to meet any situation which might confront him. He was as much at home in the Bishop's study as in his own pueblo—and he was never too much at home anywhere. Father Latour felt he had gone a good way toward gaining his guide's friendship, though he did not know how.

The truth was, Jacinto liked the Bishop's way of meeting people; thought he had the right tone with Padre Gallegos, the right tone with Padre Jesus, and that he had good manners with the Indians. In his experience, white people, when they addressed Indians, always put on a false face. There were many kinds of false faces; Father Vaillant's, for example, was kindly but too vehement. The Bishop put on none at all. He stood straight and turned to the Governor of Laguna, and his face underwent no change. Jacinto thought this remarkable.

Source: *Death Comes for the Archbishop,* Willa Cather, 1927.

Analyzing Literature

1. The bishop rarely asked Jacinto about his thoughts and beliefs because
   - **A.** he did not care about Indian beliefs.
   - **B.** he knew Jacinto did not want to talk about his beliefs.
   - **C.** he knew Jacinto did not speak English well.
   - **D.** he did not think Europeans and Indians could fully understand each other.
2. Jacinto came to trust the bishop because the bishop
   - **F.** taught Jacinto how to pray.
   - **G.** always told the truth.
   - **H.** was familiar with the countryside.
   - **J.** never put on a false face.
3. **Critical Thinking Comparing** **(a)** Compare the bishop's and Jacinto's beliefs concerning the stars. **(b)** What did each man think of the other's belief?

Historical Critique

Willa Cather wrote *Death Comes for the Archbishop* in the 1920s—more than 70 years after the novel takes place. What kinds of historical sources could she have used to help her write her novel?

★ 11–2 ★ Trapped in the Sierra Nevada

Introduction In 1846, a group of settlers started over the Sierra Nevada on their way to California. They were caught by an early winter snowstorm in what is now called Donner Pass. Of the 79 people in the party, only 45 survived. The following is an excerpt from the diary of H. H. Bancroft about the rescue of the trapped Donner party.

Vocabulary Before you read the selection, find the meanings of these words in a dictionary: **emigrants, intervals, famine, provision, repletion, imperatively.**

★ ★ ★ ★ ★ ★ ★ ★ ★

Foster had told us that we should find the emigrants at or near Truckee Lake, (since called Donner Lake) and in the direction of this we journeyed. Of course we had no guide, and most of our journey was through a dense pine forest, but the lofty peak which overlooks the lake was in sight at intervals, and this and the judgment of our two leaders were our sole means of direction. . . . When we started from the fort, Capt. Sutter assured us that we should be followed by other parties as soon as the necessary preparations could be made. For the guidance of those who might follow us and as a signal to any of the emigrants who might be straggling about in the mountains as well as for our own direction on our return trip, we set fire to every dead pine on or near our trail. . . .

At sunset of the 16th day we crossed Truckee Lake on the ice and came to the spot where we had been told we should find the emigrants. We looked all around but no living thing except ourselves was in sight and we thought that all must have perished. We raised a loud hello and then we saw a woman emerge from a hole in the snow. As we approached her several others made their appearance in like manner coming out of the snow. They were gaunt with famine and I never can forget the horrible, ghastly sight they presented. The first woman spoke in a hollow voice very much agitated and said, "Are you men from California or do you come from heaven?"

They had been without food except a few work oxen since the first fall of snow, about 3 weeks. They had gathered up the bones of the slaughtered cattle and boiled them to extract the grease and had roasted some of the hides which formed the roofs of their cabins. We gave them food very sparingly and retired for the night having some one of guard until morning to keep close watch on our provision to prevent the starving emigrants from eating them, which they would have done until they died of repletion.

When these emigrants had first been stopped by snow they had built small cabins using skins of the slaughtered oxen for roofs. Storms nearly continuous had caused the snow to fall to the depth of 18 feet so that the tops of their cabins were far beneath the surface. . . .

The morning after our arrival John P. Rhoads and Tucker started for another camp distant 8 miles east, where were the Donner family, to distribute what provisions could be spared and to bring along such of the party as had sufficient strength to walk. They returned bringing four girls and two boys of the Donner family and some others.

The next morning we started on our return trip accompanied by 21 emigrants mostly women and children. John Rhoads carried a child in his arms which died the second night. On the third day, an emigrant named John Denton, exhausted by starvation and totally snow-blind, gave out. He tried to keep up a hopeful and cheerful appearance, but we knew he could not live much longer. We made a platform of saplings, built a fire on it, cut some boughs

Viewing HISTORY **A Snowy Mountain Pass**

The journey to California was long and difficult. Travelers had to navigate narrow passes through the Rocky Mountains and the Sierra Nevada before reaching their destination. This photograph shows Carson Pass in the Sierra Nevada. ★ **If you were a settler heading west in the 1840s, what emotions might you have on seeing this view?**

for him to sit upon and left him. This was imperatively necessary. The party who followed in our trail from California found his dead body a few days after we had left him, partially eaten by wolves.

Source: *Overland in 1846: Diaries and Letters of the California-Oregon Trail,* edited by Dale Morgan, 1993.

Analyzing Primary Sources

1. At what location were the Donner party survivors found?
   - **A.** California
   - **B.** a pine forest
   - **C.** Truckee Lake
   - **D.** Sutter's fort
2. How were the Donner party stranded?
   - **F.** They lost their way.
   - **G.** Their wagons broke down.
   - **H.** There was an early winter snowstorm.
   - **J.** They ran out of food.
3. **Critical Thinking Recognizing Points of View** Based on the excerpt, how do you think H. H. Bancroft viewed the Donner party survivors?

Historical Critique

What information in this selection was Bancroft able to give as an eyewitness? What information did he have to get from members of the Donner party?

★ Chapter 12 ★ The Worlds of North and South

★ 12–1 ★ Three Views of Irish Immigration

Introduction Under British rule, most farmland in Ireland was used to grow wheat and oats for sale outside of Ireland. Irish peasants depended on the potato for nourishment. Then, in 1845, disease destroyed the potato crop. To escape starvation, thousands of poor Irish families emigrated to the United States. In the first letter below, a young woman in Ireland, describes the famine to her parents in Quebec, Canada. The second and third letters were written by new immigrants in New York to their villages back home.

Vocabulary Before you read the selection, find the meanings of these words in a dictionary: **scourge, endeavor, steward, inconceivable, quarries.**

★★★★★★★★★

Mary Rush:
Ardnaglass, Ireland
September 6, 1846

Dear Father and Mother,

Pen cannot dictate the poverty of this country at present. The potato crop is quite done away all over Ireland. There is nothing expected here, only an immediate famine. If you knew what danger we and our fellow countrymen are suffering, if you were ever so much distressed, you would take us out of this poverty isle. We can only say, the scourge of God fell down on Ireland, in taking away the potatoes, they being the only support of the people. So, dear father and mother, if you don't endeavor to take us out of it, it will be the first news you will hear by some friend of me and my little family to be lost by hunger, and there are thousands dread they will share the same fate. So, I conclude with my blessings to you both. . . .

For God's sake take us out of poverty, and don't let us die with the hunger.

Viewing History **Poverty in Ireland**

Even before famine struck, many Irish peasants lived in desperate poverty. They had to pay high rents to absentee English landlords, who often evicted tenants at will. This print from the later 1800s shows an Irish family thrown off their land with just a few meager possessions. ★ **Why do you think the United States attracted so many Irish immigrants?**

★ ★ ★ ★ ★ ★ ★ ★ ★

Daniel Guiney:
Buffalo, New York
August 9, 1850

Dear Mother and Brothers,

We mean to let you know our situation at present. We arrived here at five o'clock in the afternoon of yesterday, fourteen of us together, where we were received with the greatest kindness and respectability by Matthew Leary and Denis Danihy. When we came to the house we could not state to you how we were treated. We had potatoes, meat, butter, bread, and tea for dinner....

Dear friends, if you were to see old Denis Danihy, he never was in as good health and looks better than he ever did at home.... If you were to see Denis Reen when Daniel Danihy dressed him with clothes suitable for this country, you would think him to be a boss or steward, so that we have scarcely words to state to you how happy we felt at present. And as to the girls that used to be trotting on the bogs at home, to hear them talk English would be of great astonishment to you. Mary Keefe got two dresses, one from Mary Danihy and the other from Biddy Matt.

★ ★ ★ ★ ★ ★ ★ ★ ★

William Dever:
New York, New York
September 14, 1848

My dear Uncle and Brothers,

It's inconceivable the thousands that land here every week from all the old countries flying from tyranny and oppression. Wealthy farmers with their whole families are coming here and purchasing farms, some the best land in the whole world. Germans, French, Hollanders are doing this on a large scale.

But most of the Irish come out poor, unable to purchase farms. They work digging quarries, carrying brick and mortar in scorching sun up to the fourth stories of houses, in winter nothing to do, all their money spent. They are despised and kicked about. Many write home they are happy and wealthy, when they are of that class above mentioned. I heard friends of a young man in this city enquiring if John . . . was not a banker here, as he wrote home that he was so and persuaded all his relatives to come join him. But what was he, think you? He was sweeper of the office of the bank. They were astonished when told so. And thousands are just like him.

Source: *Out of Ireland: The Story of Irish Emigration to America*, Kerby Miller and Paul Wagner, 1994.

Analyzing Primary Sources

1. Why did Mary Rush send a letter to her parents?
   A. She wanted to leave Ireland.
   B. She wanted to tell them about life in the United States.
   C. She wanted to tell them the latest news from the village.
   D. She wanted them to send her money.
2. According to William Dever, unlike German immigrants, the Irish
   F. were not good farmers.
   G. were treated with great kindness.
   H. could not afford to buy land.
   J. worked in the banking business.
3. **Critical Thinking Recognizing Points of View** Explain how you think each of the following might have reacted if they had read Daniel Guiney's letter: **(a)** Mary Rush; **(b)** William Dever.

Historical Critique

How does Dever's letter show why we cannot always take primary sources at face value?

★ 12–2 ★ The Fires of Jubilee

Introduction In 1831, Nat Turner led a group of slaves on an uprising across Southampton County, Virginia. More than 50 white people were killed. Modern writer Stephen B. Oates wrote a dramatic account of this rebellion in *The Fires of Jubilee: Nat Turner's Fierce Rebellion.* The following excerpt describes the reaction of the white community after the rebellion.

Vocabulary Before you read the selection, find the meanings of these words in a dictionary: **pummeled, insurgents, disaffection, dire, commencement, couriers, communiqués, ascertain.**

★ ★ ★ ★ ★ ★ ★ ★ ★

In September, new alarms pummeled upper North Carolina. A man from Murfreesboro, having attended a slave trial in Virginia's Sussex County, reported back that the Southampton insurgents had expected armed slave resistance "from distant neighborhoods," including the large plantations on the Roanoke. Yes, the fellow cried, testimony in the Sussex trial "proved" that a concerted uprising was to have taken place in Virginia and upper North Carolina, where Negro preachers had been spreading disaffection, and that "dire and extensive would have been the slaughter but for a mistake in the day of commencement." The plan, the man said, called for the larger rebellion to begin on the last Sunday in August. But he contended that the Southampton rebels mistook August 21 as the target Sunday, all the while their North Carolina allies were waiting for August 28!

Though no such plan had existed, the report traumatized whites in the northeastern tier of counties, especially in neighborhoods with heavy slave concentrations. Couriers rode for Raleigh to beg for muskets and ammunition. Militia outfits mustered along the Roanoke, chased after imaginary insurgents and . . . imprisoned . . . still more innocent blacks. Phantom slave columns marched out

Viewing HISTORY **Picking Cotton**

The economy of the South depended on cotton, and cotton depended on slavery. This woodcut shows enslaved African Americans picking, baling, and ginning cotton on a plantation.

★ **Compare this picture to the reading. How do they give different pictures of slave life?**

of the Dismal Swamp, only to vanish when militia units rushed out to fight them.

In mid-September came the most shattering alarm of all: couriers reported that a full-scale rebellion had blazed up in southeastern North Carolina, in Duplin and Sampson counties. . . . Such communiqués were completely false, but frantic whites were now reacting to their own shadows. Militia commanders alerted their troops and sent off exaggerated reports to the governor, which gathered additional frills as express riders bore them to the capital. Meanwhile, mass hysteria gripped the town of Wilmington down near the Atlantic Ocean. . . .

But no slave army appeared. Out of blind vengeance, whites turned on the local Negro population and . . . forced five hapless blacks into confessing that, yes, they were to meet insurgents from Sampson County. . .

Raleigh too was in turmoil, as a succession of express riders burst into the city with doomsday reports: slave rebels had allegedly set much of eastern North Carolina afire. . . .

In all the excitement, a few people managed to keep their heads. On September 16, the Raleigh *Star* corrected its initial reports and denied the disturbing news now "circulating through the country." A few days later the Raleigh *Register* admitted that its own account of insurrections in North Carolina had been "highly exaggerated." The storm had passed now, the paper declared, so that it was possible to ascertain the truth. While slaves in the southeastern part of the state had undoubtedly "talked about insurrection," none in fact had transpired.

Source: *The Fires of Jubilee: Nat Turner's Fierce Rebellion,* Stephen B. Oates, 1975.

Analyzing Literature

1. What alarmed the white community ?
- **A.** the verdict in a slave trial
- **B.** the burning of Raleigh
- **C.** the presence of militia in the towns
- **D.** talk of a slave rebellion

2. Newspapers in Raleigh
- **F.** supported a slave revolt.
- **G.** called for an end to slavery.
- **H.** ignored rumors of a slave revolt.
- **J.** corrected their earlier reports.

3. Critical Thinking Distinguishing Fact From Opinion (a) On what information did the people in North Carolina base their belief that slaves were about to rebel? **(b)** What facts in the selection contradict those beliefs?

Historical Critique

How can you tell that Stephen B. Oates did historical research before writing his book?

★ Chapter 13 ★ An Era of Reform

★ 13–1 ★ Education of a Slave

Introduction Frederick Douglass escaped from slavery in 1838 and later became a leading abolitionist. From the money he earned writing and lecturing, Douglass was able to buy his freedom. In 1845, Douglass wrote *Narrative of the Life of Frederick Douglass.* In the following excerpt, Douglass explains why learning to read and write was so important to him.

Vocabulary Before you read the selection, find the meanings of these words in a dictionary: **blighting, impudent, tranquil, irresponsible, commenced, revelation, perplexing.**

★ ★ ★ ★ ★ ★ ★ ★ ★ ★ ★

My new mistress proved to be all she appeared when I first met her at the door—a woman of the kindest heart and finest feelings. She had never had a slave under her control previously to myself, and prior to her marriage she had been dependent upon her own industry for a living. She was by trade a weaver; and by constant application to her business, she had been in a good degree preserved from the blighting and dehumanizing effects of slavery. I was utterly astonished at her goodness. . . . She did not deem it impudent or unmannerly for a slave to look her in the face. The meanest slave was put fully at ease in her presence, and none left without feeling better for having seen her. Her face was made of heavenly smiles, and her voice of tranquil music.

But, alas! this kind heart had but a short time to remain such. The fatal poison of irresponsible power was already in her hands, and soon commenced its infernal work. That

Viewing HISTORY Frederick Douglass Speaks Out

In 1845, Frederick Douglass published his Narrative. *The same year, a song celebrating his escape appeared in the North. The photograph (far left) was taken in 1848, the year after Douglass started his antislavery newspaper, the* North Star. ★ **"Expose slavery and it dies," said Frederick Douglass. How did his actions reflect this belief?**

cheerful eye, under the influence of slavery, soon became red with rage....

Very soon after I went to live with Mr. and Mrs. Auld, she very kindly commenced to teach me the A, B, C. After I had learned this, she assisted me in learning to spell words of three or four letters. Just at this point of my progress, Mr. Auld found out what was going on, and at once forbade Mrs. Auld to instruct me further, telling her, among other things, that it was unlawful, as well as unsafe, to teach a slave to read. To use his own words, further, he said, "If...you teach that nigger (speaking of myself) how to read, there would be no keeping him. It would forever unfit him to be a slave. He would at once become unmanageable, and of no value to his master. As to himself, it could do him no good, but a great deal of harm. It would make him discontented and unhappy." These words sank deep into my heart, stirred up sentiments within that lay slumbering, and called into existence an entirely new train of thought. It was a new and special revelation, explaining dark and mysterious things, with which my youthful understanding had struggled, but struggled in vain. I now understood what had been to me a most perplexing difficulty—to wit, the white man's power to enslave the black man. It was a grand achievement, and I prized it highly. From that moment, I understood the pathway from slavery to freedom. It was just what I wanted, and I got it at a time when I the least expected it. Whilst I was saddened by the thought of losing the aid of my kind mistress, I was gladdened by the invaluable instruction which, by the merest accident, I had gained from my master. Though conscious of the difficulty of learning without a teacher, I set out with high hope, and a fixed purpose, at whatever cost of trouble, to learn how to read. The very decided manner with which he spoke, and strove to impress his wife with the evil consequences of giving me instruction, served to convince me that he was deeply sensible of the truths he was uttering. It gave me the best assurance that I might rely with the utmost confidence on the results which, he said, would flow from teaching me to read. What he most dreaded, that I most desired. What he most loved, that I most hated. That which to him was great evil, to be carefully shunned, was to me a great good, to be diligently sought; and the argument which he so warmly urged, against my learning to read, only served to inspire me with a desire and determination to learn. In learning to read, I owe almost as much to the bitter opposition of my master, as to the kindly aid of my mistress. I acknowledge the benefit of both.

Source: *Narrative of the Life of Frederick Douglass, An American Slave,* Frederick Douglass, 1845.

Analyzing Primary Sources

1. Who first taught Frederick Douglass how to read?

A. Mr. Auld
B. Mrs. Auld
C. his mother
D. another slave

2. According to Douglass, Mrs. Auld changed as a result of her

F. power over her slaves.
G. disagreement with her husband.
H. inability to teach Douglass to read.
J. fear of a slave revolt.

3. **Critical Thinking Recognizing Points of View** According to the excerpt, how did Frederick Douglass view his master's opposition to educating slaves?

Historical Critique

To gain support for what cause did Douglass write his autobiography? What made him an effective witness?

★ 13–2 ★ Declaration of Sentiments

Introduction In 1848, Elizabeth Cady Stanton and Lucretia Mott led a women's rights convention in Seneca Falls, New York. The event marked the beginning of an organized women's rights movement in the United States. The women and men attending the convention adopted the following Declaration of Sentiments and a number of resolutions.

Vocabulary Before you read the selection, find the meanings of these words in a dictionary: **impel, endowed, inalienable, allegiance, prudence, transient, usurpations, evinces, despotism, constrains, tyranny, franchise, facilities, zealous.**

★ ★ ★ ★ ★ ★ ★ ★ ★

Declaration of Sentiments

When, in the course of human events, it becomes necessary for one portion of the family of man to assume among the people of the earth a position different from that which they have hitherto occupied, but one to which the laws of nature and of nature's God entitle them, a decent respect to the opinions of mankind requires that they should declare the causes that impel them to such a course.

We hold these truths to be self-evident that all men and women are created equal; that they are endowed by their Creator with certain inalienable rights; that among these are life, liberty, and the pursuit of happiness; that to secure these rights governments are instituted, deriving their just powers from the consent of the governed. Whenever any form of government becomes destructive of these ends, it is the right of those who suffer from it to refuse allegiance to it, and to insist upon the institution of a new government, laying its foundation on such principles, and organizing its powers in such form, as to them shall seem most likely to effect their safety and happiness. Prudence, indeed, will dictate that governments long established should not be changed for light and transient causes; and accordingly all experience hath shown that mankind are more disposed to suffer while evils are sufferable, than to right themselves by abolishing the forms to which they are accustomed. But when a long train of abuses and usurpations, pursuing invariably the same object, evinces a design to reduce them under absolute despotism, it is their duty to throw off such government, and to provide new guards for their future security. Such has been the patient sufferance of the women under this government, and such is now the necessity which constrains them to demand the equal station to which they are entitled.

The history of mankind is a history of repeated injuries and usurpations on the part of man toward woman, having in direct object the establishment of an absolute tyranny over her. To prove this, let facts be submitted to a candid world.

He has never permitted her to exercise her inalienable right to the elective franchise.

He has compelled her to submit to laws, in the formation of which she had no voice.

He has withheld from her rights which are given to the most ignorant and degraded men—both natives and foreigners.

Having deprived her of this first right of a citizen, the elective franchise, thereby leaving her without representation in the halls of legislation, he has oppressed her on all sides.

He has made her, if married, in the eye of the law, civilly dead.

He has taken from her all right in property, even to the wages she earns....

He has denied her the facilities for obtaining a thorough education, all colleges being closed against her....

Resolutions

Resolved, That all laws which prevent woman from occupying such a station in society as her conscience shall dictate, or which place her in a position inferior to that of man, are contrary to the great precept of nature, and therefore of no force or authority.

Resolved, That woman is man's equal—was intended to be so by the Creator, and the

Viewing HISTORY **Education for Women**

In the early 1800s, American colleges and universities admitted only men. Still, a few women did receive an education at "seminaries for young ladies." This picture by an unknown student shows women studying geography at a seminary, somewhere between 1810 and 1820. ★ **Why did many men think it was not important for women to receive an education?**

highest good of the race demands that she should be recognized as such.

Resolved, That the women of this country ought to be enlightened in regard to the laws under which they live, that they may no longer publish their degradation by declaring themselves satisfied with their present position, nor their ignorance, by asserting that they have all the rights they want....

Resolved, That the speedy success of our cause depends on the zealous and untiring efforts of both men and women....

Source: *Words That Made American History,* Volume 1, edited by Richard N. Current, 1972.

Analyzing Primary Sources

1. What is the main point of this document?
   - **A.** Men should have more rights than women.
   - **B.** Our laws are unfair to both men and women.
   - **C.** Women should have the same rights as men.
   - **D.** All men should be allowed to hold public office.
2. According to this document, women did not have the right to
   - **F.** work.
   - **G.** vote.
   - **H.** travel to a foreign country.
   - **J.** speak out against injustice.
3. **Critical Thinking Making Inferences** Why do you think that the women at the Seneca Falls Convention used the wording of the Declaration of Independence when they wrote their Declaration of Sentiments?

Historical Critique

For what purpose was this document written? Do you think it was intended to be read primarily by women, by men, or by both?

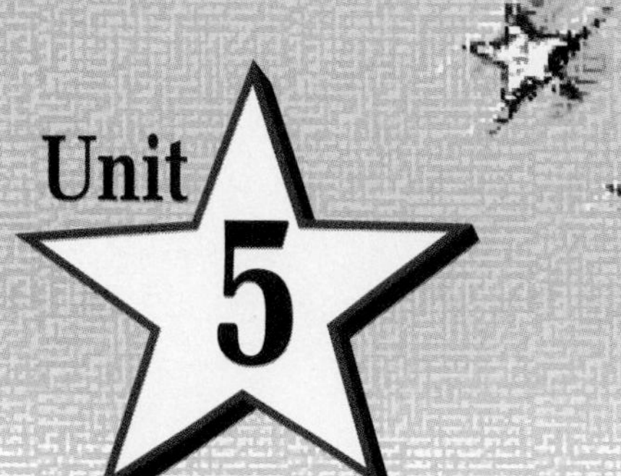

Unit 5 Division and Reunion

Chapter 14 A Dividing Nation

★ 14-1 ★ Caleb's Choice

Literature

Introduction G. Clifton Wisler's novel *Caleb's Choice* is set in the late 1850s. Young Caleb Delaney goes to northern Texas to live with his grandmother and his cousins Edith and Micah. In Caleb's new home, people are divided over the Fugitive Slave Law. Caleb is not sure how he feels about the law. In the following excerpt, Caleb helps feed two captured fugitives.

Vocabulary Before you read the selection, find the meanings of these words in a dictionary: **shackled, bounty, wretch.**

★ ★ ★ ★ ★ ★ ★ ★ ★

You had to admit that they were good at their work. They captured the two runaways from Waco not a half mile from Spring Creek, and they located three others off a Smith County plantation.

"Already wired their owners," Ulysses boasted. "Mr. Francis Leighton will meet us in Dallas to take delivery of his two. Promised us a fifty-dollar bonus, too. We'll leave the other three with Sheriff Rutherford at McKinney. They're worth two hundred dollars altogether."

I thought about that. Papa needed five hundred dollars, and here the Fitches had earned almost that much capturing runaways! The notion had a powerful pull to it. But when I followed Edith out to the well with some food for the prisoners, I realized that I would never have the heart to be a slave catcher. I recognized the two Waco slaves from the sketches on their posters, but I wasn't prepared for the other three. One was a sad-eyed girl no older than Edith, and the other two were slight-shouldered boys only a little taller than me. Not since departing Dallas had I seen people with such hollow eyes. Their feet were shackled, and their hands were bound with coarse rope that bit into the dark flesh of their wrists. The younger boy bled from the left side of his mouth. Edith gasped when she looked at the backs of the Waco runaways. The Fitches had used a whip on both.

"Fetch some water from the well," Edith told me.

"Already done," Polk Harrison announced, carrying a bucket over. "Spied them on the road."

Edith and Harrison exchanged an odd glance, and I sensed they wanted to say more. The runaways accepted cups of water gratefully, although with downcast eyes. The older ones managed to mumble a thank you when Edith promised to find some salve for their cuts. She placed slices of bread and chunks of ham in their fingers. They ate with considerable difficulty.

"We should notify the sheriff," Edith stormed. "Slaves or not, they don't deserve ill treatment."

"Its not illegal," Harrison argued. "There are slave catchers who do far worse. Fitches know better than to cut off a limb or hamstring a valuable hand. Takes away from the profit."

"They're getting a bonus," I pointed out. "Three hundred and fifty dollars in all."

"A man can always use money," Harrison admitted. "Me, I wouldn't take money earned from another man's bleeding."

"Even a slave?" I asked.

"Especially," Harrison said. "You accept a bounty for a killer, a man likely to hurt somebody else and capable of defending himself, that's one thing. But hunting down some poor wretch who only wants to be left alone?"

"That's pretty strong talk, mister," Ulysses said, walking over, rifle in hand. "You know, it wouldn't surprise me to learn somebody hereabouts hid those older ones. We looked mighty hard for 'em."

"That why you whipped them?" I asked, "To find out?"

"Oh, that was just a little message from Mr. Leighton," Ulysses explained. "Most likely they hid in a slave house at one of the big farms east of here. White men would know better than to help after that trouble on the Colorado River."

"What trouble?" I asked.

"Two years ago the authorities discovered a plot," Harrison told me. "Four hundred slaves were supposed to rise and kill their masters. . . . "

I shivered. Gazing into the eyes of those prisoners, though, I found it hard to imagine myself in much danger. Halfway starved and dressed in rags, they looked more like survivors off a Gulf shipwreck than bloodthirsty killers.

"Don't let 'em fool you, boy," Ulysses said to me in particular. "They hate us. . . . "

"Can't much blame them," Edith said, drawing me away from the well. "Lord know they've got reason enough."

"I suppose," I said, sighing. "I saw an auction in Dallas. I wouldn't want to be a slave. Desperate like that, they *could* be dangerous, though."

Viewing HISTORY **Human Beings for Sale**

In 1853, British artist Eyre Crowe visited Richmond, Virginia, a leading center of the slave trade. Crowe then painted After the Sale: South From Richmond. *It shows newly sold African Americans in a wagon, waiting to be transported to their new owner. In the lower right, two slave traders argue over the price.* ★ **Identify three details in this painting that create sympathy for the enslaved African Americans.**

"I would be," she whispered. "Let's get away from here. I can't bear seeing them that way."

All that afternoon I thought about the slaves. I couldn't get them off my mind. When I sat at the loft table composing letters to my parents for Polk Harrison to carry back south, I tried to free myself from the runaways' ghostly faces. I couldn't.

Source: *Caleb's Choice*, G. Clifton Wisler, 1996.

Analyzing Literature

1. Who were the Fitches?
   - **A.** slave catchers
   - **B.** Caleb's parents
   - **C.** Caleb's grandparents
   - **D.** abolitionists
2. Who helped the fugitives?
   - **F.** Mr. Leighton
   - **G.** Ulysses
   - **H.** Sheriff Rutherford
   - **J.** Edith
3. **Critical Thinking Drawing Conclusions** Why do you think that slave catchers were so well paid?

Historical Critique

If you were writing a report about the attitudes of white Texans toward fugitive slaves in the 1800s, could you use *Caleb's Choice* as a historical source? Why or why not?

★ 14–2 ★ Two Views of the War in Kansas

Introduction In 1856, proslavery forces attacked Lawrence, Kansas. An antislavery group led by John Brown attacked Pottawatomie Creek and killed a number of southern settlers. In the following letters, John Lawrie, a northerner, and Axalla John Hoole, a southerner, express their views of the fighting in Kansas.

Vocabulary Before you read the selection, find the meanings of these words in a dictionary: **endeavors, vengeance, propriety, molest.**

★ ★ ★ ★ ★ ★ ★ ★ ★

John Lawrie:

Dear Art,

When I left home on the fifteenth of last June I had no intention of making a home in Kansas. I intended in case I could find any organization ready to take the field against the Missourians [the proslavery settlers], to use my utmost endeavors to change the attitude of the Free-State [antislavery] settlers from a defensive to an offensive warfare. When I reached Leavenworth, I was unable to find any organization of free-state men, and could only tell one when I met him by his hanging head and subdued tone of voice....

Hearing that people held up their heads and spoke what they thought in Lawrence, I started for that point and soon found myself at home as far as a hatred of tyranny and a thirst for vengeance for the insult of the 21st of May was concerned. The people had concluded to try whether there was truth in the Border Ruffian assertion *The... Yankees won't fight!* There was quite a stir among the young men in the way of target fighting and drilling in order to prepare themselves for any emergency that might arise requiring them *to contend with superior numbers,* the only thing that thus far has held them back. I found that arms were really scarce. I expected to find plenty of improved fire-arms, and it was with the greatest difficulty I succeeded in getting an old condemned musket. I was looked upon with distrust by a great many persons in Lawrence, having the appearance of a spy in their eyes. It was complimentary, for my appearance seemed above my position to them; but it was very disagreeable. The only military company in town *(the Stubbs)* expected to attend the convention at Topeka on the second and third of July and the opening of the [antislavery] legislature on the Fourth, when it was expected they would be needed to defend the legislature against the Ruffians and troops of the U.S. I applied for admission into the company and was put off with rather evasive answers. I went up to Topeka, however, resolved to prove myself a true man when the trying time came. I found the people discussing the propriety of defending the legislature against all who might attempt to disperse it....

★ ★ ★ ★ ★ ★ ★ ★ ★ ★

Axalla John Hoole:

Dear Sister,

I fear, Sister, that coming here will do no good at last, as I begin to think that this will be made a free state at last. 'Tis true we have elected proslavery men to draft a state Constitution, but I feel pretty certain, if it is put to the vote of the people, it will be rejected, as I feel pretty confident they have a majority here at this time. The South has ceased all efforts, while the North is redoubling her exertions. We nominated a candidate for Congress last Friday—Ex-Gov. Ransom of Michigan. I must confess I have not much faith in him, though he professes to hate the abolitionists bitterly, and I have heard him say that Negroes were a great deal better off with masters. Still, I fear him, but it was the best we could do.

Viewing History **A Violent Abolitionist**

Abolitionist John Brown favored violent solutions to the evil of slavery. In 1856, he and his followers murdered five proslavery settlers in Kansas. Three years later, Brown led a raid on a gun warehouse in Harpers Ferry, Virginia. This painting shows Brown being led to his execution, as northerners imagined the scene. ★ **Why do you think many abolitionists did not support John Brown?**

Source: *America Firsthand,* Volume 1, *From Settlement to Reconstruction*, edited by Robert D. Marcus and David Burner, 1989.

Analyzing Primary Sources

1. The proslavery settlers mentioned in Lawrie's letter were from
   A. Ohio.
   B. Missouri.
   C. Kansas.
   D. Indiana.
2. Free-state settlers were supported by
   F. Border Ruffians.
   G. United States troops.
   H. southerners.
   J. northerners.
3. **Critical Thinking Recognizing Points of View** What was the point of view of each author on the issue of slavery in Kansas?

Historical Critique

Why are both of these letters reliable sources of information, even though they are written from opposing points of view?

⋆ Chapter 15 ⋆ The Civil War

★ 15–1 ★ A Nurse in the Civil War

Introduction Louisa May Alcott is best known as the author of the classic novel *Little Women.* During the Civil War, Alcott worked at the Union Hospital in the Georgetown area of Washington. She wrote letters home about her experiences as a volunteer nurse. The letters were later published under the title *Hospital Sketches.*

Vocabulary Before you read the selection, find the meanings of these words in a dictionary: **vilest, chronic, premises, fortitude, feebly, comrade, draughts, admonished, tenanted.**

★ ★ ★ ★ ★ ★ ★ ★ ★ ★

The first thing I met was a regiment of the vilest odors that ever assaulted the human nose . . . and the worst of this affliction was, everyone had assured me that it was a chronic weakness of all hospitals, and I must bear it. I did, armed with lavender water, with which I so besprinkled myself and premises, that, like my friend, Sairy, I was soon known among my patients as "the nurse with the bottle." . . . I progressed by slow stages up stairs and down, till the main hall was reached, and I paused to take breath and a survey. There they were! "our brave boys," as the papers justly call them, for cowards could hardly have been so riddled with shot and shell, so torn and shattered, nor have borne suffering for which we have no name, with an uncomplaining fortitude, which made one glad to cherish each as a brother. In they came, some on stretchers, some in men's arms, some feebly staggering along propped on rude crutches, and one lay stark and still with covered face, as a comrade gave his name to be recorded before they carried him away to the dead house. All was hurry and confusion; the hall was full of these wrecks of humanity, for the most exhausted could not reach a bed till duly ticketed and registered; the walls were lined with rows of such as could sit, the floor covered with the more disabled, the steps and doorways filled with helpers and lookers on; the sound of many feet and voices made that usually quiet hour as noisy as noon; and, in the midst of it all, the matron's motherly face brought more comfort to many a poor soul, than the cordial draughts she administered, or the cheery words that welcomed all, making of the hospital a home.

The sight of several stretchers, each with its legless, armless, or desperately wounded occupant, entering my ward, admonished me that I was there to work, not to wonder or weep; so I corked up my feelings, and returned to the path of duty, which was rather

Viewing History **Nurse and Patient**

This detail is from an engraving honoring the United States Sanitary Commission. It shows a Union nurse comforting a wounded soldier by reading to him. In the Confederacy, too, dedicated women volunteered their time to care for the wounded and the sick. ★ **In what other ways did women help the war effort?**

"a hard road to travel" just then. The house had been a hotel before hospitals were needed, and many of the doors still bore their old names; some not so inappropriate as might be imaged, for my ward was in truth a *ball-room,* if gunshot wounds could christen it. Forty beds were prepared, many already tenanted by tired men who fell down anywhere, and drowsed till the smell of food roused them. Round the great stove was gathered the dreariest group I ever saw—ragged, gaunt and pale, mud to the knees, with bloody bandages untouched since put on days before; many bundled up in blankets, coats being lost or useless; and all wearing that disheartened look which proclaimed defeat.... I pitied them so much, I dared not speak to them, though, remembering all they had been through since the roust at Fredericksburg, I yearned to serve the dreariest of them all. Presently, Miss Blank tore me from my refuge behind piles of one-sleeved shirts, odd socks, bandages and lint; put basin, sponge, towels and a block of brown soap into my hands, with these appalling directions:

"Come, my dear, begin to wash as fast as you can. Tell them to take off socks, coats, and shirts, scrub them well, put on clean shirts, and the attendants will finish them off, and lay them in bed."

Source: *Hospital Sketches,* Louisa May Alcott, 1864.

Analyzing Primary Sources

1. What did Miss Blank instruct Louisa May Alcott to do?
   A. make beds
   B. wash patients
   C. change bandages
   D. move patients
2. To handle the terrible odors, Miss Alcott
   F. used lavender water.
   G. opened windows.
   H. washed the floors.
   J. used disinfectant.
3. **Critical Thinking Recognizing Points of View** How did Louisa May Alcott view the soldiers in the hospital?

Historical Critique

Alcott was writing a letter home to her family. Do you think she included all the details of what she witnessed at the hospital? Why or why not?

★ 15–2 ★ The Gettysburg Address

Introduction At the Battle of Gettysburg in July 1863, the Union army lost more than 23,000 soldiers. The Confederates lost 28,000 men. On November 19, 1863, President Abraham Lincoln visited Gettysburg to dedicate the battlefield cemetery. The brief but stirring speech President Lincoln gave on that day became known as the "Gettysburg Address."

Vocabulary Before you read the selection, find the meanings of these words in a dictionary: **score, proposition, consecrate, hallow, detract, vain, perish.**

★ ★ ★ ★ ★ ★ ★ ★ ★ ★

Four score and seven years ago our fathers brought forth on this continent, a new nation, conceived in liberty, and dedicated to the proposition that all men are created equal. Now we are engaged in a great civil war, testing whether that nation, or any nation so conceived and so dedicated, can long endure. We are met on a great battlefield of that war. We have come to dedicate a portion of that field, as a final resting place for those

Viewing HISTORY **Honoring the Dead**

This statue stands at the Gettysburg National Military Park in Pennsylvania. This soldier looks over the now-peaceful field, where a bloody battle took place in July 1863. ★ **What was the outcome of the Battle of Gettysburg?**

who here gave their lives that that nation might live. It is altogether fitting and proper that we should do this. But, in a larger sense, we can not dedicate—we can not consecrate—we can not hallow—this ground. The brave men, living and dead. who struggled here, have consecrated it, far above our poor power to add or detract. The world will little note, nor long remember what we say here, but it can never forget what they did here. It is for us the living, rather, to be dedicated here to the unfinished work which they who fought here have thus far so nobly advanced. It is rather for us to be here dedicated to the great task remaining before us—that from these honored dead we take increased devotion to that cause for which they gave the last full measure of devotion—that we here highly resolve that these dead shall not have died in vain—that this nation, under God, shall have a new birth of freedom—and that government of the people, by the people, for the people, shall not perish from the earth.

Source: *The Annals of America,* Volume 9, *The Crisis of the Union,* 1976.

Analyzing Primary Sources

1. What is this speech mainly about?
   - **A.** the Declaration of Independence
   - **B.** our nation's founders
   - **C.** the Civil War
   - **D.** President Lincoln
2. At what occasion was this speech given?
   - **F.** the dedication of a cemetery
   - **G.** the Battle of Gettysburg
   - **H.** President Lincoln's inauguration
   - **J.** the end of the Civil War
3. **Critical Thinking Analyzing Ideas** Give examples of how Lincoln uses this speech to try to remind people of the ideals upon which the United States was founded.

Historical Critique

In addition to honoring the dead, is Lincoln trying to gain support for a particular cause? Explain.

⋆ Chapter 16 ⋆ The Reconstruction Era

⋆ 16–1 ⋆ A Southerner Looks to the Future

Introduction Susan Bradford was the daughter of a Florida planter. In November 1866, she married Nicholas Eppes, who had fought in the Confederate army. His family owned a plantation near Tallahassee. Before her marriage, she kept a diary. Later, Susan Bradford Eppes used her diary and her experiences before and after the war to write books about the South.

Vocabulary Before you read the selection, find the meanings of these words in a dictionary: **fret, invalid, dispatch, proffer, proposition, recoup, impoverished.**

★ ★ ★ ★ ★ ★ ★ ★ ★

January 1st, 1866.—A New Year but a Happy New Year? No indeed. We got up this morning to find ourselves the only occupants of Pine Hill plantation. It was a clean sweep, all were gone.... Not a servant, not one and we unused to work....

January 2nd, 1866.—I have slept well and I feel decidedly better. I am not going to fret because the negroes are gone, nor will I bother my brains as to their whereabouts. I am going to learn to do all these things that need doing and bye and bye I shall do them well....

February 17th, 1866.—The house party is a thing of the past and will be long remembered.... Mrs. Miller is a sweet old lady, a South Carolinian by birth, who married a Northern man. Her invalid son, Lieutenant Charles Miller, excited my pity to such an extent that I have tried to forget his blue [Yankee] uniform and remember only that he suffers. I think the almost constant contact with the sick and wounded soldiers in our own army has automatically made me tender of those who are ill....

Our own boys tease me about my "sick Yankee," but I think it is right or I would not do it....

March 1st, 1866.—Little Diary, I have tried hard to tell you my secret but there are some things too sacred to write about. My Soldier in Gray has held by promise for many months and, before the year is out, we expect to be married....

March 14th, 1866.—Riding horse-back with My Soldier this afternoon I told him . . . I had heard Mr. Coolidge [a Yankee officer] was related to him and if that was so I wanted to know why he did not make friends with him? He looked very serious and I was beginning to fear I had hurt him in some unknown way.

At last he spoke, "I have never mentioned my cousin, Sidney Coolidge to you; he came to Florida to visit our family prior to the war.... I loved my cousin Sidney and looked forward to the visit, which he had promised us at some future time.

"The war came on and during the whole four years of war, I was in the thickest of the fighting. After Gettysburg I was promoted and assigned to the Army of the West. One day I was sent to carry a dispatch for my general. Crossing the field of Chickamauga, I was hit by a bullet; . . . I was stunned but soon recovered, delivered the dispatch and turned to go. An officer who knew me, laid his hand on my arm and said:

" 'Your cousin, Colonel Coolidge, lies dead in that tent, don't you want to go and look at him?'....

"Now, this young lieutenant you like so much, is probably a relative . . . but this is the way I feel about it; if the Confederates had been the victorious army and I had been occupying the conquered country, if, in fact, our positions could be reversed, I should look him up, claim the tie of blood and proffer the hand of friendship. As things stand, he is the conqueror, I am the conquered and if any advances are made they must come from him...."

July 21st, 1866.—This is the anniversary of the Battle of Manassas. How hopeful we were then and it seems ages ago, so much has crowded into life in these last years....

August 26th, 1866.—We have to look ahead and plan for the fall wedding which My Soldier pleads for.... I do not want a grand wedding such as my sisters had; circumstances are so different now. Father's fortune has been swept away by the results of the war. It is true, he still has his land but that is almost valueless at present and it may never bring in anything again as land without labor is a poor proposition.

Father has aged since the surrender and he will never be able to recoup his losses. All this show and expense is wholly unnecessary. What I would like would be a pretty wedding dress, every girl wants that, but I want a quiet wedding with my family and his family present and some of his friends and some of my friends for attendants....

October 5th, 1866.—My dress has been bought....[Mother] has let all our friends know that "no wedding presents must be sent." She says the South is impoverished, there are few who can afford to give a handsome gift and yet almost every one will spend that which they can ill-afford, rather than be outdone in general giving. I am well satisfied with this arrangement....

November 1st, 1866.—My dear little friend... I am telling you goodbye. Whatever the future may bring me of weal or woe will not be recorded. This is MY DAY, my wedding day.

Source: *Through Some Eventful Years,* Susan Bradford Eppes, 1926.

Viewing History: The End of the Confederacy

In Richard Brooke's painting Furling the Flag, *Confederate soldiers weep as they roll up their flag for the last time. The end of the Civil War was a difficult time for southerners. Black and white, they had to adjust to a new world.*
★ **Compare the mood of this painting to the feelings Susan Bradford Eppes expressed in her diary. How are they similar? How are they different?**

Analyzing Primary Sources

1. Why did Susan Bradford Eppes want a simple wedding?
   A. She was marrying a Yankee officer.
   B. She was sad about the South's defeat.
   C. The family's servants had all left.
   D. The war left her family poor.
2. This passage is mainly about the
   F. effects of the Civil War on the author's life.
   G. major battles of the Civil War.
   H. author's plans for her wedding.
   J. conflicts between Yankee and Confederate officers.
3. **Critical Thinking Recognizing Points of View** How does Susan Bradford Eppes reveal her feelings about the South after the war?

Historical Critique

Eppes did not publish her diary at the time it was written. She selected certain passages to include in a book nearly 60 years later. What information would help you judge the reliability of the published diary as a source of information?

★ 16–2 ★ Out From This Place

Introduction *Out From This Place* by Joyce Hansen is a novel about African American life at the start of Reconstruction. In the final chapter, Easter, a freed slave, writes a letter to Miss Grantley, the woman who taught her how to read. Easter describes what she finally decided to do with her life. The letter also describes what life was like for freedmen in a small South Carolina town.

★ ★ ★ ★ ★ ★ ★ ★ ★ ★

March 31, 1866

Dear Miss Grantley,

I hope this letter finds you enjoying the best of health. Please forgive me for taking so long to write to you, but it took me this long to make another decision. First, let me tell you how our town is coming along. We call it New Canaan. We have a church, a school, and we are building a molasses mill and a general store. Some of the people still work for the Williams family to make extra money for the land they purchased.

Miss Fortune moved to the cabin that was built next to the school especially for the teacher. We call it the teacher's house. The men and women take turns keeping guard, though, to make certain that the buckra don't come and burn down our school as they try to do last week. Miss Fortune smelled the smoke and saw the men who set the fire riding away. She say it looked like they was wearing some kind of hood. Thank God we put the fire out before it made much damage. And to think we told her to come and live among us because we thought she would be safer with us than in the cottage near the big house!

Some bad news. Miriam and several other children died from a terrible fever. Brother Thomas still cannot talk and cannot walk by himself. But we pray that one day he'll be better.

Now for my life. I have decided, first, not to marry Julius but to go back to the old Rebel camp and find Mariah and Gabriel. Remember I tell you about them? If Obi is searching for me, he'll go to them because that's where he last left me. I went to the Freedmen's Bureau even though I said I wasn't going again, and I was told that they have a list from a colored regiment. They will write to me when they get more information.

Jason joined a medicine show. I got a letter from him and he says he is happy and fine. I miss him so much.

Now for the big news and decision: I want to go to the school in Philadelphia. We don't

PRIMARY SCHOOL FOR FREEDMEN, IN CHARGE OF MRS. GREEN, AT VICKSBURG, MISSISSIPPI.

Learning to Read

Many northern teachers, both black and white, went to the South during Reconstruction. Their first task was to teach freedmen to read and write. This engraving shows a classroom in Vicksburg, Mississippi. ★ **Why are there so many adults in this classroom?**

have enough schools or teachers to go around. Our small schoolhouse is full to overflowing, with some of the children coming from the Riverview plantation. Rose and Miss Fortune helped me to make up my mind to go to Philadelphia. Also, Miss Fortune said that I could live with her family while I attended the school. That made me feel less afraid about going. I have a welcome letter from her family already saying that I do not have to worry about my room and board.

So, my dear Miss Grantley, I hope you are happy and excited about my decision as I am. I hope it's not too late for me to attend the school. I saved a little bit of money, and Rose and a few of the other people want to help pay some of the costs too. I look forward to hearing from you soon. I am, as always,

Your Friend and Student,
Easter

Source: *Out From This Place,* Joyce Hansen, 1988.

Analyzing Literature

1. What decision does Easter make about her future?

- **A.** She wants to work for the Freedmen's Bureau.
- **B.** She wants to buy some land.
- **C.** She wants to go to school.
- **D.** She wants to work for the Williams family.

2. Where is Easter planning to go and live?

- **F.** Philadelphia
- **G.** the Williams plantation
- **H.** the Riverview plantation
- **J.** New Canaan

3. Critical Thinking Drawing Conclusions Based on this reading, what impression does the author want to create about freed slaves in the South during Reconstruction?

Historical Critique

Could you use this letter as an authentic historical document about Reconstruction in the South? Why or why not?

Unit 6 Transforming the Nation

Chapter 17 An Era of Change in the West

17–1 A Century of Dishonor

Historical Document

Introduction After Helen Hunt Jackson attended a lecture on the problems of the Native Americans, she began to research the government's mistreatment of them. In 1881, she published *A Century of Dishonor,* based on her research. The book exposes the many abuses suffered by Native Americans. As a result, Jackson was appointed to a federal commission investigating the condition of Indians living on missions. She also wrote *Ramona*, a popular novel about Indians in California. The following excerpt is from *A Century of Dishonor*.

Vocabulary Before you read the selection, find the meanings of these words in a dictionary: **influx, deftly, ingenuity, hereditary, aversion, unimpeachable, partisanship, eloquent, philanthrophy, drone, refutation, rapacity.**

★ ★ ★ ★ ★ ★ ★ ★ ★ ★

There is not among these three hundred bands of Indians [in the United States] one which has not suffered cruelly at the hands either of the government or of white settlers. The poorer, the more insignificant, the more helpless the band, the more certain the cruelty and outrage to which they have been subjected. This especially true of the bands on the Pacific slopes. These Indians found themselves of a sudden surrounded by and caught up in the great influx of gold-seeking settlers, as helpless creatures on a shore are caught up in a tidal wave. There was not time for the government to make laws. The tale of the wrongs, the oppressions, the murders of the Pacific-slope Indians in the last thirty years would be a volume by itself, and is too monstrous to be believed.

It makes little difference, however, where one opens the record of the history of the Indians; every page and every year has its dark stain. The story of one tribe is the story of all, varied only by differences of time and place;

Viewing History **Chief Joseph**

Cyrenius Hall painted this portrait of Chief Joseph in 1878. One year earlier, Chief Joseph and his Nez Percé followers had surrendered to the United States. Chief Joseph died on a Washington reservation in 1904. The reservation doctor said the chief died "of a broken heart." ★ **Do you think Helen Hunt Jackson would have sympathized with Chief Joseph? Explain.**

but neither time nor place makes any difference in the main facts. Colorado is as greedy and unjust in 1880 as was Georgia in 1830, and Ohio in 1795; and the United States government breaks promises now as deftly as then, and with added ingenuity from long practice.

One of its strongest supports in doing so is the widespread sentiment among the people of dislike to the Indian, of impatience with his presence as a "barrier to civilization," and distrust of it as a possible danger. The old tales of the frontier life, with its horrors of Indian warfare, have gradually, by two or three generations' telling, produced in the average mind something like an hereditary instinct of unquestioning and unreasoning aversion which it is almost impossible to dislodge or soften.

There are hundreds of pages of unimpeachable testimony on the side of the Indian; but it goes for nothing, is set down as sentimentalism or partisanship, tossed aside and forgotten.

President after President has appointed commission after commission to inquire into and report upon Indian affairs, and to make suggestions as to the best methods of managing them. The reports are filled with eloquent statements of wrongs done to the Indians.... These reports are bound up with the Government's Annual Report, and that it is the end of them....

In 1869 President Grant appointed a commission of nine men, representing the influence and philanthropy of six leading States, to visit the different Indian reservations, and to "examine all matters [relating] to Indian affairs."

In the report of the commission are such paragraphs as the following.

"To assert that 'the Indian will not work' is as true as it would be to say that the white man will not work.

"Why should the Indian be expected to plant corn, fence lands, build houses, or do anything but get food from day to day, when experience had taught him that the product of his labor will be seized by the white man tomorrow? The most industrious white man would become a drone under similar circumstances. Nevertheless, many of the Indians" (the commissioners might more forcibly have said 130,000 of the Indians) "are already at work, and furnish ample refutation of the assertion that 'the Indian will not work.' There is no escape from the ... logic of facts.

"The history of the government connection with the Indians is a shameful record of broken treaties and unfulfilled promises. The history of the border, white man's connection with the Indians is a sickening record of murder, outrage, robbery, and wrongs committed by the former, as the rule, and occasional savage outbreaks and unspeakable barbarous deeds of retaliation by the latter, as the exception.

"Taught by the government that they had rights entitled to respect, when those rights have been assailed by the rapacity of the white man, the arm which should have been raised to protect them has ever been ready to sustain the aggressor."...

However great perplexity and difficulty there may be in the details of any and every plan possible for doing at this late day anything like justice to the Indian, however hard it may be for good statesmen and good men to agree upon the things that ought to be done, there certainly is, or ought to be, no perplexity whatever, no difficulty whatever, in agreeing upon certain things that ought not to be done, and which must cease to be done before the first steps can be taken toward righting the wrongs, curing the ills, and wiping out the disgrace to us of the present condition of our Indians.

Cheating, robbing, breaking promises—these three are clearly things which must cease to be done. One more thing, also, and that is the refusal of the protection of the law to the Indian's rights of property, "of life, liberty, and the pursuit of happiness."

When these four things have ceased to be done, time, statesmanship, philanthropy, and Christianity can slowly and surely do the rest. Till these four things have ceased to be done, statesmanship and philanthropy alike must work in vain, and even Christianity can reap but small harvest.

Source: *A Century of Dishonor,* Helen Hunt Jackson, 1881.

Analyzing Primary Sources

1. According to Jackson, many whites believed that Indians
   - **A.** presented a barrier to civilization.
   - **B.** broke treaties with the government.
   - **C.** refused to sell their land.
   - **D.** did not cooperate with presidential commissions.
2. What is this selection mainly about?
   - **F.** the wars between Native Americans and white settlers
   - **G.** the treatment of Native Americans by the government
   - **H.** a new treaty for Native Americans
   - **J.** efforts to convert Native Americans to Christianity
3. **Critical Thinking Defending a Position** What facts does Helen Hunt Jackson use to support her position on Native American rights?

Historical Critique

Did Jackson base *A Century of Dishonor* on her own first-hand observations? If not, on what did she base it?

★ 17–2 ★ A Cowboy's Autobiography

Introduction In the following selection, Bob Kennon describes working on long cattle drives from Mexico to Montana in the late 1800s.

Vocabulary Before you read the selection, find the meanings of these words in a dictionary: **wrangling, culinary, remuda, chaps, ferried.**

★ ★ ★ ★ ★ ★ ★ ★ ★ ★

Don Luis Terrazas, the cattle king of Chihuahua, was the largest landholder and cattle breeder in the world at the time. He owned about 1,000,000 head of cattle and branded as high as 200,000 calves in one year at one time. Before the revolution later broke him, he had over 3,000 head of horses in use on his more than 11,000,000 acres of ranches.

Bill Nort, one of the foremen, gave me a job wrangling horses. He was a kindly sort of man who understood and could talk with a kid like me. Taking this job was the turning point of my life. I had only been working there a few months when Mr. Broadus and Mr. Hysham, two cowmen from Montana, together with their foreman, Mr. Baker, came down to buy steers.

They bought two thousand Mexican steers from Terrazzas, and Baker was to trail north to Montana. Baker asked Bill Nort and Tom Cottrell, a Terrazas cowhand, myself, and a few others to come along up the trail. I was willing and anxious to go up the cattle trail at any time. This had been my hope and dream for months. If a fellow had never been up to Montana on a cattle drive, he wasn't considered much of a cowman. I held back, though, until Mr. Broadus agreed to pay me a monthly wage of forty dollars for the trip. Compared with the eighteen dollars I was getting, this seemed like a fortune to me and I told him I'd go all the way.

At last everything was in readiness, the cattle gathered, tallied, and turned over to Broadus with Hysham. With the transaction closed, the wagons loaded with supplies, beds, etc., and the cook fixed out with all his culinary needs, everything was complete for the long trip north. The remuda of horses was gathered, and every cowhand had his own saddle, chaps, and war-bag where he kept his personal belongings.

Early the next morning we crossed the Rio Grande under Terrazas' supervision. After crossing into Texas, Broadus and Hysham gave the orders. We didn't travel fast nor very far in a week's time, and camped at regular intervals, holding the steers on good feed all along the way. Cattle get footsore and leg weary if crowded too hard or handled roughly, and they wanted the steers to reach Montana in good condition. . . .

Viewing History: Cowboys on a Cattle Drive

Clara McDonald Williamson captured the spirit of a cattle drive in her painting The Old Chisholm Trail. *The Chisholm Trail ran from southern Texas to Abilene, Kansas. Big profits could be made driving cattle to railheads for shipment to the East.* ★ **What geographic features does Williamson include in this painting?**

The trail itself, as I've said, was well planned for us. It lay across the tablelands, or mesas, of West Texas and into Kansas, crossed part of the Old Santa Fe Trail near Dodge City, then led onward to the North Platte, keeping clear of Ogallala, that big cow town full of fun and trouble for a bunch of cowboys on a trail drive. We skirted the Black Hills and went on into Montana. We varied somewhat in later drives as herd men found it was far better to avoid all towns unless there were stockyards there. At any rate, these shipping places were nearly all at a distance outside the towns themselves.

We unloaded the steers for the last time at Wichita, Kansas, and took them on across Kansas by trail, then across the North Platte River and the sand hills of Nebraska. On northwest of Deadwood, South Dakota, we traveled for about forty or fifty miles, going by Devil's Tower and the Belle Fourche country. Belle Fourche was a cowman's country in the brakes of the Little Missouri where there was an abundance of fine feed.

We were getting excited by this time. No one seemed tired any more. In our minds we were already spending our pay in Miles City, and nothing could dampen our spirits. We were getting mighty tired of looking at those steers, and yet we had come so far together they seemed like old friends.

We came on down Little Cottonwood and at last crossed the Powder River. We were sure happy at the sight of it, and if we hadn't been trailing those two thousand steers and afraid of stampeding them, we'd have shot into the air to celebrate our arrival, for every cowman's slogan was "Powder River or bust." Though we'd been in Montana for several days, no one could really believe it until we had crossed the Powder.

After crossing, we went over to the Broadus holdings, which were in close on the other side. The town of Broadus was established here on the old site of this ranch. We crossed the Little Powder at the Half Circle Cross Ranch, then went down the Mitzpah and on to Miles City. We were now nearing the end of our long trail and coming to the beautiful Yellowstone River. . . . We swam the herd and remuda across the Yellowstone while the wagons were ferried across, and our job was done.

Source: *From the Pecos to the Powder: A Cowboy's Autobiography,* Bob Kennon as told to Ramon F. Adams, 1965.

Analyzing Primary Sources

1. Where were the cattle being driven?
   - **A.** Mexico
   - **B.** Montana
   - **C.** Texas
   - **D.** Kansas
2. Why did the cowboys stop often?
   - **F.** to brand the cattle
   - **G.** to buy supplies
   - **H.** to feed the cattle
   - **J.** to gather stray cattle
3. **Critical Thinking Recognizing Points of View** How did Bob Kennon view the job of a cowboy on the cattle drive?

Historical Critique

Did Kennon write this account soon after this cattle drive or years later? How can you tell?

★ Chapter 18 ★ The Rise of Industry and Unions

★ 18–1 ★ The Road to Business Success

Introduction Andrew Carnegie was a self-made man. He became a successful steel manufacturer and philanthropist. The following selection is from a talk Carnegie gave to students at a business school in Pittsburgh in 1885. Carnegie advises students about how to succeed in business.

Vocabulary Before you read the selection, find the meanings of these words in a dictionary: **subordinate, salutary, perforce, speculate, revenues, expenditures, predominates, ignoble.**

★ ★ ★ ★ ★ ★ ★ ★ ★ ★

It is well that young men should begin at the beginning and occupy the most subordinate positions. Many of the leading businessmen of Pittsburgh had a serious responsibility thrust upon them at the very threshold of their career. They were introduced to the broom, and spent the first hours of their business lives sweeping out the office. I notice we have janitors and janitresses now in offices, and our young men unfortunately miss that salutary branch of a business education. But if by chance the professional sweeper is absent any morning the boy who has the genius of the future partner in him will not hesitate to try his hand at the broom. . . .

[T]he question now is how to rise from the subordinate position we have imagined you in, through the successive grades to the position for which you are, in my opinion, and, I trust, in your own, evidently intended. I can give you the secret. It lies mainly in this. Instead of the question, "What must I do for my employer?" substitute "What can I do?" Faithful and conscientious discharge of the duties assigned you is all very well, but the verdict in such cases generally is that you perform your present duties so well that you had better continue performing them. Now, young gentlemen, this will not do. It will not do for the coming partners. There must be something beyond this. We make clerks, bookkeepers, treasurers, bank tellers of this class, and there they remain to the end of the chapter. The rising man must do something exceptional, and beyond the range of his special department. He must attract attention. A shipping clerk, he may do so by discovering in an invoice an error with which he has nothing to do, and which has escaped the attention of the proper party. If a weighing clerk, he may save for the firm by doubting the adjustment of the scales and having them corrected, even if this be the province of the master mechanic. If a messenger boy, even he can lay the seed of promotion by going beyond the letter of his instructions in

Viewing HISTORY **Wealthy Shoppers**

William Glackens painted works ranging from crowded tenements to the lives of the wealthy. His 1907 painting The Shoppers *shows well-to-do women visiting a dress shop. As American industry grew, business leaders and their families could afford to enjoy lives of great luxury.* ★ **What clothing items did fashionable women of the time need?**

order to secure the desired reply. There is no service so low and simple, neither any so high, in which the young man of ability and willing disposition cannot readily and almost daily prove himself capable of greater trust and usefulness, and, what is equally important, show his invincible determination to rise. Some day, in your own department, you will be directed to do or say something which you know will prove disadvantageous to the interest of the firm. Here is your chance. Stand up like a man and say so. Say it boldly, and give your reasons, and thus prove to your employer that, while his thoughts have been engaged upon other matters, you have been studying during hours when perhaps he thought you asleep, how to advance his interests. You may be right or you may be wrong, but in either case you have gained the first condition of success. You have attracted attention. Your employer has found that he has not a mere hireling in his service, but a man; not one who is content to give so many hours of work for so many dollars in return, but one who devotes his spare hours and constant thought to the business. Such an employee must perforce be thought of, and thought of kindly and well. It will not be long before his advice is asked in his special branch, and if the advice given be sound, it will soon be asked and taken upon questions of broader bearing. This means partnership; if not with present employers then with others. Your foot, in such a case, is upon the ladder; the amount of climbing done depends entirely [on] yourself.... There is one sure mark of the coming partner, the future millionaire: his revenues always exceed his expenditures. He begins to save early, almost as soon as he begins to earn. No matter how little it may be possible to save, save that little. Invest it securely, not necessarily in bonds, but in anything which you have good reason to believe will be profitable, but no gambling with it, remember. A rare chance will soon present itself for investment. The little you have saved will prove the basis for an amount of credit utterly surprising to you. Capitalists trust the saving young man. For every hundred dollars you can produce as the result of hard-won savings, [a rich man], in search of partner, will lend or credit a thousand; for every thousand, fifty thousand. It is not capital that your seniors require, it is the man who has proved that he has the business habits which create capital, and to create it in the best of all possible ways, as far as self-discipline is concerned, is, by adjusting his habits to his means. Gentlemen, it is the first hundred dollars saved which tells. Begin at once to [save] up something. The bee predominates in the future millionaire.

Of course there are better, higher aims than saving. As an end, the acquisition of wealth is ignoble to the extreme; I assume that you save and long for wealth only as a means of enabling you the better to do some good in your day and generation. Make a note of this essential rule: Expenditure always within income. . . .

To summarize what I have said: Aim for the highest . . . make the firm's interest yours; break orders always to save owners; concentrate; put all your eggs in one basket, and watch that basket; expenditure always within revenue; lastly, be not impatient, for, as Emerson says, "no one can cheat you out of ultimate success but yourself."

Source: *The Empire of Business,* Andrew Carnegie, 1902.

Analyzing Primary Sources

1. Carnegie advises people seeking success in business to start out as
   A. small investors.
   B. janitors.
   C. executives.
   D. college students.
2. What is one thing Carnegie believes would hurt young businessmen?
   F. spending more than they earn
   G. discovering mistakes on the job
   H. giving advice to the boss
   J. spending long hours at work
3. **Critical Thinking Recognizing Points of View** Summarize Carnegie's view of how young men can succeed.

Historical Critique

Why would young people of 1885 be likely to listen to Carnegie's advice about business?

★ 18–2 ★ The Triangle Factory Fire

Introduction On March 25, 1911, a fire broke out in the shop of the Triangle Shirtwaist Company. The company was located on the eighth, ninth, and tenth floors of a "fireproof" building in New York City. In this selection, Pauline Newman, a former Triangle Shirtwaist Company worker, tells what it was like to work there. An article from the *New York World* newspaper then describes the fire.

Vocabulary Before you read the selection, find the meanings of these words in a dictionary: **negligence, incinerated, clambered, inadequate, toiling, sinisterly.**

★ ★ ★ ★ ★ ★ ★ ★ ★

Pauline Newman

I'd like to tell you about the kind of world we lived in 75 years ago because all of you probably weren't even born then. Seventy-five years is a long time, but I'd like to give you at least a glimpse of that world because it has no resemblance to the world we live in today, in any respect.

That world 75 years ago was a world of incredible exploitation of men, women, and children. I went to work for the Triangle Shirtwaist Company in 1901. The corner of a shop would resemble a kindergarten because we were young, eight, nine, ten years old. It was a world of greed; the human being didn't mean anything. The hours were from 7:30 in the morning to 6:30 at night when it wasn't busy. . . . You would go home, what kind of home did you go to? You won't find the tenements we lived in. Some of the rooms didn't have any windows. I lived in a two room tenement with my mother and two sisters and the bedroom had no windows, the facilities

Viewing HISTORY **A Tragic Fire**

Firefighters did their best to combat the blaze at the Triangle shirtwaist factory. Their hoses, however, did not have enough power and their ladders could reach only to the sixth floor of the 10-story building. The 1911 disaster focused national attention on unsafe working conditions.
★ **What changes did the Triangle fire bring about?**

were down in the yard, but that's the way it was in the factories too. In the summer the sidewalk, fire escapes, and the roof of the tenements became bedrooms just to get a breath of air.

We wore cheap clothes, lived in cheap tenements, ate cheap food. There was nothing to look forward to, nothing to expect the next day to be better.

Someone once asked me; "How did you survive?" And I told him, what alternative did we have? You stayed and you survived, that's all.

The New York World

At 4:35 o'clock yesterday afternoon fire springing from a source that may never be positively identified was discovered in the rear of the eighth floor of the ten story building at the northwest corner of Washington Place and Greene Street, the first of three floors occupied as a factory of the Triangle Shirtwaist Company.

At 11:30 o'clock Chief Croker made this statement:

"Everybody has been removed. The number taken out, which includes those who jumped from windows, is 141. . . ."

At 2 o'clock this morning Chief Croker estimated the total dead as one hundred and fifty-four. He said further: "I expect something of this kind to happen in these so-called fire-proof buildings, which are without adequate protection as far as fire-escapes are concerned. . . ."

Inspection by Acting Superintendent of Buildings Ludwig will be made the basis for charges of criminal negligence on the ground that the fire-proof doors leading to one of the enclosed tower stairways were locked. . . .

Before smoke or flame gave signs from the windows, the loss of life was fully under way. The first signs that persons in the street knew that these three top stories had turned into red furnaces in which human creatures were being caught and incinerated was when screaming men and women and boys and girls crowded out on the many window ledges and threw themselves into the streets far below. . . .

Some, about seventy, chose a successful avenue of escape. They clambered up a ladder to the roof. A few remembered the fire escape. Many may have thought of it but only as they uttered cries of dismay.

Wretchedly inadequate was this fire escape—a lone ladder running down to a rear narrow court, which was smoke filled as the fire raged, one narrow door giving access to the ladder. By the score they fought and struggled and breathed fire and died trying to make that needle-eye road to self-preservation. . . .

Concentrated, the fire burned within. The flames caught all the flimsy lace stuff and linens that go into the making of spring and summer shirtwaists and fed eagerly upon rolls of silk.

The cutting room was laden with stuff on long tables. The employees were toiling over such material at the rows and rows of machines. Sinisterly the spring day gave aid to the fire. Many of the window panes facing south and east were drawn down. Drafts had full play.

The experts say that the three floors must each have become a whirlpool of fire. Whichever way the entrapped creatures fled they met a curving sweep of flame. Many swooned and died. Others fought their way to the windows or the elevator or fell fighting for a chance at the fire escape, the single fire escape leading into the blind court that was to be reached from the upper floors by clambering over a window sill!

On all three floors, at a narrow window, a crowd met death trying to get out to that one slender fire escape ladder.

It was a fireproof building in which this enormous tragedy occurred. Save for the three stories of blackened windows at the top, you would scarcely have been able to tell where the fire had happened. The walls stood firmly. A thin tongue of flame now and then licked around a window sash. . . .

Source: *America Firsthand,* Volume II: *From Reconstruction to the Present,* edited by Robert D. Marcus and David Burner, 1992.

Analyzing Primary Sources

1. Which of the following statements would Pauline Newman agree with?
- **A.** The owners of the Triangle Company did not care about human beings.
- **B.** Children at the Triangle factory worked 8 to 10 hours a day.
- **C.** The world did not change much in the 75 years after the Triangle fire.
- **D.** Factory workers lived hard lives but looked forward to a better future.

2. According to the article in the *World,* the cause of the fire was
- **F.** a smoke-filled fire escape.
- **G.** never discovered.
- **H.** the closed windows.
- **J.** the thin factory walls.

3. Critical Thinking Analyzing Information What concerns did the authorities have about the building that contained the Triangle Shirtwaist Company?

Historical Critique

You have just read two types of primary sources: a first-person account and a newspaper report. Compare what kinds of information you can get from these two types of sources.

★ Chapter 19 ★ Immigration and the Growth of Cities

★ 19–1 ★ Coming to America: Three Views

Introduction In the late 1800s, numerous Europeans and Asians immigrated to the United States. Europeans arrived at Ellis Island in New York City. Asians arrived at Angel Island in San Francisco. Angel Island was used as an entry point for Asian immigrants awaiting admission and as a detention center for those awaiting deportation. The first two selections are the recollections of European immigrants. They describe their experiences of trying to make a living in an American city. The other selection is a poem written by an Asian immigrant who was detained on Angel Island.

Vocabulary Before you read the selection, find the meanings of these words in a dictionary: **sojourn, ordeals, discontent.**

★ ★ ★ ★ ★ ★ ★ ★ ★ ★

An Italian Immigrant:

...We came to Brooklyn, New York, to a wooden house in Adams Street that was full of Italians from Naples. Bartolo had a room on the third floor and there were fifteen men in the room, all boarding with Bartolo. He did the cooking on a stove in the middle of the room and there were beds all around the sides, one bed above another. It was very hot in the room, but we were soon asleep, for we were very tired.

The next morning, early, Bartolo told us to go out and pick rags and get bottles. He gave us bags and hooks and showed us the ash barrels. On the streets where the fine houses are the people are very careless and put out good things, like mattresses and umbrellas, clothes, bats, and boots. We brought all these to Bartolo and he made them new again and sold them on the sidewalk; but mostly we brought rags and bones. The rags we had to wash in the backyard and then we hung them to dry on lines under the ceiling in our room. The bones we kept under the beds till Bartolo could find a man to buy them.

Most of the men in our room worked at digging the sewer. Bartolo got them work and they paid him about one-quarter of their wages. Then he charged them for board and he bought the clothes for them, too. So they got little money after all.

Bartolo was always saying that the rent of the room was so high that he could not make anything, but he was really making plenty ...and is now a very rich man.

A Lithuanian Immigrant:

...[In Lithuania you paid] with sacks of rye. But here you want a hundred things. Whenever you walk out you see new things you want, and you must have money to buy everything....

The next morning my friends woke me at five o'clock and said, "Now, if you want life, liberty, and happiness," they laughed, "you must push for yourself. You must get a job. Come with us." And we went to the [Chicago stock] yards. Men and women were walking in by thousands as far as we could see. We went to the doors of one big slaughterhouse. There was a crowd of about 200 men waiting there for a job. They looked hungry and kept watching the door. At last a special policeman came out and began pointing to men, one by one. Each one jumped forward. Twenty-three were taken. Then they all went outside, and all the others turned their faces away and looked tired. I remember one boy sat down and cried, just next to me, on a pile of boards. Some policemen waved their clubs

Asian Immigrants at Angel Island

This photograph shows immigrants from Asia landing at Angel Island in San Francisco Bay. There, they lived in wooden barracks. Often they had to wait weeks or months for permission to join family or friends in the United States. ★ **Why did some Asian immigrants feel hopeless after arriving in the United States?**

and we all walked on. I found some Lithuanians to talk with, who told me they had come every morning for three weeks. Soon we met other crowds coming away from other slaughterhouses, and we all walked around and felt bad and tired and hungry.

That night I told my friends that I would not do this many days, but would go some place else. "Where?" they asked me, and I began to see then that I was in bad trouble, because I spoke no English. Then one man told me to give him $5 to give the special policeman. I did this and the next morning the policeman pointed me out, so I had a job. The union is doing another good thing. It is combining all the nationalities. The night I joined the Cattle Butchers' Union I was led into the room by a negro member. With me were Bohemians, Germans and Poles, and Mike Donnelly, the President, is an Irishman.

Poem From Angel Island:

I used to admire the land of the Flowery Flag* as a country of abundance.
I immediately raised money and started my journey.
For over a month, I have experienced enough winds and waves.
Now on an extended sojourn in jail, I am subject to the ordeals of prison life.
I look up and see Oakland so close by.
I wish to go back to my motherland to carry the farmer's hoe.
Discontent fills my belly and it is difficult for me to sleep.
I just write these few lines to express what is on my mind.

*Flowery Flag refers to the colorful flag of the United States.

Sources: *Coming to America: A New Life in a New Land,* edited by Katharine Emsden, 1993; *The American Reader: Words That Moved a Nation,* edited by Diane Ravitch, 1990.

Analyzing Primary Sources

1. What kind of work did the Italian immigrants do?
   - **A.** They sold sacks of flour.
   - **B.** They were police officers.
   - **C.** They worked in slaughterhouses.
   - **D.** They dug sewers.
2. The Lithuanian immigrant felt that he was in bad trouble because
   - **F.** he could not sleep in a crowded room.
   - **G.** his rent was too high.
   - **H.** he spoke no English.
   - **J.** he did not have five dollars.
3. **Critical Thinking Recognizing Points of View** In the poem from Angel Island, how does the writer view the United States?

Historical Critique

The first two excerpts, above, came from a series of interviews by a reporter in the early 1900s. He spoke to several immigrants, then published the interviews in a newspaper. Why is it important to know these facts when you evaluate this source?

★ 19–2 ★ Casey at the Bat

Introduction On June 3, 1888, the San Francisco *Examiner* published "Casey at the Bat," a poem by Ernest Lawrence Thayer. Thayer worked at the *Examiner* for a short time as a humor columnist. He was paid five dollars for his poem, but never published another one. "Casey at the Bat," one of the most popular poems in American literature, gives an amusing view of hometown baseball in the late 1800s.

Vocabulary Before you read the selection, find the meanings of these words in a dictionary: **patron, despair, preceded, multitude, melancholy, doffed, writhing, haughty, visage, tumult.**

★ ★ ★ ★ ★ ★ ★ ★ ★

A Ballad of the Republic, Sung in the Year 1888

The outlook wasn't brilliant for the Mudville nine that day;
The score stood four to two with but one inning more to play.
And then when Cooney died at first, and Barrows did the same,
A sickly silence fell upon the patrons of the game.

★ ★ ★

A straggling few got up to go in deep despair. The rest
Clung to that hope which springs eternal in the human breast;
They thought if only Casey could get a whack at that—
We'd put up even money now with Casey at the bat.

★ ★ ★

But Flynn preceded Casey, as did also Jimmy Blake,
And the former was a lulu and the latter was a cake;
So upon that stricken multitude grim melancholy sat,
For there seemed but little chance of Casey's getting to the bat.

★ ★ ★

But Flynn let drive a single, to the wonderment of all,
And Blake, the much despised, tore the cover off the ball;
And when the dust had lifted, and the men saw what had occurred,
There was Johnnie safe at second and Flynn a-hugging third.

★ ★ ★

Then from 5,000 throats and more there rose a lusty yell;
It rumbled through the valley, it rattled in the dell;
It knocked upon the mountain and recoiled upon the flat,
For Casey, mighty Casey, was advancing to the bat.

★ ★ ★

There was ease in Casey's manner as he stepped into his place;
There was pride in Casey's bearing and a smile on Casey's face.
And when, responding to the cheers, he lightly doffed his hat,
No stranger in the crowd could doubt 'twas Casey at the bat.

★ ★ ★

Ten thousand eyes were on him as he rubbed his hands with dirt,
Five thousand tongues applauded when he wiped them on his shirt.
Then while the writhing pitcher ground the ball into his hip,
Defiance gleamed in Casey's eye, a sneer curled Casey's lip.

★ ★ ★

And now the leather-covered sphere came hurtling through the air,
And Casey stood a-watching it in haughty grandeur there.
Close by the sturdy batsman the ball unheeded sped—
"That ain't my style," said Casey. "Strike one," the umpire said.

★ ★ ★

From the benches, black with people, there went up a muffled roar,
Like the beating of the storm-waves on a stern and distant shore.
"Kill him! Kill the umpire!" shouted some one on the stand;
And it's likely they'd have killed him had not Casey raised his hand.

★ ★ ★

With a smile of Christian charity great Casey's visage shone;
He stilled the rising tumult; he bade the game go on;

Viewing HISTORY **Baseball Players Practicing**

Artist Thomas Eakins loved to paint sporting events and scenes of outdoor life. His 1875 painting, Baseball Players Practicing, *shows a professional team warming up before a game.*

★ **Based on this painting, how were baseball players of the 1870s similar to or different from today's players?**

He signaled to the pitcher, and once more the spheroid flew;
But Casey still ignored it, and the umpire said, "Strike two."

"Fraud!" cried the maddened thousands, and echo answered fraud;
But one scornful look from Casey and the audience was awed.
They saw his face grow stern and cold, they saw his muscles strain,
And they knew that Casey wouldn't let that ball go by again.

The sneer is gone from Casey's lip, his teeth are clenched in hate;
He pounds with cruel violence his bat upon the plate.
And now the pitcher holds the ball, and now he lets it go,
And now the air is shattered by the force of Casey's blow.

Oh, somewhere in this favored land the sun is shining bright;
The band is playing somewhere, and somewhere hearts are light,
And somewhere men are laughing, and somewhere children shout;
But there is no joy in Mudville—mighty Casey has struck out.

Source: "Casey at the Bat," Ernest Lawrence Thayer, 1888.

Analyzing Literature

1. What was the situation when Casey came to bat?
   - **A.** The score was tied with no one on base.
   - **B.** Mudville was losing 4-2 with the bases loaded.
   - **C.** Mudville was losing 4-2 with two players on base.
   - **D.** Mudville was winning 4-2 with two players on base.
2. How would you describe Casey's attitude?
   - **F.** confident
   - **G.** humble
   - **H.** nervous
   - **J.** indifferent
3. **Critical Thinking Drawing Conclusions** Why do you think the poem "Casey at the Bat" became so popular?

Historical Critique

In what ways is "Casey at the Bat" a source of information about baseball in the year 1888? Why would you have to be careful about using the poem as a primary source?

Unit 7 A New Role for the Nation

★ Chapter 20 ★ Progressives and Reformers

★ 20–1 ★ Suffrage for Women

Historical Document

Introduction In the early 1900s, Carrie Chapman Catt became the head of the National American Woman Suffrage Association (NAWSA). The following excerpt is from Chapman's speech to the NAWSA in February 1902.

Vocabulary Before you read the selection, find the meanings of these words in a dictionary: **suffrage, idiosyncrasies, incapacity, egotism, tyranny, premise, perpetual, tutelage, domain.**

★ ★ ★ ★ ★ ★ ★ ★ ★

The question of woman suffrage is a very simple one. The plea is dignified, calm, and logical. Yet, great as is the victory over conservatism which is represented in the accomplishment of man suffrage, infinitely greater will be the attainment of woman suffrage. Man suffrage exists through the surrender of many a stronghold of ancient thought. . . .

Woman suffrage must meet precisely the same objections which have been urged against man suffrage, but in addition, it must combat sex-prejudice, the oldest, the most unreasoning, the most stubborn of all human idiosyncrasies. What is prejudice? An opinion, which is not based upon reason; a judgment, without having heard the argument; a feeling, without being able to trace whence it came. And sex-prejudice is a prejudgment against the rights, liberties, and

Viewing History: Casting Her First Vote

A magazine printed this cover on its September 11, 1920, issue. Less than one month earlier, the states had ratified the Nineteenth Amendment, guaranteeing American women the right to vote. ★ **Look at the Presidents of the United States on pages 752–753 of the reference section. Who was the first President elected after women won the right to vote?**

opportunities of women. A belief, without proof, in the incapacity of women to do that which they have never done. Sex-prejudice has been the chief hindrance in the rapid advance of the woman's rights movement to its present status, and still a stupendous obstacle to be overcome. . . .

Four chief causes led to the subjection of women, each the logical deduction from the theory that men were the units of the race—obedience, ignorance, the denial of personal liberty and the denial of right to property and wages. These forces united in cultivating a spirit of egotism and tyranny in men and weak dependence in women. . . . In fastening these disabilities upon women, the world acted logically when reasoning from the premise that man is the race and woman his dependent. The perpetual tutelage and subjection robbed women of all freedom of thought and action, and all incentive for growth, and they logically became the inane weaklings the world would have them, and their condition strengthened the universal belief in their incapacity. This world taught woman nothing skillful and then said her work was valueless. It permitted her no opinions and said she did not know how to think. It forbade her to speak in public, and said the sex had no orators. It denied her the schools, and said the sex had no genius. It robbed her of every vestige of responsibility, and then called her weak. . . .

Shall the woman who enjoys the right of self-government in every other department of life be permitted the right of self-government in the state? It is no more right for all men to govern all women than it was for one man to govern one woman. It is no more right for men to govern women than it was for one man to govern other men.

Source: *The American Reader: Words That Moved a Nation,* edited by Diane Ravitch, 1990.

Analyzing Primary Sources

1. According to Catt, the chief obstacle to the advancement of women was
- **A.** women's right to own property.
- **B.** prejudice toward women.
- **C.** lack of organization by women.
- **D.** the weakness of women.

2. What is this selection mainly about?
- **F.** women's suffrage
- **G.** men's suffrage
- **H.** education for women
- **J.** racial equality

3. Critical Thinking Analyzing Ideas What do you think Catt meant by the statement "It is no more right for men to govern women than it was for one man to govern other men"?

Historical Critique

Was Carrie Chapman Catt speaking to an audience who shared her viewpoint? How might this have affected what she said?

★ 20–2 ★ The Need for Education

Introduction In the 1890s, African Americans living in both the North and South faced many obstacles. In his book *Up From Slavery,* Booker T. Washington argued that before African Americans could attain political or social equality, they needed to acquire education and job training. In the following selection from *Up From Slavery,* Washington writes about his ideas for African American education.

Vocabulary Before you read this selection, find the meanings of these words in a dictionary: **heathenism, prevalent.**

★ ★ ★ ★ ★ ★ ★ ★ ★

The years from 1867 to 1878 I think may be called the period of Reconstruction. This included the time that I spent at Hampton and as a teacher in West Virginia. During the whole of the Reconstruction period two ideas were constantly agitating the minds of the colored people, or, at least, the minds of a large part of the race. One of these was the craze for Greek and Latin learning, and the other was a desire to hold office.

It could not have been expected that a people who had spent generations in slavery, and before that generations in the darkest heathenism, could at first form any proper conception of what an education meant. In every part of the South, during the Reconstruction period, schools, both day and night, were filled to overflowing with people of all ages and conditions, some being as far along in age as sixty and seventy years. The ambition to secure an education was most praiseworthy and encouraging. The idea, however, was too prevalent that, as soon as one secured a little education, in some unexplainable way he would be free from most of the hardships of the world, and, at any rate, could live without manual labor. There was a further feeling that a knowledge, however little, of the Greek and Latin languages would make one a very superior human being. . . . I remember that the first colored man whom I saw who knew something about foreign languages impressed me at that time as being a man of all others to be envied.

Naturally, most of our people who received some little education became teachers or preachers. While among these two classes there were many capable, earnest, godly men and women, still a large proportion took up teaching or preaching as an easy way to make a living. Many became teachers who could do little more than write their names. . . .

Viewing HISTORY **Students at Tuskegee Institute**

Booker T. Washington founded Tuskegee Institute in Alabama in 1881. It continues today as one of the nation's leading black colleges. This photograph shows a math class at Tuskegee in 1906. ★ **Based on the reading, why do you think Washington included mathematics in the course of study at Tuskegee?**

During the whole of the Reconstruction period our people throughout the South looked to the federal government for everything.... This was not unnatural. The central government gave them freedom, and the whole nation had been enriched for more than two centuries by the labor of the Negro. Even as a youth, and later in manhood, I had the feeling that it was cruelly wrong in the central government, at the beginning of our freedom, to fail to make some provision for the general education of our people in addition to what the states might do, so that the people would be better prepared for the duties of citizenship....

During the time I was a student in Washington, the city was crowded with colored people, many of whom had recently come from the South. A large proportion of these people had been drawn to Washington because they felt that they could lead a life of ease there. Others had secured minor government positions, and still another large class was there in the hope of securing federal positions. All this tended to make Washington an attractive place for members of the colored race. Then, too, they knew that at all times they could have the protection of the law in the District of Columbia. The public schools in Washington for colored people were better then they were elsewhere. I took great interest in studying the life of our people there closely at that time....

In Washington I saw girls whose mothers were earning their living by laundering. These girls were taught by their mothers, in a rather crude way it is true, the industry of laundering. Later these girls entered the public schools and remained there perhaps six or eight years. When the public school course was finally finished, they wanted more costly dresses, more costly hats and shoes. In a word, while their wants had been increased, their ability to supply their wants had not been increased in the same degree. On the other hand, their six or eight years of book education had weaned them away from the occupations of their mothers. The result of this was too many cases that the girls went to the bad. I often thought how much wiser it would have been to give these girls the same amount of mental training—and I favor any kind of training, whether in the languages or mathematics, that gives strength and culture to the mind—but at the same time to give them the most thorough training in the latest and best methods of laundering and other kindred occupations.

Source: *Up From Slavery,* Booker T. Washington, 1901.

Analyzing Primary Sources

1. In this selection, Booker T. Washington criticizes the federal government for failing to
   - **A.** plan for the proper education of former slaves.
   - **B.** end slavery.
   - **C.** pay African Americans for their years of labor.
   - **D.** teach Greek and Latin to African Americans.
2. According to Washington, why did many African Americans go to Washington, D.C., during Reconstruction?
   - **F.** They wanted to learn to become citizens.
   - **G.** They wanted to open their own laundries.
   - **H.** They wanted to teach in the public schools.
   - **J.** They wanted to get government jobs.
3. **Critical Thinking Recognizing Points of View** What kind of education did Booker T. Washington favor? Why?

Historical Critique

Review pages 536–537. How do you think Booker T. Washington's own background affected his viewpoint on education for African Americans?

⋆ Chapter 21 ⋆ Becoming a World Power

★ 21–1 ★ A Japanese Mission to the United States

Introduction In 1854, Matthew Perry forced Japan to open two ports to trade. Four years later, Japan sent its first mission to the United States. Among the visitors was Yukichi Fukuzawa. He had learned English and was eager to study western ways. Fukuzawa toured the United States, and later he visited Europe. Back home, he wrote articles and books explaining Western ideas and practices to the Japanese. This selection is from Fukuzawa's *Autobiography*. It recalls his impressions of his first days in San Francisco.

Vocabulary Before you read the selection, find the meanings of these words in a dictionary: **personage, dignitary, dry dock, conveyance, expelled, bewilderment, refinery, commodities, inexplicable, revered.**

★ ★ ★ ★ ★ ★ ★ ★ ★

As soon as our ship came into the port of San Francisco, we were greeted by many important personages who came on board from all over the country. Along the shores thousands of people were lined up to see the strange newcomers. . . .

As soon as we came on shore, we found we were to be driven off in carriages to a hotel. While we were resting in the hotel, city officials and various dignitaries came to offer entertainment. We were given quarters in the official residence of the Navy station on Mare Island. Our hosts knew that we Japanese were accustomed to a different diet, so they arranged that our food, instead of being served, should be prepared by our own cook. But the officials being very kind, and desiring to satisfy the Japanese love for seafood,

Viewing History **A Japanese Delegation in the United States**

Not long after Yukichi Fukuzawa visited California, another Japanese delegation arrived in Washington, D.C. Here, guests welcome the Japanese at an official reception in the nation's capital. ★ **Identify two differences between the Americans and the Japanese in this picture.**

sent fish every day. Also, on learning the Japanese custom of bathing frequently, they had baths prepared daily. Our ship had been damaged by the passing storms, so it was put in dry dock to be repaired—all expressions of American hospitality. This generous treatment in every way brought to mind an old expression of ours—"as if our host had put us on the palm of his hand to see that we lacked nothing."

On our part there were many confusing and embarrassing moments, for we were quite ignorant of the customs of American life. For instance, we were surprised even by the carriages. On seeing a vehicle with horses attached to it, we should easily have guessed what it was. But really we did not identify our mode of conveyance until the door had been opened, we were seated inside, and the horses had started off. Then we realized we were riding in a carriage behind horses.

All of us wore the usual pair of swords at our sides and the hemp [rope] sandals. So attired, we were taken to the modern hotel. There we noticed, covering the interior, the valuable carpets which in Japan only the more wealthy could buy from importers' shops at so much a square inch to make purses and tobacco pouches with. Here the carpet was laid over an entire room—something quite astounding—upon this costly fabric walked our hosts wearing the shoes with which they had come in from the streets!...

One evening our hosts said that some ladies and gentlemen were having a dancing party and that they would be glad to have us attend it. We went. To our dismay we could not make out what they were doing. The ladies and gentlemen seemed to be hopping about the room together. As funny as it was, we knew it would be rude to laugh, and we controlled our expressions with difficulty as the dancing went on. These were but a few of the instances of our bewilderment at the strange customs of American society.

When we were taking leave, our host and hostess kindly offered us horses to ride home on. This pleased us, for a chance to ride horseback again was a relief. Especially did Captain Kimura enjoy this, for he was an accomplished horseman who used to ride every day in Yedo. We touched whip to the horses and rode back to our quarters at a trot. The Americans watched us and exclaimed at the Japanese ability in riding. So neither of us really knew much about the other after all.

Our hosts in San Francisco were very considerate in showing us examples of modern industry. There was as yet no railway laid to the city, nor was there any electric light in use. But the telegraph system and also Galvani's electroplating were already in use. Then we were taken to a sugar refinery and had the principle of the operation explained to us quite minutely [in detail]. I am sure that our hosts thought they were showing us something entirely new, naturally looking for our surprise at each new device of modern engineering. But on the contrary, there was really nothing new, at least to me. I knew the principle of telegraphy even if I had not seen the actual machine before; I knew that sugar was bleached by straining the solution with bone-black, and that in boiling down the solution, the vacuum was used to better effect than heat. I had been studying nothing else but such scientific principles ever since I had entered Ogata's school.

Rather, I was suprised by entirely different things in American life. First of all, there seemed to be an enormous waste of iron everywhere. In garbage piles on the seashores—everywhere—I found lying old oil tins, empty cans, and broken tools. This was remarkable to us, for in Yedo [today Tokyo], after a fire, there would appear a swarm of people looking for nails in the ashes.

Then too, I was surprised at the high cost of daily commodities in California. We had to pay a half-dollar for a bottle of oysters, and there were only twenty or thirty in the bottle at that. In Japan the price of so many would be only a cent or two.

Things social, political, and economic proved most inexplicable. One day, on a sudden thought, I asked a gentleman where the descendants of George Washington might be. He replied, "I think there is a woman who is directly descended from Washington. I don't know where she is now, but I think I have heard she is married." His answer was so very casual that it shocked me.

Of course, I knew that America was a republic with a new president every four years, but I could not help feeling that the family of Washington would be revered above all other families. My reasoning was based on the reverence in Japan for the founders of the great lines of rulers. . . .

Source: *The Autobiography of Yukichi Fukuzawa,* revised translation by Eiichi Kiyooka, 1966.

Analyzing Primary Sources

1. What is the main topic of this selection?
   - **A.** how American customs differed from Japanese customs
   - **B.** how little respect Americans had for Japanese ways
   - **C.** why Fukuzawa liked Americans
   - **D.** why prices in America were higher than in Japan
2. How does Fukuzawa view the dance he attended?
   - **F.** with horror
   - **G.** with fear
   - **H.** with reverence
   - **J.** with amusement
3. **Critical Thinking Recognizing Points of View** Why did Fukuzawa expect Americans to treat the descendants of George Washington with great respect?

Historical Critique

Look at the source line at the end of this excerpt. What important information does it give you about this source? Explain.

★ 21–2 ★ Culebra Cut

Introduction Judith Head's 1995 novel *Culebra Cut* is set in Panama in 1911. The main character, William Thomas, moves to Culebra, Panama, when his physician father accepts a job in a local hospital. From his new home, William watches workers construct the Panama Canal.

Vocabulary Before you read the selection, find the meaning of this word in a dictionary: **isthmus, dispensary, jubilant, spewing, sheared, foliage.**

★ ★ ★ ★ ★ ★ ★ ★ ★ ★ ★

William Thomas pushed out the screen and climbed onto the windowsill. Dawn skirted the horizon and coated the sky with faint light. William grinned as he thought how close he was to his dream. Soon he would stand at the edge of Culebra Cut and watch as thousands of workers and machines carved the Panama Canal out of the mountains.

An explosion from the Cut shook the heavy, damp air. William took a breath and jumped down onto the wet grass. The screen slapped against the window frame. He froze, listening for sounds of his parents stirring, but heard nothing.

The world outside was alive with noise. A monkey's howl cracked the air. A bird warbled a melody, and another answered. A soft hum droned near William's ear. He wiped the side of his face and was relieved to find only a thin layer of sweat.

Around his feet the moist air thickened into fog. Careful to keep his eyes on the ground, he headed for the boardwalk behind the house, then quietly followed it among the other dwellings. Where the buildings and boardwalk ended, he stepped off into the thick wet grass.

Another explosion thundered in the Cut. He pictured the dirt and rock being tossed up and tried to run toward it. Matted grass grabbed at his shoes. Wet air filled his lungs. Sweat dripped from his face and tickled his back between his shoulder blades. He hardly noticed.

Where a foot-wide crack split the ground, the grass gave way to mud. William jumped the gap, and slippery, blue-black clay oozed into his shoes. He pulled his feet free and stepped back onto the grass. Ahead of him the ground disappeared under a dense mist.

"The Cut!" he said excitedly. "It's got to be."

For William being at the site of the largest construction project in history was a miracle. More than a year before, his neighbor, Mr. Fergueson, had served a stint as an engineer on the canal railroad. He had begun sending William issues of the *Canal Record,* the weekly newspaper of the Isthmian Canal Commission, or ICC, and William was hooked. He pored over facts and figures in each issue: the amount of concrete in the canal's six gigantic locks, the number of cubic yards of earth in the breakwater at Colón, the water level of the lake behind Gatun Dam. He pictured the plows scraping fill from trains of flatcars, cheered as Culebra Cut deepened, and grieved at each report of a slide sending dirt and rock tumbling into the Cut. To William an issue of the *Record* was more exciting than an adventure story by Jack London.

During the summer of 1910, when Mr. Fergueson had returned home to Maine, William's father was exhausted and ill. A hard winter traveling on skis or snowshoes tending patients had been followed by a cold, wet spring spent digging his buggy out of the mud. Deep creases lined Dr. Thomas's face, and a cough rumbled in his chest.

"Get away to a warmer place. Panama's the answer," Mr. Fergueson had suggested. "Every one of those villages along the canal has got either a dispensary or a small hospital. . . .

Viewing HISTORY **Digging the Panama Canal**

Years after the opening of the Panama Canal, Edward Laning painted TR in Panama. *It celebrates the triumph of American engineering and technology. President Theodore Roosevelt is shown walking in front of the railroad car at right.* ★ **Why do you think the artist included the two wooden crosses in the lower right corner?**

William was jubilant. "We've just got to go. It'll be as important as watching the Egyptian pyramids being built. You'd want me to see that, wouldn't you?. . . "

Now, in July 1911, on his first full day in Panama, William stood at the edge of Culebra Cut, the most challenging stretch of the whole canal. He was sure that no place on earth teemed with excitement and purpose like the spot where the Big Ditch was being carved through the mountains. . . .

For hundreds of years people had dreamed of digging a canal through the narrow Isthmus of Panama. Eliminating the long voyage around South America would make travel between the Atlantic and Pacific Oceans much faster. In 1881, a French company attempted to fulfill that dream. They made plans to dig a canal at sea-level. But almost as soon as work in Culebra Cut had started, wide sections of the bank across from the village of Culebra began sliding toward the bottom. The slides, as well as problems with money and disease, forced the French to give up the project in 1899.

Four years later the United States signed a lease for a ten-mile Canal Zone across the isthmus. The ICC scrapped the idea of a sea-level canal in favor of a lock model, which would allow digging in Culebra Cut to stop at forty feet above sea-level. Even so, the slides were getting worse.

William looked behind him. The houses were only shadows, but a shape like a giant serpent loomed close in the haze. Flatcars! William rushed to the line of train cars standing ready for loads of dirt, then hurried toward the end of the line.

A huge Bucyrus steam shovel, its massive jaws at rest, sat wrapped in fog. Beautiful, he thought, as beautiful as anything nature could produce. And it was powerful too. "Five cubic yards a bite. Ninety-five tons—so big that it takes ten men to run it," he answered to the mist. William knew why the steam shovel was there: to take off the top of the mountain so that it could not slide into the Cut.

A piercing whistle blasted, making William jump. Another joined it. He rushed back to the rim. Beneath the swirling fog, boilers popped, engines bellowed, shovels clanged. Steam merged with mist. The work day had begun.

Gradually the haze lifted to reveal the great gash. Along the opposite side of the Cut, on the sheared cliff that years before had lain deep within the mountain, layers of orange, pink, purple, and red earth blazed in the sun. Here and there, strands of deep green foliage crept down from the hilltops like fingers intent on taking back the land.

Not far below, a steam shovel lay on its side. Surrounding it was a broad wedge of dirt and rock that stretched from the wall to the middle of the Cut's floor. A slide! Just the way Mr. Fergueson had said it would look! William watched eagerly as scores of men scurried about, determining the best way to face this latest setback.

Source: *Culebra Cut,* Judith Head, 1995.

Analyzing Literature

1. Mr. Fergueson suggests that Dr. Thomas go to Panama in order to

A. see the canal being built.
B. practice medicine.
C. improve his health.
D. work on the Culebra Cut.

2. Which country was first interested in digging the Panama Canal?

F. France
G. United States
H. Panama
J. Mexico

3. Critical Thinking Evaluating Information What was the main reason for building the Panama Canal?

Historical Critique

Could you use this excerpt as a primary source in a report on the Panama Canal?

★ Chapter 22 ★ World War I

★ 22–1 ★ African Americans During World War I

Introduction During World War I, many African Americans moved from the South to northern cities. Often, these newcomers faced discrimination and even violence. At the same time, many African Americans found greater opportunity as a result of the "great migration" to the North. The first selection below is a letter written by a black southerner in response to an advertisement in a northern newspaper. The second is an excerpt from *The Big Sea,* the autobiography of writer Langston Hughes. Hughes moved with his family from Kansas to Cleveland, Ohio. He later became one of the most famous African American poets of the century.

Vocabulary Before you read the selection, find the meanings of these words in a dictionary: **foundry, references, exorbitant.**

★ ★ ★ ★ ★ ★ ★ ★ ★

Houston, Tex., 4-29-17

Dear Sir:

I am a constant reader of the "Chicago Defender"* and in your last issue I saw a want ad that appealed to me. I am a Negro, age 37, and am an all round foundry man. . . . [I] hold good references from several shops, in which I have been employed. . . . It is hard for a black man to hold a job here, as prejudice is very strong. I have never been discharged on account of dissatisfaction with

* The *Chicago Defender* was one of the most influential African American newspapers of the time. It often ran articles that urged its readers to come north to find work.

Viewing HISTORY **Cheering American Soldiers**

Like other Americans, African Americans at home helped support the American war effort during World War I. This photograph shows bystanders cheering a military parade in Chicago. ★ **Identify two ways Americans at home supported the war effort.**

my work, but I have been "let out" on account of my color. . . . I have a family and am anxious to leave here, but have not the means, and as wages are not much here, it is very hard to save enough to get away with. If you know of any firms that are in need of a core maker and whom you think would send me transportation, I would be pleased to be put in touch with them . . . If any one will send transportation, I will arrange or agree to have it taken out of my salary until full amount of fare is paid. . . . I am ready to start at any time, and would be pleased to hear something favorable.

★ ★ ★ ★ ★ ★ ★ ★ ★

Langston Hughes:

I had no sooner graduated from grammar school in Lincoln than we moved from Illinois to Cleveland. My stepfather sent for us. He was working in a steel mill during the war, and making lots of money. But it was hard work, and he never looked the same afterwards. Every day he worked several hours overtime, because they paid well for overtime. But after a while, he couldn't stand the heat of the furnaces, so he got a job as caretaker of a theater building, and after that as janitor of an apartment house.

Rents were very high for colored people in Cleveland, and the Negro district was extremely crowded, because of the great migration. It was difficult to find a place to live. We always lived, during my high school years, either in an attic or a basement, and paid quite a lot for such inconvenient quarters. White people on the east side of the city were moving out of their frame houses and renting them to Negroes at double and triple the rents they could receive from others. An eight-room house with one bath would be cut up into apartments and five or six families crowded into it, each two-room kitchenette apartment renting for what the whole house had rented for before.

But Negroes were coming in in a great tide from the South, and they had to have some place to live. Sheds and garages and store fronts were turned into living quarters. As always, the white neighborhoods resented Negroes moving closer and closer—but when the whites did give way, they gave way at very profitable rentals. So most of the colored people's wages went for rent. The landlords and the banks made it difficult for them to buy houses, so they had to pay the exorbitant rents required. When my stepfather quit the steel mill job, my mother went out to work in service to help him meet expenses. She paid a woman to take care of my little brother while she worked as a maid.

Sources: *The Journal Of Negro History,* edited by Carter G. Woodson, 1919; *The Big Sea,* Langston Hughes, 1940.

Analyzing Primary Sources

1. Why did the man from Houston write a letter to the *Chicago Defender?*
   - **A.** He wanted to protest job discrimination in the South.
   - **B.** He wanted help finding work.
   - **C.** He could not get good references.
   - **D.** He wanted to join his family in Chicago.
2. According to Langston Hughes, one problem African Americans faced when they came north was
   - **F.** lack of jobs.
   - **G.** low pay.
   - **H.** shortage of housing.
   - **J.** being fired because of prejudice.
3. **Critical Thinking Recognizing Points of View (a)** How does the man who wrote the letter feel about work? **(b)** Do you think Langston Hughes's stepfather shared this attitude?

Historical Critique

How do the two types of primary sources included above differ from one another? Would you consider both of them to be reliable sources of information?

★ 22–2 ★ A Farewell to Arms

Introduction During World War I, Ernest Hemingway worked as an ambulance driver for the Red Cross in Italy. He was 19 years old when he was sent to the front. This excerpt from his novel *A Farewell to Arms* provides a glimpse of what the war was like in Italy. The narrator is a fictional ambulance driver named Frederic Henry. The Italians were fighting against the Austrians, Croatians, and Germans.

Vocabulary Before you read the selection, find the meanings of these words in a dictionary: **bombardment, concentrated, sullen, commenced.**

★ ★ ★ ★ ★ ★ ★ ★ ★

The wind rose in the night and at three o'clock in the morning with the rain coming in sheets there was a bombardment and the Croatians came over across the mountain meadows and through patches of woods and into the front line. They fought in the dark in the rain and a counter-attack of scared men from the second line drove them back. There was much shelling and rifle fire all along the line. They did not come again and it was quieter and between the gusts and wind and rain we could hear the sound of a great bombardment far to the north.

The wounded were coming into the post, some were carried on stretchers, some walking and some were brought on the backs of men that came across the field. They were wet to the skin and all were scared. We filled two cars with stretcher cases as they came up from the cellar of the post and as I shut the door of the second car and fastened it I felt the rain on my face turn to snow. The flakes were coming heavy and fast in the rain.

When daylight came the storm was still blowing but the snow had stopped. It had melted as it fell on the wet ground and now it was raining again. There was another attack just after daylight but it was unsuccessful. We expected an attack all day but it did not come until the sun was going down. The bombardment started to the south below the long wooded ridge where the Austrian guns were concentrated. We expected a bombardment but it did not come. It was getting dark. Guns were firing from the field behind the village and the shells, going away, had a comfortable sound.

We heard that the attack to the south had been unsuccessful. They did not attack that night but we heard that they had

Viewing History **Supporting the Red Cross**

Childe Hassam painted Red Cross Drive, May 1918. *It shows a display of flags during a parade down Fifth Avenue in New York City. Donating money to the Red Cross was just one way Americans contributed to the war effort in World War I.*
★ **Some Americans who opposed the war still supported the Red Cross or served as ambulance drivers. Why do you think this was so?**

broken through to the north. In the night word came that we were to prepare to retreat. The captain at the post told me this. He had it from the Brigade. A little while later he came from the telephone and said it was a lie. The Brigade had received orders that the line of the Bainsizza should be held no matter what happened. I asked about the break through and he said that he had heard at the Brigade that the Austrians had broken through the twenty-seventh army corps up toward Caporetto. There had been a great battle in the north all day....

"It's Germans that are attacking," one of the medical officers said. The word Germans was something to be frightened of. We did not want to have anything to do with the Germans. "There are fifteen divisions of Germans," the medical officer said. "They have broken through and we will be cut off."

"At the Brigade, they say this line is to be held. They say they have not broken through badly and that we will hold a line across the mountains from Monte Maggiore."

"Where do they hear this?"

"From the Division."

"The word that we were to retreat came from the Division."

"We work under the Army Corps," I said. "But here I work under you. Naturally when you tell me to go I will go. But get the orders straight."

"The orders are that we stay here. You clear the wounded from here to the clearing station."

"Sometimes we clear from the clearing station to the field hospitals too," I said. "Tell me, I have never seen a retreat—if there is a retreat how are all the wounded evacuated?"

"They are not. They take as many as they can and leave the rest."

"What will I take in the cars?"

"Hospital equipment."

"All right," I said.

The next night the retreat started. We heard that Germans and Austrians had broken through in the north and were coming down the mountain valley toward Cividale and Udine. The retreat was orderly, wet, and sullen. In the night, going slowly along the crowded roads we passed troops marching under the rain, guns, horses pulling wagons, mules, motor trucks, all moving away from the front. There was no more disorder than in an advance.

That night we helped empty the field hospitals that had been set up in the least ruined villages of the plateau, taking the wounded down to Plava on the river-bed: and the next day hauled all day in the rain to evacuate the hospital and clearing station at Plava. It rained steadily and the army of the Bainsizza moved down off the plateau in the October rain and across the river where the great victories had commenced in the spring of that year.

Source: *A Farewell to Arms,* Ernest Hemingway, 1926.

Analyzing Literature

1. Whom did the Army Corps fear the most?
   A. Italians
   B. Croatians
   C. Austrians
   D. Germans
2. What time of day did the Croatians cross over to the front line?
   F. 3 A.M.
   G. 3 P.M.
   H. 6 P.M.
   J. 12 A.M.
3. **Critical Thinking Drawing Conclusions** Why would the ambulances be filled with hospital equipment instead of wounded soldiers during a retreat?

Historical Critique

A Farewell to Arms is a work of fiction. Do you think it could still be a useful source of some information about World War I? Why or why not?

★ Chapter 23 ★ Linking Past to Present: A Century of Change

★ 23–1 ★ "I Have a Dream"

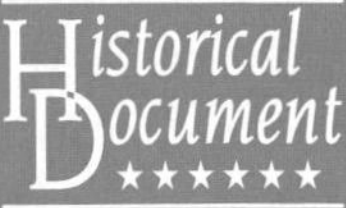

Introduction In August 1963, civil rights groups organized the March on Washington. More than 200,000 people marched to the nation's capital. By their words and massive presence, participants hoped to persuade Congress to pass civil rights laws. On that hot day in August, Martin Luther King, Jr., spoke in front of the Lincoln Memorial. The speech he gave that day became known as the "I Have a Dream" speech. His words moved a nation.

Vocabulary Before you read the selection, find the meanings of these words in a dictionary: **creed, exalted, despair, discords, prodigious, curvaceous.**

★ ★ ★ ★ ★ ★ ★ ★ ★

I have a dream that one day, this nation will rise up and live out the true meaning of its creed: "We hold these truths to be self-evident; that all men are created equal...."

I have a dream that my four little children will one day live in a nation where they will not be judged by the color of their skin but by the content of their character.

I have a dream today!

I have a dream that one day the state of Alabama... will be transformed into a situation where little black boys and black girls will be able to join hands with little white boys and white girls as sisters and brothers.

I have a dream today!

I have a dream that one day every valley shall be exalted, every hill and mountain shall be made low, the rough places shall be made plain, and the crooked places shall be made straight and the glory of the Lord will be revealed and all flesh shall see it together. This is our hope. This is the faith that I go back to the South with.

With this faith we will be able to hew out of the mountain of despair a stone of hope. With this faith we will be able to transform the jangling discords of our nation into a beautiful symphony of brotherhood.

With this faith we will be able to work together, to pray together, to struggle together, to go to jail together, to stand up for freedom together, knowing that we will be free one

Viewing History **King at Washington**

In 1963, more than 200,000 Americans marched on Washington, D.C. There, they listened to Martin Luther King, Jr., describe his dream of a nation without prejudice. A teenager who attended the march later recalled, "All around, in the faces of everyone there was this sense of hope for the future." ★ **Why do you think both black and white Americans joined the March on Washington?**

day. This will be the day when all of God's children will be able to sing with new meaning—"my country 'tis of thee; sweet land of liberty; of thee I sing; land where my fathers died, land of the pilgrim's pride, from every mountain side, let freedom ring"—and if America is to be a great nation, this must become true.

So let freedom ring from the prodigious hilltops of New Hampshire.

Let freedom ring from the mighty mountains of New York.

Let freedom ring from the heightening Alleghenies of Pennsylvania.

Let freedom ring from the snow-capped Rockies of Colorado.

Let freedom ring from the curvaceous slopes of California.

But not only that.

Let freedom ring from Stone Mountain of Georgia.

Let freedom ring from Lookout Mountain of Tennessee.

Let freedom ring from every hill and molehill of Mississippi. From every mountainside, let freedom ring.

When we let freedom ring, when we let it ring from every village and every hamlet, from every state and every city, we will be able to speed up that day when all of God's children, black men and white men, Jews and Gentiles, Protestants and Catholics, will be able to join hands and sing in the words of the old Negro spiritual: "Free at last! free at last! thank God almighty, we are free at last!"

Source: *I Have a Dream: The Life and Words of Martin Luther King, Jr.*, Jim Haskins, 1992.

Analyzing Primary Sources

1. What is Martin Luther King, Jr.'s, "dream"?
   - **A.** that whites and blacks can live together
   - **B.** that the North will no longer be segregated
   - **C.** that African Americans will be able to vote in all states
   - **D.** that all Americans can practice religious freedom
2. According to King's speech, what are the "jangling discords of our nation"?
   - **F.** religious discrimination
   - **G.** segregation laws
   - **H.** widespread unemployment
   - **J.** widespread crime throughout the country
3. **Critical Thinking Identifying the Main Idea** What is the main idea of Martin Luther King, Jr.'s, "I Have a Dream" speech?

Historical Critique

In his speech, King included quotations from the Declaration of Independence, the Bible, the song "America," and a spiritual. What effect do you think he hoped to have on his audience by including these quotations?

★ 23–2 ★ The Value of Books

Introduction *Hunger of Memory* is about the educational experiences of writer Richard Rodriguez. Rodriguez, the son of Mexican immigrants, grew up in Sacramento, California, during the 1960s. In his book, Rodriguez discusses his problems as a "minority student." In the following selection, Rodriguez discusses how he learned to become a good reader and to appreciate books.

Vocabulary Before you read the selection, find the meanings of these words in a dictionary: **reluctant, consequence, literacy, embarked, grandiose, basked, crucial, moralistic, appraisals, disheartened, constituted, earnestness.**

Viewing HISTORY **Reading: A Key to Growth**

Above, a young student reads while sitting under a giant sequoia tree. To encourage reading, the American Library Association issued posters showing well-known people with their favorite books. The poster at left features Marlee Matlin, the first deaf actor to win an Academy Award. ★ **If you appeared on a poster like this one, what book would you be holding? Why?**

★ ★ ★ ★ ★ ★ ★ ★ ★ ★

The old nun would read from her favorite books, usually biographies of early American presidents. Playfully she ran through complex sentences, calling the words alive with her voice, making it seem that the author was somehow speaking directly to me.

One day the nun concluded a session by asking me why I was so reluctant to read by myself. I tried to explain; said something about the way written words made me feel all alone—almost, I wanted to add but didn't, as when I spoke to myself in a room just emptied of furniture. She studied my face as I spoke; she seemed to be watching more than listening. In an uneventful voice she replied that I had nothing to fear. Didn't I realize that reading would open up whole new worlds? A book could open doors for me. It could introduce me to people and show me places I never imagined existed. She gestured toward the bookshelves.... I listened with respect. I was thinking then of another consequence of literacy, one I was too shy to admit but nonetheless trusted. Books were going to make me 'educated.' That confidence enabled me, several months later, to overcome my fear of the silence.

In fourth grade I embarked upon a grandiose reading program. 'Give me the names of important books,' I would say to startled teachers. They soon found out that I had in mind 'adult books.' I ignored their suggestions of anything written for children.... And whatever I read I read for extra credit. Each time I finished a book, I reported the achievement to a teacher and basked in the praise my effort earned. Despite my best efforts, however, there seemed to be more and more books I needed to read. At the library I would literally tremble as I came upon whole shelves of books I hadn't read. So I read and I read and I read: *Great Expectations;* all the short stories of Kipling; *The Babe Ruth Story;* the entire first volume of the *Encyclopedia Britannica* (A-ANSTEY); the *Iliad; Moby Dick; Gone With the Wind; The Good*

Earth; Ramona; Forever Amber; The Lives of the Saints; Crime and Punishment; The Pearl.... Librarians who initially frowned when I checked out the maximum ten books at a time started saving books they thought I might like. Teachers would say to the rest of the class. "I only wish the rest of you took reading as seriously as Richard obviously does.'...

What did I see in my books? I had the idea that they were crucial for my academic success, though I couldn't have said exactly how or why. In the sixth grade I simply concluded that what gave a book its value was some major idea or theme it contained. If that core essence could be mined and memorized, I would become learned like my teachers. I decided to record in a notebook the themes of the books that I read. After reading *Robinson Crusoe,* I wrote that its theme was 'the value of learning to live by oneself.' When I completed *Wuthering Heights,* I noted the danger of 'letting emotions get out of control.' Rereading these brief moralistic appraisals usually left me disheartened. I couldn't believe that they were really the source of reading's value. But for many more years, they constituted the only means I had of describing to myself the educational value of books.

In spite of my earnestness, I found reading a pleasurable activity. I came to enjoy the lonely good company of books. Early on weekday mornings, I'd read in my bed. I'd feel a mysterious comfort then, reading in the dawn quiet—the blue-gray silence interrupted by the occasional churning of the refrigerator motor a few rooms away or the more distant sounds of a city bus beginning its run. On weekends I'd go to the public library to read, surrounded by old men and women. Or, if the weather was fine, I would take my books to the park and read in the shade of a tree. A warm summer evening was my favorite reading time. Neighbors would leave for vacation and I would water their lawns. I would sit through the twilight on the front porches or in backyards, reading to the cool, whirling sounds of sprinklers. . . .

There were pleasures to sustain me after I'd finish my books. Carrying a volume back to the library, I would be pleased by its weight. I'd run my fingers along the edge of the pages and marvel at the breadth of my achievement. Around my room, growing stacks of paperback books reinforced my assurance.

I entered high school having read hundreds of books. My habit of reading made me a confident speaker and writer of English. Reading also enabled me to sense something of the shape, the major concerns, of Western thought. (I was able to say something about Dante and Descartes and Engels and James Baldwin in my high school term papers.) In these various ways, books brought me academic success as I hoped that they would.

Source: *Hunger of Memory: The Education of Richard Rodriguez, An Autobiography,* Richard Rodriguez, 1982.

Analyzing Primary Sources

1. In the fourth grade, Rodriguez began
   - **A.** an English program.
   - **B.** a Spanish program.
   - **C.** a reading program.
   - **D.** a writing program.
2. Richard's favorite reading time was on a
   - **F.** sunny fall day.
   - **G.** rainy spring afternoon.
   - **H.** snowy winter morning.
   - **J.** warm summer evening.
3. **Critical Thinking Recognizing Points of View** Why did Richard Rodriguez value books?

Historical Critique

In the above passage, Richard Rodriguez is retelling his own childhood experiences. Do you think his words could be used to support any particular cause? Explain.

Reference Section

★ The Declaration of Independence ★

On June 7, 1776, the Continental Congress approved the resolution that "these United Colonies are, and of right ought to be, free and independent States." Congress then appointed a committee to write a declaration of independence. The committee members were John Adams, Benjamin Franklin, Robert Livingston, Roger Sherman, and Thomas Jefferson.

Jefferson actually wrote the Declaration, but he got advice from the others. On July 2, Congress discussed the Declaration and made some changes. On July 4, 1776, it adopted the Declaration of Independence in its final form.

The Declaration is printed in black. The headings have been added to show the parts of the Declaration. They are not part of the original text. Annotations, or explanations, are on the tan side of the page. Page numbers in the annotations show where a subject is discussed in the text. Difficult words are defined.

dissolve: break ***powers of the earth:*** other nations ***station:*** place ***impel:*** force

The colonists feel that they must explain to the world the reasons why they are breaking away from England.

When in the course of human events it becomes necessary for one people to dissolve the political bands which have connected them with another and to assume, among the powers of the earth, the separate and equal station to which the laws of nature and of nature's God entitle them, a decent respect to the opinions of mankind requires that they should declare the causes which impel them to the separation.

The Purpose of Government Is to Protect Basic Rights

endowed: given ***unalienable rights:*** so basic that they cannot be taken away ***secure:*** protect ***instituted:*** set up ***deriving:*** getting ***alter:*** change ***effect:*** bring about

People set up governments to protect their basic rights. Governments get their power from the consent of the governed. If a government takes away the basic rights of the people, the people have the right to change the government.

prudence: wisdom ***transient:*** temporary, passing ***disposed:*** likely ***usurpations:*** taking and using powers that do not belong to a person ***invariably:*** always ***evinces a design to reduce them under absolute despotism:*** makes a clear plan to put them under complete and unjust control ***sufferance:*** endurance

We hold these truths to be self-evident, that all men are created equal; that they are endowed by their Creator with certain unalienable rights; that among these are life, liberty, and the pursuit of happiness. That, to secure these rights, governments are instituted among men, deriving their just powers from the consent of the governed; that, whenever any form of government becomes destructive of these ends, it is the right of the people to alter or to abolish it, and to institute a new government, laying its foundation on such principles and organizing its powers in such form, as to them shall seem most likely to effect their safety and happiness. Prudence, indeed, will dictate that governments long established should not be changed for light and transient causes; and, accordingly, all experience hath shown that mankind are more disposed to suffer, while evils are sufferable, than to right themselves by abolishing the forms to which they are accustomed. But when a long train of abuses and usurpations, pursuing invariably the same object, evinces a design to reduce them under absolute despotism, it is their right, it is their duty, to throw off such government and to provide new guards for their future security. Such has been the patient sufferance of these colonies, and such is now the necessity which constrains them to alter their former systems of government. The history of the present King of Great Britain is a history of repeated injuries and usurpations, all having, in direct object, the establishment of an absolute tyranny over these States. To prove this, let facts be submitted to a candid world:

constrains: forces ***absolute tyranny:*** harsh and unjust government ***candid:*** free from prejudice

People do not change governments for slight reasons. But they are forced to do so when a government becomes tyrannical. King George III has a long record of abusing his power.

Wrongs Done by the King

He has refused his assent to laws the most wholesome and necessary for the public good.

He has forbidden his governors to pass laws of immediate and pressing importance, unless suspended in their operation till his assent should be obtained; and, when so suspended, he has utterly neglected to attend to them.

He has refused to pass other laws for the accommodation of the large districts of people, unless those people would relinquish the right of representation in the legislature; a right inestimable to them and formidable to tyrants only.

assent: approval ***relinquish:*** give up ***inestimable:*** too great a value to be measured ***formidable:*** causing fear

This part of the Declaration spells out three sets of wrongs that led the colonists to break with Britain.

The first set of wrongs is the king's unjust use of power. The king refused to approve laws that are needed. He has tried to control the colonial legislatures.

He has called together legislative bodies at places unusual, uncomfortable, and distant from the depository of their public records, for the sole purpose of fatiguing them into compliance with his measures.

He has dissolved representative houses, repeatedly for opposing, with manly firmness, his invasions on the rights of the people.

He has refused, for a long time after such dissolutions, to cause others to be elected: whereby the legislative powers, incapable of annihilation, have returned to the people at large for their exercise; the state remaining, in the meantime, exposed to all the danger of invasion from without and convulsions within.

depository: storehouse ***fatiguing:*** tiring out ***compliance:*** giving in ***dissolved:*** broken up ***annihilation:*** total destruction ***convulsions:*** disturbances

The king has tried to force colonial legislatures into doing his will by wearing them out. He has dissolved legislatures (such as those of Massachusetts). (See page 90.)

He has endeavored to prevent the population of these States; for that purpose, obstructing the laws for naturalization of foreigners, refusing to pass others to encourage their migration hither, and raising the conditions of new appropriations of lands.

He has obstructed the administration of justice by refusing his assent to laws for establishing judiciary powers.

He has made judges dependent on his will alone for the tenure of their offices and the amount and payment of their salaries.

He has erected a multitude of new offices and sent hither swarms of officers to harass our people and eat out their substance.

endeavored: tried ***obstructing:*** blocking ***naturalization:*** process of becoming a citizen ***migration:*** moving ***hither:*** here ***appropriations:*** grants ***obstructed the administration of justice:*** prevented justice from being done ***judiciary powers:*** system of law courts ***tenure:*** term (of office) ***erected:*** set up ***multitude:*** large number ***swarms:*** huge crowds ***harass:*** cause trouble ***render:*** make

Among other wrongs, he has refused to let settlers move west to take up new land. He has prevented justice from being done. Also, he has sent large numbers of customs officials to cause problems for the colonists.

He has kept among us, in time of peace, standing armies, without the consent of our legislatures.

He has affected to render the military independent of, and superior to, the civil power.

He has combined with others to subject us to a jurisdiction foreign to our Constitution and unacknowledged by our laws, giving his assent to their acts of pretended legislation—

jurisdiction: authority

For quartering large bodies of armed troops among us;

quartering: housing

mock: false

The king has joined with others, meaning Parliament, to make laws for the colonies. The Declaration then lists the second set of wrongs—unjust acts of Parliament.

imposing: forcing ***depriving:*** taking away ***transporting us beyond seas:*** sending colonists to England for trial ***neighboring province:*** Quebec ***arbitrary government:*** unjust rule ***fit instrument:*** suitable tool ***invested with power:*** having the power

During the years leading up to 1776, the colonists claimed that Parliament had no right to make laws for them because they were not represented in Parliament. Here, the colonists object to recent laws of Parliament, such as the Quartering Act and the blockade of colonial ports (page 90), which cut off their trade. They also object to Parliament's claim that it had the right to tax them without their consent.

abdicated: given up ***plundered:*** robbed ***ravaged:*** attacked ***mercenaries:*** hired soldiers ***desolation:*** misery ***perfidy:*** falseness ***barbarous:*** uncivilized ***constrained:*** forced ***brethren:*** brothers ***domestic insurrections:*** internal revolts

Here, the Declaration lists the third set of wrongs—warlike acts of the king. Instead of listening to the colonists, the king has made war on them. He has hired soldiers to fight in America.

oppressions: harsh rule ***petitioned:*** asked ***redress:*** relief ***unwarrantable jurisdiction over:*** unfair authority ***magnanimity:*** generosity ***conjured:*** called upon ***common kindred:*** relatives ***disavow:*** turn away from ***consanguinity:*** blood relationships, kinship ***acquiesce:*** agree ***denounces:*** speaks out against

During this time, colonists have repeatedly asked for relief. But their requests have brought only more suffering. They have appealed to the British people but received no help. So they are forced to separate.

For protecting them by a mock trial from punishment for any murders which they should commit on the inhabitants of these States;

For cutting off our trade with all parts of the world;

For imposing taxes on us without our consent;

For depriving us, in many cases, of the benefit of trial by jury;

For transporting us beyond seas to be tried for pretended offences;

For abolishing the free system of English laws in a neighboring province, establishing therein an arbitrary government, and enlarging its boundaries, so as to render it at once an example and fit instrument for introducing the same absolute rule into these colonies;

For taking away our charters, abolishing our most valuable laws, and altering, fundamentally, the powers of our governments;

For suspending our own legislatures and declaring themselves invested with power to legislate for us in all cases whatsoever.

He has abdicated government here by declaring us out of his protection and waging war against us.

He has plundered our seas, ravaged our coasts, burnt out towns, and destroyed the lives of our people.

He is, at this time, transporting large armies of foreign mercenaries to complete the works of death, desolation, and tyranny already begun with circumstances of cruelty and perfidy scarcely paralleled in the most barbarous ages, and totally unworthy, the head of a civilized nation.

He has constrained our fellow citizens, taken captive on the high seas, to bear arms against their country, to become the executioners of their friends and brethren, or to fall themselves by their hands.

He has excited domestic insurrections amongst us and has endeavored to bring on the inhabitants of our frontiers, the merciless Indian savages, whose known rule of warfare is an undistinguished destruction of all ages, sexes, and conditions.

In every state of these oppressions, we have petitioned for redress in the most humble terms; our repeated petitions have been answered only by repeated injury. A prince whose character is thus marked by every act which may define a tyrant is unfit to be the ruler of a free people.

Nor have we been wanting in attention to our British brethren. We have warned them, from time to time, of attempts made by their legislature to extend an unwarrantable jurisdiction over us. We have reminded them of the circumstances of our emigration and settlement here. We have appealed to their native justice and magnanimity, and we have conjured them, by the ties of our common kindred, to disavow these usurpations, which would inevitably interrupt our connections and correspondence. They, too, have been deaf to the voice of justice and consanguinity. We must, therefore, acquiesce in the necessity which denounces our separation, and hold them, as we hold the rest of mankind, enemies in war, in peace, friends.

Colonies Declare Independence

We, therefore, the representatives of the United States of America, in general Congress assembled, appealing to the Supreme Judge of the world for the rectitude of our intentions, do, in the name and by the authority of the good people of these colonies, solemnly publish and declare, that these united colonies are, and of right ought to be, free and independent states: that they are absolved from all allegiance to the British Crown, and that all political connection between them and the state of Great Britain is, and ought to be, totally dissolved; and that, as free and independent states, they have full power to levy war, conclude peace, contract alliances, establish commerce, and to do all other acts and things which independent states may of right do. And, for the support of this declaration, with a firm reliance on the protection of Divine Providence, we mutually pledge to each other our lives, our fortunes, and our sacred honor.

appealing: calling on ***rectitude of our intentions:*** moral rightness of our plans ***absolved from all allegiance:*** freed from loyalty ***levy war:*** declare war ***contract alliances:*** make treaties

As the representatives of the United States, they declare that the colonies are free and independent states.

The states need no longer be loyal to the British king. They are an independent nation that can make war and sign treaties.

Relying on help from Divine Providence, the signers of the Declaration promise their lives, money, and honor to fight for independence.

★ Signers of the Declaration of Independence ★

John Hancock, President
Charles Thomson, Secretary

New Hampshire
Josiah Bartlett
William Whipple
Matthew Thornton

Massachusetts
Samuel Adams
John Adams
Robert Treat Paine
Elbridge Gerry

Rhode Island
Stephen Hopkins
William Ellery

Connecticut
Roger Sherman
Samuel Huntington
William Williams
Oliver Wolcott

Delaware
Caesar Rodney
George Read
Thomas McKean

New York
William Floyd
Philip Livingston
Francis Lewis
Lewis Morris

New Jersey
Richard Stockton
John Witherspoon
Francis Hopkinson
John Hart
Abraham Clark

Georgia
Button Gwinnett
Lyman Hall
George Walton

Maryland
Samuel Chase
William Paca
Thomas Stone
Charles Carroll

North Carolina
William Hooper
Joseph Hewes
John Penn

Virginia
George Wythe
Richard Henry Lee
Thomas Jefferson
Benjamin Harrison
Thomas Nelson, Jr.
Francis Lightfoot Lee
Carter Braxton

South Carolina
Edward Rutledge
Thomas Heyward, Jr.
Thomas Lynch, Jr.
Arthur Middleton

Pennsylvania
Robert Morris
Benjamin Rush
Benjamin Franklin
John Morton
George Clymer
James Smith
George Taylor
James Wilson
George Ross

★ The Constitution ★ of the United States of America

The Constitution is printed in black. The titles of articles, sections, and clauses are not part of the original document. They have been added to help you find information in the Constitution. Some words or lines are crossed out because they have been changed by amendments or no longer apply. Annotations, or explanations, are on the tan side of the page. Page numbers in the annotations show where a subject is discussed in the text. Difficult words are defined.

Preamble

The Preamble describes the purpose of the government set up by the Constitution. Americans expect their government to defend justice and liberty and provide peace and safety from foreign enemies.

We the people of the United States, in order to form a more perfect Union, establish justice, insure domestic tranquillity, provide for the common defense, promote the general welfare, and secure the blessings of liberty to ourselves and our posterity, do ordain and establish this Constitution for the United States of America.

Article 1. The Legislative Branch

The Constitution gives Congress the power to make laws. Congress is divided into the Senate and the House of Representatives.

Section 1. A Two-House Legislature

All legislative powers herein granted shall be vested in a Congress of the United States, which shall consist of a Senate and House of Representatives.

Section 2. House of Representatives

Clause 1 ***Electors*** refers to voters. Members of the House of Representatives are elected every two years. Any citizen allowed to vote for members of the larger house of the state legislature can also vote for members of the House.

1. Election of Members The House of Representatives shall be composed of members chosen every second year by the people of the several states, and the electors in each state shall have the qualifications requisite for electors of the most numerous branch of the state legislature.

Clause 2 A member of the House of Representatives must be at least 25 years old, an American citizen for 7 years, and a resident of the state he or she represents.

2. Qualifications No person shall be a Representative who shall not have attained to the age of twenty-five years, and been seven years a citizen of the United States, and who shall not, when elected, be an inhabitant of that state in which he shall be chosen.

Clause 3 The number of representatives each state elects is based on its population. An ***enumeration,*** or census, must be taken every 10 years to determine population. Today, the number of representatives in the House is fixed at 435.

This is the famous Three-Fifths Compromise worked out at the Constitutional Convention (page 124). ***Persons bound to service*** meant indentured servants. ***All other persons*** meant slaves. All free people in a state were counted. However, only three fifths of the slaves were included in the population count. This three-fifths clause became meaningless when slaves were freed by the Thirteenth Amendment.

3. Determining Representation Representatives ~~and direct taxes~~ shall be apportioned among the several states which may be included within this Union, according to their respective numbers ~~which shall be determined by adding to the whole number of free persons, including those bound to service for a term of years, and excluding Indians not taxed, three-fifths of all other persons.~~ The actual enumeration shall be made within three years after the first meeting of the Congress of the United States, and within every subsequent term of ten years, in such manner as they shall by law direct. The number of Representatives shall not exceed one for every 30,000, but each state shall have at least one Representative; ~~and until such enumeration shall be made, the state of New Hampshire shall~~

~~be entitled to choose three; Massachusetts, eight; Rhode Island and Providence Plantations, one; Connecticut, five; New York, six; New Jersey, four; Pennsylvania, eight; Delaware, one; Maryland, six; Virginia, ten; North Carolina, five; South Carolina, five; and Georgia, three.~~

4. Filling Vacancies When vacancies happen in the representation from any state, the executive authority thereof shall issue writs of election to fill such vacancies.

Clause 4 ***Executive authority*** means the governor of a state. If a member of the House leaves office before his or her term ends, the governor must call a special election to fill the seat.

5. Selection of Officers; Power of Impeachment The House of Representatives shall choose their Speaker and other officers; and shall have the sole power of impeachment.

Clause 5 The House elects a speaker. Today, the speaker is usually chosen by the party that has a majority in the House. Also, only the House has the power to ***impeach,*** or accuse, a federal official of wrongdoing.

Section 3. The Senate

1. Selection of Members The Senate of the United States shall be composed of two Senators from each state ~~chosen by the legislature thereof,~~ for six years, and each Senator shall have one vote.

Clause 1 Each state has two senators. Senators serve for six-year terms. The Seventeenth Amendment changed the way senators were elected.

2. Alternating Terms; Filling Vacancies Immediately after they shall be assembled in consequence of the first election, they shall be divided as equally as may be into three classes. ~~The seats of the Senators of the first class shall be vacated at the expiration of the second year, of the second class at the expiration of the fourth year, and of the third class at the expiration of the sixth year,~~ so that one-third may be chosen every second year; ~~and if vacancies happen by resignation, or otherwise, during the recess of the legislature of any state, the executive thereof may make temporary appointments until the next meeting of the legislature, which shall then fill such vacancies.~~

Clause 2 Every two years, one third of the senators run for reelection. Thus, the makeup of the Senate is never totally changed by any one election. The Seventeenth Amendment changed the way of filling ***vacancies,*** or empty seats. Today, the governor of a state must choose a senator to fill a vacancy that occurs between elections.

3. Qualifications No person shall be a Senator who shall not have attained to the age of thirty years, and been nine years a citizen of the United States, and who shall not, when elected, be an inhabitant of that state for which he shall be chosen.

Clause 3 A senator must be at least 30 years old, an American citizen for 9 years, and a resident of the state he or she represents.

4. President of the Senate The Vice-President of the United States shall be president of the Senate, but shall have no vote, unless they be equally divided.

Clause 4 The Vice President presides over Senate meetings, but he or she can vote only to break a tie.

5. Election of Senate Officers The Senate shall choose their other officers, and also a president *pro tempore,* in the absence of the Vice-President, or when he shall exercise the office of the President of the United States.

Clause 5 ***Pro tempore*** means temporary. The Senate chooses one of its members to serve as president pro tempore when the Vice President is absent.

6. Impeachment Trials The Senate shall have the sole power to try all impeachments. When sitting for that purpose, they shall be on oath or affirmation. When the President of the United States is tried, the Chief Justice shall preside; and no person shall be convicted without the concurrence of two-thirds of the members present.

Clause 6 The Senate acts as a jury if the House impeaches a federal official. The Chief Justice of the Supreme Court presides if the President is on trial. Two thirds of all senators present must vote for ***conviction,*** or finding the accused guilty. No President has ever been convicted. The House impeached President Andrew Johnson in 1868, but the Senate acquitted him of the charges (page 413). In 1974, President Richard Nixon resigned before he could be impeached.

Clause 7 If an official is found guilty by the Senate, he or she can be removed from office and barred from holding federal office in the future. These are the only punishments the Senate can impose. However, the convicted official can still be tried in a criminal court.

7. Penalties Upon Conviction Judgment in cases of impeachment shall not extend further than to removal from office, and disqualification to hold and enjoy any office of honor, trust, or profit under the United States; but the party convicted shall nevertheless be liable and subject to indictment, trial, judgment, and punishment, according to law.

Section 4. Elections and Meetings

Clause 1 Each state legislature can decide when and how congressional elections take place, but Congress can overrule these decisions. In 1842, Congress required each state to set up congressional districts with one representative elected from each district. In 1872, Congress decided that congressional elections must be held in every state on the same date in even-numbered years.

1. Election of Congress The times, places, and manner of holding elections for Senators and Representatives shall be prescribed in each state by the legislature thereof; but the Congress may at any time by law make or alter such regulations, except as to the places of choosing Senators.

Clause 2 Congress must meet at least once a year. The Twentieth Amendment moved the opening date of Congress to January 3.

2. Annual Sessions The Congress shall assemble at least once in every year, ~~and such meeting shall be on the first Monday in December, unless they shall by law appoint a different day.~~

Section 5. Rules for the Conduct of Business

Clause 1 Each house decides whether a member has the qualifications for office set by the Constitution. A ***quorum*** is the smallest number of members who must be present for business to be conducted. Each house can set its own rules about absent members.

1. Organization Each house shall be the judge of the elections, returns, and qualifications of its own members, and a majority of each shall constitute a quorum to do business; but a smaller number may adjourn from day to day, and may be authorized to compel the attendance of absent members, in such manner, and under such penalties, as each house may provide.

Clause 2 Each house can make rules for the conduct of members. It can only expel a member by a two-thirds vote.

2. Procedures Each house may determine the rules of its proceedings, punish its members for disorderly behavior, and with the concurrence of two-thirds, expel a member.

Clause 3 Each house keeps a record of its meetings. *The Congressional Record* is published every day with excerpts from speeches made in each house. It also records the votes of each member.

3. A Written Record Each house shall keep a journal of its proceedings, and from time to time publish the same, excepting such parts as may in their judgment require secrecy; and the yeas and nays of the members of either house on any question shall, at the desire of one-fifth of those present, be entered on the journal.

Clause 4 Neither house can ***adjourn,*** or stop meeting, for more than three days unless the other house approves. Both houses of Congress must meet in the same city.

4. Rules for Adjournment Neither house, during the session of Congress, shall, without the consent of the other, adjourn for more than three days, nor to any other place than that in which the two houses shall be sitting.

Section 6. Privileges and Restrictions

Clause 1 ***Compensation*** means salary. Congress decides the salary for its members. While Congress is in session, a member is free from arrest in civil cases and cannot be sued for anything he or she says on the floor of Congress. This allows for freedom of debate. However, a member can be arrested for a criminal offense.

1. Salaries and Immunities The Senators and Representatives shall receive a compensation for their services, to be ascertained by law and paid out of the Treasury of the United States. They shall in all cases, except treason, felony, and breach of the peace, be privileged from arrest during their attendance at the session of their respective houses, and in going to and returning from the same; and for any speech or debate in either house, they shall not be questioned in any other place.

2. Restrictions on Other Employment No Senator or Representative shall, during the time for which he was elected, be appointed to any civil office under the authority of the United States, which shall have been created, or the emoluments whereof shall have been increased, during such time; and no person holding any office under the United States shall be a member of either house during his continuance in office.

Clause 2 ***Emolument*** also means salary. A member of Congress cannot hold another federal office during his or her term. A former member of Congress cannot hold an office created while he or she was in Congress. An official in another branch of government cannot serve at the same time in Congress. This strengthens the separation of powers.

Section 7. Law-Making Process

1. Tax Bills All bills for raising revenue shall originate in the House of Representatives; but the Senate may propose or concur with amendments as on other bills.

Clause 1 ***Revenue*** is money raised by the government through taxes. Tax bills must be introduced in the House. The Senate, however, can make changes in tax bills. This clause protects the principle that people can be taxed only with their consent.

2. How a Bill Becomes a Law Every bill which shall have passed the House of Representatives and the Senate shall, before it become a law, be presented to the President of the United States; if he approve, he shall sign it, but if not, he shall return it, with his objections, to that house in which it shall have originated, who shall enter the objections at large on their journal, and proceed to reconsider it. If after such reconsideration two-thirds of that house shall agree to pass the bill, it shall be sent, together with the objections, to the other house, by which it shall likewise be reconsidered, and, if approved by two-thirds of that house, it shall become a law. But in all such cases the votes of both houses shall be determined by yeas and nays, and the names of the persons voting for and against the bill shall be entered on the journal of each house respectively. If any bill shall not be returned by the President within ten days (Sundays excepted) after it shall have been presented to him, the same bill shall be a law, in like manner as if he had signed it, unless the Congress by their adjournment prevent its return, in which case it shall not be a law.

Clause 2 A ***bill,*** or proposed law, that is passed by a majority of the House and Senate is sent to the President. If the President signs the bill, it becomes law.

A bill can also become law without the President's signature. The President can refuse to act on a bill. If Congress is in session at the time, the bill becomes law 10 days after the President receives it.

The President can ***veto,*** or reject, a bill by sending it back to the house where it was introduced. Or if the President refuses to act on a bill and Congress adjourns within 10 days, then the bill dies. This way of killing a bill without taking action is called the ***pocket veto.***

Congress can override the President's veto if each house of Congress passes the bill again by a two-thirds vote. This clause is an important part of the system of checks and balances (page 130).

3. Resolutions Passed by Congress Every order, resolution, or vote to which the concurrence of the Senate and House of Representatives may be necessary (except on a question of adjournment) shall be presented to the President of the United States; and before the same shall take effect, shall be approved by him, or being disapproved by him, shall be repassed by two-thirds of the Senate and House of Representatives, according to the rules and limitations prescribed in the case of a bill.

Clause 3 Congress can pass resolutions or orders that have the same force as laws. Any such resolution or order must be signed by the President (except on questions of adjournment). Thus, this clause prevents Congress from bypassing the President simply by calling a bill by another name.

Section 8. Powers Delegated to Congress

The Congress shall have the power

1. Taxes To lay and collect taxes, duties, imposts, and excises, to pay the debts and provide for the common defense and general welfare of the United States; but all duties, imposts, and excises shall be uniform throughout the United States;

Clause 1 ***Duties*** are tariffs. ***Imposts*** are taxes in general. ***Excises*** are taxes on the production or sale of certain goods. Congress has the power to tax and spend tax money. Taxes must be the same in all parts of the country.

2. Borrowing To borrow money on the credit of the United States;

Clause 2 Congress can borrow money for the United States. The government often borrows money by selling ***bonds,*** or certificates that promise to pay the holder a certain sum of money on a certain date (page 174).

Clause 3 Only Congress has the power to regulate foreign and ***interstate trade,*** or trade between states. Disagreement over interstate trade was a major problem with the Articles of Confederation (pages 117–118).

3. Commerce To regulate commerce with foreign nations, and among the several states, and with the Indian tribes;

Clause 4 ***Naturalization*** is the process whereby a foreigner becomes a citizen. ***Bankruptcy*** is the condition in which a person or business cannot pay its debts. Congress has the power to pass laws on these two issues. The laws must be the same in all parts of the country.

4. Naturalization; Bankruptcy To establish a uniform rule of naturalization, and uniform laws on the subject of bankruptcies throughout the United States;

Clause 5 Congress has the power to coin money and set its value. Congress has set up the National Bureau of Standards to regulate weights and measures.

5. Coins; Weights; Measures To coin money, regulate the value thereof, and of foreign coin, and fix the standard of weights and measures;

Clause 6 ***Counterfeiting*** is the making of imitation money. ***Securities*** are bonds. Congress can make laws to punish counterfeiters.

6. Counterfeiting To provide for the punishment of counterfeiting the securities and current coin of the United States;

Clause 7 Congress has the power to set up and control the delivery of mail.

7. Post Offices To establish post offices and post roads;

Clause 8 Congress may pass copyright and patent laws. A ***copyright*** protects an author. A patent makes an inventor the sole owner of his or her work for a limited time.

8. Copyrights; Patents To promote the progress of science and useful arts by securing for limited times to authors and inventors the exclusive right to their respective writings and discoveries;

Clause 9 Congress has the power to set up ***inferior,*** or lower, federal courts under the Supreme Court.

9. Federal Courts To constitute tribunals inferior to the Supreme Court;

Clause 10 Congress can punish ***piracy,*** or the robbing of ships at sea.

10. Piracy To define and punish piracies and felonies committed on the high seas and offenses against the law of nations;

Clause 11 Only Congress can declare war. Declarations of war are granted at the request of the President. ***Letters of marque and reprisal*** were documents issued by a government allowing merchant ships to arm themselves and attack ships of an enemy nation. They are no longer issued.

11. Declarations of War To declare war, ~~grant letters of marque and reprisal,~~ and make rules concerning captures on land and water;

Clauses 12, 13, 14 These clauses place the army and navy under the control of Congress. Congress decides on the size of the armed forces and the amount of money to spend on the army and navy. It also has the power to write rules governing the armed forces.

12. Army To raise and support armies, but no appropriation of money to that use shall be for a longer term than two years;

13. Navy To provide and maintain a navy;

14. Rules for the Military To make rules for the government and regulation of the land and naval forces;

Clauses 15, 16 The ***militia*** is a body of citizen soldiers. Congress can call up the militia to put down rebellions or fight foreign invaders. Each state has its own militia, today called the National Guard. Normally, the militia is under the command of a state's governor. However, it can be placed under the command of the President.

15. Militia To provide for calling forth the militia to execute the laws of the Union, suppress insurrections, and repel invasions;

16. Rules for the Militia To provide for organizing, arming, and disciplining the militia, and for governing such part of them as may be employed in the service of the United States, reserving to the states, respectively, the appointment of the officers, and the authority of training the militia according to the discipline prescribed by Congress;

17. National Capital To exercise exclusive legislation in all cases whatsoever, over such district (not exceeding ten miles square) as may, by cession of particular states, and the acceptance of Congress, become the seat of government of the United States, and to exercise like authority over all places purchased by the consent of the legislature of the state in which the same shall be, for the erection of forts, magazines, arsenals, dock-yards, and other needful buildings;—and

Clause 17 Congress controls the district around the national capital. In 1790, Congress made Washington, D.C., the nation's capital (page 175). In 1973, it gave residents of the District the right to elect local officials.

18. Necessary Laws To make all laws which shall be necessary and proper for carrying into execution the foregoing powers, and all other powers vested by this Constitution in the government of the United States, or in any department or officer thereof.

Clause 18 Clauses 1–17 list the powers delegated to Congress. The writers of the Constitution added Clause 18 so that Congress could deal with the changing needs of the nation. It gives Congress the power to make laws as needed to carry out the first 17 clauses. Clause 18 is sometimes called the elastic clause because it lets Congress stretch the meaning of its power.

Section 9. Powers Denied to the Federal Government

1. The Slave Trade ~~The migration or importation of such persons as any of the states now existing shall think proper to admit shall not be prohibited by the Congress prior to the year 1808; but a tax or duty may be imposed on such importation, not exceeding $10 for each person.~~

Clause 1 ***Such persons*** means slaves. This clause resulted from a compromise between the supporters and the opponents of the slave trade (page 125). In 1808, as soon as Congress was permitted to abolish the slave trade, it did so. The $10 import tax was never imposed.

2. Writ of Habeas Corpus The privilege of the writ of habeas corpus shall not be suspended, unless when in cases of rebellion or invasion the public safety may require it.

Clause 2 A ***writ of habeas corpus*** is a court order requiring government officials to bring a prisoner to court and explain why he or she is being held. A writ of habeas corpus protects people from unlawful imprisonment. The government cannot suspend this right except in times of rebellion or invasion.

3. Bills of Attainder and Ex Post Facto Laws No bill of attainder or *ex post facto* law shall be passed.

Clause 3 A ***bill of attainder*** is a law declaring that a person is guilty of a particular crime. An ***ex post facto law*** punishes an act which was not illegal when it was committed. Congress cannot pass a bill of attainder or *ex post facto* laws.

4. Apportionment of Direct Taxes ~~No capitation or other direct tax shall be laid, unless in proportion to the census or enumeration herein before directed to be taken.~~

Clause 4 A ***capitation tax*** is a tax placed directly on each person. ***Direct taxes*** are taxes on people or on land. They can be passed only if they are divided among the states according to population. The Sixteenth Amendment allowed Congress to tax income without regard to the population of the states.

5. Taxes on Exports No tax or duty shall be laid on articles exported from any state.

Clause 5 This clause forbids Congress to tax exports. In 1787, southerners insisted on this clause because their economy depended on exports.

6. Special Preference for Trade No preference shall be given any regulation of commerce or revenue to the ports of one state over those of another; nor shall vessels bound to, or from, one state, be obliged to enter, clear, or pay duties in another.

Clause 6 Congress cannot make laws that favor one state over another in trade and commerce. Also, states cannot place tariffs on interstate trade.

7. Spending No money shall be drawn from the Treasury, but in consequence of appropriations made by law; and a regular statement and account of the receipts and expenditures of all public money shall be published from time to time.

Clause 7 The federal government cannot spend money unless Congress ***appropriates*** it, or passes a law allowing it. This clause gives Congress an important check on the President by controlling the money he or she can spend. The government must publish a statement showing how it spends public funds.

Clause 8 The government cannot award titles of nobility, such as Duke or Duchess. American citizens cannot accept titles of nobility from foreign governments without the consent of Congress.

8. Creation of Titles of Nobility No title of nobility shall be granted by the United States; and no person holding any office of profit or trust under them, shall, without the consent of the Congress, accept of any present, emolument, office, or title, of any kind whatever, from any king, prince, or foreign state.

Section 10. Powers Denied to the States

Clause 1 The writers of the Constitution did not want the states to act like separate nations. So they prohibited states from making treaties or coining money. Some powers denied to the federal government are also denied to the states. For example, states cannot pass *ex post facto* laws.

1. Unconditional Prohibitions No state shall enter into any treaty, alliance, or confederation; grant letters of marque and reprisal; coin money; emit bills of credit; make anything but gold and silver coin a tender in payment of debts; pass any bill of attainder, *ex post facto* law, or law impairing the obligation of contracts, or grant any title of nobility.

Clauses 2, 3 Powers listed here are forbidden to the states, but Congress can lift these prohibitions by passing laws that give these powers to the states.

Clause 2 forbids states from taxing imports and exports without the consent of Congress. States may charge inspection fees on goods entering the states. Any profit from these fees must be turned over to the United States Treasury.

Clause 3 forbids states from keeping an army or navy without the consent of Congress. States cannot make treaties or declare war unless an enemy invades or is about to invade.

2. Powers Conditionally Denied No state shall, without the consent of the Congress, lay any imposts or duties on imports or exports, except what may be absolutely necessary for executing its inspection laws; and the net produce of all duties and imposts, laid by any state on imports or exports, shall be for the use of the Treasury of the United States; and all such laws shall be subject to the revision and control of the Congress.

3. Other Denied Powers No state shall, without the consent of Congress, lay any duty of tonnage, keep troops, or ships of war in time of peace, enter into any agreement or compact with another state, or with a foreign power, or engage in war, unless actually invaded, or in such imminent danger as will not admit of delay.

Article 2. The Executive Branch

Section 1. President and Vice-President

Clause 1 The President is responsible for ***executing,*** or carrying out, laws passed by Congress.

1. Chief Executive The executive power shall be vested in a President of the United States of America. He shall hold his office during the term of four years, and together with the Vice-President, chosen for the same term, be elected as follows:

Clauses 2, 3 Some writers of the Constitution were afraid to allow the people to elect the President directly (page 130). Therefore, the Constitutional Convention set up the electoral college. Clause 2 directs each state to choose electors, or delegates to the electoral college, to vote for President. A state's electoral vote is equal to the combined number of senators and representatives. Each state may decide how to choose its electors. Members of Congress and federal officeholders may not serve as electors. This much of the original electoral college system is still in effect.

Clause 3 called upon each elector to vote for two candidates. The candidate who received a majority of the electoral votes would become President. The runner-up would become Vice President. If no candidate won a majority, the House would choose the President. The Senate would choose the Vice President.

The election of 1800 showed a problem with the original electoral college system (page 189). Thomas Jefferson was the Republican candidate

2. Selection of Electors Each state shall appoint, in such manner as the legislature thereof may direct, a number of electors, equal to the whole number of Senators and Representatives to which the state may be entitled in the Congress; but no Senator or Representative, or person holding an office or trust or profit under the United States, shall be appointed an elector.

3. Electoral College Procedures ~~The electors shall meet in their respective states, and vote by ballot for two persons, of whom one at least shall not be an inhabitant of the same state with themselves. And they shall make a list of all the persons voted for, and of the number of votes for each; which list they shall sign and certify, and transmit sealed to the seat of the government of the United States, directed to the president of the Senate. The president of the Senate shall, in the presence of the Senate and House of Representatives, open all the certificates, and the votes shall then be counted. The person having the greatest number of votes shall be President, if such number be a majority of the whole number of electors appointed; and if~~

~~there be more than one who have such majority, and have an equal number of votes, then the House of Representatives shall immediately choose by ballot one of them for President; and if no person have a majority, then from the five highest on the list the said House shall in like manner choose the President. But in choosing the President the votes shall be taken by states, the representation from each state having one vote. A quorum for this purpose shall consist of a member or members from two-thirds of the states, and a majority of all the states shall be necessary to a choice. In every case, after the choice of the President, the person having the greatest number of votes of the electors shall be the Vice-President. But if there should remain two or more who have equal votes, the Senate shall choose from them by ballot the Vice-President.~~

for President, and Aaron Burr was the Republican candidate for Vice President. In the electoral college, the vote ended in a tie. The election was finally decided in the House, where Jefferson was chosen President. The Twelfth Amendment changed the electoral college system so that this could not happen again.

4. Time of Elections The Congress may determine the time of choosing the electors, and the day on which they shall give their votes; which day shall be the same throughout the United States.

Clause 4 By a law passed in 1792, electors are chosen on the Tuesday after the first Monday of November every four years. Electors from each state meet to vote in December.

Today, voters in each state choose ***slates,*** or groups, of electors who are pledged to a candidate for President. The candidate for President who wins the popular vote in each state wins that state's electoral vote.

5. Qualifications for President No person except a natural-born citizen ~~or a citizen of the United States, at the time of the adoption of this Constitution,~~ shall be eligible to the office of the President; neither shall any person be eligible to that office who shall not have attained to the age of thirty-five years, and been fourteen years a resident within the United States.

Clause 5 The President must be a citizen of the United States from birth, at least 35 years old, and a resident of the country for 14 years. The first seven Presidents of the United States were born under British rule, but they were allowed to hold office because they were citizens at the time the Constitution was adopted.

6. Presidential Succession In case of the removal of the President from office, or of his death, resignation, or inability to discharge the powers and duties of the said office, the same shall devolve on the Vice-President, and the Congress may by law provide for the case of removal, death, resignation, or inability, both of the President and Vice-President, declaring what officer shall then act as President, and such officer shall act accordingly, until the disability be removed, or a President shall be elected.

Clause 6 The powers of the President pass to the Vice President if the President leaves office or cannot discharge his or her duties. The wording of this clause caused confusion the first time a President died in office. When President William Henry Harrison died, it was uncertain whether Vice President John Tyler should remain Vice President and act as President or whether he should be sworn in as President. Tyler persuaded a federal judge to swear him in. So he set the precedent that the Vice President assumes the office of President when it becomes vacant. The Twenty-fifth Amendment replaced this clause.

7. Salary The President shall, at stated times, receive for his services, a compensation, which shall neither be increased nor diminished during the period for which he shall have been elected, and he shall not receive within that period any other emolument from the United States, or any of them.

Clause 7 The President is paid a salary. It cannot be raised or lowered during his or her term of office. The President is not allowed to hold any other federal or state position while in office. Today, the President's salary is $200,000 a year.

8. Oath of Office Before he enter on the execution of his office, he shall take the following oath or affirmation:—"I do solemnly swear (or affirm) that I will faithfully execute the office of President of the United States, and will to the best of my ability, preserve, protect, and defend the Constitution of the United States."

Clause 8 Before taking office, the President must promise to protect and defend the Constitution. Usually, the Chief Justice of the Supreme Court gives the oath of office to the President.

THE CONSTITUTION

Section 2. Powers of the President

1. Commander in Chief of the Armed Forces The President shall be Commander in Chief of the Army and Navy of the United States, and of the militia of the several states, when called into the actual service of the United States; he may require the opinion, in writing, of the principal officer in each of the executive departments, upon any subject relating to the duties of their respective offices, and he shall have power to grant reprieves and pardons for offenses against the United States, except in cases of impeachment.

Clause 1 The President is head of the armed forces and the state militias when they are called into national service. So the military is under ***civilian,*** or nonmilitary, control.

The President can get advice from the heads of executive departments. In most cases, the President has the power to grant a reprieve or pardon. A ***reprieve*** suspends punishment ordered by law. A ***pardon*** prevents prosecution for a crime or overrides the judgment of a court.

2. Making Treaties and Nominations He shall have power, by and with the advice and consent of the Senate, to make treaties, provided two-thirds of the Senators present concur; and he shall nominate, and by and with the advice and consent of the Senate, shall appoint ambassadors, other public ministers and consuls, judges of the Supreme Court, and all other officers of the United States, whose appointments are not herein otherwise provided for, and which shall be established by law; but the Congress may by law vest the appointment of such inferior officers, as they think proper, in the President alone, in the courts of law, or in the heads of departments.

Clause 2 The President has the power to make treaties with other nations. Under the system of checks and balances, all treaties must be approved by two thirds of the Senate. Today, the President also makes agreements with foreign governments. These executive agreements do not need Senate approval.

The President has the power to appoint ambassadors to foreign countries and to appoint other high officials. The Senate must ***confirm,*** or approve, these appointments.

3. Temporary Appointments The President shall have power to fill up all vacancies that may happen during the recess of the Senate, by granting commissions which shall expire at the end of their next session.

Clause 3 If the Senate is in ***recess,*** or not meeting, the President may fill vacant government posts by making temporary appointments.

Section 3. Duties

He shall from time to time give to the Congress information of the state of the Union, and recommend to their consideration such measures as he shall judge necessary and expedient; he may, on extraordinary occasions, convene both houses, or either of them, and in case of disagreement between them, with respect to the time of adjournment, he may adjourn them to such time as he shall think proper; he shall receive ambassadors and other public ministers; he shall take care that the laws be faithfully executed, and shall commission all the officers of the United States.

The President must give Congress a report on the condition of the nation every year. This report is now called the State of the Union Address. Since 1913, the President has given this speech in person each January.

The President can call a special session of Congress and can adjourn Congress if necessary. The President has the power to receive, or recognize, foreign ambassadors.

The President must carry out the laws. Today, many government agencies oversee the execution of laws.

Section 4. Impeachment and Removal From Office

The President, Vice-President, and all civil officers of the United States, shall be removed from office on impeachment for, and conviction of, treason, bribery, or other high crimes or misdemeanors.

Civil officers include federal judges and members of the Cabinet. ***High crimes*** are major crimes. ***Misdemeanors*** are lesser crimes. The President, Vice President, and others can be forced out of office if impeached and found guilty of certain crimes. Andrew Johnson is the only President to have been impeached.

Article 3. The Judicial Branch

Section 1. Federal Courts

The judicial power of the United States shall be vested in one Supreme Court, and in such inferior courts as the Congress may from time to time ordain and establish. The judges, both of the Supreme and inferior courts, shall hold their offices during good behavior, and shall, at stated times, receive for their services a compensation, which shall not be diminished during their continuance in office.

Judicial power is the right of the courts to decide legal cases. The Constitution creates the Supreme Court but lets Congress decide the size of the Supreme Court. Congress has the power to set up inferior, or lower, courts. The Judiciary Act of 1789 (page 173) set up district and circuit courts, or courts of appeal. Today, there are 94 district courts and 13 courts of appeal. All federal judges serve for life.

Section 2. Jurisdiction of Federal Courts

1. Scope of Judicial Power The judicial power shall extend to all cases, in law and equity, arising under this Constitution, the laws of the United States, and treaties made or which shall be made, under their authority; to all cases affecting ambassadors, other public ministers and consuls; to all cases of admiralty and maritime jurisdiction; to controversies to which the United States shall be a party; to controversies between two or more states; ~~between a state and citizens of another state;~~ between citizens of the same state claiming lands under grants of different states, and between a state or the citizens thereof, and foreign states, citizens, or subjects.

Clause 1 ***Jurisdiction*** refers to the right of a court to hear a case. Federal courts have jurisdiction over cases that involve the Constitution, federal laws, treaties, foreign ambassadors and diplomats, naval and maritime laws, disagreements between states or between citizens from different states, and disputes between a state or citizen and a foreign state or citizen.

In *Marbury* v. *Madison,* the Supreme Court established the right to judge whether a law is constitutional (page 197).

2. The Supreme Court In all cases affecting ambassadors, other public ministers and consuls, and those in which a state shall be a party, the Supreme Court shall have original jurisdiction. In all the other cases before mentioned, the Supreme Court shall have appellate jurisdiction, both as to law and fact, with such exceptions, and under such regulations as the Congress shall make.

Clause 2 ***Original jurisdiction*** means the power of a court to hear a case where it first arises. The Supreme Court has original jurisdiction over only a few cases, such as those involving foreign diplomats. More often, the Supreme Court acts as an appellate court. An ***appellate court*** does not decide guilt. It decides whether the lower court trial was properly conducted and reviews the lower court's decision.

3. Trial by Jury The trial of all crimes, except in cases of impeachment, shall be by jury; and such trial shall be held in the state where the said crimes shall have been committed; but when not committed within any state, the trial shall be at such place or places as the Congress may by law have directed.

Clause 3 This clause guarantees the right to a jury trial for anyone accused of a federal crime. The only exceptions are impeachment cases. The trial must be held in the state where the crime was committed.

Section 3. Treason

1. Definition Treason against the United States shall consist only in levying war against them, or in adhering to their enemies, giving them aid and comfort. No person shall be convicted of treason unless on the testimony of two witnesses to the same overt act, or on confession in open court.

Clause 1 Treason is clearly defined. An ***overt act*** is an actual action. A person cannot be convicted of treason for what he or she thinks. A person can be convicted of treason only if he or she confesses or two witnesses testify to it.

2. Punishment The Congress shall have power to declare the punishment of treason, but no attainder of treason shall work corruption of blood or forfeiture except during the life of the person attainted.

Clause 2 Congress has the power to set the punishment for traitors. Congress may not punish the children of convicted traitors by taking away their civil rights or property.

Article 4. Relations Among the States

Section 1. Official Records and Acts

Full faith and credit shall be given in each state to the public acts, records, and judicial proceedings of every other state. And the Congress may by general laws prescribe the manner in which such acts, records, and proceedings shall be proved, and the effect thereof.

Each state must recognize the official acts and records of any other state. For example, each state must recognize marriage certificates issued by another state. Congress can pass laws to ensure this.

Section 2. Privileges of Citizens

1. Privileges The citizens of each state shall be entitled to all privileges and immunities of citizens in the several states.

Clause 1 All states must treat citizens of another state in the same way it treats its own citizens. However, the courts have allowed states to give residents certain privileges, such as lower tuition rates.

2. Extradition A person charged in any state with treason, felony, or other crime, who shall flee from justice, and be found in another state, shall on demand of the executive authority of the state from which he fled, be delivered up, to be removed to the state having jurisdiction of the crime.

Clause 2 **Extradition** means the act of returning a suspected criminal or escaped prisoner to a state where he or she is wanted. State governors must return a suspect to another state. However, the Supreme Court has ruled that a governor cannot be forced to do so if he or she feels that justice will not be done.

3. Return of Fugitive Slaves ~~No person held to service or labor in one state, under the laws thereof, escaping into another, shall in consequence of any law or regulation therein, be discharged from such service or labor, but shall be delivered up on claim of the party to whom such service or labor may be due.~~

Clause 3 ***Persons held to service or labor*** refers to slaves or indentured servants. This clause required states to return runaway slaves to their owners. The Thirteenth Amendment replaces this clause.

Section 3. New States and Territories

1. New States New states may be admitted by the Congress into this Union; but no new state shall be formed or erected within the jurisdiction of any other state; nor any state be formed by the junction of two of more states, or parts of states, without the consent of the legislatures of the states concerned as well as of the Congress.

Clause 1 Congress has the power to admit new states to the Union. Existing states cannot be split up or joined together to form new states unless both Congress and the state legislatures approve. New states are equal to all other states.

2. Federal Lands The Congress shall have power to dispose of and make all needful rules and regulations respecting the territory or other property belonging to the United States; and nothing in this Constitution shall be so construed as to prejudice any claims of the United States, or of any particular state.

Clause 2 Congress can make rules for managing and governing land owned by the United States. This includes territories not organized into states, such as Puerto Rico and Guam, and federal lands within a state.

Section 4. Guarantees to the States

The United States shall guarantee to every state in this Union a republican form of government, and shall protect each of them against invasion; and on application of the legislature, or of the executive (when the legislature cannot be convened) against domestic violence.

In a ***republic,*** voters choose representatives to govern them. The federal government must protect the states from foreign invasion and from ***domestic,*** or internal, disorder if asked to do so by a state.

Article 5. Amending the Constitution

The Congress, whenever two-thirds of both houses shall deem it necessary, shall propose amendments to this Constitution, or, on the application of the legislatures of two-thirds of the several states, shall call a convention for proposing amendments, which, in either case, shall be valid to all intents and purposes, as part of this Constitution, when ratified by the legislatures of three-fourths of the several states, or by conventions in three-fourths thereof, as the one or the other mode of ratification may be proposed by the Congress; provided that ~~no amendments which may be made prior to the year 1808 shall in any manner affect the first and fourth clauses in the Ninth Section of the First Article; and that~~ no state, without its consent, shall be deprived of its equal suffrage in the Senate.

The Constitution can be ***amended,*** or changed, if necessary. An amendment can be proposed by (1) a two-thirds vote of both houses of Congress or (2) a national convention called by Congress at the request of two thirds of the state legislatures. (This second method has never been used.) An amendment must be ***ratified,*** or approved, by (1) three fourths of the state legislatures or (2) special conventions in three fourths of the states. Congress decides which method will be used.

Article 6. National Supremacy

Section 1. Prior Public Debts

All debts contracted and engagements entered into, before the adoption of this Constitution, shall be as valid against the United States under this Constitution, as under the Confederation.

The United States government promised to pay all debts and honor all agreements made under the Articles of Confederation.

Section 2. Supreme Law of the Land

This Constitution, and the laws of the United States which shall be made in pursuance thereof, and all treaties made, or which shall be made, under the authority of the United States, shall be the supreme law of the land; and the judges in every state shall be bound thereby, anything in the constitution or laws of any state to the contrary notwithstanding.

The Constitution, federal laws, and treaties that the Senate has ratified are the supreme, or highest, law of the land. Thus, they outweigh state laws. A state judge must overturn a state law that conflicts with the Constitution or with a federal law.

Section 3. Oaths of Office

The Senators and Representatives before mentioned, and the members of the several state legislatures, and all executive and judicial officers, both of the United States and of the several states, shall be bound by oath or affirmation, to support this Constitution; but no religious test shall ever be required as a qualification to any office or public trust under the United States.

State and federal officeholders take an oath, or solemn promise, to support the Constitution. However, this clause forbids the use of religious tests for officeholders. During the colonial period, every colony except Rhode Island required a religious test for officeholders.

Article 7. Ratification

The ratification of the convention of nine states shall be sufficient for the establishment of the Constitution between the states so ratifying the same.

During 1787 and 1788, states held special conventions. By October 1788, the required nine states had ratified the Constitution.

Done in convention, by the unanimous consent of the states present, the seventeenth day of September, in the year of our Lord one thousand seven hundred and eighty-seven, and of the independence of the United States of America the twelfth. In Witness *whereof, we have hereunto subscribed our names.*

Attest: William Jackson
Secretary

George Washington
President and deputy from Virginia

New Hampshire
John Langdon
Nicholas Gilman

Massachussetts
Nathaniel Gorham
Rufus King

Connecticut
William Samuel Johnson
Roger Sherman

New York
Alexander Hamilton

New Jersey
William Livingston
David Brearley
William Paterson
Jonathan Dayton

Pennsylvania
Benjamin Franklin
Thomas Mifflin
Robert Morris
George Clymer
Thomas Fitzsimons
Jared Ingersoll
James Wilson
Gouverneur Morris

Delaware
George Read
Gunning Bedford, Jr.
John Dickinson
Richard Bassett
Jacob Broom

Maryland
James McHenry
Dan of St. Thomas Jennifer
Daniel Carroll

Virginia
John Blair
James Madison, Jr.

North Carolina
William Blount
Richard Dobbs Spaight
Hugh Williamson

South Carolina
John Rutledge
Charles Cotesworth Pinckney
Charles Pinckney
Pierce Butler

Georgia
William Few
Abraham Baldwin

★ Amendments to the Constitution ★

The first 10 amendments, which were added to the Constitution in 1791, are called the Bill of Rights. Originally, the Bill of Rights applied only to actions of the federal government. However, the Supreme Court has used the due process clause of the Fourteenth Amendment to extend many of the rights to protect individuals against action by the states.

Amendment 1

Freedoms of Religion, Speech, Press, Assembly, and Petition

Congress shall make no law respecting an establishment of religion, or prohibiting the free exercise thereof; or abridging the freedom of speech, or of the press; or the right of the people peaceably to assemble, and to petition the government for a redress of grievances.

Congress cannot set up an established, or official, church or religion for the nation. During the colonial period, most colonies had established churches. However, the authors of the First Amendment wanted to keep government and religion separate.

Congress may not ***abridge,*** or limit, the freedom to speak and write freely. The government may not censor, or review, books and newspapers before they are printed. This amendment also protects the right to assemble, or hold public meetings. ***Petition*** means ask. ***Redress*** means to correct. ***Grievances*** are wrongs. The people have the right to ask the government for wrongs to be corrected.

Amendment 2

Right to Bear Arms

A well-regulated militia, being necessary to the security of a free state, the right of the people to keep and bear arms shall not be infringed.

State militias, such as the National Guard, have the right to bear arms, or keep weapons. Courts have generally ruled that the government can regulate the ownership of guns by private citizens.

Amendment 3

Lodging Troops in Private Homes

No soldier shall, in time of peace, be quartered in any house, without the consent of the owner; nor in time of war, but in a manner to be prescribed by law.

During the colonial period, the British quartered, or housed, soldiers in private homes without the permission of the owners (page 90). This amendment limits the government's right to use private homes to house soldiers.

Amendment 4

Search and Seizure

The right of the people to be secure in their persons, houses, papers, and effects, against unreasonable searches and seizures, shall not be violated; and no warrants shall issue but upon probable cause, supported by oath or affirmation, and particularly describing the place to be searched, and the persons or things to be seized.

This amendment protects Americans from unreasonable searches and seizures. Search and seizure are permitted only if a judge has issued a ***warrant,*** or written court order. A warrant is issued only if there is probable cause. This means an officer must show that it is probable, or likely, that the search will produce evidence of a crime. A search warrant must name the exact place to be searched and the things to be seized. In some cases, courts have ruled that searches can take place without a warrant. For example, police may search a person who is under arrest. However, evidence found during an unlawful search cannot be used in a trial.

Amendment 5

Rights of the Accused

No person shall be held to answer for a capital, or otherwise infamous, crime, unless on a presentment or indictment of a grand jury, except in cases arising in the land or naval forces, or in the militia, when in actual service in time of war or public danger; nor shall any person be subject for the same offense to be twice put in jeopardy of life and limb; nor shall be compelled, in any criminal case, to be a witness against himself; nor be

This amendment protects the rights of the accused. ***Capital crimes*** are those that can be punished with death. ***Infamous crimes*** are those that can be punished with prison or loss of rights. The federal government must obtain an ***indictment,*** or formal accusation, from a grand jury to prosecute anyone for such crimes. A ***grand jury*** is a panel of between 12 and 23 citizens who deprived of life, liberty, or property, without due process of law; nor shall private property be taken for public use, without just compensation.

decide if the government has enough evidence to justify a trial. This procedure prevents prosecution with little or no evidence of guilt. (Soldiers and the militia in wartime are not covered by this rule.)

Double jeopardy is forbidden. This means that a person cannot be tried twice for the same crime—unless a court sets aside a conviction because of a legal error. A person on trial cannot be forced to testify, or give evidence, against himself or herself. A person accused of a crime is entitled to ***due process of law,*** or a fair hearing or trial. Finally, the government cannot seize private property for public use without paying the owner a fair price for it.

Amendment 6

Right to Speedy Trial by Jury

In all criminal prosecutions, the accused shall enjoy the right to a speedy and public trial, by an impartial jury of the state and district wherein the crime shall have been committed, which district shall have been previously ascertained by law, and to be informed of the nature and cause of the accusation; to be confronted with the witnesses against him; to have compulsory process for obtaining witnesses in his favor, and to have the assistance of counsel for his defense.

In criminal cases, the jury must be ***impartial,*** or not favor either side. The accused is guaranteed the right to a trial by jury. The trial must be speedy. If the government purposely postpones the trial so that it becomes hard for the person to get a fair hearing, the charge may be dismissed. The accused must be told the charges against him or her and be allowed to question prosecution witnesses. Witnesses who can help the accused can be ordered to appear in court.

The accused must be allowed a lawyer. Since 1942, the federal government has been required to provide a lawyer if the accused cannot afford one. In 1963, the Supreme Court decided that states must also provide lawyers for a defendant too poor to pay for one.

Amendment 7

Jury Trial in Civil Cases

In suits at common law, where the value in controversy shall exceed $20, the right of trial by jury shall be preserved, and no fact tried by a jury shall be otherwise re-examined in any court of the United States than according to the rules of the common law.

Common law refers to rules of law established by judges in past cases. This amendment guarantees the right to a jury trial in lawsuits where the sum of money at stake is more than $20. An appeals court cannot change a verdict because it disagrees with the decision of the jury. It can set aside a verdict only if legal errors made the trial unfair.

Amendment 8

Bail and Punishment

Excessive bail shall not be required, nor excessive fines imposed, nor cruel and unusual punishments inflicted.

Bail is money the accused leaves with the court as a pledge to appear for trial. If the accused does not appear for trial, the court keeps the money. ***Excessive*** means too high. This amendment forbids courts to set unreasonably high bail. The amount of bail usually depends on the seriousness of the charge and whether the accused is likely to appear for the trial. The amendment also forbids cruel and unusual punishments such as mental and physical abuse.

Amendment 9

Powers Reserved to the People

The enumeration in the Constitution, of certain rights, shall not be construed to deny or disparage others retained by the people.

People have rights not listed in the Constitution. This amendment was added because some people feared that the Bill of Rights would be used to limit rights to those actually listed.

Amendment 10

Powers Reserved to the States

The powers not delegated to the United States by the Constitution, nor prohibited by it to the states, are reserved to the states respectively, or to the people.

This amendment limits the power of the federal government. Powers that are not given to the federal government belong to the states. The powers reserved to the states are not listed in the Constitution.

Amendment 11

Suits Against States

Passed by Congress on March 4, 1794. Ratified on January 23, 1795.

The judicial power of the United States shall not be construed to extend to any suit in law or equity, commenced or prosecuted against one of the United States, by citizens of another state, or by citizens or subjects of any foreign state.

This amendment changed part of Article 3, Section 2, Clause 1. As a result, a private citizen from one state cannot sue the government of another state in federal court. However, a citizen can sue a state government in a state court.

This amendment changed the way the electoral college voted. Before the amendment was adopted, each elector simply voted for two people. The candidate with the most votes became President. The runner-up became Vice President. In the election of 1800, however, a tie vote resulted between Thomas Jefferson and Aaron Burr (page 189).

In such a case, the Constitution required the House of Representatives to elect the President. Federalists had a majority in the House. They tried to keep Jefferson out of office by voting for Burr. It took 35 ballots in the House before Jefferson was elected President.

To keep this from happening again, the Twelfth Amendment was passed and ratified in time for the election of 1804.

This amendment provides that each elector choose one candidate for President and one candidate for Vice President. If no candidate for President receives a majority of electoral votes, the House of Representatives chooses the President. If no candidate for Vice President receives a majority, the Senate elects the Vice President. The Vice President must be a person who is eligible to be President.

This system is still in use today. However, it is possible for a candidate to win the popular vote and lose in the electoral college. This happened in 1876 (pages 419–420).

Amendment 12

Election of President and Vice-President

Passed by Congress on December 9, 1803. Ratified on June 15, 1804.

The electors shall meet in their respective states, and vote by ballot for President and Vice-President, one of whom, at least, shall not be an inhabitant of the same state with themselves; they shall name in their ballots the person voted for as President, and in distinct ballots the person voted for as Vice-President, and they shall make distinct lists of all persons voted for as President, and of all persons voted for as Vice-President, and of the number of votes for each, which lists they shall sign and certify, and transmit, sealed, to the seat of government of the United States, directed to the President of the Senate; the President of the Senate shall, in the presence of the Senate and House of Representatives, open all the certificates and the votes shall then be counted; the person having the greatest number of votes for President shall be the President, if such number be a majority of the whole number of electors appointed; and if no person have such majority, then from the persons having the highest numbers not exceeding three on the list of those voted for as President, the House of Representatives shall choose immediately, by ballot, the President. But in choosing the President, the votes shall be taken by the states, the representation from each state having one vote; a quorum for this purpose shall consist of a member or members from two-thirds of the states, and a majority of all the states shall be necessary to a choice. And if the House of Representatives shall not choose a President whenever the right of choice shall devolve upon them, before the fourth day of March next following, then the Vice-President shall act as President, as in the case of the death or other constitutional disability of the President. The person having the greatest number of votes as Vice-President, shall be the Vice-President, if such number be a majority of the whole number of electors appointed, and if no person have a majority, then, from the two highest numbers on the list, the Senate shall choose the Vice-President; a quorum for the purpose shall consist of two-thirds of the whole number of Senators, and a majority of the whole number shall be necessary to a choice. But no person constitutionally ineligible to the office of President shall be eligible to that of Vice-President of the United States.

The Emancipation Proclamation (1863) freed slaves only in areas controlled by the Confederacy (pages 387–388). This amendment freed all slaves. It also forbids ***involuntary servitude,*** or labor done against one's will. However, it does not prevent prison wardens from making prisoners work.

Section 2 says that Congress can pass laws to carry out this amendment.

Amendment 13

Abolition of Slavery

Passed by Congress on January 31, 1865. Ratified on December 6, 1865.

Section 1. Neither slavery nor involuntary servitude, except as a punishment for crime whereof the party shall have been duly convicted, shall exist within the United States, or any place subject to their jurisdiction.

Section 2. Congress shall have power to enforce this article by appropriate legislation.

Section 1 defines citizenship for the first time in the Constitution, and it extends citizenship to

Amendment 14

Rights of Citizens

Passed by Congress on June 13, 1866. Ratified on July 9, 1868.

Section 1. Citizenship All persons born or naturalized in the United States and subject to the jurisdiction thereof, are citizens of the United States and of the state wherein they reside. No state shall make or enforce any law which shall abridge the privileges or immunities of citizens of the United States; nor shall any state deprive any person of life, liberty, or property, without due process of law; nor deny to any person within its jurisdiction the equal protection of the laws.

blacks. It also prohibits states from denying the rights and privileges of citizenship to any citizen. This section also forbids states to deny due process of law.

Section 1 guarantees all citizens "equal protection under the law." For a long time, however, the Fourteenth Amendment did not protect blacks from discrimination. After Reconstruction, separate facilities for blacks and whites sprang up (page 423). In 1954, the Supreme Court ruled that separate facilities for blacks and whites were by their nature unequal. This ruling, in the case of *Brown* v. *Board of Education,* made school segregation illegal.

Section 2. Apportionment of Representatives Representatives shall be apportioned among the several states according to their respective numbers, counting the whole number of persons in each state, excluding Indians not taxed. But when the right to vote at any election for the choice of electors for President and Vice-President of the United States, Representatives in Congress, the executive and judicial officers of a state, or the members of the legislature thereof, is denied to any of the male inhabitants of such state, being twenty-one years of age and citizens of the United States, or in any way abridged, except for participation in rebellion, or other crime, the basis of representation therein shall be reduced in the proportion which the number of such male citizens shall bear to the whole number of male citizens twenty-one years of age in such state.

Section 2 replaced the three-fifths clause. It provides that representation in the House of Representatives is decided on the basis of the number of people in the state. It also provides that states which deny the vote to male citizens over age 21 will be punished by losing part of their representation in the House. This provision has never been enforced.

Despite this clause, black citizens were often prevented from voting. In the 1960s, federal laws were passed to end voting discrimination.

Section 3. Former Confederate Officials No person shall be a Senator or Representative in Congress, or elector of President and Vice-President, or hold any office, civil or military, under the United States, or under any state, who, having previously taken an oath, as a member of Congress, or as an officer of the United States, or as a member of any state legislature, or as an executive or judicial officer of any state, to support the Constitution of the United States, shall have engaged in insurrection or rebellion against the same, or given aid or comfort to the enemies thereof. But Congress may, by vote of two-thirds of each house, remove such disability.

This section prohibited people who had been federal or state officials before the Civil War and who had joined the Confederate cause from serving again as government officials. In 1872, Congress restored the rights of former Confederate officials.

Section 4. Government Debt The validity of the public debt of the United States, authorized by law, including debts incurred for payment of pensions and bounties for services in suppressing insurrection or rebellion, shall not be questioned. But neither the United States nor any state shall assume or pay any debt or obligation incurred in aid of insurrection or rebellion against the United States or any claim for the loss or emancipation of any slave; but all such debts, obligations, and claims shall be held illegal and void.

This section recognized that the United States must repay its debts from the Civil War. However, it forbade the repayment of debts of the Confederacy. This meant that people who had loaned money to the Confederacy would not be repaid. Also, states were not allowed to pay former slave owners for the loss of slaves.

Section 5. Enforcement The Congress shall have power to enforce, by appropriate legislation, the provisions of this article.

Congress can pass laws to carry out this amendment.

Amendment 15

Voting Rights

Passed by Congress on February 26, 1869. Ratified on February 2, 1870.

Section 1. Extending the Right to Vote The right of citizens of the United States to vote shall not be denied or abridged by the United States or any state on account of race, color, or previous condition of servitude.

Previous condition of servitude refers to slavery. This amendment gave blacks, both former slaves and free blacks, the right to vote. In the late 1800s, southern states used grandfather clauses, literacy tests, and poll taxes to keep blacks from voting (pages 421–422).

Congress can pass laws to carry out this amendment. The Twenty-fourth Amendment barred the use of poll taxes in national elections. The Voting Rights Act of 1965 gave federal officials the power to register voters in places where there was voting discrimination.

Section 2. Enforcement The Congress shall have power to enforce this article by appropriate legislation.

Amendment 16

The Income Tax

Passed by Congress on July 12, 1909. Ratified on February 3, 1913.

Congress has the power to collect taxes on people's income. An income tax can be collected without regard to a state's population. This amendment changed Article 1, Section 9, Clause 4.

The Congress shall have power to lay and collect taxes on incomes, from whatever source derived, without apportionment among the several states, and without regard to any census or enumeration.

Amendment 17

Direct Election of Senators

Passed by Congress on May 13, 1912. Ratified on April 8, 1913.

This amendment replaced Article 1, Section 2, Clause 1. Before it was adopted, state legislatures chose senators. This amendment provides that senators are directly elected by the people of each state.

Section 1. Method of Election The Senate of the United States shall be composed of two Senators from each state, elected by the people thereof, for six years; and each Senator shall have one vote. The electors in each state shall have the qualifications requisite for electors of the most numerous branch of the state legislatures.

When a Senate seat becomes vacant, the governor of the state must order an election to fill the seat. The state legislature can give the governor power to fill the seat until an election is held.

Section 2. Vacancies When vacancies happen in the representation of any state in the Senate, the executive authority of such state shall issue writs of election to fill such vacancies: *Provided* that the legislature of any state may empower the executive thereof to make temporary appointments until the people fill the vacancies by election as the legislature may direct.

Senators who had already been elected by the state legislatures were not affected by this amendment.

Section 3. Exception ~~This amendment shall not be so construed as to affect the election or term of any Senator chosen before it becomes valid as part of the Constitution.~~

Amendment 18

Prohibition of Alcoholic Beverages

Passed by Congress on December 18, 1917. Ratified on January 16, 1919.

This amendment, known as ***Prohibition,*** banned the making, selling, or transporting of alcoholic beverages in the United States. Later, the Twenty-first Amendment ***repealed,*** or canceled, this amendment.

Section 1. Ban on Alcohol ~~After one year from the ratification of this article the manufacture, sale, or transportation of intoxicating liquors within, the importation thereof into, or the exportation thereof from, the United States and all territory subject to the jurisdiction thereof for beverage purposes is hereby prohibited.~~

Both the states and the federal government had the power to pass laws to enforce this amendment.

Section 2. Enforcement ~~The Congress and the several states shall have concurrent power to enforce this article by appropriate legislation.~~

This amendment had to be approved within seven years. The Eighteenth Amendment was the first amendment to include a time limit for ratification.

Section 3. Method of Ratification ~~This article shall be inoperative unless it shall have been ratified as an amendment to the Constitution by the legislatures of the several states, as provided in the Constitution, within seven years from the date of the submission hereof to the states by the Congress.~~

Amendment 19

Women's Suffrage

Passed by Congress on June 4, 1919. Ratified on August 18, 1920.

Neither the federal government nor state governments can deny the right to vote on account of sex. Thus, women won ***suffrage,*** or the right to vote. Before 1920, some states had allowed women to vote in state elections.

Section 1. The Right to Vote The right of citizens of the United States to vote shall not be denied or abridged by the United States or by any state on account of sex.

Congress can pass laws to carry out this amendment.

Section 2. Enforcement Congress shall have power to enforce this article by appropriate legislation.

Amendment 20

Presidential Terms; Sessions of Congress

Passed by Congress on March 2, 1932. Ratified on January 23, 1933.

Section 1. Beginning of Term The terms of the President and Vice-President shall end at noon on the 20th day of January, and the terms of Senators and Representatives at noon on the 3rd day of January, of the years in which such terms would have ended if this article had not been ratified; and the terms of their successors shall then begin.

The date for the President and Vice President to take office is January 20. Members of Congress begin their terms of office on January 3. Before this amendment was adopted, these terms of office began on March 4.

Section 2. Congressional Sessions The Congress shall assemble at least once in every year, and such meeting shall begin at noon on the 3rd day of January, unless they shall by law appoint a different day.

Congress must meet at least once a year. The new session of Congress begins on January 3. Before this amendment, members of Congress who had been defeated in November continued to hold office until the following March. Such members were known as ***lame ducks.***

Section 3. Presidential Succession If at the time fixed for the beginning of the term of the President, the President-elect shall have died, the Vice-President-elect shall become President. If a President shall not have been chosen before the time fixed for the beginning of his term, or if the President-elect shall have failed to qualify, then the Vice-President-elect shall act as President until a President shall have qualified; and the Congress may by law provide for the case wherein neither a President-elect nor a Vice-President-elect shall have qualified, declaring who shall then act as President, or the manner in which one who is to act shall be selected, and such person shall act accordingly until a President or Vice-President shall have qualified.

By Section 3, if the President-elect dies before taking office, the Vice President-elect becomes President. If no President has been chosen by January 20 or if the elected candidate fails to qualify for office, the Vice President-elect acts as President, but only until a qualified President is chosen.

Finally, Congress can choose a person to act as President if neither the President-elect nor Vice President-elect is qualified to take office.

Section 4. Elections Decided by Congress The Congress may by law provide for the case of the death of any of the persons from whom the House of Representatives may choose a President whenever the right of choice shall have devolved upon them, and for the case of the death of any of the persons from whom the Senate may choose a Vice-President whenever the right of choice shall have devolved upon them.

Congress can pass laws in cases where a presidential candidate dies while an election is being decided in the House. Congress has similar power in cases where a candidate for Vice President dies while an election is being decided in the Senate.

Section 5. Date of Effect ~~Sections 1 and 2 shall take effect on the 15th day of October following the ratification of this article.~~

Section 5 sets the date for the amendment to become effective.

Section 6. Ratification Period ~~This article shall be inoperative unless it shall have been ratified as an amendment to the Constitution by the legislatures of three-fourths of the several states within seven years from the date of its submission.~~

Section 6 sets a time limit for ratification.

Amendment 21

Repeal of Prohibition

Passed by Congress on February 20, 1933. Ratified on December 5, 1933.

Section 1. Repeal of National Prohibition The eighteenth article of amendment to the Constitution of the United States is hereby repealed.

The Eighteenth Amendment is repealed, making it legal to make and sell alcoholic beverages. Prohibition ended December 5, 1933.

Section 2. State Laws The transportation or importation into any state, territory, or possession of the United States for delivery or use therein of intoxicating liquors, in violation of the laws thereof, is hereby prohibited.

Each state was free to ban the making and selling of alcoholic drink within its borders. This section makes bringing liquor into a "dry" state a federal offense.

Section 3. Ratification Period ~~This article shall be inoperative unless it shall have been ratified as an amendment to the Constitution by conventions in the several states, as provided in the Constitution, within seven years from the date of the submission hereof to the states by the Congress.~~

Special state conventions were called to ratify this amendment. This is the only time an amendment was ratified by state conventions rather than state legislatures.

Amendment 22

Limit on Number of President's Terms

Passed by Congress on March 12, 1947. Ratified on March 1, 1951.

Before Franklin Roosevelt became President, no President served more than two terms in office. Roosevelt broke with this custom and was elected to four terms. This amendment provides that no President may serve more than two terms. A President who has already served more than half of someone else's term can serve only one more full term. However, the amendment did not apply to Harry Truman, who had become President after Franklin Roosevelt's death in 1945.

Section 1. Two-Term Limit No person shall be elected to the office of the President more than twice, and no person who has held the office of President, or acted as President, for more than two years of a term to which some other person was elected President shall be elected to the office of the President more than once. ~~But this Article shall not apply to any person holding the office of President when this Article was proposed by the Congress, and shall not prevent any person who may be holding the office of President, or acting as President, during the term within which this Article becomes operative from holding the office of President or acting as President during the remainder of such term.~~

A seven-year time limit is set for ratification.

Section 2. Ratification Period ~~This Article shall be inoperative unless it shall have been ratified as an amendment to the Constitution by the legislatures of three-fourths of the several states within seven years from the date of its submission to the states by the Congress.~~

Amendment 23

Presidential Electors for District of Columbia

Passed by Congress on June 16, 1960. Ratified on April 3, 1961.

This amendment gives residents of Washington, D.C., the right to vote in presidential elections. Until this amendment was adopted, people living in Washington, D.C., could not vote for President because the Constitution had made no provision for choosing electors from the nation's capital. Washington, D.C., has three electoral votes.

Section 1. Determining the Number of Electors The District constituting the seat of Government of the United States shall appoint in such manner as the Congress may direct: A number of electors of President and Vice-President equal to the whole number of Senators and Representatives in Congress to which the District would be entitled if it were a State, but in no event more than the least populous State; they shall be in addition to those appointed by the States, but they shall be considered, for the purposes of the election of President and Vice-President, to be electors appointed by a State; and they shall meet in the District and perform such duties as provided by the twelfth article of amendment.

Congress can pass laws to carry out this amendment.

Section 2. Enforcement The Congress shall have power to enforce this article by appropriate legislation.

Amendment 24

Abolition of Poll Tax in National Elections

Passed by Congress on August 27, 1962. Ratified on January 23, 1964.

A ***poll tax*** is a tax on voters. This amendment bans poll taxes in national elections. Some states used poll taxes to keep blacks from voting. In 1966, the Supreme Court struck down poll taxes in state elections, also.

Section 1. Poll Tax Banned The right of citizens of the United States to vote in any primary or other election for President or Vice-President, for electors for President or Vice-President, or for Senator or Representative in Congress, shall not be denied or abridged by the United States or any state by reason of failure to pay any poll tax or other tax.

Congress can pass laws to carry out this amendment.

Section 2. Enforcement The Congress shall have the power to enforce this article by appropriate legislation.

Amendment 25

Presidential Succession and Disability

Passed by Congress on July 6, 1965. Ratified on February 11, 1967.

If the President dies or resigns, the Vice President becomes President. This section clarifies Article 2, Section 1, Clause 6.

Section 1. President's Death or Resignation In case of the removal of the President from office or his death or resignation, the Vice-President shall become President.

Section 2. Vacancies in Vice-Presidency Whenever there is a vacancy in the office of the Vice-President, the President shall nominate a Vice-President who shall take the office upon confirmation by a majority vote of both houses of Congress.

When a Vice President takes over the office of President, he or she appoints a Vice President who must be approved by a majority vote of both houses of Congress. This section was first applied after Vice President Spiro Agnew resigned in 1973. President Richard Nixon appointed Gerald Ford as Vice President.

Section 3. Disability of the President Whenever the President transmits to the President pro tempore of the Senate and the Speaker of the House of Representatives his written declaration that he is unable to discharge the powers and duties of his office, and until he transmits to them a written declaration to the contrary, such powers and duties shall be discharged by the Vice-President as Acting President.

If the President declares in writing that he or she is unable to perform the duties of office, the Vice President serves as Acting President until the President recovers.

Section 4. Whenever the Vice-President and a majority of either the principal officers of the executive departments or of such other body as Congress may by law provide, transmit to the President *pro tempore* of the Senate and the Speaker of the House of Representatives their written declaration that the President is unable to discharge the powers and duties of his office, the Vice-President shall immediately assume the powers and duties of the office as Acting President.

Thereafter, when the President transmits to the President *pro tempore* of the Senate and the Speaker of the House of Representatives his written declaration that no inability exists, he shall resume the powers and duties of his office unless the Vice-President and a majority of either the principal officers of the executive department or of such other body as Congress may by law provide, transmit within four days to the President *as* of the Senate and the Speaker of the House of Representatives their written declaration that the President is unable to discharge the powers and duties of his office. Thereupon Congress shall decide the issue, assembling within 48 hours for that purpose if not in session. If the Congress, within 21 days after receipt of the latter written declaration, or, if Congress is not in session, within 21 days after Congress is required to assemble, determines by two-thirds vote of both houses that the President is unable to discharge the powers and duties of his office, the Vice-President shall continue to discharge the same as Acting President; otherwise, the President shall assume the powers and duties of his office.

Two Presidents, Woodrow Wilson and Dwight Eisenhower, have fallen gravely ill while in office. The Constitution contained no provision for this kind of emergency.

Section 3 provided that the President can inform Congress that he or she is too sick to perform the duties of office. However, if the President is unconscious or refuses to admit to a disabling illness, Section 4 provides that the Vice President and Cabinet may declare the President disabled. The Vice President becomes Acting President until the President can return to the duties of office. In case of a disagreement between the President and the Vice President and Cabinet over the President's ability to perform the duties of office, Congress must decide the issue. A two-thirds vote of both houses is needed to decide that the President is disabled or unable to fulfill the duties of office.

Amendment 26

Voting Age

Passed by Congress on March 23, 1971. Ratified on July 1, 1971.

Section 1. Lowering of Voting Age The right of citizens of the United States, who are 18 years of age or older, to vote shall not be denied or abridged by the United States or any state on account of age.

In 1970, Congress passed a law allowing 18-year-olds to vote. However, the Supreme Court decided that Congress could not set a minimum age for state elections. So this amendment was passed and ratified.

Section 2. Enforcement The Congress shall have the power to enforce this article by appropriate legislation.

Congress can pass laws to carry out this amendment.

Amendment 27

Congressional Pay Increases

Ratified on May 7, 1992.

No law varying the compensation for the services of the Senators and Representatives shall take effect, until an election of Representatives shall have intervened.

If members of Congress vote themselves a pay increase, it cannot go into effect until after the next congressional election.

★ Presidents of the United States ★

1 George Washington
(1732–1799)

Years in office:
1789–1797
Party:
none
Elected from:
Virginia
Vice President:
John Adams

2 John Adams
(1735–1826)

Years in office:
1797–1801
Party:
Federalist
Elected from:
Massachusetts
Vice President:
Thomas Jefferson

3 Thomas Jefferson
(1743–1826)

Years in office:
1801–1809
Party:
Democratic Republican
Elected from:
Virginia
Vice President:
1) Aaron Burr,
2) George Clinton

4 James Madison
(1751–1836)

Years in office:
1809–1817
Party:
Democratic Republican
Elected from:
Virginia
Vice President:
1) George Clinton,
2) Elbridge Gerry

5 James Monroe
(1758–1831)

Years in office:
1817–1825
Party:
Democratic Republican
Elected from:
Virginia
Vice President:
Daniel Tompkins

6 John Quincy Adams
(1767–1848)

Years in office:
1825–1829
Party:
National Republican
Elected from:
Massachusetts
Vice President:
John Calhoun

7 Andrew Jackson
(1767–1845)

Years in office:
1829–1837
Party:
Democratic
Elected from:
Tennessee
Vice President:
1) John Calhoun,
2) Martin Van Buren

8 Martin Van Buren
(1782–1862)

Years in office:
1837–1841
Party:
Democratic
Elected from:
New York
Vice President:
Richard Johnson

9 William Henry Harrison*
(1773–1841)

Years in office:
1841
Party:
Whig
Elected from:
Ohio
Vice President:
John Tyler

10 John Tyler
(1790–1862)

Years in office:
1841–1845
Party:
Whig
Elected from:
Virginia
Vice President:
none

11 James K. Polk
(1795–1849)

Years in Office:
1845–1849
Party:
Democratic
Elected from:
Tennessee
Vice President:
George Dallas

12 Zachary Taylor*
(1784–1850)

Years in office:
1849–1850
Party:
Whig
Elected from:
Louisiana
Vice President:
Millard Fillmore

***Died in office**

13 Millard Fillmore
(1800–1874)

Years in office: 1850–1853
Party: Whig
Elected from: New York
Vice President: none

14 Franklin Pierce
(1804–1869)

Years in office: 1853–1857
Party: Democratic
Elected from: New Hampshire
Vice President: William King

15 James Buchanan
(1791–1868)

Years in office: 1857–1861
Party: Democratic
Elected from: Pennsylvania
Vice President: John Breckinridge

16 Abraham Lincoln**
(1809–1865)

Years in office: 1861–1865
Party: Republican
Elected from: Illinois
Vice President: 1) Hannibal Hamlin, 2) Andrew Johnson

17 Andrew Johnson
(1808–1875)

Years in office: 1865–1869
Party: Republican
Elected from: Tennessee
Vice President: none

18 Ulysses S. Grant
(1822–1885)

Years in office: 1869–1877
Party: Republican
Elected from: Illinois
Vice President: 1) Schuyler Colfax, 2) Henry Wilson

19 Rutherford B. Hayes
(1822–1893)

Years in office: 1877–1881
Party: Republican
Elected from: Ohio
Vice President: William Wheeler

20 James A. Garfield**
(1831–1881)

Years in office: 1881
Party: Republican
Elected from: Ohio
Vice President: Chester A. Arthur

21 Chester A. Arthur
(1830–1886)

Years in office: 1881–1885
Party: Republican
Elected from: New York
Vice President: none

22 Grover Cleveland
(1837–1908)

Years in office: 1885–1889
Party: Democratic
Elected from: New York
Vice President: Thomas Hendricks

23 Benjamin Harrison
(1833–1901)

Years in office: 1889–1893
Party: Republican
Elected from: Indiana
Vice President: Levi Morton

24 Grover Cleveland
(1837–1908)

Years in office: 1893–1897
Party: Democratic
Elected from: New York
Vice President: Adlai Stevenson

**Assassinated

25 William McKinley**
(1843–1901)

Years in office: 1897–1901
Party: Republican
Elected from: Ohio
Vice President: 1) Garret Hobart, 2) Theodore Roosevelt

26 Theodore Roosevelt
(1858–1919)

Years in office: 1901–1909
Party: Republican
Elected from: New York
Vice President: Charles Fairbanks

27 William Howard Taft
(1857–1930)

Years in office: 1909–1913
Party: Republican
Elected from: Ohio
Vice President: James Sherman

28 Woodrow Wilson
(1856–1924)

Years in office: 1913–1921
Party: Democratic
Elected from: New Jersey
Vice President: Thomas Marshall

29 Warren G. Harding*
(1865–1923)

Years in office: 1921–1923
Party: Republican
Elected from: Ohio
Vice President: Calvin Coolidge

30 Calvin Coolidge
(1872–1933)

Years in office: 1923–1929
Party: Republican
Elected from: Massachusetts
Vice President: Charles Dawes

31 Herbert C. Hoover
(1874–1964)

Years in office: 1929–1933
Party: Republican
Elected from: California
Vice President: Charles Curtis

32 Franklin D. Roosevelt*
(1882–1945)

Years in office: 1933–1945
Party: Democratic
Elected from: New York
Vice President: 1) John Garner, 2) Henry Wallace, 3) Harry S. Truman

33 Harry S. Truman
(1884–1972)

Years in office: 1945–1953
Party: Democratic
Elected from: Missouri
Vice President: Alben Barkley

34 Dwight D. Eisenhower
(1890–1969)

Years in office: 1953–1961
Party: Republican
Elected from: New York
Vice President: Richard M. Nixon

35 John F. Kennedy**
(1917–1963)

Years in office: 1961–1963
Party: Democratic
Elected from: Massachusetts
Vice President: Lyndon B. Johnson

36 Lyndon B. Johnson
(1908–1973)

Years in office: 1963–1969
Party: Democratic
Elected from: Texas
Vice President: Hubert Humphrey

*Died in office
**Assassinated

37 Richard M. Nixon***
(1913–1994)

Years in office: 1969–1974
Party: Republican
Elected from: New York
Vice President: 1) Spiro Agnew, 2) Gerald R. Ford

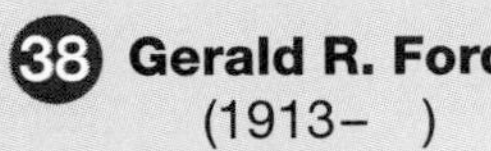

38 Gerald R. Ford
(1913–)

Years in office: 1974–1977
Party: Republican
Elected from: Michigan
Vice President: Nelson Rockefeller

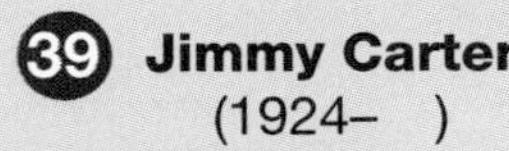

39 Jimmy Carter
(1924–)

Years in office: 1977–1981
Party: Democratic
Elected from: Georgia
Vice President: Walter Mondale

40 Ronald W. Reagan
(1911–)

Years in office: 1981–1989
Party: Republican
Elected from: California
Vice President: George H.W. Bush

41 George H.W. Bush
(1924–)

Years in office: 1989–1993
Party: Republican
Elected from: Texas
Vice President: J. Danforth Quayle

42 William J. Clinton
(1946–)

Years in office: 1993–
Party: Democratic
Elected from: Arkansas
Vice President: Albert Gore, Jr.

***Resigned

★ The Fifty States ★

State	Date of Entry to Union (Order of Entry)	Land Area in Square Miles	Population (In Thousands)	Number of Representatives in House	Capital	Largest City
Alabama	1819 (22)	50,750	4,219	7	Montgomery	Birmingham
Alaska	1959 (49)	570,374	606	1	Juneau	Anchorage
Arizona	1912 (48)	113,642	4,075	6	Phoenix	Phoenix
Arkansas	1836 (25)	52,075	2,453	4	Little Rock	Little Rock
California	1850 (31)	155,973	31,431	52	Sacramento	Los Angeles
Colorado	1876 (38)	103,730	3,656	6	Denver	Denver
Connecticut	1788 (5)	4,845	3,275	6	Hartford	Bridgeport
Delaware	1787 (1)	1,955	706	1	Dover	Wilmington
Florida	1845 (27)	53,997	13,953	23	Tallahassee	Jacksonville
Georgia	1788 (4)	57,919	7,055	11	Atlanta	Atlanta
Hawaii	1959 (50)	6,423	1,179	2	Honolulu	Honolulu
Idaho	1890 (43)	82,751	1,133	2	Boise	Boise
Illinois	1818 (21)	55,593	11,752	20	Springfield	Chicago
Indiana	1816 (19)	35,870	5,752	10	Indianapolis	Indianapolis
Iowa	1846 (29)	55,875	2,829	5	Des Moines	Des Moines
Kansas	1861 (34)	81,823	2,554	4	Topeka	Wichita
Kentucky	1792 (15)	39,732	3,827	6	Frankfort	Louisville
Louisiana	1812 (18)	43,566	4,315	7	Baton Rouge	New Orleans
Maine	1820 (23)	30,865	1,240	2	Augusta	Portland
Maryland	1788 (7)	9,775	5,006	8	Annapolis	Baltimore
Massachusetts	1788 (6)	7,838	6,041	10	Boston	Boston
Michigan	1837 (26)	56,809	9,496	16	Lansing	Detroit
Minnesota	1858 (32)	79,617	4,567	8	St. Paul	Minneapolis
Mississippi	1817 (20)	46,914	2,669	5	Jackson	Jackson
Missouri	1821 (24)	68,898	5,278	9	Jefferson City	Kansas City
Montana	1889 (41)	145,556	856	1	Helena	Billings
Nebraska	1867 (37)	76,878	1,623	3	Lincoln	Omaha
Nevada	1864 (36)	109,806	1,457	2	Carson City	Las Vegas
New Hampshire	1788 (9)	8,969	1,137	2	Concord	Manchester
New Jersey	1787 (3)	7,419	7,904	13	Trenton	Newark
New Mexico	1912 (47)	121,365	1,654	3	Santa Fe	Albuquerque
New York	1788 (11)	47,224	18,169	31	Albany	New York
North Carolina	1789 (12)	48,718	7,070	12	Raleigh	Charlotte
North Dakota	1889 (39)	68,994	638	1	Bismarck	Fargo
Ohio	1803 (17)	40,953	11,102	19	Columbus	Columbus
Oklahoma	1907 (46)	68,679	3,258	6	Oklahoma City	Oklahoma City
Oregon	1859 (33)	96,003	3,086	5	Salem	Portland
Pennsylvania	1787 (2)	44,820	12,052	21	Harrisburg	Philadelphia
Rhode Island	1790 (13)	1,045	997	2	Providence	Providence
South Carolina	1788 (8)	30,111	3,664	6	Columbia	Columbia
South Dakota	1889 (40)	75,898	721	1	Pierre	Sioux Falls
Tennessee	1796 (16)	41,220	5,175	9	Nashville	Memphis
Texas	1845 (28)	261,914	18,378	30	Austin	Houston
Utah	1896 (45)	82,168	1,908	3	Salt Lake City	Salt Lake City
Vermont	1791 (14)	9,249	580	1	Montpelier	Burlington
Virginia	1788 (10)	39,598	6,552	11	Richmond	Virginia Beach
Washington	1889 (42)	66,582	5,343	9	Olympia	Seattle
West Virginia	1863 (35)	24,087	1,822	3	Charleston	Charleston
Wisconsin	1848 (30)	54,314	5,082	9	Madison	Milwaukee
Wyoming	1890 (44)	97,105	476	1	Cheyenne	Cheyenne
District of Columbia		61	570	1 (nonvoting)		

Self-Governing Areas, Possessions, and Dependencies	Land Area in Square Miles	Population (In Thousands)	Capital
Puerto Rico	3,515	3,522	San Juan
Guam	209	133	Agana
U.S. Virgin Islands	132	102	Charlotte Amalie
American Samoa	77	52	Pago Pago

Sources: *Department of Commerce, Bureau of the Census, 1997 Information Please Almanac*

★ State Flags ★

Alabama
Alaska
Arizona
Arkansas
California
Colorado
Connecticut
Delaware
Florida
Georgia
Hawaii
Idaho
Illinois
Indiana
Iowa
Kansas
Kentucky
Louisiana
Maine
Maryland
Massachusetts
Michigan
Minnesota
Mississippi
Missouri
Montana
Nebraska
Nevada
New Hampshire
New Jersey
New Mexico
New York
North Carolina
North Dakota
Ohio
Oklahoma
Oregon
Pennsylvania
Rhode Island
South Carolina
South Dakota
Tennessee
Texas
Utah
Vermont
Virginia
Washington
West Virginia
Wisconsin
Wyoming

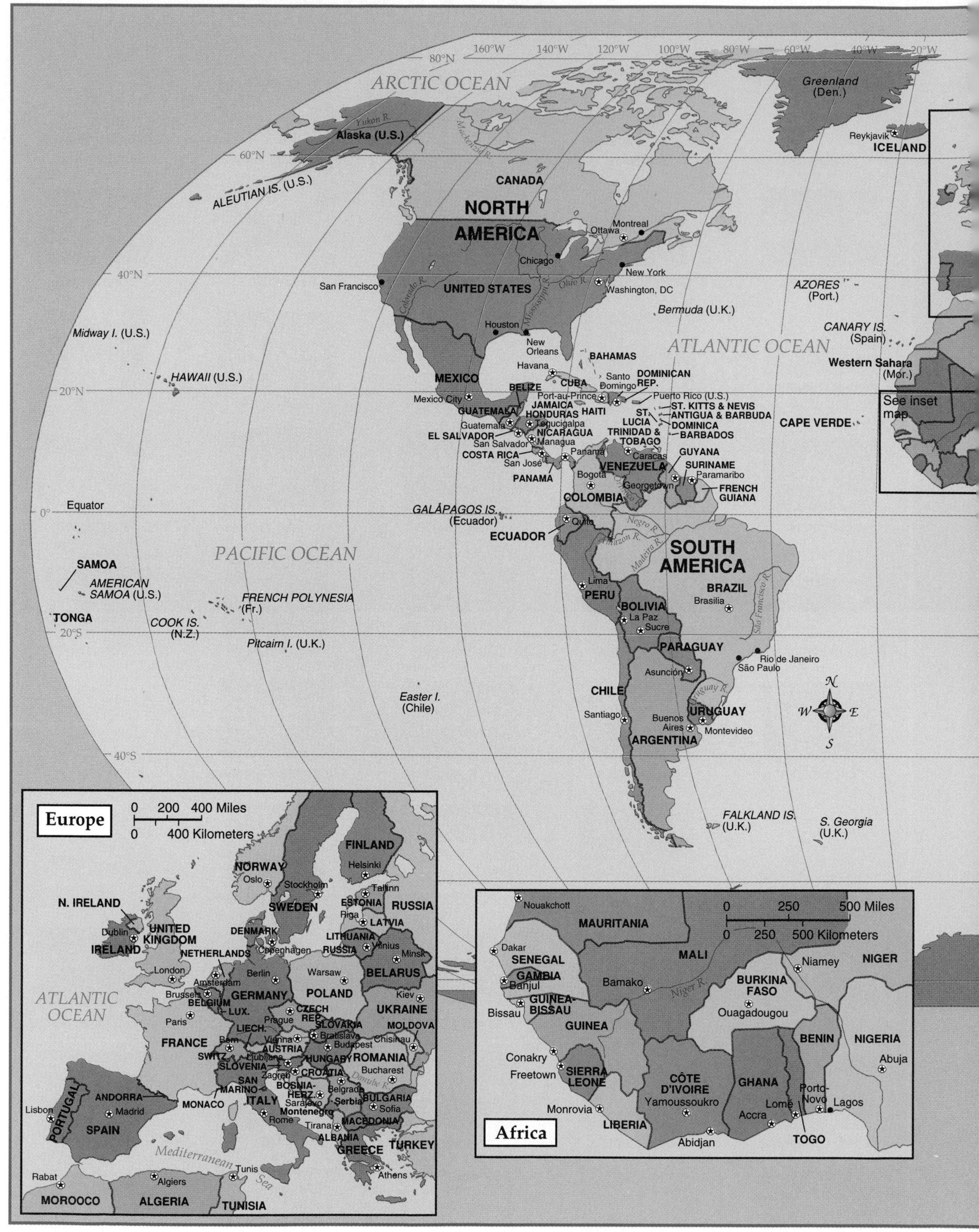
ARCTIC OCEAN
Greenland (Den.)
Reykjavik
ICELAND
Alaska (U.S.)
Yukon R.
ALEUTIAN IS. (U.S.)
CANADA
NORTH AMERICA
Ottawa
Montreal
Chicago
New York
Washington, DC
San Francisco
UNITED STATES
Houston
New Orleans
Bermuda (U.K.)
AZORES (Port.)
CANARY IS. (Spain)
Western Sahara (Mor.)
ATLANTIC OCEAN
Midway I. (U.S.)
HAWAII (U.S.)
BAHAMAS
Havana
CUBA
MEXICO
Mexico City
Santo Domingo
DOMINICAN REP.
BELIZE
Port-au-Prince
HAITI
Puerto Rico (U.S.)
JAMAICA
ST. KITTS & NEVIS
ANTIGUA & BARBUDA
DOMINICA
BARBADOS
ST. LUCIA
GUATEMALA
HONDURAS
Guatemala
Tegucigalpa
EL SALVADOR
NICARAGUA
San Salvador
Managua
TRINIDAD & TOBAGO
COSTA RICA
San José
PANAMA
Panama
Caracas
GUYANA
SURINAME
Paramaribo
FRENCH GUIANA
VENEZUELA
Bogotá
Georgetown
COLOMBIA
CAPE VERDE
See inset map.
Equator
GALÁPAGOS IS. (Ecuador)
Quito
ECUADOR
PACIFIC OCEAN
SOUTH AMERICA
BRAZIL
Brasília
SAMOA
AMERICAN SAMOA (U.S.)
FRENCH POLYNESIA (Fr.)
TONGA
COOK IS. (N.Z.)
Pitcairn I. (U.K.)
Lima
PERU
BOLIVIA
La Paz
Sucre
PARAGUAY
Asunción
Rio de Janeiro
São Paulo
Easter I. (Chile)
CHILE
Santiago
Buenos Aires
URUGUAY
Montevideo
ARGENTINA
N
W
E
S
FALKLAND IS. (U.K.)
S. Georgia (U.K.)
80°N
60°N
40°N
20°N
0°
20°S
40°S
160°W
140°W
120°W
100°W
80°W
60°W
40°W
20°W
Europe
0 200 400 Miles
0 400 Kilometers
FINLAND
Helsinki
NORWAY
Oslo
Stockholm
Tallinn
N. IRELAND
SWEDEN
ESTONIA
RUSSIA
Riga
LATVIA
Dublin
UNITED KINGDOM
DENMARK
LITHUANIA
IRELAND
NETHERLANDS
Copenhagen
RUSSIA
Vilnius
Minsk
London
Berlin
Warsaw
BELARUS
Amsterdam
ATLANTIC OCEAN
Brussels
BELGIUM
GERMANY
POLAND
LUX.
CZECH REP.
UKRAINE
Kiev
Paris
Prague
SLOVAKIA
MOLDOVA
LIECH.
Vienna
Bratislava
Chisinau
FRANCE
Bern
AUSTRIA
Budapest
SWITZ.
Ljubljana
HUNGARY
ROMANIA
SLOVENIA
Zagreb
CROATIA
Bucharest
SAN MARINO
BOSNIA-HERZ.
Belgrade
ANDORRA
Serbia
BULGARIA
Madrid
MONACO
ITALY
Sarajevo
Sofia
Lisbon
PORTUGAL
Montenegro
SPAIN
Rome
Tirana
MACEDONIA
ALBANIA
GREECE
TURKEY
Mediterranean Sea
Tunis
Athens
Rabat
Algiers
MOROOCO
ALGERIA
TUNISIA
Africa
0 250 500 Miles
0 250 500 Kilometers
Nouakchott
MAURITANIA
Dakar
SENEGAL
MALI
Niamey
NIGER
GAMBIA
Banjul
Bamako
Niger R.
BURKINA FASO
GUINEA-BISSAU
Bissau
Ouagadougou
GUINEA
BENIN
NIGERIA
Conakry
Abuja
Freetown
SIERRA LEONE
CÔTE D'IVOIRE
GHANA
Porto-Novo
Yamoussoukro
Lagos
Monrovia
Lomé
LIBERIA
Accra
Abidjan
TOGO

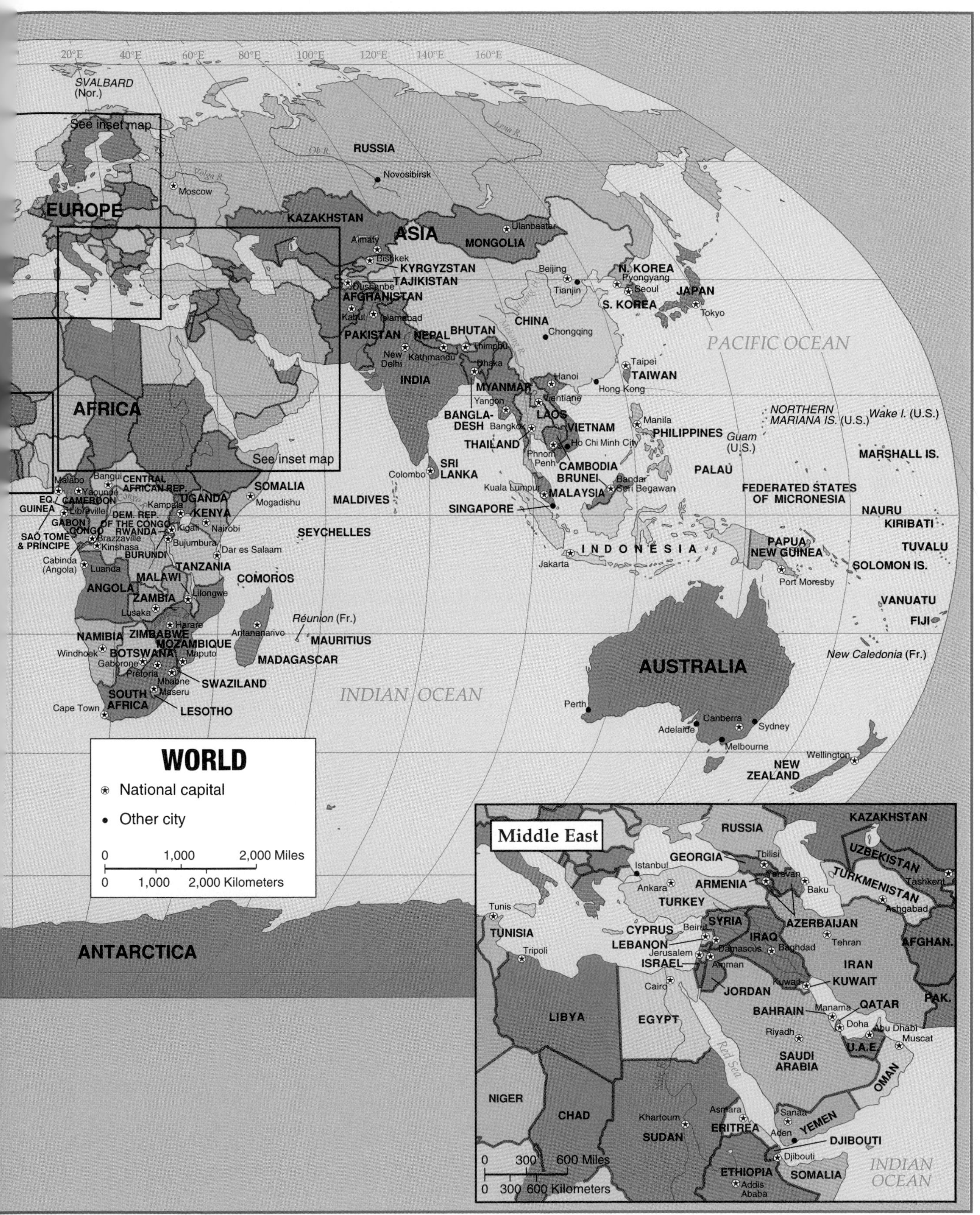

WORLD
National capital
Other city
0 1,000 2,000 Miles
0 1,000 2,000 Kilometers
RUSSIA
EUROPE
ASIA
AFRICA
AUSTRALIA
ANTARCTICA
PACIFIC OCEAN
INDIAN OCEAN
See inset map
Middle East

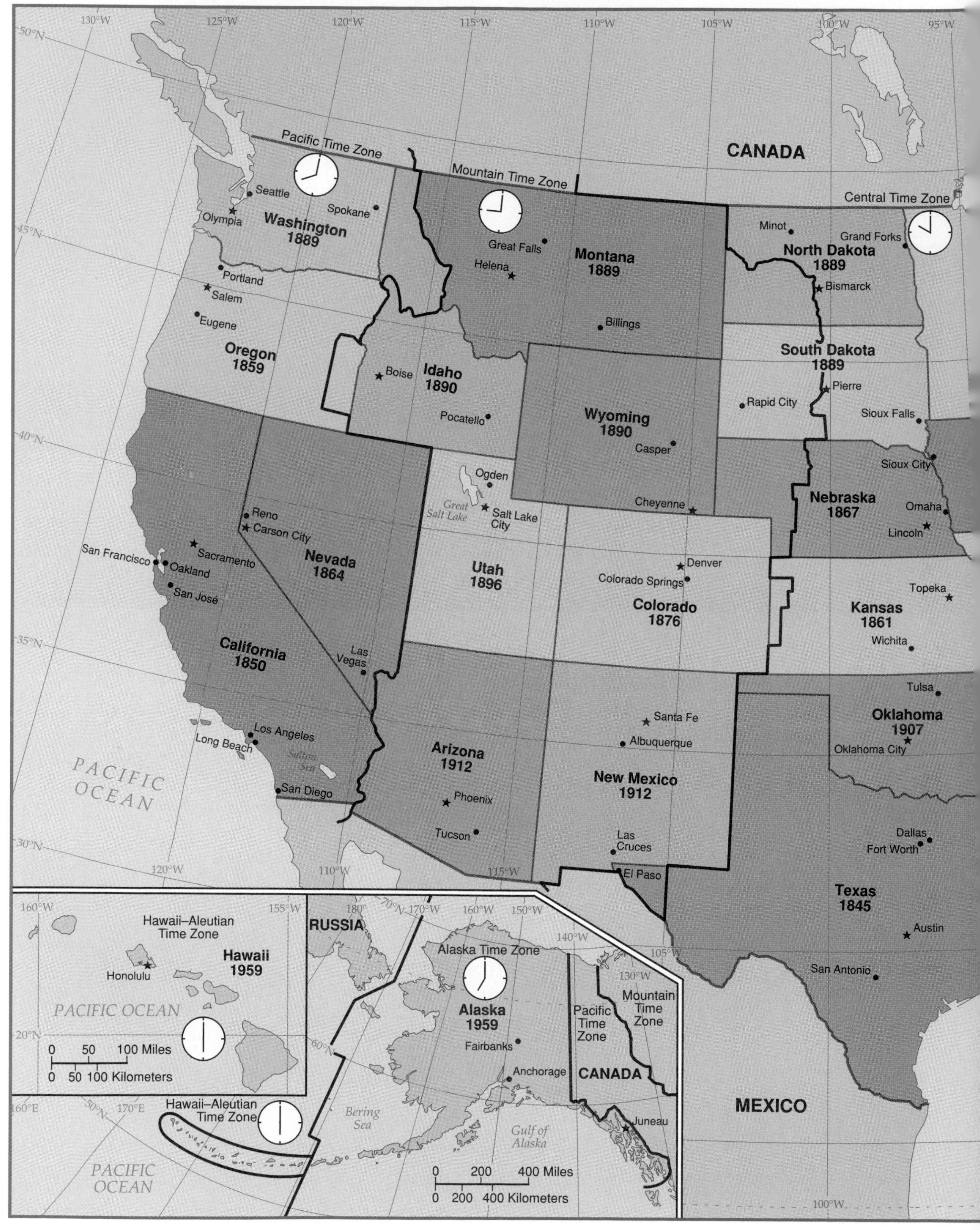

CANADA
Pacific Time Zone
Mountain Time Zone
Central Time Zone
Seattle
Olympia
Spokane
Washington 1889
Portland
Salem
Eugene
Oregon 1859
Great Falls
Helena
Montana 1889
Billings
Minot
Grand Forks
North Dakota 1889
Bismarck
South Dakota 1889
Pierre
Rapid City
Sioux Falls
Boise
Idaho 1890
Pocatello
Wyoming 1890
Casper
Cheyenne
Sioux City
Nebraska 1867
Omaha
Lincoln
Ogden
Great Salt Lake
Salt Lake City
Reno
Carson City
Nevada 1864
San Francisco
Oakland
Sacramento
San José
Utah 1896
Denver
Colorado Springs
Colorado 1876
Topeka
Kansas 1861
Wichita
California 1850
Las Vegas
Los Angeles
Long Beach
Salton Sea
San Diego
PACIFIC OCEAN
Arizona 1912
Phoenix
Tucson
Santa Fe
Albuquerque
New Mexico 1912
Las Cruces
El Paso
Tulsa
Oklahoma 1907
Oklahoma City
Dallas
Fort Worth
Texas 1845
Austin
San Antonio
MEXICO
Hawaii–Aleutian Time Zone
Hawaii 1959
Honolulu
PACIFIC OCEAN
0 50 100 Miles
0 50 100 Kilometers
RUSSIA
Alaska Time Zone
Alaska 1959
Fairbanks
Anchorage
Pacific Time Zone
Mountain Time Zone
CANADA
Juneau
Bering Sea
Gulf of Alaska
Hawaii–Aleutian Time Zone
PACIFIC OCEAN
0 200 400 Miles
0 200 400 Kilometers

THE UNITED STATES
National capital
State capital
Other city
1787 Year of admission to the Union
Boundaries of time zones
0 150 300 Miles
0 150 300 Kilometers
CANADA
Atlantic Time Zone
Eastern Time Zone
ATLANTIC OCEAN
Gulf of Mexico
Lake Superior
Lake Michigan
Lake Huron
Lake Ontario
Lake Erie
Lake Pontchartrain
Lake Okeechobee
Tropic of Cancer
Minnesota 1858
Wisconsin 1848
Michigan 1837
Iowa 1846
Illinois 1818
Indiana 1816
Ohio 1803
Missouri 1821
Kentucky 1792
Tennessee 1796
Arkansas 1836
Mississippi 1817
Alabama 1819
Georgia 1788
Louisiana 1812
Florida 1845
South Carolina 1788
North Carolina 1789
Virginia 1788
West Virginia 1863
Pennsylvania 1787
New York 1788
Vermont 1791
Maine 1820
New Hampshire 1788
Massachusetts 1788
Rhode Island 1790
Connecticut 1788
New Jersey 1787
Delaware 1787
Maryland 1788
Duluth
St. Paul
Minneapolis
Green Bay
Milwaukee
Madison
Des Moines
Chicago
Gary
Peoria
Springfield
Fort Wayne
Indianapolis
Grand Rapids
Lansing
Detroit
Toledo
Cleveland
Akron
Columbus
Cincinnati
Kansas City
St. Louis
Jefferson City
Springfield
Louisville
Frankfort
Lexington
Huntington
Charleston
Nashville
Knoxville
Memphis
Fort Smith
Little Rock
Birmingham
Montgomery
Jackson
Shreveport
Baton Rouge
New Orleans
Houston
Mobile
Pensacola
Tallahassee
Atlanta
Macon
Columbus
Savannah
Jacksonville
Tampa
Miami
Columbia
Charleston
Charlotte
Winston-Salem
Greensboro
Raleigh
Richmond
Norfolk
Washington, DC
Baltimore
Annapolis
Dover
Wilmington
Philadelphia
Harrisburg
Pittsburgh
Trenton
Newark
Jersey City
New York
Hartford
Providence
Boston
Albany
Rochester
Buffalo
Burlington
Montpelier
Concord
Manchester
Augusta
Lewiston
Portland
Bangor
90°W
85°W
80°W
75°W
70°W
65°W
60°W
95°W
50°N
45°N
40°N
35°N
30°N
25°N
20°N

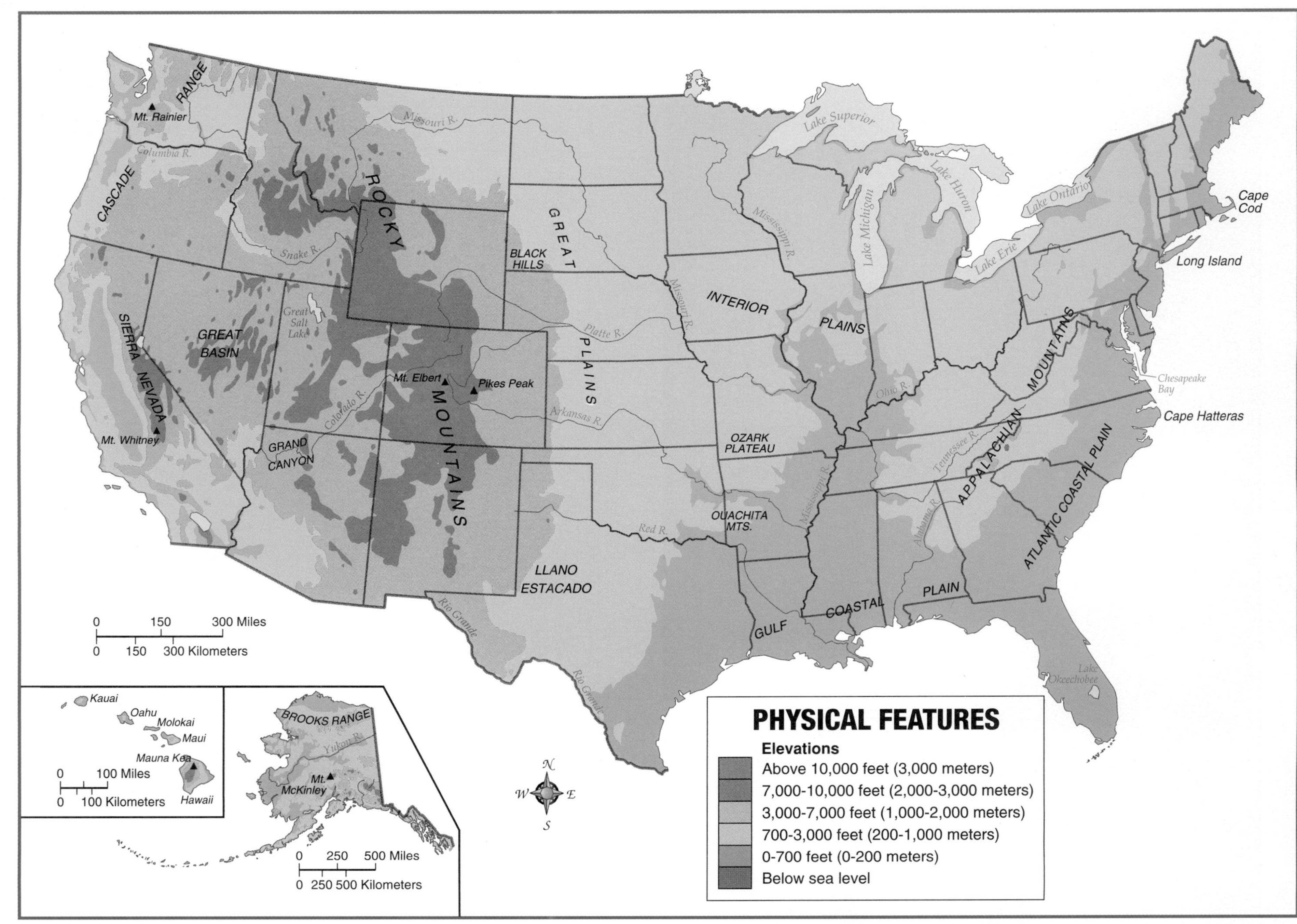
PHYSICAL FEATURES
Elevations
Above 10,000 feet (3,000 meters)
7,000-10,000 feet (2,000-3,000 meters)
3,000-7,000 feet (1,000-2,000 meters)
700-3,000 feet (200-1,000 meters)
0-700 feet (0-200 meters)
Below sea level
CASCADE RANGE
Mt. Rainier
Columbia R.
Missouri R.
Snake R.
ROCKY MOUNTAINS
Mt. Elbert
Pikes Peak
Great Salt Lake
GREAT BASIN
SIERRA NEVADA
Mt. Whitney
Colorado R.
GRAND CANYON
BLACK HILLS
GREAT PLAINS
Platte R.
Arkansas R.
LLANO ESTACADO
Rio Grande
Red R.
INTERIOR PLAINS
Mississippi R.
Lake Superior
Lake Michigan
Lake Huron
Lake Erie
Lake Ontario
OZARK PLATEAU
OUACHITA MTS.
Ohio R.
Tennessee R.
Alabama R.
APPALACHIAN MOUNTAINS
ATLANTIC COASTAL PLAIN
GULF COASTAL PLAIN
Cape Cod
Long Island
Chesapeake Bay
Cape Hatteras
Lake Okeechobee
0 150 300 Miles
0 150 300 Kilometers
N W E S
Kauai
Oahu
Molokai
Maui
Mauna Kea
Hawaii
0 100 Miles
0 100 Kilometers
BROOKS RANGE
Yukon R.
Mt. McKinley
0 250 500 Miles
0 250 500 Kilometers

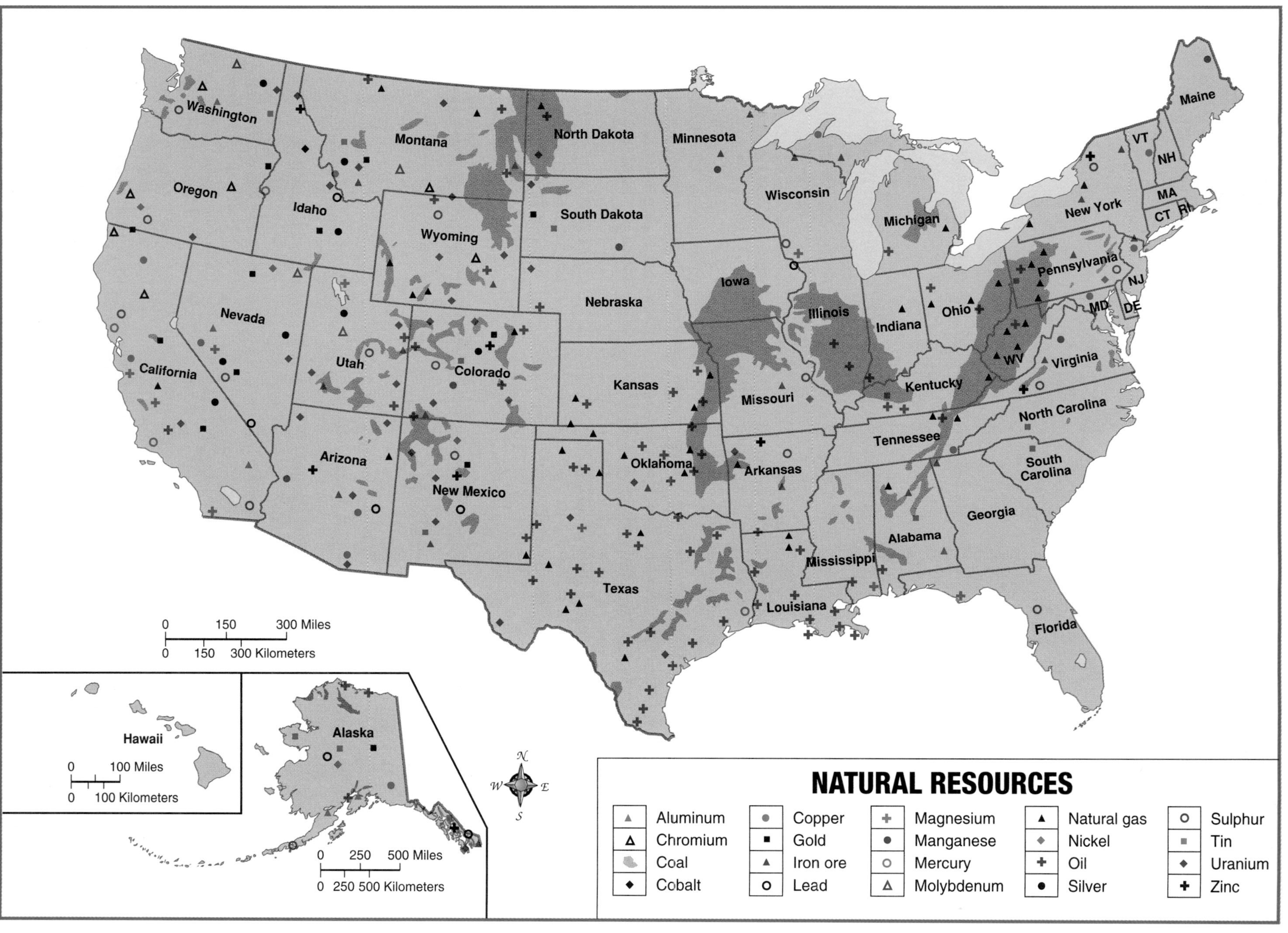

Washington
Oregon
California
Nevada
Idaho
Montana
Wyoming
Utah
Arizona
Colorado
New Mexico
North Dakota
South Dakota
Nebraska
Kansas
Oklahoma
Texas
Minnesota
Iowa
Missouri
Arkansas
Louisiana
Wisconsin
Illinois
Michigan
Indiana
Ohio
Kentucky
Tennessee
Mississippi
Alabama
Georgia
Florida
South Carolina
North Carolina
Virginia
WV
Pennsylvania
New York
MD
DE
NJ
VT
NH
MA
CT
RI
Maine
0 150 300 Miles
0 150 300 Kilometers
Hawaii
0 100 Miles
0 100 Kilometers
Alaska
0 250 500 Miles
0 250 500 Kilometers
N
W
E
S
NATURAL RESOURCES
Aluminum
Chromium
Coal
Cobalt
Copper
Gold
Iron ore
Lead
Magnesium
Manganese
Mercury
Molybdenum
Natural gas
Nickel
Oil
Silver
Sulphur
Tin
Uranium
Zinc

★ Gazetteer of American History ★

This gazetteer, or geographic dictionary, lists places that are important in American history. The approximate latitude and longitude are given for cities, towns, and other specific locations. See text page 10 for information about latitude and longitude. In the Gazetteer, after the description of each place, there are usually two numbers in parentheses. The first number refers to the text page where you can find out more about the place. The second appears in slanted, or *italic,* type and refers to a map *(m)* where the place is shown.

A

Abilene (39°N/97°W) Former cow town in Kansas at the end of the Chisholm Trail. (p. 441, *m438*)
Africa Second largest continent in the world. (p. 12, *m10*)
Alabama 22nd state. Nicknamed the Heart of Dixie or the Cotton State. (p. 756, *m760–761*)
Alamo (29°N/99°W) Mission in San Antonio, Texas, where 183 rebels died during the Texas war for independence. (p. 280, *m280*)
Alaska 49th state. Purchased from Russia in 1867. (p. 756, *m760–761*)
Amiens (50°N/2°E) World War I battle site in northeastern France. (p. 585, *m585*)
Appalachian Mountains Heavily forested mountain chain that stretches from Georgia to Maine and Canada. (p. 16, *m19*)
Appomattox Courthouse (37°N/79°W) Town in Virginia where Lee surrendered to Grant on April 9, 1865. (p. 401, *m400*)
Argentina Country in South America. Gained independence from Spain in 1816. (p. 241, *m242*)
Argonne Forest (49°N/6°E) World War I battle site in northeastern France (p. 588, *m585*)
Arizona 48th state. Nicknamed the Grand Canyon State. (p. 756, *m760–761*)
Arkansas 25th state. Nicknamed the Land of Opportunity. (p. 756, *m760–761*)
Armenia Country in southwest Europe. (p. 486, *m758–759*)
Asia Largest of the world's continents. (p. 12, *m10*)
Atlanta (34°N/84°W) Capital and largest city of Georgia. Burned by Sherman during the Civil War. (p. 400, *m388*)
Atlantic Ocean World's second largest ocean. (p. 14, *m10*)
Austria-Hungary One of the Central Powers in World War I. Divided into several countries after 1918. (p. 570, *m574*)

B

Baltimore (39°N/77°W) Port city in Maryland. (p. 215, *m214*)
Belleau Wood (49°N/3°E) World War I battle site in northeastern France. (p. 586, *m585*)
Boston (42°N/71°W) Seaport and industrial city in Massachusetts. (p. 17, *m68*)
Brazil Largest country in South America. Gained independence from Portugal in 1822. (p. 241, *m242*)
Buena Vista (26°N/101°W) Site of an American victory in the Mexican War. (p. 290, *m289*)
Buffalo (43°N/79°W) City in New York State on Lake Erie. (p. 235, *m234*)

C

California 31st state. Nicknamed the Golden State. Ceded to the United States by Mexico in 1848. (p. 756, *m760–761*)
Canada Northern neighbor of the United States. Second largest nation in the world. (p. 46, *m758–759*)
Canadian Shield Lowland region that lies mostly in eastern Canada. (p. 17, *m19*)
Caribbean Sea Tropical sea in the Western Hemisphere (p. 38, *m39*)
Chancellorsville (38°N/78°W) Site of a Confederate victory in 1863. (p. 386, *m382*)
Château-Thierry (49°N/3°E) World War I battle site in northeastern France. (p. 585, *m585*)
Chesapeake Bay Large inlet of the Atlantic Ocean in Virginia and Maryland. (p. 215, *m214*)
Chicago (42°N/88°W) City in Illinois on Lake Michigan. (p. 5, *m760–761*)
China Country in East Asia. (p. 488, *m758–759*)
Chisholm Trail Cattle trail from Texas to the railroad at Abilene, Kansas. (p. 440, *m438*)
Coastal Plains Region consisting of the Atlantic Plain and the Gulf Plain along the Gulf of Mexico. (p. 17, *m19*)
Colombia Country in South America. (p. 559, *m563*)
Colorado 38th state. Nicknamed the Centennial State. (p. 756, *m760–761*)
Colorado River Begins in Rocky Mountains and flows into Gulf of California. Forms border between California and Arizona. (p. 18, *m19*)
Columbia River Chief river of the Pacific Northwest. (p. 203, *m201*)
Connecticut One of the original 13 states. Nicknamed the Constitution State or the Nutmeg State. (p. 756, *m760–761*)

Cuba (22°N/79°W) Island nation in the Caribbean. Gained independence from Spain in 1898. (p. 552, *m554*)

D

Delaware One of the original 13 states. Nicknamed the First State or the Diamond State. (p. 756, *m760–761*)
Delaware River Flows into the Atlantic Ocean through Delaware Bay. (p. 100, *m106*)
Detroit (42°N/83°W) Largest city in Michigan. (p. 213, *m214*)
District of Columbia Located on the Potomac River. Seat of the federal government of the United States. (p. 175, *m760–761*)
Dominican Republic Country in the Caribbean. Invaded by the United States in 1916. (p. 564, *m563*)

E

England Part of Great Britain. (p. 37, *m47*)
Equator Line of latitude labeled 0°. Separates the Northern and Southern Hemispheres. (p. 10, *m10*)
Erie Canal Linked the Hudson and Mohawk rivers with Buffalo and Lake Erie. Built between 1817 and 1825. (p. 234, *m234*)
Europe World's second smallest continent. (p. 12, *m10*)

F

Florida 27th state. Nicknamed the Sunshine State. (p. 756, *m760–761*)
Fort Donelson (37°N/88°W) Located in Tennessee. Captured by Grant in 1862. (p. 386, *m398*)
Fort Henry (37°N/88°W) Located in Tennessee. Captured by Grant in 1862. (p. 386, *m398*)
Fort Sumter (33°N/80°W) Guarded Charleston harbor in South Carolina. First shots of the Civil War fired there in 1861. (p. 371, *m398*)
Fort Ticonderoga (44°N/74°W) Fort at the south end of Lake Champlain. Captured from the British by Ethan Allen in 1775. (p. 92, *m106*)
France Country in Western Europe. (p. 37, *m758–759*)
Fredericksburg (38°N/78°W) Located in eastern Virginia. Site of a Confederate victory in 1862. (p. 385, *m382*)

G

Gadsden Purchase Land purchased from Mexico in 1853. Now part of Arizona and New Mexico. (p. 291, *m291*)
Georgia One of the original 13 states. Nicknamed the Peach State or the Empire State of the South. (p. 756, *m760–761*)
Germany Country in central Europe. (p. 570, *m574*)
Gettysburg (40°N/77°W) Town in southern Pennsylvania. Site of a Union victory in 1863 and Lincoln's Gettysburg Address. (p. 397, *m382*)
Goliad (29°N//97°W) Texas town where Mexicans killed several hundred Texans during the Texas war for independence (p. 283, *m280*)
Gonzales (29°N/97°W) City in Texas near San Antonio. Site of the first Texan victory over Mexico in 1835. (p. 280, *m280*)
Great Britain Island nation of Western Europe. Includes England, Scotland, Wales, and Northern Ireland. (p. 82, *m758–759*)
Great Lakes Group of freshwater lakes in the heart of the United States. (p. 18, *m19*)
Great Plains Western part of the Interior Plains. (p. 16, *m19*)
Great Wagon Road Early pioneer route across the Appalachians. (p. 229, *m231*)
Greece Country in southeastern Europe. (p. 487, *m758–759*)
Guam (14°N/143°E) Territory of the United States. Acquired from Spain in 1898. (p. 556, *m548*)
Gulf of Mexico Body of water along the southern coast of the United States. (p. 17, *m19*)

H

Haiti Country in the West Indies. Won independence from France in the early 1800s. (p. 198, *m758–759*)
Harpers Ferry (39°N/78°W) Town in West Virginia. John Brown raided the arsenal there in 1859. (p. 366, *m382*)
Hawaii Newest of the 50 states. Nicknamed the Aloha State. (p. 756, *m760–761*)
Hawaiian Islands Region in the Pacific Ocean composed of a group of eight large islands and many small islands. (p. 17, *m19*)
Hudson River Largest river in New York State. (p. 61, *m68*)

I

Idaho 43rd state. Nicknamed the Gem State. Acquired as part of the Oregon Territory. (p. 756, *m760–761*)
Illinois 21st state. Nicknamed the Inland Empire. Settled as part of the Northwest Territory. (p. 756, *m760–761*)
Indiana 19th state. Nicknamed the Hoosier State. Settled as part of the Northwest Territory. (p. 756, *m760–761*)
Interior Plains Region of the central United States that stretches from the Rockies to the Appalachians. (p. 16, *m19*)
Intermountain Region Rugged and mostly dry region from the Rocky Mountains to the Sierra Nevada and coastal mountains of the western United States. (p. 15, *m19*)
Iowa 29th state. Nicknamed the Hawkeye State. Acquired as part of the Louisiana Purchase. (p. 756, *m760–761*)
Isthmus of Panama Narrow strip of land joining North and South America. (p. 559, *m560*)

Italy Country in southern Europe. (p. 489, *m758–759*)

J

Jamestown (37°N/77°W) First successful English colony in North America. (p. 56, *m68*)
Japan Nation in East Asia. Opened up to trade with the West by Commodore Matthew Perry. (p. 544, *m548*)

K

Kansas 34th state. Nicknamed the Sunflower State. Acquired as part of the Louisiana Purchase. (p. 756, *m760–761*)
Kentucky 15th state. Nicknamed the Bluegrass State. (p. 756, *m760–761*)

L

Lake Erie One of the Great Lakes. Site of an American victory in the War of 1812. (p. 213, *m214*)
Lancaster Turnpike Road built in the 1790s linking Philadelphia and Lancaster, Pennsylvania. (p. 230, *m231*)
Latin America Name for those parts of the Western Hemisphere where Latin languages such as Spanish, French, and Portuguese are spoken. Includes Mexico, Central and South America, and the West Indies. (p. 240, *m242*)
Lexington (42°N/71°W) Site of the first clash between minutemen and British troops in 1775. (p. 91, *m106*)
Liberia Country in West Africa. Set up in 1822 as a colony for free African Americans. (p. 331, *m758–759*)
Little Bighorn Site of a Lakota and Cheyenne victory over Custer in 1876. (p. 447, *m446*)
Long Island Located in New York. Site of a British victory in the Revolution. (p. 100, *m106*)
Los Angeles (34°N/118°W) City in southern California. First settled by Spanish missionaries. (p. 15, *m39*)
Louisiana 18th state. Nicknamed the Pelican State. First state created out of the Louisiana Purchase. (p. 756, *m760–761*)

M

Maine 23rd state. Nicknamed the Pine Tree State. Originally part of Massachusetts. (p. 756, *m760–761*)
Marne River (48°N/4°E) Located in France. Site of heavy fighting in World War I. (p. 585, *m585*)
Maryland One of the original 13 states. Nicknamed the Old Line State or the Free State. (p. 756, *m760–761*)
Massachusetts One of the original 13 states. Nicknamed the Bay State or the Old Colony. (p. 756, *m760–761*)
Memphis (35°N/90°W) City in Tennessee on the Mississippi River. Captured by Union forces in 1862. (p. 386, *m398*)
Mexican Cession Lands acquired from Mexico under the Treaty of Guadalupe Hidalgo in 1848. (p. 291, *m291*)
Mexico Southern neighbor of the United States. Gained independence from Spain in 1821. (p. 240, *m758–759*)
Mexico City (19°N/99°W) Capital of Mexico. (p. 362, *m361*)
Michigan 26th state. Nicknamed the Great Lake State or the Wolverine State. Settled as part of the Northwest Territory. (p. 756, *m760–761*)
Middle East Region at the eastern end of the Mediterranean Sea. (p. 36, *m758–759*)
Minnesota 32nd state. Nicknamed the Gopher State. Most of it was acquired as part of the Louisiana Purchase. (p. 756, *m760–761*)
Mississippi 20th state. Nicknamed the Magnolia State. (p. 756, *m760–761*)
Mississippi River Longest river in the United States. Links the Great Lakes with the Gulf of Mexico. (p. 17, *m19*)
Missouri 24th state. Nicknamed the Show Me State. Acquired as part of the Louisiana Purchase. (p. 756, *m760–761*)
Missouri Compromise line Line drawn across the Louisiana Purchase at latitude 36°/30°N to divide free states from slave states. (p. 352, *m359*)
Missouri River Second longest river in the United States. Rises in the northern Rocky Mountains and joins the Mississippi River near St. Louis. (p. 17, *m19*)
Montana 41st state. Nicknamed the Treasure State. Acquired in part through the Louisiana Purchase. (p. 756, *m760–761*)

N

National Road Early road to the West that began in Cumberland, Maryland. (p. 231, *m231*)
Nauvoo (41°N/91°W) Town founded by the Mormons in Illinois in the 1840s. (p. 293, *m294*)
Nebraska 37th state. Nicknamed the Cornhusker State. Acquired as part of the Louisiana Purchase. (p. 756, *m760–761*)
Nevada 36th state. Nicknamed the Sagebrush State or the Battle Born State. Acquired at the end of the Mexican War. (p. 756, *m760–761*)
New France Colony established by France in North America. (p. 48, *m47*)
New Hampshire One of the original 13 states. Nicknamed the Granite State. (p. 756, *m760–761*)
New Jersey One of the original 13 states. Nicknamed the Garden State. (p. 756, *m760–761*)

New Mexico 47th state. Nicknamed the Land of Enchantment. Acquired at the end of the Mexican War. (p. 756, *m760–761*)
New Orleans (30°N/90°W) Port city in Louisiana near the mouth of the Mississippi River. Settled by the French in the 1600s. (p. 50, *m47*)
New York One of the original 13 states. Nicknamed the Empire State. (p. 756, *m760–761*)
New York City (41°N/74°W) Port city at the mouth of the Hudson River. (p. 17, *m68*)
North America World's third largest continent. (p. 14, *m10*)
North Carolina One of the original 13 states. Nicknamed the Tar Heel State or the Old North State. (p. 756, *m760–761*)
North Dakota 39th state. Nicknamed the Sioux State or the Flickertail State. Acquired as part of the Louisiana Purchase. (p. 756, *m760–761*)
Northwest Territory Name for lands north of the Ohio River and east of the Mississippi River. Acquired by the Treaty of Paris in 1783. (p. 118, *m119*)
Nueces River Claimed by Mexico in the Mexican War as the southern border of Texas. (p. 289, *m289*)

O

Ohio 17th state. Nicknamed the Buckeye State. Settled as part of the Northwest Territory. (p. 756, *m760–761*)
Oklahoma 46th State. Nicknamed the Sooner State. Acquired as part of the Louisiana Purchase. (p. 756, *m760–761*)
Oregon 33rd state. Nicknamed the Beaver State. Acquired as part of the Oregon Territory. (p. 756, *m760–761*)
Oregon Country Area in the Pacific Northwest. Claimed by the United States, Britain, Spain, and Russia in the early 1800s. (p. 274, *m275*)
Oregon Trail Overland route from Independence, Missouri, to the Columbia River valley. (p. 277, *m275*)

P

Pacific Coast Highest and most rugged region of the United States. Includes the Cascades and the Sierra Nevada. (p. 15, *m19*)
Pacific Ocean World's largest ocean. (p. 14, *m10*)
Panama Country on the isthmus separating North and South America. Gained independence from Colombia in 1903. (p. 559, *m563*)
Panama Canal Canal dug through the Isthmus of Panama to link the Atlantic and Pacific oceans. (p. 560, *m560*)
Pennsylvania One of the original 13 states. Nicknamed the Keystone State. (p. 756, *m760–761*)
Petersburg (37°N/78°W) City in Virginia. Union forces kept the city under siege for nine months during the Civil War. (p. 400, *m400*)
Philadelphia (40°N/75°W) Major port and chief city in Pennsylvania. (p. 175, *m68*)
Philippine Islands (14°N/125°E) Group of islands in the Pacific Ocean. Acquired by the United States in 1898. Gained independence in 1946. (p. 554, *m554*)
Pikes Peak (39°N/105°W) Mountain located in the Rocky Mountains of central Colorado. (p. 203, *m201*)
Plymouth (42°N/71°W) New England colony founded in 1620 by Pilgrims. (p. 57, *m68*)
Portugal Country in Western Europe. (p. 37, *m42*)
Potomac River Forms part of the Maryland-Virginia border. Flows through Washington, D.C., and into Chesapeake Bay. (p. 383, *m382*)
Prime Meridian Line of longitude labeled 0°. (p. 10, *m10*)
Princeton (40°N/75°W) City in New Jersey. Site of an American victory during the Revolution. (p. 100, *m106*)
Promontory Point (42°N/112°W) Place where the Central Pacific and Union Pacific railroads were joined to form the first transcontinental railroad. (p. 439, *m448*)
Puerto Rico (18°N/67°W) Island in the Caribbean Sea. A self-governing commonwealth of the United States. (p. 552, *m554*)

Q

Quebec (47°N/71°W) City in eastern Canada on the St. Lawrence River. (p. 48, *m47*)

R

Rhode Island One of the original 13 states. Nicknamed Little Rhody or the Ocean State. (p. 756, *m760–761*)
Richmond (38°N/78°W) Capital of Virginia. Capital of the Confederacy during the Civil War. (p. 381, *m382*)
Rio Grande River that forms the border between the United States and Mexico. (p. 18, *m19*)
Rocky Mountains Mountains extending through the western United States. (p. 16, *m19*)
Russia Largest country in the world, spanning Europe and Asia. (p. 486, *m758–759*)

S

Sacramento (39°N/122°W) Capital of California. Developed as a gold rush boom town. (p. 295, *m294*)

St. Augustine (30°N/81°W) City in Florida. Founded by Spain in 1565. Oldest European settlement in the United States. (p. 39, *m39*)
St. Lawrence River Waterway from the Great Lakes to the Atlantic Ocean. Forms part of the border between the United States and Canada. (p. 18, *m47*)
St. Louis (38°N/90°W) City in Missouri on the Mississippi River. Lewis and Clark began their expedition there. (p. 200, *m201*)
Salt Lake City (41°N/112°W) Largest city in Utah. Founded in 1847 by Mormons. (p. 294, *m294*)
Samoa Chain of islands in the South Pacific. (p. 548, *m548*)
San Antonio (29°N/99°W) City in southern Texas. Site of the Alamo. (p. 280, *m280*)
San Diego (33°N/117°W) City in southern California. Founded as the first Spanish mission in California. (p. 285, *m294*)
San Francisco (38°N/122°W) City in northern California. Boom town of the California gold rush. (p. 287, *m294*)
Santa Fe (35°N/106°W) Capital of New Mexico. First settled by the Spanish. (p. 284, *m294*)
Santa Fe Trail Overland trail from Independence to Santa Fe. Opened in 1821. (p. 284, *m294*)
Sarajevo (44°N/18°E) Site of the shooting of the Archduke Franz Ferdinand in 1914. (p. 571, *m574*)
Saratoga (43°N/75°W) City in eastern New York. The American victory there in 1777 was a turning point in the Revolution. (p. 101, *m106*)
Serbia Balkan country in southeastern Europe. Involved in the beginning of World War I. (p. 571, *m574*)
Sierra Nevada Mountain range mostly in California. (p. 15, *m19*)
South America World's fourth largest continent. (p. 12, *m10*)
South Carolina One of the original 13 states. Nicknamed the Palmetto State. (p. 756, *m760–761*)
South Dakota 40th state. Nicknamed the Coyote State or the Sunshine State. Acquired as part of the Louisiana Purchase. (p. 756, *m760–761*)
Spain Country in southwestern Europe. (p. 37, *m47*)
Spanish Florida Part of New Spain. Purchased by the United States in 1821. (p. 210, *m201*)

T

Tennessee 16th state. Nicknamed the Volunteer State. Gained statehood after North Carolina ceded its western lands to the United States. (p. 756, *m760–761*)
Texas 28th state. Nicknamed the Lone Star State. Proclaimed independence from Mexico in 1836. Was a separate republic until 1845. (p. 756, *m760–761*)
Trenton (41°N/74°W) Capital of New Jersey. Site of an American victory in the Revolution. (p. 100, *m106*)

U

Utah 45th state. Nicknamed the Beehive State. Settled by Mormons. (p. 756, *m760–761*)

V

Valley Forge (40°N/76°W) Winter headquarters for the Continental Army in 1777–1778. Located near Philadelphia. (p. 102, *m106*)
Veracruz (19°N/96°W) Port city in Mexico on the Gulf of Mexico. (p. 290, *m289*)
Vermont 14th state. Nicknamed the Green Mountain State. (p. 756, *m760–761*)
Vicksburg (42°N/86°W) City in Mississippi. Site of a Union victory in 1863. (p. 396, *m398*)
Vincennes (39°N/88°W) City in Indiana. British fort there was captured by George Rogers Clark in 1779. (p. 103)
Virgin Islands (18°N/64°W) Territory of the United States. Purchased from Denmark in 1917. (p. 756, *m758–759*)
Virginia One of the original 13 states. Nicknamed the Old Dominion. (p. 756, *m760–761*)
Virginia City (39°N/120°W) City in Nevada. Boom town in 1800s because of Comstock Lode mines. (p. 436, *m438*)

W

Washington 42nd state. Nicknamed the Evergreen State. Acquired as part of Oregon Territory. (p. 756, *m760–761*)
Washington, D.C. (39°N/77°W) Capital of the United States since 1800. (p. 215, *m214*)
Western Hemisphere Western half of the world. Includes North and South America. (p. 12, *m10*)
West Virginia 35th state. Nicknamed the Mountain State. Separated from Virginia early in the Civil War. (p. 756, *m760–761*)
Willamette River Flows across fertile farmlands in northern Oregon to join the Columbia River. (p. 274, *m275*)
Wisconsin 30th state. Nicknamed the Badger State. Settled as part of the Northwest Territory. (p. 756, *m760–761*)
Wounded Knee (43°N/102°W) Site of a massacre of Indians in 1890. Located in what is now South Dakota. (p. 448, *m446*)
Wyoming 44th state. Nicknamed the Equality State. (p. 756, *m760–761*)

Y

Yorktown (37°N/76°W) Town in Virginia. Site of the British surrender in 1781. (p. 106, *m106*)

★ Glossary ★

This glossary defines all vocabulary words and many important historical terms and phrases. These words and terms appear in blue or boldfaced type the first time that they are used in the text. The page number(s) after each definition refers to the page on which the word or phrase is first discussed in the text. For other references, see the index.

Pronunciation Key

When difficult names or terms first appear in the text, they are respelled to help you with pronunciation. A syllable printed in SMALL CAPITAL LETTERS receives the greatest stress. The pronunciation key below lists the letters and symbols that will help you pronounce the word. It also includes examples of words using each sound and showing how they would be pronounced.

Symbol	Example	Respelling
a	hat	(hat)
ay	pay, late	(pay), (layt)
ah	star, hot	(stahr), (haht)
ai	air, dare	(air), (dair)
aw	law, all	(law), (awl)
eh	met	(meht)
ee	bee, eat	(bee), (eet)
er	learn, sir, fur	(lern), (ser), (fer)
ih	fit	(fiht)
i	mile	(mīl)
ir	ear	(ir)
oh	no	(noh)
oi	soil, boy	(soil), (boi)
oo	root, rule	(root), (rool)
or	born, door	(born), (dor)
ow	plow, out	(plow), (owt)

Symbol	Example	Respelling
u	put, book	(put), (buk)
uh	fun	(fuhn)
yoo	few, use	(fyoo), (yooz)
ch	chill, reach	(chihl), (reech)
g	go, dig	(goh), (dihg)
j	jet, gently bridge	(jeht), (JEHNT lee), (brihj)
k	kite, cup	(kīt), (kuhp)
ks	mix	(mihks)
kw	quick	(kwihk)
ng	bring	(brihng)
s	say, cent	(say), (sehnt)
sh	she, crash	(shee), (krash)
th	three	(three)
y	yet, onion	(yeht), (UHN yuhn)
z	zip, always	(zihp), (AWL wayz)
zh	treasure	(TREH zher)

★ GLOSSARY ★

A

abdicate to give up power (p. 589)
abolitionist person who wanted to end slavery in the United States (p. 332)
Adams-Onís Treaty (1821) agreement by which Spain sold Florida to the United States (p. 242)
affirmative action program in areas such as employment and college admissions to provide equal opportunities for members of groups that faced discrimination in the past (p. 616)
Alien Act (1789) law that allowed the President to expel foreigners thought to be dangerous to the country (p. 187)
Allied Powers in World War I, the side that included France, Britain, Russia, and the United States (p. 572)
altitude height above sea level (p. 19)
amend to change (p. 136)
amendment formal written change (p. 150)
American Federation of Labor (AFL) association of trade unions, founded in 1886 (p. 478)
American Indian Movement (AIM) organization that pushed for better treatment of American Indians (p. 622)
American System plan proposed by Henry Clay that called for high tariffs and internal improvements (p. 238)
Americans With Disabilities Act (1990) law that banned discrimination in hiring people with physical or mental disabilities (p. 623)
amnesty government pardon (p. 407)
anarchist person who opposes organized government (p. 478)
annex to add on (pp. 283, 545)
Antifederalist person who opposed ratification of the Constitution (p. 133)
appeal to request that a decision be reviewed by a higher court (p. 159)
apprentice (uh PREHN tihs) person who learns a trade or craft from a master (p. 76)
appropriate to set aside money for a special purpose (p. 154)
armistice agreement to stop fighting (pp. 555, 588)
arsenal gun warehouse (p. 366)
Articles of Confederation first constitution of the United States (p. 117)
artisan worker who has learned a trade, such as carpentry

assembly line method of production in which workers add parts to a product as it moves along on a belt (p. 474)
assimilation process of becoming part of another culture (p. 490)

B

baby boom increased birth rate in United States during the late 1940s and 1950s (p. 606)
backcountry area of land along the eastern slopes of the Appalachian Mountains (p. 65)
Bank of the United States national bank set up by Congress in 1791 (p. 175)
barrio neighborhood of Spanish-speaking people (p. 538)
Bessemer process method of making strong steel at a low cost, developed in the 1850s (p. 464)
bilingual in two languages (p. 621)
bill proposed law (pp. 131, 149)
bill of rights list of freedoms that a government promises to protect (p. 73)
Bill of Rights first 10 amendments to the Constitution (p. 136)
birth rate number of births per year for every thousand, or other number, of a population (p. 606)
black codes laws that severely limited the rights of freedmen after the Civil War (p. 410)
Bleeding Kansas name for the Kansas Territory because of the violence there over slavery in the 1850s (p. 361)
Bolsheviks communist group that seized power in Russia in November 1917 (p. 584)
bond certificate that promises to repay money loaned, plus interest, on a certain date (p. 174)
Border Ruffians proslavery bands from Missouri that battled antislavery forces in Kansas in the 1850s (p. 360)
Boston Massacre (1770) shooting of five colonists by British soldiers (p. 88)
Boston Tea Party (1773) protest in which colonists dressed as Indians dumped British tea into Boston harbor (p. 90)
Boxer Rebellion (1900) uprising against foreigners in China (p. 551)
boycott to refuse to buy certain goods or services (p. 85)
Brown* v. *Board of Education of Topeka (1954) Supreme Court ruling that ordered schools to be desegregated (p. 613)
building code laws regulating the building of new structures in order to improve the health and safety of residents (p. 494)
Bull Moose party supporters of Theodore Roosevelt in the election of 1912 (p. 529)
bureaucracy system of managing government through departments run by appointed officials (p. 580)

C

Cabinet group of officials who head government departments and advise the President (pp. 152, 173)
canal artificial channel filled with water to allow boats to cross a stretch of land (p. 233)
capitalist person who invests in a business to make a profit (p. 224)
caravan group of traders and their animals journeying together across a long distance (p. 43)
carpetbagger name for a northerner who came south after the Civil War seeking personal gain (p. 414)
cartographer person who makes maps (p. 8)
cash crop crop sold for money (p. 65)
cattle drive herding and moving of cattle, usually to railroad lines (p. 440)
Cattle Kingdom area from Texas north across the Plains, where cattle grazed in the 1870s (p. 443)
caucus private meeting of political party leaders to choose a candidate (p. 255)
cede to give up (p. 291)
Central Powers in World War I, the side that included Germany, Austria-Hungary, and the Ottoman Empire (p. 572)
charter legal document giving certain rights to a person or company (p. 56)
Chautauqua Society in the late 1800s and early 1900s, a group that offered adult education throughout the United States (p. 505)
checks and balances system by which each branch of government can check, or control, the action of the other branches (p. 130)
Chicano Mexican American (p. 621)
Chinese Exclusion Act (1882) act barring the immigration of Chinese laborers (p. 491)
Chivington Massacre (1864) attack by Colonel John Chivington and his militia unit against a peaceful Cheyenne village (p. 444)
city-state a large town that has its own independent government (p. 43)
civil disobedience nonviolent opposition to a government policy or law by refusing to comply with it (p. 614)
civil rights constitutional rights belonging to all American citizens (p. 613)
Civil Rights Act of 1964 law protecting the right of all citizens to vote—also outlawed discrimination in hiring and segregation in public places (p. 615)
civil service all federal jobs except elected positions and the armed forces (p. 517)
civil war war between people of the same country (p. 356)
civilian person not in the military (p. 391)
climate average weather of a place over a period of 20 to 30 years (p. 19)
clipper ship fast-sailing ship of the mid-1800s (p. 305)
collective bargaining right of unions to negotiate with management for workers as a group (p. 479)
colony group of people who settle in a distant land and are ruled by the government of their native land (p. 37)
Columbian Exchange worldwide exchange of goods and ideas that began with Columbus's voyages to the Americas (p. 39)
Commerce Clause section of the Constitution that gives Congress the power to regulate trade with other nations and between the states (p. 152)
committee of correspondence group of colonists who wrote letters and pamphlets reporting on British actions (p. 88)
common open field where cattle grazed (p. 64)
compensation repayment for losses (p. 629)
compromise settlement in which each side gives up some of its demands in order to reach an agreement (p. 122)
Compromise of 1850 agreement over slavery under which California

joined the Union as a free state and a strict fugitive slave law was passed (p. 356)
Comstock Lode rich vein of gold and silver discovered in the Sierra Nevada in 1859 (p. 435)
Confederate States of America nation formed in 1861 by the southern states that seceded from the Union (p. 370)
confederation alliance of independent states (p. 117)
conquistador (kahn KEES tuh dor) Spanish word for conqueror (p. 38)
conservation protection of natural resources (p. 528)
conservative person who wants to keep conditions as they are or return them to the way they used to be. (p. 415)
consolidate to combine, such as businesses (p. 461)
constituent person who elected a representative to office (p. 156)
constitution document that sets out the laws and principles of a government (p. 116)
Constitutional Convention (1787) meeting of delegates from 12 states who wrote the United States Constitution (p. 121)
Continental Army army established by the Second Continental Congress to fight the British (p. 93)
continental divide mountain ridge that separates river systems flowing toward opposite sides of a continent (p. 202)
cooperative group in which individuals pool their money to buy goods at lower prices (p. 454)
Copperheads northerners who opposed using force to keep the South in the Union (p. 391)
corduroy road road made of logs (p. 230)
corporation business that is owned by investors (p. 466)
corral enclosure for animals (p. 433)
Cotton Kingdom name for the cotton-growing area of the South in the 1850s (p. 312)
cottonocracy name for the wealthy planters who made their money from cotton in the mid-1800s (p. 316)
coureur de bois (koo ryoor duh BWAH) phrase meaning runner of the woods; trapper or trader in New France (p. 48)
cow town settlement that grew up at the end of a cattle trail (p. 441)
cowhand worker who tended cattle and drove herds (p. 440)
creole person born in Spain's American colonies to Spanish parents (p. 240)
Crusades wars fought by Christians in the Middle Ages to gain control of the Middle East (p. 36)
culture entire way of life developed by a people (p. 30)
czar Russian emperor (p. 577)

D

dame school private school for girls in the New England colonies (p. 76)
Daughters of Liberty group of colonial women who protested British policies (p. 87)
Dawes Act (1887) law that encouraged Native Americans to become farmers (p. 449)
Declaration of Independence (1776) document stating that the colonies were a free and independent nation (p. 96)
democratic ensuring that all people have the same rights (p. 194)
Democratic Republicans political party led by Thomas Jefferson; forerunner of today's Democratic party (p. 184)
Democrats political party formed in the 1830s by supporters of Andrew Jackson (p. 255)
deport to expel from a country (p. 625)
depression period when business slows, prices and wages fall, and unemployment rises (pp. 120, 266)
dime novels low-priced paperback books offering adventure stories, popular in the late 1800s (p. 505)
discrimination policy or attitude that denies equal rights and treatment to certain groups of people (pp. 309, 389)
dissenting opinion statement explaining why a Supreme Court justice disagrees with the opinion of the majority (p. 159)
dividend share of a corporation's profits (p. 466)
dollar diplomacy policy of building economic ties to Latin America in the early 1900s (p. 563)
domestic tranquillity peace at home (p. 143)
draft law requiring some to serve in the military (pp. 392, 578)
Dred Scott decision (1857) Supreme Court decision that enslaved persons were not citizens and that Congress did not have the power to outlaw slavery in any territory (p. 362)
due process principle that government must follow the same fair rules in all cases brought to trial (pp. 137, 160)
dumping selling of goods in another country at very low prices (p. 238)

E

Eighteenth Amendment (1919) amendment that made it illegal to make or sell alcoholic drinks in the United States (p. 535)
Elastic Clause section of the Constitution that gives Congress the power to make all "necessary and proper" laws (p. 152)
electoral college group of electors from every state who meet every four years to vote for the President and Vice President of the United States (p. 130)
elevation height above sea level (p. 14)
emancipate to set free (p. 387)
Emancipation Proclamation (1863) President Lincoln's declaration freeing slaves in the Confederacy (p. 388)
embargo ban on trade with another country (p. 278)
Embargo Act (1807) law that forbade Americans to export or import goods (p. 206)
English Bill of Rights (1689) document guaranteeing the rights of English citizens (pp. 72, 127)
Enlightenment movement in Europe in the late 1600s and 1700s that emphasized the use of reason (pp. 77, 127)
epidemic rapid spread of a contagious disease among large numbers of people (p. 589)
Equator imaginary line that lies at 0° latitude (p. 8)
established church religion that has the official support of the government (p. 74)
ethnic group group of people who share a common culture (p. 489)
execute to carry out (p. 116)
executive agreement informal agreement made by the President with another head of state (p. 157)

executive branch branch of government that carries out laws (p. 122)
Exodusters African Americans who moved to Kansas in the late 1800s (p. 450)
expansionism policy of extending a nation's boundaries (p. 544)
expedition long journey or voyage of exploration (p. 200)
extended family close-knit family group that includes grandparents, parents, children, aunts, uncles, and cousins (p. 321)

F

faction a group inside a political party or other group (p. 181)
factory system method of producing goods that brought workers and machinery together in one place (p. 224)
famine severe food shortage and starvation (p. 309)
Farmers' Alliance farmers' organization that began in Texas in the 1870s and spread through the South and into the Plains states (p. 454)
federal having to do with the national government (p. 143)
Federal Reserve Act (1913) act that set up a nationwide system of federal banks (p. 530)
federalism division of power between the states and the national government (p. 128)
Federalists supporters of the Constitution and a strong national government in the ratification debate in 1787 (pp. 133, 185)
Fifteenth Amendment (1870) constitutional amendment that forbade any state to deny African Americans the right to vote because of their race (p. 413)
First Continental Congress (1774) meeting of delegates from 12 colonies in Philadelphia (p. 91)
Foraker Act (1900) act that gave Puerto Ricans only a limited say in their own affairs (p. 558)
foreign policy actions that a nation takes in relation to other nations (p. 179)
Fort Laramie Treaty (1851) agreement in which Native Americans promised to keep to limited areas (p. 444)
forty-niner person who headed to California in search of gold during the Gold Rush of 1849 (p. 295)
Fourteen Points President Wilson's goals for peace after World War I (p. 590)
Fourteenth Amendment (1868) constitutional amendment that granted citizenship to all persons born in the United States (p. 411)
free enterprise system economic system in which businesses are owned by private citizens (p. 468)
Free Soil party political party founded in 1848 to keep slavery out of the western territories (p. 354)
freedmen men and women who had been slaves (p. 407)
Freedmen's Bureau agency that helped former slaves after the Civil War (p. 408)
fugitive runaway (p. 356)
Fugitive Slave Law of 1850 law that required all citizens to help catch runaway slaves (p. 357)

G

general welfare well-being of all the people (p. 144)
Gentlemen's Agreement (1907) agreement between the United States and Japan limiting the number of Japanese immigrants to the United States (p. 539)
gentry highest social class in the 13 English colonies (p. 68)
geography the study of people, their environments, and their resources (p. 4)
Gettysburg Address (1863) speech by President Lincoln after the Battle of Gettysburg (p. 398)
Ghost Dance religious ceremony that celebrated the time when Native Americans lived freely on the Plains (p. 447)
Gibbon* v. *Ogden (1824) Supreme Court ruling that upheld the power of the federal government to regulate commerce (p. 239)
Gideon* v. *Wainwright (1963) Supreme Court ruling that a lawyer must be appointed for any defendant who cannot afford one (p. 160)
glacier thick sheet of ice (p. 30)
globe sphere with a map of the Earth printed on it (p. 8)
Glorious Revolution (1688) movement that brought William and Mary to the throne of England and strengthened the rights of English citizens (p. 72)
graduated income tax tax on earnings that charges different rates for different income levels (p. 524)
grandfather clause law that excused a voter from a literacy test if his grandfather had been eligible to vote on January 1, 1867—protected the voting rights of southern whites but not those of southern blacks (p. 421)
Great Awakening religious movement in the English colonies in the early 1700s (p. 74)
Great Compromise plan at the Constitutional Convention that settled the differences between large and small states (p. 124)
Great Depression worst period of economic decline in United States history, beginning in 1929 and lasting until World War II (p. 601)
Great White Fleet name for the large and powerful American navy in the late 1890s (p. 548)
guerrilla warfare use of hit-and-run tactics (p. 361)
Gullah language spoken by African Americans in coastal South Carolina (p. 69)

H

habeas corpus right to have charges filed or a hearing before being jailed (p. 392)
Hartford Convention (1814) meeting of New Englanders to protest the War of 1812 (p. 217)
Haymarket Riot (1886) violent incident in Chicago involving strikers, strikebreakers, and police; led to anti-labor feeling (p. 478)
hemisphere half of the Earth (p. 8)
hill area of raised land that is lower and more rounded than a mountain (p. 14)
Hispanic-American Alliance organization founded in 1894 to protect the rights of Mexicanos in Arizona (p. 451)
history account of what has happened in the lives of different peoples (p. 4)
Homestead Act (1862) law promising 160 acres of land in the West to anyone who farmed it for five years (p. 450)
House of Burgesses representative assembly in colonial Virginia (pp. 57, 127)
House of Representatives larger house of Congress, in which each

state is represented according to its population (p. 153)
Hudson River School group of American artists who painted landscapes of New York's Hudson River region in the mid-1800s (p. 343)
Hull House Chicago settlement house opened by Jane Addams in 1889 (p. 496)

I

illegal alien someone who enters a country without legal permission (p. 610)
illiterate unable to read or write (p. 579)
immigrant person who enters a country in order to settle there (p. 187)
Immigration Reform and Control Act (1986) act that allowed people who had arrived illegally before 1982 to apply for citizenship (p. 610)
impeach to bring a formal charge of wrongdoing against the President or another public official (pp. 131, 156, 412)
imperialism policy of powerful countries seeking to control the economic and political affairs of weaker countries or regions (p. 546)
impressment act of forcing someone to serve in the navy (p. 205)
inauguration ceremony at which the President officially takes the oath of office (p. 172)
income tax tax on people's earnings (p. 394)
indentured servant person who agreed to work without wages for some time in exchange for passage to the colonies (p. 68)
Indian Removal Act (1830) law that forced many Native Americans to move west of the Mississippi (p. 265)
Industrial Revolution process by which machines replaced hand tools, and steam and other new sources of power replaced human and animal power (p. 222)
inflation rise in prices and decrease in the value of money (p. 394)
initiative process by which voters can put a bill directly before the state legislature by collecting signatures on a petition (pp. 524,627)
injunction court order to do or not to do something (p. 481)
interchangeable parts identical, machine-made parts for a tool or instrument (p. 227)
intern to detain or confine, usually in a compound (p. 628)
International Ladies' Garment Workers' Union (ILGWU) union organized to represent workers in the garment industry (p. 479)
interstate commerce trade between different states (p. 239)
intervention direct involvement in another country (p. 243)
Intolerable Acts (1774) laws passed by Parliament to punish colonists for the Boston Tea Party (p. 90)
irrigate to bring water to an area (p. 6)
isolationism policy of having little to do with the political affairs of foreign nations (p. 544)
isthmus narrow strip of land (pp. 14, 559)

J

Jay's Treaty (1795) agreement that settled differences between Britain and the United States (p. 180)
jerky dried meat (p. 433)
Jim Crow laws laws that separated people of different races in public places in the South (p. 423)
joint committee congressional committee that includes both House and Senate members (p. 154)
judicial branch branch of government that decides if laws are carried out fairly (p. 122)
judicial review power of the Supreme Court to decide whether acts of a President or laws passed by Congress are constitutional (pp. 152, 197)
Judiciary Act (1789) law that organized the federal court system (p. 173)
justice fairness (p. 143)

K

kachina masked dancer at religious ceremonies of the Southwest Indians (p. 33)
kaiser German emperor (p. 572)
Kansas-Nebraska Act (1854) law that divided Nebraska Territory into two territories in which the slavery issue would be decided by popular sovereignty (p. 359)
Kentucky and Virginia resolutions (1798, 1799) declarations that a state had the right to declare a federal law unconstitutional (p. 188)
kinship network close ties among family members (p. 43)
kitchen cabinet group of unofficial advisers to President Andrew Jackson (p. 259)
Knights of Labor workers' union formed in 1869 that later included skilled and unskilled workers, immigrants, blacks, and women (p. 477)
Know-Nothing party political party organized by nativists in the 1850s (p. 309)
Ku Klux Klan (KKK) secret society formed by white southerners after the Civil War; used threats and violence to keep African Americans from voting (p. 415)

L

laissez faire (lehs ay FAYR) idea that government should play as small a role as possible in economic affairs (pp. 195, 267)
Land Ordinance of 1785 law that set up a system for settling the Northwest Territory (p. 118)
latitude distance north or south from the Equator (p. 4)
lawsuit legal case brought by one person or group against another to settle a dispute (p. 362)
League of Nations association of nations proposed by President Wilson and formed after World War I (p. 590)
legislative branch branch of government that passes laws (p. 122)
legislature group of people who have the power to make laws (p. 72)
liberty freedom to live as you please provided you obey the laws and respect the rights of others (p. 145)
Liberty Bonds bonds sold during World War I to help the government pay for the war (p. 580)
life expectancy average number of years a person is expected to live (p. 608)
line item veto power of the President to veto part of a bill and sign the rest into law (p. 149)
literacy test examination to see if a voter can read and write (p. 421)

local color speech and habits of a particular region (p. 506)
locomotive engine that uses steam or another power source to pull a railroad train (p. 304)
longitude distance east or west from the Prime Meridian (p. 4)
Louisiana Purchase (1803) vast territory west of the Mississippi purchased from France (p. 200)
Loyalist colonist who remained loyal to Britain (p. 99)
lynching illegal seizure and execution of someone by a mob (p. 423)

M

Magna Carta (1215) document that guaranteed rights to English nobles (pp. 70, 126)
mainstream to place children with disabilities into regular school classes (p. 623)
majority more than half (p. 252)
Manifest Destiny belief that the United States had the right and the duty to expand to the Pacific (p. 287)
map projection a way of drawing the Earth on a flat surface (p. 8)
Marbury* v. *Madison (1803) Supreme Court decision that established the precedent of judicial review (p. 197)
martial law rule by the army instead of the elected government (p. 376)
martyr person who dies for his or her beliefs (p. 366)
mass production making large quantities of a product quickly and cheaply (p. 475)
Mayflower Compact (1620) agreement for ruling the Plymouth Colony, signed by Pilgrims before they landed at Plymouth (pp. 57, 127)
McCarran-Walter Act (1952) law that ended racial restrictions on naturalization (p. 625)
McCulloch* v. *Maryland (1819) Supreme Court ruling that states have no right to interfere with federal institutions within their borders (p. 239)
middle class in the 13 English colonies, class that included skilled craftsworkers, farmers, and some tradespeople (p. 68)
Middle Passage ocean trip from Africa to the Americas in which thousands of enslaved Africans died (p. 45)
migrant worker worker who moves with the seasons, planting or harvesting crops (p. 621)
militarism policy of building up strong armed forces to prepare for war (p. 570)
militia army of citizens who serve as soldiers in an emergency. (p. 91)
minuteman colonial volunteer who trained to fight the British (p. 91)
mission religious settlement run by Catholic priests and friars (p. 39)
Missouri Compromise (1819) plan proposed by Henry Clay to keep the number of slave and free states equal (p. 352)
mobilize to prepare for war (p. 571)
monopoly company that controls all or nearly all the business of an industry (p. 468)
Monroe Doctrine (1823) President Monroe's foreign policy statement warning European nations not to interfere in Latin America (p. 243)
moral diplomacy foreign policy proposed by President Wilson to condemn imperialism, spread democracy, and promote peace (p. 564)
mountain high, steep, rugged land, usually at least 1,000 feet (300 m) above the surrounding land (p. 14)
mountain man fur trapper who lived in the western mountains in the early 1800s (p. 275)
muckraker journalist who exposed corruption and other problems of the late 1800s and early 1900s (p. 521)
mudslinging political tactic of using insults to attack an opponent's reputation (p. 269)
mutualista Mexican American mutual aid group (p. 538)

N

NAACP (National Association for the Advancement of Colored People) organization formed in 1909 to gain equal rights for African Americans (p. 537)
national debt total sum of money a government owes (p. 173)
National Grange organization of farmers formed in 1867 to improve conditions for farmers (p. 454)
national park a natural or historic area set aside and run by the federal government for people to visit (p. 528)
nationalism pride in one's nation (pp. 210, 570)
nativist person who wanted to limit immigration and preserve the United States for native-born white Protestants (pp. 309, 490)
natural rights rights that belong to all people from birth (p. 96)
naturalization legal process of becoming a citizen (p. 624)
Navigation Acts laws that governed trade between England and its colonies (p. 83)
network system of connected lines, as in a network of railroad lines (p. 460)
neutral not taking sides in a war (pp. 103, 210)
New Deal program of President Franklin D. Roosevelt to end the Great Depression (p. 601)
New Freedom President Wilson's program to break up trusts and restore competition (p. 530)
Nineteenth Amendment (1920) constitutional amendment that gave women the right to vote (p. 533)
nominating convention meeting at which a political party chooses a candidate (p. 255)
nonimportation agreements promise by American colonists not to import goods taxed by the Townshend Acts (p. 87)
Nonintercourse Act (1809) law that replaced the Embargo Act; permitted trade with any nation but Britain and France (p. 206)
Northwest Ordinance (1787) law that set up a government for the Northwest Territory and a plan for admitting new states to the United States (p. 119)
northwest passage waterway through or around North America (p. 46)
nullification idea that a state had the right to cancel a federal law it considered unconstitutional (p. 261)
nullify to cancel (p. 188)

O

Olive Branch Petition (1775) final attempt by the Second Continental Congress to reach a peaceful settlement with Britain (p. 94)

Open Door Policy (1899) policy toward China that allowed a nation to trade in any other nation's sphere of influence (p. 551)
opinion a judge's official statement regarding the laws bearing on a case (p.159)
ordinance law (p. 118)
override to overrule or set aside (pp. 131, 149)

P

pacifist person who opposes all wars and refuses to fight in a war (p. 583)
Panic of 1837 economic crisis that led to a depression (p. 266)
Parliament representative assembly in England (p. 70)
Patriot colonist who supported independence from British rule (p. 98)
patronage practice of giving jobs to loyal supporters (p. 517)
penal system system of prisons (p. 327)
pet bank state bank in which President Jackson and Secretary of the Treasury Taney deposited federal money (p. 260)
Pilgrims in the 1600s, English settlers who sought religious freedom in the Americas (p. 57)
Pinckney Treaty (1795) agreement by which Spain agreed to keep the port of New Orleans open (p. 198)
plain broad area of fairly level land (p. 14)
plantation large estate farmed by many workers (p. 44)
plateau raised plain (p. 14)
Platt Amendment amendment to the Cuban constitution that allowed the United States to intervene in Cuba (p. 556)
Plessy* v. *Ferguson (1896) Supreme Court ruling that segregation was legal as long as facilities for blacks and whites were equal (p. 423)
pogrom in Eastern Europe, an organized attack on a Jewish community (p. 486)
poll tax tax required before a person can vote (p. 421)
pool group of companies that divided up business in an area and fixed prices (p. 463)
popular sovereignty idea that the people hold the final authority in government (p. 146), allowing each territory to decide whether to allow slavery (p. 354)
Populist party political party formed by farmers and union members in 1891 (p. 454)
Preamble opening statement of the Constitution (p. 142)
precedent (PREHS uh dehnt) act or decision that sets an example for others to follow (pp. 152, 172)
precipitation (pree sihp uh TAY shuhn) water that falls as rain, sleet, hail, or snow (p. 19)
predestination belief that God decided in advance which people will gain salvation in heaven (p. 326)
presidio (prih SIHD ee oh) fort where soldiers lived in the Spanish colonies (p. 39)
primary election in which voters choose their party's candidate for the general election (p. 524)
Prime Meridian imaginary line that lies at 0° longitude (p. 8)
productivity measure of how much a given number of workers can produce in a given time (p. 600)
profiteer person who takes advantage of a crisis to make money (p. 394)
Progressives reformers who wanted to improve American life in the late 1800s and early 1900s (p. 521)
propaganda spreading of ideas that help a cause or hurt an opposing cause (p. 574)
proprietary colony (proh PRI uh tər ee) English colony in which the king gave land to proprietors in exchange for a yearly payment (p. 60)
proprietor owner of a proprietary colony (p. 60)
protective tariff tax on imported goods to protect a country's industry from foreign competition (p. 175)
protectorate nation whose independence is limited by the control of a more powerful country (p. 558)
Protestant Reformation movement to reform the Roman Catholic Church in the 1500s; led to creation of many different Christian churches (p. 47)
public interest the good of the people (p. 523)
public school school supported by taxes (p. 76)
pueblo town in the Spanish colonies (p. 39)
pull factor condition that attracts people to a new area (p. 486)
Pure Food and Drug Act (1906) law requiring food and drug makers to list all ingredients on their packages (p. 528)
Puritans group of English Protestants who settled the Massachusetts Bay Colony (p. 58)
push factor condition that encourages people to move away from their homeland (p. 486)

Q

Quakers Protestant reformers who settled in Pennsylvania (p. 61)
quarter to provide housing for (p. 90)
quota system system that limited immigration by allowing only a certain number of people from each country to immigrate to the United States (p. 609)

R

racism belief that one race is superior to another (p. 376)
radical person who wants to make drastic changes in society (p. 410)
Radical Reconstruction period after the Civil War when Republicans controlled Congress and passed strict laws affecting the South (p. 411)
Radical Republicans group of Republicans after the Civil War who wanted to keep southern planters out of power and protect the rights of freedmen (p. 410)
ragtime popular music of the late 1800s that had a lively, rhythmic sound (p. 501)
ratify to approve (pp. 107, 132)
realist writer or artist who shows life as it really is (p. 506)
rebate discount on services or merchandise (p. 462)
recall process by which voters can remove an elected official from office (p. 524)
recession mild depression in which business slows and some workers lose their jobs (p. 602)
Reconstruction rebuilding of the South after the Civil War (p. 407)
Reconstruction Act (1867) law that disbanded southern state governments and divided the South into five military districts (p. 412)
referendum process by which people vote directly on a bill (p. 524)

refugee person who flees his or her homeland to seek safety elsewhere (p. 610)
Renaissance (REHN uh sahns) French word meaning rebirth; burst of learning in Europe from the late 1300s to about 1600 (p. 39)
rendezvous (RAHN day voo) French word meaning get-together; yearly meeting where mountain men traded furs (p. 276)
reparations after a war, payments from a defeated nation to a victorious nation to pay for losses suffered during the war (p. 591)
repeal to cancel or undo (p. 85)
representative government government in which voters elect representatives to make laws for them (pp. 57, 146)
republic nation in which voters elect representatives to govern them (p. 126)
Republican party political party formed in 1854 by Free Soilers, northern Democrats, and antislavery Whigs (p. 363)
reservation limited area set aside for Native Americans by the government (p. 445)
revival huge meeting held to stir religious feelings (p. 326)
Roosevelt Corollary (1904) President Theodore Roosevelt's addition to the Monroe Doctrine, claiming the right of the United States to intervene in Latin America to preserve law and order (p. 562)

S

sachem tribal chief of an Eastern Woodlands Native American people (p. 35)
scalawag white southerner who supported the Republicans during Reconstruction (p. 414)
secede to withdraw from membership in a group (pp. 263, 355)
Second Great Awakening religious movement that swept the United States in the early 1800s (p. 326)
sectionalism loyalty to a state or section rather than to the whole country (pp. 238, 353)
sedition stirring up rebellion against a government (p. 187)
Sedition Act (1789) law that allowed citizens to be fined or jailed for criticizing public officials (p. 187)
segregation separation of people of different races (p. 423)
Selective Service Act (1917) law requiring all men 21 to 30 to register for the military draft (p. 578)
self-determination right of national groups to their own territory and forms of government (p. 590)
Senate smaller house of Congress, in which each state has two senators (p. 153)
Seneca Falls Convention (1848) meeting at which leaders of the women's rights movement called for equality for women (p. 337)
separation of powers principle that the powers of government be divided among separate branches (p. 128)
service industry business in which workers provide a service rather than produce goods (p. 605)
settlement house community center that offers services to the poor (p. 496)
sharecropper person who farms land owned by another in exchange for a share of the crops (p. 418)
Shays' Rebellion (1786) revolt of Massachusetts farmers against increased taxes (p. 120)
Sherman Antitrust Act (1890) act that prohibited trusts or other businesses from limiting competition (pp. 469, 519)
siege military blockade of an enemy town or position in order to force it to surrender (pp. 282, 396)
slave code laws that controlled the lives of enslaved African Americans and denied them basic rights (pp. 73, 318)
smuggler person who violates trade laws by illegally taking goods into or out of a country (p. 206)
social reform organized attempt to improve what is unjust or imperfect in society (p. 326)
socialist person who supports community ownership of property and the sharing of all profits (p. 583)
Society of American Indians group formed in the early 1900s to work for social justice for Native Americans (p. 539)
sod house house built of soil held together by grass roots (p. 452)
sodbuster nickname for a Plains farmer (p. 452)
Sons of Liberty group of colonial men who protested British policies (p. 87)
speculator person who invests in a risky venture in the hope of making a large profit (pp. 174, 266)
sphere of influence area in which a foreign nation had special trading privileges and made laws for its own citizens (p. 551)
spinning jenny machine developed in the 1760s that could spin several threads at once (p. 222)
spoils system practice of rewarding supporters with government jobs (p. 259)
Square Deal Theodore Roosevelt's promise that all groups should have an equal opportunity to succeed (p. 527)
stalemate deadlock in which neither side is strong enough to defeat the other (p. 572)
Stamp Act (1765) British law that required colonists to pay a tax on legal documents, newspapers, and other materials (p. 85)
standard of living an index based on the amount of goods, services, education, and leisure time that people have (p. 602)
standard time zone one of 24 divisions of the Earth, each an hour apart (p. 12)
standing committee permanent congressional committee assigned to study a specific issue (p. 154)
states' rights idea that states have the right to limit the power of the federal government (p. 261)
steerage on a ship, the cramped quarters for passengers paying the lowest fares (p. 487)
stock share in a corporation (p. 466)
strike refusal by workers to do their jobs until their demands are met (p. 307)
strikebreaker worker hired as a replacement for a striking worker (p. 478)
subsidy financial aid or a land grant from the government (p. 437)
suffrage right to vote (p. 254)
suffragist person who campaigned for women's right to vote (p. 532)
Sun Dance religious ceremony of the Plains Indians (p. 433)
Sunbelt band of states from Florida to California that have mild climates (p. 609)
Supreme Court highest court in the United States (p. 159)
sweatshop workplace where people labor long hours in poor conditions for low pay (p. 476)

T

tariff tax on foreign goods brought into a country (p. 175)
Tariff of Abominations name southerners gave to the tariff passed in 1828 (p. 261)
Tea Act (1773) law that let the British East India Company sell tea directly to colonists (p. 89)
telegraph communication device that sends electrical signals along a wire (p. 303)
temperance movement campaign against the sale or drinking of alcohol (pp. 329, 535)
tenement small apartment in a city slum building (p. 493)
tepee (TEE pee) tent made by stretching buffalo skins on tall poles (p. 432)
Thirteenth Amendment (1865) constitutional amendment that banned slavery in the United States (p. 409)
Three-Fifths Compromise agreement at the Constitutional Convention that three fifths of the slaves in any state be counted in its population (p. 124)
toleration willingness to let others practice their own customs and beliefs (p. 74)
total war all-out war that affects civilians as well as soldiers (p. 399)
Townshend Acts (1767) British laws that taxed goods such as glass, paper, paint, lead, and tea (p. 85)
trade union association of trade workers formed to gain higher wages and better working conditions (p. 307)
Trail of Tears (1838) forced march of Native Americans to lands west of the Mississippi (p. 265)
traitor person who betrays his or her country (p. 96)
transcendentalism belief that the most important truths in life go beyond human reason (p. 341)
transcontinental railroad railroad that stretches across a continent (p. 437)
travois (truh VOI) sled pulled by a dog or horse (p. 432)
Treaty of Ghent (1814) agreement ending the War of 1812 between Britain and the United States (p. 217)
Treaty of Greenville (1795) agreement by which Indian nations gave up land in the Northwest Territory (p. 207)
Treaty of Kanagawa (1854) treaty that opened two Japanese ports to trade (p. 545)
Treaty of Paris (1783) agreement that ended the American Revolution (p. 107)
Treaty of Versailles (1919) treaty that ended World War I (p. 591)
trench warfare type of fighting in which both sides dig trenches and attempt to overrun the enemy's trenches (p. 572)
triangular trade colonial trade route between New England, the West Indies, and Africa (p. 84)
tribe group of Native American people sharing the same customs, languages, and rituals (p. 30)
tributary stream or smaller river that flows into a bigger river (p. 17)
trust group of corporations run by a single board of directors (p. 468)
trustbuster person who wanted to end all trusts (p. 526)
turnpike road built by a private company that charges a toll to use it (p. 230)

U

U-boat German submarine in World War I (p. 575)
unconstitutional not permitted by the Constitution (pp. 149, 182)
underground railroad network of abolitionists who helped runaway slaves reach freedom in the North or Canada (p. 333)
urbanization movement of population from farms to cities (pp. 228, 492)

V

vaquero (vah KEHR oh) Spanish or Mexican cowhand (p. 440)
vaudeville variety show that included comedians, song-and-dance routines, and acrobats (p. 501)
vertical integration control of all phases of an industry, from raw materials to finished product (p. 465)
veto to reject (pp. 131, 149)
viceroy person who rules in the place of a king or queen (p. 39)
vigilante (vihj uh LAN tee) self-appointed law enforcer who deals out punishment without a trial (pp. 296, 436)
Voting Rights Act of 1965 law that ended literacy tests for voting and allowed federal officials to register voters in states that practiced discrimination (p. 615)

W

War Hawks members of Congress who wanted war with Britain in 1812 (p. 210)
warmonger person who tries to stir up war (p. 576)
weather condition of the Earth's atmosphere at any given time and place (p. 19)
Whigs (1830s) political party formed by supporters of John Quincy Adams who wanted government to promote economic growth (p. 254)
Whiskey Rebellion (1794) revolt of farmers to protest the tax on whiskey (p. 177)
wholesale buying or selling of goods in large quantities at lower prices (p. 454)
Wilmot Proviso (1846) proposal made in Congress to ban slavery in lands won from Mexico (p. 352)
Wisconsin Idea program of reforms introduced in 1900 by Wisconsin Governor Robert La Follette (p. 523)
women's rights movement campaign to win equality for women (p. 338)

X

XYZ Affair (1797) incident in which French agents asked American diplomats in Paris for a bribe (p. 186)

Y

Yankee nickname for a person from New England (p. 64)
yellow journalism sensational style of reporting used by some newspapers in the late 1800s (pp. 500, 553)

Z

Zimmermann telegram (1917) secret message from Germany urging Mexico to attack the United States if the United States declared war on Germany (p. 577)

★ Index ★

Page numbers that are italicized refer to illustrations or quotations. An m, p, c, g, go, or q before a page number refers to a map (m), picture (p), chart (c), graph (g), graphic organizer (go), or quotation (q) on that page.

A

B

★ INDEX ★

C

★ INDEX ★

F

★ INDEX ★

G

H

M

O

P

T

U

V

★ INDEX ★

★ Credits ★

Text Credits

Grateful acknowledgment is made to the following for copyrighted material:

Page 110 Excerpts from "Valley Forge" by Maxwell Anderson from *America on Stage*, edited by Stanley Richards. Copyright © 1976. **Page 166** From *The Great Little Madison* by Jean Fritz. Copyright © 1989 by Jean Fritz. Used by permission of G. P. Putnam's Sons, a division of Penguin Putnam Inc. **Page 346** From *Nightjohn* by Gary Paulsen. Copyright © 1993 by Gary Paulsen. Used by permission of Delacorte Press, a division of Bantam Doubleday Dell Publishing Group, Inc. **Page 510** From *My Antonia* by Willa Cather, published by Houghton Mifflin Company. **Page 596** From *The Picture Bride* by Yoshiko Uchida, Copyright © 1987 by Yoshiko Uchida. Published by Northland Press, 1987. Reprinted courtesy of The Bancroft Library, University of California, Berkeley. **Page 632** From "The Circuit" by Francisco Jiménez. Copyright by Francisco Jiménez. Reprinted by permission of the author. **Page 640** From "Spider Woman Story" from *Sweet Salt: Navajo Folk Tales and Mythology* by Raymond Friday Locke. Copyright © 1990 by Raymond Friday Locke. Reprinted by permission of the author. **Page 658** From *Who Cares? Millions Do...* by Milton Meltzer. Copyright©1994 by Milton Meltzer. Reprinted with permission from Walker and Company, 435 Hudson Street, New York, NY 10014. 1-800-289-2553. All Rights Reserved. **Page 674** From *Death Comes for the Archbishop* by Willa Cather. Copyright 1927 by Willa Cather and renewed 1955 by the Executors of the Estate of Willa Cather. Reprinted by permission of Alfred A. Knopf, Inc. **Page 680** From *The Fires of Jubilee, Nat Turner's Fierce Rebellion* by Stephen B. Oates, Harper and Row, Publishers. Copyright©1975 by Stephen B. Oates. All rights reserved. **Page 686** From *Caleb's Choice* by G. Clifton Wisler. Copyright ©1996 by G. Clifton Wisler. Published by Lodestar Books, an affiliate of Dutton Children's Books, a division of Penguin Putnam Inc. **Page 695** From *Out From This Place* by Joyce Hansen. Copyright©1988 by Joyce Hansen Reprinted with permission from Walker and Company, 435 Hudson Street, New York, NY 10014. 1-800-289-2553. All Rights Reserved. **Page 703** From *We Were There: The Story of Working Women in America* by Barbara Wertheimer. Copyright©1977 by Barbara Wertheimer. Reprinted by permission of Pantheon Books, a division of Random House, Inc. **Page 714** From *The Autobiography of Yukichi Fukuzawa*, translated by Eiichi Kiyooka. Copyright©1980, Columbia University Press. Reprinted with permission of the publisher, Columbia University Press. **Page 716** From *Culebra Cut* by Judith Head. Copyright © 1995 by Carolrhoda Books, Inc. Used by permission of the publisher, Carolrhoda Books, Inc. All rights reserved. **Page 719** From *The Big Sea* by Langston Hughes. Copyright 1940, ©1963. Reprinted by permission of Hill and Wang, a division of Farrar, Straus & Giroux, Inc. **Page 721** Excerpt from *A Farewell to Arms* by Ernest Hemingway is reprinted with permission of Scribner, a division of Simon & Schuster. Copyright 1929 by Charles Scribner's Sons. Copyright renewed 1957 by Ernest Hemingway. **Page 724** From *Hunger of Memory* by Richard Rodriguez. Copyright©1982 by Richard Rodriguez. Reprinted by permission of David R. Godine, Publisher, Inc.

Note: Every effort has been made to locate the copyright owner of material used in this textbook. Omissions brought to our attention will be corrected in subsequent editions.

Acknowledgments

Photo Research: Photo*Search,* Inc., LaShonda Williams, Vickie Menanteaux, Katty Gavilanes, Diane Alimena

Illustration Credits

Cover and Title Page Wolfgang Kaehler; Day Williams/Photo Researchers, Inc. **iv** *t* The Granger Collection, New York; *b* *Sugar Harvest in Louisiana & Texas,* 1856–1860, #65.39.120, Collection: Glenbow Museum, Calgary, Alberta **v** *t* Leif Skoogfors/Woodfin Camp & Associates; *l* Architect of the Capitol; *br* Courtesy, Independence National Historical Park Collection **vi** *t* American Textile History Museum, Lowell, MA; *l* Courtesy of the Library of Congress; *br* O. C. Seltzer, *Lewis and Clark with Sacajawea at the Great Falls of the Missouri,* From the Collection of Gilcrease Museum, Tulsa **vii** *t* Becker Collection, Smithsonian Institution, Division of Political History, 564–97; *b* Corel Professional Photos CD-ROM™ **viii** *t* North Carolina Museum of History; *l* Chicago Historical Society; *b* Courtesy of the Library of Congress **ix** *t* Denver Art Museum; *l* Collection of Picture Research Consultants, Inc. Photo ©Rob Huntley/Lightstream; *br* ©1999 Michael Freeman **x** *t* The Museum of American Political Life, University of Hartford; photo by Sally Anderson-Bruce; *b* ©Copyright 1997 PhotoDisc, Inc. **xi** *l* ©Robert E. Daemmrich/Tony Stone Images; *r* East Bay Municipal Utility District **xii** Jim Zuckerman/West Light **xiv** Lynn Saville **xx** George Catlin, *LaSalle Claiming Louisiana for France, April 9, 1682,* 1847/1848, Paul Mellon Collection, ©1998 Board of Trustees, National Gallery of Art, Washington **3** NOAA **6** Vito Palmisano/Tony Stone Images **8** Silver Burdett Ginn **12** Map Division, New York Public Library. Astor, Lenox and Tilden Foundations. **14** Daniel J. Cox/Gamma Liaison **15** Jeff Gnass Photography **16** *l* ©François Gohier/Photo Researchers, Inc.; *r* Robert Farber/The Image Bank **17** *l* Siegfried Layda/Tony Stone Images; *r* ©Jeff LePore/Photo Researchers, Inc. **18** *l* Courtesy National Archives, photo no. NWDNS-79-AA_F09; *r* UPI/Corbis-Bettmann **20** East Bay Municipal Utility District **21** *l* Duricux/SIPA; *r* Weather Graphics Courtesy of AccuWeather, Inc., 619 West College Avenue, State College, PA 16801, (814) 237–0309; Other Educational Weather Products Available ©1997 **29** New York Public Library, Rare Book Division; Astor, Lenox and Tilden Foundations **33** *l* *Kachina Doll,* The Brooklyn Museum, 05.588.7193, Museum Expedition 1905, Museum Collection Fund; *r* *Butterfly Maiden, Kachina,* Courtesy of the Denver Art Museum, Denver Art Museum, Denver, CO **34** Courtesy of The New York State Museum, Albany, NY, Lewis Henry Morgan collection **36** Victoria & Albert Museum, London/The Bridgeman Art Library, London **37** *Christopher Columbus,* Sebastiano del Piombo, All rights reserved, The Metropolitan Museum of Art **38** *b* ©Brent Winebrenner/International Stock Photography, Ltd.; *t* Luis Castaneda/The Image Bank **42** All rights reserved, The Metropolitan Museum of Art, Louis V. Bell and Rogers Funds, 1972 (1972.63ab) **43** *Atlas Catalan,* detail, Photo Bibliothèque Nationale, Paris **44** *b* *Sugar Harvest in Louisiana & Texas,* 1856–1860, #65.39.120, Collection: Glenbow Museum, Calgary, Alberta; *t* Photo Bibliothèque Nationale, Paris **48** *b* Minnesota Historical Society; *l* North Wind Picture Archives **50** New York Public Library, Rare Book Division; Astor, Lenox and Tilden Foundations **55** Courtesy of the Pilgrim Society, Plymouth, Massachusetts **57** National Portrait Gallery, Smithsonian Institution/Art Resource, NY **58** *l* Eliot Elisofon/LIFE Magazine©TIME Inc.; *r* The Puritan, Augustus Saint-Gaudens, All Rights Reserved, The Metropolitan Museum of Art, Bequest of Jacob Ruppart, 1939 (39.65.53) **60** *The Landing of William Penn,* Thomas Birch, Courtesy, Museum of Fine Arts, Boston, Gift of Mrs. Maxim Karolik for the Karolik Collection of American Paintings, 1815–1865 **61** *l* Courtesy of the Library of Congress; *r* Kelly Mooney/Corbis **62** New York Public Library, Arents Collection; Astor, Lenox and Tilden Foundations **64** Courtesy of the Peabody Essex Museum, Salem, MA. Photo by Mark Sexton **65** *Mrs. Elizabeth Freake and Baby Mary,* unknown artist, Worcester Art Museum, Worcester, Massachusetts, Gift of Mr. and Mrs. Albert W. Rice **67** Gibbes Museum of Art, Carolina Art Association **71** John Lei/Omni-Photo Communications, Inc., for Prentice Hall **73** Courtesy, American Antiquarian Society **74** *George Whitefield,* 1742, John Wollaston, By Courtesy of the National Portrait Gallery, London **75** *l* New York Public Library, Rare Book Division; Astor, Lenox and Tilden Foundations; *r* Yale University Art Gallery **76** *l* ©Andre Jenny, 1994/Stock South; *r* Richard T. Nowitz/Corbis **81** *Surrender of Lord Cornwallis at Yorktown,* John Trumbull, Yale University Art Gallery **85** *Mrs. James Warren (Mercy Otis)* c. 1763, detail, John Singleton Copley, Bequest of Winslow Warren, Courtesy, Museum of Fine Arts, Boston **86** *b* Corel Professional Photos CD-ROM™; *t* Chuck Nacke/Woodfin Camp & Associates **87** Courtesy, American Antiquarian Society **88** *Samuel Adams,* detail, John Singleton Copley, Deposited by the City of Boston, Courtesy, Museum of Fine Arts, Boston **89** Courtesy of The Bostonian Society Old State House **90** Courtesy of the Library of Congress **91** *l* Anthony Stewart/National Geographic Society; *r* The Granger Collection, New York **93** *b* Courtesy of The Bostonian Society Old State House; *t Attack on Bunker's Hill, with the Burning of Charles Town,* Gift of Edgar William and Bernice Chrysler Garbisch, ©Board of Trustees, National Gallery of Art, Washington **94** Fort Ticonderoga Museum **96** *b* Boston Athenaeum; *t* John Wesley Jarvis, *Thomas Paine,* Gift of Marian B. Maurice, ©Board of Trustees, National Gallery of Art, Washington **97** *l* Courtesy of the United States Capitol Historical Society; *r* Courtesy of the Library of Congress **98** William Walcutt, *Pulling Down the Statue of George III at Bowling Green,* 1857, oil on canvas, 51 5/8" x 77 5/8", Lafayette College Art Collection **101** The Historical Society of Pennsylvania **103** *l* Fraunces Tavern Museum, New York City; *r* ©Les Stone/Sygma **104** Collections of The Virginia State Historical Society, Richmond, VA **107** John Lewis Stage/The Image Bank **111** Courtesy of The Valley Forge Historical Society **112** From the collections of Henry Ford Museum & Greenfield Village, MI/#63.41 **115** Architect of the Capitol **116** *The National Archives of the United States* by Herman Viola. Publisher, Harry N. Abrams, Inc. Photograph by Jonathan Wallen **121** Leif Skoogfors/Woodfin Camp & Associates **122** Yale University Art Gallery, gift of Roger Sherman White, B. A. 1859, M.A. **123** Courtesy, Independence National Historical Park Collection **124** *r* Michael Bryant/Woodfin Camp & Associates; *l* Leif Skoogfors/Corbis **127** Bulloz/Art Resource, NY **133** Courtesy of the Library of Congress **134** The Granger Collection, New York **135** *b* John Ficara/Woodfin Camp & Associates; *t* Pat & Tom Lesson/Photo Researchers, Inc. **136** *l* Virginia Historical Society, Richmond, VA; *r* Alan Klehr/Tony Stone Images **141** Mark Hess/The Image Bank **142** Joseph Sohm/ChromoSohm, Inc./Corbis **144** Food and Drug Administration **146** Image copyright© 1997 PhotoDisc, Inc. **147** George Hall/Woodfin Camp & Associates **153** U.S. House of Representatives **156** *b* Corel Professional Photos CD-ROM™; *t* C. L. Chryslin/The Image Bank **157** *l* Dirck Halstead/Gamma Liaison; *r* Wally McNamee/Woodfin Camp & Associates **158** Collection, The Supreme Court of the United States, courtesy The Supreme Court Historical Society. Photo by Richard Strauss, Smithsonian Institution **160** Corbis **161** *l* Jack Bender/Waterloo Courier/Rothco; *r* ©Alon Reininger/Contact/Stock Market; *br* ©The Stock Market/A. Reininger/Contact **162** PEOPLE weekly ©1997 Andrew Kaufman **167** *l* Shelburne Museum, Shelburne, Vermont (27.1.1–24) Photograph by Ken Burris; *r* Mead Art Museum, Amherst College **168** John Lewis Krimmel, *Election Day in Philadelphia,* 1815, Courtesy, The Henry Francis du Pont Winterthur Museum **171** Courtesy, The Henry Francis du Pont Winterthur Museum **173** *t* Private Collection; *b* The Museum of American Political Life, University of Hartford; photo by Sally Anderson-Bruce **174** Courtesy of the Art Commission of the City of New York **176** David Young Wolff/Tony Stone Images **179** *b* Roger-Viollet; *t* Giraudon/Art Resource, NY **180** Courtesy of The Mount Vernon Ladies' Association **182** *l* Unknown, American, Pennsylvania, *He That Tilleth His Land Shall be Satisfied,* detail, Philadelphia Museum of Art: The Edgar William and Bernice Chrysler Garbisch Collection; *r* John Neagle, *Pat Lyon at the Forge,* Henry M. and Zoë Oliver Sherman Fund, Courtesy, Museum of Fine Arts, Boston **183** Corel Professional Photos CD-ROM™ **187** *l* The Huntington Library, San Marino, California; *r* The Granger Collection, New York **188** *l* National Park Service, Adams National Historic Site; *m* Gilbert Stuart, *Abigail Smith Adams* (Mrs. John Adams), detail, Gift of Mrs. Robert Homans, ©1997 Board of Trustees, National Gallery of Art, Washington, Photo by: Richard Carafelli; *r John Adams,* c. 1800, James Sharples, The Museum of Fine Arts, Houston; The Bayou Bend Collection, gift of Miss Ima Hogg **190** The Granger Collection, New York **193** *Lewis and Clark on the Lower Columbia,* Charles M. Russell, 1905, 1961.195, gouache, watercolor and graphite on paper, Amon Carter Museum, Fort Worth **195** *l* Robert Llewellyn Photography; *r* Rembrandt Peale, *Thomas Jefferson,* detail, Collection of The New-York Historical Society **196** *b* ©Junebug Clark/Photo Researchers, Inc.; *t* Silver Burdett Ginn **198** Missouri Historical Society, St. Louis **199** Chicago Historical Society **202** *b* John Woodhouse Audubon, *Antelope Americana,* detail, Neg./Trans. no. 3267 (2)(Photo by: P. Hollembeak/ Bauer) Courtesy Department of Library Services, American Museum of Natural History; *t* O. C. Seltzer, *Lewis and Clark with Sacajawea at the Great Falls of the Missouri,* From the Collection of Gilcrease Museum, Tulsa **204** The Granger Collection, New York **207** Ohio State Historical Society, Jim Roese, photographer, courtesy Historic Waynesborough **208** Collection of Cranbrook Institute of Science, #CIS 2207. ©Robert Hensleigh, Photographer **209** *l* The Field Museum, Neg.# A93851.1c, Chicago; *r* Courtesy of the Library of Congress **211** Courtesy Scott Baker, Ohio Society War of 1812 **213** U.S. Navy Photo **215** *l* From the collection of Mac G. and Janelle C. Morris; *r* Ted Baker/The Image Bank **216** Courtesy of the Library of Congress **221** Leon Pomarede, *View of St. Louis,* 1835, The Saint Louis Art Museum, Private collection of Dorothy Ziern Hanon & Joseph B. Hanon **223** James Higgins; Use courtesy of Lowell National Historical Park **225** American Textile History Museum, Lowell, MA **226** Reprinted with permission of the News-Press of Fort Myers **229** Dean Beason, *Settlers' Wagon,* National Gallery of Art, Washington **230** Pavel Petrovich Svinin, *Travel by Stagecoach near Trenton, New Jersey,* All rights reserved, The Metropolitan Museum of Art, Rogers Fund, 1942. (42.95.11) **232** Silver Burdett Ginn and Colonial Williamsburg Foundation **233** *l* Courtesy Erie Canal Village; *r* Courtesy Erie Canal Museum **237** *l* Architect of the Capitol; *m* Francis Alexander, *Daniel Webster,* 1835, Hood Museum of Art, Dartmouth College, Hanover, New Hampshire; gift of Dr. George C. Shattuck, Class of 1803; *r* Charles Bird King, *John Caldwell Calhoun,* National Portrait Gallery, Smithsonian Institution, Transfer from the National Gallery of Art; Gift of Andrew W. Mellon, 1942 **241** *b* Coleccion Museo Nacional de Colombia, Bogotá; *t* Anne S.K. Brown Military Collection **247** John Quidor, *Return of Rip Van Winkle,* 1829, Andrew W. Mellon Collection, ©1998 Board of Trustees, National Gallery of Art, Washington **248** Scotts Bluff National Monument **251** George Caleb Bingham, *The County Election,* 1851–52, oil on canvas, The Saint Louis Art Museum **254** Eunice Pinney, *Two Women,* c. 1815, New York State Historical Association, Cooperstown **255** *l* Courtesy of the Library of Congress; *r* D. Walker/Gamma Liaison **257** Anna Claypoole Peale, *Andrew Jackson,* Yale University Art Gallery **259** The Granger Collection, New York **261** Courtesy of Salem Maritime NHS **262** Lynn Saville **263** Courtesy of the Library of Congress **267** Becker Collection, Division of Political History, National Museum of American History, Smithsonian Institution, #564-97 **268** ©Robert E. Daemmrich/Tony Stone Images

273 Courtesy of Bexar County and The Witte Museum, San Antonio, Texas **276** Alfred Jacob Miller, *Fort Laramie,* 1837, Walters Art Gallery, Baltimore **277** *t* Handtinting by Ladleton Studio/Culver Pictures, Inc.; *b* Courtesy of the Lane County Historical Museum **279** Courtesy Local History Programs **281** Corel Professional Photos CD-ROM™ **282** *l* Courtesy of the Texas Memorial Museum; *r* Archives Division, Texas State Library **285** *r* Courtesy of The Oakland Museum History Department; *l* Jim Zuckerman/West Light **288** Bill Pogue/The Stockhouse, Inc. **289** Courtesy of the Costume Department, Chicago Historical Society, 1920.38 **292** *Nuestra Señora del Rosario / Our Lady of the Rosary,* by Santo Nino Santero, New Mexico, 1830–60. Gesso, cloth, tin, wood, and water soluble paint. H: 40 1/2 inches. Courtesy Museum of New Mexico Collections at the Museum of International Folk Art, Santa Fe. Photo by Blair Clark **296** *l* North Wind Picture Archives; *r* California State Library **301** *b* The Warner Collection of Gulf States Paper Corporation, Tuscaloosa, Alabama; *t* American Steel Foundries **302** National Museum of History and Technology, Smithsonian Institution, Photo No. 90-4210. **307** *l* State Historical Society of Wisconsin; *r* American Textile History Museum, Lowell, MA **308** Michael Newman/PhotoEdit **310** Aaron E. Darling, *John Jones,* 1865, Chicago Historical Society, #1904.0018 **311** National Museum of American History, Smithsonian Institution, Photo No. 73-11287 **312** ©Robert Finken/Photo Researchers, Inc. **315** The Old Print Shop **317** *b* Courtesy Rosedown Plantation and Historic Garden *t* D. Donne Bryant Stock Photography **319** *b* Bob Daemmrich/Stock, Boston; *t* Maynard Frank Wolfe/Globe Photos **320** John Antrobus, *Plantation Burial,* 1860, The Historic New Orleans Collection, Museum/Research Center, Acc. No. 1960.46 **325** Museum of Art, Rhode Island School of Design, Gift of Miss Lucy T. Aldrich **327** Courtesy of the Library of Congress **328** Tony Freeman/PhotoEdit **329** *bl* Victor R. Boswell, Jr./National Geographic Society; *t* Richard T. Nowitz 1991; *r* Winslow Homer, *Homework,* 1874, watercolor, Canajoharie Library and Art Gallery, Canajoharie, New York **331** The Trustees of the Wedgwood Museum, Barlaston, Staffordshire, England **332** *b* Courtesy of the Massachusetts Historical Society; *t* Southworth and Hawes, *William Lloyd Garrison,* All Rights Reserved, The Metropolitan Museum of Art, Gift of I.N. Phelps Stokes, Edward S. Hawes, Alice Mary Hawes, Marion Augusta Hawes, 1937. (37.14.37) **333** Sophia Smith Collection, Smith College **334** C. T. Webber, *The Underground Railroad,* Cincinnati Art Museum, Subscription Fund Purchase **337** *l* Library of Congress/Corbis; *r* Sophia Smith Collection, Smith College **339** Photograph courtesy of the American Medical Women's Association, photograph by Silver Burdett Ginn **341** *l* Culver Pictures, Inc.; *r* The Kobal Collection **342** The Warner Collection of Gulf States Paper Corporation, Tuscaloosa, Alabama **347** Illustration from the cover of the book *NIGHTJOHN* copyright ©1993 by Jerry Pinkney. Written by Gary Paulsen. Published by Delacorte Press. All rights reserved. Used with permission. **348** Winslow Homer, *Prisoners from the Front,* 1866, All rights reserved, The Metropolitan Museum of Art, Gift of Mrs. Frank B. Porter, 1922 (22.207) **351** Theodor Kaufmann, *On to Liberty,* 1867, All rights reserved, The Metropolitan Museum of Art, Gift of Erving and Joyce Wolf, 1982/95 (1982.443.3) **353** *l* Edwin Taylor, *American Slave Market,* 1852, Chicago Historical Society, 1954.15; *r* Sovfoto/Eastfoto **356** *l* State Historical Society of Wisconsin; *r* North Wind Pictures **360** *l* Kansas State Historical Society; *r* Anne S.K. Brown Military Collection **361** Missouri Historical Society (S-126 E) **363** Ontario County Historical Society **364** Courtesy of the Illinois State Historical Library **365** Carolyn Schaefer/Gamma Liaison **367** Corbis-Bettmann **370** *b* Fort Sumter National Monument; *t* Emory Kristoff/National Geographic Society **375** Winslow Homer, *A Rainy Day in Camp,* All Rights Reserved, The Metropolitan Museum of Art, Gift of Mrs. William F. Milton, 1923. (23.77.1) **376** North Carolina Museum of History **381** Chicago Historical Society **383** E.B.D. Julio, *The Last Meeting of Lee and Jackson,* detail, The Museum of the Confederacy, Richmond, Virginia, Photography by Katherine Wetzel **385** Courtesy of the Library of Congress **387** Chicago Historical Society **388** Courtesy of the Library of Congress **389** ©The Greenwich Workshop Press **391** Photography by Larry Sherer/High Impact Photography, Time-Life Books, Inc. **392** Cook Collection Valentine Museum, Richmond, Virginia **393** *b* Courtesy of the American Red Cross. All Rights Reserved in all Countries. Photo by Silver Burdett Ginn; *t* Courtesy National Archives **394** Architect of the Capitol **397** *r* John Elk III/Stock, Boston; *l* ©The Stock Market/Lance Nelson **401** Appomattox Court House NHP, National Park Service, USDI **405** Dennis Malone Carter, Lincoln's Drive Through Richmond, Chicago Historical Society, Gift of Mr. Philip K. Wrigley, 1955.398 **407** *l* Courtesy of the Library of Congress; *r* Richard T. Nowitz / Virginia Division of Tourism **408** Moorland-Spingarn Research Center, Howard University **409** Culver Pictures, Inc. **411** Courtesy of the Library of Congress **414** The Children's Museum of Indianapolis **415** detail, Chicago Historical Society, P&S-1904.0018 **416** *b* Old Court House Museum, Vicksburg, Photo by Bob Pickett; *t* The Granger Collection, New York **417** New York Public Library, Print Collection. Miriam and Ira D. Wallach Division of Art, Prints and Photographs; Astor, Lenox and Tilden Foundations **418** Brown Brothers **421** The Granger Collection, New York **422** Courtesy of Jim Osborn **427** West Point Museum Collections, United States Military Academy, West Point, New York **428** Collection of The New-York Historical Society **431** SuperStock **433** *l* Charles M. Russell, *Following the Buffalo Run,* c. 1894, oil on canvas, 1961.134, Amon Carter Museum, Fort Worth; *r* Collection of the Flint Institute of Arts. FIA 85.27 Photograph ©Dirk Bakker **434** Denver Art Museum **437** Sandra Baker/Gamma Liaison **439** Special Collections Division, University of Washington Libraries **440** Seaver Center for Western History Research, Museum of Natural History, Photo by Henry Groskinsky **441** James Walker, *California Vaqueros,* The Anshutz Collection **442** J. Pat Carter/Gamma Liaison **445** *l* Smithsonian Institution, 36891; *r* G. R. Roberts **448** Culver Pictures, Inc. **449** Courtesy of The National Museum of the American Indian/Smithsonian Institution (neg. #2/1133) **451** Courtesy of the Library of Congress **452** Nebraska State Historical Society **453** Bob Daemmrich/Stock, Boston **454** Kansas State Historical Society **459** ©C.C.I. 1998 **461** *b* Brown Brothers; *t* Courtesy of the Library of Congress **462** Courtesy of the Library of Congress **465** *Andrew Carnegie,* The National Portrait Gallery, Smithsonian Institution, Gift of Mrs. Margaret Carnegie Miller/Art Resource, NY **467** *b* Corel Professional Photos CD-ROM™; *m* Larry Lee/Westlight; *t* Silver Burdett Ginn **468** *l* Brown Brothers; *r* Jonathan Kirn/Gamma Liaison **470** ©1999 Michael Freeman **471** *l* ©1999 Michael Freeman; *m* National Park Service, U.S. Dept. of Interior, Edison National Historic Site; *r* Breton Littlehales/National Geographic Society **474** From the collections of Henry Ford Museum & Greenfield Village **476** The George Meany Memorial Archives **477** *l* Courtesy of the Library of Congress **479** Corbis-Bettmann **485** The Saint Louis Art Museum, Bequest of Marie Setz Hertslet **488** *b* Photo by John Lei/Omni Photo Communications; *t* Bob Krist/Corbis **490** *bl* Bancroft Library, University of California; *t* ©C.C.I. 1998 **492** Collection of Picture Research Consultants, Inc. Photo ©Rob Huntley/Lightstream **494** *r* Cooper-Hewitt Museum, Smithsonian Institution/Art Resource, NY; *tl* Eastman Johnson, *The Brown Family,* 1869, The Fine Arts Museum of San Francisco **495** Brown Brothers **496** *r* International Museum of Photography at George Eastman House; *tl* National Portrait Gallery, Smithsonian Institution/Art Resource, NY **499** Chicago Historical Society, ICHI-01066 **500** North Wind Picture Archives **501** *tl* ©Frank Driggs/Archive Photos; *tr* New York Public Library at Lincoln Center **502** Rebus Inc. **504** *b* Spencer Grant/Stock, Boston; *tr* Image copyright ©1997 PhotoDisc, Inc. **505** *l* Culver Pictures, Inc.; *r* Brown Brothers **506** Los Angeles County Museum of Art, *Mother About to Wash Her Sleepy Child,* Mary Cassatt, Mrs. Fred Hathaway Bixby Bequest **515** Collection of The New-York Historical Society **516** From the collection of Roger Lathbury; photo by SBG **517** Courtesy of the Library of Congress **518** Collection of The New-York Historical Society **521** *b* Courtesy George Eastman House; *t* The Jacob A. Riis Collection 157, Museum of the City of New York **522** *b* Terry Vine/Tony Stone Images; *t* Bob Daemmrich/Stock, Boston **525** The Museum of American Political Life, University of Hartford, photo by Sally Anderson-Bruce **526** *l* Courtesy of the Library of Congress; *r* National Museum of American History, Smithsonian Institution **527** *b* Silver Burdett Ginn; *t* Culver Pictures, Inc. **529** *b* Guido Alberto Rossi/The Image Bank; *t* ©The Stock Market/John M. Roberts **530** Collection of The New-York Historical Society **531–532** The Granger Collection, New York **533** *l* Corbis-Bettmann; *r* Sally Anderson-Bruce **537** *b* Schomburg Center for Research in Black Culture, Prints and Photographs Division, The New York Public Library, Astor, Lenox and Tilden Foundations; *t* Courtesy of the NAACP National Headquarters **538** Courtesy Museum of New Mexico **539** ©The Burns Archive **543** Courtesy United States Naval Academy Museum **545** *b* Courtesy of the Library of Congress Manuscript Division; *t* Courtesy United States Naval Academy Museum **546** ©Jeff Greenberg/Photo Researchers, Inc. **547** Courtesy of The Oakland Museum History Department **549** *b* Seth Joel/ Bishop Museum; *t* Bishop Museum **550** Culver Pictures, Inc. **552** Theodore Roosevelt Birthplace **553** New York Journal and Advertiser **555** Courtesy of the Library of Congress **556** *r* Theodore Roosevelt Birthplace; *t* Courtesy National Archives, photo no. 111-RB-2939 **557** ©Klaus Reisinger, 1992/Black Star PNI **559** National Postal Museum, Smithsonian Institution, Washington, D.C. **561** Lynn Saville **562** *l* UPI/Corbis-Bettmann; *r* Archives Center National Museum of American History, Smithsonian Institution Photo No. 95-5305 **569** Smithsonian Institution, Photo No. 57043 **571** ©John McCutchson/The Chicago Tribune, 1914, Chicago Tribune Company **573** Culver Pictures, Inc. **575** The Granger Collection, New York **576** The Museum of American Political Life, University of Hartford; photo by Sally Anderson-Bruce **578** *l* Courtesy of the Library of Congress; *r* UPI/Corbis-Bettmann **579** Culver Pictures, Inc. **581** *b* Culver Pictures, Inc.; *l* Courtesy National Archives, photo no. 86-G-11F-7 **582** Courtesy of the Library of Congress **584** Collection of Colonel Stuart S. Corning, Jr. Photo ©Rob Huntley/Lightstream **586** *b* Musée de Verdun/Luc Joubert/Tallandier; *t* The Imperial War Museum London, John Singer Sargent, *Gassed* **587** Jack Kurtz/Impact Visuals **589** UPI/Corbis-Bettmann **590** *Woodrow Wilson,* 1919, John Christen Johansen, The National Portrait Gallery, Smithsonian Institution, Art Resource, NY **591** The Imperial War Museum, London **597** Museum of Fine Arts, Boston/Laurie Platt Winfrey, Inc. **599** Tsing-fang Chen, *Liberty States,* Chen Foundation/Lucia Gallery **600** Library of Congress/Corbis **602** *l* Courtesy of the Library of Congress; *r* ©1993, Willinger/FPG International Corp. **603** University of North Carolina at Wilmington **605** ©1991 The Stock Market/John Madere **606** *r* National Museum of American History, Smithsonian Institution, Washington, D.C. #90-15751 **606** *mr* Photofest **608** *r* Michael Kaufman/Impact Visuals; *l* Dennis Brack/Black Star (PNI) **611** ©Alon Reininger/Contact Press Images **612** The Granger Collection, New York **614** Ed Clark, Life Magazine ©Time Inc. **615** *l* Porterfield/Chickering/Photo Researchers, Inc.; *r* Corbis **616** *t* Bob Krist/Corbis; *b* Bob Takis, American Airlines **618** National Organization for Women, Copyright ©1992 **620** ©Carol Simpson/Rothco **621** *l* Silver Burdett Ginn; *r* ©Bill Nation/Sygma **622** *l* Phil Schermeister/Corbis; *r* Courtesy of The National Museum of the American Indian/Smithsonian Institution, (neg #89/2943) James P. Farnham Collection **623** Corel Professional Photos CD-ROM™ **624** Joseph Sohm/ChromoSohm, Inc./Corbis **628** *r* San Francisco School Volunteers **633** *Los Jovenes con Bicicleta,* 1993, Tony Ortega, Courtesy of Tony Ortega **635** *r* Thomas Eakins, *Baseball Players Practicing,* 1875, Museum of Art, Rhode Island School of Design; *l* North Wind Picture Archives **637** Albert Bierstadt, *Landscape,* Columbus Museum of Art, Ohio: Bequest of Rutherford H. Platt **639** ©Adam Jones/Photo Researchers, Inc. **641** Courtesy of the School of American Research, Santa Fe, New Mexico: Gift of Mrs. Chandler Hale, Santa Fe, N.M., Catalog Number IAF.T670 **643** National Maritime Museum, London **644, 646** Collection of The New-York Historical Society **649** ©Kennedy Galleries, Inc. **650** Peabody Essex Museum of Salem **652** Leif Skoogfors/Woodfin Camp & Associates **655** Courtesy of the Library of Congress **656** Thomas Rowlandson, *House of Commons,* All Rights Reserved, The Metropolitan Museum of Art Rogers Fund, 1921 **658** Paul S. Conklin **660** *George Washington banner,* c. 1939, Index of American Design, ©Board of Trustees, National Gallery of Art, Washington **662** Max Mackenzie ©Uniphoto, Inc. **664** Missouri Historical Society, St. Louis **666** North Wind Picture Archives **668** Courtesy of the Library of Congress **670** Laurie Platt Winfrey, Inc. **671** White House Collection, copyright ©White House Historical Association **673** Woolaroc Museum, Bartlesville, Oklahoma **675** Unknown artist, *Oriana Day-Mission Francisco Solano de Sonoma,* c. 1838–1886, The Fine Arts Museum of San Francisco, Gift of Eleanor Martin, 37573 **677** Dan Suzio/Photo Researchers, Inc. **679** Mary Evans Picture Library **681** North Wind Picture Archives **682** *l* Chester County Historical Society, West Chester, PA; *r* UPI/Corbis-Bettmann **685** Artist Unknown, *Scenes from a Seminary for Young Ladies* (detail), Purchase and Funds Given by Decorative Arts Society 89:1976, The Saint Louis Art Museum (Decorative Arts and Design) **687** Eyre Crowe, *After the Sale: South from Richmond,* Chicago Historical Society, P&S-1957.0027 **689** Thomas Hovenden, *The Last Moments of John Brown,* All Rights Reserved, By the Metropolitan Museum of Art, Gift of Mr. & Mrs. Carl Stoeckel, 1897 **690** Thomas Nast, *Heroes and Heroines of the War,* detail, c. 1863, Chicago Historical Society, Gift of Dr. Otto L. Schmidt, ICHi-22101 **692** National Geographic Society **694** Richard Norris Brooke, *Furling the Flag,* West Point Museum Collections, United States Military Academy, West Point, NY **696** North Wind Picture Archives **697** *Chief Joseph* (detail), 1878, Cyrenius Hall, National Portrait Gallery, Smithsonian Institution, Washington, D.C./Art Resource, NY **700** Wichita Art Museum, Wichita, KS **702** The Chrysler Museum, Norfolk, VA, Gift of Walter P. Chrysler, Jr. 71.651 **704** Archive Photos **706** Courtesy National Archives, Rudolph Vetter **709** Museum of Art, Rhode Island School of Design **710** New York Public Library: *Leslie's Illustrated Newspaper,* Sept. 11, 1920 **712** Courtesy Library of Congress **714** The Granger Collection, New York **717** National Museum of American Art, Smithsonian Institution **719** Underwood and Underwood/Corbis-Bettmann **721** Los Angeles Museum of Art, *Red Cross Drive,* Childe Hassam, The Eleanor & C. Thomas May Trust for Christopher, Sterling, Meredith, & Laura May **723** Corbis-Bettmann **725** *r* David Young-Wolff/PhotoEdit; *l* American Library Association (ALA Graphics) **727** *t* Pat & Tom Leson/Photo Researchers, Inc.; *r* Joseph Sohm/ChromoSohm, Inc./Corbis; *l* Courtesy of Bexar County and The Witte Museum, San Antonio, TX **752–755** Portrait nos. 1, 2, 4, 5, 6, 9, 10, 12, 14, 15, 18, 20, 21, 25, 26, 27, 35, National Portrait Gallery, Smithsonian Institution/Art Resource, NY; Portrait nos. 3, 7, 8, 11, 13, 16, 17, 19, 22–24, 28–34, 36–42, White House Collection, Copyright White House Historical Association **755** *b* John Ficara/Woodfin Camp & Associates **796** David Young Wolff/Tony Stone Images

Stop the Presses

Not so long ago, publishers had to stop the presses to get late-breaking information into their books. Today, Prentice Hall can use the Internet to quickly and easily update you on the most recent developments in Social Studies.

Visit Prentice Hall on the Internet at

http://www.phschool.com

for the Prentice Hall Social Studies Update.

There you will find periodic updates in the following areas:

- ★ **United States History**
- ★ **World Studies**
- ★ **American Government**

Each update topic provides you with background information as well as carefully selected links to guide you to related content on the Internet.